Oxford Primary Dictionary

Editors: Robert Allen
Andrew Delahunty

OXFORD
UNIVERSITY PRESS

Great Clarendon Street, Oxford OX2 6DP

Oxford University Press is a department of the University of Oxford. It furthers the University's objective of excellence in research, scholarship, and education by publishing worldwide in

Oxford New York
Auckland Cape Town Dar es Salaam Hong Kong Karachi
Kuala Lumpur Madrid Melbourne Mexico City Nairobi New Delhi
Shanghai Taipei Toronto

with offices in

Argentina Austria Brazil Chile Czech Republic France Greece
Guatemala Hungary Italy Japan South Korea Poland Portugal
Switzerland Thailand Turkey Ukraine Vietnam

Oxford is a registered trade mark of Oxford University Press in the UK and in certain other countries

First published 1993
Second edition 1998
Revised second edition 2002
This edition 2006

Database right Oxford University Press (maker)

British Library cataloguing in Publication Data available

ISBN 13: 978-0-19-911523-5

ISBN 10: 0-19-911523-0

Primary Dictionary with Primary Dictionary Activities CD-ROM

ISBN 13: 978-0-19-911544-0

ISBN 10: 0-19-911544-3

10 9 8 7 6 5 4 3 2 1

Typeset in OUP Argo and OUP Swift

Printed in India

Preface

This dictionary has been specially written for children aged 7 to 11 years. Special attention has been given to covering words children will encounter in literacy classes, such as *assonance*, *grapheme*, *mnemonic*, and *topic sentence*. Many common words, such as *scroll*, *search*, and *text*, have a particular meaning in ICT contexts, and many of these meanings are included in the dictionary.

Definitions are expressed clearly and in simple language. Definitions of verbs and many adjectives are given in context to clarify such aspects of their use as transitivity and typical subjects and objects. For example, one definition of *scan* is 'to scan a piece of writing is to look over it quickly', which tells you that *scan* is transitive in this meaning and shows you the typical sort of object. Another definition of *scan* is 'poetry scans when it has a fixed rhythm', which tells you that *scan* is intransitive in this meaning and shows you the typical sort of subject of the verb.

Definitions of some nouns are also given in contextualized form when this clarifies important aspects of their use, such as countability. This can be seen at *choice*, where one sense, 'choice is the process of choosing or the power to choose', is uncountable and another, 'a choice is what someone chooses', is countable.

Definitions are given for all items, including derivative words added at the end of entries. Indeed, the fuller treatment of derivatives is one of the most distinctive features of this edition. In many cases they have been given special treatment within word family panels, which highlight words derived from or closely related in form or meaning to the headword.

Most definitions are supported by example sentences showing words in use, including a generous selection of quotations from published children's authors.

The text includes 50 specially written panels on a variety of key language topics such as *adjectives*, *apostrophes*, *homophones*, *plurals*, *setting*, and *similes and metaphors*. These panels support children both as readers and as writers. For readers, the panels give additional information about aspects of word, sentence and text level literacy objectives which children often find particularly puzzling. Children as writers can use the panels before they begin their writing in order to clarify ideas and explore more successful ways of achieving an effect. While children are writing, they can make use of the dictionary as a source of ideas and related words, as well as for spelling.

Dictionaries are traditionally used to help with reading, but we hope that this dictionary will support children when they are writing too. Features such as the language panels, illustrative quotations from published writers, and the contextualized defining style are all designed to help children in their writing.

Andrew Delahunty - dictionary editor

Kate Ruttle - literacy consultant

How to use the dictionary

Dictionary entries

Words defined are arranged in alphabetical order. The words derived from each word (derivatives) are often included at the end of an entry, sometimes with short definitions, sometimes grouped together in word family panels.

Words with the same spelling but with a different meaning or origin (homographs) are given separate entries with space between them, and are numbered with a raised figure, e.g. *lean*[1] (bend your body) and *lean*[2] (not fat).

Pronunciation

Help is given with pronouncing words when they are difficult in some way, when two words with the same spelling are pronounced differently (such as several words spelt *bow*), and when the same word is pronounced differently in its different word classes or parts of speech (as with *abstract* and *record*).

The pronunciation is given in brackets, introduced by '*rhymes with* ...' (when possible) or '*say* ...' followed by a simple scheme that uses ordinary letters, e.g.

draught *NOUN* (**draughts**) (*rhymes with* **craft**)
acre *NOUN* (**acres**) (*say* **ay**- ker)

Words are divided into syllables, and the main stress is shown by bold type (thick black letters).

The following special sounds should be noted:

oo shows the sound as in s**oo**n
uu shows the sound as in b**oo**k
th shows the sound as in **th**in
th shows the sound as in *th*is
zh shows the sound as in vi**s**ion

Word classes

Word classes are printed in italic capital letters (e.g. *NOUN, ADJECTIVE, VERB*) after the word and before its definition. When a word has more than one word class, the entries are grouped together, e.g.

pause *NOUN* (**pauses**)
a short stop before continuing with something

pause *VERB* (**pauses**, **pausing**, **paused**)
1 to pause is to make a short stop before continuing with something **2** to pause (for example) a video recorder, DVD player, or CD player is to make the tape or disc stop for a short time

Inflections and plurals

The parts of verbs, plurals of nouns, and some comparatives and superlatives and adverbs are given after the word class, e.g.

cancel *VERB* (**cancels**, **cancelling**, **cancelled**)
camp *NOUN* (**camps**)
calm *ADJECTIVE* (**calmer**, **calmest**)

Meanings

Many words have more than one meaning. Each meaning is numbered separately.

Labels

Words or meanings that are only used informally or in spoken English are marked informal or slang. Subject labels are given for certain meanings that are used in, say, grammar, mathematics, or science.

Examples

Examples of words in use are given in italic or sloping print *like this* to help make a meaning clearer.

A selection of these example sentences are quotations from published children's authors.

gigantic *ADJECTIVE*
huge; enormous • *Suddenly the boy let out a gigantic belch which rolled around the Assembly Hall like thunder.* — Roald Dahl, *Matilda*

Information boxes

The dictionary includes many special panels, which give extra information at individual entries on words and the ways they are used, especially on word origins and grammar. Word family panels are often used to show the connection between a headword and its derivatives (e.g. *lamely* and *lameness* under *lame, mockery* under *mock*) and between a headword and other related words (e.g. *eat* and *edible*).

Language panels

Over 50 language panels deal with a variety of key language topics such as *adjectives*, *homophones*, *plurals*, *punctuation*, *setting*, *similes and metaphor*, and *suffixes*.

Dictionary Features

headwords are in bold to find words more easily

forget-me-not *NOUN* **(forget-me-nots)**
a plant with small blue flowers

irregular or unusual spellings for verb forms are given in full

forgive *VERB* **(forgives, forgiving, forgave, forgiven)**
to forgive someone is to stop being angry with them for something they have done
▷ **forgiveness** *NOUN* forgiving someone

words that are derived from headwords are given at the end of entries

fork *NOUN* **(forks)**
1 a small device with prongs for lifting food to your mouth **2** a large device with prongs used for digging or lifting things **3** a place where a road or river divides into two or more parts

definitions are clear and accurate

fork *VERB* **(forks, forking, forked)**
1 to fork something is to dig or lift it with a fork **2** to fork is to divide into two or more branches • *The tunnel suddenly forked into two. One passage was nice and wide, the other narrow.* — Enid Blyton, *Five On a Secret Trail*
to fork out (*informal*) is to pay out money

set phrases and idioms are defined

example sentences from children's authors show headwords in use

form *NOUN* **(forms)**
1 a form is a kind or type of thing • *What is your favourite form of transport?* **2** the form of something is its shape and general appearance • *They could see a shadowy form in front of them.* **3** a form is also a class in a school **4** a form is also a piece of paper with printed questions and spaces for the answers

labels are given to encourage accurate use of language

form *VERB* **(forms, forming, formed)**
1 to form something is to shape or make it **2** to form is to come into existence or develop • *Icicles formed on the window.*

Dictionary Features

formal *ADJECTIVE*
1 strictly following the accepted rules or customs; not casual •*She has a formal manner and never calls me by my first name.* **2** official or ceremonial •*The formal opening of the bridge takes place tomorrow.*

different meanings of one word are numbered

WORD FAMILY
To do something **formally** is to do it in a formal way.

word families show how words are related to each other

FORMAL LANGUAGE
Duplicate is a more formal word than *copy* and *Your participation was appreciated* is a more formal way of saying *Thank you for taking part.* Formal language can often be used to create a distance between writers and the texts they write. The passive is often used in formal language because it contributes to the distancing of the author, as does the use of longer, more complex sentences and unusual vocabulary. Legal documents are usually written in formal language. Look also at the panel on **Informal language**.

special language panels focus on key topics to support reading and writing

former *ADJECTIVE*
earlier; in the past •*In former times the house had been an inn.* •*He is a former President of the US.*
the former the first of two people or things just mentioned •*If it's a choice between a picnic or a swim I prefer the former.*
See also **latter**

cross references link key words

foyer *NOUN* (**foyers**) (*say* **foi**- ay)
the entrance hall of a cinema, theatre, or hotel

pronunciation guides to help with words that cause difficulty

fritter[1] *NOUN* (**fritters**)
a slice of meat, potato, or fruit that is covered in batter and fried

fritter[2] *VERB* (**fritters, frittering, frittered**)
to fritter something or fritter it away is to waste it gradually •*He frittered all his money on comics.*

headwords are numbered when they have different meanings or origins

Aa

a *DETERMINER* (called the *indefinite article*)
1 one; any •*I would like a holiday.* **2** each; every •*I go there twice a month.*

aback *ADVERB*
to be taken aback is to be surprised and slightly shocked by something someone says or does •*We were taken aback by this silly idea.*

abacus *NOUN* (**abacuses**)
a frame with rows of beads that slide on wires, used for counting and doing sums

abandon *VERB* (**abandons**, **abandoning**, **abandoned**)
to abandon something or someone is to go away and leave them, without intending to go back for them •*He abandoned his family and went off to Australia.*
abandon ship passengers abandon a sinking ship when they get into the lifeboats to save their lives

abbey *NOUN* (**abbeys**)
1 a group of buildings where monks or nuns live and work **2** a community of monks or nuns **3** a church which is or was part of an abbey, such as Westminster Abbey in London

abbot *NOUN* (**abbots**)
the head of an abbey of monks

abbreviate *VERB* (**abbreviates**, **abbreviating**, **abbreviated**)
to abbreviate a word or phrase is to write it with fewer letters so that it is shorter

abbreviation *NOUN* (**abbreviations**)
a word or group of letters that is a shorter form of something longer •*BBC is an abbreviation of 'British Broadcasting Corporation'.*

> ABBREVIATIONS
> An abbreviation is a shorter form of a word or group of words. With some abbreviations, you take the first letter of a word or the first letters of a group of words. You sometimes end abbreviations like this with a full stop. With other abbreviations, you take the first letter and one or more other letters of the word. You sometimes put full stops in between these letters. Examples of abbreviations are: cm (centimetre), Dr (Doctor), ICT (information and communication technology), Ltd (limited), MP (Member of Parliament), Mr (Mister), p.t.o. (please turn over), Sat. (Saturday).

ABC *NOUN*
a name for the alphabet •*We know our ABC.*

abdomen *NOUN* (**abdomens**)
1 the part of the human body where the stomach is **2** the back part of the body of an insect or spider

abdominal *ADJECTIVE*
in the part of the body where the abdomen is •*an abdominal pain*

abide *VERB* (**abides**, **abiding**, **abode** or **abided**)
1 you cannot abide something or someone when you don't like them at all •*I can't abide blackcurrants.* **2** (*old meaning*) to abide in a place is to be living or working in it
to abide by a promise is to keep it

ability *NOUN* (**abilities**)
1 ability is the skill or talent to do something •*They have a lot of ability at games.* **2** an ability is a special skill or talent •*a person of many abilities*

ablaze *ADJECTIVE*
a building or other large thing is ablaze when it is on fire and burning strongly

able *ADJECTIVE* (**abler**, **ablest**)
1 having the power or skill or opportunity to do something •*They were not able to find our house.* **2** having a special talent or skill •*John is a very able musician.*
▷ **ably** *ADVERB* to do something ably is to do it well and use skill or talent •*They did the work very ably.*

abnormal *ADJECTIVE*
unusual or peculiar, not normal
▷ **abnormality** *NOUN* something unusual or abnormal •*a physical abnormality*

aboard *ADVERB & PREPOSITION*
someone is aboard when they have got on on a train, ship, or aircraft •*The passengers were now all aboard.* •*It's time to get aboard the train.*

abode *NOUN* (**abodes**)
a formal word for the place where someone lives

abolish *VERB* (**abolishes**, **abolishing**, **abolished**)
to abolish a rule or custom is to get rid of it •*Some people would like to abolish homework.*

abolition *NOUN* (*say* ab- o- **lish**- on)
getting rid of something

abominable *ADJECTIVE*
very shocking, dreadful •*It was an abominable crime.*

aboriginal *NOUN*
one of the original inhabitants of a country

> SPELLING
> When **Aboriginal** refers to Australia you spell it with a capital A.

Aborigines *PLURAL NOUN* (*say* ab- er- **ij**- in- eez)
the people who lived in Australia before the European settlers arrived there

abort *VERB* (**aborts**, **aborting**, **aborted**)
to abort a plan or mission is to cancel it after it has begun

abortion *NOUN* (**abortions**)
an operation to remove an unborn child (foetus) from a woman's womb before it has developed fully enough to live

abound *VERB* (**abounds**, **abounding**, **abounded**)
things abound when there is a lot of them • *Fish abound in the river.*

about *PREPOSITION*
1 to do with, connected with • *The story is about animals.* **2** approximately, roughly • *She's about five feet tall.*

about *ADVERB*
1 in various directions or places • *They were running about.* **2** somewhere near by • *There were wild animals about.*
to be about to do something is to be just going to do it • *He was about to leave.*

above *PREPOSITION*
1 higher than, over • *There was a window above the door.* **2** more than • *The temperature was just above freezing.*

above *ADVERB*
at a higher point, or to a higher point • *Look at the stars above.*

abrasive *ADJECTIVE*
an abrasive material is rough and is used to clean or scrape something hard

abreast *ADVERB*
side by side • *They walked three abreast.*
to be abreast of something is to know all about it • *We must be abreast of modern discoveries.*

abroad *ADVERB*
in a foreign country • *They live abroad now.*

abrupt *ADJECTIVE*
1 sudden and unexpected • *It was the same for years and then there was an abrupt change.* **2** rude and unfriendly • *He gave an abrupt reply.*

abscess *NOUN* (**abscesses**)
a painful swelling on the body containing pus

abseil *VERB* (**abseils**, **abseiling**, **abseiled**)
to abseil is to lower yourself down a steep cliff or rock by sliding down a rope

absence *NOUN* (**absences**)
not being in a place where you are expected, for example school or work

absent *ADJECTIVE*
not present; away

absentee *NOUN* (**absentees**)
someone who is away, for example not at school or work

absent-minded *ADJECTIVE*
forgetting things easily
▷ **absent-mindedly** *ADVERB* to do something absent-mindedly is to do it without thinking about it much • *Lydia absent-mindedly put too much sugar in her tea.*

absolute *ADJECTIVE*
total, complete, not restricted • *The king had absolute power.*

absolutely *ADVERB*
1 completely **2** (*informal*) definitely • *'Are you going to Beth's party?' 'Absolutely!'*

absorb *VERB* (**absorbs**, **absorbing**, **absorbed**)
1 to absorb something like liquid is to soak it up **2** to be absorbed in something is to be interested in it and give it all your attention • *He was very absorbed in his book.*
▷ **absorption** *NOUN* absorption is the process of soaking up liquid

absorbent *ADJECTIVE*
an absorbent material soaks up liquid easily

abstract *ADJECTIVE* (*say* **ab**- strakt)
to do with ideas and not with physical things • *abstract patterns*

abstract *VERB* (**abstracts**, **abstracting**, **abstracted**) (*say* ab- **strakt**)
to abstract something is to take it out of something else • *Water is abstracted from the river.*

abstract *NOUN* (**abstracts**) (*say* **ab**- strakt)
a summary of a longer piece of writing

absurd *ADJECTIVE*
silly or ridiculous • *It was an absurd thing to say.*

absurdity *NOUN* (**absurdities**)
something that is silly or ridiculous

abundance *NOUN*
a large amount, plenty • *There was an abundance of good things.*

abundant *ADJECTIVE*
large in amount, plentiful

abuse *VERB* (**abuses**, **abusing**, **abused**) (*say* a- **bewz**)
1 to abuse something is to treat it badly and harm it **2** to abuse someone is to say unpleasant things about them **3** to abuse someone also means to hurt them or treat them cruelly

abuse *NOUN* (**abuses**) (*say* a- **bewss**)
1 treating something badly **2** unpleasant words said about someone • *She got a lot of abuse from her so-called friends.* **3** physical harm or cruelty done to someone

abusive *ADJECTIVE*
saying unpleasant things about someone

abysmal *ADJECTIVE*
(*informal*) very bad • *The weather was abysmal.*

abyss *NOUN* (**abysses**)
a deep dark hole that seems to go on for ever

acacia *NOUN* (**acacias**) (*say* a-**kay**-sha)
a tree with small yellow or white flowers, which grows in warm countries

academic *ADJECTIVE*
1 to do with learning in a school or university • *an academic subject* **2** not really important, because it doesn't really matter • *It was academic who won now.*

academy *NOUN* (**academies**)
1 a college or school **2** a society of scholars or scientists who meet to discuss their work

accelerate *VERB* (**accelerates**, **accelerating**, **accelerated**)
to accelerate is to go faster

acceleration *NOUN*
an increase of speed, going faster

accelerator *NOUN* (**accelerators**)
a pedal that you press down to make a motor vehicle go faster

accent *NOUN* (**accents**) (*say* **ak**- sent)
1 your accent is the way you pronounce words **2** an accent is the way that people in different parts of a country pronounce words differently • *He has a Yorkshire accent.* **3** the accent in a word is the part you speak more strongly than the rest of it • *The accent in 'dinner' is on the first syllable, din-.* **4** an accent is a special mark put over a letter, usually when it's a foreign word, to show its pronunciation • *The word 'resumé' has an accent on the second 'e'.*

accent *VERB* (**accents**, **accenting**, **accented**) (*say* **ak**- **sent**)
to accent part of a word is to speak it more strongly than the rest of it

accept *VERB* (**accepts**, **accepting**, **accepted**)
1 to accept something is to take it when someone offers it to you **2** to accept an invitation is to say 'yes' to it **3** to accept an idea or suggestion is to agree that it is true or worth thinking about

> SPELLING
> Take care not to confuse **accept** with **except**, which is a preposition meaning 'not including'.

acceptable *ADJECTIVE*
1 good enough to accept • *We think it is an acceptable offer.* **2** all right, satisfactory • *Their behaviour was not acceptable.*

acceptance *NOUN*
taking something that someone offers you

access *NOUN* (**accesses**)
a way to reach a place • *This road is the only access to the house.*

access *VERB* (**accesses**, **accessing**, **accessed**)
(*in ICT*) to access data is to find it on a computer and be able to use it

> SPELLING
> Take care not to confuse **access** with **excess**, which means 'too much of something'.

accessible *ADJECTIVE*
easy to reach or approach
▷ **accessibility** *NOUN* accessibility is how easy a place is to reach • *The library has good accessibility for disabled people.*

accession *NOUN* (**accessions**)
the time when a new king or queen begins ruling • *We saw a painting of Henry VIII at his accession.*

accessory *NOUN* (**accessories**)
1 an extra or spare part that goes with something bigger **2** an item like a piece of jewellery or a handbag that goes with clothes

accident *NOUN* (**accidents**)
something unexpected that happens, especially when something is broken, or someone is hurt or killed
by accident by chance, not intentionally

accidental *ADJECTIVE*
something is accidental when it happens by chance and not because someone wants it to happen • *accidental damage*
▷ **accidentally** *ADVERB* to do something accidentally is to do it by mistake or without meaning to • *Anthony accidentally dropped a tin on his foot.*

acclaim *VERB* (**acclaims**, **acclaiming**, **acclaimed**)
to acclaim someone is to welcome or praise them warmly

accommodate *VERB* (**accommodates**, **accommodating**, **accommodated**)
1 to accommodate someone or something is to provide them with a place to stay or find space for them **2** to accommodate someone also means to do what you can to please them

accommodation *NOUN*
accommodation is a place to live or stay • *They were looking for cheap accommodation.*

accompaniment *NOUN* (**accompaniments**)
the music played on a piano or another instrument while a singer sings

accompanist *NOUN* (**accompanists**)
a person who plays the piano or another instrument while a singer sings

accompany *VERB* (**accompanies**, **accompanying**, **accompanied**)
1 to accompany someone is to go somewhere with them **2** to accompany a singer is to play the piano or another instrument while they sing

accomplish *VERB* (**accomplishes**, **accomplishing**, **accomplished**)
to accomplish something is to do it successfully

accomplished *ADJECTIVE*
good at doing something, skilful

accomplishment *NOUN* (**accomplishments**)
something you do well

accord *NOUN* (**accords**)
to do something of your own accord is to do it willingly and without being told to

according to *PREPOSITION*
1 You say **according to someone** to show where a piece of information comes from • *According to Katie, there is a party tomorrow.* **2** You say **according to something** when you are comparing two things • *The shop has priced the apples according to their size.*

accordingly *ADVERB*
1 consequently; therefore **2** in a way that is suitable • *You are older now and must behave accordingly.*

accordion *NOUN* (**accordions**)
a portable musical instrument like a large concertina with a set of keys like a piano's at one end. You play it by squeezing it in and out and pressing the keys

account *NOUN* (**accounts**)
1 a description or story about something that happened **2** an amount of money someone has in a bank or building society **3** a statement of the money someone owes or has received, a bill • *We will send you an account next week.*
on account of something because of it
on no account certainly not
to take something into account is to consider it along with other things

account *VERB* (**accounts**, **accounting**, **accounted**)
to account for something is to be an explanation of it • *They lost the game and that accounts for their sad feelings.*

accountant *NOUN* (**accountants**)
a person whose job is to write and organize the money accounts of a person or organization
▷ **accountancy** *NOUN* accountancy is the job an accountant does

accumulate *VERB* (**accumulates**, **accumulating**, **accumulated**)
1 to accumulate things is to collect them or pile them up **2** things accumulate when they form a heap or pile

accumulation *NOUN*
1 a heap or pile, a collection **2** accumulating things

accuracy *NOUN*
accuracy is being exactly right or correct

accurate *ADJECTIVE*
correct, done exactly and carefully • *She does accurate work.*
▷ **accurately** *ADVERB* to do something accurately is to do it carefully and exactly • *You have to measure the room accurately.*

accusation *NOUN* (**accusations**)
a statement accusing someone of something

accuse *VERB* (**accuses**, **accusing**, **accused**)
to accuse someone is to say that they did something wrong

accustomed *ADJECTIVE*
to be accustomed to something is to be used to it • *I am accustomed to having lunch at twelve o'clock.*

ace *NOUN* (**aces**)
1 the four aces in a pack of cards are the cards with an A in the corner and a large emblem of the suit in the centre **2** someone or something very clever or skilful

ace *ADJECTIVE*
(*informal*) very good or clever

ache *NOUN* (**aches**)
a dull steady pain

ache *VERB* (**aches**, **aching**, **ached**)
to ache is to feel a dull steady pain

achieve *VERB* (**achieves**, **achieving**, **achieved**)
to achieve something is to succeed in doing it or getting it

achievement *NOUN* (**achievements**)
something someone has succeeded in doing
• *Winning the prize was a fine achievement.*

acid *NOUN* (**acids**)
a substance that contains hydrogen and causes chemical change. Acids are the opposite of alkalis

acid *ADJECTIVE*
sour or bitter to taste

> WORD FAMILY
> Something that is **acidic** contains a lot of acid; **acidity** is the level of acid in a substance.

acid rain *NOUN*
rain that contains harmful acids because it has mixed with waste gases from the air

acknowledge *VERB* (**acknowledges**, **acknowledging**, **acknowledged**)
1 to acknowledge something is to admit that it is true **2** to acknowledge a letter is to say that you have received it **3** to acknowledge a debt or favour is to say you are grateful for it

acknowledgement *NOUN* (**acknowledgements**)
1 something that you admit or confess **2** thanks you give for a letter you have received • *When we receive your form we will send you an acknowledgement.*

acne *NOUN* (*say* **ak**- ni)
a skin disease with red pimples on the face. It is common among teenagers

acorn *NOUN* (**acorns**)
the seed of an oak tree; it is oval with a stem ending in the shape of a cup

acoustic *ADJECTIVE* (*say* a- **koo**- stik)
1 to do with sound or hearing **2** an acoustic guitar or other musical instrument uses its own shape to make the sound, and does not have an electrical amplifier

acoustics *PLURAL NOUN* (*say* a- **koo**- stiks)
1 the acoustics of a place are the qualities that make it good or bad for sound **2** (*singular noun*) the science of sound

acquaint *VERB* (**acquaints**, **acquainting**, **acquainted**)
1 to acquaint someone with something is to tell them something about it, so they know what it is **2** to be acquainted with someone is to know them slightly

acquaintance *NOUN* (**acquaintances**)
someone you know slightly
to make someone's acquaintance is to get to know them

acquire *VERB* (**acquires**, **acquiring**, **acquired**)
to acquire something is to obtain it, usually with some effort or difficulty

acquisition *NOUN* (**acquisitions**)
something that you buy or that someone gives you. Usually it is something valuable or interesting

acquit *VERB* (**acquits**, **acquitting**, **acquitted**)
to acquit someone is to decide that they are not guilty of a crime, especially in a law trial
to acquit yourself well is to do a job or piece of work well

acquittal *NOUN* (**acquittals**)
the decision of a jury or judge that someone is not guilty of a crime

acre *NOUN* (**acres**) (*say* **ay**- ker)
an acre is the area of a piece of land containing 4,840 square yards

acrobat *NOUN* (**acrobats**) (*say* **ak**- ro- bat)
an entertainer who gives displays of jumping and balancing
▷ **acrobatic** *ADJECTIVE*
to do with an acrobat; like what an acrobat does • *They were amazed at her acrobatic skills.*

acrobatics *PLURAL NOUN*
exercises of jumping and balancing that an acrobat does.

acronym *NOUN* (**acronyms**) (*say* **ak**- ro- nim)
a word or name that is formed from the first letters of other words, for example *UFO* is an acronym of *unidentified flying object*

across *ADVERB & PREPOSITION*
1 from one side of something to the other • *The table measures 1.5 metres across.* **2** to the other side of something • *How can we get across the busy road?*

acrylic *ADJECTIVE*
an acrylic fibre is one that is made from an organic acid

act *NOUN* (**acts**)
1 something that someone does **2** an individual performance in a programme of entertainment, for example a juggling act or a comic act **3** one of the main sections of a play or opera **4** a new law that a government makes
to put on an act is to show off or pretend to be something that you are not

act *VERB* (**acts**, **acting**, **acted**)
1 to act is to do something useful or necessary • *We need to act straight away.* **2** to act stupid or act clever is to behave stupidly or cleverly **3** to act in a play or film is to take part in it

action *NOUN* (**actions**)
1 an action is something that someone does **2** action is fighting in a battle • *He was killed in action.* **3** the action of a gun or a musical instrument is the part that makes it work
out of action not working properly
to take action is to do something decisive

activate *VERB* (**activates**, **activating**, **activated**)
to activate a machine or device is to start it working

active *ADJECTIVE*
1 busy, taking part in lots of activities **2** doing things, working • *an active volcano* **3** (*in grammar*) describing a verb in which the subject does the action, for example in the sentence *We made a cake*, the subject is *We* and *made* is an active verb

activity *NOUN* (**activities**)
1 activity is doing things **2** an activity is something special that someone does • *They enjoy outdoor activities.*

actor *NOUN* (**actors**)
someone who takes part in a play or film

actress *NOUN* (**actresses**)
a girl or woman who takes part in a play or film

actual *ADJECTIVE*
really there or really happening

actually *ADVERB*
really, in fact • *Actually, I think you are wrong.*

acupuncture *NOUN*
acupuncture is a way of curing disease or taking away pain by pricking parts of the body with needles

acute *ADJECTIVE*
1 sharp or intense • *She has an acute pain.* **2** severe • *The explorers were suffering from an acute shortage of food.* **3** clever, quick to understand something **4** an acute accent is the mark ´ put over a letter, as in *resumé* **5** an acute angle is an angle of less than 90 degrees

AD
short for *Anno Domini*, used with dates that come after the birth of Jesus Christ, for example AD 1492 is the year Columbus reached America

Adam's apple *NOUN* (**Adam's apples**)
the lump at the front of a man's neck

adapt *VERB* (**adapts**, **adapting**, **adapted**)
1 to adapt something is to change it so you can use it for something different **2** to adapt to something is to make yourself cope with it • *They adapted to life in the country very quickly.*
▷ **adaptation** *NOUN* an adaptation is something someone has adapted, for example a book they have made into a film

adaptable *ADJECTIVE*
able to adapt to or become suitable for different things

adaptor *NOUN* (**adaptors**)
a device for connecting different pieces of equipment

add *VERB* (**adds**, **adding**, **added**)
1 to add one number to another is to put them together to get a bigger number **2** to add one thing to another is to mix them together, for

example the different things in a recipe
to add up is what numbers do to make a bigger number, called a total; **to add up** (*informal*) also means to make sense • *The things they said just don't add up.*
to add numbers up is to make them into a bigger number

adder *NOUN* (**adders**)
a small poisonous snake

addict *NOUN* (**addicts**)
someone with a habit they can't give up, for example taking drugs or drinking alcohol

> WORD FAMILY
> Someone who is **addicted** to a habit can't give it up • *He was addicted to chocolate*; something is **addictive** when people can't give it up • *They were taking addictive drugs.*

addiction *NOUN* (**addictions**)
a habit that someone can't give up

addition *NOUN* (**additions**)
1 addition is the process of adding numbers together, or adding other things **2** an addition is something or someone that has been added • *James is an addition to the class.*
in addition also, as well

additional *ADJECTIVE*
extra, added on

additive *NOUN* (**additives**)
something that is added to food or to something else in small amounts

address *NOUN* (**addresses**)
1 the details of the place where someone lives • *My address is 29 High Street, Newtown* **2** (*in computing*) a set of words and symbols that tells you where you can find something using a computer, for example on the Internet • *What's your email address?* **3** a speech

address *VERB* (**addresses, addressing, addressed**)
1 to address a letter or parcel is to write the address on it before sending it **2** to address a person or a group of people is to make an important remark or speech to them • *The judge addressed the prisoner*

adenoids *PLURAL NOUN*
your adenoids are the spongy flesh at the back of your nose, which can become swollen making it difficult to breathe

adequate *ADJECTIVE*
enough, sufficient

adhere *VERB* (**adheres, adhering, adhered**)
1 to adhere to something is to stick to it • *The stamp would not adhere easily to the envelope.* **2** you adhere to a promise or rule when you keep it • *Each country must adhere to the decisions of the majority.*

adhesive *NOUN* (**adhesives**)
something such as glue that you use to stick things together

adhesive *ADJECTIVE*
causing things to stick together

Adi Granth *NOUN* (*say* ah- di **grunt**)
the holy book of the Sikhs

adjacent *ADJECTIVE*
near or next to something • *Her house is adjacent to the shop.*

adjective *NOUN* (**adjectives**)
a word that describes a noun or adds to its meaning, for example *big*, *honest*, *red*

> ADJECTIVES
> Adjectives are words that describe a noun and add to its meaning, such as ***large*** and ***yellow***. Adjectives can come before a noun *a* ***large*** *balloon* (*a* ***yellow*** *bird*) or they can come after a verb like ***be*** or ***become*** or ***grow*** *The balloon grew* ***large***. *The bird was* ***yellow***.Some adjectives describe a quality that something has (*a* ***long*** *film*) and some adjectives give your opinion about something (*a* ***brilliant*** *film*). You can make **comparative** and **superlative** forms of some adjectives. Comparative adjectives are useful when you want to compare two things (the ***higher*** mountain, the ***more careful*** person). Superlative adjectives are useful when you want to say that something is the most of whatever it is (the ***highest*** mountain, the ***most careful*** person). Look also at the panel on **Comparatives and superlatives**.

adjust *VERB* (**adjusts, adjusting, adjusted**)
1 to adjust something is to change it slightly or change its position **2** to adjust to something is to try to get used to it • *They found it hard to adjust to life in the city.*

adjustment *NOUN* (**adjustments**)
a small change you make to something

ad lib *ADJECTIVE & ADVERB*
without any rehearsal or preparation

ad lib *VERB* (**ad libs, ad libbing, ad libbed**)
to ad lib is to say or do something without any rehearsal or preparation

administer *VERB* (**administers, administering, administered**)
1 to administer a country is to govern it **2** to administer something like a medicine is to give it to someone

administrate *VERB* (**administrates, administrating, administrated**)
to administrate a country or business is to govern it or run it
▷ **administrative** *ADJECTIVE* to do with running a business or country • *the chief education officer and his administrative staff*
▷ **administrator** *NOUN* someone who helps to run a business or organization

administration *NOUN* (**administrations**)
1 administration is running a business or governing a country **2** in the USA, an administration is a government that is holding office • *the Bush administration*

admirable *ADJECTIVE*
worth admiring; excellent • *You have done an admirable piece of work.*
▷ **admirably** *ADVERB* in an admirable way • *The note is written in admirably clear handwriting.*

admiral *NOUN* (**admirals**)
an officer of the highest rank in the navy

admiration *NOUN*
admiration is a feeling you have for someone or something when you think they are very good or very beautiful • *He was filled with admiration for his sister.*

admire *VERB* (**admires, admiring, admired**)
1 to admire someone or something is to think they are very good or very beautiful **2** to admire something is also to look at it and enjoy it • *They went to the top of the hill to admire the view.*

admirer *NOUN* (**admirers**)
someone who thinks that a particular person or thing is very good or beautiful • *Madonna has many admirers.*

admission *NOUN* (**admissions**)
1 admission is being allowed to go into a place • *Admission to the show is by ticket only.* **2** an admission is something that someone admits or confesses • *He is guilty by his own admission.*

admit *VERB* (**admits, admitting, admitted**)
1 to admit someone is to let them come into a place **2** to admit something is to say that it has happened or that you have done it

admittance *NOUN*
admittance is being allowed to go into a private place

admittedly *ADVERB*
as an agreed fact; without denying it • *Admittedly I was teasing the dog, but I didn't expect it to bite.*

ado *NOUN*
without more ado without wasting any more time

adolescent *NOUN* (**adolescents**)
a young person who is older than a child and not yet an adult, from about 15 to 18
▷ **adolescence** *NOUN* the time between being a child and being an adult

adopt *VERB* (**adopts, adopting, adopted**)
1 to adopt a child is to take them into your family and bring them up as your own **2** to adopt a system or method is to start using it
▷ **adoption** *NOUN* adoption is adopting someone or something

WORD FAMILY
An **adopted** child is one that someone has adopted; **adoptive** parents are parents who have adopted a child.

adorable *ADJECTIVE*
lovely, worth adoring

adore *VERB* (**adores, adoring, adored**)
to adore someone or something is to love them or admire them very much
▷ **adoration** *NOUN* adoration is adoring someone or something

adorn *VERB* (**adorns, adorning, adorned**)
to adorn something is to decorate it or make it pretty
▷ **adornment** *NOUN* adornment is making something pretty

adrenalin *NOUN*
a hormone that stimulates your nervous system and makes you feel ready to do something

adrift *ADVERB & ADJECTIVE*
something such as a boat is adrift when it is loose and drifting about

adult *NOUN* (**adults**)
a fully grown person or animal

adultery *NOUN* (*say* a-**dul**-ter-i)
adultery is having a lover in addition to a husband or wife

advance *NOUN* (**advances**)
1 an advance is a forward movement **2** advance is improvement or progress **3** an advance of money is a loan **4** an advance warning is a warning given beforehand
in advance beforehand

advance *VERB* (**advances, advancing, advanced**)
1 to advance is to move forward **2** to advance is also to make progress

advanced *ADJECTIVE*
1 a long way forward **2** an advanced course or exam is one at a higher level

advantage *NOUN* (**advantages**)
something useful or helpful
to take advantage of someone is to treat them unfairly when they are not likely to complain
to take advantage of something is to make good use of it

Advent *NOUN*
in the Christian Church, the period before Christmas

a b c d e f g h i j k l m n o p q r s t u v w x y z

adventure *NOUN* (**adventures**)
1 an adventure is something exciting or interesting that someone does **2** adventure is doing bold and exciting things • *She enjoys a bit of adventure.*
▷ **adventurous** *ADJECTIVE* an adventuorus person likes to do interesting or exciting things

adverb *NOUN* (**adverbs**)
a word that tells you how or when or where or why something happens. In these sentences, the words in italics are adverbs: They moved *slowly*. Come back *soon*. I *only* want a drink.

> ADVERBS
> Adverbs are words that tell you how, where, when, why, or how often something happens. They often tell you more about a verb. *She climbed **quickly** up the tree.* (tells you how) *'I won! I won!' he said **excitedly**.* (tells you how) ***Tomorrow** we're going to see a film.* (tells you when) *We could hear a lot of noise **outside**.* (tells you where) *Let's go **together**.* (tells you how) *You **always** have the last potato.* (tells you how often) You can often make an adverb by adding the suffix *-ly* to the end of an adjective. For example, the adverb *slowly* comes from the adjective *slow*.

adversary *NOUN* (**adversaries**) (*say* **ad- ver- sa- ri**)
an opponent or enemy

adverse *ADJECTIVE*
not good; harmful • *The drug had adverse effects.*

adversity *NOUN* (**adversities**)
adversity is bad things that happen to someone

advert *NOUN* (**adverts**)
(*informal*) an advertisement

advertise *VERB* (**advertises, advertising, advertised**)
1 to advertise something that you do or that you have made is to praise it in a newspaper or on television so that people will want it **2** to advertise an event is to tell people when it will take place • *Have you advertised the concert?*

advertisement *NOUN* (**advertisements**)
a public notice or short television film that tries to persuade people to buy something

advice *NOUN*
advice is something you say to someone to help them decide what to do

advisable *ADJECTIVE*
sensible, worth doing

advise *VERB* (**advises, advising, advised**)
to advise someone is to tell them what you think they should do

> WORD FAMILY
> Take care not to confuse **advice**, which is a noun, with **advise**, which is a verb. An **adviser** is a person who gives advice, usually as their job; an **advisory** group or service is one that gives people advice.

advocate *NOUN* (**advocates**) (*say* **ad- vo- kat**)
a person who speaks in favour of someone or something

advocate *VERB* (**advocates, advocating, advocated**) (*say* **ad- vo- kayt**)
to advocate something is to speak in favour of it • *We advocate changing the law.*

aerial *NOUN* (**aerials**)
a wire or metal rod for receiving or sending radio or television signals

> BRITISH AND AMERICAN
> In America, the word **antenna** is used.

aerial *ADJECTIVE*
from or in the air, or from aircraft • *They showed us an aerial photograph of our school.*

aerobatics *PLURAL NOUN*
an exciting display by flying aircraft
▷ **aerobatic** *ADJECTIVE* to do with aerobatics • *They went to see an aerobatic display.*

aerobics *PLURAL NOUN*
aerobics are energetic exercises that strengthen your heart and lungs

aeronautics *PLURAL NOUN*
the study of aircraft and flying
▷ **aeronautical** *ADJECTIVE* to do with aeronautics

aeroplane *NOUN* (**aeroplanes**)
a flying machine with wings

> BRITISH AND AMERICAN
> In America, the word **airplane** is also used.

aerosol *NOUN* (**aerosols**)
a device that holds a liquid under pressure and lets it out in a fine spray

aesthetic *ADJECTIVE*
to do with beauty, especially in art or music

affair *NOUN* (**affairs**)
1 something interesting that happens, an event **2** a temporary relationship between two people who are not married to each other **3** someone's affairs are their private business • *She needs to sort out her business affairs.*

affect *VERB* (**affects, affecting, affected**)
to affect someone or something is to cause them to change or to harm them • *The dampness might affect his health.*

> SPELLING
> Take care not to confuse **affect** with **effect**, which is a noun as in *that had a good effect on them.*

affected *ADJECTIVE*
not real, pretended • *'Really, Daisy!' said Chloe, clutching her ears in an affected way. 'You practically deafened me.'* — Jacqueline Wilson, *Sleepovers.*

affection *NOUN* (**affections**)
affection or an affection is love or fondness •*I have a great affection for my nephew.*
▷ **affectionate** *ADJECTIVE* an affectionate person or animal is one that shows love or fondness

affix *NOUN*
(*in grammar*) a prefix or suffix, such as *re-* and *-ness*

afflict *VERB* (**afflicts**, **afflicting**, **afflicted**)
to be afflicted by something unpleasant, like an illness, is to suffer from it
▷ **affliction** *NOUN* a great illness or problem that makes someone suffer

affluence *NOUN* (*say* **af**- loo- ens)
having a lot of money or wealth •*There is more affluence in the bigger cities.*

affluent *ADJECTIVE* (*say* **af**- loo- ent)
having a lot of money or wealth

afford *VERB* (**affords**, **affording**, **afforded**)
1 to be able to afford something is to have enough money to pay for it **2** to be unable to afford the time to do something is not to have enough time for it **3** to afford someone pleasure is to please them

afforestation *NOUN*
the process of covering an area of land with trees

afloat *ADJECTIVE & ADVERB*
floating; on a boat •*Do you enjoy life afloat?*

afraid *ADJECTIVE*
frightened
I'm afraid I am sorry; I regret •*I'm afraid I've burnt the cakes.*

afresh *ADVERB*
again; in a new way •*We must start afresh.*

African *ADJECTIVE*
coming from or to do with Africa

African *NOUN* (**Africans**)
a person from Africa

aft *ADVERB* (*say* ahft)
at the back of a ship or aircraft

after *PREPOSITION & ADVERB*
meaning 'later' or 'later than' •*Come after dinner.* •*I'll do it after.*

> GRAMMAR
> **After** is also used in special ways: •*Will you run after them?* •*After all I did for him, he never thanked me.* •*She was named after her aunt.*

afternoon *NOUN* (**afternoons**)
the time from midday or lunchtime until evening

afterwards *ADVERB*
at a later time

again *ADVERB*
1 once more; another time **2** as before •*You will soon be well again.*
again and again lots of times

against *PREPOSITION*
1 touching or hitting •*He was leaning against the wall.* **2** opposed to, not liking •*Are you against smoking?*

age *NOUN* (**ages**)
1 your age is how old you are **2** an age is a period of history •*the Elizabethan age* **3** age is the last part of someone's life •*She had the wisdom that comes with age.*
ages (*informal*) a long time •*We've been waiting ages.*

age *VERB* (**ages**, **ageing**, **aged**)
to age is to become old

aged *ADJECTIVE*
1 (*say* ayjd) having the age of •*The girl was aged 9.*
2 (*say* **ay**- jid) very old •*We saw an aged man.*

age group *NOUN* (**age groups**)
people who are the same age

agency *NOUN* (**agencies**)
the office or business of someone who organizes things

agenda *NOUN* (**agendas**) (*say* a- **jen**- da)
a list of things that people have to do or talk about, for example at a business meeting

agent *NOUN* (**agents**)
1 someone whose job is to organize things for other people •*We booked our holiday with a travel agent.* **2** a spy •*He is a secret agent.*

aggravate *VERB* (**aggravates**, **aggravating**, **aggravated**)
1 to aggravate something is to make it worse
2 (*informal*) to aggravate someone is to annoy them

aggravation *NOUN*
1 (*informal*) aggravation or an aggravation is something troublesome or annoying
2 aggravation is also making something worse •*the aggravation of the problem*

aggression *NOUN*
starting a war or attack; being aggressive
▷ **aggressor** *NOUN* someone who starts an attack

aggressive *ADJECTIVE*
1 an aggressive person or group of people is one that is likely to attack or use violence **2** an aggressive activity is one that people do with energy and that has a strong effect •*They began an aggressive sales campaign.*

agile *ADJECTIVE*
able to move quickly and easily
▷ **agility** *NOUN* agility is being agile

agitate *VERB* (**agitates**, **agitating**, **agitated**)
1 to agitate someone is to make them feel worried and anxious **2** to agitate is to make a fuss so that something gets done **3** to agitate something is to shake it about
▷ **agitation** *NOUN* agitation is getting worried or anxious •*He could not hide his agitation.*

agitator *NOUN* (**agitators**)
a person who makes a lot of fuss to get something done

agnostic *NOUN* (**agnostics**) (*say* ag- **nos**- tik)
someone who believes that we cannot know if there is a God

ago *ADVERB*
in the past • *She died long ago.*

agonizing *ADJECTIVE*
1 an agonizing pain is one that hurts terribly **2** an agonizing choice or decision is one that you find very difficult to make

agony *NOUN* (**agonies**)
severe pain or suffering

agree *VERB* (**agrees**, **agreeing**, **agreed**)
1 to agree with someone is to think the same as them **2** to agree to do something is to say that you are willing to • *She agreed to go with him.*
3 something agrees with someone when it suits them or does them good • *Spicy food doesn't agree with her.*

agreeable *ADJECTIVE*
1 willing to do something that someone suggests • *We shall go if you are agreeable.* **2** (*rather old use*) pleasant • *It is a very agreeable little place.*

agreement *NOUN* (**agreements**)
1 agreement is thinking the same • *Are we in agreement?* **2** an agreement is an arrangement that people have agreed on

agriculture *NOUN*
agriculture is farming, or growing food on the land
▷ **agricultural** *ADJECTIVE* to do with agriculture

aground *ADVERB*
stuck on the bottom of a river or the sea in shallow water • *The ship has run aground.*

ah *INTERJECTION*
a word you shout out when you are surprised or pleased

ahead *ADVERB*
forwards, in front • *Sheila went ahead to show us the way.*

ahoy *INTERJECTION*
a shout used by sailors to attract attention

aid *NOUN* (**aids**)
1 aid is help you give someone **2** aid is also money or food or other help that a country sends to a poorer country **3** an aid is something that helps someone to do something better • *He was wearing a hearing aid.*
in aid of something or **someone** so as to help them

aid *VERB* (**aids**, **aiding**, **aided**)
to aid someone is to help them

Aids or **AIDS** *NOUN*
a disease caused by a virus, which destroys the body's immunity to other diseases

ailing *ADJECTIVE*
suffering, in a bad way

ailment *NOUN* (**ailments**)
a minor illness

aim *VERB* (**aims**, **aiming**, **aimed**)
1 to aim a gun at someone or something is to point it at them so as to shoot them **2** to aim something like a ball is to throw it or kick it in a particular direction **3** to aim to do something is to try to do it

aim *NOUN* (**aims**)
1 a person's aim is what they intend to do **2** aim is also pointing a weapon in a particular direction

aimless *ADJECTIVE*
not having any definite aim or purpose • *He led an aimless life.*
▷ **aimlessly** *ADVERB* to do something aimlessly is to do it without knowing why or what for • *They wandered around aimlessly.*

air *NOUN* (**airs**)
1 air is the mixture of gases which surrounds the earth and which everyone breathes **2** an air is a tune **3** an air of mystery or secrecy is a feeling that things are mysterious or secret
to go by air is to travel in an aeroplane
to be in the air is to be just an idea, and not something certain • *Our plans are still in the air.*
to be on the air is to be on the radio or television
to put on airs is to behave grandly, as if you are important

air *VERB* (**airs**, **airing**, **aired**)
1 to air clothes or washing is to put them in a warm place to finish drying **2** to air a room is to let fresh air into it **3** to air views or opinions is to say them so that people know them

airborne *ADJECTIVE*
1 flying in an aircraft **2** carried by the air • *an airborne virus*

air-conditioning *NOUN*
a system for controlling the temperature and freshness of the air in a building, so that it is kept cool in hot weather and warm in cold weather
▷ **air-conditioned** *ADJECTIVE* an air-conditioned building or room is one that has air-conditioning

aircraft *NOUN* (**aircraft**)
an aeroplane or a helicopter • *The two aircraft passed each other over the Atlantic.*

aircraft carrier *NOUN* (**aircraft carriers**)
a large ship with a flat deck on which aircraft can take off and land

Airedale *NOUN* (**Airedales**)
a large terrier dog with rough hair

airfield *NOUN* (**airfields**)
a place where aircraft can take off and land

air force *NOUN* (**air forces**)
the part of a country's fighting force that uses aircraft

airgun *NOUN* (**airguns**)
a gun that works with compressed air

airline *NOUN* (**airlines**)
a company that takes people to places by aircraft.

airliner *NOUN* (**airliners**)
a large aircraft for carrying passengers

airlock *NOUN* (**airlocks**)
1 a bubble of air that forms in liquid and stops it flowing through a pipe **2** a compartment with airtight doors at each end

airmail *NOUN*
airmail is mail that is sent by air

airman *NOUN* (**airmen**)
a man who is a member of an air force or one of the crew of an aircraft

airport *NOUN* (**airports**)
a place where aircraft land and take off, with passenger terminals and other buildings

air raid *NOUN* (**air raids**)
an attack by bombs dropped from aircraft

airship *NOUN* (**airships**)
a large balloon with engines, designed to carry passengers or cargo

airstream *NOUN* (**airstreams**)
a current of air, especially one that affects the weather

airstrip *NOUN* (**airstrips**)
a strip of land prepared for aircraft to take off and land

airtight *ADJECTIVE*
not letting air get in or out

airy *ADJECTIVE* (**airier**, **airiest**)
1 with plenty of fresh air **2** vague and insincere • *They were just airy promises.* **3** like air
▷ **airily** *ADVERB* to do something airily is to do it in a casual or light-hearted way • *He replied airily that he didn't want to know.*

aisle *NOUN* (**aisles**) (*rhymes with* **mile**)
1 a part at the side of a church **2** a passage between or beside rows of seats or pews

ajar *ADVERB & ADJECTIVE*
slightly open • *Please leave the door ajar.*

akela *NOUN* (**akelas**) (*say* ah- kay- la)
an adult leader of a group of Cub Scouts

alarm *VERB* (**alarms**, **alarming**, **alarmed**)
to alarm someone is to make them frightened or anxious

alarm *NOUN* (**alarms**)
1 a warning sound or signal **2** a feeling of fear or anxiety • *He cried out in alarm.* **3** an alarm clock

alarm clock *NOUN* (**alarm clocks**)
a clock with a loud ring or bleep, which can be set to wake someone who is asleep

alas *INTERJECTION*
(*old use*) something you say when you are sad

albatross *NOUN* (**albatrosses**)
a large seabird with long wings

album *NOUN* (**albums**)
1 a book in which you keep things like photographs or stamps or autographs **2** a collection of songs on a CD, record, or tape

alcohol *NOUN*
1 a colourless liquid made by fermenting sugar or starch **2** drinks containing this liquid (for example beer, wine, gin), which affects people's behaviour and can make them drunk if they have too much

alcoholic *ADJECTIVE*
containing alcohol

alcoholic *NOUN* (**alcoholics**)
someone who is constantly ill from drinking too much alcohol
▷ **alcoholism** *NOUN* alcoholism is an illness caused by drinking too much alcohol

alcove *NOUN* (**alcoves**)
a part of a room where the wall is set back from the main part

ale *NOUN* (**ales**)
ale is a kind of beer, especially when it is made and stored in a traditional way

alert *ADJECTIVE*
watching for something; ready to act

alert *VERB* (**alerts**, **alerting**, **alerted**)
to alert someone to a danger or problem is to warn them about it

alert *NOUN* (**alerts**)
an alarm
on the alert on the lookout for danger or attack

A level *NOUN* (**A levels**)
a higher standard of examination that is taken after the GCSE, especially by pupils who want to go to university

algebra *NOUN* (*say* al- ji- bra)
mathematics in which letters and symbols are used to represent numbers
▷ **algebraic** *ADJECTIVE* to do with algebra, or using algebra

alias *NOUN* (**aliases**) (*say* ay- li- as)
a false or different name that someone uses instead of their real name

alias *ADVERB*
also named • *Clark Kent, alias Superman*

alibi *NOUN* (**alibis**) (*say* al- i- by)
evidence that someone accused of a crime was not there when the crime was committed

alien *NOUN* (**aliens**) (*say* ay- li- en)
1 someone who is not a citizen of the country where they are living **2** in science fiction, a being from another world

alien *ADJECTIVE*
1 foreign **2** not in keeping, quite unlike • *Lying was alien to his nature.*

alienate *VERB* (**alienates**, **alienating**, **alienated**)
to alienate someone is to make them unfriendly to you
▷ **alienation** *NOUN* alienation is making someone unfriendly

alight *ADJECTIVE*
on fire, burning

alike *ADJECTIVE*
similar, like each other

alike *ADVERB*
in the same way • *He treats everybody alike.*

alimentary canal *NOUN* (**alimentary canals**)
the tube along which food passes through the body

alive *ADJECTIVE*
living, existing • *Is he alive?*
alive to something well aware of it • *She is alive to all the dangers.*

alkali *NOUN* (**alkalis**) (*say* **al**- ka- ly)
a substance that neutralizes acids or that combines with acids to form salts

> **WORD FAMILY**
> Something that is **alkaline** contains an alkali; the **alkalinity** of something is the amount of an alkali it contains.

all *DETERMINER, ADVERB & NOUN*
meaning 'everything' or 'everyone' • *That is all I know.* • *All my books are in the desk.* • *She was dressed all in white.*
to be all in (*informal*) is to be exhausted • *I'm all in after that run.*
to do something all out (*informal*) is to use all your ability to do it • *Go all out to win.*
to be all there (*informal*) is to be intelligent or clever
all the same nevertheless; making no difference • *It was raining but I went out all the same.*

Allah
the Muslim name of God

all-clear *NOUN*
a signal that a danger has passed

allegation *NOUN* (**allegations**) (*say* a- li- **gay**- shun)
you make an allegation when you accuse someone of doing something wrong.

allege *VERB* (**alleges**, **alleging**, **alleged**) (*say* a- **lej**)
to allege that someone has done something is to accuse them of it, usually without proof • *He alleged that I stole his ring.*

allegedly *ADVERB* (*say* a- **lej**- idli)
something is allegedly true when there is no proof but someone says it is • *The man allegedly threatened them with a kinfe.*

allegiance *NOUN* (**allegiances**) (*say* a- **lee**- jans)
loyalty shown to a person or organization

allegory *NOUN* (**allegories**)
a story or poem with made-up people and places that are meant to stand for real people and places
▷ **allegorical** *ADJECTIVE* an allegorical story or poem is one that uses allegory

allergy *NOUN*
a condition that some people have that makes their body react badly to things they eat or drink or touch or breathe in, for example dust, milk, or some kinds of food
▷ **allergic** *ADJECTIVE* someone is allergic to something if they become ill or uncomfortable when they eat it or touch it • *She must be allergic to goat's milk.*

alley *NOUN* (**alleys**)
1 a narrow street or passage **2** a place where you can play at skittles or tenpin bowling

alliance *NOUN* (**alliances**)
an agreement between countries to support each other and have the same enemies

allied *ADJECTIVE*
having an alliance; on the same side • *The allied countries declared war.*

alligator *NOUN* (**alligators**)
a large reptile like a crocodile

all-in *ADJECTIVE*
including or allowing everything • *This is the all-in price.*

alliteration *NOUN*
alliteration is when the same letter or sound occurs several times in a group of words, for special effect, e.g. *sing a song of sixpence*

allot *VERB* (**allots**, **allotting**, **allotted**)
to allot shares or jobs is to give them to various people

allotment *NOUN* (**allotments**)
a small rented piece of ground used for growing vegetables

allow *VERB* (**allows**, **allowing**, **allowed**)
1 to allow someone to do something is to let them do it • *We will allow you to leave now.* • *Smoking is not allowed.* **2** to allow an amount of money is to provide it for some reason • *She was allowed $7 for books.*

allowance *NOUN* (**allowances**)
a sum of money given regularly to someone
to make allowances is to be considerate • *We must make allowances for his age.*

alloy *NOUN* (**alloys**)
a metal formed from a mixture of other metals

all right *ADJECTIVE*
satisfactory; in good condition • *She fixed my bike, so it's all right.*

> **GRAMMAR**
> You can also use **all right** as an exclamation • *All right, I'm coming!*

all-round *ADJECTIVE*
having many skills • *She's a good all-round athlete.*
▷ **all-rounder** *NOUN* a person with many skills

ally *NOUN* (**allies**) (*say* al- I)
1 a country in alliance with another country **2** a person who helps or cooperates with you

ally *VERB* (**allies**, **allying**, **allied**)
to ally oneself with someone else is to form an alliance with them

almighty *ADJECTIVE*
1 having a lot of power **2** (*informal*) very great • *They were making an almighty din.*

almond *NOUN* (**almonds**) (*say* **ah**- mond)
an oval nut that you can eat

almost *ADVERB*
very close to but not quite • *I am almost ready.*

aloft *ADVERB*
high up • *The sailors climbed aloft.*

alone *ADJECTIVE & ADVERB*
without any other people or other things • *The food alone took us all morning to prepare.*

along *PREPOSITION & ADVERB*
1 from one end of something to the other **2** on; onwards • *Move along, please!* **3** accompanying someone • *I have brought my brother along.*

alongside *PREPOSITION & ADVERB*
next to something

aloud *ADVERB*
in a voice that can be heard

alphabet *NOUN* (**alphabets**)
the letters used in a language, usually arranged in a set order
▷ **alphabetical** *ADJECTIVE* to do with the alphabet
▷ **alphabetically** *ADVERB* something is arranged alphabetically when it is in the order of the alphabet

> ALPHABETICAL ORDER
> Many reference books are organized in alphabetical order. This can make it easier to find information quickly, especially if you can find the letter quickly. Some people think of the alphabet as divided into quarters, or quartiles: *a-f*, *g-m*, *n-s*, and *t-z*. You can use these quartiles to predict where to find words in an alphabetically ordered book.

alpine *ADJECTIVE*
to do with the Alps in Switzerland

already *ADVERB*
by or before now • *I've already told you once.*

Alsatian *NOUN* (**Alsatians**) (*say* al- **say**- shan)
a large strong dog

> BRITISH AND AMERICAN
> In America, the name **German shepherd** is used.

also *ADVERB*
as an extra, besides • *We also need some bread.*

altar *NOUN* (**altars**)
a table or raised surface used in religious ceremonies

alter *VERB* (**alters**, **altering**, **altered**)
to alter something is to change it
▷ **alteration** *NOUN* a change you make to something

alternate *ADJECTIVE* (*say* ol- **ter**- nat)
1 happening on every other one • *In the Doldrums, laughter is frowned upon and smiling is permitted only on alternate Thursdays.* — Norton Juster, *The Phantom Tollbooth.* **2** coming in turns, one after the other • *alternate laughter and tears*
▷ **alternately** *ADVERB* one after the other in turn • *The weather was alternately fine and wet.*

> SPELLING
> Take care not to confuse **alternate** with **alternative. Alternative** means that you have a choice between two or more things.

alternate *VERB* (**alternates**, **alternating**, **alternated**) (*say* **ol**- ter- nayt)
to alternate is to happen in turns

alternating current *NOUN*
electric current that continually reverses its direction

alternative *NOUN* (**alternatives**) (*say* ol- **ter**- na- tiv)
something you can choose instead of something else • *If you don't like this book there is an alternative.*

alternative *ADJECTIVE*
for you to choose instead of something else • *The cafe has an alternative menu for vegetarians.*

> SPELLING
> Take care not to confuse **alternative** with the adjective **alternate**. **Alternate** means that first one thing and then the other happens.

alternator *NOUN* (**alternators**)
a generator that produces alternating current

although *CONJUNCTION*
in spite of the fact that • *Although they like parties, they prefer a trip to the zoo.*

altitude *NOUN* (**altitudes**)
the height of something, especially above sea level

alto *NOUN* (**altos**)
1 a female singer with a low voice **2** a male singer with a voice higher than a tenor's

> OTHER WORD
> The female singer is also called a **contralto**.

altogether *ADVERB*
1 completely • *He is altogether wrong.* **2** on the whole • *Altogether, it wasn't a bad holiday.*

> SPELLING
> Take care not to confuse **altogether** with **all together**, which means together in a group • *They wanted to be all together for the photographs*

aluminium *NOUN*
a silver-coloured metal that is light in weight

always *ADVERB*
1 all the time, at all times **2** often, constantly • *You are always crying.* **3** whatever happens • *You can always sleep on the floor.*

am
1st person singular present tense of **be**

a.m.
short for Latin *ante meridiem* which means 'before midday'

amalgamate *VERB* (**amalgamates, amalgamating, amalgamated**)
1 to amalgamate things is to mix them or join them together **2** to amalgamate is to join together to form one thing

amalgamation *NOUN* (**amalgamations**)
1 amalgamation is mixing or joining things together **2** an amalgamation is a mixture of things put together

amateur *NOUN* (**amateurs**) (*say* **am**- a- ter)
someone who does something because they like it, without being paid for it

amateur *ADJECTIVE*
done by amateurs

amateurish *ADJECTIVE*
1 not done very well • *It was an amateurish piece of work.* **2** not very good at something • *He was rather amateurish at swimming.*

amaze *VERB* (**amazes, amazing, amazed**)
to amaze someone is to surprise them greatly
▷ **amazement** *NOUN* amazement is a feeling of great surprise

ambassador *NOUN* (**ambassadors**)
someone sent to a foreign country to represent their own government

amber *NOUN*
1 a hard, clear, yellowish substance used for making ornaments **2** a yellowish colour, the one used in traffic lights as a signal for caution

ambiguity *NOUN* (**ambiguities**)
1 ambiguity is uncertainty about what something means **2** an ambiguity is something that has more than one possible meaning

ambiguous *ADJECTIVE*
having more than one possible meaning, uncertain • *His reply was ambiguous.*

ambition *NOUN* (**ambitions**)
1 ambition is a strong desire to be successful in life **2** an ambition is something you want to do very much • *His ambition is to run his own airline.*

ambitious *ADEJCTIVE*
1 an ambitious person wants very much to be successful in life **2** an ambitious idea or plan is difficult or challenging

amble *VERB* (**ambles, ambling, ambled**)
to amble along is to walk slowly

ambulance *NOUN* (**ambulances**)
a vehicle for carrying sick or injured people

ambush *NOUN* (**ambushes**)
a surprise attack from a hidden place

ambush *VERB* (**ambushes, ambushing, ambushed**)
to ambush someone is to attack them suddenly from a hidden place

amen *INTERJECTION*
a word used by Christians at the end of a prayer or hymn, meaning 'let it be so'

amend *VERB* (**amends, amending, amended**)
to amend something like a piece of writing is to change or improve it
▷ **amendment** *NOUN* a change to a piece of writing or a law

amenity *NOUN* (**amenities**)
a pleasant or useful feature that a place has, such as a park, a shopping centre, or a swimming pool

American *ADJECTIVE*
coming from America, or to do with America

American *NOUN* (**Americans**)
a person from America

amiable *ADJECTIVE*
friendly, good-tempered
▷ **amiability** *NOUN* friendliness
▷ **amiably** *ADVERB* in a pleasant and friendly way

amicable *ADJECTIVE*
friendly
▷ **amicably** *ADVERB* in a friendly way

amid or **amidst** *PREPOSITION*
in the middle of, among

amidships *ADVERB*
in the middle of a ship

amino acid *NOUN* (**amino acids**)
an acid found in proteins

ammeter *NOUN* (**ammeters**)
an instrument for measuring electric current

ammonia *NOUN*
a gas or liquid with a strong smell

ammunition *NOUN*
bullets, bombs, and other explosive objects used in fighting

amnesty *NOUN* (**amnesties**)
a decision to pardon people who have broken the law

amoeba *NOUN* (**amoebas**) (*say* a- **mee**- ba)
a tiny creature made of one cell. It can change shape and split itself in two

among or **amongst** *PREPOSITION*
1 surrounded by, in the middle of • *She was hiding among the bushes.* **2** between • *Let's divide the money amongst ourselves.*

amount *NOUN* (**amounts**)
a quantity or total

amount *VERB* (**amounts**, **amounting**, **amounted**)
to amount to something is to reach it as a total • *The bill amounted to $25.*

ampere *NOUN* (**amperes**) (*say* am- pair)
a unit for measuring the rate of flow of an electric current

ampersand *NOUN* (**ampersands**)
the sign &, which means 'and'

amphibian *NOUN*
1 an animal that can live on land and in water **2** a vehicle that can travel on land and in water
▷ **amphibious** *ADJECTIVE* an amphibious animal or vehicle is able to live or travel on land and in water

ample *ADJECTIVE* (**ampler**, **amplest**)
1 large, having plenty of space • *This car has an ample boot.* **2** more than enough • *We had ample provisions.*
▷ **amply** *ADVERB* generously; with as much as you need or even more • *They were amply rewarded.*

amplifier *NOUN* (**amplifiers**)
an electronic device for making music or other sounds louder

amplify *VERB* (**amplifies**, **amplifying**, **amplified**)
1 to amplify sounds is to make them louder or stronger **2** to amplify something you say is to give more details about it
▷ **amplification** *NOUN* amplification is making voices or other sounds louder

amputate *VERB* (**amputates**, **amputating**, **amputated**)
to amputate an arm or a leg is to cut it off when it is diseased
▷ **amputation** *NOUN* amputation is cutting off an arm or a leg

amuse *VERB* (**amuses**, **amusing**, **amused**)
1 to amuse someone is to make them laugh or smile **2** to amuse yourself is to find pleasant things to do

amusement *NOUN* (**amusements**)
1 an amusement is something that amuses you
2 amusement is being amused; laughing or smiling

amusing *ADJECTIVE*
making you laugh or smile • *It was an amusing story.*

an *DETERMINER* (called the *indefinite article*)
a word used instead of **a** when the next word begins with a vowel-sound or a silent **h** • *Take an apple.* • *You can hire boats for $3 an hour.*

anaemia *NOUN* (*say* a- nee- mi- a)
a poor condition of the blood that makes someone look pale
▷ **anaemic** *ADJECTIVE* an anaemic person suffers from anaemia

anaesthesia *NOUN* (*say* an- iss- thee- zi- a)
having no feeling of pain

anaesthetic *NOUN* (**anaesthetics**) (*say* an- iss- thet- ik)
a drug or gas that makes you unable to feel pain

anaesthetize *VERB* (**anaesthetizes**, **anaesthetizing**, **anaesthetized**) (*say* an- ees- thit- ize)
to anaesthetize a person or an animal is to give them an anaesthetic
▷ **anaesthetist** *NOUN* a doctor who gives patients things to make them stop feeling pain

anagram *NOUN* (**anagrams**)
a word or phrase made by rearranging the letters of another word or phrase, for example *carthorse* is an anagram of *orchestra*

analogue *ADJECTIVE*
an analogue clock or watch has hands and a dial to indicate numbers (the opposite of *digital*)

analogy *NOUN* (**analogies**)
a comparison or similarity between two things that are fairly like each other • *There is an analogy between the human heart and a pump.*
▷ **analogous** *ADJECTIVE* two things are analogous when they are like each other in some way

> ANALOGY
> Analogy is especially useful when you are trying to spell a word. For example, you can use the analogy with *catch* if you want to spell the word *hatch*. Knowing how to spell *was* can help you to spell *wasp*.

analyse *VERB* (**analyses**, **analysing**, **analysed**)
1 to analyse something is to examine it carefully
2 to analyse a substance is to divide it into its parts

analysis *NOUN* (**analyses**)
a detailed study or examination of something

analyst *NOUN* (**analysts**)
a person who analyses things and works out the best ways of doing them

anarchist *NOUN* (**anarchists**)
someone who thinks that governments and laws are bad and should be abolished
▷ **anarchism** *NOUN* anarchism is having no government or laws

anarchy *NOUN*
1 anarchy is having no government or controls, leading to a breakdown in law and order
2 complete disorder or confusion

anatomy *NOUN*
the study of the parts of the body
▷ **anatomical** *ADJECTIVE* to do with anatomy

ancestor *NOUN* (**ancestors**)
a person who lived in the past and was in the same family as someone alive now

> WORD FAMILY
> An **ancestral** home is one that has belonged to a family for a long time; a person's **ancestry** is the list of all their ancestors.

anchor *NOUN* (**anchors**)
a heavy object joined to a ship by a chain or rope and dropped to the bottom of the sea to stop the ship from moving

anchorage *NOUN* (**anchorages**)
a place where ships can stay, held by their anchors

ancient *ADJECTIVE*
1 belonging to times that were long ago **2** very old • *They came from an ancient family.*

and *CONJUNCTION*
linking words and phrases • *We had cakes and lemonade.* • *Touch that and you'll get burnt.* • *Go and buy a pen.*

anecdote *NOUN* (**anecdotes**)
a short amusing or interesting story about a real person or thing

anemone *NOUN* (**anemones**) (*say* a- nem- on- i)
1 a small flower with the shape of a cup **2** a sea anemone

angel *NOUN* (**angels**)
1 a being that some people believe in, who is a messenger or attendant of God **2** a very kind or beautiful person

angelic *ADJECTIVE*
kind and beautiful, like an angel

anger *NOUN*
a strong feeling that you do not like what someone has said or done, making you want to quarrel or fight with them

angle *NOUN* (**angles**)
1 the space between two lines or surfaces that meet **2** a point of view • *What is your angle on this?*

angle *VERB* (**angles, angling, angled**)
1 to angle something is to put it in a slanting position **2** to angle news or a story is to tell it in a special way • *The report was angled so that the robbers looked like heroes.*

angler *NOUN* (**anglers**)
someone who fishes with a fishing rod

Anglican *ADJECTIVE*
belonging to the Church of England

Anglican *NOUN* (**Anglicans**)
a member of the Church of England

Anglo-Saxon *NOUN* (**Anglo-Saxons**)
1 an English person, especially of the time before the Norman Conquest in 1066 **2** the old form of English spoken before 1066

angry *ADJECTIVE* (**angrier, angriest**)
feeling or showing anger
▷ **angrily** *ADVERB* to say something angrily is to be angry when saying it • *He spoke angrily.*

anguish *NOUN*
great suffering or unhappiness
▷ **anguished** *ADJECTIVE* suffering or unhappy

angular *ADJECTIVE*
1 having sharp corners **2** bony • *She has a thin, angular face.*

animal *NOUN* (**animals**)
a living thing that can move and feel

> **MEANING**
> Strictly speaking, humans are animals, but the word **animal** is normally used to mean creatures that are not humans.

animate *ADJECTIVE* (*say* an- im- at)
having life

animated *ADJECTIVE*
1 lively and excited **2** an animated film is one made by photographing a series of still pictures and showing them rapidly one after another, so they appear to move

animation *NOUN*
1 being lively or excited **2** a way of making films from still pictures so they appear to move

animosity *NOUN* (**animosities**)
a feeling of being an enemy towards someone • *There was a lot of animosity in his voice.*

aniseed *NOUN*
a seed with a strong sweet taste like liquorice

ankle *NOUN* (**ankles**)
the part of your leg where it is joined to your foot

annex *VERB* (**annexes, annexing, annexed**) (*say* a- neks)
1 to annex something is to add it to something larger **2** to annex territory is to take it from someone else and add it to your own

annexe *NOUN* (**annexes**) (*say* an- eks)
a building added to a larger building

annihilate *VERB* (**annihilates, annihilating, annihilated**) (*say* a- ny- il- ayt)
to annihilate something is to destroy it completely
▷ **annihilation** *NOUN* annihilation is destroying something completely

anniversary *NOUN* (**anniversaries**)
a day when you remember something special that happened on the same date in an earlier year

announce *VERB* (**announces, announcing, announced**)
to announce something is to say it publicly
▷ **announcer** *NOUN* someone who announces something, especially on radio or television

announcement *NOUN* (**announcements**)
something that is made known publicly, especially in a newspaper or on radio or television

annoy *VERB* (**annoys, annoying, annoyed**)
to annoy someone is to give them a feeling of not being pleased

annoyance *NOUN* (**annoyances**)
1 annoyance is the feeling of being annoyed **2** an annoyance is something that annoys you • *Wasps are a great annoyance at a picnic.*

annual *ADJECTIVE*
happening or coming every year
▷ **annually** *ADVERB* once every year • *A new book comes out annually.*

annual *NOUN* (**annuals**)
1 a children's book of stories or comic strips that comes out once a year **2** a plant that dies when winter comes

anon.
short for **anonymous**

anonymous *ADJECTIVE*
an anonymous book or letter is one with the name of the writer unknown
▷ **anonymity** *NOUN* anonymity is keeping your name secret
▷ **anonymously** *ADVERB* with the name unknown

anorak *NOUN* (**anoraks**)
a thick warm jacket with a hood

anorexia *NOUN* (*say* an- er- **eks**- ee- a)
an illness that makes someone not want to eat
▷ **anorexic** *ADJECTIVE* an anorexic person is suffering from anorexia • *She has an anorexic daughter.*

another *DETERMINER & PRONOUN*
a different person or thing • *Have another look.* • *May I have another?*

answer *NOUN* (**answers**)
1 an answer is what you say when someone asks you a question **2** the answer to a problem is something that solves it

answer *VERB* (**answers**, **answering**, **answered**)
1 to answer someone is to give them an answer
2 to answer a telephone is to pick it up when it rings
to answer back is to say something rude or cheeky as an answer
to answer for something is to be responsible for it

ant *NOUN* (**ants**)
a tiny insect

antagonism *NOUN*
antagonism is a feeling of being someone's enemy
▷ **antagonistic** *ADJECTIVE* feeling antagonism

antagonize *VERB* (**antagonizes**, **antagonizing**, **antagonized**)
to antagonize someone is to make them feel you are their enemy

Antarctic or **Antarctica** *NOUN*
the area round the South Pole

anteater *NOUN* (**anteaters**)
an animal with a long tongue that lives by eating ants

antelope *NOUN* (**antelope** or **antelopes**)
an animal like a deer, that lives in Africa and parts of Asia

antenna *NOUN*
1 (**antennae**) a long thin feeler on the head of an insect or shellfish **2** (**antennas**) an aerial

anthem *NOUN* (**anthems**)
a religious or patriotic song, usually sung by a choir or group of people

anthill *NOUN* (**anthills**)
a mound of earth over an ants' nest

anthology *NOUN* (**anthologies**)
a collection of poems, stories, or songs in one book

anthracite *NOUN*
a kind of hard coal

anthropology *NOUN*
the study of human beings and the way they live
▷ **anthropological** *ADJECTIVE* to do with anthropology
▷ **anthropologist** *NOUN* someone who studies anthropology

anti- *PREFIX*
against something or someone, as in *antibiotic* and *anti-school*

> GRAMMAR
> **Anti-** is joined to lots of words, and you can make up your own words with it. It comes from a Greek word *anti* meaning 'against'.

antibiotic *NOUN* (**antibiotics**)
a drug that kills bacteria. Penicillin is an antibiotic

anticipate *VERB* (**anticipates**, **anticipating**, **anticipated**)
1 to anticipate something is to expect it and be ready for it • *The police were anticipating trouble.*
2 to anticipate someone is to act before they do • *They anticipated us in getting the early train.*

anticipation *NOUN*
looking forward to doing something

anticlimax *NOUN* (**anticlimaxes**)
a disappointing ending or result after something exciting

anticlockwise *ADVERB & ADJECTIVE*
moving in the opposite direction to the hands of a clock

anticyclone *NOUN* (**anticyclones**)
an area where air pressure is high, usually causing fine weather

antidote *NOUN* (**antidotes**)
something which takes away the bad effects of a poison or disease

antifreeze *NOUN*
a liquid you add to water to make it less likely to freeze

antipodes *PLURAL NOUN* (*say* an- **ti**- po- deez)
the Antipodes Australia and New Zealand in relation to Britain and Europe

antiquated *ADJECTIVE*
old-fashioned

antique *NOUN* (**antiques**) (*say* an- **teek**)
something that is valuable because it is very old

antiseptic *NOUN* (**antiseptics**)
a chemical that kills germs

antler *NOUN* (**antlers**)
the horn of a deer, which divides into several branches

a b c d e f g h i j k l m n o p q r s t u v w x y z

antonym *NOUN* (**antonyms**) (*say* **ant**-o-nim)
a word that is opposite in meaning to another • *'Soft' is an antonym of 'hard'.*

> ANTONYMS
> A word that means the opposite of another word is called an antonym. The antonym of *win* is *lose*, the antonym of *soft* is *hard*, the antonym of *above* is *below*. You can often make an antonym of a word by adding a prefix like *un-* or *dis-* or *in-*. So *untrue* means the opposite of *true*, *dislike* means the opposite of *like*, and *insincere* means the opposite of *sincere*. You often find the antonyms of words given in a thesaurus. Look also at the panel on **Synonyms**.

anus *NOUN* (**anuses**)
the opening at the lower end of the intestines, through which solid waste leaves the body

anvil *NOUN* (**anvils**)
a large block of iron on which a blacksmith hammers metal into shape

anxiety *NOUN* (**anxieties**)
1 anxiety is a feeling of being worried **2** an anxiety is something that worries you

anxious *ADJECTIVE*
1 worried and nervous **2** eager to do something • *They were anxious to help us.*

any *DETERMINER*
1 one or some • *Have you any wool?* **2** no matter which • *Come any day you like.* **3** every • *Any fool knows that!*

any *ADVERB*
at all; in some degree • *Is it any good?*

anybody *NOUN & PRONOUN*
anyone

anyhow *ADVERB*
1 anyway **2** (*informal*) carelessly, without much thought • *He does his work anyhow.*

anyone *NOUN & PRONOUN*
any person

anything *NOUN & PRONOUN*
any thing

anyway *ADVERB*
whatever happens; whatever the situation may be • *If it rains, we'll go anyway.*

anywhere *ADVERB*
in any place or to any place

apart *ADVERB*
1 away from each other; separately • *Keep your desks apart.* **2** into pieces • *It fell apart.* **3** excluded • *Joking apart, what do you think?*

apartment *NOUN* (**apartments**)
1 a set of rooms **2** (*in America*) a flat

apathy *NOUN*
not having much interest in something
▷ **apathetic** *ADJECTIVE* not having much interest

ape *NOUN* (**apes**)
a monkey without a tail, such as a gorilla or a chimpanzee

aphid or **aphis** *NOUN* (**aphids**)
a tiny insect that sucks juices from plants

apiece *ADVERB*
(*old use*) each • *She gave us an apple apiece.*

apologetic *ADJECTIVE*
saying you are sorry for something
▷ **apologetically** *ADVERB* in a way that shows you are sorry • *He replied apologetically.*

apologize *VERB* (**apologizes, apologizing, apologized**)
to apologize to someone is to tell them you are sorry

apology *NOUN* (**apologies**)
a statement that you are sorry for doing something wrong

apostle *NOUN* (**apostles**)
in Christianity, one of the twelve men sent out by Christ to tell people about God

apostrophe *NOUN* (**apostrophes**) (*say* a-**pos**-tro-fi)
a punctuation mark (') used to show that letters have been left out, as in *can't* and *he'll*. It is also used with *s* to show who owns something, as in *the boy's books* (one boy), *the boys' books* (more than one boy)

> APOSTROPHES
> You use an apostrophe (the possessive apostrophe) with an *s* to show that something belongs to someone. *Jack's shirt* is the shirt that belongs to Jack. *The players' shirts* are the shirts that belong to the players. You also use an apostrophe to show that letters have been left out of a word. The apostrophe takes the place of the missing letters. So *I'm coming* means *I am coming* and *she doesn't like it* means *she does not like it*. Don't use an apostrophe to show that a noun is in the plural. The plural of *carrot* is *carrots*, not *carrot's*.

appal *VERB* (**appals, appalling, appalled**)
to appal someone is to shock them a lot • *The violence appalled everyone.*

appalling *ADJECTIVE*
dreadful, shocking • *The room was in an appalling mess.*

apparatus *NOUN* (**apparatuses**)
an apparatus is a set of equipment for a special use

apparent *ADJECTIVE*
1 clear, obvious • *He burst out laughing for no apparent reason.* **2** appearing to be true • *They were not put off by their apparent failure.*

apparently *ADVERB*
as it seems, so it appears • *The door had apparently been locked.*

appeal *VERB* (**appeals**, **appealing**, **appealed**)
1 to appeal for something is to ask for it when you need it badly • *They are appealing for money to rebuild the church roof.* **2** to appeal to someone is to interest or attract them • *Football appeals to them.* **3** to appeal against a decision is to ask for it to be changed • *He decided to appeal against his prison sentence.*

appeal *NOUN* (**appeals**)
1 an appeal is asking for something you need **2** appeal is what makes something interesting • *Adventure stories have a lot of appeal for older children.* **3** an appeal is asking for a decision to be changed

appear *VERB* (**appears**, **appearing**, **appeared**)
1 to appear is to become visible **2** to appear is also to seem • *They appeared very anxious.* **3** to appear in a film or play is to take part in it

appearance *NOUN* (**appearances**)
1 coming into sight **2** taking part in a play, film, show, etc. **3** what someone looks like **4** what something seems to be

appease *VERB* (**appeases**, **appeasing**, **appeased**)
to appease someone is to make them peaceful or calm, often by giving them what they want
▷ **appeasement** *NOUN* appeasement is making someone happier or calmer

appendicitis *NOUN*
an inflammation or disease of the appendix

appendix *NOUN*
1 (**appendixes**) a small tube leading off from the intestines in the body **2** (**appendices**) an extra section at the end of a book

appetite *NOUN* (**appetites**)
a desire for something, especially for food

appetizer *NOUN* (**appetizers**)
something you eat or drink before a meal, to give you an appetite

appetizing *ADJECTIVE*
looking good to eat

applaud *VERB* (**applauds**, **applauding**, **applauded**)
to applaud someone or something is to show that you like them, especially by clapping

applause *NOUN*
clapping or cheering after someone has given a speech or given a performance

apple *NOUN* (**apples**)
a round fruit with skin that is red, green, or yellow

appliance *NOUN* (**appliances**)
a device or gadget

applicable *ADJECTIVE*
1 that applies to someone • *This rule is now applicable to everyone.* **2** relevant • *Ignore any questions which are not applicable.*

applicant *NOUN* (**applicants**)
someone who applies for something, for example a job

application *NOUN* (**applications**)
1 an application is a letter or form you use to ask for something important, such as a job **2** application is when you make a lot of effort to do something

applied *ADJECTIVE*
used for something practical • *Engineering is an applied science.*

apply *VERB* (**applies**, **applying**, **applied**)
1 to apply something is to put it on something else • *You need to apply a patch to the puncture.* **2** to apply for a job is to write formally and ask for it **3** to apply to someone is to concern them • *These rules apply to everybody.* **4** to apply yourself to something is to give it all your attention

appoint *VERB* (**appoints**, **appointing**, **appointed**)
1 to appoint someone is to choose them for a job **2** to appoint a time and place for a meeting is to decide when and where to have it

appointment *NOUN* (**appointments**)
1 an arrangement to meet or visit someone **2** choosing someone for a job **3** a job or position

apposition *NOUN*
apposition is placing a word next to one that it describes. In the phrase *Elizabeth, our Queen*, *our Queen* is in apposition to *Elizabeth*

appraise *VERB* (**appraises**, **appraising**, **appraised**)
to appraise something or someone is to estimate their quality or value
▷ **appraisal** *NOUN* appraisal is estimating or valuing something

appreciation *NOUN*
1 appreciation is showing that you enjoy or value something **2** appreciation is also an increase in the money value of something, such as a house or a work of art

appreciate *VERB* (**appreciates**, **appreciating**, **appreciated**)
1 to appreciate something is to enjoy or value it **2** to appreciate a fact is to understand it • *You don't seem to appreciate how lucky we are.* **3** to appreciate is to increase in value

appreciative *ADJECTIVE*
an appreciative person or group shows how much they enjoy or value something • *I enjoy playing to an appreciative audience.*

apprehension *NOUN* (**apprehensions**)
nervous fear or worry
▷ **apprehensive** *ADJECTIVE* nervous and worried

apprentice *NOUN* (**apprentices**)
someone who is learning a trade or craft
▷ **apprenticeship** *NOUN* the time when someone is an apprentice

a b c d e f g h i j k l m n o p q r s t u v w x y z

approach *VERB* (**approaches**, **approaching**, **approached**)
1 to approach a place is to come near to it **2** to approach someone is to go to them with a request or offer **3** to approach a problem or difficulty is to start solving it

approach *NOUN* (**approaches**)
1 coming near to a place **2** going to someone with a request or offer **3** a way of tackling a problem **4** a way or road leading up to a building • *The approach to the house had trees on each side.* **5** the final part of an aircraft's flight as it comes in to land

approachable *ADJECTIVE*
friendly and easy to talk to

appropriate *ADJECTIVE*
suitable

approval *NOUN*
thinking well of someone or something

approve *VERB* (**approves**, **approving**, **approved**)
to approve of someone or something is to think they are good or suitable

approximate *ADJECTIVE*
roughly correct but not exact • *The approximate size of the playground is half an acre.*
▷ **approximately** *ADVERB* roughly but not exactly • *It will cost approximately twenty pounds.*

approximation *NOUN* (**approximations**)
something that is a rough estimate and not exact

apricot *NOUN* (**apricots**)
a juicy, orange-coloured fruit like a small peach, with a stone in it

April *NOUN*
the fourth month of the year

April Fool *NOUN*
someone who is fooled on April Fool's Day (1 April)

apron *NOUN* (**aprons**)
1 a piece of clothing worn over the front of your body to protect your clothes **2** the part of an airfield where aircraft are loaded and unloaded

apt *ADJECTIVE*
1 likely to do something • *He is apt to be careless.* **2** suitable • *I need to find an apt quotation.* **3** quick at learning • *She is an apt pupil.*

aptitude *NOUN* (**aptitudes**)
aptitude or an aptitude is a talent in something

aquarium *NOUN* (**aquariums**)
a tank or building for keeping live fish

aquatic *ADJECTIVE*
to do with water and swimming • *They enjoy aquatic sports.*

aqueduct *NOUN* (**aqueducts**)
a bridge that carries water across a valley

Arab *NOUN* (**Arabs**)
a member of a people inhabiting Arabia and other parts of the Middle East and North Africa
▷ **Arabian** *ADJECTIVE* to do with the Arabs

Arabic *NOUN*
the language of the Arabs

arabic figures or **arabic numerals** *PLURAL NOUN*
the figures 1, 2, 3, 4, and so on (compare *Roman numerals*)

arable *ADJECTIVE*
to do with the growing of crops

arbitrary *ADJECTIVE* (*say* **ar**- bi- trer- i)
done or chosen at random or without a proper reason • *It was an arbitrary decision.*

arbitrate *VERB* (**arbitrates**, **arbitrating**, **arbitrated**)
to arbitrate is to settle someone else's quarrel

arbitration *NOUN*
settling a quarrel between two people or two sides by someone who is impartial
▷ **arbitrator** *NOUN* someone who settles a quarrel

arc *NOUN* (**arcs**)
part of the circumference of a circle, a curve

arcade *NOUN* (**arcades**)
a covered place to walk, with shops down each side

arch *NOUN* (**arches**)
a curved structure that helps to support a bridge or building

arch *VERB* (**arches**, **arching**, **arched**)
to curve • *The wind itself had ceased and a brilliant, deep blue sky arched high over the moorland.*
— Frances Hodgson Burnett, *The Secret Garden*

archaeology *NOUN* (*say* ar- ki- **ol**- o- ji)
the study of ancient people from the remains of their buildings

> WORD FAMILY
> An **archaeological** site or discovery is one to do with people from the past; an **archaeologist** is someone who studies archaeology or digs ancient places to find remains.

archbishop *NOUN* (**archbishops**)
the chief bishop of a region

archer *NOUN* (**archers**)
someone who shoots with a bow and arrows

archery *NOUN*
the sport of shooting with a bow and arrows

architect *NOUN* (**architects**) (*say* **ar**- ki- tekt)
someone whose work is to design buildings

architecture *NOUN*
1 the work of designing buildings **2** a style of building • *Victorian architecture*

Arctic *NOUN*
the area round the North Pole

are
plural and 2nd person singular present tense of **be**

area *NOUN* (**areas**)
1 part of a country, place, etc. **2** the space occupied by something • *The area of this room is 20 square metres.*

arena *NOUN* (**arenas**) (*say* a- **ree**- na)
1 the level space in the middle of a stadium or sports ground **2** the place where a sports event takes place

aren't
short for *am not* or *are not*

argue *VERB* (**argues**, **arguing**, **argued**)
1 to argue with someone is to quarrel with them **2** to argue is also to give reasons for something • *She argued that the housework should be shared.*

argument *NOUN* (**arguments**)
1 a quarrel **2** a reason or set of reasons someone gives to try to convince someone about something

arid *ADJECTIVE*
dry and barren
▷ **aridity** *NOUN* a thing's aridity is how dry it is

arise *VERB* (**arises**, **arising**, **arose**, **arisen**)
1 to arise is to appear or to come into existence **2** (*old meaning*) to rise; to stand up

aristocracy *NOUN* (**aristocracies**)
the aristocracy are the people from important families who often have titles like *Lord* and *Lady*

aristocrat *NOUN* (**aristocrats**) (*say* a- ris- to- krat)
a nobleman or noblewoman
▷ **aristocratic** *ADJECTIVE* to do with aristocrats

arithmetic *NOUN*
the study of using numbers and working things out with them
▷ **arithmetical** *ADJECTIVE* to do with arithmetic, or using arithmetic

ark *NOUN* (**arks**)
1 in the Bible, the ship in which Noah and his family escaped the Flood **2** a model of Noah's ark

arm *NOUN* (**arms**)
1 the part of your body between your shoulder and your hand **2** the sleeve of a coat or dress **3** the side part of a chair, on which you can rest your arm

arm *VERB* (**arms**, **arming**, **armed**)
1 to arm people is to give them weapons **2** to arm is to prepare for war

armada *NOUN* (**armadas**) (*say* ar- **mah**- da)
a fleet of warships, especially the Spanish Armada which attacked England in 1588

armadillo *NOUN* (**armadillos**)
a South American animal whose body is covered with a shell of bony plates

armaments *PLURAL NOUN*
weapons

armchair *NOUN* (**armchairs**)
a chair with parts on either side to rest your arms on

armed forces *PLURAL NOUN*
the army, navy, and air force of a country

armful *NOUN* (**armfuls**)
as much of something as you can hold in your arms • *He had an armful of hay.*

armistice *NOUN* (**armistices**)
an agreement to stop fighting in a war or battle

armour *NOUN*
armour is a metal covering to protect people or things in battle
▷ **armoured** *ADJECTIVE* having armour

armpit *NOUN* (**armpits**)
the hollow part under your arm at your shoulder

arms *PLURAL NOUN*
1 weapons • *Lay down your arms.* **2** a coat of arms

army *NOUN* (**armies**)
1 a large number of soldiers ready to fight **2** a large group • *They had an army of supporters.*

aroma *NOUN* (**aromas**) (*say* a- **roh**- ma)
a pleasant smell, for example of food
▷ **aromatic** *ADJECTIVE* having a pleasant smell

arose
past tense of **arise**

around *ADVERB & PREPOSITION*
1 round • *They stood around the pond.* **2** about • *Stop running around.*

arouse *VERB* (**arouses**, **arousing**, **aroused**)
1 to arouse someone is to make them wake up **2** to arouse feelings in someone is to cause them to have those feelings

arrange *VERB* (**arranges**, **arranging**, **arranged**)
1 to arrange things is to put them all in the position you want **2** to arrange a meeting or event is to organize it **3** to arrange to do something is to make sure someone does it

arrangement *NOUN* (**arrangements**)
1 arrangement is how you arrange or display something, for example flowers or a table setting **2** an arrangement is something you agree with someone else • *We made an arrangement to meet at the clock tower.*

array *NOUN* (**arrays**)
a display of things for people to see • *There was a huge array of books.*

arrears *PLURAL NOUN*
money that someone owes and ought to have paid earlier
in arrears owing money • *He's in arrears with his rent.*

arrest *VERB* (**arrests**, **arresting**, **arrested**)
1 to arrest someone is to take hold of them by the power of the law **2** to arrest something is to stop it • *The doctors were trying to arrest the spread of disease.*

arrest *NOUN* (**arrests**)
taking hold of someone by the power of the law
under arrest taken by the police into custody

arrival *NOUN* (**arrivals**)
1 an arrival is when someone or something arrives at a place **2** an arrival is also someone who is new or has just arrived • *Have you met the new arrivals?*

arrive *VERB* (**arrives**, **arriving**, **arrived**)
1 to arrive at a place is to get there at the end of a journey **2** to arrive is also to happen • *The great day arrived.*

arrogance *NOUN*
arrogance is a feeling someone has that they are more important than anyone else

arrogant *ADJECTIVE*
an arrogant person is unpleasantly proud and thinks they are more important than anyone else

arrow *NOUN* (**arrows**)
1 a pointed stick shot from a bow **2** a sign used to show direction or position

arsenal *NOUN* (**arsenals**)
a place where bullets, shells, and weapons are made or stored

arsenic *NOUN*
a strong poison made from a metallic element and used in insecticides

arson *NOUN*
the crime of deliberately setting fire to a building

art *NOUN* (**arts**)
1 art is producing something by drawing or painting or sculpture **2** the arts are subjects such as history and languages, as distinct from the sciences such as physics and chemistry **3** an art is also a skill in something, such as sewing or public speaking

artefact *NOUN* (**artefacts**)
an object made by humans, especially one from the past that is studied by archaeologists

artery *NOUN* (**arteries**)
a tube carrying blood from the heart to parts of the body

artful *ADJECTIVE*
clever at getting what you want by fooling people
▷ **artfully** *ADVERB* in a clever but deceitful way

arthritic *ADJECTIVE* (*say* arth- **rit**- ik)
suffering from arthritis

arthritis *NOUN* (*say* arth- **ry**- tiss)
a disease that makes joints in the body painful and stiff

article *NOUN* (**articles**)
1 an object or thing that you can touch or pick up **2** a piece of writing published in a newspaper or magazine **3** (*in grammar*) the word 'a' or 'an' (called the *indefinite article*) or the word 'the' (called the *definite article*)

articulate *ADJECTIVE* (*say* ar- **tik**- yoo- lat)
an articulate person is able to speak clearly and fluently

articulate *VERB* (**articulates**, **articulating**, **articulated**) (*say* ar- **tik**- yoo- layt)
to articulate a word or phrase is to pronounce it clearly
▷ **articulation** *NOUN* your articulation is how clearly you speak and pronounce words

articulated lorry *NOUN* (**articulated lorries**)
a large lorry with a cab that is connected to the main part by a joint that bends, so that it can turn more easily

artificial *ADJECTIVE*
made by human beings and not by nature
▷ **artificially** *ADVERB* to make something artificially is to make it in ways that humans have invented

artificial intelligence *NOUN*
the use of computers to do things that humans do, for example thinking and making decisions

artificial respiration *NOUN*
helping someone to start breathing again, especially after an accident

artillery *NOUN* (**artilleries**)
1 artillery is a collection of large guns **2** the artillery is the part of the army that uses large guns

artist *NOUN* (**artists**)
1 someone who produces art, especially a painter **2** an entertainer

artiste *NOUN* (**artistes**)
someone whose work is to entertain people, especially by singing, dancing, or telling stories

artistic *ADJECTIVE*
1 to do with art and artists **2** showing skill and beauty • *an artistic flower arrangement*

artistry *NOUN*
the skill of an artist • *The carving showed great artistry.*

as *CONJUNCTION, ADVERB, & PREPOSITION*
linking words and phrases • *As you were late, you had better stay behind.* • *Leave it as it is.* • *She slipped as she got off the bus.* • *It is not as hard as you think.* • *He was dressed as a sailor.*

> GRAMMAR
> **As** is used to make similes, for example • *as flat as a pancake* • *as old as the hills* • *as right as rain.* There are lots more you can use.

asbestos *NOUN*
a fireproof material that is made up of fine soft fibres

ascend *VERB* (**ascends**, **ascending**, **ascended**)
to ascend something like a hill or staircase is to go up it

ascent *NOUN* (**ascents**)
an ascent is a climb, usually a hard or long one

ash[1] *NOUN* (**ashes**)
ash is the powder that is left after something has been burned

ash[2] *NOUN* (**ashes**)
an ash or ash tree is a tree with silvery bark and winged seeds

ashamed *ADJECTIVE*
feeling shame
ashamed of something is feeling shame because of something

ashen *ADJECTIVE*
grey and pale • *Her face was ashen.*

ashore *ADVERB*
on the shore

ashtray *NOUN* (**ashtrays**)
a small bowl for putting cigarette ash in

Asian *ADJECTIVE*
to do with Asia

Asian *NOUN* (**Asians**)
a person from Asia

aside *ADVERB*
to or at one side; away • *Step aside and let them pass.*

aside *NOUN* (**asides**)
something said so that only some people will hear

ask *VERB* (**asks**, **asking**, **asked**)
1 to ask someone something is to speak to them so as to find out or get something **2** to ask someone to something like a party is to invite them
to ask for it or **to ask for trouble** (*informal*) is to do something that will bring trouble

asleep *ADVERB & ADJECTIVE*
sleeping

aspect *NOUN* (**aspects**)
1 one way of looking at a problem or situation • *Perhaps the worst aspect of winter is the dark mornings.* **2** the appearance of someone or something **3** the direction a building faces • *This room has a southern aspect.*

asphalt *NOUN* (*say* ass- falt)
a sticky black stuff like tar. It is mixed with gravel to make a surface for roads and areas such as playgrounds

aspirin *NOUN* (**aspirins**)
1 aspirin is a drug used to relieve pain or reduce fever **2** an aspirin is a tablet of this drug

ass *NOUN* (**asses**)
1 a donkey **2** (informal) a fool • *Shaun, you are an ass!*

assassin *NOUN* (**assassins**)
a person who assassinates someone

assassinate *VERB* (**assassinates**, **assassinating**, **assassinated**)
to assassinate someone such as a ruler or leader is to murder them to stop them having power

assassination *NOUN* (**assassinations**)
the murder of a ruler or leader

assault *NOUN* (**assaults**)
a violent or illegal attack on someone

assault *VERB* (**assaults**, **assaulting**, **assaulted**)
to assault someone is to attack them violently

assemble *VERB* (**assembles**, **assembling**, **assembled**)
1 to assemble people or things is to bring them together in one place **2** to assemble is to come together in one place • *Please assemble in the playground.*

assembly *NOUN* (**assemblies**)
1 an assembly is when a lot of people come together and someone speaks to them, for example in a school **2** an assembly is also a group of people who meet together, such as a parliament **3** assembly of a machine or piece of furniture is putting the parts together to make it

assent *NOUN*
assent is agreement or permission to do something • *Have your parents given their assent?*

assert *VERB* (**asserts**, **asserting**, **asserted**)
to assert something is to say it strongly and clearly
▷ **assertion** *NOUN* something you say clearly and strongly

assertive *ADJECTIVE*
speaking or behaving strongly and firmly

assess *VERB* (**assesses**, **assessing**, **assessed**)
to assess someone or something is to decide how good or useful they are
▷ **assessor** *NOUN* a person who assesses someone or something

assessment *NOUN* (**assessments**)
an opinion about something after thinking about it carefully

asset *NOUN* (**assets**)
something useful or valuable to someone

assets *PLURAL NOUN*
the property of a person or company that they could sell to raise money if they wanted to

assign *VERB* (**assigns**, **assigning**, **assigned**)
to assign something to someone is to give it to them as their share or duty • *Teachers assign homework to their pupils every day.*

assignment *NOUN* (**assignments**)
a piece of work that someone is given to do

assist *VERB* (**assists**, **assisting**, **assisted**)
to assist someone is to help them, usually in a practical way

assistance *NOUN*
help someone gets when they need information or support

assistant *NOUN* (**assistants**)
1 someone whose job is to help another person in their work **2** someone who serves in a shop

associate *VERB* (**associates**, **associating**, **associated**) (*say* a- **soh**- shi- ayt)
1 to associate one thing with another is to connect them in your mind • *I associate Christmas with ice and snow.* **2** to associate with someone is to be friendly with them or work together • *The people we associate with all have young children.*

associate *NOUN* (**associates**) (*say* a- **soh**- shi- at)
someone you are friendly with or work with

association *NOUN* (**associations**)
1 an association is an organization for people sharing an interest or doing the same work **2** association is being friendly with someone

a b c d e f g h i j k l m n o p q r s t u v w x y z

Association Football *NOUN*
a game played on a field between two teams of eleven players using a round ball that may only be handled by the goalkeepers

assonance *NOUN* (*say* ass- on- ans)
assonance is when the same vowel sound is repeated, for special effect, e.g. *the bright kite flies high in the sky*

assorted *ADJECTIVE*
of various kinds; mixed and different • *A large wooden trunk stood open at the foot of his bed, revealing a cauldron, broomstick, black robes and assorted spellbooks.* — J. K. Rowling, *Harry Potter and the Goblet of Fire.*

assortment *NOUN* (**assortments**)
a mixture of different things or people

assume *VERB* (**assumes, assuming, assumed**)
to assume something is to think it is true or likely without being sure of it • *I assume you will be coming tomorrow.*
▷ **assumed** *ADJECTIVE* an assumed name is one that is not the person's real name

assumption *NOUN* (**assumptions**)
something you assume or take for granted

assurance *NOUN* (**assurances**)
1 assurance is a feeling of certainty about something **2** an assurance is a promise or guarantee **3** assurance is also a kind of life insurance

assure *VERB* (**assures, assuring, assured**)
to assure someone is to tell someone something definite • *I can assure you that we will make every effort to help.*

asterisk *NOUN* (**asterisks**)
a star-shaped sign * used in printing and writing to draw attention to something

asteroid *NOUN* (**asteroids**)
one of the small planets found mainly between the orbits of Mars and Jupiter

asthma *NOUN* (*say* ass- ma)
a disease which makes breathing difficult

asthmatic *ADJECTIVE*
suffering from asthma

asthmatic *NOUN* (**asthmatics**)
someone who is suffering from asthma

astonish *VERB* (**astonishes, astonishing, astonished**)
to astonish someone is to surprise them very much
▷ **astonishment** *NOUN* a feeling of great surprise

astound *VERB* (**astounds, astounding, astounded**)
to astound someone is to amaze or shock them very much

astride *ADVERB*
with one leg on each side of something • *She was sitting astride a big horse.*

astrology *NOUN*
astrology is studying how the planets and stars may affect people's lives

> **WORD FAMILY**
> An **astrological** sign or chart is one that is to do with astrology; an **astrologer** is someone who studies astrology.

astronaut *NOUN* (**astronauts**)
someone who travels in a spacecraft

astronomical *ADJECTIVE*
1 to do with astronomy **2** (*informal*) extremely large • *The cost of the party was astronomical.*

astronomy *NOUN*
astronomy is studying the sun, moon, planets, and stars
▷ **astronomer** *NOUN* someone who studies astronomy

at *PREPOSITION*
showing where someone or something is • *I was at the hospital.* • *They are looking at their new books.*

ate
past tense of **eat**

atheist *NOUN* (**atheists**)
someone who does not believe in a God
▷ **atheism** *NOUN* a belief that there is no God

athlete *NOUN* (**athletes**)
someone who is good at athletics or other sports

athletic *ADJECTIVE*
1 to do with athletics • *an athletic competition*
2 good at sports; strong

athletics *PLURAL NOUN*
physical exercises and sports such as running and jumping

atlas *NOUN* (**atlases**)
a book of maps

atmosphere *NOUN* (**atmospheres**)
1 the earth's atmosphere is the air around it **2** an atmosphere is a feeling you get in a room or at a place • *There was a happy atmosphere at the fairground.*

atmospheric *ADJECTIVE*
1 to do with the earth's atmosphere **2** having a strong atmosphere

atoll *NOUN* (**atolls**)
a ring-shaped island of coral in the sea

atom *NOUN* (**atoms**)
1 the smallest possible part of a chemical element
2 a tiny part of something

atom bomb or **atomic bomb** *NOUN* (**atom bombs** or **atomic bombs**)
a bomb that uses atomic energy to make the explosion, and has nuclear fallout

atomic *ADJECTIVE*
involving atoms; nuclear

at once *ADVERB*
immediately • *Come here at once!*

atrocious *ADJECTIVE* (*say* a- **troh**- shus)
awful, terrible

atrocity *NOUN* (**atrocities**)
a terrible and cruel act, such as the killing of a large number of people

attach *VERB* (**attaches**, **attaching**, **attached**)
to attach one thing to another is to fix or fasten it

attached *ADJECTIVE*
to be attached to someone is to be fond of them

attachment *NOUN* (**attachments**)
1 an extra part you fix to a device so that it can do a special kind of work • *The garden hose has an attachment for washing cars* **2** a fondness or friendship • *The boys felt a real attachment to their pet hamster* **3** (*in computing*) a document that you send to someone with an email message

attack *NOUN* (**attacks**)
1 an attempt to hurt someone with violence **2** an attempt to harm someone or something by using unfriendly words **3** a sudden illness or pain

attack *VERB* (**attacks**, **attacking**, **attacked**)
to attack someone is to try to hurt them with violence, or to harm them with unfriendly words

attain *VERB* (**attains**, **attaining**, **attained**)
to attain something is to reach or achieve it • *I have attained Grade 3 on the violin.*
▷ **attainment** *NOUN* something you have achieved

attempt *VERB* (**attempts**, **attempting**, **attempted**)
to attempt to do something is to make an effort to do it

attempt *NOUN* (**attempts**)
an attempt at something is making an effort to do it

attend *VERB* (**attends**, **attending**, **attended**)
1 to attend something like a meeting or a wedding is to be there **2** to attend school or college is to be a pupil or student there **3** to attend to someone is to look after them, especially when they are ill **4** to attend to something is to spend time dealing with it • *She had some business to attend to.*

attendance *NOUN* (**attendances**)
1 attendance is being somewhere where you are supposed to be **2** the attendance at an event is the number of people who are there to see it

attendant *NOUN* (**attendants**)
someone who helps or goes with another person

attention *NOUN*
giving care or thought to someone or something **to stand to attention** is to stand with your feet together and your arms straight down, like soldiers on parade

attentive *ADJECTIVE*
listening closely

attic *NOUN* (**attics**)
a room or space under the roof of a house

attitude *NOUN* (**attitudes**)
1 your attitude is the way you think or feel about something, and the way you behave **2** your attitude is also the position of your body

attract *VERB* (**attracts**, **attracting**, **attracted**)
1 to attract someone is to seem pleasant to them and get their attention or interest **2** to attract something unwelcome is to make it come • *Empty bottles of drink attract wasps.* **3** to attract something is also to pull it by a physical force like magnetism • *Magnets attract metal pins.*

attraction *NOUN* (**attractions**)
1 attraction is the power to attract someone **2** an attraction is something pleasant that people like to see, such as a fair or a rock concert

attractive *ADJECTIVE*
1 interesting or welcome • *They made us an attractive offer of a free holiday.* **2** pleasant, good-looking

auburn *ADJECTIVE*
auburn hair is a reddish-brown colour

auction *NOUN* (**auctions**)
a sale at which things are sold to the person who offers the most money for them
▷ **auctioneer** *NOUN* an official in charge of an auction

audible *ADJECTIVE*
loud enough to be heard
▷ **audibility** *NOUN* audibility is how well you can hear something

audience *NOUN* (**audiences**)
1 the people who have come to see or hear an event like a concert or film **2** a formal interview with an important person

audiovisual *ADJECTIVE*
using both sound and pictures to give information • *Audiovisual aids include films and video recordings.*

audition *NOUN* (**auditions**)
a test to see if a performer is suitable to act in a play or sing in a choir

auditorium *NOUN* (**auditoriums**) (*say* aw- dit- **or**- i- um)
the part of a building where the audience sits

August *NOUN*
the eighth month of the year

aunt *NOUN* (**aunts**)
1 the sister of your mother or father **2** your uncle's wife

auntie or **aunty** *NOUN* (**aunties**)
(*informal*) an aunt

au pair *NOUN* (**au pairs**) (*say* oh- **pair**)
a person from another country, usually a girl or young woman, who works for a time in someone's home

aural *ADJECTIVE*
using the sense of hearing • *The children had an aural comprehension test.*

> SPELLING
> Take care not to confuse **aural** with **oral**, which means spoken, or using your mouth.

austere *ADJECTIVE*
1 not having much comfort or luxury **2** an austere person is severe and strict

austerity *NOUN*
1 a plain or simple way of living, without much comfort or luxury **2** strictness

Australian *ADJECTIVE*
to do with Australia

Australian *NOUN* (**Australians**)
a person from Australia

authentic *ADJECTIVE*
real, genuine
▷ **authenticity** *NOUN* authenticity is being authentic

author *NOUN* (**authors**)
the writer of a book or something like a poem or article

authority *NOUN* (**authorities**)
1 authority is the power to give orders to other people **2** the authorities are the people who have the power to make decisions **3** an authority on a subject is an expert on it or a book that gives you reliable information about it

authorize *VERB* (**authorizes**, **authorizing**, **authorized**)
1 to authorize something is to give official permission for it **2** to authorize someone to do something is to give them permission to do it

autistic *ADJECTIVE*
having a disability that makes someone unable to communicate with other people

autobiography *NOUN* (**autobiographies**)
the story of someone's life that they have written themselves

> WORD FAMILY
> **Autobiographical** writing is written by a person about their own life.

autograph *NOUN* (**autographs**)
the signature of a famous person

automate *VERB* (**automates**, **automating**, **automated**)
to automate something is to make it work by an automatic process

automatic *ADJECTIVE*
1 an automatic process is one that works on its own, without needing attention or control by humans **2** an automatic action is one that you do without specially thinking about it
▷ **automatically** *ADVERB* by automatic means; without having to use controls all the time

automation *NOUN* (*say* aw- tom- ay- shun)
making processes automatic, and using machines instead of people to do work

automobile *NOUN* (**automobiles**)
(*in America*) a motor car

autumn *NOUN* (**autumns**) (*say* **aw**- tum)
the season when leaves fall off the trees, between summer and winter

> BRITISH AND AMERICAN
> In America, the word **fall** is more often used.

autumnal *ADJECTIVE* (*say* aw- **tum**- nal)
in autumn; to do with autumn

auxiliary *ADJECTIVE*
helping, extra • *The boat had an auxiliary engine.*

auxiliary *NOUN* (**auxiliaries**)
(*in grammar*) a type of verb that is used in forming parts of other verbs • *In 'I have finished', the auxiliary is 'have'.*

available *ADJECTIVE*
able to be found or used • *Fresh strawberries are available in June.*
▷ **availability** *NOUN* availability is how easily you can find or get something

avalanche *NOUN* (**avalanches**) (*say* av- a- lahnsh)
a sudden heavy fall of rocks or snow down the side of a mountain

avenue *NOUN* (**avenues**)
a wide street, usually with trees along each side

average *NOUN* (**averages**)
1 an average is the number you get by adding several amounts together and dividing the total by the number of amounts • *The average of 2, 4, 6, and 8 is 5.* **2** the average is the usual or ordinary standard • *Their work is well above the average.*

average *ADJECTIVE*
of the usual or ordinary standard

average *VERB* (**averages**, **averaging**, **averaged**)
to average is to have as an average • *We averaged 50 runs last season.*

avert *VERB* (**averts**, **averting**, **averted**)
1 to avert something is to turn it away • *People averted their eyes from the accident.* **2** to avert something is also to stop it happening • *The train driver's quick reaction had averted a disaster.*

aviary *NOUN* (**aviaries**)
a place where birds are kept

aviation *NOUN*
aviation is flying in aircraft

avid *ADJECTIVE*
keen, eager • *She is an avid reader.*

avocado *NOUN* (**avocados**) (*say* av-o-**kah**-doh)
a fruit like a pear, with a rough skin and thick smooth flesh

avoid *VERB* (**avoids**, **avoiding**, **avoided**)
1 to avoid something or someone is to keep yourself away from them • *They try to avoid their relations at Christmas.* **2** to avoid something is also to find a way of not doing it • *They wanted to avoid extra homework.*
▷ **avoidance** *NOUN* avoidance is avoiding something

await *VERB* (**awaits**, **awaiting**, **awaited**)
to await someone or something is to wait for them

awake *ADJECTIVE*
not sleeping

awake *VERB* (**awakes**, **awaking**, **awoke**, **awoken**)
1 to awake is to wake up **2** to awake someone is to wake them up

> GRAMMAR
> Notice that **awake** and **awaken** are not followed by **up**, although **wake** usually is.

awaken *VERB* (**awakens**, **awakening**, **awakened**)
1 to awaken is to wake up **2** to awaken someone is to wake them up

award *NOUN* (**awards**)
something such as a prize given to a person who has done something successful

award *VERB* (**awards**, **awarding**, **awarded**)
to award something to someone is to give it to them as an award

aware *ADJECTIVE*
to be aware of something is to know about it or realize it is there • *They soon became aware of the danger.*
▷ **awareness** *NOUN* awareness is knowing about something

awash *ADJECTIVE*
flooded with waves or water • *The sink has overflowed, and the kitchen floor is awash!*

away *ADVERB*
at a distance or somewhere else • *I wish those people would go away.* • *The ice cream melted so I threw it away.*

> MEANING
> Notice that you can use **away** with special meanings • *They are working away at their exams.* • *The noise gradually died away.*

away *ADJECTIVE*
an away match is one that is played at the opponents' ground

awe *NOUN*
fear and wonder • *The mountains filled him with awe.*
▷ **awed** filled with fear and wonder

awful *ADJECTIVE*
1 (*informal*) very bad; very great • *I've been an awful fool.* **2** causing fear or horror • *It was an awful sight.*

awfully *ADVERB*
(*informal*) very, extremely • *It's awfully hot in June.*

awhile *ADVERB*
for a short time

awkward *ADJECTIVE*
1 difficult to use or cope with • *The box was an awkward shape.* **2** embarrassed and uncomfortable • *The boy felt awkward in the smart hotel.*

awoke
past tense of **awake** *VERB*

awoken
past participle of **awake** *VERB*

axe *NOUN* (**axes**)
a tool for chopping

axe *VERB* (**axes**, **axing**, **axed**)
(*informal*) to axe something is to cancel or abolish it

axis *NOUN* (**axes**)
1 a line through the centre of a spinning object **2** a line dividing something in half

axle *NOUN* (**axles**)
the rod through the centre of a wheel, on which it turns

ay or **aye** *INTERJECTION* (*say* **I**)
(*in dialects or old uses*) yes

azalea *NOUN* (**azaleas**) (*say* a- **zay**- li- a)
a flowering shrub like a rhododendron

Aztec *NOUN* (**Aztecs**)
one of a native Indian people who lived in Mexico before the Spanish conquest of 1521

azure *ADJECTIVE*
sky-blue

Bb

babble *VERB* (**babbles**, **babbling**, **babbled**)
1 to babble is to talk quickly, without making much sense **2** to babble is also to make a murmuring or bubbling sound • *They came across a babbling brook.*

baboon *NOUN* (**baboons**)
a large kind of monkey with a long muzzle

baby *NOUN* (**babies**)
a very young child

> WORD FAMILY
> You can also talk about a **baby elephant** and other young animals using this word.

babyish *ADJECTIVE*
silly and childish

babysit *VERB* (**babysits**, **babysitting**, **babysat**)
to babysit is to look after a child while its parents are out

babysitter *NOUN* (**babysitters**)
someone who babysits

a b c d e f g h i j k l m n o p q r s t u v w x y z

bachelor *NOUN* (**bachelors**)
a man who has not married

back *NOUN* (**backs**)
1 the part of your body between your shoulders and your bottom **2** the upper part of a four-legged animal's body **3** the part of a thing that is furthest away from the front • *The back of the house faces a river.*

back *ADJECTIVE*
placed at or near the back • *Let's sit in the back row.*

back *ADVERB*
1 backwards or towards the back • *Go back!* **2** to where someone or something was before • *When will you be coming back?* **3** to an earlier time • *Think back to when you were little.*

back *VERB* (**backs**, **backing**, **backed**)
1 to back a vehicle is to move it backwards **2** to back a horse is to bet on it winning a race **3** to back someone is to support them or give them help
to back down is to admit you were wrong about something
to back out is to decide not to get involved in something
to back someone up is to give them support or help

backache *NOUN* (**backaches**)
a pain in your back, usually lasting for a long time

backbone *NOUN* (**backbones**)
your backbone is your spine

background *NOUN* (**backgrounds**)
1 the background of a picture or view is the part that is farthest away from you, behind the main subject **2** the background to an event or situation is all the things that help to explain why it happened **3** a person's background is their family, education and what they have done in their life
in the background not noticeable or obvious

backing *NOUN*
1 backing is support or help • *Our firm will give you financial backing.* **2** backing is also the material that forms a support or back for something **3** the backing on a pop song is the music that is played or sung to support the main singer or tune

backlash *NOUN* (**backlashes**)
a strong and often angry reaction to something

backlog *NOUN* (**backlogs**)
a backlog is work that should have been finished but still has to be done

backside *NOUN* (**backsides**)
(*informal*) your backside is your bottom

backstroke *NOUN*
a stroke you use when swimming on your back

backward *ADJECTIVE*
1 facing or aimed towards the back • *She walked past him without a backward glance.* **2** slow in learning or developing

backward *ADVERB*
backwards

backwards *ADVERB*
1 towards the back **2** with the back end going first **3** in the opposite order to the usual one • *Can you say the alphabet backwards?*

backyard *NOUN* (**backyards**)
an open area at the back of a building

bacon *NOUN*
smoked or salted meat from the back or sides of a pig

bacteria *PLURAL NOUN*
tiny organisms that can cause diseases
▷ **bacterial** *ADJECTIVE* to do with bacteria

bad *ADJECTIVE* (**worse**, **worst**)
1 not good or well done • *We were watching a very bad film on television.* **2** someone who is bad is wicked or naughty **3** someone is bad at something when they can't do it very well • *Tracy is bad at maths.* **4** serious or unpleasant • *That was a bad mistake.* **5** harmful to your health • *Eating fatty foods is bad for you.*
not bad fairly good, all right

baddy *NOUN* (**baddies**)
(*informal*) a bad person, especially in a story or a film

badge *NOUN* (**badges**)
a small piece of metal, plastic or cloth that you pin or sew on your clothes to tell people something about you, such as what club or school you belong to or what kind of thing you like

badger *NOUN* (**badgers**)
a grey animal with a black and white head, which lives underground and comes out at night to feed

badger *VERB* (**badgers**, **badgering**, **badgered**)
to badger someone is to keep asking them to do something • *He kept badgering his mother for his pocket money.*

badly *ADVERB*
1 not well • *They did the work badly.* **2** seriously • *He was badly wounded.* **3** very much • *I need a drink badly.*
badly off poor or unfortunate

badminton *NOUN*
a game in which players use rackets to hit a light object called a *shuttlecock* backwards and forwards across a high net

bad-tempered *ADJECTIVE*
a bad-tempered person is one who often becomes angry

baffle *VERB* (**baffles**, **baffling**, **baffled**)
to baffle someone is to puzzle or confuse them completely

bag *NOUN* (**bags**)
a container made of soft material, for holding or carrying things
bags of something (*informal*) plenty • *There's bags of room.*

bag *VERB* (**bags**, **bagging**, **bagged**)
to bag something is to get hold of it or take it •*I bagged the best seat.*

bagel *NOUN* (**bagels**)
a hard ring-shaped bread roll

baggage *NOUN*
baggage is the suitcases and bags you take on a journey

baggy *ADJECTIVE* (**baggier**, **baggiest**)
baggy clothes hang loosely from your body

bagpipes *PLURAL NOUN*
bagpipes are a musical instrument you play by squeezing air out of a bag into a set of pipes

bail [1] *NOUN*
bail is money that has to be paid or promised so that a person accused of a crime will not be kept in prison before their trial

bail [2] *NOUN* (**bails**)
bails are the two small pieces of wood placed on top of the stumps in cricket

> SPELLING
> Take care not to confuse **bail** with **bale**, which means a large bundle.

bail *VERB* (**bails**, **bailing**, **bailed**)
to bail water out of a boat is to scoop it over the side

Bairam *NOUN* (**Bairams**) (*say* by- **ram**)
either of two Muslim festivals, one in the tenth month and one in the twelfth month of the Islamic year

Baisakhi *NOUN*
a Sikh festival held in April

bait *NOUN*
bait is a small amount of food put on a hook or in a trap to catch fish or animals

bait *VERB* (**baits**, **baiting**, **baited**)
1 to bait a hook or trap is to put the bait on it or in it, to catch fish or animals

bake *VERB* (**bakes**, **baking**, **baked**)
1 to bake food is to cook it in an oven, especially bread or cakes **2** to bake something like clay is to make it hard by heating it in an oven **3** to bake is to become very hot, especially in the sun

baker *NOUN* (**bakers**)
someone who makes or sells bread and cakes

bakery *NOUN* (**bakeries**)
a place where bread is made or sold

baking powder *NOUN*
baking powder is a special powder used to make cakes rise

balance *NOUN* (**balances**)
1 a person's balance is their feeling of being steady •*He lost his balance and fell over.* **2** a balance is a device for weighing things, with two trays hanging from the ends of a horizontal bar **3** the balance of a bank account is the difference between the money paid into it and the money taken out of it **4** a balance is also an amount of money that someone owes •*I will pay you the balance on Saturday.*

balance *VERB* (**balances**, **balancing**, **balanced**)
1 to balance something is to keep it steady •*He was balancing a tray on one hand.* **2** a balanced diet is one that has all the right kinds of food for being healthy

balcony *NOUN* (**balconies**)
1 a platform built out from the wall of a building, with a railing round it **2** the upstairs part of a cinema or theatre

bald *ADJECTIVE* (**balder**, **baldest**)
a bald person does not have much hair or any hair on their head

bale [1] *NOUN* (**bales**)
a large bundle of something like hay or straw, usually tied up tightly

> SPELLING
> Take care not to confuse **bale** with **bail** meaning a sum of money, or **bail** meaning a piece of wood placed on top of cricket stumps.

bale [2] *VERB* (**bales**, **baling**, **baled**)
to bale out is to jump out of an aircraft with a parachute

ball *NOUN* (**balls**)
1 a round object used in many games **2** anything that is made into a round shape •*a ball of string* **3** a grand or formal party where people dance

ballad *NOUN* (**ballads**)
a simple song or poem that tells a story

ballerina *NOUN* (**ballerinas**) (*say* bal- e- **ree**- na)
a female ballet dancer

ballet *NOUN* (**ballets**) (*say* **bal**- ay)
a form of dancing in which a group of dancers perform special steps and movements to tell a story to music

ballet dancer *NOUN* (**ballet dancers**)
someone who performs ballet

ballistic missile *NOUN* (**ballistic missiles**)
a type of rocket that goes up into the air by its own power and falls freely

balloon *NOUN* (**balloons**)
1 a small rubber pouch that you fill up with air or gas and use as a toy or for decoration **2** a large round or pear-shaped bag filled with a light gas or hot air, so that it can carry people into the air **3** an outline in a strip cartoon containing the words the characters are saying

ballot *NOUN* (**ballots**) (*say* **bal**- ot)
a method of voting in secret by making a mark on a piece of paper and putting it into a box

ballpoint *NOUN* (**ballpoints**)
a pen with a tiny ball at the tip, round which the ink flows

ballroom *NOUN* (**ballrooms**)
a large room where dances are held

balsa *NOUN* (*say* bol- sa)
a kind of lightweight wood used to make models

bamboo *NOUN* (**bamboos**)
a tall tropical plant with hard hollow stems, used for making furniture

ban *VERB* (**bans, banning, banned**)
to ban something is to forbid people to do it

banana *NOUN* (**bananas**)
a long curved fruit with a yellow skin

band *NOUN* (**bands**)
1 a group of people playing music together **2** an organized group of people doing something together **3** a circular strip of something

band *VERB* (**bands, banding, banded**)
to band together is to join together to form an organized group

bandage *NOUN* (**bandages**) (*say* ban- dij)
a strip of material that you wrap round a wound to protect it

bandanna *NOUN* (**bandannas**)
a brightly coloured scarf worn round your head or neck

bandit *NOUN* (**bandits**)
a member of a gang of robbers who attack travellers

bandstand *NOUN* (**bandstands**)
a platform for a band playing music outdoors, usually in a park

bandwagon *NOUN* (**bandwagons**)
to jump or **climb on the bandwagon** (*informal*) is to join in something that looks like being successful

bandy *ADJECTIVE* (**bandier, bandiest**)
bandy legs curve outwards at the knees

bang *NOUN* (**bangs**)
1 a sudden loud noise **2** a heavy blow or knock

bang *VERB* (**bangs, banging, banged**)
1 to bang something is to hit or shut it noisily •*Don't bang the door when you go out.* **2** to bang something is to knock it hard against something else •*She banged her knee on the desk.*

banger *NOUN* (**bangers**)
1 (*informal*) a firework that explodes noisily **2** (*informal*) a sausage **3** (*informal*) a noisy old car

banish *VERB* (**banishes, banishing, banished**)
to banish someone is to punish them by sending them away and ordering them not to return •*The wicked witch Duchess shall be banished for seven years to the tiny Isle of Stones where nothing grows and the sea-current is strong.* — Alan Temperley, *The Brave Whale.*
▷ **banishment** *NOUN* banishment is being banished

banisters *PLURAL NOUN*
banisters are a rail with upright supports at the side of a staircase

banjo *NOUN* (**banjos**)
a musical instrument like a small guitar with a round body

bank *NOUN* (**banks**)
1 a business which looks after people's money **2** the ground beside a river or lake **3** a piece of raised or sloping ground **4** a place where something is stored and collected •*a blood bank* **5** a bank of clouds is a mass of them **6** a bank of lights or switches is a row of them

bank *VERB* (**banks, banking, banked**)
1 to bank money is to put it in a bank **2** to bank is to lean over while changing direction •*The plane banked as it turned to land.*
to bank on something is to rely on it •*We're banking on the weather being good.*

bank holiday *NOUN* (**bank holidays**)
a public holiday, when the banks are closed

banknote *NOUN* (**banknotes**)
a piece of paper money

bankrupt *ADJECTIVE*
not able to pay your debts
▷ **bankruptcy** *NOUN* bankruptcy is when a person or business can't pay their debts

banner *NOUN* (**banners**)
a large strip of cloth with writing on it, carried on a pole or between two poles in a procession or demonstration

banquet *NOUN* (**banquets**) (*say* bank- wit)
a large formal dinner, often with speeches

baobab *NOUN* (**baobabs**) (*say* **bay**-oh-bab)
an African tree with a large trunk and fruit that can be eaten

baptism *NOUN* (**baptisms**)
baptism is the ceremony of baptizing someone

Baptist *NOUN* (**Baptists**)
a Christian who believes that a person should not be baptized as a baby but only when he or she is old enough to understand what baptism means

baptize *VERB* (**baptizes, baptizing, baptized**)
to baptize someone is to sprinkle them with water, or dip them in water, in a ceremony welcoming them into the Christian Church

bar *NOUN* (**bars**)
1 a long piece of something hard **2** a counter or room where drinks and refreshments are served **3** one of the small equal sections into which music is divided •*A waltz has three beats in a bar.*

bar *VERB* (**bars, barring, barred**)
1 to bar something is to fasten it with a bar **2** to bar someone from something is to prevent them from taking part in it **3** to bar someone's way is to stop them getting past

barb *NOUN* (**barbs**)
a backward-curving point on a fish hook or spear, which makes it stick in more firmly

barbarian *NOUN* (**barbarians**)
an uncivilized or savage person

barbaric or **barbarous** *ADJECTIVE*
savage and cruel

> WORD FAMILY
> The nouns **barbarism** and **barbarity** both mean savage cruelty.

barbecue *NOUN* (**barbecues**)
1 a metal frame used for grilling food over a charcoal fire outdoors **2** a party at which food is cooked outdoors on a barbecue

barbed wire *NOUN*
wire with sharp twisted spikes on it, used to make fences

barber *NOUN* (**barbers**)
someone whose job is to cut men's hair

bar chart *NOUN* (**bar charts**)
a diagram showing amounts as bars of equal width but different heights

bar code *NOUN* (**bar codes**)
a set of black lines that are printed on goods, library books, etc. so that they can be identified by a computer

bard *NOUN* (**bards**)
(*old use*) a poet or minstrel

bare *ADJECTIVE* (**barer**, **barest**)
1 not covered with anything • *The trees were bare.* **2** empty or almost empty • *The cupboard was bare.* **3** only just enough • *They just had the bare necessities of life.*

bareback *ADJECTIVE* & *ADVERB*
riding on a horse without a saddle

barely *ADVERB*
only just; with difficulty • *They were barely able to see in the fog.*

bargain *NOUN* (**bargains**)
1 something that you buy cheaply **2** an agreement between two people to do something for each other • *I expect you to keep your side of the bargain.*
into the bargain as well • *He lost all his money and got lost into the bargain.*

bargain *VERB* (**bargains**, **bargaining**, **bargained**)
to bargain over something is to argue over its price
to get more than you bargained for is to get an unwelcome surprise

barge *NOUN* (**barges**)
a long flat-bottomed boat used especially on canals

barge *VERB* (**barges**, **barging**, **barged**)
to barge into someone is to bump clumsily into them or push them out of the way

baritone *NOUN* (**baritones**)
a male singer with a voice between a tenor and a bass

bark *NOUN* (**barks**)
1 a bark is the sound made by a dog or a fox **2** bark is the outer covering of a tree's branches or trunk

bark *VERB* (**barks**, **barking**, **barked**)
1 a dog or fox barks when it makes its special sound **2** you can say a person barks when they speak loudly or sharply

barley *NOUN*
a kind of grain which is used for food and to make beer

barley sugar *NOUN*
a sweet made from boiled sugar

barman *NOUN* (**barmen**)
a man who serves drinks in a bar

bar mitzvah *NOUN* (**bar mitzvahs**)
a religious ceremony for Jewish boys who have reached the age of 13, when they accept some of the responsibilities of an adult

> WORD FAMILY
> The ceremony for a girl is called a **bat mitzvah**.

barn *NOUN* (**barns**)
a building on a farm used to store things such as grain or hay

barnacle *NOUN* (**barnacles**)
a shellfish that attaches itself to rocks and the bottoms of ships

barn dance *NOUN* (**barn dances**)
a type of country dance, or an informal gathering of people for dancing

barnyard *NOUN* (**barnyards**)
a farmyard

barometer *NOUN* (**barometers**) (*say* ba-**rom**-it-er)
an instrument that measures air pressure, used in forecasting the weather

baron *NOUN* (**barons**)
a member of the lowest rank of noblemen

baroness *NOUN* (**baronesses**)
a female baron or a baron's wife

barrack *VERB* (**barracks**, **barracking**, **barracked**)
to barrack someone is to jeer at them in public

barracks *NOUN* (**barracks**)
the buildings where soldiers live

barrage *NOUN* (**barrages**) (*say* **ba**-rahzh)
1 heavy gunfire **2** a large amount of something • *We received a barrage of complaints.* **3** a dam or barrier built across a river to make the water deeper

barrel *NOUN* (**barrels**)
1 a large container for liquids, with curved sides and flat ends **2** the metal tube of a gun, through which the shot is fired

barrel organ *NOUN* (**barrel organs**)
a musical instrument which you play by turning a handle

barren *ADJECTIVE*
barren land or plants cannot produce any crops or fruit

barricade *NOUN* (**barricades**)
a barrier, especially one put up quickly to block a street

barricade *VERB* (**barricades**, **barricading**, **barricaded**)
to barricade a place is to block or defend it with a barrier

barrier *NOUN* (**barriers**)
1 a fence or wall put up to stop people getting past **2** something that stops you doing something • *Lack of confidence can be a barrier to success.*

barrister *NOUN* (**barristers**)
a lawyer who argues legal cases in the higher courts

barrow *NOUN* (**barrows**)
1 a small cart **2** an ancient mound of earth over a grave

barter *VERB* (**barters**, **bartering**, **bartered**)
to barter is to exchange goods for other goods, without using money

base *NOUN* (**bases**)
1 the lowest part of something, or the part on which something stands **2** a place from which an organization like an army or business is controlled **3** (*in science*) a substance (such as an alkali) that combines with an acid to form a salt

base *VERB* (**bases**, **basing**, **based**)
to base one thing on another thing is to use the second thing as the starting point for the first • *She based the story on an event in her own childhood.*

> SPELLING
> Take care not to confuse **base** with **bass**, which means the lowest sounds in music.

baseball *NOUN* (**baseballs**)
1 baseball is an American game like rounders, in which the players hit a ball and run round a series of four 'bases' to score points **2** a baseball is the ball used in this game

basement *NOUN* (**basements**)
a room or part of a building below ground level

bash *VERB* (**bashes**, **bashing**, **bashed**)
(*informal*) to bash someone or something is to hit them hard

bash *NOUN* (**bashes**)
(*informal*) a hard hit
to have a bash at something (*informal*) is to try it even though it is difficult and you think you might not succeed

bashful *ADJECTIVE*
shy

basic *ADJECTIVE*
forming the first or most important part • *He has a basic knowledge of French.* • *Food is a basic human need.*

basically *ADVERB*
in the most important ways; essentially • *She is basically lazy.*

basin *NOUN* (**basins**)
1 a deep bowl for mixing food in **2** a large container to hold water for washing your face and hands in **3** a river basin is the area of land where the river's water comes from **4** an area of water enclosed by land, where ships can stay safely

basis *NOUN* (**bases**)
1 the basis of something is what you start from or add to • *These players will be the basis of a new team.* **2** a basis is the way in which something is arranged or organized • *You will be paid on a monthly basis.*

bask *VERB* (**basks**, **basking**, **basked**)
to bask is to lie or sit comfortably warming yourself in the sun

basket *NOUN* (**baskets**)
a container made of strips of wood, cane or wire woven together

basketball *NOUN* (**basketballs**)
1 basketball is a team game in which players try to throw a large ball through a high net hanging from a hoop **2** a basketball is the ball used in this game

basketful *NOUN* (**basketfuls**)
as much of something as you can hold in a basket • *They brought her a basketful of apples.*

bass *ADJECTIVE* (*say* bayss)
forming the lowest sounds in music

bass *NOUN* (**basses**) (*say* bayss)
a bass singer or instrument

> SPELLING
> Take care not to confuse **bass** with **base**, which means the bottom part of something.

bassoon *NOUN* (**bassoons**)
a woodwind instrument that plays low notes

bastard *NOUN* (**bastards**)
an old word for a person whose parents were not married

bat[1] *NOUN* (**bats**)
a shaped piece of wood used to hit the ball in cricket, baseball, and other games
to do something off your own bat (*informal*) is to do it without any help from other people

bat *VERB* (**bats**, **batting**, **batted**)
to bat is to take a turn at using a bat in cricket, baseball and other games

bat[2] *NOUN* (**bats**)
a flying mammal that looks like a mouse with wings. Bats come out at night to feed

batch *NOUN* (**batches**)
a set of things made at one time or dealt with together

bated *ADJECTIVE*
with bated breath waiting anxiously

bath *NOUN* (**baths**)
1 a bath is a large container you fill with water and get into to wash yourself **2** a bath sometimes means the water in a bath • *Your bath is getting cold.* **3** the baths are also a public swimming pool

bath *VERB* (**baths**, **bathing**, **bathed**)
1 to bath someone is to give them a bath **2** to bath is to have a bath

bathe *VERB* (**bathes**, **bathing**, **bathed**)
1 to bathe is to go swimming in the sea or a river **2** to bathe a sore part of your body is to wash it gently

bathe *NOUN* (**bathes**)
a bathe is a swim

bathroom *NOUN* (**bathrooms**)
a room for having a bath or wash in

bat mitzvah *NOUN* (**bat mitzvahs**)
a religious ceremony for Jewish girls who have reached the age of 12, when they accept some of the responsibilities of an adult

> WORD FAMILY
> The ceremony for a boy is called a **bar mitzvah**.

baton *NOUN* (**batons**)
a short stick, especially one you use to conduct an orchestra or in a relay race

batsman *NOUN* (**batsmen**)
a player who uses a bat in cricket

battalion *NOUN* (**battalions**)
an army unit consisting of two or more companies

batten *NOUN* (**battens**)
a flat strip of wood used to hold something in place

batten *VERB*
to batten something down is to fix it securely

batter *VERB* (**batters**, **battering**, **battered**)
to batter someone or something is to hit them hard and often • *The huge waves battered the rocks.*

batter *NOUN*
batter is a mixture of flour, eggs, and milk beaten together and used to make pancakes or to coat food before you fry it

battering ram *NOUN* (**battering rams**)
(*historical*) a heavy pole used to break through the walls and gates of a city or fort

battery *NOUN* (**batteries**)
1 a portable device for storing and supplying electricity **2** a series of cages in which animals are kept close together on a farm • *Free-range hens are not kept in batteries.* **3** a set of devices that are used together, especially a group of large guns

battle *NOUN* (**battles**)
1 a fight between two armies **2** a struggle

battlefield *NOUN* (**battlefields**)
a place where a battle is or was fought

battlements *PLURAL NOUN*
the top of a castle wall, usually with gaps through which people defending the castle could fire arrows at the enemy

battleship *NOUN* (**battleships**)
a large warship armed with powerful guns

bawl *VERB* (**bawls**, **bawling**, **bawled**)
to bawl is to shout or cry loudly

bay *NOUN* (**bays**)
1 a place by the sea or a lake where the shore curves inwards **2** an area that is marked out to be used for parking vehicles, storing things, etc.
to keep someone at bay is to prevent them from coming near you

bayonet *NOUN* (**bayonets**)
a steel blade that can be fixed to the end of a rifle and used for stabbing

bay window *NOUN* (**bay windows**)
a window that sticks out from the wall of a house

bazaar *NOUN* (**bazaars**)
1 a sale held to raise money for charity **2** a covered market in an Eastern country

BBC
short for *British Broadcasting Corporation*

BC
short for *before Christ*, used with dates that come before the birth of Jesus Christ • *Julius Caesar came to Britain in 55 BC.*

be *VERB* (**I am**; **you are**; **he, she,** or **it is**; **they are**; **I, he, she,** or **it was**, **you were**, **they were**; **I, you,** or **they have been**; **he, she,** or **it has been**)
1 to be is to live or exist • *Three boys were in the classroom.* • *There is a bus stop at the corner.* **2** to be someone or something is to have that position or quality • *She is my teacher.* • *You are very tall.*

> GRAMMAR
> The verb **be** can also be used as an 'auxiliary' verb to help make other verbs • *They are having a good time.* • *A man was killed on the motorway.* It can also be used instead of **go** in questions and in statements with **not** • *Have you been to Paris?* • *No, I've never been there.*

beach *NOUN* (**beaches**)
the strip of pebbles or sand close to the sea

beacon *NOUN* (**beacons**)
a light or fire used as a warning signal

bead *NOUN* (**beads**)
1 a small piece of glass, wood, or plastic with a hole through it, threaded on a string or wire to make a necklace or bracelet **2** a small drop of liquid • *She had beads of sweat on her face.*

beady *ADJECTIVE* (**beadier**, **beadiest**)
beady eyes are small and bright

beagle *NOUN* (**beagles**)
a type of dog with long ears, used for hunting hares

beak *NOUN* (**beaks**)
the hard, horny part of a bird's mouth

beaker *NOUN* (**beakers**)
1 a tall drinking mug, usually without a handle **2** (*in science*) a glass container used for pouring liquids in a laboratory

beam *NOUN* (**beams**)
1 a long, thick bar of wood or metal **2** a ray of light or other radiation

beam *VERB* (**beams, beaming, beamed**)
1 to beam is to send out a beam of light or radio waves **2** you can say a person beams when they smile very happily

bean *NOUN* (**beans**)
1 a kind of plant with seeds growing in pods **2** the seed or pod of this kind of plant, eaten as food

bear[1] *VERB* (**bears, bearing, bore, born** or **borne**)
1 to bear something is to carry or support it **2** to bear something such as a signature or mark is to have or show it • *The letter bore her signature.* **3** to bear something is to put up with it or suffer it • *I can't bear all this noise.* **4** a woman bears children when she gives birth to them • *She was born in 1950.* • *She has borne three sons.*

> GRAMMAR
> See the note at **born**.

bear[2] *NOUN* (**bears**)
a large heavy animal with thick fur and sharp hooked claws

bearable *ADJECTIVE*
something that is bearable is something you are able to put up with • *His toothache was hardly bearable.*

beard *NOUN* (**beards**)
hair on the lower part of a man's face
▷ **bearded** *ADJECTIVE* a bearded man is a man with a beard

bearing *NOUN* (**bearings**)
1 your bearing is the way you stand and walk **2** the direction or position of something in relation to something else
to lose your bearings is to forget where you are in relation to other things

beast *NOUN* (**beasts**)
1 any large four-footed animal **2** (*informal*) a person you think is cruel or unkind

beastly *ADJECTIVE*
(*informal*) cruel or unkind • *Don't be so beastly to your sister.*

beat *VERB* (**beats, beating, beat, beaten**)
1 to beat someone or something is to hit them repeatedly, especially with a stick **2** to beat someone in a game or match is to do better than them and win it **3** to beat a cooking mixture is to stir it quickly so that it becomes thicker **4** to beat something is to shape or flatten it by hitting it many times **5** to beat is also to make regular movements like your heart does
to beat someone up is to attack them very violently

beat *NOUN* (**beats**)
1 a regular rhythm or stroke, like your heart makes **2** a strong rhythm in pop music **3** the regular route of a police officer

Beaufort scale *NOUN* (*say* **boh**- fert skayl)
a scale for wind speed ranging from 0 (calm) to 12 (hurricane)

beautiful *ADJECTIVE*
very pleasing to look at or listen to
▷ **beautifully** *ADVERB* you do something beautifully when you do it in a beautiful or pleasing way

beauty *NOUN* (**beauties**)
1 beauty is a quality that gives delight or pleasure, especially to your senses • *They enjoyed the beauty of the sunset.* **2** a beauty is a particularly beautiful person or thing

beauty queen *NOUN* (**beauty queens**)
a woman chosen as the most beautiful in a contest

beaver *NOUN* (**beavers**)
1 a brown furry animal with strong teeth and a long flat tail, which builds dams in rivers **2** a member of the most junior section of the Scout Association

becalmed *ADJECTIVE*
a becalmed sailing ship can't sail on because the wind has dropped

became
past tense of **become**

because *CONJUNCTION*
for the reason that • *We were happy because it was a holiday.*
because of someone or **something** for that reason; on account of them • *He limped because of his bad leg.*

beckon *VERB* (**beckons, beckoning, beckoned**)
to beckon to someone is to make a sign asking them to come to you

become *VERB* (**becomes, becoming, became, become**)
1 to become is to start being something described • *It gradually became darker.* **2** to become someone is to make them look attractive • *That dress becomes you.*
to ask **what became of someone** or **something** is to wonder what happened to them in the end • *Whatever became of Jim?*

bed *NOUN* (**beds**)
1 a bed is a piece of furniture for sleeping on **2** bed is the place where you sleep • *I'm going to bed now.* **3** a bed is also a part of a garden where plants are grown **4** the bed of the sea or of a river is the bottom of it

bedclothes *PLURAL NOUN*
sheets, blankets, and duvets for using on a bed

bedding *NOUN*
things for making a bed, such as sheets, blankets, and duvets

bedlam *NOUN*
a loud noise or disturbance • *There was bedlam at the playgroup.*

bedraggled *ADJECTIVE* (*say* bi- **drag**- uld)
wet and dirty

bedridden *ADJECTIVE* (*say* **bed**- rid- en)
too ill or injured to get out of bed

bedroom *NOUN* (**bedrooms**)
a room where you sleep

bedside *NOUN*
the space beside a bed, especially the bed of someone who is ill • *He sat by his son's bedside all night.*

bedspread *NOUN* (**bedspreads**)
a covering put over the top of a bed

bedstead *NOUN* (**bedsteads**)
the framework of a bed

bedtime *NOUN*
the time when you are supposed to go to bed

bee *NOUN* (**bees**)
a stinging insect that makes honey

beech *NOUN* (**beeches**)
a tree with smooth bark and glossy leaves

beef *NOUN*
the meat of an ox, bull, or cow

beefburger *NOUN* (**beefburgers**)
a hamburger

beefeater *NOUN* (**beefeaters**)
a guard at the Tower of London

beefy *ADJECTIVE* (**beefier**, **beefiest**)
(*informal*) a beefy person is big, with strong muscles

beehive *NOUN* (**beehives**)
a container for bees to live in

beeline *NOUN*
to make a beeline for something is to go quickly and directly towards it

been
past participle of **be**

beer *NOUN* (**beers**)
beer is an alcoholic drink made from malt and hops

beet *NOUN* (**beet** or **beets**)
beet is a plant used as a vegetable or for making sugar

beetle *NOUN* (**beetles**)
an insect with hard, shiny covers over its wings

beetroot *NOUN* (**beetroot**)
the dark red root of beet used as a vegetable

before *ADVERB & PREPOSITION*
1 earlier, or earlier than • *Have you been here before?* • *They came the day before yesterday.* **2** in front of • *He stood up before the whole school.*

beforehand *ADVERB*
earlier, or before something else happens • *She had tried to phone me beforehand.* • *Let me know beforehand if you want to come on the picnic.*

beg *VERB* (**begs**, **begging**, **begged**)
1 to beg is to ask people to give you money or food **2** to beg someone is to ask them seriously or desperately • *He begged me not to tell the teacher.*
I beg your pardon I didn't hear or understand what you said; I apologize

began
past tense of **begin**

beggar *NOUN* (**beggars**)
someone who lives by begging in the street

begin *VERB* (**begins**, **beginning**, **began**, **begun**)
to begin something is to start doing it

beginner *NOUN* (**beginners**)
someone who is just starting to learn or is still learning a subject

beginning *NOUN* (**beginnings**)
the start of something

begrudge *VERB* (**begrudges**, **begrudging**, **begrudged**)
to begrudge something is to feel unhappy because someone else has it and you don't feel they deserve it • *She begrudged her brother's good luck.*

begun
past participle of **begin**

behalf *NOUN*
on behalf of something to help a cause • *They were collecting money on behalf of cancer research.*
on someone's behalf for them or in their name • *Will you accept the prize on my behalf?*

behave *VERB* (**behaves**, **behaving**, **behaved**)
1 to behave well or badly is to act in a good or bad way • *They behaved very badly at the party.* **2** to show good manners • *Why can't you behave?*

behaviour *NOUN*
1 your behaviour is the way you behave **2** animal behaviour is the way animals normally behave and treat one another

behead *VERB* (**beheads**, **beheading**, **beheaded**)
to behead someone is to cut off their head, as a form of execution

behind *ADVERB & PREPOSITION*
1 at or to the back • *The others are a long way behind.* • *She hid behind a tree.* **2** not making good progress • *He's behind the rest of the class in French.* **3** supporting or encouraging • *We're all behind you.*
behind someone's back without them knowing about it

behind *NOUN* (**behinds**)
your behind is your bottom • *He kicked me on the behind.*

beige *NOUN & ADJECTIVE* (*say* bayzh)
a light yellowish-brown colour

being *NOUN* (**beings**)
a being is a person or creature of any kind

belch *VERB* (**belches**, **belching**, **belched**)
1 to belch is to make a noise by letting air come up from your stomach through your mouth **2** a chimney or factory belches smoke or fumes when it sends out thick smoke or fumes into the air

belch *NOUN* (**belches**)
the act or sound of belching

belfry *NOUN* (**belfries**)
the top part of a tower or steeple, in which bells hang

belief *NOUN* (**beliefs**)
1 a belief is something you believe • *They have very few beliefs.* **2** belief is when you believe something

believe *VERB* (**believes**, **believing**, **believed**)
1 to believe something is to think that it is true **2** to believe someone is to think that they are telling the truth **3** to believe in something is to think it is real or important • *Do you believe in ghosts?*

> WORD FAMILY
> Something is **believable** when you are able to believe it; a **believer** is someone who believes in God.

bell *NOUN* (**bells**)
a device that makes a ringing sound, especially a cup-shaped metal object with a clapper

bellow *VERB* (**bellows**, **bellowing**, **bellowed**)
to bellow is to roar or shout loudly and deeply

bellows *PLURAL NOUN*
bellows are a device for blowing out air, especially into a fire to make it burn more strongly

belly *NOUN* (**bellies**)
1 the abdomen or the stomach of a human **2** the under part of a four-legged animal

belong *VERB* (**belongs**, **belonging**, **belonged**)
1 to belong to someone is to be their property • *The pencil belongs to me.* **2** to belong to a club or group is to be a member of it • *We both belong to the tennis club.* **3** to belong somewhere is to have a special place where it goes • *The butter belongs in the fridge.*

belongings *PLURAL NOUN*
your belongings are the things that you own

beloved *ADJECTIVE* (*say* bi- **luvd** or bi- **luv**- id)
greatly loved

below *PREPOSITION*
lower than, under • *We have nice neighbours in the flat below us.*

below *ADVERB*
at a lower point, or to a lower point • *I'll have the top bunk, and you can sleep below.*

belt *NOUN* (**belts**)
1 a strip of material, often leather or cloth, that you wear round your waist **2** a long narrow area • *As we went further north we met a belt of rain.*

belt *VERB* (**belts**, **belting**, **belted**)(*informal*)
1 to belt someone is to hit them hard **2** to belt along is to move very fast

bench *NOUN* (**benches**)
1 a long seat **2** a long table for working at

bend *VERB* (**bends**, **bending**, **bent**)
1 to bend something is to make it curved or crooked **2** to bend is to become curved or crooked • *The trees were bending in the wind.* **3** to bend is also to move the top of your body downwards • *She bent down to pick up the cat.*

bend *NOUN* (**bends**)
a part where something curves or turns

beneath *PREPOSITION & ADVERB*
under • *Beneath the soil there is clay.*

benefactor *NOUN* (**benefactors**)
someone who gives money or other help to a person or organization that needs it

beneficial *ADJECTIVE*
something is beneficial when it is useful or helpful

benefit *NOUN* (**benefits**)
1 a benefit is something that is useful or helpful • *Television is one of the benefits of modern science.* **2** benefit is money that the government pays to help people who are poor, sick, or out of work **3** a benefit concert or match is one organized to raise money for a good cause
to give someone the benefit of the doubt is to believe them even though you cannot be sure

benefit *VERB* (**benefits**, **benefiting**, **benefited**)
you benefit from something, or it benefits you, when it helps you

benevolent *ADJECTIVE*
kind and helpful
▷ **benevolence** *NOUN* benevolence is kindness or being helpful

bent *ADJECTIVE*
1 curved or crooked **2** (*slang*) dishonest
to be bent on something is to be determined to do it

bent *NOUN*
a bent is a liking or talent for something • *She has quite a bent for acting.*

bequeath *VERB* (**bequeaths**, **bequeathing**, **bequeathed**) (*rhymes with* **breathe**)
to bequeath something to someone is to leave it to them in a will

bequest *NOUN* (**bequests**)
a gift of money or property that someone leaves to a person in their will

bereaved *ADJECTIVE*
a bereaved person is someone with a close relative who has recently died
▷ **bereavement** *NOUN* someone suffers bereavement when a close relative dies

bereft *ADJECTIVE*
to be bereft of something is to be deprived of it • *He was bereft of hope.*

beret *NOUN* (**berets**) (*say* **bair**- ay)
a soft, round, flat cap

berry *NOUN* (**berries**)
a small, juicy fruit

berserk *ADJECTIVE*
to go berserk is to become extremely angry or lose control • *The man went berserk and started flinging things around.*

berth *NOUN* (**berths**)
1 a sleeping place on a ship or train **2** a place where a ship is tied up

> SPELLING
> Take care not to confuse **berth** with **birth**, which means being born.

beside *PREPOSITION*
next to; close to • *A house beside the sea.*
to be beside the point is to have nothing to do with what is being talked about • *All your excuses are beside the point.*
to be beside yourself is to be very excited or upset • *He was beside himself with anger.*

besides *PREPOSITION*
in addition to • *Who came besides you?*

besides *ADVERB*
also; in addition to this • *The coat cost too much. Besides, it's the wrong colour.*

besiege *VERB* (**besieges**, **besieging**, **besieged**)
(*say* bi- **seej**)
1 to besiege a place is to surround it until the people inside surrender **2** to besiege someone famous is to crowd round them • *The rock group was besieged by hundreds of fans.*

best *ADJECTIVE* superlative of **good** and **well**
most excellent; most able to do something • *She's the best swimmer in the class.*

best *ADVERB*
1 in the best way; most • *We'll do what suits you best.* **2** most usefully; most wisely • *He is best ignored.*

best *NOUN*
the best person or thing, or the best people or things • *She was the best at tennis.* • *These apples are the best you can buy.*
to do your best is to do as well as you can
to make the best of something is to accept it and enjoy it as much as you can, even though it is not very good

best man *NOUN*
someone who helps the bridegroom at his wedding

best-seller *NOUN* (**best-sellers**)
a book or other product that has sold in very large numbers

bet *NOUN* (**bets**)
1 an agreement that you will receive money if you are correct in choosing the winner of a race or in saying something will happen, and will lose money if you are not correct **2** the money you risk losing in a bet

bet *VERB* (**bets**, **betting**, **bet** or **betted**)
1 to bet, or to bet money, is to make a bet
2 (*informal*) to bet something is to say you are sure about it • *I bet I'm right.*

betray *VERB* (**betrays**, **betraying**, **betrayed**)
1 to betray someone is to do them harm when they are expecting your support **2** to betray something like a secret is to give it away
▷ **betrayal** *NOUN* betrayal is betraying someone

better *ADJECTIVE* comparative of **good** and **well**
1 more excellent • *I need a better bike.* **2** to be better is to feel well again after an illness • *Are you better?*

better *NOUN* (**betters**)
a better person or thing
to get the better of someone is to defeat or outwit them

better *ADVERB*
in a better way • *Try to do it better next time.*
I had better do something it would be better for me to do it (you can use **we, you,** and so on, instead of **I**)
to be better off is to be more fortunate in some way, for example by having more money

better *VERB* (**betters**, **bettering**, **bettered**)
to better something is to improve on it • *She hopes to better her own record time.*

between *PREPOSITION & ADVERB*
within two or more points; among • *Call me between Tuesday and Friday.* • *The train runs between London and Glasgow.* • *What is the difference between butter and margarine?* • *Divide the sweets between the children.* • *The two houses are side by side with a fence between.*

beware *VERB* (*only in the form* **beware**)
a warning to be careful • *Beware of pickpockets.*

bewilder *VERB* (**bewilders**, **bewildering**, **bewildered**)
to bewilder someone is to puzzle them completely
▷ **bewilderment** *NOUN* bewilderment is being bewildered or puzzled

bewitch *VERB* (**bewitches**, **bewitching**, **bewitched**)
1 to bewitch someone is to put a spell on them **2** to bewitch someone is also to delight them very much • *He was completely bewitched by her beauty.*

beyond *PREPOSITION & ADVERB*
farther on • *Don't go beyond the end of the street.* • *You can see the next valley and the mountains beyond.*

bias *NOUN* (**biases**)
1 bias is a strong feeling in favour of one person or side and against another • *The referee was accused of bias.* **2** bias is also a tendency for a ball to swerve, especially in a game of bowls
▷ **biased** *ADJECTIVE* someone is biased when they show that they prefer one person or side over another

bib *NOUN* (**bibs**)
a piece of cloth or plastic you put under a baby's chin during meals to protect its clothes from stains

Bible *NOUN* (**Bibles**)
the holy book of Christianity and Judaism
▷ **biblical** *ADJECTIVE* to do with the Bible

a
b
c
d
e
f
g
h
i
j
k
l
m
n
o
p
q
r
s
t
u
v
w
x
y
z

bibliography (*say* bib-lee-og-ra-fee) *NOUN* (**bibliographies**)
a list of books about a subject or by a particular author

bicycle *NOUN* (**bicycles**)
a two-wheeled vehicle that you ride by pushing down on pedals with your feet

bid *NOUN* (**bids**)
1 offering an amount you will pay for something, especially at an auction **2** an attempt • *He will make a bid for the world record tomorrow.*

bid *VERB* (**bids, bidding, bid**)
to bid an amount of money is to offer it for something at an auction

bide *VERB* (**bides, biding, bided**)
to bide your time is to wait, expecting something to happen that will help you

big *ADJECTIVE* (**bigger, biggest**)
1 more than the normal size; large **2** important • *This is a big decision.* **3** elder • *Have you met my big sister?*

bigamy *NOUN*
bigamy is when a person has more than one wife or husband at the same time

bike *NOUN* (**bikes**)
(*informal*) a bicycle or motor cycle

bikini *NOUN* (**bikinis**)
a woman's two-piece swimsuit

bile *NOUN*
a bitter greenish-brown fluid produced in the liver, that helps the body to digest fat

bilge *NOUN* (**bilges**)
bilge is the water that collects inside the bottom of a ship

bilingual *ADJECTIVE*
speaking two languages well

bill[1] *NOUN* (**bills**)
1 a piece of paper that tells you how much money you owe for something **2** a plan for a new law in parliament **3** a poster **4** a programme of entertainment • *There's a magician on the bill.*

bill[2] *NOUN* (**bills**)
a bird's beak

billiards *NOUN*
a game played with long sticks (called *cues*) and three balls on a cloth-covered table

billion *NOUN* (**billions**)
a thousand million (1,000,000,000)
▷ **billionth** *ADJECTIVE & NOUN* a thousand-millionth

> BRITISH AND AMERICAN
> In Britain, but not in America, **billion** can also mean a million million (1,000,000,000,000). People often say **billions**, meaning very many, and then the exact number is not important.

billow *VERB* (**billows, billowing, billowed**)
to billow is to rise up or move like waves on the sea • *As she floated gently down, Mrs Twit's petticoat billowed out like a parachute, showing her long knickers.* — Roald Dahl, *The Twits.*

billy goat *NOUN* (**billy goats**)
a male goat

bin *NOUN* (**bins**)
a large or deep container, especially one that you put rubbish or litter in

binary *ADJECTIVE*
having two parts • *a binary star*

binary number *NOUN* (**binary numbers**)
a number that uses only the digits 0 and 1. Binary numbers are used in computer programming.

binary system *NOUN*
a system of expressing numbers by using the digits 0 and 1 only. For example, 21 is written 10101

bind *VERB* (**binds, binding, bound**)
1 to bind things is to tie them up or tie them together **2** to bind something is to wrap a piece of material round it **3** to bind a book is to fasten the pages inside a cover **4** to bind someone is to make them do something or promise something

bingo *NOUN*
a game played with cards with numbered squares. These are covered or crossed out as the numbers are called out, and the first person to complete the card wins the game

binoculars *PLURAL NOUN*
a device with lenses for both eyes, for making distant objects seem nearer

biodegradable *ADJECTIVE*
able to be broken down by bacteria in the environment • *All our packaging is biodegradable.*

biography *NOUN* (**biographies**)
the story of a person's life

> WORD FAMILY
> A **biographer** is someone who writes a biography; a **biographical** story or history is one that is about a person's life.

biology *NOUN*
the science or study of living things
▷ **biological** *ADJECTIVE* to do with biology
▷ **biologist** *NOUN* a person who studies biology

> WORD FAMILY
> A **biologist** is someone who studies biology; a **biological** science or experiment is one that has to do with living things.

bionic *ADJECTIVE*
worked by electronic devices, and imitating a living being

biosphere *NOUN*
the parts of the earth's surface and its atmosphere where living things are found

birch *NOUN* (**birches**)
a thin tree with shiny bark and slender branches

bird *NOUN* (**birds**)
a feathered animal with two wings, two legs, and a beak

bird of prey *NOUN*
a bird that feeds on animal flesh, such as an eagle or hawk

birdseed *NOUN*
seeds for caged birds to eat

bird's-eye view *NOUN*
a general view of something, seen from above

Biro *NOUN* (**Biros**)
(*trademark*) a kind of ballpoint pen

birth *NOUN* (**births**)
birth is the beginning of a person's or animal's life, when they come out of their mother's body

SPELLING
Take care not to confuse **birth** with **berth**, which means a sleeping place, or a place where a ship is tied up.

birth certificate *NOUN* (**birth certificates**)
a document showing where and when you were born

birth control *NOUN*
the use of contraceptives to prevent women from becoming pregnant

WORD FAMILY
This is also called **family planning**.

birthday *NOUN* (**birthdays**)
the anniversary of the day on which you were born

birthmark *NOUN* (**birthmarks**)
a coloured mark which has been on someone's skin since they were born

birthplace *NOUN* (**birthplaces**)
the place where someone was born

birth rate *NOUN*
the number of children born in one year for every 1,000 of the population

biscuit *NOUN* (**biscuits**)
a small flat kind of cake that has been baked until it is hard

bisect *VERB* (**bisects**, **bisecting**, **bisected**)
to bisect something is to divide it into two equal parts

bishop *NOUN* (**bishops**)
1 a senior priest in the Christian Church who is in charge of all the churches in a city or district **2** a chess piece shaped like a bishop's mitre

bison *NOUN* (**bison**)
a wild ox with shaggy hair

bit *NOUN* (**bits**)
1 a small piece or amount of somethin **2** the part of a horse's bridle that is put into its mouth **3** the part of a tool that cuts or grips **4** (*in computing*) the smallest unit of data or memory
a bit slightly • *I'm a bit worried.*
bit by bit gradually
bits and pieces small things of various kinds

bit
past tense of **bite** *VERB*

bitch *NOUN* (**bitches**)
a female dog, fox, or wolf

bitchy *ADJECTIVE* (**bitchier**, **bitchiest**)
nasty or spiteful • *Stop making bitchy remarks about Rebecca!*

bite *VERB* (**bites**, **biting**, **bit**, **bitten**)
1 to bite something is to cut it or hold it with your teeth **2** to bite into something is to penetrate it • *The tyres bit into the mud.* **3** to accept bait • *The fish are biting.* **4** to sting or hurt • *a biting wind*

bite *NOUN* (**bites**)
1 to give a person or animal a bite is to bite them **2** a mark or spot made by biting • *You've had an insect bite.* **3** a snack • *Would you like a bite?*

bitter *ADJECTIVE*
1 tasting sour and unpleasant **2** feeling angry and resentful because you are disappointed about something • *She is very bitter about losing her place in the team.* **3** extremely cold • *There was a bitter wind.*

black *ADJECTIVE* (**blacker**, **blackest**)
1 of the darkest colour, like coal or soot **2** having dark skin **3** dismal; not hopeful • *The outlook is black.* **4** very dirty

black *NOUN* (**blacks**)
1 a black colour **2** a person with dark skin

blackberry *NOUN* (**blackberries**)
a sweet black berry

blackbird *NOUN* (**blackbirds**)
a dark European songbird

blackboard *NOUN* (**blackboards**)
a dark board for writing on with chalk

blacken *VERB* (**blackens**, **blackening**, **blackened**)
1 to blacken something is to make it black **2** to blacken someone's name is to say bad things about them

black eye *NOUN* (**black eyes**)
an eye with heavy bruises round it

black hole *NOUN* (**black holes**)
(*in astronomy*) a region in space with such strong gravity that no light escapes

black ice *NOUN*
thin transparent ice on roads

blackmail *VERB* (**blackmails**, **blackmailing**, **blackmailed**)
to blackmail someone is to get money from them by threatening to tell people something that they want to keep secret

black market *NOUN*
a black market in goods is illegal trading in them

a b c d e f g h i j k l m n o p q r s t u v w x y z

blackout *NOUN* (**blackouts**)
1 when a person becomes unconscious for a short time **2** a time when lights are kept hidden or turned off

blacksmith *NOUN* (**blacksmiths**)
someone who makes and repairs things made of iron, and fits shoes on horses

bladder *NOUN* (**bladders**)
1 the bladder is the bag-like part of your body where urine collects **2** a bladder is also an inflatable bag inside a football

blade *NOUN* (**blades**)
1 the sharp part of a device for cutting, such as a knife or sword **2** the flat, wide part of an oar or propeller **3** a long narrow leaf of grass

blame *VERB* (**blames, blaming, blamed**)
to blame someone is to say that they have done something wrong • *My brother broke the window but they blamed me.*

blame *NOUN*
to get the blame for something is to be blamed for it
to be to blame is to be the person who has done something wrong

blancmange *NOUN* (**blancmanges**) (*say* bla- **monj**)
blancmange is a pudding like a jelly made with milk

blank *ADJECTIVE*
1 not written, drawn, or printed on • *The piece of paper was blank.* **2** showing no expression or interest • *His face looked blank.*
to go blank is to suddenly forget everything • *When he asked me the way, my mind went blank.*

blank *NOUN* (**blanks**)
1 an empty space **2** a blank cartridge
to draw a blank is to fail to achieve what you wanted

blank cartridge *NOUN* (**blank cartridges**)
a cartridge for a gun which makes a noise but does not fire a bullet

blanket *NOUN* (**blankets**)
a large piece of thick cloth, used as a warm covering for a bed

blank verse *NOUN*
verse which does not rhyme at the ends of lines

blare *VERB* (**blares, blaring, blared**)
to blare is to make a harsh, loud sound

blaspheme *VERB* (**blasphemes, blaspheming, blasphemed**)
to blaspheme is to talk without respect about God or a religion

> **WORD FAMILY**
> A **blasphemous** person is disrespectful about God or a religion; **blasphemy** is talking without respect about God or a religion.

blast *NOUN* (**blasts**)
1 a strong rush of wind or air **2** a sharp or loud noise • *The referee gave a long blast of his whistle.*

blast *VERB* (**blasts, blasting, blasted**)
to blast something is to blow it up with explosives

blast-off *NOUN*
the launch of a spacecraft

blaze *NOUN* (**blazes**)
1 a very bright fire **2** a very bright colour or light

blaze *VERB* (**blazes, blazing, blazed**)
1 to blaze is to burn or shine brightly **2** to blaze with a feeling is to feel it very strongly • *He was blazing with anger.*
to blaze a trail is to show the way for others to follow

blazer *NOUN* (**blazers**)
a kind of jacket, often with a badge on the front

bleach *NOUN* (**bleaches**)
a substance used to clean things or make clothes white

bleach *VERB* (**bleaches, bleaching, bleached**)
to bleach something is to make it white

bleak *ADJECTIVE* (**bleaker, bleakest**)
1 bare and cold • *The village school for younger children was a bleak brick building called Crunchem Hall Primary School.* — Roald Dahl, *Matilda.*
2 dreary and miserable • *The future looks bleak.*

bleary *ADJECTIVE* (**blearier, bleariest**)
bleary eyes are tired and do not see clearly
▷ **blearily** *ADVERB* with bleary eyes • *He looked at me blearily.*

bleat *NOUN* (**bleats**)
the cry of a sheep or goat

bleat *VERB* (**bleats, bleating, bleated**)
a sheep or goat bleats when it makes a bleat

bleed *VERB* (**bleeds, bleeding, bled**)
1 to bleed is to lose blood from your body, for example if you are injured **2** to bleed a person or animal is to take blood from them

bleep *NOUN* (**bleeps**)
a small, high sound like the sound some digital watches make

blemish *NOUN* (**blemishes**)
1 a mark or stain on something **2** a fault or weakness

blend *VERB* (**blends, blending, blended**)
to blend things is to mix them together smoothly or easily

blend *NOUN* (**blends**)
a smooth mixture

bless *VERB* (**blesses, blessing, blessed**)
1 to bless someone is to wish or bring them happiness **2** to bless someone is also to ask God to look after them

blessing *NOUN* (**blessings**)
1 a prayer or act of blessing someone **2** something you are glad of or happy about • *It's a blessing that they are safe.*

blew
past tense of **blow** *VERB*

blight *NOUN* (**blights**)
1 blight is a plant disease **2** a blight is a thing that spoils or damages something

blind *ADJECTIVE* (**blinder**, **blindest**)
1 not able to see **2** without thought or understanding

blind *VERB* (**blinds**, **blinding**, **blinded**)
1 to blind someone is to make them blind **2** a bright light blinds you when it makes you unable to see for a time

blind *NOUN* (**blinds**)
a screen for a window

blind alley *NOUN* (**blind alleys**)
a road which is closed at one end

blindfold *NOUN* (**blindfolds**)
a piece of cloth used to cover someone's eyes so that they cannot see where they are or what is happening

blindfold *VERB* (**blindfolds**, **blindfolding**, **blindfolded**)
to blindfold someone is to cover their eyes with a blindfold

blindfold *ADJECTIVE*
with a blindfold over the eyes

blink *VERB* (**blinks**, **blinking**, **blinked**)
to blink is to shut and open your eyes quickly

bliss *NOUN*
bliss is great happiness
▷ **blissful** *ADJECTIVE* very happy
▷ **blissfully** *ADVERB* very happily

blister *NOUN* (**blisters**)
a swelling like a bubble on your skin

blitz *NOUN* (**blitzes**)
a sudden violent attack, especially from aircraft

blizzard *NOUN* (**blizzards**)
a severe snowstorm

bloated *ADJECTIVE*
swollen or puffed out

blob *NOUN* (**blobs**)
a small round lump of something like paint or ice cream

block *NOUN* (**blocks**)
1 a solid piece of something hard such as wood **2** a large building or group of buildings with streets all around it **3** something that stops people getting through • *They came to a road block and had to turn back.*

block *VERB* (**blocks**, **blocking**, **blocked**)
1 to block something is to get in the way of it • *Tall buildings blocked our view.* **2** to block something like a pipe or drain is to prevent water flowing through it

blockade *NOUN* (**blockades**)
when a city or port is surrounded to stop people or goods from getting in or out

blockage *NOUN* (**blockages**)
1 something that stops up a pipe or drain **2** a blocked state • *Roadworks are causing blockages in the traffic.*

block capitals or **block letters** *PLURAL NOUN*
large capital letters

blond or **blonde** *ADJECTIVE* (**blonder**, **blondest**)
fair-haired

blonde *NOUN* (**blondes**)
a fair-haired girl or woman

blood *NOUN*
1 blood is the red liquid that flows through your veins and arteries **2** someone who is of noble or royal blood has ancestors who were noble or royal • *He is of royal blood.*
to do something in cold blood is to do it deliberately and cruelly

blood donor *NOUN* (**blood donors**)
someone who gives some blood for use in transfusions

bloodhound *NOUN* (**bloodhounds**)
a large breed of dog which can track people over long distances by following their scent

bloodshed *NOUN*
bloodshed is the killing and injuring of people

bloodshot *ADJECTIVE*
eyes are bloodshot when they are streaked with red from being strained or tired

bloodstream *NOUN*
the bloodstream is the blood flowing round your body

bloodthirsty *ADJECTIVE* (**bloodthirstier**, **bloodthirstiest**)
enjoying killing and violence

bloody *ADJECTIVE* (**bloodier**, **bloodiest**)
1 bleeding **2** covered in blood **3** a bloody fight or battle is one in which a lot of people are killed or badly hurt

bloody-minded *ADJECTIVE*
deliberately awkward or unhelpful

bloom *VERB* (**blooms**, **blooming**, **bloomed**)
to bloom is to produce flowers • *Look! The roses have bloomed!*

bloom *NOUN* (**blooms**)
a bloom is a flower
in bloom trees and plants are in bloom when they are producing flowers

blossom *NOUN* (**blossoms**)
1 a blossom is a flower, especially on a fruit tree **2** blossom is a mass of flowers on a tree

blossom *VERB* (**blossoms**, **blossoming**, **blossomed**)
1 a tree or bush blossoms when it produces flowers **2** to blossom is also to develop into something very fine or good • *She has blossomed into a lovely singer.*

blot *NOUN* (**blots**)
1 a spot or blob of ink **2** a flaw or fault

blot *VERB* (**blots, blotting, blotted**)
1 to blot something is to make a blot on it **2** to blot paper is to dry it with blotting paper
to blot something out is to remove it or make it invisible
to blot your copybook is to spoil your good reputation

blotch *NOUN* (**blotches**)
an untidy patch of colour
▷ **blotchy** *ADJECTIVE* having lots of blotches

blotting paper *NOUN*
blotting paper is thick, soft paper for soaking up ink blots on paper

blouse *NOUN* (**blouses**)
a loose piece of clothing like a shirt that girls and women wear

blow *NOUN* (**blows**)
1 a hard knock or hit **2** a shock or disappointment • *Losing so much money was a terrible blow.* **3** the action of blowing

blow *VERB* (**blows, blowing, blew, blown**)
1 to blow is to force out air from your mouth or nose • *He blew on his cold hands to warm them up.* **2** to move in the wind • *Her hat blew off.* **3** to blow something is to form it by blowing • *Let's blow bubbles.* **4** to blow something such as a whistle is to make a sound with it **5** a fuse or light bulb blows when it melts or breaks
to blow something up is to destroy it with an explosion
to blow up is to be destroyed in an explosion

blowlamp or **blowtorch** *NOUN* (**blowlamps** or **blowtorches**)
a device for aiming a strong flame at a surface, especially to remove old paint

blue *ADJECTIVE* (**bluer, bluest**)
1 of the colour of a bright cloudless sky **2** sad and miserable • *I'm feeling blue.* **3** rude or obscene • *They were telling blue jokes.*

blue *NOUN* (**blues**)
a blue colour
out of the blue with no warning • *My friend turned up out of the blue.*

bluebell *NOUN* (**bluebells**)
a blue wild flower

bluebottle *NOUN* (**bluebottles**)
a large blue fly that makes a loud buzz

blueprint *NOUN* (**blueprints**)
a detailed plan of something that is going to be built

blues *PLURAL NOUN*
blues is a type of music that is often sad
to get the blues is to feel sad and miserable

bluff *VERB* (**bluffs, bluffing, bluffed**)
to bluff someone is to make them think that you will do something that you don't intend to do or that you know something that you don't really know

bluff *NOUN* (**bluffs**)
a bluff is something that someone says or does to bluff someone else, for example an empty promise or threat • *He said he'd report us, but that was just a bluff.*
to call someone's bluff is to challenge them to do what they have threatened to do

blunder *NOUN* (**blunders**)
a careless mistake

blunt *ADJECTIVE* (**blunter, bluntest**)
1 having an edge that is smooth and not good for cutting **2** saying what you mean without trying to be polite or tactful

blur *VERB* (**blurs, blurring, blurred**)
to blur something is to make it unclear or smeared

blur *NOUN* (**blurs**)
an unclear shape with no definite outline • *Without her glasses on, everything was a blur.*

blurb *NOUN* (**blurbs**)
a short description of a book that is printed on the back and meant to attract your attention and make you want to buy it

blurt *VERB* (**blurt, blurting, blurted**)
to blurt something out is to say it suddenly, without thinking

blush *VERB* (**blushes, blushing, blushed**)
to blush is to have a strong pink tinge in your face because you are embarrassed or ashamed

bluster *VERB* (**blusters, blustering, blustered**)
to bluster is to boast or make threats that don't mean very much

blustery *ADJECTIVE*
blustery weather is when the wind is blowing in gusts

boa or **boa constrictor** *NOUN* (**boas** or **boa constrictors**)
a large South American snake that coils round its prey and crushes it

boar *NOUN* (**boars**)
1 a wild pig **2** a male pig

board *NOUN* (**boards**)
1 a board is a flat piece of wood, used in building **2** a board is also a flat piece of wood or cardboard used to play games with, for example a dartboard or a chess board **3** a board is also a group of people who run a company or organization **4** board is daily meals supplied in return for money or work • *The price of the holiday includes full board.*
on board aboard a ship

board *VERB* (**boards, boarding, boarded**)
1 to board a ship or train or aircraft is to get on it for a journey **2** to board is to get meals and accommodation
to board something up is to cover it with boards

boarder *NOUN* (**boarders**)
1 a child who lives at a boarding school during the term **2** a lodger

board game *NOUN* (**board games**)
a game played on a board, such as chess or draughts

boarding school *NOUN* (**boarding schools**)
a school in which the pupils live during the term

boast *VERB* (**boasts**, **boasting**, **boasted**)
to boast about something that you own or that you have done is to talk proudly about it, often in order to impress people

boastful *ADJECTIVE*
a boastful person likes to talk a lot about the things they own or the things they have done
▷ **boastfully** *ADVERB* in a boasting way

boat *NOUN* (**boats**)
a vehicle designed to float and travel on water
to be in the same boat is to share the same problems or difficulties

bob *VERB* (**bobs**, **bobbing**, **bobbed**)
to bob is to move gently up and down, like something floating on water

bobble *NOUN* (**bobbles**)
a small round ball of something soft such as wool, used as a decoration on a hat or clothing

bobsleigh or **bobsled** *NOUN* (**bobsleighs** or **bobsleds**)
a large sledge with two sets of runners

bodice *NOUN* (**bodices**)
the upper part of a woman's dress

bodily *ADJECTIVE*
to do with your body

bodily *ADVERB*
by taking hold of someone's body • *He was picked up bodily and bundled into the car.*

body *NOUN* (**bodies**)
1 the body is the flesh and bones and other parts of a person or animal **2** the body is also the main part of a person or animal, not including the head, arms, or legs **3** a body is a dead person or corpse **4** the body of something is the main part of it **5** a body of people is a group of them in one place **6** a body is a distinct object or piece of matter • *Stars and planets are heavenly bodies.*

bodyguard *NOUN* (**bodyguards**)
a guard who protects someone from being attacked

bog *NOUN* (**bogs**)
bog or a bog is an area of wet, spongy ground
▷ **boggy** *ADJECTIVE* boggy ground is wet and spongy

bogus *ADJECTIVE*
false; not real or genuine • *He gave a name that turned out to be bogus.*

boil[1] *VERB* (**boils**, **boiling**, **boiled**)
1 to boil a liquid is to heat it until it starts to bubble and give off vapour **2** to boil is to start bubbling, like water **3** to boil food is to cook it in boiling water
to be boiling (*informal*) is to be very hot, like the weather • *It's boiling outside.*
to bring a liquid to the boil is to heat it until it boils

boil[2] *NOUN* (**boils**)
a painful red swelling on the skin

boiler *NOUN* (**boilers**)
a container for heating water or making steam

boiling point *NOUN* (**boiling points**)
the temperature at which something boils

boisterous *ADJECTIVE*
noisy and lively

bold *ADJECTIVE* (**bolder**, **boldest**)
1 brave and adventurous **2** clear and easy to see **3** printed in thick black type

bollard *NOUN* (**bollards**)
1 a short thick post put up on a road, used to keep out traffic **2** a short thick post on a ship or quay, that ropes are tied to

bolster *VERB* (**bolsters**, **bolstering**, **bolstered**)
to bolster something such as a feeling is to increase it • *Her win last week has really bolstered her confidence.*
to bolster something up is to support it when it is weak

bolt *NOUN* (**bolts**)
1 a sliding bar for fastening a door or window **2** a thick metal pin for fastening things together **3** a flash of lightning
a bolt from the blue an unwelcome surprise

bolt *VERB* (**bolts**, **bolting**, **bolted**)
1 to bolt a door or window is to fasten it with a bolt **2** to bolt is to run away in panic, as a horse does **3** to bolt food is to swallow it too quickly

bomb *NOUN* (**bombs**)
a container with explosives, which blows up when it is detonated

bomb *VERB* (**bombs**, **bombing**, **bombed**)
to bomb a place is to attack it with bombs

bombard *VERB* (**bombards**, **bombarding**, **bombarded**)
1 to bombard a place is to attack it with heavy gunfire **2** to bombard someone with questions or complaints is to direct a large number of questions or complaints at them
▷ **bombardment** *NOUN* a bombardment is a heavy attack with guns

bomber *NOUN* (**bombers**)
1 an aircraft built to drop bombs **2** a person who plants or sets off a bomb

bond *NOUN* (**bonds**)
1 a shared experience or feeling that brings people close together **2** bonds are ropes or chains used to tie people up

bondage *NOUN*
bondage is being a slave

a
b
c
d
e
f
g
h
i
j
k
l
m
n
o
p
q
r
s
t
u
v
w
x
y
z

bone *NOUN* (**bones**)
a bone is one of the hard pieces of a skeleton
to have a bone to pick with someone is to have a reason to argue with them about something

bonfire *NOUN* (**bonfires**)
a large fire lit out of doors

bonnet *NOUN* (**bonnets**)
1 the hinged cover over the front part of a car **2** a baby's or woman's hat with strings that tie under the chin

> BRITISH AND AMERICAN
> In America, the word **hood** is used for the first meaning.

bonus *NOUN* (**bonuses**)
1 an extra payment that someone gets for their work **2** an extra advantage or reward

bony *ADJECTIVE* (**bonier**, **boniest**)
1 bony people or animals have bones without much flesh on them **2** full of bones **3** thin and hard, like a bone

boo *VERB* (**boos**, **booing**, **booed**)
to boo is to shout out that you don't like what someone has said or done, like an angry audience in a theatre

booby prize *NOUN* (**booby prizes**)
a prize given as a joke to someone who comes last in a contest

booby trap *NOUN* (**booby traps**)
something designed to hit or injure someone when they do not expect it

book *NOUN* (**books**)
a set of sheets of paper, usually with printing or writing on, fastened together inside a cover

book *VERB* (**books**, **booking**, **booked**)
1 to book something such as a seat in a theatre or on a train, or a room in a hotel, is to arrange for it to be kept for you **2** to book something is to record it in a book or list
to book in is to record that you have arrived in a place such as a hotel

bookcase *NOUN* (**bookcases**)
a piece of furniture with shelves for holding books

bookkeeping *NOUN*
bookkeeping is recording details of all the money that a business receives and spends

booklet *NOUN* (**booklets**)
a small book with paper covers

bookmaker *NOUN* (**bookmakers**)
a person whose business is taking bets, especially bets made on horse races

bookmark *NOUN* (**bookmarks**)
something you use to mark a place in a book

boom *NOUN* (**booms**)
1 a deep hollow sound **2** a time when people are well off **3** a long pole at the bottom of a sail to keep it stretched **4** a long pole carrying a microphone

boom *VERB* (**booms**, **booming**, **boomed**)
1 to boom is to make a deep hollow sound, like a heavy gun **2** to boom is also to speak in a loud deep voice **3** to boom is also to grow quickly or be prosperous • *Business is booming.*

boomerang *NOUN* (**boomerangs**)
a curved stick which moves in a curve and comes back to you when you throw it.

boost *VERB* (**boosts**, **boosting**, **boosted**)
to boost something is to increase its size or value or power • *Being in the drama group has really boosted his confidence.*

booster *NOUN* (**boosters**)
1 something that increases the power of a system, especially a radio or television transmitter **2** an additional engine or rocket for a spacecraft **3** an additional dose of a vaccine

boot *NOUN* (**boots**)
1 a heavy shoe that covers the ankle and sometimes part of your leg **2** the space for luggage at the back of a car

> BRITISH AND AMERICAN
> In America, the word **trunk** is used for the second meaning.

boot *VERB* (**boots**, **booting**, **booted**)
1 to boot someone is to kick them hard **2** to boot up a computer is to switch it on and start it

booth *NOUN* (**booths**)
a small compartment for a special purpose, such as making a telephone call or having your photo taken

border *NOUN* (**borders**)
1 the border between two countries is the line where they meet • *We're about to cross the Scottish border.* **2** an edge • *There is a black border around the poster.* **3** a flower bed

borderline *ADJECTIVE*
only just acceptable or valid

bore [1] *VERB* (**bores**, **boring**, **bored**)
1 to bore someone is to make them feel tired and uninterested **2** to bore a hole is to drill it through something

bore *NOUN* (**bores**)
a dull or uninteresting person or thing

bore [2]
past tense of **bear** *VERB*

boredom *NOUN*
a feeling of tiredness and lack of interest

borehole *NOUN* (**boreholes**)
a deep narrow hole that engineers make in the ground when they are looking for water or oil

boring *ADJECTIVE*
dull and uninteresting • *The book was really boring.*

born or **borne**
past participle of **bear** *VERB*

GRAMMAR
Born is used in sentences where the child is the subject, such as • *Their son was born on the 17th of December*; **borne** is used in sentences where the mother is the subject, such as • *She has borne three children.*

borough *NOUN* (**boroughs**) (*say* **bu**- ro)
an important town or district with its own local council

borrow *VERB* (**borrows**, **borrowing**, **borrowed**)
to borrow something is to have it for a time and then return it to its owner

bosom *NOUN* (**bosoms**)
a woman's breasts

boss *NOUN* (**bosses**)
(*informal*) a person who is in charge of a business or group of workers

boss *VERB* (**bosses**, **bossing**, **bossed**)
(*informal*) to boss someone is to order them around

bossy *ADJECTIVE* (**bossier**, **bossiest**)
(*informal*) a bossy person is fond of ordering people about

botany *NOUN*
botany is the study of plants

WORD FAMILY
A **botanist** is someone who studies botany; a **botanical** garden is one that has a lot of interesting plants that the public can go and see.

both *DETERMINER & PRONOUN*
the two of them, not just one • *I want them both in the team.*

both *ADVERB*
you use **both** with **and** to say two things about something or someone • *He is both friendly and helpful.*

bother *VERB* (**bothers**, **bothering**, **bothered**)
1 to bother someone is to cause them trouble or worry **2** to be bothered to do something is to take trouble over it

bother *NOUN*
bother is trouble or worry

bottle *NOUN* (**bottles**)
a glass or plastic container with a narrow neck for holding liquids

bottle *VERB* (**bottles**, **bottling**, **bottled**)
to bottle something is to put it in a bottle
to bottle something up is to keep something you are worried about to yourself

bottle bank *NOUN* (**bottle banks**)
a large tank or drum for putting glass bottles and jars in for recycling

bottleneck *NOUN* (**bottlenecks**)
a place where traffic is slowed down or stuck by a blockage or hazard

bottom *NOUN* (**bottoms**)
1 the bottom of something is its lowest point **2** the bottom of a garden is the farther end of it, away from the house **3** your bottom is the part of you that you sit on, also called your buttocks

bottomless *ADJECTIVE*
1 very deep **2** not seeming to have any limit • *I don't have a bottomless purse.*

bougainvillea *NOUN* (**bougainvilleas**) (*say* boo-gan-**vil**-ia)
a brightly coloured tropical shrub

bough *NOUN* (**boughs**) (*rhymes with* **cow**)
a large branch of a tree that reaches out from the trunk

bought
past tense and past participle of **buy** *VERB*

boulder *NOUN* (**boulders**)
a very large smooth stone

bounce *VERB* (**bounces**, **bouncing**, **bounced**)
1 to bounce is to spring back when thrown against something, like a rubber ball **2** to bounce something like a ball is to throw it so that it bounces

bounce *NOUN* (**bounces**)
1 a bounce is the action of bouncing **2** bounce is liveliness, such as a young child or puppy has
▷ **bouncy** *ADJECTIVE* a bouncy person is lively and full of energy

bouncing *ADJECTIVE*
a bouncing baby is lively and healthy

bound [1]
past tense and past participle of **bind** *VERB*

bound [2] *ADJECTIVE*
to be bound for a place is to be travelling towards it • *This train is bound for London.*
to be bound to do something is to have to do it or be likely to do it • *He is bound to come.*

bound [3] *VERB* (**bounds**, **bounding**, **bounded**)
to bound is to leap or to run with leaping steps

bound *NOUN* (**bounds**)
a leaping movement

boundary *NOUN* (**boundaries**)
1 a line that marks a limit **2** a hit to the outer edge of a cricket field

bounds *PLURAL NOUN*
a place that is **out of bounds** is somewhere you are not allowed to go • *The teachers' common room is out of bounds to pupils.*

bouquet *NOUN* (**bouquets**) (*say* boo- **kay** or boh- **kay**)
an attractively arranged bunch of flowers

bout *NOUN* (**bouts**) (*say* bowt)
1 a period of illness • *I've just had a bout of flu.* **2** a boxing or wrestling fight

boutique *NOUN* (**boutiques**) (*say* boo- **teek**)
a small shop, especially one that sells fashionable clothes

bow[1] *NOUN* (**bows**) (*rhymes with* **go**)
1 a knot made with loops **2** the stick used for playing a stringed musical instrument such as a violin or cello **3** a long curved piece of wood with a tight string joining its ends, used for shooting arrows

bow[2] *NOUN* (**bows**) (*rhymes with* **cow**)
the front part of a ship

bow[3] *VERB* (**bows**, **bowing**, **bowed**) (*rhymes with* **cow**)
to bow is to bend your body forwards to show respect or as a greeting

bow *NOUN* (**bows**) (*rhymes with* **cow**)
a movement of bowing your body • *The pianist stood up to take a bow.*

bowels *PLURAL NOUN*
the bowels are the intestines

bowl[1] *NOUN* (**bowls**)
1 a deep round dish for eating from **2** the rounded part of a spoon **3** a heavy ball used in the game of bowls or tenpin bowling

bowl[2] *VERB* (**bowls, bowling, bowled**)(*in cricket*)
1 to bowl is to send the ball towards the batsman **2** to bowl someone is to get them out by hitting the wicket with the ball

bow-legged *ADJECTIVE*
a bow-legged person has legs that curve outwards at the knees

bowler *NOUN* (**bowlers**)
1 someone who bowls in cricket **2** a hat with a rounded top and a narrow brim

bowling *NOUN*
1 bowling is the game of bowls **2** bowling is also another game, in which you have to knock down skittles with a ball you roll down an alley **3** the action of throwing a cricket ball

bowls *PLURAL NOUN*
a game played on a smooth piece of grass, in which you roll heavy balls towards a small target ball called the 'jack'

bow tie *NOUN* (**bow ties**)
a tie in the form of a bow, worn by men as part of formal dress

box *NOUN* (**boxes**)
1 a container made of wood or cardboard, often with a lid **2** a small rectangle that you fill in on a form or computer screen **3** a special compartment or booth, such as a phone box or a witness box in a lawcourt **4** an evergreen shrub

box *VERB* (**boxes**, **boxing**, **boxed**)
1 to box is to fight with the fists **2** to box something is to put it into a box

boxer *NOUN* (**boxers**)
1 someone who boxes **2** a breed of dog that looks like a bulldog

Boxing Day *NOUN* (**Boxing Days**)
the first weekday after Christmas Day

box office *NOUN* (**box offices**)
a place where you can buy seats for the theatre or cinema

boy *NOUN* (**boys**)
a male child

> WORD FAMILY
> A man's **boyhood** is the time when he was a boy; you call someone **boyish** when they look or behave like a boy.

boycott *VERB* (**boycotts**, **boycotting**, **boycotted**)
to boycott something is to refuse to buy it or have anything to do with it • *They boycotted the buses when the fares went up.*

boyfriend *NOUN* (**boyfriends**)
someone's boyfriend is the male friend they have a romantic relationship with

bra *NOUN* (**bras**)
(*informal*) a piece of underwear women wear to support their breasts

> GRAMMAR
> The more formal word is **brassière**, which comes from a French word meaning 'vest'.

brace *NOUN* (**braces**)
1 a device for holding something in place **2** a wire device for straightening the teeth

bracelet *NOUN* (**bracelets**)
a small band or chain you wear round your wrist

braces *PLURAL NOUN*
braces are a pair of stretching straps worn over the shoulders to hold trousers up

> BRITISH AND AMERICAN
> In America, the word **suspenders** is used.

bracken *NOUN*
bracken is a kind of large fern that grows in open country

bracket *NOUN* (**brackets**)
1 a kind of punctuation mark used in pairs round words or figures to separate them from what comes before and after. Brackets are round ( ) or square [ ] **2** a support attached to a wall to hold up a shelf or light fitting

> BRACKETS
> You put brackets round words or numbers to separate them from what comes before and after. The most common kind are round brackets, which look like this (). They surround a comment or piece of information which isn't part of the main flow of the sentence and which you could leave out without changing the meaning of the sentence. *Oscar (my cat) was looking hungry. Two goslings (young geese) swam up to the boat. Roald Dahl (1916-1990) wrote many books including The BFG, Matilda, and James and the Giant Peach.*

brag *VERB* (**brags**, **bragging**, **bragged**)
to brag is to boast

braid *NOUN* (**braids**)
1 a plait **2** a decorative ribbon or band

braille *NOUN*
braille is a system of writing or printing using raised dots, which blind people can read by touch

brain *NOUN* (**brains**)
1 your brain is the part inside the top of your head that controls your body **2** brain also means a person's mind or intelligence • *He's got a good brain.*

brainy *ADJECTIVE* (**brainier**, **brainiest**)
(*informal*) clever, intelligent • *She's the brainiest child in the school.*

brake *NOUN* (**brakes**)
a device for making a vehicle stop or slow down

bramble *NOUN* (**brambles**)
a bramble is a blackberry bush or a prickly bush like it

branch *NOUN* (**branches**)
1 a part that sticks out from the trunk of a tree **2** a part of a railway or river or road that leads off from the main part **3** a part of a large organization

branch *VERB* (**branches**, **branching**, **branched**)
to branch is to form a branch
to branch out is to start doing something new

brand *NOUN* (**brands**)
a particular make or kind of goods • *Just get a cheap brand of tea.*

brand *VERB* (**brands**, **branding**, **branded**)
to brand sheep or cattle is to mark them with a hot iron

brandish *VERB* (**brandishes**, **brandishing**, **brandished**)
to brandish something is to wave it about • *Before Eddie knew what was happening, Mad Uncle Jack had leapt to his feet and was brandishing a small ceremonial sword.* — Philip Ardagh, *Terrible Times.*

brand-new *ADJECTIVE*
completely new

brandy *NOUN* (**brandies**)
brandy is a kind of strong alcoholic drink

brass *NOUN*
1 brass is an alloy made from copper and zinc
2 brass also means the wind instruments made of brass, such as trumpets and trombones

brass band *NOUN* (**brass bands**)
a musical band made up of brass instruments

brassière *NOUN* (**brassières**) (*say* **braz- i- er**)
a piece of underwear worn by women to support their breasts

> WORD FAMILY
> The more usual word for this is **bra**.

brassy *ADJECTIVE* (**brassier**, **brassiest**)
1 having the colour of brass **2** loud and harsh • *We heard a brassy laugh.* **3** cheeky and showy

brave *ADJECTIVE* (**braver**, **bravest**)
ready to face danger or suffering

brave *NOUN* (**braves**)
a Native American warrior
▷ **bravery** *NOUN* bravery is being brave
▷ **bravely** *ADVERB* in a brave way

brawl *NOUN* (**brawls**)
a noisy fight or quarrel

brawn *NOUN*
brawn is physical strength

brawny *ADJECTIVE* (**brawnier**, **brawniest**)
a brawny person has a strong body and muscles

bray *VERB* (**brays**, **braying**, **brayed**)
to bray is to make a noise like a donkey

brazen *ADJECTIVE*
1 shameless or cheeky **2** made of brass

brazier *NOUN* (**braziers**) (*say* **bray- zi- er**)
a metal container holding hot coals

breach *NOUN* (**breaches**)
1 the breaking of an agreement or rule **2** a gap or broken place in something like a wall

bread *NOUN*
1 bread is food made by baking flour and water, usually with yeast **2** (*slang*) bread is also money

breadth *NOUN* (**breadths**)
a thing's breadth is its width from side to side

breadwinner *NOUN* (**breadwinners**)
the member of a family who earns most of the money

break *VERB* (**breaks**, **breaking**, **broke**, **broken**)
1 to break something is to make it go into several pieces by hitting it or dropping it **2** to break is to stop working properly • *I think my watch must have broken.* **3** to break a law or rule or promise is to fail to keep it or observe it **4** the weather breaks when it changes after being hot **5** waves break over rocks when they fall and froth over them **6** a boy's voice breaks when it starts to go deeper at about the age of 14 **7** to break a record is to do better than the previous holder, for example in athletics
to break down a machine or vehicle breaks down when it stops working properly
to break off is to stop doing something for a time • *We broke off for lunch.*
to break out is to start and spread rapidly, like a disease or fighting
to break the news is to make it known
to break up 1 people break up when they leave one another after a long time together **2** is to finish school at the end of term

break *NOUN* (**breaks**)
1 a broken place; a gap **2** a sudden dash or attempt to escape **3** a short rest from work **4** (*informal*) a piece of luck; a fair chance • *Give me a break.*

breakable *ADJECTIVE*
easy to break • *Be careful with that box—there are breakable things in it.*

breakage *NOUN* (**breakages**)
something that is broken • *All breakages must be paid for.*

a b c d e f g h i j k l m n o p q r s t u v w x y z

breakdown *NOUN* (**breakdowns**)
1 a sudden failure to work, especially by a car • *We had a breakdown on the motorway.* **2** a failure or collapse of an organization or arrangement • *There has been a breakdown of communications.* **3** a period of mental illness caused by anxiety or depression **4** a detailed look at the parts of something to make it easier to understand • *Here's a breakdown of last season's football results.*

breaker *NOUN* (**breakers**)
a wave breaking on the shore

breakfast *NOUN* (**breakfasts**)
breakfast is the first meal of the day

breakneck *ADJECTIVE*
dangerously fast • *He drove at breakneck speed.*

breakthrough *NOUN* (**breakthroughs**)
an important piece of progress, for example in medical research

breakwater *NOUN* (**breakwaters**)
a wall built out into the sea to protect a harbour or coast against heavy waves

breast *NOUN* (**breasts**)
1 one of the two parts on the front of a woman's body where milk is produced after she has had a baby **2** a person's or animal's chest

breaststroke *NOUN*
a stroke you use when swimming on your front, by pushing your arms forward and bringing them round and back

breath *NOUN* (**breaths**) (*say* breth)
the air that you take into your lungs and send out again
to be out of breath is to gasp for air after exercise
to take someone's breath away is to surprise or delight them

breathalyser *NOUN* (**breathalysers**)
a device to measure the amount of alcohol in someone's breath
▷ **breathalyse** *VERB* to breathalyse someone is to test their breath with a breathalyser

breathe *VERB* (**breathes**, **breathing**, **breathed**)
(*say* breeth)
to breathe is to take air into your lungs through your nose or mouth and send it out again

> SPELLING
> Take care not to confuse **breathe** with **breath**, which is a noun.

breather *NOUN* (**breathers**)
(*informal*) a pause for a rest • *We all need a breather.*

breathless *ADJECTIVE*
short of breath

breathtaking *ADJECTIVE*
extremely beautiful or delightful

bred
past tense and past participle of **breed** *VERB*

breech *NOUN* (**breeches**)
the part of a gun barrel where the bullets are put in

breeches *PLURAL NOUN* (*say* brich-iz)
short trousers that fit tightly at the knee

breed *VERB* (**breeds**, **breeding**, **bred**)
1 to breed is to produce offspring **2** to breed animals is to keep them in order to get young ones from them **3** to breed something like illness or poverty is to cause it

breed *NOUN* (**breeds**)
a variety of similar animals

breeder *NOUN* (**breeders**)
someone who breeds animals

breeder reactor *NOUN* (**breeder reactors**)
a nuclear reactor that creates more radioactive material than it uses

breeze *NOUN* (**breezes**)
a gentle wind

breeze-block *NOUN* (**breeze-blocks**)
a lightweight building-block made of cinders and cement

breezy *ADJECTIVE* (**breezier**, **breeziest**)
1 slightly windy **2** bright and cheerful

brethren *PLURAL NOUN*
(*old use*) brothers

brevity *NOUN*
brevity is being brief or short • *I was surprised by the brevity of her answer.*

brew *VERB* (**brews**, **brewing**, **brewed**)
1 to brew beer or tea is to make it **2** to be brewing is to start or develop • *Trouble is brewing.*

brewer *NOUN* (**brewers**)
someone whose work is to make beer

brewery *NOUN* (**breweries**)
a place where beer is made

briar *NOUN* (**briars**)
another spelling of **brier**

bribe *NOUN* (**bribes**)
a bribe is money or a gift offered to someone to make them do something

bribe *VERB* (**bribes**, **bribing**, **bribed**)
to bribe someone is to give them a bribe
▷ **bribery** *NOUN* bribery is offering someone a bribe

brick *NOUN* (**bricks**)
1 a small hard block of baked clay used in building **2** a rectangular block of something

bricklayer *NOUN* (**bricklayers**)
a worker who builds with bricks

bridal *ADJECTIVE*
to do with brides

bride *NOUN* (**brides**)
a woman on her wedding day

bridegroom *NOUN* (**bridegrooms**)
a man on his wedding day

bridesmaid *NOUN* (**bridesmaids**)
a girl or unmarried woman who helps the bride at her wedding

bridge *NOUN* (**bridges**)
1 a bridge is a structure built over a river, railway, or road, to allow people to cross it **2** the bridge of a ship is the high platform above the deck, from where the ship is controlled **3** the bridge of your nose is the bony upper part of your nose **4** bridge is a card game rather like whist

bridle *NOUN* (**bridles**)
the part of a horse's harness that fits over its head

bridle path *NOUN* (**bridle paths**)
a path for people on horseback

brief *ADJECTIVE* (**briefer**, **briefest**)
lasting a short time or using only a few words
in brief in a few words

brief *NOUN* (**briefs**)
a brief is a set of instructions about a job to be done, especially one given to a lawyer about a case

brief *VERB* (**briefs**, **briefing**, **briefed**)
to brief someone is to give them instructions about a job to be done

briefcase *NOUN* (**briefcases**)
a flat case for keeping documents and papers in

briefs *PLURAL NOUN*
short underpants

brier *NOUN* (**briers**)
a thorny bush, especially a wild rose bush

brigade *NOUN* (**brigades**)
1 an army unit usually consisting of three battalions **2** a group of people in uniform, for example the fire brigade

brigadier *NOUN* (**brigadiers**)
an army officer who commands a brigade and is higher in rank than a colonel

brigand *NOUN* (**brigands**)
an old word for a robber or outlaw • *The chief brigand was a ferocious-looking man, with two belts full of bullets criss-cross over his shoulders.* — Philip Pullman, *The Scarecrow and his Servant.*

bright *ADJECTIVE* (**brighter**, **brightest**)
1 giving out a strong light; shining **2** a bright colour is strong and vivid **3** clever • *He's a bright lad.* **4** cheerful

brighten *VERB* (**brightens**, **brightening**, **brightened**)
1 to brighten something is to make it brighter **2** to brighten is to become brighter, like the sky when the weather improves

brilliance *NOUN*
1 brilliance is bright light • *the brilliance of the summer sky* **2** brilliance is also being very intelligent or clever

brilliant *ADJECTIVE*
1 a brilliant person is very intelligent or clever **2** (*informal*) really good or enjoyable • *That was a brilliant film!* **3** very bright and sparkling

brim *NOUN* (**brims**)
1 the edge round the top of a container **2** the bottom edge of a hat that sticks out

brimming *ADJECTIVE*
completely full
brimming over overflowing

brine *NOUN*
brine is salty water

bring *VERB* (**brings**, **bringing**, **brought**)
to bring someone or something is to make them come with you to a place
to bring someone round is to make them conscious again after they have fainted
to bring someone up is to look after them and educate them as a child
to bring something about is to make it happen
to bring something off is to achieve something difficult or unexpected
to bring something up is to mention it in a conversation

brink *NOUN*
the edge of a steep or dangerous place

brisk *ADJECTIVE* (**brisker**, **briskest**)
quick and lively

bristle *NOUN* (**bristles**)
a short, stiff hair
▷ **bristly** *ADJECTIVE* having lots of bristles

British *ADJECTIVE*
to do with Great Britain

Briton *NOUN* (**Britons**)
someone born in Great Britain

brittle *ADJECTIVE* (**brittler**, **brittlest**)
hard but likely to break or snap

broad *ADJECTIVE* (**broader**, **broadest**)
1 wide and open • *They walked down a broad avenue.* **2** broad daylight is clear and full daylight **3** general, not detailed • *a broad outline*

broad bean *NOUN* (**broad beans**)
a large flat bean

broadcast *NOUN* (**broadcasts**)
a radio or television programme

broadcast *VERB* (**broadcasts**, **broadcasting**, **broadcast**)
to broadcast a radio or television programme is to transmit it or take part in it
▷ **broadcaster** *NOUN* a person who takes part in a radio or television programme

broaden *VERB* (**broadens**, **broadening**, **broadened**)
to broaden something is to make it broader

broadly *ADVERB*
in general terms • *They were broadly right.*

broad-minded *ADJECTIVE*
tolerant of other people's views and opinions and not easily shocked

broadside *NOUN* (**broadsides**)
a round of firing by all the guns on one side of a ship

broccoli *NOUN*
a vegetable with green or purple heads on green stalks

brochure *NOUN* (**brochures**)
a booklet containing information, especially about a place

brogue *NOUN* (**brogues**)
1 a strong kind of shoe **2** a strong accent • *He spoke with an Irish brogue.*

broke[1]
past tense of **break** *VERB*

broke[2] *ADJECTIVE*
(*informal*) not having any money

broken
past participle of **break** *VERB*

broken *ADJECTIVE*
1 broken English is English spoken with a strong foreign accent and lots of mistakes **2** a broken home is a home in which the parents have separated

bronchitis *NOUN* (*say* brong- ky- tiss)
bronchitis is a disease of the lungs

bronze *NOUN*
1 bronze is an alloy of copper and tin **2** bronze is also a yellowish-brown colour

bronze medal *NOUN* (**bronze medals**)
a medal made of bronze, usually awarded as the third prize

brooch *NOUN* (**brooches**) (*rhymes with* **coach**)
a piece of jewellery that can be pinned on to clothes

brood *NOUN* (**broods**)
a brood is a number of young birds hatched together

brood *VERB* (**broods**, **brooding**, **brooded**)
1 birds such as chickens brood when they sit on eggs to hatch them **2** to brood over something is to keep on thinking and worrying about it

broody *ADJECTIVE* (**broodier**, **broodiest**)
1 a broody hen is one that wants to hatch its eggs **2** a broody person is one who keeps on thinking and worrying about things

brook *NOUN* (**brooks**)
a small stream

broom *NOUN* (**brooms**)
1 a broom is a brush with a long handle, for sweeping **2** broom is a shrub with yellow, white, or pink flowers

broomstick *NOUN* (**broomsticks**)
the handle of a broom

broth *NOUN* (**broths**)
broth is a thin kind of soup

brother *NOUN* (**brothers**)
your brother is a man or boy who has the same parents as you

brother-in-law *NOUN* (**brothers-in-law**)
a person's brother-in-law is the brother of their husband or wife, or the husband of their sister

brought
past tense and past participle of **bring**

brow *NOUN* (**brows**)
1 your brow is your forehead **2** your brows are your eyebrows **3** the brow of a hill is the top of it

brown *ADJECTIVE* (**browner**, **brownest**)
1 of the colour of earth, wood, or toast **2** suntanned

brown *NOUN*
a brown colour

brownie *NOUN* (**brownies**)
a small chocolate cake with nuts

Brownie *NOUN* (**Brownies**)
a junior member of the Guides

browse *VERB* (**browses**, **browsing**, **browsed**)
1 to browse is to read or look at something casually **2** animals browse when they feed on grass or leaves

bruise *NOUN* (**bruises**)
a dark mark that appears on your skin when it is hit or hurt

bruise *VERB* (**bruises**, **bruising**, **bruised**)
to bruise your skin or a part of your body is to get a bruise on it

brunette *NOUN* (**brunettes**)
a woman with dark brown or black hair

brush *NOUN* (**brushes**)
1 a device with hairs or bristles for sweeping, painting, or arranging the hair **2** a fox's bushy tail

brush *VERB* (**brushes**, **brushing**, **brushed**)
1 to brush something is to use a brush on it • *Have you brushed your hair yet?* **2** to brush against someone is to touch them gently as you pass them
to brush something aside is to ignore it
to brush something up is to improve your knowledge of it

Brussels sprout *NOUN* (**Brussels sprouts**)
a green vegetable like a tiny cabbage

brutal *ADJECTIVE*
savage and cruel
▷ **brutality** *NOUN* brutality is savage cruelty
▷ **brutally** *ADVERB* with savage cruelty

brute *NOUN* (**brutes**)
1 a cruel person **2** an animal

BSE
short for **bovine spongiform encephalopathy**, a fatal disease of cattle that attacks their nervous system and makes them stagger about. Also called **mad cow disease**.

bubble *NOUN* (**bubbles**)
1 a thin transparent ball of liquid filled with air or gas **2** a small ball of air in a liquid or a solid

bubble *VERB* (**bubbles**, **bubbling**, **bubbled**)
a liquid bubbles when it produces bubbles, as it does when it boils

bubble gum *NOUN*
bubble gum is a kind of chewing gum that you can blow into a bubble out of the front of your mouth

bubbly *ADJECTIVE* (**bubblier**, **bubbliest**)
1 full of bubbles, like fizzy water **2** a bubbly person is cheerful and lively

buccaneer *NOUN* (**buccaneers**)
an old word for a pirate

buck *NOUN* (**bucks**)
a male deer, rabbit, or hare

buck *VERB* (**bucks**, **bucking**, **bucked**)
a horse bucks when it jumps with its back arched
to buck up (*informal*) is to start hurrying

bucket *NOUN* (**buckets**)
a container with a handle, for carrying liquids or something such as sand

bucketful *NOUN* (**bucketfuls**)
as much of something as you can carry in a bucket

buckle *NOUN* (**buckles**)
a clip at the end of a belt or strap for fastening it

buckle *VERB* (**buckles**, **buckling**, **buckled**)
1 to buckle something is to fasten it with a buckle **2** to buckle is to bend or give way under a strain • *The arm of the crane was beginning to buckle.*
to buckle down is to start work

bud *NOUN* (**buds**)
a flower or leaf before it has opened

Buddhism *NOUN* (*say* **buud**- izm)
Buddhism is a religion that started in Asia and follows the teachings of Buddha
▷ **Buddhist** *NOUN* someone who practises Buddhism

budding *ADJECTIVE*
showing great promise • *The new class had several budding musicians.*

budge *VERB* (**budges**, **budging**, **budged**)
to budge is to move slightly • *The door was stuck and wouldn't budge.*

budgerigar *NOUN* (**budgerigars**) (*say* **bud**- jer- i- gar)
an Australian bird often kept as a pet in a cage

budget *NOUN* (**budgets**)
1 the money someone plans to spend on something **2** a plan for earning and spending money

budget *VERB* (**budgets**, **budgeting**, **budgeted**)
to budget is to plan how much you are going to spend

budgie *NOUN* (**budgies**)
(*informal*) a budgerigar

buff *ADJECTIVE*
of a dull yellow colour

buffalo *NOUN* (**buffalo** or **buffaloes**)
a wild ox with long curved horns

buffer *NOUN* (**buffers**)
1 something that softens a blow or collision, especially a device on a railway engine or wagon or at the end of a railway line **2** (*in computing*) a memory in which data can be stored for a time, especially while being sent from one device to another

buffet *NOUN* (**buffets**) (*say* **buu**- fay)
1 a cafe or place for buying drinks and snacks **2** a meal where guests serve themselves

bug *NOUN* (**bugs**)
1 a tiny insect **2** (*informal*) a germ that causes illness • *I may have a tummy bug.* **3** (*informal*) a hidden microphone **4** a fault or problem in a computer program that stops it working properly

bug *VERB* (**bugs**, **bugging**, **bugged**)
1 (*informal*) to bug a place is to put a hidden microphone into it **2** (*slang*) to bug someone is to annoy them • *This loud music is really beginning to bug me.*

bugle *NOUN* (**bugles**) (*say* **byoo**- gul)
a brass instrument like a small trumpet
▷ **bugler** *NOUN* someone who plays the bugle

build *VERB* (**builds**, **building**, **built**)
to build something is to make it by putting the parts together
to build something up is to make it larger or stronger • *Regular exercise will build up your health.*
to build up is to become larger or stronger • *The work was starting to build up.*

build *NOUN* (**builds**)
your build is the shape of your body

builder *NOUN* (**builders**)
someone who puts up buildings

building *NOUN* (**buildings**)
1 a building is a structure that someone has built, such as a house or a block of flats **2** building is the business of making houses and other structures

building society *NOUN* (**building societies**)
an organization that lends money to people for them to buy houses

build-up *NOUN*
1 a gradual increase in the amount of something **2** the part of a story or series of events which is before the most important part and leads up to it

built-in *ADJECTIVE*
made into a permanent part of something • *The house had built-in kitchen units.*

built-up *ADJECTIVE*
a built-up area is one with lots of houses and other buildings

bulb *NOUN* (**bulbs**)
1 the glass part of an electric light, with a wire inside that glows when you switch it on **2** an onion-shaped root which grows into a plant or flower when it is put in the ground

bulge *NOUN* (**bulges**)
a part that sticks out; a swelling

bulge *VERB* (**bulges**, **bulging**, **bulged**)
to bulge is to stick out or swell

bulk *NOUN*
1 a thing's bulk is its size, especially when it is large **2** the bulk of something is most of it • *He spends the bulk of his time on the computer.*
in bulk in large quantities

a
b
c
d
e
f
g
h
i
j
k
l
m
n
o
p
q
r
s
t
u
v
w
x
y
z

bulky *ADJECTIVE* (**bulkier**, **bulkiest**)
taking up a lot of space

bull *NOUN* (**bulls**)
1 the male of the cattle family **2** a male seal, whale, or elephant

bulldog *NOUN* (**bulldogs**)
a breed of dog with a short thick neck

bulldozer *NOUN* (**bulldozers**)
a heavy vehicle with caterpillar tracks and a wide metal blade in front, used to clear or flatten land
▷ **bulldoze** *VERB* to bulldoze land is to clear it with a bulldozer

bullet *NOUN* (**bullets**)
a piece of shaped metal shot from a rifle or pistol

bulletin *NOUN* (**bulletins**)
a short announcement of news on radio or television

bullet point *NOUN* (**bullet points**)
an important item in a list, often printed with a black dot (called a *bullet*) in front of it

bulletproof *ADJECTIVE*
able to stop bullets getting through

bullfight *NOUN* (**bullfights**)
in Spain, a public entertainment in which people challenge bulls, and sometimes kill them
▷ **bullfighter** *NOUN* someone who takes part in a bullfight

bullion *NOUN*
gold or silver in the form of bars

bullock *NOUN* (**bullocks**)
a young bull

bull's-eye *NOUN* (**bull's-eyes**)
1 the centre of a target **2** a hard peppermint sweet

bully *VERB* (**bullies**, **bullying**, **bullied**)
to bully someone is to hurt or frighten them when they are weaker

bully *NOUN* (**bullies**)
someone who bullies people

bulrush *NOUN* (**bulrushes**)
a tall reed which grows in water or on boggy land

bulwark *NOUN* (**bulwarks**) (*say* **buul**- werk)
a strong defending wall

bulwarks *PLURAL NOUN*
a ship's side above the level of the deck

bum *NOUN* (**bums**)(*slang*)
1 your bum is your bottom **2** (*in America*) a bum is a tramp

bumble-bee *NOUN* (**bumble-bees**)
a large kind of bee with a loud buzz

bump *VERB* (**bumps**, **bumping**, **bumped**)
1 to bump something is to knock against it accidentally **2** to bump along is to move along unsteadily, like an old car
to bump into someone (*informal*) is to meet them unexpectedly
to bump someone off (*slang*) is to kill them

bump *NOUN* (**bumps**)
1 an accidental knock **2** a swelling or lump

bumper[1] *NOUN* (**bumpers**)
a bar along the front or back of a motor vehicle to protect it in collisions

> BRITISH AND AMERICAN
> In America, the word **fender** is used.

bumper[2] *ADJECTIVE*
unusually large or fine • *We had a bumper crop of apples this year.*

bumpy *ADJECTIVE* (**bumpier**, **bumpiest**)
having lots of bumps

bun *NOUN* (**buns**)
1 a small round sweet cake **2** a round bunch of hair that some women make at the back of their head

bunch *NOUN* (**bunches**)
a number of things joined or tied together, such as fruit or flowers or keys • *He was eating a bunch of grapes.*

bundle *NOUN* (**bundles**)
a number of things tied or wrapped loosely together, such as clothes or papers

bundle *VERB* (**bundles**, **bundling**, **bundled**)
1 to bundle things together is to tie or wrap them loosely **2** to bundle someone into a room or car is to push them there hurriedly • *They bundled him into the back of a taxi.*

bung *VERB* (**bungs**, **bunging**, **bunged**)
(*slang*) to bung something somewhere is to throw or pass it carelessly • *Bung that pencil over here.*
to bung something up is to block it

bung *NOUN* (**bungs**)
a stopper for a bottle or barrel

bungalow *NOUN* (**bungalows**)
a house with all the rooms on one floor

bungle *VERB* (**bungles**, **bungling**, **bungled**)
to bungle something is to do it badly and clumsily
▷ **bungler** *NOUN* someone who bungles something

bunk *NOUN* (**bunks**)
a narrow bed like a shelf, as on a ship
to do a bunk (*slang*) is to run away

bunk bed *NOUN* (**bunk beds**)
a single bed with another bed above it or below it

bunker *NOUN* (**bunkers**)
1 a container for storing fuel such as coal **2** a hollow filled with sand, made as an obstacle on a golf course **3** an underground shelter

bunny *NOUN* (**bunnies**)
(*informal*) a rabbit

bunsen burner *NOUN* (**bunsen burners**)
a gas burner with a flame you can adjust, used in laboratories

buoy *NOUN* (**buoys**) (*say* boi)
a floating object anchored to the bottom of the sea and used to mark a channel or a stretch of shallow water

buoyant *ADJECTIVE*
1 able to float **2** lively and cheerful • *He was in a buoyant mood.*
▷ **buoyancy** *NOUN* buoyancy is being able to float

bur *NOUN* (**burs**)
part of a plant that clings to your clothes or hair

burden *NOUN* (**burdens**)
1 a heavy load **2** something troublesome that you have to put up with
▷ **burdensome** *ADJECTIVE* something that is burdensome is hard to put up with

bureau *NOUN* (**bureaux**) (*say* **bewr**- oh)
1 a writing desk with drawers **2** an office or department • *They will tell you at the Information Bureau.*

burger *NOUN* (**burgers**)
a hamburger

burglar *NOUN* (**burglars**)
someone who breaks into a building to steal things
▷ **burglary** *NOUN* burglary is the crime of stealing things from a building

burgle *VERB* (**burgles**, **burgling**, **burgled**)
to burgle someone is to steal from their house

burial *NOUN* (**burials**)
putting a dead body in a grave

burly *ADJECTIVE* (**burlier**, **burliest**)
a burly person is big and strong

burn[1] *VERB* (**burns**, **burning**, **burnt** or **burned**)
1 to burn something is to damage or destroy it by fire or strong heat **2** to burn is to be damaged or destroyed by fire or heat **3** to be burning is to be on fire **4** to be burning is also to feel very hot

burn *NOUN* (**burns**)
1 an injury or mark caused by fire or strong heat **2** the firing of a spacecraft's rocket

burn[2] *NOUN* (**burns**)
(*in Scotland*) a small stream

burner *NOUN* (**burners**)
the part of a lamp or cooker that forms the flame

burning *ADJECTIVE*
a burning wish or desire is one that is very strong

burp *VERB* (**burps**, **burping**, **burped**)
to burp is to make a noise through your mouth by letting air come up from your stomach

burp *NOUN* (**burps**)
the act or sound of burping

burrow *NOUN* (**burrows**)
a hole dug by an animal such as a rabbit or fox

burrow *VERB* (**burrows**, **burrowing**, **burrowed**)
1 an animal burrows when it digs a burrow **2** to burrow is also to dig or search deeply • *He burrowed in his pockets to find a pound coin.*

burst *VERB* (**bursts**, **bursting**, **burst**)
1 to burst is to break apart suddenly **2** to burst something is to make it break apart **3** to be bursting with energy or excitement is to have a lot of energy or to be very excited
to burst in is to rush in noisily or clumsily
to burst into tears is to suddenly start crying
to burst out laughing is to start laughing noisily

burst *NOUN* (**bursts**)
1 a split caused by something bursting • *There's a burst in one of the pipes.* **2** something short and quick • *a burst of gunfire*

bury *VERB* (**buries**, **burying**, **buried**)
1 to bury something is to put it under the ground **2** to bury someone is to put them in a grave when they are dead
to bury the hatchet is to agree to stop quarrelling or fighting

bus *NOUN* (**buses**)
a large road vehicle for carrying passengers

bush *NOUN* (**bushes**)
1 a bush is a plant like a small tree with a lot of stems or branches **2** the bush is wild land, especially in Australia or Africa

bushy *ADJECTIVE* (**bushier**, **bushiest**)
thick and hairy • *His dad has bushy eyebrows.*

busily *ADVERB*
in a busy way

business *NOUN* (**businesses**) (*say* **biz**- niss)
1 a business is an organization that makes money by selling goods or services • *His uncle worked in a garage business.* **2** business is what an organization does to make money • *She has made a career in business.* **3** a person's business is what concerns them and no one else • *Mind your own business.* **4** a business is also an affair or subject • *I am tired of the whole business.*
to get down to business is to start working or talking seriously
to go out of business is to stop trading because you are not making enough money

businesslike *ADJECTIVE*
efficient and practical

busker *NOUN* (**buskers**)
someone who plays music in the street, hoping for money from people passing by

bus stop *NOUN* (**bus stops**)
a place where a bus regularly stops

bust[1] *NOUN* (**busts**)
1 a sculpture of a person's head and shoulders **2** a woman's breasts

bust[2] *ADJECTIVE* (*informal*)
1 broken • *My watch is bust.* **2** bankrupt

bustle *VERB* (**bustles**, **bustling**, **bustled**)
to bustle is to be in a hurry or rushing about busily • *Mum bustled into the kitchen, stuffing papers into her briefcase.* — Catherine MacPhail, *Granny Nothing*

busy *ADJECTIVE* (**busier**, **busiest**)
1 a busy person is one with a lot to do **2** a busy place is one with a lot going on **3** a busy telephone line is one that someone is already using

a
b
c
d
e
f
g
h
i
j
k
l
m
n
o
p
q
r
s
t
u
v
w
x
y
z

busybody *NOUN* (**busybodies**)
someone who interferes in other people's affairs

but *CONJUNCTION*
you use **but** to join two words or statements that say different or opposite things • *I wanted to go but I couldn't.*

but *PREPOSITION*
except • *There's no one here but me.*

butcher *NOUN* (**butchers**)
1 someone who runs a shop that cuts and sells meat **2** a person who kills people cruelly

butchery *NOUN*
butchery is the cruel killing of many people

butler *NOUN* (**butlers**)
a male servant in charge of other servants in a large private house

butt[1] *NOUN* (**butts**)
1 the thicker end of a weapon or tool **2** a large barrel **3** someone people often make fun of • *James always seems to be the butt of your jokes.*

butt[2] *VERB* (**butts, butting, butted**)
to butt someone is to hit them hard with your head
to butt in is to interrupt suddenly or rudely

butter *NOUN*
butter is a fatty yellow food made from cream

buttercup *NOUN* (**buttercups**)
a yellow wild flower

butter-fingers *NOUN* (**butter-fingers**)
(*informal*) someone who is clumsy and keeps dropping things

butterfly *NOUN* (**butterflies**)
1 an insect with a thin body and large white or brightly coloured wings **2** a stroke you use when swimming on your front, by raising both arms together over your head

butterscotch *NOUN* (**butterscotches**)
butterscotch is a kind of hard toffee

buttocks *PLURAL NOUN*
your buttocks are the part of the body on which you sit, your bottom

button *NOUN* (**buttons**)
1 a flat plastic or metal disc sewn on clothes and passed through a buttonhole to fasten them **2** a small knob you press to work an electric device

button *VERB* (**buttons, buttoning, buttoned**)
to button clothes or to button up clothes is to fasten them with buttons

buttonhole *NOUN* (**buttonholes**)
1 a slit for a button to pass through **2** a flower worn on a lapel

buttress *NOUN* (**buttresses**)
a support built against a wall

buy *VERB* (**buys, buying, bought**)
to buy something is to get it by paying for it • *I bought a CD yesterday.*
▷ **buyer** *NOUN* someone who buys something

buy *NOUN* (**buys**)
something you buy • *That was a good buy.*

buzz *NOUN* (**buzzes**)
a sharp humming sound, like bees make
to get a buzz from something (*slang*) is to find it exciting

buzz *VERB* (**buzzes, buzzing, buzzed**)
to buzz is to make a buzzing sound
to buzz off (*slang*) is to go away

buzzard *NOUN* (**buzzards**)
a bird of prey like a large hawk

buzzer *NOUN* (**buzzers**)
an alarm or signalling device that makes a buzzing noise

by *PREPOSITION & ADVERB*
1 near, close • *Sit by me.* **2** using; by means of • *I fixed the tyre by sticking on a patch.* **3** before • *Do your homework by tomorrow.* **4** past • *She went by the window.* • *I can't get by.*
by and large mostly, on the whole
by the way a phrase you use to begin a new topic

bye *NOUN* (**byes**)
a run scored in cricket when the batsman has not touched the ball

bye-bye *INTERJECTION*
(*informal*) goodbye

by-election *NOUN* (**by-elections**)
an election in one district only, when an MP has died or resigned

by-law *NOUN* (**by-laws**)
a law which only applies to a particular town, district, etc.

bypass *NOUN* (**bypasses**)
a road that takes traffic round the edge of a town or city rather than going through the centre

by-product *NOUN* (**by-products**)
something useful that is made while something else is being made

bystander *NOUN* (**bystanders**)
someone who sees something happening but takes no part in it

byte *NOUN*
(*in computing*) a unit that measures data or memory

C
1 short for centigrade **2** 100 in Roman numerals

CAB
short for *Citizens' Advice Bureau*

cab *NOUN* (**cabs**)
1 a taxi **2** the place for the driver in a lorry, bus, train, or crane

cabaret *NOUN* (**cabarets**) (*say* kab- a- ray)
a show in a nightclub or restaurant, with singers and dancers

cabbage *NOUN* (**cabbages**)
a large round green vegetable with layers of closely packed leaves

cabin *NOUN* (**cabins**)
1 a hut or shelter **2** one of the small rooms on a ship for sleeping in **3** the part of an aircraft where the passengers sit

cabin crew *NOUN*
the people on an aircraft whose job is to look after the passengers

cabinet *NOUN* (**cabinets**)
1 a cupboard with shelves and doors, used for storing things **2** the group of chief ministers who run the government

cable *NOUN* (**cables**)
1 a thick rope, wire, or chain used for lifting heavy loads or tying up ships **2** a telegram sent overseas

cable car *NOUN*
a small cabin that hangs from a moving cable, used for carrying people up and down the side of a mountain.

cable television *NOUN*
a television system in which programmes are transmitted along underground cables into people's houses

cackle *NOUN* (**cackles**)
1 a cackle is the clucking of a hen **2** a cackle is also a loud, silly laugh **3** cackle is stupid chattering

cactus *NOUN* (**cacti**)
a fleshy plant that grows in hot, dry places

CAD *ABBREVIATION*
computer-asisted design, a system of using computers to draw plans for buildings and machines

caddie *NOUN* (**caddies**)
someone whose job is to help a golfer by carrying the clubs and giving advice

caddy *NOUN* (**caddies**)
a small box for holding tea leaves

cadet *NOUN* (**cadets**)
a young person who is being trained for the armed forces or the police

cadge *VERB* (**cadges**, **cadging**, **cadged**)
to cadge something is to get it by asking for it in a blunt or direct way

cafe *NOUN* (**cafes**) (*say* kaf- ay)
a place that sells hot and cold drinks and light meals

cafeteria *NOUN* (**cafeterias**) (*say* kaf- e- **teer**- i- a)
a cafe where customers serve themselves from a counter

caffeine *NOUN*
caffeine is a substance in tea and coffee and some other drinks, which keeps you awake and makes you feel active

caftan *NOUN* (**caftans**)
a long loose jacket or dress with wide sleeves

cage *NOUN* (**cages**)
an enclosure made of bars or wires, for keeping birds or animals so that they can't get away

cagey *ADJECTIVE* (**cagier**, **cagiest**)
(*informal*) cautious about what you say

cagoule *NOUN* (**cagoules**)
a lightweight waterproof jacket

cake *NOUN* (**cakes**)
1 a sweet food made from a baked mixture of flour, eggs, fat, and sugar **2** something made into a lump rather like a cake, such as soap
a piece of cake (*informal*) something very easy to do
to have your cake and eat it is to get the benefit of two things that are normally alternatives

caked *ADJECTIVE*
covered with something that has dried hard, like mud

calamine *NOUN*
a pink powder used to make a soothing liquid to put on your skin

calamity *NOUN* (**calamities**)
a disaster
▷ **calamitous** *ADJECTIVE* disastrous

calcium *NOUN*
a greyish-white element contained in teeth, bones, and lime

calculate *VERB* (**calculates**, **calculating**, **calculated**)
1 to calculate something is to work it out by arithmetic or with a calculator **2** to calculate on something is to plan round it • *They were calculating on a fine day for the picnic.*

calculation *NOUN* (**calculations**)
something you work out by using numbers or other information

calculator *NOUN* (**calculators**)
a machine for adding up figures and doing other calculations with numbers

calendar *NOUN* (**calendars**)
a chart or display that shows the days of the year

calf[1] *NOUN* (**calves**)
1 a young cow or ox **2** a young seal, whale, or elephant

calf[2] *NOUN* (**calves**)
the back part of your leg below your knee

call *NOUN* (**calls**)
1 a shout or cry • *They heard a call for help.* **2** a short visit • *She decided to pay her father a call.* **3** a telephone conversation with someone

call *VERB* (**calls**, **calling**, **called**)
1 to call is to shout out **2** to call someone is to telephone them •*I'll call you at the weekend.* **3** to call someone near you is to ask them to come to you **4** to call on someone is to visit them **5** to be called something is to have it as your name •*His friend was called Damon.* **6** to call something a certain thing is to describe it that way •*I call that a swindle.*
to call it a day is to stop working for a while
to call someone names is to be rude to them or insult them
to call something off is to cancel it

calligram *NOUN* (**calligrams**)
a poem written or printed in a special way that shows the meaning of the words. For example, the word *bigger* might be printed with the letters themselves getting bigger from left to right.

calling *NOUN* (**callings**)
someone's calling is their profession or trade

callipers *PLURAL NOUN*
a device for measuring the width of tubes or of round objects

callous *ADJECTIVE*
a callous person is very unkind and doesn't care about other people's feelings

calm *ADJECTIVE* (**calmer**, **calmest**)
1 quiet and still, like the sea or the weather
2 someone is calm when they are not excited or agitated •*Please keep calm.*
▷ **calmly** *ADVERB* in a calm way, without any great excitement
▷ **calmness** *NOUN* being calm

calorie *NOUN* (**calories**)
a unit for measuring the amount of heat or the energy produced by food

calves
plural of **calf**

calypso *NOUN* (**calypsos**)
a West Indian folk song which is made up as the singer goes along

camcorder *NOUN* (**camcorders**)
a video camera that can record pictures and sound

came
past tense of **come**

camel *NOUN* (**camels**)
a large animal with a long neck and one or two humps on its back •*Arabian camels have one hump, and Bactrian camels have two.*

camera *NOUN* (**cameras**)
a device for taking photographs, films, or television pictures

camouflage *NOUN* (*say* kam-o-flahzh)
a way of hiding things by making them look like part of their surroundings

camp *NOUN* (**camps**)
a place where people live in tents or huts or caravans for a short time

camp *VERB* (**camps**, **camping**, **camped**)
1 to camp or go camping is to have a holiday in a tent **2** to camp is also to put up a tent or tents •*Let's camp here for the night.*

> **WORD FAMILY**
> A **camper** is a person who goes to a camp; **camping** is what you do when you go to a camp.

campaign *NOUN* (**campaigns**)
1 a planned series of actions, especially to get people to support you or become interested in something •*a campaign for human rights* **2** a series of battles in one area or with one aim

campaign *VERB* (**campaigns**, **campaigning**, **campaigned**)
to campaign is to carry out a plan of action to raise people's interest in something such as a good cause •*They are campaigning to stop the destruction of the rainforests.*

campsite *NOUN* (**campsites**)
a place for camping

campus *NOUN* (**campuses**)
the buildings of a college or university and the land around them

can[1] *VERB* (*present tense* **can**; *past tense* **could**)
1 to be able to do something or to know how to do it •*Can you lift this stone?* •*They can speak French.* **2** (*informal*) to be allowed to do something •*Can I go home?*

can[2] *NOUN* (**cans**)
a sealed metal container holding food or drink

can *VERB* (**cans**, **canning**, **canned**)
to can food is to put it into cans and seal it

canal *NOUN* (**canals**)
1 a long channel specially dug and filled with water for boats to travel along **2** a tube in the body of a human being or animal •*The canals in your ears help you balance.*

canary *NOUN* (**canaries**)
a small yellow bird that sings, often kept in a cage as a pet

cancel *VERB* (**cancels**, **cancelling**, **cancelled**)
1 to cancel something planned is to say that it will not be done or not take place after all **2** to cancel an order or instruction is to stop it **3** to cancel a stamp or ticket is to mark it so that it cannot be used again
▷ **cancellation** *NOUN* something that someone has cancelled, especially a theatre or travel booking that can then be sold to someone else

cancer *NOUN* (**cancers**)
a serious disease in which a harmful growth forms in the body

candidate *NOUN* (**candidates**)
1 someone who has applied for a job or position
2 someone who is taking an exam

candle *NOUN* (**candles**)
a stick of wax with a wick through it, giving light when it is burning

candlelight *NOUN*
candlelight is the light given out by a candle

candlestick *NOUN* (**candlesticks**)
a holder for a candle or candles

candy *NOUN* (**candies**)
1 candy is crystallized sugar **2** a candy is a sweet

candyfloss *NOUN*
candyfloss is a fluffy mass of sugar that has been spun into fine threads

cane *NOUN* (**canes**)
a cane is the hollow stem of a reed or tall grass

cane *VERB* (**canes**, **caning**, **caned**)
to cane someone is to beat them with a cane

canine *ADJECTIVE*
to do with dogs

canine tooth *NOUN* (**canine teeth**)
a pointed tooth at the front of the mouth. Human beings have four of these

cannabis *NOUN* (*say* kan- a- bis)
a drug made from the plant that also produces hemp

cannibal *NOUN* (**cannibals**)
1 a person who eats human flesh **2** an animal that eats animals of its own kind
▷ **cannibalism** *NOUN* cannibalism is eating other people, or animals of the same kind

cannon *NOUN* (**cannon** or **cannons**)
a large gun that fires heavy balls made of metal or stone

cannonball *NOUN* (**cannonballs**)
a heavy metal or stone ball fired from a cannon

cannot
can not • *I cannot believe it.*

canoe *NOUN* (**canoes**)
a light narrow boat driven with paddles

canoe *VERB* (**canoes**, **canoeing**, **canoed**)
to canoe is to travel in a canoe
▷ **canoeist** *NOUN* someone who uses a canoe

canopy *NOUN* (**canopies**)
a covering that hangs over something

can't
short for **cannot** • *We can't see them.*

canteen *NOUN* (**canteens**)
a restaurant in a factory or office or school, where the people working there can get a meal or snack

canter *VERB* (**canters**, **cantering**, **cantered**)
to canter is to go at a gentle gallop

canvas *NOUN* (**canvases**)
1 canvas is strong, coarse cloth **2** a canvas is a piece of this kind of cloth used for painting on

canvass *VERB* (**canvasses**, **canvassing**, **canvassed**)
to canvass people is to visit them to ask them for their support, especially in an election

> SPELLING
> Take care not to confuse **canvass** with **canvas**, which means a kind of material.

canyon *NOUN* (**canyons**)
a deep valley with a river running through it

cap *NOUN* (**caps**)
1 a soft hat without a brim but often with a peak **2** a cover or top

cap *VERB* (**caps**, **capping**, **capped**)
1 to cap something is to cover it **2** to cap a story or joke is to tell one that is better

capable *ADJECTIVE*
able to do something
▷ **capability** *NOUN* being able to do something
▷ **capably** *ADVERB* to do something capably is to do it well

capacity *NOUN* (**capacities**)
1 ability to do something • *He has a great capacity for work.* **2** the amount that something can hold **3** the position someone occupies • *He was there in his capacity as our leader.*

cape [1] *NOUN* (**capes**)
a piece of high land sticking out into the sea

cape [2] *NOUN* (**capes**)
a cloak

caper *VERB* (**capers**, **capering**, **capered**)
to caper is to jump about playfully

caper *NOUN* (**capers**)
1 a leap or jump **2** (*informal*) an activity or adventure

capital *NOUN* (**capitals**)
1 the capital of a country is the most important city in it **2** capital is money or property that can be used to make more wealth **3** a capital is the top part of a pillar

capitalism *NOUN* (*say* kap- i- ta- lizm)
capitalism is a system in which the wealth of a country is owned by private individuals and not by the state
▷ **capitalist** *NOUN* someone who supports capitalism

capital letter *NOUN* (**capital letters**)
a large letter of the kind used at the start of a name or a sentence, such as A, B, C

capital punishment *NOUN*
capital punishment is when someone is killed as a punishment for a crime, such as murder or treason

capsize *VERB* (**capsizes**, **capsizing**, **capsized**)
to capsize is to overturn in a boat in the water

capsule *NOUN* (**capsules**)
1 a hollow pill containing medicine **2** a small spacecraft or pressurized cabin

captain *NOUN* (**captains**)
1 an officer in charge of a ship or aircraft **2** an officer in the army or navy **3** the leader in a sports team

caption *NOUN* (**captions**)
1 the words printed beside a picture to describe it **2** a heading in a newspaper or magazine

captivate *VERB*
to captivate someone is to charm them or make them interested
▷ **captivating** *ADJECTIVE* charming and attractive

captive *NOUN* (**captives**)
a prisoner

captive *ADJECTIVE*
imprisoned; unable to escape

captivity *NOUN*
1 captivity is being held prisoner **2** an animal in captivity is one kept in a zoo or wildlife park rather than living in the wild

captor *NOUN* (**captors**)
someone who has captured a person or animal

capture *VERB* (**captures**, **capturing**, **captured**)
1 to capture an animal or person is to catch or imprison them **2** (*in computing*) to capture data is to put it into a form that a computer can accept

capture *NOUN*
catching or imprisoning an animal or person

car *NOUN* (**cars**)
1 a private motor vehicle **2** a railway carriage • *The train has a dining car.*

caramel *NOUN* (**caramels**)
1 caramel is burnt sugar used to give a sweet taste to food **2** a caramel is a sweet made from butter, milk, and sugar

carat *NOUN* (**carats**)
1 a measure of weight for precious stones **2** a measure of the purity of gold

caravan *NOUN* (**caravans**)
1 a vehicle towed by a car and used for living in, especially by people on holiday **2** a large number of people travelling together, especially across a desert

> BRITISH AND AMERICAN
> In America, the word **trailer** is used for the first meaning.

carbohydrate *NOUN* (**carbohydrates**)
a compound of carbon, oxygen, and hydrogen • *Sugar and starch are carbohydrates.*

carbon *NOUN*
carbon is an element found in charcoal, graphite, diamonds, and other substances

carbon dioxide *NOUN*
a colourless gas made by humans and animals breathing

carbon monoxide *NOUN*
a colourless, poisonous gas found especially in the exhaust fumes of motor vehicles

car-boot sale *NOUN* (**car-boot sales**)
an outdoor sale where people sell things which they have brought by car

carburettor *NOUN* (**carburettors**)
a device for mixing fuel and air in an internal-combustion engine

carcass *NOUN* (**carcasses**)
the dead body of an animal or bird

card *NOUN* (**cards**)
1 card is thick stiff paper **2** a card is a piece of thick paper that you use to put information on or to send greetings to someone, for example a business card or a birthday card **3** a card is also a playing card **4** a card is also a small piece of plastic that a bank or building society issues to a customer, with an electronic strip recording details of their account
cards is a game with playing cards
something is **on the cards** when it is likely to happen

cardboard *NOUN*
cardboard is thick stiff paper

cardigan *NOUN* (**cardigans**)
a knitted jumper fastened with buttons down the front

cardinal *NOUN* (**cardinals**)
one of the most senior priests in the Roman Catholic Church

cardinal number *NOUN* (**cardinal numbers**)
a number for counting things, for example 1, 2, 3 (compare *ordinal number*)

care *NOUN* (**cares**)
1 care is worry or trouble • *She was free from care.* **2** care is also serious thought or attention • *Take more care with your homework.* **3** care is also protection or supervision • *You can leave your dog in my care.*
to take care is to be especially careful
to take care of someone or **something** is to look after them • *Please could you take care of the cat while I'm away?*
to write to someone care of someone else is to write to the first person at the address of the second • *While I'm away, write to me care of my father.*

care *VERB* (**cares**, **caring**, **cared**)
to care about something or someone is to feel interested or concerned about them
to care for someone is to look after them • *He cared for his wife when she was ill.*
to care for something is to like it or want it • *I don't much care for fried food.*

career *NOUN* (**careers**)
a person's career is what they have been trained to do to earn a living and make progress during their lives

career *VERB* (**careers**, **careering**, **careered**)
to career along or down somewhere is to rush along wildly • *The beast was careering through the tunnels, crashing, bellowing, thundering through the maze.* — Alan Gibbons, *Shadow of Minotaur*

carefree *ADJECTIVE*
not having any worries or responsibilities

careful *ADJECTIVE*
making sure that you do something well without any mistakes and without causing any danger • *She is a careful driver.* • *He was careful to read the instructions first.*
▷ **carefully** *ADVERB* to do something carefully is to do it with a lot of care and attention

careless *ADJECTIVE*
not taking care; clumsy
▷ **carelessly** *ADVERB* to do something carelessly is to do it without much care and make a lot of mistakes
▷ **carelessness** *NOUN* carelessness is not taking care

caress *NOUN* (**caresses**) (*say* ka- **ress**)
a gentle and loving touch

caress *VERB* (**caresses**, **caressing**, **caressed**)
to caress someone is to touch them gently and fondly

caretaker *NOUN* (**caretakers**)
someone who looks after a large building

cargo *NOUN* (**cargoes**)
cargo or a cargo is the goods carried in a ship or aircraft

Caribbean *ADJECTIVE* (*say* ka- ri- **bee**- an)
to do with the West Indies

caricature *NOUN* (**caricatures**)
a drawing or description of someone that exaggerates their features and makes them look funny or absurd

carnation *NOUN* (**carnations**)
a garden flower with a sweet smell

carnival *NOUN* (**carnivals**)
a festival or celebration with a procession of people in fancy dress

carnivore *NOUN* (**carnivores**)
an animal that eats meat
▷ **carnivorous** *ADJECTIVE* a carnivorous animal is one that eats meat

carol *NOUN* (**carols**)
a hymn or song that you sing at Christmas time
▷ **caroller** *NOUN* someone who sings carols, often as part of a group of singers
▷ **carolling** *NOUN* carolling is singing carols at Christmas time, usually in the street or going from house to house

carp *NOUN* (**carp**)
a freshwater fish

carpenter *NOUN* (**carpenters**)
someone who makes things, especially parts of buildings, out of wood
▷ **carpentry** making things from wood

carpet *NOUN* (**carpets**)
a thick soft covering for a floor

carriage *NOUN* (**carriages**)
1 a carriage is one of the separate sections of a train where passengers sit **2** a carriage is also a passenger vehicle pulled by horses **3** carriage is taking goods from one place to another • *You will have to pay extra for carriage.*

carriageway *NOUN* (**carriageways**)
the part of a road that vehicles travel on

carrier bag *NOUN* (**carrier bags**)
a large bag for holding shopping

carrot *NOUN* (**carrots**)
a long thin orange-coloured vegetable

carry *VERB* (**carries**, **carrying**, **carried**)
1 to carry something is to lift it and take it somewhere **2** to carry something is also to have it with you • *He is carrying a gun.* **3** a sound carries when it can be heard a long way away
to be carried away is to become very excited
to carry on is to continue doing something • *They carried on chatting.*
to carry something out is to put it into practice • *Will you please carry out my orders?*

cart *NOUN* (**carts**)
a small vehicle for carrying loads
to put the cart before the horse is to do things in the wrong order

cart *VERB* (**carts**, **carting**, **carted**)
(*informal*) to cart something somewhere is to carry or transport it, especially when it is heavy or tiring • *I've been carting these books around the school all afternoon.*

carthorse *NOUN* (**carthorses**)
a large heavy horse

cartilage *NOUN* (*say* **kar**- ti- lij)
cartilage is tough and flexible tissue attached to one of the bones in the nose or ear

carton *NOUN* (**cartons**)
a lightweight cardboard box

cartoon *NOUN* (**cartoons**)
1 a drawing that is funny or tells a joke **2** a series of drawings that tell a story **3** an animated film
▷ **cartoonist** *NOUN* someone who draws cartoons

cartridge *NOUN* (**cartridges**)
1 a container holding film to be put into a camera or ink to be put into a pen **2** the case containing the explosive for a bullet or shell

cartwheel *NOUN* (**cartwheels**)
a somersault done sideways, with your arms and legs spread wide

carve *VERB* (**carves**, **carving**, **carved**)
1 to carve wood or stone is to make something artistic by cutting it carefully **2** to carve meat is to cut it into slices

cascade *NOUN* (**cascades**)
a waterfall or a series of waterfalls

cascade *VERB* (**cascades**, **cascading**, **cascaded**)
to cascade is to tumble down like the water in a waterfall

case [1] *NOUN* (**cases**)
1 a container **2** a suitcase

case [2] *NOUN* (**cases**)
1 an example of something existing or happening • *We've had four cases of chickenpox.* • *It's just a case of being patient.* **2** a crime or incident that the police or a lawcourt are investigating • *The next case was a murder.*
in any case anyway
in case because something may happen • *Take an umbrella in case it rains.*

cash *NOUN*
cash is coins and banknotes that you use to pay for something

cash *VERB* (**cashes**, **cashing**, **cashed**)
to cash a cheque is to exchange it for coins and banknotes
to cash in on something (*informal*) is to take advantage of it

cash dispenser *NOUN* (**cash dispensers**)
a machine from which customers of a bank or building society can get money

cashew *NOUN* (**cashews**) (*say* **kash**-oo)
a small nut with a curved shape, which grows on a tropical tree

cashier *NOUN* (**cashiers**)
someone in charge of the money in a bank, office, or shop

cash register *NOUN* (**cash registers**)
a machine that records and stores money received in a shop

cask *NOUN* (**casks**)
a barrel

casket *NOUN* (**caskets**)
a small box for jewellery or other small objects

cassava *NOUN* (**cassavas**) (*say* ka-**sah**-va)
a fleshy root from a tropical tree, used for food

casserole *NOUN* (**casseroles**)
1 a covered dish in which food is cooked **2** the food cooked in a dish of this kind

cassette *NOUN* (**cassettes**)
a small sealed case containing recording tape or film on spools that turn when it is put in a tape recorder or camera

cassette recorder *NOUN* (**cassette recorders**)
a tape recorder that uses cassettes

cast *VERB* (**casts**, **casting**, **cast**)
1 to cast something is to throw it **2** to cast a vote is to make your vote in an election **3** to cast something made of metal or plaster is to make it in a mould **4** to cast a play or film is to choose the performers for it
to cast off is to untie a boat and start sailing in it

cast *NOUN* (**casts**)
1 a shape you make by pouring liquid metal or plaster into a mould **2** the performers in a play or film

castanets *PLURAL NOUN*
two pieces of wood or ivory held in one hand and clapped together to make a clicking sound, as in Spanish dancing

castaway *NOUN* (**castaways**)
someone who has been left in a deserted place, especially after a shipwreck

castle *NOUN* (**castles**)
1 a large old building with heavy stone walls and battlements, made to protect people in it from attack **2** a piece in chess, also called a *rook*

castor *NOUN* (**castors**) (*say* **kah**-ster)
a small wheel on the leg of a piece of furniture

castor oil *NOUN*
a yellowish oil made from the seeds of a tropical plant, used as medicine

castor sugar *NOUN*
finely ground white sugar

casual *ADJECTIVE*
1 not deliberate or planned • *It was just a casual remark.* **2** casual clothes are informal clothes that you wear for leisure time **3** not regular or permanent • *His dad was doing casual work.*
▷ **casually** *ADVERB* in a casual way

casualty *NOUN* (**casualties**)
someone killed or injured in war or in an accident

cat *NOUN* (**cats**)
1 a small furry animal, usually kept as a pet and known for catching mice **2** a larger member of the same family, for example a lion, tiger, or leopard
to let the cat out of the bag is to give away a secret

catalogue *NOUN* (**catalogues**)
a list of goods for sale or of books in a library

catalyst *NOUN* (**catalysts**) (*say* **kat**-a-list)
1 something that starts or speeds up a chemical reaction **2** something important that results in a change

catamaran *NOUN* (**catamarans**)
a sailing boat with two hulls fixed side by side

catapult *NOUN* (**catapults**)
a small weapon made from a forked stick with elastic attached to each fork, used for shooting pellets or small stones

catastrophe *NOUN* (**catastrophes**) (*say* ka-**tas**-tro-fi)
a great or sudden disaster
▷ **catastrophic** *ADJECTIVE* absolutely disastrous or dreadful • *The tornado did catastrophic damage.*

catch *VERB* (**catches**, **catching**, **caught**)
1 to catch something is to get hold of it, for example a ball that is coming towards you **2** to catch an animal is to capture it and not let it escape **3** to catch someone is to discover them doing

something wrong • *He was caught going home early.* **4** to catch an illness is to get it from someone else **5** to catch a bus or train is to get on it before it leaves **6** to catch something someone says is to manage to hear it • *I'm afraid I didn't catch your question.* **7** to catch your clothes is to get them entangled in something • *I've caught my sleeve on a bramble.*
to catch fire is to start burning
to catch on (*informal*) is to become popular, as a craze or fashion does
to catch someone out is to show that they are wrong or mistaken
to catch up with someone is to reach them when they have been ahead of you

catch *NOUN* (**catches**)
1 something caught or worth catching • *They had a large catch of fish.* **2** a hidden difficulty or snag • *The car was so cheap there had to be a catch.* **3** a device for fastening a door or window

catching *ADJECTIVE*
a disease is catching when people catch it easily, so that it spreads quickly

catchment area *NOUN*
1 the area in which pupils go to a particular school **2** the area in which rainwater drains into a river or reservoir

catchphrase *NOUN* (**catchphrases**)
a phrase that someone famous has used and a lot of people now use

catchy *ADJECTIVE* (**catchier**, **catchiest**)
pleasant and easy to remember, like a tune

category *NOUN* (**categories**)
a group or division of similar people or things • *I'm going to enter the competition in the under-twelves category.*

cater *VERB* (**caters**, **catering**, **catered**)
to cater for someone or something is to give them what they need

caterer *NOUN* (**caterers**)
someone whose job is to provide food for people, especially at an important function

caterpillar *NOUN* (**caterpillars**)
a long, creeping creature that turns into a butterfly or moth

cathedral *NOUN* (**cathedrals**)
a large and important church in a major city, with a bishop in charge of it

Catherine wheel *NOUN* (**Catherine wheels**)
a round flat firework that spins round and throws out sparks as it burns

cathode *NOUN* (**cathodes**)
the electrode by which electric current leaves a device (the opposite of *anode*)

Catholic *ADJECTIVE*
belonging to the Roman Catholic Church

Catholic *NOUN* (**Catholics**)
a member of the Roman Catholic Church

catkin *NOUN* (**catkins**)
a tiny flower hanging down from a willow or hazel

Catseye *NOUN* (**Catseyes**)
(*trademark*) a stud containing small pieces of glass or plastic that reflect the lights of vehicles, set in a row in the road to help drivers see their way at night

cattle *PLURAL NOUN*
cattle are cows and bulls and other large grass-eating animals

caught
past tense and past participle of **catch** *VERB*

cauldron *NOUN* (**cauldrons**)
a large round iron cooking pot used especially by witches in stories

cauliflower *NOUN* (**cauliflowers**)
a kind of cabbage with a large head of white flowers

cause *NOUN* (**causes**)
1 what makes something happen, a reason • *You have no cause for complaint.* **2** the aim or purpose that a group of people are working for • *They were raising money for a good cause.*

cause *VERB* (**causes**, **causing**, **caused**)
to cause something is to make it happen

caution *NOUN* (**cautions**)
1 caution is being careful to avoid danger or mistakes **2** a caution is a warning
▷ **cautionary** *ADJECTIVE*
a cautionary story is one that gives a warning about a danger or difficulty

cautious *ADJECTIVE*
careful to avoid a risk or difficulty
▷ **cautiously** *ADVERB* to act cautiously is to be careful in what you do

Cavalier *NOUN* (**Cavaliers**)
a supporter of King Charles I in the English Civil War

cavalry *NOUN*
soldiers who fight on horseback or in armoured vehicles

cave *NOUN* (**caves**)
a large hole in the side of a hill or cliff, or under the ground

cave *VERB* (**caves**, **caving**, **caved**)
to cave or go caving is to explore caves
to cave in is to collapse

caveman or **cavewoman** *NOUN* (**cavemen** or **cavewomen**)
a person who lived in a cave in prehistoric times

cavern *NOUN* (**caverns**)
a cave, especially a deep or dark cave

cavity *NOUN* (**cavities**)
a hollow or hole

CD (**CD's**)
short for **compact disc**

CD player *NOUN* (**CD players**)
a machine for playing compact discs

CD-ROM
short for *compact disc read-only memory*, a system for storing information that can be viewed on the VDU screen of a computer

cease *VERB* (**ceases, ceasing, ceased**)
to cease doing something is to stop doing it

ceasefire *NOUN* (**ceasefires**)
an agreement to stop using weapons, made by people who are fighting a war

ceaseless *ADJECTIVE*
going on all the time, not stopping

cedar *NOUN* (**cedars**)
an evergreen tree with hard sweet-smelling wood

ceiling *NOUN* (**ceilings**) (*say* see- ling)
1 the flat surface along the top of a room **2** the highest limit that something can reach • *They agreed to put a ceiling on taxes.*

celebrate *VERB* (**celebrates, celebrating, celebrated**)
to celebrate a day or event is to do something special to show that it is important

celebrated *ADJECTIVE*
famous, well known • *He won a prize to meet a celebrated film star.*

celebration *NOUN* (**celebrations**)
a celebration is a party or other special event to celebrate something

celebrity *NOUN* (**celebrities**)
a famous person, especially in show business or on television

celery *NOUN*
a vegetable with crisp white or green stems

cell *NOUN* (**cells**)
1 a small room, especially in a prison **2** a tiny part of a living creature or plant **3** a device for producing electric current chemically

cellar *NOUN* (**cellars**)
an underground room for storing things

cello *NOUN* (**cellos**) (*say* chel- oh)
a large stringed musical instrument, which you play by placing it upright between the knees and using a bow
▷ **cellist** someone who plays the cello

cellular *ADJECTIVE*
1 made of cells, or having cells • *the cellular structure of living things* **2** a cellular telephone is one that uses a network of radio stations to allow messages to be sent over a wide area

celluloid *NOUN*
celluloid is a transparent plastic

cellulose *NOUN*
cellulose is a tissue that forms the main part of all plants and trees

Celsius *ADJECTIVE*
using a scale for measuring temperature in which water freezes at 0 degrees and boils at 100 degrees

Celt *NOUN* (**Celts**) (*say* kelt)
one of the people who lived in Britain before the Romans came

Celtic *ADJECTIVE* (*say* kel- tik)
to do with the Celts, or the people descended from them and now living in Wales, Scotland, and Ireland

cement *NOUN*
1 cement is a mixture of lime and clay used in building to make floors and join bricks together **2** cement is also a strong glue

cemetery *NOUN* (**cemeteries**) (*say* sem- e- tri)
a place where dead people are buried

censor *VERB* (**censors, censoring, censored**)
to censor films, plays, or books is to look at them to make sure that they are suitable for people to see, and to take out any parts that do not seem suitable

censor *NOUN* (**censors**)
someone whose job is to censor films, plays, and books
▷ **censorship** *NOUN* the job or process of censoring films, plays, or books

census *NOUN* (**censuses**)
an official count or survey of the number of people or the volume of traffic in a place

cent *NOUN* (**cents**)
a coin and unit of money in America and some other countries
not to have a cent (*informal*) to have no money

centenary *NOUN* (**centenaries**)
the hundredth anniversary of something special or important

centigrade *ADJECTIVE*
a non-technical word for **Celsius**

centimetre *NOUN* (**centimetres**)
one-hundredth of a metre, about four-tenths of an inch

centipede *NOUN* (**centipedes**)
a small, long creature with many pairs of legs

central *ADJECTIVE*
1 at or near the centre of something **2** most important • *She will have a central role in our plans.*
▷ **centrally** *ADVERB* in a central position

central heating *NOUN*
central heating is a system of heating a building by sending hot water, hot air, or steam round it in pipes

centre *NOUN* (**centres**)
1 the middle of something **2** an important place • *Vienna is one of the great music centres of Europe.* **3** a building or place for a special purpose, such as a sports centre or a shopping centre

centre forward *NOUN* (**centre forwards**)
the middle player in the front line of a team in football or hockey

centre of gravity *NOUN* (**centres of gravity**)
the point in an object around which its mass is perfectly balanced

centrifugal force *NOUN*
centrifugal force is a force that affects something that is turning or spinning and makes it move out from the centre

centurion *NOUN* (**centurions**)
an officer in the ancient Roman army, originally commanding a hundred men

century *NOUN* (**centuries**)
1 a period of a hundred years **2** a hundred runs scored by one batsman in an innings at cricket

ceramics *PLURAL NOUN*
ceramics is the art of making pottery

cereal *NOUN* (**cereals**)
1 a grass that produces seeds which are used as food **2** a breakfast food made from seeds of this kind

ceremony *NOUN* (**ceremonies**) (*say* se- ri- mo- ni)
1 ceremony is the formal actions carried out at a wedding, funeral, or other important occasion **2** a ceremony is a formal event such as a wedding or funeral

> **WORD FAMILY**
> A **ceremonial** event or duty is one to do with a ceremony; **ceremonious** behaviour is formal and dignifed.

certain *ADJECTIVE*
1 something is certain when it is definitely true or is going to happen **2** you are certain about something when you know it is definitely true
for certain definitely, for sure
to make certain is to make sure

certainly *ADVERB*
as a fact, without any doubt • *They were certainly here last night.*

certainty *NOUN* (**certainties**)
1 a certainty is something that is sure to happen **2** certainty is being sure

certificate *NOUN* (**certificates**)
an official document that records an important event or achievement, such as someone's birth or passing an exam

certify *VERB* (**certifies**, **certifying**, **certified**)
to certify something is to say in writing that it is true

CFC
short for *chlorofluorocarbon*, a chemical that can damage the earth's ozone layer, and was once used in refrigerators and aerosols

chaffinch *NOUN* (**chaffinches**)
a small bird

chain *NOUN* (**chains**)
1 a row of metal rings fastened together **2** a line of people **3** a connected series of things • *The story told of a strange chain of events.*

chain letter *NOUN* (**chain letters**)
a letter someone sends you asking you to copy it and send it to several other people, who are supposed to do the same

chain reaction *NOUN* (**chain reactions**)
a series of happenings, each causing the next

chain saw *NOUN* (**chain saws**)
a saw with teeth on a chain that is moved round very fast by a motor

chair *NOUN* (**chairs**)
1 a seat with a back for one person **2** the person who is in charge of a meeting

chairlift *NOUN* (**chairlifts**)
a set of seats hanging from a moving cable, carrying people up the side of a mountain

chairman or **chairperson** *NOUN* (**chairmen** or **chairpersons**)
the person who is in charge of a meeting

chalet *NOUN* (**chalets**) (*say* shal- ay)
a small house, usually built of wood

chalk *NOUN* (**chalks**)
1 a kind of soft white rock **2** a soft white or coloured stick of a similar rock, used for writing on blackboards
▷ **chalky** *ADJECTIVE* white or powdery like chalk

challenge *VERB* (**challenges**, **challenging**, **challenged**)
to challenge someone is to demand that they perform some feat or take part in a fight
▷ **challenger** *NOUN* a person who makes a challenge, especially for a sports title

challenge *NOUN* (**challenges**)
something difficult that someone has to do

chamber *NOUN* (**chambers**)
1 (*old use*) a room **2** a hall used for meetings of a parliament or council

chamber music *NOUN*
classical music for a small group of players

chameleon *NOUN* (**chameleons**) (*say* ka- **mee**- li- on)
a small lizard that can change the colour of its skin to match its surroundings and appear almost invisible

champagne *NOUN* (*say* sham- **payn**)
a bubbly white French wine

champion *NOUN* (**champions**)
1 the best person in a sport or competition **2** someone who supports a cause by fighting or speaking for it • *Martin Luther King was a champion of human rights.*

championship *NOUN* (**championships**)
a contest to decide who is the best player or competitor in a game or sport

chance *NOUN* (**chances**)
1 a chance is a possibility or opportunity • *This is your only chance to see them.* **2** chance is the way things happen accidentally • *It was pure chance that*

we met.
by chance accidentally, without any planning • *We found the place by chance.*
to take a chance is to take a risk

chancel *NOUN* (**chancels**)
the part of a church round the altar

chancellor *NOUN* (**chancellors**)
1 an important government or legal official **2** the chief minister of the government in some European countries

Chancellor of the Exchequer *NOUN*
the minister in charge of a country's finances and taxes

chandelier *NOUN* (**chandeliers**) (*say* shan- de- **leer**)
a light fitting that hangs from the ceiling and has a lot of bright bulbs

change *VERB* (**changes, changing, changed**)
1 to change something or someone is to make them different **2** to change is to become different • *My gran said I'd changed since she'd last seen me.* **3** to change one thing for another is to exchange them • *I'm going to change my bike for a new one.* **4** to change money is to give coins or notes of small values in exchange for higher value money • *Can you change a $5 bill?* **5** to change trains or buses is to get off one and get on another • *Change at York for the train to Durham.*

change *NOUN* (**changes**)
1 change is the process of changing **2** your change is the money you get back when you give more money than the price of something you are buying, for example if you don't have the right money **3** a change of clothes is a set of fresh clothes
to do something for a change is to do it because it is different or unusual • *Let's walk home for a change.*

changeable *ADJECTIVE*
likely to change, often changing • *The weather has been very changeable.*

channel *NOUN* (**channels**)
1 a stretch of water joining two seas, like the English Channel between Britain and France **2** a television or radio station that transmits on a particular frequency **3** a way for water to flow along **4** the part of a river or sea that is deep enough for ships to sail on

chant *NOUN* (**chants**)
a tune, especially one that is often repeated

chant *VERB* (**chants, chanting, chanted**)
to chant words is to say them or call them out in a special rhythm

chaos *NOUN* (*say* **kay**- oss)
chaos is complete disorder or confusion • *The room was in chaos.*

chaotic *ADJECTIVE* (*say* kay- **ot**- ik)
completely confused or in a mess

chap *NOUN* (**chaps**)
(*informal*) a man or boy • *What a funny chap he is.*

chapatti *NOUN* (**chapattis**)
a flat thin cake of Indian bread made without yeast

chapel *NOUN* (**chapels**)
1 a small church or part of a large church **2** a room in a large house, used for worship

chapped *ADJECTIVE*
having rough, cracked skin

chapter *NOUN* (**chapters**)
a section of a book

char *VERB* (**chars, charring, charred**)
to char something is to scorch it or blacken it with fire

character *NOUN* (**characters**)
1 the special nature and qualities of a person or thing **2** a person in a story or play

characteristic *NOUN* (**characteristics**)
something that makes a person or thing noticeable or different from others

characteristic *ADJECTIVE*
typical, what you would expect of someone

characterize *VERB* (**characterizes, characterizing, characterized**)
1 to characterize something is to provide it with its special character or qualities • *Stony beaches and grey seas characterize the south coast of England.* **2** to characterize someone is to describe their character in a certain way • *His friends characterized him as boastful.*

charades *NOUN* (*say* sha- **rahdz**)
charades is a game in which people have to guess a word or the title of a book or film when other people act it out

charcoal *NOUN*
charcoal is a black substance made by burning wood slowly

charge *NOUN* (**charges**)
1 the price asked for something **2** an accusation that someone committed a crime • *He is facing three charges of burglary.* **3** an attack in a battle **4** the amount of explosive needed to fire a weapon **5** the amount of an electric current
to be in charge of something or **someone** is to be the one who decides what will happen to them

charge *VERB* (**charges, charging, charged**)
1 to charge a price for something is to ask people to pay it **2** to charge someone is to accuse them of committing a crime **3** to charge in a battle is to rush to attack the enemy

chariot *NOUN* (**chariots**)
a horse-drawn vehicle with two wheels, used in ancient times for fighting and racing
▷ **charioteer** *NOUN* someone who drove a chariot

charitable *ADJECTIVE*
1 a charitable person or act is one that is kind and generous **2** a charitable organization is one that gives money or other kinds of help to those who need it

charity *NOUN* (**charities**)
1 charity is giving money and help to other people **2** a charity is an organization that helps those in need

charm *NOUN* (**charms**)
1 charm is being pleasant and attractive **2** a charm is a magic spell **3** a charm is also something small worn or carried to bring good luck

charm *VERB* (**charms**, **charming**, **charmed**)
1 to charm someone is to give them pleasure or delight **2** to charm someone is also to put a spell on them

charming *ADJECTIVE*
pleasant and attractive

chart *NOUN* (**charts**)
1 a large plan or map **2** a diagram or list with information set out in columns or rows **3** a list of the most popular CDs and records that are sold

charter *NOUN* (**charters**)
1 an official document explaining people's rights or privileges **2** the hire of an aircraft or vehicle for a special purpose

charter *VERB* (**charters**, **chartering**, **chartered**)
to charter an aircraft or vehicle is to hire it for a special journey

charter flight *NOUN* (**charter flights**)
a flight by an aircraft specially hired by the holiday companies

charwoman *NOUN* (**charwomen**)
(*old use*) a woman whose job is to clean inside houses or offices

chase *VERB* (**chases**, **chasing**, **chased**)
to chase someone is to go quickly after them to try to catch them up

chase *NOUN* (**chases**)
a chase is when you chase someone

chasm *NOUN* (**chasms**) (*say* ka- zum)
a deep opening in the ground

chassis *NOUN* (**chassis**) (*say* shass- i)
the frame and wheels of a vehicle, which support the body

chat *NOUN* (**chats**)
a friendly or informal talk with someone

chat *VERB* (**chats**, **chatting**, **chatted**)
to chat to someone is to talk to them in a friendly or informal way
▷ **chatty** *ADJECTIVE* liking to chat to people in a friendly way

château *NOUN* (**châteaux**) (*say* shat- oh)
a castle or large house in France

chatter *VERB* (**chatters**, **chattering**, **chattered**)
1 to talk quickly or stupidly; to talk too much **2** to make a rattling noise

chauffeur *NOUN* (**chauffeurs**) (*say* shoh- fer)
someone who is paid to drive a large smart car for someone important

chauvinism *NOUN* (*say* shoh- vin- izm)
1 chauvinism is believing your country is always better than any other **2** male chauvinism is believing men are always better or more important than women
▷ **chauvinist** *NOUN* someone who believes their own country or their own sex is superior

cheap *ADJECTIVE* (**cheaper**, **cheapest**)
1 something cheap does not cost much **2** you call something cheap when it is shoddy or inferior

cheat *VERB* (**cheats**, **cheating**, **cheated**)
1 to cheat someone is to trick them so they lose something **2** to cheat is to try to do well in an examination or game by breaking the rules

cheat *NOUN* (**cheats**)
someone who cheats

check *VERB* (**checks**, **checking**, **checked**)
1 to check something is to make sure that it is correct or all right **2** to check someone or something is to make them stop or slow down
to check in is to sign your name to show you have arrived at a hotel or to show your ticket at an airport
to check on something or **check up on something** is to look at it carefully to see if it is correct or suitable
to check out is to pay your bill and leave a hotel

check *NOUN* (**checks**)
1 a check is when you check something **2** check in chess is when the king is threatened by another piece **3** a check is a pattern of squares

> SPELLING
> Take care not to confuse **check** with **cheque**, which means a piece of paper telling your bank to pay money out of your account.

checkmate *NOUN* (**checkmates**)
checkmate in chess is when one side wins by trapping the other side's king

checkout *NOUN* (**checkouts**)
the place where you pay for your shopping in a supermarket or a large shop

check-up *NOUN* (**check-ups**)
a careful check or examination

cheek *NOUN* (**cheeks**)
1 your cheek is the side of your face below your eye **2** cheek, or a cheek, is being rude or impolite

cheek *VERB* (**cheeks**, **cheeking**, **cheeked**)
to cheek someone is to be rude to them

cheeky *ADJECTIVE* (**cheekier**, **cheekiest**)
rude or impolite, without being unpleasant or nasty
▷ **cheekily** *ADVERB* in a rude or cheeky way

cheer *NOUN* (**cheers**)
a shout praising or supporting someone

cheer *VERB* (**cheers**, **cheering**, **cheered**)
1 to cheer someone is to support them by cheering **2** to cheer someone is to comfort or encourage them
to cheer someone up is to make them more cheerful
to cheer up is to become more cheerful

cheerful *ADJECTIVE*
happy and bright

cheerio *INTERJECTION*
(*informal*) goodbye

cheese *NOUN* (**cheeses**)
a white or yellow food made from milk. Cheese can be hard like cheddar or soft like some French cheeses
▷ **cheesy** *ADJECTIVE* tasting or smelling like cheese

cheetah *NOUN* (**cheetahs**)
a large spotted animal of the cat family, which can run very fast

chef *NOUN* (**chefs**) (*say* shef)
the chief cook in a hotel or restaurant

chemical *NOUN* (**chemicals**)
a substance used in or made by chemistry

chemical *ADJECTIVE*
to do with chemistry or made by chemistry

chemist *NOUN* (**chemists**)
1 someone who makes or sells medicines **2** an expert in chemistry

chemistry *NOUN*
chemistry is the study of the way substances combine and react with one another

cheque *NOUN* (**cheques**)
a written form instructing a bank to pay money out of an account

> SPELLING
> Take care not to confuse **cheque** with **check**, which means the action of making sure that something is correct or in good condition.

chequered *ADJECTIVE*
marked with a pattern of squares

cherish *VERB* (**cherishes**, **cherishing**, **cherished**)
to cherish something is to look after it lovingly

cherry *NOUN* (**cherries**)
a small bright red fruit with a large stone

chess *NOUN*
a game for two players played with sixteen pieces each on a board of 64 squares

> WORD FAMILY
> The pieces are called **chessmen** and the board is called a **chessboard.** Each player has a **king** and **queen**, two pieces called **castle** (or **rook**), two pieces called **bishop**, two pieces called **knight** (which can hop over other pieces), and eight pieces called **pawn.**

chest *NOUN* (**chests**)
1 a chest is a large strong box **2** your chest is the front part of your body between your neck and your waist
to get something off your chest (*informal*) is to admit something you are worried about or feel bad about

chestnut *NOUN* (**chestnuts**)
1 a hard brown nut **2** the tree that produces this kind of nut

chest of drawers *NOUN* (**chests of drawers**)
a piece of furniture with drawers for holding clothes

chew *VERB* (**chews**, **chewing**, **chewed**)
to chew food is to grind it into pieces between your teeth
▷ **chewy** *ADJECTIVE* chewy food is tough and needs a lot of chewing

chewing gum *NOUN*
a sticky flavoured gum for chewing

chick *NOUN* (**chicks**)
a young bird

chicken *NOUN* (**chickens**)
1 a chicken is a young hen **2** chicken is the meat of a hen used as food

chicken *ADJECTIVE*
(*informal*) cowardly

chicken *VERB* (**chickens**, **chickening**, **chickened**)
to chicken out of something (*informal*) is to avoid it because you are afraid

chickenpox *NOUN*
a disease that produces red itchy spots on your skin

chief *NOUN* (**chiefs**)
1 a leader or ruler **2** the most important person, the boss

chief *ADJECTIVE*
1 having the highest rank or power **2** most important

chiefly *ADVERB*
mainly, mostly • *Peter is the one who is chiefly to blame.*

chieftain *NOUN* (**chieftains**)
the chief of a tribe or clan

chilblain *NOUN* (**chilblains**)
a sore place on a hand or foot, caused by cold weather

child *NOUN* (**children**)
1 a young person, a boy or girl **2** someone's son or daughter • *Whose child is that?*

childhood *NOUN* (**childhoods**)
the time when you are a child

childish *ADJECTIVE*
silly and immature • *Don't be childish!*

childminder *NOUN* (**childminders**)
a person who is paid to look after children while their parents are out at work

childproof *ADJECTIVE*
not able to be opened or operated by small children • *The car has childproof door locks.*

chill *NOUN* (**chills**)
1 chill is an unpleasant feeling of being cold **2** a chill is a cold that makes you shiver

chill *VERB* (**chills**, **chilling**, **chilled**)
to chill something is to make it cold

chilli *NOUN* (**chillies**)
the hot-tasting pod of a red pepper

chilly *ADJECTIVE* (**chillier**, **chilliest**)
1 slightly cold **2** unfriendly • *They went to see the head and got a chilly reception.*

chime *NOUN* (**chimes**)
a ringing sound made by a bell

chime *VERB* (**chimes**, **chiming**, **chimed**)
to chime is to ring • *The clock chimes every quarter-hour.*

chimney *NOUN* (**chimneys**)
a tall pipe or passage that carries away smoke from a fire

chimney pot *NOUN* (**chimney pots**)
the piece of pipe at the top of a chimney

chimney sweep *NOUN* (**chimney sweeps**)
someone who cleans the soot out of chimneys

chimpanzee *NOUN* (**chimpanzees**)
an small African ape with black fur and large eyes

chin *NOUN* (**chins**)
your chin is the part of your face under your mouth

china *NOUN*
china is thin and delicate pottery

chink *NOUN* (**chinks**)
1 a narrow opening • *He looked through a chink in the curtains.* **2** a clinking sound • *They heard the chink of coins.*

chip *NOUN* (**chips**)
1 a small piece of something **2** a place where a small piece has been knocked off something **3** a small piece of fried potato **4** a small counter used in gambling games **5** a silicon chip
to have a chip on your shoulder is to feel defensive and resentful about something • *He's got a chip on his shoulder about rich people.*

chip *VERB* (**chips**, **chipping**, **chipped**)
to chip something is to knock a small piece off it by accident
to chip in is to make a suggestion or comment during a conversation that other people are having

chirp *VERB* (**chirps**, **chirping**, **chirped**)
to chirp is to make short sharp sounds like a small bird

chirpy *ADJECTIVE* (**chirpier**, **chirpiest**)
(*informal*) lively and cheerful

chisel *NOUN* (**chisels**)
a tool with a sharp end for shaping wood or stone

chisel *VERB* (**chisels**, **chiselling**, **chiselled**)
to chisel wood or stone is to shape or cut it with a chisel

chivalry *NOUN*
being ready to help people who are less strong than you are
▷ **chivalrous** *ADJECTIVE* kind and helpful to people who are less strong

chlorine *NOUN*
a chemical used to disinfect water

chlorophyll *NOUN*
the substance that makes plants green

choc *NOUN* (**chocs**)
(*informal*) a chocolate

chock-a-block or **chock-full** *ADJECTIVE & ADVERB*
a place that is chock-a-block is completely full so there is hardly any room to move

chocolate *NOUN* (**chocolates**)
1 chocolate is a sweet brown food **2** a chocolate is a sweet made of or covered with chocolate
3 chocolate is also a sweet powder used for making drinks

choice *NOUN* (**choices**)
1 choice is the process of choosing or the power to choose • *I'm afraid we have no choice.* **2** a choice is what someone chooses • *Let me know your choice of book.*

choir *NOUN* (**choirs**)
a group of singers, especially in a church

> WORD FAMILY
> A **choirboy** or **choirgirl** is a boy or girl singer in a choir. Note that you do not say **choirman** or **choirwoman**, but **chorister**. A choir is also called a **chorus**. The music a choir sings is called **choral** music.

choke *VERB* (**chokes**, **choking**, **choked**)
1 to choke on something is to be unable to breathe properly because it is stuck in your throat **2** to choke someone is to stop them breathing properly
3 to choke something is to block it up

choke *NOUN* (**chokes**)
a valve in a motor vehicle that controls the mixture of air and petrol

cholera *NOUN* (*say* kol- er- a)
cholera is a severe infectious disease that affects the intestines

cholesterol *NOUN* (*say* ko- less- te- rol)
cholesterol is a substance found in the cells of your body which helps to carry fat in the bloodstream

choose *VERB* (**chooses, choosing, chose, chosen**)
to choose something or someone is to decide that you want them rather than any of the others

choosy *ADJECTIVE* (**choosier**, **choosiest**)
(*informal*) a choosy person is fussy and difficult to please

chop *VERB* (**chops**, **chopping**, **chopped**)
1 to chop something up is to cut it into small pieces **2** to chop something is to cut or hit it with a heavy blow

chop *NOUN* (**chops**)
1 a chopping blow **2** a small thick slice of meat

chopper *NOUN* (**choppers**)
1 a small axe **2** (*informal*) a helicopter

chopping board *NOUN* (**chopping boards**)
a board made of wood or plastic, used for cutting meat or vegetables on

choppy *ADJECTIVE* (**choppier**, **choppiest**)
a choppy sea is fairly rough with lots of small waves

chopsticks *PLURAL NOUN*
a pair of thin sticks used for eating Chinese or Japanese food

choral *ADJECTIVE* (*say* kor- al)
for a choir or chorus

chord *NOUN* (**chords**) (*say* kord)
a number of musical notes sounded together

> SPELLING
> Take care not to confuse **chord** with **cord**, which means a piece of thin rope.

chore *NOUN* (**chores**) (*say* chor)
a tedious or difficult task

chorister *NOUN* (**choristers**) (*say* kor- is- ter)
someone who sings in a choir

chorus *NOUN* (**choruses**) (*say* kor- us)
1 a group of people singing or speaking together **2** a piece of music sung by a group of people **3** the words repeated after every verse of a song or poem

chose
past tense of **choose**

chosen
past participle of **choose**

christen *VERB* (**christens**, **christening**, **christened**)
to christen a child is to baptize it and give it a name
▷ **christening** *NOUN* the ceremony at which a child is baptized

Christian *NOUN* (**Christians**)
someone who believes in Christ

Christian *ADJECTIVE*
to do with Christ or Christians

Christianity *NOUN*
the religion of Christians

Christian name *NOUN* (**Christian names**)
a first name, for example *John* and *Mary*

Christmas *NOUN* (**Christmases**)
the time of celebrating the birth of Christ on 25 December

chrome or **chromium** *NOUN*
a shiny silvery metal

chromosome *NOUN* (**chromosomes**)
in living things, the part of a cell that contains the genes

chronic *ADJECTIVE*
1 a chronic illness or problem is one that lasts for a long time **2** (*informal*) very bad or unpleasant • *He was telling us chronic stories about his holidays.*
▷ **chronically** *ADVERB* to be chronically ill is to have a very long illness

chronicle *NOUN* (**chronicles**)
a list of events with their dates

chronological *ADJECTIVE*
a chronological list of events is arranged in the order in which the events happened
▷ **chronologically** *ADVERB* in the order in which things happen

chronology *NOUN*
the arrangement of events in the order in which they happened, especially in history or geology

chrysalis *NOUN* (**chrysalises**) (*say* kris- a- lis)
the hard cover a caterpillar makes round itself before it turns into a butterfly or moth

chrysanthemum *NOUN* (**chrysanthemums**)
a garden flower that blooms in autumn

chubby *ADJECTIVE* (**chubbier**, **chubbiest**)
plump and healthy

chuck *VERB* (**chucks**, **chucking**, **chucked**)
(*informal*) to chuck something is to throw it roughly • *He chucked a brick through the window.*

chuckle *VERB* (**chuckles**, **chuckling**, **chuckled**)
to chuckle is to laugh quietly

chuckle *NOUN* (**chuckles**)
a quiet laugh

chug *VERB* (**chugs**, **chugging**, **chugged**)
to chug is to move with the sound of a slow-running engine

chum *NOUN* (**chums**)
(*informal*) a friend
▷ **chummy** *ADJECTIVE* friendly

chunk *NOUN* (**chunks**)
a thick lump of something
▷ **chunky** *ADJECTIVE* big and thick

church *NOUN* (**churches**)
1 a church is a building where Christians worship **2** a church is also a particular Christian religion, for example the Church of England

churchyard *NOUN* (**churchyards**)
the ground round a church, used as a graveyard

churn *NOUN* (**churns**)
1 a large container for milk **2** a machine for making butter

churn *VERB* (**churns**, **churning**, **churned**)
1 to churn butter is to make it in a churn **2** to churn something is to stir it vigorously
to churn something out (*informal*) is to produce lots of it very quickly

chute *NOUN* (**chutes**) (*say* shoot)
a steep channel for people or things to slide down

chutney *NOUN*
chutney is a spicy mixture of fruit and peppers in a sauce, eaten with meat or cheese

cider *NOUN* (**ciders**)
cider is an alcoholic drink made from apples

cigar *NOUN* (**cigars**)
a roll of compressed tobacco leaves for smoking

cigarette *NOUN* (**cigarettes**)
a small, thin roll of shredded tobacco in thin paper for smoking

cinder *NOUN* (**cinders**)
a small piece of coal or wood that is partly burned

cine camera *NOUN* (**cine cameras**)
a camera used for taking moving pictures on film

cinema *NOUN* (**cinemas**)
1 a cinema is a place where people go to see films **2** cinema is the art or business of making films • *recent trends in British cinema*

cinnamon *NOUN*
a yellowish-brown spice

cinquain *NOUN* (**cinquains**) (*say* sin- kayn)
an American form of short poem, with five lines and 22 syllables in the pattern 2,4,6,8,2

circle *NOUN* (**circles**)
1 a round flat shape, the shape of a coin or wheel **2** a balcony in a cinema or theatre **3** a number of people who have the same interests • *She belongs to a writers' circle.*

circle *VERB* (**circles**, **circling**, **circled**)
1 to circle is to move in a circle • *Vultures circled overhead.* **2** to circle a place is go round it • *The space probe circled Mars.*

circuit *NOUN* (**circuits**) (*say* ser- kit)
1 a circular line or journey **2** a racecourse **3** the path of an electric current

circular *ADJECTIVE*
round like a circle

circular *NOUN* (**circulars**)
a letter or advertisement sent to a lot of people

circulate *VERB* (**circulates**, **circulating**, **circulated**)
1 to circulate is to move around and come back to the beginning • *Blood circulates in the body.* **2** to circulate something like a letter or notice is to send it to a lot of people

circulation *NOUN* (**circulations**)
1 the movement of blood around your body **2** the number of copies of each issue of a newspaper or magazine that are sold

circumference *NOUN* (**circumferences**)
the line or distance round something, especially round a circle

circumstance *NOUN* (**circumstances**)
1 a circumstance is a fact or event that makes a difference to something • *He won under difficult circumstances.* **2** a person's circumstances are how much money they have, where they live, and the sort of life they lead

circus *NOUN* (**circuses**)
an entertainment with clowns, acrobats, and animals, usually performed in a large tent

cistern *NOUN* (**cisterns**)
a water tank

citizen *NOUN* (**citizens**)
a citizen of a place is someone who was born there or who lives there

citizenship *NOUN*
1 the citizenship of a country is the right to live there and be a citizen of it • *She has applied for American citizenship.* **2** citizenship is also the duties a person has when they are the citizen of a country • *The school has lessons in citizenship.*

citric acid *NOUN*
a weak acid found in fruits like lemons and limes

citrus fruit *NOUN*
citrus fruits are juicy fruits with a tough skin, such as oranges, lemons, limes, and grapefruit

city *NOUN* (**cities**)
a large and important town, often having a cathedral

civic *ADJECTIVE*
to do with a city or its citizens

civil *ADJECTIVE*
1 to do with the citizens of a place **2** to do with the ordinary people and not those who are in the armed forces **3** a civil person is polite and courteous to other people

civil engineering *NOUN*
civil engineering is the designing and making of roads, bridges, and large buildings

civilian *NOUN* (**civilians**)
someone who is an ordinary citizen and not in the armed forces

civilization *NOUN* (**civilizations**)
1 a civilization is a society or culture at a particular time in history • *They were learning about the Bronze Age civilization.* **2** civilization is a developed or organized way of life • *We are studying a primitive society with little civilization.*

civilize *VERB* (**civilizes**, **civilizing**, **civilized**)
to civilize someone is to improve their education and manners

civil rights *PLURAL NOUN*
people's civil rights are their rights as citizens to have freedom and fair treatment, and to vote in elections

civil service *NOUN*
the civil service is all the officials who do the work the government needs to do to run the country

civil war *NOUN* (**civil wars**)
a war fought between people of the same country, such as the English Civil War (1642–51) or the American Civil War (1861–65)

clad *ADJECTIVE*
clothed or covered • *The story was about a knight clad in shining armour.*

claim *VERB* (**claims, claiming, claimed**)
1 to claim something is to ask for it when you think it belongs to you • *I'd like to claim the three weeks' money you owe me.* **2** to claim something is to state or assert it • *They claimed they had been at home all evening.*

claim *NOUN* (**claims**)
1 an act of claiming **2** something claimed

claimant *NOUN* (**claimants**)
someone who makes a claim, especially for a right or benefit

clam *NOUN* (**clams**)
a large shellfish

clamber *VERB* (**clambers, clambering, clambered**)
to clamber is to climb up or over something difficult using your hands and feet • *We clambered over the slippery rocks.*

clammy *ADJECTIVE* (**clammier, clammiest**)
damp and slimy

clamp *NOUN* (**clamps**)
a device for holding things together

clamp *VERB* (**clamps, clamping, clamped**)
to clamp something is to fit a clamp on it
to clamp down on something is to be strict about it • *The teachers decided to clamp down on homework.*

clan *NOUN* (**clans**)
a number of families with the same ancestor • *The Scottish clans include the Campbells and the MacDonalds.*

clang *VERB* (**clangs, clanging, clanged**)
to clang is to make a loud ringing sound

clank *VERB* (**clanks, clanking, clanked**)
to clank is to make a loud sound like heavy pieces of metal banging together

clap *VERB* (**claps, clapping, clapped**)
to clap is to make a noise by hitting the palms of your hands together, especially to show you like something

clap *NOUN* (**claps**)
1 a round of clapping, especially to show you like something • *They gave the winners a loud clap.* **2** a clap of thunder is a sudden sound of loud thunder

clapper *NOUN* (**clappers**)
the piece that swings inside a bell and makes it ring when the bell is moved

clarify *VERB* (**clarifies, clarifying, clarified**)
to clarify something is to explain it and make it easier to understand
▷ **clarification** *NOUN* clarification is making something clear and easier to understand

clarinet *NOUN* (**clarinets**)
a woodwind instrument with a low tone
▷ **clarinettist** *NOUN* someone who plays the clarinet

clarity *NOUN*
clarity is a clear quality • *They spoke with clarity.*

clash *VERB* (**clashes, clashing, clashed**)
1 to clash is to make a loud sound like cymbals banging together **2** two events clash when they happen inconveniently at the same time • *My favourite TV programmes clash at 8 o'clock tonight.* **3** two or more people clash when they have a fight or argument • *Gangs of rival supporters clashed outside the ground.*

clash *NOUN* (**clashes**)
1 a clashing sound **2** a fight or argument

clasp *VERB* (**clasps, clasping, clasped**)
to clasp someone or something is to hold them tightly

clasp *NOUN* (**clasps**)
1 a device for fastening things **2** a tight grasp

class *NOUN* (**classes**)
1 a class is a group of similar people, animals, or things **2** a class is also a division according to how good or important something is • *Send the letter by first class post.* **3** a class is also a group of children or students who are taught together **4** class is a system of different ranks in society
to have class (*informal*) is to look smart or behave elegantly

class *VERB* (**classes, classing, classed**)
to class things is to put them in classes or groups

classic *NOUN* (**classics**)
a book, film, or story that is well known and thought to be very good and important

classic *ADJECTIVE*
1 a classic story is one that most people think is very good and important **2** very typical or common • *They made the classic mistake of leaving things to the last moment.*
classics the study of the ancient Greek and Latin languages and writers

classical *ADJECTIVE*
1 to do with Greek and Latin literature **2** classical music is serious music, often written in the past and still played

classified *ADJECTIVE*
1 classified advertisements in newspapers are organized into types or subjects **2** classified information is officially secret and not told to the public

classify *VERB* (**classifies, classifying, classified**)
to classify things is to put them in classes or groups
▷ **classification** *NOUN* a system of classifying things or putting them into groups

classmate *NOUN* (**classmates**)
your classmates are the people in the same class as you at school

classroom *NOUN* (**classrooms**)
a room where lessons are given at a school

clatter *NOUN*
a loud noise of things being rattled or banged

clatter *VERB* (**clatters**, **clattering**, **clattered**)
to clatter is to make a clatter

clause *NOUN* (**clauses**)
1 (*in grammar*) a part of a sentence that has its own verb **2** a part of a contract, treaty, or law

> GRAMMAR
> A clause can be a main clause or a subordinate clause. In the sentence *I was four when I ate my first ice cream*, the main clause is *I was four* and the subordinate clause is *when I ate my first ice cream*. A sentence can have more than one main clause, for example *I was four and I had a birthday party*.

claw *NOUN* (**claws**)
one of the hard sharp nails that some birds and animals have on their feet

claw *VERB* (**claws**, **clawing**, **clawed**)
to claw something is to grasp or scratch it with a claw or hand

clay *NOUN*
clay is a sticky kind of earth, and is used for making bricks and pottery
▷ **clayey** *ADJECTIVE* soft or sticky like clay

clean *ADJECTIVE* (**cleaner**, **cleanest**)
1 something is clean when it does not have any dirt or stains on it **2** fresh, not yet used • *Start on a clean page.* **3** not rude or offensive • *I hope your jokes are clean ones.* **4** fair and honest • *They wanted a clean fight.*

clean *VERB* (**cleans**, **cleaning**, **cleaned**)
to clean something is to make it clean

clean *ADVERB*
(*informal*) completely • *I clean forgot.*

cleaner *NOUN* (**cleaners**)
1 someone who cleans rooms or offices
2 something used for cleaning
the cleaners a firm which cleans clothes

cleanliness *NOUN* (*say* **klen- li- nes**)
the practice of keeping things clean

cleanly *ADVERB*
neatly, exactly • *He cut the brick cleanly in two.*

cleanse *VERB* (**cleanses**, **cleansing**, **cleansed**) (*say* klenz)
to cleanse something is to clean it and make it pure
▷ **cleanser** *NOUN* something you use to make a thing clean

clear *ADJECTIVE* (**clearer**, **clearest**)
1 easy to see or hear or understand • *He spoke with a clear voice.* **2** free from things that get in the way or aren't wanted • *Make sure the table's clear for dinner.*

clear *ADVERB*
1 clearly • *Speak loud and clear.* **2** completely • *He got clear away.* **3** at a distance from something • *You'd better stand clear of the gates.*

clear *VERB* (**clears**, **clearing**, **cleared**)
1 to clear something is to make it free of unwanted things • *Will you clear the table for dinner?* **2** to clear is to become clearer • *After the storm, the sky slowly cleared.* **3** to clear someone is to find out that they are not to blame for something people thought they had done **4** to clear something is to jump over it without touching it
to clear off or **clear out** (*informal*) is to go away
to clear something out is to empty or tidy it
to clear up is to make things tidy

clearance *NOUN* (**clearances**)
1 clearance between two things is how close together they are when one passes the other or comes near it • *There was not much clearance between the bridge and the top of the bus.* **2** clearance to do something is official permission for it to happen • *The pilot wanted clearance for takeoff.* **3** clearance is moving away things that are in the way or not wanted

clearing *NOUN* (**clearings**)
an open space in a wood or forest

clearly *ADVERB*
1 in a clear way • *We could see the house clearly.*
2 obviously • *They were clearly going to win.*

clef *NOUN* (**clefs**)
a sign that shows the pitch of a stave in music

clench *VERB* (**clenches**, **clenching**, **clenched**)
to clench your teeth or fingers is to close them tightly

clergy *PLURAL NOUN*
the clergy are the priests and other officials of a Christian Church

clergyman *NOUN* (**clergymen**)
a man who is one of the clergy

clergywoman *NOUN* (**clergywomen**)
a woman who is one of the clergy

clerical *ADJECTIVE*
1 to do with the routine work in an office, such as filing and writing letters **2** to do with the clergy

clerihew *NOUN* (**clerihews**) (*say* **kle- ri- hyew**)
a short comical rhyme about a person. Clerihews have uneven lines and are often very silly.

> CLERIHEWS
> Here is an example of a clerihew: Sir Christopher Wren Said, 'I'm going to dine with some men. If anybody calls Say I'm designing St Paul's.'

clerk *NOUN* (**clerks**) (*say* klark)
someone who works in an office to keep records and accounts and file papers

clever *ADJECTIVE* (**cleverer**, **cleverest**)
quick to learn and understand things; skilful

cliché *NOUN* (**clichés**) (*say* klee- shay)
a phrase that people use a lot, so that it doesn't mean very much

CLICHÉS
Here are some well-known clichés:
At this moment in time
Have a nice day
In this day and age
Taking everything into consideration.

click *NOUN* (**clicks**)
a short sharp sound • *She heard a click as someone turned on the light.*

client *NOUN* (**clients**)
someone who gets help or advice from a professional person such as a lawyer or architect; a customer

cliff *NOUN* (**cliffs**)
a steep rock face, especially on the coast

cliffhanger *NOUN* (**cliffhangers**)
a story or situation that is exciting because you do not know what will happen next

climate *NOUN* (**climates**)
the usual sort of weather in a particular area
▷ **climatic** *ADJECTIVE* to do with the climate

climax *NOUN* (**climaxes**)
the most important or exciting part of a story or series of events

climb *VERB* (**climbs**, **climbing**, **climbed**)
1 to climb or climb up something is go up it **2** to climb down something is to go down it **3** to climb is to grow or rise upwards, like a tall plant or a building
to climb down is to admit that you have been wrong about something or have had to change your mind

climb *NOUN* (**climbs**)
an act of climbing • *It's a long climb to the top of the hill.*

climber *NOUN* (**climbers**)
someone who climbs hills and mountains for sport

cling *VERB* (**clings**, **clinging**, **clung**)
to cling to someone or something is to hold on tightly • *The child was clinging to its mother.*

clingfilm *NOUN*
clingfilm is a thin clear sheet of plastic that sticks to itself easily and is used for wrapping food

clinic *NOUN* (**clinics**)
a place where people see doctors for treatment or advice

clink *VERB* (**clinks**, **clinking**, **clinked**)
to clink is to make a short ringing sound, like a coin being dropped

clip *NOUN* (**clips**)
a fastener for keeping things together

clip *VERB* (**clips**, **clipping**, **clipped**)
1 to clip things together is to fasten them with a clip **2** to clip something is to cut it with shears or scissors

clipboard *NOUN* (**clipboards**)
a board that you can carry around, with a clip at the top to hold papers

clipper *NOUN* (**clippers**)
an old type of fast sailing ship

clippers *PLURAL NOUN*
clippers are large scissors for clipping

clipping *NOUN* (**clippings**)
a piece cut from a newspaper or magazine

cloak *NOUN* (**cloaks**)
a piece of outdoor clothing, usually without sleeves, that hangs loosely from your shoulders

cloakroom *NOUN* (**cloakrooms**)
1 a place where you can leave coats and bags while you are visiting a building **2** a lavatory

clobber *VERB* (**clobbers**, **clobbering**, **clobbered**)
(*informal*) to clobber someone is to hit them very hard

clock *NOUN* (**clocks**)
an instrument that shows what the time is

clockwise *ADVERB & ADJECTIVE*
moving round a circle in the same direction as the hands of a clock

clockwork *ADJECTIVE*
worked by a spring which you wind up

clog *VERB* (**clogs**, **clogging**, **clogged**)
to clog something is to block it up accidentally

clog *NOUN* (**clogs**)
a shoe with a wooden sole

cloister *NOUN* (**cloisters**)
a covered path that is open on one side and goes round a courtyard or along the side of a cathedral or monastery

clone *NOUN* (**clones**)
an animal or plant made from the cells of another animal or plant

clone *VERB* (**clones**, **cloning**, **cloned**)
to clone something is to produce a clone of it

close[1] *ADJECTIVE* (**closer**, **closest**) (*say* klohss)
1 near, either in time or place • *They were close to finding the answer.* • *The shops were quite close to their new house.* **2** careful and detailed • *Please pay close attention.* **3** tight; with little empty space • *They got the wardrobe in but it was a close fit.* **4** a close race or finish is one in which competitors are nearly equal at the end **5** stuffy; without fresh air • *It's very close in this room.*

close *ADVERB* (**closer**, **closest**) (*say* klohss)
at a close distance • *The children were following close behind.*

close *NOUN* (**closes**) (*say* klohss)
1 a street that is closed at one end **2** an enclosed area, especially round a cathedral

close[2] *VERB* (**closes**, **closing**, **closed**) (*say* klohz)
1 to close something is to shut it **2** to close an event or meeting is to finish it
to close down is to stop doing business • *Several shops in the High Street have closed down recently.*
to close in is to get nearer • *The police closed in around the house.*

closely *ADVERB* (*say* **klohss**- li)
1 carefully, with attention • *His friends were watching closely.* **2** tightly • *The box was closely packed with toys.*

close-up *NOUN* (**close-ups**) (*say* **klohss**- up)
a photograph or film taken at short range

closure *NOUN* (**closures**) (*say* **kloh**- *zher*)
the closure of a business is when it closes down

clot *NOUN* (**clots**)
1 a mass of thick liquid like blood or cream that has become nearly solid **2** (*informal*) a stupid person

clot *VERB* (**clots**, **clotting**, **clotted**)
to clot is to form into clots, like blood or cream

cloth *NOUN* (**cloths**)
1 cloth is material woven from wool, cotton, or some other fabric **2** a cloth is a piece of this material **3** a cloth is also a tablecloth

clothe *VERB* (**clothes**, **clothing**, **clothed**)
to clothe someone is to put clothes on them

clothes *PLURAL NOUN*
clothes are the things you wear to cover your body

clothing *NOUN*
clothing is the clothes you wear

cloud *NOUN* (**clouds**)
1 a mass of water vapour floating in the air **2** a mass of smoke or something else dense in the air

cloud *VERB* (**clouds**, **clouding**, **clouded**)
to cloud or cloud over is to become full of clouds
• *In the afternoon the sky clouded over.*
▷ **cloudless** *ADJECTIVE* a cloudless sky does not have any clouds

cloudburst *NOUN* (**cloudbursts**)
a sudden heavy downpour of rain

cloudy *ADJECTIVE* (**cloudier**, **cloudiest**)
1 full of clouds **2** hard to see through • *The glass contained a cloudy liquid.*

clout *VERB* (**clouts**, **clouting**, **clouted**)
to clout someone is to give them a hard blow

clove *NOUN* (**cloves**)
the dried bud of a tropical tree used as a spice, especially to flavour apples

clover *NOUN*
a small wild plant, usually with leaves in three parts

clown *NOUN* (**clowns**)
1 a circus performer who dresses up and wears bright face paint and does silly things to make people laugh **2** an amusing or silly person

clown *VERB* (**clowns**, **clowning**, **clowned**)
to clown is to behave like a clown

cloze test *NOUN* (**cloze tests**)
a test in which you have to fill in the missing words that have been taken out of a sentence

club *NOUN* (**clubs**)
1 a heavy stick **2** a stick for playing golf **3** a group of people who meet together because they are interested in the same thing **4** a playing card with a black cloverleaf printed on it

club *VERB* (**clubs**, **clubbing**, **clubbed**)
to club someone is to hit them hard with a heavy stick
to club together is to join with other people in doing something, especially raising money

cluck *VERB* (**clucks**, **clucking**, **clucked**)
to cluck is to make a noise like a hen

clue *NOUN* (**clues**)
something that helps you to solve a puzzle or a mystery

clueless *ADJECTIVE*
(*informal*) stupid, having no idea how to do something

clump *NOUN* (**clumps**)
a cluster of trees or plants

clumsy *ADJECTIVE* (**clumsier**, **clumsiest**)
a clumsy person is careless and awkward, and likely to knock things over or drop things
▷ **clumsily** *ADVERB* in a clumsy way
▷ **clumsiness** *NOUN* being clumsy

clung
past tense and past participle of **cling**

cluster *NOUN* (**clusters**)
a group of people or things close together

clutch[1] *VERB* (**clutches**, **clutching**, **clutched**)
to clutch something or clutch at something is to grab hold of it

clutch *NOUN* (**clutches**)
1 a tight grasp **2** a device for disconnecting the engine of a motor vehicle from its gears and wheels

clutch[2] *NOUN* (**clutches**)
a set of eggs in a nest

clutter *VERB* (**clutters**, **cluttering**, **cluttered**)
to clutter a place up is to make it untidy or messy

clutter *NOUN*
clutter is a lot of things left around untidily

cm
short for **centimetre** or **centimetres**

Co.
short for **company**

c/o
short for **care of**

a b **c** d e f g h i j k l m n o p q r s t u v w x y z

coach *NOUN* (**coaches**)
1 a comfortable single-deck bus used for long journeys **2** a carriage of a railway train **3** a carriage pulled by horses **4** a person who trains or instructs people in a sport or skill

coach *VERB* (**coaches, coaching, coached**)
to coach someone is to instruct or train them in a sport or skill

coal *NOUN*
coal is a hard black mineral used as fuel

coarse *ADJECTIVE* (**coarser, coarsest**)
1 rough, not delicate or smooth **2** rude or offensive • *You have a very coarse sense of humour.*

coast *NOUN* (**coasts**)
the seashore and the land close to it
the coast is clear there is no one about to catch you or stop you doing something

coast *VERB* (**coasts, coasting, coasted**)
to coast is to ride downhill without using power • *They stopped pedalling and coasted down the slope.*

coastal *ADJECTIVE*
by the coast or near the coast

coastguard *NOUN* (**coastguards**)
someone whose job is to keep watch on coasts to prevent smuggling

coastline *NOUN*
the edge of the land by the sea

coat *NOUN* (**coats**)
1 a piece of clothing with sleeves that covers most of the body and is worn outdoors over other clothes **2** a layer of paint

coat *VERB* (**coats, coating, coated**)
to coat something is to cover it with a coating

coating *NOUN* (**coatings**)
a covering or layer, especially of paint

coat of arms *NOUN* (**coats of arms**)
a design on a shield or building, representing a historic family or town

coax *VERB* (**coaxes, coaxing, coaxed**)
to coax someone is to persuade them gently or patiently

cobalt *NOUN*
cobalt is a silvery-white metal

cobbler *NOUN* (**cobblers**)
someone whose job is to mend shoes

cobbles *PLURAL NOUN*
cobbles are a surface of cobblestones on a road
▷ **cobbled** paved with cobbles

cobblestone *NOUN* (**cobblestones**)
a small smooth and rounded stone sometimes used in large numbers to pave roads in towns

cobra *NOUN* (**cobras**) (*say* koh-bra)
a poisonous snake

cobweb *NOUN* (**cobwebs**)
a net of thin sticky threads that spiders spin to catch insects

cock *NOUN* (**cocks**)
a male bird, especially a male fowl

cock *VERB* (**cocks, cocking, cocked**)
1 to cock your eye or ear is to turn it in a particular direction **2** to cock a gun is to make it ready to fire

cockerel *NOUN* (**cockerels**)
a young male fowl

cocker spaniel *NOUN* (**cocker spaniels**)
a kind of small spaniel with a golden brown coat and long hanging ears

cockle *NOUN* (**cockles**)
an edible shellfish

cockney *NOUN* (**cockneys**)
1 a cockney is someone born in the East End of London **2** cockney is a kind of English spoken by people from this part of London

cockpit *NOUN* (**cockpits**)
the place in an aircraft where the pilot sits

cockroach *NOUN* (**cockroaches**)
a dark brown insect

cocky *ADJECTIVE* (**cockier, cockiest**)
(*informal*) conceited and cheeky

cocoa *NOUN* (**cocoas**)
1 a hot drink that tastes of chocolate **2** the powder from which you make this drink

coconut *NOUN* (**coconuts**)
a large round nut containing a milky juice, that grows on palm trees

cocoon *NOUN* (**cocoons**)
the covering round a chrysalis

cod *NOUN* (**cod**)
a large edible sea fish

code *NOUN* (**codes**)
1 a set of signs and letters for sending messages secretly **2** a set of rules • *the Highway Code* • *a code of behaviour*

code *VERB* (**codes, coding, coded**)
1 to code a message is to use special signs and letters, so that other people cannot understand it **2** to code data is to put it into a form that can be accepted by a computer

co-education *NOUN*
the teaching of boys and girls together
▷ **co-educational** *ADJECTIVE* a co-educational school or system is one that teaches boys and girls together

coffee *NOUN* (**coffees**)
1 a hot drink made from the roasted and crushed beans of a tropical plant **2** the powder from which you make this drink

coffin *NOUN* (**coffins**)
a long box in which a dead body is buried or cremated

cog *NOUN* (**cogs**)
one of a number of pieces sticking out from the edge of a wheel and allowing it to drive another wheel

cohort *NOUN* (**cohorts**)
in the ancient Roman army, one of the ten parts of a legion

coil *NOUN* (**coils**)
a circle or spiral of rope or wire

coil *VERB* (**coils**, **coiling**, **coiled**)
to coil something is to wind it into circles or spirals

coin *NOUN* (**coins**)
a piece of metal money

coin *VERB* (**coins**, **coining**, **coined**)
1 to coin money is to manufacture it **2** to coin a new word is to invent it

coinage *NOUN* (**coinages**)
1 a country's coinage is the system of money that it uses **2** a coinage is also a new word or phrase that someone has invented

coincide *VERB* (**coincides**, **coinciding**, **coincided**)
to coincide is to happen at the same time as something else • *The end of term coincides with my birthday.*

coincidence *NOUN* (**coincidences**)
coincidence, or a coincidence, is when two things can happen by chance at the same time

coir *NOUN* (*say* coy- er)
coir is rough fibre made from coconut shells, used to make ropes and mats

coke *NOUN*
coke is a solid fuel made out of coal

cola *NOUN* (**colas**)
cola is a sweet brown fizzy drink

colander *NOUN* (**colanders**) (*say* kul- an- der)
a bowl with holes, for draining water from vegetables

cold *ADJECTIVE* (**colder**, **coldest**)
1 low in temperature, not hot or warm **2** a cold person is unfriendly and distant

cold *NOUN* (**colds**)
1 cold weather or temperature **2** a cold is an illness that makes your nose run and gives you a sore throat
▷ **coldly** *ADVERB* to act coldly is to be very unfriendly
▷ **coldness** *NOUN* coldness is being unfriendly

cold-blooded *ADJECTIVE*
1 having blood that changes temperature according to the surroundings **2** cruel, ruthless

coleslaw *NOUN*
a salad made of chopped cabbage covered in mayonnaise

collaborate *VERB* (**collaborates**, **collaborating**, **collaborated**)
1 people collaborate when they work together or share their information **2** to collaborate with an enemy is to work secretly on their side
▷ **collaboration** *NOUN* working with someone or sharing information with them

collaborator *NOUN*
1 someone who works with someone else or shares ideas with them **2** someone who betrays their country during a war by sharing information with the enemy

collage *NOUN* (**collages**) (*say* kol- ah*zh* or kol- ah*zh*)
a picture made by arranging scraps of paper and other things on a card

collapse *VERB* (**collapses**, **collapsing**, **collapsed**)
1 to collapse is to fall or break into pieces because of too much weight **2** someone collapses when they fall from being very weak or ill

collapse *NOUN* (**collapses**)
1 an act of collapsing **2** a breakdown

collapsible *ADJECTIVE*
a collapsible piece of furniture or equipment can be folded up into a smaller space

collar *NOUN* (**collars**)
1 the part of a piece of clothing that goes round your neck **2** a band that goes round an animal's neck

collate *VERB* (**collates**, **collating**, **collated**)
to collate pieces of information is to collect and arrange them in an organized way • *They had to collate the results in the form of a graph.*

colleague *NOUN* (**colleagues**)
someone's colleague is a person they work with

collect *VERB* (**collects**, **collecting**, **collected**)
1 to collect things is to get them together from various places, especially as a hobby • *She collects stamps, and I collect coins.* **2** to collect someone or something is to go and get them
▷ **collector** *NOUN* someone who collects things for a hobby

collection *NOUN* (**collections**)
1 things you have collected as a hobby **2** money given by people at a meeting or concert or church service

collective *ADJECTIVE*
involving several people or things • *It was a collective decision.*

collective noun *NOUN* (**collective nouns**)
a singular noun that is a name for a group of things or people, for example *choir, flock, government*

college *NOUN* (**colleges**)
a place where people continue to study after they have left school

collide *VERB* (**collides, colliding, collided**)
to collide with something is to hit it while moving • *The bicycle collided with the car.*

collie *NOUN* (**collies**)
a breed of dog with a long pointed muzzle and long hair

collision *NOUN* (**collisions**)
a crash between moving vehicles • *There has been a collision on the motorway.*

colloquial *ADJECTIVE*
colloquial language is used for conversation but not for formal speech or writing • *'Chuck' is a colloquial word for 'throw'.*

colon *NOUN* (**colons**)
a punctuation mark (:) used to separate parts of a sentence or before items in a list

> COLON
> You use a colon before giving a list of things or before explaining something you have just written. *To make a spaceship you will need: a cardboard tube, an empty washing-up liquid bottle, a sheet of thick paper, and some silver foil. There are two things I love about my room: the walls are bright yellow and you can see the sea out of the window.*

colonel *NOUN* (**colonels**) (*say* **ker**- nel)
a senior army officer

colonial *ADJECTIVE*
from or to do with a country's colonies abroad

colonist *NOUN* (**colonists**)
a person who goes to live in a colony abroad

colony *NOUN* (**colonies**)
1 a country that another another country governs and sends people out to live there **2** a group of people or animals living together

colossal *ADJECTIVE*
huge, enormous • *The monster did not laugh. He set off, up from the earth, beating his colossal wings.* — Ted Hughes, *The Iron Man*

colour *NOUN* (**colours**)
1 the quality of being red, green, blue, and so on, produced by rays of light of different wavelengths **2** the use of all colours, not just black and white • *Is this film in colour?* **3** the colour of someone's skin **4** a substance used to give colour to things **5** the special flag of a ship or regiment

colour *VERB* (**colours, colouring, coloured**)
to colour something is to give it a colour or colours with paints or crayons

colour-blind *ADJECTIVE*
not able to see or distinguish between some colours, usually red and green

coloured *ADJECTIVE*
having a particular colour

colourful *ADJECTIVE*
1 having a lot of bright colours **2** lively • *The film was a colourful story of life on board a pirate ship.*

colouring *NOUN*
1 colouring is a substance you add to something to give it a special colour **2** a person's colouring is the colour and appearance of their skin and hair

colourless *ADJECTIVE*
not having any colour • *Many gases are colourless.*

colt *NOUN* (**colts**)
a young male horse

column *NOUN* (**columns**)
1 a pillar **2** something long and narrow • *They could see a column of smoke in the distance.* **3** a strip of printing in a book or newspaper **4** a regular feature in a newspaper • *He always read the sports column.*

coma *NOUN* (**comas**) (*say* **koh**- ma)
someone is in a coma when they are unconscious for a long time

comb *NOUN* (**combs**)
1 a tool with teeth for making the hair tidy **2** the red, fleshy crest on a fowl's head

comb *VERB* (**combs, combing, combed**)
1 to comb the hair is to tidy it with a comb **2** to comb an area is to search it carefully for something lost • *We combed the woods all day but couldn't find our dog.*

combat *NOUN* (**combats**)
a fight or contest

combat *VERB* (**combats, combating, combated**)
to combat something bad or unpleasant is to fight it and try to get rid of it • *The police force combats crime.*

combination *NOUN* (**combinations**)
1 combination is joining or mixing things **2** a combination is a group of things that have been joined or mixed together

combination lock *NOUN* (**combination locks**)
a lock that you open by moving a dial to the correct positions shown by numbers or letters

combine *VERB* (**combines, combining, combined**) (*say* kom- **byn**)
to combine things is to join them or mix them together

combine harvester *NOUN* (**combine harvesters**)
a machine that cuts and threshes the grain in the fields

combustible *ADJECTIVE*
a combustible substance is one that can catch fire and burn

combustion *NOUN*
combustion is what happens when something burns

come *VERB* (**comes**, **coming**, **came**, **come**)
1 to come is to move towards the person or place that is here, and is the opposite of **go** • *Do you want to come to my house?* • *Has that letter come yet?* **2** to come is also to occur or be present • *The pictures come at the end of the book.*
to come about is to happen
to come across someone is to meet them by chance
to come by something is to get it • *How did you come by that watch?*
to come round or **come to** is to revive after being unconscious
to come to something is to add up to it • *The bill came to $30.*
to come true is to actually happen • *Their holiday was a dream come true.*

comeback *NOUN* (**comebacks**)
someone makes a comeback when they start doing something again that they have been famous for in the past

comedian *NOUN* (**comedians**)
someone who entertains people with humour and jokes

comedy *NOUN* (**comedies**)
1 a comedy is a play or film that makes people laugh **2** comedy is using humour to make people laugh

comet *NOUN* (**comets**)
an object moving across the sky with a bright tail of light

comfort *NOUN*
1 comfort is a feeling of relief from worry or pain **2** your comforts are the things you have around you that you enjoy and that make life pleasant

comfort *VERB* (**comforts**, **comforting**, **comforted**)
to comfort someone is to make them feel happier when they are feeling sad or worried

comfortable *ADJECTIVE*
1 pleasant to use or wear • *a comfortable chair* **2** free from worry or pain • *The nurse made the patient comfortable.*
▷ **comfortably** *ADVERB* in a comfortable way • *We can sit more comfortably in the living room.*

comic *NOUN* (**comics**)
1 a children's magazine that has stories with pictures **2** a comedian

comic or **comical** *ADJECTIVE*
funny, making people laugh
▷ **comically** *ADVERB* in a funny way

comic strip *NOUN* (**comic strips**)
a series of drawings that tell a story

comings and goings *PLURAL NOUN*
a lot of busy things happening, such as people arriving and leaving

comma *NOUN* (**commas**)
a punctuation mark (,) used to mark a pause in a sentence or between items in a list

> COMMA
> You use a comma to separate one part of a sentence from another. When you are reading something, a comma marks where you should pause slightly: *It's a story about ghosts and goblins, but it's not scary.* Commas are also used around a piece of information which isn't part of the main flow of the sentence and which you could leave out without changing the meaning of the sentence: *The cheetah, a large spotted animal of the cat family, is the fastest animal on land.* You also use commas to separate items in a list: *She put on her football shirt, shorts, socks, and boots.* You don't have to put a comma before the word *and* in a list like this and many people prefer to leave it out (*her football shirt, shorts, socks and boots*). Some publishers like to keep it, though, and you will find a comma before the *and* in their books.

command *NOUN* (**commands**)
1 a command is an instruction telling someone to do something **2** command is authority or control • *Who has command of these soldiers?* **3** a command of a subject is the skill or ability to understand it • *She has a good command of Spanish.*

command *VERB* (**commands**, **commanding**, **commanded**)
1 to command someone is to tell them to do something **2** to command a group of people is to be in charge of them • *A centurion commanded a hundred soldiers.*

commander *NOUN* (**commanders**)
someone who commands, especially a senior naval officer

commandment *NOUN* (**commandments**)
a sacred command, especially one of the Ten Commandments of Moses

commando *NOUN* (**commandos**)
a soldier trained for making dangerous raids

commemorate *VERB* (**commemorates**, **commemorating**, **commemorated**)
to commemorate a past event is to do something special so that people remember it
▷ **commemoration** *NOUN* a ceremony or religious service to remember a person or a past event

commence *VERB* (**commences**, **commencing**, **commenced**)
to commence something is to begin it
▷ **commencement** *NOUN* the beginning of something

a b c d e f g h i j k l m n o p q r s t u v w x y z

commend *VERB* (**commends**, **commending**, **commended**)
to commend someone is to praise them • *He was commended for bravery.*
▷ **commendable** *ADJECTIVE* deserving praise
▷ **commendation** *NOUN* praise or an honour for something someone has done

comment *NOUN* (**comments**)
a remark or opinion

commentary *NOUN* (**commentaries**)
a description of an event by someone who is watching it, especially for radio or television

commentator *NOUN* (**commentators**)
a person who gives a commentary, especially of a sports event
▷ **commentate** *VERB* to commentate is to give a commentary

commerce *NOUN*
commerce is trade, or buying and selling goods

commercial *ADJECTIVE*
1 connected with trade and making money **2** paid for by advertising • *a commercial radio station*

commercial *NOUN* (**commercials**)
an advertisement, especially on television or radio
▷ **commercially** *ADVERB* in a commercial or profitable way

commit *VERB* (**commits**, **committing**, **committed**)
to commit a crime is to do something against the law
to commit yourself to something is to decide to do it or to promise that you will do it

commitment *NOUN* (**commitments**)
1 commitment is being determined to do something **2** a commitment is something you have promised to do

committee *NOUN* (**committees**)
a group of people who meet to organize or discuss something

commodity *NOUN* (**commodities**)
something that can be bought and sold

common *ADJECTIVE* (**commoner**, **commonest**)
1 ordinary or usual • *The dandelion is a common plant.* **2** happening or used often • *Traffic jams are common where we live.* **3** shared by many people • *The story was common knowledge.* • *Music was their common interest.*

common *NOUN* (**commons**)
a piece of open land that anyone can use

commonplace *ADJECTIVE*
ordinary, familiar

common room *NOUN* (**common rooms**)
a room for teachers or pupils to relax in at a school or college

commonwealth *NOUN* (**commonwealths**)
a group of countries cooperating together
the Commonwealth an association of Britain and various other countries, such as Canada, Australia, and New Zealand

commotion *NOUN* (**commotions**)
an uproar • *The cocker spaniel heard the commotion and he ran out from the barn to join in the chase.* — E. B. White, *Charlotte's Web*

communal *ADJECTIVE*
shared by several people

commune *NOUN* (**communes**)
a group of people who live in the same house and share the money and work

communicate *VERB* (**communicates**, **communicating**, **communicated**)
to communicate news or information is to pass it on to other people
▷ **communicative** *ADJECTIVE* a communicative person is willing to talk to people and give them information

communication *NOUN* (**communications**)
1 communication is giving people useful information and telling them about things that have happened **2** a communication is a message or piece of information that someone gives you **3** communication is also a form of technology for passing on information, for example television and text messaging

Communion *NOUN*
Communion is the Christian ceremony in which holy bread and wine are given to worshippers

communism *NOUN*
communism is a political belief that everyone should share the wealth of a country and the state should control its industry and resources

communist *NOUN* (**communists**)
someone who believes in communism

community *NOUN* (**communities**)
the people living in one area

commuter *NOUN* (**commuters**)
someone who travels from their home to work every morning and back again in the evening
▷ **commute** *VERB* to commute is to travel to work every day

compact *ADJECTIVE*
small and neat

compact disc *NOUN* (**compact discs**)
a small plastic and metal disc on which music or information is stored as digital signals and is read by a laser beam. Usually called **CD**

companion *NOUN* (**companions**)
a companion is someone who spends a lot of time with you
▷ **companionship** *NOUN* companionship is being with someone and enjoying their friendship

company *NOUN* (**companies**)
1 a company is a group of people, especially a business firm **2** company is having people with you • *Jill was lonely and longed for some company.* **3** a company is an army unit consisting of two or more platoons

comparable *ADJECTIVE* (*say* kom- per- a- bul)
able to be compared, similar

comparative *ADJECTIVE*
compared with something else • *After the noise of her own house she enjoyed the comparative peace of her friend's place.*

comparative *NOUN* (**comparatives**)
the form of an adjective or adverb that expresses 'more' • *The comparative of 'big' is 'bigger', and the comparative of 'bad' is 'worse'.*

COMPARATIVES
Adjectives and adverbs can be made comparative or superlative in the following ways:

positive	**comparative**	**superlative**
stiff	*stiffer*	*stiffest*
quick	*quicker*	*quickest*
funny	*funnier*	*funniest*
late	*later*	*latest*

For longer adjectives, and for most adverbs, the comparative and superlative are formed by putting *more* or *most* in front of them.

positive	**comparative**	**superlative**
terrible	*more terrible*	*most terrible*
quickly	*more quickly*	*most quickly*

But watch out for exceptions:

bad	*worse*	*worst*
badly	*worse*	*worst*

If in doubt, look them up in the dictionary. Look also at the panel on **Adjectives**.

comparatively *ADVERB*
in comparison, relatively • *They all went to bed comparatively late.*

compare *VERB* (**compares**, **comparing**, **compared**)
1 to compare things is to see how they are similar • *Compare your answers.* **2** to compare with something is to be as good as it • *Our football pitch cannot compare with Wembley Stadium.*

comparison *NOUN* (**comparisons**)
comparison, or a comparison, is thinking about several things and seeing how they are similar or different

compartment *NOUN* (**compartments**)
a special place or section where you can put something • *The coach had a luggage compartment under the floor.*

compass *NOUN* (**compasses**)
an instrument with a magnetized needle that shows which direction you are facing
compasses or **pair of compasses** a device for drawing circles

compassion *NOUN*
compassion is pity or mercy you show to people who are suffering
▷ **compassionate** *ADJECTIVE* a compassionate person shows pity or mercy to people who are suffering

compatible *ADJECTIVE*
1 people are compatible when they are able to live or exist together without trouble **2** machines and devices are compatible when they can be used together

compel *VERB* (**compels**, **compelling**, **compelled**)
to compel someone to do something is to force them to do it

compensate *VERB* (**compensates**, **compensating**, **compensated**)
to compensate someone is to give them something to make up for something they have lost or suffered
▷ **compensation** *NOUN* compensation is something given to someone to make up for a loss or injury

compère *NOUN* (**compères**) (*say* kom- pair)
someone who introduces the performers in a show or broadcast

compete *VERB* (**competes**, **competing**, **competed**)
to compete in a competition is to try to win it by being better than other people

competent *ADJECTIVE*
having the skill or knowledge to do something well • *He is not competent to teach French.*
▷ **competence** *NOUN* the ability to do something well

competition *NOUN* (**competitions**)
a game or race in which you try to do better than other people

WORD FAMILY
A **competitive** person enjoys competing with other people; a **competitor** is someone who competes in a game or race, or a rival in business.

compile *VERB* (**compiles**, **compiling**, **compiled**)
to compile information is to collect and arrange it, especially in a book • *She compiled a collection of children's poems.*

WORD FAMILY
A **compilation** is a collection of information, stories, or poems, that someone has compiled; a **compiler** is someone who compiles something.

complacent *ADJECTIVE*
smugly satisfied with the way things are, without wanting to improve them

complain *VERB* (**complains**, **complaining**, **complained**)
to complain about something is to say that you are not pleased about it

complaint *NOUN* (**complaints**)
1 you make a complaint when you are not pleased about something **2** you suffer from a complaint when you are slightly ill

complement *NOUN* (**complements**)
1 the amount needed to fill or complete something • *This ship has a full complement of sailors.* **2** (*in grammar*) a word or words used after a verb to complete the meaning • *In 'She is brave' and 'He was made king', the complements are 'brave' and 'king'.*
▷ **complementary** *ADJECTIVE* acting as a complement

> SPELLING
> Take care not to confuse **complement** with **compliment**, which means words or actions that show approval.

complementary *ADJECTIVE*
1 complementary colours and designs go well together **2** complementary parts together make up a whole **3** in geometry, complementary angles add up to 90°

complementary medicine *NOUN*
ways of treating illness and injury that are not the usual ones doctors practise, e.g. acupuncture and homoeopathy

complete *ADJECTIVE*
1 having all its parts, with nothing missing • *I hope the tool kit is complete.* **2** finished, achieved • *By evening the jigsaw puzzle was complete.* **3** utter, total • *It came as a complete surprise.*

complete *VERB* (**completes, completing, completed**)
to complete something is to finish it or make it complete
▷ **completion** *NOUN* the completing of something, the finish • *The work is nearing completion.*

completely *ADVERB*
totally, utterly • *You are completely wrong.*

complex *ADJECTIVE*
difficult and complicated
▷ **complexity** *NOUN* being difficult or complicated

complex *NOUN* (**complexes**)
1 a group of buildings, such as a sports centre **2** something that someone has a strange attitude or obsession about • *He has a complex about winning.*

complexion *NOUN* (**complexions**)
the colour or appearance of your skin

complicate *VERB* (**complicates, complicating, complicated**)
to complicate something is to make it difficult or awkward

complicated *ADJECTIVE*
difficult to understand or cope with because it has so many parts or details

complication *NOUN* (**complications**)
1 a difficult or awkward situation **2** a difficulty that makes something worse

compliment *NOUN* (**compliments**)
words or actions that show you approve of a person or thing

> SPELLING
> Take care not to confuse **compliment** with **complement**, which means the amount needed to complete something, or the words that come after a verb.

complimentary *ADJECTIVE*
1 praising someone or saying good things about them • *She liked Neil's work and was very complimentary about him.* **2** given to someone free of charge • *Every adult received a complimentary drink.*

comply *VERB* (**complies, complying, complied**)
to comply with a law or rule is to obey it

> WORD FAMILY
> **Compliance** is obeying laws or rules.

component *NOUN* (**components**)
one of the parts that a machine is made of

compose *VERB* (**composes, composing, composed**)
1 to compose music or poetry is to write it **2** to be composed of several people or things is to be made up of them • *The class is composed of children up to the age of 8.*
▷ **composer** *NOUN* someone who writes music

composition *NOUN* (**compositions**)
1 composition is composing or writing something **2** a composition is a piece of music or an essay

compost *NOUN*
compost is a mixture of decayed leaves, grass, and other natural refuse, and is used as manure

compound[1] *NOUN* (**compounds**)
1 a substance that is made of two or more parts or ingredients **2** (*grammar*) a word that is made from two or more other words, such as *bathroom* and *newspaper*

> COMPOUND WORDS
> A compound word is a word made of two other words put together. There are three different ways of writing a compound word. You can join the two words together to make one word (*motorcycle*) or keep the words separate (*no one*) or put a hyphen between them (*cross-section*). There isn't a rule to tell you which of these ways you should use when you are writing a particular compound word. If you are not sure, look the word up in the dictionary.

compound[2] *NOUN* (**compounds**)
a fenced area containing buildings

comprehend *VERB* (**comprehends, comprehending, comprehended**)
to comprehend something is to understand it

comprehension *NOUN* (**comprehensions**)
1 comprehension is understanding **2** a comprehension is an exercise that tests or helps your understanding of a language

comprehensive *ADJECTIVE*
including everything or everyone • *a comprehensive list*

comprehensive school *NOUN* (**comprehensive schools**)
a secondary school for children of all abilities

compress *VERB* (**compresses**, **compressing**, **compressed**)
1 to compress something is to press it or squeeze it together **2** to be compressed is to be forced into a small space
▷ **compression** *NOUN* compression is pressing or squeezing something

comprise *VERB* (**comprises**, **comprising**, **comprised**)
to comprise several people or things is to include them • *A football team comprises eleven players.*

> GRAMMAR
> Take care not to use **comprise** with 'of'.

compromise *VERB* (**compromises**, **compromising**, **compromised**) (*say* kom- pro- myz)
to compromise is to accept less than you really wanted, especially so as to settle a disagreement

compromise *NOUN* (**compromises**) (*say* kom- pro- myz)
accepting less than you really wanted

compulsory *ADJECTIVE*
something is compulsory when you have to do it • *Wearing seat belts is compulsory.*

compute *VERB* (**computes**, **computing**, **computed**)
to compute something is to calculate it

computer *NOUN* (**computers**)
an electronic machine that does word processing, sorts data, and does rapid calculations

comrade *NOUN* (**comrades**)
a friend or companion
▷ **comradeship** *NOUN* enjoying other people's company, friendship

con *VERB* (**cons**, **conning**, **conned**)
(*informal*) to con someone is to swindle them

concave *ADJECTIVE*
a concave surface is curved like the inside of a circle or ball. The opposite of **convex**.

conceal *VERB* (**conceals**, **concealing**, **concealed**)
to conceal something is to hide it carefully or cleverly
▷ **concealment** *NOUN* concealment is hiding something carefully

conceit *NOUN*
conceit is thinking a lot about how clever or attractive you are
▷ **conceited** *ADJECTIVE* a conceited person thinks a lot of themselves and is vain and proud

conceive *VERB* (**conceives**, **conceiving**, **conceived**)
1 to conceive an idea or plan is to form it in your mind **2** a woman conceives when she becomes pregnant

concentrate *VERB* (**concentrates**, **concentrating**, **concentrated**)
1 to concentrate on something is to think hard about it **2** to concentrate people or things is to bring them together in one place

concentrated *ADJECTIVE*
a liquid is concentrated when it is made stronger by having water removed from it

concentration *NOUN*
concentration is thinking hard about something

concentric *ADJECTIVE*
circles that are concentric are placed one inside another and have the same centre

concept *NOUN* (**concepts**)
a new idea about something

conception *NOUN* (**conceptions**)
1 conception is forming an idea in your mind **2** conception is also when a woman becomes pregnant

concern *VERB* (**concerns**, **concerning**, **concerned**)
1 to concern someone is to be important or interesting to them **2** to concern something is to be about a particular subject • *This story concerns a shipwreck.* **3** to worry someone

concern *NOUN* (**concerns**)
1 something that matters to someone • *I think that is my concern.* **2** a business

concerning *PREPOSITION*
on the subject of; in connection with • *The council wrote to everyone concerning their refuse collection.*

concert *NOUN* (**concerts**)
a performance of music

concertina *NOUN* (**concertinas**)
a portable musical instrument that you squeeze to push air past reeds

concerto *NOUN* (**concertos**) (*say* kon- cher- toh)
a piece of music for a solo instrument and an orchestra • *a violin concerto*

concession *NOUN* (**concessions**)
something that someone allows you to have or do, to be helpful or to reach an a greement • *As a special concession, parents may park in the teachers' car park on Sports Day.*

concise *ADJECTIVE*
giving a lot of information in a few words

a b **c** d e f g h i j k l m n o p q r s t u v w x y z

conclude *VERB* (**concludes**, **concluding**, **concluded**)
1 to conclude something is to end it **2** to conclude something is also to decide about it • *The jury concluded that he was not guilty.*

conclusion *NOUN* (**conclusions**)
1 the ending of something **2** a decision that you reach after a lot of thought

concrete *NOUN*
cement mixed with water and gravel or sand and used in building

concrete *ADJECTIVE*
real, definite • *We must have concrete evidence.*

concrete poem *NOUN* (**concrete poems**)
a poem printed in a special way, so that the words form a pattern on the page that has something to do with the meaning of the poem

concussion *NOUN*
a temporary injury to the brain that is caused by a hard knock and leaves you feeling dizzy or unconscious

condemn *VERB* (**condemns**, **condemning**, **condemned**)
1 to condemn someone or something is to say that you strongly disapprove of them **2** to condemn criminals is to sentence them to a punishment • *He was condemned to death.* **3** to condemn a building is to declare that it is not fit to be used
▷ **condemnation** *NOUN* condemnation is saying that you blame someone or something or do not approve of them

condensation *NOUN*
drops of liquid formed from vapour that has condensed

condense *VERB* (**condenses**, **condensing**, **condensed**)
1 to condense a piece of writing is to make it shorter **2** to condense is to change into water or other liquid • *Steam condenses on cold windows.*

condensed *ADJECTIVE*
a condensed liquid, such as milk, is one that is made stronger or thicker

condition *NOUN* (**conditions**)
1 the state in which a person or thing is • *This bike is in good condition.* **2** something that must happen if something else is to happen • *Learning to swim is a condition of going sailing.* • *You can come on condition that you bring your sister too.*

condom *NOUN* (**condoms**)
a rubber covering that a man can wear on his penis during sexual intercourse, as a contraceptive and as protection against disease

conduct *VERB* (**conducts**, **conducting**, **conducted**) (*say* kon-**dukt**)
1 to conduct someone is to lead or guide them **2** to conduct something is to organize or manage it **3** to conduct an orchestra or band is to direct it in a piece of music **4** to conduct electricity or heat is to allow it to pass along • *Copper conducts electricity well.*

conduct *NOUN* (*say* **kon**-dukt)
a person's conduct is their behaviour

conduction *NOUN*
the conducting of electricity or heat

conductor *NOUN* (**conductors**)
1 someone who conducts an orchestra or band **2** something that conducts electricity or heat **3** someone who collects the fares on a bus or coach

cone *NOUN* (**cones**)
1 an object which is circular at one end and pointed at the other end **2** an ice cream cornet **3** the fruit of a pine, fir, or cedar

confectioner *NOUN* (**confectioners**)
someone who makes or sells sweets
▷ **confectionery** *NOUN* confectionery is sweets and cakes that a shop sells

confer *VERB* (**confers**, **conferring**, **conferred**)
1 to confer a title or honour on someone is to give it to them **2** to confer is to have a discussion

conference *NOUN* (**conferences**)
a meeting for discussion

confess *VERB* (**confesses**, **confessing**, **confessed**)
to confess to something wrong is to admit that you have done it

confession *NOUN* (**confessions**)
an act of admitting that you have committed a crime or done wrong • *The burglar made a full confession.*

confetti *PLURAL NOUN*
tiny bits of coloured paper thrown at the bride and bridegroom after a wedding

confide *VERB* (**confides**, **confiding**, **confided**)
to confide in someone is to tell them a secret

confidence *NOUN*
1 you have confidence when you are sure that you are right or can do something **2** confidence in someone is trusting or believing them
in confidence as a secret • *He told me all this in confidence.*

confidence trick *NOUN* (**confidence tricks**)
a trick to get money out of someone by deceiving them into giving their trust

confident *ADJECTIVE*
1 being sure that you are right or can do something **2** certain that something will happen • *We are confident it will be an enjoyable day.*

confidential *ADJECTIVE*
information is confidential when it has to be kept secret
▷ **confidentially** *ADVERB* in confidence, as a secret

confine *VERB* (**confines**, **confining**, **confined**)
1 to confine something is to restrict or limit it • *Please confine your comments to points of fact.* **2** to confine someone is to lock them up or shut them in a place
▷ **confinement** *NOUN* confinement is being locked up or shut in

confirm *VERB* (**confirms**, **confirming**, **confirmed**)
1 to confirm something is to say that it is true or to show that it is true **2** to confirm an arrangement is to make it definite • *Please write to confirm your order.* **3** to confirm someone is to make them a full member of a Christian Church

confirmation *NOUN*
a fact or piece of information that shows something is true or has happened • *You will receive confirmation of your booking by email.*
Confirmation a Christian ceremony that makes them a full member of a Christian Church

confiscate *VERB* (**confiscates**, **confiscating**, **confiscated**)
to confiscate something is to take it away from someone as a punishment
▷ **confiscation** *NOUN* confiscation is taking something from someone as a punishment

conflict *NOUN* (**conflicts**) (*say* kon- flikt)
a fight or disagreement • *the conflict in the Middle East* • *a conflict between the unions and the bosses*

conflict *VERB* (**conflicts**, **conflicting**, **conflicted**) (*say* kon- **flikt**)
two things conflict when they contradict or disagree with one another • *The two accounts of the incident conflict.*

conform *VERB* (**conforms**, **conforming**, **conformed**)
to conform is to follow other people's rules or ideas about something

confront *VERB* (**confronts**, **confronting**, **confronted**)
1 to confront someone is to challenge them face to face for a fight or argument • *The police decided to confront the criminals there and then.* **2** to confront a problem or difficulty is to deal with it firmly and positively
▷ **confrontation** *NOUN* meeting someone face to face for a fight or argument

confuse *VERB* (**confuses**, **confusing**, **confused**)
1 to confuse someone is to make them puzzled or muddled **2** to confuse things is to mistake one thing for another
▷ **confusing** *ADJECTIVE* difficult to understand, muddling
▷ **confusion** *NOUN* confusion is being confused or muddled

congested *ADJECTIVE*
crowded, especially with people or traffic
▷ **congestion** *NOUN* congestion is when there are lots of crowds and traffic in a place

congratulate *VERB* (**congratulates**, **congratulating**, **congratulated**)
to congratulate someone is to tell them how pleased you are about something they have done
▷ **congratulations** *PLURAL NOUN* congratulations are words that tell someone how well they have done

congregation *NOUN* (**congregations**)
the people who take part in a church service

congress *NOUN* (**congresses**)
a large meeting or conference
Congress the parliament or government of the USA

congruent *ADJECTIVE*
(*in mathematics*) having exactly the same shape and size • *The two triangles are congruent.*
▷ **congruence** *NOUN* congruence is being congruent

conical *ADJECTIVE*
shaped like a cone

conifer *NOUN* (**conifers**) (*say* kon- i- fer)
an evergreen tree with cones
▷ **coniferous** *ADJECTIVE* a coniferous tree has cones

conjunction *NOUN* (**conjunctions**)
a word that joins other words and parts of a sentence, e.g. *and*, *but*, and *whether*

> CONJUNCTIONS
> Conjunctions are words that link parts of a sentence together. For example, *and* is a conjunction in *fish and chips*, and *because* is a conjunction in *We stayed inside because it was raining*. Other conjuctions include *but, or, so, since, although, however, yet,* and *until*.

conjure *VERB* (**conjures**, **conjuring**, **conjured**)
to conjure is to perform tricks that look like magic
▷ **conjurer** *NOUN* someone who performs magic tricks

conker *NOUN* (**conkers**)
a hard and shiny brown nut that grows on a horse chestnut tree
conkers a game played with conkers threaded on pieces of string

connect *VERB* (**connects**, **connecting**, **connected**)
to connect things is to join them together

connection *NOUN* (**connections**)
1 a link between things **2** joining together

a b **c** d e f g h i j k l m n o p q r s t u v w x y z

connective *NOUN* (**connectives**)
(*in grammar*) a word or phrase that links clauses or sentences. Connectives can be conjunctions (e.g. *because*), connecting adverbs (e.g. *however*), or adverbial phrases (e.g. *on the other hand*)

> CONNECTIVES
> Connectives are words which connect or link ideas within texts. Common connectives include: **conjunctions** like *because*, *so*, and *but*, which link ideas within a sentence and **adverbial connectives** like *moreover*, *furthermore*, and *finally*, which link ideas within a text.

conquer *VERB* (**conquers, conquering, conquered**)
to conquer a people or country is to defeat them and take them over • *William I conquered England.* • *He managed to conquer all his fears.*
▷ **conqueror** *NOUN* someone who conquers a country and takes it over

conquest *NOUN* (**conquests**)
a victory over another country or people

conscience *NOUN* (*say* **kon**- shens)
a feeling people have about what is right or wrong

conscientious *ADJECTIVE* (*say* kon- shee- **en**- shus)
careful and hard-working
▷ **conscientiously** *ADVERB* to do something conscientiously is to take care over it and do it well

conscious *ADJECTIVE* (*say* **kon**- shus)
1 awake and knowing what is happening **2** aware of something • *Are you conscious of the danger you are in?* **3** deliberate • *She has made a conscious effort to improve.*

> WORD FAMILY
> To do something **consciously** is to know that you are doing it and want to do it; **consciousness** is being aware of what is happening.

conscription *NOUN*
conscription is a system of making young people join the army for a time

consecutive *ADJECTIVE*
things are consecutive when they come one after another in a list or sequence

consensus *NOUN*
an agreement between most people about something • *There was a consensus that the law should be changed.*

consent *NOUN*
consent is agreement or permission

consent *VERB* (**consents, consenting, consented**)
to consent to something is to agree to it or permit it

consequence *NOUN* (**consequences**)
1 a consequence is something which happens because of an event or action • *His injury was the consequence of an accident.* **2** consequence is the importance that something has • *It is of no consequence.*
consequences is a game in which two or more people make a story by passing it from one to the other to continue
to take or **suffer the consequences** is to accept any unpleasant results from something you do
▷ **consequently** *ADVERB* as a result

conservation *NOUN*
conservation is keeping buildings and natural surroundings in a good state
▷ **conservationist** *NOUN* someone who takes an interest in conservation

conservative *ADJECTIVE*
1 a conservative person doesn't like change and wants things to stay the same **2** a conservative estimate or guess is a careful or cautious one

Conservative *NOUN* (**Conservatives**)
someone who supports the Conservative Party, a British political party

conservatory *NOUN* (**conservatories**)
a room built on the back or side of a house, with glass walls and a glass roof

conserve *VERB* (**conserves, conserving, conserved**)
to conserve something is to keep it from being changed or spoilt

consider *VERB* (**considers, considering, considered**)
1 to consider something is to think carefully about it **2** to consider something is also to believe it • *We consider that people should be allowed to follow their own religion.*

considerable *ADJECTIVE*
large or important • *The journey takes a considerable time.*
▷ **considerably** *ADVERB* very much • *Her new house is considerably larger.*

considerate *ADJECTIVE*
kind and thoughtful towards other people

consideration *NOUN* (**considerations**)
1 consideration is careful thought or attention **2** a consideration is a serious thought or reason • *Money is a major consideration in this plan.*
to take something into consideration is to think carefully about it when you are making a decision

considering *PREPOSITION*
in view of • *The car goes well, considering its age.*

consist *VERB* (**consists, consisting, consisted**)
to consist of something is to be made from it • *The meal consisted of pasta and cheese.*

consistency *NOUN* (**consistencies**)
1 consistency is being the same **2** the consistency of a liquid is how thick it is

consistent *ADJECTIVE*
1 always the same, regular **2** always acting in the same way
▷ **consistently** *ADVERB* in the same way, without changing • *He consistently misspells 'accommodation'.*

consolation *NOUN* (**consolations**)
consolation is comfort or sympathy given to someone

consolation prize *NOUN* (**consolation prizes**)
a prize given to someone who does not win a main prize

console *VERB* (**consoles**, **consoling**, **consoled**)
to console someone is to give them comfort or sympathy

consonant *NOUN* (**consonants**)
a letter that is not a vowel

> ENGLISH CONSONANTS
> The consonants in the English alphabet are b, c, d, f, g, h, j, k, l, m, n, p, q, r, s, t, v, w, x, y, z. Notice that y is a consonant in *yacht* and a vowel in *rhythm*.

conspicuous *ADJECTIVE*
something conspicuous stands out and is easy to see or notice

conspiracy *NOUN* (**conspiracies**)
a plot to do something bad or illegal
▷ **conspirator** *NOUN* someone who joins a conspiracy

conspire *VERB* (**conspires**, **conspiring**, **conspired**)
to conspire is to plot together

constable *NOUN* (**constables**)
an ordinary member of the police

constant *ADJECTIVE*
1 not changing; continual **2** a constant person is loyal and faithful

constant *NOUN* (**constants**)
(*in science and mathematics*) a number or quantity that does not change
▷ **constancy** *NOUN* constancy is beng loyal and faithful
▷ **constantly** *ADVERB* continually, all the time • *They are constantly complaining.*

constellation *NOUN* (**constellations**)
a group of stars that you can see in the sky at night

constipated *ADJECTIVE*
someone is constipated when they cannot empty their bowels easily to get rid of the waste in their body
▷ **constipation** *NOUN* being constipated

constituency *NOUN* (**constituencies**)
a district of the country that chooses its own Member of Parliament

constituent *NOUN* (**constituents**)
1 a part of something **2** someone who lives in the district of a particular Member of Parliament

constitute *VERB* (**constitutes**, **constituting**, **constituted**)
to constitute something is to form it or make it up • *50 states constitute the USA.*

constitution *NOUN* (**constitutions**)
1 the set of principles or laws by which a country is governed **2** a person's condition or state of health
▷ **constitutional** *ADJECTIVE* to do with a constitution

construct *VERB* (**constructs**, **constructing**, **constructed**)
to construct something is to build it

construction *NOUN* (**constructions**)
1 construction is the process of building **2** a construction is something that someone has built

constructive *ADJECTIVE*
helpful and positive • *Their criticism was very constructive.*

consul *NOUN* (**consuls**)
an official representative of one country, living in another country

consult *VERB* (**consults**, **consulting**, **consulted**)
to consult a person or book is to look for information or advice
▷ **consultation** *NOUN* a meeting with someone for information or advice

consultant *NOUN* (**consultants**)
1 a person who provides professional advice **2** a senior hospital doctor

consume *VERB* (**consumes**, **consuming**, **consumed**)
1 to consume food or drink is to eat or drink it **2** to consume something is to use it up or destroy it • *The building was consumed by fire.*

consumer *NOUN* (**consumers**)
someone who buys goods or services

consumption *NOUN*
the using up of food or fuel • *The consumption of oil has increased.*

contact *NOUN* (**contacts**)
1 contact is touching someone or something **2** contact is also communication • *I've lost contact with my uncle.* **3** a contact is a person to communicate with

contact *VERB* (**contacts**, **contacting**, **contacted**)
to contact someone is to get in touch with them

contact lens *NOUN* (**contact lenses**)
a small plastic lens worn against the eyeball instead of glasses

contagious *ADJECTIVE* (*say* kon-tay-jus)
you catch a contagious disease by having contact with people or things that are already infected with it

contain *VERB* (**contains**, **containing**, **contained**)
to contain something is to have it inside • *This book contains a great deal of information.*

a b c d e f g h i j k l m n o p q r s t u v w x y z

container *NOUN* (**containers**)
1 something that is designed to contain things **2** a large box-shaped container for taking goods abroad by sea

contaminate *VERB* (**contaminates, contaminating, contaminated**)
to contaminate something is to make it dirty or impure
▷ **contamination** *NOUN* contamination is making something dirty or impure

contemplate *VERB* (**contemplates, contemplating, contemplated**)
1 to contemplate something is to look hard at it or think about it **2** to contemplate doing something is to plan or intend to do it
▷ **contemplation** *NOUN* contemplation is thinking hard and seriously about something

contemporary *ADJECTIVE*
1 people or things are contemporary when they belong to the same time • *Florence Nightingale was contemporary with Queen Victoria.* **2** modern or up to date • *We like contemporary furniture.*

contempt *NOUN*
a feeling of strong disapproval when you despise someone or something

> **WORD FAMILY**
> Someone or something is **contemptible** when people strongly disapprove of them or despise them; to be **contemptuous** of someone or something is to disapprove strongly of them.

contend *VERB* (**contends, contending, contended**)
1 to contend is to struggle or compete **2** to contend something is to state or claim it • *We contend that the company was guilty of negligence.*
▷ **contender** *NOUN* someone who takes part in a competition

content[1] *NOUN* (*say* kon- tent)
1 the amount of a substance that there is in something • *Drink milk with a low fat content.* **2** the content of a book, magazine, or piece of writing is what you read in it

content[2] *ADJECTIVE* (*say* kon- **tent**)
happy and willing • *Are you content to stay behind?*
▷ **contentment** *NOUN* contentment is being happy

contented *ADJECTIVE* (*say* kon- **tent**- id)
happy and satisfied • *After his big dinner he looked very contented.*

contents *PLURAL NOUN* (*say* **kon**- tents)
1 the contents of a box or other container are what is inside it **2** the contents of a book or magazine are the things you read in it

contest *NOUN* (**contests**) (*say* **kon**- test)
a competition

contest *VERB* (**contests, contesting, contested**) (*say* kon- **test**)
to contest something is to argue about it • *After her death, relatives contested her will.*

contestant *NOUN* (**contestants**) (*say* kon- **test**- ant)
someone who takes part in a contest or competition

context *NOUN* (**contexts**)
the context of a word or phrase is the words that come before or after it and help to tell you what it means

continent *NOUN* (**continents**)
one of the main masses of land in the world
the Continent the mainland of Europe from the pont of view of people living in Britain

> **CONTINENTS**
> The continents are Africa, Antarctica, Asia, Australia, Europe, North America, and South America.

continental *ADJECTIVE*
on a continent, especially Europe from the point of view of people living in Britain • *We thought we'd have a continental holiday this year.*

continual *ADJECTIVE*
happening repeatedly • *I get fed up with his continual shouting.*
▷ **continually** *ADVERB* repeatedly, often

continue *VERB* (**continues, continuing, continued**)
to continue something, or to continue to do something, is to go on doing it
▷ **continuation** *NOUN* continuing something

continuous *ADJECTIVE*
going on all the time; without a break • *We could hear a continuous hum from the fridge.*

> **WORD FAMILY**
> **Continuity** is the process of going on without any breaks or changes. Something that is **continuous** goes on all the time without a break, and something that is **continual** happens repeatedly with breaks in between. Something happens **continuously** when it goes on all the time.

contour *NOUN* (**contours**)
1 the contour of something is its shape or outline **2** a line on a map joining points that are the same height above sea level

contraception *NOUN*
contraception is using contraceptives to prevent a woman from becoming pregnant

contraceptive *NOUN* (**contraceptives**)
something, such as a condom, that is used to prevent a woman from becoming pregnant

contract *NOUN* (**contracts**) (*say* **kon**- trakt)
a legal agreement

contract *VERB* (**contracts, contracting, contracted**) (*say* kon- **trakt**)
1 to contract is to become smaller • *Heated metal contracts as it cools.* **2** to contract to do something is

to make a contract about it **3** to contract an illness is to catch it • *She contracted pneumonia.*
▷ **contraction** *NOUN* contraction is getting smaller or shorter

CONTRACTIONS
In speech and informal language, you sometimes join two words together by leaving out some of the letters. An apostrophe shows where you have missed out the letters. For example: *I'm = I am, you're = you are, he's = he has* or *he is*. Common mistakes with contractions include *would've = would have* (not *would of*) and confusing *it's = it is* (*It's cold today*) and *its* which is a pronoun (*My cat has hurt its paw*). Look also at the panel on **Apostrophes**.

contractor *NOUN* (**contractors**)
a company or firm that does a piece of work for someone else, especially in the building industry

contradict *VERB* (**contradicts**, **contradicting**, **contradicted**)
to contradict someone or something is to say they are wrong or untrue

WORD FAMILY
A **contradiction** is saying that someone or something is wrong or untrue; a **contradictory** statement says the opposite of something someone has just said.

contraflow *NOUN* (**contraflows**)
a special arrangement of traffic when a motorway is being repaired, with some traffic using the carriageway on the other side

contraption *NOUN* (**contraptions**)
a clumsy or strange-looking device or machine

contrary *ADJECTIVE*
1 (*say* **kon**- tra- ri) one thing is contrary to another when they are opposites or contradict one another • *The two sisters had contrary views about marriage.* **2** (*say* kon- **trair**- i) someone who is contrary is obstinate and difficult to deal with • *Mary, Mary, quite contrary.*
on the contrary the opposite is true • *Are you pleased? On the contrary, I'm very annoyed.*

contrast *VERB* (**contrasts**, **contrasting**, **contrasted**) (*say* kon- **trahst**)
1 to contrast two things is to show they are different **2** one thing contrasts with another when it is clearly different

contrast *NOUN* (**contrasts**) (*say* **kon**- trahst)
1 the action of contrasting **2** a clear difference **3** the amount of difference between colours or tones

contribute *VERB* (**contributes**, **contributing**, **contributed**)
1 to contribute to something is to give money to help it **2** to contribute to a result is to help cause it • *His tiredness contributed to the accident.*

WORD FAMILY
A **contribution** is money or help that someone gives towards something; a **contributor** is someone who gives money or help.

contrivance *NOUN* (**contrivances**)
a weird or unusual device or machine

contrive *VERB* (**contrives**, **contriving**, **contrived**)
1 to contrive something is to plan or invent it in a clever way **2** to contrive to do something is to manage to do it though it is probably foolish or dangerous • *He contrived to get stuck in the lift near the fifth floor.*

control *NOUN* (**controls**)
1 control is the power to make someone or something do what you want **2** the controls of a machine are the switches and levers that make it work
to be in control is to have power or control over people or things

control *VERB* (**controls**, **controlling**, **controlled**)
to control something or someone is to have power over what they do
▷ **controller** *NOUN* someone who controls or organizes something

control tower *NOUN* (**control towers**)
the building at an airport where air traffic controllers direct the movements of aircraft by radio

controversial *ADJECTIVE*
a controversial action or statement is one that is likely to cause people to have strong opinions and disagree about it

controversy *NOUN* (**controversies**) (*say* **kon**- tro- ver- si or kon- **trov**- er- si)
a long argument or disagreement

conundrum *NOUN* (**conundrums**)
a riddle

convalescent *ADJECTIVE*
recovering from an illness
▷ **convalescence** *NOUN* a period of recovery after an illness

convection *NOUN*
heating by moving air or liquid
▷ **convector** *NOUN* a heater that works by convection

a b c d e f g h i j k l m n o p q r s t u v w x y z

convenience *NOUN* (**conveniences**)
1 convenience is usefulness and comfort **2** a convenience is something that is useful, such as central heating **3** a convenience is also a public lavatory
to do something at your convenience is to do it when it suits you

convenience food *NOUN* (**convenience foods**)
food that is easy to use and partly prepared in a factory

convenient *ADJECTIVE*
easy to use or reach
▷ **conveniently** *ADVERB* in a convenient way

convent *NOUN* (**convents**)
a group of buildings where nuns live and work

convention *NOUN* (**conventions**)
an accepted way of doing things

conventional *ADJECTIVE*
done in the accepted way; usual, traditional
▷ **conventionally** *ADVERB* in a conventional way, traditionally

converge *VERB* (**converges, converging, converged**)
to converge is to come together • *The two roads converge at the pub.* • *Thousands of fans converged on the football ground.*

conversation *NOUN* (**conversations**)
conversation, or a conversation, is when you talk to someone for a while
▷ **conversational** *ADJECTIVE* to do with conversation, like conversation • *Use a conversational style of writing.*

converse[1] *VERB* (**converses, conversing, conversed**) (*say* kon- **verss**)
to converse is to talk together • *They conversed in low voices.*

converse[2] *NOUN* (*say* **kon**- verss)
the converse of something is the opposite of it

conversion *NOUN* (**conversions**)
conversion, or a conversion, is changing or converting something

convert *VERB* (**converts, converting, converted**) (*say* kon- **vert**)
1 to convert something is to change it for a new purpose **2** to convert someone is to persuade them to change their religion or beliefs **3** (*in rugby football*) to convert a try is to kick a goal after scoring

convert *NOUN* (**converts**) (*say* **kon**- vert)
someone who has changed their beliefs
▷ **convertible** *ADJECTIVE* something is convertible when it can be changed from one form or shape to another

convex *ADJECTIVE*
a convex surface is curved like the outside of a circle or ball. The opposite of **concave**.

convey *VERB* (**conveys, conveying, conveyed**)
1 to convey someone or something is to take them somewhere **2** to convey a message or idea is to get someone to understand it

conveyor belt *NOUN* (**conveyor belts**)
a long belt or chain for carrying goods in a factory

convict *NOUN* (**convicts**) (*say* **kon**- vikt)
a criminal in a prison

convict *VERB* (**convicts, convicting, convicted**) (*say* kon- **vikt**)
to convict someone of a crime is to decide at their trial that they are guilty of it and punish them

conviction *NOUN* (**convictions**)
1 being convicted of a crime **2** being convinced of something; a strong opinion

convince *VERB* (**convinces, convincing, convinced**)
to convince someone is to persuade them about something

convoy *NOUN* (**convoys**)
a group of ships or vehicles travelling together

cook *VERB* (**cooks, cooking, cooked**)
to cook food is to make it ready to eat by heating it
to cook something up (*informal*) is to make it up hurriedly • *They cooked up a clever excuse for being late.*

cook *NOUN* (**cooks**)
someone who cooks, especially as their job

cooker *NOUN* (**cookers**)
a device with an oven and hotplates for cooking food

cookery *NOUN*
the art or skill of cooking food

cool *ADJECTIVE* (**cooler, coolest**)
1 not very warm; fairly cold **2** a cool person is calm and not easily excited **3** (*informal*) good or fashionable • *He looks cool in those glasses.*
▷ **coolly** *ADVERB* calmly
▷ **coolness** *NOUN* being cool

cool *VERB* (**cools, cooling, cooled**)
1 to cool something is to make it cool **2** to cool is to become cool
▷ **cooler** *NOUN* a device for making something cool

coop *NOUN* (**coops**)
a cage for poultry

cooped up *ADJECTIVE*
having to stay in a place which is small and uncomfortable • *The children felt cooped up in their tiny classroom.*

cooperate *VERB* (**cooperates, cooperating, cooperated**)
to cooperate with people is to work helpfully with them
▷ **cooperative** *ADJECTIVE* someone who is cooperative is helpful and willing to do what people ask them

cooperation *NOUN*
1 cooperation is working together to achieve something **2** you give someone your cooperation when you do what they ask and help them

coordinate *VERB* (**coordinates**, **coordinating**, **coordinated**) (*say* koh- **or**- din- ayt)
to coordinate people or things is to get them to work well together

coordinate *NOUN* (**coordinates**) (*say* koh- **or**- din- at)
a quantity used to fix the position of something • *The coordinates of point P are (4,2).*

coordination *NOUN*
1 coordination is organizing people or things so that they work well together **2** the coordination of parts of your body, for example your hands and your eyes, is making them help each other and work well together

coot *NOUN* (**coots**)
a waterbird with a horny white plate on its forehead

cop *VERB* (**cops**, **copping**, **copped**)
(*informal*) to cop something is to get or catch it, especially when you don't want it • *Her brother copped most of the blame.*
to cop it is to get into trouble
to cop out of something is to avoid it because you are afraid

cop *NOUN* (**cops**)
(*informal*) a police officer
not much cop not very good

cope *VERB* (**copes**, **coping**, **coped**)
to cope with something awkward or difficult is to deal with it successfully

copper *NOUN* (**coppers**)
1 copper is a reddish-brown metal used for making wire and pipes **2** copper is also a reddish-brown colour **3** a copper is a coin made of copper or bronze **4** (*informal*) a copper is a police officer

copper sulphate *NOUN*
blue-green crystals that are a compound of copper and sulphur

copy *NOUN* (**copies**)
1 something made to look exactly like something else **2** something written out a second time **3** one newspaper, magazine, or book • *We each have a copy of 'Alice in Wonderland'*

copy *VERB* (**copies**, **copying**, **copied**)
1 to copy something is to make a copy of it **2** to copy someone is to do the same as them **3** to copy a computer file or program or piece of text is to make another one that is exactly the same, usually one that you store somewhere else
▷ **copier** *NOUN* a machine for copying pages

coral *NOUN*
coral is a hard substance made of the skeletons of tiny sea creatures

cord *NOUN* (**cords**)
a cord is a piece of thin rope

> **SPELLING**
> Take care not to confuse **cord** with **chord**, which means a number of musical notes sounded together.

cordial *ADJECTIVE*
warm and friendly • *We got a cordial welcome.*
▷ **cordiality** *NOUN* cordiality is being friendly ▷ **cordially** *ADVERB* in a friendly way

cordial *NOUN* (**cordials**)
a sweet drink

corduroy *NOUN* (*say* **kor**- der- oi)
thick cotton cloth with ridges along it

core *NOUN* (**cores**)
the part in the middle of something

corgi *NOUN* (**corgis**)
a small breed of dog with short legs and large upright ears

cork *NOUN* (**corks**)
1 cork is the lightweight bark of a kind of oak tree **2** a cork is a piece of this bark used to close a bottle

corkscrew *NOUN* (**corkscrews**)
1 a device for removing corks from bottles **2** a spiral

cormorant *NOUN* (**cormorants**)
a large black seabird

corn [1] *NOUN*
grain • *a field of corn*

corn [2] *NOUN* (**corns**)
a small, hard lump on your toe or foot

corned beef *NOUN*
tinned beef preserved with salt

corner *NOUN* (**corners**)
1 the point where two lines, roads, or walls meet **2** a kick from the corner of a football field; a hit from the corner of a hockey field

corner *VERB* (**corners**, **cornering**, **cornered**)
1 to corner someone is to trap them • *The police cornered the escaped prisoner.* **2** to corner is to go round a corner • *The car cornered slowly and accelerated up the road.*

cornet *NOUN* (**cornets**)
1 a long cone-shaped biscuit open at the top for ice cream **2** a musical instrument like a trumpet

cornfield *NOUN* (**cornfields**)
a field where corn grows

cornflakes *PLURAL NOUN*
toasted maize flakes eaten for breakfast

cornflour *NOUN*
fine flour used for making puddings

cornflower *NOUN* (**cornflowers**)
a blue wild flower

Cornish *ADJECTIVE*
from or to do with Cornwall

a b c d e f g h i j k l m n o p q r s t u v w x y z

Cornish pasty *NOUN* (**Cornish pasties**)
a small pie containing meat and vegetables

corny *ADJECTIVE* (**cornier**, **corniest**)
(*informal*) a corny joke is one that is feeble and often repeated

coronation *NOUN* (**coronations**)
the ceremony of crowning a king or queen

coroner *NOUN* (**coroners**)
an official who holds an inquiry into the cause of an unnatural death

corporal *NOUN* (**corporals**)
a soldier just below sergeant in rank

corporal *ADJECTIVE*
to do with the human body

corporal punishment *NOUN*
punishment by hitting or beating someone

corporation *NOUN* (**corporations**)
a group of people elected to govern a town

corps *NOUN* (**corps**) (*say* kor)
1 a large unit of soldiers **2** a special army unit • *He is in the Medical Corps.*

> SPELLING
> Take care not to confuse **corps** with **corpse**, which is the next word in this dictionary.

corpse *NOUN* (**corpses**)
a dead body

corpuscle *NOUN* (**corpuscles**) (*say* kor- pu- sul)
one of the many red or white cells in the blood

corral *NOUN* (**corrals**) (*say* ko- rahl)
an enclosure for horses or cattle

correct *ADJECTIVE*
1 true or accurate; without any mistakes • *Your answers are all correct.* **2** proper, suitable • *Is that the correct way to talk to your parents?*
▷ **correctly** *ADVERB* to do something correctly is to do it the right way and without any mistakes

correct *VERB* (**corrects**, **correcting**, **corrected**)
to correct a piece of work is to mark the mistakes in it, or to put them right

correction *NOUN* (**corrections**)
1 correction is correcting something **2** a correction is a change made to something in order to correct it

correspond *VERB* (**corresponds**, **corresponding**, **corresponded**)
1 to correspond with something is to agree with it or match it • *Your story corresponds with what I heard.* **2** to correspond with someone is to exchange letters with them

correspondence *NOUN*
1 similarity or agreement **2** letters or writing letters

correspondent *NOUN* (**correspondents**)
1 someone who writes letters **2** someone employed to send news or articles to a newspaper or magazine

corridor *NOUN* (**corridors**)
1 a long narrow passage from which doors open into rooms or compartments **2** a route an aircraft follows

corrode *VERB* (**corrodes**, **corroding**, **corroded**)
to corrode is to wear away by rust or chemical action
▷ **corrosion** *NOUN* corrosion is the process of corroding
▷ **corrosive** *ADJECTIVE* a corrosive substance is likely to corrode

corrugated *ADJECTIVE*
shaped into folds or ridges • *The roof was made of corrugated iron.*

corrupt *ADJECTIVE*
a corrupt person is dishonest in carrying out their responsibilities or duties, for example by taking bribes

corrupt *VERB*
1 to corrupt someone is to make them dishonest, especially when they have important responsibilities **2** in a computer, a bug or other problem corrupts a file when it makes it impossible to read or use

corruption *NOUN*
corruption is dishonest beahviour by people who are in authority or have important responsibilities

corset *NOUN* (**corsets**)
a tight piece of underwear worn round the hips and waist

cosmetics *PLURAL NOUN*
substances like lipstick and face powder, for making the skin or hair look beautiful or different

cosmic *ADJECTIVE* (*say* koz- mik)
to do with the universe

cosmonaut *NOUN* (**cosmonauts**)
a Russian astronaut

cost *VERB* (**costs**, **costing**, **cost**)
to cost a certain amount is to have that amount as its price • *The book only cost $3 last year.*

cost *NOUN* (**costs**)
what you have to spend to do or get something
at all costs or **at any cost** no matter what the cost or difficulty may be

costly *ADJECTIVE* (**costlier**, **costliest**)
expensive

cost of living *NOUN*
the average amount each person in a country spends on food, clothing, and housing

costume *NOUN* (**costumes**)
clothes, especially for a particular purpose or of a particular period

cosy *ADJECTIVE* (**cosier**, **cosiest**)
warm and comfortable

cosy *NOUN* (**cosies**)
a cover put over a teapot or boiled egg to keep it hot

cot *NOUN* (**cots**)
a baby's bed with high sides

cottage *NOUN* (**cottages**)
a small house, especially in the country

cottage cheese *NOUN*
soft white cheese made from skimmed milk

cottage pie *NOUN* (**cottage pies**)
minced meat covered with mashed potato and baked

cotton *NOUN*
1 a soft white substance covering the seeds of a tropical plant **2** thread made from this substance **3** cloth made from cotton thread

couch *NOUN* (**couches**)
a long soft seat or sofa

couch potato *NOUN* (**couch potatoes**)
(*informal*) a person who spends a lot of time watching television

cough *VERB* (**coughs**, **coughing**, **coughed**) (*say* kof)
to cough is to push air suddenly out of your lungs with a harsh noise
to cough up (*informal*) is to give someone money or information

cough *NOUN* (**coughs**)
1 the action or sound of coughing **2** an illness which makes you cough a lot

could
past tense of **can**[1] *VERB*

couldn't
short for *could not*

council *NOUN* (**councils**)
a group of people chosen to organize or discuss something, especially to plan the affairs of a town

> SPELLING
> Take care not to confuse **council** with **counsel**, which means advice.

council house *NOUN* (**council houses**)
a house owned and let by a council

councillor *NOUN* (**councillors**)
a member of a council

> SPELLING
> Take care not to confuse **councillor** with **counsellor**, which means someone who gives advice.

council tax *NOUN*
a tax paid to the local council by owners of houses

counsel *NOUN* (**counsels**)
1 advice **2** the barrister or barristers involved in a case in a lawcourt

counsel *VERB* (**counsels**, **counselling**, **counselled**)
to counsel someone is to give them advice

counsellor *NOUN* (**counsellors**)
someone who gives advice, especially as their job

count[1] *VERB* (**counts**, **counting**, **counted**)
1 to count is to use numbers to find out how many people or things there are in a place **2** to count or count out is to say numbers in their proper order **3** to count someone or something is to include them in a total • *There are 30 in the class, counting the teacher.* **4** to count is to have a particular value or importance • *Playing well counts a lot even if you lose.*
to count on someone or **something** is to rely on them

count *NOUN* (**counts**)
1 the total reached by counting **2** one of the things that someone is accused of • *He was found guilty on all counts.*

count[2] *NOUN* (**counts**)
a foreign nobleman

countable *ADJECTIVE*
able to be counted

countdown *NOUN* (**countdowns**)
a counting down to 0, especially before launching a rocket

countenance *NOUN* (**countenances**)
someone's face or the expression on their face

counter *NOUN* (**counters**)
1 a long table where customers are served in a shop or café **2** a small plastic disc used in board games

counterfeit *ADJECTIVE* (*say* kown- ter- fit)
faked to deceive or swindle people • *They were using counterfeit money.*

countess *NOUN* (**countesses**)
the wife or widow of a count or earl; a female earl

countless *ADJECTIVE*
too many to count; very many

country *NOUN* (**countries**)
1 a country is a part of the world where a particular nation of people lives **2** the country is the countryside

countryman or **countrywoman** *NOUN* (**countrymen** or **countrywomen**)
1 a man or woman who lives in the countryside **2** a fellow countryman is someone who lives in the same country

countryside *NOUN*
an area with fields, woods, and villages, away from towns

county *NOUN* (**counties**)
one of the areas that a country is divided into, for example Kent in England, Fife in Scotland, and Powys in Wales

couple *NOUN* (**couples**)
a couple is two people or things

couple *VERB* (**couples**, **coupling**, **coupled**)
to couple things is to join them together

couplet *NOUN* (**couplets**)
a pair of lines in rhyming verse

coupling *NOUN* (**couplings**)
a link or fastening, especially for vehicles

coupon *NOUN* (**coupons**)
a piece of paper that gives you the right to receive or do something

courage *NOUN*
being courageous

courageous *ADJECTIVE*
ready to face danger or pain

courgette *NOUN* (**courgettes**)
a kind of vegetable like a small marrow

> BRITISH AND AMERICAN
> In America, the word **zucchini** (plural) is used.

courier *NOUN* (**couriers**) (*say* koor- i- er)
1 someone who carries a message **2** someone employed to guide and help holidaymakers, especially abroad

course *NOUN* (**courses**)
1 the direction in which something moves along • *The ship's course was to the west.* **2** a series of lessons or exercises in learning something • *My Mum's starting a cookery course at last.* **3** a part of a meal, such as the meat course or the pudding course **4** a racecourse or golf course
in due course eventually; at the right time
in the course of something while it is happening
of course naturally; certainly • *Of course they will help us .* • *'Will you help us?' 'Of course!'*

court *NOUN* (**courts**)
1 a lawcourt **2** an enclosed place for games like tennis or netball **3** a courtyard **4** the place where a king or queen lives **5** the people who are usually at a king's or queen's court

court *VERB* (**courts**, **courting**, **courted**)
to court someone is to try to win their love or support

courteous *ADJECTIVE* (*say* ker- ti- us)
friendly and polite towards other people
▷ **courteously** *ADVERB* to behave courteously is to be friendly and polite towards other people
▷ **courtesy** *NOUN* courtesy is polite behaviour towards other people

court martial *NOUN* (**courts martial**)
1 a court for trying offenders against military law **2** a trial in this court

courtship *NOUN*
courting someone, especially a boyfriend or girlfriend

courtyard *NOUN* (**courtyards**)
a paved area surrounded by walls or buildings

cousin *NOUN* (**cousins**)
your cousin is a child of your uncle or aunt

cove *NOUN* (**coves**)
a small bay

cover *VERB* (**covers**, **covering**, **covered**)
1 to cover something is to put something else over it to hide or protect it **2** to cover a distance is to travel over it • *We managed to cover ten miles a day.* **3** to cover a subject is to deal with it or include it • *This book covers everything you need to know about stamp collecting.* **4** to cover something is to be enough money for it • *I expect $2 will cover my fare.* **5** to cover someone is to aim a gun at or near them • *I've got you covered.*
to cover something up is to make sure no one knows about something wrong or illegal

cover *NOUN* (**covers**)
1 a cover is something used for covering something else; a lid or wrapper **2** cover is a place where someone can hide or take shelter

coverage *NOUN*
the amount of time or space given to reporting an event on radio, on television, or in a newspaper

cover-up *NOUN* (**cover-ups**)
a cover-up is when people in power prevent other people knowing about something wrong or illegal • *The government were accused of a cover-up of their mistakes.*

cow *NOUN* (**cows**)
a large female animal kept by farmers for its milk and beef

coward *NOUN* (**cowards**)
someone who has no courage and runs away from danger and difficulties
▷ **cowardice** *NOUN* cowardice is being a coward
▷ **cowardly** *ADJECTIVE* behaving like a coward

cowboy *NOUN* (**cowboys**)
1 a man who rides round looking after the cattle on a large farm in America **2** (*informal*) a person who uses dishonest methods in business, especially in building

cowslip *NOUN* (**cowslips**)
a wild plant that has yellow flowers in spring

cox *NOUN* (**coxes**)
someone who steers a racing boat

coxswain *NOUN* (**coxswains**) (*say* kok- swayn or kok- sun)
a person who steers a boat or is in charge of the crew of a small ship

coy *ADJECTIVE*
shy; pretending to be shy or modest
▷ **coyly** *ADVERB* in a coy way

crab *NOUN* (**crabs**)
a shellfish with ten legs

crab apple *NOUN* (**crab apples**)
a small sour apple

crack *NOUN* (**cracks**)
1 a line on the surface of something where it has broken but not come completely apart; a narrow gap • *There's a crack in this cup.* **2** a sudden sharp noise • *They heard the crack of a pistol shot.* **3** a sudden sharp blow • *He got a crack on the head.*

crack *VERB* (**cracks**, **cracking**, **cracked**)
1 to crack something is to make a crack in it **2** something cracks when it splits without breaking • *The plate has cracked.* **3** to crack is to make a sudden sharp noise **4** to crack a joke is to tell it
to get cracking (*informal*) is to start work

cracker *NOUN* (**crackers**)
1 a pretty paper tube with a small gift inside it, which bangs when two people pull it apart **2** a thin biscuit

crackle *VERB* (**crackles**, **crackling**, **crackled**)
to crackle is to make small cracking sounds, like a fire

crackling *NOUN*
the hard skin of roast pork

cradle *NOUN* (**cradles**)
1 a cot for a baby **2** a supporting frame for something

craft *NOUN* (**crafts**)
1 a craft is an activity which needs skill with the hands **2** a boat **3** craft is cunning or trickery

craftsman or **craftswoman** *NOUN* (**craftsmen** or **craftswomen**)
someone who is skilled at making things with the hands
▷ **craftsmanship** *NOUN* the skill of a craftsman or craftswoman

crafty *ADJECTIVE* (**craftier**, **craftiest**)
cunning and clever
▷ **craftily** *ADVERB* in a crafty way
▷ **craftiness** *NOUN* being crafty

crag *NOUN* (**crags**)
a steep piece of rough rock
▷ **craggy** *ADJECTIVE* steep and rocky

cram *VERB* (**crams**, **cramming**, **crammed**)
1 to cram things is to force them into a small space **2** to cram is to study very hard for an examination

cramp *NOUN* (**cramps**)
pain caused by a muscle tightening suddenly

cramp *VERB* (**cramps**, **cramping**, **cramped**)
to cramp someone is to hinder their freedom or growth

cramped *ADJECTIVE*
in a space that is too small or tight • *We felt very cramped sleeping three in the same room.*

crane *NOUN* (**cranes**)
1 a machine for lifting and moving heavy objects **2** a large bird with long legs and neck

crane *VERB* (**cranes**, **craning**, **craned**)
to crane your neck is to stretch it so that you can see something

crane-fly *NOUN* (**crane-flies**)
an insect with long thin legs

crank *NOUN* (**cranks**)
1 an L-shaped rod used to turn or control something **2** a person with weird or unusual ideas

crank *VERB* (**cranks**, **cranking**, **cranked**)
to crank something like an engine is to turn it by using an L-shaped rod

cranky *ADJECTIVE* (**crankier**, **crankiest**)
weird or unusual

cranny *NOUN* (**crannies**)
a crevice; a narrow hole or space

crash *NOUN* (**crashes**)
1 the loud noise of something falling or breaking **2** a collision between road vehicles, causing damage

crash *VERB* (**crashes**, **crashing**, **crashed**)
1 to crash is to collide or fall violently **2** to crash a vehicle is to have a crash while driving it **3** to crash along or through something is to move violently and loudly

crash helmet *NOUN* (**crash helmets**)
a padded helmet worn by cyclists and motorcyclists

crash landing *NOUN* (**crash landings**)
an emergency landing of an aircraft, causing it damage

crate *NOUN* (**crates**)
a container in which goods are transported

crater *NOUN* (**craters**)
1 the mouth of a volcano **2** a hole in the ground made by a bomb

crave *VERB* (**craves**, **craving**, **craved**)
to crave something is to want it very badly

crawl *VERB* (**crawls**, **crawling**, **crawled**)
1 to crawl is to move along on your hands and knees **2** to crawl is also to move slowly in a vehicle **3** to be crawling with something unpleasant is to be full of it or covered in it • *This room's crawling with cockroaches.*

crawl *NOUN*
1 a crawling movement **2** a powerful swimming stroke with the arms hitting the water alternately

crayon *NOUN* (**crayons**)
a coloured pencil for drawing or writing

craze *NOUN* (**crazes**)
a brief enthusiasm for something

crazy *ADJECTIVE* (**crazier**, **craziest**)
mad or weird
▷ **crazily** *ADVERB* in a crazy way
▷ **craziness** *NOUN* being crazy

crazy paving *NOUN*
paving made of odd pieces of stone fitted together

creak *NOUN* (**creaks**)
a sound like the noise made by a stiff door opening

creak *VERB* (**creaks**, **creaking**, **creaked**)
to make a creak
▷ **creaky** *ADJECTIVE* old and creaking

cream *NOUN* (**creams**)
1 the rich fatty part of milk **2** a yellowish-white colour **3** a food containing or looking like cream **4** something that looks like cream, for example face cream
▷ **creamy** *ADJECTIVE* smooth and thick like cream

crease *NOUN* (**creases**)
1 a line made in something by folding or pressing it **2** a line on a cricket pitch showing where the batsman should stand

crease *VERB* (**creases**, **creasing**, **creased**)
to crease something is to make a crease in it

create *VERB* (**creates**, **creating**, **created**)
to create something is to make it exist
▷ **creation** *NOUN* creating something

creative *ADJECTIVE*
showing imagination and thought as well as skill • *The older children have started some creative writing.*
▷ **creativity** *NOUN* the ability to use the imagination to create things

creator *NOUN* (**creators**)
someone who creates something
the Creator a name for God

creature *NOUN* (**creatures**)
a living animal or person

crèche *NOUN* (**crèches**) (*say* kresh)
a place where babies or small children are looked after while their parents are busy

credibility *NOUN*
being credible

credible *ADJECTIVE*
able to be believed; trustworthy
▷ **credibly** *ADVERB* in a credible way

> USING THIS WORD
> Take care not to confuse **credible** with **creditable**, which means deserving praise.

credit *NOUN*
1 honour or approval • *Give her credit for her honesty.* **2** a system of allowing someone to pay for something later on • *Do you want cash now or can I have it on credit?* **3** an amount of money in an account at a bank or building society
credits the list of people who have helped to produce a film, television programme, etc.
to do someone credit is to earn them praise • *Your topic work does you credit.*

credit *VERB* (**credits**, **crediting**, **credited**)
1 to credit something is to believe it • *Can you credit that?* **2** to credit someone with something is to enter it as a credit in their bank account • *We will credit you with a £50 refund.*

creditable *ADJECTIVE*
deserving praise
▷ **creditably** *ADVERB* in a creditable way

> USING THIS WORD
> Take care not to confuse **creditable** with **credible**, which means trustworthy.

credit card *NOUN* (**credit cards**)
a card allowing someone to buy goods on credit

creditor *NOUN* (**creditors**)
someone to whom you owe money

creed *NOUN* (**creeds**)
a set or statement of beliefs

creek *NOUN* (**creeks**)
1 a narrow inlet **2** (*in Australia, New Zealand, or America*) a small stream
up the creek (*informal*) in trouble

creep *VERB* (**creeps**, **creeping**, **crept**)
1 to creep is to move along with the body close to the ground **2** to creep about is to move quietly or secretly
to creep up on someone is to go up to them quietly from behind

creep *NOUN* (**creeps**)
1 a creeping movement **2** (*informal*) a nasty or unpleasant person
the creeps (*informal*) a feeling of fear or disgust

creeper *NOUN* (**creepers**)
a plant that grows close to the ground or up walls

creepy *ADJECTIVE* (**creepier**, **creepiest**)
(*informal*) weird and slightly frightening

cremate *VERB* (**cremates**, **cremating**, **cremated**)
to cremate a dead body is to burn it into fine ashes instead of burying it
▷ **cremation** *NOUN* the cremating of a dead body

crematorium *NOUN* (**crematoria**) (*say* krem- a- **tor**- i- um)
a place where dead bodies are cremated

creole *NOUN* (**creoles**) (*say* kree- ohl)
a language that is formed over time from a mixture of a local language (especially an African one) and a European language and that has become the main language in a place
Creole a person of mixed European and African race, especially someone who lives in the West Indies; a person descended from the Europeans who first settled in the West Indies

creosote *NOUN* (*say* **kree**- o- soht)
a brown oily liquid painted on wood to prevent it from rotting

crêpe *NOUN* (**crêpes**) (*say* krayp)
1 cloth or paper with a wrinkled surface **2** a kind of thin French pancake

crept
past tense and past participle of **creep** *VERB*

crescendo *NOUN* (**crescendos**) (*say* kri- **shen**- doh)
music that gets gradually louder

crescent *NOUN* (**crescents**)
1 a narrow curved shape, pointed at both ends, like a new moon **2** a curved street

cress *NOUN*
a green plant used in salads and sandwiches

crest *NOUN* (**crests**)
1 a tuft of hair, feathers, or skin on an animal's head **2** the top of a hill or wave

crevasse *NOUN* (**crevasses**)
a deep crack in a glacier

crevice *NOUN* (**crevices**)
a crack in rock or in a wall

crew *NOUN* (**crews**)
the people who work on a ship or aircraft

crib *NOUN* (**cribs**)
1 a baby's cot **2** a framework containing fodder for animals **3** a translation of a book written in another language **4** something copied

crib *VERB* (**cribs**, **cribbing**, **cribbed**)
to crib someone else's work is to copy it

cricket[1] *NOUN*
a game played outdoors by two teams with a ball, two bats, and two wickets
▷ **cricketer** *NOUN* someone who plays cricket

cricket[2] *NOUN* (**crickets**)
an insect like a grasshopper

cried
past tense and past participle of **cry** *VERB*

crime *NOUN* (**crimes**)
an act that breaks the law

criminal *NOUN* (**criminals**)
someone who has committed one or more crimes

criminal *ADJECTIVE*
to do with crime or criminals

crimson *NOUN* and *ADJECTIVE*
a dark red colour

crinkle *VERB* (**crinkles**, **crinkling**, **crinkled**)
to crinkle something is to crease or wrinkle it
▷ **crinkly** *ADJECTIVE* full of creases, wrinkled

cripple *NOUN* (**cripples**)
someone who cannot walk properly

cripple *VERB* (**cripples**, **crippling**, **crippled**)
1 to cripple someone is to make them a cripple **2** to cripple something is to damage it so it won't work properly

crisis *NOUN* (**crises**) (*say* **kry**- sis)
an important or difficult time or situation

crisp *ADJECTIVE* (**crisper**, **crispest**)
1 very dry so that it breaks easily **2** firm and fresh • *I'd like a nice crisp apple.* **3** cold and frosty • *We woke up to a crisp winter morning.*

crisp *NOUN* (**crisps**)
a thin fried slice of potato, sold in packets

> BRITISH AND AMERICAN
> In America, **potato chip** is used.

crispy *ADJECTIVE* (**crispier**, **crispiest**)
crispy food is pleasantly crisp

criss-cross *ADJECTIVE & ADVERB*
with crossing lines

critic *NOUN* (**critics**)
1 a person who criticizes someone or something **2** someone who gives opinions on books, plays, films, music, or other performances

critical *ADJECTIVE*
1 criticizing **2** to do with critics or criticism **3** serious, amounting to a crisis
▷ **critically** *ADVERB* in a critical way; seriously

criticism *NOUN* (**criticisms**) (*say* **krit**- i- si- zum)
an opinion or judgement about something, usually pointing out its faults

criticize *VERB* (**criticizes**, **criticizing**, **criticized**)
(*say* **krit**- i- syz)
to criticize something or someone is to give an opinion pointing out their faults

croak *NOUN* (**croaks**)
a deep sound, like a frog makes

croak *VERB* (**croaks**, **croaking**, **croaked**)
to make a croak

crochet *NOUN* (*say* **kroh**- shay)
a kind of needlework done with a hooked needle

crock *NOUN* (**crocks**)
(*informal*) an old or worn-out person or thing

crockery *NOUN*
dishes, plates, and cups and saucers used for eating

crocodile *NOUN* (**crocodiles**)
a large reptile living in hot countries, with a thick skin, long tail, and huge jaws

crocodile tears *PLURAL NOUN*
sorrow that is not genuine

crocus *NOUN* (**crocuses**)
a small spring flower that is yellow, purple, or white

croft *NOUN* (**crofts**)
a small farm in Scotland
▷ **crofter** *NOUN* someone who lives and works on a croft

croissant *NOUN* (**croissants**) (*say* **krwa**- sahn)
a crescent-shaped roll of rich pastry, first made in France and usually eaten for breakfast

crook *NOUN* (**crooks**)
1 (*informal*) someone who cheats or robs people; a criminal **2** a shepherd's or bishop's stick with a curved end

crook *VERB* (**crooks**, **crooking**, **crooked**)
to crook something is to bend it into a hook shape

crooked *ADJECTIVE* (*say* **kruuk**- id)
1 bent or twisted **2** (*informal*) dishonest or criminal

croon *VERB* (**croons**, **crooning**, **crooned**)
to croon is to sing softly or sentimentally

crop *NOUN* (**crops**)
1 something grown for food, especially in a field • *They had a good crop of wheat last year.* **2** a riding whip with a loop instead of a lash

crop *VERB* (**crops**, **cropping**, **cropped**)
to crop something is to cut or bite the top off it • *They could see sheep in a field, cropping the grass.*
to crop up is to happen or appear unexpectedly

cross *NOUN* (**crosses**)
1 a mark or shape like + or x **2** an upright post with another post across it, used in ancient times for crucifixions **3** an animal produced by mixing one breed with another • *A mule is a cross between a donkey and a horse.*
the Cross the cross on which Christ was crucified, used as a symbol of Christianity

cross *VERB* (**crosses**, **crossing**, **crossed**)
1 to cross something is to go across it • *She crossed the room to meet him.* **2** to cross your fingers or legs is to put one over the other
to cross something out is to draw a line across something because it is unwanted or wrong

cross *ADJECTIVE*
1 angry or bad-tempered **2** going from one side to another • *There were cross winds on the bridge.*
▷ **crossly** *ADVERB* angrily
▷ **crossness** *NOUN* being cross

crossbar *NOUN* (**crossbars**)
a horizontal bar between two upright bars

crossbow *NOUN* (**crossbows**)
a kind of bow used for shooting arrows, held like a gun and fired by pulling a trigger

cross-country *NOUN*
a running race through fields and country

cross-examine *VERB* (**cross-examines**, **cross-examining**, **cross-examined**)
to cross-examine someone is to question them about information they have given, usually in a lawcourt
▷ **cross-examination** *NOUN* the cross-examining of a witness in a lawcourt

cross-eyed *ADJECTIVE*
having eyes that appear to look in different directions

crossing *NOUN* (**crossings**)
a place where people can cross a road or railway

cross-legged *ADVERB & ADJECTIVE*
having crossed legs

crossroads *NOUN* (**crossroads**)
a place where two or more roads cross one another

cross-section *NOUN* (**cross-sections**)
1 a drawing of something as if it has been cut through **2** a typical sample • *A cross-section of parents said they wanted an after-school club.*

crosswise *ADVERB & ADJECTIVE*
with one thing crossing another

crossword *NOUN* (**crosswords**)
a puzzle with blank squares in which you put the letters of words worked out from clues

crotchet *NOUN* (**crotchets**) (*say* kroch- it)
a musical note equal to half a minim, written .

crouch *VERB* (**crouches**, **crouching**, **crouched**)
to crouch is to lower your body, with your arms and legs bent

crow *NOUN* (**crows**)
a large black bird
as the crow flies in a straight line

crow *VERB* (**crows**, **crowing**, **crowed**)
1 to make a noise like a cock **2** to boast; to be proudly triumphant

crowbar *NOUN* (**crowbars**)
an iron bar used as a lever

crowd *NOUN* (**crowds**)
a large number of people in one place

crowd *VERB* (**crowds**, **crowding**, **crowded**)
1 to crowd or crowd round is to form a crowd **2** to crowd a place is to make it uncomfortably full of people • *The town is crowded with tourists in summer.*

crown *NOUN* (**crowns**)
1 a crown is an ornamental headdress worn by a king or queen **2** the crown is the king or queen of a country • *This land belongs to the crown.* **3** the top of the head **4** the middle part of a road, which is higher than the sides

crown *VERB* (**crowns**, **crowning**, **crowned**)
1 to crown someone is to make them king or queen **2** to crown something is to form the top of it **3** to crown an achievement is to finish it happily • *Their efforts were crowned with success.*

crow's-nest *NOUN* (**crow's-nests**)
a look-out position at the top of a ship's mast

crucial *ADJECTIVE* (*say* kroo- shal)
extremely important

crucifix *NOUN* (**crucifixes**)
a model of the Cross or of Christ on the Cross

crucify *VERB* (**crucifies**, **crucifying**, **crucified**)
to crucify someone is to execute them by fixing their hands and feet to a cross and leaving them to die. The Romans used this method of executing criminals.
▷ **crucifixion** *NOUN* the execution of someone by crucifying them

crude *ADJECTIVE* (**cruder**, **crudest**)
1 natural; not purified • *The country exported crude oil.* **2** rough and simple • *They stayed in a crude hut in the mountains.* **3** rude or dirty • *The boys were telling each other crude jokes.*

cruel *ADJECTIVE* (**crueller**, **cruellest**)
causing pain and suffering to others • *They were ruled by a cruel tyrant.* • *War is cruel.*
▷ **cruelly** *ADVERB* in a cruel way
▷ **cruelty** *NOUN* cruelty is cruel acts or treatment

cruise *NOUN* (**cruises**)
a holiday on a ship, usually visiting different places

cruise *VERB* (**cruises**, **cruising**, **cruised**)
1 to cruise is to sail or travel at a gentle speed **2** to cruise is also to have a cruise on a ship

cruiser *NOUN* (**cruisers**)
1 a fast warship **2** a large motor boat

crumb *NOUN* (**crumbs**)
a tiny piece of bread or cake

crumble *VERB* (**crumbles**, **crumbling**, **crumbled**)
1 to crumble something is to break it into small pieces **2** to crumble is to be broken into small pieces
▷ **crumbly** *ADJECTIVE* soft and likely to crumble

crumpet *NOUN* (**crumpets**)
a soft flat cake made with yeast, toasted and eaten with butter

crumple *VERB* (**crumples, crumpling, crumpled**)
1 to crumple something is to make it creased **2** to crumple is to become creased

crunch *NOUN* (**crunches**)
the noise made by chewing hard food or walking on gravel
the crunch (*informal*) a crucial event; a crisis

crunch *VERB* (**crunches, crunching, crunched**)
to crunch something is to chew or crush it with a crunch
▷ **crunchy** *ADJECTIVE* making a crunching sound

crusade *NOUN* (**crusades**)
1 a military expedition to Palestine made by Christians in the Middle Ages **2** a campaign against something that you think is bad
▷ **crusader** *NOUN* someone who takes part in a crusade

crush *VERB* (**crushes, crushing, crushed**)
1 to crush something is to press it so that it gets broken or damaged **2** to crush an enemy is to defeat them

crush *NOUN* (**crushes**)
1 a crowd; a crowded place **2** a fruit-flavoured drink **3** (*informal*) a sudden liking you have for someone

crust *NOUN* (**crusts**)
1 the hard outside part of something, especially of a loaf **2** the rocky outer part of a planet

crustacean *NOUN* (**crustaceans**) (*say* krus- tay- shan)
a shellfish

crutch *NOUN* (**crutches**)
a stick that fits under the arm, used as a support in walking

cry *VERB* (**cries, crying, cried**)
1 to cry is to shout **2** to cry is also to let tears fall from your eyes
to cry off is to change your mind and not do something you were going to do • *George was going to come on holiday with us, but he cried off at the last minute.*

cry *NOUN* (**cries**)
1 a loud shout **2** a period of weeping

crypt *NOUN* (**crypts**)
a large room underneath a church

crystal *NOUN* (**crystals**)
1 a clear mineral rather like glass **2** a small solid piece of a substance with a symmetrical shape, such as snow and ice
▷ **crystalline** *ADJECTIVE* made of crystals, having the structure of crystals

crystallize *VERB* (**crystallizes, crystallizing, crystallized**)
to crystallize is to form into crystals

cub *NOUN* (**cubs**)
a young animal, especially a lion, tiger, fox, or bear
Cub a junior Scout

cubbyhole *NOUN* (**cubbyholes**)
a small compartment or snug place

cube *NOUN* (**cubes**)
1 an object that has six square sides, like a box or dice **2** the result of multiplying something by itself twice • *The cube of 3 is 3 x 3 x 3 = 27.*

cube *VERB* (**cubes, cubing, cubed**)
1 to cube a number is to multiply it by itself twice • *4 cubed is 4 x 4 x 4 = 64.* **2** to cube something is to cut it into small cubes

cube root *NOUN* (**cube roots**)
a number that gives another number if it is multiplied by itself twice • *2 is the cube root of 8.*

cubic *ADJECTIVE*
1 shaped like a cube **2** a cubic metre or foot is the volume of a cube with sides that are one metre or foot long

cubicle *NOUN* (**cubicles**)
a small division of a room

cuboid *NOUN* (**cuboids**)
an object with six rectangular sides

cuckoo *NOUN* (**cuckoos**)
a bird that makes a sound like 'cuck-oo', and lays its eggs in other birds' nests

cucumber *NOUN* (**cucumbers**)
a long green vegetable, eaten raw

cud *NOUN*
half-digested food that a cow brings back from its first stomach to chew again

cuddle *VERB* (**cuddles, cuddling, cuddled**)
to cuddle someone is to put your arms closely round them and squeeze them in a loving way
▷ **cuddly** *ADJECTIVE* a cuddly person is nice to cuddle

cue[1] *NOUN* (**cues**)
something that tells an actor when to start speaking or come on the stage

cue[2] *NOUN* (**cues**)
a long stick used to strike the ball in billiards or snooker

cuff *NOUN* (**cuffs**)
1 the end of a sleeve that fits round your wrist **2** a blow given to someone with your hand

cuff *VERB* (**cuffs, cuffing, cuffed**)
to cuff someone is to hit them with the hand

cul-de-sac *NOUN* (**cul-de-sacs**)
a street that is closed at one end

culminate *VERB* (**culminates**, **culminating**, **culminated**)
to reach the end or the most important part • *Their long struggle for freedom culminated in victory.*
▷ **culmination** *NOUN* the end or most important part of something

culprit *NOUN* (**culprits**)
someone who is to blame for something

cult *NOUN* (**cults**)
1 a religion **2** being extremely keen on someone or something • *They enjoyed the cult of rock music.*

cultivate *VERB* (**cultivates**, **cultivating**, **cultivated**)
1 to cultivate land is to grow crops on it **2** to cultivate something is to try to make it grow or develop
▷ **cultivation** *NOUN* cultivation is the cultivating of land

cultivated *ADJECTIVE*
having good manners and education

culture *NOUN* (**cultures**)
1 culture is the development of the mind by education and learning **2** a culture is the customs and traditions of a people • *They were studying Greek culture.*

> WORD FAMILY
> A **cultural** activity is one to do with education and learning; a **cultured** person is well educated and knowledgeable.

cunning *ADJECTIVE*
clever at deceiving people • *Said the cunning Spider to the Fly, 'Dear Friend, what can I do, / To prove the warm affection I've always felt for you?'* — Mary Howitt, *The Spider and the Fly.*

cup *NOUN* (**cups**)
1 a small container with a handle, from which you drink liquid **2** a prize in the form of a silver cup, usually with two handles

cup *VERB* (**cups**, **cupping**, **cupped**)
to cup your hands is to form them into the shape of a cup • *John lifted up one of the eggs, cupping it carefully in his hands.* — Alexander McCall Smith, *Akimbo and the Crocodile Man*

cupboard *NOUN* (**cupboards**) (*say* **kub**- erd)
a compartment or piece of furniture with a door, for storing things

cupful *NOUN* (**cupfuls**)
as much as a cup will hold

curate *NOUN* (**curates**) (*say* **kewr**- at)
a member of the clergy who helps a vicar

curator *NOUN* (**curators**) (*say* kewr- **ay**- ter)
someone in charge of a museum or art gallery

curb *VERB* (**curbs**, **curbing**, **curbed**)
to curb a feeling is to hold it back or hide it • *You must curb your anger.*

curd *NOUN* (**curds**)
a thick substance formed when milk turns sour

curdle *VERB* (**curdles**, **curdling**, **curdled**)
to curdle is to form into curds

cure *VERB* (**cures**, **curing**, **cured**)
1 to cure someone who is ill is to make them better **2** to cure something bad is to stop it **3** to cure food is to treat it so as to preserve it • *Fish can be cured in smoke.*

cure *NOUN* (**cures**)
something that cures a person or thing • *They are still trying to find a cure for cancer.*

curfew *NOUN* (**curfews**)
a time or signal after which people must stay indoors until the next day

curiosity *NOUN* (**curiosities**)
1 curiosity is being curious **2** a curiosity is something strange or interesting

curious *ADJECTIVE*
1 wanting to find out about things **2** strange or unusual • *Whenever Auntie moves around, / Her dresses make a curious sound; / They trail behind her up the floor, / And trundle after through the door.* — Robert Louis Stevenson, *A Child's Garden of Verses*
▷ **curiously** *ADVERB* in a curious way

curl *NOUN* (**curls**)
a curve or coil, especially of hair

curl *VERB* (**curls**, **curling**, **curled**)
to curl is to form into curls
to curl up is to sit or lie with your knees drawn up

curly *ADJECTIVE* (**curlier**, **curliest**)
full of curls

currant *NOUN* (**currants**)
1 a small black fruit made from dried grapes **2** a small juicy berry, or the bush that produces it

> SPELLING
> Take care not to confuse **currant** with **current**, which means a flow.

currency *NOUN* (**currencies**)
money that is in use in a place • *You can pay with Russian currency.*

current *NOUN* (**currents**)
a flow of water, air, or electricity

> SPELLING
> Take care not to confuse **current** with **currant**, which means a dried fruit or a juicy berry.

current *ADJECTIVE*
happening or used now
▷ **currently** *ADVERB* now, at the moment • *The admission charge is currently $7.*

curriculum *NOUN* (**curriculums** or **curricula**)
a course of study

curry[1] *NOUN* (**curries**)
food cooked with spices that make it taste hot

curry[2] *VERB* (**curries**, **currying**, **curried**)
to curry a horse is to groom it
to curry favour is to try to win favour or approval

curse *NOUN* (**curses**)
1 a call or prayer for someone to be harmed or killed **2** something very unpleasant **3** an angry word or words

curse *VERB* (**curses**, **cursing**, **cursed**)
to curse someone is to use a curse against them

cursor *NOUN* (**cursors**)
a movable flashing signal on a VDU screen, showing where new data will go

curtain *NOUN* (**curtains**)
a piece of material hung at a window or door, or at the front of a stage

curtsy *NOUN* (**curtsies**)
a bow made by bending the knees, done by women as a mark of respect

curtsy *VERB* (**curtsies**, **curtsying**, **curtsied**)
to curtsy is to make a curtsy

curvature *NOUN* (**curvatures**)
a curving or bending, especially of the earth's horizon

curve *NOUN* (**curves**)
a line that bends smoothly

curve *VERB* (**curves**, **curving**, **curved**)
to curve is to bend smoothly

cushion *NOUN* (**cushions**)
a fabric cover filled with soft material so that it is comfortable to sit on or rest against

cushion *VERB* (**cushions**, **cushioning**, **cushioned**)
to cushion someone is to protect them from harm • *When he fell down the stairs, the rug at the bottom cushioned his fall.*

custard *NOUN*
a sweet yellow sauce eaten with puddings

custom *NOUN* (**customs**)
1 the usual way of doing things • *It is the custom to go on holiday in the summer.* **2** regular business from customers • *That rude man at the corner shop won't get my custom any more.*
customs are the group of officials at a port or airport to whom people coming into a country declare what goods they have with them

customary *ADJECTIVE*
something that is customary is usually done or done according to a custom

customer *NOUN* (**customers**)
someone who uses a shop, bank, or business

customize *NOUN* (**customizes**, **customizing**, **customized**)
to customize something is to alter it for a special use

cut *VERB* (**cuts**, **cutting**, **cut**)
1 to cut something is to divide it or make a slit in it with a knife or scissors **2** to cut something like prices or taxes is to reduce them **3** to cut a pack of playing cards is to divide it **4** to cut a corner is to go across it rather than round it **5** to cut a meeting or lesson is to stay away from it **6** a baby cuts a tooth when it has a new tooth coming
to cut and paste is to remove text on a computer screen from one place and put it in another place
to cut someone off is to interrupt them • *She cut me off before I could finish my sentence*
to cut something out (*informal*) is to stop doing it • *Cut out the talking!*

cut *NOUN* (**cuts**)
1 an act of cutting; the result of cutting • *Your hair could do with a cut* **2** a small wound caused by something sharp **3** (*informal*) a share • *I want a cut of the profits*

cut and dried *ADJECTIVE*
already organized or decided • *By the time we arrived the plans were all cut and dried.*

cute *ADJECTIVE* (**cuter**, **cutest**)
(*informal*) attractive in a quaint or simple way

cutlass *NOUN* (**cutlasses**)
a short sword with a wide curved blade

cutlery *NOUN*
knives, forks, and spoons used for eating

cutlet *NOUN* (**cutlets**)
a thick slice of meat still on the bone

cut-out *NOUN* (**cut-outs**)
something cut out of paper or cardboard

cut-price *ADJECTIVE*
sold at a reduced price

cutter *NOUN* (**cutters**)
a sailing ship with one mast

cutting *NOUN* (**cuttings**)
1 something cut from a newspaper or magazine **2** a piece cut off a plant to grow as a new plant **3** a deep passage cut through high ground for a railway or road

cycle *NOUN* (**cycles**)
1 a bicycle **2** a series of events that are regularly repeated • *Rainfall is part of the water cycle.*

cycle *VERB* (**cycles**, **cycling**, **cycled**)
to cycle is to ride a bicycle
▷ **cyclist** *NOUN* someone who rides a bicycle

cyclone *NOUN* (**cyclones**)
a strong wind rotating round a calm central area
▷ **cyclonic** *ADJECTIVE* like a cyclone

cygnet *NOUN* (**cygnets**) (*say* **sig-** nit)
a young swan

cylinder *NOUN* (**cylinders**)
1 an object with straight sides and circular ends **2** part of an engine in which a piston moves

cylindrical *ADJECTIVE*
shaped like a cylinder

cymbal *NOUN* (**cymbals**)
a cymbal is a round, slightly hollowed metal plate that you hit to make a ringing sound in music

cynic *NOUN* (**cynics**) (*say* sin- ik)
someone who doubts that anything is good or worthwhile

> **WORD FAMILY**
> A **cynical** person believes that nothing is good or valuable; **cynicism** is being cynical and doubting that anything can be good or valuable.

cypress *NOUN* (**cypresses**)
an evergreen tree with dark leaves

Dd

dab *NOUN* (**dabs**)
a gentle touch with something soft

dab *VERB* (**dabs, dabbing, dabbed**)
to dab something is to touch it gently with something soft • *I dabbed my eyes with a handkerchief.*

dabble *VERB* (**dabbles, dabbling, dabbled**)
1 to dabble something is to splash it about in water **2** to dabble in something is to do it as a hobby or not very seriously • *She likes to dabble in photography.*

dachshund *NOUN* (**dachshunds**) (*say* daks- huund or daks- huunt)
a small dog with a long body and short legs

dad *NOUN* (**dads**)
(*informal*) father

daddy *NOUN* (**daddies**)
(*informal*) father

daddy-long-legs *NOUN* (**daddy-long-legs**)
a crane-fly

daffodil *NOUN* (**daffodils**)
a yellow flower that grows from a bulb

daft *ADJECTIVE* (**dafter, daftest**)
silly or stupid

dagger *NOUN* (**daggers**)
a pointed knife with two sharp edges, used as a weapon

dahlia *NOUN* (**dahlias**) (*say* day- li- a)
a garden plant with brightly-coloured flowers

daily *ADJECTIVE & ADVERB*
something that happens daily happens every day

dainty *ADJECTIVE* (**daintier, daintiest**)
small and delicate

> **WORD FAMILY**
> You do something **daintily** when you do it in a dainty way; **daintiness** is being dainty.

dairy *NOUN* (**dairies**)
a place where milk, butter, cream, and cheese are made or sold

dairy *ADJECTIVE*
dairy products are made with or contain milk

daisy *NOUN* (**daisies**)
a small flower with white petals and a yellow centre

dale *NOUN* (**dales**)
a valley

Dalmatian *NOUN* (**Dalmatians**)
a large dog that is white with black or brown spots

dam *NOUN* (**dams**)
a wall built across a river to hold the water back

dam *VERB* (**dams, damming, dammed**)
to dam a river is to build a dam across it

damage *VERB* (**damages, damaging, damaged**)
to damage something is to injure or harm it

damage *NOUN*
damage is injury or harm • *The storm caused a lot of damage.*

damages *PLURAL NOUN*
damages are money paid to someone to make up for an injury or loss

Dame *NOUN* (**Dames**)
the title of a lady who has been given the equivalent of a knighthood

dame *NOUN* (**dames**)
a comic middle-aged woman in a pantomime, usually played by a man

damn *VERB* (**damns, damning, damned**)
to damn something is to say it is bad or wrong

damned *ADJECTIVE*
(*informal*) hateful or annoying

damp *ADJECTIVE* (**damper, dampest**)
slightly wet; not quite dry

damp *NOUN*
damp or the damp is wetness in the air or on something

dampen *VERB* (**dampens, dampening, dampened**)
1 to dampen something is to make it damp **2** to dampen sound or noise is to make it softer

damson *NOUN* (**damsons**)
a small purple plum

dance *VERB* (**dances, dancing, danced**)
to dance is to move about in time to music

dance *NOUN* (**dances**)
1 a piece of music or set of movements for dancing **2** a party or gathering where people dance

> **WORD FAMILY**
> A **dancer** is someone who dances.

dandelion *NOUN* (**dandelions**)
a yellow wild flower with jagged leaves

dandruff *NOUN*
dandruff is small white flakes of dead skin in a person's hair

danger *NOUN* (**dangers**)
something that is dangerous

dangerous *ADJECTIVE*
likely to harm you

dangle *VERB* (**dangles, dangling, dangled**)
to dangle is to swing or hang down loosely

dappled *ADJECTIVE*
marked with patches of different colours • *She was a strong, well-made animal, of a bright dun colour, beautifully dappled, and with a dark-brown mane and tail.*
— Anna Sewell, *Black Beauty*

dare *VERB* (**dares, daring, dared**)
1 to dare to do something is to be brave or bold enough to do it **2** to dare someone to do something is to challenge them to do it • *I dare you to climb that tree.*

dare *NOUN* (**dares**)
(*informal*) a challenge to do something risky

daredevil *NOUN* (**daredevils**)
a person who enjoys doing dangerous things

daring *ADJECTIVE*
bold or brave

dark *ADJECTIVE* (**darker, darkest**)
1 with little or no light **2** deep and rich in colour • *She wore a dark green coat.*

dark *NOUN*
1 dark or the dark is when there is no light • *Cats can see in the dark.* **2** dark is also the time when it becomes dark just after sunset • *Be home before dark.*

> WORD FAMILY
> **Darkness** is when there is no light.

darken *VERB* (**darkens, darkening, darkened**)
1 to darken something is to make it dark **2** to darken is to become dark • *The sky suddenly darkened.*

darkroom *NOUN* (**darkrooms**)
a room kept dark for developing and printing photographs

darling *NOUN* (**darlings**)
someone who is loved very much

darn *VERB* (**darns, darning, darned**)
to darn a hole is to mend it by sewing across it

dart *NOUN* (**darts**)
an object with a sharp point that you throw at a dartboard in the game of **darts**

dartboard *NOUN* (**dartboards**)
a round target at which you throw darts

dash *NOUN* (**dashes**)
1 a quick rush or a hurry • *They made a dash for the door.* **2** a dash of something is a small amount of it **3** a short line (–) used in writing or printing

> DASH
> You can use a single dash to add a comment or explanation to what you have just written: *She hopes to win a medal at the Olympics one day – and perhaps she will.* You can use a pair of dashes to mark off words that don't belong to the main part of the sentence: *Ben – my dog – was waiting for me by the door.* Using a pair of dashes is a bit like using a pair of brackets or a pair of commas, but you should only use dashes in informal writing, such as letters to friends and emails.

dash *VERB* (**dashes, dashing, dashed**)
1 to dash somewhere is to rush there **2** to dash something is to hurl it and smash it • *In her anger she dashed the cup against the wall.*

dashboard *NOUN* (**dashboards**)
a panel with dials and controls in front of the driver of a car

data *PLURAL NOUN* (*say* **day**- ta)
data is pieces of information

> GRAMMAR
> Strictly speaking, **data** is a plural noun, but it is often used as if it were singular, so you can say *Here is the data* or *Here are the data.*

database *NOUN* (**databases**)
a store of information held in a computer

date[1] *NOUN* (**dates**)
1 the day of the month, or the year, when something happens or happened **2** an appointment to go out with someone

date *VERB* (**dates, dating, dated**)
1 to date something that happened is to give it a date **2** to date from a time is to have existed from then • *The church dates from the 15th century.* **3** to date is also to seem old-fashioned • *Some fashions date very quickly.*

date[2] *NOUN* (**dates**)
a sweet brown fruit that grows on a palm tree

daughter *NOUN* (**daughters**)
a girl or woman who is someone's child

dawdle *VERB* (**dawdles, dawdling, dawdled**)
to dawdle is to walk or do something too slowly

dawn *NOUN* (**dawns**)
the time of the day when the sun rises

dawn *VERB* (**dawns, dawning, dawned**)
1 to dawn is to begin to become light in the morning **2** something dawns on you when you begin to realize it

day *NOUN* (**days**)
1 the 24 hours between midnight and the next midnight **2** the light part of the day **3** a period in time • *Write about what it was like in Queen Victoria's day.*

a b c **d** e f g h i j k l m n o p q r s t u v w x y z

daybreak *NOUN*
the first light of day; dawn

daydream *VERB* (**daydreams**, **daydreaming**, **daydreamed**)
to daydream is to have pleasant thoughts about things you would like to happen

daylight *NOUN*
1 the light of day **2** dawn • *They left before daylight.*

day-to-day *ADJECTIVE*
ordinary; happening every day

daze *NOUN*
to be in a daze is to be unable to think or see clearly

dazed *ADJECTIVE*
someone is dazed when they can't think or see clearly

dazzle *VERB* (**dazzles**, **dazzling**, **dazzled**)
a light dazzles you when it shines so brightly in your eyes that you are blinded for a moment

dead *ADJECTIVE*
1 no longer alive **2** no longer working or active • *The phone went dead.* **3** a dead place is not at all lively • *This town is dead at the weekend.* **4** complete, sure • *It was a dead loss.*

deaden *VERB* (**deadens**, **deadening**, **deadened**)
to deaden pain or noise is to make it weaker

dead end *NOUN* (**dead ends**)
a road or passage that is closed at one end

dead heat *NOUN* (**dead heats**)
a race in which two or more winners finish exactly together

deadline *NOUN* (**deadlines**)
the time by which you must finish doing something

deadlock *NOUN*
a situation in which people cannot agree or settle an argument

deadly *ADJECTIVE* (**deadlier**, **deadliest**)
likely to kill • *The liquid in the glass was a deadly poison.*

deaf *ADJECTIVE* (**deafer**, **deafest**)
unable to hear

> WORD FAMILY
> **Deafness** is being deaf.

deafen *VERB* (**deafens**, **deafening**, **deafened**)
to be deafening is to be very loud • *The noise from the party upstairs was deafening.*

deal *VERB* (**deals**, **dealing**, **dealt**)
1 to deal something is to hand it out **2** to deal in something is to buy and sell it • *He deals in scrap metal.* **3** to deal playing cards is to give them to players in a card game
to deal with someone or **something** is to spend time sorting them out • *I'll deal with you later.*
to deal with something is to be concerned with it • *This book deals with cacti.*

deal *NOUN* (**deals**)
1 an agreement or bargain **2** someone's turn to give out playing cards • *Whose deal is it?*
a good deal or **a great deal** a large amount

dealer *NOUN* (**dealers**)
1 someone who buys and sells things **2** the person dealing at cards

dean *NOUN* (**deans**)
1 an important member of the clergy in a cathedral or large church **2** the head of part of a college or university

dear *ADJECTIVE* (**dearer**, **dearest**)
1 loved very much **2** you use dear as the usual way of beginning a letter • *Dear Mary* **3** expensive

death *NOUN* (**deaths**)
dying; the end of life

deathly *ADJECTIVE*
like death; very quiet or spooky

debatable *ADJECTIVE*
something is debatable when it is not certain and can be argued about

debate *NOUN* (**debates**)
a formal discussion about a subject

debate *VERB* (**debates**, **debating**, **debated**)
to debate is to discuss or argue about something

debris *NOUN* (*say* **deb**- ree)
debris is scattered pieces that are left after something has been destroyed

debt *NOUN* (**debts**) (*say* det)
something that someone owes
to be in debt is to owe money

debtor *NOUN* (**debtors**) (*say* **det**- er)
someone who owes money

debug *VERB* (**debugs**, **debugging**, **debugged**) (*informal*)
1 to debug a computer program is to remove faults from it **2** to debug a room is to remove listening devices from it

début *NOUN* (**débuts**) (*say* **day**- bew or **day**- boo)
someone's first public appearance as a performer

decade *NOUN* (**decades**)
a period of ten years

decant *VERB* (**decants**, **decanting**, **decanted**)
to decant a liquid is to pour it gently from one container into another without disturbing any solid matter that was in the first container

decathlon *NOUN* (**decathlons**) (*say* dek- **ath**- lon)
an athletics competition in which you take part in ten different events

decay *VERB* (**decays**, **decaying**, **decayed**)
to decay is to rot or go bad

decay *NOUN*
decay is going bad or rotting

deceased *ADJECTIVE* (*say* di- **seest**)
a formal word for dead

deceit *NOUN* (*say* di- **seet**)
deceit is telling lies or doing something dishonest

> WORD FAMILY
> Someone who is **deceitful** tells lies or does something dishonest; doing things **deceitfully** is doing them in a deceitful way.

deceive *VERB* (**deceives**, **deceiving**, **deceived**) (*say* di- **seev**)
to deceive someone is to make them believe something that is not true

December *NOUN*
the last month of the year

decent *ADJECTIVE*
1 respectable and honest **2** of good enough quality • *Was it a decent film?*

> WORD FAMILY
> **Decency** is respectable and honest behaviour; behaving **decently** is behaving in a respectable and honest way.

deception *NOUN* (**deceptions**)
1 deception is making someone believe something that is not true **2** a deception is a trick or a lie

deceptive *ADJECTIVE*
not what it seems to be • *The sunshine was deceptive and the wind made it very cold.*

decibel *NOUN* (**decibels**)
a unit for measuring how loud a sound is

decide *VERB* (**decides**, **deciding**, **decided**)
1 to decide something is to make up your mind about it or make a choice **2** to decide a contest or argument is to settle it

> WORD FAMILY
> Something is a **decided** advantage when it is a definite and clear advantage; **decidedly** means very much • *She was looking decidedly worried.*

deciduous *ADJECTIVE*
a deciduous tree loses its leaves in autumn

decimal *ADJECTIVE*
a decimal system uses tens or tenths to count things

decimal *NOUN* (**decimals**)
a decimal fraction

decimal fraction *NOUN* (**decimal fractions**)
a fraction with tenths shown as numbers after a dot ($\frac{1}{3}$ is 0.3; 1$\frac{1}{2}$ is 1.5)

decimalize *VERB* (**decimalizes**, **decimalizing**, **decimalized**)
to decimalize measurements or currency is to change them to a decimal system
▷ **decimalization** *NOUN* changing to a decimal system

decimal point *NOUN* (**decimal points**)
the dot in a decimal fraction

decipher *VERB* (**deciphers**, **deciphering**, **deciphered**) (*say* di- **sy**- fer)
to decipher writing is to work out what it means when it is in code or difficult to read

decision *NOUN* (**decisions**)
a decision is what someone has decided

decisive *ADJECTIVE*
1 ending or deciding something important • *The decisive battle of the war was fought here.* **2** a decisive person decides things quickly and firmly

> WORD FAMILY
> To do something **decisively** is to do it quickly and firmly.

deck *NOUN* (**decks**)
1 a floor on a ship or bus **2** the part of a record player where the record is put for playing

deckchair *NOUN* (**deckchairs**)
a folding chair with a seat of canvas or plastic material

declaration *NOUN* (**declarations**)
an official or public statement

declare *VERB* (**declares**, **declaring**, **declared**)
1 to declare something is to say it clearly and openly **2** a cricket team declares when it ends its innings before all the batsmen are out
to declare war is to announce a state of war with another country

decline *VERB* (**declines**, **declining**, **declined**)
1 to decline is to become weaker or smaller **2** to decline an offer is to refuse it politely **3** to decline a noun or adjective is to give its grammatical forms

decode *VERB* (**decodes**, **decoding**, **decoded**)
to decode something written in code is to work out its meaning

decompose *VERB* (**decomposes**, **decomposing**, **decomposed**)
to decompose is to decay or rot
▷ **decomposition** *NOUN* when something decays or rots

decompression *NOUN*
decompression is when air pressure is reduced

decontamination *NOUN*
removing poisonous chemicals or radioactive material from a place

decorate *VERB* (**decorates**, **decorating**, **decorated**)
1 to decorate something is to make it look more beautiful or colourful **2** to decorate a room or building is to put fresh paint or paper on the walls **3** to decorate someone is to give them a medal for bravery

> WORD FAMILY
> Something **decorative** is made to look colourful and pretty.

a b c **d** e f g h i j k l m n o p q r s t u v w x y z

decoration *NOUN* (**decorations**)
1 decorations are the paint, wallpaper, and ornaments that make a place look more attractive **2** decoration is making something look more attractive or colourful **3** a decoration is a medal

decorator *NOUN* (**decorators**)
a person whose job is to paint rooms and buildings and to put up wallpaper

decoy *NOUN* (**decoys**) (*say* dee- koi or di- **koi**)
something used to tempt a person or animal into a trap

decrease *VERB* (**decreases**, **decreasing**, **decreased**) (*say* di- **kreess**)
1 to decrease something is to make it smaller or less **2** to decrease is to become smaller or less

decrease *NOUN* (**decreases**) (*say* **dee**- kreess)
the amount by which something decreases

decree *NOUN* (**decrees**)
an official order or decision

decree *VERB* (**decrees**, **decreeing**, **decreed**)
to decree something is to give an official order that it must happen

decrepit *ADJECTIVE* (*say* dik- **rep**- it)
old and weak

dedicate *VERB* (**dedicates**, **dedicating**, **dedicated**)
1 to dedicate yourself or your life to something is to spend all your time doing it • *She dedicated her life to nursing.* **2** to dedicate a book to someone is to name them at the beginning, as a sign of friendship or thanks

dedication *NOUN* (**dedications**)
1 dedication is hard work and effort **2** a dedication is a message at the beginning of a book in which you name someone as a sign of friendship or thanks

deduce *VERB* (**deduces**, **deducing**, **deduced**)
to deduce a fact or answer is to work it out from what you already know is true • *She deduced from my smile that I had won the prize.*

> USING THIS WORD
> Take care not to confuse **deduce** with **deduct**, which is the next word in this dictionary.

deduct *VERB* (**deducts**, **deducting**, **deducted**)
to deduct an amount is to subtract it from a total • *His Dad deducted 50 pence from his pocket money for breaking a window.*

deduction *NOUN* (**deductions**)
1 something that you work out by reasoning **2** an amount taken away from a total

deed *NOUN* (**deeds**)
1 something that someone has done **2** a legal document that shows who owns something

deep *ADJECTIVE* (**deeper**, **deepest**)
1 going down or back a long way from the top or front **2** measured from top to bottom or from front to back • *The hole was two metres deep.* **3** intense or strong • *The room was painted a deep blue.* **4** a deep voice is very low in pitch
▷ **deeply** *ADVERB* very, extremely • *She was deeply upset.*

> WORD FAMILY
> The noun from **deep** is **depth**. There is a noun **deepness**, but it is not often used now. You use the adverb **deeply** about people's feelings to mean 'very, extremely' • *They were deeply upset.*

deepen *VERB* (**deepens**, **deepening**, **deepened**)
to deepen is to become deeper • *The pool deepened to 2 metres half way along.*

deep-freeze *NOUN* (**deep-freezes**)
a freezer for food

deer *NOUN* (**deer**)
a fast-running, graceful animal. The male has antlers

deface *VERB* (**defaces**, **defacing**, **defaced**)
to deface something is to spoil its appearance by writing or drawing on it

default *NOUN* (**defaults**)
(*in computing*) what a computer does unless you give it another command

defeat *VERB* (**defeats**, **defeating**, **defeated**)
to defeat someone is to beat them in a game or battle

defeat *NOUN* (**defeats**)
1 defeat is losing a game or battle **2** a defeat is a lost game or battle

defecate *VERB* (**defecates**, **defecating**, **defecated**)
to defecate is a formal word for getting rid of faeces from the body

defect *NOUN* (**defects**) (*say* **dee**- fekt)
a flaw or weakness

defect *VERB* (**defects**, **defecting**, **defected**) (*say* di- **fekt**)
to defect is to desert a country or cause and join the other side

> WORD FAMILY
> **Defection** is when someone deserts a country or cause and joins the other side; a **defector** is a person who does this.

defective *ADJECTIVE*
something is faulty when it has flaws or faults or doesn't work properly

defence *NOUN* (**defences**)
1 something that protects you • *High walls were built around the city as a defence against enemy attacks.* **2** protecting yourself or a place from an attack or from criticism • *In her defence, she thought she was acting for the best.* **3** the players whose job is to stop the other team scoring in football and other games
▷ **defenceless** *ADJECTIVE* someone who is defenceless can't protect themselves

defend *VERB* (**defends**, **defending**, **defended**)
1 to defend someone or something is to protect them from an attack **2** to defend an idea, belief, or person is to argue in support of them **3** to defend an accused person is to try to prove that they are innocent
▷ **defender** *NOUN* someone who defends something

defendant *NOUN* (**defendants**)
a person accused of something in a lawcourt

defensive *ADJECTIVE*
1 used to defend something • *We need to take defensive measures.* **2** a defensive person is anxious about being criticized

defer *VERB* (**defers**, **deferring**, **deferred**)
to defer something is to put it off until later • *She deferred her departure until Saturday.*

defiant *ADJECTIVE*
openly showing that you refuse to obey someone

> WORD FAMILY
> **Defiance** is openly showing that you refuse to obey someone; to do something **defiantly** is to do it in a way that shows this.

deficiency *NOUN* (**deficiencies**)
a lack or shortage
▷ **deficient** *ADJECTIVE* to be deficient in something is not to have enough of it

deficit *NOUN* (**deficits**) (*say* def- i- sit)
the amount by which a sum of money is too small

defile *VERB* (**defiles**, **defiling**, **defiled**)
to defile something is to make it dirty or impure

define *VERB* (**defines**, **defining**, **defined**)
1 to define a word is to explain what it means **2** to define an idea or problem is to show exactly what it is

definite *ADJECTIVE*
fixed or certain • *Is it definite that we are going to move?*

definite article *NOUN* (**definite articles**)
the word **the**

definitely *ADVERB & INTERJECTION*
certainly, without doubt • *We are definitely going to the party.*

definition *NOUN* (**definitions**)
an explanation of what a word means

deflate *VERB* (**deflates**, **deflating**, **deflated**)
1 to deflate a tyre or balloon is to let air out of it **2** to deflate someone is to make them feel less confident or proud

deflect *VERB* (**deflects**, **deflecting**, **deflected**)
to deflect something that is moving is to make it go in a different direction
▷ **deflection** *NOUN* a deflection is a sudden change in direction of something that is moving

deforestation *NOUN*
the cutting down of a large number of trees in an area

deformed *ADJECTIVE*
not properly shaped
▷ **deformity** *NOUN* a deformity is a part of someone's body that is deformed

defrost *VERB* (**defrosts**, **defrosting**, **defrosted**)
1 to defrost a refrigerator or freezer is to remove the ice from it **2** to defrost frozen food is to thaw it out

deft *ADJECTIVE* (**defter**, **deftest**)
skilful and quick • *Presently a mouse ran out of a pile of ropes, and with a deft pat of his paw Gobbolino killed it.* — Ursula Moray Williams, *Gobbolino the Witch's Cat*
▷ **deftly** *ADVERB* to do something deftly is to do it in a skilful and quick way

defuse *VERB* (**defuses**, **defusing**, **defused**)
1 to defuse a bomb is to remove its fuse so that it won't blow up **2** to defuse a situation is to make it less dangerous or tense

defy *VERB* (**defies**, **defying**, **defied**)
1 to defy someone is to refuse to obey them **2** to defy something is to prevent it happening • *The door defied all attempts to open it.* **3** to defy someone to do something is to challenge them • *I defy you to find anything cheaper.*

degenerate *VERB* (**degenerates**, **degenerating**, **degenerated**)
to degenerate is to become worse • *The game degenerated into a succession of fouls.*

degrade *VERB* (**degrades**, **degrading**, **degraded**)
to degrade someone is to humiliate them
▷ **degradation** *NOUN* degradation is humiliation or embarrassment

degree *NOUN* (**degrees**)
1 a unit for measuring temperature • *Water boils at 100 degrees centigrade, or 100°C.* **2** a unit for measuring angles • *There are 90 degrees (90°) in a right angle.* **3** the level or amount of something • *I agree with you to a large degree.* **4** an award to someone at a university or college who has successfully finished a course • *She has a degree in English.*

dehydrated *ADJECTIVE*
dried up, with all the water removed
▷ **dehydration** *NOUN* someone suffers from dehydration when they lose too much water from their body

de-ice *VERB* (**de-ices**, **de-icing**, **de-iced**)
to de-ice a windscreen is to remove ice from its surface
▷ **de-icer** *NOUN* a substance that de-ices

deity *NOUN* (**deities**) (*say* dee- i- ti or day- i- ti)
a god or goddess

dejected *ADJECTIVE*
sad or depressed
▷ **dejection** *NOUN* dejection is being sad or depressed

a b c **d** e f g h i j k l m n o p q r s t u v w x y z

delay *VERB* (**delays**, **delaying**, **delayed**)
1 to delay someone is to make them late **2** to delay something is to put it off until later **3** to delay is to wait before doing something

delay *NOUN* (**delays**)
1 delaying or waiting • *Do it without delay.* **2** the period you have to wait when something happens late • *There will be a delay of 20 minutes.*

delegate *VERB* (**delegates**, **delegating**, **delegated**) (*say* del- i- gayt)
to delegate someone is to choose them to do a job that you are responsible for

delegate *NOUN* (**delegates**) (*say* del- i- gat)
a person who represents other people at a meeting or conference
▷ **delegation** *NOUN* a delegation is a group of delegates

delete *VERB* (**deletes**, **deleting**, **deleted**)
to delete something is to cross it out or remove it
▷ **deletion** *NOUN* a deletion is something that has been crossed out or removed

deliberate *ADJECTIVE* (*say* di- lib- er- at)
1 done on purpose • *It was a deliberate lie.* **2** slow and careful • *He has a deliberate way of talking.*
▷ **deliberately** *ADVERB* to do something deliberately is to do it on purpose

deliberate *VERB* (**deliberates**, **deliberating**, **deliberated**) (*say* di- **lib**- er- ayt)
to deliberate is to think carefully about something
▷ **deliberation** *NOUN* deliberation is thinking carefully about something

delicacy *NOUN* (**delicacies**)
1 delicacy is being delicate **2** a delicacy is something small and tasty to eat

delicate *ADJECTIVE*
1 fine and graceful • *The cloth had delicate embroidery.* **2** fragile and easily damaged
3 becoming ill easily **4** a delicate situation needs great care
▷ **delicately** *ADVERB* to do something delicately is to do it in a delicate way

delicatessen *NOUN* (**delicatessens**)
a shop that sells cooked or prepared food such as meat and cheese

delicious *ADJECTIVE*
tasting or smelling very pleasant
▷ **deliciously** *ADVERB* in a delicious way • *a deliciously creamy sauce*

delight *VERB* (**delights**, **delighting**, **delighted**)
to delight someone is to please them a lot

delight *NOUN* (**delights**)
great pleasure

> **WORD FAMILY**
> Something is **delightful** when it gives great pleasure; **delightfully** means in a delightful way.

delinquent *NOUN* (**delinquents**)
a young person who breaks the law
▷ **delinquency** *NOUN* delinquency is criminal behaviour by young people

delirious *ADJECTIVE*
1 in a confused state of mind because you are ill or have a high fever **2** extremely excited or enthusiastic
▷ **deliriously** *ADVERB* in a delirious way

delirium *NOUN* (**deliriums**)
1 the confused state of mind of people who are ill or have a high fever **2** wild excitement

deliver *VERB* (**delivers**, **delivering**, **delivered**)
1 to deliver letters, milk, or newspapers is to take them to a house or office **2** to deliver a speech or lecture is to give it to an audience **3** to deliver a baby is to help with its birth

delivery *NOUN* (**deliveries**)
1 delivery is when letters or goods are taken to a house or office **2** a person's delivery is the way they give a speech or lecture **3** giving birth to a baby

delphinium *NOUN* (**delphiniums**)
a garden plant with tall spikes of flowers, usually blue

delta *NOUN* (**deltas**)
a triangular area at the mouth of a river where it spreads into branches

delude *VERB* (**deludes**, **deluding**, **deluded**)
to be deluded is to believe something that isn't true

deluge *NOUN* (**deluges**)
1 a large flood **2** a heavy fall of rain **3** something coming in great numbers • *After the speech there was a deluge of questions.*

deluge *VERB* (**deluges**, **deluging**, **deluged**)
to be deluged with something is to get a huge amount of it • *We have been deluged with replies.*

delusion *NOUN* (**delusions**)
a false belief

de luxe *ADJECTIVE*
of very high quality

demand *VERB* (**demands**, **demanding**, **demanded**)
to demand something is to ask for it forcefully

demand *NOUN* (**demands**)
1 a demand is a very firm request for something
2 demand is a desire to have something • *There's not much demand for ice cream at this time of year.*
to be in demand is to be wanted or popular

demanding *ADJECTIVE*
1 asking for many things • *Toddlers can be very demanding.* **2** needing a lot of time or effort • *She has a demanding job.*

demerara *NOUN* (*say* dem- er- air- a)
light-brown cane sugar

demist *VERB* (**demists**, **demisting**, **demisted**)
to demist a window or windscreen is to remove misty condensation from it

demo *NOUN* (**demos**)
(*informal*) a demonstration

democracy *NOUN* (**democracies**)
1 democracy is government by leaders elected by the people **2** a democracy is a country governed in this way

democrat *NOUN* (**democrats**)
a person who believes in or supports democracy
Democrat a supporter of the Democratic Party in the USA

democratic *ADJECTIVE*
a democratic idea or process is one that involves ordinary people and takes account of their views
▷ **democratically** *ADVERB* to do something democratically is to take account of ordinary people and their views

demolish *VERB* (**demolishes**, **demolishing**, **demolished**)
to demolish a building is to knock it down and break it up
▷ **demolition** *NOUN* the demolition of a building is when it is knocked down and broken up

demon *NOUN* (**demons**)
1 a devil or evil spirit **2** a fierce or forceful person

demonstrate *VERB* (**demonstrates**, **demonstrating**, **demonstrated**)
1 to demonstrate something is to show or prove it **2** to demonstrate is to take part in a demonstration

demonstration *NOUN* (**demonstrations**)
1 showing how to do or work something **2** a march or meeting to show everyone what you think about something • *There will be a demonstration against the new motorway.*

demonstrator *NOUN* (**demonstrators**)
1 someone who takes part in a demonstration or meeting **2** someone who demonstrates something

demoralize *VERB* (**demoralizes**, **demoralizing**, **demoralized**)
to demoralize someone is to make them lose confidence or courage

demote *VERB* (**demotes**, **demoting**, **demoted**)
to demote someone is to reduce them to a lower position or rank

den *NOUN* (**dens**)
1 the home of a wild animal • *a lion's den* **2** a place where something illegal happens • *a gambling den* **3** a hiding place, especially for children

denial *NOUN* (**denials**)
saying that something is not true

denim *NOUN*
strong cotton cloth, used to make jeans

denomination *NOUN* (**denominations**)
1 a religious group with a special name **2** a unit of money • *The purse contained coins and notes of various denominations*

denominator *NOUN* (**denominators**)
the number below the line in a fraction • *In $\frac{1}{4}$ the 4 is the denominator.*

denote *VERB* (**denotes**, **denoting**, **denoted**)
to denote something is to indicate or mean it • *In road signs, P denotes a car park.*

denounce *VERB* (**denounces**, **denouncing**, **denounced**)
to denounce someone or something is to speak strongly against them, or accuse them of something • *They denounced him as a spy.*
▷ **denunciation** *NOUN* denouncing someone or something

dense *ADJECTIVE* (**denser**, **densest**)
1 thick • *The fog was getting very dense.* **2** packed close together • *They walked through a dense forest.* **3** (*informal*) stupid
▷ **densely** *ADVERB* thickly, close together • *a densely populated area*

density *NOUN* (**densities**)
1 how thick or tightly packed something is **2** (*in science*) the proportion of mass to volume • *Water has greater density than air.*

dent *NOUN* (**dents**)
a hollow made in a surface by hitting it or pressing it

dent *VERB* (**dents**, **denting**, **dented**)
to dent something is to make a dent in it

dental *ADJECTIVE*
to do with the teeth or dentistry

dentist *NOUN* (**dentists**)
a person who is trained to treat teeth, fill them or take them out, and fit false ones

> WORD FAMILY
> **Dentistry** is the work of a dentist.

denture *NOUN* (**dentures**)
a set of false teeth

deny *VERB* (**denies**, **denying**, **denied**)
1 to deny something is to say that it is not true **2** to deny a request is to refuse it

deodorant *NOUN* (**deodorants**)
a powder or liquid that removes unpleasant smells

depart *VERB* (**departs**, **departing**, **departed**)
to depart is to go away or leave
▷ **departure** *NOUN* a departure is when someone or something leaves a place

department *NOUN* (**departments**)
one part of a large organization or shop

department store *NOUN* (**department stores**)
a large shop that sells many different kinds of goods

depend *VERB* (**depends**, **depending**, **depended**)
to depend on someone or **something** is to rely on them • *We depend on you for help.*
to depend on something is to be decided or controlled by it • *Whether we can have a picnic depends on the weather.*

dependable *ADJECTIVE*
that you can depend on; reliable

dependant *NOUN* (**dependants**)
a person who depends on someone else, especially for money • *She has two dependants, a son and a daughter.*

> **SPELLING**
> Notice that the spelling of the noun ends in *-ant* but the spelling of the adjective ends in *-ent*.

dependent *ADJECTIVE*
depending or relying on someone • *He was dependent on his father.* • *She has two dependent children.*
▷ **dependence** *NOUN* dependence is being dependent on someone

depict *VERB* (**depicts**, **depicting**, **depicted**)
1 to depict something is to show it in a painting or drawing **2** to depict a scene is to describe it • *The story depicted a small village in Austria.*

deplorable *ADJECTIVE*
extremely bad; shocking • *Their rudeness was deplorable.*

deplore *VERB* (**deplores**, **deploring**, **deplored**)
to deplore something is to dislike it very much because it upsets or annoys you

deport *VERB* (**deports**, **deporting**, **deported**)
to deport someone is to send them out of a country
▷ **deportation** *NOUN* deportation is when someone is sent out of a country

deposit *NOUN* (**deposits**)
1 an amount of money you pay into a bank or building society **2** a sum of money paid as a first instalment **3** a layer of solid matter in or on the earth

deposit *VERB* (**deposits**, **depositing**, **deposited**)
1 to deposit something is to put it down somewhere **2** to deposit money is to pay it into a bank or building society

depot *NOUN* (**depots**) (*say* dep- oh)
1 a place where things are stored **2** a place where buses or trains are kept and repaired

depress *VERB* (**depresses**, **depressing**, **depressed**)
to depress someone is to make them very sad

depressed *ADJECTIVE*
someone who is depressed feels very sad and without hope

depression *NOUN* (**depressions**)
1 a feeling of great sadness and hopelessness **2** a long period when there is less trade and business than usual and many people have no work **3** a shallow hollow or dip in the ground **4** an area of low air pressure which may bring rain

deprive *VERB* (**deprives**, **depriving**, **deprived**)
to deprive someone of something is to take it away from them • *Prisoners are deprived of their freedom.*

deprived *ADJECTIVE*
without all the things you need to live a happy and comfortable life, like enough food and good housing

depth *NOUN* (**depths**)
how deep something is • *What is the depth of the river here?*
in depth thoroughly
out of your depth 1 in water that is too deep to stand in **2** trying to do something that is too difficult for you

deputize *VERB* (**deputizes**, **deputizing**, **deputized**)
to deputize for someone is to act as their deputy

deputy *NOUN* (**deputies**)
a person who acts as a substitute or chief assistant for someone and does that person's job when they are away

derail *VERB* (**derails**, **derailing**, **derailed**)
a train is derailed when something causes it to leave the track

derby *NOUN* (**derbies**)
a sports match between two teams from the same city or area

derelict *ADJECTIVE* (*say* de- re- likt)
abandoned and left to fall into ruin • *The factory is now completely derelict.*

deride *VERB* (**derides**, **deriding**, **derided**)
to deride someone or something is to treat them with scorn • *He was derided for his beliefs.*

derision *NOUN*
scorn or ridicule • *They treated him with derision.*

derivation *NOUN* (**derivations**)
where a word comes from

> **DERIVATIONS**
> The words we use today come from many other languages, some of which, like Latin, no longer exist. A lot of English words come from an old form of English called Anglo-Saxon, for example *eat*, *drink*, and *house*. Others, especially since 1066, have come from Latin and French words, for example *face* and *table*, and longer more technical words such as *emission* and *receive*. *Egg*, *window*, and some other words, come from the language of the Vikings, called Old Norse. More recently, we have words from Dutch (*yacht*), Finnish (*sauna*), Indian languages (*bungalow*), Persian (*kiosk*), and many others.

derive *VERB* (**derives**, **deriving**, **derived**)
to get something from another person or thing • *She derived a lot of pleasure from music.* • *Many English words are derived from Latin.*

derrick *NOUN* (**derricks**)
1 a kind of large crane for lifting things **2** a tall framework that holds the machinery used for drilling an oil well

derv *NOUN*
diesel fuel for heavy vehicles

descant *NOUN* (**descants**)
a tune sung or played above another tune

descend *VERB* (**descends**, **descending**, **descended**)
to descend something like a hill or staircase is to go down it
to be descended from someone is to be in the same family as them but living at a later time

descendant *NOUN* (**descendants**)
a person's descendants are the people who are descended from them

descent *NOUN* (**descents**)
a descent is a climb down, usually a hard or long one

describe *VERB* (**describes**, **describing**, **described**)
to describe something or someone is to say what they are like

description *NOUN* (**descriptions**)
1 description is saying what someone or something is like • *She's a writer who's very good at description.* **2** a description is something you write or say that describes what someone or something is like • *He gave the police a description of the robbers.*
▷ **descriptive** *ADJECTIVE* a descriptive word or piece of writing describes someone or something • *a descriptive poem*

desert *NOUN* (**deserts**) (*say* **dez**- ert)
a large area of very dry, often sandy, land

desert *VERB* (**deserts**, **deserting**, **deserted**) (*say* di- **zert**)
to desert someone or something is to leave them without intending to return
▷ **desertion** *NOUN* desertion is when a soldier runs away from the army

> SPELLING
> Take care not to confuse **desert** with **dessert**, which means food eaten at the end of a meal.

deserted *ADJECTIVE*
a place is deserted when there is nobody there

deserter *NOUN* (**deserters**)
a soldier who runs away from the army

desert island *NOUN* (**desert islands**)
a tropical island where nobody lives

deserts *PLURAL NOUN* (*say* di- **zerts**)
someone's deserts are what they deserve • *He got his deserts.*

deserve *VERB* (**deserves**, **deserving**, **deserved**)
to deserve something is to be worthy of it or to have a right to it
▷ **deservedly** *ADVERB* rightly, because it is deserved • *This restaurant is deservedly popular.*

design *NOUN* (**designs**)
1 the way that something is made or arranged **2** a drawing that shows how something is to be made **3** lines and shapes forming a pattern

design *VERB* (**designs**, **designing**, **designed**)
to design something is to make a design or plan for it
▷ **designer** *NOUN* someone who designs things, especially clothes

designate *VERB* (**designates**, **designating**, **designated**)
to designate something is to choose it to be used for a special purpose • *The meadow was designated a picnic area.*

desirable *ADJECTIVE*
worth having or doing • *It is desirable for you to come with us.*
▷ **desirability** *NOUN* the desirability of something is the fact that it is worth having or doing

desire *VERB* (**desires**, **desiring**, **desired**)
to desire something is to want it very much

desire *NOUN* (**desires**)
a feeling of wanting something very much

desk *NOUN* (**desks**)
1 a piece of furniture with a flat top and drawers, used for writing, reading, or working at **2** a counter at which a cashier or receptionist sits

desktop *ADJECTIVE*
small enough to use on a desk • *I've bought a desktop computer.*

desolate *ADJECTIVE*
1 lonely and sad **2** a desolate place is empty, with no people living there • *They had come to the edge of a clearing in the wood, a desolate place like a quarry strewn with boulders, with stagnant pools of water between the rocks.* — Elizabeth Goudge, *The Little White Horse*
▷ **desolation** *NOUN* feeling desolate

despair *NOUN*
despair is a complete loss of hope

despair *VERB* (**despairs**, **despairing**, **despaired**)
to despair is to lose hope completely

despatch *NOUN* (**despatches**) and *VERB* (**despatches**, **despatching**, **despatched**)
a different spelling of *dispatch*

desperate *ADJECTIVE*
1 extremely serious or hopeless • *We were in a desperate situation.* **2** ready to do anything to get out of a difficulty • *There are three desperate criminals at large.* **3** needing or wanting something very much • *She was desperate to go home.*
▷ **desperately** *ADVERB* seriously; recklessly
▷ **desperation** *NOUN* desperation is being desperate

despicable *ADJECTIVE*
very unpleasant or evil

despise *VERB* (**despises**, **despising**, **despised**)
to despise someone is to hate them and have no respect at all for them

despite *PREPOSITION*
in spite of • *They went out despite the rain.*

a b c d e f g h i j k l m n o p q r s t u v w x y z

dessert *NOUN* (**desserts**) (*say* di-zert)
fruit or a sweet food eaten at the end of a meal

> SPELLING
> Take care not to confuse **dessert** with **desert**, which means an area of very dry land.

dessertspoon *NOUN* (**dessertspoons**)
a medium-sized spoon used for eating puddings

destination *NOUN* (**destinations**)
the place you are travelling to

destined *ADJECTIVE*
intended by fate; meant to happen •*They felt they were destined to win.*

destiny *NOUN* (**destinies**)
your destiny is what is intended for you in the future; your fate •*His destiny was to travel the world.*

destroy *VERB* (**destroys**, **destroying**, **destroyed**)
to destroy something is to ruin it or put an end to it

> WORD FAMILY
> **Destruction** is destroying something; something that is **destructive** causes a lot of damage.

destroyer *NOUN* (**destroyers**)
a fast warship

detach *VERB* (**detaches**, **detaching**, **detached**)
to detach something is to remove it or separate it •*Detach the coupon from the bottom of the page.*
▷ **detachable** *ADJECTIVE* something that is detachable can be detached

detached *ADJECTIVE*
1 able to stand back from a situation and not get emotionally involved in it •*I was just a detached observer.* **2** a detached house is one that is not joined to another house

detachment *NOUN* (**detachments**)
1 detachment is the ability to stand back from a situation and not get emotionally involved in it **2** a detachment is a special group of people, especially soldiers

detail *NOUN* (**details**)
1 a small piece of information **2** a small part of a design or picture or piece of decoration
in detail describing or dealing with everything fully

detain *VERB* (**detains**, **detaining**, **detained**)
1 to detain someone is to keep them in a place **2** to detain someone is also to keep them waiting •*I'll try not to detain you for long.*

detect *VERB* (**detects**, **detecting**, **detected**)
to detect something is to discover or notice it
▷ **detection** *NOUN* detection is detecting something
▷ **detector** *NOUN* a detector is a device that detects something

detective *NOUN* (**detectives**)
a person, especially a police officer, who investigates crimes

detention *NOUN* (**detentions**)
detention is when someone is made to stay in a place, especially made to stay late in school as a punishment

deter *VERB* (**deters**, **deterring**, **deterred**)
to deter someone is to put them off doing something

detergent *NOUN* (**detergents**)
a kind of washing powder or liquid

deteriorate *VERB* (**deteriorates**, **deteriorating**, **deteriorated**)
to deteriorate is to become worse •*The weather was starting to deteriorate.*
▷ **deterioration** *NOUN* deterioration is when something becomes worse

determination *NOUN*
a strong intention to achieve something, even though it is difficult

determine *VERB* (**determines**, **determining**, **determined**)
to determine something is to decide it or work it out •*The task was to determine the height of the mountain.*

determined *ADJECTIVE*
having your mind firmly made up

determiner *NOUN* (**determiners**)
(*in grammar*) a word (such as *a*, *the*, and *many*) that introduces a noun or noun phrase

> DETERMINERS
> Determiners are words that introduce nouns or noun phrases and give you some information about them. For example: *I saw **a** boy* – the word 'a' tells the reader that they don't yet know anything about this boy. *I saw **the** boy* – the word 'the' tells the reader that they already know about the boy. Other determiners include *this, that, all, every, my, your, one, two, three,* and so on.

deterrent *NOUN* (**deterrents**)
something that is meant to put people off doing something, such as a powerful weapon
▷ **deterrence** *NOUN* deterrence is being a deterrent

detest *VERB* (**detests**, **detesting**, **detested**)
to detest something is to dislike it very much •*I truly detested that Jamie. He was just the most annoying person in the whole world to have to sit next to.* — Jacqueline Wilson, *The Lottie Project*
▷ **detestable** *ADJECTIVE* horrid

detonate *VERB* (**detonates**, **detonating**, **detonated**)
to detonate a bomb is to make it explode
▷ **detonation** *NOUN* detonation is making a bomb explode
▷ **detonator** *NOUN* a device that makes a bomb explode

detour *NOUN* (**detours**)
a roundabout route you use instead of the normal route

deuce *NOUN*
a tennis score when each player has 40 points and needs two more points in a row to win the game

devastate *VERB* (**devastates**, **devastating**, **devastated**)
to devastate a place is to ruin or destroy it, making it impossible to live in
▷ **devastation** *NOUN* devastation is destruction of a place

devastated *ADJECTIVE*
someone is devastated when they are extremely shocked and upset

develop *VERB* (**develops**, **developing**, **developed**)
1 to develop something is to make it bigger or better **2** to develop is to become bigger or better **3** to develop land is to put up new buildings on it **4** to develop photographic film is to treat it with chemicals so that pictures appear on it

developing country *NOUN* (**developing countries**)
a poor country that is building up its industry and trying to improve its living conditions

development *NOUN* (**developments**)
1 a development is something interesting that has happened • *Have there been any further developments since I last saw you?* **2** development is putting up new buildings • *Extensive development has taken place around the village.*

device *NOUN* (**devices**)
a piece of equipment used for a particular purpose • *We need a device for opening tins.*
to leave someone to their own devices is to leave them alone to do as they wish and not tell them what to do

> SPELLING
> Take care not to confuse **device**, which is a noun, with **devise**, which is a verb meaning to invent or plan something.

devil *NOUN* (**devils**)
an evil spirit or person
▷ **devilish** *ADJECTIVE* cruel or wicked, like a devil

devious *ADJECTIVE*
1 using unfair and dishonest methods • *He got rich by devious means.* **2** not straight or direct • *The coach took us by a devious route to avoid the traffic jams.*

devise *VERB* (**devises**, **devising**, **devised**)
to devise a plan or idea is to think it up

devolution *NOUN*
handing over power from a central government to a local or regional government

devote *VERB* (**devotes**, **devoting**, **devoted**)
to devote yourself or your time to something is to spend all your time doing it • *They devote all their free time to sport.*

> WORD FAMILY
> A **devotee** is a person who is enthusiastic about something; **devotion** is great love or loyalty.

devoted *ADJECTIVE*
loving and loyal • *They are devoted parents.*

devour *VERB* (**devours**, **devouring**, **devoured**)
to devour something is to eat or swallow it greedily • *Latch and the beasts sat round the kitchen table drinking tea and devouring an overlooked packet of digestive biscuits.* — Debi Gliori, *Pure Dead Wicked*

devout *ADJECTIVE*
deeply religious

dew *NOUN*
tiny drops of water that form during the night on the ground and other surfaces out of doors
▷ **dewy** *ADJECTIVE* wet with dew or like dew

dhoti *NOUN* (**dhotis**) (*say* **doh**- ti)
a long piece of cloth worn by Hindu men around the lower part of their bodies

diabetes *NOUN* (*say* dy- a- **bee**- teez)
a disease in which there is too much sugar in a person's blood

> WORD FAMILY
> A **diabetic** is a person suffering from diabetes; you can also say that someone is **diabetic**.

diabolical *ADJECTIVE*
like a devil; very wicked

diagnose *VERB* (**diagnoses**, **diagnosing**, **diagnosed**)
to diagnose a disease is to find out what it is and what treatment is needed

diagnosis *NOUN* (**diagnoses**)
a doctor makes a diagnosis when they decide what disease someone has

diagonal *NOUN* (**diagonals**)
a straight line joining opposite corners
▷ **diagonally** *ADVERB* across from one corner to another

diagram *NOUN* (**diagrams**)
a drawing or picture that shows the parts of something or how it works

dial *NOUN* (**dials**)
a circular piece of plastic or card with numbers or letters round it

dial *VERB* (**dials**, **dialling**, **dialled**)
to dial a telephone number is to choose it by pressing numbered buttons

dialect *NOUN* (**dialects**)
the form of a language used by people in one area of the country but not in the rest of the country

dialogue *NOUN* (**dialogues**)
talk between people, especially in a play, film or book

diameter *NOUN* (**diameters**)
1 a line drawn from one side of a circle to the other, passing through the centre **2** the length of this line

diamond *NOUN* (**diamonds**)
1 a very hard jewel that looks like clear glass **2** a shape which has four equal sides but which is not a square **3** a playing card with red diamond shapes on it

diaphragm *NOUN* (**diaphragms**) (*say* dy- a- fram)
1 the muscular layer inside your body between your chest and your abdomen, used when you breathe **2** a thin sheet or membrane that keeps things apart

diarrhoea *NOUN* (*say* dy- a- **ree**- a)
an illness that makes you have to keep going to the toilet and the waste matter you empty from your bowels is very watery

diary *NOUN* (**diaries**)
a book with a separate space to write in for each day of the year, in which you write down what happens each day or to plan what you need to do in the future

dice *NOUN* (**dice**)
a small cube marked with one to six dots on each side, thrown to give a number in some games

> GRAMMAR
> **Dice** was once the plural of a word **die**, but nowadays it is used in the singular as well.

dictate *VERB* (**dictates**, **dictating**, **dictated**)
1 to dictate something is to speak or read it aloud for someone else to write down **2** to dictate to someone is to give them orders in a bossy way
▷ **dictation** *NOUN* dictation, or a dictation, is an exercise in writing down what someone reads out

dictator *NOUN* (**dictators**)
a ruler who has complete power over the people of a country

> WORD FAMILY
> Someone who is **dictatorial** is always telling people what to do and ignoring their views; a **dictatorship** is a country ruled by a dictator.

dictionary *NOUN* (**dictionaries**)
a book with words listed in alphabetical order, so that you can find out what a word means and how to spell it

did
past tense of **do**

diddle *VERB* (**diddles**, **diddling**, **diddled**)
(*informal*) to cheat someone • *We've been diddled! He's charged us $10 too much.*

didn't
short for *did not*

die *VERB* (**dies**, **dying**, **died**)
to die is to stop living
to die down is to gradually become less strong • *The wind died down at last.*
to die out is to gradually disappear • *The tiger is beginning to die out.*

diesel *NOUN* (**diesels**)
1 a diesel is an engine that works by burning oil in compressed air **2** diesel is fuel for this kind of engine

diet *NOUN* (**diets**)
1 a diet is special meals that someone eats to be healthy or to lose weight • *Mum's on a diet.*
2 someone's diet is the food they normally eat

diet *VERB* (**diets**, **dieting**, **dieted**)
to diet is to keep to a special diet, especially in order to lose weight

differ *VERB* (**differs**, **differing**, **differed**)
1 to differ from something is to be not the same as it **2** to differ is to disagree • *The two writers differ on this point.*

difference *NOUN* (**differences**)
1 the way in which something is different from something else **2** the amount between two numbers • *The difference between 8 and 3 is 5.*

different *ADJECTIVE*
one person or thing is different from another when they are not the same
▷ **differently** *ADVERB* in a different way

> GRAMMAR
> You can say **different from** or **different to**, although some people prefer **different from**.

differential *NOUN* (**differentials**)
1 a difference in wages between groups of workers **2** a system of gears that allows a vehicle's driving wheels to turn at slightly different speeds when going round corners

difficult *ADJECTIVE*
needing a lot of effort or skill; not easy

difficulty *NOUN* (**difficulties**)
1 difficulty is not being easy, trouble • *I had difficulty answering most of the questions.* **2** a difficulty is something that causes a problem • *She has learning difficulties.*

diffuse *VERB* (**diffuses**, **diffusing**, **diffused**)
to diffuse something is to spread it widely or thinly • *The building had diffused lighting.*
▷ **diffusion** *NOUN* diffusion is when something like light spreads widely or thinly

dig *VERB* (**digs**, **digging**, **dug**)
1 to dig soil or the ground is to break it up and move it **2** to dig a hole is to make it **3** to dig someone is to poke them • *He dug me in the ribs.*
▷ **digger** *NOUN* a machine for digging

dig *NOUN* (**digs**)
1 a place where archaeologists dig to look for ancient remains **2** a sharp thrust or poke • *She gave me a dig in the ribs with her elbow.* **3** an unpleasant remark • *What he said was clearly a dig at me.*

digest *VERB* (**digests**, **digesting**, **digested**)
to digest food is to soften and change it in the stomach and intestine so that the body can absorb it
▷ **digestible** *ADJECTIVE* easy to digest
▷ **digestion** *NOUN* the way your body digests food

digestive *ADJECTIVE*
to do with digesting food

digit *NOUN* (**digits**) (*say* **dij**- it)
1 any of the numbers from 0 to 9 **2** a finger or toe

digital *ADJECTIVE*
1 to do with or using digits **2** a digital clock or watch has a row of digits to indicate numbers (the opposite of *analogue*) **3** a digital computer or recording stores the data or sound as a series of binary digits

dignified *ADJECTIVE*
having dignity

dignity *NOUN*
a calm and serious manner

digraph *NOUN* (**digraphs**)
a combination of two letters that are used to represent one sound or phoneme, e.g. in the word *ship* the digraph *sh* represents one sound or phoneme

dike *NOUN* (**dikes**)
1 a long wall or embankment to hold back water and prevent flooding **2** a ditch for draining water from land

dilemma *NOUN* (**dilemmas**)
an awkward choice between two possible actions, either of which would cause difficulties

dilute *VERB* (**dilutes**, **diluting**, **diluted**)
to dilute a liquid is to make it weaker by mixing it with water
▷ **dilution** *NOUN* diluting a liquid

dim *ADJECTIVE* (**dimmer**, **dimmest**)
only faintly lit and difficult to see
▷ **dimly** *ADVERB* to see something dimly is to find it hard to see clearly

dim *VERB* (**dims**, **dimming**, **dimmed**)
a light dims when it becomes less bright • *As the curtain rose, the lights dimmed.*

dimension *NOUN* (**dimensions**)
1 a measurement such as length, width, area, or volume • *What are the dimensions of the box?* **2** size or extent

diminish *VERB* (**diminishes**, **diminishing**, **diminished**)
1 to diminish something is to make it smaller **2** to diminish is to become smaller

diminutive (*say* dim- **in**- yoo- tiv) *ADJECTIVE*
very small

diminutive *NOUN* (**diminutives**)
a word, name, or ending of a word that shows that something is small, e.g. the name *Tiny Tim* or the word *piglet*

dimple *NOUN* (**dimples**)
a small hollow on a person's cheek or chin

din *NOUN*
a loud noise

dine *VERB* (**dines**, **dining**, **dined**)
to dine is to have dinner
▷ **diner** *NOUN* someone eating a meal in a restaurant or hotel

dinghy *NOUN* (**dinghies**) (*say* **ding**- i)
a kind of small boat

dingy *ADJECTIVE* (**dingier**, **dingiest**) (*say* **din**- ji)
shabby and dirty-looking

dinner *NOUN* (**dinners**)
the main meal of the day, eaten either in the middle of the day or in the evening

dinosaur *NOUN* (**dinosaurs**)
a prehistoric reptile, often of enormous size

dioxide *NOUN* (**dioxides**)
an oxide with two atoms of oxygen and one atom of another element, as in carbon dioxide

dip *VERB* (**dips**, **dipping**, **dipped**)
1 to dip something is to put it into a liquid and then take it out again • *Dip the brush in the paint.* **2** to dip is to go or slope downwards • *The road dips steeply after the hill.* **3** to dip a vehicle's headlights is to lower the beam so that they do not dazzle other drivers

dip *NOUN* (**dips**)
1 dipping **2** a downward slope **3** a quick swim **4** a mixture into which things are dipped

diphtheria *NOUN* (*say* dif- **theer**- i- a)
a serious disease of the throat

diploma *NOUN* (**diplomas**)
a certificate awarded for skill in a particular subject

diplomacy *NOUN*
1 the business of keeping friendly with other nations **2** dealing with other people without upsetting or offending them

diplomatic *ADJECTIVE*
1 to do with diplomacy **2** tactful and courteous

> WORD FAMILY
> A **diplomat** is someone who works in diplomacy; to do something **diplomatically** is to do it in a tactful and courteous way.

dire *ADJECTIVE* (**direr**, **direst**)
dreadful or serious • *The refugees are in dire need of food and shelter.*

direct *ADJECTIVE*
1 as straight or quick as possible **2** frank and honest
▷ **directness** *NOUN* directness is being frank and honest

direct *VERB* (**directs**, **directing**, **directed**)
1 to direct someone is to show them the way **2** to direct a film or play is to decide how it should be made or performed

direct current *NOUN*
electric current flowing only in one direction

direction *NOUN* (**directions**)
1 a direction is the way you go to get somewhere
2 direction is directing something
directions information on how to use or do something or how to get somewhere

directly *ADVERB*
1 by a direct route • *Go directly to the shop.*
2 immediately • *I want you to come directly.*

direct object *NOUN* (**direct objects**)
the word that receives the action of the verb. In *she hit him*, the direct object is *him*.

director *NOUN* (**directors**)
1 a person who is in charge of something, especially one of a group of people managing a company **2** a person who decides how a film or play should be made or performed

directory *NOUN* (**directories**)
a book containing a list of people with their telephone numbers and addresses

direct speech *NOUN*
someone's words written down exactly in the way they were said

> DIRECT SPEECH
> Direct speech is when you show exactly what someone's words were. *'I want to go home,' said Josh.* Indirect speech or reported speech is when you just describe what someone said, without using their exact words. You don't use speech marks in indirect speech, only in direct speech. *Josh said that he wanted to go home.*

dirt *NOUN*
earth or soil; anything that is not clean

dirty *ADJECTIVE* (**dirtier**, **dirtiest**)
1 covered with dirt; not clean **2** rude or offensive • *Someone has written dirty words on the wall.*
3 unfair or mean • *That was a dirty trick.*
▷ **dirtily** *ADVERB* in a dirty way
▷ **dirtiness** *NOUN* being dirty

dis- *PREFIX*
1 showing the opposite of something, as in *dishonest* **2** showing that something has been taken away or apart, as in *disarm* or *dismantle*

disability *NOUN* (**disabilities**)
something that prevents someone from using their body in the usual way

disabled *ADJECTIVE*
having a disease or injury that makes it difficult for someone to use their body properly

disadvantage *NOUN* (**disadvantages**)
something that hinders you or makes things difficult

disagree *VERB* (**disagrees**, **disagreeing**, **disagreed**)
1 to disagree with someone is to have or express a different opinion from them **2** to disagree with someone is also to have a bad effect on them • *Rich food disagrees with me.*
▷ **disagreement** *NOUN* disagreement, or a disagreement, is when people don't agree about something or argue about it

disagreeable *ADJECTIVE*
unpleasant

disappear *VERB* (**disappears**, **disappearing**, **disappeared**)
1 to disappear is to become impossible to see; to vanish **2** to disappear is also to stop happening or existing • *Her nervousness soon disappeared.*
▷ **disappearance** *NOUN* a person's or thing's disappearance is when they disappear

disappoint *VERB* (**disappoints**, **disappointing**, **disappointed**)
to disappoint someone is to fail to do what they want
▷ **disappointing** *ADJECTIVE* causing someone to be disappointed
▷ **disappointment** *NOUN* a feeling of being disappointed

disapprove *VERB* (**disapproves**, **disapproving**, **disapproved**)
to disapprove of someone or something is to have a bad opinion of them
▷ **disapproval** *NOUN* having a bad opinion

disarm *VERB* (**disarms**, **disarming**, **disarmed**)
1 to disarm is to reduce the size of armed forces
2 to disarm someone is to take away their weapons
▷ **disarmament** *NOUN* disarmament is reducing the number of weapons a country has

disaster *NOUN* (**disasters**)
1 a very bad accident or misfortune, often one where many people are killed or injured **2** a complete failure • *The first night of the play was a disaster.*
▷ **disastrous** *ADJECTIVE* causing great misfortune; going completely wrong
▷ **disastrously** *ADVERB* in a disastrous way

disc *NOUN* (**discs**)
1 a round flat object **2** a round, flat piece of plastic on which sound or data is recorded; a CD

discard *VERB* (**discards**, **discarding**, **discarded**)
to discard something is to throw it away

discharge *VERB* (**discharges**, **discharging**, **discharged**)
1 to release someone • *She was discharged from hospital yesterday.* **2** to send something out • *Vehicles must not discharge excessive smoke.*

disciple *NOUN* (**disciples**)
a follower of a political or religious leader, especially one of Christ's first followers

discipline *NOUN*
1 training people to obey rules and punishing them if they don't **2** the control you have over how you behave • *You need lots of discipline to learn the piano.*

disc jockey *NOUN* (**disc jockeys**)
someone who introduces and plays records on the radio or at a club

disclose *VERB* (**discloses**, **disclosing**, **disclosed**)
to disclose information or a secret is to tell someone about it
▷ **disclosure** *NOUN* disclosure is telling people information that is secret

disco *NOUN* (**discos**)
a place or party where records are played for dancing

discolour *VERB* (**discolours**, **discolouring**, **discoloured**)
to discolour something is to spoil its colour

discomfort *NOUN*
being uncomfortable

disconnect *VERB* (**disconnects**, **disconnecting**, **disconnected**)
to disconnect something is to break its connection or detach it
▷ **disconnection** *NOUN* disconnecting something

discontented *ADJECTIVE*
unhappy and not satisfied
▷ **discontent** *NOUN* discontent is a feeling of being unhappy or not satisfied

discount *NOUN* (**discounts**)
an amount by which a price is reduced

discourage *VERB* (**discourages**, **discouraging**, **discouraged**)
1 to discourage someone is to take away their enthusiasm or confidence **2** to discourage someone from doing something is to try to persuade them not to do it
▷ **discouragement** *NOUN* a feeling of being discouraged

discover *VERB* (**discovers**, **discovering**, **discovered**)
to discover something is to find it or learn about it, especially by chance or for the first time

discovery *NOUN* (**discoveries**)
1 finding or learning about something, especially by chance or for the first time • *Columbus is famous for the discovery of America.* **2** something that is found or learned about for the first time • *This drug was an important discovery in the history of medicine.*

discreet *ADJECTIVE*
being careful in what you say and do, especially when you have a secret to keep
▷ **discreetly** *ADVERB* in a discreet way

discriminate *VERB* (**discriminates**, **discriminating**, **discriminated**)
1 to discriminate between things is to notice the differences between them, or to prefer one thing to another **2** to discriminate between people is to treat them differently or unfairly because of their race, sex, or religion

discrimination *NOUN*
1 discrimination is treating people differently or unfairly because of their race, sex, or religion
2 discrimination is also the ability to notice the differences between things

discus *NOUN* (**discuses**) (*say* **dis**- kuss)
a thick heavy disc thrown in an athletic contest

discuss *VERB* (**discusses**, **discussing**, **discussed**)
(*say* dis- **kuss**)
to discuss a subject is to talk with other people about it or to write about it in detail

discussion *NOUN* (**discussions**)
1 a conversation about a subject **2** a piece of writing in which the writer examines a subject from different points of view

disease *NOUN* (**diseases**)
1 a disease is an illness or sickness
▷ **diseased** *ADJECTIVE* someone or something is diseased when they have a disease

disembark *VERB* (**disembarks**, **disembarking**, **disembarked**)
to disembark is to get out of a boat or aircraft

disgrace *NOUN*
1 disgrace is shame • *You have brought disgrace to your family.* **2** a disgrace is a person or thing that is so bad that people should feel ashamed • *This room is an absolute disgrace.*
▷ **disgraceful** *ADJECTIVE* so bad that people should feel ashamed about it
▷ **disgracefully** *ADVERB* in a disgraceful way

disgrace *VERB* (**disgraces**, **disgracing**, **disgraced**)
to disgrace someone or something is to bring them shame

disguise *VERB* (**disguises**, **disguising**, **disguised**)
to disguise someone or something is to make them look different so that other people won't recognize them

disguise *NOUN* (**disguises**)
clothes or make-up you put on to change the way you look so that people won't recognize you

disgust *NOUN*
a strong feeling of dislike or contempt

disgust *VERB* (**disgusts**, **disgusting**, **disgusted**)
to disgust someone is to make them feel disgust

> **WORD FAMILY**
> Someone is **disgusted** when they dislike someone or something very much; you say something is **disgusting** when it is very unpleasant and makes you feel disgust.

dish *NOUN* (**dishes**)
1 a plate or bowl for food **2** food that has been prepared for eating

dish *VERB* (**dishes**, **dishing**, **dished**)
to dish something out (*informal*) is to give it to people

dishcloth *NOUN* (**dishcloths**)
a cloth you use for washing or drying dishes

dishevelled *ADJECTIVE*
untidy in appearance

dishonest *ADJECTIVE*
not honest or truthful
▷ **dishonesty** *NOUN* dishonesty is being dishonest

dishwasher *NOUN* (**dishwashers**)
a machine for washing dishes automatically

disinfect *VERB* (**disinfects**, **disinfecting**, **disinfected**)
to disinfect something is to treat it to kill all the germs in it

disinfectant *NOUN* (**disinfectants**)
a liquid used to disinfect things

disintegrate *VERB* (**disintegrates**, **disintegrating**, **disintegrated**)
to disintegrate is to break up into small pieces
▷ **disintegration** *NOUN* the disintegration of something is when it disintegrates

disinterested *ADJECTIVE*
not favouring one side more than the other; impartial

> USING THIS WORD
> Take care not to confuse **disinterested** with **uninterested**, which means 'not interested' or 'bored'.

disk *NOUN* (**disks**)
a disc, especially one used to store computer data

dislike *VERB* (**dislikes**, **disliking**, **disliked**)
to dislike someone or something is not to like them

dislike *NOUN* (**dislikes**)
a feeling of not liking someone or something

dislocate *VERB* (**dislocates**, **dislocating**, **dislocated**)
to dislocate a bone or joint in your body is to make it come out of its proper place by accident
▷ **dislocation** *NOUN* dislocating something

dislodge *VERB* (**dislodges**, **dislodging**, **dislodged**)
to dislodge something is to move it from its place

disloyal *ADJECTIVE*
not loyal

dismal *ADJECTIVE*
gloomy and sad
▷ **dismally** *ADVERB* in a dismal way

dismantle *VERB* (**dismantles**, **dismantling**, **dismantled**)
to dismantle something is to take it to pieces

dismay *NOUN*
a feeling of strong disappointment and surprise
▷ **dismayed** *ADJECTIVE* disappointed and surprised

dismiss *VERB* (**dismisses**, **dismissing**, **dismissed**)
1 to dismiss someone is to tell them that they have to leave, especially to leave their job **2** to dismiss an idea or suggestion is to reject it

> WORD FAMILY
> **Dismissal** is telling someone that they have to leave their job.

dismount *VERB* (**dismounts**, **dismounting**, **dismounted**)
to dismount is to get off a horse or bicycle

disobey *VERB* (**disobeys**, **disobeying**, **disobeyed**)
to disobey someone is to refuse to do what they tell you to do

> WORD FAMILY
> **Disobedience** is refusing to obey someone; someone who is **disobedient** doesn't do what they are told to do.

disorder *NOUN* (**disorders**)
1 disorder is confusion or disturbance **2** a disorder is an illness
▷ **disorderly** *ADJECTIVE* behaving in a wild and noisy way

dispatch *NOUN* (**dispatches**)
a report or message

dispatch *VERB* (**dispatches**, **dispatching**, **dispatched**)
1 to dispatch something or someone is to send them somewhere **2** to dispatch someone is to kill them

dispense *VERB* (**dispenses**, **dispensing**, **dispensed**)
1 to dispense something is to give it out to people • *The machine dispenses drinks and snacks.* **2** to dispense medicine is to prepare it for patients
to dispense with something is to do without it

dispenser *NOUN* (**dispensers**)
a device that gives you things, especially in special amounts • *There is a soap dispenser above each washbasin.*

disperse *VERB* (**disperses**, **dispersing**, **dispersed**)
1 to disperse people is to send them away in various directions • *The police dispersed the crowd.* **2** to disperse is to go off in various directions
▷ **dispersal** *NOUN* dispersal is when people go off in different directions

displace *VERB* (**displaces**, **displacing**, **displaced**)
1 to displace something is to move it from its place • *Some roof tiles had been displaced by the wind.* **2** to displace someone is to take their place • *Last year she displaced him as captain.*

displacement *NOUN*
1 displacing **2** the amount of water displaced by a ship

display *VERB* (**displays**, **displaying**, **displayed**)
to display something is to arrange it so that it can be clearly seen

display *NOUN* (**displays**)
1 a show or exhibition **2** the showing of information on a computer screen

displease *VERB* (**displeases**, **displeasing**, **displeased**)
to displease someone is to annoy them

disposable *ADJECTIVE*
something that is disposable is made to be thrown away after it has been used

disposal *NOUN*
getting rid of something
at your disposal ready for you to use

dispose *VERB* (**disposes**, **disposing**, **disposed**)
to be disposed to do something is to be ready and willing to do it • *They were not at all disposed to help us.*
to dispose of something is to get rid of it

disposition *NOUN* (**dispositions**)
a person's nature or qualities • *He has a cheerful disposition.*

disprove *VERB* (**disproves**, **disproving**, **disproved**)
to disprove something is to prove that it is not true

dispute *NOUN* (**disputes**)
a quarrel or disagreement

disqualify *VERB* (**disqualifies**, **disqualifying**, **disqualified**)
to disqualify someone is to remove them from a race or competition because they have broken the rules
▷ **disqualification** *NOUN* disqualification, or a disqualification, is when someone is disqualified

disregard *VERB* (**disregards**, **disregarding**, **disregarded**)
to disregard someone or something is to take no notice of them

disrespect *NOUN*
lack of respect; rudeness
▷ **disrespectful** *ADJECTIVE* showing disrespect ▷ **disrespectfully** *ADVERB* in a disrespectful way

disrupt *VERB* (**disrupts**, **disrupting**, **disrupted**)
to disrupt something is to stop it running smoothly or throw it into confusion • *Floods have disrupted local traffic.*

> WORD FAMILY
> **Disruption** is when something stops running smoothly; someone is **disruptive** when they cause so much disorder that a meeting or lesson can't continue.

dissatisfied *ADJECTIVE*
not satisfied or pleased
▷ **dissatisfaction** *NOUN* dissatisfaction is being dissatisfied

dissect *VERB* (**dissects**, **dissecting**, **dissected**)
to dissect something is to cut it up so that you can examine it
▷ **dissection** *NOUN* dissecting something

dissolve *VERB* (**dissolves**, **dissolving**, **dissolved**)
1 to dissolve something is to mix it with a liquid so that it becomes part of the liquid **2** to dissolve is to melt or become liquid • *As the book sank into the green sea the ink dissolved from its pages. And as each page washed blank, the spell written upon it was broken.* — Alan Temperley, *The Brave Whale*

dissuade *VERB* (**dissuades**, **dissuading**, **dissuaded**)
to dissuade someone is to persuade them not to do something

distance *NOUN* (**distances**)
the amount of space between two places or things
in the distance a long way off but able to be seen

distant *ADJECTIVE*
1 far away **2** a person who is distant is not friendly or sociable

distil *VERB* (**distils**, **distilling**, **distilled**)
to distil a liquid is to purify it by boiling it and condensing the vapour

distillery *NOUN* (**distilleries**)
a place where spirits such as whisky are produced
▷ **distiller** *NOUN* a person or firm that makes spirits

distinct *ADJECTIVE*
1 easily heard or seen; clear or definite • *You have made a distinct improvement.* **2** clearly separate or different • *A rabbit is quite distinct from a hare.*
▷ **distinctly** *ADVERB* clearly or noticeably

distinction *NOUN* (**distinctions**)
1 a distinction is a clear difference between two things **2** distinction is excellence or honour • *She is a writer of distinction.* **3** a distinction is also a high mark in an examination

distinctive *ADJECTIVE*
clearly different from all the others and easy to recognize or notice • *The school has a distinctive blue football strip.*

distinguish *VERB* (**distinguishes**, **distinguishing**, **distinguished**)
1 to distinguish things is to notice the differences between them **2** to distinguish something is to see or hear it clearly

distinguished *ADJECTIVE*
famous, successful, and much admired by other people • *There was a distinguished writer staying at the same hotel.*

a b c **d** e f g h i j k l m n o p q r s t u v w x y z

distort *VERB* (**distorts, distorting, distorted**)
1 to distort something is to change it into a strange shape • *His face was distorted with anger.* **2** to distort facts is to change them so that they are untrue or misleading
▷ **distortion** *NOUN* distortion is distorting something

distract *VERB* (**distracts, distracting, distracted**)
to distract someone is to take their attention away from what they are doing • *Don't distract the bus driver.*
▷ **distraction** *NOUN* distraction, or a distraction, is when you are distracted

distress *NOUN*
great sorrow, suffering or trouble
in distress a ship or plane is in distress when it is in difficulty and needs help

distress *VERB* (**distresses, distressing, distressed**)
to distress someone is to make them feel very upset or worried

distribute *VERB* (**distributes, distributing, distributed**)
1 to distribute things is to give them out or deliver them • *The teacher distributed textbooks to the class.* **2** to distribute something is to share it among a number of people • *The money was distributed among all the local schools.* **3** to distribute something is also to spread or scatter it around • *Make sure your weight is evenly distributed.*
▷ **distribution** *NOUN* distribution is distributing things
▷ **distributor** someone who distributes things
▷ **distributor** *NOUN* someone who distributes things

district *NOUN* (**districts**)
part of a town or country

distrust *NOUN*
lack of trust; suspicion
▷ **distrustful** *ADJECTIVE* not trusting people

distrust *VERB* (**distrusts, distrusting, distrusted**)
to think that someone or something can't be trusted

disturb *VERB* (**disturbs, disturbing, disturbed**)
1 to disturb someone is to interrupt them or spoil their peace **2** to disturb someone is also to worry or upset them **3** to disturb something is to move it from its right position
▷ **disturbance** *NOUN* a disturbance is something that disturbs someone

disused *ADJECTIVE*
no longer used • *The house was next to a disused warehouse.*

ditch *NOUN* (**ditches**)
a narrow trench to hold or carry away water

dither *VERB* (**dithers, dithering, dithered**)
to dither is to hesitate nervously

ditto *NOUN*
the same again

> **PUNCTUATION**
> Ditto marks (") are sometimes used in lists or bills to show where something is repeated.

divan *NOUN* (**divans**)
a bed or couch without a raised back or sides

dive *VERB* (**dives, diving, dived**)
1 to dive is to go into water head first **2** to dive is also to move downwards quickly • *The aeroplane then dived.*

diver *NOUN* (**divers**)
1 a swimmer who dives **2** someone who works under water using special breathing equipment **3** a bird that dives for its food

diverse *ADJECTIVE*
very different from each other and of several different kinds • *He has a diverse collection of rocks.*
▷ **diversity** *NOUN* diversity is variety

diversify *VERB* (**diversifies, diversifying, diversified**)
to diversify is to try out different things

diversion *NOUN* (**diversions**)
1 a different way for traffic to go when the usual road is closed **2** something amusing or entertaining

divert *VERB* (**diverts, diverting, diverted**)
1 to divert something is to change the direction it is moving in **2** to divert someone is to amuse or entertain them

divide *VERB* (**divides, dividing, divided**)
1 to divide something is to separate it into smaller parts or shares **2** (*in mathematics*) to divide a number by another number is to find out how many times the second number is contained in the first • *Divide six by two and you get three (6 ÷ 2 = 3).*

dividend *NOUN* (**dividends**)
1 (*in mathematics*) an amount to be divided **2** a share in the profit a business makes

dividers *PLURAL NOUN*
dividers are a pair of compasses for measuring distances

divine *ADJECTIVE*
1 belonging to God or coming from God **2** like a god **3** (*informal*) excellent; extremely beautiful
▷ **divinely** *ADVERB* in a divine or excellent way
▷ **divinity** *NOUN* divinity is the fact of being a god or like God

divine *VERB* (**divines, divining, divined**)
to divine is to find hidden water or metal by holding a Y-shaped stick called a **divining rod**

division *NOUN* (**divisions**)
1 the process of dividing numbers or things **2** a dividing line or partition **3** one of the parts into which something is divided
▷ **divisible** *ADJECTIVE* able to be divided, or divided exactly

divisor *NOUN* (**divisors**)
(*in mathematics*) a number that you divide into another number

divorce *NOUN* (**divorces**)
the legal ending of a marriage

divorce *VERB* (**divorces**, **divorcing**, **divorced**)
a husband and wife divorce when they end their marriage by law

Diwali *NOUN* (*say* di- **wah**- li)
a Hindu festival held in October or November

DIY
short for **do-it-yourself**

dizzy *ADJECTIVE* (**dizzier**, **dizziest**)
giddy and feeling confused
▷ **dizzily** *ADVERB* in a dizzy way
▷ **dizziness** *NOUN* feeling dizzy

DJ
short for **disc jockey**

do *VERB* (**does**, **doing**, **did**, **done**)
1 to do something is to perform it or deal with it • *Are you doing your work?* • *I can't do this sum.* **2** to do well is to manage; to do badly is not to manage very well **3** you say that something will do when it is all right or suitable • *I'd really like some football boots but trainers will do.* **4** you also use **do** with other verbs in special ways • *Do you want this?* • *He does not want it.* • *I do like crisps.* • *We work as hard as they do.*
to do away with something or **someone** (*informal*) is to get rid of them or kill them
to do something up is to fasten it • *Do up your coat.*
to do without something is to manage without having it

docile *ADJECTIVE*
gentle and obedient

dock[1] *NOUN* (**docks**)
a part of a harbour where ships are loaded, unloaded, or repaired

dock *VERB* (**docks**, **docking**, **docked**)
1 a ship docks when it comes into a dock
2 spacecraft dock when they join together in orbit

dock[2] *NOUN* (**docks**)
a place for the prisoner on trial in a lawcourt

dock[3] *VERB* (**docks**, **docking**, **docked**)
1 to dock an animal's tail is to cut it short **2** to dock someone's pay is to take something off it as a penalty

dock[4] *NOUN*
a weed with broad leaves

docker *NOUN* (**dockers**)
a person whose job is loading and unloading ships

dockyard *NOUN* (**dockyards**)
an open area with docks and equipment for building or repairing ships

doctor *NOUN* (**doctors**)
a person trained to heal sick or injured people

doctrine *NOUN* (**doctrines**)
a religious or political belief
▷ **doctrinal** *ADJECTIVE* to do with doctrine

document *NOUN* (**documents**)
1 an important written or printed piece of paper
2 (*in computing*) something stored in a computer or on a disk, such as a piece of text or a picture
▷ **documentation** *NOUN* a collection of documents

documentary *NOUN* (**documentaries**)
a film or a television programme that tells you about real events or situations

doddery *ADJECTIVE*
someone who is doddery is shaking or unsteady because they are old

doddle *NOUN*
(*informal*) you say that something is a doddle when it is very easy to do

dodge *VERB* (**dodges**, **dodging**, **dodged**)
to dodge something is to move quickly to avoid it

dodge *NOUN* (**dodges**)
1 a dodging movement **2** a trick; a clever way of doing something

dodgem *NOUN* (**dodgems**)
a small electrically driven car at a funfair, in which you drive round an enclosure, dodging and bumping other cars

dodgy *ADJECTIVE* (**dodgier**, **dodgiest**) (*informal*)
1 awkward or tricky **2** dishonest or unreliable

doe *NOUN* (**does**)
a female deer, rabbit, or hare

does
3rd singular present tense of **do** • *She does what she likes.*

doesn't
short for *does not* • *He doesn't understand.*

dog *NOUN* (**dogs**)
a four-legged animal that barks, often kept as a pet

dog-eared *ADJECTIVE*
a dog-eared book has the corners of its pages bent or worn because it has been read so much

dogged *ADJECTIVE* (*say* **dog**- id)
not giving up in spite of difficulties; obstinate
▷ **doggedly** *ADVERB* in a dogged way

do-it-yourself *ADJECTIVE*
suitable for anyone to make or use at home, rather than paying for someone else to do it

doldrums *PLURAL NOUN*
the ocean regions near the equator, where there is little or no wind
in the doldrums bored and unhappy

dole *NOUN*
(*informal*) the dole is money paid by the government to unemployed people

doll *NOUN* (**dolls**)
a toy model of a person, especially a baby or child

dollar *NOUN* (**dollars**)
a unit of money in the United States and some other countries

dolly *NOUN* (**dollies**)
(*informal*) a doll

dolphin *NOUN* (**dolphins**)
a sea mammal like a small whale with a snout like a beak

domain *NOUN* (**domains**)
an area that is ruled or controlled by someone • *No sooner had the Fairy reached her own domain than she made herself visible.* — Andrew Lang, *The Yellow Fairy Book*

dome *NOUN* (**domes**)
a roof shaped like the top half of a ball

domestic *ADJECTIVE*
1 to do with the home **2** a domestic animal is tame and kept at home

domesticated *ADJECTIVE*
1 a domesticated animal is trained to live with people **2** a domesticated person enjoys household work and home life

dominant *ADJECTIVE*
most powerful or important
▷ **dominance** *NOUN* being dominant

dominate *VERB* (**dominates**, **dominating**, **dominated**)
to dominate people is to control them by being the most powerful
▷ **domination** *NOUN* dominating people

dominion *NOUN* (**dominions**)
1 rule or authority **2** an area ruled by one ruler

domino *NOUN* (**dominoes**)
a small flat oblong piece of wood or plastic with dots (1 to 6) or a blank space at each end, used in the game of **dominoes**

> IDIOM
> If you set up a row of upright dominoes and then knock the first one over, they all fall over one after the other. This is why people talk about the **domino effect** when one event causes a whole string of events of the same kind.

donate *VERB* (**donates**, **donating**, **donated**)
to donate something, especially money, is to give it to a charity or organization
▷ **donation** *NOUN* a donation is something that is donated

done
past participle of **do**

donkey *NOUN* (**donkeys**)
an animal that looks like a small horse with long ears

donor *NOUN* (**donors**)
someone who gives something • *New blood donors are needed.*

don't
short for *do not* • *Don't cycle on the pavement.*

doodle *NOUN* (**doodles**)
a quick drawing or scribble

doodle *VERB* (**doodles**, **doodling**, **doodled**)
to doodle is to draw a doodle

doom *NOUN*
a grim fate like ruin or death

doom *VERB* (**dooms**, **dooming**, **doomed**)
to be doomed to something is to have a grim fate you can't avoid

door *NOUN* (**doors**)
a movable panel that opens and closes the entrance to a room, building, or cupboard

doorstep *NOUN* (**doorsteps**)
the step or piece of ground outside a door

doorway *NOUN* (**doorways**)
the opening into which a door fits

dope *NOUN* (**dopes**)(*informal*)
1 dope is a narcotic drug **2** a dope is a fool

dopey *ADJECTIVE* (**dopier**, **dopiest**)(*informal*)
1 half asleep **2** stupid

dormitory *NOUN* (**dormitories**)
a room for several people to sleep in, especially in a school

dose *NOUN* (**doses**)
the amount of a medicine that you are meant to take at one time

dossier *NOUN* (**dossiers**) (*say* **doss**- i- er or doss- i- ay)
a set of documents with information about a person or event

dot *NOUN* (**dots**)
a tiny spot

dot *VERB* (**dots**, **dotting**, **dotted**)
to dot something is to mark it with dots

dotty *ADJECTIVE* (**dottier**, **dottiest**)
(*informal*) crazy or silly
▷ **dottiness** *NOUN* being dotty

double *ADJECTIVE*
1 twice as much or twice as many **2** having two of something • *a double-barrelled shotgun* **3** suitable for two people • *a double bed*

double *NOUN* (**doubles**)
1 double is twice the amount or cost **2** a double is someone who looks like someone else **3** you play doubles in tennis when you play with someone else against another pair of players

double *VERB* (**doubles**, **doubling**, **doubled**)
1 to double something is to make it twice as big **2** to double is to become twice as big
to double up is to bend over because you are in pain or laughing so much

double bass *NOUN* (**double basses**)
a musical instrument with strings, like a large cello

double-cross *VERB* (**double-crosses**, **double-crossing**, **double-crossed**)
to double-cross someone is to cheat or betray them when you are supposed to be supporting them

double-decker *NOUN* (**double-deckers**)
a bus with two floors, one above the other

doubly *ADVERB*
twice as much • *It's doubly important that you should go.*

doubt *NOUN* (**doubts**)
not feeling sure about something

doubt *VERB* (**doubts**, **doubting**, **doubted**)
to doubt something is to feel unsure about it • *I doubt whether he is telling the truth.*

doubtful *ADJECTIVE*
1 having doubts • *She looked doubtful.* **2** making you feel doubt • *Their story was very doubtful.*
▷ **doubtfully** *ADVERB* in a doubtful way

doubtless *ADVERB*
certainly; without any doubt

dough *NOUN*
1 a thick mixture of flour and water used for making bread or pastry **2** (*slang*) money
▷ **doughy** *ADJECTIVE* thick and sticky like dough

doughnut *NOUN* (**doughnuts**)
a round or ring-shaped bun that has been fried and covered with sugar

dove *NOUN* (**doves**)
a kind of pigeon, often used as a symbol of peace

dovetail *NOUN* (**dovetails**)
a wedge-shaped joint used to join two pieces of wood

dovetail *VERB* (**dovetails**, **dovetailing**, **dovetailed**)
1 to dovetail two pieces of wood is to join them with a dovetail **2** to dovetail is to fit neatly together • *My plans dovetailed with hers.*

dowel *NOUN* (**dowels**)
a headless wooden or metal pin for holding together two pieces of wood or stone

down[1] *ADVERB & PREPOSITION*
1 to or in a lower place • *It fell down.* • *Run down the hill.* **2** along • *Go down to the shops.*

down[2] *NOUN*
very soft feathers or hair • *Ducks are covered with down.*
▷ **downy** *ADJECTIVE* covered in something very soft like feathers or hair

downcast *ADJECTIVE*
1 looking downward • *Her eyes were downcast.*
2 sad or dejected

downfall *NOUN* (**downfalls**)
1 a person's downfall is their ruin or fall from power
2 a heavy fall of rain or snow

downhill *ADVERB*
down a slope

downpour *NOUN* (**downpours**)
a heavy fall of rain

downright *ADJECTIVE & ADVERB*
very, completely • *I felt downright angry about it.*

downs *PLURAL NOUN*
grass-covered hills • *Let's have a picnic on the downs.*

downstairs *ADVERB & ADJECTIVE*
to or on a lower floor

downstream *ADVERB*
in the direction that a river or stream flows

downward or **downwards** *ADVERB*
towards a lower place

doze *VERB* (**dozes**, **dozing**, **dozed**)
to doze is to sleep lightly
▷ **dozy** *ADJECTIVE* someone is dozy when they are feeling sleepy

dozen *NOUN* (**dozens**)
a set of twelve

Dr
short for **Doctor**

drab *ADJECTIVE* (**drabber**, **drabbest**)
1 dull and without colour • *His clothes were drab.*
2 dreary and uninteresting

draft *NOUN* (**drafts**)
a rough plan for something you are going to write

draft *VERB* (**drafts**, **drafting**, **drafted**)
to draft something you are going to write is to make a rough plan of it

> SPELLING
> Take care not to confuse **draft** with **draught**, which means a current of air.

drag *VERB* (**drags**, **dragging**, **dragged**)
1 to drag something heavy is to pull it along **2** to drag a river or lake is to search it with nets and hooks

drag *NOUN*
(*informal*) something annoying or tedious

dragon *NOUN* (**dragons**)
a winged lizard-like monster that breathes fire in stories

dragonfly *NOUN* (**dragonflies**)
an insect with a long body and two pairs of transparent wings

drain *NOUN* (**drains**)
1 a pipe or ditch for taking away water or sewage
2 something that uses up your strength or money

drain *VERB* (**drains**, **draining**, **drained**)
1 to drain water is to take it away with drains **2** to drain is to flow or trickle away **3** to drain a glass or bottle is to empty liquid out of it **4** to drain food is to pour off liquid in which it has been cooked • *Drain the pasta thoroughly* **5** to drain someone is to exhaust them
▷ **drainage** *NOUN* drainage is a system of drains

draining board *NOUN* (**draining boards**)
a sloping surface beside a sink where you put washed dishes

drake *NOUN* (**drakes**)
a male duck

a b c d e f g h i j k l m n o p q r s t u v w x y z

drama *NOUN* (**dramas**)
1 drama is writing or performing plays **2** a drama is a play **3** a drama is also a series of exciting events

dramatic *ADJECTIVE*
1 to do with drama **2** exciting and impressive • *A dramatic change has taken place.*
▷ **dramatically** *ADVERB* in a dramatic way

dramatics *PLURAL NOUN*
performing plays

dramatist *NOUN* (**dramatists**)
someone who writes plays

dramatize *VERB* (**dramatizes**, **dramatizing**, **dramatized**)
1 to dramatize a story is to make it into a play **2** to dramatize an event is to exaggerate it • *Why do you always dramatize everything?*
▷ **dramatization** *NOUN* a dramatization is a play made from a story

drank
past tense of **drink** *VERB*

drape *VERB* (**drapes**, **draping**, **draped**)
to drape something like cloth is to hang it loosely over something

drastic *ADJECTIVE*
having a strong or violent effect
▷ **drastically** *ADVERB* in a drastic way

draught *NOUN* (**draughts**) (*rhymes with* **craft**)
a current of cold air indoors
▷ **draughty** *ADJECTIVE* a draughty room has lots of draughts

> **SPELLING**
> Take care not to confuse **draught** with **draft**, which means a rough plan.

draughts *NOUN*
a game played with 24 round pieces on a chessboard

> **BRITISH AND AMERICAN**
> In America, the word **checkers** is used.

draughtsman *NOUN* (**draughtsmen**)
1 someone who makes drawings **2** a piece used in the game of draughts

draw *VERB* (**draws**, **drawing**, **drew**, **drawn**)
1 to draw a picture or outline is to form it with a pencil or pen **2** to draw something is to pull it • *She drew her chair up to the table.* **3** to draw people is to attract them • *The fair drew large crowds.* **4** to draw is to end a game or contest with the same score on both sides • *They drew 2-2 last Saturday.* **5** to draw the curtains is to open or close them **6** to draw near is to come nearer • *The ship was drawing nearer.*

draw *NOUN* (**draws**)
1 a raffle or similar competition in which the winner is chosen by picking tickets or numbers at random **2** a game that ends with the same score on both sides **3** an attraction

drawback *NOUN* (**drawbacks**)
a disadvantage

drawbridge *NOUN* (**drawbridges**)
a bridge over a moat, hinged at one end so that it can be raised or lowered

drawer *NOUN* (**drawers**)
a sliding box-like container in a piece of furniture

drawing *NOUN* (**drawings**)
something drawn with a pencil or pen

drawing pin *NOUN* (**drawing pins**)
a short pin with a large flat top that you use for fixing paper to a surface

drawl *VERB* (**drawls**, **drawling**, **drawled**)
to drawl is to speak very slowly or lazily

dread *VERB* (**dreads**, **dreading**, **dreaded**)
to dread something is to fear it very much

dread *NOUN*
great fear

dreadful *ADJECTIVE*
very bad • *We've had dreadful weather.*
▷ **dreadfully** *ADVERB* very badly

dreadlocks *PLURAL NOUN*
hair in long tightly-curled ringlets, worn especially by Rastafarians

dream *NOUN* (**dreams**)
1 things you seem to see while you are sleeping **2** something you imagine; an ambition or ideal • *His dream is to be famous.*
▷ **dreamy** *ADJECTIVE* like a dream; not real

dream *VERB* (**dreams**, **dreaming**, **dreamt** or **dreamed**)
1 to dream is to have a dream **2** to dream is also to want something badly • *She dreams of being a ballet dancer.* **3** to dream something is to think it may happen • *I never dreamt she would leave.*

dreary *ADJECTIVE* (**drearier**, **dreariest**)
1 dull or boring **2** gloomy
▷ **drearily** *ADVERB* in a dreary way
▷ **dreariness** *NOUN* being dreary

dredge *VERB* (**dredges**, **dredging**, **dredged**)
to dredge something is to drag it up, especially mud from the bottom of water
▷ **dredger** *NOUN* a machine for clearing mud from the bottom of a river

drench *VERB* (**drenches**, **drenching**, **drenched**)
to drench someone or something is to soak them • *They got drenched in the rain.*

dress *NOUN* (**dresses**)
1 a dress is a woman's or girl's piece of clothing, having a top and skirt in one **2** dress is clothes or costume • *We have to wear fancy dress.*

dress *VERB* (**dresses**, **dressing**, **dressed**)
1 to dress is to put clothes on **2** to dress a wound is to put a bandage or plaster it **3** to dress food is to prepare it for cooking or eating

dresser *NOUN* (**dressers**)
a sideboard with shelves at the top

dressing *NOUN* (**dressings**)
1 a sauce of oil, vinegar, and spices for a salad **2** a bandage or plaster used to cover a wound

dressing gown *NOUN* (**dressing gowns**)
a loose light indoor coat you wear over pyjamas or a nightdress

dressmaker *NOUN* (**dressmakers**)
a person whose job is to make clothes for women

drew
past tense of **draw** *VERB*

dribble *VERB* (**dribbles**, **dribbling**, **dribbled**)
1 to dribble is to let saliva trickle out of your mouth **2** to dribble is also to kick a ball gently in front of you as you run forward

dried
past tense and past participle of **dry** *VERB*

drier *NOUN* (**driers**)
a device for drying hair or washing

drift *VERB* (**drifts**, **drifting**, **drifted**)
1 to drift is to be carried gently along by water or air **2** to drift is also to live casually or wander about without any real plan or purpose

drift *NOUN* (**drifts**)
1 a drifting movement **2** a mass of snow or sand piled up by the wind **3** the general meaning of what someone says • *Do you get my drift?*

driftwood *NOUN*
wood floating on the sea or washed ashore

drill *NOUN* (**drills**)
1 a tool for making holes **2** repeated exercises in military training, gymnastics, or sport **3** a set way of doing something • *Do you know the drill?*

drill *VERB* (**drills**, **drilling**, **drilled**)
1 to drill a hole is to make a hole with a drill **2** to drill is to do repeated exercises

drink *VERB* (**drinks**, **drinking**, **drank**, **drunk**)
1 to drink is to swallow liquid **2** to drink can also mean to have a lot of alcohol • *Don't drink and drive.*
▷ **drinker** *NOUN* someone who drinks

drink *NOUN* (**drinks**)
1 a liquid for drinking **2** an alcoholic drink

drip *VERB* (**drips**, **dripping**, **dripped**)
1 to drip is to fall in drops **2** to drip is also to let liquid fall in drops • *The tap was dripping.*

drip *NOUN* (**drips**)
a falling drop of liquid

dripping *NOUN*
fat that melts from roasted meat and is allowed to set

drive *VERB* (**drives**, **driving**, **drove**, **driven**)
1 to drive a vehicle is to operate it **2** to drive someone or something is to make them move **3** to drive someone into a state or feeling is to force them into it • *That music is driving me mad!*
to be driving at something is to be trying to say it • *What is he driving at?*
▷ **driver** *NOUN* someone who drives a vehicle

drive *NOUN* (**drives**)
1 a drive is a journey in a vehicle **2** drive is energy and enthusiasm **3** a drive is a road leading to a house **4** a drive is a powerful stroke of the ball in cricket, golf, and other games

drizzle *NOUN*
gentle rain

drizzle *VERB* (**drizzles**, **drizzling**, **drizzled**)
to rain gently

drone *VERB* (**drones**, **droning**, **droned**)
1 to drone is to make a low humming sound **2** you can also say that someone drones when they talk in a boring voice

drone *NOUN* (**drones**)
1 a droning sound **2** a male bee

drool *VERB* (**drools**, **drooling**, **drooled**)
to drool is to dribble continuously
to drool over something is to look at it with longing • *He's been drooling over car catalogues all afternoon.*

droop *VERB* (**droops**, **drooping**, **drooped**)
to droop is to hang down weakly

drop *NOUN* (**drops**)
1 a tiny amount of liquid **2** a fall or decrease • *There has been a sharp drop in prices.*
▷ **droplet** *NOUN* a small drop

drop *VERB* (**drops**, **dropping**, **dropped**)
1 to drop is to fall **2** to drop something is to let it fall **3** to drop is also to become less or lower • *The temperature suddenly dropped.*
to drop in is to visit someone casually
to drop out is to stop taking part in something

drought *NOUN* (**droughts**) (*rhymes with* **out**)
a long period of dry weather

drove
past tense of **drive** *VERB*

drown *VERB* (**drowns**, **drowning**, **drowned**)
1 to drown is to die from being under water and unable to breathe **2** to drown a person or animal is to kill them by forcing them to stay under water **3** to drown sounds is to make so much noise that they cannot be heard

drowsy *ADJECTIVE* (**drowsier**, **drowsiest**)
sleepy
▷ **drowsily** *ADVERB* in a drowsy way
▷ **drowsiness** *NOUN* being drowsy

drug *NOUN* (**drugs**)
1 a substance that kills pain or cures a disease **2** a substance that people take because it affects their senses or their mind. Some drugs cause addiction or are illegal

drug *VERB* (**drugs**, **drugging**, **drugged**)
to drug someone is to make them unconscious with drugs

Druid *NOUN* (**Druids**)
a priest of an ancient Celtic religion in Britain and France

a b c d e f g h i j k l m n o p q r s t u v w x y z

drum *NOUN* (**drums**)
1 a musical instrument made of a cylinder with a thin skin stretched over one end or both ends **2** a cylindrical container • *There was a row of oil drums along the side of the road.*

drum *VERB* (**drums**, **drumming**, **drummed**)
1 to drum is to play a drum or drums **2** to drum on something is to tap it repeatedly • *He drummed his fingers on the table.*
▷ **drummer** *NOUN* someone who plays the drums

drumstick *NOUN* (**drumsticks**)
1 a stick used for hitting a drum **2** the lower part of a cooked bird's leg

drunk [1] *ADJECTIVE*
not able to control your behaviour through drinking too much alcohol

drunk *NOUN* (**drunks**)
someone who is drunk
▷ **drunkard** *NOUN* a person who is often drunk

drunk [2]
past participle of **drink** *VERB*

dry *ADJECTIVE* (**drier**, **driest**)
1 not wet or damp **2** boring and dull • *The book I'm reading is rather dry.* **3** funny in a clever and sarcastic way • *He has a very dry sense of humour.*
▷ **drily** *ADVERB* you speak drily when you say something funny in a clever and sarcastic way
▷ **dryness** *NOUN* being dry

dry *VERB* (**dries**, **drying**, **dried**)
1 to dry is to become dry **2** to dry something is to make it dry
to dry up (*informal*) is to stop talking

dry-cleaning *NOUN*
a method of cleaning clothes using chemicals rather than water

dry dock *NOUN*
a dock which can be emptied of water, for repairing ships

dual *ADJECTIVE*
having two parts or aspects; double • *This building has a dual purpose.*

> SPELLING
> Take care not to confuse **dual** with **duel**, which is a noun meaning a fight between two people.

dual carriageway *NOUN* (**dual carriageways**)
a road with several lanes in each direction

dub *VERB* (**dubs**, **dubbing**, **dubbed**)
1 to change or add new sound to the sound on a film • *It's a Japanese film but has been dubbed into English.* **2** to give someone a name or title

dubious *ADJECTIVE*
1 feeling doubtful or uncertain • *I'm dubious about our chances of winning.* **2** probably not honest or not good

duchess *NOUN* (**duchesses**)
a duke's wife or widow

duck *NOUN* (**ducks**)
1 a web-footed water bird with a flat beak **2** a batsman's score of nought at cricket

duck *VERB* (**ducks**, **ducking**, **ducked**)
1 to duck is to bend down quickly to avoid something **2** to duck someone is to push them under water quickly

duckling *NOUN* (**ducklings**)
a young duck

duct *NOUN* (**ducts**)
a tube or pipe

dud *NOUN* (**duds**)
(*slang*) something that is useless or that fails to work

due *ADJECTIVE*
1 expected to arrive • *The train is due in five minutes.*
2 needing to be paid • *Payment for the trip is due next week.*
due to something or **someone** because of something or someone • *The traffic jam was due to an accident.*
in due course eventually; at the expected time

due *ADVERB*
directly • *The camp is due north.*

duel *NOUN* (**duels**)
a fight between two people, especially with pistols or swords

> SPELLING
> Take care not to confuse **duel** with **dual**, which is an adjective meaning double.

duet *NOUN* (**duets**)
a piece of music for two players or two singers

duff *ADJECTIVE*
(*slang*) useless or broken

duffel coat *NOUN* (**duffel coats**)
a thick overcoat with a hood

dug
past tense and past participle of **dig** *VERB*

dugout *NOUN* (**dugouts**)
1 an underground shelter **2** a canoe made by hollowing out a tree trunk

duke *NOUN* (**dukes**)
a member of the highest rank of noblemen

dull *ADJECTIVE* (**duller**, **dullest**)
1 not bright or clear; gloomy • *It was a dull day.*
2 boring • *What a dull programme.* **3** not sharp • *I had a dull pain.* **4** stupid • *You are a dull boy.*
▷ **dully** *ADVERB* in a dull way
▷ **dullness** *NOUN* being dull

duly *ADVERB*
rightly; as expected • *They promised to come, and later they duly arrived.*

dumb *ADJECTIVE* (**dumber**, **dumbest**)
1 unable to speak; silent **2** (*informal*) stupid

dumbfounded *ADJECTIVE*
unable to say anything because you are so astonished

dummy *NOUN* (**dummies**)
1 something made to look like a person or thing; an imitation **2** an imitation teat for a baby to suck

dump *NOUN* (**dumps**)
1 a place where something, especially rubbish, is left or stored **2** (*informal*) a place you don't like

dump *VERB* (**dumps**, **dumping**, **dumped**)
1 to dump something is to get rid of it when you don't want it **2** to dump something somewhere is to put it down carelessly

dumpling *NOUN* (**dumplings**)
a lump of boiled or baked dough

dumpy *ADJECTIVE* (**dumpier**, **dumpiest**)
short and fat

dune *NOUN* (**dunes**)
a hill of loose sand formed by the wind

dung *NOUN*
solid waste matter from an animal

dungarees *PLURAL NOUN*
trousers with a piece in front covering your chest, held up by straps over your shoulders

dungeon *NOUN* (**dungeons**) (*say* **dun**- jon)
an underground prison cell

dunk *VERB* (**dunks**, **dunking**, **dunked**)
to dunk something is to dip it into a liquid

duo *NOUN* (**duos**)
a pair of people, especially playing music

duplicate *NOUN* (**duplicates**) (*say* **dew**- pli- kat)
something that is exactly the same as something else; an exact copy

duplicate *VERB* (**duplicates**, **duplicating**, **duplicated**) (*say* **dew**- pli- kayt)
to duplicate something is to make an exact copy of it
▷ **duplication** *NOUN* duplication is making an exact copy of something

durable *ADJECTIVE*
lasting and strong
▷ **durability** *NOUN* something has durability when it is strong and lasts a long time

duration *NOUN*
the time something lasts

during *PREPOSITION*
while something else is going on • *Let's meet in the cafe during the interval.*

dusk *NOUN*
the time of the day just after sunset when it is starting to get dark

dust *NOUN*
a fine powder made up of tiny pieces of dry earth or other material

dust *VERB* (**dusts**, **dusting**, **dusted**)
1 to dust things is to clear the dust off them **2** to dust something is to sprinkle it with dust or powder • *You can dust the cake with sugar.*

dustbin *NOUN* (**dustbins**)
a bin for household rubbish

duster *NOUN* (**dusters**)
a cloth for dusting things

dustman *NOUN* (**dustmen**)
a person whose job is to empty dustbins

dustpan *NOUN* (**dustpans**)
a pan into which you brush dust

dusty *ADJECTIVE* (**dustier**, **dustiest**)
covered with or full of dust

dutiful *ADJECTIVE*
doing your duty; obedient
▷ **dutifully** *ADVERB* in a dutiful way

duty *NOUN* (**duties**)
1 your duty is what you have to do, perhaps as part of your job **2** a duty is a kind of tax

duvet *NOUN* (**duvets**) (*say* **doo**- vay)
a kind of quilt used instead of other bedclothes

DVD short for *digital video disc* or *digital versatile disc*, a disc on which large amounts of sound and pictures can be stored, especially films

DVD player *NOUN* (**DVD players**)
a machine for playing DVDs

dwarf *NOUN* (**dwarfs** or **dwarves**)
a very small person or thing

dwarf *VERB* (**dwarfs**, **dwarfing**, **dwarfed**)
to dwarf something is to make it seem very small • *The skyscraper dwarfs all the buildings round it.*

dwell *VERB* (**dwells**, **dwelling**, **dwelt**)
to dwell in a place is to live there
to dwell on something is to think or talk about it constantly

dwelling *NOUN* (**dwellings**)
a house or other place to live in

dwindle *VERB* (**dwindles**, **dwindling**, **dwindled**)
to dwindle is to get smaller gradually • *A trickle of woodsmoke from the Schloss chimneys slowly dwindled to a thin line, etching a message of embers and ash across the night sky.* — Debi Gliori, *Pure Dead Magic*

dye *VERB* (**dyes**, **dyeing**, **dyed**)
to dye something is to change its colour by putting it in a special liquid

dye *NOUN* (**dyes**)
a liquid used to dye things

dying
present participle of **die** *VERB*

dyke *NOUN* (**dykes**)
another spelling of **dike**

dynamic *ADJECTIVE*
energetic and active

dynamite *NOUN*
1 a powerful explosive **2** (*informal*) something that will make people angry or excited

dynamo *NOUN* (**dynamos**)
a machine that makes electricity

dynasty *NOUN* (**dynasties**) (*say* **din**- a- sti)
a series of kings and queens from the same family

dyslexia *NOUN* (*say* dis- **lek**- si- a)
special difficulty in being able to read and spell words
▷ **dyslexic** *ADJECTIVE* someone is dyslexic when they have dyslexia

dystrophy *NOUN* (*say* **dis**- tro- fi)
a disease that badly weakens the muscles

Ee

each *DETERMINER & PRONOUN*
each person or thing in a group is every one of them when you think of them separately • *Each film lasts an hour.* • *You get ten marks for each of these questions.* • *We all knew each other.*

eager *ADJECTIVE*
badly wanting to do something or to have something; enthusiastic
▷ **eagerly** *ADVERB* in an eager way
▷ **eagerness** *NOUN* eagerness is being eager to do something

eagle *NOUN* (**eagles**)
a large bird of prey with strong eyesight

ear [1] *NOUN* (**ears**)
1 the part of your body that you hear with **2** an ear, or a good ear, for something is the ability to hear something clearly and understand it well • *She has an unusually good ear for music.*

> **WORD FAMILY**
> A word meaning to do with the ear or hearing is **aural**: for example, an *aural memory* is something you remember from hearing it.

ear [2] *NOUN* (**ears**)
the spike of seeds at the top of a stalk of corn

earache *NOUN*
a pain inside your ear

eardrum *NOUN* (**eardrums**)
a membrane in the ear that vibrates when sound reaches it

earl *NOUN* (**earls**)
a British nobleman

earlobe *NOUN* (**earlobes**)
the rounded part that hangs down at the bottom of your ear

early *ADVERB & ADJECTIVE* (**earlier**, **earliest**)
1 arriving or happening before the usual or expected time • *Jane caught a bus and got home early.* **2** happening near the beginning • *The team was helped by an early goal.* • *They became friends early in their lives.*

earmark *VERB* (**earmarks**, **earmarking**, **earmarked**)
to earmark something, especially money, is to put it aside for a special purpose

earn *VERB* (**earns**, **earning**, **earned**)
1 to earn money is to get it by working for it **2** to earn a reward or praise is to do something good so that you deserve it

earnest *ADJECTIVE*
serious about something you want to do or about something important • *Inside the shop, Mrs Brown was having an earnest conversation with the store detective.* — Michael Bond, *A Bear Called Paddington*
▷ **earnestly** *ADVERB* in an earnest way

earnings *PLURAL NOUN*
earnings are money that someone earns

earphones *PLURAL NOUN*
earphones are a set of two small flat speakers joined by a band that fits over your ears so that you can listen to music without other people hearing it

earplugs *PLURAL NOUN*
earplugs are a pair of small plugs that fit into your ears to cut out loud sounds

earring *NOUN* (**earrings**)
an ornament worn on the ear

earshot *NOUN*
a sound is in earshot when it is close enough for you to be able to hear it

earth *NOUN* (**earths**)
1 the earth is the planet that we live on **2** earth is soil or the ground **3** an earth is a hole or burrow where a fox or badger lives **4** an earth is also a connection to the ground to complete an electric circuit
you use **on earth** with words like *what*, *who*, and *where* to make the point stronger • *What on earth are you doing?*
to cost the earth (*informal*) is to cost a lot

earthenware *NOUN*
earthenware is crockery made of baked clay

earthly *ADJECTIVE*
to do with life on earth

earthquake *NOUN* (**earthquakes**)
a violent movement of part of the earth's surface caused by pressure that has built up underneath

> **WORD FAMILY**
> A word meaning 'to do with earthquakes' is **seismic**: for example *seismic activity* is movement under the earth that can make a volcano erupt.

earthworm *NOUN* (**earthworms**)
a common worm that is found in the soil

earthy *ADJECTIVE* (**earthier**, **earthiest**)
1 an earthy colour is dark like earth or soil **2** earthy humour is rather crude or vulgar

earwig *NOUN* (**earwigs**)
a crawling garden insect with pincers at the end of its body

ease *NOUN*
to do something with ease is to do it without any difficulty or trouble
to be at ease is to be comfortable and relaxed • *She liked Tony and felt at ease with him.*

ease *VERB* (**eases**, **easing**, **eased**)
1 to ease something unpleasant is to make it easier or less troublesome **2** a pain or problem eases when it becomes less severe or troublesome **3** to ease something is to move it gently into position

easel *NOUN* (**easels**)
a stand or frame for holding a blackboard or a painting

easily *ADVERB*
1 without difficulty; with ease • *Pencil marks can be easily rubbed out afterwards.* **2** by far • *This was easily the best victory of his career.* **3** very likely • *They could easily be wrong.*

east *NOUN*
1 the direction in which the sun rises **2** the part of a country or city that is in this direction

> WORD FAMILY
> A word sometimes used in literature for eastern countries is **the Orient**.

east *ADJECTIVE & ADVERB*
1 towards the east or in the east **2** coming from the east • *An east wind made the day very cold.*

> WORD FAMILY
> A word describing things in the east is **oriental**: *oriental languages* are languages that are spoken in eastern countries.

Easter *NOUN*
a Christian festival in spring, commemorating Christ's rising from the dead

easterly *ADJECTIVE*
an easterly wind is one that blows from the east

eastern *ADJECTIVE*
coming from or to do with the east

eastward or **eastwards** *ADJECTIVE & ADVERB*
towards the east

easy *ADJECTIVE* (**easier**, **easiest**)
something easy can be done or understood without trouble • *He started with easy questions.* • *The machine is easy to use.*
to take it easy is to relax or go carefully

eat *VERB* (**eats**, **eating**, **ate**, **eaten**)
to eat food is to chew it and swallow it
to eat something up or **eat something away** is to use it up or destroy it • *Acid rain has eaten away the forests.* • *The sun gradually ate up the mist.* • *Letter writing ate up most of her free time.*

> WORD FAMILY
> A word describing things you can eat is **edible**: *edible plants* are plants that you can use as food.

eatable *ADJECTIVE*
food is eatable when it is good and pleasant to eat

eaves *PLURAL NOUN*
eaves are the overhanging edges of a roof

ebb *NOUN*
the movement of the tide when it is going out
to be at a low ebb is to be in a poor or weak condition

ebb *VERB* (**ebbs**, **ebbing**, **ebbed**)
1 the tide ebbs when it goes away from the land **2** a good feeling ebbs or ebbs away when it becomes much weaker • *When he saw his opponent his courage ebbed away.*

ebony *NOUN*
ebony is a hard black wood

eccentric *ADJECTIVE* (*say* ik- **sen**- trik)
behaving strangely
▷ **eccentricity** *NOUN* eccentricity is strange or unusual behaviour

echo *NOUN* (**echoes**)
a second sound that you hear when the original sound is reflected off a hard surface such as walls or high rocks

echo *VERB* (**echoes**, **echoing**, **echoed**)
1 to echo is to make an echo **2** to echo something said is to repeat it

éclair *NOUN* (**éclairs**) (*say* ay- **klair**)
a finger-shaped cake of pastry with a cream filling

eclipse *NOUN* (**eclipses**)
the blocking of light from the sun or moon, causing a short period of darkness. An eclipse of the sun happens when the moon comes between the sun and the earth and blocks out the light from the sun; and an eclipse of the moon happens when the earth comes between the moon and the sun and casts a dark shadow on the surface of the moon

ecology *NOUN* (*say* ee- **kol**- o- ji)
ecology is the study of living creatures and plants in their surroundings

economic *ADJECTIVE* (*say* eek- o- **nom**- ik or ek- o- **nom**- ik)
1 to do with economics or the economy • *Coal no longer dominates the country's economic scene.*
2 making money, profitable • *It is not normally economic to get drinking water from the sea.*

economical *ADJECTIVE* (*say* eek- o- **nom**- ik- al)
using money and resources carefully
▷ **economically** *ADVERB* to do something economically is to use money and resources carefully when you do it

economics *NOUN* (*say* eek- o- **nom**- iks or ek- o- **nom**- iks)
economics is the study of how money is used and how goods and services are provided and used

economist *NOUN* (**economists**) (*say* i- **kon**- o- mist)
someone who studies economics

economize *VERB* (**economizes**, **economizing**, **economized**) (*say* i- **kon**- o- myz)
to economize is to use money more carefully

economy *NOUN* (**economies**) (*say* i- **kon**- o- mi)
1 an economy is a country's or family's income and the way it is spent **2** economy is being careful with money **3** economies are ways of saving money

ecstasy *NOUN* (**ecstasies**)
1 ecstasy is a feeling of great delight or joy
2 ecstasy is also a name for an illegal drug that gives people extra energy and can cause hallucinations
▷ **ecstatic** *ADJECTIVE* delighted and joyful about something

eczema *NOUN* (*say* **ek**- si- ma)
eczema is a skin disease that causes rough itching patches

edge *NOUN* (**edges**)
1 the part along the side or end of something **2** the sharp part of a knife or other cutting device
to be on edge is to feel nervous and irritable

edge *VERB* (**edges**, **edging**, **edged**)
1 to edge is to move gradually and carefully • *He edged carefully round the puddles in the garden.* **2** to edge something is to form a border to it

edgeways *ADVERB*
with the edge outwards or forwards

edgy *ADJECTIVE* (**edgier**, **edgiest**)
nervous and irritable

edible *ADJECTIVE*
an edible substance is one that you can eat, and is not poisonous

edit *VERB* (**edits**, **editing**, **edited**)
1 to edit a book, newspaper, or magazine is to get it ready for publishing **2** to edit a film or tape recording is to choose parts of it and put them in the right order

> WORD FAMILY
> **Editorial** means to do with editing or editors.

edition *NOUN* (**editions**)
1 the form in which something is published • *There is a special illustrated edition of the book.* **2** all the copies of a newspaper, magazine, or book issued at the same time

editor *NOUN* (**editors**)
1 someone who prepares a book, newspaper, or magazine for publishing **2** the person who manages a newspaper and is in charge of everything that is published in it

educate *VERB* (**educates**, **educating**, **educated**)
to educate someone is to teach them and give them knowledge and skills

education *NOUN*
education, or an education, is the process of teaching people and giving them knowledge and skills

> WORD FAMILY
> Something **educational** teaches you things, for example *an educational television programme.* Another word describing things you learn is **academic**: *academic subjects* are subjects like history, maths, and science, that you learn in a classroom.

eel *NOUN* (**eels**)
a long thin fish that looks like a snake

eerie *ADJECTIVE* (**eerier**, **eeriest**)
weird and frightening • *It was dark outside and there was an eerie silence.*
▷ **eerily** *ADVERB* in an eerie way • *Her voice echoed eerily in the cold air.*
▷ **eeriness** *NOUN* eeriness is being eerie

effect *NOUN* (**effects**)
1 something that happens because of something else • *The drink had a strange effect on Alice.* **2** a general impression • *The lights made a cheerful effect.*

> SPELLING
> Take care not to confuse **effect** with **affect**, which is a verb meaning to have an effect on or to harm.

effective *ADJECTIVE*
producing what you want; successful • *The program is much more effective if it is linked to the Internet.*
▷ **effectively** *ADVERB* in an effective way
▷ **effectiveness** *NOUN* being effective

effervescent *ADJECTIVE* (*say* ef- er- **vess**- ent)
an effervescent liquid is fizzy and gives off bubbles
▷ **effervescence** *NOUN* effervescence is being fizzy or effervescent

efficient *ADJECTIVE*
doing work well; effective
▷ **efficiency** *NOUN* efficiency is being efficient and doing work well
▷ **efficiently** *ADVERB* in an efficient way

effort *NOUN* (**efforts**)
1 effort is using energy or hard work **2** an effort is an attempt

effortless *ADJECTIVE*
something that is effortless doesn't need much work or effort • *The team won another effortless victory.*

e.g.
for example • *There are lots of ways of finding out, e.g. ask a teacher.*

egg[1] *NOUN* (**eggs**)
1 an oval or round object with a thin shell that birds, fish, reptiles, and insects lay, and in which their offspring develop **2** a hen's or duck's egg used as food

> WORD FAMILY
> An egg in a woman or female mammal is called an **ovum**; an egg shape is sometimes called **ovoid**.

egg[2] *VERB* (**eggs**, **egging**, **egged**)
to egg someone on is to encourage them with taunts or dares • *He didn't want to dance but his friends egged him on.*

Eid *NOUN* (*say* eed)
a Muslim festival that marks the end of the fast of Ramadan

eiderdown *NOUN* (**eiderdowns**) (*say* I- der- down)
a quilt stuffed with soft material

eight *NOUN* (**eights**)
the number 8

> WORD FAMILY
> A word for a group of eight people, especially musicians playing together, is **octet**.

eighteen *NOUN* (**eighteens**)
the number 18
▷ **eighteenth** *ADJECTIVE & NOUN* 18th

eighth *ADJECTIVE & NOUN*
the next after the seventh
▷ **eighthly** *ADVERB* in the eighth place; as the eighth one

eighty *NOUN* (**eighties**)
the number 80
▷ **eightieth** *ADJECTIVE & NOUN* 80th

either *DETERMINER & PRONOUN*
1 one or the other of two people or things • *Either road will take us there.* • *Either of them might have seen the killer.* **2** both of two things • *The houses on either side were all boarded up.*

either *ADVERB*
also; similarly • *I didn't rush, but I didn't hang about either.*

either *CONJUNCTION*
either ... or ... one thing or another, but not both • *You can choose either a CD or a DVD .* • *The soldiers were all either killed or badly injured.*

eject *VERB* (**ejects**, **ejecting**, **ejected**)
1 to eject something is to send it out with force **2** to eject someone is to make them leave
▷ **ejection** *NOUN* ejection is ejecting something or someone

elaborate *ADJECTIVE* (*say* i- lab- er- at)
complicated or detailed

elaborate *VERB* (**elaborates**, **elaborating**, **elaborated**) (*say* i- lab- er- ayt)
to elaborate something is to describe it or work it out in detail

elastic *NOUN*
cord or material with strands of rubber in it so that it can stretch

elastic *ADJECTIVE*
able to stretch and then return to its original shape or length
▷ **elasticity** *NOUN* elasticity is when something stretches easily

elated *ADJECTIVE*
very pleased and excited

elbow *NOUN* (**elbows**)
the joint in the middle of your arm, where it bends

elbow *VERB* (**elbows**, **elbowing**, **elbowed**)
to elbow someone is to push or prod them with your elbow

elder *ADJECTIVE*
older • *Apparently Arthur has an elder brother.*

elderberry *NOUN*
a small black berry from a tree with white flowers called an *elder*

elderly *ADJECTIVE*
rather old

eldest *ADJECTIVE*
oldest • *Their eldest son George was born in 1660.*

elect *VERB* (**elects**, **electing**, **elected**)
to elect someone is to choose them by voting

election *NOUN* (**elections**)
the process of voting for people, especially for Members of Parliament

electorate *NOUN*
a country's electorate is all the people who can vote in an election

electric or **electrical** *ADJECTIVE*
to do with electricity, or worked by electricity
▷ **electrically** *ADVERB* by using electricity

electrician *NOUN* (**electricians**)
someone whose job is to fit and repair electrical equipment

electricity *NOUN*
electricity is a kind of energy used to produce light and heat, and to make machines work

electrify *VERB* (**electrifies**, **electrifying**, **electrified**)
1 to electrify something is to make it work by electricity, or to give it an electric charge **2** to electrify someone is to excite or startle them • *Her singing electrified the audience.*
▷ **electrification** *NOUN* electrification is making something work by electricity

electrocute *VERB* (**electrocutes, electrocuting, electrocuted**)
to electrocute someone is to kill them when a large charge of electricity passes through them
▷ **electrocution** *NOUN* electrocution is electrocuting someone

electromagnet *NOUN* (**electromagnets**)
a magnet worked by electricity

electron *NOUN* (**electrons**)
a particle of matter that is smaller than an atom and has a negative electric charge

electronic *ADJECTIVE*
electronic equipment uses transistors and silicon chips, which are worked by electrons
▷ **electronically** *ADVERB* by means of electronic devices

electronic mail *NOUN*
a system of sending messages from one computer to another by means of a network

electronics *PLURAL NOUN*
electronics are the use or study of electronic devices

elegant *ADJECTIVE*
graceful and smart
▷ **elegance** *NOUN* elegance is being graceful and smart
▷ **elegantly** *ADVERB* in an elegant way

element *NOUN* (**elements**)
1 (*in science*) a substance that cannot be split up into simpler substances, for example copper and oxygen **2** a part of something **3** the elements of a subject are the basic facts to do with it • *Next term you will learn the elements of algebra.* **4** the elements are forces that make the weather, such as rain and wind **5** a wire or coil that gives out heat in an electric heater or cooker
to be in your element is to be doing something you enjoy

elementary *ADJECTIVE*
dealing with the simplest stages of something; easy

elephant *NOUN* (**elephants**)
a very large animal found in Africa and India, with a thick grey skin, large ears, a trunk, and tusks

elevate *VERB* (**elevates, elevating, elevated**)
to elevate something is to lift it or raise it to a higher position

elevation *NOUN* (**elevations**)
1 a drawing of a building or large object seen from the side **2** the height of land or a large object in relation to sea level

elevator *NOUN* (**elevators**)
a lift for carrying people from one floor to another in a large building

eleven *NOUN* (**elevens**)
1 the number 11 **2** a team of eleven people in cricket, football, and other sports
▷ **eleventh** *ADJECTIVE & NOUN* 11th

elf *NOUN* (**elves**)
a tiny mischievous fairy in stories

eligible *ADJECTIVE*
a person is eligible for something when they are qualified or suitable for it
▷ **eligibility** *NOUN* eligibility is being eligible for something

eliminate *VERB* (**eliminates, eliminating, eliminated**)
to eliminate someone or something is to get rid of them
▷ **elimination** *NOUN* elimination is getting rid of someone or something

elite *NOUN* (**elites**)
a group of people with special privileges

elk *NOUN* (**elk** or **elks**)
a large kind of deer

ellipse *NOUN* (**ellipses**)
an oval shape

elliptical *ADJECTIVE*
oval-shaped

elm *NOUN* (**elms**)
a tall tree with large rough leaves

elocution *NOUN*
elocution is the art of speaking clearly and correctly

elongated *ADJECTIVE*
made longer; lengthened

eloquent *ADJECTIVE*
speaking well and expressing ideas clearly
▷ **eloquence** *NOUN* eloquence is speaking well and clearly

else *ADVERB*
besides; instead • *Nobody else knows.*
or else otherwise • *Run or else you'll be late.*

elsewhere *ADVERB*
somewhere else

elude *VERB* (**eludes, eluding, eluded**)
1 to elude someone is to escape from them or avoid being caught by them **2** something eludes you when you cannot find it or remember it

elusive *ADJECTIVE*
difficult to find or catch • *Deer are elusive animals.*

elves
plural of **elf**

email
short for **electronic mail**

emancipate *VERB* (**emancipates, emancipating, emancipated**)
to emancipate someone is to set them free from slavery

> **WORD FAMILY**
> **Emancipation** is being set free from slavery.

embankment *NOUN* (**embankments**)
a long wall or bank of earth that holds back water or supports a road or railway

embark *VERB* (**embarks**, **embarking**, **embarked**)
to embark is to go on board a ship
to embark on something is to begin something important
▷ **embarkation** *NOUN* embarkation is going on board a ship

embarrass *VERB* (**embarrasses**, **embarrassing**, **embarrassed**)
to embarrass someone is to make them feel shy or awkward
▷ **embarrassment** *NOUN* embarrassment is feeling awkward or embarrassed

embassy *NOUN* (**embassies**)
a building where an ambassador from another country lives and has an office

embellish *VERB* (**embellishes**, **embellishing**, **embellished**)
to embellish something is to decorate it or add extra details to it
▷ **embellishment** *NOUN* an extra piece of decoration or a detail that makes something more attractive or interesting

embers *PLURAL NOUN*
the embers of a fire are small pieces of coal or wood that keep glowing when the fire is going out

emblem *NOUN* (**emblems**)
a symbol that stands for something • *The dove is an emblem of peace.*

embrace *VERB* (**embraces**, **embracing**, **embraced**)
1 to embrace someone is to hold them closely in your arms **2** to embrace a cause or belief is to adopt it • *Many Roman soldiers embraced Christianity.* **3** to embrace several things is to include them • *The trade association embraces seventeen countries of central and east Africa.*

embroider *VERB* (**embroiders**, **embroidering**, **embroidered**)
to embroider cloth is to decorate it by stitching in designs or pictures
▷ **embroidery** *NOUN* embroidery is the art of embroidering

embryo *NOUN* (**embryos**)
a baby or young animal that is growing in the womb

emerald *NOUN* (**emeralds**)
1 a green jewel **2** a bright green colour

emerge *VERB* (**emerges**, **emerging**, **emerged**)
to emerge is to come out or appear
▷ **emergence** *NOUN* the emergence of something is when it first appears

emergency *NOUN* (**emergencies**)
a sudden dangerous event that needs to be dealt with very quickly

emery paper *NOUN*
a gritty paper like sandpaper

emigrant *NOUN* (**emigrants**)
someone who leaves their own country and goes to live in another country

emigrate *VERB* (**emigrates**, **emigrating**, **emigrated**)
to emigrate is to leave your own country and go and live in another country
▷ **emigration** *NOUN* emigration is going to live in another country

> SPELLING
> Be careful not to confuse **emigrate** with **immigrate**, which means to come into a country to live there.

eminent *ADJECTIVE*
famous and respected • *Britain's most eminent woman mountaineer died ten years ago.*
▷ **eminence** *NOUN* eminence is being famous

emission *NOUN* (**emissions**)
1 the action of sending something out
2 something that is emitted, for example fumes or radiation

emit *VERB* (**emits**, **emitting**, **emitted**)
to emit something such as smoke or fumes is to send it out

emotion *NOUN* (**emotions**)
1 an emotion is a strong feeling in your mind, such as love or fear **2** emotion is being excited or upset • *Tears of emotion flooded his eyes.*

> WORD FAMILY
> An **emotional** person expresses feelings openly; an **emotional** event or experience is one that excites strong feelings in people; you behave **emotionally** when you show your feelings openly.

emperor *NOUN* (**emperors**)
the ruler of an empire

> WORD FAMILY
> The word **emperor** normally means man. A female emperor, or the wife of an emperor, is called an **empress**. A word describing things to do with emperors and empires is **imperial**: an *imperial guard* protects the emperor.

emphasis *NOUN* (**emphases**)
special importance given to something

emphatic *ADJECTIVE*
an emphatic statement or expression is one that you make very firmly or strongly • *He agreed, with an emphatic nod of the head.*
▷ **emphatically** *ADVERB* you say something emphatically when you are very firm and definite about it

emphasize *VERB* (**emphasizes**, **emphasizing**, **emphasized**)
to emphasize something is to give it special importance

a b c d e f g h i j k l m n o p q r s t u v w x y z

empire *NOUN* (**empires**)
1 a group of countries ruled by one person or group of people **2** a large group of businesses or shops under the control of one person or group of people

employ *VERB* (**employs**, **employing**, **employed**)
1 to employ someone is to pay them to work for you **2** to employ something is to use it

employee *NOUN* (**employees**) (*say* im- **ploi**- ee)
someone who works for another person or group of people

employer *NOUN* (**employers**)
a person or organization that has people working for them

employment *NOUN*
1 employment is having paid work **2** an employment is a paid job

empress *NOUN* (**empresses**)
a female emperor, or the wife of an emperor

empty *ADJECTIVE* (**emptier**, **emptiest**)
an empty place or container has nothing or no one in it • *The shop had an empty flat above it.* • *Diana waved her empty glass, hoping for more.*
▷ **emptiness** *NOUN* emptiness is being empty

empty *VERB* (**empties**, **emptying**, **emptied**)
1 to empty something is to make it empty **2** to empty is to become empty • *After the show the hall quickly emptied.*

emu *NOUN* (**emus**) (*say* ee- mew)
a large Australian bird that cannot fly, like an ostrich but smaller

emulate *VERB* (**emulates**, **emulating**, **emulated**)
to emulate someone is to do what they do because you respect or admire them

emulsion *NOUN* (**emulsions**)
1 emulsion is a creamy or slightly oily liquid
2 emulsion, or emulsion paint, a kind of water paint used for decorating buildings

enable *VERB* (**enables**, **enabling**, **enabled**)
to enable someone to do something is to make it possible for them • *A calculator will enable you to multiply and divide quickly.*

enamel *NOUN* (**enamels**)
1 enamel is a shiny glassy substance that is baked on to metal or pottery to form a hard bright surface **2** enamel is also the hard shiny surface of teeth **3** an enamel paint is a hard glossy paint

encampment *NOUN* (**encampments**)
a military camp

enchant *VERB* (**enchants**, **enchanting**, **enchanted**)
1 to enchant someone is to delight or please them
2 to enchant someone is also to put a magic spell on them in stories

> WORD FAMILY
> An **enchanted** place is one that has come under a magic spell in stories; something is **enchanting** when it is beautiful or delightful; **enchantment** is a feeling of wonder or delight.

encircle *VERB* (**encircles**, **encircling**, **encircled**)
to encircle something or someone is to surround them • *The lake was completely encircled by a road.*

enclose *VERB* (**encloses**, **enclosing**, **enclosed**)
1 to enclose an area is to put a fence or wall round it **2** to enclose something is to put it in an envelope or packet with a letter

enclosure *NOUN* (**enclosures**)
1 a piece of ground with a fence or wall round it
2 something you put in an envelope or packet together with a letter

encore *NOUN* (**encores**) (*say* **on**- kor)
an extra item performed at a concert or show when the audience has clapped or cheered the main items

encounter *VERB* (**encounters**, **encountering**, **encountered**)
1 to encounter someone is to meet them unexpectedly **2** to encounter something is to experience it • *We have encountered difficulties.*

encourage *VERB* (**encourages**, **encouraging**, **encouraged**)
1 to encourage someone is to give them confidence or hope • *We were encouraged by your support.* **2** to encourage someone to do something is to urge and help them to do it • *They try to encourage schools to take part in these road safety schemes.* • *This behaviour should not be encouraged.*
▷ **encouragement** *NOUN* encouragement is supporting someone or something in what they do • *The crowd shouted their encouragement.*

encyclopedia *NOUN* (**encyclopedias**)
a book or set of books containing a lot of information on a particular subject, or on all subjects, often with headings arranged in alphabetical order like a dictionary
▷ **encyclopedic** *ADJECTIVE* an encyclopedic book is one that gives you a lot of information

end *NOUN* (**ends**)
1 the end of something is the last part of it or the point where it stops • *Holly stood at the end of the pier.* • *Kenny thought he would never reach the end of his work.* **2** each end of a sports pitch is the part defended by one team or player **3** an end is an aim or purpose • *They used the money for their own ends.*
on end 1 upright • *His hair stood on end.*
2 continuously • *She spoke for two hours on end.*

end *VERB* (**ends**, **ending**, **ended**)
1 to end something is to finish it **2** to end is to finish

endanger *VERB* (**endangers**, **endangering**, **endangered**)
to endanger someone or something is to cause them danger, especially of being injured

endangered species *NOUN*
a type of animal or plant that has become so rare that it is in danger of becoming extinct

endeavour *VERB* (**endeavours**, **endeavouring**, **endeavoured**)
to endeavour to do something is to try hard to do it •*He endeavoured to get the job finished that day.*

ending *NOUN* (**endings**)
the last part of something •*They all wanted a story with a happy ending.*

endless *ADJECTIVE*
never stopping •*Top athletes need endless training.*
▷ **endlessly** *ADVERB* without ending

endure *VERB* (**endures**, **enduring**, **endured**)
1 to endure pain or suffering is to put up with it **2** to endure is to continue or last
▷ **endurance** *NOUN* endurance is suffering or putting up with something unpleasant

enemy *NOUN* (**enemies**)
1 someone who is opposed to someone else and wants to harm them **2** a nation or army that is at war with another country

WORD FAMILY
Someone who is an enemy is **hostile**: *a hostile attitude* is very unfriendly, and *a hostile force* is an army that might attack someone.

energetic *ADJECTIVE*
1 an energetic person has a lot of energy **2** an energetic activity needs a lot of energy •*They then performed an energetic dance.*
▷ **energetically** *ADVERB* with a lot of energy

energy *NOUN* (**energies**)
1 energy is the ability to do work or provide power, for example electrical energy **2** a person's energy is the strength they have to do things

enforce *VERB* (**enforces**, **enforcing**, **enforced**)
to enforce a law or order is to make people obey it
▷ **enforcement** *NOUN* enforcement is making people obey laws

engage *VERB* (**engages**, **engaging**, **engaged**)
1 to engage someone is to give them a job **2** to engage someone in conversation is to talk to them **3** to engage the enemy is to start a battle

engaged *ADJECTIVE*
1 someone is engaged when they have promised to marry someone **2** a telephone line or lavatory is engaged when someone is already using it

engagement *NOUN* (**engagements**)
1 a promise to marry someone **2** an appointment to meet someone or do something **3** a battle

engine *NOUN* (**engines**)
1 a machine that turns energy into motion **2** a vehicle that pulls a railway train

engineer *NOUN* (**engineers**)
a person who designs and builds machines, roads, and bridges

engineering *NOUN*
engineering is the designing and building of machines, roads, bridges, and other large buildings

engrave *VERB* (**engraves**, **engraving**, **engraved**)
to engrave a surface is to carve figures or words on it
▷ **engraver** *NOUN* someone who is skilled in engraving

engrossed *ADJECTIVE*
to be engrossed in something is to concentrate on it and ignore other things around you •*He was so engrossed in his work that he didn't hear her come in.*

engulf *VERB* (**engulfs**, **engulfing**, **engulfed**)
to engulf something is to flow over it and swamp it •*The town was engulfed by smoke from a huge forest fire.*

enhance *VERB* (**enhances**, **enhancing**, **enhanced**)
to enhance something is to make it more valuable or attractive •*There is a simple trick that enhances the flavour of vegetables during cooking.*
▷ **enhancement** *NOUN* something that improves a thing or makes it more attractive

enjoy *VERB* (**enjoys**, **enjoying**, **enjoyed**)
1 to enjoy something is to get pleasure from it **2** to enjoy yourself is to have a good time
▷ **enjoyable** *ADJECTIVE* able to be enjoyed; pleasant
▷ **enjoyment** *NOUN* enjoyment is a feeling of great pleasure

enlarge *VERB* (**enlarges**, **enlarging**, **enlarged**)
to enlarge something is to make it larger
▷ **enlargement** *NOUN* enlargement is making something larger

enlist *VERB* (**enlists**, **enlisting**, **enlisted**)
1 to enlist is to join the army, navy, or air force **2** to enlist someone's help is to ask them to help you
▷ **enlistment** *NOUN* enlistment is joining the army, navy, or air force

enormity *NOUN*
something very wicked or harmful •*People don't realize the enormity of the disaster created by this war.*

USING THIS WORD
Enormity is also used to mean 'huge size', but it is better to use **enormousness** for this •*We were astonished by the enormousness of the house.*

enormous *ADJECTIVE*
very large; huge
▷ **enormously** *ADVERB* hugely; a lot •*I enjoyed the party enormously.*
▷ **enormousness** *NOUN* enormousness is huge size

enough *DETERMINER, NOUN, & ADVERB*
as much or as many as you need or can cope with

enquire *VERB* (**enquires**, **enquiring**, **enquired**)
to enquire about something is to ask for information about it •*He enquired if I was well.*
▷ **enquiry** *NOUN* a question that asks for information

enquiry *NOUN* (**enquiries**)
a question you ask when you want information •*Her enquiry was about the time of the next train.*

enrage *VERB* (**enrages**, **enraging**, **enraged**)
to enrage a person or animal is to make them very angry

enrich *VERB* (**enriches**, **enriching**, **enriched**)
to enrich something is to make it richer
▷ **enrichment** *NOUN* enrichment is making something richer

enrol *VERB* (**enrols**, **enrolling**, **enrolled**)
1 to enrol in a society or class is to become a member of it **2** to enrol someone is to make them a member
▷ **enrolment** *NOUN* enrolment is becoming a member or making someone a member

ensue *VERB* (**ensues**, **ensuing**, **ensued**)
to ensue is to happen or come after something else, often as a result of it

ensure *VERB* (**ensures**, **ensuring**, **ensured**)
to ensure that something happens or has happened is to make sure of it • *Please ensure that you leave the room tidy when you go.*

> SPELLING
> Take care not to confuse **ensure** with **insure**, which means to protect yourself or your property with insurance.

entangle *VERB* (**entangles**, **entangling**, **entangled**)
to entangle something is to get it tangled or caught up
▷ **entanglement** *NOUN* entanglement is becoming tangled

enter *VERB* (**enters**, **entering**, **entered**)
1 to enter a place is to come into it or go into it **2** to enter something in a list or book is to write or record it there **3** to enter data in a computer is to key it in **4** to enter for a competition or examination is to take part in it

enterprise *NOUN* (**enterprises**)
1 enterprise is being bold and adventurous **2** an enterprise is a difficult or important task or project

enterprising *ADJECTIVE*
an enterprising person or activity is one that is exciting or adventurous

entertain *VERB* (**entertains**, **entertaining**, **entertained**)
1 to entertain someone is to amuse them or give them pleasure, as a singer or comedian does **2** to entertain people is to have them as guests and give them food and drink
▷ **entertainer** *NOUN* someone such as a singer or comedian who entertains people
▷ **entertainment** *NOUN* entertainment is something that entertains or amuses people

enthusiasm *NOUN* (**enthusiasms**)
1 enthusiasm is a feeling of excitement and interest you show for something **2** an enthusiasm is a strong liking or interest

enthusiast *NOUN* (**enthusiasts**)
a person who has a strong interest in something • *Her brother is a hockey enthusiast.*

enthusiastic *ADJECTIVE*
full of enthusiasm • *She is very enthusiastic about breeding mice.*
▷ **enthusiastically** *ADVERB* in an enthusiastic way

entire *ADJECTIVE*
whole or complete • *The entire school gathered in the field for a photograph.*
▷ **entirely** *ADVERB* completely; in every way • *The brothers look entirely different.*
▷ **entirety** *NOUN* the entirety of something is all of it

entitle *VERB* (**entitles**, **entitling**, **entitled**)
to entitle someone to something is to give them a right to it • *The voucher entitles you to a free drink with your pizza.*
▷ **entitlement** *NOUN* a right you have to something

entrance [1] *NOUN* (**entrances**) (*say* **en**- transs)
1 the way into a place **2** coming into a room or on to a stage or arena • *Everyone clapped when the clowns made their entrance.*

entrance [2] *VERB* (**entrances**, **entrancing**, **entranced**) (*say* in- **trahnss**)
to entrance someone is to delight or enchant them

entrant *NOUN* (**entrants**)
someone who goes in for a competition or examination

entreat *VERB* (**entreats**, **entreating**, **entreated**)
to entreat someone is to ask them seriously or earnestly
▷ **entreaty** *NOUN* a serious or earnest request

entrust *VERB* (**entrusts**, **entrusting**, **entrusted**)
to entrust someone with something, or to entrust something to someone, is to give it to them to look after

entry *NOUN* (**entries**)
1 an entrance **2** something written in a list or diary

envelop *VERB* (**envelops**, **enveloping**, **enveloped**) (*say* in- **vel**- op)
to envelop something is to cover or wrap it completely • *The mountain was enveloped in mist.*

envelope *NOUN* (**envelopes**) (*say* **en**- ve- lohp or **on**- ve- lohp)
a wrapper or covering, especially for a letter

envious *ADJECTIVE*
you are envious of someone when they have something you would like to have too
▷ **enviously** *ADVERB* in an envious way

environment *NOUN* (**environments**)
1 surroundings, especially as they affect people and other living things • *Some animals and plants can die out if their environment is damaged.* **2** the

environment is the natural world of the land and sea and air
▷ **environmental** *ADJECTIVE* to do with the environment

> WORD FAMILY
> Another word to do with the environment is **green**.

envy *NOUN*
an unhappy feeling you have when you want something that someone else has got

envy *VERB* (**envies**, **envying**, **envied**)
to envy someone is to feel envy about them

enzyme *NOUN* (**enzymes**)
a chemical substance that humans, animals, and plants produce and that sets off processes of change such as the digestion of food

epic *NOUN* (**epics**)
1 a story or poem about heroes **2** an exciting or spectacular film

epidemic *NOUN* (**epidemics**)
a disease that spreads quickly among the people of an area

epilepsy *NOUN*
epilepsy is a disease of the nervous system, which causes periods of unconsciousness and convulsions

epileptic *ADJECTIVE*
to do with epilepsy • *an epileptic fit*

epileptic *NOUN* (**epileptics**)
someone who suffers from epilepsy

epilogue *NOUN* (**epilogues**) (*say* **ep**- i- log)
words written or spoken at the end of a story or a play

episode *NOUN* (**episodes**)
1 one event that is part of a series of happenings or forms part of a story **2** one programme in a radio or television serial

epitaph *NOUN* (**epitaphs**)
words written on a tomb or describing a person who has died

epoch *NOUN* (**epochs**) (*say* ee- pok)
a long period of time in the past, during which important events happened

equal *ADJECTIVE*
things are equal when they are the same in amount, size, or value
to be equal to something is to have the strength or ability to do it • *She was equal to the task.*

equal *NOUN* (**equals**)
a person or thing that is equal to another • *He thought he was his sister's equal at maths.*

equal *VERB* (**equals**, **equalling**, **equalled**)
to equal something is to be the same in amount, size, or value

equality *NOUN*
equality is being equal

equalize *VERB* (**equalizes**, **equalizing**, **equalized**)
to equalize things is to make them equal

equalizer *NOUN* (**equalizers**)
a goal or point that makes the scores in a game equal

equally *ADVERB*
in the same way or to the same extent • *You are all equally to blame.*

equation *NOUN* (**equations**) (*say* i- **kway**- zhon)
(*in mathematics*) a statement that two amounts are equal, for example 3 + 4 = 2 + 5

equator *NOUN* (*say* i- **kway**- ter)
an imaginary line round the earth at an equal distance from the North and South Poles
▷ **equatorial** *ADJECTIVE* to do with the equator or near the equator

equestrian *ADJECTIVE*
to do with horse-riding

equilateral *ADJECTIVE* (*say* ee- kwi- **lat**- er- al)
an equilateral triangle has all its sides equal

equilibrium *NOUN* (**equilibria**) (*say* ee- kwi- **lib**- ri- um)
equilibrium is a state of even balance

equinox *NOUN* (**equinoxes**)
the time of year when day and night are equal in length (about 20 March in spring and about 22 September in autumn)

equip *VERB* (**equips**, **equipping**, **equipped**)
to equip someone or something is to supply them with what is needed • *Are you equipped for mountaineering?*

equipment *NOUN*
equipment is a set of things needed for a special purpose

equivalent *ADJECTIVE*
things are equivalent when they are equal in value, importance, or meaning
▷ **equivalence** *NOUN* equivalence is being equivalent

era *NOUN* (**eras**) (*say* **eer**- a)
a long period of history

erase *VERB* (**erases**, **erasing**, **erased**)
1 to erase something written is to rub it out **2** to erase a recording on magnetic tape is to wipe it out
▷ **eraser** *NOUN* a piece of rubber or plastic for rubbing out writing

erect *ADJECTIVE*
standing straight up

erect *VERB* (**erects**, **erecting**, **erected**)
to erect something is to set it up or build it
▷ **erection** *NOUN* something that has been built or erected

erode *VERB* (**erodes**, **eroding**, **eroded**)
to erode something is to wear it away • *Water has eroded the rocks.*

a b c d **e** f g h i j k l m n o p q r s t u v w x y z

erosion *NOUN*
erosion is the wearing away of the earth's surface by the action of water and wind

errand *NOUN* (**errands**)
a short journey to take a message or fetch something

erratic *ADJECTIVE* (*say* i- **rat**- ik)
not reliable or regular
▷ **erratically** *ADVERB* in an erratic way

error *NOUN* (**errors**)
a mistake
in error by mistake

erupt *VERB* (**erupts**, **erupting**, **erupted**)
1 a volcano erupts when it shoots out lava
2 something powerful or violent erupts when it suddenly happens • *An argument erupted over a disputed goal.*
▷ **eruption** *NOUN* eruption, or an eruption, is when a volcano erupts

escalate *VERB* (**escalates**, **escalating**, **escalated**)
to escalate is to become gradually greater or more serious • *The riots escalated into a war.*
▷ **escalation** *NOUN* escalation is when something becomes greater or more serious

escalator *NOUN* (**escalators**)
a staircase with a revolving band of steps moving up or down

escape *VERB* (**escapes**, **escaping**, **escaped**)
1 to escape is to get free or get away **2** to escape something is to avoid it • *He escaped the washing-up.*

escape *NOUN* (**escapes**)
1 an act of escaping • *an escape of prisoners* **2** a way to escape • *He suddenly saw his escape, and ran for it.*

escort *NOUN* (**escorts**) (*say* **ess**- kort)
1 a person or group who accompanies someone, especially to give protection **2** a group of vehicles, ships, or aircraft accompanying someone or something

escort *VERB* (**escorts**, **escorting**, **escorted**) (*say* i- **skort**)
to escort someone or something is to act as an escort to them

Eskimo *NOUN* (**Eskimos** or **Eskimo**)
one of the people who live in very cold parts of North America, Greenland, and Siberia

> **USING THIS WORD**
> The official name of the people who live in the far north of North America is **Inuit**.

especially *ADVERB*
chiefly; more than anything else • *I like cheese, especially strong cheese.*

espionage *NOUN* (*say* **ess**- pi- on- ahzh)
espionage is spying on other countries or people

esplanade *NOUN* (**esplanades**)
a flat open area for walking, especially by the sea

Esq.
a title sometimes put after a man's surname on letters, when no title is used before his name, for example John Smith Esq.

-ess *SUFFIX*
used to make feminine forms of words, for example *lioness* and *actress*

essay *NOUN* (**essays**)
a short piece of writing on one subject

essence *NOUN* (**essences**)
1 the most important quality or ingredient of something **2** a concentrated liquid

essential *ADJECTIVE*
something is essential when it is very important and you must have it or do it • *A car is essential in the country.*
▷ **essentially** *ADVERB* basically; in many ways • *The two stories are essentially the same.*

essential *NOUN* (**essentials**)
something you must have or do

establish *VERB* (**establishes**, **establishing**, **established**)
1 to establish a business, government, or relationship is to start it on a firm basis **2** to establish a fact is to show that it is true • *He managed to establish his innocence.*

establishment *NOUN* (**establishments**)
1 a place where people do business **2** establishing something
the Establishment the people in positions of power and influence

estate *NOUN* (**estates**)
1 an area of land with a set of houses or factories on it **2** a large area of land belonging to one person **3** everything that a person owns when they die

estate agent *NOUN* (**estate agents**)
someone whose business is selling or letting buildings and land

estate car *NOUN* (**estate cars**)
a car with a door or doors at the back, and rear seats that can be removed or folded away

esteem *VERB* (**esteems**, **esteeming**, **esteemed**)
to esteem someone or something is to think they are excellent

estimate *NOUN* (**estimates**) (*say* **ess**- ti- mat)
a rough calculation or guess about an amount or value

estimate *VERB* (**estimates**, **estimating**, **estimated**) (*say* **ess**- ti- mayt)
to estimate is to make an estimate

estimation *NOUN*
1 estimation is making a rough estimate **2** a person's estimation is their opinion • *It is very good in my estimation.*

estuary *NOUN* (**estuaries**) (*say* **ess**- tew- er- i)
the mouth of a large river where it flows into the sea

etc.
short for **et cetera**

et cetera
and other similar things; and so on

etch *VERB* (**etches**, **etching**, **etched**)
to etch a picture is to make it by engraving on a metal plate with an acid
▷ **etching** *NOUN* a picture made by engraving

eternal *ADJECTIVE*
lasting for ever; not ending or changing
▷ **eternally** *ADVERB* for ever
▷ **eternity** *NOUN* eternity is time that goes on for ever

ether *NOUN* (*say* **ee**- ther)
1 ether is a colourless liquid that evaporates easily, and is used as an anaesthetic or a solvent **2** the ether is the upper air

ethnic *ADJECTIVE*
belonging to a particular national or racial group

etymology *NOUN* (**etymologies**)
1 etymology is the study of words and where they come from **2** a word's etymology is a description of where it came from

EU
short for **European Union**

eucalyptus *NOUN* (**eucalyptuses**) (*say* yoo- ka- **lip**- tus)
an evergreen tree from which an oil is obtained

euphemism *NOUN* (**euphemisms**)
a word or phrase which is used instead of an impolite or less tactful one; 'pass away' is a euphemism for 'die'

Eurasian *ADJECTIVE*
having European and Asian parents or ancestors

euro *NOUN* (**euros** or **euro**)
the single currency introduced in the European Union in 1999

European *ADJECTIVE*
coming from Europe or to do with Europe

European *NOUN* (**Europeans**)
a European person

euthanasia *NOUN* (*say* yooth- an- **ay**- zi- a)
euthanasia is causing someone to die gently and without pain when they are suffering from an incurable disease

evacuate *VERB* (**evacuates**, **evacuating**, **evacuated**)
to evacuate people is to move them away from a dangerous place
▷ **evacuation** *NOUN* evacuation is moving people away, especially during a war or when there is a danger
▷ **evacuee** *NOUN* someone who is evacuated, especially during a war

evade *VERB* (**evades**, **evading**, **evaded**)
to evade someone or something is to make an effort to avoid them

evaluate *VERB* (**evaluates**, **evaluating**, **evaluated**)
to evaluate something is to estimate its value
▷ **evaluation** *NOUN* evaluation is estimating the value of something

evaporate *VERB* (**evaporates**, **evaporating**, **evaporated**)
to evaporate is to change from liquid into steam or vapour
▷ **evaporation** *NOUN* evaporation is when a liquid changes into steam or vapour

evasion *NOUN* (**evasions**)
1 evasion is evading something **2** an evasion is an answer that tries to avoid the question being asked

evasive *ADJECTIVE*
trying to avoid answering something; not honest or straightforward

eve *NOUN* (**eves**)
the day or evening before an important day, for example Christmas Eve

even *ADJECTIVE*
1 level and smooth **2** calm and stable • *He has a very even temper.* **3** equal • *Our scores were even.* **4** (*in mathematics*) able to be divided exactly by two • *6 and 14 are even numbers.*
to get even with someone is to take revenge on them
▷ **evenly** *ADVERB* in an even way • *Spread the varnish evenly over the surface.* • *The money will be shared out evenly.*
▷ **evenness** *NOUN* evenness is when something is level and smooth

even *VERB* (**evens**, **evening**, **evened**)
1 to even something is to make it even **2** to even or even out is to become even

even *ADVERB*
used to emphasize another word • *You haven't even started your work!* • *I ran fast, but she ran even faster.* • *She even ignored her mother.*
even so although that is correct

evening *NOUN* (**evenings**)
the time at the end of the day before night time

event *NOUN* (**events**)
1 something that happens, especially something important **2** an item in an athletics contest • *The next event will be the long jump.*
at all events or **in any event** anyway

eventful *ADJECTIVE*
full of happenings, especially remarkable or exciting ones • *They had an eventful train journey across the USA.*

eventual *ADJECTIVE*
happening at last or as a result • *Many failures preceded his eventual success.*

eventually *ADVERB*
finally, in the end • *We eventually managed to get the door open.*

ever *ADVERB*
1 at any time • *It's the best present I've ever had.* **2** always • *ever hopeful* **3** (*informal*) used for emphasis • *Why ever didn't you tell me?*
ever so or **ever such** (*informal*) very much • *I'm ever so pleased.* • *She's ever such a nice girl.*

evergreen *ADJECTIVE*
having green leaves all through the year

evergreen *NOUN* (**evergreens**)
an evergreen tree

everlasting *ADJECTIVE*
lasting for ever or for a long time

every *DETERMINER*
all the people or things of a particular kind; each • *Every child should learn to swim.*
every other each alternate one; every second one • *Every other house had a garage.*

everybody *PRONOUN*
everyone

everyday *ADJECTIVE*
happening or used every day; ordinary • *Just wear your everyday clothes.*

everyone *PRONOUN*
every person; all people • *Everyone likes her.*

everything *PRONOUN*
1 all things; all • *Everything you need is here.* **2** the only or most important thing • *Beauty is not everything.*

everywhere *ADVERB*
in all places

evict *VERB* (**evicts**, **evicting**, **evicted**)
to evict someone is to make them move out of their house
▹ **eviction** *NOUN* eviction is making someone move out of their house

evidence *NOUN*
evidence is facts and information that give people reason to believe something

evident *ADJECTIVE*
obvious; clearly seen • *It is evident that he is lying.*
▹ **evidently** *ADVERB* clearly; obviously • *His mother had evidently changed her mind.*

evil *ADJECTIVE*
an evil person or action is one that is wicked and harmful

evil *NOUN* (**evils**)
evil, or an evil, is something wicked or harmful

evolution *NOUN* (*say* ee-vo-**loo**-shon)
1 gradual change into something different **2** the development of animals and plants from earlier or simpler forms of life

evolve *VERB* (**evolves**, **evolving**, **evolved**)
to develop gradually or naturally

ewe *NOUN* (**ewes**) (*say* yoo)
a female sheep

ex- *PREFIX*
meaning something or someone that used to be, as in *ex-husband*

exact *ADJECTIVE*
1 completely correct **2** giving all the details • *He gave an exact description of the robbers.*
▹ **exactly** *ADVERB* in an exact way; correctly
▹ **exactness** *NOUN* being correct

exaggerate *VERB* (**exaggerates**, **exaggerating**, **exaggerated**)
to exaggerate something is to make it seem bigger or better or worse than it really is
▹ **exaggeration** *NOUN* exaggeration, or an exaggeration, is making something seem more than it really is

exalt *VERB* (**exalts**, **exalting**, **exalted**)
1 to exalt someone is to make them higher in rank **2** to exalt someone is also to praise them highly

exam *NOUN* (**exams**)
(*informal*) an examination

examination *NOUN* (**examinations**)
1 a test of someone's knowledge or skill **2** a close inspection of something

examine *VERB* (**examines**, **examining**, **examined**)
to examine something is to look at it closely or in detail

examiner *NOUN* (**examiners**)
a person who sets and marks an examination to test students' knowledge

example *NOUN* (**examples**)
1 a single thing or event that shows what others of the same kind are like **2** a person or thing that you should copy or learn from
for example as an example

exasperate *VERB* (**exasperates**, **exasperating**, **exasperated**)
to exasperate someone is to make them very annoyed
▹ **exasperation** *NOUN* exasperation is a feeling of being very annoyed

excavate *VERB* (**excavates**, **excavating**, **excavated**)
to excavate a piece of land is to dig in it, especially in building or archaeology
▹ **excavation** *NOUN* excavation, or an excavation, is digging in land
▹ **excavator** *NOUN* a person or machine that excavates

exceed *VERB* (**exceeds**, **exceeding**, **exceeded**)
1 to exceed an amount or achievement is to be more than it or do better than it **2** to exceed a rule or limit is to go beyond it when you are not supposed to • *The driver was exceeding the speed limit.*

exceedingly *ADVERB*
extremely; very much

excel *VERB* (**excels**, **excelling**, **excelled**)
to excel at something is to be very good at it, and better than everyone else

excellent *ADJECTIVE*
extremely good; of the best kind
▷ **excellence** *NOUN* excellence is being extremely good

except *PREPOSITION*
not including; apart from • *Everyone got a prize except me.*

> SPELLING
> Take care not to confuse **except** with **accept**, which is a verb meaning to take something which is offered, or to agree with something.

exception *NOUN* (**exceptions**)
1 something or someone that does not follow the normal rule **2** something that is left out
to take exception to something is to complain about it

exceptional *ADJECTIVE*
unusual • *She has exceptional skill.*
▷ **exceptionally** *ADVERB* to an unusual degree

excerpt *NOUN* (**excerpts**)
a piece taken from a book or story or film

excess *NOUN* (**excesses**)
excess, or an excess, is too much of something • *We have an excess of food.*

> SPELLING
> Take care not to confuse **excess** with **access**, which means a way to reach something.

excessive *ADJECTIVE*
too much or too great
▷ **excessively** *ADVERB* too; by too much • *They are excessively greedy.*

exchange *VERB* (**exchanges**, **exchanging**, **exchanged**)
to exchange something is to give it and receive something else for it

exchange *NOUN* (**exchanges**)
1 a place where telephone lines are connected to each other when a call is made **2** a place where company shares are bought and sold **3** a process of exchanging things

excite *VERB* (**excites**, **exciting**, **excited**)
to excite someone is to make them eager and enthusiastic about something • *The thought of the outing excited them.*

> WORD FAMILY
> A person who is **excitable** is easily excited; to behave **excitedly** is to be very excited about something.

excitement *NOUN* (**excitements**)
1 excitement is being excited **2** an excitement is something that excites you

exclaim *VERB* (**exclaims**, **exclaiming**, **exclaimed**)
to exclaim is to shout or cry out

exclamation *NOUN* (**exclamations**)
1 exclamation is shouting or crying out **2** an exclamation is a word or phrase you say out loud that expresses a strong feeling such as surprise or pain

exclamation mark *NOUN* (**exclamation marks**)
the punctuation mark (!) placed after an exclamation

> EXCLAMATION MARK
> You use an exclamation mark at the end of a sentence which expresses a strong feeling such as anger (*I'll get you for that!*) surprise (*What a strange creature!*) pain (*Ow, that hurt!*) dismay (*Oh no!*). You also use an exclamation mark after a command (*Come here!*) or warning (*Look out!*). In informal writing people sometimes use several exclamation marks together (*I was so angry!!!*), but you should avoid doing this in serious or formal writing.

exclude *VERB* (**excludes**, **excluding**, **excluded**)
1 to exclude someone or something is to keep them out **2** to exclude something is to leave it out • *Do not exclude the possibility of rain.*
▷ **exclusion** *NOUN* exclusion is keeping someone or something out or leaving them out

exclusive *ADJECTIVE*
1 not shared with others • *Today's newspaper has an exclusive report about the match.* **2** allowing only a few people to be involved • *They joined an exclusive club.*
▷ **exclusively** *ADVERB* in an exclusive way

excrement *NOUN*
excrement is waste matter expelled from the body

excrete *VERB* (**excretes**, **excreting**, **excreted**)
to excrete is to pass waste matter out of your body
▷ **excretion** *NOUN* excretion is excreting waste matter

excursion *NOUN* (**excursions**)
a short journey or outing made for pleasure

excuse *NOUN* (**excuses**) (*say* iks-**kewss**)
a reason given to explain why something wrong has been done

excuse *VERB* (**excuses**, **excusing**, **excused**) (*say* iks-**kewz**)
1 to excuse someone is to forgive them **2** to excuse someone something is to allow them not to do it • *Please may I be excused swimming?*
excuse me a polite apology for interrupting or disagreeing
▷ **excusable** *ADJECTIVE* excusable behaviour can be forgiven or excused

execute *VERB* (**executes**, **executing**, **executed**)
1 to execute someone is to put them to death as a punishment **2** to execute something is to perform or produce it • *She executed the somersault perfectly.*
▷ **execution** *NOUN* execution, or an execution, is executing someone or something
▷ **executioner** *NOUN* someone who executes people

executive *NOUN* (**executives**)
a senior person with authority in a business or government organization

exempt *ADJECTIVE*
not having to do something that others have to do • *Old people are sometimes exempt from paying bus fares.*
▷ **exemption** *NOUN* exemption is being exempt from having to do something

exercise *NOUN* (**exercises**)
1 exercise is using your body to make it strong and healthy **2** an exercise is a piece of work done for practice

exercise *VERB* (**exercises**, **exercising**, **exercised**)
1 to exercise is to do exercises **2** to exercise an animal is to give it exercise **3** to exercise something is to use it • *You will have to exercise patience.*

exercise book *NOUN* (**exercise books**)
a book for writing in

exert *VERB* (**exerts**, **exerting**, **exerted**)
to exert oneself or one's ability is to make an effort to get something done • *He exerted all his strength to bend the bar.*
▷ **exertion** *NOUN* exertion is making a big effort

exhale *VERB* (**exhales**, **exhaling**, **exhaled**)
to exhale is to breathe out
▷ **exhalation** *NOUN* exhalation is breathing out

exhaust *NOUN* (**exhausts**)
1 the waste gases from an engine **2** the pipe these gases are sent out through

exhaust *VERB* (**exhausts**, **exhausting**, **exhausted**)
1 to exhaust someone is to make them very tired **2** to exhaust something is to use it up completely
▷ **exhaustion** *NOUN* exhaustion is being very tired

exhibit *VERB* (**exhibits**, **exhibiting**, **exhibited**)
to exhibit something is to show it in public, especially in a gallery or museum
▷ **exhibitor** *NOUN* someone who exhibits something in a gallery or museum

exhibit *NOUN* (**exhibits**)
something displayed in a gallery or museum

exhibition *NOUN* (**exhibitions**)
a collection of things put on display for people to look at

exile *VERB* (**exiles**, **exiling**, **exiled**)
to exile someone is to send them away from their country

exile *NOUN* (**exiles**)
1 exile is having to live away from your own country • *He was in exile for ten years.* **2** an exile is a person who is exiled

exist *VERB* (**exists**, **existing**, **existed**)
1 to exist is to have life or be real • *Do ghosts exist?* **2** to exist is also to stay alive • *They existed on biscuits and water.*

existence *NOUN* (**existences**)
1 existing or being **2** staying alive • *It was a real struggle for existence.*

exit *NOUN* (**exits**)
1 the way out of a place **2** going out of a room or going off a stage or arena • *The clowns then made their exit.*

exit *VERB* (**exits**, **exiting**, **exited**)
to exit is to leave a stage or arena

> USING THIS WORD
> **Exit** is also used as a stage direction: **Exit Hamlet** means 'Hamlet leaves the stage'.

exorcize *VERB* (**exorcizes**, **exorcizing**, **exorcized**)
to exorcize a spirit is to get rid of it, usually with a special ceremony
▷ **exorcism** *NOUN* exorcism is exorcizing a spirit
▷ **exorcist** *NOUN* someone who exorcizes a spirit

exotic *ADJECTIVE*
unusual and colourful, especially because it comes from another part of the world

expand *VERB* (**expands**, **expanding**, **expanded**)
1 to expand something is to make it larger **2** to expand is to become larger
▷ **expansion** *NOUN* expansion is becoming larger or making something larger

expanse *NOUN* (**expanses**)
a wide area

expect *VERB* (**expects**, **expecting**, **expected**)
1 to expect something is to think that it will probably happen • *We expected it would rain.* **2** to be expecting someone is to be waiting for them to arrive **3** to expect something is to think that it ought to happen • *She expects us to be quiet.*

expectant *ADJECTIVE*
1 full of expectation or hope **2** an expectant mother is a woman who is pregnant

expectation *NOUN* (**expectations**)
1 expectation is expecting something or being hopeful **2** an expectation is something you hope to get

expecting *ADJECTIVE*
a woman is expecting when she is pregnant

expedition *NOUN* (**expeditions**)
a journey made in order to do something • *They are going on a climbing expedition.*

expel *VERB* (**expels**, **expelling**, **expelled**)
1 to expel something is to send or force it out • *The fan expels stale air and fumes.* **2** to expel someone is to make them leave a school or country • *He was expelled for bullying.*

expenditure *NOUN*
expenditure is when you spend money or use effort • *We must reduce our expenditure.*

expense *NOUN* (**expenses**)
expense, or an expense, is the cost of doing something

expensive *ADJECTIVE*
costing a lot of money

experience *NOUN* (**experiences**)
1 experience is what you learn from doing and seeing things **2** an experience is something that has happened to you

experience *VERB* (**experiences**, **experiencing**, **experienced**)
to experience something is to have it happen to you

experienced *ADJECTIVE*
having skill or knowledge from much experience

experiment *NOUN* (**experiments**)
a test made in order to study what happens
▷ **experimental** *ADJECTIVE* to do with experiments ▷ **experimentally** *ADVERB* as an experiment

experiment *VERB* (**experiments**, **experimenting**, **experimented**)
to experiment is to carry out experiments
▷ **experimentation** *NOUN* doing experiments

> WORD FAMILY
> Something is **experimental** when it is being tried out to see how good or successful it is; you do something **experimentally** when you are trying it out; **experimentation** is when you are doing experiments to try things out.

expert *NOUN* (**experts**)
someone who has skill or special knowledge in something

expert *ADJECTIVE*
having great knowledge or skill

expertise *NOUN*
expertise is expert ability or knowledge

expire *VERB* (**expires**, **expiring**, **expired**)
1 to expire is to come to an end or to stop being usable • *Your TV licence has expired.* **2** to expire is also to die
▷ **expiry** *NOUN* the time when something expires

explain *VERB* (**explains**, **explaining**, **explained**)
1 to explain something is to make it clear to someone else **2** to explain a fact or event is to show why it happens • *That explains his absence.*

explanation *NOUN* (**explanations**)
something you say that explains something or gives reasons for it • *He gave an explanation for what had happened.*
▷ **explanatory** *ADJECTIVE* an explanatory statement is one that explains something

explode *VERB* (**explodes**, **exploding**, **exploded**)
1 to explode is to burst or suddenly release energy with a loud bang **2** to explode a bomb is to set it off **3** to explode is to increase suddenly or quickly • *The city's population exploded to 3 million in a year.*

exploit *NOUN* (**exploits**) (*say* eks- ploit)
a brave or exciting deed

exploit *VERB* (**exploits**, **exploiting**, **exploited**) (*say* iks- **ploit**)
1 to exploit resources is to use or develop them **2** to exploit someone is to use them selfishly
▷ **exploitation** *NOUN* exploitation is exploiting something or someone

explore *VERB* (**explores**, **exploring**, **explored**)
1 to explore a place is to travel through it to find out more about it **2** to explore a subject is to examine it carefully • *We need to explore all the possibilities.*
▷ **exploration** *NOUN* exploration is exploring a place
▷ **explorer** *NOUN* someone who explores a remote country to find out more about it

explosion *NOUN* (**explosions**)
1 the exploding of a bomb or other weapon **2** a sudden or quick increase • *There was a population explosion after the war.*

explosive *NOUN* (**explosives**)
explosive, or an explosive, is a substance that can explode

explosive *ADJECTIVE*
likely to explode; able to cause an explosion

export *VERB* (**exports**, **exporting**, **exported**) (*say* iks- **port**)
to export goods is to send them abroad to be sold
▷ **exporter** *NOUN* someone who exports goods

export *NOUN* (**exports**) (*say* **eks**- port)
something that is sent abroad to be sold

expose *VERB* (**exposes**, **exposing**, **exposed**)
1 to expose something is to reveal or uncover it **2** to expose someone is to show that they are to blame for something **3** to expose a photographic film is to let light reach it in a camera, so as to take a picture

exposure *NOUN* (**exposures**)
1 exposure is being harmed by the weather when in the open without enough protection **2** an exposure is a single photograph or frame on a film

express *ADJECTIVE*
going or sent quickly

express *NOUN* (**expresses**)
a fast train stopping at only a few stations

express *VERB* (**expresses**, **expressing**, **expressed**)
to express an idea or feeling is to put it into words

a b c d **e** f g h i j k l m n o p q r s t u v w x y z

expression *NOUN* (**expressions**)
1 the look on a person's face that shows what they are thinking or feeling **2** a word or phrase **3** a way of speaking or performing music that expresses feelings
▷ **expressive** *ADJECTIVE* an expressive look or statement is one that shows your feelings

expulsion *NOUN* (**expulsions**)
expulsion, or an expulsion, is when someone is driven away or made to leave

exquisite *ADJECTIVE*
very delicate or beautiful • *Next came a tall, beautiful woman clothed in a splendid trailing gown, trimmed with exquisite lace as fine as cobweb.* — L. Frank Baum, *The Road to Oz*
▷ **exquisitely** *ADVERB* in an exquisite way

extend *VERB* (**extends**, **extending**, **extended**)
1 to extend is to stretch out **2** to extend something is to make it longer or larger **3** to extend a greeting or welcome is to offer it

extension *NOUN* (**extensions**)
1 extension is extending or being extended **2** an extension is something added on, especially to a building **3** an extension is also an extra telephone in an office or house

extensive *ADJECTIVE*
covering a large area • *The bomb caused extensive damage.*
▷ **extensively** *ADVERB* over a large area • *She travelled extensively with her children.*

extent *NOUN* (**extents**)
1 the area or length of something **2** an amount or level • *The extent of the damage was enormous.*

exterior *NOUN* (**exteriors**)
the outside of something

exterminate *VERB* (**exterminates**, **exterminating**, **exterminated**)
to exterminate a people or breed of animal is to kill all the members of it
▷ **extermination** *NOUN* extermination is killing all the people or animals in a place

external *ADJECTIVE*
outside
▷ **externally** *ADVERB* on the outside

extinct *ADJECTIVE*
1 an animal or bird is extinct when there are no more examples of it alive **2** a volcano is extinct when it is not burning or active any more
▷ **extinction** *NOUN* extinction is when something no longer exists or is no longer active

extinguish *VERB* (**extinguishes**, **extinguishing**, **extinguished**)
to extinguish a fire or light is to put it out
▷ **extinguisher** *NOUN* a device for putting out a fire

extra *ADJECTIVE*
more than usual; added • *There is an extra charge for taking a bicycle on the train.*

extra *NOUN* (**extras**)
1 an extra person or thing **2** someone acting as part of the crowd in a film or play

extra- *PREFIX*
1 more than usual, as in *extra-special* **2** outside or beyond something, as in *extraterrestrial*

extract *NOUN* (**extracts**) (*say* **eks- trakt**)
1 a piece taken from a book, play, or film
2 something obtained from something else
• *a plant extract*

extract *VERB* (**extracts**, **extracting**, **extracted**) (*say* **iks- trakt**)
to extract something is to remove it or take it out of something else

extraction *NOUN*
1 a person's extraction is the place or people they come from • *She is of Indian extraction.* **2** extraction is taking something out

extraordinary *ADJECTIVE*
unusual or very strange
▷ **extraordinarily** *ADVERB* in an extraordinary way

extrasensory *ADJECTIVE*
beyond the range of the ordinary senses

extraterrestrial *ADJECTIVE*
existing in or coming from another planet

extraterrestrial *NOUN* (**extraterrestrials**)
a living thing from another planet, especially in science fiction

extravagant *ADJECTIVE*
spending or using too much of something
▷ **extravagance** *NOUN* extravagance is being extravagant
▷ **extravagantly** *ADVERB* in an extravagant way

extreme *ADJECTIVE*
1 very great or strong • *They were suffering from extreme cold.* **2** farthest away • *She lives in the extreme north of the country.*

extreme *NOUN* (**extremes**)
1 something very great, strong, or far away **2** either end of something

extremely *ADVERB*
as much or as far as possible; very much • *They are extremely pleased.*

extremity *NOUN* (**extremities**) (*say* **iks- trem- it- ee**)
an extreme point; the very end of something

exuberant *ADJECTIVE*
very cheerful or lively
▷ **exuberance** *NOUN* exuberance is being exuberant

exult *VERB* (**exults**, **exulting**, **exulted**)
to exult is to rejoice or be very pleased
▷ **exultant** *ADJECTIVE* rejoicing
▷ **exultation** *NOUN* exultation is rejoicing or being very pleased

eye *NOUN* (**eyes**)
1 the organ of your body used for seeing **2** the small hole in a needle **3** the centre of a storm

eye *VERB* (**eyes**, **eyeing**, **eyed**)
to eye someone or something is to look at them closely

> WORD FAMILY
> Words for parts of the eye are **iris** and **pupil**. A surgeon who treats the eyes is called an **ophthalmic surgeon**.

eyeball *NOUN* (**eyeballs**)
the ball-shaped part of your eye, inside your eyelids

eyebrow *NOUN* (**eyebrows**)
the curved fringe of hair growing above each eye

eyelash *NOUN* (**eyelashes**)
one of the short hairs that grow on your eyelids

eyelid *NOUN* (**eyelids**)
the upper or lower fold of skin that can close over your eyeball

eyepiece *NOUN* (**eyepieces**)
the lens of a telescope or microscope that you put to your eye

eyesight *NOUN*
a person's eyesight is their ability to see

eyesore *NOUN* (**eyesores**)
something that is ugly to look at

eyewitness *NOUN* (**eyewitnesses**)
someone who actually saw something happen, especially an accident or crime

F
short for **Fahrenheit**

fable *NOUN* (**fables**)
a short story which teaches a lesson about how people should behave, often with animals as characters

fabric *NOUN* (**fabrics**)
cloth

fabricate *VERB* (**fabricates**, **fabricating**, **fabricated**)
1 to fabricate something is to make it, especially in a factory **2** to fabricate a story or excuse is to make it up

fabulous *ADJECTIVE*
1 very great • *The prince enjoyed fabulous wealth.* **2** (*informal*) wonderful; marvellous **3** spoken of or described in fables and myths • *Dragons are fabulous creatures.*

face *NOUN* (**faces**)
1 the front part of your head **2** the look on a person's face • *She had a friendly face.* **3** the front or upper side of something • *Put the cards face down.* **4** a surface • *A cube has six faces.*
face to face looking directly at someone

> WORD FAMILY
> **Facial** means on or to do with a person's face • *He had some facial injuries.*

face *VERB* (**faces**, **facing**, **faced**)
1 to face in a certain direction is to look there or have the front in that direction • *Please face the front.* • *The church faces the school.* **2** to face a problem or danger is to accept that you have to deal with it

facet *NOUN* (**facets**) (*say* fass- it)
1 one aspect or view of something **2** one side of a many-sided object like a diamond

facetious *ADJECTIVE* (*say* fa- **see**- shus)
trying to be funny at an unsuitable time
▷ **facetiously** *ADVERB* in a facetious way

facilitate *VERB* (**facilitates**, **facilitating**, **facilitated**)
to facilitate something is to make it easier

facility *NOUN* (**facilities**) (*say* fa- **sil**- i- ti)
1 something that helps you to do things • *The youth club has facilities for dancing and sport.* **2** the ability to do something easily • *She has a facility for writing songs.*

fact *NOUN* (**facts**)
fact, or a fact, is something that is true or certain
as a matter of fact or **in fact** really
the facts of life knowledge of how humans have sex and produce babies

factor *NOUN* (**factors**)
1 something that helps to bring about a result or situation • *Hard work has been a factor in her success.* **2** a number by which a larger number can be divided exactly • *2 and 3 are factors of 6.*

factory *NOUN* (**factories**)
a large building where machines are used to make things in large quantities

factual *ADJECTIVE*
based on or containing facts • *Write down a factual account of what happened.*
▷ **factually** *ADVERB* in a factual way

fad *NOUN* (**fads**)
1 something that is popular for only a short time • *There used to be a fad for jogging.*

faddy (**faddier**, **faddiest**) *ADJECTIVE*
someone is faddy when they are fussy about which foods they like and which foods they don't like • *Stephen is a faddy eater.*

fade *VERB* (**fades**, **fading**, **faded**)
1 to fade is to lose colour, freshness, or strength **2** to fade or fade away is to disappear gradually **3** to fade in a sound is to make it gradually louder, and to fade out a sound is to make it gradually softer

a b c d e **f** g h i j k l m n o p q r s t u v w x y z

faeces *PLURAL NOUN* (*say* fee- seez)
solid waste that is passed out of the body

fag *NOUN* (**fags**) (*informal*)
1 something that is tiring or boring **2** a cigarette

faggot *NOUN* (**faggots**)
a meat ball made of baked chopped liver

Fahrenheit *ADJECTIVE* (*say* fa- ren- hyt)
using a scale for measuring temperature that gives 32 degrees for freezing water and 212 degrees for boiling water

fail *VERB* (**fails**, **failing**, **failed**)
1 to fail is to try to do something but not be able to do it **2** to fail an exam or test is not to pass it **3** to fail is also to become weak or useless or to come to an end • *The batteries are failing.* • *The crops failed last year.* **4** to fail to do something is not to do it when you should • *He failed to warn me of the danger.*

fail *NOUN* (**fails**)
not being successful in an examination • *She has five passes and one fail.*
without fail definitely or always • *I'll be there without fail.*

failing *NOUN* (**failings**)
a fault or weakness

failure *NOUN* (**failures**)
1 failure is not being successful **2** a failure is someone or something that has failed

faint *ADJECTIVE* (**fainter**, **faintest**)
1 weak; not clear or distinct **2** nearly unconscious, often because you are exhausted or very hungry

> WORD FAMILY
> Something is heard or seen **faintly** when it is heard or seen weakly or not clearly; **faintness** is being faint.

faint *VERB* (**faints**, **fainting**, **fainted**)
to faint is to become unconscious for a short time

faint-hearted *ADJECTIVE*
not having much courage or confidence

fair[1] *ADJECTIVE* (**fairer**, **fairest**)
1 right or just; honest • *It was a fair fight.* **2** light in colour • *The sisters both had fair hair.* **3** quite good • *We've got a fair chance of winning.* **4** weather is fair when it is fine and not raining
▷ **fairness** *NOUN* fairness is being fair

fair[2] *NOUN* (**fairs**)
1 an outdoor entertainment with rides, amusements, and stalls. Fairs move from town to town **2** an exhibition or market • *a craft fair*

fairground *NOUN* (**fairgrounds**)
a place where a fair is held

fairly *ADVERB*
1 quite or rather • *It is fairly hard.* **2** honestly; justly • *He promised to treat everyone fairly.*

fairy *NOUN* (**fairies**)
an imaginary small creature with wings and magic powers

fairyland *NOUN*
a place where fairies live; an imaginary place

fairy story or **fairy tale** *NOUN* (**fairy stories** or **fairy tales**)
a story about fairies or magic

faith *NOUN* (**faiths**)
1 faith is strong belief or trust • *We have great faith in her.* **2** a faith is a religion
to do something in good faith is to do it believing that it is right and honest

faithful *ADJECTIVE*
loyal and trustworthy
▷ **faithfully** *ADVERB* in a faithful way
▷ **faithfulness** *NOUN* being faithful

fake *NOUN* (**fakes**)
a copy of something made to deceive people into thinking it is real

fake *ADJECTIVE*
not real or genuine • *fake diamonds*

fake *VERB* (**fakes**, **faking**, **faked**)
1 to fake something is to make it look real in order to deceive people **2** to fake something is also to pretend to have it • *He was always faking illness so he could miss games.*

> WORD FAMILY
> A **faker** is someone who fakes something.

falcon *NOUN* (**falcons**)
a small kind of hawk

> WORD FAMILY
> **Falconry** is the sport of training falcons to hunt other birds.

fall *VERB* (**falls**, **falling**, **fell**, **fallen**)
1 to fall is to come down quickly towards the ground **2** numbers or prices fall when they get lower or smaller **3** a city or stronghold falls when it is captured **4** soldiers fall when they die in battle **5** when silence falls it becomes quiet **6** to fall sick or ill is to become ill **7** a look or glance falls on someone when it is directed at them
to fall back on something or **someone** is to rely on them in a difficulty
to fall for someone is to start loving them
to fall for something is to be tricked into believing it
to fall in is to collapse • *The roof fell in.*
to fall out is to quarrel and stop being friends
to fall through is to fail to happen • *Our plans have fallen through.*

fall *NOUN* (**falls**)
1 a time when a person or thing falls • *My grandma had a bad fall.* **2** (*in America*) autumn

fallacy *NOUN* (**fallacies**)
a false idea or belief

> WORD FAMILY
> An idea or belief is **fallacious** if it is false.

fallout *NOUN*
fallout is radioactive dust that is carried in the air after a nuclear explosion

fallow *ADJECTIVE*
land that is fallow has been ploughed but not sown with crops • *The field was left fallow every three years.*

falls *PLURAL NOUN*
a waterfall

false *ADJECTIVE* (**falser**, **falsest**)
1 untrue or incorrect **2** faked; not genuine **3** treacherous or deceitful
▷ **falsely** *ADVERB* in a false way
▷ **falseness** *NOUN* falseness is being false

falsehood *NOUN* (**falsehoods**)
1 falsehood is telling lies **2** a falsehood is a lie

falter *VERB* (**falters**, **faltering**, **faltered**)
1 to falter is to hesitate when you move or speak **2** to falter is also to become weaker • *His courage began to falter.*

fame *NOUN*
fame is being famous
▷ **famed** *ADJECTIVE* a person or thing is famed when they are very well known

familiar *ADJECTIVE*
1 well-known; often seen or experienced • *It was a familiar sight.* **2** knowing something well • *Are you familiar with this story?* **3** very friendly
▷ **familiarity** *NOUN* familiarity with something is being familiar with it

family *NOUN* (**families**)
1 parents and their children, sometimes including grandchildren and other relations **2** a group of animals, plants, or things that are alike in some way • *The tiger is a member of the cat family.*

family planning *NOUN*
the use of contraceptives to control pregnancies

> OTHER WORDS
> This is also called **birth control**.

family tree *NOUN* (**family trees**)
a diagram showing how people in a family are related

famine *NOUN* (**famines**)
famine, or a famine, is a severe shortage of food that causes many people to die

famished *ADJECTIVE*
extremely hungry

famous *ADJECTIVE*
known to a lot of people • *Her uncle is a famous scientist.*

fan[1] *NOUN* (**fans**)
a device for making the air move about, in order to cool people or things

fan *VERB* (**fans**, **fanning**, **fanned**)
to fan something is to send a draught of air at it • *She fanned her face with her hand.*
to fan out is to spread out in the shape of a fan • *Lloyd could see the men in brown overalls fanning out across the Dome, like hounds searching for a scent.* — Gillian Cross, *The Revenge of the Demon Headmaster*

fan[2] *NOUN* (**fans**)
an enthusiastic follower or supporter of someone or something

fanatic *NOUN* (**fanatics**) (*say* fa- **nat**- ik)
someone who is too enthusiastic about something

> WORD FAMILY
> To be **fanatical** about something is to be too enthusiastic about it; to do something **fanatically** is to do it in a fanatical way.

fan belt *NOUN* (**fan belts**)
a belt driving the fan that cools a vehicle's radiator

fanciful *ADJECTIVE*
imagined rather than based on facts or reason

fancy *NOUN* (**fancies**)
1 fancy is imagination **2** a fancy is a liking or desire for something

fancy *ADJECTIVE* (**fancier**, **fanciest**)
decorated; not plain

fancy *VERB* (**fancies**, **fancying**, **fancied**)
1 to fancy something is to want it • *Does anyone fancy an ice cream?* **2** to fancy something unusual is to imagine or think of it • *Just fancy him riding a horse!*

fancy dress *NOUN*
unusual costume that you wear to a party or dance, often to make you look like someone else

fanfare *NOUN* (**fanfares**)
a short burst of music, often with trumpets and to announce something

fang *NOUN* (**fangs**)
a long, sharp tooth

fantastic *ADJECTIVE*
1 strange or unusual • *Some of my companions pass the time by carving sea monsters' teeth into fantastic shapes, or by engraving pictures on them.* — Richard Platt, *Pirate Diary* **2** (*informal*) excellent
▷ **fantastically** *ADVERB* strangely or unusually

fantasy *NOUN* (**fantasies**)
1 something pleasant that you imagine but isn't likely to happen • *His fantasy is to play football for England.* **2** a very imaginative story

far *ADVERB* (**farther**, **farthest**)
1 a long way • *We didn't go far.* **2** much; by a great amount • *She's a far better singer than I am.*
so far up to now

far *ADJECTIVE* (**farther**, **farthest**)
distant; opposite • *She swam to the far side of the river.*

far-away *ADJECTIVE*
distant • *I'd love to go to far-away places.*

a b c d e **f** g h i j k l m n o p q r s t u v w x y z

farce *NOUN* (**farces**)
1 a farce is a far-fetched or absurd kind of comedy **2** farce, or a farce, is a series of ridiculous events • *The meeting ended up in farce.* • *The trial was a complete farce.*

> **WORD FAMILY**
> A situation is **farcical** when it is absurd and ridiculous.

fare *NOUN* (**fares**)
the money you pay to travel on a bus, train, ship, or aircraft

fare *VERB* (**fares**, **faring**, **fared**)
to fare is to get on or make progress • *How did you fare in your exam?*

farewell *INTERJECTION*
goodbye

far-fetched *ADJECTIVE*
unlikely to be true; difficult to believe

farm *NOUN* (**farms**)
1 an area of land where someone grows crops and keeps animals for food **2** the buildings on land of this kind **3** a farmhouse

farm *VERB* (**farms**, **farming**, **farmed**)
1 to farm is to grow crops and raise animals for food **2** to farm land is to use it for growing crops

farmer *NOUN* (**farmers**)
someone who owns or looks after a farm

farmhouse *NOUN* (**farmhouses**)
the house where a farmer lives

farmyard *NOUN* (**farmyards**)
the open area surrounded by farm buildings

farther *ADVERB & ADJECTIVE*
at or to a greater distance; more distant • *She lives farther from the school than I do.*

farthest *ADVERB & ADJECTIVE*
at or to the greatest distance; most distant

farthing *NOUN* (**farthings**)
an old British coin that was worth a quarter of a penny

fascinate *VERB* (**fascinates**, **fascinating**, **fascinated**)
to fascinate someone is to attract or interest them very much

> **WORD FAMILY**
> To have a **fascination** with something is to have a great interest in it.

Fascist *NOUN* (**Fascists**) (*say* **fash**- ist)
a person who supports a type of government in which a country is ruled by a powerful dictator and people are not allowed to have opposing views

> **WORD FAMILY**
> **Fascism** is this type of government.

fashion *NOUN* (**fashions**)
1 fashion, or a fashion, is the style of clothes or other things that most people like at a particular time **2** a way of doing something • *Please continue in the same fashion.*

fashion *VERB* (**fashions**, **fashioning**, **fashioned**)
to fashion something is to make it in a particular shape or style

fashionable *ADJECTIVE*
something is fashionable when it follows a style that is popular at a particular time

fast [1] *ADJECTIVE* (**faster**, **fastest**)
1 moving or done quickly • *He's a fast runner.* **2** allowing fast movement • *This is a fast road.* **3** a watch or clock is fast when it shows a time later than the correct time **4** firmly fixed • *Make the boat fast.* **5** a fast colour is one that is not likely to fade

fast *ADVERB*
1 quickly **2** firmly
fast asleep deeply asleep

fast [2] *VERB* (**fasts**, **fasting**, **fasted**)
to fast is to go without food

fasten *VERB* (**fastens**, **fastening**, **fastened**)
to fasten something is to join it firmly to something else

> **WORD FAMILY**
> A **fastener** or **fastening** is a device used to fasten something.

fat *NOUN* (**fats**)
1 the white greasy part of meat **2** an oily or greasy substance used in cooking

fat *ADJECTIVE* (**fatter**, **fattest**)
1 having a very thick round body **2** thick • *What a fat book!* **3** fat meat is meat with a lot of fat

fatal *ADJECTIVE*
1 causing someone's death • *There has been a fatal accident on the motorway.* **2** likely to have bad results • *He then made a fatal mistake.*

> **WORD FAMILY**
> Someone is **fatally** injured or wounded when they die as a result of their injuries.

fatality *NOUN* (**fatalities**)
a death caused by war or an accident

fate *NOUN* (**fates**)
1 a power that is thought to make things happen **2** someone's fate is what has happened or will happen to them

father *NOUN* (**fathers**)
a male parent

father-in-law *NOUN* (**fathers-in-law**)
the father of your husband or wife

fathom *VERB* (**fathoms**, **fathoming**, **fathomed**)
to fathom something difficult or tricky is to work it out • *I can't fathom how you did it.*

fathom *NOUN* (**fathoms**)
a unit used in measuring the depth of water, equal to 1.83 metres or 6 feet

fatigue *NOUN* (*say* fa- teeg)
1 extreme tiredness **2** weakness in metals, caused by stress

> WORD FAMILY
> Someone is **fatigued** when they are extremely tired.

fatten *VERB* (**fattens**, **fattening**, **fattened**)
1 to fatten something is to make it fat **2** to fatten is to become fat

fattening *ADJECTIVE*
fattening food is food that is likely to make you fat

fatty *ADJECTIVE* (**fattier**, **fattiest**)
containing a lot of fat

fault *NOUN* (**faults**)
1 something wrong that spoils a person or thing; a flaw or mistake **2** the responsibility or blame for something •*It's my fault we are late.*
to be at fault is to be in the wrong or responsible for a mistake

> WORD FAMILY
> Something is **faultless** when it is perfect and has nothing wrong with it.

fault *VERB* (**faults**, **faulting**, **faulted**)
to fault something is to find faults in it

faulty *ADJECTIVE* (**faultier**, **faultiest**)
having a fault or faults; not working properly

fauna *NOUN* (*say* faw- na)
the animals of an area or of a period of time

> OTHER WORD
> See also **flora**, which refers to plants.

favour *NOUN* (**favours**)
1 a favour is something kind that you do for someone •*Will you do me a favour?* **2** favour is approval or goodwill •*The idea found favour with most people.*
to be in favour of someone or **something** is to like or support them

favour *VERB* (**favours**, **favouring**, **favoured**)
to favour someone or something is to like or support them, or prefer them to others

favourable *ADJECTIVE*
1 helpful or advantageous **2** showing approval
▹ **favourably** *ADVERB* in a favourable way

favourite *ADJECTIVE*
liked more than others •*This is my favourite book.*

favourite *NOUN* (**favourites**)
the person or thing that you like best •*This book is my favourite.*

favouritism *NOUN*
favouritism is when someone is unfairly kinder to one person than to others

fawn *NOUN* (**fawns**)
1 a young deer **2** a light brown colour

fax *NOUN* (**faxes**)
1 a machine that sends copies of documents by electronic means through a telephone line **2** a copy made by this process

fax *VERB* (**faxes**, **faxing**, **faxed**)
to fax a document is to send a copy of it using a fax machine

fear *NOUN* (**fears**)
fear, or a fear, is a feeling that something unpleasant may happen

fear *VERB* (**fears**, **fearing**, **feared**)
1 to fear someone or something is to be afraid of them **2** to fear something is also to be anxious or sad about it •*I fear we may be too late.*

fearful *ADJECTIVE*
1 frightened •*Within a dozen paces I came upon what I perceived to be a wolf pup. I was not fearful for I could see that he was too weak to do me harm.* — Michael Morpurgo, *The Last Wolf* **2** (*informal*) awful or horrid •*They had a fearful quarrel.*
▹ **fearfully** *ADVERB* in a fearful way

fearless *ADJECTIVE*
having no fear •*The great knights were fearless when it came to anything you could stick your sword into.* — Martyn Beardsley, *Sir Gadabout and the Ghost*
▹ **fearlessly** *ADVERB* in a fearless way

fearsome *ADJECTIVE*
frightening •*'As I was saying,' the Scarecrow went on, 'the brigands were a fearsome crew. Armed to the teeth, every single one.'* — Philip Pullman, *The Scarecrow and his Servant*

feasible *ADJECTIVE*
able to be done; possible or likely

feast *NOUN* (**feasts**)
a large and splendid meal for a lot of people

feast *VERB* (**feasts**, **feasting**, **feasted**)
to feast is to have a feast
to feast your eyes on something is to gaze at it with pleasure

feat *NOUN* (**feats**)
a brave or clever deed

feather *NOUN* (**feathers**)
a bird's feathers are the very light coverings that grow from its skin

> WORD FAMILY
> Something is **feathery** when it is soft or light like feathers.

feature *NOUN* (**features**)
1 your features are the different parts of your face •*He has rugged features.* **2** an important or noticeable part of something; a characteristic **3** a newspaper article or television programme on a particular subject

feature *VERB* (**features**, **featuring**, **featured**)
1 to feature something is to make it an important part of something **2** to feature in something is to be an important part of it • *Sport features a lot in the Sunday papers.*

February *NOUN*
the second month of the year

fed
past tense and past participle of **feed** *VERB*

federal *ADJECTIVE*
to do with a system in which several states are ruled by a central government but make some of their own laws

> WORD FAMILY
> A **federation** is a group of several states that have joined together under a central government.

fed up *ADJECTIVE*
(*informal*) depressed or unhappy

fee *NOUN* (**fees**)
a payment or charge

feeble *ADJECTIVE* (**feebler**, **feeblest**)
weak; not having much strength or force • *Years went over, and the Giant grew very old and feeble.* — Oscar Wilde, *The Selfish Giant*
▷ **feebly** *ADVERB* in a feeble way

feed *VERB* (**feeds**, **feeding**, **fed**)
1 to feed a person or animal is to give them food **2** to feed on something is to eat it • *Sheep feed on grass.* **3** to feed a machine is to put coins or other things into it

feed *NOUN* (**feeds**)
1 a feed is a meal **2** feed is food for animals

feedback *NOUN*
information from someone about something you have done for them

feel *VERB* (**feels**, **feeling**, **felt**)
1 to feel something is to touch it to find out what it is like **2** to feel a feeling or emotion is to experience it • *I feel very angry about it.*
to feel like something is to want it

feel *NOUN*
what something is like when you touch it • *Her dress has a funny feel about it.*

feeler *NOUN* (**feelers**)
1 an insect's feelers are the two long thin parts that extend from the front of its body and are used for feeling **2** a cautious question or suggestion

feeling *NOUN* (**feelings**)
1 feeling is the ability to feel or touch things • *She lost the feeling in her right hand.* **2** feeling is also what a person feels in the mind, such as love or fear • *I have hurt her feelings.* **3** a feeling is what you think about something • *My feeling is that he's right.*

feet
plural of **foot**

feline *ADJECTIVE*
to do with cats; like a cat

fell [1]
past tense of **fall** *VERB*

fell [2] *VERB* (**fells**, **felling**, **felled**)
1 to fell a tree is to cut it down **2** to fell someone is to knock them down

fell [3] *NOUN* (**fells**)
a piece of wild hilly country in the north of England

fellow *NOUN* (**fellows**)
1 a friend or companion; someone who belongs to the same group **2** (*informal*) a man or boy • *He's a clever fellow.*

fellow *ADJECTIVE*
of the same group or kind • *She arranged a meeting with her fellow teachers.*

fellowship *NOUN* (**fellowships**)
1 fellowship is friendship **2** a fellowship is a group of friends; a society

felt [1]
past tense and past participle of **feel**

felt [2] *NOUN*
thick woollen material

felt-tip pen or **felt-tipped pen** *NOUN* (**felt-tip pens** or **felt-tipped pens**)
a pen with a tip made of felt or fibre

female *ADJECTIVE*
of the sex that can produce offspring

female *NOUN* (**females**)
a female person or animal

feminine *ADJECTIVE*
1 to do with women or like women; suitable for women **2** in some languages, belonging to the class of words that includes words referring to women

> WORD FAMILY
> **Femininity** is being feminine.

feminist *NOUN* (**feminists**)
someone who believes that women should have the same rights and opportunities as men

> WORD FAMILY
> **Feminism** is the belief that women should have the same rights and opportunities as men.

fen *NOUN* (**fens**)
an area of low-lying marshy or flooded land

fence *NOUN* (**fences**)
1 a wooden or metal barrier round an area of land **2** (*slang*) someone who buys stolen goods and sells them again
to sit on the fence is to avoid taking sides in an argument

fence *VERB* (**fences**, **fencing**, **fenced**)
1 to fence something or to fence it in is to put a fence round it **2** to fence is to fight with long narrow swords called *foils*, as a sport

> WORD FAMILY
> A **fencer** is someone who fences; **fencing** is the sport of fighting with swords as a sport.

fend *VERB* (**fends**, **fending**, **fended**)
to fend for yourself is to take care of yourself **to fend someone** or **something off** is to keep them away from yourself when they are attacking you

fender *NOUN* (**fenders**)
1 a low guard placed round a fireplace to stop coal from falling into the room **2** (*in America*) bumper

ferment *VERB* (**ferments**, **fermenting**, **fermented**) (*say* fer- **ment**)
beer or wine ferments when it bubbles and changes chemically by the action of yeast or bacteria. This makes the sugar turn into alcohol

> WORD FAMILY
> **Fermentation** is the process of fermenting.

ferment *NOUN* (*say* **fer**- ment)
a state of great excitement or agitation • *The crowd was in a ferment.*

fern *NOUN* (**ferns**)
a plant with feathery leaves and no flowers

ferocious *ADJECTIVE*
fierce or savage • *Stig looked up, and for a moment Barney felt quite frightened at the ferocious scowl on his face, and was glad to be high up out of his reach.* — Clive King, *Stig of the Dump*

> WORD FAMILY
> To do something **ferociously** is to do it fiercely or savagely; **ferocity** is fierceness.

ferret *NOUN* (**ferrets**)
a small fierce animal with a long thin body, used for catching rabbits and rats

ferret *VERB* (**ferrets**, **ferreting**, **ferreted**)
to ferret, or ferret about, is to search busily for something

ferry *NOUN* (**ferries**)
a boat that takes people or things across a river or other stretch of water

ferry *VERB* (**ferries**, **ferrying**, **ferried**)
to ferry people or things is to take them from one place to another, especially by boat or car

fertile *ADJECTIVE*
1 land that is fertile is good for growing crops and plants **2** people or animals that are fertile can produce babies or young animals

> WORD FAMILY
> **Fertility** is being fertile.

fertilize *VERB* (**fertilizes**, **fertilizing**, **fertilized**)
1 to fertilize the soil is to add chemicals or manure to it so that crops and plants grow better **2** to fertilize an egg or plant is to put sperm or pollen into it so that it develops its young or seeds
▷ **fertilization** *NOUN* fertilizing the soil or an egg or plant

fertilizer *NOUN* (**fertilizers**)
chemicals or manure added to the soil to make crops and plants grow better

fervent *ADJECTIVE*
very enthusiastic or passionate about something • *He is a fervent supporter of reform.*

> WORD FAMILY
> To do something **fervently** is to do it very enthusiastically or passionately; **fervour** is great enthusiasm or passion.

festival *NOUN* (**festivals**)
1 a time of celebration, especially for religious reasons **2** an organized set of concerts, shows, or other events, especially one that is arranged every year

festive *ADJECTIVE*
to do with joyful celebrating

> WORD FAMILY
> **Festivities** are the parties and other events that are held to celebrate something.

festoon *VERB* (**festoons**, **festooning**, **festooned**)
to festoon a place is to decorate it with chains of flowers or ribbons

fetch *VERB* (**fetches**, **fetching**, **fetched**)
1 to fetch something or someone is to go and get them **2** something fetches a particular price when it is sold for that price • *My old bike fetched £10.*

fête *NOUN* (**fêtes**) (*say* fayt)
an outdoor event with stalls, games, and things for sale, often held to raise money

fetlock *NOUN* (**fetlocks**)
the part of a horse's leg above and behind its hoof

fetters *PLURAL NOUN*
fetters are chains put round a prisoner's ankles

feud *NOUN* (**feuds**) (*say* fewd)
a bitter quarrel between two people or families that lasts a long time

feud *VERB* (**feuds**, **feuding**, **feuded**)
people feud when they keep up a quarrel for a long time

feudal *ADJECTIVE* (*say* **few**- dal)
in the Middle Ages, the feudal system was a system in which people could farm land in exchange for working or fighting for the owner

> WORD FAMILY
> **Feudalism** is the feudal system.

a b c d e **f** g h i j k l m n o p q r s t u v w x y z

a b c d e **f** g h i j k l m n o p q r s t u v w x y z

fever *NOUN* (**fevers**)
1 a person has a fever when their body temperature is higher than usual because they are ill **2** fever is excitement or agitation

feverish *ADJECTIVE*
1 someone is feverish when they have a slight fever **2** excited or frantic • *There was feverish activity getting the hall ready for the show.*
▷ **feverishly** *ADVERB* in a feverish way

few *DETERMINER* (**fewer**, **fewest**)
not many

few *NOUN*
a small number of people or things
a good few or **quite a few** a fairly large number

fez *NOUN* (**fezzes**)
a tall round hat with a flat top and a tassel, worn especially by Muslim men

fiancé *NOUN* (**fiancés**) (*say* fee- **ahn**- say)
a woman's fiancé is the man who she is engaged to be married to

fiancée *NOUN* (**fiancées**) (*say* fee- **ahn**- say)
a man's fiancée is the woman who he is engaged to be married to

fiasco *NOUN* (**fiascos**) (*say* fi- **ass**- koh)
a complete failure • *The party turned into a fiasco.*

fib *NOUN* (**fibs**)
a lie about something unimportant

fib *VERB* (**fibs**, **fibbing**, **fibbed**)
to fib is to tell a lie about something unimportant
▷ **fibber** *NOUN* someone who tells fibs

fibre *NOUN* (**fibres**) (*say* **fy**- ber)
1 a fibre is a very thin thread **2** fibre is a substance made up of thin threads **3** fibre is also a substance in food that your body can't digest but that moves the rest of the food quickly through your body and helps you to digest it

> WORD FAMILY
> Something that is **fibrous** is made up of lots of fibres.

fibreglass *NOUN*
a kind of lightweight plastic containing glass fibres

fickle *ADJECTIVE*
someone is fickle when they often change their mind or do not stay loyal to one person or group

fiction *NOUN* (**fictions**)
1 fiction is writings about events that have not really happened; stories and novels **2** a fiction is something untrue or made up

> WORD FAMILY
> A **fictional** character or event exists only in a story, not in real life; something is **fictitious** when it is made up by someone and is not true.

fiddle *NOUN* (**fiddles**)
1 a violin **2** (*informal*) a swindle

fiddle *VERB* (**fiddles**, **fiddling**, **fiddled**)
1 to fiddle is to play the violin **2** to fiddle with something is to keep touching or playing with it with your fingers • *Stop fiddling with the CD player.* **3** (*informal*) to fiddle something is to be dishonest about it • *Her dad was fiddling his company's expenses.*
▷ **fiddler** *NOUN* someone who plays the violin

fiddling *ADJECTIVE*
unimportant but tedious • *The job involves a lot of fiddling details.*

fiddly *ADJECTIVE*
(*informal*) awkward to use or do because it involves handling small objects • *Making the model of the ship was quite a fiddly job.*

fidelity *NOUN* (*say* fi- **del**- i- ti)
1 fidelity is being faithful or loyal **2** the exactness with which sound is reproduced

fidget *VERB* (**fidgets**, **fidgeting**, **fidgeted**)
to fidget is to make small restless movements because you are bored or nervous

> WORD FAMILY
> Someone is **fidgety** when they fidget a lot.

field *NOUN* (**fields**)
1 a piece of land with crops or grass growing on it, often surrounded by a hedge or fence **2** an area of grass where people play a sport **3** an area of interest or study • *The book describes important developments in the field of science.* **4** all the people or animals that take part in a race

field *VERB* (**fields**, **fielding**, **fielded**)
1 to field a ball in cricket or other games is to stop it or catch it **2** to be fielding in cricket is to be on the side that is not batting

> WORD FAMILY
> A **fielder** or **fieldsman** is a player who is fielding.

Field Marshal *NOUN* (**Field Marshals**)
an army officer of the highest rank

field trip *NOUN* (**field trips**)
a visit to a place with your school to study something in its natural environment • *We went to North Wales on a geology field trip.*

fieldwork *NOUN*
practical work or research that is done in various places, not in a school, library, or laboratory • *We went to the coast to do some geography fieldwork.*

fiend *NOUN* (**fiends**) (*say* feend)
1 a devil or evil spirit **2** a wicked or cruel person

fiendish *ADJECTIVE*
1 wicked or cruel **2** very difficult or complicated • *That was a fiendish puzzle.*
▷ **fiendishly** *ADVERB* to be fiendishly difficult or complicated is to be very difficult or complicated indeed

fierce *ADJECTIVE* (**fiercer**, **fiercest**)
1 angry and violent and likely to attack you
2 strong or intense • *The heat from the fire was fierce.*

> WORD FAMILY
> To do something **fiercely** is to do it in an angry and violent way; **fierceness** is being angry and violent.

fiery *ADJECTIVE* (**fierier**, **fieriest**)
1 full of flames or heat • *The building looked like a fiery ghost, with great bursts of flame coming from the windows.* — Lemony Snicket, *A Series of Unfortunate Events* **2** easily made angry • *He had a fiery temper.*

fifteen *NOUN* (**fifteens**)
the number 15
▷ **fifteenth** *ADJECTIVE & NOUN* 15th

fifth *ADJECTIVE & NOUN*
the next after the fourth
▷ **fifthly** *ADVERB* in the fifth place; as the fifth one

fifty *NOUN* (**fifties**)
the number 50
▷ **fiftieth** *ADJECTIVE & NOUN* 50th

fifty-fifty *ADJECTIVE & ADVERB*
to share something fifty-fifty is to share it equally between two people or groups • *Let's split the money fifty-fifty.*

fig *NOUN* (**figs**)
a soft fruit full of small seeds

fight *NOUN* (**fights**)
1 a struggle against someone, using hands or weapons **2** an attempt to achieve or overcome something • *We can all help in the fight against crime.*

fight *VERB* (**fights**, **fighting**, **fought**)
1 to fight someone is to have a fight with them **2** to fight something is to try to stop it • *They fought the fire all night.*

fighter *NOUN* (**fighters**)
1 someone who fights **2** a fast military plane that attacks other aircraft

figurative *ADJECTIVE*
figurative language uses words for special effect and not in their literal meanings, often in order to describe what something is like. For example *flood* in *a flood of letters* is a figurative meaning of the word

> FIGURATIVE USES
> Using figurative language can help to create strong images in your reader's mind. You can strengthen images made with similes, metaphors, and personification by carefully choosing powerful verbs: *Quiet as a mouse, she scuttled across the floor. He marched across the room like a soldier on parade.* Look also at the panel on **Similes and metaphors**.

figure *NOUN* (**figures**)
1 one of the symbols that stand for numbers, such as 1, 2, and 3 **2** the shape of someone's body **3** a diagram or illustration in a book or magazine **4** a pattern or shape • *He drew a figure of eight.*

figure *VERB* (**figures**, **figuring**, **figured**)
1 to appear or take part in something • *His name does not figure in the list of entrants.* **2** to think that something is probably true • *I figure the best thing to do is to wait.*
to figure something out is to work it out • *Can you figure out the answer?*

figure of speech *NOUN* (**figures of speech**)
a special way of using words that makes what you say or write interesting, such as a metaphor or a simile

filament *NOUN* (**filaments**)
a thread or thin wire

file[1] *NOUN* (**files**)
a metal tool with a rough surface that you rub on things to make them smooth or shape them

file *VERB* (**files**, **filing**, **filed**)
to file something is to make it smooth or shape it with a file

file[2] *NOUN* (**files**)
1 a box or folder for keeping papers in **2** (*in computing*) a set of data that has been stored under one name in a computer
to walk in single file is to walk one behind the other

file *VERB* (**files**, **filing**, **filed**)
1 to file a paper or document is to put it in a box or folder **2** to file is to walk one behind the other

filings *PLURAL NOUN*
tiny pieces of metal

fill *VERB* (**fills**, **filling**, **filled**)
1 to fill something is to make it full **2** to fill is to become full • *The room was filling quickly.* **3** to fill a tooth is to put a filling in it
to fill in a form is to write answers to all the questions on it
to fill something up is to fill it completely

fill *NOUN* (**fills**)
enough to make you full • *Eat your fill.*

filler *NOUN* (**fillers**)
filler is material used to fill holes in wood or plaster

fillet *NOUN* (**fillets**)
a piece of fish or meat without bones

filling *NOUN* (**fillings**)
1 a piece of metal put in a tooth to replace a decayed part **2** food you put inside a pie, sandwich, or cake

filling station *NOUN* (**filling stations**)
a place where petrol is sold

filly *NOUN* (**fillies**)
a young female horse

film *NOUN* (**films**)
1 a series of moving pictures that tells a story, such as those shown in a cinema or on television **2** a roll or piece of thin plastic coated with a chemical that is sensitive to light, that you put in a camera to take photographs **3** a very thin layer of something • *The table was covered in a film of grease.*
▷ **filmy** *ADJECTIVE* thin and transparent

film *VERB* (**films, filming, filmed**)
to film a book or story is to make a film of it

filter *NOUN* (**filters**)
1 a device for removing dirt or other unwanted things from a liquid or gas that passes through it **2** a system allowing a line of traffic to move in one direction while other lines are held up

filter *VERB* (**filters, filtering, filtered**)
1 to filter something is to pass it through a filter **2** to filter is to move gradually • *People started to filter into the hall.* **3** traffic filters when it moves in one direction while other traffic is held up

filth *NOUN*
disgusting dirt

> **WORD FAMILY**
> Someone is **filthy** when they are extremely dirty.

fin *NOUN* (**fins**)
1 a thin flat part that sticks out from a fish's body and helps it to swim **2** a small part that sticks out from an aircraft or rocket and helps it to balance

final *ADJECTIVE*
1 coming at the end; last **2** a decision is final when it puts an end to argument or doubt • *You must not go, and that's final!*
▷ **finality** *NOUN* finality is being final or last

final *NOUN* (**finals**)
the last of a series of contests, that decides the overall winner

finale *NOUN* (**finales**) (*say* fin-**ah**-li)
the last part of a show or piece of music

finalist *NOUN* (**finalists**)
a person or team taking part in a final

finally *ADVERB*
1 after a long time, at last • *We finally got there around midnight.* **2** as the last thing • *Finally, I would like to thank my parents.*

finance *NOUN*
1 finance is the use and control of money
2 someone's finances are the amount of money or funds they have

finance *VERB* (**finances, financing, financed**)
to finance something is to provide money for it

> **WORD FAMILY**
> A **financier** is someone who provides money.

financial *ADJECTIVE*
to do with money

finch *NOUN* (**finches**)
a small bird with a short thick beak

find *VERB* (**finds, finding, found**)
1 to find something is to see or get it by chance or by looking for it **2** to find something is also to learn it by experience • *He found that digging is hard work*
to find and replace is to use a computer to find a word or phrase in a piece of text and then replace it with another word or phrase
to find someone out is to discover them doing wrong
to find something out is to get information about it
▷ **finder** *NOUN* someone who finds something

findings *PLURAL NOUN*
things someone has found out

fine [1] *ADJECTIVE* (**finer, finest**)
1 of high quality; excellent • *They saw some fine pictures at the show.* **2** the weather is fine when it is sunny and not raining **3** very thin or delicate • *The curtains were made of a fine material.* **4** made of small particles • *The sand on the beach was very fine.*
▷ **finely** *ADVERB* into fine or small parts • *Slice the tomato finely.*

fine [2] *NOUN* (**fines**)
money that someone must pay as a punishment

fine *VERB* (**fines, fining, fined**)
to fine someone is to make them pay money as a punishment

finger *NOUN* (**fingers**)
1 one of the long thin parts that stick out on your hand **2** something that is shaped like a finger

finger *VERB* (**fingers, fingering, fingered**)
to finger something is to touch it with your fingers

fingernail *NOUN* (**fingernails**)
the hard covering at the end of your finger

fingerprint *NOUN* (**fingerprints**)
a mark made by the pattern of curved lines on the tip of your finger

finicky *ADJECTIVE*
fussy or hard to please

finish *VERB* (**finishes, finishing, finished**)
1 to finish something is to bring it to an end **2** to finish is to come to an end

finish *NOUN* (**finishes**)
the end of something

fiord *NOUN* (**fiords**) (*say* fi-**ord**)
in Norway, an inlet of the sea between high cliffs

fir *NOUN* (**firs**)
an evergreen tree with leaves like needles

fire *NOUN* (**fires**)
1 fire, or a fire, is the flames, heat, and light that come from burning things **2** coal or wood burning in a grate or furnace to give heat **3** a device using electricity or gas to heat a room **4** the shooting of guns • *Hold your fire!*
to be on fire is to be burning
to set fire to something is to start it burning

fire *VERB* (**fires**, **firing**, **fired**)
1 to fire a gun is to shoot it **2** (*informal*) to fire someone is to dismiss them from their job **3** to fire pottery or bricks is to bake them in an oven to make them hard

firearm *NOUN* (**firearms**)
a gun or rifle

fire brigade *NOUN* (**fire brigades**)
a team of people whose job is to put out fires and rescue people from fires

fire drill *NOUN* (**fire drills**)
a practice of what you must do if a fire breaks out

fire engine *NOUN* (**fire engines**)
a large vehicle that carries firefighters and equipment to fight fires

fire escape *NOUN* (**fire escapes**)
a special staircase or exit for people to use if there is a fire

fire extinguisher *NOUN* (**fire extinguishers**)
a metal cylinder containing water or foam for spraying over a fire to put it out

firefighter *NOUN* (**firefighters**)
a member of a fire brigade

fireman *NOUN* (**firemen**)
a man who is a member of a fire brigade

fireplace *NOUN* (**fireplaces**)
an open space for a fire in the wall of a room

fireproof *ADJECTIVE*
something is fireproof when it can stand great heat without burning

fireside *NOUN* (**firesides**)
the part of a room near the fire

fire station *NOUN* (**fire stations**)
the headquarters of a fire brigade

firewood *NOUN*
wood suitable for burning as fuel

firework *NOUN* (**fireworks**)
a cardboard tube containing chemicals that give off pretty sparks and lights and sometimes make loud noises

firm *NOUN* (**firms**)
a business organization • *She works for a clothing firm.*

firm *ADJECTIVE* (**firmer**, **firmest**)
1 fixed or solid so that it will not move **2** definite and not likely to change • *She has made a firm decision to go.*

> WORD FAMILY
> **Firmly** means in a strong or definite way; **firmness** is being firm.

first *ADJECTIVE*
1 coming before all others **2** the most important • *He plays football in the first team at school.*

first *ADVERB*
before everything else • *Finish your work first.*

first *NOUN*
a person or thing that is first
at first at the beginning; to start with

first aid *NOUN*
simple medical treatment that is given to an injured person before a doctor comes

first-class *ADJECTIVE*
1 belonging to the best part of a service • *Send the letter by first-class post.* **2** excellent

first floor *NOUN* (**first floors**)
the next floor above the ground floor

first-hand *ADJECTIVE & ADVERB*
you get first-hand information directly, rather than from other people or from books

firstly *ADVERB*
as the first thing • *Firstly, let me tell you about our holiday.*

first-rate *ADJECTIVE*
excellent

fish *NOUN* (**fish** or **fishes**)
an animal that lives and breathes in water

fish *VERB* (**fishes**, **fishing**, **fished**)
1 to fish is to try to catch fish **2** to fish for something is to try and get it • *He is only fishing for compliments.*
to fish something out is to get it out of something after searching for it

fisherman *NOUN* (**fishermen**)
someone who tries to catch fish

fishmonger *NOUN* (**fishmongers**)
a shopkeeper who sells fish

fishy *ADJECTIVE* (**fishier**, **fishiest**)
1 smelling or tasting of fish **2** (*informal*) suspicious or doubtful • *His excuse was rather fishy.*

fission *NOUN* (*say* **fish**-on)
splitting something, especially the nucleus of an atom to produce energy

fist *NOUN* (**fists**)
a tightly closed hand with the fingers bent into the palm

fit[1] *ADJECTIVE* (**fitter**, **fittest**)
1 healthy and strong because you get a lot of exercise **2** suitable or good enough • *It was a meal fit for a king.* **3** ready or likely • *They worked till they were fit to collapse.*
to see fit or **think fit to do something** is to decide or choose to do it

fit *VERB* (**fits**, **fitting**, **fitted**)
1 to fit someone or something is to be the right size and shape for them **2** to fit something is to put it into place • *We need to fit a new lock on the door.* **3** to fit something is to be suitable for it • *Her speech fitted the occasion perfectly.*
to fit in is to be suitable for something • *Does this fit in with your plans?*

fit *NOUN*
the way something fits • *The coat is a good fit.*

fit[2] *NOUN* (**fits**)
1 a sudden illness, especially one that makes you move violently or become unconscious **2** (*informal*) a sudden outburst • *He rushed off in a fit of rage.*
in fits and starts in short bursts; now and then

fitness *NOUN*
being healthy and strong because of doing a lot of exercise

fitted *ADJECTIVE*
made to fit something exactly • *The room has a fitted carpet.*

fitter *NOUN* (**fitters**)
someone who fits clothes or machinery

fitting *ADJECTIVE*
suitable or proper

fitting *NOUN* (**fittings**)
fittings are pieces of furniture or equipment in a room or building

five *NOUN* (**fives**)
the number 5

fiver *NOUN* (**fivers**)
(*informal*) a five-pound note; £5

fix *VERB* (**fixes, fixing, fixed**)
1 to fix something is to join it firmly to something else or to put it where it will not move **2** to fix something is also to decide or settle it • *We have fixed a date for the party.* **3** to fix something that is broken is to mend it • *He's fixing my bike.*
to fix something up is to arrange or organize something

fix *NOUN* (**fixes**)
1 (*informal*) an awkward situation • *I'm in a fix.*
2 finding the position of something, especially by using a compass

fixture *NOUN* (**fixtures**)
1 a sports event planned for a particular day
2 something fixed in its place, like a cupboard or a washbasin

fizz *VERB* (**fizzes, fizzing, fizzed**)
1 to fizz is to make a hissing or spluttering sound
2 liquid fizzes when it produces a lot of small bubbles

> **WORD FAMILY**
> A **fizzy** drink has a lot of bubbles.

fizzle *VERB* (**fizzles, fizzling, fizzled**)
to fizzle is to make a slight hissing sound
to fizzle out is to end in a disappointing or unsuccessful way

flabbergasted *ADJECTIVE*
(*informal*) completely astonished

flabby *ADJECTIVE* (**flabbier, flabbiest**)
fat and soft; not firm

flag[1] *NOUN* (**flags**)
1 a piece of material with a coloured pattern or shape on it, often used as the symbol of a country or organization

flag *VERB* (**flags, flagging, flagged**)
1 to flag is to become weak or droop
to flag a vehicle down is to make the driver stop by waving your hand

flag[2] *NOUN* (**flags**)
a flat slab of paving stone

flagpole *NOUN* (**flagpoles**)
a pole that a flag is attached to

flagship *NOUN* (**flagships**)
the main ship in a navy's fleet, which has the commander of the fleet on board

flagstaff *NOUN* (**flagstaffs**)
a flagpole

flagstone *NOUN* (**flagstones**)
a flat slab of paving stone

flake *NOUN* (**flakes**)
1 a very light thin piece of something **2** a piece of falling snow

> **WORD FAMILY**
> Something is **flaky** when it is likely to break into light thin pieces.

flake *VERB* (**flakes, flaking, flaked**)
to flake is to come off in light thin pieces
to flake out (*informal*) is to faint or fall asleep

flame *NOUN* (**flames**)
a bright strip of fire that flickers and leaps

flame *VERB* (**flames, flaming, flamed**)
to flame is to produce flames or become bright red

flamingo *NOUN* (**flamingos**)
a large wading bird with long legs, a long neck, and pale pink feathers

flammable *ADJECTIVE*
that can be set alight

flan *NOUN* (**flans**)
a pie without any pastry on top

flank *NOUN* (**flanks**)
the side of something, especially an animal's body or an army

flannel *NOUN* (**flannels**)
1 a flannel is a piece of soft cloth you use to wash yourself **2** flannel is a soft woollen material

flap *NOUN* (**flaps**)
1 a part that hangs down from one edge of something, usually to cover an opening **2** the action or sound of flapping **3** (*informal*) a panic or fuss • *Don't get in a flap.*

flap *VERB* (**flaps, flapping, flapped**)
1 to flap something is to move it up and down or from side to side • *The bird flapped its wings.* **2** to flap is to wave about • *The sails were flapping in the breeze.* **3** (*informal*) to panic or fuss

flapjack *NOUN* (**flapjacks**)
a cake made from oats and syrup

flare *VERB* (**flares**, **flaring**, **flared**)
1 to flare is to burn with a sudden bright flame **2** to flare is also to become suddenly angry **3** things flare when they get gradually wider

flare *NOUN* (**flares**)
1 a bright light fired into the sky as a signal **2** a gradual widening, especially in skirts or trousers

flash *NOUN* (**flashes**)
1 a sudden bright burst of light **2** a device for making a brief bright light when you take a photograph **3** a sudden display of anger or humour
to happen in a flash is to happen immediately or very quickly

flash *VERB* (**flashes**, **flashing**, **flashed**)
1 to flash is to make a sudden bright burst of light **2** to flash past or across is to approach and go past very fast • *The train flashed past into the distance.*

flashback *NOUN* (**flashbacks**)
going back in a film or story to something that happened earlier • *The hero's childhood was shown in flashbacks.*

flashy *ADJECTIVE* (**flashier**, **flashiest**)
showy and expensive

flask *NOUN* (**flasks**)
1 a bottle with a narrow neck **2** a vacuum flask

flat *ADJECTIVE* (**flatter**, **flattest**)
1 having no curves or bumps; smooth and level **2** spread out; lying at full length • *Lie flat on the ground.* **3** dull or uninteresting • *He spoke in a flat voice.* **4** complete; not changing • *We got a flat refusal.* **5** a liquid is flat when it is no longer fizzy **6** a tyre is flat when it is punctured and has lost its air **7** feet are flat when they do not have the normal arch underneath **8** below the proper musical pitch • *The clarinet was flat.*
▷ **flatness** *NOUN* flatness is being flat

flat *ADVERB*
exactly and no more • *He won the race in ten seconds flat.*
flat out as fast as possible • *They all worked flat out to get everything ready in time.*

flat *NOUN* (**flats**)
1 a set of rooms for living in, usually on one floor of a building **2** (*in music*) the note that is a semitone lower than the natural note; the sign (♭) that indicates this

> BRITISH AND AMERICAN
> In America, the word **apartment** is used for the first meaning of the noun.

flatly *ADVERB*
in a definite way, leaving no room for doubt • *They flatly refused to go.*

flatten *VERB* (**flattens**, **flattening**, **flattened**)
1 to flatten something is to make it flat **2** to flatten is to become flat

flatter *VERB* (**flatters**, **flattering**, **flattered**)
1 to flatter someone is to praise them more than they deserve, often because you want to please them **2** to flatter someone is also to make them seem better or more attractive than they really are • *The portrait flatters him, don't you think?*

> WORD FAMILY
> A **flatterer** is someone who is often flattering people; **flattery** is flattering people.

flaunt *VERB* (**flaunts**, **flaunting**, **flaunted**)
to flaunt something is to show it off too proudly • *He is always flaunting his expensive clothes.*

flavour *NOUN* (**flavours**)
flavour, or a flavour, is the taste and smell of something

flavour *VERB* (**flavours**, **flavouring**, **flavoured**)
to flavour something is to give it a particular taste and smell

> WORD FAMILY
> **Flavouring** is something added to food or drink to give it a particular flavour.

flaw *NOUN* (**flaws**)
a fault that stops a person or thing from being perfect • *The diamond had a flaw.*

> WORD FAMILY
> Something that is **flawed** has a fault that stops it being perfect; something that is **flawless** is perfect, with no faults.

flax *NOUN*
a plant that produces fibres from which cloth is made and seeds from which oil is obtained

flea *NOUN* (**fleas**)
a small jumping insect that sucks blood

fleck *NOUN* (**flecks**)
a small piece or speck • *There were flecks of dirt on the table.*

fled
past tense and past participle of **flee**

flee *VERB* (**flees**, **fleeing**, **fled**)
to flee is to run away from something

fleece *NOUN* (**fleeces**)
1 a sheep's fleece is the wool that covers its body **2** a piece of clothing made from a soft warm material

> WORD FAMILY
> **Fleecy** material is soft and warm like a fleece.

fleece *VERB* (**fleeces**, **fleecing**, **fleeced**)
1 to fleece a sheep is to shear it **2** to fleece someone is to swindle them

fleet *NOUN* (**fleets**)
a number of ships, aircraft, or vehicles owned by one country or company

fleeting *ADJECTIVE*
very brief; passing quickly • *I caught a fleeting glimpse of him.*

flesh *NOUN*
the soft substance of the bodies of people and animals, made of muscle and fat

> WORD FAMILY
> Part of your body is **fleshy** when there is a lot of flesh on it.

flew
past tense of **fly** *VERB*

flex *NOUN* (**flexes**)
flexible insulated wire for carrying an electric current

flex *VERB* (**flexes**, **flexing**, **flexed**)
to flex something is to move or bend it • *Try flexing your muscles.*

flexible *ADJECTIVE*
1 easy to bend or stretch **2** able to be changed • *Our plans are flexible.*

> WORD FAMILY
> Something that has **flexibility** can bend or stretch easily.

flick *NOUN* (**flicks**)
a quick light hit or movement

flick *VERB* (**flicks**, **flicking**, **flicked**)
to flick something is to hit or move it with a flick

flicker *VERB* (**flickers**, **flickering**, **flickered**)
to flicker is to burn or shine unsteadily

flight[1] *NOUN* (**flights**)
1 flight is the action of flying • *She looked up to see a flock of birds in flight.* **2** a flight is a journey in an aircraft or rocket **3** a flight is also a group of flying birds or aircraft **4** a flight of stairs is one set of stairs **5** a flight on a dart or arrow is its feathers or fins

flight[2] *NOUN* (**flights**)
running away; escape

flimsy *ADJECTIVE* (**flimsier**, **flimsiest**)
light and thin; fragile

flinch *VERB* (**flinches**, **flinching**, **flinched**)
to flinch is to make a sudden movement because you are frightened or in pain

fling *VERB* (**flings**, **flinging**, **flung**)
to fling something is to throw it violently or carelessly • *He flung his shoes under the bed.*

flint *NOUN* (**flints**)
1 flint is a very hard kind of stone **2** a flint is a piece of this stone or hard metal used to produce sparks

> WORD FAMILY
> Something is **flinty** when it is hard like flint.

flip *VERB* (**flips**, **flipping**, **flipped**)
to flip something is to turn it over quickly • *We were flipping pancakes in the kitchen.*

flippant *ADJECTIVE*
not being serious when you should be • *Don't be flippant about his illness.*

> WORD FAMILY
> **Flippancy** is not being serious when you should be; to say something **flippantly** is to say it in a flippant way.

flipper *NOUN* (**flippers**)
1 a limb that water animals use for swimming **2** a flat rubber shoe shaped like a duck's foot, that you wear on your feet to help you swim

flirt *VERB* (**flirts**, **flirting**, **flirted**)
to flirt with someone is to talk to them as if you wanted to get them to love you, not seriously but just for fun

flit *VERB* (**flits**, **flitting**, **flitted**)
to flit is to fly or move lightly and quickly • *A moth flitted across the room.*

float *VERB* (**floats**, **floating**, **floated**)
1 to float is to stay or move on the surface of a liquid or in the air **2** to float something is to make it stay on the surface of a liquid

float *NOUN* (**floats**)
1 a device designed to float • *She learned to swim with the help of floats.* **2** a vehicle with a platform used for delivering milk or for carrying a display in a parade **3** a small amount of money kept for paying small bills or giving change

flock *NOUN* (**flocks**)
a group of sheep, goats, or birds

flock *VERB* (**flocks**, **flocking**, **flocked**)
to flock is to gather or move in a crowd • *And everywhere thousands of folks flocked to see / And laugh at the elephant up in a tree.* — Dr Seuss, *Horton Hatches the Egg*

flog *VERB* (**flogs**, **flogging**, **flogged**)
1 to flog someone is to beat them severely with a whip or stick **2** (*slang*) to flog something is to sell it

flood *NOUN* (**floods**)
1 a large amount of water spreading over a place that is usually dry **2** a great amount of something • *They received a flood of complaints.*

flood *VERB* (**floods**, **flooding**, **flooded**)
1 to flood something is to cover it with a large amount of water **2** a river floods when it flows over its banks **3** to arrive in large amounts • *Offers of help came flooding in from all over the country.*

floodlight *NOUN* (**floodlights**)
a lamp that gives a broad bright beam, used to light up a public building or a sports ground at night

> WORD FAMILY
> Something that is **floodlit** is lit up by floodlights.

floor *NOUN* (**floors**)
1 the part of a room that people walk on **2** all the rooms on the same level in a building • *The sports department is on the top floor.*

floor *VERB* (**floors**, **flooring**, **floored**)
1 to floor someone is to knock them down **2** to floor someone is also to baffle them • *One of the exam questions floored everyone.*

floorboard *NOUN* (**floorboards**)
one of the long flat boards in a wooden floor

flop *VERB* (**flops**, **flopping**, **flopped**)
1 to flop, or flop down, is to fall or sit down heavily **2** to flop is also to fall or hang loosely or heavily • *Her hair flopped over her eyes.* **3** (*informal*) to flop is to be a failure

flop *NOUN* (**flops**)
1 the movement or sound of sudden falling or sitting down **2** (*informal*) a failure or disappointment • *The play was a complete flop.*

floppy *ADJECTIVE* (**floppier**, **floppiest**)
hanging loosely or heavily • *Our dog has huge floppy ears.*

floppy disk *NOUN* (**floppy disks**)
a flat disc in a plastic cover that is used to store computer data

flora *NOUN* (*say* flor- a)
the plants of an area or of a period of time

> OTHER WORD
> See also **fauna**, which refers to animals.

floral *ADJECTIVE*
made of flowers or to do with flowers

florist *NOUN* (**florists**)
a shopkeeper who sells flowers

floss *NOUN*
silky thread or fibres

flounder *VERB* (**flounders**, **floundering**, **floundered**)
to flounder is to move or struggle clumsily because you are in difficulties • *The animals floundered in the shallows at the river's edge, trampling the banks to mud, treading on each other.* — Ted Hughes, *How the Whale Became and Other Stories*

flour *NOUN*
a fine powder made from corn or wheat and used for making bread, cakes, and pastry

> WORD FAMILY
> Something that is **floury** is powdery like flour.

flourish *VERB* (**flourishes**, **flourishing**, **flourished**)
1 to flourish is to grow or develop strongly; to be successful **2** to flourish something is to wave it about

flow *VERB* (**flows**, **flowing**, **flowed**)
1 to flow is to move along smoothly, like a river does **2** to flow is also to hang loosely • *She had golden flowing hair.*

flow *NOUN* (**flows**)
a continuous steady movement of something

flow chart *NOUN* (**flow charts**)
a diagram that shows how the different stages of a process or parts of a system are connected

flower *NOUN* (**flowers**)
1 the part of a plant from which the seed or fruit develops **2** a plant with a flower
to be in flower is to be producing flowers

flower *VERB* (**flowers**, **flowering**, **flowered**)
a plant flowers when it produces flowers

flowerpot *NOUN* (**flowerpots**)
a pot in which plants are grown

flowery *ADJECTIVE*
1 decorated with flowers or pictures of them • *The room had flowery wallpaper.* **2** using fancy words • *He had a flowery style of writing.*

flown
past participle of **fly** *VERB*

flu *NOUN*
influenza

fluctuate *VERB* (**fluctuates**, **fluctuating**, **fluctuated**)
to fluctuate is to keep changing • *Oil prices fluctuate all the time.*
▷ **fluctuation** *NOUN* fluctuation, or a fluctuation, is when something keeps changing

flue *NOUN* (**flues**)
a pipe that takes smoke and fumes away from a stove or boiler

fluent *ADJECTIVE*
skilful at speaking, especially a foreign language

> WORD FAMILY
> To have **fluency** in a language or to speak it **fluently** is to be speak it very well.

fluff *NOUN*
fluff is the small soft bits that come off wool and cloth

> WORD FAMILY
> Something that is **fluffy** is soft like fluff.

fluid *NOUN* (**fluids**)
a substance that flows easily, like liquids and gases

fluke *NOUN* (**flukes**)
a success that you achieve by unexpected good luck

flung
past tense and past participle of **fling**

fluorescent *ADJECTIVE*
a fluorescent light or lamp is one that produces a bright light by means of radiation

fluoridation *NOUN*
adding fluoride to drinking water

fluoride *NOUN*
a chemical that is thought to help prevent tooth decay

flurry *NOUN* (**flurries**)
a sudden gust of wind or rain or snow

flush[1] *VERB* (**flushes, flushing, flushed**)
1 to flush is to go slightly red in the face **2** to flush something is to clean or remove it with a fast flow of liquid

flush *NOUN* (**flushes**)
1 a slight blush **2** a fast flow of water

flush[2] *ADJECTIVE*
1 level; without any part sticking out • *The doors are flush with the walls.* **2** (*slang*) having a lot of money

flustered *ADJECTIVE*
nervous and confused • *Aunty Rose looked around her like a flustered hen. 'What are you all talking about?' she asked.* — Michael Morpurgo, *Tom's Sausage Lion*

flute *NOUN* (**flutes**)
a musical instrument consisting of a long pipe with holes that are covered by fingers or keys. You play it by holding it to one side of your mouth and blowing over a hole at one end

flutter *VERB* (**flutters, fluttering, fluttered**)
1 to flutter is to move with a quick flapping of wings • *A butterfly fluttered in through the window.* **2** to flutter is to move or flap quickly and lightly • *The flags fluttered in the breeze.*

flutter *NOUN* (**flutters**)
1 a fluttering movement **2** (*informal*) a small bet • *Let's have a flutter.*
to be in a flutter is to be nervous and excited

fly *VERB* (**flies, flying, flew, flown**)
1 to fly is to move through the air with wings or in an aircraft **2** to fly is also to wave in the air • *Flags were flying.* **3** to fly something is to make it move through the air • *They were flying model aircraft.* **4** to fly is to move or pass quickly • *The door flew open.* • *The weeks just flew by.*

fly *NOUN* (**flies**)
1 a small flying insect with two wings **2** a real or artificial insect used as bait in fishing **3** the front opening of a pair of trousers

flying saucer *NOUN* (**flying saucers**)
a saucer-shaped flying object believed to come from outer space, especially in science fiction stories

flyleaf *NOUN* (**flyleaves**)
a blank page at the beginning or end of a book

flyover *NOUN* (**flyovers**)
a bridge that carries one road over another

flywheel *NOUN* (**flywheels**)
a heavy wheel fixed to a turning part of a machine, helping it to run smoothly

foal *NOUN* (**foals**)
a young horse

foam *NOUN*
1 a mass of tiny bubbles on a liquid **2** a spongy kind of rubber or plastic

> WORD FAMILY
> A **foamy** liquid produces a mass of tiny bubbles.

foam *VERB* (**foams, foaming, foamed**)
to foam is to form a mass of tiny bubbles

focal point *NOUN* (**focal points**)
1 the focal point on a lens is the point where rays seem to meet **2** a focal point is also the thing that people pay most attention to

focus *NOUN* (**focuses** or **foci**)
1 the distance at which something appears most clearly to your eye or in a lens **2** the point at which rays seem to meet **3** the part of something that people pay most attention to
to be in focus is to appear clearly and not blurred
to be out of focus is to appear blurred

focus *VERB* (**focuses, focusing, focused**)
1 to focus your eye or a camera lens is to adjust it so that objects appear clearly **2** to focus your attention on something is to concentrate on it

fodder *NOUN*
fodder is food for horses and farm animals

foe *NOUN* (**foes**)
(*old use*) an enemy

foetus *NOUN* (**foetuses**) (*say* **fee**- tus)
a developing embryo, especially an unborn human baby

> WORD FAMILY
> **Foetal** means to do with a foetus.

fog *NOUN* (**fogs**)
thick mist which makes it difficult to see

> WORD FAMILY
> It is **foggy** when there is a lot of fog.

foghorn *NOUN* (**foghorns**)
a loud horn for warning ships in fog

fogy *NOUN* (**fogies**)
a person with old-fashioned ideas

foil[1] *NOUN* (**foils**)
a very thin sheet of metal

foil[2] *NOUN* (**foils**)
a long narrow sword you use in fencing

foil[3] *VERB* (**foils, foiling, foiled**)
to foil someone or something is to prevent them from succeeding • *Police foiled the kidnapping plan.*

fold[1] *VERB* (**folds, folding, folded**)
1 to fold something is to bend it so that one part lies over another part **2** to fold is to bend or move in this way • *The table folds up when we are not using it.* **3** to fold your arms is to put one of your arms over the other one and hold them against your chest **4** to fold ingredients in cooking is to mix them together gently, turning one part over another

fold *NOUN* (**folds**)
a line where something has been folded

fold[2] *NOUN* (**folds**)
an enclosure for sheep

folder *NOUN* (**folders**)
1 a folding cardboard or plastic cover you use to keep loose papers in **2** (*in computing*) a place where a set of files are grouped together in a computer

foliage *NOUN*
the leaves of a tree or plant

folk *PLURAL NOUN*
people

folk dance *NOUN* (**folk dances**)
a dance in the traditional style of a country

folklore *NOUN*
old beliefs and legends

folk song *NOUN* (**folk songs**)
a song in the traditional style of a country

follow *VERB* (**follows**, **following**, **followed**)
1 to follow someone or something is to go or come after them, or to do something after they have **2** to follow someone's instructions or advice is to obey them **3** to follow a road or path is to go along it **4** to follow a sport or team is to take an interest in them or support them • *Which football team do you follow?* **5** to follow someone is to understand them • *Do you follow me?* **6** to follow is to happen as a result • *Who knows what trouble may follow?*

follower *NOUN* (**followers**)
a person who follows or supports someone or something

following *PREPOSITION*
after or as a result of • *Following the break-in we had new locks fitted.*

fond *ADJECTIVE* (**fonder**, **fondest**)
1 kind and loving • *She wished me a fond farewell.*
to be fond of someone or **something** is to like them very much

> WORD FAMILY
> To do something **fondly** is to do it in a way that shows you love someone or something very much; **fondness** for someone or something is loving or liking them.

font *NOUN* (**fonts**)
a stone or wooden basin in a church, to hold water for baptism

food *NOUN* (**foods**)
anything that a plant or animal can take into its body to make it grow or give it energy

food chain *NOUN* (**food chains**)
a series of plants and animals, each of which is eaten as food by the one above in the series

fool *NOUN* (**fools**)
1 a silly or stupid person **2** a jester or clown • *Stop playing the fool.* **3** a pudding made of fruit mixed with custard or cream

fool *VERB* (**fools**, **fooling**, **fooled**)
to fool someone is to trick or deceive them
to fool about or **fool around** is to behave in a silly or stupid way

foolhardy *ADJECTIVE* (**foolhardier**, **foolhardiest**)
bold but foolish; reckless
▷ **foolhardiness** *NOUN* being foolhardy

foolish *ADJECTIVE*
stupid or unwise

> WORD FAMILY
> To do something **foolishly** is to be stupid or unwise when you do it; **foolishness** is being stupid or unwise.

foolproof *ADJECTIVE*
a plan or method is foolproof when it is easy to follow and can't easily go wrong

foot *NOUN* (**feet**)
1 the lower part of your leg below your ankle **2** the lowest part of something • *They met up at the foot of the hill.* **3** a measure of length, 12 inches or about 30 centimetres
on foot walking

football *NOUN* (**footballs**)
1 a game played by two teams which try to kick an inflated ball into their opponents' goal **2** the ball used in this game

> WORD FAMILY
> A **footballer** is someone who plays football.

foothill *NOUN* (**foothills**)
a low hill near the bottom of a mountain or range of mountains

foothold *NOUN* (**footholds**)
1 a place where you can put your foot when you are climbing **2** a good start in achieving something • *Our win has given us a foothold in the championship.*

footing *NOUN*
1 your footing is the position of your feet when you are standing firmly on something • *He lost his footing and slipped.* **2** the relationship between two people or groups • *We must try to get on a more friendly footing with our neighbours.*

footlights *PLURAL NOUN*
a row of lights along the front of the stage in a theatre

footnote *NOUN* (**footnotes**)
a note printed at the bottom of the page

footpath *NOUN* (**footpaths**)
a path for people to walk along, especially one in the countryside

footprint *NOUN* (**footprints**)
a mark made by a foot or shoe

footstep *NOUN* (**footsteps**)
the sound made each time your foot touches the ground when they are walking or running

for *PREPOSITION*
used to show **1** purpose or direction • *This letter is for you.* • *We set out for home.* • *Let's go for a walk.* **2** length of time or distance • *We've been waiting for hours.* • *They walked for three miles.* **3** price or cost • *She bought it for $2.* **4** an alternative • *New lamps for old!* **5** cause or reason • *He was rewarded for*

bravery. •*I only did it for the money.* **6** reference •*She has a good ear for music.* **7** support •*Are you for us or against us?*
for ever always

for *CONJUNCTION*
because •*They paused, for they heard a noise.*

forbid *VERB* (**forbids, forbidding, forbade, forbidden**)
1 to forbid someone to do something is to tell them that they must not do it **2** to forbid something is not to allow it •*Smoking is forbidden in this station.*

forbidding *ADJECTIVE*
looking stern or unfriendly

force *NOUN* (**forces**)
1 strength or power **2** (*in science*) an influence that can be measured and that tends to cause things to move **3** an organized team of soldiers or police
in force having effect •*Is the rule still in force?*

force *VERB* (**forces, forcing, forced**)
1 to force someone to do something is to use your power or strength to make them do it **2** to force something is to break it open using your strength

forceful *ADJECTIVE*
strong and effective
▷ **forcefully** *ADVERB* in a forceful way

forceps *PLURAL NOUN* (*say* for- seps)
a pair of pincers or tongs that a dentist or surgeon uses

forcible *ADJECTIVE*
done by force
▷ **forcibly** *ADVERB* with force

ford *NOUN* (**fords**)
a shallow place where you can wade or drive across a river

fore *ADJECTIVE*
at or towards the front

fore *NOUN*
the front part
to the fore to or at the front; in a leading position

forecast *NOUN* (**forecasts**)
a statement about what is likely to happen, especially what the weather is likely to be

forecast *VERB* (**forecasts, forecasting, forecast** or **forecasted**)
to forecast something is to say what is likely to happen •*The weather report forecasts snow for tomorrow.*

forecourt *NOUN* (**forecourts**)
an area in front of a petrol station or large building

forefathers *PLURAL NOUN*
your forefathers are your ancestors

forefinger *NOUN* (**forefingers**)
the finger next to your thumb

foregone conclusion *NOUN*
a result that is certain to happen

foreground *NOUN* (**foregrounds**)
the part of a scene or view that is nearest to you

forehead *NOUN* (**foreheads**) (*say* for- hed or fo- rid)
the part of your face above your eyes

foreign *ADJECTIVE*
1 belonging to or coming from another country **2** strange or unnatural •*Lying is foreign to her nature.*

> **FOREIGN WORDS IN ENGLISH**
> We use many words in English that come from foreign languages. Here are some examples: French *cafe*, *charades*, Italian *pasta*, *spaghetti*, Japanese *karaoke*, Hindi *guru*. See if you can find some more. A lot of them are names of food.

foreigner *NOUN* (**foreigners**)
a person from another country

foreman *NOUN* (**foremen**)
someone in charge of a group of workers

foremost *ADJECTIVE*
most important •*Holly became the LEP's foremost expert in the Artemis Fowl cases, and was invaluable in the fight against the People's most feared enemy.* — Eoin Colfer, *Artemis Fowl*

forename *NOUN* (**forenames**)
a person's first name

foresee *VERB* (**foresees, foreseeing, foresaw, foreseen**)
to foresee something is to realize that it is likely to happen

> **WORD FAMILY**
> A **foreseeable** event is one that you should realize is likely to happen.

foresight *NOUN*
the ability to realize that something is likely to happen in the future and prepare for it

forest *NOUN* (**forests**)
a large area of trees growing close together

> **WORD FAMILY**
> A **forester** is a worker in a forest.

forestry *NOUN*
the science of planting forests and looking after them

foretell *VERB* (**foretells, foretelling, foretold**)
to foretell something is to say it will happen •*Among other things the witch told her that she understood all magic arts, and that she could foretell the future, and knew the healing powers of herbs and plants.* — Andrew Lang, *The Red Fairy Book*

forever *ADVERB*
continually or always •*He is forever complaining.*

forfeit *NOUN* (**forfeits**)
something that you lose or have to pay as a penalty

forfeit *VERB* (**forfeits, forfeiting, forfeited**)
to forfeit something is to lose it as a penalty

forgave
past tense of **forgive**

forge[1] *NOUN* (**forges**)
a place where metal is heated and shaped; a blacksmith's workshop

forge *VERB* (**forges, forging, forged**)
1 to forge metal is to shape it by heating and hammering **2** to forge money or a signature is to copy it in order to deceive people

forge[2] *VERB* (**forges, forging, forged**)
to forge ahead is to make progress with a strong effort

forgery *NOUN* (**forgeries**)
1 forgery is copying something in order to deceive people **2** a forgery is a copy of something made to deceive people

forget *VERB* (**forgets, forgetting, forgot, forgotten**)
1 to forget something is to fail to remember it **2** to forget something is also to stop thinking about it • *Try to forget your worries.*
to forget yourself is to behave rudely or thoughtlessly

forgetful *ADJECTIVE*
tending to forget things
▷ **forgetfulness** *NOUN* being forgetful

forget-me-not *NOUN* (**forget-me-nots**)
a plant with small blue flowers

forgive *VERB* (**forgives, forgiving, forgave, forgiven**)
to forgive someone is to stop being angry with them for something they have done
▷ **forgiveness** *NOUN* forgiving someone

fork *NOUN* (**forks**)
1 a small device with prongs for lifting food to your mouth **2** a large device with prongs used for digging or lifting things **3** a place where a road or river divides into two or more parts

fork *VERB* (**forks, forking, forked**)
1 to fork something is to dig or lift it with a fork **2** to fork is to divide into two or more branches • *The tunnel suddenly forked into two. One passage was nice and wide, the other narrow.* — Enid Blyton, *Five On a Secret Trail*
to fork out (*informal*) is to pay out money

fork-lift truck *NOUN* (**fork-lift trucks**)
a truck with two metal bars at the front for lifting and moving heavy loads

forlorn *ADJECTIVE*
looking sad and lonely

form *NOUN* (**forms**)
1 a form is a kind or type of thing • *What is your favourite form of transport?* **2** the form of something is its shape and general appearance • *They could see a shadowy form in front of them.* **3** a form is also a class in a school **4** a form is also a piece of paper with printed questions and spaces for the answers

form *VERB* (**forms, forming, formed**)
1 to form something is to shape or make it **2** to form is to come into existence or develop • *Icicles formed on the window.*

formal *ADJECTIVE*
1 strictly following the accepted rules or customs; not casual • *She has a formal manner and never calls me by my first name.* **2** official or ceremonial • *The formal opening of the bridge takes place tomorrow.*

WORD FAMILY
To do something **formally** is to do it in a formal way.

FORMAL LANGUAGE
Duplicate is a more formal word than *copy* and *Your participation was appreciated* is a more formal way of saying *Thank you for taking part.* Formal language can often be used to create a distance between writers and the texts they write. The passive is often used in formal language because it contributes to the distancing of the author, as does the use of longer, more complex sentences and unusual vocabulary. Legal documents are usually written in formal language. Look also at the panel on **Informal language**.

formality *NOUN* (**formalities**)
1 formality is formal behaviour **2** a formality is something done to obey a rule or custom

format *NOUN* (**formats**)
1 the shape and size of a book or magazine **2** the way something is arranged or organized • *What will the format of the lesson be?*

formation *NOUN* (**formations**)
1 the action of forming something • *This chapter is about the formation of ice crystals.* **2** something that is formed • *We were studying formations of rock.* **3** a special pattern or arrangement • *The aircraft were flying in formation.*

former *ADJECTIVE*
earlier; in the past • *In former times the house had been an inn.* • *He is a former President of the US.*
the former the first of two people or things just mentioned • *If it's a choice between a picnic or a swim I prefer the former.*
See also **latter**

formerly *ADVERB*
once; previously

formidable *ADJECTIVE* (*say* **for**- mid- a- bul)
1 deserving respect because of being so powerful or impressive • *The Sheepdog was a formidable Twilight Barker. Tonight, with the most important news in Dogdom to send out, he surpassed himself.* — Dodie Smith, *The Hundred and One Dalmatians*

2 very difficult to deal with or do • *This is a formidable task.*

WORD FAMILY
To be **formidably** difficult is to be very difficult indeed.

formula *NOUN* (**formulas** or **formulae**)
1 a set of chemical symbols showing what a substance consists of • *H_2O is the formula for water.* **2** a rule or statement expressed in symbols or numbers **3** a list of what you need to make something **4** one of the groups into which racing cars are placed according to their engine size, for example Formula 1

formulate *VERB* (**formulates, formulating, formulated**)
to formulate an idea or plan is to work it out and express it clearly and exactly

forsake *VERB* (**forsakes, forsaking, forsook, forsaken**)
to forsake someone is to abandon them

fort *NOUN* (**forts**)
a building that has been strongly built against attack

forth *ADVERB*
forwards or onwards

fortification *NOUN* (**fortifications**)
a tower or wall that is built to help defend a place against attack

fortify *VERB* (**fortifies, fortifying, fortified**)
1 to fortify a place is to make it strong against attack **2** to fortify someone is to make them feel stronger • *A bowl of hot soup will fortify you.*

fortnight *NOUN* (**fortnights**)
a period of two weeks

WORD FAMILY
Something that happens **fortnightly** happens every two weeks.

fortress *NOUN* (**fortresses**)
a castle or town that has been strongly built against attack

fortunate *ADJECTIVE*
lucky

WORD FAMILY
You say **fortunately** when it is lucky that something happened • *Fortunately the train hadn't left when we got to the station.*

fortune *NOUN* (**fortunes**)
1 fortune is luck or chance **2** a fortune is a large amount of money

fortune-teller *NOUN* (**fortune-tellers**)
someone who tells you what will happen to you in the future

forty *NOUN* (**forties**)
the number 40
▷ **fortieth** *ADJECTIVE & NOUN* 40th

forward *ADJECTIVE*
1 going towards the front **2** placed in the front **3** too eager or bold

forward *ADVERB*
forwards

forward *NOUN* (**forwards**)
a player in an attacking position in a team at football, hockey, and other games

forwards *ADVERB*
to or towards the front; in the direction you are facing

fossil *NOUN* (**fossils**)
the remains of a prehistoric animal or plant that has been in the ground for a very long time and become hardened in rock

WORD FAMILY
A **fossilized** animal or plant has been formed into a fossil.

foster *VERB* (**fosters, fostering, fostered**)
to foster someone is to look after someone else's child as if they were your own, but without adopting them

foster child *NOUN* (**foster children**)
a child brought up by foster parents

foster parent *NOUN* (**foster parents**)
a parent who is fostering a child

fought
past tense and past participle of **fight** *VERB*

foul *ADJECTIVE* (**fouler, foulest**)
1 disgusting; tasting or smelling unpleasant **2** breaking the rules of a game • *That was a foul shot.*
▷ **foulness** *NOUN* being foul

foul *NOUN* (**fouls**)
an action that breaks the rules of a game

foul *VERB* (**fouls, fouling, fouled**)
to foul a player in a game is to commit a foul against them

found [1] *VERB* (**founds, founding, founded**)
to found an organization or society is to start it or set it up • *When was the hospital founded?*

found [2]
past tense and past participle of **find**

foundation *NOUN* (**foundations**)
1 a building's foundations are the solid base under the ground on which it is built **2** the basis for something **3** the founding of something

founder [1] *NOUN* (**founders**)
someone who founds something • *Guru Nanak was the founder of the Sikh religion.*

founder[2] *VERB* (**founders**, **foundering**, **foundered**)
1 to founder is to fill with water and sink • *The ship foundered on the rocks.* **2** to founder is to fail completely • *Their plans have foundered.*

foundry *NOUN* (**foundries**)
a factory or workshop where metal or glass is made

fountain *NOUN* (**fountains**)
an outdoor structure in which jets of water shoot up into the air

fountain pen *NOUN* (**fountain pens**)
a pen that can be filled with a cartridge or a supply of ink

four *NOUN* (**fours**)
the number 4
to be on all fours is to be on your hands and knees

fourteen *NOUN* (**fourteens**)
the number 14
▷ **fourteenth** *ADJECTIVE & NOUN* 14th

fourth *ADJECTIVE & NOUN*
the next after the third
▷ **fourthly** *ADVERB* in the fourth place; as the fourth one

fowl *NOUN* (**fowl** or **fowls**)
a bird, such as a chicken or duck, that is kept for its eggs or meat

fox *NOUN* (**foxes**)
a wild animal that looks like a dog with a long furry tail

> WORD FAMILY
> Someone is **foxy** when they are cunning.

fox *VERB* (**foxes**, **foxing**, **foxed**)
to fox someone is to puzzle them

foxglove *NOUN* (**foxgloves**)
a tall plant with flowers like the fingers of gloves

foyer *NOUN* (**foyers**) (*say* foi- ay)
the entrance hall of a cinema, theatre, or hotel

fraction *NOUN* (**fractions**)
1 a number that is not a whole number, for example $\frac{1}{2}$ and 0.5 **2** a tiny part or amount of something

fractionally *ADVERB*
by a small amount; very slightly • *The ball was fractionally over the line.*

fracture *VERB* (**fractures**, **fracturing**, **fractured**)
to fracture something, especially a bone, is to break it

fracture *NOUN* (**fractures**)
the breaking of something, especially a bone

fragile *ADJECTIVE* (*say* fra- jyl)
easy to break or damage

> WORD FAMILY
> **Fragility** is being easy to break or damage.

fragment *NOUN* (**fragments**)
1 a small piece broken off something **2** a small part • *She overheard fragments of conversation.*

> WORD FAMILY
> Something is **fragmentary** when it is not complete but consists of small pieces.

fragrant *ADJECTIVE* (*say* fray- grant)
having a sweet or pleasant smell

> WORD FAMILY
> A thing's **fragrance** is the sweet or pleasant smell it has.

frail *ADJECTIVE* (**frailer**, **frailest**)
weak or fragile

> WORD FAMILY
> **Frailty** is being weak or fragile.

frame *NOUN* (**frames**)
1 a set of wooden or metal strips that fit round the outside of a picture or mirror to hold it **2** a rigid structure that supports something • *I've broken the frame of my glasses.* **3** a human body • *He has a small frame.*
your frame of mind is the way you think or feel for a while • *Wait till he's in a better frame of mind.*

frame *VERB* (**frames**, **framing**, **framed**)
1 to frame a picture is to put a frame round it **2** to frame laws or proposals is to put them together **3** (*informal*) to frame someone is to make them seem guilty of a crime by giving false evidence against them

framework *NOUN* (**frameworks**)
1 a structure that supports something **2** a basic plan or system

franc *NOUN* (**francs**)
a former unit of money in France, Switzerland, and some other countries

franchise *NOUN* (**franchises**)
1 the franchise is the right to vote in elections **2** a franchise is a licence to sell a firm's goods or services in a certain area

frank *ADJECTIVE* (**franker**, **frankest**)
honest and saying exactly what you think • *I'll be frank with you.*

> WORD FAMILY
> To say something **frankly** is to say it honestly and openly; **frankness** is being honest and open.

frank *VERB* (**franks**, **franking**, **franked**)
to frank a letter or parcel is to mark it with a postmark

frantic *ADJECTIVE*
wildly anxious or excited
▷ **frantically** *ADVERB* in a frantic way

fraud *NOUN* (**frauds**)
1 fraud is the crime of getting money by tricking people; a fraud is a swindle **2** a fraud is also someone who is not what they pretend to be

> WORD FAMILY
> To be **fraudulent** is to be dishonest.

fraught *ADJECTIVE*
1 someone is fraught when they are tense and upset **2** a situation is fraught when it is full of problems and makes you worried

frayed *ADJECTIVE*
1 frayed material is worn and ragged at the edge • *Your shirt collar is frayed.* **2** tempers or nerves are frayed when people feel strained or upset • *Tempers were becoming frayed.*

freak *NOUN* (**freaks**)
1 a very strange or abnormal person, animal, or thing **2** (*informal*) someone who is a keen fan of something • *She is a fitness freak.*

> WORD FAMILY
> Something that is **freakish** is very unusual.

freckle *NOUN* (**freckles**)
a small brown spot on someone's skin

> WORD FAMILY
> Part of your body is **freckled** when it is covered in freckles.

free *ADJECTIVE* (**freer**, **freest**)
1 able to do what you want to do or go where you want to go **2** not costing any money • *Entrance to the museum is free.* **3** available; not being used or occupied • *Is this seat free?* **4** not busy doing something • *Are you free tomorrow morning?* **5** generous • *She is very free with her money.*
to be free of something is not to have it or be affected by it • *The roads are free of ice.*

> WORD FAMILY
> To do something **freely** is to do it as you want, without anyone or anything stopping you.

free *VERB* (**frees**, **freeing**, **freed**)
to free someone or something is to make them free

freedom *NOUN*
the right to go where you like or do what you like

freehand *ADJECTIVE & ADVERB*
to draw something freehand is to do it without using a ruler or compasses

free-range *ADJECTIVE*
1 free-range hens are allowed to move about freely in the open instead of being caged **2** free-range eggs are those laid by free-range hens

free verse *NOUN*
free verse is poetry that does not rhyme and does not have a regular rhythm

freewheel *VERB* (**freewheels**, **freewheeling**, **freewheeled**)
to freewheel is to ride a bicycle without pedalling

freeze *VERB* (**freezes**, **freezing**, **froze**, **frozen**)
1 to freeze is to turn into ice or another solid, or to become covered with ice • *The pond froze last night.* **2** to be freezing or to be frozen is to be very cold • *My hands are frozen.* **3** to freeze food is to store it at a low temperature to preserve it **4** a person or animal freezes when they suddenly stand still with fright **5** to freeze wages or prices is to keep them at a fixed level

freezer *NOUN* (**freezers**)
a large refrigerator for keeping food frozen

freezing point *NOUN* (**freezing points**)
the temperature at which a liquid freezes

freight *NOUN* (*say* frayt)
goods carried by road or in a ship or aircraft

freighter *NOUN* (**freighters**)
a ship or aircraft for carrying goods

French window *NOUN* (**French windows**)
a long window that reaches down to the ground and is used as a door

frenzy *NOUN* (**frenzies**)
to be in a frenzy is to be wildly excited or angry about something
▷ **frenzied** *ADJECTIVE* wildly excited or angry about something

frequency *NOUN* (**frequencies**)
1 how often something happens **2** being frequent **3** the number of vibrations made each second by a wave of sound or light

frequent *ADJECTIVE* (*say* free- kwent)
happening often

> WORD FAMILY
> To happen **frequently** is to happen often.

frequent *VERB* (**frequents**, **frequenting**, **frequented**) (*say* fri- kwent)
to frequent a place is to visit it often • *They frequented the youth club.*

fresh *ADJECTIVE* (**fresher**, **freshest**)
1 newly made or produced; not old or used • *We need fresh bread.* **2** not tinned or preserved • *Would you like some fresh fruit?* **3** cool and clean • *It's nice to be in the fresh air.* **4** fresh water is water that is not salty

> WORD FAMILY
> To be **freshly** done is to be newly or recently done • *Here are some freshly made biscuits.*; **freshness** is being fresh.

freshen *VERB* (**freshens**, **freshening**, **freshened**)
1 to freshen something is to make it fresh **2** to freshen is to become fresh

freshwater *ADJECTIVE*
freshwater fish live in rivers or lakes and not the sea

fret *VERB* (**frets**, **fretting**, **fretted**)
to fret is to worry or be upset about something

WORD FAMILY
Someone is **fretful** when they are worried and upset; to do something **fretfully** is to be worried and upset when you are doing it.

fret *NOUN*
frets are the bars on the neck of a guitar where you press the strings

friar *NOUN* (**friars**)
a man who is a member of a Roman Catholic order and has vowed to live a life of poverty

WORD FAMILY
A **friary** is a place where friars live.

friction *NOUN*
1 the rubbing of one thing against another
2 disagreement and quarrelling

Friday *NOUN* (**Fridays**)
the sixth day of the week

fridge *NOUN* (**fridges**)
(*informal*) a refrigerator

friend *NOUN* (**friends**)
1 someone you like and who likes you **2** a helpful or kind person

WORD FAMILY
Someone who is **friendless** has no friends. • *A friendless, bitter old man, Roxanne's grandfather was interested in nothing unless there was some money in it.*
— Michael Morpurgo, *The Dancing Bear*

friendly *ADJECTIVE* (**friendlier**, **friendliest**)
kind and pleasant
▷ **friendliness** *NOUN* friendliness is being friendly

friendship *NOUN* (**friendships**)
friendship, or a friendship, is being friends with someone

frieze *NOUN* (**friezes**) (*say* freez)
a strip of designs or pictures along the top of a wall

frigate *NOUN* (**frigates**)
a small fast warship

fright *NOUN* (**frights**)
1 a sudden feeling of fear
to look a fright (*informal*) is to look ridiculous

frighten *VERB* (**frightens**, **frightening**, **frightened**)
to frighten someone is to make them afraid

frightful *ADJECTIVE*
awful; very great or bad • *It's a frightful shame.*

WORD FAMILY
Frightfully means awfully or very • *I'm frightfully sorry.*

frill *NOUN* (**frills**)
1 a strip of pleated material used to decorate the edge of a dress or curtain **2** an unnecessary extra • *We lead a simple life with no frills.*

WORD FAMILY
Frilly material is decorated with frills.

fringe *NOUN* (**fringes**)
1 a straight line of short hair that hangs down over your forehead **2** a decorative edge of hanging threads on something like a piece of clothing or a curtain **3** the edge of something • *We walked around on the fringe of the crowd.*

WORD FAMILY
To be **fringed** with something is to have a fringe.

frisk *VERB* (**frisks**, **frisking**, **frisked**)
(*informal*) to frisk someone is to search them by moving your hands over their body

frisky *ADJECTIVE* (**friskier**, **friskiest**)
playful or lively

WORD FAMILY
To do something **friskily** is to do it in a playful or lively way; **friskiness** is being playful or lively.

fritter [1] *NOUN* (**fritters**)
a slice of meat, potato, or fruit that is covered in batter and fried

fritter [2] *VERB* (**fritters**, **frittering**, **frittered**)
to fritter something or fritter it away is to waste it gradually • *He frittered all his money on comics.*

frivolous *ADJECTIVE*
light-hearted and playful; not serious

WORD FAMILY
Frivolity is playfulness; to do something **frivolously** is to do it in a light-hearted and playful way.

frizzy *ADJECTIVE* (**frizzier**, **frizziest**)
frizzy hair has tight short curls

fro *ADVERB*
to and fro backwards and forwards

frock *NOUN* (**frocks**)
a girl's or woman's dress

frog *NOUN* (**frogs**)
a small jumping animal that can live both in water and on land
to have a frog in your throat is to be hoarse

frogman *NOUN* (**frogmen**)
a swimmer equipped with a rubber suit and flippers and breathing apparatus for swimming under water

frolic *VERB* (**frolics**, **frolicking**, **frolicked**)
to frolic is to spend time playing in a lively and cheerful way

a b c d e f g h i j k l m n o p q r s t u v w x y z

frolic *NOUN* (**frolics**)
a lively cheerful game or entertainment

> WORD FAMILY
> To be **frolicsome** is to be lively and cheerful.

from *PREPOSITION*
used to show **1** a beginning or starting point • *She comes from London.* • *Buses run from 8 o'clock.* **2** distance • *We are a mile from home.* **3** separation • *Get the gun from him.* **4** origin or source • *Get water from the tap.* **5** cause • *I suffer from headaches.* **6** difference • *Can you tell margarine from butter?*

front *NOUN* (**fronts**)
1 the part of a person or thing that faces forwards • *The front of the house is blue.* **2** the part of a thing or place that is furthest forward • *Go to the front of the class.* **3** a road or promenade that runs alongside the seashore **4** the place where fighting is happening in a war • *More troops were moved to the front.* **5** in weather systems, the forward edge of an approaching mass of air • *There is a warm front out in the Atlantic.*
in front at or near the front

front *ADJECTIVE*
placed at or near the front • *We sat in the front row.*

frontier *NOUN* (**frontiers**)
the boundary between two countries or regions

frost *NOUN* (**frosts**)
1 powdery ice that forms on things in freezing weather **2** weather with a temperature below freezing point

frost *VERB* (**frosts**, **frosting**, **frosted**)
to frost up is to become covered with frost

frostbite *NOUN*
harm done to a person's body by very cold weather

> WORD FAMILY
> Part of your body is **frostbitten** when it is suffering from frostbite.

frosted glass *NOUN*
glass that is made cloudy so that you cannot see clearly through it

frosting *NOUN*
sugar icing you put on cakes

frosty *ADJECTIVE*
1 so cold that there is frost • *It was a frosty morning.* **2** unfriendly • *She gave us a frosty look.*

froth *NOUN*
a white mass of tiny bubbles on or in a liquid

> WORD FAMILY
> A **frothy** liquid has froth on top.

froth *VERB* (**froths**, **frothing**, **frothed**)
to froth is to form a froth

frown *VERB* (**frowns**, **frowning**, **frowned**)
to frown is to wrinkle your forehead because you are angry or worried

frown *NOUN* (**frowns**)
the wrinkling of your forehead when you frown

froze
past tense of **freeze**

frozen
past participle of **freeze**

frugal *ADJECTIVE* (*say* froo- gal)
1 spending very little money • *The girls tried to be frugal with their pocket money.* **2** costing little money • *They ate a frugal meal.*

> WORD FAMILY
> Someone who shows **frugality** spends very little money.

fruit *NOUN* (**fruit** or **fruits**)
1 the seed-container that grows on a tree or plant and is often used as food, such as apples, oranges, and bananas **2** the result of doing something • *He lived to see the fruits of his efforts.*

fruitful *ADJECTIVE*
1 something is fruitful when it is successful or has good results • *Their talks were fruitful.*
▷ **fruitfully** *ADVERB* in a fruitful way

fruitless *ADJECTIVE*
something is fruitless when it is unsuccessful or has no results • *It was a fruitless search.*
▷ **fruitlessly** *ADVERB* without success

fruity *ADJECTIVE* (**fruitier**, **fruitiest**)
1 tasting like fruit **2** full and rich • *She sang with a fruity voice.*

frustrate *VERB* (**frustrates**, **frustrating**, **frustrated**)
to frustrate someone is to prevent them from doing something or from succeeding in something, in a way that annoys them

> WORD FAMILY
> **Frustration** is the feeling of annoyance you have when you can't do what you want to do.

fry *VERB* (**fries**, **frying**, **fried**)
to fry food is to cook it in hot fat

frying pan *NOUN* (**frying pans**)
a shallow pan in which things are fried
out of the frying pan into the fire from a bad situation to something worse

fudge *NOUN*
a soft sweet made with milk, sugar, and butter

fuel *NOUN* (**fuels**)
something that is burnt to make heat or power, such as coal and oil

fuel *VERB* (**fuels**, **fuelling**, **fuelled**)
to fuel something is to provide it with material to burn to make heat or power

fugitive *NOUN* (**fugitives**) (*say* few- ji- tiv)
a person who is running away from something, especially from the police

fulcrum *NOUN* (**fulcra** or **fulcrums**)
the point on which something turns or balances

fulfil *VERB* (**fulfils**, **fulfilling**, **fulfilled**)
1 to fulfil something is to achieve it or carry it out • *She fulfilled her promise to come.* **2** to fulfil a prophecy is to make it come true

> WORD FAMILY
> **Fulfilment** is the feeling that you have achieved something.

full *ADJECTIVE*
1 containing as much or as many as possible • *The cinema was full.* **2** having many people or things • *You are full of ideas.* **3** complete • *Tell me the full story.* **4** the greatest possible • *They drove at full speed.* **5** fitting loosely; having many folds • *She's wearing a full skirt.*
in full not leaving anything out
to the full completely; thoroughly

> WORD FAMILY
> **Fullness** is being full; to do something **fully** is to do it completely.

full *ADVERB*
completely; very • *You knew full well what I wanted.*

full moon *NOUN* (**full moons**)
the moon when you can see the whole of it as a bright disc

full stop *NOUN* (**full stops**)
the dot used as a punctuation mark at the end of a sentence or an abbreviation

> FULL STOP
> You use a full stop at the end of a sentence which is a statement, not a question or an exclamation. A sentence that comes after a full stop always begins with a capital letter. Full stops are also used in some abbreviations like *e.g.*, *p.t.o.*, and *Thurs.* Look also at the panel on **Abbreviations**.

full-time *ADJECTIVE & ADVERB*
you do something full-time when you do it for all the normal working hours of the day • *She has a full-time job.* • *She works full-time.*

fumble *VERB* (**fumbles**, **fumbling**, **fumbled**)
to fumble is to handle or feel for something clumsily • *He fumbled in the dark for the light switch.*

fume *VERB* (**fumes**, **fuming**, **fumed**)
1 to fume is to give off strong-smelling smoke or gas **2** to be fuming is to be very angry

fumes *PLURAL NOUN*
strong-smelling smoke or gas

fun *NOUN*
amusement or enjoyment
to make fun of someone or **something** is to make them look silly or make people laugh at them

function *NOUN* (**functions**)
1 what someone or something does or ought to do • *The function of a doctor is to cure sick people.* **2** an important event or party **3** a basic operation of a computer or calculator

function *VERB* (**functions**, **functioning**, **functioned**)
to function is to work properly or perform a function • *The chair also functions as a small table.*

functional *ADJECTIVE*
1 working properly • *The drinks machine is fully functional again.* **2** designed to be practical and useful • *I like furniture that's functional rather than stylish.*
▷ **functionally** *ADVERB* in a functional way

fund *NOUN* (**funds**)
a fund is an amount of money collected or kept for a special purpose • *They started a fund for refugees.*

fundamental *ADJECTIVE*
basic and necessary • *Let me explain the fundamental rules of the game.*
▷ **fundamentally** *ADVERB* basically

funeral *NOUN* (**funerals**)
the ceremony where a person who has died is buried or cremated

fungus *NOUN* (**fungi**)
a plant without leaves or flowers that grows on other plants or on decayed material, such as mushrooms and toadstools

funnel *NOUN* (**funnels**)
1 a tube that is wide at the top and narrow at the bottom, to help you pour things into bottles or other containers **2** a chimney on a ship or steam engine

funny *ADJECTIVE* (**funnier**, **funniest**)
1 that makes you laugh or smile • *We heard a funny joke.* **2** strange or odd • *There's a funny smell in here.*
▷ **funnily** *ADVERB* in a funny way

funny bone *NOUN* (**funny bones**)
part of your elbow which gives you a strange tingling feeling if you knock it

fur *NOUN* (**furs**)
1 the soft hair that covers some animals **2** animal skin with the hair on it, used for clothing; fabric that looks like animal skin with hair on it • *She was wearing a fur hat.*

furious *ADJECTIVE*
1 very angry **2** violent or extreme • *They were travelling at a furious speed.*

> WORD FAMILY
> To say something **furiously** is to say it very angrily; to do something **furiously** is to put a lot of effort into doing it • *We worked furiously to get it finished in time.*

furl *VERB* (**furls**, **furling**, **furled**)
to furl a sail or flag or umbrella is to roll it up and fasten it • *Pegasus snorted, then calmly furled his wings as he chomped.* — Francesca Simon, *Helping Hercules*

furlong *NOUN* (**furlongs**)
one-eighth of a mile, 220 yards or about 201 metres

a b c d e f g h i j k l m n o p q r s t u v w x y z

a b c d e f g h i j k l m n o p q r s t u v w x y z

furnace *NOUN* (**furnaces**)
an oven in which great heat can be produced for making glass or heating metals

furnish *VERB* (**furnishes, furnishing, furnished**)
to furnish a room or building is to put furniture in it

furniture *NOUN*
tables, chairs, beds, cupboards, and other movable things that you need inside a building

furrow *NOUN* (**furrows**)
1 a long cut in the ground made by a plough **2** a deep wrinkle on the skin

furry *ADJECTIVE* (**furrier, furriest**)
1 soft and hairy like fur **2** covered with fur

further *ADVERB* and *ADJECTIVE*
1 at or to a greater distance; more distant • *I can't walk any further.* **2** more • *We need further information.*

further *VERB* (**furthers, furthering, furthered**)
to further something is to help it make progress • *We want to further the cause of peace.*

further education *NOUN*
education for people above school age

furthermore *ADVERB*
also; moreover

furthest *ADVERB* and *ADJECTIVE*
at or to the greatest distance; most distant

furtive *ADJECTIVE*
cautious, trying not to be seen • *He gave a furtive glance and helped himself to the biscuits.*

fury *NOUN* (**furies**)
violent or extreme anger

fuse[1] *NOUN* (**fuses**)
a safety device containing a short piece of wire that melts if too much electricity passes through it

fuse *VERB* (**fuses, fusing, fused**)
1 a piece of electrical equipment fuses when it stops working because a fuse has melted • *The lights have fused.* **2** to fuse things is to blend them together, especially through melting

fuse[2] *NOUN* (**fuses**)
a device for setting off an explosive

fuselage *NOUN* (**fuselages**) (*say* few- ze- lahzh)
the main body of an aircraft

fusion *NOUN* (*say* few- zhon)
1 the action of blending or joining together **2** the joining together of the nuclei of atoms, usually releasing energy

fuss *NOUN* (**fusses**)
fuss, or a fuss, is unnecessary excitement or worry about something that is not important
to make a fuss of someone is to pay a lot of attention to them in a kind way

fuss *VERB* (**fusses, fussing, fussed**)
to fuss is to be excited or worried about something that is not important

fussy *ADJECTIVE* (**fussier, fussiest**)
1 worrying too much about something that is not important **2** full of unnecessary details or decorations
▷ **fussily** *ADVERB* in a fussy way
▷ **fussiness** *NOUN* being fussy

futile *ADJECTIVE* (*say* few- tyl)
useless or having no purpose

> WORD FAMILY
> **Futility** is being useless or having no purpose.

futon *NOUN* (**futons**) (*say* foo- ton)
a seat with a mattress that you can roll out to form a bed

future *NOUN*
1 the time that will come **2** what is going to happen in the time that will come
in future from now onwards

future tense *NOUN*
the form of a verb that shows that something is going to happen in the time that will come. In English, the future tense uses 'will' and 'shall' in front of the verb, for example *I shall come tomorrow*

fuzz *NOUN*
something soft and fluffy like soft hair

fuzzy *ADJECTIVE* (**fuzzier, fuzziest**)
1 blurred or not clear **2** soft and fluffy
▷ **fuzzily** *ADVERB* in a fuzzy way
▷ **fuzziness** *NOUN* being fuzzy

g
short for **gram** or **grams**

gabble *VERB* (**gabbles, gabbling, gabbled**)
to gabble is to talk so quickly that it is difficult to hear the words

gable *NOUN* (**gables**)
the three-sided part of a wall between two sloping roofs

> WORD FAMILY
> A **gabled** house is one that has a gable.

gadget *NOUN* (**gadgets**) (*say* gaj- it)
a small device or tool that helps you with a particular task

Gaelic *NOUN* (*say* gay- lik (in Ireland) or gal- ik (in Scotland))
a Celtic language that is spoken in Ireland and (in a different form) in the Highlands of Scotland

gag *NOUN* (**gags**)
1 something put over someone's mouth to stop them from speaking **2** (*informal*) a joke

gag *VERB* (**gags**, **gagging**, **gagged**)
to gag someone is to put a gag over their mouth

gaiety *NOUN*
gaiety is being cheerful and having fun

gaily *ADVERB*
in a cheerful way

gain *VERB* (**gains**, **gaining**, **gained**)
1 to gain something is to get it when you did not have it before **2** a clock or watch gains when it goes ahead of the correct time
to gain on someone is to come closer to them when you are following them

gain *NOUN* (**gains**)
something you have got that you did not have before; profit

gala *NOUN* (**galas**) (*say* gah- la)
1 a festival **2** a series of sports contests, especially in swimming

galaxy *NOUN* (**galaxies**) (*say* gal- ak- si)
a very large group of stars
▷ **galactic** *ADJECTIVE* to do with a galaxy

gale *NOUN* (**gales**)
a very strong wind

gallant *ADJECTIVE*
brave or courteous
▷ **gallantly** *ADVERB* in a gallant way
▷ **gallantry** *NOUN* gallantry is being gallant

galleon *NOUN* (**galleons**)
a large Spanish sailing ship used in the 16th and 17th centuries

gallery *NOUN* (**galleries**)
1 a platform sticking out from the inside wall of a building **2** the highest set of seats in a cinema or theatre **3** a long room or passage **4** a building or room for showing works of art

galley *NOUN* (**galleys**)
1 an ancient type of long ship driven by oars **2** the kitchen in a ship

gallon *NOUN* (**gallons**)
a measure of liquid, 8 pints or about 4.5 litres

gallop *NOUN* (**gallops**)
1 the fastest pace that a horse can go **2** a fast ride on a horse

gallop *VERB* (**gallops**, **galloping**, **galloped**)
to gallop is to ride fast on a horse

gallows *PLURAL NOUN*
gallows are a framework with a noose for hanging criminals

galore *ADJECTIVE*
in large amounts • *The players were scoring runs galore.*

galvanize *VERB* (**galvanizes**, **galvanizing**, **galvanized**)
1 to galvanize iron is to coat it with zinc to protect it from rust **2** to galvanize someone is to stimulate or shock them into doing something

gamble *VERB* (**gambles**, **gambling**, **gambled**)
1 to gamble is to play a betting game for money **2** to gamble with something is to take great risks • *The government is gambling with the nation's future.*
▷ **gambler** *NOUN* someone who gambles

gamble *NOUN* (**gambles**)
1 a bet or chance • *His idea of a gamble was a pound on the lottery.* **2** a risk • *We were taking a bit of a gamble on the weather being good.*

game *NOUN* (**games**)
1 something that you can play, usually with rules • *She could get a good game of Scrabble out of a tin of alphabet soup.* • *Children zap human figures on their electronic games.* **2** a section of a long game like tennis or whist **3** a trick or scheme • *It was difficult to know what their game might be.* **4** wild animals or birds hunted for sport or food
to give the game away is to reveal a secret

game *ADJECTIVE*
1 able and willing to do something • *Are you game for a swim?* **2** brave • *She's a game lass.*

gamekeeper *NOUN* (**gamekeepers**)
someone whose job is to protect game birds and animals, especially from poachers

gammon *NOUN*
gammon is a kind of ham or thick bacon

gander *NOUN* (**ganders**)
a male goose

gang *NOUN* (**gangs**)
1 a group of people who do things together **2** a group of criminals

gang *VERB* (**gangs**, **ganging**, **ganged**)
to gang up on someone is to form a group to oppose them or frighten them

gangplank *NOUN* (**gangplanks**)
a plank for walking on to or off a ship

gangster *NOUN* (**gangsters**)
a member of a gang of violent criminals

gangway *NOUN* (**gangways**)
1 a gap left for people to move along between rows of seats or through a crowd **2** a movable bridge for getting on or off a ship

gaol *NOUN* and *VERB*
a different spelling of **jail**

gaoler *NOUN*
a different spelling of **jailer**

gap *NOUN* (**gaps**)
1 an opening or break in something **2** an interval

gape *VERB* (**gapes**, **gaping**, **gaped**)
1 to gape is to open your mouth wide **2** to gape is also to stare in amazement

garage *NOUN* (**garages**) (*say* ga- rahzh or ga- rij)
1 a building for keeping motor vehicles in **2** a place where motor vehicles are serviced and repaired and where petrol is sold

garbage *NOUN*
garbage is household refuse or rubbish

a b c d e f g h i j k l m n o p q r s t u v w x y z

garden *NOUN* (**gardens**)
a piece of ground where flowers, fruit, or vegetables are grown • *He jumped over the fence into the next-door garden.*

gardener *NOUN* (**gardeners**)
someone who looks after gardens, especially as a job

gardening *NOUN*
gardening is looking after a garden

gargle *VERB* (**gargles**, **gargling**, **gargled**)
to gargle is to wash your throat by holding liquid at the back of your mouth and breathing air through it

gargoyle *NOUN* (**gargoyles**)
an ugly or comical carving of a face on a building, especially one that sticks out from a gutter and sends out rainwater through its mouth

garland *NOUN* (**garlands**)
a wreath of flowers worn as a decoration

garlic *NOUN*
a plant with a bulb divided into sections (called cloves), which have a strong smell and taste and are used in cooking

garment *NOUN* (**garments**)
a piece of clothing

garnish *VERB* (**garnishes**, **garnishing**, **garnished**)
to garnish a dish of food is to decorate it with extra items such as salad

garrison *NOUN* (**garrisons**)
troops who stay in a town or fort to defend it

garter *NOUN* (**garters**)
a band of elastic to hold up a sock or stocking

gas *NOUN* (**gases**)
1 gas, or a gas, is a substance, such as oxygen, that can move freely and is not liquid or solid at normal temperatures **2** a gas that burns and is used for heating or cooking
▷ **gaseous** *ADJECTIVE* in the form of a gas

gas *VERB* (**gasses**, **gassing**, **gassed**)
to gas someone is to kill or injure them with a poisonous gas

gash *NOUN* (**gashes**)
a long deep cut or wound

gasket *NOUN* (**gaskets**)
a flat ring or strip of soft material for sealing a joint between metal surfaces

gasoline *NOUN*
(*in America*) petrol

gasometer *NOUN* (**gasometers**) (*say* gas-**om**-it-er)
a large round tank in which gas is stored

gasp *VERB* (**gasps**, **gasping**, **gasped**)
1 to gasp is to breathe in suddenly when you are shocked or surprised **2** to gasp is also to struggle to breathe when you are ill or tired **3** to gasp something is to say it in a breathless way

gastric *ADJECTIVE*
to do with the stomach

gate *NOUN* (**gates**)
1 a movable barrier, usually on hinges, used as a door in a wall or fence **2** a barrier used to control the flow of water in a dam or lock **3** a place where you wait before you board an aircraft **4** the number of people attending a football match

gateau *NOUN* (**gateaux**) (*say* gat-oh)
a rich cream cake

gateway *NOUN* (**gateways**)
an opening containing a gate

gather *VERB* (**gathers**, **gathering**, **gathered**)
1 to gather is to come together **2** to gather people or things is to bring them together **3** to gather flowers or fruit is to pick them **4** to gather a piece of information is to hear or read about it • *I gather you went to the same school as me?*
to gather speed is to move gradually faster

gathering *NOUN* (**gatherings**)
an assembly or meeting of people; a party

gaudy *ADJECTIVE* (**gaudier**, **gaudiest**)
very showy and bright

gauge *NOUN* (**gauges**) (*say* gayj)
1 a measuring instrument, such as a fuel gauge **2** one of the standard sizes of something **3** the distance between a pair of railway lines

gauge *VERB* (**gauges**, **gauging**, **gauged**)
to gauge something is to measure it or estimate it • *We can gauge the size of the cave from the time it takes for an echo to reach us.*

gaunt *ADJECTIVE*
a gaunt person is thin and tired-looking

gauntlet [1] *NOUN* (**gauntlets**)
a glove with a wide covering for the wrist
to throw down the gauntlet is to offer a challenge

gauntlet [2] *NOUN*
to run the gauntlet is to face a lot of criticism or risks

gauze *NOUN*
gauze is thin transparent material

gave
past tense of **give**

gay *ADJECTIVE* (**gayer**, **gayest**)
1 cheerful **2** brightly coloured **3** (*informal*) homosexual

gaze *VERB* (**gazes**, **gazing**, **gazed**)
to gaze at something or someone is to look at them hard for a long time

gaze *NOUN* (**gazes**)
a long steady look

gazetteer *NOUN* (**gazetteers**)
a list of the names of cities, towns, and other places, usually with some information about them

GCSE
short for **General Certificate of Secondary Education**

gear *NOUN* (**gears**)
1 a gear is a set of toothed wheels working together in a machine, especially those connecting the engine to the wheels of a vehicle **2** gear is equipment or clothes • *He had left all his fishing gear behind by the river.*
in gear with the gears connected
out of gear with the gears not connected

gee *INTERJECTION*
1 a command to a horse to go on or go faster • *Gee up!* **2** an exclamation of surprise or disappointment

geese
plural of **goose**

Geiger counter *NOUN* (**Geiger counters**)
a device that detects and measures radioactivity

gel *NOUN* (**gels**)
gel is a substance like jelly, especially one used to give a style to hair

gelatine *NOUN*
gelatine is a clear tasteless substance used to make jellies

gem *NOUN* (**gems**)
1 a precious stone or jewel **2** an excellent person or thing • *Her auntie's a real gem.*

gender *NOUN* (**genders**) (*say* **jen**- der)
the group to which a noun or pronoun belongs in some languages (masculine, feminine, and neuter)

> MASCULINE AND FEMININE WORDS
> In English there are not many words that are masculine or feminine, and hardly any that are neuter. There are the pronouns *he*, *she*, and *it*; some special words ending in *-ess* that mean females, such as *actress* and *lioness*, and some animal names such as *bitch* and *hen*. Sometimes we refer informally to things as *she* and *her*, especially machines like cars, for example • *She won't start this morning.*

gene *NOUN* (**genes**) (*say* jeen)
the part of a living cell that controls which characteristics (such as the colour of your hair or eyes) you inherit from your parents

genealogy *NOUN* (**genealogies**) (*say* jeen- ee- **al**- o- jee)
1 genealogy is the study of the history of families **2** a genealogy is a list or diagram of the members of a family

general *ADJECTIVE*
1 to do with most people or things • *The general opinion is that there needs to be a new bypass.* **2** not detailed or specialized • *That is the general idea.*
in general usually; to do with most people

general *NOUN* (**generals**)
an army officer of high rank

general election *NOUN* (**general elections**)
an election of Members of Parliament for the whole country

generalize *VERB* (**generalizes**, **generalizing**, **generalized**)
to generalize is to say things about people or things generally
▷ **generalization** *NOUN* a statement about people or things generally

generally *ADVERB*
usually; to do with most people

general practitioner *NOUN* (**general practitioners**)
a doctor who treats all kinds of diseases and sends people to specialists if necessary

generate *VERB* (**generates**, **generating**, **generated**)
to generate something is to produce or create it

generation *NOUN* (**generations**)
1 a single stage in a family • *Three generations were included: children, parents, and grandparents.* **2** all the people born about the same time • *His generation grew up during the war.*

generator *NOUN* (**generators**)
a machine for producing electricity

generous *ADJECTIVE*
ready to give or share what you have

> WORD FAMILY
> Being generous and ready to give a lot is **generosity**; someone behaves **generously** when they are kind and generous towards other people.

genetic *ADJECTIVE* (*say* ji- **net**- ik)
to do with genes and with characteristics inherited from parents
▷ **genetically** *ADVERB* by means of genes

genetics *PLURAL NOUN*
genetics are the study of genes and genetic behaviour

genial *ADJECTIVE*
kind and pleasant
▷ **genially** *ADVERB* in a genial way

genie *NOUN* (**genies**)
a magical being in stories who can grant wishes

genitals *PLURAL NOUN*
the genitals are the parts of the body used for sexual intercourse

genius *NOUN* (**geniuses**)
1 an unusually clever person **2** an unusually great ability

gent *NOUN* (**gents**)
(*informal*) a gentleman; a man

gentle *ADJECTIVE* (**gentler**, **gentlest**)
kind and quiet; not rough or severe
▷ **gentleness** *NOUN* gentleness is being gentle
▷ **gently** *ADVERB* in a gentle way • *Will kissed her again and gently unfastened her arms from his neck.*

a b c d e f **g** h i j k l m n o p q r s t u v w x y z

gentleman *NOUN* (**gentlemen**)
1 a man **2** a well-mannered or honest man • *He's a real gentleman.*
▷ **gentlemanly** *ADJECTIVE* polite and courteous

genuine *ADJECTIVE*
1 something is genuine when it is real and not fake **2** a person is genuine when they are honest and sincere
▷ **genuinely** *ADVERB* really; in a genuine way

genus *NOUN* (**genera**) (*say* **jee**- nus)
a group of similar animals or plants

geography *NOUN*
geography is the science or study of the world and its climate, peoples, and products

> WORD FAMILY
> A **geographer** is someone who studies geography. A **geographical** area is a region of the earth that you can see on a map.

geology *NOUN* (*say* ji- **ol**- o- ji)
geology is the study of the earth's crust and its layers

> WORD FAMILY
> A **geologist** is someone who studies geology. A **geological** era or period is a time in the past that you can see in the layers of the earth.

geometry *NOUN*
geometry is the study of lines, angles, surfaces, and solids in mathematics

> WORD FAMILY
> **Geometric** or **geometrical** shapes and patterns have regular lines and angles.

geranium *NOUN* (**geraniums**) (*say* je- **ray**- ni- um)
a plant with red, pink, or white flowers

gerbil *NOUN* (**gerbils**) (*say* **jer**- bil)
a small brown animal with long back legs

germ *NOUN* (**germs**)
a tiny living thing, especially one that causes a disease

germinate *VERB* (**germinates**, **germinating**, **germinated**)
a seed germinates when it starts growing and developing
▷ **germination** *NOUN* germination is the process of germinating

gesticulate *VERB* (**gesticulates**, **gesticulating**, **gesticulated**)
to gesticulate is to make movements with your hands and arms while you are talking

gesture *NOUN* (**gestures**) (*say* **jes**- cher)
a movement or action which expresses what you feel

get *VERB* (**gets**, **getting**, **got**)This word has many meanings, depending on the words that go with it
1 to get something is to obtain or receive it • *I got a new bike yesterday.* **2** to get (for example) angry or upset is to become angry or upset **3** to get to a place is to reach it • *We had to borrow money to get home.* **4** to get something (for example) on or off is take it on or off • *I can't get my shoe on.* **5** to get (for example) a meal is to prepare it **6** to get an illness is to catch it • *I think she's got measles.* **7** to get someone to do something is to persuade or order them to do it • *Lara might get him to say yes.*
8 (*informal*) to get something is to understand it • *Do you get what I mean?*
to get by is to manage
to get on is to make progress, or to be friendly with someone
to get out of something is to avoid having to do it
to get over something is to recover from an illness or shock
to get your own back is to have your revenge
to have got to do something is to have no choice about it

getaway *NOUN* (**getaways**)
an escape

geyser *NOUN* (**geysers**) (*say* **gee**- zer or **gy**- zer)
a natural spring that shoots up columns of hot water

ghastly *ADJECTIVE* (**ghastlier**, **ghastliest**)
horrible; awful

ghetto *NOUN* (**ghettos**) (*say* **get**- oh)
an area of a city, often a slum area, where a group of people live who are treated unfairly compared with other people

ghost *NOUN* (**ghosts**)
the spirit of a dead person seen by a living person

> WORD FAMILY
> A **ghostly** place or feeling is one that is unreal or frightening • *The moon gave a ghostly light to the scene.*

ghoulish *ADJECTIVE* (*say* **gool**- ish)
enjoying looking at things to do with death and suffering

giant *NOUN* (**giants**)
1 a creature in stories, like a huge man **2** something that is much larger than the usual size

giant *ADJECTIVE*
huge

giddy *ADJECTIVE* (**giddier**, **giddiest**)
feeling unsteady or dizzy
▷ **giddily** *ADVERB* in a giddy way
▷ **giddiness** *NOUN* giddiness is being giddy

gift *NOUN* (**gifts**)
1 a present **2** a talent • *She has a special gift for drawing.*

gifted *ADJECTIVE*
a gifted person has a special talent or ability

gigantic *ADJECTIVE*
huge; enormous • *Suddenly the boy let out a gigantic belch which rolled around the Assembly Hall like thunder.* — Roald Dahl, *Matilda*

giggle *VERB* (**giggles**, **giggling**, **giggled**)
to giggle is to laugh in a silly way

giggle *NOUN* (**giggles**)
1 a silly laugh **2** (*informal*) something amusing; a joke • *We did it for a giggle.*
the giggles (*informal*) are a fit of giggling

gild *VERB* (**gilds**, **gilding**, **gilded**)
to gild something is to cover it with a thin layer of gold paint or gold

> SPELLING
> Take care not to confuse **gild** with **guild**, which is a noun meaning a society of people.

gills *PLURAL NOUN*
the gills are the part of a fish's body that it breathes through

gimmick *NOUN* (**gimmicks**)
something unusual done or used to attract people's attention

gin *NOUN*
gin is a strong alcoholic drink

ginger *NOUN*
1 ginger is a hot-tasting tropical root, used as a flavouring for food **2** ginger is also a reddish-yellow colour
▷ **gingery** *ADJECTIVE* reddish-yellow like ginger

gingerbread *NOUN*
a cake or biscuit flavoured with ginger

gingerly *ADVERB*
you do something gingerly when you do it carefully and cautiously because you are not sure about it • *Paddington stepped gingerly off the table and, with a last look at the sticky remains of his bun, climbed down onto the floor.* — Michael Bond, *A Bear Called Paddington*

gipsy *NOUN* (**gipsies**)
a different spelling of **gypsy**

giraffe *NOUN* (**giraffes**)
a tall African animal with a very long neck

girder *NOUN* (**girders**)
a metal beam supporting part of a building or bridge

girdle *NOUN* (**girdles**)
a belt or cord worn around your waist

girl *NOUN* (**girls**)
1 a female child **2** a young woman

> WORD FAMILY
> A woman's **girlhood** is the time when she was a girl; you call someone **girlish** when they look or behave like a girl.

girlfriend *NOUN* (**girlfriends**)
a person's regular female friend or lover

giro *NOUN* (**giros**)
a system of sending money directly from one bank account or Post Office account to another

girth *NOUN* (**girths**)
1 the measurement round something **2** a band fastened round a horse's belly to keep its saddle in place

gist *NOUN* (*say* jist)
the main points or general meaning of a speech or conversation

give *VERB* (**gives**, **giving**, **gave**, **given**)
1 to give someone something is to let them have it • *She gave me a sweet.* **2** to give (for example) a laugh or shout is to laugh or shout out **3** to give a performance is to present or perform something • *They gave a concert to raise money.* **4** something gives if it bends or goes down under a strain • *Will this branch give if I sit on it?*
to give in is to surrender
to give up is to stop doing or trying something
to give way is to break or collapse
▷ **giver** *NOUN* a person who gives something

given *ADJECTIVE*
stated or agreed in advance • *Work out how much you can do in a given time.*

glacial *ADJECTIVE* (*say* **glay**- shal)
made of ice or formed by glaciers

glacier *NOUN* (**glaciers**) (*say* **glas**- i- er)
a mass of ice moving slowly along a valley

glad *ADJECTIVE* (**gladder**, **gladdest**)
happy and pleased
to be glad of something is to be grateful for it

> WORD FAMILY
> You do something **gladly** when you are pleased to do it; **gladness** is being glad.

gladden *VERB* (**gladdens**, **gladdening**, **gladdened**)
to gladden someone is to make them glad

gladiator *NOUN* (**gladiators**)
a man who fought with a sword or other weapons at public shows in ancient Rome

glamorize *VERB* (**glamorizes**, **glamorizing**, **glamorized**)
to glamorize something is to make it attractive and exciting

glamorous *ADJECTIVE*
attractive and exciting

glamour *NOUN*
1 the glamour of something is what makes it attractive or exciting • *Just think of the glamour of competing in the Olympics.* **2** a person's glamour is their beauty or attractiveness • *The Basic Brown was the most common type of dragon, a serviceable beast but without much glamour.* — Cressida Cowell, *How to Train Your Dragon*

glance *VERB* (**glances**, **glancing**, **glanced**)
1 to glance at something is to look at it quickly **2** to glance off something is to hit it and slide off • *The ball glanced off his bat.*

glance *NOUN* (**glances**)
a quick look

gland *NOUN* (**glands**)
an organ of the body that separates substances from the blood, so that they can be used or passed out of the body

> WORD FAMILY
> **Glandular** fever is a disease that affects glands in the body called the lymph glands.

glare *VERB* (**glares, glaring, glared**)
1 to glare is to shine with a bright or dazzling light **2** to glare at someone is to look angrily at them • *The bald man glared down at the children and spoke to them in a frightening whisper.* — Lemony Snicket, *A Series of Unfortunate Events*

glare *NOUN* (**glares**)
1 a strong light **2** an angry stare

glaring *ADJECTIVE*
1 very bright **2** very obvious and embarrassing • *Fortunately there were no glaring mistakes in their work.*

glass *NOUN* (**glasses**)
1 glass is a hard brittle substance that lets light through **2** a glass is a container made of glass, for drinking out of **3** a glass is also a mirror or a lens

glasses *PLURAL NOUN*
spectacles or binoculars

glassful *NOUN* (**glassfuls**)
as much as a glass will hold

glassy *ADJECTIVE* (**glassier, glassiest**)
1 like glass **2** dull; without liveliness or expression • *He gave a glassy stare.*

glaze *VERB* (**glazes, glazing, glazed**)
1 to glaze something is to cover or fit it with glass **2** to glaze pottery is to give it a shiny surface **3** to glaze is to become glassy • *Her eyes glazed and she fainted.*

glaze *NOUN* (**glazes**)
a shiny surface

glazier *NOUN* (**glaziers**)
someone whose job is to fit glass into windows and doors

gleam *NOUN* (**gleams**)
1 a beam of soft light, especially one that comes and goes **2** a clear sign of something • *She could see the gleam of excitement in his eyes.*

gleam *VERB* (**gleams, gleaming, gleamed**)
to gleam is to shine with beams of soft light

glee *NOUN*
glee is when you feel happy and excited about something • *Then he stuffed all the food up the chimney with glee. / 'And NOW!' grinned the Grinch, 'I will stuff up the tree!'* — Dr. Seuss, *How the Grinch Stole Christmas*

> WORD FAMILY
> You are **gleeful**, or you act **gleefully**, when you are happy and excited.

glen *NOUN* (**glens**)
a narrow valley, especially in Scotland

glide *VERB* (**glides, gliding, glided**)
1 to glide is to fly or move smoothly **2** to glide is also to fly without using an engine

glider *NOUN* (**gliders**)
an aircraft that does not use an engine and floats on air currents

glimmer *NOUN* (**glimmers**)
a faint light

glimmer *VERB* (**glimmers, glimmering, glimmered**)
to glimmer is to shine with a faint light

glimpse *VERB* (**glimpses, glimpsing, glimpsed**)
to glimpse something is to see it briefly

glimpse *NOUN* (**glimpses**)
a brief view of something

glint *VERB* (**glints, glinting, glinted**)
to glint is to shine with a flash of light • *High upon the slope to our right, in among the trees, a little frozen waterfall glinted brilliantly.* — Philip Pullman, *Count Karlstein*

glint *NOUN* (**glints**)
a brief flash of light

glisten *VERB* (**glistens, glistening, glistened**)
to glisten is to shine like something wet or oily

glitter *VERB* (**glitters, glittering, glittered**)
to glitter is to shine with tiny flashes of light • *There was the dragon she had longed for and dreamed of. His green scales glittered, his eyes were bright and black.* — Helen Cresswell, *Dragon Ride*

gloat *VERB* (**gloats, gloating, gloated**)
to gloat is to be pleased in an unkind way that you have succeeded or that someone else has been hurt or upset

global *ADJECTIVE*
to do with the whole world

> WORD FAMILY
> Something happens or exists **globally** when it is all over the world.

global warming *NOUN*
global warming is the gradual increase in the average temperature of the earth's climate, caused by the greenhouse effect

globe *NOUN* (**globes**)
1 a globe is something shaped like a ball, especially one with a map of the world on it **2** the globe is the world

gloom *NOUN*
gloom is a depressed condition or feeling

gloomy *ADJECTIVE* (**gloomier, gloomiest**)
1 almost dark; not well lit **2** sad or depressed
▷ **gloomily** *ADVERB* in a gloomy way
▷ **gloominess** *NOUN* gloominess is being gloomy

glorify *VERB* (**glorifies**, **glorifying**, **glorified**)
1 to glorify someone is to praise them highly **2** to glorify something is to make it seem splendid
▷ **glorification** *NOUN* glorification is glorifying someone or something

glorious *ADJECTIVE*
splendid or magnificent

> WORD FAMILY
> You say that (for example) the weather is **gloriously** warm when it makes you feel very pleased and happy.

glory *NOUN* (**glories**)
1 glory is fame and honour **2** a thing's glory is its splendour or beauty

gloss *NOUN* (**glosses**)
the shine on a smooth surface

glossary *NOUN* (**glossaries**)
a list of words with their meanings explained • *Your Science book has a glossary of technical terms.*

glossy *ADJECTIVE* (**glossier**, **glossiest**)
smooth and shiny

glove *NOUN* (**gloves**)
a covering for the hand, with a separate division for each finger

glow *NOUN*
1 a brightness and warmth without flames • *They sat and finished their drinks in the glow from the fire.* **2** a warm or cheerful feeling • *Sarah felt a deep glow of satisfaction at her win.*

glow *VERB* (**glows**, **glowing**, **glowed**)
to glow is to shine with a soft light

glower *VERB* (**glowers**, **glowering**, **glowered**)
(*rhymes with* **flower**)
to glower is to stare with an angry look

glow-worm *NOUN* (**glow-worms**)
an insect with a tail that gives out a green light

glucose *NOUN*
glucose is a type of sugar found in fruits and honey

glue *NOUN* (**glues**)
glue is a thick liquid for sticking things together
▷ **gluey** *ADJECTIVE* sticky like glue

glue *VERB* (**glues**, **gluing**, **glued**)
to glue something is to stick it with glue

glum *ADJECTIVE* (**glummer**, **glummest**)
sad or depressed
▷ **glumly** *ADVERB* in a glum way

glutton *NOUN* (**gluttons**)
someone who is greedy and enjoys eating too much

> WORD FAMILY
> Someone is **gluttonous** when they eat too much; **gluttony** is eating too much.

gnarled *ADJECTIVE* (*say* narld)
twisted and knobbly, like an old tree

gnash *VERB* (**gnashes**, **gnashing**, **gnashed**) (*say* nash)
to gnash your teeth is to grind them together

gnat *NOUN* (**gnats**) (*say* nat)
a tiny fly that bites

gnaw *VERB* (**gnaws**, **gnawing**, **gnawed**) (*say* naw)
to gnaw something hard is to keep biting it

gnome *NOUN* (**gnomes**) (*say* nohm)
a kind of dwarf in fairy tales that usually lives underground

go *VERB* (**goes**, **going**, **went**, **gone**)
1 to go is to move or lead from one place to another • *Let's go in and see Mrs Cooper.* • *We'll have to go soon.* • *This road goes to Bristol.* **2** a machine or device goes when it is working • *My watch isn't going.* • *A car that doesn't go is not much use.* **3** you say that someone or something has gone when they are no longer there and you can't find them • *All her money had gone.*
Go also has many special uses shown in these examples • *The milk went sour.* • *The plates go on that shelf.* • *The party went well.* • *The gun went bang.*
to be going to do something is to be ready to do it
to go in for something is to take part in it
to go off is to explode
to go off someone or **something** is to stop liking them
to go on is to happen or continue • *What's going on?*

go *NOUN* (**goes**)
1 a go is a turn or try • *May I have a go?* **2** (*informal*) a go is also a successful try • *They made a go of it.* **3** (*informal*) go is energy or liveliness • *She's full of go.*
on the go always working or moving

go-ahead *NOUN*
permission to do something • *The Council has given the go-ahead to introduce a waste recycling scheme in the area.*

go-ahead *ADJECTIVE*
adventurous and keen to try out new methods

goal *NOUN* (**goals**)
1 the two posts that the ball must go between to score a point in football, hockey, and other games **2** a point scored in football, hockey, netball, and other games **3** something that you try to do or to achieve • *Her goal is to become a pilot.*

> SPELLING
> Take care not to confuse **goal** with **gaol**, which means prison.

goalie *NOUN* (**goalies**)
(*informal*) a goalkeeper

goalkeeper *NOUN* (**goalkeepers**)
the player who guards the goal in football and hockey

a b c d e f **g** h i j k l m n o p q r s t u v w x y z

goalpost *NOUN* (**goalposts**)
each of the upright posts of a goal in sports

goat *NOUN* (**goats**)
an animal with horns, belonging to the same family as sheep

gobble *VERB* (**gobbles**, **gobbling**, **gobbled**)
to gobble something is to eat it quickly and greedily

gobbledegook or **gobbledygook** *NOUN*
the pompous technical language used by officials that is difficult to understand

goblet *NOUN* (**goblets**)
a drinking glass with a long stem and a base

goblin *NOUN* (**goblins**)
an evil or mischievous fairy in stories

God *NOUN*
the creator of the Universe in Christian, Jewish, and Muslim belief

god *NOUN* (**gods**)
a male being that is worshipped

godchild *NOUN* (**godchildren**)
a child that a godparent promises to see brought up as a Christian. A boy is a **godson** and a girl is a **god-daughter**

goddess *NOUN* (**goddesses**)
a female being that is worshipped

godparent *NOUN* (**godparents**)
a person at a child's christening who promises to see that it is brought up as a Christian

> **WORD FAMILY**
> A man is a **godfather** and a woman is a **godmother**.

goggles *PLURAL NOUN*
goggles are large glasses that you wear to protect your eyes from wind, water, or dust

going *NOUN*
good going is quick progress • *It was good going to get home before dark.*

gold *NOUN*
1 gold is a precious yellow metal **2** gold is also a bright yellow colour

golden *ADJECTIVE*
1 made of gold **2** coloured like gold **3** precious or excellent • *It was a golden opportunity.*

golden wedding *NOUN* (**golden weddings**)
the 50th anniversary of a wedding

goldfinch *NOUN* (**goldfinches**)
a small, brightly-coloured bird with yellow feathers in its wings

goldfish *NOUN* (**goldfish**)
a small red or orange fish, often kept as a pet

golf *NOUN*
golf is an outdoor game played on a prepared course by hitting a small ball into a series of small holes, using a club

> **WORD FAMILY**
> A person who plays golf is a **golfer**, and the sport is called **golfing**.

golf course *NOUN* (**golf courses**)
an area of land where golf is played

gondola *NOUN* (**gondolas**) (*say* gon- do- la)
a boat with high pointed ends, used on the canals in Venice

> **WORD FAMILY**
> A **gondolier** is the person who stands at the back of a gondola and moves it along with a pole.

gone
past participle of **go** *VERB*

gong *NOUN* (**gongs**)
a large metal disc that makes a deep hollow sound when it is hit

good *ADJECTIVE* (**better**, **best**)
1 of the kind that people like, want, or praise • *They wanted to have a good time.* **2** kind • *It was good of you to come.* **3** well-behaved • *Be a good boy.*
4 healthy; giving benefit • *Exercise is good for you.*
5 thorough; large enough • *Let's give it a good clean.*
6 quite large or long • *It's a good walk to the station.*

good *NOUN*
1 something good or right • *Do good to others.*
2 benefit or advantage • *I'm telling you for your own good.*
for good for ever
no good useless

goodbye *INTERJECTION*
a word you use when you leave someone or at the end of a telephone call

Good Friday *NOUN*
the Friday before Easter, when Christians remember Christ's death on the Cross

good-looking *ADJECTIVE*
attractive or handsome

good-natured *ADJECTIVE*
kind

goodness *NOUN*
1 goodness is being good **2** a thing's goodness is the good it does

goods *PLURAL NOUN*
goods are things that people buy and sell

goodwill *NOUN*
goodwill is a kindly and helpful feeling towards people

gooey *ADJECTIVE*
sticky or slimy

goose *NOUN* (**geese**)
a water bird with webbed feet, larger than a duck

gooseberry *NOUN* (**gooseberries**)
a small green fruit that grows on a prickly bush

goose pimples *PLURAL NOUN*
goose pimples are lots of tiny bumps you get on the skin when you are cold or afraid

gore *VERB* (**gores, goring, gored**)
to gore a person or animal is to wound them savagely with a horn or tusk • *Several dogs had been gored by a wild boar.*

gorge *NOUN* (**gorges**)
a narrow valley with steep sides

gorgeous *ADJECTIVE*
magnificent; beautiful
▷ **gorgeously** *ADVERB* in a gorgeous way

gorilla *NOUN* (**gorillas**)
a large strong African ape

> SPELLING
> Take care not to confuse **gorilla** with **guerrilla**, which means a type of fighter.

gorse *NOUN*
gorse is a prickly bush with small yellow flowers

gory *ADJECTIVE* (**gorier, goriest**)
1 covered in blood **2** involving a lot of killing

gosh *INTERJECTION*
(*informal*) an exclamation of surprise

gosling *NOUN* (**goslings**)
a young goose

gospel *NOUN* (**gospels**)
1 the gospel is the teachings of Jesus Christ
2 gospel is something you can safely believe • *You can take what she says as gospel.*
the Gospels the first four books of the New Testament

gossip *VERB* (**gossips, gossiping, gossiped**)
to gossip is to talk a lot about other people

gossip *NOUN* (**gossips**)
1 gossip is talk or rumours about other people **2** a gossip is someone who likes talking about other people

got
past tense and past participle of **get**

gouge *VERB* (**gouges, gouging, gouged**) (*say* gowj)
to gouge something is to press or scoop it out

gourd *NOUN* (**gourds**)
1 the hard-skinned fruit of a climbing plant **2** this fruit hollowed out to make a bowl or container

govern *VERB* (**governs, governing, governed**)
to govern a country or organization is to be in charge of it

government *NOUN* (**governments**)
the group of people who are in charge of a country

governor *NOUN* (**governors**)
someone who governs or runs a place

gown *NOUN* (**gowns**)
a loose flowing piece of clothing

GP
short for **general practitioner**

grab *VERB* (**grabs, grabbing, grabbed**)
to grab something is to take hold of it firmly or suddenly

grace *NOUN* (**graces**)
1 grace is beauty, especially in movement
2 someone behaves with grace when they are kind and friendly to people

graceful *ADJECTIVE*
beautiful and elegant in movement or shape
▷ **gracefully** *ADVERB* in a graceful way

gracious *ADJECTIVE*
1 kind and pleasant to other people **2** merciful

> WORD FAMILY
> You do something **graciously** when you do it in a kind and generous way.

grade *NOUN* (**grades**)
a step in a scale of quality, value, or rank

grade *VERB* (**grades, grading, graded**)
to grade things is to sort or divide them into grades

gradient *NOUN* (**gradients**) (*say* gray- di- ent)
1 a slope **2** the amount that a road or railway slopes

gradual *ADJECTIVE*
happening slowly but steadily

> WORD FAMILY
> Something happens **gradually** when it takes a long time and it is done in stages.

graduate *NOUN* (**graduates**) (*say* grad- yoo- at)
someone who has a degree from a university or college

graduate *VERB* (**graduates, graduating, graduated**) (*say* grad- yoo- ayt)
1 to graduate is to get a university degree **2** to graduate something is to divide it into graded sections, or to mark it so that it can be used for measuring • *The ruler was graduated in millimetres.*
▷ **graduation** *NOUN* graduation is graduating from a university or college

graffiti *PLURAL NOUN* (*say* gra- fee- tee)
graffiti are words or drawings scribbled on a wall

grain *NOUN* (**grains**)
1 grain is cereals when they are growing or after they have been harvested **2** a grain is the hard seed of a cereal **3** a grain of something is a small amount of it • *The story had a grain of truth in it.* **4** the grain on a piece of wood is the pattern of lines going through it
▷ **grainy** *ADJECTIVE* having a distinct grain

gram *NOUN* (**grams**)
a unit of weight in the metric system, a thousandth of a kilogram

grammar *NOUN* (**grammars**)
1 grammar is the rules for using words **2** a grammar is a book that gives the rules for using words

> WORD FAMILY
> Something you say or write is **grammatical**, or **grammatically** correct, when it follows the rules of grammar.

grammar school *NOUN* (**grammar schools**)
a kind of secondary school

gramophone *NOUN* (**gramophones**)
(*old use*) a record player

grand *ADJECTIVE* (**grander**, **grandest**)
1 great or splendid **2** a grand total is one that includes everything
▷ **grandly** *ADVERB* in a grand way

grandad *NOUN* (**grandads**)
(*informal*) grandfather

grandchild *NOUN* (**grandchildren**)
a child of a person's son or daughter

> WORD FAMILY
> A girl is a **granddaughter**, and a boy is a **grandson**.

grandeur *NOUN*
grandeur is greatness and splendour

grandfather *NOUN* (**grandfathers**)
the father of a person's mother or father

grandfather clock *NOUN* (**grandfather clocks**)
a clock in a tall wooden case

grandma *NOUN* (**grandmas**)
(*informal*) grandmother

grandmother *NOUN* (**grandmothers**)
the mother of a person's mother or father

grandpa *NOUN* (**grandpas**)
(*informal*) grandfather

grandparent *NOUN* (**grandparents**)
a grandmother or grandfather

grand piano *NOUN* (**grand pianos**)
a large piano that extends at the back and has its strings arranged horizontally

grandstand *NOUN* (**grandstands**)
a building at a racecourse or sports ground, that is open at the front with rows of seats for spectators

granite *NOUN*
granite is a very hard kind of rock

granny *NOUN* (**grannies**)
(*informal*) grandmother

granny knot *NOUN* (**granny knots**)
a reef knot with the strings crossed the wrong way

grant *VERB* (**grants**, **granting**, **granted**)
to grant someone something is to give or allow them what they have asked for
to take something for granted is to assume that it is true or will happen

grant *NOUN* (**grants**)
something given, especially a sum of money

granulated sugar *NOUN*
sugar in the form of hard grains

grape *NOUN* (**grapes**)
a small green or purple fruit that grows in bunches on a vine

grapefruit *NOUN* (**grapefruit**)
a large round yellow citrus fruit with a soft juicy pulp

grapevine *NOUN* (**grapevines**)
1 a climbing plant on which grapes grow **2** to hear something on the grapevine is to be told it by friends and people you know • *We heard the rumour on the grapevine.*

graph *NOUN* (**graphs**)
a diagram that shows how two amounts are related

grapheme *NOUN* (**graphemes**)
a letter or combination of letters, which can be used to represent a sound. For example, the grapheme 'c' can be used to represent the sound at the beginning of the word 'cat' or the sound at the beginning of the word 'ceiling'

graphic *ADJECTIVE*
1 short and lively • *He gave a graphic account of the journey.* **2** to do with drawing or painting • *She is a graphic artist.*
▷ **graphically** *ADVERB* in a graphic way

graphics *PLURAL NOUN*
graphics are diagrams, lettering, and drawings, especially pictures that are produced by a computer

graphite *NOUN*
graphite is a soft kind of carbon used for the lead in pencils

graph paper *NOUN*
paper covered with small squares, used for making graphs

grapple *VERB* (**grapples**, **grappling**, **grappled**)
1 to grapple someone or grapple with someone is to fight them **2** to grapple something is to hold it tightly **3** to grapple with a problem is to try to deal with it

grasp *VERB* (**grasps**, **grasping**, **grasped**)
1 to grasp someone or something is to hold them tightly **2** to grasp something is to understand it

grasp *NOUN*
1 a firm hold **2** a person's grasp of something is how well they understand it • *His grasp of English was obviously limited.*

grasping *ADJECTIVE*
greedy for money or possessions

grass *NOUN* (**grasses**)
1 grass is a green plant with thin stalks **2** a piece of grass is an area of ground covered with grass

> WORD FAMILY
> A **grassy** piece of land is one that is covered in grass.

grasshopper *NOUN* (**grasshoppers**)
a jumping insect that makes a shrill noise

grate [1] *NOUN* (**grates**)
1 a metal framework that keeps fuel in the fireplace **2** a fireplace

grate [2] *VERB* (**grates, grating, grated**)
1 to grate something is to shred it into small pieces **2** to grate is to make an unpleasant noise by rubbing something • *The chalk grated on the blackboard.*

grateful *ADJECTIVE*
feeling glad that someone has done something for you • *I was grateful for their kindness in giving me food and drink.*
▷ **gratefully** *ADVERB* in a grateful way

grating *NOUN* (**gratings**)
a framework of metal bars placed across an opening

gratitude *NOUN*
you show gratitude when you are grateful or thankful for something

grave [1] *NOUN* (**graves**)
the place where a dead body is buried

grave [2] *ADJECTIVE* (**graver, gravest**)
serious or solemn • *We've had grave news.*

> WORD FAMILY
> You speak **gravely** when you are quiet and serious in what you say.

gravel *NOUN*
gravel is small stones mixed with coarse sand, used to make paths

> WORD FAMILY
> A road or area is **gravelled** when it is covered in gravel; something is **gravelly** when it looks or feels like small stones.

gravestone *NOUN* (**gravestones**)
a stone monument over a grave

graveyard *NOUN* (**graveyards**)
a place where dead bodies are buried

gravity *NOUN*
1 gravity is the force that pulls all objects in the universe towards each other **2** the earth's gravity is the force that pulls everything towards itself **3** a person's gravity is when they look serious and worried

> WORD FAMILY
> The earth's **gravitation**, or its **gravitational** pull, is the force that pulls objects towards it.

gravy *NOUN*
a hot brown sauce made from meat juices

graze *VERB* (**grazes, grazing, grazed**)
1 to graze is to feed on growing grass **2** to graze your skin is to scrape it slightly against something rough

graze *NOUN* (**grazes**)
a sore place where skin has been scraped

grease *NOUN*
grease is thick fat or oil
▷ **greasy** *ADJECTIVE* oily like grease

great *ADJECTIVE* (**greater, greatest**)
1 very large **2** very important or distinguished • *She was a great writer.* **3** (*informal*) very good or enjoyable • *It's great to see you again.* **4** older or younger by one generation, as in *great-grandmother* and *great-grandson*

> WORD FAMILY
> You like something **greatly** when you like it a lot; a person's **greatness** is how important and famous they are.

greed *NOUN*
greed is being greedy and wanting too much

greedy *ADJECTIVE* (**greedier, greediest**)
wanting more food or money than you need
▷ **greedily** *ADVERB* in a greedy way

green *ADJECTIVE* (**greener, greenest**)
1 of the colour of grass and leaves **2** concerned with protecting the natural environment

green *NOUN* (**greens**)
1 green is a green colour **2** a green is an area of grass

greenery *NOUN*
green leaves or plants

greengage *NOUN* (**greengages**)
a green kind of plum

greengrocer *NOUN* (**greengrocers**)
someone who keeps a shop that sells fruit and vegetables
▷ **greengrocery** *NOUN* a greengrocer's shop

greenhouse *NOUN* (**greenhouses**)
a glass building that is kept warm inside for growing plants

greenhouse effect *NOUN*
the warming of the earth's surface by gases (called **greenhouse gases**) such as methane and carbon dioxide, which trap heat in the earth's atmosphere

greens *PLURAL NOUN*
greens are green vegetables, such as cabbage and spinach

greet *VERB* (**greets, greeting, greeted**)
1 to greet someone is to welcome them when they arrive • *His cat Moxie greeted him with a soft miaow.* **2** to greet something is to respond to it in a certain way • *They greeted the news with loud cheering.*

greeting *NOUN* (**greetings**)
a greeting is the words or actions used to greet someone
greetings are good wishes when you meet someone or talk to them

grenade *NOUN* (**grenades**)
a small bomb, usually thrown by hand

grew
past tense of **grow**

grey *ADJECTIVE* (**greyer**, **greyest**)
of the colour between black and white, like ashes or dark clouds

grey *NOUN*
a grey colour

greyhound *NOUN* (**greyhounds**)
a slim dog with smooth hair, used in racing

grid *NOUN* (**grids**)
a framework or pattern of bars or lines crossing each other

grief *NOUN*
grief is deep sadness or sorrow people feel when someone has died
to come to grief is to have an accident or misfortune

grievance *NOUN* (**grievances**)
something that people are unhappy or angry about

grieve *VERB* (**grieves**, **grieving**, **grieved**)
1 to grieve is to feel sad or sorrowful **2** to grieve someone is to make them feel very sad • *It grieves me to have to tell you this.*

grievous *ADJECTIVE*
1 causing great sadness **2** serious • *We have suffered a grievous loss.*

> WORD FAMILY
> Something upsets you **grievously** when it makes you very sad and unhappy.

> SPELLING
> Notice that the word is spelt **grievous** and not *grievious*.

grill *NOUN* (**grills**)
1 an element or burner on a cooker, that sends heat downwards **2** grilled food **3** a grating

grill *VERB* (**grills**, **grilling**, **grilled**)
1 to grill food is to cook it under a grill **2** to grill someone is to question them closely and severely • *The police grilled him for several hours.*

grim *ADJECTIVE* (**grimmer**, **grimmest**)
1 stern or severe **2** frightening or unpleasant • *They had a grim experience.*

> WORD FAMILY
> Someone speaks or looks **grimly** when they look very stern and severe; **grimness** is being grim.

grimace *NOUN* (**grimaces**)
a strange or twisted expression on your face

grime *NOUN*
grime is a layer of dirt on a surface

> WORD FAMILY
> Something is **grimy** when it is very dirty.

grin *NOUN* (**grins**)
a smile showing your teeth

grin *VERB* (**grins**, **grinning**, **grinned**)
to grin is to smile showing your teeth
to grin and bear it is to put up with something without complaining

grind *VERB* (**grinds**, **grinding**, **ground**)
1 to grind something is to crush it into a powder
2 to grind something hard is to sharpen or polish it by rubbing it on a rough surface
to grind to a halt is to stop suddenly with a lot of noise
▷ **grinder** *NOUN* something that grinds things

grindstone *NOUN* (**grindstones**)
a rough round revolving stone used for grinding things
to keep your nose to the grindstone is to keep working hard

grip *VERB* (**grips**, **gripping**, **gripped**)
1 to grip something is to hold it tightly **2** a story, film, game, or other activity grips you when you find it very interesting or exciting

grip *NOUN* (**grips**)
1 a firm hold on something **2** a handle

grisly *ADJECTIVE* (**grislier**, **grisliest**)
disgusting or horrible • *He met a grisly end by being stabbed to death in a park.*

gristle *NOUN*
gristle is the tough rubbery part of meat

> WORD FAMILY
> Meat is **gristly** when it is tough and full of gristle.

grit *NOUN*
1 grit is tiny pieces of stone or sand **2** a person's grit is their courage and determination to do something difficult
▷ **gritty** *ADJECTIVE* rough like grit

grit *VERB* (**grits**, **gritting**, **gritted**)
1 to grit your teeth is to clench them tightly when in pain or trouble **2** to grit a road or path is to put grit on it

grizzly bear *NOUN* (**grizzly bears**)
a large bear of North America

groan *VERB* (**groans**, **groaning**, **groaned**)
to groan is to make a long deep sound when in pain or distress

groan *NOUN* (**groans**)
a long deep sound of pain or distress

grocer *NOUN* (**grocers**)
someone who keeps a shop that sells food, drink, and other goods for the house

grocery *NOUN* (**groceries**)
a grocer's shop
groceries goods sold by a grocer

groggy *ADJECTIVE* (**groggier**, **groggiest**)
dizzy or unsteady, especially from illness or injury

groin *NOUN* (**groins**)
the flat part between your thighs and your trunk

groom *NOUN* (**grooms**)
1 someone whose job is to look after horses **2** a bridegroom

groom *VERB* (**grooms**, **grooming**, **groomed**)
1 to groom a horse or other animal is to clean and brush it **2** to groom the hair or a beard is to make it neat and trim

groove *NOUN* (**grooves**)
a long narrow channel cut in the surface of something

grope *VERB* (**gropes**, **groping**, **groped**)
to grope for something is to feel about for it when you cannot see it

gross *ADJECTIVE* (**grosser**, **grossest**)
1 fat and ugly **2** having bad manners; crude or vulgar **3** very bad or shocking • *They showed gross stupidity.* **4** a person's gross income or the gross profits of a business are the total amount before taxes and other amounts have been taken off

WORD FAMILY
Someone **grossly** exaggerates something, or people are **grossly** overpaid, when they exaggerate a lot or get far too much money.

gross *NOUN* (**gross**)
a gross is twelve dozen or 144

grotesque *ADJECTIVE* (*say* groh- **tesk**)
strange and ugly
▷ **grotesquely** *ADVERB* in a grotesque way

grotty *ADJECTIVE* (**grottier**, **grottiest**)
(*informal*) unpleasant or dirty

ground[1] *NOUN* (**grounds**)
1 the ground is the surface of the earth **2** a ground is a sports field

ground[2]
past tense and past participle of **grind**

grounded *ADJECTIVE*
1 aircraft are grounded when they are prevented from flying, for example because of the weather **2** (*informal*) someone is grounded when they are not allowed to go out

ground floor *NOUN* (**ground floors**)
in a building, the floor that is level with the ground

groundnut *NOUN* (**groundnuts**)
a peanut

grounds *PLURAL NOUN*
1 the grounds for something are the reasons that explain it or justify it • *There are grounds for suspecting that a crime has been committed.* **2** the gardens of a large house **3** bits of coffee or dregs at the bottom of a cup

groundsheet *NOUN* (**groundsheets**)
a piece of waterproof material for spreading on the ground, especially in a tent

groundsman *NOUN* (**groundsmen**)
someone whose job is to look after a sports ground

group *NOUN* (**groups**)
a number of people, animals, or things that belong together in some way

group *VERB* (**groups**, **grouping**, **grouped**)
to group people or things is to make them into a group

grouse[1] *VERB* (**grouses**, **grousing**, **groused**)
to grouse is to grumble or complain

grouse[2] *NOUN* (**grouse**)
a large bird with feathered feet, hunted as game

grove *NOUN* (**groves**)
a group of trees; a small wood

grovel *VERB* (**grovels**, **grovelling**, **grovelled**)
1 to grovel is to crawl on the ground **2** to grovel is to be extremely humble and obedient towards someone, usually because you want something from them

grow *VERB* (**grows**, **growing**, **grew**, **grown**)
1 a person grows when they become bigger with age **2** a plant or seed grows when it develops in the ground **3** to grow something is to plant it in the ground and look after it • *She grows lovely roses.* **4** to grow is also to become • *By now it was growing dark on the moor.* • *He grew richer and richer.*
to grow on someone is to become more attractive to them • *This music grows on you.*
to grow out of something is to become too big or too old for it
to grow up is to become an adult
▷ **grower** *NOUN* someone who grows things

growl *VERB* (**growls**, **growling**, **growled**)
to growl is to make a deep rough sound, like an angry dog

growl *NOUN* (**growls**)
a deep rough sound

grown-up *NOUN* (**grown-ups**)
an adult

growth *NOUN* (**growths**)
1 growth is growing or development **2** a growth is something that has grown, especially something unwanted in the body such as a tumour

grub *NOUN* (**grubs**)
1 a grub is a tiny creature that will become an insect; a larva **2** (*slang*) grub is food

grubby *ADJECTIVE* (**grubbier**, **grubbiest**)
rather dirty

grudge *NOUN* (**grudges**)
a dislike of someone because you think they have harmed you, or because you are jealous

grudge *VERB* (**grudges**, **grudging**, **grudged**)
to grudge someone something is to feel unwilling to let them have it

WORD FAMILY
You do something **grudgingly** when you don't really want to do it, and only do it because you have to.

gruelling *ADJECTIVE*
a gruelling test or journey or other experience is one that is very hard and tiring

gruesome *ADJECTIVE*
horrible or disgusting to look at

gruff *ADJECTIVE* (**gruffer**, **gruffest**)
having a rough unfriendly voice or manner
▷ **gruffly** *ADVERB* in a gruff way

grumble *VERB* (**grumbles**, **grumbling**, **grumbled**)
to grumble is to complain in a bad-tempered way
▷ **grumbler** *NOUN* someone who grumbles

grumpy *ADJECTIVE* (**grumpier**, **grumpiest**)
bad-tempered
▷ **grumpily** *ADVERB* in a grumpy way
▷ **grumpiness** *NOUN* grumpiness is being grumpy

grunt *VERB* (**grunts**, **grunting**, **grunted**)
to grunt is to make a snorting sound like a pig

grunt *NOUN* (**grunts**)
a snort like that of a pig

guarantee *NOUN* (**guarantees**)
a formal promise to do something, especially to repair something you have sold someone if it goes wrong

guarantee *VERB* (**guarantees**, **guaranteeing**, **guaranteed**)
to guarantee something is to make a promise to do it

guard *VERB* (**guards**, **guarding**, **guarded**)
1 to guard something or someone is to keep them safe **2** to guard a prisoner is to prevent them from escaping
to guard against something is to be careful to prevent it happening

guard *NOUN* (**guards**)
1 guard is protecting or guarding people or things • *He was kept on constant guard after several attempts to escape.* **2** a guard is someone who protects a person or place, or a group of people guarding a prisoner **3** a guard is also an official in charge of a railway train **4** a guard is a shield or device protecting people from the dangers of a fire or machinery
on guard protecting; acting as a guard

guardian *NOUN* (**guardians**)
1 someone who protects something **2** someone who is legally in charge of a child instead of the child's parents
▷ **guardianship** *NOUN* guardianship is being a guardian

guerrilla *NOUN* (**guerrillas**) (*say* ge- **ril**- a)
a member of a small army or band that fights by means of surprise attacks

SPELLING
Take care not to confuse **guerrilla** with **gorilla**, which is a kind of ape.

guess *NOUN* (**guesses**)
an opinion or answer that you give without working it out in detail or being sure of it

guess *VERB* (**guesses**, **guessing**, **guessed**)
to guess is to make a guess

guesswork *NOUN*
guesswork is something you do or think by guessing • *The police had a few facts but the rest was guesswork.*

guest *NOUN* (**guests**) (*say* gest)
1 a person who is invited to visit or stay at someone's house **2** someone staying at a hotel **3** a performer in a show in which someone else is the main performer

guest house *NOUN* (**guest houses**)
a kind of small hotel

guidance *NOUN*
guidance is giving help or information to someone, or telling them how to do something

guide *NOUN* (**guides**)
1 someone who shows people the way, helps them, or points out interesting sights **2** a book that tells you about a place
Guide a member of the Girl Guides Association, an organization for girls

guide *VERB* (**guides**, **guiding**, **guided**)
to guide someone is to show them the way or help them do something • *He guided her into the sitting room where the piano was.*

guide dog *NOUN* (**guide dogs**)
a dog specially trained to lead a blind person

guided missile *NOUN* (**guided missiles**)
an explosive rocket that is guided to its target from the ground

guidelines *PLURAL NOUN*
guidelines are rules and information about how to do something

guild *NOUN* (**guilds**) (*say* gild)
a society of people, especially in the Middle Ages, with similar skills or interests

SPELLING
Take care not to confuse **guild** with **gild**, which is a verb meaning to cover something with gold.

guillotine *NOUN* (**guillotines**) (*say* **gil**- o- teen)
1 a machine once used in France for beheading people **2** a device with a sharp blade for cutting paper

guilt *NOUN*
1 guilt is an unpleasant feeling you have when you have done something wrong **2** a person's guilt is the fact that they have done something wrong • *Everyone was convinced of their guilt.*

guilty *ADJECTIVE* (**guiltier**, **guiltiest**)
1 someone is guilty when they have done wrong **2** someone feels guilty when they know they have done wrong

guinea *NOUN* (**guineas**)
a British gold coin worth 21 shillings or £1.05, no longer in use

guinea pig *NOUN* (**guinea pigs**)
1 a small furry animal without a tail, kept as a pet **2** a person who is used in an experiment

guitar *NOUN* (**guitars**)
a musical instrument played by plucking its strings
▷ **guitarist** *NOUN* someone who plays the guitar

gulf *NOUN* (**gulfs**)
a large area of sea partly surrounded by land

gull *NOUN* (**gulls**)
a seagull

gullet *NOUN* (**gullets**)
the tube from the throat to the stomach

gullible *ADJECTIVE*
someone is gullible when they can be easily fooled about something

gully *NOUN* (**gullies**)
a narrow channel that carries water

gulp *VERB* (**gulps**, **gulping**, **gulped**)
1 to gulp something is to swallow it quickly or greedily **2** to gulp is to make a loud swallowing noise, especially out of fear

gulp *NOUN* (**gulps**)
a loud swallowing noise

gum[1] *NOUN* (**gums**)
the firm fleshy part of the mouth that holds the teeth

gum[2] *NOUN* (**gums**)
1 a sticky substance used as glue **2** chewing gum
▷ **gummy** *ADJECTIVE* sticky like gum

gum *VERB* (**gums**, **gumming**, **gummed**)
to gum something is to cover it or stick it with gum

gum tree *NOUN* (**gum trees**)
a eucalyptus tree
up a gum tree (*slang*) in great difficulties

gun *NOUN* (**guns**)
1 a weapon that fires shells or bullets from a metal tube **2** a pistol fired to signal the start of a race **3** a device that forces a substance such as grease out of a tube

gun *VERB* (**guns**, **gunning**, **gunned**)
to gun someone down is to shoot them with a gun

gunboat *NOUN* (**gunboats**)
a small warship

gunfire *NOUN*
gunfire is the firing of guns, or the noise they make

gunman *NOUN* (**gunmen**)
a man armed with a gun

gunner *NOUN* (**gunners**)
someone who works with guns, especially in the army

gunpowder *NOUN*
gunpowder is a type of explosive

gunshot *NOUN* (**gunshots**)
gunshot is the shot that some guns fire

gurdwara *NOUN* (**gurdwaras**)
a building where Sikhs worship

gurgle *VERB* (**gurgles**, **gurgling**, **gurgled**)
to gurgle is to make a bubbling sound • *Water gurgled down the waste pipe.* • *Anna's clear voice gurgled with laughter.*

guru *NOUN* (**gurus**)
1 a Hindu religious teacher **2** a wise and respected teacher

Guru Granth Sahib *NOUN*
the holy book of the Sikh religion

gush *VERB* (**gushes**, **gushing**, **gushed**)
1 to gush is to flow quickly **2** to gush is also to talk quickly and with excitement

gust *NOUN* (**gusts**)
a sudden rush of wind or rain

> WORD FAMILY
> The weather is **gusty** when there is a strong wind.

gut *NOUN* (**guts**)
the lower part of the digestive system; the intestine

gut *VERB* (**guts**, **gutting**, **gutted**)
1 to gut a dead fish or animal is to remove its insides before cooking it **2** to gut a place is to remove or destroy the inside of it • *Flames gutted the bedroom and bathroom of a first-floor flat in the High Street.*

guts *PLURAL NOUN*
1 your guts are your insides, especially your stomach and intestines **2** (*informal*) a person has guts when they show courage and determination to do something difficult

gutter *NOUN* (**gutters**)
a long narrow channel at the side of a street or along the edge of a roof, to carry away rainwater

guy[1] *NOUN* (**guys**)
1 a figure in the form of Guy Fawkes, burnt on or near 5 November in memory of the Gunpowder Plot to blow up Parliament in 1605 **2** (*informal*) a man

guy[2] or **guy-rope** *NOUN* (**guys** or **guy-ropes**)
a rope used to hold something in place, especially a tent

guzzle *VERB* (**guzzles**, **guzzling**, **guzzled**)
to guzzle food or drink is to eat or drink it greedily

gym *NOUN* (**gyms**) (*say* jim) (*informal*)
1 a gym is a gymnasium **2** gym is gymnastics

gymkhana *NOUN* (**gymkhanas**) (*say* jim- kah- na)
a show of horse-riding contests and other events

gymnasium *NOUN* (**gymnasiums**)
a place equipped for gymnastics

gymnast *NOUN* (**gymnasts**)
an expert in gymnastics

gymnastics *PLURAL NOUN*
gymnastics are exercises and movements that show the body's agility and strength

gypsy *NOUN* (**gypsies**)
a member of a community of people, also called **travellers**, who live in caravans or similar vehicles and travel from place to place

gyroscope *NOUN* (**gyroscopes**)
a device used in navigation, that keeps steady because of a heavy wheel spinning inside it

habit *NOUN* (**habits**)
something that you do often and almost without thinking

> WORD FAMILY
> Something is **habitual** when you do it regularly, as a habit; to do something **habitually** is to do it in a habitual way.

habitat *NOUN* (**habitats**)
an animal's or plant's habitat is the place where it naturally lives or grows

hack *VERB* (**hacks**, **hacking**, **hacked**)
to hack something is to chop or cut it roughly

hacker *NOUN* (**hackers**)
someone who uses a computer to get access to a company's or government's computer system without permission

hacksaw *NOUN* (**hacksaws**)
a saw with a thin blade for cutting metal

had
past tense and past participle of **have**

haddock *NOUN* (**haddock**)
a sea fish used for food

hadn't
short for *had not*

hag *NOUN* (**hags**)
an ugly old woman

haggard *ADJECTIVE*
looking ill or very tired

haggis *NOUN* (**haggises**)
a Scottish food made from some of the inner parts of a sheep mixed with oatmeal

haggle *VERB* (**haggles**, **haggling**, **haggled**)
to haggle is to argue about a price or agreement

haiku *NOUN* (**haiku**) (*say* hy- koo)
a Japanese short poem, with three lines and 17 syllables in the pattern 5,7,5

hail [1] *NOUN*
frozen drops of rain

hail *VERB* (**hails**, **hailing**, **hailed**)
it hails or it is hailing when hail falls

hail [2] *VERB* (**hails**, **hailing**, **hailed**)
to hail someone is to call out or wave to them to get their attention

hailstone *NOUN* (**hailstones**)
a piece of hail

hair *NOUN* (**hairs**)
1 hair is the soft covering that grows on the heads and bodies of people and animals **2** a hair is one of the fine threads that makes up this soft covering

hairbrush *NOUN* (**hairbrushes**)
a brush for tidying your hair

haircut *NOUN* (**haircuts**)
cutting a person's hair when it gets too long; the style into which it is cut

hairdresser *NOUN* (**hairdressers**)
someone whose job is to cut and arrange people's hair

hairpin *NOUN* (**hairpins**)
a pin for keeping your hair in place

hairpin bend *NOUN* (**hairpin bends**)
a very sharp bend in a road

hair-raising *ADJECTIVE*
terrifying or dangerous

hairstyle *NOUN* (**hairstyles**)
a way or style of arranging your hair

hairy *ADJECTIVE* (**hairier**, **hairiest**)
1 having a lot of hair **2** (*slang*) dangerous or risky

hake *NOUN* (**hake**)
a sea fish used for food

halal *ADJECTIVE*
halal meat is prepared according to Muslim law

half *NOUN* (**halves**)
each of the two equal parts that something is or can be divided into

half *ADVERB*
partly; not completely • *This meat is only half cooked.*
not half (*slang*) very much • *Was she cross? Not half!*

half-baked *ADJECTIVE*
(*informal*) a half-baked plan or idea has not been properly worked out

half-hearted *ADJECTIVE*
not very enthusiastic
▷ **half-heartedly** *ADVERB* not very enthusiastically

half-life *NOUN* (**half-lives**)
the time it takes for radioactivity to fall to half the original amount

half-mast *NOUN*
a flag is at half-mast when it is lowered to halfway down its flagpole, as a sign that someone important has died

halfpenny *NOUN* (**halfpennies** or **halfpence**) (*say* hayp- ni)
an old British coin that was worth half a penny

> GRAMMAR
> The plural is **halfpennies** when you mean individual coins, and **halfpence** when you mean a sum of money.

half-term *NOUN* (**half-terms**)
a short holiday from school in the middle of a school term

half-time *NOUN* (**half-times**)
a short break in the middle of a game

halfway *ADVERB & ADJECTIVE*
at a point half the distance or amount between two places or times

halibut *NOUN* (**halibut**)
a large flat sea fish used for food

hall *NOUN* (**halls**)
1 a space or passage inside the front door of a house **2** a very large room for meetings, concerts, or other large gatherings of people **3** a large important building or house, such as a town hall

hallo *INTERJECTION*
a word used to greet someone or to attract their attention

Hallowe'en *NOUN*
the night of 31 October, when people used to think that ghosts and witches might appear

hallucination *NOUN* (**hallucinations**)
something you think you can see or hear when it isn't really there

halo *NOUN* (**haloes**)
a circle of light, especially one shown round the head of a saint or angel in a painting

halt *VERB* (**halts**, **halting**, **halted**)
to halt is to stop

halt *NOUN*
to call a halt is to stop something
to come to a halt is to stop

halter *NOUN* (**halters**)
a rope or strap put round a horse's head so that it can be controlled

halting *ADJECTIVE*
slow and uncertain • *He has a halting walk.*

halve *VERB* (**halves**, **halving**, **halved**)
1 to halve something is to divide it into halves **2** to halve something is to reduce to half its size or amount • *If the shop had another checkout it would halve the queues.*

halves
plural of **half** *NOUN*

ham *NOUN* (**hams**)
1 ham is meat from a pig's leg **2** (*informal*) a ham is an actor who is not very good and acts in a very exaggerated way **3** a ham is also someone who sends and receives radio messages as a hobby

hamburger *NOUN* (**hamburgers**)
a round flat cake of minced beef that is fried and usually eaten in a bread roll

hammer *NOUN* (**hammers**)
a tool with a heavy metal head at the end of a handle, used for hitting nails in or beating out things

hammer *VERB* (**hammers**, **hammering**, **hammered**)
1 to hammer something is to hit it with a hammer **2** to hammer is to knock loudly • *We heard someone hammering on the door.* **3** (*informal*) to hammer someone in a game or contest is to defeat them completely

hammock *NOUN* (**hammocks**)
a bed made of a strong net or piece of cloth hung up above the ground or floor

hamper[1] *NOUN* (**hampers**)
a large box-shaped basket with a lid

hamper[2] *VERB* (**hampers**, **hampering**, **hampered**)
to hamper someone or something is to get in their way or make it difficult for them to work

hamster *NOUN* (**hamsters**)
a small furry animal with cheek pouches, often kept as a pet

hand *NOUN* (**hands**)
1 the part of your body at the end of your arm **2** a pointer on a clock or watch **3** the cards held by one player in a card game **4** a worker, especially a member of a ship's crew **5** side or direction • *the right-hand side* • *on the other hand*
at hand near or close by
to do or make something by hand is to do or make it using your hands
to give someone a hand is to help them
hands down winning easily or completely
on hand ready and available
to get out of hand is to get out of control

hand *VERB* (**hands**, **handing**, **handed**)
to hand something to someone is to give or pass it to them
something is handed down when it is passed on from one generation to the next

handbag *NOUN* (**handbags**)
a small bag for holding money, keys, and other personal items

handbook *NOUN* (**handbooks**)
a book that gives useful facts about something

handcuffs *PLURAL NOUN*
a pair of metal rings joined by a chain, used for locking a person's wrists together

handful *NOUN* (**handfuls**)
1 as much as you can carry in one hand **2** a small number of people or things • *There were only a handful of people in the audience.* **3** (*informal*) a troublesome person

handicap *NOUN* (**handicaps**)
1 a disadvantage **2** a disability affecting a person

handicapped *ADJECTIVE*
1 suffering from a disadvantage **2** suffering from a disability

handicraft *NOUN* (**handicrafts**)
artistic work done with your hands, such as woodwork and pottery

handiwork *NOUN*
something you have done or made using your artistic skill

handkerchief *NOUN* (**handkerchiefs**) (*say* hang- ker- cheef)
a square piece of material for wiping your nose

handle *NOUN* (**handles**)
the part of a thing by which you can hold or control it or pick it up

handle *VERB* (**handles**, **handling**, **handled**)
1 to handle something is to touch or feel it with your hands **2** to handle a task or problem is to deal with it • *I thought you handled the situation very well.*

handlebars *PLURAL NOUN*
a bar with a handle at each end, used to steer a bicycle or motor cycle

handrail *NOUN* (**handrails**)
a rail for holding on to for support

handsome *ADJECTIVE* (**handsomer**, **handsomest**)
1 attractive or good-looking • *I have no children of my own, and as you are the cleverest and handsomest young man I've ever met, I think I would like to make you the Prince of Narnia.* — C. S. Lewis, *The Lion, The Witch and the Wardrobe* **2** large or generous • *They have made a handsome offer.*

hands-on *ADJECTIVE*
involving actual experience of doing something, rather than just watching other people do it or reading about it

handstand *NOUN* (**handstands**)
an exercise in which you balance on your hands with your feet in the air

handwriting *NOUN*
writing done by hand; a person's style of writing

> WORD FAMILY
> Something is **handwritten** when it is written by hand, not typed or printed.

handy *ADJECTIVE* (**handier**, **handiest**)
useful or convenient

handyman *NOUN* (**handymen**)
someone who does small jobs or repairs in the house

hang *VERB* (**hangs**, **hanging**, **hung**)
1 to hang something is to fix the top part of it to a hook or nail • *Hang your coat on one of the pegs.* **2** something hangs when it is supported from the top and does not touch the ground • *The bat was hanging by its feet.* **3** to hang wallpaper is to paste it in strips on to a wall **4** to hang is to float in the air **5** (in this meaning, the past tense and past participle are **hanged**) to hang someone is to execute them by hanging them from a rope that tightens around their neck • *He was hanged in 1950.*
to hang about or **hang around** is to wait around doing nothing
to hang on (*informal*) is to wait • *Hang on! I'm not ready yet.*
to hang on to something is to hold it tightly
to hang up is to end a telephone conversation by putting back the receiver

hangar *NOUN* (**hangars**)
a large shed where aircraft are kept

> SPELLING
> Take care not to confuse **hangar** with **hanger**, which is the next word in this dictionary.

hanger *NOUN* (**hangers**)
a curved piece of wood, plastic, or wire with a hook at the top, that you use to hang clothes up on

hang-glider *NOUN* (**hang-gliders**)
a frame like a large kite on which a person can glide through the air

> WORD FAMILY
> **Hang-gliding** is the sport of using a hang-glider.

hangman *NOUN* (**hangmen**)
a person whose job is to execute people by hanging them

hangover *NOUN* (**hangovers**)
an unpleasant feeling that someone can have after drinking too much alcohol

hank *NOUN* (**hanks**)
a coil or piece of wool or thread

hanker *VERB* (**hankers**, **hankering**, **hankered**)
to hanker after something is to want it badly • *The penguin, who had always hankered after the good life, recognized that this was as near to it as any penguin could decently hope for.* — Alan Rusbridger, *The Coldest Day in the Zoo*

hanky *NOUN* (**hankies**)
(*informal*) a handkerchief

Hanukkah *NOUN*
a Jewish festival held in December

haphazard *ADJECTIVE* (*say* hap- haz- erd)
done or chosen at random, with no particular order or plan • *The books were arranged on the shelf in a haphazard way.*
▷ **haphazardly** *ADVERB* in a haphazard way • *Mrs*

Weasley was clattering around, cooking breakfast a little haphazardly, throwing dirty looks at her sons as she threw sausages into the frying pan. — J. K. Rowling, *Harry Potter and the Chamber of Secrets*

happen *VERB* (**happens**, **happening**, **happened**)
to happen is to take place or occur
to happen to do something is to do it by chance without planning it • *I happened to see him in the street.*

happening *NOUN* (**happenings**)
something that happens; an unusual event

happy *ADJECTIVE* (**happier**, **happiest**)
1 pleased or contented **2** satisfied that something is good • *My teacher is happy with my work this term.* **3** lucky or fortunate • *By a happy coincidence, we met Jenny in town.*

> WORD FAMILY
> To do something **happily** is to do it in a happy way; **happiness** is being happy.

happy-go-lucky *ADJECTIVE*
being cheerful and not worrying about the future

harass *VERB* (**harasses**, **harassing**, **harassed**) (*say* ha- ras)
to harass someone is to annoy or trouble them a lot

> WORD FAMILY
> Someone is **harassed** when they feel anxious because they have so much to do; **harassment** is being harassed.

> SPELLING
> Notice that **harass** has only one *r*.

harbour *NOUN* (**harbours**)
a place where ships can shelter or unload

harbour *VERB* (**harbours**, **harbouring**, **harboured**)
to harbour a criminal is to give them shelter

hard *ADJECTIVE* (**harder**, **hardest**)
1 firm or solid; not soft • *The ground was hard.* **2** difficult • *These sums are quite hard.* **3** severe or harsh • *There has been a hard frost.* **4** energetic; using great effort • *She is a hard worker.*
hard up short of money
▷ **hardness** *NOUN* being hard

hard *ADVERB* (**harder**, **hardest**)
1 with great effort • *We must work hard.* **2** with a lot of force • *It was raining hard.*

hardboard *NOUN*
stiff board made of compressed wood pulp

hard-boiled *ADJECTIVE*
a hard-boiled egg is one that has been boiled until it is hard

hard disk *NOUN* (**hard disks**)
a disk fitted inside a computer, able to store large amounts of data

harden *VERB* (**hardens**, **hardening**, **hardened**)
1 to harden is to become hard • *Wait for the varnish to harden.* **2** to harden something is to make it hard • *What's the best way to harden a conker?*

hardly *ADVERB*
only just; only with difficulty • *She was hardly able to walk.*

hardship *NOUN* (**hardships**)
1 hardship is suffering or difficulty **2** a hardship is something that causes suffering

hardware *NOUN*
1 tools and other pieces of equipment you use in the house and garden **2** the machinery and electronic parts of a computer, not the software

hard-wearing *ADJECTIVE*
able to stand a lot of wear

hardwood *NOUN* (**hardwoods**)
hard heavy wood from deciduous trees, such as oak and teak

hardy *ADJECTIVE* (**hardier**, **hardiest**)
able to endure cold or difficult conditions

hare *NOUN* (**hares**)
a fast-running animal like a large rabbit

hark *VERB* (**harks**, **harking**, **harked**)
(*old-fashioned use*) to hark is to listen
to hark back is to return to an earlier subject

harm *VERB* (**harms**, **harming**, **harmed**)
to harm someone or something is to hurt or damage them

harm *NOUN*
injury or damage

> WORD FAMILY
> Something is **harmful** when it causes injury or damage; something is **harmless** when it is not at all dangerous.

harmonica *NOUN* (**harmonicas**)
a mouth organ

harmonious *ADJECTIVE*
1 music is harmonious when it is pleasant to listen to **2** peaceful and friendly

> WORD FAMILY
> To live or work **harmoniously** with other people is to do it in a friendly way without disagreeing.

harmonize *VERB* (**harmonizes**, **harmonizing**, **harmonized**)
1 musicians or singers harmonize when they play or sing together with notes that combine in a pleasant way with the main tune **2** to harmonize is to combine together in an effective or pleasant way
▷ **harmonization** *NOUN* harmonizing

harmony *NOUN* (**harmonies**)
1 a pleasant combination of musical notes played or sung at the same time **2** agreement or friendship • *They live in perfect harmony.*

> WORD FAMILY
> **Harmonic** means to do with musical harmony.

harness *NOUN* (**harnesses**)
the straps put over a horse's head and round its neck to control it

harness *VERB* (**harnesses**, **harnessing**, **harnessed**)
1 to harness a horse is to put a harness on it **2** to harness something is to control it and make use of it • *They tried to harness the power of the wind to make electricity.*

harp *NOUN* (**harps**)
a musical instrument made of a frame with strings stretched across it that you pluck with your fingers

> WORD FAMILY
> A **harpist** is someone who plays the harp.

harp *VERB* (**harps**, **harping**, **harped**)
to harp on about something is to keep on talking about it in an annoying way • *He keeps harping on about all the work he has to do.*

harpoon *NOUN* (**harpoons**)
a spear attached to a rope, fired from a gun to catch whales and large fish

harpsichord *NOUN* (**harpsichords**)
a musical instrument like a piano but with the strings plucked and not struck

harrow *NOUN* (**harrows**)
a heavy device pulled over the ground to break up the soil

harsh *ADJECTIVE* (**harsher**, **harshest**)
1 rough and unpleasant **2** cruel or severe
▷ **harshly** *ADVERB* in a harsh way
▷ **harshness** *NOUN* being harsh

harvest *NOUN* (**harvests**)
1 the time when farmers gather in the corn, fruit, or vegetables they have grown **2** the crop that is gathered in

harvest *VERB* (**harvests**, **harvesting**, **harvested**)
to harvest crops is to gather them in

has
3rd person singular of **have**

hash *NOUN* (**hashes**)
a mixture of small pieces of meat and vegetables, usually fried
to make a hash of something is to make a real mess of it

hasn't
short for *has not*

hassle *NOUN* (**hassles**)
(*informal*) hassle or a hassle is something that is difficult or causes problems

hassle *VERB* (**hassles**, **hassling**, **hassled**)
to hassle someone is to annoy them or cause them problems

haste *NOUN*
hurry or speed
to make haste is to hurry

hasten *VERB* (**hastens**, **hastening**, **hastened**)
1 to hasten is to hurry **2** to hasten something is to speed it up

hasty *ADJECTIVE* (**hastier**, **hastiest**)
hurried; done too quickly • *a hasty decision*
▷ **hastily** *ADVERB* in a hurried way
▷ **hastiness** *NOUN* being hasty

hat *NOUN* (**hats**)
a covering for the head
to keep something under your hat is to keep it as a secret

hatch[1] *NOUN* (**hatches**)
an opening in a floor, wall, or door, usually with a covering

hatch[2] *VERB* (**hatches**, **hatching**, **hatched**)
1 to hatch is to break out of an egg • *The chicks hatched this morning.* **2** to hatch an egg is to keep it warm until a young bird hatches from it **3** to hatch a plan is to form it

hatchback *NOUN* (**hatchbacks**)
a car with a sloping rear door hinged at the top

hatchet *NOUN* (**hatchets**)
a small axe

hate *VERB* (**hates**, **hating**, **hated**)
to hate someone or something is to dislike them very much

hate *NOUN* (**hates**)
1 hate is a feeling of great dislike **2** (*informal*) a hate is someone or something that you dislike very much • *Sweetcorn is one of my hates.*

hateful *ADJECTIVE*
hated; very nasty
▷ **hatefully** *ADVERB* in a hateful way

hatred *NOUN* (*say* hay-trid)
a strong feeling of great dislike

hat trick *NOUN* (**hat tricks**)
getting three goals, wickets, or victories one after another

haughty *ADJECTIVE* (**haughtier**, **haughtiest**) (*say* haw-ti)
proud of yourself and looking down on other people
▷ **haughtily** *ADVERB* in a haughty way
▷ **haughtiness** *NOUN* being haughty

haul *VERB* (**hauls**, **hauling**, **hauled**)
to haul something is to pull it using a lot of power or strength • *The topmen hurried aloft while on the deck the rest of us hauled the thick anchor cable from its locker.* — Richard Platt, *Pirate Diary*

haul *NOUN* (**hauls**)
an amount that someone has gained; a catch or booty • *The thieves made a haul of over $6 million.* • *The trawler brought home a large haul of fish.*

haunt *VERB* (**haunts**, **haunting**, **haunted**)
1 a ghost haunts a place or person when it appears often **2** to haunt a place is to visit it often **3** an idea or memory haunts someone when they are always thinking of it

WORD FAMILY
A **haunted** place is one that people think is visited by ghosts.

have *VERB* (**has**, **having**, **had**)
This word has many meanings, depending on the words that go with it **1** to have something is to own or possess it •*We haven't any money.* **2** to have something in it is to contain it •*I thought this tin had biscuits in it.* **3** to have (for example) a party is to organize it **4** to have (for example) a shock or accident is to experience it •*I'm afraid she has had an accident.* **5** to have to do something is to be obliged or forced to do it •*We really have to go now.* **6** to have something (for example) mended or built is to get someone to mend or build it •*I'm having my watch mended.* **7** to have (for example) a letter is to receive it •*I had a letter from my cousin.*
to have someone on (*informal*) is to fool them

GRAMMAR
The verb **have** can also be used as an 'auxiliary' verb to help make other verbs. •*They have gone.* •*Has he seen my book?* •*We had eaten them.*

haven *NOUN* (**havens**) (*say* hay- ven)
1 a safe place **2** a harbour

haven't
short for *have not*

haversack *NOUN* (**haversacks**)
a strong bag you carry on your back

hawk[1] *NOUN* (**hawks**)
a bird of prey with very strong eyesight and a hooked beak

hawk[2] *VERB* (**hawks**, **hawking**, **hawked**)
to hawk things is to go from place to place selling them

WORD FAMILY
A **hawker** is someone who calls at houses to sell things.

hawthorn *NOUN* (**hawthorns**)
a thorny tree with small red berries

hay *NOUN*
cut grass that is dried and used to feed to animals

hay fever *NOUN*
an allergy to pollen that makes you sneeze and makes your eyes water or itch

haystack *NOUN* (**haystacks**)
a large neat pile of stored hay

hazard *NOUN* (**hazards**)
a risk or danger

WORD FAMILY
Something is **hazardous** when it is dangerous or risky. •*Cold and hunger drove me to ever more desperate and hazardous escapades.* — Michael Morpurgo, *The Last Wolf*

haze *NOUN* (**hazes**)
thin mist

hazel *NOUN* (**hazels**)
1 a type of small nut tree **2** a nut from this tree **3** a light brown colour

hazy *ADJECTIVE* (**hazier**, **haziest**)
1 misty •*hazy sunshine* **2** vague and unclear •*I have a hazy memory of the party.*
▹ **hazily** *ADVERB* in a hazy way
▹ **haziness** *NOUN* being hazy

H-bomb *NOUN* (**H-bombs**)
a hydrogen bomb

he *PRONOUN & NOUN*
a male person or animal: used as the subject of a verb

head *NOUN* (**heads**)
1 the part of the body containing the brains, eyes, and mouth **2** brains or intelligence •*Use your head!* **3** a talent or ability •*He has a good head for sums.* **4** the side of a coin on which someone's head is shown **5** a person •*It costs $3 per head.* **6** the top or front of something, such as a pin or nail **7** the person in charge •*She's the head of this school.*
to come to a head is to reach a point of crisis
to keep your head is to stay calm
off the top of your head (*informal*) without preparation or thinking carefully •*He gave an estimate off the top of his head.*

head *VERB* (**heads**, **heading**, **headed**)
1 to head a group or organization is to lead it or be the person in charge **2** to head a ball is to hit it with your head **3** to head in a particular direction is to start going there •*They headed for home.*
to head someone off is to get in front of them in order to turn them aside

headache *NOUN* (**headaches**)
1 a pain in your head that goes on hurting **2** (*informal*) a problem or difficulty

headdress *NOUN* (**headdresses**)
a decorative covering for the head

header *NOUN* (**headers**)
the act of hitting the ball with your head in football

head first *ADVERB*
with your head at the front •*I dived in head first.*

heading *NOUN* (**headings**)
a word or words at the top of a piece of printing or writing

WORD FAMILY
A **sub-heading** is a heading given to one of the sections into which a piece of printing or writing has been divided

a b c d e f g h i j k l m n o p q r s t u v w x y z

headland *NOUN* (**headlands**)
a piece of high land sticking out into the sea

headlight *NOUN* (**headlights**)
a strong light at the front of a vehicle

headline *NOUN* (**headlines**)
a heading in a newspaper, printed in large type

headlong *ADVERB & ADJECTIVE*
1 falling head first **2** in a hasty or thoughtless way • *He's always rushing headlong into trouble.*

headmaster *NOUN* (**headmasters**)
a male headteacher

headmistress *NOUN* (**headmistresses**)
a female headteacher

head-on *ADVERB & ADJECTIVE*
with the front parts hitting each other • *They had a head-on collision.*

headphones *PLURAL NOUN*
a listening device that fits over the top of your head

headquarters *NOUN* (**headquarters**)
the place from which an organization is controlled

headteacher *NOUN* (**headteachers**)
the person in charge of a school

headway *NOUN*
to make headway is to make progress

heal *VERB* (**heals, healing, healed**)
1 to heal someone is to make them healthy **2** a wound or injury heals when it gets better • *The cut soon healed.* **3** to heal a disease is to cure it
▷ **healer** *NOUN* someone who heals people who are ill

health *NOUN*
1 the condition of a person's body or mind • *His health is bad.* **2** being healthy • *in sickness and in health*

health food *NOUN* (**health foods**)
food that contains only natural substances and is thought to be good for your health

healthy *ADJECTIVE* (**healthier, healthiest**)
1 free from illness; having good health **2** good for you • *Fresh air is healthy.*
▷ **healthily** *ADVERB* in a healthy way
▷ **healthiness** *NOUN* being healthy

heap *NOUN* (**heaps**)
a pile, especially an untidy pile
heaps (*informal*) a large amount • *We've got heaps of time.*

heap *VERB* (**heaps, heaping, heaped**)
1 to heap things is to pile them up **2** to heap something is to put large amounts on it • *She heaped his plate with food.*

hear *VERB* (**hears, hearing, heard**)
1 to hear is to take in sounds through the ears **2** to hear something is to take in its sound through the ear **3** to hear news or information is to receive it **4** you hear from someone when they write to you or phone you

hearing *NOUN* (**hearings**)
1 the ability to hear **2** a chance to be heard • *Please give me a fair hearing.* **3** a trial in court

hearing aid *NOUN* (**hearing aids**)
a device to help a deaf person to hear

hearse *NOUN* (**hearses**)
a vehicle for taking a coffin to a funeral

heart *NOUN* (**hearts**)
1 the part of the body inside your chest that pumps blood around your body **2** a person's feelings or emotions • *She has a kind heart.* **3** courage or enthusiasm • *We must take heart.* **4** the middle or most important part of something **5** a curved shape representing a heart, or a playing card with this shape on it
to break someone's heart is to make them very unhappy
by heart by using your memory

heart attack *NOUN* (**heart attacks**)
a sudden failure of the heart to work properly, causing pain and sometimes death

hearth *NOUN* (**hearths**) (*say* harth)
the floor of a fireplace or the area near it

heartless *ADJECTIVE*
cruel or without pity

hearty *ADJECTIVE* (**heartier, heartiest**)
1 strong and healthy **2** enthusiastic or sincere • *Hearty congratulations!* **3** a hearty meal is large and filling
▷ **heartily** *ADVERB* in a hearty way
▷ **heartiness** *NOUN* being hearty

heat *NOUN* (**heats**)
1 being hot; great warmth **2** a race or contest to decide who will take part in the final

heat *VERB* (**heats, heating, heated**)
1 to heat something, or heat something up, is to make it hot **2** to heat, or heat up, is to become hot

heater *NOUN* (**heaters**)
a device for heating a place, especially a room or a car

heath *NOUN* (**heaths**)
wild flat land often covered with heather or bushes

heathen *NOUN* (**heathens**)
someone who does not believe in any of the world's chief religions

heather *NOUN*
a low bush with small purple, pink, or white flowers

heatwave *NOUN* (**heatwaves**)
a long period of hot weather

heave *VERB* (**heaves, heaving, heaved**)
1 to heave something is to lift or move it with great effort **2** (*informal*) to heave something is to throw it
to heave a sigh is to sigh deeply

heaven *NOUN*
1 the place where, in some religions, good people are thought to go when they die and where God and the angels are thought to live **2** a very pleasant place or condition
the heavens the sky

heavenly *ADJECTIVE*
1 to do with the sky or in the sky **2** (*informal*) pleasing or delicious • *The cake is heavenly.*

heavy *ADJECTIVE* (**heavier**, **heaviest**)
1 weighing a lot; hard to lift or carry **2** you talk about how heavy something is when you are talking about how much it weighs **3** strong or severe • *Heavy rain was falling.* **4** hard or difficult • *The climb up the hill was heavy going.*
with a heavy heart unhappily • *I left my home town with a heavy heart.*
▷ **heavily** *ADVERB* with a lot of weight or force
▷ **heaviness** *NOUN* being heavy

heavyweight *NOUN* (**heavyweights**)
1 a heavy person **2** a boxer or wrestler of the heaviest weight

Hebrew *NOUN*
the language of the ancient Jews, with a modern form used in Israel

hectare *NOUN* (**hectares**) (*say* **hek**- tar)
a unit of area equal to 10,000 square metres or nearly $2\frac{1}{2}$ acres

hectic *ADJECTIVE*
very active or busy • *It's been a hectic morning.*

he'd
short for *he had, he should,* or *he would*

hedge *NOUN* (**hedges**)
a row of bushes forming a barrier or boundary

hedge *VERB* (**hedges**, **hedging**, **hedged**)
1 to hedge a field or other area is to surround it with a hedge **2** to hedge is also to avoid giving a definite answer • *He wasn't sure, so he tried to hedge.*

hedgehog *NOUN* (**hedgehogs**)
a small animal covered with prickles

hedgerow *NOUN* (**hedgerows**)
a row of bushes forming a hedge

heed *VERB* (**heeds**, **heeding**, **heeded**)
to heed something is to pay attention to it

heed *NOUN*
attention given to something

> WORD FAMILY
> To be **heedless** of something is to take no notice of it.

heel *NOUN* (**heels**)
1 the back part of your foot **2** the part of a sock or shoe round or under the back part of your foot
to take to your heels is to run away

heel *VERB* (**heels**, **heeling**, **heeled**)
to heel a shoe is to mend its heel

hefty *ADJECTIVE* (**heftier**, **heftiest**)
big and strong

heifer *NOUN* (**heifers**) (*say* **hef**- er)
a young cow

height *NOUN* (**heights**)
1 how high someone or something is **2** a high place • *She's afraid of heights.* **3** the highest or most important part of something • *We shall be going at the height of the holiday season.*

heighten *VERB* (**heightens**, **heightening**, **heightened**)
1 to heighten something is to make it higher or more intense **2** to heighten is to become higher or more intense • *Their excitement heightened as the kick-off approached.*

heir *NOUN* (**heirs**) (*say* air)
someone who inherits money or a title

> WORD FAMILY
> An **heiress** is a female heir.

held
past tense and past participle of **hold** *VERB*

helicopter *NOUN* (**helicopters**)
a kind of aircraft without wings, lifted by a large horizontal propeller on top

helium *NOUN* (*say* **hee**- li- um)
a colourless gas that is lighter than air and is sometimes used in balloons

helix *NOUN* (**helices**)
a three-dimensional spiral, shaped like a screw

hell *NOUN*
1 a place where, in some religions, wicked people are thought to be punished after they die and where the Devil is thought to live **2** a very unpleasant place or situation
hell for leather at great speed

he'll
short for *he will*

hellish *ADJECTIVE*
very unpleasant or difficult

hello *INTERJECTION*
a word used to greet someone or to attract their attention

helm *NOUN* (**helms**)
the handle or wheel used to steer a ship

helmet *NOUN* (**helmets**)
a strong covering that you wear to protect your head

help *VERB* (**helps**, **helping**, **helped**)
1 to help someone is to do something useful for them or make things easier for them **2** when you cannot help doing something, you cannot avoid doing it • *I can't help coughing.* **3** to help someone to food is to give them some

> WORD FAMILY
> A **helper** is someone who helps another person.

help *NOUN* (**helps**)
1 doing something useful for someone **2** someone who does something, especially housework, for someone

helpful *ADJECTIVE*
giving help; useful
▷ **helpfully** *ADVERB* in a helpful way

helping *NOUN* (**helpings**)
a portion of food at a meal

helpless *ADJECTIVE*
not able to do things or look after yourself
▷ **helplessly** *ADVERB* in a helpless way

helter-skelter *NOUN* (**helter-skelters**)
a spiral slide at a fair

hem *NOUN* (**hems**)
the edge of a piece of cloth that has been folded over and sewn down

hem *VERB* (**hems**, **hemming**, **hemmed**)
to hem material is to fold it over and sew down its edge
to hem someone in is to surround them or restrict their movements

hemisphere *NOUN* (**hemispheres**)
1 half a sphere **2** half the earth • *Australia is in the southern hemisphere.*

hemp *NOUN*
a plant that produces coarse fibres from which cloth and ropes are made

hen *NOUN* (**hens**)
a female bird, especially a chicken

hence *ADVERB*
1 from this time on **2** therefore

henceforth *ADVERB*
from now on; from this time on

her *PRONOUN*
a word used for *she* when it is the object of a verb, or when it comes after a preposition • *I can see her.* • *He took the books from her.*

her *DETERMINER*
belonging to her • *That is her book.*

herald *NOUN* (**heralds**)
1 an official who in the past used to make announcements or carry messages for a king or queen **2** someone or something that is a sign of things to come

herald *VERB* (**heralds**, **heralding**, **heralded**)
to herald something or someone is to say or show that they are coming

heraldry *NOUN*
the study of coats of arms

> WORD FAMILY
> **Heraldic** means to do with heraldry.

herb *NOUN* (**herbs**)
a plant used for flavouring or for making medicines

> WORD FAMILY
> **Herbal** means to do with herbs or using herbs.

herbivore *NOUN* (**herbivores**)
an animal that only eats plants

herd *NOUN* (**herds**)
a large group of animals, especially cattle

herd *VERB* (**herds**, **herding**, **herded**)
to herd animals or people is to gather them together or move them in a large group

here *ADVERB*
in or to this place
here and there in various places or directions

hereditary *ADJECTIVE*
passed down to a child from a parent

heredity *NOUN* (*say* hi-red-i-ti)
the passing down of characteristics from parents to children through their genes

heritage *NOUN* (**heritages**)
things that have been passed from one generation to another; a country's history and traditions • *Music is part of our cultural heritage.*

hermit *NOUN* (**hermits**)
someone who lives alone and keeps away from people, often for religious reasons

> WORD FAMILY
> A **hermitage** is a place where a hermit lives.

hero *NOUN* (**heroes**)
1 a man or boy who has done something very brave **2** the most important man or boy in a story, film, or play

> WORD FAMILY
> Someone who is **heroic** is very brave, like a hero; to act **heroically** is to act bravely; **heroism** is being a hero or great bravery.

heroine *NOUN* (**heroines**)
1 a woman or girl who has done something very brave **2** the most important woman or girl in a story, film, or play

heron *NOUN* (**herons**)
a wading bird with long legs and a long neck

herring *NOUN* (**herring** or **herrings**)
a sea fish that swims in large groups and is used for food

hers *DETERMINER*
belonging to her • *Those books are hers.*

herself *PRONOUN*
she or her and nobody else, used to refer back to the subject of a verb • *She has hurt herself.*
by herself on her own; alone • *She did the work all by herself.*

he's
short for *he is* and (before a verb in the past tense) *he has*

hesitant *ADJECTIVE*
being slow or uncertain when you speak or move
▷ **hesitantly** *ADVERB* in a hesitant way

hesitate *VERB* (**hesitates**, **hesitating**, **hesitated**)
to hesitate is to be slow or uncertain when you speak or move

> WORD FAMILY
> **Hesitation** is when you hesitate; a **hesitation** is a pause.

hexagon *NOUN* (**hexagons**)
a flat shape with six sides

> WORD FAMILY
> Something that is **hexagonal** has six sides.

hey *INTERJECTION*
an exclamation used to express surprise or to call someone's attention

hi *INTERJECTION*
an exclamation used to greet someone or to call their attention

hibernate *VERB* (**hibernates**, **hibernating**, **hibernated**) (*say* hy- ber- nayt)
animals hibernate when they sleep for a long time during cold weather
▷ **hibernation** *NOUN* hibernating

hiccup *NOUN* (**hiccups**)
a high gulping sound made when your breath is briefly interrupted

hiccup *VERB* (**hiccups**, **hiccupping**, **hiccupped**)
to make this high gulping sound

hide *VERB* (**hides**, **hiding**, **hidden**, **hid**, **hidden**)
1 to hide is to get into a place where you cannot be seen or found • *I hid behind a tree.* **2** to hide someone or something is to keep them from being seen • *The gold was hidden in a cave.* **3** to hide information is to keep it secret • *Are you hiding the truth from me?*

hide-and-seek *NOUN*
a game in which one person looks for others who are hiding

hideous *ADJECTIVE*
very ugly or unpleasant • *Aunt Sponge had a long-handled mirror on her lap and she kept picking it up and gazing at her own hideous face.* — Roald Dahl, *James and the Giant Peach*
▷ **hideously** *ADVERB* in a hideous way

hideout *NOUN* (**hideouts**)
a place where someone hides

hiding [1] *NOUN*
to go into hiding is to hide yourself so that people can't find you

hiding [2] *NOUN* (**hidings**)
a thrashing or beating

hieroglyphics *PLURAL NOUN* (*say* hyr- o- glif- iks)
pictures or symbols used in ancient Egypt to represent words

hi-fi *NOUN* (**hi-fis**) (*say* hy- fy)(*informal*)
a piece of equipment that reproduces sound well

higgledy-piggledy *ADVERB & ADJECTIVE*
in disorder; completely mixed up

high *ADJECTIVE* (**higher**, **highest**)
1 reaching a long way up • *They could see a high building.* **2** far above the ground or above sea level • *The clouds were high in the sky.* **3** measuring from top to bottom • *The post is two metres high.* **4** above average in amount or importance • *They are people of a high rank.* • *Prices are high.* **5** lively; happy • *They are in high spirits.* **6** a high note is one at the top end of a musical scale **7** going bad • *This meat is high.*

high *ADVERB* (**higher**, **highest**)
1 far above the ground or a long way up • *She jumped high into the air.* **2** at a high level • *The temperature is going to rise even higher this week.*
it is high time to do something when you should do it at once • *It's high time you started work.*

higher education *NOUN*
education at a university or college

high explosive *NOUN* (**high explosives**)
a very strong explosive

high jump *NOUN*
an athletic contest in which competitors jump over a high bar

highland *ADJECTIVE*
in the highlands; to do with the highlands

highlands *PLURAL NOUN*
mountainous country, especially in Scotland

> WORD FAMILY
> A **highlander** is someone who lives in the highlands.

highlight *NOUN* (**highlights**)
the most interesting part of something • *We watched the highlights of the match on the TV.*

highlight *VERB* (**highlights**, **highlighting**, **highlighted**)
to highlight something is to draw attention to it

highlighter *NOUN* (**highlighters**)
a pen with bright coloured ink that you spread over words on paper to draw attention to them

highly *ADVERB*
extremely • *He is highly amusing.*
to think highly of someone is to admire them very much

highly-strung *ADJECTIVE*
very sensitive or nervous

Highness *NOUN* (**Highnesses**)
a title of a prince or princess • *His Royal Highness, the Prince of Wales.*

high-pitched *ADJECTIVE*
high in sound

high-rise *ADJECTIVE*
a high-rise building is a tall one with many storeys

high school *NOUN* (**high schools**)
a secondary school

highway *NOUN* (**highways**)
an important road or route

highwayman *NOUN* (**highwaymen**)
a man who in earlier times robbed travellers on highways

hijack *VERB* (**hijacks, hijacking, hijacked**)
to hijack an aircraft or vehicle is to take control of it by force during a journey

> WORD FAMILY
> A **hijacker** is someone who hijacks an aircraft or vehicle.

hike *NOUN* (**hikes**)
a long walk in the countryside

hike *VERB* (**hikes, hiking, hiked**)
to hike is to go for a long walk in the countryside

> WORD FAMILY
> A **hiker** is someone who goes for long walks in the countryside.

hilarious *ADJECTIVE*
very funny

> WORD FAMILY
> To be **hilariously** funny is to be extremely funny; **hilarity** is loud laughter.

hill *NOUN* (**hills**)
a piece of ground that is higher than the ground around it

> WORD FAMILY
> A **hillside** is the side of a hill; a **hilly area** has lots of hills.

hilt *NOUN* (**hilts**)
the handle of a sword or dagger
up to the hilt completely

him *PRONOUN*
a word used for *he* when it is the object of a verb, or when it comes after a preposition • *I like him.* • *I gave it to him.*

himself *PRONOUN*
he or him and nobody else, used to refer back to the subject of a verb • *He has hurt himself.*
by himself on his own; alone • *He did the work all by himself.*

hind [1] *ADJECTIVE* (*say* hynd)
at the back • *The donkey had hurt one of its hind legs.*

hind [2] *NOUN* (**hinds**) (*say* hynd)
a female deer

hinder *VERB* (**hinders, hindering, hindered**) (*say* hin-der)
to hinder someone is to get in their way, or to make it difficult for them to do something

> WORD FAMILY
> A **hindrance** is something that gets in your way, or makes it difficult for you to do something.

Hindi *NOUN*
a language spoken in northern India

Hindu *NOUN* (**Hindus**)
someone who believes in **Hinduism**, one of the religions of India

hinge *NOUN* (**hinges**)
a joining device on which a door, gate, or lid swings when it opens

hinge *VERB* (**hinges, hinging, hinged**)
to hinge on something is to depend on it • *It all hinges on the weather.*

hinged *ADJECTIVE*
a hinged door, window, or lid is fixed on a hinge

hint *NOUN* (**hints**)
1 a slight indication or suggestion • *Give me a hint of what you want for your birthday.* **2** a useful piece of advice • *He was always giving us hints on model-making.*

hint *VERB* (**hints, hinting, hinted**)
to hint is to suggest something without actually saying it • *She hinted that she'd like to have a puppy.*

hip [1] *NOUN* (**hips**)
your hips are the bony parts at the side of your body between your waist and your thighs

hip [2] *INTERJECTION*
a word that you say when you give a cheer • *Hip, hip, hooray!*

hippo *NOUN* (**hippos**)
(*informal*) a hippopotamus

hippopotamus *NOUN* (**hippopotamuses**)
a very large African animal that lives near water

hire *VERB* (**hires, hiring, hired**)
to hire something is to pay to use it for a time

hire *NOUN*
something is for hire when you can hire it

hire purchase *NOUN*
buying something by paying for it in instalments

his *DETERMINER*
belonging to him • *That is his book.*

hiss *VERB* (**hisses, hissing, hissed**)
to hiss is to make a sound like a continuous *s*, as some snakes do

histogram *NOUN* (**histograms**)
a chart showing amounts as bars of different heights and widths

historian *NOUN* (**historians**)
someone who writes or studies history

historic *ADJECTIVE*
famous or important in history

historical *ADJECTIVE*
1 to do with history **2** that really happened in the past • *The story is based on historical events.*

history *NOUN* (**histories**)
1 what happened in the past **2** the study of past events **3** a description of important events

hit *VERB* (**hits**, **hitting**, **hit**)
1 to hit someone or something is to come up against them with force, or to give them a blow **2** something hits you when you suddenly realize or feel it • *The answer suddenly hit me.* **3** to hit a place or people is to have a bad effect on them • *Famine hit the poorer countries.* **4** to hit a note is to reach it when you are singing
to hit it off with someone is to get on well with them when you meet them
to hit on something is to think of an idea suddenly

hit *NOUN* (**hits**)
1 a knock or stroke **2** a shot that hits the target **3** a successful song or show

hitch *VERB* (**hitches**, **hitching**, **hitched**)
1 to hitch something is to tie it up with a loop **2** (*informal*) to hitch a lift is to hitch-hike
to hitch something up is to pull it up quickly or with a jerk • *He hitched up his trousers.*

hitch *NOUN* (**hitches**)
1 a slight difficulty or delay **2** a knot

hitch-hike *VERB* (**hitch-hikes**, **hitch-hiking**, **hitch-hiked**)
to hitch-hike is to travel by getting lifts in other people's vehicles

> WORD FAMILY
> A **hitch-hiker** is someone who hitch-hikes.

hi-tech *ADJECTIVE*
(*informal*) using the most advanced technology, such as computers

hither *ADVERB*
(*old use*) to or towards this place

hitherto *ADVERB*
up to now

HIV
short for *human immunodeficiency virus*, a virus that weakens a person's resistance to disease and causes the disease Aids

hive *NOUN* (**hives**)
1 a beehive **2** a very busy place • *The office was a hive of activity.*

HMS
short for *His or Her Majesty's Ship*

ho *INTERJECTION*
an exclamation of triumph or surprise, etc.

hoard *NOUN* (**hoards**)
a hidden store of something valuable

> SPELLING
> Take care not to confuse **hoard** with **horde**, which means a large group or crowd.

hoard *VERB* (**hoards**, **hoarding**, **hoarded**)
to hoard things is to collect them and store them away

> WORD FAMILY
> A **hoarder** is someone who likes saving things and keeping them rather than throwing them out.

hoarding *NOUN* (**hoardings**)
a tall fence covered with advertisements

hoar frost *NOUN*
white frost

hoarse *ADJECTIVE* (**hoarser**, **hoarsest**)
having a rough or croaking voice • *He was hoarse from shouting.*

hoax *NOUN* (**hoaxes**)
a trick played on someone in which they are told about something but it isn't true • *The bomb scare was hoax.*

hoax *VERB* (**hoaxes**, **hoaxing**, **hoaxed**)
to hoax someone is to trick them by telling them about something that isn't true

hobble *VERB* (**hobbles**, **hobbling**, **hobbled**)
to hobble is to walk with unsteady steps, especially because your feet are sore

hobby *NOUN* (**hobbies**)
something that you enjoy doing in your spare time

hockey *NOUN*
an outdoor game played by two teams with long curved sticks and a small hard ball

hoe *NOUN* (**hoes**)
a gardening tool with a long handle and a metal blade, used for scraping up weeds and making soil loose

hoe *VERB* (**hoes**, **hoeing**, **hoed**)
to hoe ground is to scrape it or dig it with a hoe

hog *NOUN* (**hogs**)
1 a male pig **2** (*informal*) a greedy person
to go the whole hog (*informal*) is to do something completely or thoroughly

hog *VERB* (**hogs**, **hogging**, **hogged**)
(*informal*) to hog something is to take more than your fair share of it

Hogmanay *NOUN*
New Year's Eve in Scotland

hoist *VERB* (**hoists**, **hoisting**, **hoisted**)
to hoist something is to lift it up using ropes or pulleys

hold *VERB* (**holds**, **holding**, **held**)
1 to hold something is to have it in your hands **2** to hold something is also to possess it or be the owner of it • *She holds the world high jump record.* **3** to hold

a party, meeting, or event is to organize it • *The 2004 Olympic Games were held in Athens.* **4** a container holds an amount when that is what you can put in it • *This jug holds a litre.* **5** to hold someone or something is to support them • *This plank won't hold my weight.* **6** to hold someone is to keep them and stop them getting away • *They held the thief until help arrived.* **7** something like the weather holds when it stays the same • *Will this good weather hold?* **8** to hold an opinion is to believe it

hold it (*informal*) stop; wait a minute
to hold on (*informal*) is to wait • *Hold on! I'm not ready yet.*
to hold on to something is to keep holding it
to hold out is to last or continue
to hold someone up is to rob them with threats of force
to hold someone or **something up** is to hinder or delay them • *We were held up by the traffic.*

hold *NOUN* (**holds**)
1 holding something • *Don't lose hold of the rope.* **2** the part of a ship where cargo is stored
to get hold of someone is to make contact with them • *I want to invite Jane to the party but I can't get hold of her.*
to get or **take hold of something** is to grasp it

holdall *NOUN* (**holdalls**)
a large portable bag or case

holder *NOUN* (**holders**)
a person or thing that holds something

hold-up *NOUN* (**hold-ups**)
1 a delay **2** a robbery with threats or force

hole *NOUN* (**holes**)
1 a gap or opening made in something **2** an animal's burrow • *a rabbit hole*

> WORD FAMILY
> Something is **holey** when it is full of holes.

Holi *NOUN*
a Hindu festival held in the spring

holiday *NOUN* (**holidays**)
a day or time when you do not go to work or school; a time when you go away to enjoy yourself
to be on holiday is to be away from work or school enjoying yourself

hollow *ADJECTIVE*
having an empty space inside; not solid

hollow *VERB* (**hollows, hollowing, hollowed**)
to hollow something is to make it hollow • *We always hollow out a pumpkin at Halloween.*

hollow *NOUN* (**hollows**)
1 a hollow or sunken place **2** a small valley

holly *NOUN*
an evergreen bush with shiny prickly leaves and red berries

holocaust *NOUN* (**holocausts**) (*say* hol- o- kawst)
great destruction, especially because of a fire
the Holocaust the mass murder of Jews by the Nazis from the 1930s until 1945

hologram *NOUN* (**holograms**)
a type of photograph made by laser beams, that appears to have depth as well as height and width

holster *NOUN* (**holsters**)
a leather case for a pistol, usually attached to a belt

holy *ADJECTIVE* (**holier, holiest**)
1 to do with God and treated with religious respect **2** a holy person is devoted to God or a religion
▷ **holiness** *NOUN* being holy

home *NOUN* (**homes**)
1 the place where you live **2** the place where you were born or where you feel you belong **3** a place where people are looked after • *She went to a home for the elderly.* **4** the place that you try to reach in a game • *The far end of the gym is home.*
to feel at home is to feel comfortable and happy

home *ADVERB*
1 to or at the place where you live • *Go home!* • *Is she home yet?* **2** to the place aimed at • *Push the bolt home.*
to bring something home to someone is to make them realize it

home *VERB* (**homes, homing, homed**)
to home in on something is to aim for it

home economics *PLURAL NOUN*
studying how to run a home

homeless *ADJECTIVE*
not having a place to live

homely *ADJECTIVE*
simple or ordinary

home-made *ADJECTIVE*
made at home and not bought from a shop

homesick *ADJECTIVE*
sad or upset because you are away from home

> WORD FAMILY
> **Homesickness** is the feeling of being homesick.

homestead *NOUN* (**homesteads**)
a farmhouse and the land around it

homeward or **homewards** *ADVERB*
towards home

homework *NOUN*
school work that you have to do at home

homograph *NOUN* (**homographs**)
a word spelt the same as another word but with a different meaning, such as *lead* (the metal) and *lead* (for a dog)

homing *ADJECTIVE*
trained to fly home • *He kept homing pigeons.*

homonym *NOUN* (**homonyms**)
a word spelt or sounding the same as another word but with a different meaning, such as *bat* (the flying animal) and *bat* (for hitting a ball)

homophone *NOUN* (**homophones**)
a word with the same sound as another word but with a different spelling and meaning, such as *son* and *sun*

> HOMOPHONES
> Homophones are words that have the same sound as one another but have different spellings and have completely different meanings. Some common pairs of homophones include *break* and *brake*, *flour* and *flower*, *hear* and *here*, *night* and *knight*, *piece* and *peace*, *right* and *write*, and *their* and *there*. Homographs are words that are spelt the same as one another but have different meanings. They may have different sounds, such as *bow* (knot made with loops) and *bow* (bending your body forwards), or have the same sound, such as *calf* (part of your leg) and *calf* (young cow). Homonyms are words that have the same spelling or the same sound as one another but have completely different meanings, such as *light* (not heavy) and *light* (not dark) or *hair* and *hare*. Homophones and homographs are different types of homonym.

homosexual *ADJECTIVE* (*say* hoh- mo- **seks**- yoo- al or hom- o- **seks**- yoo- al)
loving or attracted to people of the same sex

homosexual *NOUN* (**homosexuals**)
a homosexual person

honest *ADJECTIVE*
1 truthful and able to be trusted; not stealing, cheating, or telling lies

> WORD FAMILY
> **Honesty** is being honest and truthful.

honestly *ADVERB*
1 to say something honestly is to say it truthfully **2** to do something honestly is to do it without stealing or cheating

honey *NOUN*
a sweet sticky food made by bees

honeycomb *NOUN* (**honeycombs**)
a wax framework made by bees to hold their honey and eggs

honeymoon *NOUN* (**honeymoons**)
a holiday that a newly-married couple spend together

honeysuckle *NOUN*
a climbing plant with sweet-smelling yellow or pink flowers

honk *NOUN* (**honks**)
a loud sound like the one made by a car horn or a wild goose

honk *VERB* (**honks**, **honking**, **honked**)
to make a honking sound

honour *NOUN* (**honours**)
1 honour is great respect or reputation **2** an honour is something given to a person who deserves it because of the good work they have done **3** an honour is also something a person is proud to do • *It is an honour to meet you.*

honour *VERB* (**honours**, **honouring**, **honoured**)
1 to honour someone is to show you respect them or to give them an honour **2** to honour a promise or agreement is to keep it

honourable *ADJECTIVE*
someone is honourable when they can be trusted and always try to do the right thing
▷ **honourably** *ADVERB* in an honourable way

hood *NOUN* (**hoods**)
1 a covering of soft material for the head and neck, usually part of a coat or sweatshirt **2** a folding roof or cover

> WORD FAMILY
> A **hooded** person is wearing a hood.

hoof *NOUN* (**hoofs**)
the hard, bony part of the foot of horses, cattle, or deer

hook *NOUN* (**hooks**)
a piece of bent or curved metal or plastic for hanging things on or catching hold of something

> WORD FAMILY
> A **hooked** nose has a curved shape like a hook.

hook *VERB* (**hooks**, **hooking**, **hooked**)
1 to hook something is to fasten it with or on a hook **2** to hook a fish is to catch it with a hook

hooligan *NOUN* (**hooligans**)
a rough or noisy person

hoop *NOUN* (**hoops**)
a large ring made of metal, wood, or plastic

hoopla *NOUN*
a game in which you try to throw hoops round an object, which you then win as a prize

hooray *INTERJECTION*
a shout of joy or approval; a cheer

hoot *NOUN* (**hoots**)
1 a sound like the one made by an owl or a car horn **2** a jeer

hoot *VERB* (**hoots**, **hooting**, **hooted**)
to hoot is to make a sound like an owl or a car horn

hooter *NOUN* (**hooters**)
a horn or other device that makes a hoot

hop[1] *VERB* (**hops**, **hopping**, **hopped**)
1 to hop is to jump on one foot **2** animals hop when they move in jumps **3** (*informal*) to hop is also to move quickly • *Hop in and I'll give you lift.*
hop it (*slang*) go away

hop *NOUN* (**hops**)
a jump you make on one foot

hop[2] *NOUN* (**hops**)
a climbing plant used to give beer its flavour

a b c d e f g h i j k l m n o p q r s t u v w x y z

hope *NOUN* (**hopes**)
1 the feeling of wanting something to happen, and thinking that it will happen **2** a person or thing that makes you feel like this • *She is our big hope for a gold medal.*

hope *VERB* (**hopes**, **hoping**, **hoped**)
to hope for something is to want it and expect it to happen

hopeful *ADJECTIVE*
1 having hope **2** likely to be good or successful • *The future did not seem very hopeful.*

hopefully *ADVERB*
1 in a hopeful way **2** I hope that ... • *Hopefully we can all go to the sea tomorrow.*

> USING THIS WORD
> Some people don't like the second meaning ('I hope that ... '), but it is very common, especially in conversation.

hopeless *ADJECTIVE*
1 without hope **2** very bad at something • *I'm hopeless at cricket.*
▷ **hopelessly** *ADVERB* in a hopeless way

hopscotch *NOUN*
a game in which you hop into squares drawn on the ground

horde *NOUN* (**hordes**)
a large group or crowd

> SPELLING
> Take care not to confuse **horde** with **hoard**, which means a hidden store of something.

horizon *NOUN* (**horizons**) (*say* ho- **ry**- zon)
the line where the sky appears to meet the land or sea

horizontal *ADJECTIVE* (*say* ho- ri- **zon**- tal)
level or flat; going across from left to right
▷ **horizontally** *ADVERB* in a horizontal direction

hormone *NOUN* (**hormones**)
a substance made in glands in the body and sent directly into the blood to stimulate other organs in the body

horn *NOUN* (**horns**)
1 a kind of pointed bone that grows on the head of a bull, cow, ram, and other animals **2** a brass musical instrument that you blow **3** a device for making a warning sound

hornet *NOUN* (**hornets**)
a large kind of wasp

horoscope *NOUN* (**horoscopes**)
an astrologer's forecast of future events

horrible *ADJECTIVE*
very unpleasant or nasty
▷ **horribly** *ADVERB* in a horrible way

horrid *ADJECTIVE*
nasty or unkind

horrific *ADJECTIVE*
shocking or terrifying
▷ **horrifically** *ADVERB* in a horrific way

horrify *VERB* (**horrifies**, **horrifying**, **horrified**)
to horrify someone is to make them feel shocked and disgusted

horror *NOUN* (**horrors**)
1 horror is great fear or disgust **2** a horror is a person or thing you really dislike

horse *NOUN* (**horses**)
1 a four-legged animal used for riding on or pulling carts **2** a tall box that you jump over when you are doing gymnastics

horseback *NOUN*
to be on horseback is to be riding a horse

horse chestnut *NOUN* (**horse chestnuts**)
a large tree that produces dark brown nuts called conkers

horseman *NOUN* (**horsemen**)
a man who rides a horse, especially a skilful rider

> WORD FAMILY
> **Horsemanship** is the art of riding.

horsepower *NOUN* (**horsepower**)
a unit for measuring the power of an engine, equal to 746 watts

horseshoe *NOUN* (**horseshoes**)
a U-shaped piece of metal nailed as a shoe to a horse's hoof

horsewoman *NOUN* (**horsewomen**)
a woman who rides a horse, especially a skilful rider

horticulture *NOUN*
the art of planning and looking after gardens

hose *NOUN* (**hoses**)
a long flexible tube through which liquids or gases can travel

hospitable *ADJECTIVE*
welcoming to people; liking to give hospitality
▷ **hospitably** *ADVERB* in a hospitable way

hospital *NOUN* (**hospitals**)
a place where sick or injured people are given medical treatment

hospitality *NOUN*
welcoming people and giving them food and entertainment

host [1] *NOUN* (**hosts**)
someone who has guests and looks after them

host [2] *NOUN* (**hosts**)
a large number of people or things

hostage *NOUN* (**hostages**)
someone who is held prisoner until the people who are holding them get what they want

hostel *NOUN* (**hostels**)
a building with rooms where students or other people can stay cheaply

hostess *NOUN* (**hostesses**)
a woman who has guests and looks after them

hostile *ADJECTIVE*
1 unfriendly and angry • *The crowd outside was hostile.* **2** opposed to someone or something

> WORD FAMILY
> **Hostility** is unfriendliness and strong dislike.

hot *ADJECTIVE* (**hotter**, **hottest**)
1 having a high temperature; very warm **2** having a burning taste like pepper or mustard **3** excited or angry • *He has a hot temper.*
to be in hot water (*informal*) is to be in trouble or difficulty

hot *VERB* (**hots**, **hotting**, **hotted**)
to hot up (*informal*) is to become hotter or more exciting

hot cross bun *NOUN* (**hot cross buns**)
a spicy bun with a cross marked on it, eaten at Easter

hot dog *NOUN* (**hot dogs**)
a hot sausage in a bread roll

hotel *NOUN* (**hotels**)
a building where people pay to stay for the night and have meals

hothouse *NOUN* (**hothouses**)
a heated greenhouse

hotly *ADVERB*
strongly or forcefully • *He hotly denied that he'd done it.*

hotpot *NOUN* (**hotpots**)
a kind of stew

hot-water bottle *NOUN* (**hot-water bottles**)
a container that you fill with hot water to make a bed warm

hound *NOUN* (**hounds**)
a dog used for hunting or racing

hound *VERB* (**hounds**, **hounding**, **hounded**)
to hound someone is to keep on chasing and bothering them • *The family was hounded by newspaper reporters.*

hour *NOUN* (**hours**)
1 one of the twenty-four parts into which a day is divided **2** a particular time • *Why are you up at this hour?*

hourglass *NOUN* (**hourglasses**)
an old-fashioned device for telling the time, with sand running from one half of a glass container into the other through a narrow middle part

hourly *ADJECTIVE & ADVERB*
every hour; done once an hour

house *NOUN* (**houses**) (*say* howss)
1 a building where people live, usually designed for one family **2** a building used for a special purpose • *They passed the opera house.* **3** a building for a government assembly, or the assembly itself, for example the Houses of Parliament and the House of Commons **4** one of the divisions in some schools for sports competitions and other events

house *VERB* (**houses**, **housing**, **housed**) (*say* howz)
to house someone or something is to provide a house or room for them

houseboat *NOUN* (**houseboats**)
a boat for living in

household *NOUN* (**households**)
all the people who live together in the same house

householder *NOUN* (**householders**)
someone who owns or rents a house

housekeeper *NOUN* (**housekeepers**)
a person employed to look after a household

house-proud *ADJECTIVE*
very careful to keep a house clean and tidy

house-trained *ADJECTIVE*
an animal that is house-trained is trained to be clean in the house

house-warming *NOUN* (**house-warmings**)
a party you have to celebrate moving into a new home

housewife *NOUN* (**housewives**)
a woman who stays at home to look after her children and do the housework rather than doing a paid job

housework *NOUN*
the work like cooking and cleaning that has to be done in a house

housing *NOUN* (**housings**)
1 housing is accommodation or houses **2** a housing is a cover or guard for a piece of machinery

hove
see **heave**

hover *VERB* (**hovers**, **hovering**, **hovered**)
1 to hover is to stay in one place in the air **2** to hover round someone is to wait near them to watch what they do

hovercraft *NOUN* (**hovercraft**)
a vehicle that travels just above the surface of water or land, supported by a strong current of air sent downwards by its engines

how *ADVERB*
1 in what way • *How did you do it?* **2** to what extent • *How much do you want?* **3** in what condition • *How are you?*
how about ... would you like ... ? • *How about a game of football?*
how do you do? a more formal greeting when you meet someone

however *ADVERB*
1 no matter how; in whatever way • *You will never catch him, however hard you try.* **2** nevertheless • *It was snowing; however, he went out.*

however *CONJUNCTION*
in any way • *You can do it however you like.*

howl *NOUN* (**howls**)
a long loud cry like an animal in pain

howl *VERB* (**howls**, **howling**, **howled**)
to howl is to make a long loud cry like an animal in pain, or to weep loudly

howler *NOUN* (**howlers**)
(*informal*) a silly mistake

HQ
short for **headquarters**

hub *NOUN* (**hubs**)
the centre of a wheel

huddle *VERB* (**huddles**, **huddling**, **huddled**)
to huddle is to crowd together with other people for warmth or comfort • *Behind the village was a stony field where a flock of thin sheep huddled together under the shadow of a few spindly apple trees.* — Vivian French, *Under the Moon*

hue [1] *NOUN* (**hues**)
a colour or tint

huff *NOUN*
to be in a huff is to be annoyed or offended

hug *VERB* (**hugs**, **hugging**, **hugged**)
1 to hug someone is to clasp them tightly in your arms **2** to hug something is to keep close to it • *The ship hugged the shore.*

hug *NOUN* (**hugs**)
clasping someone tightly in your arms

huge *ADJECTIVE* (**huger**, **hugest**)
extremely large
▷ **hugely** *ADVERB* greatly; very

hulk *NOUN* (**hulks**)
1 the remains of an old decaying ship **2** a large clumsy person or thing

> WORD FAMILY
> Someone or something that is **hulking** is large, heavy, and clumsy.

hull *NOUN* (**hulls**)
the main part or framework of a ship

hullabaloo *NOUN* (**hullabaloos**)
an uproar • *Quite a hullabaloo was breaking out upstairs, and most of the sounds were by no means pleasant.* — Alan Garner, *The Weirdstone of Brisingamen*

hullo *INTERJECTION*
a word used to greet someone or to attract their attention

hum *VERB* (**hums**, **humming**, **hummed**)
1 to hum is to sing a tune with your lips closed **2** to hum is also to make a low continuous sound like a bee

hum *NOUN* (**hums**)
a humming sound

human *NOUN* (**humans**)
a man, woman, or child; a human being

human *ADJECTIVE*
to do with humans

human being *NOUN* (**human beings**)
a man, woman, or child; a human

humane *ADJECTIVE* (*say* hew- **mayn**)
showing kindness and a wish to cause as little suffering or pain as possible
▷ **humanely** *ADVERB* in a way that causes as little suffering or pain as possible

humanitarian *ADJECTIVE* (*say* hew- man- i- **tair**- i- an)
concerned with helping humanity and relieving suffering

humanity *NOUN*
1 all the people in the world **2** being human **3** kindness and sympathy to other people

> WORD FAMILY
> The **humanities** are arts subjects such as history and English, not sciences.

humble *ADJECTIVE* (**humbler**, **humblest**)
modest and not proud
▷ **humbly** *ADVERB* in a humble way

> GRAMMAR
> The noun from **humble** is **humility**, although **humbleness** is sometimes used.

humid *ADJECTIVE* (*say* **hew**- mid)
damp and warm in the air

> WORD FAMILY
> **Humidity** is how damp it is in the air.

humiliate *VERB* (**humiliates**, **humiliating**, **humiliated**)
to humiliate someone is to make them feel ashamed or foolish in front of other people

> WORD FAMILY
> **Humiliation** is a feeling of shame because you have been made to look foolish in front of other people.

humility *NOUN*
being humble

hummingbird *NOUN* (**hummingbirds**)
a small tropical bird that makes a humming sound by beating its wings rapidly

humorous *ADJECTIVE*
amusing or funny

humour *NOUN*
1 being amusing; what makes people laugh **2** being able to enjoy things that are funny • *He has a good sense of humour.* **3** a person's mood • *Keep him in a good humour.*

humour *VERB* (**humours**, **humouring**, **humoured**)
to humour someone is to keep them happy by doing what they want

hump *NOUN* (**humps**)
1 a rounded lump or mound **2** a lump on a person's back

hump *VERB* (**humps**, **humping**, **humped**)
to hump something heavy is to carry it with difficulty on your back

humpback bridge *NOUN* (**humpback bridges**)
a small bridge that rises steeply in the middle

humus *NOUN* (*say* hew-mus)
rich earth made by decayed plants

hunch[1] *NOUN* (**hunches**)
a feeling that you can guess what will happen • *I have a hunch that she won't come.*

hunch[2] *VERB* (**hunches**, **hunching**, **hunched**)
to hunch your shoulders is to bring them up and forward so that your back is rounded

hunchback *NOUN* (**hunchbacks**)
someone with a hump on their back
▷ **hunchbacked** *ADJECTIVE* having a hunchback

hundred *NOUN* (**hundreds**)
the number 100
▷ **hundredth** *ADJECTIVE & NOUN* 100th

hundredweight *NOUN* (**hundredweights**)
a unit of weight equal to 112 pounds or 50.8 kilograms

hung
past tense and past participle of **hang**

hunger *NOUN*
the feeling you get when you want or need to eat

hunger strike *NOUN* (**hunger strikes**)
a hunger strike is when someone refuses to eat, as a way of making a protest

hungry *ADJECTIVE* (**hungrier**, **hungriest**)
you are hungry when you want or need to eat
▷ **hungrily** *ADVERB* in a hungry way

hunk *NOUN* (**hunks**)
a large piece or chunk of something

hunt *VERB* (**hunts**, **hunting**, **hunted**)
1 to hunt animals is to chase and kill them for food or sport **2** to hunt for something is to look hard for it

hunt *NOUN* (**hunts**)
1 a time when a group of people chase and kill animals for food or sport **2** a group of people who go hunting

hunter or **huntsman** *NOUN* (**hunters** or **huntsmen**)
someone who hunts for sport

hurdle *NOUN* (**hurdles**)
1 an upright frame that runners jump over in hurdling **2** a problem or difficulty

hurdling *NOUN*
racing in which the runners run and jump over hurdles

> WORD FAMILY
> A **hurdler** is someone who goes hurdling.

hurl *VERB* (**hurls**, **hurling**, **hurled**)
to hurl something is to throw it as far as you can

hurrah or **hurray** *INTERJECTION*
a shout of joy or approval; a cheer

hurricane *NOUN* (**hurricanes**)
a severe storm with a strong wind

hurry *VERB* (**hurries**, **hurrying**, **hurried**)
1 to hurry is to move or act quickly **2** to hurry someone is to try to make them be quick
▷ **hurriedly** *ADVERB* in a hurry • *We hurriedly got dressed.*

hurry *NOUN*
moving quickly; doing something quickly
in a hurry hurrying or impatient • *They were in a hurry to catch their train.*

hurt *VERB* (**hurts**, **hurting**, **hurt**)
1 to hurt a person or animal is to harm them or cause them pain **2** part of your body hurts when you feel pain there **3** to hurt someone is also to upset them by doing or saying something unkind

hurt *NOUN*
pain or injury

> WORD FAMILY
> A **hurtful** remark upsets someone because it is unkind.

hurtle *VERB* (**hurtles**, **hurtling**, **hurtled**)
to hurtle is to move quickly or dangerously • *The front three rows of students drew backwards as the carriage hurtled ever lower, coming in to land at a tremendous speed.* — J. K. Rowling, *Harry Potter and the Goblet of Fire*

husband *NOUN* (**husbands**)
the man that a woman is married to

hush *VERB* (**hushes**, **hushing**, **hushed**)
to hush someone is to make them be quiet
to hush something up is to prevent people knowing about it

hush *NOUN*
silence or quiet • *Let's have a bit of hush.*

hush-hush *ADJECTIVE*
(*informal*) very secret

husk *NOUN* (**husks**)
the dry outer covering of a seed

a b c d e f g h i j k l m n o p q r s t u v w x y z

husky[1] *ADJECTIVE* (**huskier, huskiest**)
1 you say a voice is husky when it is deep and rough • *She has a husky voice.*
▷ **huskily** *ADVERB* with a husky voice
▷ **huskiness** *NOUN* being husky

husky[2] *NOUN* (**huskies**)
a large strong dog used in the Arctic for pulling sledges

hustle *VERB* (**hustles, hustling, hustled**)
1 to hustle is to hurry **2** to hustle someone is to push them rudely

hut *NOUN* (**huts**)
a small roughly made house or shelter

hutch *NOUN* (**hutches**)
a box or cage for a rabbit or other pet animal

hyacinth *NOUN* (**hyacinths**)
a sweet-smelling flower that grows from a bulb

hybrid *NOUN* (**hybrids**)
1 an animal or plant that combines two different species • *A mule is a hybrid of a donkey and a mare.* **2** something that is a mixture of two things

hydrangea *NOUN* (**hydrangeas**) (*say* hy- **drayn**- ja)
a shrub with large pink, blue, or white flowers

hydrant *NOUN* (**hydrants**)
an outdoor water-tap connected to the main water supply, for fixing a hose to

hydraulic *ADJECTIVE*
worked by the movement of water or other liquid

hydroelectric *ADJECTIVE*
using water-power to make electricity

hydrofoil *NOUN* (**hydrofoils**)
a boat designed to skim over the surface of the water

hydrogen *NOUN*
a very light gas which with oxygen makes water

hydrogen bomb *NOUN* (**hydrogen bombs**)
a very powerful bomb using energy from the joining of hydrogen nuclei

hyena *NOUN* (**hyenas**) (*say* hy- ee- na)
a wild animal that looks like a wolf and makes a shrieking howl

hygiene *NOUN* (*say* **hy**- jeen)
keeping clean and healthy and free of germs

hygienic *ADJECTIVE*
clean and healthy and free of germs
▷ **hygienically** *ADVERB* in a hygienic way

hymn *NOUN* (**hymns**)
a Christian religious song, especially one that praises God

hyperactive *ADJECTIVE*
unable to relax and always moving about or doing things

hypermarket *NOUN* (**hypermarkets**)
a very large supermarket, usually outside a town

hyphen *NOUN* (**hyphens**)
a short dash used to join words or parts of words together, for example in *house-proud*

> WORD FAMILY
> A word is **hyphenated** when it is spelt with a hyphen.

> HYPHENS
> You use a hyphen to join separate words to make a single word, such as *mix-up, one-way, red-handed, self-service, tongue-twister, two-year-old*. You also use a hyphen when you can't fit the whole of a word at the end of a line and have to split it into two parts. You put a hyphen on the end of the first part. Look also at the panel on **Compound words**.

hypnosis *NOUN* (*say* hip- **noh**- sis)
to be under hypnosis is to be in a condition like a deep sleep in which a person follows the instructions of another person

hypnotism *NOUN* (*say* **hip**- no- tizm)
hypnotizing people

> WORD FAMILY
> A **hypnotist** is someone who hypnotizes people.

hypnotize *VERB* (**hypnotizes, hypnotizing, hypnotized**)
to hypnotize someone is to put them to sleep by hypnosis

hypocrite *NOUN* (**hypocrites**) (*say* **hip**- o- krit)
someone who pretends to be a better person than they really are

> WORD FAMILY
> **Hypocrisy** is pretending to be a better person than you really are; someone is being **hypocritical** when they are pretending to be a better person than they really are.

hypodermic *ADJECTIVE* (*say* hy- po- **der**- mik)
a hypodermic needle or syringe is one used to inject something under the skin

hypotenuse *NOUN* (**hypotenuses**) (*say* hy- **pot**- i- newz)
the side opposite the right angle in a right-angled triangle

hypothermia *NOUN*
a person suffers from hypothermia when they become so cold that their body temperature falls well below normal

hypothesis *NOUN* (**hypotheses**) (*say* hy- **poth**- i- sis)
a suggestion or theory that tries to explain something but has not been proved right

hypothetical *ADJECTIVE*
a hypothetical situation or example is one that you imagine, not a real one

hysteria *NOUN*
wild uncontrollable excitement or emotion

hysterical *ADJECTIVE*
1 suffering from hysteria **2** very excited **3** (*informal*) very funny
▷ **hysterically** *ADVERB* in a hysterical way

hysterics *PLURAL NOUN*
a fit of hysteria
to be in hysterics (*informal*) is to be laughing a lot

I *PRONOUN*
a word used by someone to speak about himself or herself

ice *NOUN* (**ices**)
1 ice is frozen water **2** an ice is an ice cream

ice *VERB* (**ices**, **icing**, **iced**)
1 to ice or ice up is to become covered in ice **2** to ice a cake is to put icing on it

ice age *NOUN*
a time in the past when ice covered large areas of the earth's surface

iceberg *NOUN* (**icebergs**)
a large mass of ice floating in the sea, with most of it under water

ice cream *NOUN* (**ice creams**)
1 ice cream is a sweet creamy frozen food **2** an ice cream is a portion of this

ice hockey *NOUN*
ice hockey is a game like hockey played on ice

ice lolly *NOUN* (**ice lollies**)
a piece of flavoured ice on a stick

ice-skating *NOUN*
ice-skating is moving on ice wearing special boots with blades on the bottom

icicle *NOUN* (**icicles**)
a thin pointed piece of hanging ice formed from dripping water

icing *NOUN*
icing is a sugary substance for decorating cakes

icon *NOUN* (**icons**)
1 a small picture or symbol standing for a program on a computer screen **2** a painting of a holy person

ICT
short for *information and communication technology*

icy *ADJECTIVE* (**icier**, **iciest**)
1 an icy road has ice on it **2** an icy wind is very cold **3** very unfriendly; hostile • *He gave them an icy stare.*

> **WORD FAMILY**
> To say or do something **icily** is to say or do it in an unfriendly way.

I'd
short for *I had*, *I should*, or *I would*

idea *NOUN* (**ideas**)
something that you have thought of; a plan
to have no idea is to not know something

ideal *ADJECTIVE*
exactly what you want; perfect
▷ **ideally** *ADVERB* if things were perfect • *Ideally, I'd like to live by the sea.*

ideal *NOUN* (**ideals**)
something that is perfect or the best thing to have; a very high standard

identical *ADJECTIVE*
exactly the same • *Daniel and Sammy are identical twins.*
▷ **identically** *ADVERB* in exactly the same way • *They were identically dressed.*

identification *NOUN*
1 identification is any document, such as a passport, that proves who you are **2** identification is the process of discovering who someone is or what something is

identify *VERB* (**identifies**, **identifying**, **identified**)
to identify someone or something is to discover who or what they are • *The police have identified the car used in the robbery.*
to identify with someone is to understand or share their feelings or opinions

identity *NOUN* (**identities**)
who someone is or what something is • *Can you discover the identity of our mystery guest?*

idiom *NOUN* (**idioms**) (*say* **id**- i- om)
a phrase or group of words that together have a special meaning that is not obvious from the words themselves, for example *to be in hot water* means to be in trouble or difficulty

> **IDIOMS**
> Every language has its idioms, which people who speak the language use to make it more descriptive, but which often don't make sense to people who are learning the language. For example, what does *he let the cat out of the bag* really mean? Think about phrases like *keep something under your hat, bury the hatchet, have a whale of a time.* You know what they mean, and you can use them to make your writing more exciting, but the phrases don't mean exactly what the words in them mean.

a b c d e f g h i j k l m n o p q r s t u v w x y z

idiomatic *ADJECTIVE*
a person's language is idiomatic when it is natural and uses a lot of idioms

idiot *NOUN* (**idiots**)
(*informal*) a stupid or foolish person

> WORD FAMILY
> **Idiocy** is being stupid or foolish.

idiotic *ADJECTIVE*
(*informal*) stupid or foolish • *That was an idiotic thing to do.*
▷ **idiotically** *ADVERB* in a stupid or foolish way

idle *ADJECTIVE* (**idler**, **idlest**)
1 a person is idle when they are lazy or doing nothing **2** a machine is idle when it is not being used **3** idle talk or gossip is talk that is silly or pointless

idle *VERB* (**idles**, **idling**, **idled**)
a machine or engine idles when it is working slowly
▷ **idly** *ADVERB* in a lazy way

idol *NOUN* (**idols**)
1 a famous person who is admired by a lot of people **2** a statue or image that people worship as a god

> WORD FAMILY
> **Idolatory** is the worship of idols.

idolize *VERB* (**idolizes**, **idolizing**, **idolized**)
to idolize someone is to admire them very much

i.e.
short for the Latin *id est*, which means 'that is', used to explain something • *The world's highest mountain (i.e. Mount Everest) is in the Himalayas.*

if *CONJUNCTION*
1 on condition that • *I'll tell you what happened if you promise to keep it secret.* **2** although; even though • *I'll finish this job if it kills me!* **3** whether • *Do you know if lunch is ready?*
if only ... I wish ... • *If only I could go with you!*

igloo *NOUN* (**igloos**)
an Inuit round house made of blocks of hard snow

igneous *ADJECTIVE* (*say* **ig**- ni- us)
igneous rocks are formed by the action of a volcano

ignite *VERB* (**ignites**, **igniting**, **ignited**)
1 to ignite something is to set fire to it **2** to ignite is to catch fire

ignition *NOUN*
1 igniting **2** ignition is the system in a motor engine that starts the fuel burning

ignorant *ADJECTIVE*
not knowing about something; knowing very little

> WORD FAMILY
> **Ignorance** is not knowing about something or knowing very little.

ignore *VERB* (**ignores**, **ignoring**, **ignored**)
to ignore someone or something is to take no notice of them

I'll
short for *I shall* or *I will*

ill *ADJECTIVE*
1 not well; in bad health **2** bad or harmful • *There were no ill effects.*

ill *ADVERB*
badly • *She was ill-treated.*

illegal *ADJECTIVE*
something is illegal when it is against the law

> WORD FAMILY
> To do something **illegally** is to do it when it is against the law.

illegible *ADJECTIVE* (*say* i- **lej**- i- bul)
illegible writing is not clear enough to read

> WORD FAMILY
> Something written **illegibly** is not clear enough to read.

illegitimate *ADJECTIVE* (*say* il- i- **jit**- i- mat)
(*old use*) someone is illegitimate when they are born to parents who are not married to each other

illiterate *ADJECTIVE* (*say* i- **lit**- er- at)
unable to read or write

> WORD FAMILY
> **Illiteracy** is not being able to read or write.

illness *NOUN* (**illnesses**)
1 illness is being ill **2** an illness is something that makes people ill; a disease

illogical *ADJECTIVE*
not logical or having any good reason

> WORD FAMILY
> To think or behave **illogically** is to do so in a way that is not logical.

illuminate *VERB* (**illuminates**, **illuminating**, **illuminated**)
1 to illuminate a place or street is to light it up or decorate it with lights **2** to illuminate something difficult is to make it clearer

> WORD FAMILY
> **Illuminations** are lights put up to decorate a place or street.

illusion *NOUN* (**illusions**)
1 something that you think is real or happening but is not **2** an idea or belief you have that isn't true

illustrate *VERB* (**illustrates**, **illustrating**, **illustrated**)
1 to illustrate something is to show it with pictures or examples **2** to illustrate a book is to put pictures in it

illustration *NOUN* (**illustrations**)
1 an illustration is a picture in a book **2** an illustration is also an example that helps to explain something

illustrator *NOUN* (**illustrators**)
a person who produces the illustrations in a book

illustrious *ADJECTIVE* (*say* i- lus- tri- us)
famous

I'm
short for *I am*

image *NOUN* (**images**)
1 a picture or statue of a person or thing **2** what you see in a mirror or through a lens **3** a person who looks very much like another • *She is the image of her mother.* **4** the way that people think of a person or thing

imagery *NOUN*
imagery is the use of words to produce pictures in the mind of the reader

imaginary *ADJECTIVE*
not real; existing only in your mind

imagination *NOUN* (**imaginations**)
your ability to form pictures and ideas in your mind

imaginative *ADJECTIVE*
showing that you are good at thinking of new and exciting ideas • *Her stories are always very imaginative.*

imagine *VERB* (**imagines**, **imagining**, **imagined**)
to imagine something or someone is to form a picture of them in your mind

> WORD FAMILY
> Something is **imaginable** when it is possible to imagine it.

imam *NOUN* (**imams**)
a Muslim religious leader

imbecile *NOUN* (**imbeciles**) (*say* im- bi- seel)
(*informal*) a very stupid person

imitate *VERB* (**imitates**, **imitating**, **imitated**)
to imitate someone or something is to do the same as them

> WORD FAMILY
> **Imitation**, or an **imitation**, is copying someone or something; an **imitator** is someone who copies someone or something else.

immature *ADJECTIVE*
1 not fully grown or developed **2** behaving in a silly or childish way

> WORD FAMILY
> **Immaturity** is being immature.

immediate *ADJECTIVE*
1 happening or done without any delay **2** nearest; with nothing or no one between • *The Smiths are our immediate neighbours.*

immediately *ADVERB*
without any delay; at once • *You must come immediately.*

immense *ADJECTIVE*
huge • *'ME on your egg? Why, that doesn't make sense / Your egg is so small, ma'am, and I'm so immense!'* — Dr Seuss, *Horton Hatches the Egg*
▷ **immensely** *ADVERB* extremely
▷ **immensity** *NOUN* immensity is being immense

immerse *VERB* (**immerses**, **immersing**, **immersed**)
1 to immerse something is to put it completely into a liquid **2** to be immersed in something is to be very interested or involved in it
▷ **immersion** *NOUN* the immersion of something is when you put it into a liquid

immersion heater *NOUN* (**immersion heaters**)
a device that heats water with an electric element immersed in the water in a tank

immigrant *NOUN* (**immigrants**)
someone who has come into a country to live there

immigrate *VERB* (**immigrates**, **immigrating**, **immigrated**)
to immigrate is to come into a country to live there

> WORD FAMILY
> **Immigration** is people coming into a country to live there.

> SPELLING
> Do not confuse **immigrate** with **emigrate**, which means to go and live in another country.

immobile *ADJECTIVE*
not moving • *After a few minutes, the crocodiles became quite immobile, their giant heads resting in the warm sand, their tails stretched out behind them.* — Alexander McCall Smith, *Akimbo and the Crocodile Man*

> WORD FAMILY
> **Immobility** is being immobile.

immobilize *VERB* (**immobilizes**, **immobilizing**, **immobilized**)
to immobilize something is to stop it moving or working

immoral *ADJECTIVE*
not following the usual standards of right and wrong

> WORD FAMILY
> **Immorality** is behaviour that does not follow the usual standards of right and wrong.

immortal *ADJECTIVE*
someone who is immortal lives for ever and never dies

> WORD FAMILY
> **Immortality** is living for ever.

immune *ADJECTIVE*
someone is immune to a disease if they cannot catch it

> WORD FAMILY
> **Immunity** is being immune.

a b c d e f g h i j k l m n o p q r s t u v w x y z

immunize *VERB* (**immunizes**, **immunizing**, **immunized**)
to immunize someone is to make them safe from a disease, usually by giving them an injection
▷ **immunization** *NOUN* immunization is immunizing someone

imp *NOUN* (**imps**)
1 a small devil **2** a naughty child
▷ **impish** *ADJECTIVE* naughty, like an imp

impact *NOUN* (**impacts**)
1 the force of one thing hitting another **2** a strong influence or effect • *The internet is having a big impact on our lives.*

impair *VERB* (**impairs**, **impairing**, **impaired**)
to impair something is to harm or weaken it • *The accident has impaired his health.*

impale *VERB* (**impales**, **impaling**, **impaled**)
to impale something is to push a sharp pointed object through it

impartial *ADJECTIVE*
fair and not supporting one side more than the other • *A referee must be impartial.*

WORD FAMILY
Someone shows **impartiality** when they are fair and do not support one side more than the other; to do something **impartially** is to do it in an impartial way.

impassable *ADJECTIVE*
an impassable road is one that you cannot get through

impatient *ADJECTIVE*
annoyed because you can't wait for something to happen

WORD FAMILY
Impatience is being annoyed because you can't wait for something to happen; to do something **impatiently** is to do it in an impatient way.

impede *VERB* (**impedes**, **impeding**, **impeded**)
to impede someone or something is to hinder them or get in their way

imperative *ADJECTIVE*
1 essential • *Speed is imperative.* **2** in grammar, an imperative word expresses a command, like *come* in *Come here!*

imperceptible *ADJECTIVE*
too small or gradual to be noticed • *The change in the weather was imperceptible.*

WORD FAMILY
Something happens **imperceptibly** when it happens so gradually that it cannot be noticed.

imperfect *ADJECTIVE*
not perfect or complete

WORD FAMILY
Imperfection is being imperfect; to do something **imperfectly** is to do it in an imperfect way.

imperial *ADJECTIVE*
1 belonging to an empire or its rulers **2** an imperial unit or measure is one fixed by British law, such as gallon, ounce or yard. These are non-metric units

impersonal *ADJECTIVE*
1 not showing friendly human feelings • *The letter was a bit impersonal.* **2** not referring to a particular person

impersonate *VERB* (**impersonates**, **impersonating**, **impersonated**)
to impersonate someone is to pretend to be them

WORD FAMILY
An **impersonation** is an act in which you impersonate someone, and an **impersonator** is a person who impersonates someone else.

impertinent *ADJECTIVE*
rude to someone and not showing them respect

WORD FAMILY
Impertinence is being impertinent.

implement *NOUN* (**implements**) (*say* **im**- pli- ment)
a tool or device you use to do something

implement *VERB* (**implements**, **implementing**, **implemented**) (*say* im- pli- **ment**)
to implement a plan or idea is to put it into action

implication *NOUN* (**implications**)
1 an implication is something that someone suggests without actually saying it **2** an implication is also a possible effect or result

implore *VERB* (**implores**, **imploring**, **implored**)
to implore someone to do something is to beg them to do it

imply *VERB* (**implies**, **implying**, **implied**)
to imply something is to suggest it without actually saying it • *Are you implying that I'm lazy?*

USING THIS WORD
Do not confuse **imply** with **infer**, which means to form an opinion from something said

impolite *ADJECTIVE*
not having good manners; not respectful and thoughtful towards other people

import *VERB* (**imports**, **importing**, **imported**) (*say* im- **port**)
to import goods is to bring them in from another country to sell them

WORD FAMILY
An **importer** is someone who imports goods.

import *NOUN* (**imports**) (*say* **im**- port)
something brought in from another country to be sold

important *ADJECTIVE*
1 needing to be taken seriously; having a great effect • *This is an important decision.* **2** an important person is powerful or influential

> WORD FAMILY
> **Importance** is being important; **importantly** means seriously • *Try to win the match but, more importantly, don't lose.*

impose *VERB* (**imposes**, **imposing**, **imposed**)
1 to impose something on someone is to make them have to put up with it • *The building plans were imposed on the village against everyone's wishes.* **2** to impose a charge or tax is to make people pay it
to impose on someone is to take unfair advantage of them

imposing *ADJECTIVE*
looking important and impressive

imposition *NOUN* (**impositions**)
something that someone is made to suffer, especially as a punishment

impossible *ADJECTIVE*
1 not possible **2** (*informal*) very annoying • *He is impossible!*

> WORD FAMILY
> An **impossibility** is something that is not possible; you say that (for example) a problem is **impossibly** difficult when it is not possible to solve it.

impostor *NOUN* (**impostors**)
someone who is not what he or she pretends to be

impracticable *ADJECTIVE*
not able to be done or used

impractical *ADJECTIVE*
1 impractical people are not good at making or doing things **2** not likely to work or be useful • *Their ideas are impractical.*

impress *VERB* (**impresses**, **impressing**, **impressed**)
1 to impress someone is to make them admire you **2** to impress something on someone is to make them realize or remember it

impression *NOUN* (**impressions**)
1 a vague idea that you have about something **2** the effect that something has on your mind or feelings **3** an imitation of a person or a sound

impressive *ADJECTIVE*
something is impressive when it makes you admire it
▷ **impressively** *ADVERB* in an impressive way

imprison *VERB* (**imprisons**, **imprisoning**, **imprisoned**)
to imprison someone is to put them in prison

> WORD FAMILY
> **Imprisonment** is being put in prison.

improbable *ADJECTIVE*
unlikely
▷ **improbability** *NOUN* being improbable

impromptu *ADJECTIVE & ADVERB* (*say* im-**promp**-tew)
done without any rehearsal or preparation

improper *ADJECTIVE*
1 not proper; wrong **2** rude or indecent

improve *VERB* (**improves**, **improving**, **improved**)
to improve something is to make it better; to improve is to become better

> WORD FAMILY
> An **improvement** is something that is better or makes a thing better.

improvise *VERB* (**improvises**, **improvising**, **improvised**)
1 to improvise is to do something without any rehearsal or preparation, especially to play music without rehearsing **2** to improvise something is to make it quickly with what is to hand
▷ **improvisation** *NOUN* improvisation is improvising something

impudent *ADJECTIVE*
not respectful; rude

> WORD FAMILY
> **Impudence** is being impudent.

impulse *NOUN* (**impulses**)
1 a sudden desire to do something **2** a push; a driving force **3** (*in science*) a force acting for a very short time

impulsive *ADJECTIVE*
doing things suddenly without much thought

> WORD FAMILY
> To do something **impulsively** is to do it suddenly without much thought.

impure *ADJECTIVE*
not pure

> WORD FAMILY
> An **impurity** is something in a substance that makes it not pure.

in *PREPOSITION & ADVERB*
1 showing position at or inside something • *They live in London.* • *Please come in.* • *She fell in the water.* • *Then the others fell in.* **2 in** also has some special uses, shown by the following examples • *We came in April.* • *I paid in cash.* • *They are watching a serial in four parts.* • *He is in the army.* • *We knocked on the door but no one was in.*
in all including everything • *The bill comes to $120 in all.*
to be in for something is to be likely to get it • *You're in for a shock.*
to be in on something is to take part in something • *I want to be in on this game.*

in- *PREFIX*
meaning 'not', as in *inefficient*

inability *NOUN*
inability is being unable to do something

inaccessible *ADJECTIVE*
an inaccessible place is impossible to reach

inaccurate *ADJECTIVE*
not accurate
▷ **inaccuracy** *NOUN* inaccuracy is being inaccurate
▷ **inaccurately** *ADVERB* in an inaccurate way

inaction *NOUN*
inaction is lack of action

inactive *ADJECTIVE*
not working or doing anything
▷ **inactivity** *NOUN* inactivity is being inactive

inadequate *ADJECTIVE*
not enough
▷ **inadequacy** *NOUN* inadequacy is being inadequate
▷ **inadequately** *ADVERB* in an inadequate way

inanimate *ADJECTIVE* (*say* in-**an**-im-at)
not living or moving

inappropriate *ADJECTIVE*
not appropriate or suitable
▷ **inappropriately** *ADVERB* in an inappropriate way

inattentive *ADJECTIVE*
not listening or paying attention
▷ **inattention** *NOUN* inattention is being inattentive

inaudible *ADJECTIVE*
not able to be heard

> **WORD FAMILY**
> To say something **inaudibly** is to say it so quietly that it cannot be heard.

incapable *ADJECTIVE*
unable to do something • *They are incapable of understanding the problem.*

incapacity *NOUN*
incapacity is inability or disability

incendiary *ADJECTIVE*
an incendiary bomb or device is one that starts a fire

incense *NOUN* (*say* **in**-senss)
incense is a substance that makes a spicy smell when it is burnt

incense *VERB* (**incenses, incensing, incensed**) (*say* in-**senss**)
to incense someone is to make them very angry

incentive *NOUN* (**incentives**)
something that encourages a person to do something or to work harder

incessant *ADJECTIVE*
going on without stopping, usually in an annoying way • *They were bothered by the incessant noise.*

> **WORD FAMILY**
> Something goes on **incessantly** when it goes on without stopping.

inch *NOUN* (**inches**)
a measure of length, one twelfth of a foot or about $2\frac{1}{2}$ centimetres

incident *NOUN* (**incidents**)
an event, usually a strange or unusual one

incidental *ADJECTIVE*
happening along with something else; not so important
▷ **incidentally** *ADVERB* by the way

incinerator *NOUN* (**incinerators**)
a device for burning rubbish

incisor *NOUN* (**incisors**) (*say* in-**sy**-zer)
each of the sharp-edged front teeth in the upper and lower jaws

inclination *NOUN* (**inclinations**)
a feeling that makes you want to do something • *He suddenly had an inclination to look through the keyhole.*

incline *VERB* (**inclines, inclining, inclined**) (*say* in-**klyn**)
to incline is to lean or bend
to be inclined to do something is to feel like doing it • *I'm inclined to wait until later.*

incline *NOUN* (**inclines**) (*say* **in**-klyn)
a slope

include *VERB* (**includes, including, included**)
to include something or someone is to make or consider them as part of a group of things • *Did you include Peter in the party?*

> **WORD FAMILY**
> **Inclusion** is being included.

inclusive *ADJECTIVE*
including everything; including all the things mentioned • *We want to stay from Monday to Thursday inclusive.*

income *NOUN* (**incomes**)
the money that a person earns regularly

income tax *NOUN*
income tax is a tax people have to pay on their income

incompatible *ADJECTIVE*
1 not able to live or exist together without trouble **2** machines and devices are incompatible when they cannot be used together

incompetent *ADJECTIVE*
unable to do something properly

> **WORD FAMILY**
> **Incompetence** is the inability to do something properly; to do something **incompetently** is to do it in an incompetent way.

incomplete *ADJECTIVE*
not complete
▷ **incompletely** *ADVERB* not completely

incomprehensible *ADJECTIVE*
not able to be understood

incongruous *ADJECTIVE* (*say* in- kong- roo- us)
not suitable and out of place
▷ **incongruity** *NOUN* incongruity is being incongruous
▷ **incongruously** *ADVERB* in an incongruous way

inconsiderate *ADJECTIVE*
not thinking of other people

inconsistent *ADJECTIVE*
not consistent
▷ **inconsistency** *NOUN* inconsistency is being inconsistent
▷ **inconsistently** *ADVERB* in an inconsistent way

inconspicuous *ADJECTIVE*
not noticeable or remarkable

inconvenient *ADJECTIVE*
not convenient; awkward

> WORD FAMILY
> **Inconvenience** is when something is inconvenient •*Sorry for the inconvenience.*

incorporate *VERB* (**incorporates, incorporating, incorporated**)
to incorporate something is to include it as a part of something else
▷ **incorporation** *NOUN* the incorporation of something is when it is incorporated in something else

incorrect *ADJECTIVE*
not correct; wrong

> WORD FAMILY
> To do something **incorrectly** is to do it wrongly.

increase *VERB* (**increases, increasing, increased**) (*say* in- kreess)
1 to increase something is to make it bigger **2** to increase is to become bigger
▷ **increasingly** *ADVERB* more and more •*They were becoming increasingly angry.*

increase *NOUN* (**increases**) (*say* **in**- kreess)
1 increasing **2** the amount by which something increases

incredible *ADJECTIVE*
unbelievable
▷ **incredibly** *ADVERB* in an incredible way

> USING THIS WORD
> Do not confuse **incredible** with **incredulous**, which is the next word in this dictionary.

incredulous *ADJECTIVE*
finding it difficult to believe someone

> WORD FAMILY
> **Incredulity** is disbelief.

incubate *VERB* (**incubates, incubating, incubated**)
to incubate eggs is to hatch them by keeping them warm
▷ **incubation** *NOUN* incubation is the hatching of eggs

incubator *NOUN* (**incubators**)
1 a specially heated container for keeping newly born babies warm and well supplied with oxygen **2** a container for hatching eggs

indebted *ADJECTIVE*
owing something to someone

indecent *ADJECTIVE*
not decent; improper
▷ **indecency** *NOUN* indecency is being indecent
▷ **indecently** *ADVERB* in an indecent way

indeed *ADVERB*
used for emphasis •*He was very wet indeed.*

indefinite *ADJECTIVE*
not definite; vague and unclear

indefinite article *NOUN* (**indefinite articles**)
the word *a* or *an*

indefinitely *ADVERB*
for an indefinite or unlimited time

indelible *ADJECTIVE*
impossible to rub out or remove

> WORD FAMILY
> To **indelibly** stain something is to leave a stain that is impossible to remove.

indent *VERB* (**indents, indenting, indented**)
to indent a line of print or writing is to begin it further to the right than usual

indentation *NOUN* (**indentations**)
a dent or hollow made in something

independent *ADJECTIVE*
1 free from the control of another person or country **2** not needing help from other people

> WORD FAMILY
> **Independence** is being independent; to do something **independently** is to do it without help from other people.

index *NOUN* (**indexes**)
1 a list of names or topics, usually in alphabetical order at the end of a book **2** a number showing how much prices or wages have changed

index finger *NOUN* (**index fingers**)
the finger next to the thumb

Indian summer *NOUN* (**Indian summers**)
a period of warm weather in early autumn

indicate *VERB* (**indicates, indicating, indicated**)
to indicate something is to point it out or show that it is there

> WORD FAMILY
> An **indication** is a sign of something.

indicative *ADJECTIVE*
being a sign of something

indicator *NOUN* (**indicators**)
1 something that tells you what is happening **2** a flashing light on a vehicle, to show that it is turning left or right

a b c d e f g h **i** j k l m n o p q r s t u v w x y z

indifferent *ADJECTIVE*
1 you are indifferent to something when you have no interest in it at all **2** not very good; ordinary • *He is an indifferent cricketer.*

> WORD FAMILY
> You show **indifference** when you have no interest at all in something; to do something **indifferently** is not to do it well.

indigestible *ADJECTIVE*
not easy to digest

indigestion *NOUN*
indigestion is pain caused by difficulty in digesting food

indigenous *ADJECTIVE* (*say* in- **dij**- in- us)
an indigenous people, animal, or plant is one that has always lived or grown in a particular country and not come from somewhere else • *The kangaroo is indigenous to Australia*

indignant *ADJECTIVE*
angry at something that seems wrong or unjust • *'Stupid things!' Alice began in a loud, indignant voice.* — Lewis Carroll, *Alice's Adventures in Wonderland*
▷ **indignantly** *ADVERB* in an indignant way
▷ **indignation** *NOUN* indignation is a feeling of being indignant

indigo *NOUN*
a deep blue colour

indirect *ADJECTIVE*
not direct or straight
▷ **indirectly** *ADVERB* in an indirect way

indirect speech *NOUN*
indirect speech is when someone's words are given in a changed form reported by someone else, as in *He said that he would come* (reporting the words 'I will come')

indispensable *ADJECTIVE*
essential

indistinct *ADJECTIVE*
not clear
▷ **indistinctly** *ADVERB* in an indistinct way

indistinguishable *ADJECTIVE*
impossible to see or hear, or to tell apart from something else

individual *ADJECTIVE*
1 of or for one person **2** single or separate
▷ **individually** *ADVERB* separately; one by one

individual *NOUN* (**individuals**)
an individual is one person

individuality *NOUN*
individuality is the things that make one person or thing different from another

indoctrinate *VERB* (**indoctrinates, indoctrinating, indoctrinated**)
to indoctrinate someone is to fill their mind with particular ideas or beliefs, so that they accept them without thinking
▷ **indoctrination** *NOUN* indoctrination is indoctrinating someone

indoor *ADJECTIVE*
placed or done inside a building • *We like indoor sports.*

indoors *ADVERB*
inside a building

induce *VERB* (**induces, inducing, induced**)
1 to induce someone to do something is to persuade them to do it **2** to induce a pregnant woman is to start the birth of her baby artificially

> WORD FAMILY
> An **inducement** is something given or done to persuade someone to do something.

indulge *VERB* (**indulges, indulging, indulged**)
to indulge someone is to let them have or do what they want
to indulge in something is to have or do something that you really like

indulgent *ADJECTIVE*
kind and allowing people to do what they want
▷ **indulgence** *NOUN* indulgence is being indulgent

industrial *ADJECTIVE*
to do with industry

industrial action *NOUN*
industrial action is ways for workers to protest, such as striking or working to rule

industrialist *NOUN* (**industrialists**)
someone who runs an industry

industrialize *VERB* (**industrializes, industrializing, industrialized**)
to industrialize a country is to increase or develop its industry
▷ **industrialization** *NOUN* industrialization is when a country is industrialized

industrious *ADJECTIVE*
hard-working
▷ **industriously** *ADVERB* in an industrious way

industry *NOUN* (**industries**)
1 industry is making or producing goods to sell, especially in factories **2** an industry is a branch of this, such as the motor industry **3** industry is also working hard

ineffective *ADJECTIVE*
not effective; not working well
▷ **ineffectively** *ADVERB* in an ineffective way

ineffectual *ADJECTIVE*
not achieving anything
▷ **ineffectually** *ADVERB* in an ineffectual way

inefficient *ADJECTIVE*
not working well and wasting time or energy

> WORD FAMILY
> **Inefficiency** is being inefficient; to do something **inefficiently** is to do it in a way that wastes time or energy.

inequality *NOUN* (**inequalities**)
inequality is not being equal

inert *ADJECTIVE*
not moving or reacting

inertia *NOUN* (*say* in- **er**- sha)
1 inertia is being inert or slow to take action **2** (*in science*) inertia is the tendency for a moving thing to keep moving in a straight line

inevitable *ADJECTIVE*
something is inevitable when it can't be avoided
▷ **inevitability** *NOUN* inevitability is being inevitable
▷ **inevitably** *ADVERB* in an inevitable way

inexhaustible *ADJECTIVE*
that you cannot use up completely; never-ending

inexpensive *ADJECTIVE*
not expensive; cheap
▷ **inexpensively** *ADVERB* cheaply

inexperience *NOUN*
inexperience is lack of experience

> WORD FAMILY
> Someone is **inexperienced** when they don't have much experience.

inexplicable *ADJECTIVE*
impossible to explain

> WORD FAMILY
> Something happens **inexplicably** when it is impossible to explain.

infallible *ADJECTIVE*
1 never wrong **2** always working • *They have an infallible way of winning the lottery.*
▷ **infallibility** *NOUN* infallibility is being infallible
▷ **infallibly** *ADVERB* in an infallible way

infamous *ADJECTIVE* (*say* **in**- fa- mus)
well-known for being bad or wicked

> WORD FAMILY
> **Infamy** is being infamous.

infant *NOUN* (**infants**)
a baby or young child

> WORD FAMILY
> **Infancy** is the time when someone is a baby or young child.

infantile *ADJECTIVE*
1 childish and silly **2** to do with babies or young children

infantry *NOUN*
infantry are soldiers trained to fight on foot

infect *VERB* (**infects**, **infecting**, **infected**)
to infect someone is to pass on a disease to them

infection *NOUN* (**infections**)
1 infection is infecting someone **2** an infection is an infectious disease

infectious *ADJECTIVE*
1 an infectious disease is one that can spread from one person to another **2** something like laughter or fear is infectious when it spreads to other people

infer *VERB* (**infers**, **inferring**, **inferred**)
to infer something is to work it out from what someone says or does • *I infer from your uniform that you are the postman.*

> WORD FAMILY
> An **inference** is something that you can work out from what someone says or does.

> USING THIS WORD
> Do not confuse **infer** with **imply**, which means to suggest something without actually saying it.

inferior *ADJECTIVE*
not as good or important as something else; lower in position or quality

> WORD FAMILY
> **Inferiority** is being inferior.

inferior *NOUN* (**inferiors**)
a person who is lower in position or rank than someone else

infernal *ADJECTIVE*
1 like hell or to do with hell **2** (*informal*) awful; very annoying

inferno *NOUN* (**infernos**) (*say* in- **fer**- noh)
a fierce fire

infested *ADJECTIVE*
a place is infested with (for example) insects or rats when it is full of them

infiltrate *VERB* (**infiltrates**, **infiltrating**, **infiltrated**)
to infiltrate a place or organization is to get into it without being noticed
▷ **infiltration** *NOUN* infiltration is infiltrating a place

infinite *ADJECTIVE* (*say* **in**- fi- nit)
endless; too large to be measured or imagined
▷ **infinitely** *ADVERB* to an infinite extent

infinitive *NOUN* (**infinitives**) (*say* in- **fin**- i- tiv)
the form of a verb that does not change to indicate a particular person or tense. In English it often comes after *to*, as in *to go* and *to hit*

infinity *NOUN* (*say* in- **fin**- i- ti)
infinity is an infinite number or distance

infirm *ADJECTIVE*
someone is infirm when they are weak because they are ill or old

> WORD FAMILY
> **Infirmity** is being infirm.

a b c d e f g h **i** j k l m n o p q r s t u v w x y z

infirmary *NOUN* (**infirmaries**)
a place for sick people; a hospital

inflame *VERB* (**inflames**, **inflaming**, **inflamed**)
1 a part of the body is inflamed when it has become red and sore **2** to inflame someone is to make them angry

inflammable *ADJECTIVE*
an inflammable material can be set alight

OTHER WORDS
The opposite of **inflammable** is **non-flammable** and not **flammable**, which is a technical word meaning the same as **inflammable.**

inflammation *NOUN* (**inflammations**)
a painful swelling or sore place on the body

inflammatory *ADJECTIVE*
likely to make people angry

inflate *VERB* (**inflates**, **inflating**, **inflated**)
1 to inflate something is to fill it with air or gas so that it swells up **2** a claim or statement is inflated when it is exaggerated

WORD FAMILY
Something is **inflatable** when it can be filled with air to make it swell up.

inflation *NOUN*
inflation is a general rise in prices

inflect *VERB* (**inflects**, **inflecting**, **inflected**)
1 (*in grammar*) to inflect a word is to change it slightly to make it fit with other words, for example *make*, *makes*, *making* **2** to inflect your voice is to change the sound of it when you speak

inflection *NOUN* (**inflections**)
(*in grammar*) the change you make to a word when you inflect it

inflexible *ADJECTIVE*
that you cannot bend or change • *There are a lot of inflexible rules.*
▷ **inflexibility** *NOUN* inflexibility is being inflexible
▷ **inflexibly** *ADVERB* in an inflexible way

inflict *VERB* (**inflicts**, **inflicting**, **inflicted**)
to inflict something on someone is to make them suffer it • *She inflicted a severe blow on him.*

influence *NOUN* (**influences**)
the power to affect someone or something

influence *VERB* (**influences**, **influencing**, **influenced**)
to influence someone or something is to have an effect on what they are or do • *The tides are influenced by the moon.*

influential *ADJECTIVE*
having a big influence; important

influenza *NOUN* (*say* in- floo- **en**- za)
influenza is an infectious disease that causes fever, catarrh, and pain

OTHER WORD
The more usual word for this is **flu.**

inform *VERB* (**informs**, **informing**, **informed**)
to inform someone of something is to tell them about it
to inform against or **on someone** is to give information about them, especially to the police

informal *ADJECTIVE*
not formal; casual and relaxed
▷ **informality** *NOUN* informality is being informal
▷ **informally** *ADVERB* in an informal way

INFORMAL LANGUAGE
Informal language is the kind of language you use when you are talking or writing to your friends or members of your family. Words and phrases are called 'informal' in dictionaries when they can be used in ordinary conversation but are less suitable in writing, for example *hanky, hassle,* and *hold on.* Look also at the panel on **Formal language.**

informant *NOUN* (**informants**)
a person who gives information

information *NOUN*
information is facts or what someone tells you

information technology *NOUN*
information technology is ways of storing, arranging, and giving out information, especially the use of computers and telecommunications

informative *ADJECTIVE* (*say* in- **form**- a- tiv)
containing a lot of helpful information

informed *ADJECTIVE*
you are informed about something when you know about it

informer *NOUN* (**informers**)
a person who tells the police about someone else

infrequent *ADJECTIVE*
not frequent

WORD FAMILY
To happen **infrequently** is to happen only now and then.

infuriate *VERB* (**infuriates**, **infuriating**, **infuriated**)
to infuriate someone is to make them very angry

ingenious *ADJECTIVE*
1 clever at doing things **2** cleverly made or done
▷ **ingeniously** *ADVERB* in an ingenious way
▷ **ingenuity** *NOUN* ingenuity is being ingenious

ingot *NOUN* (**ingots**)
a lump of gold or silver that has been cast in the form of a brick

ingrained *ADJECTIVE*
deeply fixed • *She was accused of ingrained idleness.*

ingratitude *NOUN*
ingratitude is not showing that you are grateful for something that someone has done for you

ingredient *NOUN* (**ingredients**) (*say* in- **greed**- i- ent)
1 one of the parts of a mixture **2** one of the things used in a recipe

inhabit *VERB* (**inhabits**, **inhabiting**, **inhabited**)
to inhabit a place is to live in it

> WORD FAMILY
> An **inhabitant** of a place is someone who lives there.

inhale *VERB* (**inhales**, **inhaling**, **inhaled**)
1 to inhale is to breathe in **2** to inhale something is to breathe it in

inhaler *NOUN* (**inhalers**)
a device for taking medicine by inhaling it

inherent *ADJECTIVE* (*say* in- **heer**- ent)
naturally or permanently part of something
▷ **inherently** *ADVERB* in an inherent way

inherit *VERB* (**inherits**, **inheriting**, **inherited**)
1 to inherit money, property, or a title is to receive it when its previous owner dies **2** to inherit qualities or characteristics is to get them from your parents or ancestors

> WORD FAMILY
> An **inheritance** is something you inherit; an **inheritor** is a person who inherits something.

inhibited *ADJECTIVE*
not relaxed enough to show or talk about your feelings

inhospitable *ADJECTIVE* (*say* in- hos- **pit**- a- bul or in- **hos**- pit- a- bul)
1 unfriendly to visitors **2** an inhospitable place is difficult to live in because it gives no shelter • *They reached an inhospitable rocky island.*

inhuman *ADJECTIVE*
cruel; without pity or kindness

> WORD FAMILY
> **Inhumanity** is cruel behaviour.

initial *NOUN* (**initials**)
the first letter of a word or name, especially of someone's forename

initial *ADJECTIVE*
first; of the beginning • *the initial stages of the work*
▷ **initially** *ADVERB* at the beginning

initiate *VERB* (**initiates**, **initiating**, **initiated**) (*say* in- **ish**- i- ayt)
1 to initiate something is to start it **2** to initiate someone is to admit them as a member of a society or group, often with special ceremonies

> WORD FAMILY
> Someone's **initiation** into a society or group is when they are initiated.

initiative *NOUN* (**initiatives**) (*say* in- **ish**- a- tiv)
1 the action that starts something • *She took the initiative in planning the party.* **2** initiative is the ability or power to start things or to get them done on your own

inject *VERB* (**injects**, **injecting**, **injected**)
1 to inject someone is to put a medicine or drug through their skin using a hollow needle **2** to inject something is to add it • *Try to inject some humour into the story.*

> WORD FAMILY
> An **injection** is injecting someone with medicine.

injure *VERB* (**injures**, **injuring**, **injured**)
to injure someone is to harm or hurt them

injury *NOUN* (**injuries**)
injury, or an injury, is harm or damage done to someone

injustice *NOUN* (**injustices**)
injustice, or an injustice, is unjust action or treatment

ink *NOUN* (**inks**)
ink is a black or coloured liquid used for writing and printing

> WORD FAMILY
> **Inky** fingers or pages are covered in ink.

inkling *NOUN*
a slight idea or suspicion • *I had an inkling that we'd find them in here.*

inland *ADVERB*
in or towards a place on land and away from the coast

in-laws *PLURAL NOUN*
a person's in-laws are the relatives of their husband or wife • *We're going to visit the in-laws at Easter.*

inlet *NOUN* (**inlets**)
a strip of water reaching into the land from a sea or lake

inn *NOUN* (**inns**)
a hotel or public house, especially in the country

> WORD FAMILY
> An **innkeeper** is someone who runs an inn.

inner *ADJECTIVE*
inside; nearer the centre
▷ **innermost** *ADJECTIVE* furthest inside • *'Ask for the High Priest,' said the Phoenix. 'Say that you have a secret to unfold that concerns my worship, and he will lead you to the innermost sanctuary.'* — Edith Nesbit, *The Phoenix and the Carpet*

innings *NOUN* (**innings**)
the time when a cricket team or player is batting

innocence *NOUN*
1 innocence is when someone is not guilty of doing something wrong **2** innocence is also lack of experience of the world and the evil things in it

innocent *ADJECTIVE*
1 not guilty of doing something wrong **2** not knowing much about the world and the evil things in it
▷ **innocently** *ADVERB* in an innocent way

a b c d e f g h i j k l m n o p q r s t u v w x y z

innocuous *ADJECTIVE*
harmless

innovation *NOUN* (**innovations**)
1 innovation is inventing or using new things **2** an innovation is something new that you have just invented or started using

> **WORD FAMILY**
> An **innovative** design or way of doing something is new and clever; an **innovator** is someone who innovates something.

innumerable *ADJECTIVE*
too many to be counted • *Innumerable candles were hovering in mid-air over four long, crowded tables, making the golden plates and goblets sparkle.* — J. K. Rowling, *Harry Potter and the Chamber of Secrets*

inoculate *VERB* (**inoculates, inoculating, inoculated**)
to inoculate someone is to inject them to protect them against a disease
▷ **inoculation** *NOUN* inoculation is being inoculated

in-patient *NOUN* (**in-patients**)
someone who stays at a hospital for treatment

input *NOUN* (**inputs**)
what you put into something, especially data put into a computer

input *VERB* (**inputs, inputting, input**)
(*in computing*) to input data or programs is to put them into a computer

inquest *NOUN* (**inquests**)
an official investigation to decide why someone died

inquire *VERB* (**inquires, inquiring, inquired**)
1 to inquire about something is to ask about it **2** to inquire into something is to make an official investigation of it

inquiry *NOUN* (**inquiries**)
an official investigation

inquisitive *ADJECTIVE*
always trying to find out things, especially about other people • *Goldipig was a very inquisitive little swine, always poking her snout into other people's business.* — Dick King-Smith, *Goldipig and the Three Bears*
▷ **inquisitively** *ADVERB* in an inquisitive way

insane *ADJECTIVE*
not sane; mad
▷ **insanely** *ADVERB* in an insane way
▷ **insanity** *NOUN* insanity is being insane

insanitary *ADJECTIVE*
not clean or healthy

inscribe *VERB* (**inscribes, inscribing, inscribed**)
to inscribe something is to write or carve it on a surface

inscription *NOUN* (**inscriptions**)
words written or carved on a monument, stone, or coin, or written in the front of a book

insect *NOUN* (**insects**)
a small animal with six legs and a body divided into three parts

insecticide *NOUN* (**insecticides**)
a poisonous chemical used for killing insects

insecure *ADJECTIVE*
1 not safe or protected properly **2** not feeling safe or confident

> **WORD FAMILY**
> Something is **insecurely** fastened or fixed when it is not firm or safe; **insecurity** is not feeling safe or confident.

insensitive *ADJECTIVE*
not sensitive or thinking about the feelings of other people
▷ **insensitively** *ADVERB* in an insensitive way
▷ **insensitivity** *NOUN* being insensitive

inseparable *ADJECTIVE*
1 unable to be separated **2** people are inseparable when they are very good friends and always together • *The two girls were inseparable during the summer.*

> **WORD FAMILY**
> Two things are **inseparably** linked when they are so closely linked that they can't be separated.

insert *VERB* (**inserts, inserting, inserted**)
to insert something is to put it into something else
▷ **insertion** *NOUN* the insertion of something is when it is inserted into something else

inshore *ADJECTIVE & ADVERB*
on the sea near or nearer to the shore

inside *NOUN* (**insides**)
1 the middle or centre of something; the part nearest to the middle **2** (*informal*) your insides are your stomach or abdomen
inside out with the inside turned so that it faces outwards

inside *ADJECTIVE*
placed on the inside of something • *Look on an inside page.*

inside *ADVERB & PREPOSITION*
in or to the inside of something • *Come inside.* • *It's inside that box.*

insight *NOUN* (**insights**)
1 insight is being able to see the truth about things **2** an insight is an understanding of something

insignificant *ADJECTIVE*
not important or influential
▷ **insignificance** *NOUN* insignificance is being insignificant

insincere *ADJECTIVE*
not sincere
▷ **insincerely** *ADVERB* in an insincere way
▷ **insincerity** *NOUN* insincerity is being insincere

insist *VERB* (**insists, insisting, insisted**)
to insist something is to be very firm in saying it • *He insisted that he was innocent.*
to insist on something is to demand it • *We insist on seeing the manager.*

insistent *ADJECTIVE*
insisting on doing or having something
▷ **insistence** *NOUN* insistence is being insistent

insolent *ADJECTIVE*
very rude and insulting • *Malfoy gave Professor Lupin an insolent stare.* — J. K. Rowling, *Harry Potter and the Prisoner of Azkaban*

> WORD FAMILY
> Someone shows **insolence** when they speak to someone rudely and without respect.

insoluble *ADJECTIVE*
1 impossible to solve • *It is an insoluble problem.* **2** impossible to dissolve • *Some chemicals are insoluble.*
▷ **insolubility** *NOUN* insolubility is being insoluble

insomnia *NOUN* (*say* in- som- ni- a)
insomnia is being unable to sleep

inspect *VERB* (**inspects, inspecting, inspected**)
to inspect something or someone is to look carefully at them, especially to check them

> WORD FAMILY
> An **inspection** is a close or careful look at something to check it.

inspector *NOUN* (**inspectors**)
1 someone employed to inspect things or people **2** a police officer next in rank above a sergeant

inspire *VERB* (**inspires, inspiring, inspired**)
to inspire someone is to fill them with ideas or enthusiasm

> WORD FAMILY
> An **inspiration** is a person or thing that encourages you and fills you with ideas.

install *VERB* (**installs, installing, installed**)
1 to install something is to put it in position ready for use • *We want to install central heating.* **2** to install someone is to put them into an important position with a ceremony • *He was installed as pope.*
▷ **installation** *NOUN* installation is being installed

instalment *NOUN* (**instalments**)
one of the parts into which something is divided so that it is spread over a period of time • *He is paying for his bike in monthly instalments.* • *The story was in three instalments.*

instance *NOUN* (**instances**)
an example
for instance for example

instant *ADJECTIVE*
1 happening immediately • *It has been an instant success.* **2** that can be made very quickly • *Do you like instant coffee?*

instant *NOUN* (**instants**)
a moment • *I don't believe it for an instant.*
this instant at once • *Come here this instant!*

instantaneous *ADJECTIVE*
happening or done in an instant, or without any delay • *Mrs. Cobb had taken an instantaneous and illogical dislike to the Rev. Mr. Burch in the afternoon.* — Kate Douglas Wiggin, *Rebecca of Sunnybrook Farm*
▷ **instantaneously** *ADVERB* in an instant; immediately

instantly *ADVERB*
to do something instantly is to do it without any delay

instead *ADVERB*
in place of something else; as a substitute • *There were no potatoes, so we had rice instead.*

instep *NOUN* (**insteps**)
the top of your foot between the toes and the ankle

instinct *NOUN* (**instincts**)
a natural tendency to do or feel something without being taught • *Spiders spin webs by instinct.*

> WORD FAMILY
> **Instinctive** behaviour follows instinct, not thought; to do something **instinctively** is to do it in an instinctive way • *He knew instinctively that something was wrong.*

institute *NOUN* (**institutes**)
an organization set up to study something or for some other purpose, or the building used by it

institute *VERB* (**institutes, instituting, instituted**)
to institute something is to establish it or start it

institution *NOUN* (**institutions**)
1 a large organization **2** something that is an established habit or custom • *Going for a swim on Sunday was a family institution.*

instruct *VERB* (**instructs, instructing, instructed**)
1 to instruct someone is to teach them a subject or skill **2** to instruct someone is also to give them information or orders

instruction *NOUN* (**instructions**)
1 instruction is teaching a subject or skill **2** an instruction is an order or piece of information • *Follow the instructions carefully.*

instrument *NOUN* (**instruments**)
1 a device for making musical sounds **2** a device for delicate or scientific work

instrumental *ADJECTIVE*
1 instrumental music uses musical instruments without any singing **2** to be instrumental in something is to be helpful in making it happen • *She was instrumental in getting him a job.*

insufficient *ADJECTIVE*
not enough

a b c d e f g h i j k l m n o p q r s t u v w x y z

insulate *VERB* (**insulates**, **insulating**, **insulated**)
to insulate something is to cover it to stop heat, cold, or electricity from passing in or out
▷ **insulation** *NOUN* insulation is insulating something

insulin *NOUN*
insulin is a chemical that controls how much sugar there is in the blood

insult *VERB* (**insults**, **insulting**, **insulted**) (*say* **in-sult**)
to insult someone is to speak or behave in a rude way that offends them

insult *NOUN* (**insults**) (*say* **in-** sult)
a rude remark or action that offends someone

insurance *NOUN*
insurance is a business agreement to receive money or compensation if you suffer a loss or injury, in return for a regular payment called a premium

insure *VERB* (**insures**, **insuring**, **insured**)
to insure yourself or your goods is to protect them with insurance

> SPELLING
> Do not confuse **insure** with **ensure**, which means to make sure.

intact *ADJECTIVE*
complete and undamaged • *Despite the storm our tent was still intact.*

intake *NOUN* (**intakes**)
1 taking something in **2** the number of people or things taken in • *The school had a high intake of pupils this year.*

integer *NOUN* (**integers**) (*say* **in**- ti- jer)
a whole number, such as 0, 1, 24, and not a fraction

integral *ADJECTIVE* (*say* **in**- ti- gral)
1 that is an essential part of something • *Your heart is an integral part of your body.* **2** whole or complete

integrate *VERB* (**integrates**, **integrating**, **integrated**) (*say* **in**- ti- grayt)
1 to integrate different things or parts is to make them into a whole **2** to integrate people, especially of different origins, is to bring them together into a single community
▷ **integration** *NOUN* integration is being integrated

integrity *NOUN* (*say* in- **teg**- ri- ti)
integrity is being honest and behaving well

intellect *NOUN* (**intellects**)
the ability to think and work things out with your mind

intellectual *ADJECTIVE*
1 involving the intellect **2** able to think effectively; keen to study and learn
▷ **intellectually** *ADVERB* in an intellectual way

intellectual *NOUN* (**intellectuals**)
an intellectual person

intelligence *NOUN*
1 your intelligence is your ability to think and learn
2 intelligence is also information, especially of military value

intelligent *ADJECTIVE*
good at thinking and learning
▷ **intelligently** *ADVERB* in an intelligent way

intelligible *ADJECTIVE*
able to be understood • *The message was barely intelligible.*

> WORD FAMILY
> **Intelligibility** is being intelligible; to write or speak **intelligibly** is to do so in a way that can be understood.

intend *VERB* (**intends**, **intending**, **intended**)
1 to intend to do something is to have it in mind as a plan • *She was intending to go swimming.* **2** to intend someone to do something is to want them to do it

intense *ADJECTIVE*
1 very strong or great • *The heat was intense.*
2 having or showing strong feelings
▷ **intensely** *ADVERB* very strongly

intensify *VERB* (**intensifies**, **intensifying**, **intensified**)
1 to intensify something is to make it more intense
2 to intensify is to become more intense
▷ **intensification** *NOUN* intensification is intensifying something or becoming more intense

intensity *NOUN* (**intensities**)
the intensity of something is how strong or great it is

intensive *ADJECTIVE*
using a lot of effort; thorough • *We have made an intensive search.*
▷ **intensively** *ADVERB* in an intensive way

intent *ADJECTIVE*
showing a lot of attention and interest
to be intent on something is to be eager or determined to do it

> WORD FAMILY
> To listen or look **intently** is to do so with a lot of attention and interest. • *For a moment everything was quiet as Milo, Tock, and the Humbug looked intently at the bottle, wondering what Dr Dischord would do next.* — Norton Juster, *The Phantom Tollbooth*

intent *NOUN* (**intents**)
a person's intent is what they intend to do

intention *NOUN* (**intentions**)
what you intend to do; a plan

intentional *ADJECTIVE*
done on purpose; deliberate

> WORD FAMILY
> To do something **intentionally** is to do it on purpose.

inter- *PREFIX*
meaning between two or more people or things, as in *interchangeable* and *inter-school*

interact *VERB* (**interacts**, **interacting**, **interacted**)
two people or things interact when they have an effect on one another • *It is interesting to watch how young children interact.*
▷ **interaction** *NOUN* interaction is the process of interacting

interactive *ADJECTIVE*
(*in computing*) allowing information to be sent in either direction between a computer system and its user

intercept *VERB* (**intercepts**, **intercepting**, **intercepted**)
to intercept someone or something is to stop them going from one place to another
▷ **interception** *NOUN* interception is intercepting someone or something

interchange *NOUN* (**interchanges**)
a place where you can move from one main road or motorway to another

interchangeable *ADJECTIVE*
things are interchangeable when they can be changed or swapped round

intercom *NOUN* (**intercoms**)
a device for communicating by radio or telephone

intercourse *NOUN*
1 intercourse is communication or dealings between people **2** intercourse is also sexual intercourse

interdependent *ADJECTIVE*
depending or relying on each another

> WORD FAMILY
> **Interdependence** is when two or more people or groups depend or rely on each another.

interest *VERB* (**interests**, **interesting**, **interested**)
to interest someone is to make them want to look or listen or take part in something

interest *NOUN* (**interests**)
1 interest is being interested **2** an interest is a thing that interests you **3** interest is also money a borrower has to pay regularly for a loan

interface *NOUN* (**interfaces**)
a connection between two parts of a computer system

interfere *VERB* (**interferes**, **interfering**, **interfered**)
1 to interfere in something is to become involved in it when it has nothing to do with you **2** to interfere is to get in the way

interference *NOUN*
1 interference is interfering in something **2** interference is also a crackling or distorting of a radio or television signal

interior *NOUN* (**interiors**)
the inside of something

interjection *NOUN* (**interjections**)
an exclamation, such as *oh!*

interlock *VERB* (**interlocks**, **interlocking**, **interlocked**)
to interlock is to fit into one another • *The gearwheels interlocked.*

interlude *NOUN* (**interludes**)
1 an interval **2** music played during an interval

intermediate *ADJECTIVE*
coming between two things in place, order, or time

interminable *ADJECTIVE* (*say* in- **ter**- min- a- bul)
seeming to go on for ever
▷ **interminably** *ADVERB* in an interminable way

intermission *NOUN* (**intermissions**)
an interval in a play or film

intermittent *ADJECTIVE*
happening at intervals
▷ **intermittently** *ADVERB* at intervals

intern *VERB* (**interns**, **interning**, **interned**)
to intern someone is to imprison them in a special camp or building, usually during a war

> WORD FAMILY
> An **internee** is someone who is interned; **internment** is being interned.

internal *ADJECTIVE*
of or in the inside of something
▷ **internally** *ADVERB* on the inside

internal-combustion engine *NOUN* (**internal-combustion engines**)
an engine that produces power by burning fuel inside the engine itself

international *ADJECTIVE*
to do with more than one country • *Interpol is an international police organization.*
▷ **internationally** *ADVERB* for or in more than one country

Internet *NOUN*
the Internet is a computer network that allows people all over the world to share information and send messages

interplanetary *ADJECTIVE*
between planets

interpret *VERB* (**interprets**, **interpreting**, **interpreted**)
1 to interpret something is to explain what it means **2** to interpret a foreign language is to translate it into another language

> WORD FAMILY
> **Interpretation** is the way someone explains what something means.

interpreter *NOUN* (**interpreters**)
a person who translates what someone says into another language

a b c d e f g h **i** j k l m n o p q r s t u v w x y z

interrogate *VERB* (**interrogates, interrogating, interrogated**)
to interrogate someone is to question them closely in order to get information

> WORD FAMILY
> An **interrogation** is when someone is interrogated, and an **interrogator** is someone who interrogates.

interrogative *ADJECTIVE*
expressing a question • *'Are they here?' is an interrogative sentence.*

interrupt *VERB* (**interrupts, interrupting, interrupted**)
1 to interrupt someone is to stop them talking **2** to interrupt something is to stop it continuing

> WORD FAMILY
> An **interruption** is when someone or something is interrupted.

intersect *VERB* (**intersects, intersecting, intersected**)
to intersect something is to cross or divide it • *The cloth had a design of intersecting lines.*

intersection *NOUN* (**intersections**)
a place where lines or roads cross each other

interval *NOUN* (**intervals**)
a time between two events or between two parts of a play or film
at intervals with some time or distance between each one; not continuously

intervene *VERB* (**intervenes, intervening, intervened**)
1 to intervene is to come between two events • *During the intervening years they went abroad.* **2** to intervene in an argument or fight is to interrupt it in order to stop it or affect the result
▷ **intervention** *NOUN* an intervention is when someone intervenes in something

interview *NOUN* (**interviews**)
a meeting with someone to ask them questions or discuss something

interview *VERB* (**interviews, interviewing, interviewed**)
to interview someone is to have an interview with them

interviewer *NOUN* (**interviewers**)
a person who interviews someone, especially on radio or television

intestine *NOUN* or **intestines** *PLURAL NOUN*
the long tube along which food passes from the stomach to the anus
▷ **intestinal** *ADJECTIVE* to do with the intestine

intimate *ADJECTIVE* (*say* **in**- ti- mat)
1 very friendly with someone **2** intimate thoughts are thoughts that are private or personal **3** detailed • *They have an intimate knowledge of the town.*

> WORD FAMILY
> **Intimacy** is having a very close friendship; to know something **intimately** is to know it in a detailed way.

intimate *VERB* (**intimates, intimating, intimated**) (*say* **in**- ti- mayt)
to intimate something is to hint at it or suggest it • *He has not yet intimated what his plans are.*

> WORD FAMILY
> An **intimation** is a hint or suggestion.

intimidate *VERB* (**intimidates, intimidating, intimidated**)
to frighten a person with threats into doing something
▷ **intimidation** *NOUN* intimidation is intimidating someone

into *PREPOSITION*
1 expressing movement to the inside of something • *Go into the house.* **2 Into** also has some special uses, shown by the following examples • *He got into trouble.* • *She went into acting.* • *3 into 12 goes 4 times.*

intolerable *ADJECTIVE*
unbearable • *The noise outside was intolerable.*
▷ **intolerably** *ADVERB* to an intolerable degree

intolerant *ADJECTIVE*
not tolerant or willing to put up with people
▷ **intolerance** *NOUN* intolerance is being intolerant
▷ **intolerantly** *ADVERB* in an intolerant way

intonation *NOUN* (**intonations**)
1 the pitch or tone of a voice or musical instrument **2** when you speak, your intonation is the way you use the pitch of your voice to alter the meaning of what you are saying, for example when asking a question

intoxicate *VERB* (**intoxicates, intoxicating, intoxicated**)
1 a person is intoxicated when they are drunk **2** a person is intoxicated by something when they are very excited by it
▷ **intoxication** *NOUN* intoxication is being drunk

intransitive *ADJECTIVE*
(*in grammar*) a verb is intransitive when it is used without a direct object, for example *ran* in *they ran away* (but not in *they ran a paper shop*)

intrepid *ADJECTIVE*
brave or fearless • *'Perhaps most of the brave defenders were killed quite early in the siege and all the provisions eaten, and now there are only a few intrepid survivors.'* — Edith Nesbit, *Five Children and It*
▷ **intrepidly** *ADVERB* in an intrepid way

intricate *ADJECTIVE*
an intricate pattern or design is detailed and complicated
▷ **intricacy** *NOUN* intricacy is being intricate
▷ **intricately** *ADVERB* in an intricate way

intrigue *VERB* (**intrigues**, **intriguing**, **intrigued**) (*say* in- **treeg**)
to intrigue someone is to interest them very much and make them curious
▷ **intriguing** *ADJECTIVE*
very interesting because it is unusual

intrigue (*say* **in**- treeg) *NOUN* (**intrigues**)
a secret plot

introduce *VERB* (**introduces**, **introducing**, **introduced**)
1 to introduce someone is to make them known to other people **2** to introduce something is to get it into general use

introduction *NOUN* (**introductions**)
1 introducing someone or something **2** a piece at the beginning of a book, explaining what it is about
▷ **introductory** *ADJECTIVE* coming at the beginning of something

intrude *VERB* (**intrudes**, **intruding**, **intruded**)
to intrude is to come in or join in without being wanted

> WORD FAMILY
> An **intrusion** is coming in where you are not wanted; something is **intrusive** when it is not wanted and gets in the way.

intruder *NOUN* (**intruders**)
someone who forces their way into a place where they are not supposed to be

intuition *NOUN* (*say* in- tew- **ish**- on)
intuition is the power to know or understand things without having to think hard
▷ **intuitive** *ADJECTIVE* using intuition

Inuit *NOUN* (**Inuit** or **Inuits**)
one of the people who live in very cold parts of North America

inundate *VERB* (**inundates**, **inundating**, **inundated**)
to inundate someone is to overwhelm them with a large number of things • *We've been inundated with complaints.*
▷ **inundation** *NOUN* an inundation of things is a large number of them that overwhelm you

invade *VERB* (**invades**, **invading**, **invaded**)
to invade a country or place is to attack and enter it

> WORD FAMILY
> **Invaders** are people who invade a place.

invalid[1] *NOUN* (**invalids**) (*say* **in**- va- leed or **in**- va- lid)
someone who is ill or weakened by a long illness

invalid[2] *ADJECTIVE* (*say* in- **val**- id)
not valid • *This passport is invalid.*

invaluable *ADJECTIVE*
very valuable

invariable *ADJECTIVE*
never changing; always the same

invariably *ADVERB*
always

invasion *NOUN* (**invasions**)
when an army or a large number of people attack and enter a place

invent *VERB* (**invents**, **inventing**, **invented**)
1 to invent something is to be the first person to make it or think of it **2** to invent a story or excuse is to make it up

> WORD FAMILY
> An **invention** is something invented; someone is being **inventive** when they cleverly think of new ideas; an **inventor** is a person who invents things.

inverse *ADJECTIVE*
reversed or opposite
▷ **inversely** *ADVERB* in an inverse or opposite way

inverse *NOUN*
the opposite of something

invert *VERB* (**inverts**, **inverting**, **inverted**)
to invert something is to turn it upside down
▷ **inversion** *NOUN* inversion is inverting things

invertebrate *NOUN* (**invertebrates**) (*say* in- **vert**- i- brat)
an animal without a backbone, such as a worm or an amoeba

inverted commas *PLURAL NOUN*
punctuation marks (“ ”) or (‘ ’) that you put round spoken words and quotations

invest *VERB* (**invests**, **investing**, **invested**)
1 to invest money is to use it to earn interest or make a profit **2** to invest someone is to give them an honour or medal or special title • *He was invested as Prince of Wales.*

> WORD FAMILY
> An **investor** is someone who invests money.

investigate *VERB* (**investigates**, **investigating**, **investigated**)
to investigate something or someone is to find out as much as you can about them • *Police are investigating the robbery.*

> WORD FAMILY
> An **investigation** is a careful search for information; an **investigator** is a person who investigates someone or something.

investiture *NOUN* (**investitures**)
a ceremony in which someone is given an official title

investment *NOUN* (**investments**)
1 money someone invests **2** something someone invests money in • *Houses are a safe investment.*

a b c d e f g h **i** j k l m n o p q r s t u v w x y z

invigilate *VERB* (**invigilates**, **invigilating**, **invigilated**)
to supervise the people taking an examination
▷ **invigilation** *NOUN* invigilation is invigilating an examination
▷ **invigilator** *NOUN* someone who invigilates

invigorate *VERB* (**invigorates**, **invigorating**, **invigorated**)
to fill someone with energy
▷ **invigorating** *ADJECTIVE* filling you with energy

invincible *ADJECTIVE*
not able to be defeated

invisible *ADJECTIVE*
not visible; not able to be seen

> WORD FAMILY
> **Invisibility** is being invisible; to do something **invisibly** is to do it so that you can't be seen.

invitation *NOUN* (**invitations**)
a request for someone to do something, such as come to a party

invite *VERB* (**invites**, **inviting**, **invited**)
1 to invite someone is to ask them to come to a party or do something special **2** to invite something unwelcome is to make it likely to happen by your actions • *You are inviting trouble by doing that.*

inviting *ADJECTIVE*
attractive or tempting
▷ **invitingly** *ADVERB* in an inviting way

invoice *NOUN* (**invoices**)
a list of goods sent or of work done, with the prices charged

involuntary *ADJECTIVE*
not deliberate; done without thinking

involve *VERB* (**involves**, **involving**, **involved**)
1 to involve something is to need it or result in it • *The job involved a lot of effort.* **2** to be involved in something is to take part in it • *We are involved in charity work.*
▷ **involvement** *NOUN* involvement is being involved in something

involved *ADJECTIVE*
long and complicated

inward *ADJECTIVE*
on the inside, or facing the inside

inward *ADVERB*
inwards

inwardly *ADVERB*
in your thoughts; privately • *Titus shut his eyes like a clam and inwardly vowed never to grow old.* — Debi Gliori, *Pure Dead Magic*

inwards *ADVERB*
towards the inside

iodine *NOUN* (*say* I- o- deen or I- o- dyn)
iodine is a chemical used to kill germs

ion *NOUN* (**ions**) (*say* I- on)
an electrically-charged particle

IQ *NOUN* (**IQs**)
a measure of someone's intelligence, calculated from the results of a test

iris *NOUN* (**irises**)
1 the coloured part of your eyeball **2** a flower with long pointed leaves

iron *NOUN* (**irons**)
1 iron is a strong heavy metal **2** an iron is a device that you heat up and press on clothes to make them smooth **3** an iron is also a tool made of iron

iron *VERB* (**irons**, **ironing**, **ironed**)
to iron clothes is to smooth them with an iron
to iron something out is to solve a difficulty gradually and carefully

ironic or **ironical** *ADJECTIVE* (*say* I- **ron**- ik or I- **ron**- ikal)
1 an ironic situation is strange because the opposite happens to what you might expect **2** you are being ironic when you say the opposite of what you mean
▷ **ironically** *ADVERB* in an ironic way

ironmonger *NOUN* (**ironmongers**)
someone who keeps a shop that sells tools, nails, and other metal things

> WORD FAMILY
> **Ironmongery** is things that an ironmonger sells.

irony *NOUN* (**ironies**) (*say* I- ro- ni)
1 irony is saying the opposite of what you mean in order to emphasize it or be funny, for example *What a lovely day* when it is pouring with rain **2** an irony is an unexpected or strange event or situation • *The irony is that she had sold all her jewels the day before the burglars broke in.*

irrational *ADJECTIVE*
not rational
▷ **irrationally** *ADVERB* in an irrational way

irregular *ADJECTIVE*
1 not regular; not usual **2** against the rules
▷ **irregularity** *NOUN* irregularity is being irregular or unusual
▷ **irregularly** *ADVERB* in an irregular way

irrelevant *ADJECTIVE* (*say* i- **rel**- i- vant)
not relevant; not having anything to do with what is being discussed

> WORD FAMILY
> An **irrelevance** is something irrelevant.

irresistible *ADJECTIVE*
too strong or attractive or tempting to resist

irresponsible *ADJECTIVE*
not thinking enough about the effects of your actions

> WORD FAMILY
> Someone shows **irresponsibility** when they act without thinking enough about the effects of their actions; you can say that they act **irresponsibly**.

irreverent *ADJECTIVE*
not reverent or respectful
▷ **irreverence** *NOUN* irreverence is being irreverent
▷ **irreverently** *ADVERB* in an irreverent way

irrigate *VERB* (**irrigates**, **irrigating**, **irrigated**)
to irrigate land is to supply it with water so that crops can grow

> WORD FAMILY
> **Irrigation** is irrigating land.

irritable *ADJECTIVE*
easily annoyed; bad-tempered

> WORD FAMILY
> **Irritability** is being irritable; to say something **irritably** is to say it in a bad-tempered way.

irritate *VERB* (**irritates**, **irritating**, **irritated**)
1 to irritate someone is to annoy them **2** to irritate a part of your body is to make it itch or feel sore

> WORD FAMILY
> An **irritant** is something that makes you sore.

irritation *NOUN* (**irritations**)
1 irritation is being annoyed **2** an irritation is something that annoys you

is
3rd person singular present tense of **be**

-ish *SUFFIX*
meaning 'somewhat; rather like something', as in *boyish* and *reddish*

Islam *NOUN* (*say* **iz**- lahm)
Islam is the religion of Muslims
▷ **Islamic** *ADJECTIVE* to do with Islam

island *NOUN* (**islands**)
a piece of land surrounded by water

> WORD FAMILY
> An **islander** is someone who lives on an island.

isle *NOUN* (**isles**)
an island

-ism *SUFFIX*
meaning a belief or a system of thought, such as *Hinduism*

isn't
short for *is not*

isobar *NOUN* (**isobars**) (*say* **I**- so- bar)
a line on a map connecting places that have the same atmospheric pressure

isolate *VERB* (**isolates**, **isolating**, **isolated**)
to isolate someone or something is to keep them apart from others • *Patients with the disease need to be isolated.*

> WORD FAMILY
> **Isolation** is being isolated or alone.

isosceles triangle *NOUN* (**isosceles triangles**) (*say* I- **sos**- i- leez)
a triangle with two sides the same length

isotope *NOUN* (**isotopes**) (*say* **I**- so- tohp)
(*in science*) a form of an element that is different from other forms in the structure of its nucleus, but has the same chemical properties as the other forms

issue *VERB* (**issues**, **issuing**, **issued**)
1 to issue something is to send it or give it out to people • *They issued blankets to the refugees.* **2** to issue a book or piece of information is to publish it **3** to issue is to come out of something • *Smoke was issuing from the chimney.*

issue *NOUN* (**issues**)
1 an issue is a subject that people are discussing • *What are the most important issues?* **2** an issue of a magazine or newspaper is the edition sold on a particular day • *There's a good poster in this week's issue of my football magazine.* **3** the issue of documents is making them available to people

-ist *SUFFIX*
meaning someone who does a particular job, such as *anaesthetist*

isthmus *NOUN* (**isthmuses**) (*say* **iss**- mus)
a narrow strip of land connecting two larger pieces of land

it *PRONOUN*
1 the thing being talked about, used as the subject or object of a verb **2 It** also has some special uses, as in • *It is raining.* • *We must go it alone.*

italic *ADJECTIVE*
printed with sloping letters *like this*

italics *PLURAL NOUN* (*say* it- **al**- iks)
letters printed with a slant, *like this*

itch *NOUN* (**itches**)
1 a tickling feeling in your skin that makes you want to scratch it **2** a longing to do something • *He has an itch to go to America.*

> WORD FAMILY
> A part of your body is **itchy** when it makes you want to scratch it.

itch *VERB* (**itches**, **itching**, **itched**)
a part of your body itches when it makes you want to scratch it

item *NOUN* (**items**)
one thing in a list or group of things

itinerary *NOUN* (**itineraries**) (*say* I- **tin**- er- er- i)
a list of places to be visited on a journey

-itis *SUFFIX*
used in names of diseases in which part of the body is inflamed, such as *bronchitis*

it'll
short for *it will*

its *DETERMINER & PRONOUN*
of it; belonging to it • *The cat hurt its paw.*

it's
short for *it is* and (before a verb in the past tense) *it has* • *It's raining.* • *It's been raining.*

itself *PRONOUN*
it and nothing else, used to refer back to the subject of a verb • *I think the cat has hurt itself.*
by itself on its own, alone • *The house stands by itself in a wood.*

ITV
short for *Independent Television*

I've
short for *I have*

ivory *NOUN*
1 ivory is the hard creamy-white substance that forms elephants' tusks **2** a creamy-white colour

ivy *NOUN*
ivy is a climbing evergreen plant with shiny leaves

Jj

jab *VERB* (**jabs, jabbing, jabbed**)
1 to jab someone or something is to poke them roughly • *Eddie felt something jab him in the back. He turned to find that it was Malcolm the stuffed stoat's nose.* — Philip Ardagh, *Terrible Times* **2** to jab something is to push it roughly into something else

jab *NOUN* (**jabs**)
1 a quick hit with something pointed or a fist **2** (*informal*) an injection

jabber *VERB* (**jabbers, jabbering, jabbered**)
to jabber is to chatter a lot or to speak quickly and not clearly

jack *NOUN* (**jacks**)
1 a piece of equipment for lifting something heavy off the ground, especially a car **2** a playing card with a picture of a young man **3** a small white ball that you aim at in the game of bowls

jack *VERB* (**jacks, jacking, jacked**)
to jack something is to lift it with a jack

jackal *NOUN* (**jackals**)
a wild animal rather like a dog

jackass *NOUN* (**jackasses**)
1 a male donkey **2** a stupid person

jackdaw *NOUN* (**jackdaws**)
a bird like a small crow

jacket *NOUN* (**jackets**)
1 a short coat covering the top half of the body **2** a paper cover for a book **3** a wrapping round a boiler to insulate it

jacket potato *NOUN* (**jacket potatoes**)
a potato that is baked without being peeled

jack-in-the-box *NOUN* (**jack-in-the-boxes**)
a toy figure that springs out of a box when you lift the lid

jackknife *VERB* (**jackknifes, jackknifing, jackknifed**)
an articulated lorry jackknifes when it goes out of control, with the trailer skidding round towards the cab

jackpot *NOUN* (**jackpots**)
an amount of prize money that increases until someone wins it

jacuzzi *NOUN* (**jacuzzis**) (*say* ja- **koo**- zi)
a large bath with jets of water that massage the body under the water

jade *NOUN*
jade is a hard green stone which is carved to make ornaments

jaded *ADJECTIVE*
tired and bored because you have had too much of something

jagged *ADJECTIVE* (*say* **jag**- id)
having an uneven edge with sharp points

jaguar *NOUN* (**jaguars**)
a large fierce South American animal of the cat family rather like a leopard

jail *NOUN* (**jails**)
a prison

jail *VERB* (**jails, jailing, jailed**)
to jail someone is to put them in prison

jailer *NOUN* (**jailers**)
a person in charge of a jail

Jain *NOUN* (**Jains**) (*rhymes with* **main**)
a believer in an Indian religion rather like Buddhism

jam *NOUN* (**jams**)
1 a sweet food made of fruit boiled with sugar until it is thick **2** a lot of people or cars or other things crowded together so that it is difficult to move
to be in a jam (*informal*) is to be in a difficult situation

jam *VERB* (**jams, jamming, jammed**)
1 to jam something is to make it stuck and difficult to move **2** to jam is to become stuck • *The door has jammed.* **3** to jam something is to push or squeeze it with force • *I jammed on the brakes.*

jamboree *NOUN* (**jamborees**)
1 a large party or celebration **2** a rally of Scouts

jammy *ADJECTIVE* (**jammier, jammiest**)
1 covered with jam **2** (*informal*) very lucky

jangle *VERB* (**jangles, jangling, jangled**)
to jangle is to make a harsh ringing sound

January *NOUN*
the first month of the year

jar[1] *NOUN* (**jars**)
a container made of glass or pottery

jar[2] *VERB* (**jars, jarring, jarred**)
1 to jar is to give you an unpleasant shock or jolt • *I jarred every bone in my body.* **2** to jar is also to make a harsh sound • *All that shrieking really jars on my ears.*

jargon *NOUN*
jargon is words used by people in a particular profession, that are difficult for other people to understand • *The guide is full of computer jargon.*

jaundice *NOUN*
jaundice is a disease that makes the skin turn yellow

jaunt *NOUN* (**jaunts**)
a short trip for fun

jaunty *ADJECTIVE* (**jauntier**, **jauntiest**)
lively and cheerful
▷ **jauntily** *ADVERB* in a jaunty way
▷ **jauntiness** *NOUN* jauntiness is being jaunty

javelin *NOUN* (**javelins**)
a light spear used for throwing in athletics competitions

jaw *NOUN* (**jaws**)
1 one of the two bones that hold the teeth **2** the lower part of the face; the mouth and teeth of a person or animal **3** the part of a tool that grips something

jay *NOUN* (**jays**)
a noisy brightly-coloured bird

jazz *NOUN*
jazz is a kind of music with strong rhythm

> WORD FAMILY
> Something is **jazzy** when it is bright and colourful.

jealous *ADJECTIVE*
1 unhappy or resentful because you feel that someone is better or luckier than you **2** upset because you think that someone you love is loved by someone else more

> WORD FAMILY
> You behave **jealously** when you behave in a jealous way; **jealousy** is being jealous.

jeans *PLURAL NOUN*
casual trousers made of denim

Jeep *NOUN* (**Jeeps**)
(*trademark*) a small sturdy motor car that can be driven over rough ground

jeer *VERB* (**jeers**, **jeering**, **jeered**)
to jeer is to laugh rudely at someone and shout insults at them

jelly *NOUN* (**jellies**)
1 a soft sweet food with a fruit flavour **2** any soft slippery substance

> WORD FAMILY
> **Jellied** food is prepared or cooked in jelly.

jellyfish *NOUN* (**jellyfish**)
a sea animal with a body like jelly and tentacles that can sting

jerk *VERB* (**jerks**, **jerking**, **jerked**)
1 to jerk is to make a sudden sharp movement **2** to jerk something is to pull it suddenly

jerk *NOUN* (**jerks**)
1 a sudden sharp movement **2** (*slang*) a fool

jerky *ADJECTIVE* (**jerkier**, **jerkiest**)
moving with sudden sharp movements
▷ **jerkily** *ADVERB* to move jerkily is to move in a jerky way

jersey *NOUN* (**jerseys**)
a pullover with sleeves

jest *NOUN* (**jests**)
a joke

jest *VERB* (**jests**, **jesting**, **jested**)
to jest is to make jokes
to say something **in jest** is to be joking

jester *NOUN* (**jesters**)
a professional entertainer at a royal court in the Middle Ages

jet [1] *NOUN* (**jets**)
1 a stream of liquid, gas, or flame forced out of a narrow opening **2** a narrow opening from which a jet comes out **3** an aircraft driven by jet engines

jet *VERB* (**jets**, **jetting**, **jetted**)
1 to jet is to come out in a strong stream
2 (*informal*) to jet around is to travel a lot in jet aircraft

jet [2] *NOUN*
1 jet is a hard black mineral **2** a deep glossy black colour

jet engine *NOUN* (**jet engines**)
an engine that drives an aircraft forward by sending out a powerful jet of hot gas at the back

jet lag *NOUN*
jet lag is extreme tiredness that someone feels after a long plane journey because they have not got used to the different time zones

jet-propelled *ADJECTIVE*
driven by jet engines

jetty *NOUN* (**jetties**)
a small landing stage for boats

Jew *NOUN* (**Jews**)
1 a member of the race of people descended from the ancient tribes of Israel **2** someone who believes in Judaism

> WORD FAMILY
> A **Jewish** person is a Jew; **Jewish** also means to do with Judaism.

jewel *NOUN* (**jewels**)
1 a precious stone **2** an ornament containing precious stones

> WORD FAMILY
> Something that is **jewelled** is decorated with jewels • *a jewelled box*

jeweller *NOUN* (**jewellers**)
someone who sells or makes jewellery

jewellery *NOUN*
jewellery is jewels or ornaments that people wear

jib *NOUN* (**jibs**)
1 a triangular sail of a ship, stretching forward from the mast **2** the arm of a crane that lifts things

a b c d e f g h i **j** k l m n o p q r s t u v w x y z

jiffy *NOUN*
(*informal*) a moment • *I won't be a jiffy.*

jig *NOUN* (**jigs**)
1 a lively jumping dance **2** a device that holds something in place while you work on it with tools

jig *VERB* (**jigs, jigging, jigged**)
to jig is to move up and down with quick jerks

jigsaw *NOUN* (**jigsaws**)
1 a saw that can cut curved shapes **2** a jigsaw puzzle

jigsaw puzzle *NOUN* (**jigsaw puzzles**)
a puzzle made of differently shaped pieces that you fit together to make a picture

jingle *VERB* (**jingles, jingling, jingled**)
to jingle is to make a tinkling or clinking sound

jingle *NOUN* (**jingles**)
1 a tinkling or clinking sound • *Just as I was getting ready to go to sleep I heard a jingle of harness and a grunt, and a mule passed me shaking his wet ears.* — Rudyard Kipling, *The Jungle Book* **2** a simple tune or song that is used in an advertisement

job *NOUN* (**jobs**)
1 work that someone does regularly to earn a living • *He got a job as a postman.* **2** a piece of work that needs to be done • *We'll have tea when we've finished this job.* **3** (*informal*) a difficult task • *You'll have a job to lift that box.* **4** (*informal*) a situation or state of affairs • *It's a good job you're here.*
to be **just the job** (*informal*) is to be exactly what you want

jobcentre *NOUN* (**jobcentres**)
a government office with information about jobs that are available

jockey *NOUN* (**jockeys**)
someone who rides horses in races

jodhpurs *PLURAL NOUN* (*say* **jod**- perz)
jodhpurs are trousers for riding a horse, fitting closely from the knee to the ankle

jog *VERB* (**jogs, jogging, jogged**)
1 to jog is to run slowly, especially for exercise **2** to jog someone is to give them a slight knock or push
to jog someone's memory is to help them remember something
▷ **jogger** *NOUN* someone who goes jogging

join *VERB* (**joins, joining, joined**)
1 to join things together, or join one thing to another, is to put or fix them together **2** two or more things join when they come together **3** to join a society or group is to become a member of it
to join in is to take part in something

join *NOUN* (**joins**)
a place where things join

joiner *NOUN* (**joiners**)
someone whose job is to make furniture and other things out of wood

> **WORD FAMILY**
> **Joinery** is the work of making furniture and other things out of wood.

joint *NOUN* (**joints**)
1 a place where things are fixed together **2** the place where two bones fit together **3** a large piece of meat

joint *ADJECTIVE*
shared or done by two or more people or groups • *The song was a joint effort.*

> **WORD FAMILY**
> Two or more people **jointly** do something when they do it together.

joist *NOUN* (**joists**)
a long beam supporting a floor or ceiling

jojoba *NOUN* (*say* hoh- **hoh**- ba)
jojoba is oil from the seeds of a desert plant, used in making shampoo and cosmetics

joke *NOUN* (**jokes**)
1 something that you say or do to make people laugh

joke *VERB* (**jokes, joking, joked**)
to joke is to make jokes, or to talk in a way that is not serious

joker *NOUN* (**jokers**)
1 someone who makes jokes **2** an extra playing card with a picture of a jester on it

jollity *NOUN*
jollity is being happy and cheerful; enjoyment

jolly *ADJECTIVE* (**jollier, jolliest**)
happy and cheerful

jolly *ADVERB*
(*informal*) very • *That film was jolly good!*

jolly *VERB* (**jollies, jollying, jollied**)
to jolly someone along is to make them more cheerful

jolt *VERB* (**jolts, jolting, jolted**)
1 to jolt something or someone is to hit them or move them suddenly and sharply **2** to jolt is to make a sudden sharp movement • *The bus jolted to a halt.*

jolt *NOUN* (**jolts**)
1 a sudden sharp movement • *The plane landed with a jolt.* **2** a surprise or shock

jostle *VERB* (**jostles, jostling, jostled**)
to jostle someone is to push them roughly

jot *NOUN*
a tiny amount • *I don't care a jot.*

jot *VERB* (**jots, jotting, jotted**)
to jot something down is to write it quickly

jotter *NOUN* (**jotters**)
a notebook

joule *NOUN* (**joules**)
(*in science*) a unit of work or energy

journal *NOUN* (**journals**)
1 a newspaper or magazine **2** a diary

journalist *NOUN* (**journalists**)
someone whose job is to write news stories for a newspaper or magazine or on television or radio

> WORD FAMILY
> **Journalism** is the job of writing news stories for a newspaper or magazine or on television or radio; **journalistic** writing is writing of this kind.

journey *NOUN* (**journeys**)
1 going from one place to another **2** the distance or time you take to travel somewhere • *The town is a day's journey away.*

journey *VERB* (**journeys, journeying, journeyed**)
to journey is to go from one place to another

joust *VERB* (**jousts, jousting, jousted**)
to joust is to fight on horseback with lances, as knights did in medieval times

jovial *ADJECTIVE*
cheerful and jolly • *Half a dozen jovial lads were talking about skates in another part of the room.* — Louisa May Alcott, *Little Women*

> WORD FAMILY
> **Joviality** is being cheerful; to say something **jovially** is to say it in a cheerful way.

joy *NOUN* (**joys**)
1 joy is great happiness or pleasure **2** a joy is something that gives happiness

joyful *ADJECTIVE*
very happy
▷ **joyfully** *ADVERB* in a joyful way

joyous *ADJECTIVE*
full of joy; causing joy • *The following days were some of the most joyous that Clara had spent on the mountain.* — Johanna Spyri, *Heidi*
▷ **joyously** *ADVERB* in a joyous way

joyride *NOUN* (**joyrides**)
(*informal*) a ride in a stolen car for amusement

joystick *NOUN* (**joysticks**)
1 (*informal*) the lever that controls the movement of an aircraft **2** a lever for controlling the cursor on a VDU screen, especially in computer games

jubilant *ADJECTIVE* (*say* **joo**- bi- lant)
very happy because you have won or succeeded • *Long lines of pelicans went clanging out to sea; the hum of the insects hushed, and a thousand birds burst into jubilant song.* — Charles Kingsley, *Westward Ho!*

> WORD FAMILY
> To say something **jubilantly** is to say it happily because you have won or succeeded; **jubilation** is rejoicing because you have won or succeeded.

jubilee *NOUN* (**jubilees**)
a special anniversary of an important event

> USING THIS WORD
> A **silver jubilee** is the 25th anniversary, a **golden jubilee** is the 50th anniversary, and a **diamond jubilee** is the 60th anniversary.

Judaism *NOUN* (*say* **joo**- day- izm)
Judaism is the religion of the Jewish people

judge *NOUN* (**judges**)
1 someone who hears cases in a lawcourt and decides what should be done **2** someone who decides who has won a contest or competition **3** someone who is good at forming opinions or making decisions about things • *She's a good judge of musical ability.*

judge *VERB* (**judges, judging, judged**)
1 to judge something is to act as judge in a law case or a competition **2** to judge an amount is to estimate or guess what it is **3** to judge something is to form an opinion about it

judgement *NOUN* (**judgements**)
1 judgement is acting as judge for a law case or a contest **2** a judgement is the decision made by a lawcourt **3** judgement is also the ability to make decisions wisely **4** someone's judgement is their opinion • *In my judgement, you're making a big mistake.*

judicial *ADJECTIVE* (*say* joo- **dish**- al)
to do with lawcourts, judges, or decisions made in lawcourts

judicious *ADJECTIVE* (*say* joo- **dish**- us)
showing good sense or judgement

judo *NOUN* (*say* **joo**- doh)
judo is a Japanese form of unarmed combat for sport

jug *NOUN* (**jugs**)
a container for pouring liquids, with a handle and lip

juggernaut *NOUN* (**juggernauts**)
a very large articulated lorry

juggle *VERB* (**juggles, juggling, juggled**)
to juggle objects is to keep tossing and catching them so that you keep them moving in the air without dropping any
▷ **juggler** *NOUN* someone who juggles at a fair or circus

juice *NOUN* (**juices**)
1 the liquid from fruit, vegetables, or other food **2** a liquid produced by the body, such as the digestive juices
▷ **juicy** *ADJECTIVE* juicy fruit or meat is full of juice

jukebox *NOUN* (**jukeboxes**)
a machine that automatically plays a record of your choice when you put a coin in

July *NOUN*
the seventh month of the year

a b c d e f g h i j k l m n o p q r s t u v w x y z

jumble *VERB* (**jumbles, jumbling, jumbled**)
to jumble things is to mix them up in a confused way

jumble *NOUN*
a confused mixture of things; a muddle

jumble sale *NOUN* (**jumble sales**)
a sale of second-hand goods to raise money

jumbo jet *NOUN* (**jumbo jets**)
a large jet aircraft for carrying a lot of passengers

jump *VERB* (**jumps, jumping, jumped**)
1 to jump is to move suddenly from the ground into the air **2** to jump a fence or other obstacle is to go over it by jumping **3** to jump up or out is to move quickly or suddenly • *He jumped out of his seat.* **4** to jump in or out of a vehicle is to get in or out quickly
to jump at something (*informal*) is to accept it eagerly
to jump the gun is to start something before the right time
to jump the queue is to go in front of people before it is your turn

jump *NOUN* (**jumps**)
1 a sudden movement into the air **2** an obstacle to jump over

jumper *NOUN* (**jumpers**)
a pullover with sleeves

jump suit *NOUN* (**jump suits**)
a piece of clothing made in one piece and covering the whole body

jumpy *ADJECTIVE* (**jumpier, jumpiest**)
nervous and anxious

junction *NOUN* (**junctions**)
a place where roads or railway lines join

June *NOUN*
the sixth month of the year

jungle *NOUN* (**jungles**)
a thick tangled forest, especially in tropical countries

junior *ADJECTIVE*
1 younger **2** for young children • *She goes to a junior school.* **3** lower in rank or importance

junior *NOUN* (**juniors**)
1 a younger person • *Peter is my junior.* **2** a person of lower rank or importance

junk[1] *NOUN*
1 junk is old worthless things that should be thrown away • *The garage is full of junk.* **2** junk is also rubbish

junk[2] *NOUN* (**junks**)
a Chinese sailing boat

junk food *NOUN*
junk food is food that is not nourishing, usually containing a lot of sugar and starch

juror *NOUN* (**jurors**)
a member of a jury

jury *NOUN* (**juries**)
a group of people (usually twelve) chosen to make a decision about a case in a lawcourt, especially whether a person accused of a crime is innocent or guilty

just *ADJECTIVE*
1 fair and right; giving proper thought to everybody **2** deserved • *He got his just reward.*
▷ **justly** *ADVERB* in a just or fair way

just *ADVERB*
1 exactly • *It's just what I wanted.* **2** only; simply • *I just wanted another cake.* **3** barely; by only a short amount • *The ball hit her just below the knee.* **4** a short time ago • *They had just gone.*

justice *NOUN* (**justices**)
1 justice is being just or having fair treatment **2** justice is also the actions of the law • *They were tried in a court of justice.* **3** a justice is a judge or magistrate

justify *VERB* (**justifies, justifying, justified**)
to justify something is to show that it is reasonable or necessary • *Do you think that you were justified in taking such a risk?*

> **WORD FAMILY**
> Something **justifiable** is able to be justified; a **justification** for something is a good reason for doing it.

jut *VERB* (**juts, jutting, jutted**)
to jut, or to jut out, is to stick out

juvenile *ADJECTIVE* (*say* **joo**- vi- nyl)
to do with young people

juvenile *NOUN* (**juveniles**)
a young person who is not yet an adult

Kk

kaleidoscope *NOUN* (**kaleidoscopes**) (*say* kal- **I**- dos- kohp)
a tube that you look through to see brightly-coloured patterns which change as you turn the end of the tube

kangaroo *NOUN* (**kangaroos**)
an Australian animal that moves by jumping on its strong back legs

karaoke *NOUN* (*say* ka- ri- **oh**- ki)
karaoke is a party entertainment in which people sing songs with a recorded background played from a special machine

karate *NOUN* (*say* ka- **rah**- ti)
karate is a Japanese method of self-defence using the hands, arms, and feet

kayak *NOUN* (**kayaks**) (*say* ky- ak)
a small canoe with a covering that fits round the canoeist's waist

kebab *NOUN* (**kebabs**)
small pieces of meat or vegetables grilled on a skewer

keel *NOUN* (**keels**)
the long piece of wood or metal along the bottom of a boat
to be on an even keel is to be steady

keel *VERB* (**keels, keeling, keeled**)
to keel over is to fall sideways or overturn

keen *ADJECTIVE* (**keener, keenest**)
1 enthusiastic or eager • *She is keen on swimming.* • *We are keen to go.* **2** strong or sharp • *The knife had a keen edge.* • *There was a keen wind.*

> WORD FAMILY
> A **keenly** fought contest is one in which people are competing very hard; **keenness** is being keen.

keep *VERB* (**keeps, keeping, kept**)
1 to keep something is to have it and not get rid of it **2** to keep something in a place is to put it there when you aren't using it **3** to keep (for example) well or still is to continue to be well or still **4** to keep someone (for example) warm or happy is to cause them to continue to be warm or happy
5 something keeps when it lasts without going bad • *Will the milk keep until tomorrow?* **6** to keep doing something is to continue to do it • *They kept laughing at her.* **7** to keep your word or promise is to honour it and not break it **8** to keep animals or pets is to have them and look after them
to keep something up is to continue doing it • *Keep up the good work!*
to keep up with someone is to go as fast as them

keep *NOUN* (**keeps**)
1 someone's keep is the food or money they need to live • *They have to earn their keep.* **2** a keep is a strong tower in a castle
for keeps (*informal*) to keep; permanently • *Is this football mine for keeps?*

keeper *NOUN* (**keepers**)
1 someone who looks after the animals in a zoo **2** a goalkeeper

keeping *NOUN*
something is in your keeping when you are looking after it • *The diaries are in safe keeping.*
to be in keeping with something is to fit in with it or be suitable

keg *NOUN* (**kegs**)
a small barrel

kennel *NOUN* (**kennels**)
a shelter for a dog

kenning *NOUN* (**kennings**)
an type of expression or riddle from Anglo-Saxon times, in which something is described without using its name. For example, a *tail-wagger* could be a dog and a *life-taker* could be a sword

kept
past tense and past participle of **keep** *VERB*

kerb *NOUN* (**kerbs**)
the edge of a pavement

kerbstone *NOUN* (**kerbstones**)
a long square stone used to make a kerb

kernel *NOUN* (**kernels**)
the part inside the shell of a nut

kestrel *NOUN* (**kestrels**)
a kind of small falcon

ketchup *NOUN*
ketchup is a thick sauce made from tomatoes

kettle *NOUN* (**kettles**)
a container with a spout and handle, used for boiling water in

kettledrum *NOUN* (**kettledrums**)
a drum made of skin stretched over a large metal bowl

key *NOUN* (**keys**)
1 a piece of metal shaped so that it opens a lock **2** a small lever that you press with your finger, on a piano or keyboard **3** a device for winding up a clock or clockwork toy **4** a scale of musical notes • *It is played in the key of C major.* **5** something that solves a problem or mystery • *Police think they have found the key to the crime.*

keyboard *NOUN* (**keyboards**)
a set of keys on a piano, typewriter, or computer

keyhole *NOUN* (**keyholes**)
the hole through which you put a key into a lock

keynote *NOUN* (**keynotes**)
1 the note on which a key in music is based • *The keynote of C major is C.* **2** the main idea in something that is said, written, or done

key word or **key phrase** *NOUN* (**key words** or **key phrases**)
1 one of the most important words or phrases in a text, that helps you to understand what the text is about **2** a word or phrase that you type into a computer when you are searching for information

kg
short for **kilogram** or **kilograms**

khaki *NOUN* (*say* kah- ki)
a dull yellowish-brown colour, often used for army uniforms

kibbutz *NOUN* (**kibbutzim**)
a farming commune in Israel

kick *VERB* (**kicks, kicking, kicked**)
1 to kick someone or something is to hit them with your foot **2** to kick is to move your legs about vigorously **3** a gun kicks when it moves back sharply as it is fired

to kick off is to start a football match, or (*informal*) to start doing something
to kick someone out is to get rid of them
to kick up a fuss or row (*informal*) is to make a loud fuss or noise

kick *NOUN* (**kicks**)
1 a kicking movement **2** the sudden backwards movement a gun makes when it is fired **3** (*informal*) an interest or activity •*He's on a health kick.*
to get a kick out of something (*informal*) is to enjoy it very much

kick-off *NOUN* (**kick-offs**)
the start of a football match

kid *NOUN* (**kids**)
1 a young goat **2** (*informal*) a child

kid *VERB* (**kids, kidding, kidded**)
(*informal*) to kid someone is to deceive or tease them

kidnap *VERB* (**kidnaps, kidnapping, kidnapped**)
to kidnap someone is to capture them by force, usually to get a ransom

> WORD FAMILY
> A **kidnapper** is a person who kidnaps someone.

kidney *NOUN* (**kidneys**)
each of two organs in your body that remove waste products from your blood and send them as urine to your bladder

kill *VERB* (**kills, killing, killed**)
1 to kill a person or animal is to make them die **2** to kill something like an idea or plan is to make sure it doesn't happen

> WORD FAMILY
> A **killer** is a person who kills someone.

kiln *NOUN* (**kilns**)
an oven for hardening or drying pottery or bricks

kilo *NOUN* (**kilos**)
a kilogram

kilobyte *NOUN* (**kilobytes**)
(*in computing*) a unit that measures data or memory, equal to 1,024 bytes

kilogram *NOUN* (**kilograms**)
a unit of weight equal to 1,000 grams or about 2.2 pounds

kilometre *NOUN* (**kilometres**) (*say* kil- o- mee- ter or kil- **om**- i- ter)
a unit of length equal to 1,000 metres or about $\frac{3}{5}$ of a mile

kilowatt *NOUN* (**kilowatts**)
a unit of electrical power equal to 1,000 watts

kilt *NOUN* (**kilts**)
a kind of pleated skirt worn by men as part of traditional Scottish dress
▷ **kilted** *ADJECTIVE* wearing a kilt

kin *NOUN*
a person's family or relatives
your next of kin is your closest relative

kind [1] *NOUN* (**kinds**)
a type or sort of something •*What kind of food do you like?*
kind of (*informal*) in a way, to some extent •*We kind of hoped you would come.*

kind [2] *ADJECTIVE* (**kinder, kindest**)
helpful and friendly

> WORD FAMILY
> To show **kindness** is to be helpful and friendly.

kindergarten *NOUN* (**kindergartens**) (*say* kin- der- gar- ten)
a school or class for very young children

kind-hearted *ADJECTIVE*
kind and generous

kindle *VERB* (**kindles, kindling, kindled**)
1 to kindle something is to get it to burn **2** to kindle is to start burning

kindling *NOUN*
kindling is small pieces of wood for lighting fires

kindly *ADVERB*
1 in a kind way **2** please •*Kindly close the door.*

kindly *ADJECTIVE* (**kindlier, kindliest**)
kind •*She gave a kindly smile.*
▷ **kindliness** *NOUN* kindliness is being kindly

kinetic *ADJECTIVE* (*say* kin- **et**- ik)
to do with movement, or produced by movement, as in *kinetic energy*

king *NOUN* (**kings**)
1 a man who has been crowned as the ruler of a country **2** a piece in chess that has to be captured to win the game **3** a playing card with a picture of a king
▷ **kingly** *ADJECTIVE* like a king

kingdom *NOUN* (**kingdoms**)
a country that is ruled by a king or queen

kingfisher *NOUN* (**kingfishers**)
a brightly-coloured bird that lives near water and catches fish

king-size or **king-sized** *ADJECTIVE*
larger than the usual size

kink *NOUN* (**kinks**)
a short twist in a rope, wire, or piece of hair

kinky *ADJECTIVE* (**kinkier, kinkiest**)
having odd sexual habits

kiosk *NOUN* (**kiosks**) (*say* **kee**- osk)
1 a telephone box **2** a small hut or stall where you can buy newspapers, sweets, and drinks

kipper *NOUN* (**kippers**)
a smoked herring

kiss *NOUN* (**kisses**)
touching someone with your lips as a sign of affection or greeting

a b c d e f g h i j k l m n o p q r s t u v w x y z

kiss *VERB* (**kisses**, **kissing**, **kissed**)
to kiss someone is to give them a kiss

kiss of life *NOUN*
blowing air from your mouth into someone else's to help them to start breathing again, especially after an accident

kit *NOUN* (**kits**)
1 equipment or clothes that you need to do a sport, a job, or some other activity **2** a set of parts sold to be fitted together to make something • *a model aircraft kit*

kitchen *NOUN* (**kitchens**)
a room where food is prepared and cooked

kite *NOUN* (**kites**)
a light frame covered with cloth or paper that you fly in the wind at the end of a long piece of string

kitten *NOUN* (**kittens**)
a very young cat

kitty[1] *NOUN* (**kitties**)
1 an amount of money that you can win in a card game **2** an amount of money that you put aside for a special purpose

kitty[2] *NOUN* (**kitties**)
(*informal*) a kitten

kiwi *NOUN* (**kiwis**) (*say* kee- wee)
a New Zealand bird that cannot fly

kiwi fruit *NOUN* (**kiwi fruits**)
a fruit with thin hairy skin, soft green flesh, and black seeds

km
short for **kilometre** or **kilometres**

knack *NOUN*
a special skill or talent • *There's a knack to putting up a deckchair.*

knapsack *NOUN* (**knapsacks**)
a bag carried on the back by hikers or soldiers

knave *NOUN* (**knaves**)(*old use*)
1 a dishonest man **2** a jack in a pack of playing cards

knead *VERB* (**kneads**, **kneading**, **kneaded**)
to knead dough or something else soft is to press and stretch it with your hands

knee *NOUN* (**knees**)
the joint in the middle of your leg

kneecap *NOUN* (**kneecaps**)
the bony part at the front of your knee

kneel *VERB* (**kneels**, **kneeling**, **knelt**)
to kneel is to bend your legs so you are resting on your knees

knew
past tense of **know**

knickers *PLURAL NOUN*
underpants worn by women or girls

knife *NOUN* (**knives**)
a cutting instrument made of a short blade set in a handle

knife *VERB* (**knifes**, **knifing**, **knifed**)
to knife someone is to stab them with a knife

knight *NOUN* (**knights**)
1 a man who has been given the honour that lets him put 'Sir' before his name **2** a warrior who had been given the rank of a nobleman, in the Middle Ages **3** a piece in chess, with a horse's head

> **WORD FAMILY**
> A man receives a **knighthood** when he is made a knight.

knight *VERB* (**knights**, **knighting**, **knighted**)
to knight someone is to make them a knight

knit *VERB* (**knits**, **knitting**, **knitted**)
to knit something is to make it by looping together threads of wool or other material, using long needles or a machine

knitting *NOUN*
1 knitting is the activity of making things by knitting **2** knitting is also something that is being made this way

knitting needle *NOUN* (**knitting needles**)
a long large needle used in knitting

knives
plural of **knife** *NOUN*

knob *NOUN* (**knobs**)
1 the round handle of a door or drawer **2** a control to adjust a radio or television set **3** a lump of something

> **WORD FAMILY**
> Something **knobbly** has many lumps or bumps. • *His head was made of a great knobbly turnip, with a broad crack for a mouth and a long thin sprout for a nose and two bright little stones for eyes.* — Philip Pullman, *The Scarecrow and his Servant*

knock *VERB* (**knocks**, **knocking**, **knocked**)
1 to knock something is to hit it hard or bump into it • *Oops, I knocked the vase over.* **2** to knock is to hit something with your hand or fist • *Who's knocking at the door?* **3** (*slang*) to knock someone or something is to criticize them
to knock off (*informal*) is to stop working
to knock someone out is to hit them so that they become unconscious
to knock something off (*slang*) is to steal it

knock *NOUN* (**knocks**)
the act or sound of hitting something

knocker *NOUN* (**knockers**)
a device for knocking on a door

knockout *NOUN* (**knockouts**)
1 knocking someone out **2** a game or contest in which the loser in each round has to drop out **3** (*slang*) an amazing person or thing

a
b
c
d
e
f
g
h
i
j
k
l
m
n
o
p
q
r
s
t
u
v
w
x
y
z

knot *NOUN* (**knots**)
1 a fastening made by tying or looping two ends of string, rope, or ribbon together **2** a round spot on a piece of wood where a branch once joined it **3** a unit for measuring the speed of ships and aircraft, 2,025 yards (or 1,852 metres) per hour **4** a knot of people is a small group of them standing close together

knot *VERB* (**knots, knotting, knotted**)
to knot something is to tie or fasten it with a knot

knotty *ADJECTIVE* (**knottier, knottiest**)
1 full of knots **2** difficult or puzzling • *It's a knotty problem.*

know *VERB* (**knows, knowing, knew, known**)
1 to have something in your mind that you have learned or discovered **2** to know a person or place is to recognize it or be familiar with it • *I've known him for years.*

know-all *NOUN* (**know-alls**)
someone who behaves as if they know everything

know-how *NOUN*
know-how is the skill or knowledge you need for a particular job

knowing *ADJECTIVE*
a knowing look is one that shows that you know something

knowingly *ADVERB*
1 in a knowing way • *He winked at me knowingly.* **2** deliberately • *She would never have done such a thing knowingly.*

knowledge *NOUN* (*say* **nol**- ij)
knowledge is what someone or everybody knows

knowledgeable *ADJECTIVE* (*say* **nol**- ij- a- bul)
knowing a lot about something
▷ **knowledgeably** *ADVERB* in a knowledgeable way

knuckle *NOUN* (**knuckles**)
a joint in your finger

koala *NOUN* (**koalas**) (*say* koh- **ah**- la)
a furry Australian animal that looks like a small bear

kookaburra *NOUN* (**kookaburras**) (*say* **kuuk**- a- bu- ra)
a large Australian kingfisher that makes a laughing or shrieking noise

Koran *NOUN* (*say* kor- **ahn**)
the holy book of Islam, believed by Muslims to contain the words of Allah

kosher *ADJECTIVE* (*say* **koh**- sher)
kosher food is food prepared according to Jewish religious law

kung fu *NOUN* (*say* kuung- **foo**)
kung fu is a Chinese method of self-defence rather like karate

Ll

L
short for **learner**

label *NOUN* (**labels**)
a piece of paper, cloth, or metal fixed on or beside something to show what it is or to give other information about it such as its price

label *VERB* (**labels, labelling, labelled**)
to label something is to put a label on it

laboratory *NOUN* (**laboratories**) (*say* la- **bo**- ra- ter- i)
a room or building equipped for scientific work

laborious *ADJECTIVE*
needing a lot of effort; very hard

> **WORD FAMILY**
> To do something **laboriously** is to use a lot of effort doing it.

labour *NOUN*
1 labour is hard work **2** labour is also the movements of a woman's womb when a baby is born
Labour the Labour Party, a socialist political party

labourer *NOUN* (**labourers**)
someone who does hard work with their hands, especially outdoors

Labrador *NOUN* (**Labradors**)
a large black or light-brown dog

laburnum *NOUN* (**laburnums**)
a tree with hanging yellow flowers

labyrinth *NOUN* (**labyrinths**)
a complicated set of passages or paths; a maze • *McDougal's cave was but a vast labyrinth of crooked aisles that ran into each other and out again and led nowhere.* — Mark Twain, *The Adventures of Tom Sawyer*

lace *NOUN* (**laces**)
1 lace is thin material with decorative patterns of holes in it **2** a lace is a piece of thin cord used to tie up a shoe or boot
▷ **lacy** *ADJECTIVE* like lace or made of lace

lace *VERB* (**laces, lacing, laced**)
1 to lace up a shoe or boot is to fasten it with a lace **2** to lace a drink is to add strong spirits to it

lack *NOUN*
there is a lack of something when there isn't any of it or there isn't enough of it • *The trip was cancelled because of lack of interest.*

lack *VERB* (**lacks, lacking, lacked**)
to lack something is to be without it • *He lacks courage.*

lacquer *NOUN*
lacquer is a kind of varnish

lacrosse *NOUN*
lacrosse is a game using a stick with a net on it (called a *crosse*) to catch and throw a ball

lad *NOUN* (**lads**)
a boy or young man

ladder *NOUN* (**ladders**)
1 a device to help you climb up or down something, made of upright pieces of wood, metal, or rope with crosspieces called rungs **2** a run of damaged stitches in tights or a stocking

laden *ADJECTIVE*
carrying a heavy load

ladle *NOUN* (**ladles**)
a large deep spoon with a long handle, which you use for serving soup or other liquids

lady *NOUN* (**ladies**)
1 a polite name for a woman **2** a well-mannered woman, or a woman of high social standing
Lady the title of a noblewoman

ladybird *NOUN* (**ladybirds**)
a small flying beetle, usually red with black spots

ladylike *ADJECTIVE*
polite and quiet, as a lady is supposed to be

ladyship *NOUN*
a title for a woman of high social standing

lag [1] *VERB* (**lags, lagging, lagged**)
to lag is to go too slowly and not keep up with others • *The little boy was lagging behind.*

lag [2] *VERB* (**lags, lagging, lagged**)
to lag pipes or boilers is to wrap them with insulating material to keep in the heat

lager *NOUN* (**lagers**) (*say* lah-ger)
a light beer

lagoon *NOUN* (**lagoons**)
1 a lake separated from the sea by sandbanks or reefs **2** (*in Australia and New Zealand*) a pond, often one that is stagnant

laid
past tense and past participle of **lay** [1] *VERB*

lain
past participle of **lie** [1] *VERB*

lair *NOUN* (**lairs**)
the place where a wild animal lives

lake *NOUN* (**lakes**)
a large area of water completely surrounded by land

lama *NOUN* (**lamas**)
a Buddhist priest or monk in Tibet and Mongolia

lamb *NOUN* (**lambs**)
1 a lamb is a young sheep **2** lamb is the meat from young sheep

lame *ADJECTIVE* (**lamer, lamest**)
1 not able to walk normally **2** weak and not very convincing • *What a lame excuse.*

> WORD FAMILY
> To say something **lamely** is to say it in a weak and unconvincing way; **lameness** is being lame.

lament *VERB* (**laments, lamenting, lamented**)
to lament something is to express grief or disappointment about it

> WORD FAMILY
> **Lamentation** is expressing grief or disappointment about something.

lament *NOUN* (**laments**)
a song or poem that expresses grief or regret

laminated *ADJECTIVE*
1 made of layers joined together **2** permanently covered in a kind of plastic for protection

lamp *NOUN* (**lamps**)
a device for producing light from electricity, gas, or oil

lamp-post *NOUN* (**lamp-posts**)
a tall post in a street or public place, with a lamp at the top

lampshade *NOUN* (**lampshades**)
a cover for the bulb of an electric lamp, to soften the light

lance *NOUN* (**lances**)
a long spear

lance corporal *NOUN* (**lance corporals**)
a soldier between a private and a corporal in rank

land *NOUN* (**lands**)
1 land or the land is all the dry parts of the world's surface **2** land is an area of ground **3** a land is a country or nation

land *VERB* (**lands, landing, landed**)
1 to land is to come down to the ground from the air • *Where did the arrow land?* **2** to land is also to arrive in a ship or aircraft **3** to land someone or something is to bring them to a place by means of a ship or aircraft **4** (*informal*) to land someone in difficulty or trouble is to cause them difficulty or trouble
to land up (*informal*) is to get to a particular place or situation • *They landed up in France.*

landing *NOUN* (**landings**)
the floor at the top of a flight of stairs

landing stage *NOUN* (**landing stages**)
a platform used for taking people and things on or off a boat

landlady *NOUN* (**landladies**)
1 a woman who lets rooms to lodgers **2** a woman who looks after a pub

landlord *NOUN* (**landlords**)
1 a person who rents a house or land to someone else, or lets rooms to lodgers **2** a person who looks after a pub

a b c d e f g h i j k l m n o p q r s t u v w x y z

landmark *NOUN* (**landmarks**)
an object on land that you can easily see from a distance

landowner *NOUN* (**landowners**)
a person who owns a large amount of land

landscape *NOUN* (**landscapes**)
1 a view of a particular area of town or countryside
2 a picture of the countryside

landscape gardening *NOUN*
laying out gardens to imitate natural scenery

landslide *NOUN* (**landslides**)
1 a landslide is when earth or rocks slide down the side of a hill **2** a landslide is also an overwhelming victory in an election

lane *NOUN* (**lanes**)
1 a narrow road, especially in the country **2** a strip of road for a single line of traffic **3** a strip of track or water for one runner or swimmer in a race

language *NOUN* (**languages**)
1 language is the use of words in speech and writing **2** a language is the words used in a particular country or by a particular group of people **3** a language is also a system of signs or symbols giving information, especially in computing

lanky *ADJECTIVE* (**lankier**, **lankiest**)
awkwardly tall and thin
▷ **lankiness** *NOUN* lankiness is being lanky

lantern *NOUN* (**lanterns**)
a transparent case for holding a light and shielding it from the wind

lap[1] *NOUN* (**laps**)
1 the flat area from the waist to the knees, formed when a person is sitting down **2** going once round a racecourse

lap *VERB* (**laps**, **lapping**, **lapped**)
to lap someone in a race is to be more than one lap ahead of them

lap[2] *VERB* (**laps**, **lapping**, **lapped**)
1 to lap liquid is to drink it with the tongue, as a cat or dog does **2** waves lap when they make a gentle splash on rocks or the shore

lapel *NOUN* (**lapels**) (*say* la- **pel**)
the flap folded back at each front edge of a coat or jacket

lapse *NOUN* (**lapses**)
1 a slight mistake or fault **2** the passing of time •*After a lapse of three months work began again.*

lapse *VERB* (**lapses**, **lapsing**, **lapsed**)
1 to lapse into a state is to pass gradually into it •*He lapsed into unconsciousness.* **2** a contract or document lapses when it is no longer valid •*My passport has lapsed.*

laptop *NOUN* (**laptops**)
a computer small enough to be held and used on your lap, especially while you are travelling

lapwing *NOUN* (**lapwings**)
a black and white bird with a crest on its head and a shrill cry

larch *NOUN* (**larches**)
a tall deciduous tree that produces small cones

lard *NOUN*
lard is white greasy fat from pigs, used in cooking

larder *NOUN* (**larders**)
a cupboard or small room for storing food

large *ADJECTIVE* (**larger**, **largest**)
more than the ordinary or average size; big
to be at large is to be free and dangerous •*The escaped prisoners were still at large.*
▷ **largeness** *NOUN* largeness is being large

largely *ADVERB*
mainly; mostly •*His success is largely a matter of hard work.*

lark[1] *NOUN* (**larks**)
a small sandy-brown bird; a skylark

lark[2] *NOUN* (**larks**)
(*informal*) something amusing; a bit of fun •*They just did it for a lark.*

lark *VERB* (**larks**, **larking**, **larked**)
to lark about is to have fun or play tricks

larva *NOUN* (**larvae**)
an insect in the first stage of its life, after it comes out of the egg

lasagne *NOUN* (*say* la- **zan**- ya)
lasagne is pasta in the form of flat sheets, cooked with minced meat or vegetables and a white sauce

laser *NOUN* (**lasers**) (*say* **lay**- zer)
a device that makes a very strong narrow beam of light

lash *NOUN* (**lashes**)
1 an eyelash **2** a stroke with a whip

lash *VERB* (**lashes**, **lashing**, **lashed**)
1 to lash someone or something is to hit them with a whip or like a whip •*Rain lashed the window.* **2** to lash something is to tie it tightly •*During the storm they lashed the boxes to the mast.*
to lash out is to speak or hit out angrily

lass *NOUN* (**lasses**)
a girl or young woman

lasso *NOUN* (**lassos**) (*say* la- **soo**)
a rope with a loop at the end which tightens when you pull the rope, used for catching cattle

last[1] *ADJECTIVE*
1 coming after all the others; final •*Try not to miss the last bus.* **2** most recent or latest •*Where were you last night?*
the last straw a final or added thing that makes a problem unbearable

last *ADVERB*
at the end; after everything or everyone else •*He came last in the race.*

last *NOUN*
a person or thing that is last • *I think I was the last to arrive.*
at last finally; at the end

last[2] *VERB* (**lasts, lasting, lasted**)
1 to continue • *The journey lasts for two hours.* **2** to go on without being used up • *How long will our supplies last?*

lastly *ADVERB*
in the last place; finally

latch *NOUN* (**latches**)
a small bar fastening a gate or door

late *ADJECTIVE & ADVERB* (**later, latest**)
1 after the proper or expected time **2** near the end of a period of time • *They came late in the afternoon.* **3** recent • *Do you have the latest news?* **4** no longer alive • *They saw the tomb of the late king.*
▷ **lateness** *NOUN* lateness is being late

lately *ADVERB*
recently • *She has been very tired lately.*

latent *ADJECTIVE* (*say* **lay**- tent)
existing but not yet active, developed, or visible

lateral *ADJECTIVE*
to do with the sides of something

lateral thinking *NOUN*
lateral thinking is thinking of unusual ways to solve problems or achieve things

lathe *NOUN* (**lathes**) (*say* layth)
a machine for holding and turning pieces of wood or metal while you shape them

lather *NOUN* (**lathers**)
the thick foam you get when you mix soap with water

Latin *NOUN*
Latin is the language of the ancient Romans

latitude *NOUN* (**latitudes**)
1 the distance of a place north or south of the equator, measured in degrees **2** freedom to do what you want or make decisions

latter *ADJECTIVE*
later • *We'd like a holiday in the latter part of the year.*
the latter the second of two people or things just mentioned • *If it's a choice between a picnic or a swim I prefer the latter.*
See also **former**

latterly *ADVERB*
recently

lattice *NOUN* (**lattices**)
a framework of crossed strips with spaces between

laugh *VERB* (**laughs, laughing, laughed**)
to laugh is to make sounds that show you are happy or that you think something is funny

laugh *NOUN* (**laughs**)
1 the sound you make when you laugh **2** (*informal*) something that is fun or amusing • *Yesterday's party was quite a laugh.*

laughable *ADJECTIVE*
silly and deserving to be laughed at

laughter *NOUN*
laughter is laughing or the sound of laughing

launch[1] *VERB* (**launches, launching, launched**)
1 to launch a ship is to send it into the water for the first time **2** to launch a rocket is to send it into space **3** to launch a new idea or product is to make it available for the first time

launch *NOUN* (**launches**)
the launching of a ship or spacecraft

launch[2] *NOUN* (**launches**)
a large motor boat

launch pad *NOUN* (**launch pads**)
a platform from which rockets are sent into space

launder *VERB* (**launders, laundering, laundered**)
to launder clothes is to wash and iron them

launderette *NOUN* (**launderettes**)
a shop with washing machines that people pay to use

laundry *NOUN* (**laundries**)
1 laundry is clothes to be washed **2** a laundry is a place where clothes are sent or taken to be washed and ironed

laurel *NOUN* (**laurels**)
an evergreen bush with smooth shiny leaves

lava *NOUN*
lava is molten rock that flows from a volcano, or the solid rock formed when it cools

lavatory *NOUN* (**lavatories**)
a place for getting rid of waste from the body

lavender *NOUN*
1 lavender is a shrub with pale purple flowers that smell very sweet **2** a pale purple colour

lavish *ADJECTIVE*
1 generous • *They are lavish with their gifts.*
2 plentiful • *What a lavish meal!*

law *NOUN* (**laws**)
1 a rule or set of rules that everyone must keep **2** something that always happens, for example the law of gravity

lawcourt *NOUN* (**lawcourts**)
a room or building where a judge and jury or a magistrate decide whether someone has broken the law

lawful *ADJECTIVE*
allowed or accepted by the law

> **WORD FAMILY**
> To do something **lawfully** is to do it in a way that is allowed or accepted by the law.

lawless *ADJECTIVE*
a lawless place doesn't have any proper laws • *It was a lawless country.*

lawn *NOUN* (**lawns**)
an area of mown grass in a garden

lawnmower *NOUN* (**lawnmowers**)
a machine with revolving blades for cutting grass

lawsuit *NOUN* (**lawsuits**)
a dispute or claim that is brought to a lawcourt to be settled

lawyer *NOUN* (**lawyers**)
a person whose job is to help people with the law

lax *ADJECTIVE*
not strict; tolerant • *Discipline was very lax.*

laxative *NOUN* (**laxatives**)
a medicine that you take to empty your bowels

lay[1] *VERB* (**lays, laying, laid**)
1 to lay something somewhere is to put it down in a particular place or in a particular way **2** to lay a table is to arrange things on it for a meal **3** to lay an egg is to produce it **4** to lay plans is to form or prepare them
to lay someone off is to stop employing them
to lay something on is to supply or provide it
to lay something out is to arrange or prepare it

> GRAMMAR
> Take care not to confuse **lay** with **lie**[1], as in *Don't lie on the floor*, which doesn't have an object. Remember that **lay** can also be the past tense of **lie**[1], as in • *The dog lay in front of the fire; he had been lying there all night.*

lay[2]
past tense of **lie**[1] *VERB*

layabout *NOUN* (**layabouts**)
a lazy person

layer *NOUN* (**layers**)
something flat that lies on or under something else • *The cake had a layer of icing on top and a layer of jam inside.*

> SPELLING
> Take care not to confuse **layer** with **lair**, which is the place where a wild animal lives.

layman *NOUN* (**laymen**)
a person who does not have special knowledge of a subject

layout *NOUN* (**layouts**)
the arrangement or design of something

laze *VERB* (**lazes, lazing, lazed**)
to laze is to spend time in a lazy way

lazy *ADJECTIVE* (**lazier, laziest**)
not wanting to work; doing as little as possible

> WORD FAMILY
> To do something **lazily** is to do it in a lazy way; **laziness** is being lazy.

lb.
short for **pound** or **pounds** in weight

l.b.w.
short for **leg before wicket**

lead[1] *VERB* (**leads, leading, led**) (*say* leed)
1 to lead a person or animal is to guide them, especially by going in front **2** to lead an activity is to be in charge of it **3** to lead in a race or contest is to be winning it **4** a road or path leads somewhere when it goes in that direction • *This road leads to the beach.* **5** to lead is to play the first card in a card game
to lead to something is to cause it • *Their carelessness led to the accident.*

lead *NOUN* (**leads**) (*say* leed)
1 the first or front place or position • *Who's in the lead now?* **2** help or guidance • *Just follow my lead.* **3** a strap or cord for leading a dog **4** an electric wire • *Don't trip over that lead.*

lead[2] *NOUN* (**leads**) (*say* led)
1 lead is a soft heavy grey metal **2** a lead is the writing substance (graphite) in the middle of a pencil

leader *NOUN* (**leaders**)
1 someone who leads or is in charge **2** an article in a newspaper, giving the editor's opinion

> WORD FAMILY
> **Leadership** is being a leader.

leaf *NOUN* (**leaves**)
1 a flat and usually green growth on a tree or plant, growing from its stem **2** a page of a book **3** a very thin sheet of metal, such as gold leaf **4** a flap that makes a table larger
to turn over a new leaf is to make a fresh start and improve your behaviour

> WORD FAMILY
> A **leafy** tree or plant has a lot of leaves.

leaflet *NOUN* (**leaflets**)
a piece of paper printed with information

league *NOUN* (**leagues**) (*say* leeg)
1 a group of teams that play matches against each other **2** a group of countries that have agreed to work together for a particular reason
to be in league with someone is to work or plot together

leak *NOUN* (**leaks**)
1 a hole or crack through which liquid or gas escapes **2** the revealing of some secret information

> WORD FAMILY
> A **leaky** pipe or tap has a leak.

leak *VERB* (**leaks, leaking, leaked**)
1 something leaks when it lets something out through a hole or crack • *The sink is leaking.* **2** liquid or gas leaks out when it escapes from a container **3** to leak secret information is to reveal it

> WORD FAMILY
> A **leakage** is an escape of liquid or gas from a container.

lean[1] *VERB* (**leans**, **leaning**, **leaned** or **leant**)
1 to lean is to bend your body towards something or over it **2** to lean something is to put it into a sloping position • *Do not lean bicycles against the window.* **3** to lean against something is to rest against it

lean[2] *ADJECTIVE* (**leaner**, **leanest**)
1 lean meat has little fat **2** a lean person is thin

leap *NOUN* (**leaps**)
1 a high or long jump **2** a sudden increase or advance

leap *VERB* (**leaps**, **leaping**, **leapt** or **leaped**)
1 to leap is to jump high or a long way **2** to leap is also to increase or advance suddenly

leapfrog *NOUN*
a game in which each player jumps with legs apart over another player who is bending down

leap year *NOUN* (**leap years**)
a year with an extra day in it, on 29 February

learn *VERB* (**learns**, **learning**, **learnt** or **learned**)
1 to learn something is to find out about it and gain knowledge or skill in it • *She's learning to play the guitar.* **2** to learn something is to discover some news • *I was sorry to learn that he was ill.*

learned *ADJECTIVE* (*say* ler- nid)
clever and knowledgeable

learner *NOUN* (**learners**)
someone who is learning something, for example how to drive a car

learning *NOUN*
learning is knowledge you get by studying

lease *NOUN* (**leases**)
an agreement to let someone use a building or land for a fixed period in return for a payment
a new lease of life is a chance to go on being active or useful

leash *NOUN* (**leashes**)
a strap or cord for leading a dog

least *ADJECTIVE & ADVERB*
smallest; less than all the others • *I'll get the least expensive bike.* • *I like this one least.*
at least 1 not less than what is mentioned • *It will cost at least £50.* **2** anyway • *He's at home; at least I think he is.*

least *NOUN*
the smallest amount

leather *NOUN* (**leathers**)
leather is a strong material made from animals' skins

> **WORD FAMILY**
> Something **leathery** is tough like leather.

leave *VERB* (**leaves**, **leaving**, **left**)
1 to leave a person, place, or group is to go away from them **2** to leave something is to let it stay where it is or remain as it is • *You can leave your bags by the door.* **3** to leave something to someone is to give it to them in a will
to leave something or **someone out** is not to include them
to be left over is to remain when other things have been used

leave *NOUN*
1 permission, especially to be away from work
2 the time when someone is allowed to be away from work • *They get 30 days' leave.*

leaves
plural of **leaf**

lectern *NOUN* (**lecterns**)
a stand to hold a Bible or other large book from which you read

lecture *NOUN* (**lectures**)
1 a talk about a subject to an audience or a class **2** a long or serious warning given to someone • *We got a lecture about closing the windows.*

lecture *VERB* (**lectures**, **lecturing**, **lectured**)
to lecture is to give a lecture
▷ **lecturer** *NOUN* someone who gives a lecture

led
past tense and past participle of **lead** *VERB*

ledge *NOUN* (**ledges**)
a narrow shelf

lee *NOUN*
the sheltered side of something, away from the wind

leek *NOUN* (**leeks**)
a long green and white vegetable like an onion with broad leaves

leer *VERB* (**leers**, **leering**, **leered**)
to leer at someone is to look at them in an unpleasant or evil way

leeward *ADJECTIVE*
facing away from the wind

left[1] *ADJECTIVE & ADVERB*
1 on or towards the west if you think of yourself as facing north **2** in favour of political and social change

left *NOUN*
the left side

left[2]
past tense and past participle of **leave** *VERB*

left-hand *ADJECTIVE*
on the left side of something

left-handed *ADJECTIVE*
using the left hand more than the right hand

leftovers *PLURAL NOUN*
food that has not been eaten by the end of a meal

leg *NOUN* (**legs**)
1 one of the parts of a human's or animal's body on which they stand or move **2** one of the parts of a pair of trousers that cover your leg **3** each of the supports of a chair or other piece of furniture **4** one part of a journey **5** each of a pair of matches between the same teams in a competition
to be on your last legs is to be exhausted

a b c d e f g h i j k **l** m n o p q r s t u v w x y z

legacy *NOUN* (**legacies**)
something given to someone in a will

legal *ADJECTIVE*
1 allowed by the law **2** to do with the law or lawyers

> **WORD FAMILY**
> The **legality** of something is whether it is legal or not; to do something **legally** is to do it in a way that is allowed by law.

legalize *VERB* (**legalizes**, **legalizing**, **legalized**)
to legalize something is to make it legal

legend *NOUN* (**legends**) (*say* **lej**- end)
an old story handed down from the past

> **WORD FAMILY**
> Something or someone **legendary** is mentioned in legends or is very famous. • *the legendary knight Sir Galahad*

legible *ADJECTIVE*
clear enough to read • *Make sure your writing is legible.*

> **WORD FAMILY**
> The **legibility** of a piece of writing is how easy it is to read; to write something **legibly** is to write it in a way that is easy to read.

legion *NOUN* (**legions**)
1 a division of the ancient Roman army **2** a group of soldiers, or men who used to be soldiers

legislate *VERB* (**legislates**, **legislating**, **legislated**)
to legislate is to make laws

> **WORD FAMILY**
> **Legislation** is making laws; a **legislator** is someone who makes laws.

legitimate *ADJECTIVE* (*say* li- **jit**- i- mat)
1 allowed by a law or rule **2** (*old use*) born of parents who were married to each other

> **WORD FAMILY**
> The **legitamacy** of something is whether or not it is allowed by a law or rule; to do something **legitimately** is to do it in a legitimate way.

legume *NOUN* (**legumes**) (*say* **leg**- yewm)
a plant that has seeds in long pods, such as peas and beans

leisure *NOUN*
leisure is free time, when you can do what you like
to do something at leisure is to do it without hurrying

leisurely *ADJECTIVE*
done with plenty of time, without hurrying • *They took a leisurely stroll down to the river.*

lemon *NOUN* (**lemons**)
1 a yellow citrus fruit with a sour taste **2** a pale yellow colour

lemonade *NOUN* (**lemonades**)
a drink with a lemon flavour

lend *VERB* (**lends**, **lending**, **lent**)
1 to lend something to someone is to let them have it for a short time **2** to lend someone money is to give them money which they must pay back plus an extra amount called interest
to lend a hand is to help someone

length *NOUN* (**lengths**)
1 how long something is **2** a piece of something cut from a longer piece, for example rope, wire, or cloth **3** the distance of a swimming pool from one end to the other
at length after a while; eventually

lengthen *VERB* (**lengthens**, **lengthening**, **lengthened**)
1 to lengthen something is to make it longer **2** to lengthen is to become longer

lengthways or **lengthwise** *ADVERB*
from end to end; along the longest part of something • *Slice the carrots lengthways.*

lengthy *ADJECTIVE* (**lengthier**, **lengthiest**)
going on for a long time • *He gave a lengthy speech.*

lenient *ADJECTIVE* (*say* **lee**- ni- ent)
not as strict as expected, especially when punishing someone

> **WORD FAMILY**
> To show **leniency** is to be not as strict as expected; to punish someone **leniently** is to do so without being too strict.

lens *NOUN* (**lenses**)
1 a curved piece of glass or plastic used to focus images of things, or to concentrate light **2** the transparent part of the eye, behind the pupil

Lent *NOUN*
Lent is a period of about six weeks before Easter when some Christians give up something they enjoy

lent
past tense and past participle of **lend**

lentil *NOUN* (**lentils**)
a kind of small bean

leopard *NOUN* (**leopards**) (*say* **lep**- erd)
a large spotted wild animal of the cat family

leotard *NOUN* (**leotards**) (*say* **lee**- o- tard)
a close-fitting piece of clothing worn by acrobats and dancers

leper *NOUN* (**lepers**)
someone who has leprosy

leprosy *NOUN*
leprosy is an infectious disease that affects the skin and nerves, and causes parts of the body to waste away

less *ADJECTIVE & ADVERB*
smaller; not so much • *Make less noise.* • *It is less important.*

less *NOUN*
a smaller amount • *I have less than you.*

less *PREPOSITION*
minus; deducting • *She earned $100, less tax.*

-less *SUFFIX*
forming adjectives meaning 'lacking something' or 'free from something', such as *smokeless* and *useless*

lessen *VERB* (**lessens**, **lessening**, **lessened**)
1 to lessen something is to make it smaller or not so much **2** to lessen is to become smaller or not so much

lesser *ADJECTIVE*
the smaller or less great of two things • *This is the lesser evil.*

lesson *NOUN* (**lessons**)
1 the time when someone is teaching you
2 something that you have to learn **3** a passage from the Bible read aloud as part of a church service

lest *CONJUNCTION*
so that something should not happen • *He ran away lest he should be seen.*

let *VERB* (**lets**, **letting**, **let**)
1 to let someone do something is to allow them to do it **2** to let something happen is to cause it or not prevent it • *Don't let your bike slide into the ditch.*
3 to let a house or room or building is to allow someone to use it in return for payment **4** to let someone in or out is to allow them to go in or out
to let on (*informal*) is to reveal a secret • *If I tell you, don't let on.*
to let someone down is to disappoint them
to let someone off is to excuse them from a punishment or duty
to let something off is to make it explode
to let up is to relax or do less work

lethal *ADJECTIVE*
something that is lethal can kill you

let's *VERB*
(*informal*) shall we? • *Let's go to the park.*

letter *NOUN* (**letters**)
1 one of the symbols used for writing words, such as a, b, or c **2** a written message sent to another person

letter box *NOUN* (**letter boxes**)
a box or slot into which letters are delivered or posted

lettering *NOUN*
lettering is letters drawn or painted

lettuce *NOUN* (**lettuces**)
a green vegetable with crisp leaves used in salads

leukaemia *NOUN* (*say* lew- **kee**- mi- a)
leukaemia is a disease in which there are too many white cells in the blood

level *ADJECTIVE*
1 flat or horizontal • *The ground is level near the house.* **2** at the same height or position • *Are these pictures level?*

level *VERB* (**levels**, **levelling**, **levelled**)
1 to level something is to make it flat or horizontal
2 to level, or to level out, is to become horizontal
3 to level a gun at a target is to aim it

level *NOUN* (**levels**)
1 height or position • *Fix the shelf at eye level.* **2** a standard or grade of achievement • *She has reached level 3 in gymnastics.* **3** a device that shows if something is horizontal **4** a flat or horizontal surface
to be on the level (*informal*) is to be honest

level crossing *NOUN* (**level crossings**)
a place where a road crosses a railway at the same level

lever *NOUN* (**levers**)
a bar that is pushed or pulled to lift something heavy, force something open, or make a machine work

leverage *NOUN*
leverage is the force you need when you use a lever

lexical *ADJECTIVE*
to do with the words of a language

liability *NOUN* (**liabilities**)
1 liability is being legally liable for something **2** a liability is a debt or obligation **3** a liability is also a disadvantage or handicap

liable *ADJECTIVE*
1 likely to do or get something • *Parking on the yellow lines makes you liable to a fine.* **2** responsible for something

liar *NOUN* (**liars**)
someone who tells lies

liberal *ADJECTIVE*
1 tolerant of other people's point of view
2 generous • *She is liberal with her money.*
Liberal a supporter of the Liberal Party, now part of the Liberal Democrats

> WORD FAMILY
> To do something **liberally** is to do it in large amounts or generously • *Pour the cream on liberally.*

liberate *VERB* (**liberates**, **liberating**, **liberated**)
to liberate someone is to set them free

> WORD FAMILY
> **Liberation** is setting someone free.

liberty *NOUN* (**liberties**)
liberty is freedom
to take liberties is to behave too casually or informally

librarian *NOUN* (**librarians**)
someone who looks after a library or works in one

> WORD FAMILY
> **Librarianship** is the work of a librarian.

library *NOUN* (**libraries**)
a place where books are kept for people to use or borrow

lice
plural of **louse**

a b c d e f g h i j k **l** m n o p q r s t u v w x y z

licence *NOUN* (**licences**)
an official document allowing someone to do or use or own something

> SPELLING
> Take care not to confuse **licence**, which is a noun, with **license**, which is a verb and is the next word in this dictionary.

license *VERB* (**licenses, licensing, licensed**)
to license someone to do something is to give them a licence to do it • *We are not licensed to sell alcoholic drinks.*

lichen *NOUN* (**lichens**) (*say* **ly**- ken)
a dry-looking plant that grows on rocks, walls, trees, and other surfaces

lick *VERB* (**licks, licking, licked**)
1 to lick something is to move your tongue over it **2** (*informal*) to lick someone is to defeat them

lick *NOUN* (**licks**)
the act of moving your tongue over something
to do something at a lick (*informal*) is to do it very fast

lid *NOUN* (**lids**)
1 a cover for a box or jar **2** an eyelid

lie[1] *VERB* (**lies, lying, lay, lain**)
1 to lie is to be in or get into a flat position, especially to rest with your body flat as it is in bed • *He lay on the grass.* • *The cat has lain here all night.* **2** to lie is also to be or remain a certain way • *The castle was lying in ruins.* • *The valley lay before us.*
to lie low is to keep yourself hidden

> GRAMMAR
> Take care not to confuse **lie** *VERB* with **lay** *VERB*, which takes an object as in *laying an egg* and *laying something down.*

lie[2] *VERB* (**lies, lying, lied**)
to lie is to say something that you know is not true

lie *NOUN* (**lies**)
something you say that you know is not true

lieutenant *NOUN* (**lieutenants**) (*say* lef- **ten**- ant)
an officer in the army or navy

life *NOUN* (**lives**)
1 a person's or animal's life is the time between their birth and death **2** life is being alive and able to grow **3** life is also all living things • *Is there life on Mars?* **4** life is also liveliness • *She is full of life.* **5** the life of a famous person is the story of what they have done

lifebelt *NOUN* (**lifebelts**)
a large ring that will float, used to support someone's body in water

lifeboat *NOUN* (**lifeboats**)
a boat for rescuing people at sea

life cycle *NOUN* (**life cycles**)
the series of changes in the life of a living thing • *The diagram shows the life cycle of a frog.*

lifeguard *NOUN* (**lifeguards**)
someone whose job is to rescue swimmers who are in difficulty

life jacket *NOUN* (**life jackets**)
a jacket of material that will float, used to support a person in water

lifeless *ADJECTIVE*
1 without life **2** unconscious

lifelike *ADJECTIVE*
looking exactly like a real person or thing

lifelong *ADJECTIVE*
lasting throughout someone's life

lifespan *NOUN* (**lifespans**)
how long a person or animal or plant lives

lifestyle *NOUN* (**lifestyles**)
the way of life of a person or a group of people

lifetime *NOUN* (**lifetimes**)
the period of time during which someone is alive

lift *VERB* (**lifts, lifting, lifted**)
1 to lift something is to pick it up or move it to a higher position **2** to lift is to rise or go upwards **3** (*informal*) to lift something is to steal it

lift *NOUN* (**lifts**)
1 a movement upwards **2** a device for taking people or goods from one floor to another in a building **3** a ride in someone else's car or other vehicle

lift-off *NOUN* (**lift-offs**)
the vertical take-off of a rocket or spacecraft

light[1] *NOUN* (**lights**)
1 light is the form of energy that makes things visible, the opposite of darkness • *There was not enough light to see the garden.* **2** a light is something that provides light or a flame, especially an electric lamp • *Switch on the light.*

light *ADJECTIVE* (**lighter, lightest**)
1 full of light; not dark **2** pale • *The house was painted light blue.*

light *VERB* (**lights, lighting, lit** or **lighted**)
1 to light something is to start it burning **2** to light is to begin to burn • *The fire won't light.* **3** to light a place is to give it light • *The streets were lit by gaslamps.*
to light up is to become bright with lights
to light something up is to make it bright with lights

light[2] *ADJECTIVE* (**lighter, lightest**)
1 not heavy; weighing little **2** not large or strong • *There is a light wind.* **3** not needing much effort • *They were doing some light work in the garden.* **4** pleasant and entertaining rather than serious • *We prefer light music.*

> WORD FAMILY
> **Lightly** means gently or only a little. • *He kissed her lightly on the cheek.* • *It began to snow lightly.*

lighten *VERB* (**lightens, lightening, lightened**)
1 to lighten something is to make it lighter or brighter **2** to lighten is to become lighter

lighter *NOUN* (**lighters**)
a device for lighting something like a cigarette or a fire

light-hearted *ADJECTIVE*
1 cheerful; free from worry **2** not serious
▷ **light-heartedly** *ADVERB* in a light-hearted way
▷ **light-heartedness** *NOUN* light-heartedness is being light-hearted

lighthouse *NOUN* (**lighthouses**)
a tower with a bright light at the top to guide ships and warn them of danger

lighting *NOUN*
lighting is lamps or the light they provide

lightning *NOUN*
lightning is a flash of bright light in the sky during a thunderstorm

lightning conductor *NOUN* (**lightning conductors**)
a metal wire or rod fixed on a building to divert lightning into the earth

lightweight *ADJECTIVE*
less than average weight

light year *NOUN* (**light years**)
the distance that light travels in one year (about 9.5 million million kilometres or 6 million million miles)

like [1] *VERB* (**likes, liking, liked**)
to like someone or something is to think they are pleasant or satisfactory
should like or **would like** to want • *I should like to see him.*

like [2] *PREPOSITION*
1 resembling; similar to; in the manner of • *He cried like a baby.* **2** such as • *We need things like knives and forks.* **3** typical of • *It was like her to forgive him.*
like anything (*informal*) very much • *She wanted like anything to become a doctor.*

likeable *ADJECTIVE*
pleasant and easy to like

likely *ADJECTIVE* (**likelier, likeliest**)
probable; expected to happen or to be true or suitable • *It's likely that it will rain this afternoon.*

liken *VERB* (**likens, likening, likened**)
to liken one thing to another is to compare them or show that they are similar

likeness *NOUN* (**likenesses**)
a resemblance

likewise *ADVERB*
similarly; in the same way

liking *NOUN* (**likings**)
a feeling that you like something or someone • *She has a great liking for chocolate.*
to be to someone's liking is to be what they like • *These shoes are not to my liking.*

lilac *NOUN* (**lilacs**)
1 lilac is a bush with sweet-smelling purple or white flowers **2** a pale purple colour

lily *NOUN* (**lilies**)
a trumpet-shaped flower grown from a bulb

limb *NOUN* (**limbs**)
a leg, arm, or wing

limber *VERB* (**limbers, limbering, limbered**)
to limber up is to do exercises to be ready for a sport or athletic activity

lime [1] *NOUN* (**limes**)
a green fruit like a small round lemon

lime [2] *NOUN* (**limes**)
a tree with yellow blossom

lime [3] *NOUN*
lime is a white chalky powder (calcium oxide) used in making cement or as a fertilizer

limelight *NOUN*
to be in the limelight is to get a lot of publicity and attention

limerick *NOUN* (**limericks**) (*say* **lim**- er- ik)
an amusing poem with five lines and a strong rhythm

> USING THIS WORD
> Limericks usually start 'There was a young lady (or man, and so on) from Leeds (or Paris, and so on), who ...' You will find lots of examples in poetry books. See if you can make up your own.

limestone *NOUN*
limestone is rock from which lime (calcium oxide) is made, used in building and in making cement

limit *NOUN* (**limits**)
1 a line or point that you cannot or should not pass • *You must obey the speed limit.* **2** a line or edge where something ends • *The white line marks the limit of the road.*

> WORD FAMILY
> Something that is **limitless** has no limit.

limit *VERB* (**limits, limiting, limited**)
to limit something or someone is to keep them within a limit • *You are limited to one choice each.*

> WORD FAMILY
> A **limitation** is a thing that stops something or someone from going beyond a certain point.

limited *ADJECTIVE*
kept within limits; not great • *The choice was limited.*

limited company *NOUN* (**limited companies**)
a business company whose members are responsible for only some of its debts

limp [1] *VERB* (**limps, limping, limped**)
to limp is to walk with difficulty because something is wrong with your leg or foot

limp *NOUN* (**limps**)
a limping movement

a b c d e f g h i j k **l** m n o p q r s t u v w x y z

a b c d e f g h i j k **l** m n o p q r s t u v w x y z

limp[2] *ADJECTIVE* (**limper**, **limpest**)
not stiff or firm; without much strength • *He gave me a limp handshake.*

> **WORD FAMILY**
> Something hangs **limply** when it does so in a limp way. • *Her hair hung limply over her forehead.*

limpet *NOUN* (**limpets**)
a small shellfish that attaches itself firmly to rocks

line[1] *NOUN* (**lines**)
1 a long thin mark made on a surface **2** a row or series of people or things **3** a length of something long and thin like rope, string, or wire **4** a number of words together in a play, film, poem, or song **5** a railway or a length of railway track **6** a company operating a transport service of ships, aircraft, or buses **7** a way of working or behaving; a type of business • *What line are you in?*
in line 1 forming a straight line **2** obeying or behaving well

line *VERB* (**lines**, **lining**, **lined**)
1 to line something is to mark it with lines **2** to line a place is to form an edge or border along it • *People lined the streets to watch the race.*
to line up is to form lines or rows • *The children lined up in the playground.*
to line things up is to set them up in a line or row

line[2] *VERB* (**lines**, **lining**, **lined**)
to line material or a piece of clothing is to put a lining on it

line graph *NOUN* (**line graphs**)
a simple graph, using a line to show how two amounts are related

linen *NOUN*
1 linen is cloth made from flax, used to make shirts, sheets, tablecloths, and so on **2** linen is also things made of this cloth

liner *NOUN* (**liners**)
a large ship or aircraft, usually carrying passengers

linesman *NOUN* (**linesmen**)
an official in football, tennis, and other games who decides whether the ball has crossed a line

linger *VERB* (**lingers**, **lingering**, **lingered**)
to linger is to stay for a long time or be slow to leave • *The smell of her perfume lingered in the room.*

lingerie *NOUN* (*say* **lan**- *zher*- ee)
lingerie is women's underclothes

linguist *NOUN* (**linguists**)
an expert in languages, or someone who can speak several languages well
▷ **linguistic** *ADJECTIVE* to do with languages

linguistics *NOUN*
linguistics is the study of language

lining *NOUN* (**linings**)
a layer of material covering the inside of something

link *NOUN* (**links**)
1 one of the rings in a chain **2** a connection between two things

link *VERB* (**links**, **linking**, **linked**)
to link things is to join them together
to link up is to become connected

lino *NOUN*
lino is linoleum

linoleum *NOUN* (*say* lin- **oh**- li- um)
linoleum is a stiff shiny floor covering

lint *NOUN*
lint is a soft material for covering wounds

lion *NOUN* (**lions**)
a large strong flesh-eating animal found in Africa and India

lioness *NOUN* (**lionesses**)
a female lion

lip *NOUN* (**lips**)
1 each of the two fleshy edges of the mouth **2** the edge of something hollow such as a cup or a crater **3** the pointed part at the top of a jug or saucepan, for pouring from

lip-read *VERB* (**lip-reads**, **lip-reading**, **lip-read**)
to lip-read is to understand what someone is saying by watching the movements of their lips, not by hearing their voice

lipstick *NOUN* (**lipsticks**)
a stick of a waxy substance for colouring the lips

liquid *NOUN* (**liquids**)
a substance (such as water or oil) that can flow but is not a gas

liquid *ADJECTIVE*
in the form of a liquid; flowing freely

liquidizer *NOUN* (**liquidizers**)
a device for making food into a pulp or a liquid

liquor *NOUN* (**liquors**) (*say* **lik**- er)
liquor is alcoholic drink

liquorice *NOUN* (*say* **lik**- er- iss)
liquorice is a soft black sweet with a strong taste, which comes from the root of a plant

lisp *NOUN* (**lisps**)
a fault in speaking, in which *s* and *z* are pronounced like *th*

lisp *VERB* (**lisps**, **lisping**, **lisped**)
to lisp is to speak with a lisp

list[1] *NOUN* (**lists**)
a number of names or figures or items written or printed one after another

list *VERB* (**lists**, **listing**, **listed**)
to list things is to write or say them one after another

list[2] *VERB* (**lists**, **listing**, **listed**)
a ship lists when it leans over to one side in the water

listen *VERB* (**listens**, **listening**, **listened**)
to listen to someone or something is to pay attention so that you can hear them • *Listen to me.* • *I like listening to music.*
▷ **listener** *NOUN* someone who is listening

listless *ADJECTIVE*
too tired to be active or enthusiastic
▷ **listlessly** *ADVERB* in a listless way

lit
past tense and past participle of **light** *VERB*

literacy *NOUN* (*say* **lit**- er- a- si)
literacy is the ability to read and write

literal *ADJECTIVE*
1 meaning exactly what it says **2** word for word • *Write out a literal translation.*

literally *ADVERB*
really; exactly as stated • *The noise made me literally jump out of my seat.*

literary *ADJECTIVE* (*say* **lit**- er- er- i)
to do with literature; interested in literature

literate *ADJECTIVE* (*say* **lit**- er- at)
able to read and write

literature *NOUN*
literature is books or writings, especially the best or most famous

litmus *NOUN*
litmus is a blue substance used to show whether something is an acid or an alkali

litmus paper *NOUN*
litmus paper is paper stained with litmus

litre *NOUN* (**litres**) (*say* **lee**- ter)
a measure of liquid, 1,000 cubic centimetres or about $1\frac{3}{4}$ pints

litter *NOUN* (**litters**)
1 litter is rubbish or untidy things left lying about **2** a litter is a number of young animals born to one mother at one time

litter *VERB* (**litters**, **littering**, **littered**)
to litter a place is to make it untidy with litter

little *ADJECTIVE* (**less** or **littler**, **least** or **littlest**)
1 small; not great or not much • *She brought a little boy.* • *We have very little time.* **2** a small amount of something • *Have a little sugar.*
little by little gradually

little *ADVERB*
not much

live[1] *VERB* (**lives**, **living**, **lived**) (*rhymes with* **give**)
1 to live is to be alive **2** to live in a particular place is to have your home there • *She is living in Glasgow.* **3** to live in a certain way is to pass your life in that way • *He lived as a hermit.*
to live on something is to have it as food or income • *The islanders lived mainly on fish.* • *No one can live on £30 a week.*

live[2] *ADJECTIVE* (*rhymes with* **hive**)
1 alive **2** carrying electricity **3** broadcast while it is actually happening, not from a recording

livelihood *NOUN* (**livelihoods**) (*say* **lyv**- li- huud)
a person's livelihood is the way in which they earn a living

lively *ADJECTIVE* (**livelier**, **liveliest**)
cheerful and full of life and energy
▷ **liveliness** *NOUN* liveliness is being lively

> GRAMMAR
> There is no adverb *livelily*, because it would be too difficult to say.

liver *NOUN* (**livers**)
1 a large organ in the body that produces bile and helps keep the blood clean **2** an animal's liver used as food

livery *NOUN* (**liveries**)
the special colours used by a railway or bus company or airline

lives
plural of **life**

livestock *NOUN*
livestock is farm animals

livid *ADJECTIVE*
1 very angry **2** of a dark blue-grey colour, like bruised skin

living *NOUN* (**livings**)
1 the way that a person lives • *They have a good standard of living.* **2** a means of earning money • *What do you do for a living?*

living room *NOUN* (**living rooms**)
a room for sitting and relaxing in

lizard *NOUN* (**lizards**)
a reptile with a scaly skin, four legs, and a long tail

llama *NOUN* (**llamas**) (*say* **lah**- ma)
a South American animal with woolly fur

load *NOUN* (**loads**)
1 something that is being carried **2** an amount that can be carried **3** (*informal*) a large amount • *It's a load of nonsense.*

load *VERB* (**loads**, **loading**, **loaded**)
1 to load something is to put things into it so they can be carried • *I'll go and load the back of the car.* **2** to load someone with something is to give them large amounts of it • *They loaded him with gifts.* **3** to load a gun is to put a bullet or shell into it **4** to load a machine is to put something it needs into it, such as a film in a camera or a cassette in a tape recorder **5** to load a computer is to enter programs or data on it **6** to load dice is to put a weight into them to make them fall in a special way

loaf[1] *NOUN* (**loaves**)
a shaped mass of bread baked in one piece

loaf[2] *VERB* (**loafs**, **loafing**, **loafed**)
to loaf or loaf about is to loiter or waste time
▷ **loafer** *NOUN* someone who loafs about

loam *NOUN*
loam is rich fertile soil
▷ **loamy** *ADJECTIVE* like loam

loan *NOUN* (**loans**)
something that has been lent to someone, especially money
on loan being lent • *The books are on loan from the library.*

loan *VERB* (**loans, loaning, loaned**)
to loan something is to lend it

loath *ADJECTIVE* (*rhymes with* **both**)
unwilling • *I was loath to go.*

> SPELLING
> Take care not to confuse **loath** with **loathe**, which is a verb and is the next word in this dictionary.

loathe *VERB* (**loathes, loathing, loathed**) (*rhymes with* **clothe**)
to loathe something or someone is to dislike them very much

loathsome *ADJECTIVE*
making you feel disgusted; horrible • *'Now you've done it, you loathsome pest!' whispered the Earthworm to the Centipede.* — Roald Dahl, *James and the Giant Peach*

loaves
plural of **loaf** *NOUN*

lob *VERB* (**lobs, lobbing, lobbed**)
to lob something is to throw or hit it high into the air

lobby *NOUN* (**lobbies**)
an entrance hall

lobby *VERB* (**lobbies, lobbying, lobbied**)
to lobby politicians or officials is to try to influence them or persuade them of something

lobe *NOUN* (**lobes**)
the rounded part at the bottom of the ear

lobster *NOUN* (**lobsters**)
a large shellfish with eight legs and two claws

local *ADJECTIVE*
1 belonging to a particular place or area • *Where is your local library?* **2** affecting a certain part of the body • *You'll need a local anaesthetic.*

> WORD FAMILY
> To live or shop **locally** is to do so nearby, in the area where you are. • *Do you live locally?*

local *NOUN* (**locals**)(*informal*)
1 a local is someone who lives in a particular district **2** someone's local is the pub nearest their home

locality *NOUN* (**localities**)
a place and the area that surrounds it

locate *VERB* (**locates, locating, located**)
1 to locate something is to discover where it is • *I have located the fault.* **2** to be located in a place is to be situated there • *The cinema is located in the High Street.*

location *NOUN* (**locations**)
the place where something is • *What is the exact location of the submarine?*
when a film is filmed **on location** it is filmed in natural surroundings, not in a studio

loch *NOUN* (**lochs**)
a lake in Scotland

lock[1] *NOUN* (**locks**)
1 a fastening that is opened with a key or other device **2** a section of a canal or river with gates at each end, so that the level of water can be raised or lowered to allow boats to pass from one level to another **3** the distance that a vehicle's front wheels can turn
lock, stock, and barrel completely

lock *VERB* (**locks, locking, locked**)
1 to lock a door or window or lid is to fasten or secure it with a lock **2** to lock something somewhere is to put it in a safe place that can be fastened with a lock **3** to lock is to become fixed in one place, or to jam

lock[2] *NOUN* (**locks**)
a few strands of hair formed into a loop

locker *NOUN* (**lockers**)
a small cupboard for keeping things safe, often in a changing room

locket *NOUN* (**lockets**)
a small case holding a photograph or lock of hair, worn on a chain round the neck

locomotive *NOUN* (**locomotives**)
a railway engine

locus *NOUN* (**loci**)
(*in mathematics*) the line made by a moving point or by points placed in a certain way

locust *NOUN* (**locusts**)
an insect like a large grasshopper, that flies in swarms which eat all the plants in an area

lodge *NOUN* (**lodges**)
1 a small house **2** a room or small house at the entrance to a large house or building

lodge *VERB* (**lodges, lodging, lodged**)
1 to lodge is to become fixed or get stuck somewhere • *The ball lodged in the branches.* **2** to lodge somewhere is to stay there as a lodger **3** to lodge someone is to give them a place to sleep
to lodge a complaint is to make an official complaint

lodger *NOUN* (**lodgers**)
someone who pays to live in someone else's house

lodgings *PLURAL NOUN*
a room or set of rooms that a person rents in someone else's house

loft *NOUN* (**lofts**)
the room or space under the roof of a house

lofty *ADJECTIVE* (**loftier, loftiest**)
1 high or tall **2** noble and proud • *They have lofty ideas.*
▷ **loftily** *ADVERB* in a lofty way

log *NOUN* (**logs**)
1 a large piece of a tree that has fallen or been cut down **2** a detailed record of what happens each day, especially on a journey or voyage

log *VERB* (**logs, logging, logged**)
to log information is to put it in a log
to log in is to gain access to a computer
to log out is to finish using a computer

logbook *NOUN* (**logbooks**)
1 a book in which a log of a voyage is kept **2** the registration document of a motor vehicle

logic *NOUN*
logic is a system of thinking and working out ideas

logical *ADJECTIVE*
using logic or worked out by logic
▷ **logically** *ADVERB* in a logical way

logo *NOUN* (**logos**)
a printed symbol used by a business company or other organization as its emblem

loiter *VERB* (**loiters, loitering, loitered**)
to loiter is to stand about not doing anything

loll *VERB* (**lolls, lolling, lolled**)
to loll is to sit or lie in an untidy and lazy way

lollipop *NOUN* (**lollipops**)
a hard sticky sweet on the end of a stick

lollipop woman or **lollipop man** *NOUN* (**lollipop women** or **lollipop men**)
an official who uses a circular sign on a stick to signal traffic to stop so that children can cross the road

lolly *NOUN* (**lollies**)
1 (*informal*) a lolly is a lollipop or an ice lolly
2 (*slang*) lolly is money

lone *ADJECTIVE*
on its own; solitary • *a lone rider*

lonely *ADJECTIVE* (**lonelier, loneliest**)
1 unhappy because you are on your own **2** far from other inhabited places; not often used or visited • *They passed through a lonely village.*
▷ **loneliness** *NOUN* loneliness is being lonely

long [1] *ADJECTIVE* (**longer, longest**)
1 big when measured from one end to the other • *They walked up a long path.* **2** taking a lot of time • *I'd like a long holiday.* **3** measuring from one end to the other • *A cricket pitch is 22 yards long.*

long *ADVERB* (**longer, longest**)
1 for a long time • *Have you been waiting long?* **2** a long time before or after • *They left long ago.*
as long as or **so long as** provided that; on condition that • *I'll come as long as I can bring my dog.*

long [2] *VERB* (**longs, longing, longed**)
to long for something is to want it very much
• *Matilda longed for her parents to be good and loving and understanding and honourable and intelligent.* — Roald Dahl, *Matilda*

long division *NOUN*
long division is dividing one number by another and writing down all the calculations

longitude *NOUN* (**longitudes**) (*say* long- i- tewd or lon- ji- tewd)
longitude is the distance of a place east or west, measured in degrees from an imaginary line that passes through Greenwich in London
▷ **longitudinal** *ADJECTIVE* to do with longitude

long jump *NOUN*
an athletic contest of jumping as far as possible along the ground with one leap

long-range *ADJECTIVE*
covering a long distance or period of time

long-sighted *ADJECTIVE*
able to see things clearly when they are at a distance but not when they are close

long-term *ADJECTIVE*
to do with a long period of time

loo *NOUN* (**loos**)
(*informal*) a toilet

look *VERB* (**looks, looking, looked**)
1 to look is to use your eyes to see something, or to turn your eyes towards something **2** to look in a particular direction is to face it • *Look right and left before you cross.* **3** to look (for example) happy or sad is to appear that way
to look after something or **someone** is to protect them or take care of them
to look down on someone is to despise them
to look for something or **someone** is to try to find them
to look forward to something is to be waiting eagerly for it to happen
to look out is to be careful
to look up to someone is to admire or respect them

look *NOUN* (**looks**)
1 a look is the act of looking • *Take a look at this.*
2 the expression on someone's face • *She gave me a surprised look.* **3** the look of someone or something is their appearance • *I don't like the look of that dog.*

look-alike *NOUN* (**look-alikes**)
someone who looks very like a famous person

looking-glass *NOUN* (**looking-glasses**)
(*old use*) a glass mirror

lookout *NOUN* (**lookouts**)
1 a place from which you watch for something
2 someone whose job is to keep watch **3** watching or being watchful • *Keep a lookout for snakes.*
4 (*informal*) something that is your lookout is your concern or problem • *It's your lookout if you get hurt.*

loom [1] *NOUN* (**looms**)
a machine for weaving cloth

a b c d e f g h i j k **l** m n o p q r s t u v w x y z

loom[2] *VERB* (**looms, looming, loomed**)
to loom or loom up is to appear large and threatening •*Then a monstrous three-headed hell-hound loomed up, lashing its snake tail, with serpent heads writhing all over its back.* — Francesca Simon, *Helping Hercules*

loop *NOUN* (**loops**)
the shape made by a curve crossing itself; a piece of string, ribbon, or wire made into this shape

loop *VERB* (**loops, looping, looped**)
to loop something is to make it into a loop

loophole *NOUN* (**loopholes**)
1 a narrow opening **2** a way of getting round a law or rule without quite breaking it

loose *ADJECTIVE* (**looser, loosest**)
1 not tight or firmly fixed •*a loose tooth* **2** not tied up or shut in •*The dog got loose.*
to be at a loose end is to have nothing to do
to be on the loose is to be free after escaping

> WORD FAMILY
> You do something **loosely** when you do it in a way that is not firm or tight •*She tied the scarf loosely round her waist*; **looseness** is being loose.

> SPELLING
> Take care not to confuse the adjective **loose** with the verb **lose**.

loose-leaf *ADJECTIVE*
having a cover that allows pages to be put in or taken out

loosen *VERB* (**loosens, loosening, loosened**)
1 to loosen something is to make it loose **2** to loosen is to become loose

loot *NOUN*
loot is stolen things

loot *VERB* (**loots, looting, looted**)
to loot a place is to rob it violently, especially during a war or riot
▷ **looter** *NOUN* someone who loots a place

lopsided *ADJECTIVE*
uneven, with one side lower than the other •*She had a lopsided smile.*

lord *NOUN* (**lords**)
1 a nobleman, especially one who is allowed to use the title 'Lord' in front of his name **2** (*old use*) a master or ruler
Our Lord a name used by Christians for Jesus Christ
the Lord a name for God

lordly *ADJECTIVE*
1 relating to a lord **2** proud; haughty

Lord Mayor *NOUN*
the mayor of a large city

lordship *NOUN*
a title for a lord or a man of high social standing

lorry *NOUN* (**lorries**)
a large motor vehicle for carrying goods

> BRITISH AND AMERICAN
> In America, **truck** is used.

lose *VERB* (**loses, losing, lost**)
1 to lose something is to no longer have it, especially because you can't find it •*I've lost my hat.* **2** to lose a contest or game is to be beaten in it •*We lost last Friday's match.* **3** a clock or watch loses when it gives a time that is earlier than the correct time
to lose your way is not to know where you are
▷ **loser** *NOUN* someone who loses a game

> SPELLING
> Take care not to confuse the verb **lose** with the adjective **loose**.

loss *NOUN* (**losses**)
1 losing something **2** something you have lost
to be at a loss is to be puzzled or unable to do something

lost
past tense and past participle of **lose**

lost *ADJECTIVE*
1 not knowing where you are or not able to find your way •*I think we're lost.* **2** missing or strayed •*a lost dog*

lot *NOUN* (**lots**)
1 a lot is a large number of people or things **2** a lot can also mean very much •*Thanks a lot.* **3** a lot is a piece of land **4** at an auction, a lot is one item or group of items for sale
to draw lots is to choose one person or thing from a group by a method that depends on chance
the lot or **the whole lot** everything

lotion *NOUN* (**lotions**)
a liquid that you put on your skin

lottery *NOUN* (**lotteries**)
a way of raising money by selling numbered tickets and giving prizes to people who have the winning tickets

lotto *NOUN*
lotto is a game like bingo

loud *ADJECTIVE* (**louder, loudest**)
1 noisy; easily heard **2** bright or gaudy •*The room was painted in loud colours.*

> WORD FAMILY
> You do something **loudly** when you make a lot of noise doing it; **loudness** is being loud.

loudspeaker *NOUN* (**loudspeakers**)
a device that changes electrical impulses into sound, for reproducing music or voices

lounge *NOUN* (**lounges**)
a room in a house, hotel, or airport for sitting in and relaxing

lounge *VERB* (**lounges**, **lounging**, **lounged**)
to lounge is to sit or stand in a relaxed or lazy way •*Sirius was lounging in his chair at his ease, tilting it back on two legs.* — J. K. Rowling, *Harry Potter and the Prisoner of Azkaban*

louse *NOUN* (**lice**)
a small insect that sucks the blood of animals or the juices of plants

lousy *ADJECTIVE* (**lousier**, **lousiest**)
1 full of lice **2** (*slang*) very bad or unpleasant

lout *NOUN* (**louts**)
a bad-mannered man

love *NOUN* (**loves**)
1 love is a feeling of liking someone or something very much; great affection or kindness **2** love is also sexual feelings and great affection between two people **3** someone's love is a person that they love **4** in games, love is a score of nothing
to be in love is to love another person very deeply
to make love is to have sexual intercourse

love *VERB* (**loves**, **loving**, **loved**)
to love someone or something is to like them very much

> WORD FAMILY
> Someone is **lovable** when they are easy to love; you do something **lovingly** when you do it in a way that shows love.

lovely *ADJECTIVE* (**lovelier**, **loveliest**)
1 beautiful **2** (*informal*) very pleasant or enjoyable
▷ **loveliness** *NOUN* loveliness is being lovely

lover *NOUN* (**lovers**)
1 someone who loves something •*I am a lover of milk chocolate.* **2** a person who is having a sexual affair with someone without being married to them

low[1] *ADJECTIVE* (**lower**, **lowest**)
1 only reaching a short way up; not high **2** below average in amount or importance •*They are people of a low rank.* •*Prices are low.* **3** unhappy •*I'm feeling low.* **4** a low note is one at the bottom end of a musical scale
▷ **lowness** *NOUN* lowness is being low

low[2] *VERB* (**lows**, **lowing**, **lowed**)
to low is to make a sound like a cow

lower *VERB* (**lowers**, **lowering**, **lowered**)
to lower something is move it down

lower case *NOUN*
lower case is small letters, not capitals

lowland *ADJECTIVE*
to do with the lowlands

lowlands *PLURAL NOUN*
low-lying country, especially the south of Scotland
▷ **lowlander** *NOUN* someone who lives in the lowlands

lowly *ADJECTIVE* (**lowlier**, **lowliest**)
humble
▷ **lowliness** *NOUN* lowliness is being lowly

loyal *ADJECTIVE*
always true to your friends; faithful

> WORD FAMILY
> To **loyally** do something is to do it in a faithful way; **loyalty** is being true to your friends.

lozenge *NOUN* (**lozenges**)
1 a small sweet tablet, especially one that contains medicine **2** a diamond-shaped design

Ltd.
in names of companies, short for **limited**

lubricant *NOUN* (**lubricants**)
oil or grease for lubricating machinery

lubricate *VERB* (**lubricates**, **lubricating**, **lubricated**)
to lubricate something like machinery is to put oil or grease on it so that it moves smoothly

> WORD FAMILY
> **Lubrication** is putting oil or grease on something so that it moves smoothly.

lucid *ADJECTIVE* (*say* loo- sid)
1 something is lucid when it is clear and easy to understand **2** someone is lucid when they are able to think clearly again after being ill

> WORD FAMILY
> **Lucidity** is being clear and easy to understand; to explain something **lucidly** is to do it in a way that is clear and easy to understand.

luck *NOUN*
1 luck is the way things happen by chance, without being planned **2** luck is also good fortune

luckily *ADVERB*
by a lucky chance; fortunately •*Luckily it stayed warm all day.*

lucky *ADJECTIVE* (**luckier**, **luckiest**)
having or bringing good luck

ludicrous *ADJECTIVE* (*say* loo- di- krus)
extremely silly or absurd
▷ **ludicrously** *ADVERB* in a ludicrous way

ludo *NOUN*
ludo is a game played with dice and counters on a board

lug *VERB* (**lugs**, **lugging**, **lugged**)
to lug something heavy is to carry it or drag it with difficulty

luggage *NOUN*
luggage is the suitcases and bags you take on a journey

lukewarm *ADJECTIVE*
1 slightly warm **2** not very keen or enthusiastic •*They got a lukewarm response.*

lull *VERB* (**lulls**, **lulling**, **lulled**)
to lull someone is to soothe or calm them

lull *NOUN* (**lulls**)
a short period of quiet or rest •*There was a lull in the fighting.*

a b c d e f g h i j k **l** m n o p q r s t u v w x y z

lullaby *NOUN* (**lullabies**)
a song that you sing to send a baby to sleep

lumber *NOUN*
lumber is junk or old unwanted furniture or other things

lumber *VERB* (**lumbers, lumbering, lumbered**)
1 to lumber is to move along clumsily and heavily •*A shadow under the trees moved and came lumbering out into the sunlight towards us. A monkey, a giant monkey.* — Michael Morpurgo, *Kensuke's Kingdom* **2** (*informal*) to lumber someone is to leave them with something unpleasant or difficult to do

lumberjack *NOUN* (**lumberjacks**)
someone whose job is to cut down trees or transport them

luminous *ADJECTIVE* (*say* loo- mi- nus)
shining or glowing in the dark •*Eerie green light was provided by luminous fish that hung from the rocky walls and floated overhead.* — Alan Temperley, *The Brave Whale*
▷ **luminosity** *NOUN* luminosity is being luminous

lump[1] *NOUN* (**lumps**)
1 a solid piece of something **2** a swelling
▷ **lumpy** *ADJECTIVE* having lots of lumps

lump *VERB* (**lumps, lumping, lumped**)
to lump different things together is to put them together in the same group

lump[2] *VERB* (**lumps, lumping, lumped**)
to lump it (*informal*) is to put up with something you don't like •*You'll have to like it or lump it.*

lunacy *NOUN* (**lunacies**) (*say* loo- na- si)
lunacy is madness

lunar *ADJECTIVE*
to do with the moon

lunar month *NOUN* (**lunar months**)
a period of four weeks between one new moon and the next

lunatic *NOUN* (**lunatics**) (*say* loo- na- tik)
a mad person

lunch *NOUN* (**lunches**)
a meal eaten in the middle of the day

lung *NOUN* (**lungs**)
each of the two organs in your chest, used for breathing

lunge *VERB* (**lunges, lunging, lunged**)
to lunge is to make a sudden movement forwards •*Just as the creature lunged forwards to kill him, Hiccup was grabbed around the ankle by one of Stoick's hairy hands, and pulled back through the hole he had climbed in.* — Cressida Cowell, *How to Be a Pirate*

lupin *NOUN* (**lupins**)
a garden plant with tall spikes of flowers

lurch[1] *VERB* (**lurches, lurching, lurched**)
to lurch is to stagger or lean suddenly

lurch *NOUN* (**lurches**)
a sudden staggering or leaning movement

lurch[2] *NOUN*
to leave someone in the lurch is to desert them when they are in difficulty

lure *VERB* (**lures, luring, lured**)
to lure a person or animal is to tempt them into a trap or difficulty

lurk *VERB* (**lurks, lurking, lurked**)
to lurk is to wait threateningly where you can't be seen

luscious *ADJECTIVE* (*say* lush- us)
tasting or smelling delicious •*He would buy one luscious bar of chocolate and eat it all up, every bit of it, right then and there.* — Roald Dahl, *Charlie and the Chocolate Factory*

lush *ADJECTIVE* (**lusher, lushest**)
growing thickly and healthily •*Below the garden a green field lush with clover sloped down to the hollow where the brook ran and where scores of white birches grew.* — L. M. Montgomery, *Anne of Green Gables*

lust *NOUN* (**lusts**)
lust is a powerful or greedy desire

lustful *ADJECTIVE*
having a greedy desire for something

lustre *NOUN* (**lustres**) (*say* lus- ter)
a thing's lustre is its brightness or brilliance

> WORD FAMILY
> Something is **lustrous** when it is shiny or bright.

lute *NOUN* (**lutes**)
a musical instrument rather like a guitar but with a deeper and rounder body. It was used a lot in the Middle Ages

luxury *NOUN* (**luxuries**)
1 a luxury is something expensive that you enjoy but don't really need **2** luxury is having a very comfortable and expensive lifestyle •*They led a life of luxury.*

> WORD FAMILY
> Something, like a hotel, that is **luxurious** is very comfortable and expensive.

Lycra *NOUN*
(*trademark*) Lycra is a thin stretchy material used especially for sports clothing

lying
present participle of **lie**[1] *VERB* and **lie**[2] *VERB*

lynch *VERB* (**lynches, lynching, lynched**)
to lynch someone is to execute them without a proper trial

lyre *NOUN* (**lyres**)
an ancient musical instrument like a small harp

lyric *NOUN* (**lyrics**) (*say* li- rik)
a short poem that expresses feelings and emotions

lyrical *ADJECTIVE*
sounding like a song or a poem

lyrics *PLURAL NOUN*
the words of a popular song

Mm

m
short for **metre**, **metres**, **miles**, or **millions**

ma *NOUN* (**mas**)
(*informal*) mother

mac *NOUN* (**macs**)
(*informal*) a mackintosh

macabre *ADJECTIVE* (*say* mak- ahbr)
strange and horrible

macaroni *NOUN*
macaroni is pasta in the form of short tubes

machine *NOUN* (**machines**)
a piece of equipment made of moving parts that work together to do a job

machine-gun *NOUN* (**machine-guns**)
a gun that can keep firing bullets quickly one after another

machinery *NOUN*
1 machinery is machines generally • *farm machinery* **2** machinery is a mechanism • *The lift's machinery is faulty.* **3** machinery is also a system for doing something • *They are studying the machinery of local government.*

mackerel *NOUN* (**mackerel**)
a sea fish used as food

mackintosh *NOUN* (**mackintoshes**)
a raincoat

mad *ADJECTIVE* (**madder**, **maddest**)
1 having something wrong with your mind; not sane **2** very foolish **3** very keen • *She's mad about rock music.* **4** (*informal*) very excited or annoyed
like mad (*informal*) with great speed, energy, or enthusiasm

> WORD FAMILY
> **Madness** is being mad.

madam *NOUN*
a word sometimes used when speaking or writing politely to a woman, instead of her name • *Can I help you, madam?*

mad cow disease *NOUN*
mad cow disease is a name for BSE

madden *VERB* (**maddens**, **maddening**, **maddened**)
to madden someone is to make them mad or angry

made
past tense and past participle of **make** *VERB*

madly *ADVERB*
extremely; very much • *They are madly in love.*

madman *NOUN* (**madmen**)
a man who is mad

magazine *NOUN* (**magazines**)
1 a paper-covered publication with articles or stories, which comes out regularly **2** the part of a gun that holds the cartridges **3** a store for weapons and ammunition or for explosives **4** a device that holds film for a camera or slides for a projector

maggot *NOUN* (**maggots**)
the larva of some kinds of fly

magic *NOUN*
1 magic is the power to make impossible things happen **2** magic is also performing clever tricks

magical *ADJECTIVE*
1 done by magic or as if by magic **2** wonderful; marvellous

> WORD FAMILY
> To happen **magically** is to happen by magic or as if by magic.

magician *NOUN* (**magicians**)
1 someone who does magic tricks **2** a man with magic powers; a wizard

magistrate *NOUN* (**magistrates**)
a judge in a local court who deals with some less serious cases

magma *NOUN*
magma is a molten substance beneath the earth's crust

magnesium *NOUN*
magnesium is a silvery-white metal that burns with a very bright flame

magnet *NOUN* (**magnets**)
a piece of metal that can attract iron or steel and that points north and south when it is hung in the air

> WORD FAMILY
> **Magnetism** is the attraction of a magnet.

magnetic *ADJECTIVE*
having or using the powers of a magnet

magnetic tape *NOUN*
magnetic tape is a plastic strip coated with a magnetic substance for recording sound

magnetize *VERB* (**magnetizes**, **magnetizing**, **magnetized**)
1 to magnetize something is to make it into a magnet **2** to magnetize someone is to attract them or influence them very strongly • *Jane magnetized the audience when she began to sing.*

magnificent *ADJECTIVE*
1 looking splendid or impressive • *There was a whirr and flutter of wings and down from the dawn sky flew a magnificent white horse.* — Francesca Simon, *Helping Hercules* **2** excellent • *We had a magnificent meal.*

> WORD FAMILY
> **Magnificence** is being magnificent; **magnificently** means in a magnificent way.

magnify *VERB* (**magnifies**, **magnifying**, **magnified**)
to magnify something is to make it look bigger than it really is

magnifying glass *NOUN* (**magnifying glasses**)
a lens that magnifies things

magnitude *NOUN* (**magnitudes**)
magnitude is how large or important something is

magnolia *NOUN* (**magnolias**)
a tree with large white or pale pink flowers

magpie *NOUN* (**magpies**)
a black and white bird, related to the crow

mahogany *NOUN* (*say* ma- **hog**- a- ni)
mahogany is a hard brown wood used for making furniture

maid *NOUN* (**maids**)
1 a female servant **2** (*old use*) a girl

maiden *NOUN* (**maidens**)
(*old use*) a girl

maiden name *NOUN* (**maiden names**)
a woman's family name before she gets married

maiden over *NOUN* (**maiden overs**)
a cricket over in which no runs are scored

maiden voyage or **maiden flight** *NOUN* (**maiden voyages** or **maiden flights**)
a ship's first voyage or an aircraft's first flight

mail[1] *NOUN*
1 mail is letters and parcels sent by post **2** mail is also electronic mail

mail *VERB* (**mails**, **mailing**, **mailed**)
to mail something is to send it by post or by electronic mail

mail[2] *NOUN*
armour made of metal rings joined together

mail order *NOUN*
mail order is a system of buying goods through the post

maim *VERB* (**maims**, **maiming**, **maimed**)
to maim someone is to injure them so badly that part of their body is damaged for life

main *ADJECTIVE*
largest or most important

main or **mains** *NOUN*
the main pipe or cable in a system carrying water, gas, or electricity to a building

main clause *NOUN* (**main clauses**)
a clause which can be used as a complete sentence

mainland *NOUN*
the mainland is the main part of a country or continent, not the islands around it

mainly *ADVERB*
chiefly or usually; almost completely

maintain *VERB* (**maintains**, **maintaining**, **maintained**)
1 to maintain something is to keep it in good condition **2** to maintain a belief is to have it or state it • *I maintain that animals should not be hunted.* **3** to maintain someone is to provide money for them

maintenance *NOUN*
1 maintenance is keeping something in good condition **2** maintenace is also money for food and clothing

maisonette *NOUN* (**maisonettes**)
a small flat or house

maize *NOUN*
maize is a tall kind of corn with large seeds

majestic *ADJECTIVE*
stately and dignified
▹ **majestically** *ADVERB* in a majestic way

majesty *NOUN* (**majesties**)
1 the title of a king or queen **2** majesty is the quality of being stately and dignified

major *ADJECTIVE*
1 more important; main • *Use the major roads.* **2** of the musical scale that has a semitone between the 3rd and 4th notes and between the 7th and 8th notes

major *NOUN* (**majors**)
an army officer above captain in rank

majority *NOUN* (**majorities**) (*say* ma- **jo**- ri- ti)
1 the greatest part of a group of people or things; more than half • *The majority of the class wanted a quiz.* **2** the amount by which the winner in an election beats the loser • *She had a majority of 25 over her opponent.* **3** the age at which a person becomes legally an adult, now usually 18

make *VERB* (**makes**, **making**, **made**)
1 to make something is to build or produce it • *They are making a raft out of logs.* **2** to make someone or something do something is to cause it to happen • *The bang made him jump.* **3** to make money is to get it or earn it • *She makes £30,000 a year.* **4** in a game, to make a score is to achieve it • *He has made 20 runs so far.* **5** to make a certain point is to reach it • *The swimmer just made the shore.* **6** to make something is to estimate it or reckon it • *What do you make the time?* **7** several numbers make a total when they add up to it • *4 and 6 make 10.* **8** to make (for example) a suggestion or promise is to give it to someone **9** to make a bed is to tidy it or arrange it for use
to make someone's day is to cause them to be happy or successful
to make do is to manage with something that is not what you really want
to make for a place is to go towards it
to make off is to leave quickly
to make something or **someone out** is to manage to see or hear or understand them
to make something up is to invent a false story or excuse
to make up is to be friendly again after a disagreement
to make up for something is to give or do something in return for a loss or difficulty
to make up your mind is to decide

Writing letters

A formal letter

15 Market Street
Hilltown HT21

The Editor
Highfield Publishers
77 Broad Street
London W1

21st September 2005

Dear Sir

I am writing to enquire whether you would be interested in publishing a book I have written. The book is about the life of my grandfather, Henry Robinson, who was an explorer in the Arctic and Antarctic in the 1920s. It is based on the diary he kept on his journeys, and could be illustrated with photographs from his collection.

I have enclosed a chapter for you to read. This describes an expedition to the North Pole in 1924, in which my grandfather and his companions were stranded on the ice in bad weather for three days.

If you are interested in this proposal I can send you the rest of the manuscript. Thank you for your consideration.

Yours faithfully

James Robinson

James Robinson

When you write to an organization or a person you do not know, keep your letter short and to the point.

- your address
- the address you are writing to
- the date
- If you know the person's name, write 'Dear Mr ...', 'Miss', 'Ms', or 'Mrs'. If you do not know their name, write 'Dear Sir' or 'Madam'.
- If you have written the person's name at the top of the letter, sign off 'Yours sincerely'. If you have written 'Sir' or 'Madam', sign off 'Yours faithfully'.
- Print your name below your signature.

An informal letter

35 Main Street
Hightown

21st September 2005

Darling Auntie Susan

Thank you so much for my lovely birthday present. I've spent ages listening to the CD you gave me – it's fantastic! It was really clever of you to remember that they're my favourite band.

I had a wonderful birthday. Mum took me and some friends to the cinema, then we came back here for tea and birthday cake. We all stayed up really late! Now I'm back at school. I'm in the swimming team, so I have to practise a lot. It's great fun and I'm getting really fast!

Please come and visit us soon.

lots of love from

Sarah

When you write to a friend or relation, the language of your letter is less formal and more personal.

- your address
- the date

There is no need to write the address of the person you are writing to.

- You can sign off in many ways, such as 'love from'.

An email

Send | Save Draft | Attach | Tools | Cancel

To: sarah@puo.con

Cc:

Bcc:

Subject: Cinema

Hi Sarah
Let's meet at six at the cinema. Can't wait to see you!
love Jane

When you write an email, there are no rules about how to set it out. The language is very informal, as if you are speaking directly to the other person.

You can leave out 'Dear ...' or 'Hi ...' if you wish.

You do not have to sign your name at the bottom, as the recipient will know who the message is from, but most people do, to be friendly.

Words to do with the human body

The body

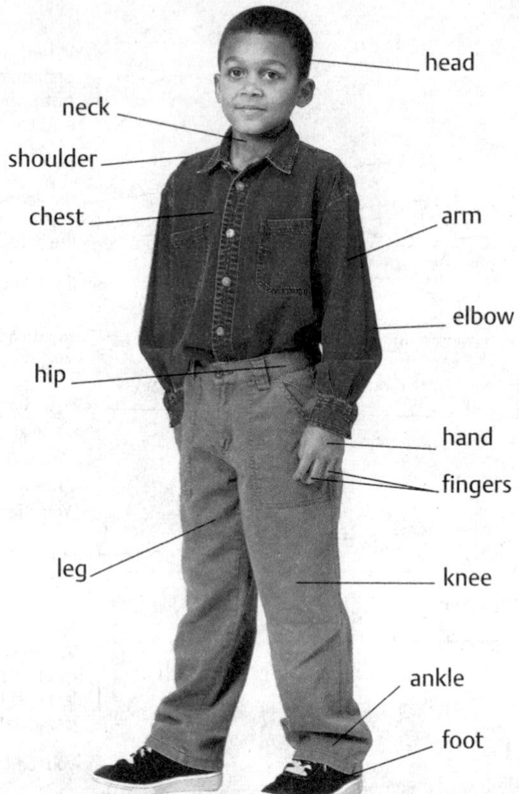

The face

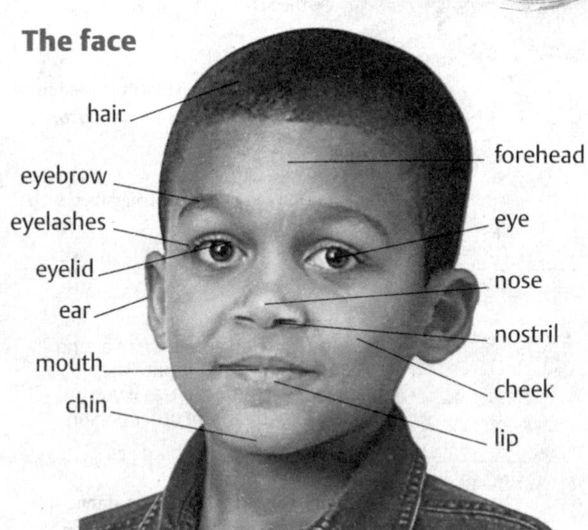

The senses

touch

sight

hearing

taste

smell

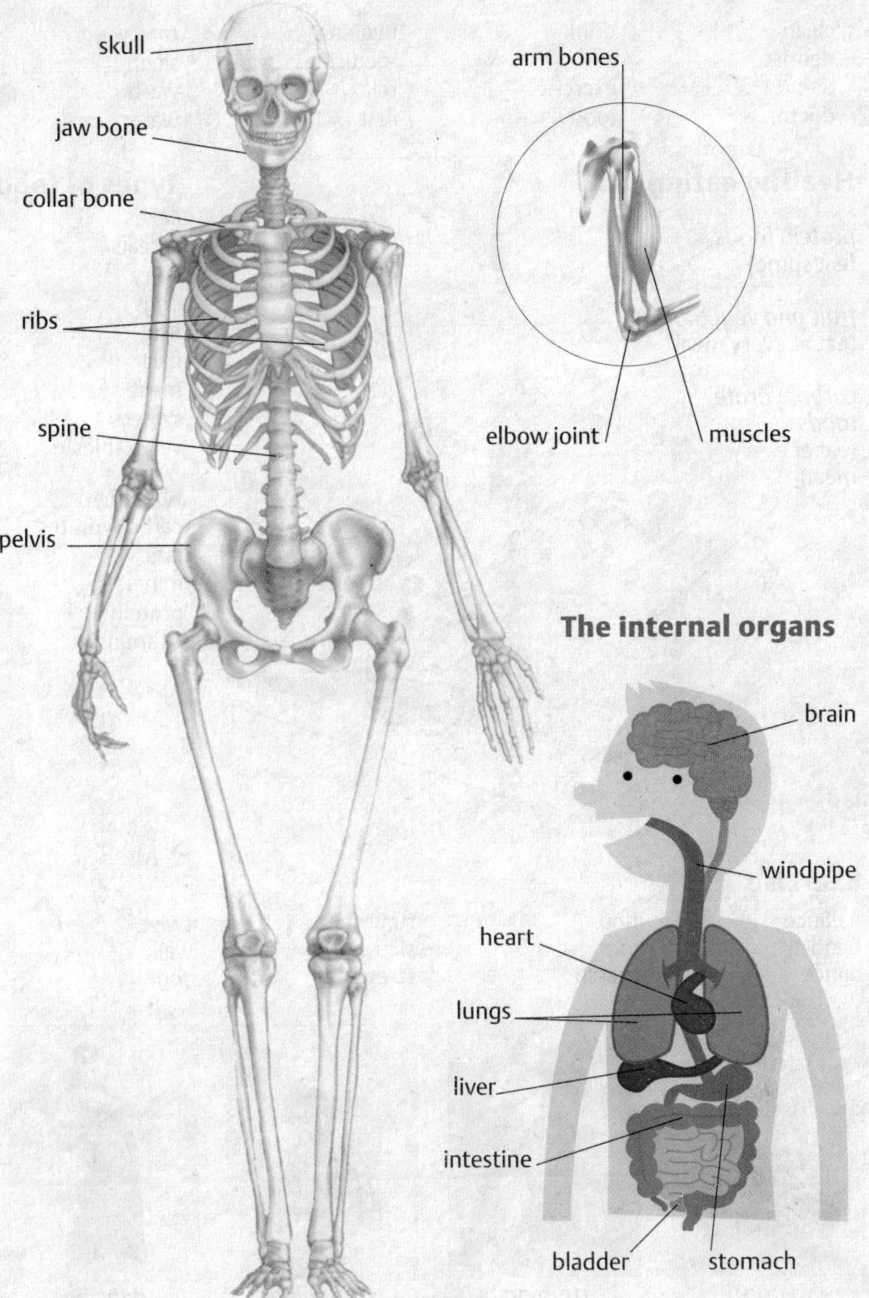
The skeleton
skull
jaw bone
collar bone
ribs
spine
pelvis
arm bones
elbow joint
muscles
The internal organs
brain
windpipe
heart
lungs
liver
intestine
bladder
stomach

Words to do with healthy living

Keeping healthy

clean
dentist
diet
doctor
drink
eat
exercise
food
hygiene
medicine
relax
rest
safety
sleep
wash
water

Healthy eating

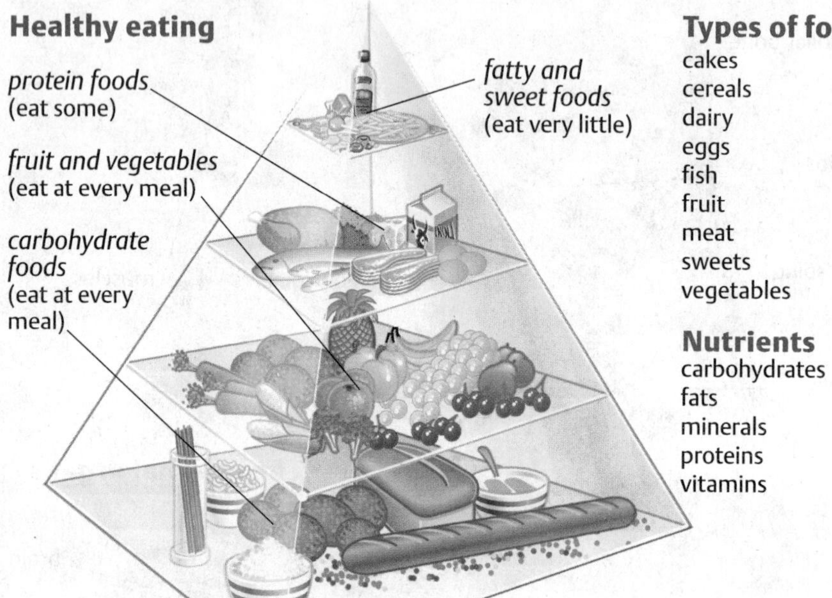

Types of food

cakes
cereals
dairy
eggs
fish
fruit
meat
sweets
vegetables

Nutrients

carbohydrates
fats
minerals
proteins
vitamins

Exercise

balance
bend
dance
hop
jog
march
run
skip
stretch
twist
walk
yoga

yoga

running

stretching

dancing

Words to do with food technology

Equipment
bowl
chopping board
cooker
dish
electricity
fork
frying pan
gas
knife
oven
plate
saucepan
sieve
spoon
whisk

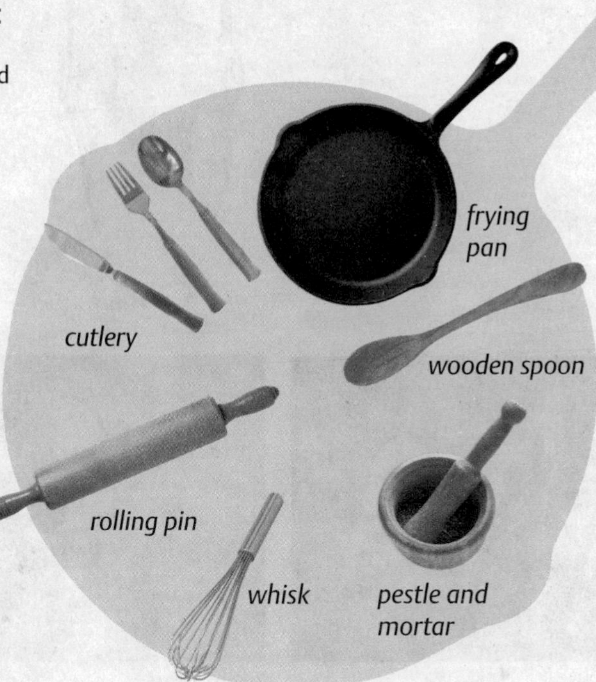

Food
chewy
crispy
crunchy
juicy
runny
sticky

Cooking verbs
beat
chop
combine
crush
drain
grate
knead
measure
mix
peel
roll
sieve
slice
spread
sprinkle
stir
strain
weigh
whisk

Tastes
bitter
peppery
salty
sharp
sour
sweet

Preparing food
boil
cook
equipment
flavour
fry
grill
ingredients
quality
roast
serve
tools
utensils

Words to do with sports

gymnastics

athletics

swimming

athletics
basketball
climbing
cricket
cycling
football
gymnastics
hockey
ice hockey
riding
rowing
rugby

basketball

sailing
scuba diving
skating
skiing
soccer
squash
surfing
swimming
tennis
volleyball
water skiing
windsurfing

climbing

cricket

football

sailing

Words to do with ICT

Equipment
CD
CD-ROM
computer
DVD
fax
keyboard
modem
monitor
mouse
screen
telephone
television
video

Using computers
bar chart
bold
calculate
copy
cut and paste
database
document
file
find and replace
folder
formula
italic
line graph
menu
move
order
pie chart
record
sort
spell check
spreadsheet
sum

Using the Internet
address
attachment
email
key word
search
surf
website
World Wide Web

Words to do with transport

By air
helicopter
plane

helicopter
plane

By water
barge
boat
canoe
ferry
hovercraft
hydrofoil
liner
ship
speedboat
tanker
yacht

tanker

ferry

By land
bicycle
bus
car
coach
motorbike
taxi
train
truck
van

car
train

Grammar

Words can be put into sets called word classes, or parts of speech. The main ones are: **noun**, **pronoun**, **verb**, **adjective**, **adverb**, **preposition**, **conjunction**, **interjection**.

Nouns

Nouns are words that are the names of things or persons, such as **child**, **danger**, **tree**. Nouns divide up into names (or **proper nouns**) and descriptions (or **common nouns**).

proper nouns	James, Africa, Shakespeare...
common nouns	dog, stream, mystery, bone, fire, danger...

Common nouns divide into those which stand for objects (**concrete nouns**) and those which stand for ideas (**abstract nouns**).

concrete nouns	dog, stream, cone, fire, steel, bread, car...
abstract nouns	mystery, danger, happiness, beauty...

Nouns also divide into those which can be made plural (**countables**) and those which cannot (**uncountables**).

countables	dog, stream, bone, car...
uncountables	bread, steel, air, clothing...

Pronouns

Pronouns are words used instead of a noun, such as **it**, **me**, **they**.

Verbs and their tenses

Some verbs express actions or feelings. For example:

I **came**. She **ate**. They **know**.

Other verbs connect words or phrases in a sentence.

It **is** late. I **am** coming. You **have** eaten. They **must** not know.

Verbs have several different forms, depending on their **tense**. For example:

present tense:	I speak, she speaks, they are speaking
past tenses:	I spoke, she has spoken, you had spoken, they have been speaking
future tense:	I will be speaking, they will be speaking

The forms of verbs are given in the dictionary in the same order every time:

speak verb (**speaks**, **speaking**, **spoke**, **spoken**)

speak:	present tense after I, you, they
speaks:	present tense after he, she or it
speaking:	present participle (used after is, are, was, has been etc.)
spoke:	simple past tense
spoken:	past participle (used after has, had etc)

You will see that some verbs are **regular**, which means that they follow a rule in the way they form their tenses. For example:

kick verb (**kicks**, **kicking**, **kicked**)

But many verbs are **irregular** and have rules of their own. For example:

throw verb (**throws**, **throwing**, **threw**, **thrown**)

The connecting verb **be** is the most irregular of all:

be verb (present tense: singular, 1st person **am**, 2nd person **are**, 3rd person **is**, plural **are**; present participle **being**; past tense: singular, 1st and 3rd persons **was**, 2nd person **were**, plural **were**; past participle **been**.

Adjectives

Adjectives are words that describe a noun and add to its meaning, such as **happy**, **important**, **old**.

Adverbs

Adverbs are words that tell you how, when, where or why something happens, such as **quickly**, **again**, **here**, **together**.

Comparison of adjectives and adverbs

Adjectives and adverbs can be made **comparative** or **superlative** in the following ways:

positive	**comparative**	**superlative**
stiff	stiffer	stiffest
quick	quicker	quickest
funny	funnier	funniest

For longer adjectives, and for most adverbs, the comparative and superlative are formed by putting **more** or **most** in front of them.

positive	**comparative**	**superlative**
terrible	more terrible	most terrible
quickly	more quickly	most quickly

But watch out for exceptions:

bad	worse	worst
badly	worse	worst

If in doubt, look them up in the dictionary.

Prepositions

Prepositions are words put in front of nouns or pronouns to show how the nouns and pronouns are connected with other words, such as **against**, **in**, **on**.

Conjunctions

Conjunctions are joining words, such as **and**, **but**, **whether**.

Interjections

Interjections are words that express surprise, pain, delight etc, such as **oh**, **ouch**, **hooray**.

Spelling

Here are some useful rules:

To make a noun plural:

Normally just add **-s**:

skirts ties pianos stars

But watch out for some words ending in **-o** that need **-es**:

echoes, heroes, potatoes, tomatoes, volcanoes etc

To words ending in **-ch**, **-s**, **-sh**, **-x** or **-z**, add **-es**:

dress – dresses box – boxes stitch – stitches

To words ending in **-f** and **-fe**, change to **-ves**:

scarf – scarves life – lives half–halves

But watch out for the exceptions: beliefs, proofs, roofs etc

To words ending in a consonant followed by **-y**, change the **y** to **i** and add **-es**:

copy – copies cry – cries party – parties

Adding -ing and -ed to verbs

Normally just add **-ing** or **-ed**:

load – loading – loaded open – opening – opened stay – staying – stayed

For short words ending in **-e** usually leave off the **e**:

race – racing – raced blame – blaming – blamed

For many short words that end with one consonant, double the last consonant:

slam – slamming – slammed tip – tipping – tipped

For longer words ending with one consonant and having the stress on the last syllable, double the last consonant:

compel – compelling – compelled prefer – preferring – preferred

For words ending in **-y** after a consonant, change the **y** to an **i** before adding **-ed**:

try – trying – tried

For words ending in **-ie**, change the **ie** to **y** before adding **-ing**:

lie – lying – lied tie – tying – tied

Watch out for these exceptions:

lay – laid pay – paid say – said

Adding -er and -est to adjectives

Normally just add **-er** and **-est**, unless the word already ends in **-e**:

cold – colder – coldest
wide – wider – widest

For many short words that end with one consonant, change to a double consonant:

wet – wetter – wettest
dim – dimmer – dimmest

If the word has two syllables and ends in **-y**, change the **y** to an **i**:

dirty – dirtier – dirtiest
happy – happier – happiest

Adding -ly

Adding **-ly** to an adjective makes it into an adverb:

slowly, badly, awkwardly

If the word ends in **-ll** just add **-y**

full – fully

For words ending in **-y** and with more than one syllable, leave off the **-y** and add **-ily**:

happy – happily
hungry – hungrily

For words ending in **-le**, leave off the **e**:

idle – idly
simple – simply

For adjectives ending in **-ic**, usually add **-ally**:

basic – basically
drastic – drastically

But watch out for other special ones:

public – publicly

Help with punctuation

These are the punctuation marks that will make your writing easier to understand:

apostrophe	'	Use an apostrophe to show that a letter has been left out of a word for example, *don't*, or to show belonging, for example, *the cat's tail*.
brackets	( )	You use brackets around things that are interesting but not necessary, for example, *the cat's tail (which was black and very long) was caught in the door*.
colon	:	You use a colon when you have a list of things coming after a heading. You also use a colon in a sentence when you have examples to list, for example, *I got a lot of birthday presents: a camera, a chess set, a skateboard, a jacket and an ink pen*. A colon is also used when you have two sentences and the second sentence explains what is meant in the first, for example, *The cat is in trouble again: it is stuck in the tree.*
comma	,	You use a comma to show a small break in a sentence.
dash	—	Dashes are useful to show an interruption or bigger break in a sentence.
exclamation mark	!	An exclamation mark shows surprise or urgency.
full stop	.	A full stop is used at the end of a sentence.
hyphen	-	A hyphen joins words or parts of words together, for example, *hard-boiled*.
question mark	?	A question mark shows a question is being asked.
semi-colon	;	You use a semi-colon to show more of a break than a comma.
speech marks	' '	You use these around the words that a person speaks, for example, '*You are in the team,' said Miss Johnson*.

Countries and nationalities

Afghanistan Afghans
Albania Albanians
Algeria Algerians
Andorra Andorrans
Angola Angolans
Antigua and Barbuda Antiguans, Barbudans
Argentina Argentinians
Armenia Armenians
Australia Australians
Austria Austrians
Azerbaijan Azerbaijanis or Azeris

Bahamas Bahamians
Bahrain Bahrainis
Bangladesh Bangladeshis
Barbados Barbadians
Belarus Belorussians
Belgium Belgians
Belize Belizians
Benin Beninese
Bhutan Bhutanese
Bolivia Bolivians
Bosnia-Herzegovina Bosnians
Botswana Batswana or Citizens of Botswana
Brazil Brazilians
Brunei Darussalam People of Brunei
Bulgaria Bulgarians
Burkina Faso Burkinans
Burundi People of Burundi

Cambodia Cambodians
Cameroon Cameroonians
Canada Canadians
Cape Verde Cape Verdeans
Central African Republic People of the Central African Republic
Chad Chadians
Chile Chileans
China, People's Republic of Chinese
Colombia Colombians
Comoros Comorans
Congo, Democratic Republic of the Congolese
Congo, Republic of the Congolese
Costa Rica Costa Ricans
Côte d'Ivoire People of the Côte d'Ivoire
Croatia Croats
Cuba Cubans
Cyprus Cypriots
Czech Republic Czechs

Denmark Danes
Djibouti Djiboutians
Dominica Dominicans
Dominican Republic Dominicans

East Timor East Timorese
Ecuador Ecuadoreans
Egypt Egyptians
El Salvador Salvadoreans
Equatorial Guinea Equatorial Guineans
Eritrea Eritreans
Estonia Estonians
Ethiopia Ethiopians

Fiji Fijians
Finland Finns
France French

Gabon Gabonese
Gambia, The Gambians
Georgia Georgians
Germany Germans
Ghana Ghanaians
Greece Greeks
Grenada Grenadians
Guatemala Guatemalans
Guinea Guineans
Guinea-Bissau People of Guinea-Bissau
Guyana Guyanese

Haiti Haitians
Honduras Hondurans
Hungary Hungarians

Iceland Icelanders
India Indians
Indonesia Indonesians
Iran Iranians
Iraq Iraqis
Ireland, Republic of Irish
Israel Israelis
Italy Italians

Jamaica Jamaicans
Japan Japanese
Jordan Jordanians

Kazakhstan Kazakhs
Kenya Kenyans
Kiribati Kiribatians
Kuwait Kuwaitis
Kyrgyzstan Kyrgyz

Laos Laotians
Latvia Latvians
Lebanon Lebanese
Lesotho Basotho
Liberia Liberians
Libya Libyans
Liechtenstein Liechtensteiners
Lithuania Lithuanians
Luxembourg Luxembourgers

Macedonia (Former Yugoslav Republic of Macedonia) Macedonians
Madagascar Malagasies
Malawi Malawians
Malaysia Malaysians
Maldives Maldivians
Mali Malians
Malta Maltese
Marshall Islands Marshall Islanders
Mauritania Mauritanians
Mauritius Mauritians
Mexico Mexicans
Micronesia Micronesians
Moldova Moldovans
Monaco Monégasques
Mongolia Mongolians
Morocco Moroccans
Mozambique Mozambicans
Myanmar (Burma) Burmese

Namibia Namibians
Nauru Nauruans
Nepal Nepalese
Netherlands Dutch
New Zealand New Zealanders
Nicaragua Nicaraguans
Niger Nigeriens
Nigeria Nigerians
North Korea (People's Democratic Republic of Korea) North Koreans
Norway Norwegians

Oman Omanis

Pakistan Pakistanis
Palau Palauans
Panama Panamanians
Papua New Guinea Papua New Guineans
Paraguay Paraguayans
Peru Peruvians
Philippines Filipinos
Poland Poles
Portugal Portuguese

Qatar Qataris

Romania Romanians
Russia (Russian Federation) Russians
Rwanda Rwandans

St Kitts and Nevis People of St Kitts and Nevis
St Lucia St Lucians
St Vincent and the Grenadines St Vincentians
Samoa Samoans
San Marino People of San Marino
São Tomé and Principe People of São Tomé and Principe
Saudi Arabia Saudi Arabians
Senegal Senegalese
Seychelles Seychellois
Sierra Leone Sierra Leoneans
Singapore Singaporeans
Slovakia Slovaks
Slovenia Slovenes
Solomon Islands Solomon Islanders
Somalia Somalis
South Africa South Africans
South Korea (Republic of Korea) South Koreans
Spain Spaniards
Sri Lanka Sri Lankans
Sudan Sudanese
Suriname Surinamers
Swaziland Swazis
Sweden Swedes
Switzerland Swiss
Syria Syrians

Taiwan Taiwanese
Tajikistan Tajiks
Tanzania Tanzanians
Thailand Thais
Togo Togolese
Tonga Tongans
Trinidad and Tobago Trinidadians and Tobagans or Tobagonians
Tunisia Tunisians
Turkey Turks
Turkmenistan Turkmens
Tuvalu Tuvaluans

Uganda Ugandans
Ukraine Ukrainians
United Arab Emirates People of the United Arab Emirates
United Kingdom British
United States of America Americans
Uruguay Uruguayans
Uzbekistan Uzbeks

Vanuatu People of Vanuatu
Vatican City Vatican citizens
Venezuela Venezuelans
Vietnam Vietnamese

Yemen Yemenis
Yugoslavia (Montenegro and Serbia) Yugoslavians (Montenegrins and Serbians)

Zambia Zambians
Zimbabwe Zimbabweans

make *NOUN* (**makes**)
1 how something is made **2** a brand of goods; something made by a particular firm • *What make of car is that?*

make-believe *NOUN*
make-believe is pretending or imagining things

maker *NOUN* (**makers**)
the person or firm that has made something

makeshift *ADJECTIVE*
used because you have nothing better • *We'll use the bed as a makeshift table.*

make-up *NOUN*
1 make-up is creams and powders for making your skin look beautiful or different **2** a person's make-up is their character

maladjusted *ADJECTIVE*
a person is maladjusted when they cannot cope with their life or with other people

malaria *NOUN* (*say* ma- **lair**- i- a)
malaria is a tropical disease spread by mosquito bites, that causes fever

male *ADJECTIVE*
of the sex that produces young by fertilizing the female's egg cells

male *NOUN* (**males**)
a male person or animal

male chauvinist *NOUN* (**male chauvinists**)
a man who believes that men are always better than women

malevolent *ADJECTIVE* (*say* ma- **lev**- o- lent)
wanting to harm other people • *'A bad idea, Professor Lockhart,' said Snape, gliding over like a large and malevolent bat.* — J. K. Rowling, *Harry Potter and the Chamber of Secrets*

> WORD FAMILY
> **Malevolence** is wanting to harm people; to do something **malevolently** is to want to harm people by doing it.

malice *NOUN*
malice is a desire to harm other people

malicious *ADJECTIVE*
intending to do harm
▷ **maliciously** *ADVERB* in a malicious way • *Inspector Hole grinned maliciously. 'Well, it looks like you two are out of a job,' he sniggered.* — Jeremy Strong, *Viking at School*

mall *NOUN* (**malls**)
a large covered shopping centre

mallet *NOUN* (**mallets**)
a large wooden hammer

malnutrition *NOUN*
malnutritian is bad health caused by not having enough food

> WORD FAMILY
> **Malnourished** people are suffering from malnutrition.

malt *NOUN*
malt is dried barley used in brewing and making vinegar

> WORD FAMILY
> A **malted** drink or food is made with malt.

mammal *NOUN* (**mammals**)
any animal of which the female gives birth to live young and can feed them with her own milk

mammoth *NOUN* (**mammoths**)
an extinct kind of hairy elephant with long curved tusks

mammoth *ADJECTIVE*
huge

man *NOUN* (**men**)
1 a man is a grown-up male human being **2** a man is also any individual person • *No man is perfect.* **3** man is all the people in the world **4** a man is one of the pieces used in a board game

man *VERB* (**mans, manning, manned**)
to man something is to supply people to work it • *Man the pumps!*

manage *VERB* (**manages, managing, managed**)
1 to manage something is to be able to do it although it is difficult **2** to manage a shop or factory or other business is to be in charge of it

manageable *ADJECTIVE*
able to be managed or done

management *NOUN*
1 management is being in charge of something **2** the management of a business is the people in charge of it

manager *NOUN* (**managers**)
a person who manages a business or part of it

manageress *NOUN* (**manageresses**)
a woman manager of a shop or restaurant

mane *NOUN* (**manes**)
the long hair along the back of the neck of a horse or lion

manger *NOUN* (**mangers**) (*say* **mayn**- jer)
a trough in a stable for animals to feed from

mangle *VERB* (**mangles, mangling, mangled**)
to mangle something is to crush or twist it so it is badly damaged

mango *NOUN* (**mangoes**)
a juicy tropical fruit with yellow pulp

manhandle *VERB* (**manhandles, manhandling, manhandled**)
to manhandle someone or something is to handle them or move them roughly

manhole *NOUN* (**manholes**)
a hole, usually with a cover, through which a person can get into a sewer or boiler to inspect or repair it

mania *NOUN* (**manias**)
1 mania is violent madness **2** a mania is a strong enthusiasm • *They have a mania for sport.*

maniac *NOUN* (**maniacs**)
a person who acts in a violent and wild way

manic *ADJECTIVE*
manic behaviour is busy and excited

manifesto *NOUN* (**manifestos**)
a public statement of a group's or person's policy or principles

manipulate *VERB* (**manipulates**, **manipulating**, **manipulated**)
1 to manipulate something is to handle it skilfully **2** to manipulate someone is to get them to do what you want by treating them cleverly

> WORD FAMILY
> **Manipulation** is manipulating something or someone; a **manipulator** is a person who manipulates something or someone.

mankind *NOUN*
mankind is all the people in the world • *This is a discovery for the good of all mankind.*

manly *ADJECTIVE* (**manlier**, **manliest**)
1 strong or brave **2** suitable for a man
▷ **manliness** *NOUN* manliness is being manly

man-made *ADJECTIVE*
made by human beings and not by nature • *This is a man-made lake*

manner *NOUN* (**manners**)
the way that something happens or is done

manners *PLURAL NOUN*
a person's manners are how they behave with other people; behaving politely

manoeuvre *NOUN* (**manoeuvres**) (*say* ma- **noo**- ver)
a skilful or clever action

manoeuvre *VERB* (**manoeuvres**, **manoeuvring**, **manoeuvred**)
1 to manoeuvre something is to move it skilfully into position **2** to manoeuvre is to move skilfully or cleverly

> WORD FAMILY
> Something is **manoeuvrable** when it is easy to move into position.

man-of-war *NOUN* (**men-of-war**)
in earlier times, a warship

manor *NOUN* (**manors**)
a large important house in the country

mansion *NOUN* (**mansions**)
a large stately house

manslaughter *NOUN* (*say* **man**- slaw- ter)
manslaughter is the crime of killing someone without meaning to

mantelpiece *NOUN* (**mantelpieces**)
a shelf above a fireplace

mantle *NOUN* (**mantles**)
1 (*old use*) a cloak **2** a covering • *There was a mantle of snow on the hills.*

manual *ADJECTIVE*
manual work is work you do with your hands; manual equipment is equipment used with your hands

> WORD FAMILY
> You do something **manually** when you use your hands to do it.

manual *NOUN* (**manuals**)
a handbook or book of instructions

manufacture *VERB* (**manufactures**, **manufacturing**, **manufactured**)
to manufacture things is to make them with machines, usually in a factory

manufacture *NOUN*
manufacture is the process of making things with machines, especially in large quantities for sale

> WORD FAMILY
> A **manufacturer** is a business that manufactures things.

manure *NOUN*
manure is animal dung added to the soil to make it more fertile

manuscript *NOUN* (**manuscripts**)
something written or typed before it has been printed

Manx *ADJECTIVE*
to do with the Isle of Man

Manx cat *NOUN* (**Manx cats**)
a breed of cat without a tail

many *DETERMINER* (**more**, **most**)
large in number • *There were many people at the party.* • *How many potatoes do you want?*

many *NOUN*
a large number of people or things • *Many were found.*

Maori *NOUN* (**Maoris**) (*say* **mow**- ri)
1 a member of the aboriginal people of New Zealand **2** their language

map *NOUN* (**maps**)
a diagram of part or all of the earth's surface, showing features such as towns, mountains, and rivers
to put a place on the map is to do something that makes it famous

map *VERB* (**maps**, **mapping**, **mapped**)
to map an area is to make a map of it
to map something out is to arrange it or organize it

maple *NOUN* (**maples**)
a tree with broad leaves

mar *VERB* (**mars**, **marring**, **marred**)
to mar something is to spoil it

marathon *NOUN* (**marathons**)
a long-distance running race on roads, usually 26 miles long

marauder *NOUN* (**marauders**)
marauders are people who attack a place and steal things from it

> WORD FAMILY
> A **marauding** army or pack of animals goes round a place attacking people or stealing things.

marble *NOUN* (**marbles**)
1 a marble is a small glass ball used in games **2** marble is a hard kind of limestone that is polished and used for building or sculpture

March *NOUN*
the third month of the year

march *VERB* (**marches**, **marching**, **marched**)
1 to march is to walk with regular steps **2** to march someone is to make them walk somewhere • *He marched them up the hill.*
▷ **marcher** *NOUN* someone who marches

march *NOUN* (**marches**)
1 a march is a large group of people marching, sometimes to protest about something **2** a march is also a piece of music suitable for marching to

mare *NOUN* (**mares**)
a female horse or donkey

margarine *NOUN* (*say* mar- ja- **reen**)
margarine is a soft creamy substance used like butter, made from animal or vegetable fats

margin *NOUN* (**margins**)
1 the empty space between the edge of a page and the writing or pictures **2** the small difference between two scores or prices • *She won by a narrow margin.*

marginal *ADJECTIVE*
a marginal difference is a very small or slight one • *The difference in price is marginal.*
▷ **marginally** *ADVERB* very slightly; by a small amount

marigold *NOUN* (**marigolds**)
a yellow or orange garden flower

marijuana *NOUN* (*say* ma- ri- **hwahna**)
marijuana is a drug made from hemp

marina *NOUN* (**marinas**) (*say* ma- **ree**- na)
a harbour for yachts and motor boats

marine *ADJECTIVE* (*say* ma- **reen**)
to do with the sea

marine *NOUN* (**marines**)
a soldier trained to serve on land and sea

mariner *NOUN* (**mariners**)
(*old use*) a sailor

marionette *NOUN* (**marionettes**)
a puppet that you work by strings or wires

mark[1] *NOUN* (**marks**)
1 a spot, dot, line, or stain on something **2** a number or letter put on a piece of work to show how good it is **3** a distinguishing feature or sign of something • *They kept a minute's silence as a mark of respect.* **4** the place from which you start a race • *On your marks, get set, go!*

mark *VERB* (**marks**, **marking**, **marked**)
1 to mark something is to put a mark on it **2** to mark a piece of work is to give it a number or letter to show how good it is **3** in football or hockey, to mark a player on the other team is to keep close to them to stop them getting the ball **4** to mark something said is to take note of it • *Mark my words!*

mark[2] *NOUN* (**marks**)
a former German unit of money

market *NOUN* (**markets**)
1 a place where things are bought and sold, usually from stalls in the open air **2** a demand for goods • *There is hardly any market for typewriters now.*

market *VERB* (**markets**, **marketing**, **marketed**)
to market a product is to put it on sale

marksman *NOUN* (**marksmen**)
an expert in shooting at a target

> WORD FAMILY
> **Marksmanship** is the skill of shooting at a target.

marmalade *NOUN*
marmalade is jam made from oranges or lemons

maroon[1] *VERB* (**maroons**, **marooning**, **marooned**)
to maroon someone is to abandon them in a place far away from other people • *'It sounds thrilling!' said George, picturing them all marooned by fierce storms, waiting to be rescued from peril and starvation!* — Enid Blyton, *Five Go to Demon's Rocks*

maroon[2] *ADJECTIVE*
dark red

marquee *NOUN* (**marquees**) (*say* mar- **kee**)
a large tent used for a party or exhibition

marriage *NOUN* (**marriages**)
1 marriage is the state of being married **2** a marriage is a wedding

marrow *NOUN* (**marrows**)
1 a marrow is a large green or yellow vegetable with a hard skin **2** marrow is the soft substance inside your bones

marry *VERB* (**marries**, **marrying**, **married**)
1 to marry someone is to become their husband or wife **2** to marry two people is to perform a marriage ceremony

marsh *NOUN* (**marshes**)
a low-lying area of very wet ground

> WORD FAMILY
> **Marshy** ground is low-lying and very wet.

a b c d e f g h i j k l **m** n o p q r s t u v w x y z

marshal *NOUN* (**marshals**)
1 an official who supervises a contest or ceremony **2** a high-ranking officer •*He is a Field Marshal.* **3** a police official in the USA

marshmallow *NOUN* (**marshmallows**)
marshmallow is a soft spongy sweet

marsupial *NOUN* (**marsupials**) (*say* mar- soo- pi- al)
an animal such as a kangaroo, wallaby, or koala. The female has a pouch for carrying her young

martial *ADJECTIVE*
to do with war or fighting

martial arts *PLURAL NOUN*
martial arts are fighting sports such as karate and judo

martial law *NOUN*
martial law is government of a country by the army during a crisis

Martian *NOUN* (**Martians**)
in stories, a creature from the planet Mars

martin *NOUN* (**martins**)
a bird rather like a swallow

martyr *NOUN* (**martyrs**) (*say* mar- ter)
someone who is killed or suffers because of their beliefs

> WORD FAMILY
> **Martyrdom** is when someone is killed or suffers because of their beliefs.

marvel *NOUN* (**marvels**)
a wonderful thing

marvel *VERB* (**marvels, marvelling, marvelled**)
to marvel at something is to be filled with wonder or astonishment by it •*When people call this beast to mind, / They marvel more and more / At such a little tail behind, / So large a trunk before.* — Hillaire Belloc, *The Elephant*

marvellous *ADJECTIVE*
wonderful
▷ **marvellously** *ADVERB* in a marvellous way

Marxism *NOUN*
Marxism is the Communist ideas of the German writer Karl Marx (1818-83)

> WORD FAMILY
> A **Marxist** is a person who believes in Marxism.

marzipan *NOUN*
marzipan is a soft sweet food made from almonds and sugar, sometimes put on the top of cakes

mascot *NOUN* (**mascots**)
a person, animal, or object that is believed to bring good luck

masculine *ADJECTIVE*
1 to do with men or like men; suitable for men **2** in some languages, belonging to the class of words that includes words referring to men

> WORD FAMILY
> **Masculinity** is being masculine.

mash *VERB* (**mashes, mashing, mashed**)
to mash something is to crush it into a soft mass

mash *NOUN*
(*informal*) mashed potatoes

mask *NOUN* (**masks**)
a covering that you wear over your face to disguise or protect it

mask *VERB* (**masks, masking, masked**)
1 to mask your face is to cover it with a mask **2** to mask something is to hide it

Mason *NOUN* (**Masons**)
a member of a secret society called the Freemasons

mason *NOUN* (**masons**)
someone who builds or works with stone

masonry *NOUN*
masonry is the stone parts of a building

Mass *NOUN* (**Masses**)
the Communion service in a Roman Catholic church

mass *NOUN* (**masses**)
1 a large amount of something **2** a lump or heap **3** (*in science*) the amount of matter in an object, measured in grams
the masses the ordinary people

mass *VERB* (**masses, massing, massed**)
to mass is to collect into a mass •*People were massing in the square.*

massacre *VERB* (**massacres, massacring, massacred**) (*say* mas- a- ker)
to massacre people is to kill a large number of them

massacre *NOUN* (**massacres**)
the killing of a large number of people

massage *VERB* (**massages, massaging, massaged**) (*say* mas- ahzh)
to massage the body is to rub and press it to make it less stiff or less painful

massage *NOUN*
massaging someone's body

massive *ADJECTIVE*
very big; large and heavy
▷ **massively** *ADVERB* hugely

mass production *NOUN*
mass production is when goods are produced in large quantities

mast *NOUN* (**masts**)
a tall pole that holds up a ship's sails or a flag or aerial

master *NOUN* (**masters**)
1 a man who is in charge of something **2** a male teacher **3** someone who is very good at what they do, such as a great artist or composer **4** something from which copies are made
Master (*old use*) a title put before a boy's name

master *VERB* (**masters, mastering, mastered**)
1 to master a subject or skill is to learn it completely **2** to master a fear or difficulty is to control it •*She succeeded in mastering her fear of heights.*

masterly *ADJECTIVE*
very clever or skilful

mastermind *NOUN* (**masterminds**)
1 a very clever person **2** someone who organizes a scheme or crime

masterpiece *NOUN* (**masterpieces**)
1 an excellent piece of work **2** someone's best piece of work

mastery *NOUN*
mastery is complete control or knowledge of something • *He has a complete mastery of the art of fencing.*

mat *NOUN* (**mats**)
1 a small piece of material that partly covers a floor **2** a small piece of material put on a table to protect the surface

matador *NOUN* (**matadors**)
someone who fights and kills the bull in a bullfight

match[1] *NOUN* (**matches**)
a small thin stick with a small amount of chemical at one end that gives a flame when rubbed on something rough

match[2] *NOUN* (**matches**)
1 a game or contest between two teams or players **2** one person or thing that is equal or similar to another • *Can you find a match for this sock?* **3** a marriage

match *VERB* (**matches, matching, matched**)
1 to match another person or thing is to be equal to them **2** one thing matches another when it goes well with it • *Your jacket matches your shoes.* **3** to match one person with another is to put them in competition

mate[1] *NOUN* (**mates**)
1 a friend or companion **2** one of a pair of animals that produce young together **3** one of the officers on a ship

mate *VERB* (**mates, mating, mated**)
1 to mate is to come together in order to have offspring **2** to mate animals is to put them together so that they will have offspring

mate[2] *NOUN* (**mates**)
checkmate in chess

material *NOUN* (**materials**)
1 anything used for making something else **2** cloth or fabric

materialistic *ADJECTIVE*
liking possessions and money more than anything else

maternal *ADJECTIVE*
to do with a mother; motherly

maternity *NOUN*
maternity is having a baby; motherhood

mathematician *NOUN* (**mathematicians**) (*say* math- em- a- **tish**- an)
an expert in mathematics

mathematics *NOUN*
mathematics is the study of numbers, measurements, and shapes

> WORD FAMILY
> A **mathematical** problem or calculation is one you need mathematics to work out, and **mathematical** ability is being able to do mathematics.

maths *NOUN*
(*informal*) maths is mathematics

matinée *NOUN* (**matinées**) (*say* **mat**- i- nay)
an afternoon performance at a theatre or cinema

matrimony *NOUN* (*say* **mat**- ri- mo- ni)
matrimony is marriage
▷ **matrimonial** *ADJECTIVE* to do with marriage

matrix *NOUN* (**matrices**)
(*in mathematics*) a set of numbers or quantities arranged in rows and columns

matron *NOUN* (**matrons**)
1 an older married woman **2** a woman in charge of health in a school

matt *ADJECTIVE*
not shiny • *The wall was decorated with matt paint.*

matted *ADJECTIVE*
tangled

matter *NOUN* (**matters**)
1 something you need to think about or do • *It is a serious matter.* **2** a substance • *Peat consists mainly of vegetable matter.*
a matter of fact something true
no matter it is not important
what's the matter? what is wrong?

matter *VERB* (**matters, mattering, mattered**)
to matter is to be important

matting *NOUN*
matting is mats; rough material for covering a floor

mattress *NOUN* (**mattresses**)
a thick layer of soft or springy material covered in cloth and used on a bed

mature *ADJECTIVE*
1 fully grown or developed **2** behaving in a sensible adult manner

> WORD FAMILY
> **Maturity** is being fully grown or behaving in a sensible adult manner.

mature (**matures, maturing, matured**)
to become fully grown or developed

mauve *ADJECTIVE* (*say* mohv)
pale purple

maximum *NOUN* (**maxima**)
the greatest number or amount possible • *The maximum is 10.*

maximum *ADJECTIVE*
the greatest possible • *The maximum speed is 60 miles per hour.*

May *NOUN*
the fifth month of the year

may *VERB* (*past tense* **might**)
1 may means to be allowed to • *May I have a sweet?* **2** may also means that something will possibly happen or has possibly happened • *He may come tomorrow.* • *He might have missed the train.*

maybe *ADVERB*
perhaps

May Day *NOUN*
the first day of May, often celebrated with sport and dancing

mayday *NOUN* (**maydays**)
an international radio signal calling for help

mayonnaise *NOUN* (*say* may- on- **ayz**)
mayonnaise is a creamy sauce made from eggs, oil, and vinegar, and used on salads

mayor *NOUN* (**mayors**)
the person in charge of the council in a town or city

mayoress *NOUN* (**mayoresses**)
a woman who is a mayor

maypole *NOUN* (**maypoles**)
a decorated pole which people dance round on May Day

maze *NOUN* (**mazes**)
a complicated arrangement of paths or lines to follow your way through as a game or puzzle

me *PRONOUN*
a word used for *I*, usually when it is the object of a sentence, or when it comes after a preposition • *She likes me.* • *She gave it to me.*

meadow *NOUN* (**meadows**)
a field of grass

meagre *ADJECTIVE* (*say* meeg- er)
very little; barely enough • *The Rev. John Whittier was the pastor of this small mission church, and had a very meagre salary.* — Eleanor H. Porter, *Pollyanna*

meal[1] *NOUN* (**meals**)
a meal is the food eaten at one time, such as breakfast, lunch, or dinner

meal[2] *NOUN*
meal is grain coarsely ground to a powder

mean[1] *VERB* (**means**, **meaning**, **meant**)
1 to mean something is to have that as its explanation or equivalent, or to convey that as its sense • *What does this word mean?* **2** to mean to do something is to intend to do it • *I meant to tell him, but I forgot.*

mean[2] *ADJECTIVE* (**meaner**, **meanest**)
1 not generous; selfish • *What a mean man.*
2 unkind or spiteful • *That was a mean trick.*
▷ **meanly** *ADVERB* in a mean way
▷ **meanness** *NOUN* meanness is being mean

mean[3] *ADJECTIVE*
(*in mathematics*) average • *Work out the mean temperature.*

meander *VERB* (**meanders**, **meandering**, **meandered**) (*say* mee- **an**- der)
a river or road meanders when it takes a winding course, with a lot of bends

meaning *NOUN* (**meanings**)
what something means

> **WORD FAMILY**
> A **meaningful** look is one that expresses a meaning; something is **meaningless** when it has no meaning or purpose.

means *NOUN*
a means of doing something is a way or method of doing it
by all means certainly
by means of something using something or with something
by no means not at all

means *PLURAL NOUN*
money or other resources for doing things

meantime *NOUN*
in the meantime meanwhile

meanwhile *ADVERB*
while something else is happening • *I'll cut the cake up; meanwhile, you get the plates out.*

measles *PLURAL NOUN*
measles is an infectious disease that causes small red spots on the skin

measly *ADJECTIVE* (**measlier**, **measliest**)
(*informal*) very small or poor • *All I got was a measly T-shirt.*

measure *VERB* (**measures**, **measuring**, **measured**)
1 to measure something is to find out how big it is **2** to measure (for example) six feet is to be six feet long

measure *NOUN* (**measures**)
1 a unit used for measuring something **2** a device used for measuring **3** the size of something **4** something done for a particular purpose; a law or rule

measurement *NOUN* (**measurements**)
1 a measurement is the size or length of something **2** measurement is when you measure something

meat *NOUN* (**meats**)
meat is animal flesh that is cooked as food

> **WORD FAMILY**
> **Meaty** food is full of meat. • *meaty sausages*

mechanic *NOUN* (**mechanics**)
someone who maintains and repairs machinery

mechanical *ADJECTIVE*
1 to do with machines **2** done without thinking about it

> **WORD FAMILY**
> You do something **mechanically** when you do it without thinking about it.

mechanics *NOUN*
1 mechanics is the study of movement and force **2** mechanics is also the study or use of machines

mechanism *NOUN* (**mechanisms**)
1 the moving parts of a machine **2** the way a machine works

medal *NOUN* (**medals**)
a piece of metal shaped like a coin, star, or cross, given to someone for bravery or for achieving something • *She won two Olympic gold medals.*

medallist *NOUN* (**medallists**)
a winner of a medal

meddle *VERB* (**meddles**, **meddling**, **meddled**)
to meddle in something is to interfere in it

> WORD FAMILY
> A **meddler** is someone who interferes with something; a **meddlesome** person likes to do this.

media *PLURAL NOUN* (*say* mee- di- a)
the plural of **medium** *NOUN*
the media newspapers and radio and television, which provide information about current events to the public

median *NOUN* (**medians**)
(*in mathematics*) the middle number in a set of numbers that have been arranged in order • *The median of 2, 3, 5, 8, 9, 14, and 15 is 8.*

medical *ADJECTIVE*
to do with the treatment of disease
▷ **medically** *ADVERB* by medical means

medicine *NOUN* (**medicines**)
1 a medicine is a substance, usually swallowed, used to try to cure an illness **2** medicine is the treatment of disease and injuries

> WORD FAMILY
> Something is **medicinal** when it helps to cure an illness.

medieval *ADJECTIVE* (*say* med- i- **ee**- val)
to do with the Middle Ages

mediocre *ADJECTIVE* (*say* meed- i- **oh**- ker)
only fairly good

> WORD FAMILY
> **Mediocrity** is being mediocre.

meditate *VERB* (**meditates**, **meditating**, **meditated**)
to meditate is to think deeply and seriously, usually in silence

> WORD FAMILY
> **Meditation** is thinking deeply and seriously, usually in silence.

Mediterranean *ADJECTIVE* (*say* med- i- ter- **ay**- ni- an)
to do with the Mediterranean Sea, which is between Europe and Africa, or the countries round it

medium[1] *ADJECTIVE*
average; of middle size

medium[2] *NOUN* (**media** or **mediums**)
1 a thing in which something exists, moves, or is expressed • *Air is the medium in which sound travels.* **2** someone who claims to communicate with the dead

> GRAMMAR
> The plural is **media** in the first meaning and **mediums** in the second meaning.

meek *ADJECTIVE* (**meeker**, **meekest**)
quiet and obedient

> WORD FAMILY
> To **meekly** do something is to do it quietly and obediently; **meekness** is being meek.

meet *VERB* (**meets**, **meeting**, **met**)
1 to meet is to come together from different places • *We all met in London* . **2** to meet someone is to come face to face with them, especially for the first time or by an arrangement • *I met her at a party.* • *I'll meet you at the station.* **3** to meet a bill or cost is to be able to pay it • *He is finding it difficult to meet all his debts.*

meeting *NOUN* (**meetings**)
a time when people come together for a special purpose, often to discuss something

megabyte *NOUN* (**megabytes**)
(*in computing*) a unit that measures data or memory, roughly equal to one million bytes

megaphone *NOUN* (**megaphones**)
a funnel-shaped device for making someone's voice sound louder

melancholy *ADJECTIVE*
sad and gloomy • *By and by there was to be heard a sound at once the most musical and the most melancholy in the world: the mermaids calling to the moon.* — J. M. Barrie, *The Adventures of Peter Pan*

mellow *ADJECTIVE* (**mellower**, **mellowest**)
having a soft rich sound or colour

melodious *ADJECTIVE*
sounding sweet; pleasant to listen to

melodrama *NOUN* (**melodramas**)
a play full of excitement and emotion

> WORD FAMILY
> A story is **melodramatic** when it is full of exciting events and lots of emotion.

melody *NOUN* (**melodies**)
a tune, especially one that is pleasant to listen to

> WORD FAMILY
> A **melodic** piece of music has a tune that is pleasant to listen to.

melon *NOUN* (**melons**)
a large juicy fruit with yellow or green skin

melt *VERB* (**melts**, **melting**, **melted**)
1 to melt something solid is to make it liquid by heating it **2** to melt is to become liquid by heating **3** to melt, or to melt away, is to go away or disappear slowly • *The crowd gradually melted away.*

member *NOUN* (**members**)
someone who belongs to a society or group

> WORD FAMILY
> A person's **membership** of a society or group is the fact that they are a member of it.

Member of Parliament *NOUN* (**Members of Parliament**)
someone who has been elected by the people of an area to speak for them in Parliament

membrane *NOUN* (**membranes**)
a thin skin or covering

memoirs *PLURAL NOUN*
a famous person's account of their own life and experiences

memorable *ADJECTIVE*
1 worth remembering • *It was a memorable holiday.*
2 easy to remember • *He has a memorable name.*

> WORD FAMILY
> Something happens **memorably** when it is so unusual or important that people will remember it.

memorial *NOUN* (**memorials**)
something set up to remind people of a person or an event • *They passed a war memorial in the High Street.*

memorize *VERB* (**memorizes**, **memorizing**, **memorized**)
to memorize something is to learn it and remember it exactly

memory *NOUN* (**memories**)
1 memory is the ability to remember things **2** a memory is something that you remember, usually something interesting or special **3** a computer's memory is the part where information is stored
to do something in memory of someone or **something** is to do it in order to remind people of a person or an event

men
plural of **man** *NOUN*

menace *VERB* (**menaces**, **menacing**, **menaced**)
to menace someone is to threaten them with harm or danger • *Rabbits avoid close woodland, where the ground is shady, damp and grassless and they feel menaced by the undergrowth.* — Richard Adams, *Watership Down*

menace *NOUN* (**menaces**)
1 something that threatens people with harm or danger **2** an annoying person or thing

menagerie *NOUN* (**menageries**) (*say* min- aj- er- i)
a small zoo

mend *VERB* (**mends**, **mending**, **mended**)
to mend something that is broken or damaged is to make it as good as it was before
to be on the mend is to be getting better after an illness
▷ **mender** *NOUN* someone who mends something

meningitis *NOUN* (*say* men-in-jI-tiss)
a serious disease caused by a virus, in which the covering of the brain becomes inflamed

menstruation *NOUN*
menstruation is the natural flow of blood from a woman's womb, normally happening every 28 days
▷ **menstrual** *ADJECTIVE* to do with menstruation

-ment *SUFFIX*
used to make nouns, as in *amusement* and *oddments*

mental *ADJECTIVE*
1 to do with the mind • *mental arithmetic.*
2 (*informal*) mad or crazy

> WORD FAMILY
> You **mentally** work something out when you do it in your head; someone who is **mentally** ill is ill in their mind.

mention *VERB* (**mentions**, **mentioning**, **mentioned**)
to mention someone or something is to speak about them briefly

mention *NOUN* (**mentions**)
when someone or something is mentioned • *Our school got a mention in the local paper.*

menu *NOUN* (**menus**) (*say* men- yoo)
1 a list of the food that is available in a restaurant or served at a meal **2** (*in computing*) a list of possible actions, displayed on a screen, from which you choose what you want a computer to do

MEP
short for *Member of the European Parliament*

mercenary *ADJECTIVE*
interested only in the money you can get for the work you do

mercenary *NOUN* (**mercenaries**)
a soldier hired to fight for a foreign country

merchandise *NOUN*
merchandise is goods for buying or selling

merchant *NOUN* (**merchants**)
someone involved in trade

merchant navy *NOUN* (**merchant navies**)
the ships and sailors that carry goods for trade

merciful *ADJECTIVE*
showing mercy
▷ **mercifully** *ADVERB* in a merciful way

merciless *ADJECTIVE*
showing no mercy; cruel
▷ **mercilessly** *ADVERB* in a merciless way

mercury *NOUN*
mercury is a heavy silvery metal that is usually liquid, used in thermometers

mercy *NOUN* (**mercies**)
1 mercy is kindness or pity shown towards someone instead of harming them or punishing them **2** a mercy is something to be thankful for • *Thank God for small mercies.*

mere [1] *ADJECTIVE*
not more than • *He's a mere child.*

mere [2] *NOUN* (**meres**)
(*poetical use*) a lake

merely *ADVERB*
only; simply • *She was merely joking.*

merge *VERB* (**merges, merging, merged**)
1 to merge things is to combine or blend them **2** to merge is to be combined

merger *NOUN* (**mergers**)
a merger is when two businesses or companies join together into one

meridian *NOUN* (**meridians**) (*say* mer- **rid**- i- an)
a line on a map or globe from the North Pole to the South Pole

meringue *NOUN* (**meringues**) (*say* mer- **rang**)
a crisp cake made from the whites of eggs mixed with sugar and baked

merit *NOUN* (**merits**)
1 to have merit is to be good or excellent **2** a merit is something that deserves praise • *I can see the merits of this argument.*

merit *VERB* (**merits, meriting, merited**)
to merit something is to deserve something good

mermaid *NOUN* (**mermaids**)
a mythical sea creature with a woman's body and a fish's tail instead of legs

merry *ADJECTIVE* (**merrier, merriest**)
happy and cheerful

> WORD FAMILY
> To do or say something **merrily** is to do so in a merry way; **merriment** is being happy and cheerful.

merry-go-round *NOUN* (**merry-go-rounds**)
a large roundabout with horses and other things to ride on

mesh *NOUN* (**meshes**)
1 mesh is material made like a net, with open spaces between the wire or threads

mess *NOUN* (**messes**)
1 something untidy or dirty **2** a difficult or confused situation **3** a place where soldiers or sailors eat their meals
to make a mess of something is to do it very badly

mess *VERB* (**messes, messing, messed**)
to mess about is to waste time behaving stupidly or doing things slowly • *Stop messing about and give me a hand.*
to mess something up is to do it very badly

message *NOUN* (**messages**)
a question or piece of information that one person sends to another

messenger *NOUN* (**messengers**)
someone who carries a message

Messiah *NOUN* (*say* mi- **sy**- a)
1 the person that the Jews expect to come as their saviour **2** Jesus Christ, who Christians believe was their saviour

messy *ADJECTIVE* (**messier, messiest**)
1 untidy or dirty **2** difficult or complicated • *I'm afraid it's a messy situation.*

> WORD FAMILY
> You do something **messily** when you make a mess doing it.

met
past tense and past participle of **meet**

metal *NOUN* (**metals**)
a hard substance that melts when it is heated, such as gold, silver, copper, and iron

> WORD FAMILY
> Something **metallic** is made of metal or shines like metal.

metallurgy *NOUN* (*say* mi- **tal**- er- ji)
1 metallurgy is the study of metals **2** metallurgy is also the craft of making and using metals
▷ **metallurgical** *ADJECTIVE* to do with metallurgy
▷ **metallurgist** *NOUN* an expert in using metals

metamorphosis *NOUN* (**metamorphoses**)
a complete change made by some living things, such as a caterpillar changing into a butterfly

metaphor *NOUN* (**metaphors**) (*say* **met**- a- fer)
using words in a way that describes one thing as if it were something else, as in *the lion, the king of beasts*, in which *king* is a metaphor. See the panel at **similes and metaphors**.

> WORD FAMILY
> **Metaphorical** language uses metaphors; you use an expression **metaphorically** when you use it in a metaphorical way.

meteor *NOUN* (**meteors**) (*say* **meet**- i- er)
a piece of rock or metal that moves through space and burns up as it enters the earth's atmosphere

meteoric *ADJECTIVE*
very fast and sudden, like a meteor • *They've had a meteoric rise to fame.*

meteorite *NOUN* (**meteorites**) (*say* **meet**- i- er- ryt)
the remains of a meteor that has landed on the earth

meteorology *NOUN* (*say* meet- i- er- **ol**- o- ji)
meteorology is the study of the weather
▷ **meteorological** *ADJECTIVE* to do with meteorology
▷ **meteorologist** *NOUN* an expert on the weather

a b c d e f g h i j k l m n o p q r s t u v w x y z

meter *NOUN* (**meters**)
a device for measuring something, especially for measuring how much of something has been used

> SPELLING
> Take care not to confuse **meter** with **metre**, which means a unit of length or a rhythm.

methane *NOUN*
methane is an inflammable gas produced when plants rot away, found mainly in mines and marshes

method *NOUN* (**methods**)
1 a method is a way of doing something **2** method is good organization or orderly behaviour • *There is method in everything she does.*

methodical *ADJECTIVE* (*say* mi- **thod**- i- kal)
done carefully and in a logical way

> WORD FAMILY
> You do something **methodically** when you do it in a careful and logical way.

Methodist *NOUN* (**Methodists**)
someone who believes in Methodism, a Christian religious movement started by John and Charles Wesley in the 18th century

meths *NOUN*
(*informal*) meths is methylated spirit

methylated spirit or **spirits** *NOUN*
methylated spirit is a liquid fuel made from alcohol

meticulous *ADJECTIVE*
very careful and precise
▷ **meticulously** *ADVERB* in a meticulous way

metre *NOUN* (**metres**) (*say* **meet**- er)
1 the main unit of length in the metric system, equal to about $39\frac{1}{2}$ inches **2** a particular type of rhythm in poetry

> SPELLING
> Take care not to confuse **metre** with **meter**, which means a machine for measuring something.

metric *ADJECTIVE*
1 to do with the metric system **2** to do with metre in poetry

metrical *ADJECTIVE*
written as poetry rather than prose

metric system *NOUN*
a measuring system based on decimal units (the metre, litre, and gram)

metronome *NOUN* (**metronomes**) (*say* **met**- ro- nohm)
a device that makes a regular clicking noise to help you keep in time when practising music

mettle *NOUN*
to be on your mettle is to be ready to do your best

mew *VERB* (**mews**, **mewing**, **mewed**)
to make a sound like a cat

miaow *VERB* (**miaows**, **miaowing**, **miaowed**) (*say* mee- **ow**)
to make a sound like a cat

mice
plural of **mouse**

microbe *NOUN* (**microbes**) (*say* **my**- krohb)
a tiny organism that can only be seen with a microscope

microchip *NOUN* (**microchips**)
a very small piece of silicon working as an electric circuit, used in computers

microcomputer *NOUN* (**microcomputers**)
a small computer that uses a microprocessor as its central processing unit

microfilm *NOUN* (**microfilms**)
film on which printing or writing is photographed in greatly reduced size

microphone *NOUN* (**microphones**)
an electrical device that picks up sound waves for recording them or making them louder

microprocessor *NOUN* (**microprocessors**)
a set of microchips that form the central processing unit of a computer

microscope *NOUN* (**microscopes**) (*say* **my**- kro- skohp)
a device with lenses that make tiny objects appear larger so you can study them

microscopic *ADJECTIVE* (*say* my- kro- **skop**- ik)
too small to be seen without a microscope; tiny

microwave *NOUN* (**microwaves**)
1 energy moving in very short waves **2** a microwave oven

microwave *VERB* (**microwaves**, **microwaving**, **microwaved**)
to microwave food is to cook it in a microwave oven

microwave oven *NOUN* (**microwave ovens**)
a kind of oven which heats things quickly by using energy in very short waves

mid *ADJECTIVE*
in the middle of • *The holiday is from mid-July to mid-August.*

midday *NOUN*
the middle of the day; noon

middle *NOUN* (**middles**)
1 the middle of something is the place or part that is at the same distance from all its sides or edges or from both its ends **2** someone's waist

middle *ADJECTIVE*
placed in the middle

middle-aged *ADJECTIVE*
aged between about forty and sixty

Middle Ages *NOUN*
the period in history from about AD 1100 to 1500

middle class *NOUN* or **middle classes** *PLURAL NOUN*
the class of people between the upper class and the working class, including business and professional people such as teachers, doctors, and lawyers

> WORD FAMILY
> **Middle-class** people belong to the middle class.

Middle East *NOUN*
the countries to the east of the Mediterranean Sea, from Egypt to Iran

middle school *NOUN* (**middle schools**)
a school for children aged from about 9 to 13

midge *NOUN* (**midges**)
a small insect like a gnat

midget *NOUN* (**midgets**)
an unusually short person

midland *ADJECTIVE*
of the middle part of a country; of the middle part of England

Midlands *PLURAL NOUN*
the central part of England

midnight *NOUN*
twelve o'clock at night

midst *NOUN*
to be in the midst of something is to be in the middle of it

midsummer *NOUN*
the middle of summer, about 21 June in the northern hemisphere

midway *ADVERB*
halfway

midwife *NOUN* (**midwives**)
a person trained to look after a woman who is giving birth to a baby

> WORD FAMILY
> **Midwifery** is the job of a midwife.

might [1]
past tense of **may** *VERB*

might [2] *NOUN*
great power or strength

mighty *ADJECTIVE* (**mightier**, **mightiest**)
very strong or powerful

> WORD FAMILY
> You are (for example) **mightily** impressed by something when you are very impressed indeed.

migraine *NOUN* (**migraines**) (*say* **mee- grayn**)
a severe kind of headache

migrant *NOUN* (**migrants**) (*say* **my- grant**)
1 a person who moves from one place to another, usually to find work **2** a bird or animal that moves from one region to another

migrate *VERB* (**migrates**, **migrating**, **migrated**) (*say* **my- grayt**)
1 to migrate is to move from one place to another, usually to find work **2** birds migrate when they fly to a warmer region for the winter

> WORD FAMILY
> **Migration** is migrating to another country; **migratory** birds migrate every year.

mike *NOUN* (**mikes**)
(*informal*) a microphone

mild *ADJECTIVE* (**milder**, **mildest**)
gentle; not harsh or severe • *Miss Jennifer Honey was a mild and quiet person who never raised her voice and was seldom seen to smile.* — Roald Dahl, *Matilda*

> WORD FAMILY
> To be **mildly** surprised or interested is to be slightly surprised or interested; **mildness** is being mild.

mile *NOUN* (**miles**)
a measure of distance, equal to 1,760 yards or about 1.6 kilometres

mileage *NOUN* (**mileages**)
the number of miles you have travelled

milestone *NOUN* (**milestones**)
1 a stone of a kind that used to be placed beside a road to mark the distance between towns **2** an important event in history or in a person's life

militant *ADJECTIVE*
aggressive; eager to fight
▷ **militancy** *NOUN* militancy is being militant

militarism *NOUN*
militarism is belief in the use of military strength and methods
▷ **militaristic** *ADJECTIVE* using military strength

military *ADJECTIVE*
to do with soldiers or the armed forces

milk *NOUN*
milk is a white liquid that female mammals produce in their bodies to feed to their young

milk *VERB* (**milks**, **milking**, **milked**)
to milk a cow or other animal is to get milk from it

milkman *NOUN* (**milkmen**)
a man who delivers milk to people's houses

milk shake *NOUN* (**milk shakes**)
a frothy drink of milk mixed with a sweet fruit flavouring

milk tooth *NOUN* (**milk teeth**)
one of the first set of teeth a child or animal has, which are later replaced by adult teeth

milky *ADJECTIVE* (**milkier**, **milkiest**)
1 like milk; white **2** made with a lot of milk

Milky Way *NOUN*
a faintly shining band of light from the stars in our galaxy

mill *NOUN* (**mills**)
1 a building with machinery for grinding corn to make flour **2** a factory for making materials, such as a paper mill or a steel mill **3** a machine for grinding something such as coffee or pepper

mill *VERB* (**mills, milling, milled**)
1 to mill something is to grind or crush it in a mill **2** people mill or mill about when they move in a confused crowd

millennium *NOUN* (**millenniums**)
a period of 1,000 years

miller *NOUN* (**millers**)
someone who runs a flour mill

millet *NOUN*
a kind of cereal with tiny seeds

milligram *NOUN* (**milligrams**)
one thousandth of a gram

millilitre *NOUN* (**millilitres**)
one thousandth of a litre

millimetre *NOUN* (**millimetres**)
one thousandth of a metre

million *NOUN* (**millions**)
a thousand thousands (1,000,000)
▷ **millionth** *ADJECTIVE & NOUN* 1,000,000th

millionaire *NOUN* (**millionaires**)
an extremely rich person who has at least a million pounds or dollars

millstone *NOUN* (**millstones**)
a large heavy stone used in grinding corn
a millstone round someone's neck a heavy burden or responsibility

milometer *NOUN* (**milometers**) (*say* my-lom-it-er)
a device for measuring how far a vehicle has travelled

mime *VERB* (**mimes, miming, mimed**)
to mime is to tell a story by using movements of the body without speaking

mime *NOUN* (**mimes**)
mime is the art of telling a story by using movements of the body without speaking

mimic *VERB* (**mimics, mimicking, mimicked**)
to mimic someone is to imitate them, especially to make people laugh

> WORD FAMILY
> **Mimicry** is imitating someone to make people laugh.

mimic *NOUN* (**mimics**)
a person who is good at imitating other people

minaret *NOUN* (**minarets**)
a tall tower on a mosque

mince *NOUN*
mince is meat that has been cut up into very small pieces

mince *VERB* (**minces, mincing, minced**)
to mince food is to cut it up into very small pieces
not to mince words is to speak frankly or bluntly

> WORD FAMILY
> A **mincer** is a device for mincing food.

mincemeat *NOUN*
mincemeat is a sweet mixture of currants, raisins, and chopped fruit, used in pies

mince pie *NOUN* (**mince pies**)
a pie containing mincemeat

mineral *NOUN* (**minerals**)
1 a hard substance that can be dug out of the ground, such as coal and iron ore **2** a natural substance needed by the human body for good health • *Vegetables are an excellent source of vitamins and minerals* **3** a cold fizzy drink

mind *NOUN* (**minds**)
the function of the brain to think, feel, understand, and remember; your thoughts and feelings
to change your mind is to have a new opinion or intention about something
to have a good mind to do something is to intend to do it

mind *VERB* (**minds, minding, minded**)
1 to mind something is to be sad or upset about it • *I don't mind missing the party.* **2** to mind someone or something is to look after them for a time • *He was minding the baby.* **3** to mind, or to mind out, is to be careful or watch out for something • *Mind the doors!*

mindless *ADJECTIVE*
done without thinking; stupid or pointless

mine[1] *ADJECTIVE & PRONOUN*
belonging to me • *That book is mine.*

mine[2] *NOUN* (**mines**)
1 a place where coal, metal, or precious stones are dug out of the ground **2** a type of bomb hidden under the ground or in the sea that explodes when people or things touch it

mine *VERB* (**mines, mining, mined**)
1 to mine something is to dig it from a mine **2** to mine a place is to lay explosives in it

minefield *NOUN* (**minefields**)
1 an area where explosive mines have been laid **2** you can say that an activity is a minefield when it has many dangers

miner *NOUN* (**miners**)
someone who works in a mine

mineral *NOUN* (**minerals**)
1 a hard substance that can be dug out of the ground, such as coal and iron ore **2** a natural substance needed by the human body for good health • *Vegetables are an excellent source of vitamins and minerals* **3** a cold fizzy drink

mineral water *NOUN*
mineral water is water that comes from a natural spring. It can be fizzy or still

mingle *VERB* (**mingles**, **mingling**, **mingled**)
1 things mingle when they become mixed together **2** to mingle things is to mix or blend them

mingy *ADJECTIVE* (**mingier**, **mingiest**) (*say* **min**- ji) (*informal*) mean or stingy

miniature *ADJECTIVE* (*say* **min**- i- cher)
very small, especially copying something larger • *When, what to my wondering / eyes should appear, / But a miniature sleigh, / and eight tiny reindeer.* — Clement Moore, *The Night Before Christmas*

minibeast *NOUN* (**minibeasts**)
a very small creature such as an insect or spider

minibus *NOUN* (**minibuses**)
a small bus with seats for about ten people

minim *NOUN* (**minims**)
a musical note equal to two crotchets or half a semibreve, written 𝅗𝅥

minimal *ADJECTIVE*
very little; as little as possible

minimize *VERB* (**minimizes**, **minimizing**, **minimized**)
to minimize something is to make it as small as possible

minimum *NOUN* (**minima**)
the smallest number or amount possible • *We want the minimum of fuss.*

minimum *ADJECTIVE*
least or smallest • *The minimum number is 3.*

minister *NOUN* (**ministers**)
1 a member of the government who is in charge of a department **2** a member of the clergy

ministry *NOUN* (**ministries**)
1 a government department • *the Ministry of Defence* **2** the work of a minister in the church

mink *NOUN* (**minks**)
1 a mink is a small animal rather like a stoat **2** mink is this animal's valuable brown fur

minnow *NOUN* (**minnows**)
a tiny freshwater fish

minor *ADJECTIVE*
1 not very important, especially when compared to something else **2** of the musical scale that has a semitone between the 2nd and 3rd notes

minority *NOUN* (**minorities**) (*say* myn- **o**- ri- ti)
1 the smaller part of a group of people or things • *There was a minority who wanted to leave.* **2** a small group that is different from others

minstrel *NOUN* (**minstrels**)
a travelling singer and musician in the Middle Ages

mint[1] *NOUN*
1 mint is a green plant with sweet-smelling leaves used for flavouring **2** a mint is a sweet flavoured with peppermint

mint[2] *NOUN* (**mints**)
a place where a country's coins are made
to be in mint condition is to be new, as if it had just been made

mint *VERB* (**mints**, **minting**, **minted**)
to mint coins is to make them

minus *PREPOSITION*
1 less; with the next number taken away • *Eight minus two equals six (8-2 = 6).* **2** less than zero • *The temperature is minus 5 degrees.*

minute[1] *NOUN* (**minutes**) (*say* **min**- it)
1 one-sixtieth of an hour **2** (*informal*) a short time • *I'll be ready in a minute!*

minute[2] *ADJECTIVE* (*say* my- **newt**)
1 tiny • *The insect was minute.* **2** very detailed • *He gave it a minute examination.*

> WORD FAMILY
> You examine something **minutely** when you do it in a very detailed way.

miracle *NOUN* (**miracles**)
a wonderful or magical happening that is unexpected

> WORD FAMILY
> Something **miraculous** is wonderful or magical; something happens **miraculously** when it seems to be a miracle. • *By lunchtime, the whole place was a seething mass of men, women, and children all pushing and shoving to get a glimpse of this miraculous fruit.* — Roald Dahl, *James and the Giant Peach*

mirage *NOUN* (**mirages**) (*say* **mi**- rahzh)
something that seems to be visible but is not really there, like a lake in a desert

mirror *NOUN* (**mirrors**)
a glass or metal surface that reflects things clearly

mirth *NOUN*
mirth is laughter or cheerfulness

mis- *PREFIX*
meaning 'wrong, wrongly', as in *misbehave* and *misunderstanding*

misbehave *VERB* (**misbehaves**, **misbehaving**, **misbehaved**)
to misbehave is to behave badly

> WORD FAMILY
> **Misbehaviour** is when someone behaves badly.

miscarriage *NOUN* (**miscarriages**)
a woman has a miscarriage when she gives birth to a baby before it is old enough to survive

miscellaneous *ADJECTIVE* (*say* mis- el- **ay**- ni- us)
a miscellaneous group is one that is made up of different kinds of thing

miscellany *NOUN* (**miscellanies**) (*say* mis- **el**- an- ee)
a mixture of different things

mischief *NOUN*
mischief is naughty or troublesome behaviour

mischievous *ADJECTIVE*
naughty or troublesome

miser *NOUN* (**misers**)
someone who stores money away and spends as little as they can

> WORD FAMILY
> A **miserly** person hates to spend money.

miserable *ADJECTIVE*
1 very unhappy • *He felt miserable.* **2** unpleasant • *What miserable weather!*

> WORD FAMILY
> To do or say something **miserably** is to do or say it in a miserable way.

misery *NOUN* (**miseries**)
1 misery is great unhappiness or suffering **2** (*informal*) a misery is someone who is always unhappy or complaining

misfire *VERB* (**misfires**, **misfiring**, **misfired**)
1 a gun misfires when it fails to fire **2** a plan or idea or joke misfires when it goes wrong

misfit *NOUN* (**misfits**)
someone who does not fit in well with other people

misfortune *NOUN* (**misfortunes**)
1 a misfortune is an unlucky event or an accident **2** misfortune is bad luck

mishap *NOUN* (**mishaps**) (*say* mis- hap)
an unfortunate accident

misjudge *VERB* (**misjudges**, **misjudging**, **misjudged**)
to misjudge someone or something is to form a wrong idea or opinion about them

mislay *VERB* (**mislays**, **mislaying**, **mislaid**)
to mislay something is to lose it for a short time

mislead *VERB* (**misleads**, **misleading**, **misled**)
to mislead someone is to give them a wrong idea or impression deliberately

misprint *NOUN* (**misprints**)
a mistake in printing, such as a spelling mistake

Miss *NOUN* (**Misses**)
a title you put before the name of a girl or unmarried woman

miss *VERB* (**misses**, **missing**, **missed**)
1 to miss something is to fail to hit, reach, catch, see, hear, or find it **2** to miss someone or something is to be sad because they are not with you • *I missed my sister when she was in hospital.* **3** to miss a train, bus, or plane is to arrive too late to catch it **4** to miss a lesson or other activity is to fail to attend it • *How many classes have you missed?* **5** to miss something is also to notice that it isn't where it should be • *When did you first miss your wallet?*

miss *NOUN* (**misses**)
not hitting, reaching, or catching something • *Was that shot a hit or a miss?*

missile *NOUN* (**missiles**)
1 a weapon that is fired a long distance and explodes when it lands **2** an object thrown at someone

missing *ADJECTIVE*
something is missing when it is lost or not in the proper place

mission *NOUN* (**missions**)
1 an important job that someone is sent to do or that someone feels they must do **2** a place or building where missionaries work

missionary *NOUN* (**missionaries**)
someone who goes to another country to spread a religious faith

misspell *VERB* (**misspells**, **misspelling**, **misspelt** or **misspelled**)
to misspell a word is to spell it wrongly

mist *NOUN* (**mists**)
1 damp cloudy air like a thin fog **2** condensed water vapour on a window or mirror

mistake *NOUN* (**mistakes**)
something done or said wrongly

mistake *VERB* (**mistakes**, **mistaking**, **mistook**, **mistaken**)
to mistake one person or thing for another is to confuse them

mistaken *ADJECTIVE*
to be mistaken is to be incorrect or wrong • *You are mistaken if you believe that.*

> WORD FAMILY
> You **mistakenly** believe or think something when you do so incorrectly or wrongly.

mister *NOUN*
1 Mr **2** (*informal*) sir • *Can you tell me the time, mister?*

mistletoe *NOUN*
mistletoe is a plant with green leaves and white berries in winter

mistreat *VERB* (**mistreats**, **mistreating**, **mistreated**)
to mistreat someone is to treat them badly or unfairly

> WORD FAMILY
> **Mistreatment** is treating someone badly or unfairly.

mistress *NOUN* (**mistresses**)
1 a woman who is in charge of something **2** a woman who teaches in a school **3** the woman owner of a dog or other animal **4** a woman who is a man's lover, although he is married to someone else

mistrust *VERB* (**mistrusts**, **mistrusting**, **mistrusted**)
to mistrust someone or something is not to trust them

misty *ADJECTIVE* (**mistier**, **mistiest**)
1 if it is misty outside there is a lot of mist **2** misty eyes are full of tears

misunderstand *VERB* (**misunderstands, misunderstanding, misunderstood**)
to misunderstand something is to get a wrong idea or impression about it • *You misunderstood what I said.*

> WORD FAMILY
> To have a **misunderstanding** is to get the wrong idea or impression about something.

misuse *VERB* (**misuses, misusing, misused**) (*say* mis-**yooz**)
to misuse something is to use it in the wrong way or treat it badly

misuse *NOUN* (*say* mis-**yooss**)
misuse is using something in the wrong way

mite *NOUN* (**mites**)
1 a tiny insect found in food **2** a small child

mitre *NOUN* (**mitres**) (*say* **my**-ter)
1 the tall tapering hat that a bishop wears **2** a joint of two tapering pieces of wood or cloth, forming a right angle

mitten *NOUN* (**mittens**)
a kind of glove without separate parts for the fingers

mix *VERB* (**mixes, mixing, mixed**)
1 to mix different things is to stir or shake them together to make one thing **2** to mix is to get on well with other people • *She mixes well.*
to mix up people or **things** is to confuse them

> WORD FAMILY
> A **mixer** is a machine for mixing food.

mixed *ADJECTIVE*
containing two or more kinds of things or people

mixing bowl *NOUN* (**mixing bowls**)
a large bowl for mixing food in

mixture *NOUN* (**mixtures**)
something made of different things mixed together

mix-up *NOUN* (**mix-ups**)
a muddle or confused situation, especially one that ruins a plan

mm
short for **millimetre** or **millimetres**

mnemonic *NOUN* (**mnemonics**) (*say* nim-**on**-ik)
a verse or saying that helps you to remember something

moan *NOUN* (**moans**)
1 a long low sound, usually of suffering **2** a complaint or grumble

moan *VERB* (**moans, moaning, moaned**)
1 to moan is to make a long low sound **2** to moan is also to complain or grumble

moat *NOUN* (**moats**)
a deep ditch round a castle, usually filled with water

mob *NOUN* (**mobs**)
1 a large disorderly crowd of people **2** a gang

mob *VERB* (**mobs, mobbing, mobbed**)
people mob someone when they crowd round them • *The singer was mobbed by her fans.*

mobile *ADJECTIVE*
able to be moved or carried about easily

> WORD FAMILY
> **Mobility** is being able to move easily from place to place.

mobile *NOUN* (**mobiles**)
1 a decoration made to be hung up from threads so that it moves about in the air **2** (*informal*) a mobile phone

mobile phone *NOUN* (**mobile phones**)
a telephone you can carry around with you

mobilize *VERB* (**mobilizes, mobilizing, mobilized**)
to mobilize people or things is to get them ready for a particular purpose, especially for war
▷ **mobilization** *NOUN* mobilization is mobilizing people

moccasin *NOUN* (**moccasins**) (*say* **mok**-a-sin)
a soft leather shoe like those worn by Native Americans

mock *VERB* (**mocks, mocking, mocked**)
to mock someone or something is to make fun of them

> WORD FAMILY
> **Mockery** is making fun of people or things.

mock *ADJECTIVE*
not real or genuine • *They fought a mock battle.*

mock-up *NOUN* (**mock-ups**)
a model of something, especially to study it or test it

mode *NOUN* (**modes**)
1 the way that something is done • *Flying is the fastest mode of transport.* **2** what is fashionable **3** (*in mathematics*) the value that occurs most often in a set of values • *The mode of 6, 5, 4, 4, 5, 4 and 3 is 4.*

model *NOUN* (**models**)
1 a small copy of an object • *He makes models of aircraft.* **2** a particular version or design of something • *We saw the latest models at the motor show.* **3** someone who displays clothes by wearing them or who poses for an artist or photographer **4** someone or something worth copying or imitating

model *ADJECTIVE*
1 being a small copy of something • *I'd like a model railway.* **2** being a good example for people to follow • *She was a model pupil.*

model *VERB* (**models, modelling, modelled**)
1 to model something is to make a small copy of it **2** to model one thing on another is to use the second thing as a pattern for the first • *The building is modelled on an Egyptian temple.* **3** to model, or to model clothes, is to work as an artist's model or a fashion model

modem *NOUN* (**modems**)
(*in computing*) a piece of equipment that links a computer to a telephone line

moderate *ADJECTIVE* (*say* mod- er- at)
1 a moderate amount or level is not too little and not too much **2** moderate opinions are not extreme

> WORD FAMILY
> Something is (for example) **moderately** hot when it is fairly but not very hot; **moderation** is being moderate, not too little and not too much.

moderate *VERB* (**moderates**, **moderating**, **moderated**) (*say* mod- er- ayt)
to moderate something is to make it less strong or severe

modern *ADJECTIVE*
belonging to the present day or recent times

modernize *VERB* (**modernizes**, **modernizing**, **modernized**)
to modernize something is to make it modern, or suitable for modern tastes

> WORD FAMILY
> The **modernization** of something is when it is made more modern.

modest *ADJECTIVE*
1 not thinking or talking too much about how good you are **2** quite small in amount •*Their needs were modest.*

> WORD FAMILY
> You say something **modestly** when you say it in a modest way; **modesty** is being modest.

modify *VERB* (**modifies**, **modifying**, **modified**)
to modify something is to change it slightly

> WORD FAMILY
> A **modification** is a slight change in something.

module *NOUN* (**modules**) (*say* mod- yool)
1 a separate section or part of something larger, such as a spacecraft or building **2** one of the parts that make up a course of learning •*This term I'm doing a Maths module.*

moist *ADJECTIVE*
slightly wet

moisten *VERB* (**moistens**, **moistening**, **moistened**) (*say* moi- sen)
1 to moisten something is to make it slightly wet **2** to moisten is to become slightly wet

moisture *NOUN*
moisture is tiny drops of water in the air or on a surface

molar *NOUN* (**molars**) (*say* moh- ler)
one of the wide teeth at the back of your mouth

mole *NOUN* (**moles**)
1 a small furry animal that digs holes under the ground **2** a small dark spot on the skin

molecule *NOUN* (**molecules**) (*say* mol- i- kewl)
1 (*in science*) the smallest part into which a substance can be divided without changing its chemical nature; a group of atoms

> WORD FAMILY
> **Molecular** means to do with molecules.

molehill *NOUN* (**molehills**)
a small pile of earth thrown up by a mole
to make a mountain out of a molehill is to give something too much importance

molest *VERB* (**molests**, **molesting**, **molested**)
1 to molest someone is to annoy or pester them in an unfriendly or violent way **2** to molest someone is also to abuse them sexually

mollusc *NOUN* (**molluscs**)
an animal with a soft body and usually a hard shell, such as a snail or an oyster

molten *ADJECTIVE*
molten rock or metal has been made into liquid by great heat •*Molten lava flowed down the side of the volcano.*

moment *NOUN* (**moments**)
1 a very short period of time •*Wait a moment.* **2** a particular time •*At that moment, all the lights went out.*
at the moment now

momentary *ADJECTIVE* (*say* moh- men- ter- i)
lasting for only a moment

> WORD FAMILY
> Something happens **momentarily** when it happens for only a moment.

momentous *ADJECTIVE* (*say* moh- ment- us)
very important

momentum *NOUN* (*say* moh- ment- um)
momentum is the amount or force of movement •*The stone gained momentum as it rolled down the hill.*

monarch *NOUN* (**monarchs**)
a king, queen, emperor, or empress ruling a country

monarchy *NOUN* (**monarchies**)
1 monarchy is rule by a monarch **2** a monarchy is a country ruled by a monarch

monastery *NOUN* (**monasteries**) (*say* mon- a- ster- i)
a building where monks live and work

> WORD FAMILY
> **Monastic** means to do with a monastery.

Monday *NOUN* (**Mondays**)
the second day of the week

money *NOUN*
money is coins and notes used by people to buy things

mongoose *NOUN* (**mongooses**)
a small animal like a large weasel, that can kill snakes

mongrel *NOUN* (**mongrels**) (*say* mung- rel)
a dog of mixed breeds

monitor *NOUN* (**monitors**)
1 a device used for checking how something is working **2** (*in computing*) a computer or television screen **3** a pupil who is given a special job to do at school

monitor *VERB* (**monitors**, **monitoring**, **monitored**)
to monitor something or someone is to watch or test them to see how they are working

monk *NOUN* (**monks**)
a member of a religious community of men

monkey *NOUN* (**monkeys**)
1 an animal with long arms, hands with thumbs, and a tail **2** a mischievous person, especially a child

mono- *PREFIX*
meaning 'having one of something', as in *monorail*

monogram *NOUN* (**monograms**)
a design made up of a letter or a group of letters

monologue *NOUN* (**monologues**) (*say* mon- o- log)
a long speech by one person or performer

monopolize *VERB* (**monopolizes**, **monopolizing**, **monopolized**)
to monopolize something is to have complete control of it and keep out everyone else

monopoly *NOUN* (**monopolies**)
control of a business or activity by one person or group

monorail *NOUN* (**monorails**)
a railway that runs on a single rail

monotonous *ADJECTIVE* (*say* mon- **ot**- on- us)
boring because it does not change • *This is monotonous work.* • *The sky became quite grey and, along with it, the whole countryside seemed to lose its colour and assume the same monotonous tone.* — Norton Juster, *The Phantom Tollbooth*

WORD FAMILY
Something happens **monotonously** when it is boring because it does not change; **monotony** is when something happens like this.

monsoon *NOUN* (**monsoons**)
a strong wind in and around the Indian Ocean, bringing heavy rain in summer

monster *NOUN* (**monsters**)
a huge frightening creature

monster *ADJECTIVE*
(*informal*) huge

monstrous *ADJECTIVE*
1 like a monster; huge **2** very shocking or cruel • *It was a monstrous crime.*

WORD FAMILY
A **monstrosity** is a monstrous thing.

month *NOUN* (**months**)
one of the twelve parts into which a year is divided

monthly *ADJECTIVE & ADVERB*
something happens monthly when it happens every month

monument *NOUN* (**monuments**)
a statue, building, or column put up to remind people of some person or event

monumental *ADJECTIVE*
1 built as a monument **2** great or huge • *It was a monumental achievement.*

moo *VERB* (**moos**, **mooing**, **mooed**)
to make the sound of a cow

mood *NOUN* (**moods**)
the way someone feels at a particular time • *She is in a cheerful mood.*

moody *ADJECTIVE* (**moodier**, **moodiest**)
1 gloomy **2** likely to have sudden changes of mood
▷ **moodily** *ADVERB* in a moody way
▷ **moodiness** *NOUN* being moody

moon *NOUN* (**moons**)
1 the natural satellite which orbits the earth and shines in the sky at night **2** a similar object which orbits another planet

moonlight *NOUN*
moonlight is the light reflected from the moon

WORD FAMILY
A moonlit **night** is one that is lit by the moon.

moor [1] *NOUN* (**moors**)
an area of rough land covered with bracken and bushes

moor [2] *VERB* (**moors**, **mooring**, **moored**)
to moor a boat is to tie it up to the land

moorhen *NOUN* (**moorhens**)
a small water bird

mooring *NOUN* (**moorings**)
a place where a boat can be moored

moose *NOUN* (**moose**)
a North American elk

mop *NOUN* (**mops**)
a piece of soft material on the end of a stick, used for cleaning floors or dishes

mop *VERB* (**mops**, **mopping**, **mopped**)
to mop something is to clean it with a mop
to mop something up is to clear away spilt liquid

mope *VERB* (**mopes**, **moping**, **moped**)
to mope is to be miserable and not interested in doing anything • *'Eeyore, who is a friend of mine, has lost his tail. And he's Moping about it. So could you very kindly tell me how to find it for him?'* — A. A. Milne, *Winnie-the-Pooh*

a b c d e f g h i j k l m n o p q r s t u v w x y z

moped *NOUN* (**mopeds**) (*say* moh- ped)
a kind of small motorcycle with pedals

moraine *NOUN* (**moraines**)
a mass of stones and earth carried down by a glacier

moral *ADJECTIVE*
1 to do with people's behaviour and what is right and wrong **2** being or doing good and what is right • *We are expected to lead moral lives.*

> WORD FAMILY
> **Morality** is moral behaviour and standards; to behave **morally** is to do so in a moral way.

moral *NOUN* (**morals**)
a lesson taught by a story or event

morale *NOUN* (*say* mo- **rahl**)
morale is confidence or courage

morals *PLURAL NOUN*
standards of behaviour

morbid *ADJECTIVE*
thinking about gloomy or unpleasant things such as death
▷ **morbidly** *ADVERB* in a morbid way

more *DETERMINER*
greater in number or amount • *We need more money.* • *She is more beautiful.*

more *NOUN*
a larger number or amount • *I want more.*

more *ADVERB*
1 to a greater extent • *You must work more.* **2** again • *I'll tell you once more.*
more or less almost; approximately • *I've more or less finished the work.* • *The repairs cost £100, more or less.*

moreover *ADVERB*
also; in addition to what has been said

Mormon *NOUN* (**Mormons**)
a member of a religious group founded in the USA

morning *NOUN* (**mornings**)
the early part of the day before noon or before lunchtime

moron *NOUN* (**morons**)
(*informal*) a stupid person
▷ **moronic** *ADJECTIVE* stupid

morose *ADJECTIVE*
bad-tempered and miserable

morpheme *NOUN* (**morphemes**)
the smallest unit of meaning that a word can be divided into. The word *like* contains one morpheme, but the word *unlikely* contains three (*un-*, *like*, and *-ly*)

morphine *NOUN* (*say* **mor**- feen)
morphine is a drug made from opium, used to relieve pain

morris dance *NOUN* (**morris dances**)
a traditional English dance performed by people in costume with ribbons and bells

Morse code *NOUN*
a code for sending radio signals, using dots and dashes to represent letters and numbers

morsel *NOUN* (**morsels**)
a small piece of food

mortal *ADJECTIVE*
1 certain to die • *All men are mortal.* **2** causing death • *He received a mortal wound.*

> WORD FAMILY
> Someone who is **mortally** wounded or ill is certain to die from their wounds or illness.

mortality *NOUN*
1 mortality can be used to talk about the number of people who die over a period of time • *There is a low rate of infant mortality.* **2** mortality is also being mortal

mortar *NOUN* (**mortars**)
1 mortar is a mixture of sand, cement, and water used in building to stick bricks together **2** a mortar is a small thick bowl for pounding food with a tool called a pestle **3** a mortar is also a small cannon

mortgage *NOUN* (**mortgages**) (*say* **mor**- gij)
an arrangement to borrow money to buy a house, repaid over many years

mortuary *NOUN* (**mortuaries**)
a place where dead bodies are kept before they are buried or cremated

mosaic *NOUN* (**mosaics**) (*say* moh- **zay**- ik)
a picture or design made from small coloured pieces of glass or stone

mosque *NOUN* (**mosques**) (*say* mosk)
a building where Muslims worship

mosquito *NOUN* (**mosquitoes**) (*say* mos- **kee**- toh)
an insect that sucks blood and carries disease

moss *NOUN* (**mosses**)
a plant that grows in damp places and has no flowers

> WORD FAMILY
> A **mossy** place is covered in moss.

most *DETERMINER*
greatest in number or amount • *Most people came by bus.*

most *NOUN*
the greatest number or amount • *They've eaten most of the food.*

most *ADVERB*
1 more than any other • *I liked this book most.*
2 very; extremely • *It was most amusing.*

mostly *ADVERB*
mainly

MOT or **MOT test** *NOUN* (**MOTs** or **MOT tests**)
a safety check that has to be made every year on road vehicles

motel *NOUN* (**motels**) (*say* moh- tel)
a hotel near a main road, with parking and rooms for motorists

moth *NOUN* (**moths**)
an insect rather like a butterfly, that usually flies around at night

mother *NOUN* (**mothers**)
your female parent

motherhood *NOUN*
motherhood is being a mother and looking after children

mother-in-law *NOUN* (**mothers-in-law**)
the mother of your husband or wife

motherly *ADJECTIVE*
kind or tender like a mother

motion *NOUN* (**motions**)
a way of moving; movement
to go through the motions is to do or say something because you have to, without much interest

motionless *ADJECTIVE*
not moving; still

motivate *VERB* (**motivates, motivating, motivated**)
to motivate someone is to make them keen to achieve something • *She is good at motivating her team.*

motive *NOUN* (**motives**)
a person's motive is what makes them do something

motor *NOUN* (**motors**)
a machine that provides power to drive machinery

motorbike *NOUN* (**motorbikes**)
(*informal*) a motorcycle

motor boat *NOUN* (**motor boats**)
a boat driven by a motor

motor car *NOUN* (**motor cars**)
a motor vehicle that can carry several people inside it

motorcycle *NOUN* (**motorcycles**)
a motor vehicle with two wheels and a saddle for the riders

> WORD FAMILY
> A **motorcyclist** is someone who rides a motorcycle.

motorist *NOUN* (**motorists**)
someone who drives a motor car

motor vehicle *NOUN* (**motor vehicles**)
a vehicle driven by a motor, for use on roads

motorway *NOUN* (**motorways**)
a wide road for fast long-distance traffic

mottled *ADJECTIVE*
marked with spots or patches of colour

motto *NOUN* (**mottoes**)
1 a short saying used as a guide for behaviour • *His motto was 'Do your best'.* **2** a short verse or riddle found inside a cracker

mould[1] *NOUN* (**moulds**)
a mould is a container for making things like jelly or plaster set in a special shape

mould *VERB* (**moulds, moulding, moulded**)
to mould something is to make it have a particular shape or character

mould[2] *NOUN* (**moulds**)
mould is a furry growth that appears on some moist surfaces, especially on something decaying

mouldy *ADJECTIVE* (**mouldier, mouldiest**)
something is mouldy when it has mould on it

moult *VERB* (**moults, moulting, moulted**) (*say* mohlt)
animals or birds moult when they lose hair or feathers

mound *NOUN* (**mounds**)
a pile of earth or stones; a small hill

mount *VERB* (**mounts, mounting, mounted**)
1 to mount a horse or bicycle is to get on it so that you can ride it **2** to mount is to increase in amount • *The cost of running a car is mounting.* **3** to mount a picture or photograph is to put it in a frame or album in order to display it

mount *NOUN* (**mounts**)
1 a mountain, especially in names such as *Mount Everest* **2** something on which a picture or photograph is mounted **3** an animal for someone to ride on

mountain *NOUN* (**mountains**)
1 a very high hill **2** a large amount • *We've got a mountain of work to do.*

> WORD FAMILY
> A **mountainous** place has a lot of mountains.

mountaineer *NOUN* (**mountaineers**)
someone who climbs mountains

mountaineering *NOUN*
mountaineering is the sport of climbing mountains

mourn *VERB* (**mourns, mourning, mourned**)
to mourn is to be sad, especially because someone has died

> WORD FAMILY
> **Mourners** are the people who go to a funeral, especially the family and friends of the person who has died.

mournful *ADJECTIVE*
sad and sorrowful • *Paddington sank down on to his case looking very mournful. Even the pom-pom on his hat seemed limp.* — Michael Bond, *A Bear Called Paddington*

> WORD FAMILY
> You look or say something **mournfully** when you do so in a sad and sorrowful way.

a b c d e f g h i j k l **m** n o p q r s t u v w x y z

mouse *NOUN* (**mice**)
1 a small animal with a long tail and a pointed nose **2** (*in computing*) a small device that you move around on a mat to control the movements of a cursor on a computer screen

mousetrap *NOUN* (**mousetraps**)
a trap for catching and killing mice

mousse *NOUN* (**mousses**) (*say* mooss)
1 a creamy pudding flavoured with chocolate or fruit **2** a frothy creamy substance used for holding hair while styling it

moustache *NOUN* (**moustaches**) (*say* mus-tahsh)
a strip of hair that a man grows above his upper lip

mousy *ADJECTIVE* (**mousier**, **mousiest**)
1 mousy hair is light brown in colour **2** a mousy person is timid and feeble

mouth *NOUN* (**mouths**)
1 the part of the face that opens for eating and speaking **2** the place where a river flows into the sea **3** an opening or outlet

mouthful *NOUN* (**mouthfuls**)
an amount of food you put in your mouth

mouth organ *NOUN* (**mouth organs**)
a small musical instrument you play by blowing and sucking while passing it along your lips

mouthpiece *NOUN* (**mouthpieces**)
the part of a musical instrument or other device that you put to your mouth

movable *ADJECTIVE*
able to be moved

move *VERB* (**moves**, **moving**, **moved**)
1 to move something is to take it from one place to another **2** to move is to go from one place to another **3** to move someone is to affect their feelings • *Their story moved us deeply.*

move *NOUN* (**moves**)
1 a movement **2** a player's turn in a game
to get a move on (*informal*) is to hurry up
to be on the move is to be moving or making progress

movement *NOUN* (**movements**)
1 movement is moving or being moved **2** a movement is a group of people working together to achieve something **3** in music, a movement is one of the main parts of a long piece such as a symphony

movie *NOUN* (**movies**)
a cinema film

moving *ADJECTIVE*
causing someone to feel strong emotion, especially sadness or pity

mow *VERB* (**mows**, **mowing**, **mowed**, **mown**)
to mow grass is to cut it with a machine
to mow people down is to knock them down and kill them

> WORD FAMILY
> A **mower** is a machine for mowing grass.

MP
short for **Member of Parliament**

m.p.h.
short for *miles per hour*

Mr *NOUN* (**Messrs**) (*say* mis- ter)
a title you put before a man's name

Mrs *NOUN* (**Mrs** or **Mesdames**) (*say* mis- iz)
a title you put before a married woman's name

Ms *NOUN* (*say* miz)
a title you put before a woman's name

much *DETERMINER*
existing in a large amount • *There is much work to do.*

much *NOUN*
a large amount of something • *£5 is not very much.*

much *ADVERB*
1 greatly; considerably • *They came, much to my surprise.* **2** about; approximately • *It's much the same.*

muck *NOUN*
1 muck is farmyard manure **2** (*informal*) muck is dirt or filth

muck *VERB* (**mucks**, **mucking**, **mucked**)
(*informal*)
to muck about or **muck around** is to behave stupidly or idly
to muck something up is to do it very badly

mucky *ADJECTIVE* (**muckier**, **muckiest**)
dirty or messy

mud *NOUN*
mud is wet soft earth

> WORD FAMILY
> Something **muddy** is covered with mud.

muddle *VERB* (**muddles**, **muddling**, **muddled**)
1 to muddle things is to mix them up **2** to muddle someone is to confuse them

muddle *NOUN* (**muddles**)
a confusion or mess • *I've got these papers in a bit of a muddle.*

mudguard *NOUN* (**mudguards**)
a curved cover fixed over a bicycle wheel to stop mud and water being thrown up on to the rider

muesli *NOUN* (*say* mooz- li)
muesli is a breakfast food made of cereals, nuts, and dried fruit

muezzin *NOUN* (**muezzins**)
a man who calls Muslims to prayer from a minaret

muffle *VERB* (**muffles**, **muffling**, **muffled**)
1 to muffle something is to cover or wrap it to protect it or keep it warm **2** to muffle a sound is to deaden it or reduce it

mug *NOUN* (**mugs**)
1 a large cup, usually used without a saucer **2** (*slang*) a fool; someone who is easily fooled or cheated **3** (*slang*) a person's face

mug *VERB* (**mugs**, **mugging**, **mugged**)
to mug someone is to attack and rob them in the street

WORD FAMILY
A **mugger** is a person who attacks and robs someone in the street.

muggy *ADJECTIVE* (**muggier**, **muggiest**)
a muggy day is unpleasantly warm and damp

mule *NOUN* (**mules**)
an animal that is the offspring of a donkey and a mare

multi- *PREFIX*
meaning 'having many of something', as in *multiracial*

multiple *ADJECTIVE*
having many parts

multiple *NOUN* (**multiples**)
a number that can be divided exactly by another number • *30 and 50 are multiples of 10.*

multiplication *NOUN*
multiplication is when you multiply numbers

multiply *VERB* (**multiplies**, **multiplying**, **multiplied**)
1 to multiply a number is to add it to itself a certain number of times • *Five multiplied by four equals twenty (5 x 4 = 20).* **2** to multiply is to increase or become many • *His doubts started to multiply.*

multiracial *ADJECTIVE* (*say* mul- ti- **ray**- shal)
a multiracial area has people living there of many different races

multitude *NOUN* (**multitudes**)
a very large number of people or things

mum *NOUN* (**mums**)
(*informal*) mother

mumble *VERB* (**mumbles**, **mumbling**, **mumbled**)
to mumble is to speak softly and unclearly

mummify *VERB* (**mummifies**, **mummifying**, **mummified**)
in ancient Egypt, to mummify a dead body was to prepare it as a mummy

mummy[1] *NOUN* (**mummies**)
(*informal*) mother

mummy[2] *NOUN* (**mummies**)
in ancient Egypt, a dead body wrapped in cloth and treated with oils for burial

mumps *NOUN*
mumps is an infectious disease that makes the neck swell painfully

munch *VERB* (**munches**, **munching**, **munched**)
to munch food is to chew it noisily

mundane *ADJECTIVE*
ordinary or dull

municipal *ADJECTIVE* (*say* mew- **nis**- i- pal)
to do with a town or city

mural *NOUN* (**murals**)
a picture painted on a wall

murder *VERB* (**murders**, **murdering**, **murdered**)
to murder someone is to kill them deliberately

murder *NOUN* (**murders**)
1 murder is the deliberate killing of someone **2** (*informal*) you can say something is murder when it is very difficult or unpleasant • *It was murder changing the wheel in the dark.*

murderer *NOUN* (**murderers**)
someone who commits murder

murderous *ADJECTIVE*
likely to commit murder; showing you are very angry

murky *ADJECTIVE* (**murkier**, **murkiest**)
dark and gloomy • *The sea was murky and choppy and uninviting. I didn't want to go in, not one bit.* — Michael Morpurgo, *The Sleeping Sword*

murmur *NOUN* (**murmurs**)
a low or soft continuous sound, especially of people speaking

murmur *VERB* (**murmurs**, **murmuring**, **murmured**)
to murmur is to speak softly with a low continuous sound • *The afternoon sun was getting low as the Rat sculled gently homewards in a dreamy mood, murmuring poetry-things over to himself, and not paying much attention to Mole.* — Kenneth Grahame, *The Wind in the Willows*

muscle *NOUN* (**muscles**)
a bundle of fibres that can stretch to cause movement of a part of the body

muscle *VERB* (**muscles**, **muscling**, **muscled**)
to muscle in on something (*informal*) is to try to take part in something that does not concern you

muscular *ADJECTIVE*
having a lot of muscles; powerful

museum *NOUN* (**museums**)
a place where interesting old or valuable objects are displayed for people to see

mushroom *NOUN* (**mushrooms**)
a fast-growing edible fungus with a dome-shaped top

mushroom *VERB* (**mushrooms**, **mushrooming**, **mushroomed**)
things mushroom when they grow or appear suddenly like mushrooms • *Blocks of flats mushroomed in the city.*

music *NOUN*
1 music is pleasant or interesting sounds made by instruments or by the voice **2** music is also a system of printed or written symbols for making this kind of sound

musical *ADJECTIVE*
1 to do with music **2** good at music or interested in it
▷ **musically** *ADVERB* in a musical way

musical *NOUN* (**musicals**)
a play or film with music and songs

musician *NOUN* (**musicians**)
someone who plays a musical instrument, especially for a living

musket *NOUN* (**muskets**)
an old type of rifle

musketeer *NOUN* (**musketeers**)
a soldier armed with a musket

Muslim *NOUN* (**Muslims**) (*say* **muuz**- lim)
someone who follows the religious teachings of Muhammad, as set out in the Koran

muslin *NOUN*
fine cotton cloth

mussel *NOUN* (**mussels**)
a black shellfish, often found sticking to rocks

must *VERB*
a word used with another verb to show **1** that someone has to do something •*I must go home soon.* **2** that something is certain •*You must be joking!*

mustard *NOUN*
mustard is a yellow paste or powder used to give food a hot taste

mustard and cress *PLURAL NOUN*
small green plants eaten in salads

muster *VERB* (**musters**, **mustering**, **mustered**)
to muster is to assemble or gather together

musty *ADJECTIVE* (**mustier**, **mustiest**)
smelling or tasting mouldy or stale
▷ **mustiness** *NOUN* mustiness is being musty

mutation *NOUN* (**mutations**)
a change in the form of a living creature because of changes in its genes

mute *ADJECTIVE*
not speaking or able to speak

> WORD FAMILY
> You do something **mutely** when you do it without speaking.

mute *NOUN* (**mutes**)
1 a person who cannot speak **2** a device fitted to a musical instrument to soften the sound

muted *ADJECTIVE*
silent or quiet •*She gave a muted reply.*

mutilate *VERB* (**mutilates**, **mutilating**, **mutilated**)
to mutilate something is to damage it by breaking or cutting off part of it

> WORD FAMILY
> **Mutilation** is when someone damages something by breaking or cutting off part of it.

mutineer *NOUN* (**mutineers**) (*say* **mew**- tin- **eer**)
someone who takes part in a mutiny

mutiny *NOUN* (**mutinies**) (*say* **mew**- tin- i)
a rebellion by sailors or soldiers against their officers
▷ **mutinous** *ADJECTIVE* rebellious

> WORD FAMILY
> **Mutinous** people take part in a mutiny or refuse to obey orders; to do something **mutinously** is to do it in a rebellious way.

mutiny *VERB* (**mutinies**, **mutinying**, **mutinied**) (*say* **mew**- tin- i)
to mutiny is to take part in a mutiny

mutter *VERB* (**mutters**, **muttering**, **muttered**)
to mutter is to murmur or grumble in a low voice •*Mildred muttered the spell under her breath – and Ethel vanished. In her place stood a small pink and grey pig.* — Jill Murphy, *The Worst Witch*

mutton *NOUN*
mutton is meat from an adult sheep

mutual *ADJECTIVE* (*say* **mew**- tew- al)
given or done to each other •*They have mutual respect for one another.*

> WORD FAMILY
> **Mutually** means felt or done equally by two or more people •*Let's arrange a mutually convenient time to meet.*

muzzle *NOUN* (**muzzles**)
1 an animal's nose and mouth **2** a cover put over an animal's nose and mouth so that it cannot bite **3** the open end of a gun

muzzle *VERB* (**muzzles**, **muzzling**, **muzzled**)
1 to muzzle an animal is to put a muzzle on it **2** to muzzle someone is to prevent them from saying what they think

my *DETERMINER*
belonging to me •*This is my book.*

myself *PRONOUN*
me and nobody else, used to refer back to the person who is speaking •*I have hurt myself.*
by myself on my own; alone •*I did the work all by myself.*

mysterious *ADJECTIVE*
full of mystery; strange and puzzling

> WORD FAMILY
> Something happens **mysteriously** when what happens is difficult to explain or understand •*My watch mysteriously disappeared.*

mystery *NOUN* (**mysteries**)
something strange or puzzling • *Exactly why the ship sank is a mystery.*

mystify *VERB* (**mystifies, mystifying, mystified**)
to mystify someone is to puzzle them very much
▹ **mystification** *NOUN* mystification is being mystified

myth *NOUN* (**myths**)
1 an old story about gods and heroes in ancient times **2** an untrue story or belief • *It is a myth that carrots make you see better.*

mythical *ADJECTIVE*
imaginary; only found in myths

mythology *NOUN*
mythology is the study of myths

> WORD FAMILY
> **Mythological** creatures or characters are found in myths.

Nn

nab *VERB* (**nabs, nabbing, nabbed**)
(*informal*) to nab someone is to catch or grab them

nag [1] *VERB* (**nags, nagging, nagged**)
to nag someone is to keep criticizing them or complaining to them

nag [2] *NOUN* (**nags**)
(*informal*) a horse

nail *NOUN* (**nails**)
1 the hard covering on the end of one of your fingers or toes **2** a small, sharp piece of metal used to fix pieces of wood together

nail *VERB* (**nails, nailing, nailed**)
1 to nail something is to fasten it with a nail or nails **2** to nail someone is to catch or trap them

naive *ADJECTIVE* (*say* ny- **eev**)
1 too ready to believe what you are told; showing a lack of experience **2** innocent and trusting

> WORD FAMILY
> You **naively** believe or do something when you are too ready to believe what you are told or show a lack of experience; **naivety** is being naive.

naked *ADJECTIVE* (*say* **nay**- kid)
without any clothes or coverings on
to look at something with the naked eye is to look at it with your eyes without the help of a telescope or microscope
▹ **nakedness** *NOUN* nakedness is being naked

name *NOUN* (**names**)
what you call a person or thing

name *VERB* (**names, naming, named**)
1 to name someone or something is to give them a name **2** to name someone or something is to say what they are called • *Can you name these plants?*

nameless *ADJECTIVE*
1 not having a name **2** not named or identified • *The culprit shall be nameless.*

namely *ADVERB*
that is to say • *I will invite two friends, namely Vicky and Tom.*

nanny *NOUN* (**nannies**)
1 a woman whose job is to look after small children **2** (*informal*) a grandmother

nanny goat *NOUN* (**nanny goats**)
a female goat

nap *NOUN* (**naps**)
a short sleep

napkin *NOUN* (**napkins**)
1 a piece of cloth or paper to keep your clothes clean or wipe your lips at meals **2** (*old use*) a nappy

nappy *NOUN* (**nappies**)
a piece of cloth or a paper pad put round a baby's bottom

narcissus *NOUN* (**narcissi**) (*say* nar- **sis**- us)
a garden flower like a daffodil

narcotic *NOUN* (**narcotics**) (*say* nar- **kot**- ik)
a drug that makes you sleepy or unconscious

narrate *VERB* (**narrates, narrating, narrated**)
to narrate a story or experiences is to tell them to someone • *She narrated her adventures in South America.*

> WORD FAMILY
> **Narration** is telling a story.

narrative *NOUN* (**narratives**)
a story or account that someone tells

narrator *NOUN* (**narrators**)
the person who is telling a story

narrow *ADJECTIVE* (**narrower, narrowest**)
1 not wide **2** with only a small margin of error or safety • *We all had a narrow escape.*

> WORD FAMILY
> You say that something **narrowly** happens when it only just happens • *She narrowly escaped injury.*

narrow-minded *ADJECTIVE*
not liking or understanding other people's ideas or beliefs

nasal *ADJECTIVE*
to do with the nose

nasturtium *NOUN* (**nasturtiums**) (*say* na- **ster**- shum)
a garden flower with round leaves

nasty *ADJECTIVE* (**nastier, nastiest**)
not pleasant; unkind
▹ **nastily** *ADVERB* in a nasty way
▹ **nastiness** *NOUN* nastiness is being nasty

a b c d e f g h i j k l m **n** o p q r s t u v w x y z

nation *NOUN* (**nations**)
1 a large number of people who have the same history, language, and customs, and live in the same part of the world under one government **2** a country and the people who live there

national *ADJECTIVE*
to do with a nation or country

> WORD FAMILY
> Something happens **nationally** when it happens all over the country.

nationalism *NOUN*
supporting your country and wanting it to be independent

> WORD FAMILY
> A **nationalist** is someone who believes in nationalism.

nationality *NOUN* (**nationalities**)
the nation someone belongs to • *What is her nationality?*

nationalize *VERB* (**nationalizes**, **nationalizing**, **nationalized**)
to nationalize an industry or organization is to put it under government control
▷ **nationalization** *NOUN* nationalization is putting industries and organizations under government control

nationwide *ADJECTIVE & ADVERB*
over the whole of a country

native *NOUN* (**natives**)
a person born in a particular place • *He is a native of Sweden.*

native *ADJECTIVE*
of the country where you were born • *English is my native language.*

Native American *NOUN* (**Native Americans**)
one of the original inhabitants of North or South America

nativity *NOUN* (**nativities**) (*say* na- tiv- i- ti)
someone's birth
the Nativity the birth of Jesus Christ

natural *ADJECTIVE*
1 made or done by nature, not by people or machines **2** normal; not surprising **3** belonging to someone from birth • *He has plenty of natural ability.* **4** in music, not sharp or flat

natural *NOUN* (**naturals**)
1 a natural note in music; a sign (♮) that shows a note is natural **2** someone who is naturally good at something • *She's a natural at juggling.*

natural gas *NOUN*
natural gas is gas that is found underground or under the sea, not made from coal

natural history *NOUN*
natural history is the study of plants and animals

naturalist *NOUN* (**naturalists**)
someone who studies natural history

naturalize *VERB* (**naturalizes**, **naturalizing**, **naturalized**)
1 to naturalize a person is to make them a full citizen of a country **2** to naturalize a plant or animal is to cause it to grow or live in a place where it is not normally found
▷ **naturalization** *NOUN* naturalizing someone or something

naturally *ADVERB*
1 in a natural way • *The gas is produced naturally.* **2** as you would expect • *Naturally I will pay your train fare.*

nature *NOUN* (**natures**)
1 nature is everything in the world that was not made by people, such as plants and animals **2** a person's or thing's nature is the qualities or characteristics they have • *She has a loving nature.* **3** a nature is a kind or sort of thing • *He likes things of that nature.*

nature reserve *NOUN* (**nature reserves**)
an area of land set aside to keep wild life

nature trail *NOUN* (**nature trails**)
a path in the country with signs telling you about the plants and wildlife you can see there

naughty *ADJECTIVE* (**naughtier**, **naughtiest**)
not behaving as you should; disobedient or rude
▷ **naughtily** *ADVERB* in a naughty way
▷ **naughtiness** *NOUN* naughtiness is being naughty

nausea *NOUN*
nausea is a feeling of sickness or disgust

nautical *ADJECTIVE*
connected with ships or sailors

naval *ADJECTIVE*
to do with a navy

nave *NOUN* (**naves**)
the main central part of a church

navel *NOUN* (**navels**)
the small hollow at the front of your stomach, where the umbilical cord was attached

navigable *ADJECTIVE*
a navigable river is suitable for ships to sail in

navigate *VERB* (**navigates**, **navigating**, **navigated**)
1 to navigate is to make sure that an aircraft, ship, or vehicle is going in the right direction **2** to navigate a sea or river is to sail a ship on it

> WORD FAMILY
> **Navigation** is making sure that an aircraft, ship, or vehicle is going in the right direction; the **navigator** is the person who does this.

navy *NOUN* (**navies**)
1 a fleet of ships and the people trained to use them **2** navy blue

navy blue *NOUN & ADJECTIVE*
dark blue

Nazi *NOUN* (**Nazis**) (*say* nah- tsi)
a member of the German National Socialist Party in Hitler's time

> WORD FAMILY
> **Nazism** was the Fascist beliefs of the Nazis.

near *ADVERB & ADJECTIVE* (**nearer**, **nearest**)
not far away
near by at a place not far away • *They live near by.*

near *PREPOSITION*
not far away from something • *She lives near the town.*

near *VERB* (**nears**, **nearing**, **neared**)
to near a place is to come close to it • *The ships were nearing the harbour.*

nearby *ADJECTIVE*
near; not far away • *We live in a nearby town.*

nearly *ADVERB*
1 almost • *It was nearly midnight.* **2** closely • *They are nearly related.*
not nearly not at all • *There is not nearly enough food.*

neat *ADJECTIVE* (**neater**, **neatest**)
1 tidy and carefully arranged **2** skilfully done • *That was a neat goal.* **3** without water added • *They were drinking neat orange juice.*

> WORD FAMILY
> You **neatly** do something when you do it in a neat way; **neatness** is being neat.

necessarily *ADVERB*
for certain; definitely • *It won't necessarily cost you a lot.*

necessary *ADJECTIVE*
needed very much; essential

necessity *NOUN* (**necessities**)
1 necessity is need • *There is no necessity for you to come too.* **2** a necessity is also something needed • *We have brought all the necessities for a picnic.*

neck *NOUN* (**necks**)
1 the part of the body that joins the head to the shoulders **2** a narrow part of something, especially of a bottle
to be neck and neck is to be almost exactly together in a race or contest
to stick your neck out is to say or do something that could get you into trouble

neckerchief *NOUN* (**neckerchiefs**)
a square of cloth worn round the neck, for example by Scouts and Cubs

necklace *NOUN* (**necklaces**)
a piece of jewellery you wear round your neck

nectar *NOUN*
nectar is a sweet liquid collected by bees from flowers

nectarine *NOUN* (**nectarines**)
a kind of peach with a smooth skin

need *VERB* (**needs**, **needing**, **needed**)
1 to need something is to be without it when you should have it **2** to need to do something is to have to do it • *I needed to get a haircut.*

need *NOUN* (**needs**)
1 a need is something that you need **2** need is a situation in which something is necessary • *There's no need to shout.*
to be in need is to need money or help

> WORD FAMILY
> Something is **needless** when it is not necessary • *That was a needless waste of time*; to **needlessly** do something is to do it even though it is not necessary.

needle *NOUN* (**needles**)
1 a very thin pointed piece of metal used for sewing **2** something long, thin, and sharp, such as a knitting needle or a pine needle **3** the pointer of a meter or compass

needlework *NOUN*
needlework is sewing or embroidery

needy *ADJECTIVE* (**needier**, **neediest**)
needy people are very poor and don't have what they need to live properly

negative *ADJECTIVE*
1 a negative statement or answer is one that says 'no' **2** not definite or helpful **3** a negative number is one that is less than nought **4** a negative electric charge is one that carries electrons
▷ **negatively** *ADVERB* in a negative way

negative *NOUN* (**negatives**)
1 something that means 'no' **2** a photograph or film with the dark parts light and the light parts dark, from which prints are made

neglect *VERB* (**neglects**, **neglecting**, **neglected**)
1 to neglect something or someone is to fail to look after them or deal with them **2** to neglect to do something is to fail to do it

neglect *NOUN*
neglect is failing to look after someone or something

neglectful *ADJECTIVE*
tending not to do things you should

negligent *ADJECTIVE*
not taking proper care or paying enough attention • *The cleaners had been negligent and left the windows open.*

> WORD FAMILY
> **Negligence** is failing to give something enough care or attention.

negligible *ADJECTIVE* (*say* neg- li- ji- bul)
not big enough or important enough to bother about • *Fortunately, the damage was negligible.*

negotiate *VERB* (**negotiates**, **negotiating**, **negotiated**) (*say* nig- **oh**- shi- ayt)
1 to negotiate is to try to reach an agreement about something by discussing it **2** to negotiate an obstacle or difficulty is to get past it or over it

> WORD FAMILY
> **Negotiations** are discussions people have to try to reach an agreement about something; one of the people doing this is a **negotiator**.

neigh *VERB* (**neighs**, **neighing**, **neighed**)
to make a high-pitched cry like a horse

neigh *NOUN* (**neighs**)
the sound of a horse neighing

neighbour *NOUN* (**neighbours**)
someone who lives next door or near to you

> WORD FAMILY
> The **neighbouring** house or family is the one next door.

neighbourhood *NOUN* (**neighbourhoods**)
the surrounding district

neighbourly *ADJECTIVE*
someone is neighbourly when they are friendly and helpful to people who live near them

neither *DETERMINER & PRONOUN* (*say* **ny**- *ther* or **nee**- *ther*)
not either • *Neither parent was there.* • *Neither of them likes cabbage.*

neither *CONJUNCTION*
neither ... nor ... not one thing and not the other • *I neither know nor care.*

neon *NOUN* (*say* **nee**- on)
neon is a gas that glows when electricity passes through it, used in street lighting and signs

nephew *NOUN* (**nephews**)
the son of a person's brother or sister

nerve *NOUN* (**nerves**)
1 a nerve is one of the fibres inside your body that carry messages to and from your brain, so that parts of your body can feel and move **2** nerve is courage and calmness in a dangerous situation • *Don't lose your nerve.* **3** (*informal*) nerve is cheek or impudence • *He had the nerve to ask for more.*
to get on someone's nerves is to irritate them
nerves nervousness • *I always suffer from nerves before an exam.*

nerve-racking *ADJECTIVE*
difficult and worrying • *We had a nerve-racking time trying to get out.*

nervous *ADJECTIVE*
1 easily upset or agitated; timid **2** to do with the nerves

> WORD FAMILY
> To do something **nervously** is to do it in a way that shows you are nervous • *He smiled nervously*; **nervousness** is being nervous.

nervous breakdown *NOUN* (**nervous breakdowns**)
a mental illness in which a person is depressed and anxious, and unable to cope with life

nest *NOUN* (**nests**)
1 the place where a bird lays its eggs and feeds its young **2** a warm place where some small animals live

nest *VERB* (**nests**, **nesting**, **nested**)
birds or animals nest when they make or have a nest • *Gulls were nesting on the cliffs.*

nestle *VERB* (**nestles**, **nestling**, **nestled**)
to nestle is to curl up comfortably • *Moomintroll stood on his doorstep and watched the valley nestle beneath its winter blanket.* — Tove Jansson, *Finn Family Moonintroll*

nestling *NOUN* (**nestlings**)
a young bird before it is old enough to leave the nest

net[1] *NOUN* (**nets**)
1 net is material made of pieces of thread, cord, or wire joined together in a criss-cross pattern with holes between **2** a net is a piece of this material **3** the net is the Internet

net[2] *ADJECTIVE*
left over after everything has been taken away • *The net weight, without the box, is 100 grams.*

netball *NOUN*
netball is a game in which two teams try to throw a ball through a high net hanging from a ring

nettle *NOUN* (**nettles**)
a wild plant with leaves that sting when you touch them

network *NOUN* (**networks**)
1 a criss-cross arrangement of lines **2** a system with many connections or parts, such as a railway or broadcasting or computer system

neuter *ADJECTIVE* (*say* **new**- ter)
1 neither male nor female **2** in some languages, belonging to the class of words that are neither masculine nor feminine

neuter *VERB* (**neuters**, **neutering**, **neutered**) (*say* **new**- ter)
to neuter an animal is to remove its sexual organs so that it cannot breed

neutral *ADJECTIVE* (*say* **new**- tral)
1 not supporting either side in a war or quarrel **2** not distinct or distinctive • *The room was painted in neutral colours.* **3** a neutral gear is one that is not connected to the driving parts of an engine

> WORD FAMILY
> **Neutrality** is not supporting either side in a war or quarrel.

neutralize *VERB* (**neutralizes**, **neutralizing**, **neutralized**)
to neutralize something is to take away its use or effect

neutron *NOUN* (**neutrons**)
a particle of matter with no electric charge

never *ADVERB*
at no time; not ever; not at all

nevertheless *CONJUNCTION & ADVERB*
in spite of this; although that is a fact

new *ADJECTIVE* (**newer**, **newest**)
1 not existing before; just bought, made, or received **2** different or unfamiliar • *That's a new idea.*
▷ **newly** *ADVERB* recently
▷ **newness** *NOUN* newness is being new

newcomer *NOUN* (**newcomers**)
someone who has recently arrived in a place

new moon *NOUN* (**new moons**)
the moon at the beginning of its cycle, when it appears as a thin crescent

news *NOUN*
1 news is new information about people or recent events • *I've got some good news.* **2** news is also a radio or television report about important events

newsagent *NOUN* (**newsagents**)
a shopkeeper who sells newspapers and magazines

newsletter *NOUN* (**newsletters**)
a short informal report sent regularly to members of an organization or club

newspaper *NOUN* (**newspapers**)
1 a newspaper is a daily or weekly publication of large sheets of printed paper folded together, containing news reports and articles **2** newspaper is the paper these are printed on • *Wrap it in newspaper.*

newt *NOUN* (**newts**)
a small animal rather like a lizard, that lives near or in water

New Testament *NOUN*
the second part of the Bible, which describes the life and teachings of Jesus Christ

newton *NOUN* (**newtons**)
(*in science*) a unit for measuring force

next *ADJECTIVE*
the nearest; following immediately after

next *ADVERB*
1 in the nearest place **2** at the nearest time • *What comes next?*

next door *ADVERB & ADJECTIVE*
in the next house or room

nib *NOUN* (**nibs**)
the pointed metal part at the end of a pen

nibble *VERB* (**nibbles**, **nibbling**, **nibbled**)
to nibble something is to take small or gentle bites at it

nice *ADJECTIVE* (**nicer**, **nicest**)
1 pleasant or kind **2** delicate or precise • *There is a nice difference between stealing and borrowing.*
▷ **nicely** *ADVERB* in a nice way • *Ask me nicely and I might say yes.*
▷ **niceness** *NOUN* niceness is being nice

nicety *NOUN* (**niceties**)
a small detail or feature

nick *NOUN* (**nicks**)
1 a small cut or notch **2** (*slang*) a prison or police station
to be in good nick (*informal*) is to be in good condition
in the nick of time only just in time

nick *VERB* (**nicks**, **nicking**, **nicked**)
1 to nick something is to make a small cut in it **2** (*slang*) to nick something is to steal it **3** (*slang*) to nick someone is to arrest them

nickel *NOUN* (**nickels**)
1 a silvery-white metal **2** (*in America*) a 5-cent coin

nickname *NOUN* (**nicknames**)
an informal name given to someone instead of their real name

nicotine *NOUN* (*say* **nik**-o-teen)
nicotine is a poisonous substance found in tobacco

niece *NOUN* (**nieces**)
the daughter of a person's brother or sister

night *NOUN* (**nights**)
the time when it is dark, between sunset and sunrise

nightclub *NOUN* (**nightclubs**)
a club or restaurant where there is entertainment at night

nightdress *NOUN* (**nightdresses**)
a loose light dress that girls and women wear in bed

nightfall *NOUN*
nightfall is the time when it becomes dark just after sunset

nightingale *NOUN* (**nightingales**)
a small brown bird that sings sweetly

nightly *ADJECTIVE*
happening every night

nightmare *NOUN* (**nightmares**)
1 a frightening or unpleasant dream **2** a terrifying experience

WORD FAMILY
You can say something is **nightmarish** when it is terrifying.

nil *NOUN*
nothing • *We lost three-nil.*

nimble *ADJECTIVE* (**nimbler**, **nimblest**)
moving quickly or easily • *As soon as the King and his huntsmen saw the Roe with the golden collar they all rode off after it, but it was far too quick and nimble for them.* — Andrew Lang, *The Red Fairy Book*

> WORD FAMILY
> To do something **nimbly** is to do it by moving quickly or easily. • *The dog approached the shield cautiously, sniffed at it once and stepped back nimbly.* — Michael Morpurgo, *The Sleeping Sword*

nine *NOUN* (**nines**)
the number 9

nineteen *NOUN* (**nineteens**)
the number 19
▷ **nineteenth** *ADJECTIVE & NOUN* 19th

ninety *NOUN* (**nineties**)
the number 90
▷ **ninetieth** *ADJECTIVE & NOUN* 90th

ninth *ADJECTIVE & NOUN*
the next after the eighth
▷ **ninthly** *ADVERB* in the ninth place; as the ninth one

nip *VERB* (**nips**, **nipping**, **nipped**)
1 to nip someone is to pinch or bite them sharply **2** (*informal*) to nip somewhere is to go quickly there • *I'll just nip into the supermarket.*

nip *NOUN* (**nips**)
1 a quick pinch or bite **2** a cold feeling • *There's a nip in the air.*

nipple *NOUN* (**nipples**)
one of the two small parts that stick out at the front of a person's chest

nippy *ADJECTIVE* (**nippier**, **nippiest**)(*informal*)
1 quick or nimble **2** cold

nit *NOUN* (**nits**)
a louse or its egg

nit-picking *NOUN*
pointing out small faults or mistakes

nitrate *NOUN* (**nitrates**)
a chemical compound containing nitrogen

nitric acid *NOUN* (*say* **ny**-trik)
nitric acid is a very strong acid containing nitrogen

nitrogen *NOUN* (*say* **ny**-tro-jen)
nitrogen is a gas that makes up about four-fifths of the air

nitty-gritty *NOUN*
(*slang*) the important or practical details or facts about something

nitwit *NOUN* (**nitwits**)
(*informal*) a stupid person

no *INTERJECTION*
a word you use to refuse something or say that you don't agree

no *DETERMINER & ADVERB*
not any • *We have no money.* • *She is no better.*

nobility *NOUN*
1 the nobility is the nobles or the aristocracy
2 nobility is being noble

noble *ADJECTIVE* (**nobler**, **noblest**)
1 of high social rank; aristocratic **2** having a good and generous nature • *He is a noble king.* **3** stately or impressive • *It was a noble building.*

> WORD FAMILY
> Someone does something **nobly** when they do it in a way that shows their good and generous nature.

noble *NOUN* (**nobles**)
a person of high social rank

nobleman or **noblewoman** *NOUN* (**noblemen** or **noblewomen**)
a man or woman of high rank

nobody *PRONOUN*
no person; not anyone • *Nobody knows.*

nobody *NOUN* (**nobodies**)
an unimportant person • *He's just a nobody.*

nocturnal *ADJECTIVE* (*say* nok-**ter**-nal)
1 active at night • *Badgers are nocturnal animals.*
2 happening at night

nod *VERB* (**nods**, **nodding**, **nodded**)
1 to nod, or nod your head, is to move your head up and down as a way of agreeing with someone or as a greeting **2** to nod is also to be drowsy

noise *NOUN* (**noises**)
a loud sound, especially one that is unpleasant or unwanted

> WORD FAMILY
> Something is **noiseless** when it doesn't make any noise; you **noiselessly** do something when you don't make any noise doing it.

noisy *ADJECTIVE* (**noisier**, **noisiest**)
making a lot of noise

> WORD FAMILY
> You **noisily** do something when you make a lot of noise doing it.

nomad *NOUN* (**nomads**) (*say* **noh**-mad)
a member of a tribe that moves from place to place looking for pasture for their animals

> WORD FAMILY
> **Nomadic** people move around from place to place.

no man's land *NOUN*
land that does not belong to anyone, especially the land between two armies at war

nominate *VERB* (**nominates**, **nominating**, **nominated**)
to nominate someone is to suggest that they should be a candidate in an election or should be given a job or award

> WORD FAMILY
> To receive a **nomination** for a job or award is to be nominated for it.

non- *PREFIX*
meaning 'not', as in *non-existent*

non-chronological *ADJECTIVE*
a non-chronological account or piece of writing is one in which the events are not arranged in the order in which they happened

none *PRONOUN*
not any; not one •*None of us went.*

none *ADVERB*
not at all •*He's none too pleased.*
none the less nevertheless

non-existent *ADJECTIVE*
not existing

non-fiction *NOUN*
non-fiction is writings that are not fiction; books about real things and true events

non-flammable *ADJECTIVE*
not able to be set on fire

nonsense *NOUN*
1 nonsense is words that do not mean anything or make any sense **2** nonsense is also absurd or silly ideas or behaviour

> WORD FAMILY
> Something is **nonsensical** when it doesn't make any sense.

non-stop *ADVERB & ADJECTIVE*
1 not stopping •*They talked non-stop all morning.* **2** not stopping until the end of a journey •*There's a non-stop train to London.*

noodles *PLURAL NOUN*
pasta made in narrow strips, used in soups

noon *NOUN*
twelve o'clock midday

no one *PRONOUN*
no person; not anyone

noose *NOUN* (**nooses**)
a loop in a rope that gets smaller when the rope is pulled

nor *CONJUNCTION*
and not •*She cannot do it; nor can I.*

normal *ADJECTIVE*
1 usual or ordinary •*It's normal to want a holiday.* **2** natural and healthy; not suffering from an illness

> WORD FAMILY
> **Normality** is being normal.

normally *ADVERB*
1 usually •*The journey normally takes an hour.* **2** in the usual way •*Just breathe normally.*

north *NOUN*
1 north is the direction to the left of a person facing east **2** north is also the part of a country or city that is in this direction

north *ADJECTIVE & ADVERB*
1 towards the north or in the north **2** coming from the north •*A north wind was blowing.*

north-east *NOUN, ADJECTIVE, & ADVERB*
midway between north and east

northerly *ADJECTIVE*
a northerly wind is one that blows from the north

northern *ADJECTIVE*
from or to do with the north

northerner *NOUN* (**northerners**)
someone who lives in the north of a country

northward or **northwards** *ADJECTIVE & ADVERB*
towards the north

north-west *NOUN, ADJECTIVE, & ADVERB*
midway between north and west

nose *NOUN* (**noses**)
1 the part of your face that you use for breathing and smelling **2** the front part of something, especially a vehicle or aircraft

nose *VERB* (**noses**, **nosing**, **nosed**)
to nose forward or through is to make progress cautiously •*The ship nosed through the ice.*
to nose about or **nose around** is to pry or interfere in someone else's affairs

nosedive *NOUN* (**nosedives**)
a steep dive, especially in an aircraft

nosedive *VERB* (**nosedives**, **nosediving**, **nosedived**)
to go suddenly downward

nostalgia *NOUN* (*say* nos-tal-ja)
you feel nostalgia when you fondly remember something that made you happy in the past

> WORD FAMILY
> You are **nostalgic** about something when you remember it fondly because it made you happy in the past.

nostril *NOUN* (**nostrils**)
each of the two openings in your nose

nosy *ADJECTIVE* (**nosier**, **nosiest**)
(*informal*) always wanting to know other people's business
▷ **nosiness** *NOUN* nosiness is being nosy

a b c d e f g h i j k l m **n** o p q r s t u v w x y z

not *ADVERB*
a word you use to change the meaning of something to its opposite

notable *ADJECTIVE*
remarkable or famous
▷ **notably** *ADVERB* especially or remarkably

notch *NOUN* (**notches**)
a small V-shaped cut or mark

note *NOUN* (**notes**)
1 something you write down as a reminder or help **2** a short letter **3** a single sound in music **4** a sound or tone that indicates something • *There was a note of anger in his voice.* **5** a banknote • *Have you got a five-pound note?*
to take note of something is to listen to it and understand it

note *VERB* (**notes**, **noting**, **noted**)
to note something is to pay attention to it, or to write it down as a reminder or help

notebook *NOUN* (**notebooks**)
a book in which you write things down

notepaper *NOUN*
notepaper is paper for writing letters

nothing *NOUN*
nothing is not anything

notice *NOUN* (**notices**)
1 a notice is something written or printed and displayed for people to see **2** to take notice of something is to pay attention to it • *It escaped my notice.* **3** a warning that something is going to happen

notice *VERB* (**notices**, **noticing**, **noticed**)
to notice something is to see it or become aware of it

noticeable *ADJECTIVE*
easy to see or notice
▷ **noticeably** *ADVERB* in a noticeable way

noticeboard *NOUN* (**noticeboards**)
a board on which notices can be displayed

notion *NOUN* (**notions**)
an idea, especially one that is vague or uncertain • *The notion that the earth is flat was disproved long ago.*

notorious *ADJECTIVE* (*say* noh- tor- i- us)
well-known for doing something bad • *He was a notorious criminal.*

> WORD FAMILY
> **Notoriety** is being well-known for doing something bad; to be **notoriously** bad is to be well-known for it • *This quiz is notoriously difficult.*

nougat *NOUN* (*say* noo- gah)
nougat is a chewy sweet made from nuts and sugar or honey

nought *NOUN* (**noughts**) (*say* nawt)
1 the figure 0 **2** nothing

noun *NOUN* (**nouns**)
a word that stands for a person, place, or thing

> GRAMMAR
> Nouns are called **common nouns** when they stand for a whole kind of people or things, for example *girl, horse, town, table*. They are called **abstract nouns** when they stand for things you can't feel or touch, for example *happiness, sport*. They are called **proper nouns** when they are the name of one person or thing, for example *Jane, Paris, Concorde*.

> NOUNS
> Nouns are words that name things. They tell you who or what a sentence is about. Nouns divide up into names (or proper nouns) and descriptions (or common nouns). Proper nouns name particular people, places, or things (*Jasmine, China, Charles Dickens, the Eiffel Tower*). Proper nouns always begin with a capital letter. Common nouns name people, places, or things in general (*girl, dog, stream, mystery, bone, fire, danger*). Common nouns divide into those which stand for objects (concrete nouns), and those which stand for ideas (abstract nouns). Examples of concrete nouns are *dog, stream, cone, fire, steel, bread*, and *car*. Examples of abstract nouns are *mystery, danger, happiness, and beauty*. Common nouns don't begin with a capital letter, unless they are the first word in a sentence.

nourish *VERB* (**nourishes**, **nourishing**, **nourished**)
to nourish someone is to give them enough good food to keep them alive and well

nourishment *NOUN*
nourishment is the food someone needs to keep them alive and well

novel *NOUN* (**novels**)
a story that fills a whole book

novel *ADJECTIVE*
unusual • *What a novel idea.*

novelist *NOUN* (**novelists**) (*say* nov- el- ist)
someone who writes novels

novelty *NOUN* (**novelties**)
1 novelty is being new or unusual • *The novelty of living in a cave soon wore off.* **2** a novelty is something new and unusual **3** a novelty is also a cheap toy or ornament

November *NOUN*
the eleventh month of the year

novice *NOUN* (**novices**)
a beginner

now *ADVERB*
1 at this time • *I am now living in Glasgow.*
2 without any delay • *Do it now!*
for now until a later time • *Goodbye for now.*
now and again or **now and then** occasionally; sometimes

now *CONJUNCTION*
since or as • *I do remember, now you mention it.*

now *NOUN*
this moment • *They should be home by now.*

nowadays *ADVERB*
at the present time

nowhere *ADVERB*
not anywhere; in no place or to no place

nozzle *NOUN* (**nozzles**)
the part at the end of a hose or pipe from which something flows

nuclear *ADJECTIVE* (*say* new- kli- er)
1 to do with a nucleus, especially of an atom
2 using the energy that is created by the splitting of atoms

nucleus *NOUN* (**nuclei**) (*say* new- kli- us)
1 the central part of an atom or cell **2** the part in the centre of something, round which other things are grouped • *The queen bee is the nucleus of the hive.*

nude *ADJECTIVE*
not wearing any clothes

nude *NOUN* (**nudes**)
a nude person, especially in a work of art

> WORD FAMILY
> **Nudity** is not wearing any clothes.

nudge *VERB* (**nudges**, **nudging**, **nudged**)
to nudge someone is to touch or push them with your elbow

nudist *NOUN* (**nudists**)
a person who believes that going naked is enjoyable and good for the health

nugget *NOUN* (**nuggets**)
a rough lump of gold from the ground

nuisance *NOUN* (**nuisances**)
an annoying person or thing

numb *ADJECTIVE*
part of your body is numb when you can't feel anything in it
▷ **numbness** *NOUN* numbness is being numb

number *NOUN* (**numbers**)
1 a symbol or word that tells you how many of something there are **2** a quantity of people or things • *Do you know the number of bones in your body?* **3** a person's number is their telephone number **4** a song or piece of music

number *VERB* (**numbers**, **numbering**, **numbered**)
1 to number things is to count them or mark them with numbers **2** to number a certain amount is to reach it • *The crowd numbered 10,000.*

numeracy *NOUN*
numeracy is the ability to understand and work with numbers

numeral *NOUN* (**numerals**)
a symbol or figure that stands for a number

numerate *ADJECTIVE*
having a good basic knowledge of mathematics

numerator *NOUN* (**numerators**)
the number above the line in a fraction.
In $\frac{1}{2}$ the 1 is the numerator

numerical *ADJECTIVE*
to do with numbers

> WORD FAMILY
> To express information **numerically** is to use numbers.

numerous *ADJECTIVE*
many • *There are numerous kinds of cat.*

nun *NOUN* (**nuns**)
a member of a religious community of women

nunnery *NOUN* (**nunneries**)
a group of nuns; a convent

nurse *NOUN* (**nurses**)
a person trained to look after people who are ill or injured

nurse *VERB* (**nurses**, **nursing**, **nursed**)
1 to nurse someone is to look after them when they are ill or injured **2** to nurse someone or something is to hold them carefully in your arms • *He was nursing a puppy.* **3** to nurse a baby is to feed it from the breast

nursery *NOUN* (**nurseries**)
1 a place where young children are looked after or play **2** a place where young plants are grown and usually offered for sale

nursery rhyme *NOUN* (**nursery rhymes**)
a simple poem or song that young children like

nursery school *NOUN* (**nursery schools**)
a school for very young children

nursing home *NOUN* (**nursing homes**)
a small or private hospital

nurture *VERB* (**nurtures**, **nurturing**, **nurtured**)
to nurture children is to look after them and educate them

nut *NOUN* (**nuts**)
1 a fruit with a hard shell **2** the eatable part of this kind of fruit **3** a hollow piece of metal for screwing on to a bolt **4** (*slang*) the head **5** (*slang*) a mad or eccentric person

> WORD FAMILY
> Something **nutty** tastes of nuts or is full of nuts.

nutcrackers *PLURAL NOUN*
pincers for cracking the shells of nuts

nutmeg *NOUN* (**nutmegs**)
a hard seed that is made into a powder and used as a spice

nutrient *NOUN* (**nutrients**) (*say* new- tri- ent)
a substance that is needed to keep a plant or animal alive and to help it to grow

nutrition *NOUN* (*say* new-**trish**-on)
nutrition is the food someone needs to keep them alive and well
▷ **nutritional** *ADJECTIVE* to do with nutrition

nutritious *ADJECTIVE* (*say* new-**trish**-us)
nutritious food helps you to grow and keep well
• *They ate a nutritious meal.*

nutshell *NOUN* (**nutshells**)
the shell of a nut
to put something in a nutshell is to state it very briefly

nuzzle *VERB* (**nuzzles**, **nuzzling**, **nuzzled**)
to nuzzle someone is to rub gently against them with the nose, in the way that some animals do
• *Bella lowered her head and turned to nuzzle Irina's hair with her warm velvety nose, then she trotted off into the barn and stood quietly in her corner on the straw.* — Magdalen Nabb, *The Enchanted Horse*

nylon *NOUN*
nylon is a lightweight synthetic cloth or fibre

nymph *NOUN* (**nymphs**)
in myths, a young goddess living in trees or rivers or the sea

Oo

oak *NOUN* (**oaks**)
a large tree that produces seeds called acorns

oar *NOUN* (**oars**)
a pole with a flat blade at one end, used for rowing a boat

oarsman or **oarswoman** *NOUN* (**oarsmen** or **oarswomen**)
a man or woman who rows a boat

oasis *NOUN* (**oases**) (*say* oh-**ay**-sis)
a fertile place with water and trees in a desert

oath *NOUN* (**oaths**)
1 a solemn promise to do something or that something is true **2** a swear word

oatmeal *NOUN*
oatmeal is ground oats

oats *PLURAL NOUN*
a cereal used to make food for humans and animals

obedient *ADJECTIVE*
doing what someone tells you to do; willing to obey

> WORD FAMILY
> **Obedience** is doing what you are told; to do something **obediently** is to do it when someone tells you to.

obey *VERB* (**obeys**, **obeying**, **obeyed**)
1 to obey someone is to do what they tell you **2** to obey a rule or law is to do what it says

obituary *NOUN* (**obituaries**) (*say* o-**bit**-yoo-er-i)
an announcement in a newspaper that someone has died, often with a short account of their life

object *NOUN* (**objects**) (*say* **ob**-jikt)
1 something that can be seen or touched **2** the purpose of something **3** (*in grammar*) the word naming the person or thing that the action of the verb affects, for example *him* in the sentence *I chased him*

object *VERB* (**objects**, **objecting**, **objected**) (*say* ob-**jekt**)
to object to something or someone is to say that you do not like them or do not agree with them

objection *NOUN* (**objections**)
1 objection is objecting to something **2** an objection is a reason for objecting • *I have three objections to your plan.*

objectionable *ADJECTIVE*
unpleasant or nasty

objective *NOUN* (**objectives**)
what you are trying to reach or do; an aim

objective *ADJECTIVE*
1 not influenced by your own beliefs or ideas • *He gave an objective account of the incident.* **2** having a real existence outside someone's mind • *No objective evidence has yet been found to prove his claims.*

obligation *NOUN* (**obligations**)
a duty

obligatory *ADJECTIVE*
something is obligatory when you must do it because of a rule or law • *Games are obligatory.*

oblige *VERB* (**obliges**, **obliging**, **obliged**)
1 to oblige someone to do something is to force them to do it **2** to oblige someone is to help and please them • *Can you oblige me with a loan?*
to be obliged to someone is to be grateful to them for helping you

oblique *ADJECTIVE* (*say* o-**bleek**)
1 an oblique line slants at an angle **2** not straightforward or direct • *They gave an oblique reply.*

> WORD FAMILY
> To (for example) cut something **obliquely** is to do it at an angle.

oblong *NOUN* (**oblongs**)
a rectangle that is longer than it is wide

oblong *ADJECTIVE*
having the shape of an oblong

obnoxious *ADJECTIVE*
really horrible

oboe *NOUN* (**oboes**) (*say* **oh**- boh)
a high-pitched woodwind instrument

> WORD FAMILY
> A person who plays the oboe is an **oboist**.

obscene *ADJECTIVE* (*say* ob- **seen**)
offensive to people's feelings, especially because of being connected with sex

> WORD FAMILY
> **Obscenity** is obscene language or behaviour.

obscure *ADJECTIVE* (**obscurer**, **obscurest**)
1 difficult to see or understand; very unclear **2** not well-known
▷ **obscurely** *ADVERB* in an obscure way
▷ **obscurity** *NOUN* obscurity is being not well-known

observance *NOUN* (**observances**)
obeying a law or keeping a custom

observant *ADJECTIVE*
quick at noticing things • *Paddington was a very observant bear, and since he had arrived in London he'd noticed lots of these shop windows.* — Michael Bond, *A Bear Called Paddington*
▷ **observantly** *ADVERB* in an observant way

observation *NOUN* (**observations**)
1 observation is noticing or watching something carefully **2** an observation is a comment or remark • *He made a few observations about the weather.*

observatory *NOUN* (**observatories**) (*say* ob- **zerv**- a- ter- i)
a building equipped with telescopes for looking at the stars or weather

observe *VERB* (**observes**, **observing**, **observed**)
1 to observe someone or something is to watch them carefully **2** to observe something is to notice it **3** to observe a law or custom is to obey it or keep it **4** to observe a fact is to state it • *She observed that she did not like ice in her drinks.*

> WORD FAMILY
> An **observer** is someone who watches something.

obsessed *ADJECTIVE*
always thinking about something • *He is obsessed with his work.*

> WORD FAMILY
> An **obsession** is something that someone thinks about too much.

obsolete *ADJECTIVE*
not used any more; out of date

obstacle *NOUN* (**obstacles**)
something that gets in your way or makes it difficult for you to do something

obstinate *ADJECTIVE*
not willing to change your ideas or ways, even though they may be wrong
▷ **obstinacy** *NOUN* obstinacy is being obstinate
▷ **obstinately** *ADVERB* in an obstinate way

obstruct *VERB* (**obstructs**, **obstructing**, **obstructed**)
to obstruct someone or something is to stop them from getting past, or to hinder them

obtain *VERB* (**obtains**, **obtaining**, **obtained**)
to obtain something is to get it or be given it
▷ **obtainable** *ADJECTIVE* able to be bought or got

obtuse *ADJECTIVE* (**obtuser**, **obtusest**)
1 slow to understand; stupid **2** an obtuse angle is an angle of between 90 and 180 degrees
▷ **obtusely** *ADVERB* in an obtuse way

obvious *ADJECTIVE*
easy to see or understand

obviously *ADVERB*
it's obvious that; clearly • *Obviously we don't want to lose.*

occasion *NOUN* (**occasions**)
1 the time when something happens • *On this occasion, we will not take any action.* **2** a special event • *The wedding was a marvellous occasion.*

occasional *ADJECTIVE*
happening from time to time, but not often and not regularly

> WORD FAMILY
> Something happens **occasionally** when it happens from time to time.

occupant *NOUN* (**occupants**)
someone who occupies a place

occupation *NOUN* (**occupations**)
1 a person's occupation is their job or profession **2** the occupation of a country or territory is when an army captures it and stays there

occupy *VERB* (**occupies**, **occupying**, **occupied**)
1 to occupy a place or building is to live in it **2** to occupy a space or position is to fill it **3** in a war, to occupy territory is to capture it and keep an army in it **4** to occupy someone is to keep them busy or interested

occur *VERB* (**occurs**, **occurring**, **occurred**)
1 an event occurs when it happens or takes place • *An earthquake occurred on the island in 1953.*
2 something occurs when it exists or is found somewhere • *These plants occur in ponds.*
3 something occurs to you when it suddenly comes into your mind • *Just then an idea occurred to me.*

occurrence *NOUN* (**occurrences**)
something that happens or exists

ocean *NOUN* (**oceans**)
1 the ocean is the area of salt water surrounding the land of the earth **2** an ocean is a large part of this water, such as the Pacific Ocean

o'clock *ADVERB*
by the clock • *Lunch is at one o'clock.*

octagon *NOUN* (**octagons**)
a flat shape with eight sides
▷ **octagonal** *ADJECTIVE* having eight sides

octave *NOUN* (**octaves**)
1 the interval between one musical note and the next note of the same name above or below it
2 these two notes played together

October *NOUN*
the tenth month of the year

octopus *NOUN* (**octopuses**)
a sea creature with eight arms (called *tentacles*)

odd *ADJECTIVE* (**odder**, **oddest**)
1 strange or unusual **2** an odd number is one that cannot be divided by 2, such as 5 and 31 **3** left over or spare • *I've got an odd sock.* **4** of various kinds; occasional • *He's doing odd jobs.*

> WORD FAMILY
> An **oddity** is something that is odd or strange; to behave **oddly** is to behave in an odd way; **oddness** is being odd.

oddments *PLURAL NOUN*
small things of various kinds

odds *PLURAL NOUN*
1 the chances that something will happen **2** the proportion of money that you will win if a bet is successful • *When the odds are 10 to 1, you will win £10 if you bet £1.*
odds and ends small things of various kinds

odour *NOUN* (**odours**)
a smell, usually an unpleasant one

> WORD FAMILY
> Something that is **odorous** has an odour.

oesophagus *NOUN* (**oesophagi** or **oesophaguses**) (*say* ee- **sof**- a- gus)
the tube leading from your throat to your stomach

of *PREPOSITION*
1 belonging to • *She is the mother of the child.*
2 coming from • *He is a native of Italy.* **3** away from • *The supermarket is two miles north of the town.*
4 about; concerning • *Is there any news of your father?* **5** from; out of • *The house is built of stone.*

off *ADVERB*
1 not on; away • *His hat blew off.* **2** not working or happening • *The heating is off.* • *The match is off because of snow.* **3** behind or at the side of a stage • *There were noises off.* **4** beginning to go bad • *I think the milk is off.*

off *PREPOSITION*
1 not on; away or down from • *He fell off his chair.*
2 not taking or wanting • *She is off her food.* **3** taken away from • *There is £5 off the normal price.*

offence *NOUN* (**offences**)
1 an offence is a crime or something illegal • *When was the offence committed?* **2** offence is a feeling of annoyance or hurt
to give offence is to hurt someone's feelings
to take offence is to be upset by what someone has said or done

offend *VERB* (**offends**, **offending**, **offended**)
1 to offend someone is to hurt their feelings or be unpleasant to them **2** to offend is to break a law or do something wrong

> WORD FAMILY
> An **offender** is someone who breaks a law or does something wrong.

offensive *ADJECTIVE*
1 insulting or causing offence **2** used for attacking • *He was arrested for carrying an offensive weapon.*
▷ **offensively** *ADVERB* in an offensive way

offer *VERB* (**offers**, **offering**, **offered**)
1 to offer something is to hold it out so that someone can take it if they want it **2** to offer to do something is to say that you are willing to do it **3** to offer a sum of money is to say how much you are willing to pay for something

offer *NOUN* (**offers**)
1 the action of offering something • *Thank you for your offer of help.* **2** an amount of money that you are willing to pay for something

offhand *ADJECTIVE*
1 said without much thought **2** rude or abrupt

office *NOUN* (**offices**)
1 a room or building where people work, often at desks **2** a place where you can go for tickets, information, or some other purpose • *a lost property office* **3** an important job or position • *He was honoured to hold the office of President.*

officer *NOUN* (**officers**)
1 someone who is in charge of other people, especially in the armed forces **2** a policeman or policewoman

official *ADJECTIVE*
1 done or said by someone with authority
2 connected with the job of someone in a position of authority • *The prime minister will make an official visit to Australia next month.*

> WORD FAMILY
> To do something **officially** is to do it in an official way.

official *NOUN* (**officials**)
someone who does a job of authority or trust

> OTHER WORD
> Take care not to confuse the adjective **official** with **officious**, which is the next word in this dictionary.

officious *ADJECTIVE* (*say* o- fish- us)
too ready to order people about; bossy and unpleasant
▷ **officiously** *ADVERB* in an officious way

off-licence *NOUN* (**off-licences**)
a shop with a licence to sell alcoholic drinks for people to take away

offset *VERB* (**offsets**, **offsetting**, **offset**)
one thing offsets another when it balances it out • *The failures were offset by some successes.*

offshore *ADJECTIVE & ADVERB*
1 from the land towards the sea • *There is an offshore breeze.* **2** in the sea some distance from the shore • *They swam to an offshore island.*

offside *ADJECTIVE*
(*in sport*) in a position which is not allowed by the rules

offspring *NOUN* (**offspring**)
a child or young animal

often *ADVERB*
many times; in many cases

ogre *NOUN* (**ogres**)
1 a cruel giant in stories **2** a frightening person

oh *INTERJECTION*
a cry of surprise, pain, or delight

ohm *NOUN* (**ohms**) (*rhymes with* **home**)
a unit of electrical resistance

oil *NOUN* (**oils**)
1 an oil is a thick slippery liquid that does not mix with water **2** oil is a kind of petroleum used as fuel

oil *VERB* (**oils**, **oiling**, **oiled**)
to oil something is to put oil on it to make it work smoothly

oilfield *NOUN* (**oilfields**)
an area where oil is found under the ground or under the sea

oil painting *NOUN* (**oil paintings**)
a painting done using paints made with oil

oil rig *NOUN* (**oil rigs**)
a structure set up to support the equipment for drilling for oil

oilskin *NOUN* (**oilskins**)
a waterproof piece of clothing worn especially by fishermen

oil well *NOUN* (**oil wells**)
a hole drilled in the ground or under the sea to get oil

oily *ADJECTIVE* (**oilier**, **oiliest**)
1 like oil or covered in oil **2** unpleasantly over-polite • *She didn't like his oily manner.*

ointment *NOUN* (**ointments**)
a cream that you put on sore skin and cuts

OK *ADVERB & ADJECTIVE*
(*informal*) all right

old *ADJECTIVE* (**older**, **oldest**)
1 not new; born or made a long time ago **2** of a particular age • *I'm ten years old.* **3** former or original • *I liked my old school better than the one I go to now.*

old age *NOUN*
old age is the time when a person is old

old-fashioned *ADJECTIVE*
of the kind that was usual a long time ago; out of date

Old Norse *NOUN*
Old Norse is the language of the Vikings, from which the modern Scandinavian languages come

Old Testament *NOUN*
the first part of the Bible, which is the holy book of the Jewish and Christian religions

olive *NOUN* (**olives**)
1 an evergreen tree with a small bitter fruit **2** the fruit of this tree, used for eating and to make olive oil

olive branch *NOUN* (**olive branches**)
something you do or say that shows you want to make peace

Olympic Games or **Olympics** *PLURAL NOUN* (*say* o- lim- pik)
a series of international sports contests held every four years in different countries

ombudsman *NOUN* (**ombudsmen**) (*say* om- budz- man)
an official who looks into people's complaints against government departments

omelette *NOUN* (**omelettes**) (*say* om- lit)
eggs beaten together and fried, often with a filling or flavouring

omen *NOUN* (**omens**)
an event that some people see as a sign that something is going to happen

ominous *ADJECTIVE*
suggesting that trouble is coming • *In winter the dragons were hibernating and the cliff fell silent, except for the ominous, low rumble of their snores.* — Cressida Cowell, *How to Train Your Dragon*
▷ **ominously** *ADVERB* in an ominous way

omission *NOUN* (**omissions**)
something left out or not done

omit *VERB* (**omits**, **omitting**, **omitted**)
1 to omit something is to leave it out **2** to omit to do something is to fail to do it

omnivorous *ADJECTIVE*
an omnivorous animal is one that feeds on plants as well as the flesh of animals

on *PREPOSITION*
1 at or over the top or surface of something • *Sit on the floor.* **2** at the time of • *Come on Monday.* **3** about; concerning • *We went to a talk on butterflies.* **4** towards or near • *They advanced on the town.*

on *ADVERB*
1 so as to be on something • *Put your hat on.* **2** forwards • *Move on.* **3** working; in action • *Is the heater on?*

once *ADVERB*
1 at one time • *I once lived in Leeds.* **2** one time only • *I've only met him once.*

once *CONJUNCTION*
as soon as • *We can get out once I open this door.*
at once immediately

one *NOUN* **(ones)**
the smallest whole number, 1

one *PRONOUN*
a person or thing on their own • *One likes to help.* • *One of my friends is ill.*
one another each other

one *ADJECTIVE*
single • *I have one packet left.*

oneself *PRONOUN*
one's own self; yourself • *One should not always think of oneself.*

one-sided *ADJECTIVE*
a one-sided contest is one where one side has a big advantage • *It will be a very one-sided game.*

one-way *ADJECTIVE*
a one-way street is one where traffic is only allowed to go in one direction

ongoing *ADJECTIVE*
continuing to exist or make progress • *It's an ongoing project.*

onion *NOUN* **(onions)**
a round vegetable with a strong flavour

onlooker *NOUN* **(onlookers)**
a spectator

only *ADJECTIVE*
being the one person or thing of a kind • *He's the only person we can trust.*

only *ADVERB*
no more than • *There are only three cakes.*

only *CONJUNCTION*
but then; however • *I want to come, only I'm busy that night.*

onomatopoeia *NOUN* (*say* on- om- at- o- **pee**- a)
onomatopoeia is forming or using words that sound like the thing they describe, such as *cuckoo, hiss*, and *plop*
▷ **onomatopoeic** *ADJECTIVE* using onomatopoeia

onset *NOUN*
1 the onset of (for example) winter or war is the beginning of it **2** the onset of a word or syllable is the consonant or group of consonants at the beginning

onshore *ADJECTIVE*
from the sea towards the land • *There is an onshore breeze.*

onto *PREPOSITION*
to a position on • *They fell onto the floor.*

onward or **onwards** *ADVERB*
forward or forwards

ooze *VERB* **(oozes, oozing, oozed)**
a thick liquid oozes when it flows out slowly, especially through a narrow opening • *Blood oozed from his wound.*

opaque *ADJECTIVE* (*say* oh- **payk**)
something that is opaque doesn't allow light through and so can't be seen through

open *ADJECTIVE*
1 allowing people or things to pass through; not shut • *The door is open .* • *The bottles need to be open.* **2** not enclosed • *There were miles of open land.* **3** not folded; spread out • *She greeted us with open arms.* **4** honest; not secret or secretive • *We all want open government.* **5** not settled or finished • *That is still an open question.*
in the open air outdoors; not inside a house or building

open *VERB* **(opens, opening, opened)**
1 to open something is to make it open **2** to open is to become open **3** to open is also to start • *The jumble sale opens at 2 o'clock.* **4** a shop opens when it starts business for the day • *What time do you open?*

opener *NOUN* **(openers)**
a device for opening a bottle or can

opening *NOUN* **(openings)**
1 a space or gap in something **2** the beginning of something **3** an opportunity, especially for a job

openly *ADVERB*
to do something openly is to do it for all to see, not secretly

open-minded *ADJECTIVE*
ready to listen to other people's ideas and opinions; not having fixed ideas

opera *NOUN* **(operas)**
opera, or an opera, is a form of drama in which the characters sing all or most of the words, with an orchestra
▷ **operatic** *ADJECTIVE* to do with opera

operate *VERB* **(operates, operating, operated)**
1 to operate something is to make it work **2** to operate is to work or be in action **3** to operate on someone is to perform a surgical operation on them

operation *NOUN* **(operations)**
1 something done to a patient's body by a surgeon to remove or repair a part of it **2** a carefully planned activity
to be in operation is to be working • *The new rules are now in operation.*

operator *NOUN* **(operators)**
someone who works something, especially a telephone switchboard or exchange

opinion *NOUN* **(opinions)**
what you think of something; a belief or judgement

opinion poll *NOUN* (**opinion polls**)
an estimate of what people think, made by questioning a certain number of them

opium *NOUN*
opium is a drug made from poppies, used to calm people and to make them unable to feel pain

opponent *NOUN* (**opponents**)
someone who is against you in a contest, war, or argument

opportunity *NOUN* (**opportunities**)
a good time to do something

oppose *VERB* (**opposes**, **opposing**, **opposed**)
to oppose someone or something is to be against them or disagree with them
as opposed to in contrast with • *We want some action, as opposed to mere talking.*
to be opposed to something is to disagree strongly with it • *We are opposed to parking in the town centre.*

opposite *ADJECTIVE & ADVERB*
1 on the other side; facing • *She lives on the opposite side of the road to me.* • *I'll sit opposite.* **2** completely different • *They went in opposite directions.*

opposite *NOUN* (**opposites**)
something that is completely different from something else • *'Happy' is the opposite of 'sad'.*

opposition *NOUN*
opposition is opposing something; resistance
the Opposition the chief political party opposing the one that has formed the government

oppress *VERB* (**oppresses**, **oppressing**, **oppressed**)
1 to oppress people is to govern them or treat them cruelly or unjustly **2** to oppress someone is to trouble them with worry or sadness

> WORD FAMILY
> **Oppression** is treating people cruelly or unjustly; an **oppressor** is someone who treats people like this.

oppressive *ADJECTIVE*
1 harsh and cruel • *They live under an oppressive regime.* **2** hot and tiring • *The weather can be very oppressive in July.*

opt *VERB* (**opts**, **opting**, **opted**)
to opt for something or to do something is to choose it • *I opted for the cash prize.* • *We opted to go abroad.*
to opt out of something is to decide not to join in with it

optical *ADJECTIVE*
to do with sight or the eyes
▷ **optically** *ADVERB* as far as sight or the eyes are concerned

optical illusion *NOUN* (**optical illusions**)
something you think you see that is not really there

optician *NOUN* (**opticians**) (*say* op-**tish**-an)
someone who tests your eyesight and makes and sells glasses and contact lenses

optimist *NOUN* (**optimists**)
someone who usually expects things to turn out well

> WORD FAMILY
> **Optimism** is the feeling that things will turn out well.

optimistic *ADJECTIVE*
expecting things to turn out well
▷ **optimistically** *ADVERB* in an optimistic way

option *NOUN* (**options**)
1 one of the things that you can choose • *Your options are to travel by bus or by train.* **2** the right to choose; choice • *You have the option of staying.*

optional *ADJECTIVE*
something is optional when you can choose whether to do it or not

opulent *ADJECTIVE* (*say* **op**-yoo-lent)
1 made or decorated with expensive things; luxurious **2** very rich
▷ **opulence** *NOUN* opulence is wealth and luxury
▷ **opulently** *ADVERB* in an opulent way

or *CONJUNCTION*
used to show that there is a choice or alternative • *Do you want a cake or a biscuit?*

oral *ADJECTIVE*
1 spoken, not written **2** to do with the mouth or using your mouth

> WORD FAMILY
> To do something **orally** is to do it by speaking or using your mouth • *This medicine must not be taken orally.*

> SPELLING
> Take care not to confuse **oral** with **aural**, which means 'of or using hearing'.

orange *NOUN* (**oranges**)
1 a round juicy fruit with thick reddish-yellow peel
2 a reddish-yellow colour

orange *ADJECTIVE*
reddish-yellow

orangeade *NOUN* (**orangeades**)
a drink with a flavour of oranges

orang-utan *NOUN* (**orang-utans**) (*say* o-rang-u-**tan**)
a large kind of ape found in Borneo and Sumatra

oration *NOUN* (**orations**)
a long formal speech

orator *NOUN* (**orators**) (*say* **o**-ra-ter)
someone who makes formal speeches

oratorio *NOUN* (**oratorios**) (*say* o-ra-**tor**-i-oh)
a piece of music for voices and orchestra, usually on a religious subject

oratory *NOUN*
oratory is the skill of making speeches in public
▷ **oratorical** *ADJECTIVE* to do with oratory

orbit *NOUN* (**orbits**)
the curved path taken by something moving round a planet or other body in space

orbit *VERB* (**orbits, orbiting, orbited**)
to orbit a planet or other body in space is to move round it • *The satellite orbited the earth.*
▷ **orbital** *ADJECTIVE* to do with the orbit of a planet or other body in space

orchard *NOUN* (**orchards**)
a piece of ground with fruit trees

orchestra *NOUN* (**orchestras**)
a group of musicians playing various instruments together

WORD FAMILY
Orchestral music is written to be played by an orchestra.

orchid *NOUN* (**orchids**) (*say* **or**- kid)
a type of brightly coloured flower

ordeal *NOUN* (**ordeals**)
a difficult or unpleasant experience

order *NOUN* (**orders**)
1 a command **2** a request for something to be supplied • *The waiter came to take our order.* **3** the way things are arranged • *The words are in alphabetical order.* **4** obedience or good behaviour • *Can we have some order please?* **5** tidiness or neatness **6** a kind or sort of thing • *They showed courage of the highest order.* **7** a group of religious monks, priests, or nuns
in order that or **in order to** for the purpose of
to be out of order is to be broken or not working

order *VERB* (**orders, ordering, ordered**)
1 to order someone to do something is to tell them to do it **2** to order something is to ask for it to be supplied to you

orderly *ADJECTIVE*
1 arranged tidily or well; methodical
2 well-behaved; obedient
▷ **orderliness** *NOUN* orderliness is being orderly

ordinal number *NOUN* (**ordinal numbers**)
a number that shows where something comes in a series, for example 1st, 2nd, 3rd (compare *cardinal number*)

ordinary *ADJECTIVE*
normal or usual; not special

WORD FAMILY
Something **ordinarily** happens when it is what normally happens • *Stanley Lambchop had noticed in the lift that Mr Dart, who was ordinarily a cheerful man, had become quite gloomy.* — Jeff Brown, *Flat Stanley*

ore *NOUN* (**ores**)
rock with metal in it, such as iron ore

organ *NOUN* (**organs**)
1 a musical instrument from which sounds are produced by air forced through pipes, played by keys and pedals **2** a part of your body with a particular function, for example the digestive organs

organic *ADJECTIVE*
1 organic food is grown or produced without using artificial chemicals to act as fertilizers or pesticides **2** made by or found in living things

organism *NOUN* (**organisms**)
a living animal or plant

organist *NOUN* (**organists**)
someone who plays the organ

organization *NOUN* (**organizations**)
1 an organization is a group of people who work together to do something **2** organization is planning or arranging things such as getting people together to do something

organize *VERB* (**organizes, organizing, organized**)
1 to organize people is to get them together to do something **2** to organize something is to plan or arrange it • *We organized a picnic.* **3** to organize things is to put them in order
▷ **organizer** *NOUN* someone who organizes something

oriental *ADJECTIVE*
to do with the countries east of the Mediterranean Sea, especially China and Japan

orienteering *NOUN* (*say* or- i- en- **teer**- ing)
orienteering is the sport of finding your way across rough country with a map and compass

origami *NOUN* (*say* o- ri- **gah**- mi)
origami is folding pieces of paper to make decorative shapes

origin *NOUN* (**origins**)
the start of something; the point where something began • *a book about the origins of life on earth*

original *ADJECTIVE*
1 existing from the start; earliest • *They were the original inhabitants.* **2** new; not a copy or an imitation • *It is an original design.* **3** producing new ideas; inventive • *He was an original thinker.*

WORD FAMILY
Originality is being original or inventive; what happened **originally** is what happened in the beginning • *My family came from Pakistan originally.*

originate *VERB* (**originates, originating, originated**)
1 to originate something is to create it or develop it **2** to originate is to start in a certain way • *The war originated in a dispute over fishing rights.*
▷ **originator** *NOUN* someone who originates something

ornament *NOUN* (**ornaments**)
an object you wear or display as a decoration

> WORD FAMILY
> Something that is **ornamental** is used to decorate something • *an ornamental fountain*; **ornamentation** is using things to decorate something.

ornithology *NOUN* (*say* or- ni- **thol**- o- ji)
ornithology is the study of birds

> WORD FAMILY
> **Ornithological** means to do with birds; an **ornithologist** is a person who studies birds.

orphan *NOUN* (**orphans**)
a child whose parents are dead

orphanage *NOUN* (**orphanages**)
a home for orphans

orthodox *ADJECTIVE*
having beliefs that are correct or generally accepted

> WORD FAMILY
> **Orthodoxy** is the belief that is generally accepted.

Orthodox Church *NOUN*
the Christian Churches of eastern Europe

oscillate *VERB* (**oscillates, oscillating, oscillated**) (*say* **oss**- il- ate)
to oscillate is to keep moving to and fro • *The hideous creature ... began to move its head backwards and forwards, with a slow oscillating motion, as if looking for something.* — George MacDonald, *The Light Princess*

> WORD FAMILY
> **Oscillation** is when something keeps moving to and fro, and an **oscillation** is a single movement from one position to another.

ostrich *NOUN* (**ostriches**)
a large long-legged bird that can run fast but cannot fly

> IDIOM
> There is an old story that the ostrich buried its head in the sand when it was trying to escape from hunters, thinking that if it couldn't see them they couldn't see it. This is why people talk about 'burying your head in the sand' or being 'ostrich-like' when they think you are fooling yourself by what you do or say.

other *DETERMINER*
not the same as this; different • *Play some other tune.* • *Try the other shoe.*
every other day every second day, for example Monday, Wednesday, and Friday
other than except • *They have no belongings other than what they are carrying.*
the other day or **the other week** a few days or weeks ago

other *NOUN* (**others**)
the other person or thing • *Where are the others?*

otherwise *ADVERB*
1 if you do not; if things happen differently • *Write it down, otherwise you'll forget it.* **2** in other ways • *It rained a lot but otherwise the holiday was good.* **3** differently • *We could not do otherwise.*

otter *NOUN* (**otters**)
an animal with thick fur, webbed feet, and a flat tail, that lives near water

ouch *INTERJECTION*
a cry of pain

ought *VERB*
used with other words to show **1** what you should or must do • *You ought to do your music practice.* **2** what is likely to happen • *With all these dark clouds it ought to rain.*

ounce *NOUN* (**ounces**)
a unit of weight equal to $\frac{1}{16}$ of a pound or about 28 grams

our *DETERMINER*
belonging to us • *This is our house.*

ours *PRONOUN*
belonging to us • *This house is ours.*

ourselves *PRONOUN*
us and nobody else, used to refer back to the subject of a verb • *We have hurt ourselves.*
by ourselves on our own; alone • *We did the work all by ourselves.*

out *ADVERB*
1 away from a place or not in it; not at home **2** into the open or outdoors • *Are you going out today?* **3** not burning or working • *The fire has gone out.* **4** loudly • *She cried out.* **5** completely • *They have sold out.* **6** dismissed from a game • *Another batsman is out.*
to be out for something is to want it badly
to be out of something is to have no more of it left
out of date old-fashioned; not used any more
out of doors in the open air
out of the way remote or distant

out and out *ADJECTIVE*
complete or thorough • *He is an out and out villain.*

outback *NOUN*
the remote inland areas of Australia

outboard motor *NOUN* (**outboard motors**)
a motor fitted to the outside of a boat's stern

outbreak *NOUN* (**outbreaks**)
the sudden start of a disease, war, or show of anger

outburst *NOUN* (**outbursts**)
the sudden beginning of anger or laughter

outcast *NOUN* (**outcasts**)
someone who has been rejected by family, friends, or society

outcome *NOUN* (**outcomes**)
the result of what happens or has happened

outcry *NOUN* (**outcries**)
a strong protest from many people • *There was an outcry over the rise in rail fares.*

outdated *ADJECTIVE*
out of date

outdo *VERB* (**outdoes, outdoing, outdid, outdone**)
to outdo someone else is to do better than them

outdoor *ADJECTIVE*
done or used outside • *You'll need your outdoor clothes.*

outdoors *ADVERB*
in the open air • *It is cold outdoors.*

outer *ADJECTIVE*
nearer the outside; external

outer space *NOUN*
outer space is the universe beyond the earth's atmosphere

outfit *NOUN* (**outfits**)
1 a set of clothes you wear together **2** a set of things you need for doing something

outgrow *VERB* (**outgrows, outgrowing, outgrew, outgrown**)
1 to outgrow something such as clothes or a habit is to grow too big or too old for them **2** to outgrow someone is to grow faster or taller than them

outhouse *NOUN* (**outhouses**)
a small building attached to a larger building or close to it

outing *NOUN* (**outings**)
a trip or short journey you make for pleasure

outlast *VERB* (**outlasts, outlasting, outlasted**)
to outlast something else is to last longer than it

outlaw *NOUN* (**outlaws**)
a robber or bandit who is hiding to avoid being caught and is not protected by the law

outlaw *VERB* (**outlaws, outlawing, outlawed**)
1 to outlaw something is to make it illegal

outlet *NOUN* (**outlets**)
1 a way for something to get out • *The tank has an outlet at the bottom.* **2** a place to sell goods • *We need to find fresh outlets for our products.*

outline *NOUN* (**outlines**)
1 a line round the outside of something; a line showing the shape of a thing **2** a summary

outline *VERB* (**outlines, outlining, outlined**)
1 to outline something is to draw a line round it to show its shape **2** to outline a story or account is to summarize or describe it briefly

outlook *NOUN* (**outlooks**)
1 a view on which people look out **2** a person's outlook is the way that they look at and think about things • *She has an odd outlook on life.* **3** what seems likely to happen in the future • *The outlook is bright.*

outlying *ADJECTIVE*
far from a town or city • *We need to visit the outlying districts.*

outnumber *VERB* (**outnumbers, outnumbering, outnumbered**)
to outnumber something else is to be greater in number than it • *The girls outnumber the boys in our team.*

outpatient *NOUN* (**outpatients**)
a patient who visits a hospital for treatment but does not stay there overnight

outpost *NOUN* (**outposts**)
a distant settlement

output *NOUN* (**outputs**)
1 the amount produced, especially by a factory or business **2** (*in computing*) information produced by a computer

output *VERB* (**outputs, outputting, output**)
(*in computing*) to output information is to get it from a computer

outrage *NOUN* (**outrages**)
1 outrage is the anger you feel when something shocking happens **2** an outrage is something very shocking or cruel

outrage *VERB* (**outrages, outraging, outraged**)
to outrage someone is to make them very shocked and angry • *The Scarecrow was outraged. He waved his road sign, he opened and shut his umbrella, and he stamped with fury.* — Philip Pullman, *The Scarecrow and his Servant*

outrageous *ADJECTIVE*
shocking or dreadful

outright *ADVERB*
1 completely • *We won outright.* **2** all at once; in one go • *They were able to buy their house outright.*

outset *NOUN*
at or **from the outset** at or from the beginning of something

outside *NOUN* (**outsides**)
the outer side or surface of a thing; the part furthest from the middle

outside *ADJECTIVE*
1 on or coming from the outside **2** the greatest possible • *£100 is the outside price.* **3** slight or remote • *There is an outside chance that he will come.*

outside *ADVERB & PREPOSITION*
on or to the outside of something • *Go outside.* • *It's outside the house.*

outside broadcast *NOUN* (**outside broadcasts**)
a broadcast made where something is happening and not in a studio

outsider *NOUN* (**outsiders**)
1 someone who is not a member of a particular group of people **2** a horse or person that people think has no chance of winning a race or contest

outskirts *PLURAL NOUN*
the parts on the outside edge of an area, especially of a town or city

outspoken *ADJECTIVE*
speaking frankly even though it might offend people

outstanding *ADJECTIVE*
1 extremely good or distinguished • *She is an outstanding athlete.* **2** not yet dealt with • *What are your outstanding debts?*

outward *ADJECTIVE*
1 going outwards **2** on the outside

outwardly *ADVERB*
on the outside; for people to see • *They were outwardly calm.*

outwards *ADVERB*
towards the outside

outweigh *VERB* (**outweighs, outweighing, outweighed**)
to outweigh something is to be more important than it • *The advantages of the plan outweigh the disadvantages.*

outwit *VERB* (**outwits, outwitting, outwitted**)
to outwit someone is to deceive or defeat them by being more clever

oval *ADJECTIVE*
shaped like an egg or a number 0

oval *NOUN* (**ovals**)
an oval shape

ovary *NOUN* (**ovaries**)
1 part of a female body where egg-cells (*ova*) are produced **2** the part of a flowering plant that produces seeds

oven *NOUN* (**ovens**)
a closed space in which things are cooked or heated

over *ADVERB*
1 down or sideways; out and down from the top or edge • *He fell over.* **2** across to a place • *We walked over to the house.* **3** so that a different side shows • *Turn it over.* **4** finished • *The lesson is over.* **5** left or remaining • *There are a few apples over.* **6** through or thoroughly • *Think it over.*
over and over repeatedly; many times

over *PREPOSITION*
1 above or covering • *There's a light over the door.* • *I'll put a cloth over the table.* **2** across • *They ran over the road.* **3** more than • *The house is over a mile away.* **4** concerning; about • *They quarrelled over money.* **5** during • *We can talk over dinner.* **6** being better than • *They won a victory over their opponents.*

over *NOUN* (**overs**)
in cricket, a series of six balls bowled by one person

over- *PREFIX*
meaning 'too much', as in *over-excited*

overall *ADJECTIVE & ADVERB*
including everything; total • *What is the overall cost?*

overalls *PLURAL NOUN*
a kind of light coat that you wear over your other clothes to protect them when you are working

overarm *ADJECTIVE & ADVERB*
with the arm lifted above shoulder level and coming down in front of the body

overboard *ADVERB*
to fall or jump overboard is to go over the side of a boat into the water

overcast *ADJECTIVE*
covered with cloud • *The sky is grey and overcast.*

overcoat *NOUN* (**overcoats**)
a warm outdoor coat

overcome *VERB* (**overcomes, overcoming, overcame, overcome**)
1 to overcome a problem or difficulty is to succeed in dealing with it or controlling it • *He overcame injury to win a gold medal.* **2** to be overcome by something is to become helpless from it • *She was overcome by the fumes.* **3** to overcome someone is to beat them

overdo *VERB* (**overdoes, overdoing, overdid, overdone**)
1 to overdo something is to do it too much **2** to overdo food is to cook it for too long

overdose *NOUN* (**overdoses**)
too large a dose of a drug or medicine

overdue *ADJECTIVE*
something is overdue when it is later than it should be • *The train is overdue.*

overflow *VERB* (**overflows, overflowing, overflowed**)
to overflow is to flow over the edges or limits of something

overgrown *ADJECTIVE*
a place is overgrown when it is thickly covered with weeds or unwanted plants

overhang *VERB* (**overhangs, overhanging, overhung**)
to overhang something is to stick out beyond and above it • *The branches of the tree overhung the pond.*

overhaul *VERB* (**overhauls, overhauling, overhauled**)
1 to overhaul a machine or vehicle is to check it thoroughly and repair it if necessary **2** to overhaul someone or something is to overtake it

overhead *ADJECTIVE & ADVERB*
above your head; in the sky

overheads *PLURAL NOUN*
the money that has to be spent to run a business

overhear *VERB* (**overhears, overhearing, overheard**)
to overhear something is to hear it accidentally or without the speaker knowing

overland *ADJECTIVE & ADVERB*
over the land, not by sea or air • *We travelled overland to Italy.* • *an overland expedition*

overlap *VERB* (**overlaps, overlapping, overlapped**)
one thing overlaps another when it lies across part of it • *The carpet overlapped the fireplace.*

overlook *VERB* (**overlooks**, **overlooking**, **overlooked**)
1 to overlook something is not to notice it **2** to overlook a mistake or offence is not to punish it **3** to overlook a place is to have a view over it • *The hotel overlooks the city park.*

overnight *ADVERB & ADJECTIVE*
of or during a night • *We stayed overnight in a hotel.* • *There will be an overnight stop in Paris.*

overpower *VERB* (**overpowers**, **overpowering**, **overpowered**)
to overpower someone is to defeat them because you are stronger

> WORD FAMILY
> Something is **overpowering** when it is very strong.

overrun *VERB* (**overruns**, **overrunning**, **overran**, **overrun**)
1 to overrun an area is to spread harmfully over it • *The place is overrun with mice.* **2** something overruns when it goes on longer than it should • *The programme overran by ten minutes.*

overseas *ADVERB*
abroad • *They travelled overseas.*

overseas *ADJECTIVE*
from abroad; foreign • *We met some overseas students.*

oversight *NOUN* (**oversights**)
a mistake you make by not noticing something

oversleep *VERB* (**oversleeps**, **oversleeping**, **overslept**)
to sleep longer than you intended to

overtake *VERB* (**overtakes**, **overtaking**, **overtook**, **overtaken**)
to overtake a moving vehicle or person is to catch them up or pass them in the same direction

overthrow *VERB* (**overthrows**, **overthrowing**, **overthrew**, **overthrown**)
to overthrow a government is to remove it from power by force

overthrow *NOUN* (**overthrows**)
the overthrow of a government is when it is forced out of power

overtime *NOUN*
overtime is time someone spends working outside their normal hours

overture *NOUN* (**overtures**)
a piece of music played at the start of a concert, opera, or ballet
overtures a friendly attempt to start a discussion with someone

overturn *VERB* (**overturns**, **overturning**, **overturned**)
1 to overturn something is to make it turn over or fall over **2** to overturn is to turn over • *The car went out of control and overturned.*

overweight *ADJECTIVE*
too heavy

overwhelm *VERB* (**overwhelms**, **overwhelming**, **overwhelmed**)
1 to overwhelm someone is to have a very strong effect on them • *I was overwhelmed by everyone's kindness.* **2** to overwhelm someone is to defeat them completely

overwork *VERB* (**overworks**, **overworking**, **overworked**)
to overwork is to become exhausted from working too hard

overwork *NOUN*
overwork is too much work, causing exhaustion

ovum *NOUN* (**ova**) (*say* **oh**-vum)
a female cell that can develop into offspring of plants and animals

owe *VERB* (**owes**, **owing**, **owed**)
1 to owe something, especially money, is to have a duty to pay or give it to someone • *I owe you a pound.* **2** to owe something to someone is to have it thanks to them • *They owed their lives to the pilot's skill.*
owing to something because of it • *The train was late owing to leaves on the line.*

owl *NOUN* (**owls**)
a bird of prey with large eyes and a short beak, usually flying at night

own *ADJECTIVE*
belonging to yourself or itself
to get your own back (*informal*) is to have your revenge
on your own by yourself; alone • *I did it all on my own.* • *I sat on my own in the empty room.*

own *VERB* (**owns**, **owning**, **owned**)
to own something is to have it as your property
to own up to something (*informal*) is to admit that you did it

owner *NOUN* (**owners**)
the person who owns something

> WORD FAMILY
> **Ownership** is owning something.

ox *NOUN* (**oxen**)
a neutered bull kept for its meat and for pulling carts

oxide *NOUN* (**oxides**)
a compound of oxygen and one other element

oxidize *VERB* (**oxidizes**, **oxidizing**, **oxidized**)
1 to oxidize something is to cause it to combine with oxygen **2** to oxidize is to be combined with oxygen

> WORD FAMILY
> **Oxidization** or **oxidation** happens when something combines with oxygen.

oxygen *NOUN*
oxygen is one of the gases in the air that people need to stay alive

oyster *NOUN* (**oysters**)
a kind of shellfish whose shell sometimes contains a pearl

oz.
short for **ounce** or **ounces**

ozone *NOUN*
ozone is a strong-smelling gas that is a form of oxygen

ozone layer *NOUN*
a layer of ozone high in the atmosphere, that absorbs harmful radiation from the sun

p
short for **penny** or **pence**

pa *NOUN* (**pas**)
(*informal*) father

pace *NOUN* (**paces**)
1 one step in walking, marching, or running **2** speed • *He set a fast pace.*

pace *VERB* (**paces**, **pacing**, **paced**)
to pace is to walk up and down with slow or regular steps • *He was pacing across the room as he spoke.*
to pace something out is to measure a distance in paces

pacemaker *NOUN* (**pacemakers**)
1 a person who sets the speed for someone else in a race **2** an electrical device put into a person by surgery, that keeps the heart beating regularly

pacifist *NOUN* (**pacifists**) (*say* pas- i- fist)
someone who believes that war is always wrong

> WORD FAMILY
> **Pacifism** is the belief that war is always wrong.

pacify *VERB* (**pacifies**, **pacifying**, **pacified**) (*say* pas- i- fy)
to pacify someone is to calm them down
▷ **pacification** *NOUN* pacification is calming someone down

pack *NOUN* (**packs**)
1 a bundle or collection of things wrapped or tied together **2** a set of playing cards **3** a strong bag carried on your back **4** a group of hounds, wolves, or other animals **5** a group of people, especially a group of Brownies or Cub Scouts

pack *VERB* (**packs**, **packing**, **packed**)
1 to pack a suitcase, bag, or box is to put things in it so that you can store them or take them somewhere **2** to pack a room or building is to fill it • *The hall was packed.*

package *NOUN* (**packages**)
1 a parcel or packet **2** a number of things offered or accepted together

package holiday *NOUN* (**package holidays**)
a holiday in which all the travel and accommodation is arranged and included in the price

packet *NOUN* (**packets**)
a small parcel

pad [1] *NOUN* (**pads**)
1 a number of sheets of blank or lined paper joined together along one edge **2** a piece of soft material used to protect or shape something **3** a piece of soft material that you wear to protect your leg in cricket and other games **4** a flat surface from which helicopters take off or rockets are launched

pad *VERB* (**pads**, **padding**, **padded**)
to pad something is to put a piece of soft material on it or into it in order to protect or shape it
to pad something out is to make a book or story longer than it needs to be

pad [2] *VERB* (**pads**, **padding**, **padded**)
to pad is to walk softly

padding *NOUN*
padding is soft material used to protect or shape things

paddle *VERB* (**paddles**, **paddling**, **paddled**)
1 to paddle is to walk about with bare feet in shallow water **2** to paddle a boat is to move it along with a short oar

paddle *NOUN* (**paddles**)
1 a time spent paddling in water **2** a short oar with a broad blade

paddock *NOUN* (**paddocks**)
a small field for keeping horses

paddy *NOUN* (**paddies**)
a field where rice is grown

padlock *NOUN* (**padlocks**)
a lock with a metal loop that you can use to fasten a gate or lock a bicycle

pagan *NOUN* (**pagans**)
a person who does not believe in any religion; a heathen

> WORD USAGE
> This word is normally used about people in the past.

page [1] *NOUN* (**pages**)
a piece of paper that is part of a book or newspaper; one side of this piece of paper

page [2] *NOUN* (**pages**)
a boy who acts as an attendant or runs errands

pageant *NOUN* (**pageants**) (*say* paj- ent)
1 a play or entertainment about historical events and people **2** a procession of people in costume

> WORD FAMILY
> **Pageantry** is elaborate display that is part of a ceremony or procession.

pagoda *NOUN* (**pagodas**) (*say* pa- **goh**- da)
a Buddhist tower or Hindu temple in the Far East

paid
past tense and past participle of **pay** *VERB*

pail *NOUN* (**pails**)
a bucket

pain *NOUN* (**pains**)
1 pain or a pain is an unpleasant feeling caused by injury or disease • *Are you in pain?* **2** pain is also mental suffering
to take pains is to make a careful effort or take trouble over something

pain *VERB* (**pains**, **paining**, **pained**)
to pain someone is to cause them pain, usually mental pain

painful *ADJECTIVE*
causing you pain • *My ankle is too painful to walk on.*

> WORD FAMILY
> To be (for example) **painfully** thin or **painfully** slow is to be extremely thin or extremely slow.

painkiller *NOUN* (**painkillers**)
a drug that reduces pain

painless *ADJECTIVE*
not causing any pain

painstaking *ADJECTIVE*
making a careful effort • *Rebecca sat down carefully, smoothing her dress under her with painstaking precision.* — Kate Douglas Wiggin, *Rebecca of Sunnybrook Farm*

paint *NOUN* (**paints**)
a liquid substance put on something to colour or cover it

paint *VERB* (**paints**, **painting**, **painted**)
1 to paint something is to put paint on it **2** to paint a picture is to make it with paints **3** to paint someone or something is to make a picture of them using paint

paintbox *NOUN* (**paintboxes**)
a box of coloured paints used in art

paintbrush *NOUN* (**paintbrushes**)
a brush used in painting

painter *NOUN* (**painters**)
1 an artist who paints pictures **2** a person whose job is painting walls and houses

painting *NOUN* (**paintings**)
1 painting is using paints to make a picture • *She likes painting.* **2** a painting is a painted picture

pair *NOUN* (**pairs**)
1 two things or people that go together or are the same kind • *I need a new pair of shoes.* **2** something made of two parts joined together • *Have you got a pair of scissors?*

pal *NOUN* (**pals**)
(*informal*) a friend

palace *NOUN* (**palaces**)
a large and splendid house where a king or queen or other important person lives

palate *NOUN* (**palates**) (*say* **pal**- at)
1 the roof of your mouth **2** a person's sense of taste • *She has a refined palate.*

> SPELLING
> Take care not to confuse **palate** with **palette**, which means a board on which an artist mixes colours.

pale *ADJECTIVE* (**paler**, **palest**)
1 almost white • *He had a pale face.* **2** not bright in colour; faint • *The sky was a pale blue.*
▷ **paleness** *NOUN* paleness is being pale

palette *NOUN* (**palettes**) (*say* **pal**- it)
a board on which an artist mixes colours

> SPELLING
> Take care not to confuse **palette** with **palate**, which means the roof of your mouth, or your sense of taste.

paling *NOUN* (**palings**)
a wooden fence

palisade *NOUN* (**palisades**)
a fence made of wooden posts or railings

pall *VERB* (**palls**, **palling**, **palled**)
something palls when it becomes dull or uninteresting after a time • *The novelty of the new computer game soon began to pall.*

pallid *ADJECTIVE*
pale, especially because of illness

pallor *NOUN*
pallor is paleness in a person's face, especially because they are ill

palm *NOUN* (**palms**)
1 the inner part of your hand, between your fingers and wrist **2** a tropical tree with large leaves and no branches

palm *VERB* (**palms**, **palming**, **palmed**)
to palm something off on someone is to fool them into taking something they don't want

palmistry *NOUN*
palmistry is fortune-telling by looking for signs in the markings of a person's hand

Palm Sunday *NOUN*
the Sunday before Easter, when Christians celebrate Christ's entry into Jerusalem on a path of palm leaves

paltry *ADJECTIVE*
not very much or not very valuable • *His reward was a paltry 50 cents.*

pampas *PLURAL NOUN*
pampas are wide grassy plains in South America

pampas grass *NOUN*
pampas grass is a tall grass with long feathery flowers

pamper *VERB* (**pampers**, **pampering**, **pampered**)
to pamper someone is to go to a lot of trouble to make someone feel comfortable and let them have whatever they want

pamphlet *NOUN* (**pamphlets**)
a thin book with a paper cover

pan *NOUN* (**pans**)
1 a pot or dish with a flat base, used for cooking **2** the bowl of a lavatory

pancake *NOUN* (**pancakes**)
a flat round cake of batter fried on both sides

panda *NOUN* (**pandas**)
a large black and white bear-like animal found in China

panda car *NOUN* (**panda cars**)
a police patrol car, which was originally white with black stripes on the sides

pandemonium *NOUN*
you say there is pandemonium when there is a loud noise or disturbance • *At this pandemonium broke loose. All the men leaped to their feet and shouted and waved their cudgels and guns.* — Elizabeth Goudge, *The Little White Horse*

pander *VERB* (**panders**, **pandering**, **pandered**)
to pander to someone is to let them have whatever they want

pane *NOUN* (**panes**)
a sheet of glass in a window

panel *NOUN* (**panels**)
1 a long flat piece of wood, metal, or other material that is part of a door, wall, or piece of furniture **2** a group of people appointed to discuss or decide something • *The winner of the contest will be decided by a panel of judges.*

pang *NOUN* (**pangs**)
a sudden feeling of pain or strong emotion

panic *NOUN*
panic is sudden fear that makes you behave wildly

> WORD FAMILY
> Someone is **panicky** when they feel or show panic.

panic *VERB* (**panics**, **panicking**, **panicked**)
to panic is to be overcome with fear or anxiety and behave wildly

pannier *NOUN* (**panniers**)
a bag or basket hung on one side of a bicycle or horse

panorama *NOUN* (**panoramas**)
a view or picture of a wide area • *I know not how to describe the glorious panorama which unfolded itself to our gaze.* — H. Rider Haggard, *King Solomon's Mines*

> WORD FAMILY
> A **panoramic** view is one that covers a wide area.

pansy *NOUN* (**pansies**)
a small brightly-coloured garden flower

pant *VERB* (**pants**, **panting**, **panted**)
you pant when you take short quick breaths, usually after running or working hard

panther *NOUN* (**panthers**)
a leopard

panties *PLURAL NOUN*
(*informal*) short knickers worn by women and girls

pantomime *NOUN* (**pantomimes**)
a Christmas entertainment based on a fairy tale

pantry *NOUN* (**pantries**)
a cupboard or small room for storing food

pants *PLURAL NOUN*
1 (*informal*) underpants or knickers **2** (*in America*) trousers

paper *NOUN* (**papers**)
1 paper is a thin substance made in sheets and used for writing or printing or drawing on, or for wrapping things **2** a paper is a newspaper **3** papers are documents

paper *VERB* (**papers**, **papering**, **papered**)
to paper a wall or room is to cover it with wallpaper

paperback *NOUN* (**paperbacks**)
a book with thin flexible covers

papier mâché *NOUN* (*say* pap- yay **mash**- ay)
papier mâché is a mixture of paper pulp and glue you use to make models or ornaments

papyrus *NOUN* (**papyri**) (*say* pa- **py**- rus)
1 papyrus is a kind of paper made from the stems of reeds, used in ancient Egypt **2** a papyrus is a document written on this paper

parable *NOUN* (**parables**)
a story told to teach people something, especially one of the stories told by Jesus Christ

parachute *NOUN* (**parachutes**)
an umbrella-shaped device on which people or things can float slowly down to the ground from an aircraft

> WORD FAMILY
> A **parachutist** is someone who uses a parachute.

parade *NOUN* (**parades**)
1 a line of people or vehicles moving forward through a place as a celebration **2** soldiers are on parade when they assemble for inspection or drill **3** a public square or row of shops

parade *VERB* (**parades**, **parading**, **paraded**)
1 to parade is to move forward through a place as a celebration **2** soldiers parade when they assemble for inspection or drill

paradise *NOUN*
1 paradise is heaven or, in the Bible, the Garden of Eden **2** you can describe a wonderful or perfect place as a paradise

a b c d e f g h i j k l m n o p q r s t u v w x y z

paradox *NOUN* (**paradoxes**) (*say* pa- ra- doks)
a statement which, because it has two opposite ideas in it, does not seem to make sense but may still be true, for example *'More haste, less speed'*

paradoxical *ADJECTIVE*
a paradoxical statement seems to contradict itself but may still be true
▷ **paradoxically** *ADVERB* in a paradoxical way

paraffin *NOUN*
paraffin is a kind of oil used as fuel

paragraph *NOUN* (**paragraphs**)
one of the group of sentences that a piece of writing is divided into, beginning on a new line

parallel *ADJECTIVE*
parallel lines are lines that are the same distance apart for their whole length, like railway lines

parallelogram *NOUN* (**parallelograms**)
a four-sided figure with its opposite sides parallel to each other and equal in length

paralyse *VERB* (**paralyses**, **paralysing**, **paralysed**)
1 to paralyse someone is to make them unable to feel anything or to move • *A few children whimpered and clung to each other; but most just stared at the lion, paralysed with terror.* — Michael Morpurgo, *Tom's Sausage Lion* **2** to paralyse something is to make it unable to move or work properly • *Train services were paralysed by the strike.*

paralysis *NOUN* (*say* pa- **ral**- i- sis)
paralysis is the loss of the ability to move or feel anything

> WORD FAMILY
> To be **paralytic** is to suffer from paralysis.

parapet *NOUN* (**parapets**)
a low wall along the edge of a balcony, bridge, or roof

paraphernalia *NOUN* (*say* pa- ra- fer- **nay**- li- a)
paraphernalia is various pieces of equipment or small possessions

paraphrase *VERB* (**paraphrases**, **paraphrasing**, **paraphrased**)
to paraphrase something that has been said or written is to give its meaning by using different words

parasite *NOUN* (**parasites**)
an animal or plant that lives in or on another and gets its food from it

> WORD FAMILY
> A **parasitic** animal or plant lives as a parasite on another.

parasol *NOUN* (**parasols**)
a lightweight umbrella you use to shade yourself from the sun

paratroops *PLURAL NOUN*
troops trained to be dropped from aircraft by parachute

> WORD FAMILY
> A **paratrooper** is a soldier in the paratroops.

parcel *NOUN* (**parcels**)
something wrapped up to be posted or carried

parched *ADJECTIVE*
very dry or thirsty

parchment *NOUN*
parchment is a kind of heavy paper originally made from animal skins

pardon *VERB* (**pardons**, **pardoning**, **pardoned**)
to pardon someone is to forgive or excuse them

pardon *NOUN* (**pardons**)
1 forgiveness; an act of pardoning someone
2 used as an exclamation to mean 'I didn't hear or understand what you said', or 'I apologize'

pardonable *ADJECTIVE*
a pardonable mistake is one that can be forgiven

parent *NOUN* (**parents**)
your parents are your father and mother

> WORD FAMILY
> **Parental** means to do with parents; **parenthood** is being a parent.

parentage *NOUN*
your parentage is who your parents are

parenthesis *NOUN* (**parentheses**) (*say* pa- **ren**- thi- sis)
1 something extra put in a sentence between brackets or dashes **2** one of a pair of brackets (like these) used in the middle of a sentence

parish *NOUN* (**parishes**)
a district that has its own church

> WORD FAMILY
> A **parishioner** is a person who regularly goes to a particular church.

park *NOUN* (**parks**)
1 a large area with grass and trees, for public use
2 a piece of ground belonging to a large country house

park *VERB* (**parks**, **parking**, **parked**)
to park a vehicle is to leave it somewhere for a time

parka *NOUN* (**parkas**)
a warm jacket with a hood attached

parking meter *NOUN* (**parking meters**)
a device that shows how long a vehicle has been parked in a street • *When you park your car, you put a coin in the parking meter.*

parliament *NOUN* (**parliaments**)
the group of people that make a country's laws
▷ **parliamentary** *ADJECTIVE* to do with a parliament • *a parliamentary election*

parody *NOUN* (**parodies**)
a play or poem that makes fun of people or things by imitating them

parole *NOUN* (*say* pa- **rohl**)
parole is letting someone out of prison before they have finished their sentence, on condition that they behave well • *He was on parole.*

parrot *NOUN* (**parrots**)
a brightly-coloured bird with a curved beak, that can learn to repeat words or sounds

parsley *NOUN*
parsley is a plant with crinkled green leaves used to flavour and decorate food

parsnip *NOUN* (**parsnips**)
a pale yellow vegetable

parson *NOUN* (**parsons**)
a member of the clergy

parsonage *NOUN* (**parsonages**)
a parson's house

part *NOUN* (**parts**)
1 some but not all of a thing or a number of things; anything that belongs to something bigger **2** the character played by an actor or actress; the words spoken by a character in a play • *She has a good part in the school play.*

part *VERB* (**parts**, **parting**, **parted**)
1 to part people or things is to separate them or divide them **2** to part is to separate **3** to part hair is to divide it so that it goes in two different directions
to part with something is to give it away or get rid of it

part exchange *NOUN* (**part exchanges**)
giving something you own as well as some money as part of the price for something else

partial *ADJECTIVE*
1 not complete or total • *There will be a partial eclipse of the sun.* **2** unfairly showing more support for one person or side than another
to be partial to something is to like it

> WORD FAMILY
> To have a **partiality** for something is to like it; **partially** means partly or not completely.

participate *VERB* (**participates**, **participating**, **participated**)
to participate in something is to take part in it

> WORD FAMILY
> A **participant** is someone who takes part in something; **participation** is taking part in something.

participle *NOUN* (**participles**)
a word formed from a verb and used as part of the verb or as an adjective, for example 'going', 'gone', 'sailed', 'sailing'

particle *NOUN* (**particles**)
a very small piece or amount

particular *ADJECTIVE*
1 only this one and no other; special; individual • *Are you looking for a particular book?* **2** fussy; hard to please • *He is very particular about his clothes.*
in particular especially; chiefly

> WORD FAMILY
> You can say something is (for example) **particularly** good or useful when it is especially good or useful.

particular *NOUN* (**particulars**)
a detail or single fact

parting *NOUN* (**partings**)
1 leaving or separation **2** the line where hair is combed in different directions

partition *NOUN* (**partitions**)
1 partition is dividing something into parts **2** a partition is a thin dividing wall

partly *ADVERB*
not completely; in some ways

partner *NOUN* (**partners**)
1 one of a pair of people who do something together, especially dancing, running a business, or playing a game **2** someone's partner is the person they are married to or live with

> WORD FAMILY
> **Partnership** is being a partner with someone.

part of speech *NOUN* (**parts of speech**)
each of the groups (also called **word classes**) into which words can be divided in grammar: noun, adjective, verb, pronoun, adverb, preposition, conjunction, interjection

partridge *NOUN* (**partridges**)
a game bird with brown feathers

part-time *ADJECTIVE & ADVERB*
working for only some of the normal hours

> WORD FAMILY
> A **part-timer** is someone who works part-time.

party *NOUN* (**parties**)
1 a time when people get together to enjoy themselves • *Come to my birthday party.* **2** a group of people working or travelling together • *They organized a search party.* **3** an organized group of people with similar political beliefs • *The Labour Party won the election.* **4** a person who is involved in an action or legal case • *He is the guilty party.*

pass *VERB* (**passes**, **passing**, **passed**)
1 to pass something or someone is to go past them **2** to pass in a certain direction is to move or go that way • *They passed over the bridge.* **3** to pass something to someone is to give it or hand it to them • *Can you pass the butter, please?* **4** to pass an examination is to be successful in it **5** to pass time is to use time doing something **6** to pass is to finish or no longer be there • *His opportunity passed.* **7** to pass a law or rule is to approve or accept it

a b c d e f g h i j k l m n o **p** q r s t u v w x y z

pass *NOUN* (**passes**)
1 when a ball is kicked, hit, or thrown from one player to another in a game **2** a success in an examination • *She got several GCSE passes.* **3** a card or ticket that allows you to go in or out of a place **4** a narrow way between mountains

passable *ADJECTIVE*
just about acceptable or all right

passage *NOUN* (**passages**)
1 a corridor or narrow space between two walls **2** a section of a piece of writing or music **3** a journey by sea or air **4** passing • *the passage of time*

passageway *NOUN* (**passageways**)
a passage or way through, especially between buildings

passenger *NOUN* (**passengers**)
someone who is travelling in a car or other vehicle and is not the driver or a member of the crew

passer-by *NOUN* (**passers-by**)
someone who is going past by chance when something happens

passion *NOUN* (**passions**)
1 passion is strong feeling or emotion **2** a passion is a great enthusiasm for something

passionate *ADJECTIVE*
full of passion or strong feeling
▷ **passionately** *ADVERB* in a passionate way

passion fruit *NOUN* (**passion fruits**)
a fruit that grows on a climbing plant in warm countries. Some people think its flowers look like the crown of thorns and other things associated with the Passion of Christ

passive *ADJECTIVE*
1 not active; not resisting or fighting against something **2** (*in grammar*) describing a verb in which the subject receives the action, for example in the sentence *She was hit by a car* the subject is *She* and *was hit* is a passive verb
▷ **passively** *ADVERB* in a passive way

Passover *NOUN*
Passover is a Jewish religious festival, celebrating the escape of the ancient Jews from slavery in Egypt

passport *NOUN* (**passports**)
an official document that allows you to travel abroad

password *NOUN* (**passwords**)
a secret word or phrase that you need to know to be allowed to go somewhere or to gain access to a computer system

past *NOUN*
the time gone by • *Try to forget the past.*

past *ADJECTIVE*
of the time gone by • *He was thinking about his past achievements.*

past *PREPOSITION*
1 beyond • *Go past the school and turn right.* **2** later than • *It is past midnight.*
to be past it (*slang*) is to be too old to be able to do something

pasta *NOUN*
pasta is an Italian food made as a dried paste of flour, water, and often eggs, formed into various shapes such as spaghetti and lasagne

paste *NOUN* (**pastes**)
a soft and moist or gluey substance

paste *VERB* (**pastes**, **pasting**, **pasted**)
to paste something is to stick it to a surface with paste

pastel *NOUN* (**pastels**)
1 a crayon that is like a slightly greasy chalk **2** a light delicate colour

pasteurize *VERB* (**pasteurizes**, **pasteurizing**, **pasteurized**) (*say* pahs- cher- ryz)
to pasteurize milk is to purify it by heating and then cooling it

> **WORD FAMILY**
> **Pasteurization** is the process of pasteurizing milk.

pastille *NOUN* (**pastilles**)
a small flavoured sweet that you suck

pastime *NOUN* (**pastimes**)
something you do to pass time pleasantly; a hobby or game

pastoral *ADJECTIVE*
to do with the country

past participle *NOUN* (**past participles**)
a form of a verb used after *has, have, had, was, were,* to describe an action that happened at a time before now, for example *done*, *overtaken*, and *written*

pastry *NOUN* (**pastries**)
1 pastry is dough made from flour, fat, and water rolled flat and baked **2** a pastry is a cake made from this dough

past tense *NOUN*
a form of a verb used to describe an action that happened at a time before now, for example *took* is the past tense of *take*

pasture *NOUN* (**pastures**)
land covered with grass that cattle, sheep, or horses can eat

pasty[1] *NOUN* (**pasties**) (*say* pas- ti)
a pastry filled with meat and vegetables, like a small pie

pasty[2] *ADJECTIVE* (**pastier**, **pastiest**) (*say* pay- sti)
looking pale and unhealthy

pat *VERB* (**pats**, **patting**, **patted**)
to pat something or someone is to tap them gently with your open hand or with something flat

pat *NOUN* (**pats**)
1 a patting movement or sound **2** a small piece of butter
a pat on the back congratulations or praise

patch *NOUN* (**patches**)
1 a piece of material put over a hole or damaged place **2** an area that is different from its surroundings • *We have a black cat with a white patch on its chest.* **3** a small area of land **4** a small piece of something • *There are patches of ice on the road.*

patch *VERB* (**patches**, **patching**, **patched**)
to patch something is to put a piece of material on it to repair it
to patch something up is to repair it roughly
to patch things up is to be friendly again after a quarrel

patchwork *NOUN*
patchwork is needlework using small pieces of different cloth which are sewn together

patchy *ADJECTIVE* (**patchier**, **patchiest**)
occurring in some areas but not others; uneven • *There may be some patchy rain.*

patent *NOUN* (**patents**) (*say* **pay**- tent or **pat**- ent)
the official right given to someone to make something they have invented and to stop other people from copying it

patent *ADJECTIVE* (*say* **pay**- tent)
1 protected by a patent **2** obvious • *What they say is a patent lie.*

patent *VERB* (**patents**, **patenting**, **patented**) (*say* **pay**- tent or **pat**- ent)
to patent an idea or invention is to get a patent for it

patent leather *NOUN*
patent leather is leather with a special glossy surface

patently *ADVERB*
clearly; obviously • *They were patently lying.*

paternal *ADJECTIVE*
to do with a father, or like a father

path *NOUN* (**paths**)
1 a narrow way to walk or ride along **2** the line along which something moves • *They were tracing the path of the meteor.*

pathetic *ADJECTIVE*
1 sad and pitiful **2** sadly or comically weak or useless • *He made a pathetic attempt to climb the tree.*
▷ **pathetically** *ADVERB* in a pathetic way

patience *NOUN* (*say* **pay**- shens)
1 patience is the ability to stay calm, especially when you have to wait for a long time **2** patience is also a card game for one person

patient *ADJECTIVE* (*say* **pay**- shent)
1 able to wait for a long time without getting anxious or angry **2** able to bear pain or trouble

> WORD FAMILY
> You do something **patiently** when you do it in a patient way • *He waited patiently for his turn.*

patient *NOUN* (**patients**) (*say* **pay**- shent)
a person who is getting treatment from a doctor or dentist

patio *NOUN* (**patios**) (*say* **pat**- i- oh)
a paved area beside a house

patois *NOUN* (**patois**) (*say* **pat**- wah)
a form of a language used by people in one region of a country, which is different from the standard language of the country; a dialect

patriot *NOUN* (**patriots**) (*say* **pay**- tri- ot or **pat**- ri- ot)
someone who loves and supports their country

> WORD FAMILY
> To be **patriotic** is to be loyal to your country; **patriotism** is loving and supporting your country.

patrol *VERB* (**patrols**, **patrolling**, **patrolled**)
to walk or travel regularly round a place or a thing to guard it and make sure that all is well

patrol *NOUN* (**patrols**)
1 a group of people or vehicles patrolling a place **2** a group of Scouts or Guides
to be on patrol is to be patrolling a place

patron *NOUN* (**patrons**) (*say* **pay**- tron)
1 someone who supports a person or cause with money or encouragement **2** a regular customer of a shop or business

> WORD FAMILY
> **Patronage** is being a patron.

patronize *VERB* (**patronizes**, **patronizing**, **patronized**)
1 to patronize someone is to treat them as an inferior **2** to patronize a shop or business is to be one of its regular customers

patron saint *NOUN* (**patron saints**)
a saint who is thought of as protecting a place or activity

patter [1] *NOUN* (**patters**)
a series of light tapping sounds

patter *VERB* (**patters**, **pattering**, **pattered**)
to patter is to make light tapping sounds • *The rain was pattering on the glass roof.*

patter [2] *NOUN*
patter is the quick talk of a performer or salesperson

pattern *NOUN* (**patterns**)
1 a decorative arrangement of lines or shapes **2** a thing that you copy so that you can make something, such as a piece of clothing

pause *NOUN* (**pauses**)
a short stop before continuing with something

pause *VERB* (**pauses**, **pausing**, **paused**)
1 to pause is to make a short stop before continuing with something **2** to pause (for example) a video recorder, DVD player, or CD player is to make the tape or disc stop for a short time

pave *VERB* (**paves**, **paving**, **paved**)
to pave a road or path is to put a hard surface on it **to pave the way** is to prepare for something

pavement *NOUN* (**pavements**)
a path with a hard surface, along the side of a street

> BRITISH AND AMERICAN
> In America, the word **sidewalk** is used.

pavilion *NOUN* (**pavilions**)
a building at a sports ground for players and spectators to use

paw *NOUN* (**paws**)
an animal's foot

paw *VERB* (**paws**, **pawing**, **pawed**)
an animal paws something when it touches or scrapes it clumsily with its paw

pawn *NOUN* (**pawns**)
1 one of the sixteen pieces in chess that are at the front on each side and are the least valuable **2** a person who is controlled by someone else

pawn *VERB* (**pawns**, **pawning**, **pawned**)
to pawn something is to leave it with a pawnbroker while borrowing money • *He had to pawn his watch.*

pawnbroker *NOUN* (**pawnbrokers**)
a shopkeeper who lends money to people in return for objects that they leave and which are sold if the money is not paid back

pay *VERB* (**pays**, **paying**, **paid**)
1 to pay for something is to give money in return for it • *Have you paid for your lunch?* **2** to pay someone is to give them money for something they have done • *Wash my car and I'll pay you £5.* **3** to pay is to be profitable or worthwhile • *It pays to be honest.* **4** to pay (for example) attention or a compliment is to give someone your attention or make them a compliment **5** to pay for something you have done wrong is to suffer for it • *I'll make you pay for this!*
to pay someone back 1 is to pay money that you owe them **2** is to get revenge on them

pay *NOUN*
pay is the money you earn when you work

payment *NOUN* (**payments**)
1 payment is when you pay someone or are paid for something **2** a payment is money you pay

PC
short for **personal computer**, **police constable**

PE
short for **physical education**

pea *NOUN* (**peas**)
a small round green seed of a climbing plant, growing inside a pod and used as a vegetable

peace *NOUN*
1 peace is a time when there is no war or violence • *At last the country was at peace.* **2** peace is also quietness and calm

peaceful *ADJECTIVE*
1 quiet and calm **2** not involving violence

> WORD FAMILY
> To happen **peacefully** is to happen in a peaceful way • *The siege ended peacefully.*

peach *NOUN* (**peaches**)
a soft round juicy fruit with a slightly furry skin and a large stone

peacock *NOUN* (**peacocks**)
a large male bird with a long brightly coloured tail that it can spread out like a fan

peak *NOUN* (**peaks**)
1 the top of a mountain **2** the highest or best point of something • *Traffic reaches its peak at 5 o'clock.* **3** the part of a cap that sticks out in front

> WORD FAMILY
> A **peaked** hat or cap is one with a peak.

peak *VERB* (**peaks**, **peaking**, **peaked**)
to reach the highest point or amount • *Prices peaked in March.*

peal *VERB* (**peals**, **pealing**, **pealed**)
bells peal when they make a loud ringing sound

peal *NOUN* (**peals**)
a loud ringing sound made by bells

> SPELLING
> Take care not to confuse **peal** with **peel**, which is the skin of fruit or vegetables.

peanut *NOUN* (**peanuts**)
a small round nut that grows in a pod in the ground

peanut butter *NOUN*
peanut butter is a paste made from crushed roasted peanuts

pear *NOUN* (**pears**)
a juicy fruit that gets narrower near the stalk

pearl *NOUN* (**pearls**)
a small shiny white ball found in the shells of some oysters and used as a jewel

> WORD FAMILY
> **Pearly** white teeth are as white and shiny as a pearl.

peasant *NOUN* (**peasants**)
a person who belongs to a farming community, especially in poor areas of the world

> WORD FAMILY
> The **peasantry** are the peasants of a region or country.

peat *NOUN*
peat is rotted plant material that can be dug out of the ground and used as fuel or fertilizer

pebble *NOUN* (**pebbles**)
a small round stone found on the beach

> WORD FAMILY
> A **pebbly** beach is one with lots of pebbles.

peck *VERB* (**pecks**, **pecking**, **pecked**)
1 when a bird pecks something, it bites it or eats it with its beak

peck *NOUN* (**pecks**)
1 a short sharp bite with a bird's beak **2** (*informal*) a quick kiss

peckish *ADJECTIVE*
(*informal*) hungry

peculiar *ADJECTIVE*
strange or unusual
to be peculiar to someone or **something** is to be restricted to them • *This species of bird is peculiar to Asia.*
▷ **peculiarly** *ADVERB* more than usually; strangely • *He is peculiarly fond of brightly coloured socks.*

peculiarity *NOUN* (**peculiarities**)
something peculiar or special

pedal *NOUN* (**pedals**)
a lever that you press with your foot to operate a bicycle, car, or machine, or to play some musical instruments

pedal *VERB* (**pedals**, **pedalling**, **pedalled**)
to pedal is to push or turn the pedals of a bicycle or other device

peddle *VERB* (**peddles**, **peddling**, **peddled**)
to peddle things is to sell them as a pedlar

pedestal *NOUN* (**pedestals**)
the base that supports a statue or pillar

pedestrian *NOUN* (**pedestrians**)
someone who is walking

pedestrian *ADJECTIVE*
ordinary and dull

pedigree *NOUN* (**pedigrees**)
a list of a person's or animal's ancestors, especially to show how well an animal has been bred

pedlar *NOUN* (**pedlars**)
someone who goes from house to house selling small things

peel *NOUN* (**peels**)
the skin of some fruit and vegetables

peel *VERB* (**peels**, **peeling**, **peeled**)
1 to peel a piece of fruit or a vegetable is to remove the peel or covering from it **2** to peel is to lose a covering or skin • *My skin is peeling.*

> SPELLING
> Take care not to confuse **peel** with **peal**, which means to make a loud ringing sound.

peep *VERB* (**peeps**, **peeping**, **peeped**)
1 to peep is to look quickly or secretly, or through a narrow opening **2** to peep or peep out is to come slowly or briefly into view • *The moon peeped out through the clouds.*

peep *NOUN* (**peeps**)
a quick look

peer [1] *VERB* (**peers**, **peering**, **peered**)
to peer at something or someone is to look at them closely or with difficulty

peer [2] *NOUN* (**peers**)
1 a noble **2** your peers are the people who are the same age as you

peerless *ADJECTIVE*
not having an equal; best

peewit *NOUN* (**peewits**)
a kind of wading bird

peg *NOUN* (**pegs**)
a clip or pin for fixing things in place or for hanging things on

peg *VERB* (**pegs**, **pegging**, **pegged**)
1 to peg something is to fix it with pegs • *We pegged out the tent.*
to peg out (*slang*) is to die

Pekingese or **Pekinese** *NOUN* (**Pekingese** or **Pekinese**) (*say* peek- i- **neez**)
a small breed of dog with short legs and long silky hair

pelican *NOUN* (**pelicans**)
a large bird with a pouch in its long beak for storing fish

pelican crossing *NOUN* (**pelican crossings**)
a place where pedestrians can cross a street by operating lights that signal the traffic to stop

pellet *NOUN* (**pellets**)
a tiny ball of metal, food, wet paper, or other substance

pelt [1] *VERB* (**pelts**, **pelting**, **pelted**)
1 to pelt someone with things is to throw a lot of things at them • *We pelted him with snowballs.* **2** it pelts down when it is raining very hard **3** to pelt is to run fast

pelt [2] *NOUN* (**pelts**)
an animal skin, especially with the fur or hair still on it

pen [1] *NOUN* (**pens**)
a device with a metal point for writing with ink

pen [2] *NOUN* (**pens**)
an enclosure for cattle or other animals

penalize *VERB* (**penalizes**, **penalizing**, **penalized**)
1 to penalize someone is to punish them **2** in a game, to penalize someone is to award a penalty against them

penalty *NOUN* (**penalties**)
1 a punishment **2** a point or advantage given to one side in a game when a member of the other side breaks a rule

pence *PLURAL NOUN*
pennies

pencil *NOUN* (**pencils**)
a device for drawing or writing, made of a thin stick of graphite or coloured chalk inside a cylinder of wood or metal

pencil *VERB* (**pencils, pencilling, pencilled**)
to pencil something is to write it or mark it with a pencil • *I'll pencil that date in my diary.*

pendant *NOUN* (**pendants**)
a piece of jewellery hung round the neck on a long chain or string

pendulum *NOUN* (**pendulums**)
a weight hung at the end of a rod so that it swings to and fro, especially to keep a clock working

penetrate *VERB* (**penetrates, penetrating, penetrated**)
to penetrate something is to find a way through it or into it

> WORD FAMILY
> **Penetration** is penetrating something.

penfriend *NOUN* (**penfriends**)
someone in another country you write to, usually without meeting them

penguin *NOUN* (**penguins**)
an Antarctic sea bird that cannot fly but uses its wings as flippers for swimming

penicillin *NOUN*
penicillin is a drug that kills bacteria, made from mould

peninsula *NOUN* (**peninsulas**)
a long piece of land that is almost surrounded by water
▷ **peninsular** *ADJECTIVE* to do with a peninsula

penis *NOUN* (**penises**)
the part of the body with which a male person or animal urinates and has sexual intercourse

penitent *ADJECTIVE*
sorry for what you have done

> WORD FAMILY
> **Penitence** is regret for something wrong you have done.

penknife *NOUN* (**penknives**)
a small folding knife

pennant *NOUN* (**pennants**)
a long pointed flag

penniless *ADJECTIVE*
having no money; very poor

penny *NOUN* (**pennies** or **pence**)
a British coin worth a hundredth of a pound

pension *NOUN* (**pensions**)
an income of regular payments made to someone who has retired or been widowed

pensioner *NOUN* (**pensioners**)
someone who receives a pension

pentagon *NOUN* (**pentagons**)
a flat shape with five sides
the Pentagon a five-sided building in Washington, headquarters of the leaders of the American armed forces

pentathlon *NOUN* (**pentathlons**) (*say* pent-ath-lon)
a sports competition that has five different events

peony *NOUN* (**peonies**) (*say* pee-o-ni)
a plant with large round red, pink, or white flowers

people *PLURAL NOUN*
1 people are human beings; men, women, and children **2** the people of a particular country or area are the men, women, and children who live there

people *NOUN* (**peoples**)
a people is a community or nation • *They are a peaceful people.*

pepper *NOUN* (**peppers**)
1 pepper is a hot-tasting powder used to flavour food **2** a pepper is a bright green, red, or yellow vegetable

> WORD FAMILY
> **Peppery** food is hot-tasting like pepper.

peppermint *NOUN* (**peppermints**)
1 peppermint is a kind of mint used for flavouring **2** a peppermint is a sweet flavoured with this mint

per *PREPOSITION*
for each • *The charge is £1 per person.*

per annum *ADVERB*
each year • *$15,000 per annum*

per capita *ADJECTIVE & ADVERB*
for each person • *The daily water consumption was thirty litres per capita.*

perceive *VERB* (**perceives, perceiving, perceived**)
to perceive something is to see or notice it or understand it

per cent *ADVERB*
for every hundred • *We pay interest at 5 per cent (5%).*

percentage *NOUN* (**percentages**)
an amount or rate expressed as a proportion of 100

perceptible *ADJECTIVE*
able to be seen or noticed
▷ **perceptibly** *ADVERB* in a perceptible way • *It was perceptibly warmer.*

perception *NOUN*
perception is the ability to see, notice, or understand something

perceptive *ADJECTIVE*
quick to notice or understand things • *It was very perceptive of you to spot that.*

perch[1] *NOUN* (**perches**)
a place where a bird sits or rests

perch *VERB* (**perches**, **perching**, **perched**)
to perch is to sit or stand on the edge of something or on something small • *Matilda, who was perched on a tall stool at the kitchen table, ate her bread and jam slowly.* — Roald Dahl, *Matilda*

perch[2] *NOUN* (**perch**)
a freshwater fish used for food

percolator *NOUN* (**percolators**)
a pot for making coffee with ground coffee beans

percussion *NOUN*
percussion is musical instruments that you play by hitting them or shaking them, such as drums and cymbals

> WORD FAMILY
> A **percussionist** is someone who plays percussion instruments; a **percussive** sound is one made by striking something.

perennial *ADJECTIVE*
lasting or occurring for many years • *It is a perennial problem.*

perennial *NOUN* (**perennials**)
a plant that lives for many years
▷ **perennially** *ADVERB* year after year

perfect *ADJECTIVE* (*say* per- fikt)
1 so good that it cannot be made any better; without any faults **2** complete • *The man is a perfect stranger.*

> WORD FAMILY
> **Perfection** is being perfect.

perfect *NOUN*
a form of a verb that describes a completed action or event in the past, in English formed with *has* and *have*, for example *I have lost my pen*

perfect *VERB* (**perfects**, **perfecting**, **perfected**) (*say* per- **fekt**)
to perfect something is to make it perfect

perfectly *ADVERB*
1 completely • *She stood perfectly still.* **2** without any faults • *The toaster works perfectly now.*

perforate *VERB* (**perforates**, **perforating**, **perforated**)
to perforate something is to make tiny holes in it, especially so that it can be torn off easily

> WORD FAMILY
> **Perforations** are the tiny holes made in something so that it can be torn off easily.

perform *VERB* (**performs**, **performing**, **performed**)
1 to perform something is to present it in front of an audience • *They performed a play in the school hall.* **2** to perform something is also to do something you have to do or ought to do • *The surgeon performed the operation on Tuesday.*

> WORD FAMILY
> A **performer** is someone who performs an entertainment.

performance *NOUN* (**performances**)
the showing of something in front of an audience

perfume *NOUN* (**perfumes**)
1 a sweet-smelling liquid that people put on their skin **2** a sweet or pleasant smell

perhaps *ADVERB*
it may be; possibly

peril *NOUN* (**perils**)
peril is danger • *She was in great peril.*

> WORD FAMILY
> A **perilous** journey or adventure is a dangerous one; to be (for example) **perilously** close to something is to be dangerously close to it • *It was a perilous climb. The rocks were slippery with snow and the other boys were thoroughly over-excited, making the ascent far too quickly.* — Cressida Cowell, *How to Train Your Dragon* • *We came perilously close to disaster.*

perimeter *NOUN* (**perimeters**) (*say* per- **im**- it- er)
1 a boundary • *A fence marks the perimeter of the airfield.* **2** the distance round the edge of something

period *NOUN* (**periods**)
1 a length of time **2** the time every month when a woman or girl bleeds from her womb in menstruation

periodic *ADJECTIVE*
occurring at regular intervals

> WORD FAMILY
> Something happens **periodically** when it happens from time to time.

periodical *NOUN* (**periodicals**)
a magazine published regularly, for example once a month

periscope *NOUN* (**periscopes**)
a device with a tube and mirrors that lets you see things at a higher level, used for example in submarines

perish *VERB* (**perishes, perishing, perished**)
1 to perish is to die or be destroyed • *Many sailors perished in the shipwreck.* **2** to perish is also to rot • *The tyres have perished.* **3** (*informal*) to be perished is to feel extremely cold • *I was perished after the long walk in the hills.*

> WORD FAMILY
> **Perishable** food is likely to go off quickly.

perm *NOUN*
(*informal*) treatment of the hair with chemicals to give it long-lasting waves

perm *VERB* (**perms, perming, permed**)
to perm hair is to treat it with chemicals to give it long-lasting waves

permanent *ADJECTIVE*
lasting for ever or for a long time • *Will there be any permanent damage?*

> WORD FAMILY
> **Permanence** is the fact of lasting for ever or for a long time; to be (for example) **permanently** damaged is to be damaged for ever or for a long time.

permissible *ADJECTIVE*
something is permissible when it is allowed

permission *NOUN*
you have permission to do something when you are allowed to do it

permissive *ADJECTIVE*
letting people do what they wish; tolerant or liberal
▷ **permissively** *ADVERB* in a permissive way
▷ **permissiveness** *NOUN* permissiveness is being permissive

permit *VERB* (**permits, permitting, permitted**)
(*say* per- **mit**)
1 to permit someone to do something is to allow them to do it **2** to permit something is to allow it to be done

permit *NOUN* (**permits**) (*say* **per**- mit)
a written or printed statement that says you are allowed to do something

perpendicular *ADJECTIVE*
upright, or at a right angle to a line or surface

perpetual *ADJECTIVE*
lasting for ever or for a long time
▷ **perpetually** *ADVERB* continually

perpetuate *VERB* (**perpetuates, perpetuating, perpetuated**)
to perpetuate something is to cause it to continue or be remembered for a long time

perplex *VERB* (**perplexes, perplexing, perplexed**)
to perplex someone is to puzzle them very much • *When Mr. McGregor returned about half an hour later he observed several things which perplexed him.* — Beatrix Potter, *The Tale of Benjamin Bunny*

> WORD FAMILY
> **Perplexity** is feeling puzzled and confused.

persecute *VERB* (**persecutes, persecuting, persecuted**)
to persecute someone is to be continually cruel to them, especially because you disagree with their beliefs

> WORD FAMILY
> **Persecution** is when someone is being persecuted; their **persecutor** is the person who is doing this to them.

persevere *VERB* (**perseveres, persevering, persevered**)
to persevere is to go on with something even though it is difficult

> WORD FAMILY
> You show **perseverence** when you go on with something even though it is difficult.

persist *VERB* (**persists, persisting, persisted**)
1 to persist is to keep on firmly or obstinately doing something • *She persists in breaking the rules.* **2** to persist is also to last for a long time • *The rain persisted all afternoon.*

> WORD FAMILY
> You show **persistence** when you keep on doing something without giving up.

persistent *ADJECTIVE*
1 refusing to give up **2** lasting for a long time • *The rain was persistent.*
▷ **persistently** *ADVERB* in a persistent way

person *NOUN* (**persons** or **people**)
1 a human being; a man, woman, or child **2** (*in grammar*) each of the parts of a verb and the pronouns that go with the verb.
The **first person** (= *I, me, we, us*) refers to the person or people speaking; the **second person** (= *you*) refers to the person or people spoken to; and the **third person** (= *he, him, she, her, it, they, them*) refers to the person or people spoken about

personal *ADJECTIVE*
1 belonging to, done by, or concerning a particular person • *The stars of the film will be making a personal appearance at the première.* **2** private • *I can't tell you about that because it's personal.*

personal computer *NOUN* (**personal computers**)
a small computer designed for a single user

personality *NOUN* (**personalities**)
1 your personality is your nature and character • *She has a cheerful personality.* **2** a well-known person • *There were several TV personalities at the party.*

personally *ADVERB*
1 in person; being actually there • *The head thanked me personally.* **2** as far as I am concerned • *Personally, I'd rather stay here.*

personify *VERB* (**personifies**, **personifying**, **personified**)
to personify a quality or idea is to represent it as if it was a person

> WORD FAMILY
> **Personification** is when a writer represents a quality or idea as if it was a person.

personnel *NOUN* (*say* per- so- **nel**)
the personnel in a business or organization are the people who work there

perspective *NOUN* (**perspectives**)
1 perspective is the impression of depth and space in a picture or scene **2** your perspective on a situation is your point of view
in perspective giving a balanced view of things • *Try to see the problem in perspective.*

perspire *VERB* (**perspires**, **perspiring**, **perspired**)
to perspire is to sweat

> WORD FAMILY
> **Perspiration** is sweat.

persuade *VERB* (**persuades**, **persuading**, **persuaded**)
to persuade someone is to get them to agree about something

> WORD FAMILY
> **Persuasion** is when you persuade someone to do or believe something; a **persuasive** person is good at persuading people.

perverse *ADJECTIVE* (*say* per- **verss**)
obstinate or unreasonable in what you do or say
▷ **perversely** *ADVERB* in a perverse way
▷ **perversity** *NOUN* perversity is being perverse

pervert *VERB* (**perverts**, **perverting**, **perverted**) (*say* per- **vert**)
1 to pervert something is to make it go wrong **2** to pervert someone is to make them behave wickedly or in a way that is not normal

> WORD FAMILY
> **Perversion**, or a **perversion**, is behaviour that most people think is not normal.

pervert *NOUN* (**perverts**) (*say* **per**- vert)
someone with odd or unnatural sexual behaviour

Pesach *NOUN*
Pesach is the Hebrew name for Passover

pessimist *NOUN* (**pessimists**)
someone who usually expects things to turn out badly

> WORD FAMILY
> **Pessimism** is the feeling that things will turn out badly.

pessimistic *ADJECTIVE*
expecting things to turn out badly
▷ **pessimistically** *ADVERB* in a pessimistic way

pest *NOUN* (**pests**)
1 a destructive insect or animal, such as a locust or a mouse **2** a nuisance

pester *VERB* (**pesters**, **pestering**, **pestered**)
to pester someone is to annoy them with frequent questions or interruptions

pesticide *NOUN* (**pesticides**)
a chemical used to kill insects and grubs

pestle *NOUN* (**pestles**)
a tool with a heavy rounded end for pounding food in a bowl called a mortar

pet *NOUN* (**pets**)
1 a tame animal that you keep at home **2** a person treated as a favourite • *She seems to be teacher's pet.*

petal *NOUN* (**petals**)
each of the separate coloured outer parts of a flower

petition *NOUN* (**petitions**)
a written request for something, usually signed by a large number of people

petrify *VERB* (**petrifies**, **petrifying**, **petrified**)
to petrify someone is to make them so terrified that they cannot move

petrochemical *NOUN* (**petrochemicals**)
a chemical substance made from petroleum or natural gas

petrol *NOUN*
petrol is a liquid made from petroleum, used as a fuel for engines

> USING THIS WORD
> In America, the word **gasoline** is used.

petroleum *NOUN* (*say* pi- **troh**- li- um)
petroleum is an oil found underground that is purified to make petrol, diesel oil, and other fuels

petticoat *NOUN* (**petticoats**)
a piece of women's clothing worn under a skirt or dress

petty *ADJECTIVE* (**pettier**, **pettiest**)
1 minor and unimportant • *There are some petty regulations.* **2** mean and small-minded
▷ **pettily** *ADVERB* in a petty way
▷ **pettiness** *NOUN* pettiness is being petty

pew *NOUN* (**pews**)
one of the long wooden seats in a church

pewter *NOUN*
pewter is a grey alloy of tin and lead

pH *NOUN*
a measure of the acidity or alkalinity of a solution. Pure water has a pH of 7; acids have a pH between 0 and 7, and alkalis have a pH between 7 and 14

phantom *NOUN* (**phantoms**)
a ghost

pharmacy *NOUN* (**pharmacies**)
a shop that sells medicines

phase *NOUN* (**phases**)
a stage in the progress or development of something

phase *VERB* (**phases**, **phasing**, **phased**)
to phase a plan or operation is to carry it out in stages • *The new buildings were phased over three years.*
to phase something in is to start it gradually
to phase something out is to stop it gradually

pheasant *NOUN* (**pheasants**) (*say* fez- ant)
a game bird with a long tail

phenomenal *ADJECTIVE* (*say* fin- **om**- in- al)
amazing or remarkable

> WORD FAMILY
> To be (for example) **phenomenally** successful is to be greatly or remarkably successful.

phenomenon *NOUN* (**phenomena**)
an event or fact, especially one that is remarkable or unusual

philately *NOUN* (*say* fil- **at**- el- i)
philately is collecting postage stamps

> WORD FAMILY
> A **philatelist** is someone who collects stamps.

philosophical *ADJECTIVE*
1 to do with philosophy **2** calmly accepting disappointment or suffering • *He was philosophical about losing.*

> WORD FAMILY
> To accept something **philosophically** is to do so calmly even though it is disappointing • *He took the bad news philosophically.*

philosophy *NOUN* (**philosophies**) (*say* fil- **os**- o- fi)
1 philosophy is the study of truths about life and human behaviour **2** a philosophy is a way of thinking or a system of beliefs

> WORD FAMILY
> A **philosopher** is someone who studies philosophy.

phobia *NOUN* (**phobias**) (*say* **foh**- bi- a)
a great or unusual fear of something

phoenix *NOUN* (**phoenixes**) (*say* **fee**- niks)
a mythical bird that was said to burn itself to death on a fire and be born again from the ashes

phone *NOUN* (**phones**)
a telephone

phone *VERB* (**phones**, **phoning**, **phoned**)
to phone someone is to telephone them

phonecard *NOUN* (**phonecards**)
a plastic card that you can use to work some kinds of public telephone

phone-in *NOUN* (**phone-ins**)
a radio or TV programme in which people telephone the studio and take part in a discussion

phoneme *NOUN* (**phoneme**) (*say* **foh**- neem)
one of the sounds used in a language, which can sometimes be written in different ways. For example, the phoneme 'n' can be written as 'n' (in the word 'new'), or it can be written as 'kn' (in the word 'knee')

phosphorescent *ADJECTIVE*
shining or glowing in the dark
▷ **phosphorescence** *NOUN* phosphorescence is being phosphorescent

phosphorus *NOUN*
phosphorus is a yellowish substance that glows in the dark

photo *NOUN* (**photos**)
(*informal*) a photograph

photocopier *NOUN* (**photocopiers**)
a machine that makes photocopies

photocopy *NOUN* (**photocopies**)
a copy of a document or page made by a machine that photographs it on special paper

photocopy *VERB* (**photocopies**, **photocopying**, **photocopied**)
to photocopy a document is to make a copy of it with a photocopier

photoelectric *ADJECTIVE*
using the electrical effects of light

photograph *NOUN* (**photographs**)
a picture made on film, using a camera

photograph *VERB* (**photographs**, **photographing**, **photographed**)
to photograph someone or something is to take a photograph of them

> WORD FAMILY
> A **photographer** is someone who takes photographs.

photography *NOUN*
photography is taking photographs with a camera

> WORD FAMILY
> **Photographic** means to do with photography.

photosynthesis *NOUN*
photosynthesis is the process by which green plants use sunlight to make their food from carbon dioxide and water

phrase *NOUN* (**phrases**)
1 a group of words that form a unit smaller than a clause, for example *in the garden* in the sentence *The Queen was in the garden* **2** a short section of a tune

PHRASE
A phrase is a group of words that have the same role in a sentence as one word. For example: **noun** - *elephant* **noun phrase** - *wild, enraged elephant* **verb** - *stamping* **verb phrase** (or **verb chain**) - *has been stamping* **preposition** - *over* **prepositional phrase** - *over my garden.*

phrase *VERB* (**phrases, phrasing, phrased**)
to phrase an idea or thought is to put it into words

physical *ADJECTIVE*
1 to do with the body rather than the mind or feelings **2** to do with things you can touch or see
▷ **physically** *ADVERB* in a way that is connected with the body rather than the mind or feelings

physical education *NOUN*
physical education is gymnastics or other exercises that you do to keep your body healthy

physician *NOUN* (**physicians**)
a doctor

physics *NOUN*
physics is the study of matter and energy, including movement, heat, light, and sound

WORD FAMILY
A **physicist** is an expert in physics.

physiology *NOUN* (*say* fiz- i- ol- o- ji)
physiology is the study of the body and how it works
▷ **physiological** *ADJECTIVE* to do with physiology
▷ **physiologist** *NOUN* an expert in physiology

pi *NOUN* (*say* pie)
pi is a number roughly equal to 3.14159, shown by the symbol p and used in calculating the circumference and area of circles. The diameter of a circle multiplied by pi gives the circumference

pianist *NOUN* (**pianists**)
someone who plays the piano

piano *NOUN* (**pianos**)
a large musical instrument with a row of black and white keys on a keyboard

piccolo *NOUN* (**piccolos**)
a small high-pitched flute

pick[1] *VERB* (**picks, picking, picked**)
1 to pick something or someone is to choose them • *Pick a card from this pack.* **2** to pick flowers or fruit is to cut or pull them off the plant or tree **3** to pick someone's pocket is to steal from it **4** to pick a lock is to open it without using a key **5** to pick bits off or out of something is to pull them away from it
to pick holes in something is to find fault with it
to pick on someone is to keep criticizing or bothering them
to pick someone up is to give them a lift in a vehicle
to pick something up 1 is to take it from the ground or a surface **2** is to collect it • *I'll pick up my bags from the station.*
to pick up is to improve or recover

pick *NOUN*
1 a choice • *Take your pick.* **2** the best part of something

pick[2] *NOUN* (**picks**)
a pickaxe

pickaxe *NOUN* (**pickaxes**)
a heavy pointed tool with a long handle, used for breaking up concrete or hard ground

picket *NOUN* (**pickets**)
a group of strikers who try to persuade other people not to go into a place of work during a strike

picket *VERB* (**pickets, picketing, picketed**)
a group of people picket a place of work when they stand outside and try to persuade other people not to go in during a strike

pickle *NOUN* (**pickles**)
1 a strong-tasting food made of vegetables preserved in vinegar **2** (*informal*) a difficulty • *Now we're in a real pickle!*

pickle *VERB* (**pickles, pickling, pickled**)
to pickle food is to preserve it in vinegar or salt water

pickpocket *NOUN* (**pickpockets**)
a thief who steals from people's pockets or bags

pick-up *NOUN* (**pick-ups**)
an open truck for carrying small loads

picnic *NOUN* (**picnics**)
a meal eaten in the open air away from home

picnic *VERB* (**picnics, picnicking, picnicked**)
to picnic is to have a picnic

WORD FAMILY
Picnickers are people who are having a picnic.

pictogram *NOUN* (**pictograms**)
a picture or symbol that stands for a word or a phrase

pictorial *ADJECTIVE*
with or using pictures

WORD FAMILY
To show something **pictorially** is to show it using pictures.

picture *NOUN* (**pictures**)
1 a painting, drawing, or photograph **2** a film at the cinema
to be in the picture is to know about something

picture *VERB* (**pictures, picturing, pictured**)
1 to picture someone or something is to show them in a picture **2** to picture someone or something in your mind is to imagine them

a b c d e f g h i j k l m n o **p** q r s t u v w x y z

picturesque *ADJECTIVE* (say pik- cher- esk)
1 a picturesque place is attractive or charming • *We drove through a picturesque village.* **2** picturesque language is clear and vivid

pie *NOUN* (**pies**)
a baked dish of meat or fruit covered with pastry

piece *NOUN* (**pieces**)
1 a part of something; a bit **2** a work of art or writing or music • *They played a piece of piano music.* **3** one of the objects you use on a board to play a game • *You've dropped a chess piece.* **4** a coin • *a 20p piece*
to be in one piece is to be not broken or injured
piece by piece gradually; one bit at a time

piece *VERB* (**pieces, piecing, pieced**)
to piece things together is to join them to make something

piecemeal *ADVERB*
you do something piecemeal when you do it gradually, a bit at a time

pie chart *NOUN* (**pie charts**)
a diagram in the form of a circle divided into slices, showing how a quantity or amount is divided up

pier *NOUN* (**piers**)
1 a long structure built out into the sea for people to walk on **2** a pillar supporting a bridge or arch

pierce *VERB* (**pierces, piercing, pierced**)
to pierce something is to make a hole through it

piercing *ADJECTIVE*
1 a piercing sound is loud and high-pitched • *We heard a piercing shriek.* **2** something piercing seems to go right through you • *The wind was cold and piercing.*

pig *NOUN* (**pigs**)
1 a fat animal with short legs and a blunt snout, kept for its meat **2** (*informal*) you can describe someone as a pig when they are greedy, dirty, or unpleasant

> WORD FAMILY
> A **piggy** is a little pig.

pigeon *NOUN* (**pigeons**)
1 a common grey bird with a small head and large chest **2** (*informal*) someone's business or responsibility • *That's his pigeon.*

pigeon-hole *NOUN* (**pigeon-holes**)
a small compartment for holding papers and letters, for someone to collect

piggyback *NOUN* (**piggybacks**)
a ride on someone's back

pig-headed *ADJECTIVE*
obstinate; stubborn

piglet *NOUN* (**piglets**)
a young pig

pigment *NOUN* (**pigments**)
a substance that colours something

pigmy *NOUN* (**pigmies**)
another spelling of **pygmy**

pigsty *NOUN* (**pigsties**)
1 a place for keeping pigs **2** (*informal*) you can describe a very untidy room or place as a pigsty

pigtail *NOUN* (**pigtails**)
a single plait of hair worn hanging at the back of the head

pike *NOUN* (**pikes**)
1 a large fish that lives in rivers and lakes **2** a heavy spear

pilchard *NOUN* (**pilchards**)
a small sea fish

pile [1] *NOUN* (**piles**)
1 a number of things on top of one another **2** (*informal*) a large amount of something, especially money

pile *VERB* (**piles, piling, piled**)
to pile things is to put them into a pile
to pile up is to become very much or very many • *The work was piling up.*

pile [2] *NOUN* (**piles**)
a heavy beam driven vertically into the ground to support something

pilfer *VERB* (**pilfers, pilfering, pilfered**)
to pilfer small or unimportant things is to steal them

pilgrim *NOUN* (**pilgrims**)
someone who goes on a journey to a holy place

pilgrimage *NOUN* (**pilgrimages**)
a journey to a holy place

pill *NOUN* (**pills**)
a small piece of medicine that you swallow
the pill a special kind of pill taken by a woman to prevent her from becoming pregnant

pillage *VERB* (**pillages, pillaging, pillaged**)
to pillage a place is to seize things from it by force and carry them off, especially in a war

pillar *NOUN* (**pillars**)
a tall stone or wooden post

pillar box *NOUN* (**pillar boxes**)
a postbox standing in a street

pillion *NOUN* (**pillions**)
a seat for a passenger behind the driver's seat on a motorcycle

pillow *NOUN* (**pillows**)
a cushion to rest your head on in bed

pillowcase *NOUN* (**pillowcases**)
a cloth cover for a pillow

pilot *NOUN* (**pilots**)
1 someone who flies an aircraft **2** someone who helps to steer a ship in and out of a port or through a difficult stretch of water

pilot *VERB* (**pilots, piloting, piloted**)
to pilot an aircraft is to be the pilot of it

pimple *NOUN* (**pimples**)
a small round swelling on your skin

> WORD FAMILY
> Someone is **pimply** when they have pimples.

pin *NOUN* (**pins**)
1 a short piece of metal with a sharp point and a rounded head, used to fasten pieces of paper or cloth together **2** a pointed device for fixing or marking something
pins and needles a tingling feeling in the skin

pin *VERB* (**pins**, **pinning**, **pinned**)
1 to pin something is to fasten it with a pin **2** to pin someone or something in a place is to keep them fixed or trapped there • *He was pinned under the wreckage for hours.*

pinafore *NOUN* (**pinafores**)
a large apron

pincer *NOUN* (**pincers**)
the claw of a shellfish such as a lobster

pincers *PLURAL NOUN*
a tool for gripping and pulling things, especially for pulling out nails

pinch *VERB* (**pinches**, **pinching**, **pinched**)
1 to pinch something is to squeeze it tightly between two things, especially between the finger and thumb **2** (*informal*) to pinch something is to steal it

pinch *NOUN* (**pinches**)
1 a firm squeezing movement **2** the amount you can pick up between the tips of your finger and thumb • *Take a pinch of salt.*
at a pinch if it is really necessary

pincushion *NOUN* (**pincushions**)
a small pad into which needles and pins are stuck to keep them ready for use

pine [1] *NOUN* (**pines**)
an evergreen tree with leaves shaped like needles

pine [2] *VERB* (**pines**, **pining**, **pined**)
1 to pine for someone or something is to feel a strong longing for them **2** to pine, or pine away, is to become weak or ill through sorrow or yearning

pineapple *NOUN* (**pineapples**)
a large tropical fruit with yellow flesh and prickly leaves and skin

ping-pong *NOUN*
ping-pong is table tennis

pink *ADJECTIVE* (**pinker**, **pinkest**)
pale red

pink *NOUN* (**pinks**)
1 a sweet-smelling garden flower **2** a pink colour

pint *NOUN* (**pints**)
a measure of liquid, an eighth of a gallon or about 568 millilitres

pioneer *NOUN* (**pioneers**)
one of the first people to go to a place or do something new

pious *ADJECTIVE*
very religious or devout
▷ **piously** *ADVERB* in a pious way

pip *NOUN* (**pips**)
1 a small hard seed of a fruit such as an apple, orange, or pear **2** a short high-pitched sound • *She heard the six pips of the time signal on the radio.*

pipe *NOUN* (**pipes**)
1 a tube for carrying water, gas, or oil from one place to another **2** a short tube with a small bowl at one end, used to smoke tobacco **3** a tubular musical instrument
the pipes bagpipes

pipe *VERB* (**pipes**, **piping**, **piped**)
1 to pipe something is to send it along pipes or wires **2** to pipe is to play music on a pipe or the bagpipes
to pipe down (*informal*) is to be quiet
to pipe up (*informal*) is to start saying something

pipe dream *NOUN* (**pipe dreams**)
a wish for something you are unlikely to get

pipeline *NOUN* (**pipelines**)
a pipe for carrying oil, water, or gas over a long distance
to be in the pipeline is to be planned and ready to happen soon

piper *NOUN* (**pipers**)
someone who plays a pipe or the bagpipes

piping *ADJECTIVE*
high-pitched; shrill
piping hot very hot, ready to eat

piping *NOUN*
piping is a length of pipes or material used for making pipes

pirate *NOUN* (**pirates**)
a sailor who attacks and robs other ships

> WORD FAMILY
> **Piracy** is being a pirate.

pistil *NOUN* (**pistils**)
the part of a flower that produces the seed

pistol *NOUN* (**pistols**)
a small gun held in the hand

piston *NOUN* (**pistons**)
a disc that moves up and down inside a cylinder in an engine or pump

pit *NOUN* (**pits**)
1 a deep hole or hollow **2** a coal mine **3** the part of a race circuit where cars are refuelled and serviced during a race

pit *VERB* (**pits**, **pitting**, **pitted**)
1 to pit something is to make deep holes or hollows in it • *The surface of the planet was pitted with craters.* **2** to pit one person against another is to arrange for them to compete with one another • *In the final he was pitted against the champion.*

a b c d e f g h i j k l m n o **p** q r s t u v w x y z

pitch[1] *NOUN* (**pitches**)
1 a pitch is a piece of ground marked out for cricket, football, or another game **2** pitch is how high or low a voice or musical note is **3** the pitch of something is also its intensity or strength • *Excitement was at a high pitch.*

pitch *VERB* (**pitches**, **pitching**, **pitched**)
1 to pitch something is to throw or fling it **2** to pitch a tent is to set it up **3** to pitch is to fall heavily • *He tripped over the doorstep and pitched headlong.* **4** a ship pitches when it moves up and down on a rough sea **5** to pitch something is to set it at a particular level • *We are pitching our hopes high.*
to pitch in is to join in and help with something • *Everyone pitched in with ideas.*

pitch[2] *NOUN*
pitch is a black sticky substance like tar

pitch-black or **pitch-dark** *ADJECTIVE*
completely black or dark, with no light at all

pitched battle *NOUN* (**pitched battles**)
a battle between armies in regular formation

pitcher *NOUN* (**pitchers**)
a large jug, usually with two handles

pitchfork *NOUN* (**pitchforks**)
a large fork with two prongs for lifting hay

pitfall *NOUN* (**pitfalls**)
a hidden danger or difficulty

pitiful *ADJECTIVE*
1 making you feel pity • *It was a pitiful sight.*
2 inadequate; feeble • *He made a pitiful attempt to make us laugh.*
▷ **pitifully** *ADVERB* in a pitiful way

pitiless *ADJECTIVE*
having or showing no pity
▷ **pitilessly** *ADVERB* in a pitiless way

pitta bread *NOUN*
pitta bread is a flat, round piece of bread that you can open and fill with food

pity *NOUN*
1 pity is the feeling of being sorry because someone is in pain or in trouble • *I feel pity for the homeless people.* **2** a pity is something that you regret • *It's a pity we can't meet.*
to take pity on someone is to help someone who is in trouble

pity *VERB* (**pities**, **pitying**, **pitied**)
to pity someone is to feel sorry for them

pivot *NOUN* (**pivots**)
a point on which something turns or balances

pivot *VERB* (**pivots**, **pivoting**, **pivoted**)
to pivot is to turn on a pivot or balance

pixel *NOUN* (**pixels**)
each of the tiny dots on a computer screen from which the image is formed

pixie or **pixy** *NOUN* (**pixies**)
a small fairy or elf

pizza *NOUN* (**pizzas**) (*say* **peet**- sa)
an Italian food made as a layer of dough covered with cheese, vegetables, and spices and baked

pizzicato *ADVERB & ADJECTIVE* (*say* pit- si- **kah**- toh)
in music, plucking the strings of an instrument such as a violin

placard *NOUN* (**placards**)
a large poster or notice put up on a wall or carried at a demonstration

place *NOUN* (**places**)
1 a particular part of space, especially where something belongs; an area or position **2** a position in a race or competition **3** a seat • *Save me a place.* **4** a person's duty or function • *It's not my place to interfere.*
in place in the proper position
in place of something or **someone** instead of them
out of place 1 in the wrong position **2** unsuitable • *Jeans and sandals are out of place in a smart restaurant.*
to take place is to happen

place *VERB* (**places**, **placing**, **placed**)
to place something somewhere is to put it in a particular place

placid *ADJECTIVE*
calm and gentle; peaceful • *a placid horse.*
▷ **placidity** *NOUN* placidity is being placid
▷ **placidly** *ADVERB* in a placid way

plague *NOUN* (**plagues**)
1 a dangerous illness that spreads very quickly
2 a large number of pests • *The crops were devastated by a plague of locusts.*

plague *VERB* (**plagues**, **plaguing**, **plagued**)
to plague someone is to pester or annoy them continuously • *They have been plagued with complaints.*

plaice *NOUN* (**plaice**)
a flat sea fish used for food

plaid *NOUN* (**plaids**) (*say* plad)
cloth with a tartan or chequered pattern

plain *ADJECTIVE* (**plainer**, **plainest**)
1 simple; not decorated **2** not pretty **3** easy to understand or see **4** frank; straightforward • *I'll be quite plain with you.*
▷ **plainness** *NOUN* plainness is being plain

plain *NOUN* (**plains**)
a large area of flat country without trees

plain clothes *PLURAL NOUN*
ordinary clothes worn instead of a uniform

plainly *ADVERB*
1 clearly or obviously • *The clock tower was plainly visible in the distance.* **2** simply • *She was plainly dressed.*

plaintiff *NOUN* (**plaintiffs**)
a person who brings a complaint against someone else to a lawcourt

plaintive *ADJECTIVE*
sounding sad • *We heard a plaintive cry.*
▷ **plaintively** *ADVERB* in a plaintive way • *'Will somebody please tell me what all this is about?' the Hemulen asked plaintively.* — Tove Jansson, *Finn Family Moonintroll*

plait *NOUN* (**plaits**) (*say* plat)
a length of hair or rope with several strands twisted together

plait *VERB* (**plaits**, **plaiting**, **plaited**) (*say* plat)
to plait hair or rope is to make it into a plait

plan *NOUN* (**plans**)
1 a way of doing something that you think out in advance **2** a drawing showing how the parts of something are arranged **3** a map of a town or district

plan *VERB* (**plans**, **planning**, **planned**)
1 to plan something is to think out in advance how you are going to do it **2** to plan to do something is to intend to do it
▷ **planner** *NOUN* someone who plans things

plane[1] *NOUN* (**planes**)
1 an aeroplane **2** a tool for making wood smooth **3** a flat or level surface

plane *VERB* (**planes**, **planing**, **planed**)
to plane wood is to smooth it with a plane

plane[2] *NOUN* (**planes**)
a tall tree with broad leaves

planet *NOUN* (**planets**)
one of the bodies that move in an orbit round the sun. The main planets of the solar system are Mercury, Venus, Earth, Mars, Jupiter, Saturn, Uranus, Neptune, and Pluto

> WORD FAMILY
> **Planetary** means to do with planets.

plank *NOUN* (**planks**)
a long flat piece of wood

plankton *NOUN*
plankton is made up of tiny creatures that float in the sea and lakes

plant *NOUN* (**plants**)
1 a living thing that grows out of the ground, including flowers, bushes, trees, and vegetables **2** a factory or its equipment

plant *VERB* (**plants**, **planting**, **planted**)
1 to plant something such as a tree or flower is to put it in the ground to grow **2** to plant something is also to put it firmly in place • *He planted his feet on the ground and took hold of the rope.* **3** to plant something such as a piece of evidence is to put it where it will be found, usually to mislead people or to cause trouble

> WORD FAMILY
> A **planter** is someone who owns a plantation.

plantation *NOUN* (**plantations**)
an area of land where a crop such as tobacco, tea, or rubber is planted

plaque *NOUN* (**plaques**) (*say* plak or plahk)
1 a plaque is a metal or porcelain plate fixed on a wall as a memorial or an ornament **2** plaque is a substance that forms a thin layer on your teeth, allowing bacteria to develop

plasma *NOUN* (*say* **plaz**- ma)
plasma is the colourless liquid part of blood, which carries the corpuscles

plaster *NOUN* (**plasters**)
1 a plaster is a small covering you put over your skin around a cut or wound to protect it **2** plaster is a mixture of lime, sand, and water, used to cover walls and ceilings

plaster *VERB* (**plasters**, **plastering**, **plastered**)
1 to plaster a surface is to cover it with plaster **2** to plaster a surface with something is to cover it thickly • *His clothes were plastered with mud.*

> WORD FAMILY
> A **plasterer** is someone who plasters walls and ceilings.

plaster of Paris *NOUN*
plaster of Paris is a white paste used for making moulds and for casts round a broken leg or arm

plastic *NOUN* (**plastics**)
a strong light synthetic substance that can be moulded into different shapes

plastic *ADJECTIVE*
made of plastic • *I need a plastic bag.*

Plasticine *NOUN*
(*trademark*) Plasticine is a soft and easily shaped substance used for making models

plastic surgery *NOUN*
plastic surgery is work done by a surgeon to alter or mend parts of someone's body

plate *NOUN* (**plates**)
1 a dish that is flat or almost flat, used for eating **2** a thin flat sheet of metal, glass, or other hard material **3** one of the large areas of rock that make up the earth's crust **4** an illustration on a separate page in a book

plate *VERB* (**plates**, **plating**, **plated**)
to plate metal is to cover it with a thin layer of gold, silver, tin, or other soft metal

plateau *NOUN* (**plateaux**) (*say* **plat**- oh)
a flat area of high land

plateful *NOUN* (**platefuls**)
as much as you can put on a plate

platform *NOUN* (**platforms**)
1 a flat raised area along the side of the line at a railway station **2** a small stage in a hall

platinum *NOUN*
platinum is a silver-coloured metal that does not lose its brightness

platoon *NOUN* (**platoons**)
a small unit of soldiers

platypus *NOUN* (**platypuses**)
an Australian animal with a beak and feet like those of a duck

play *VERB* (**plays, playing, played**)
1 to play, or play a game, is to take part in a game or other amusement **2** to play music, or a musical instrument, is to make music or sound with it **3** to play a part in a film or play is to perform it **4** to play a CD, DVD, or tape is to put it in a machine and listen to it or watch it
to play about or **around** is to have fun or be mischievous
to play someone up is to tease or annoy them

> WORD FAMILY
> A **player** is someone who plays a game or a musical instrument.

play *NOUN* (**plays**)
1 a play is a story acted on a stage or broadcast on radio or television **2** play is playing or having fun

playback *NOUN* (**playbacks**)
playing something that has been recorded

playful *ADJECTIVE*
1 wanting to play; full of fun **2** not serious
▷ **playfully** *ADVERB* in a playful way
▷ **playfulness** *NOUN* playfulness is being playful

playground *NOUN* (**playgrounds**)
a place out of doors where children can play

playgroup *NOUN* (**playgroups**)
a group of very young children who play together regularly, with adults to supervise them

playing card *NOUN* (**playing cards**)
each of a set of cards (usually 52) used for playing games

playing field *NOUN* (**playing fields**)
a grassy field for outdoor games

playmate *NOUN* (**playmates**)
someone that you play games with

play-off *NOUN* (**play-offs**)
an extra match played to decide a draw or tie

playscript *NOUN* (**playscripts**)
the text of a play

playtime *NOUN* (**playtimes**)
the time when young schoolchildren go out to play

playwright *NOUN* (**playwrights**)
someone who writes plays

plc
short for **public limited company**

plea *NOUN* (**pleas**)
1 a request or appeal **2** a statement of 'guilty' or 'not guilty' made in a lawcourt by someone accused of a crime

plead *VERB* (**pleads, pleading, pleaded**)
to plead with someone is to beg them to do something
to plead guilty or **not guilty** is to state in a lawcourt that you are guilty or not guilty of a crime

pleasant *ADJECTIVE* (**pleasanter, pleasantest**)
pleasing or enjoyable or friendly
▷ **pleasantly** *ADVERB* in a pleasant way • *I was pleasantly surprised.*

please *VERB* (**pleases, pleasing, pleased**)
1 to please someone is to make them happy or satisfied **2** used when you want to ask something politely • *Please shut the door.*
as you please as you like • *Do as you please.*

pleasurable *ADJECTIVE*
causing pleasure; enjoyable

pleasure *NOUN* (**pleasures**)
1 pleasure is being pleased **2** a pleasure is something that pleases you
with pleasure gladly; willingly

pleat *NOUN* (**pleats**)
a permanent fold made in the cloth of a piece of clothing

> WORD FAMILY
> A **pleated** (for example) skirt has pleats in it.

pledge *NOUN* (**pledges**)
a solemn promise

pledge *VERB* (**pledges, pledging, pledged**)
to pledge something is to promise it

plentiful *ADJECTIVE*
large in amount • '*On this Coast of Coromandel / Shrimps and watercresses grow, / Prawns are plentiful and cheap,' / Said the Yonghy-Bonghy-Bo.* — Edward Lear, *The Courtship of the Yonghy-Bonghy-Bo*
▷ **plentifully** *ADVERB* in a plentiful way

plenty *NOUN*
to have plenty of something is to have a lot of it or more than enough • *We have plenty of chairs.*

pliable *ADJECTIVE*
easy to bend; flexible

pliers *PLURAL NOUN*
pincers with flattened jaws for gripping something or for breaking wire

plight *NOUN* (**plights**)
a difficult and sad situation • *The programme examines the plight of the homeless.*

plod *VERB* (**plods, plodding, plodded**)
1 to plod is to walk slowly and with heavy steps • *We plodded back through the rain.* **2** to plod, or plod away, is to work slowly but steadily

> WORD FAMILY
> A **plodder** is someone who works slowly but steadily.

plop *NOUN* (**plops**)
the sound of something dropping into a liquid

plop *VERB* (**plops, plopping, plopped**)
to plop is to fall into a liquid with a plop

plot *NOUN* (**plots**)
1 a secret plan, especially to do something illegal or bad **2** what happens in a story, film, or play **3** a piece of land for a house or garden

plot *VERB* (**plots**, **plotting**, **plotted**)
1 to plot is to make a secret plan to do something **2** to plot a chart or graph is to make it, marking all the points on it

> WORD FAMILY
> **Plotters** are people who take part in a plot.

plough *NOUN* (**ploughs**) (*say* plow)
a device used on farms for turning over the soil

plough *VERB* (**ploughs**, **ploughing**, **ploughed**)
1 to plough the soil is to turn it over with a plough **2** to plough through something is to go through it with effort or difficulty •*He ploughed through the book.*

ploughman *NOUN* (**ploughmen**)
someone who uses a plough

plover *NOUN* (**plovers**) (*say* pluv- er)
a long-legged wading bird

pluck *VERB* (**plucks**, **plucking**, **plucked**)
1 to pluck a bird is to pull the feathers off it to prepare it for cooking **2** to pluck a flower or fruit is to pick it **3** to pluck something is to pull it or pull it out •*I'll try and pluck out your splinter.* **4** in music, to pluck a string is to pull it and let it go again
to pluck up courage is to be brave and overcome fear

pluck *NOUN*
pluck is courage or bravery

plucky *ADJECTIVE* (**pluckier**, **pluckiest**)
brave or courageous •*Emil was past fourteen and a plucky fellow, so he challenged Dan to a fight.* — Louisa May Alcott, *Little Men*
▷ **pluckily** *ADVERB* in a plucky way

plug *NOUN* (**plugs**)
1 something used to stop up a hole, especially in a sink or bath **2** a device that is used to connect a piece of electric equipment to a socket **3** (*informal*) a piece of publicity for something

plug *VERB* (**plugs**, **plugging**, **plugged**)
1 to plug a hole is to stop it up **2** (*informal*) to plug an event or product is to publicize it
to plug something in is to connect it to an electric socket by means of a plug

plum *NOUN* (**plums**)
a soft juicy fruit with a stone in the middle

plumage *NOUN* (*say* ploo- mij)
a bird's plumage is its feathers

plumb *VERB* (**plumbs**, **plumbing**, **plumbed**)
1 to plumb a river or the sea is to measure how deep it is **2** to plumb a mystery or puzzle is to find out what it means

plumber *NOUN* (**plumbers**)
someone who fits and mends water pipes in a building

plumbing *NOUN*
1 plumbing is the work of a plumber **2** the plumbing in a building is all the water pipes and water tanks

plume *NOUN* (**plumes**)
1 a large feather **2** something shaped like a feather •*We saw a plume of smoke in the distance.*

> WORD FAMILY
> A **plumed** hat or helmet is decorated with plumes.

plump *ADJECTIVE* (**plumper**, **plumpest**)
rounded or slightly fat

plump *VERB* (**plumps**, **plumping**, **plumped**)
to plump for something or **someone** is to choose them

plunder *VERB* (**plunders**, **plundering**, **plundered**)
to plunder a place or an enemy is to rob them violently, especially in a time of war or disorder •*The chief brigand counted out the jewels and gold coins they'd plundered and divided them all into twenty heaps.* — Philip Pullman, *The Scarecrow and his Servant*
▷ **plunderer** *NOUN* someone who plunders a place

plunder *NOUN*
1 plunder is plundering a person or place **2** plunder is also goods taken by plundering

plunge *VERB* (**plunges**, **plunging**, **plunged**)
1 to plunge into water is to jump or dive into it with force **2** to plunge something into a liquid or something soft is to put it in with force

plunge *NOUN* (**plunges**)
a sudden fall or dive

plural *NOUN* (**plurals**)
the form of a word meaning more than one person or thing, such as *cakes* and *children*

plural *ADJECTIVE*
in the plural; meaning more than one •*'Mice' is a plural noun.*

> PLURALS
> You make most nouns into a plural simply by adding an **s** on the end. *one apple, two apples.* Some nouns change their spelling in different ways when they become plural. With words that end in **ch**, **sh**, **s**, or **x** , you add **es** *watch - watches, dish - dishes, bus - buses, box - boxes.* With words that end in **y** (and the letter in front is not a vowel), you change the **y** to **ies** *baby - babies, party - parties, country - countries.* With words that end in **y** (and the letter in front is a vowel), you add **s** *donkey - donkeys.* With words that end in **f** or **fe**, you sometimes change the **f** or **fe** to **ves** *leaf - leaves, wolf - wolves, knife - knives.* With words that end in **o**, you usually add **es** *potato - potatoes, hero - heroes.* Some nouns are the same in the plural as they are in the singular, such as *aircraft*, *series*, and *sheep*. Some common words have plurals that don't follow a rule and that you need to learn, such as *child - children, woman - women, mouse - mice, foot - feet.* Look also at the panel on **Singular and plural.**

a b c d e f g h i j k l m n o **p** q r s t u v w x y z

plus *PREPOSITION*
with the next number or thing added • *2 plus 2 equals 4 (2 + 2 = 4).*

plutonium *NOUN* (*say* ploo- **toh**- ni- um)
plutonium is a radioactive element used in nuclear weapons and reactors

plywood *NOUN*
plywood is board made from thin sheets of wood glued together

p.m.
short for Latin *post meridiem* which means 'after midday'

pneumatic *ADJECTIVE* (*say* new- **mat**- ik)
filled with air or worked by compressed air • *a pneumatic tyre* • *a pneumatic drill*

pneumonia *NOUN* (*say* new- **moh**- ni- a)
pneumonia is a serious disease of the lungs

poach *VERB* (**poaches**, **poaching**, **poached**)
1 to poach food, especially fish or an egg taken out of its shell, is to cook it in or over boiling water **2** to poach animals is to hunt them illegally on someone else's land

> WORD FAMILY
> A **poacher** is someone who hunts animals illegally on someone else's land.

pocket *NOUN* (**pockets**)
1 part of a piece of clothing shaped like a small bag, for keeping things in **2** a small area in which something happens • *There will be pockets of rain in the south.* **3** a person's pocket is their supply of money • *The cost is well beyond my pocket.*
to be out of pocket is to have spent more money than you got back

pocket *ADJECTIVE*
small enough to carry in your pocket • *Use a pocket calculator.*

pocket *VERB* (**pockets**, **pocketing**, **pocketed**)
(*informal*) to pocket something is to steal it

pocketful *NOUN* (**pocketfuls**)
an amount you can put in your pocket

pocket money *NOUN*
pocket money is money given to a child to spend

pod *NOUN* (**pods**)
a long seed-container on a pea or bean plant

podgy *ADJECTIVE* (**podgier**, **podgiest**)
short and fat

poem *NOUN* (**poems**)
a piece of writing arranged in short lines, often with a particular rhythm and sometimes rhyming

poet *NOUN* (**poets**)
someone who writes poetry

poetic or **poetical** *ADJECTIVE*
like poetry; using the language of poetry
▷ **poetically** *ADVERB* in a poetic way

poetry *NOUN*
poetry is poems as a form of literature • *Do you write poetry?*

> POETRY
> Different poets choose to write in different poetic styles and have their own reasons for writing poems. For example:
> **Narrative poems** tell a story.
> **Performance poetry** is written to be performed or is able to be performed effectively.
> **Shape poems and concrete poems** make their impact on the page.
> **Syllabic poems** (like haiku, tanka, and cinquain) must have a certain number of syllables in each line and usually try to capture a moment in time.
> Some poems, like limericks, have a very definite rhythmical shape.
> Many poems have a rhyming pattern, for example rhyming couplets. **Free verse poems** usually have a 'thought' or a 'unit of meaning' on each line.

point *NOUN* (**points**)
1 the narrow or sharp end of something • *Don't hold the knife by its point.* **2** a written dot • *Put in a decimal point.* **3** a single mark in a game or quiz • *How many points did I get?* **4** a particular place or time • *They gave up at this point.* **5** something that someone says during a discussion • *That's a very good point.* **6** a detail or special feature • *He has some good points.* **7** purpose or advantage • *There's no point in hurrying.* **8** the points on a railway line are the movable parts that allow trains to change from one track to another
to come to the point is to mention the thing you really want to say

point *VERB* (**points**, **pointing**, **pointed**)
1 to point to something is to show where it is, especially by holding out your finger towards it **2** to point something is to aim it or direct it • *She pointed a gun at us.*
to point something out is to show it or explain it

point-blank *ADJECTIVE & ADVERB*
1 close to the target **2** directly and completely • *He refused point-blank.*

pointed *ADJECTIVE*
1 a pointed object has a point at the end **2** a pointed remark is clearly directed at a person, especially to criticize them • *He made a pointed remark about working hard.*

> WORD FAMILY
> To say or do something **pointedly** is to do so in a way that clearly shows what you mean • *She yawned and looked pointedly at her watch.*

pointer *NOUN* (**pointers**)
1 a stick or device you use to point at something **2** a dog that points with its muzzle at birds which it scents **3** a hint or piece of guidance • *He gave us a few pointers on the best way to make a campfire.*

pointless *ADJECTIVE*
something is pointless when it has no purpose or meaning
▷ **pointlessly** *ADVERB* in a pointless way

point of view *NOUN* (**points of view**)
1 a way of looking or thinking of something **2** the way that a writer chooses to tell a story, for example by telling it through the experiences of one of the characters

poise *NOUN*
poise is a dignified and self-confident manner

poise *VERB* (**poises**, **poising**, **poised**)
1 to poise something is to balance it or keep it steady **2** to be poised to do something is to be ready to do it

poison *NOUN* (**poisons**)
a substance that can kill or harm living things

poison *VERB* (**poisons**, **poisoning**, **poisoned**)
1 to poison someone is to kill or harm them with poison **2** to poison something is to put poison in it

WORD FAMILY
A **poisoner** is a person who kills someone using poison.

poisonous *ADJECTIVE*
1 a poisonous chemical, gas, or plant can kill or harm you if you swallow it or breathe it in
2 poisonous animals or insects can kill or harm you with poison if they bite you • *a poisonous snake*

poke [1] *VERB* (**pokes**, **poking**, **poked**)
to poke something or someone is to push or jab them hard with your finger or a pointed object
to poke about is to rummage nosily
to poke out is to stick out

poke *NOUN* (**pokes**)
a prod or jab

poke [2] *NOUN*
to buy a pig in a poke is to buy something without seeing it first

poker *NOUN* (**pokers**)
1 a poker is a metal rod for stirring a fire **2** poker is a card game in which the players bet on who has the best cards

polar *ADJECTIVE*
to do with the North or South Pole, or near one of them

polar bear *NOUN* (**polar bears**)
a powerful white bear living in Arctic regions

Polaroid *NOUN*
(*trademark*) Polaroid is a type of plastic that reduces the brightness of the light. It is used in sunglasses

Polaroid camera *NOUN* (**Polaroid cameras**)
(*trademark*) a camera that takes a picture and produces the finished photograph a few seconds later

pole [1] *NOUN* (**poles**)
a long thin piece of wood or metal

pole [2] *NOUN* (**poles**)
1 each of the two points at the ends of the earth's axis, the **North Pole** and the **South Pole** **2** each end of a magnet

pole vault *NOUN*
the pole vault is an athletic contest in which you jump over a high bar with the help of a long springy pole

police *NOUN*
the police are the people whose job is to catch criminals and make sure that people obey the law

policeman or **policewoman** *NOUN* (**policemen** or **policewomen**)
a man or woman member of the police

police officer *NOUN* (**police officers**)
a member of the police

USING THIS WORD
This is now often used instead of **policeman** and **policewoman** because it can mean both sexes.

policy *NOUN* (**policies**)
1 the aims or plans of a person or group of people **2** a plan of action • *Honesty is the best policy.*

polio *NOUN* (*say* **poh**- li- oh)
(*informal*) polio is poliomyelitis

poliomyelitis *NOUN* (*say* poh- li- oh- my- i- **ly**- tis)
poliomyelitis is a disease that paralyses the body

polish *VERB* (**polishes**, **polishing**, **polished**) (*say* **pol**- ish)
to polish something is to make its surface shiny or smooth
to polish something off (*informal*) is to finish it quickly

polish *NOUN* (**polishes**) (*say* **pol**- ish)
1 polish is a substance used in polishing **2** a polish is a shine got by polishing • *He gave his shoes a good polish.*

polished *ADJECTIVE*
1 shiny **2** well practised or rehearsed • *The choir gave a polished performance.*

polite *ADJECTIVE* (**politer**, **politest**)
having good manners; respectful and thoughtful towards other people
▷ **politely** *ADVERB* in a polite way
▷ **politeness** *NOUN* politeness is being polite

political *ADJECTIVE*
to do with the governing of a country
▷ **politically** *ADVERB* in a way that is to do with politics

politician *NOUN* (**politicians**)
someone who is involved in politics

politics *NOUN*
politics is political matters; the business of governing a country

polka *NOUN* (**polkas**)
a lively dance

poll *NOUN* (**polls**)
1 a round of voting at an election **2** an opinion poll

pollen *NOUN*
pollen is yellow powder found inside flowers, containing male seeds for fertilizing other flowers

pollen count *NOUN* (**pollen counts**)
a measurement of how much pollen there is in the air, given as a warning for people who suffer from hay fever or asthma

pollinate *VERB* (**pollinates, pollinating, pollinated**)
to pollinate a flower or plant is to put pollen into it so that it becomes fertilized

> WORD FAMILY
> **Pollination** is the process of pollinating a flower or plant.

pollute *VERB* (**pollutes, polluting, polluted**)
to pollute a place or thing is to make it dirty or impure

pollution *NOUN*
pollution is the process of making the air, water, and soil dirty or impure

polo *NOUN*
polo is a game rather like hockey, with players on horseback using long mallets

polo neck *NOUN* (**polo necks**)
a high rounded collar that is turned over at the top

poltergeist *NOUN* (**poltergeists**) (*say* pol- ter- gyst)
a noisy mischievous ghost that damages things •*Peeves was the school poltergeist, a grinning, airborne menace who lived to cause havoc and distress.* — J. K. Rowling, *Harry Potter and the Chamber of Secrets*

poly- *PREFIX*
meaning 'many', as in *polygon*

polygon *NOUN* (**polygons**)
a figure or shape with many sides, such as a hexagon or octagon

polystyrene *NOUN* (*say* pol- i- sty- reen)
polystyrene is a kind of plastic used for insulating or packing things

polythene *NOUN* (*say* pol- i- theen)
polythene is a lightweight plastic used to make bags and wrappings

pomp *NOUN*
pomp is the dignified and solemn way in which an important ceremony is carried out

pompous *ADJECTIVE*
someone is being pompous when they are thinking too much of their own importance

> WORD FAMILY
> To show **pomposity** is to show that you think you are more important than other people; to say something **pompously** is to use long and formal words to make you sound more important.

pond *NOUN* (**ponds**)
a small lake

ponder *VERB* (**ponders, pondering, pondered**)
to ponder something is to think carefully and seriously about it

ponderous *ADJECTIVE*
1 heavy and awkward **2** dull and not easy to follow •*He writes in a ponderous style.*
▷ **ponderously** *ADVERB* in a ponderous way

pony *NOUN* (**ponies**)
a small horse

ponytail *NOUN* (**ponytails**)
a bunch of long hair tied at the back of the head

pony-trekking *NOUN*
pony-trekking is travelling across country on ponies for pleasure

poodle *NOUN* (**poodles**)
a dog with long curly hair

pool[1] *NOUN* (**pools**)
1 a pond **2** a puddle **3** a swimming pool

pool[2] *NOUN* (**pools**)
1 a group of things shared by several people **2** the fund of money that can be won in a gambling game **3** pool is a game similar to snooker but played on a smaller table
the pools a system of gambling on the results of football matches

pool *VERB* (**pools, pooling, pooled**)
to pool things is to put them all together so that everyone can share them

poor *ADJECTIVE* (**poorer, poorest**)
1 having very little money •*He came from a poor family.* **2** not good or adequate •*This is poor work.* **3** unfortunate •*Poor fellow!*

poorly *ADVERB*
not adequately •*They arrived poorly dressed.*

poorly *ADJECTIVE*
unwell •*I'm feeling poorly today.*

pop[1] *NOUN* (**pops**)
1 a pop is a small explosive sound **2** pop is a fizzy drink

pop *VERB* (**pops, popping, popped**)
1 to pop is to make a small explosive sound **2** (*informal*) to pop somewhere is to go there quickly •*I'm just popping out to the shops.* **3** to pop something somewhere is to put it there quickly •*Will you pop the potatoes in the oven?*

pop[2] *NOUN*
pop is modern popular music

popcorn *NOUN*
popcorn is maize heated till it bursts and forms light fluffy balls for eating

Pope *NOUN* (**Popes**)
the Pope is the leader of the Roman Catholic Church

poplar *NOUN* (**poplars**)
a tall straight tree

poppadam or **poppadom** *NOUN* (**poppadams** or **poppadoms**)
a thin crisp pancake that you eat with Indian food

poppy *NOUN* (**poppies**)
a plant with large red flowers

popular *ADJECTIVE*
liked or enjoyed by a lot of people

> WORD FAMILY
> **Popularity** is being liked or enjoyed by a lot of people; something is (for example) **popularly** believed when it is believed by a large number of people.

popularize *VERB* (**popularizes**, **popularizing**, **popularized**)
to popularize something is to make it known and liked by a lot of people

populated *ADJECTIVE*
a place is populated when it has people living there • *The land is thinly populated.*

population *NOUN* (**populations**)
the population of a particular place is all the people who live there; the total number of people who live there • *What's the population of London?*

populous *ADJECTIVE*
a populous place is inhabited by a lot of people

porcelain *NOUN* (*say* **por**- se- lin)
porcelain is a fine kind of china

porch *NOUN* (**porches**)
a small roofed area outside the door of a building

porcupine *NOUN* (**porcupines**)
a small animal covered with long prickles

pore [1] *NOUN* (**pores**)
one of the tiny openings in your skin which sweat can pass through

pore [2] *VERB* (**pores**, **poring**, **pored**)
to pore over something is to study it closely

> SPELLING
> Take care not to confuse **pore** with **pour**, as in *I'll pour out the milk.*

pork *NOUN*
pork is meat from a pig

pornography *NOUN* (*say* por- **nog**- ra- fi)
pornography is obscene pictures or writings
▷ **pornographic** *ADJECTIVE* to do with pornography; obscene

porous *ADJECTIVE*
something is porous when it allows liquid or air to pass through • *Sandy soil is porous.*
▷ **porosity** *NOUN* porosity is being porous

porpoise *NOUN* (**porpoises**) (*say* **por**- pus)
a sea animal rather like a small whale

porridge *NOUN*
porridge is a food made by boiling oatmeal to make a thick paste

port [1] *NOUN* (**ports**)
1 a port is a harbour **2** a port is also a city or town with a harbour **3** port is the left-hand side of a ship or aircraft when you are facing forward

port [2] *NOUN*
port is a strong red Portuguese wine

portable *ADJECTIVE*
able to be carried easily

portcullis *NOUN* (**portcullises**)
a heavy grating that can be lowered to block the gateway to a castle

porter *NOUN* (**porters**)
1 someone whose job is to carry luggage or goods **2** someone whose job is to look after the entrance to a large building

porthole *NOUN* (**portholes**)
a small round window in the side of a ship or aircraft

portion *NOUN* (**portions**)
a part or share given to someone

portly *ADJECTIVE* (**portlier**, **portliest**)
rather fat • *By dinner- time we arrived at Porlock, and dined with my old friend, Master Pooke, now growing rich and portly.* — R. D. Blackmore, *Lorna Doone*

portrait *NOUN* (**portraits**)
a picture of a person

portray *VERB* (**portrays**, **portraying**, **portrayed**)
1 to portray someone is to make a portrait of them **2** to portray something or someone is to describe or show them in a certain way • *The play portrays the king as a kind man.*

> WORD FAMILY
> The **portrayal** of something or someone is how they are described or shown.

pose *NOUN* (**poses**)
1 a way of standing or sitting for a portrait or photograph to be made of you • *Just hold that pose for a second.* **2** a pretence; unnatural behaviour to impress people

pose *VERB* (**poses**, **posing**, **posed**)
1 to pose is to put your body into a special position **2** to pose someone is to put them in a particular position to be painted or photographed **3** to pose as someone is to pretend to be them • *The man posed as a police officer.* **4** to pose a question or problem is to present it • *Icy weather always poses a problem to motorists.*

poser *NOUN* (**posers**)
1 a puzzling question or problem **2** someone who behaves in an unnatural way to impress people

posh *ADJECTIVE* (**posher**, **poshest**)(*informal*)
1 very smart; high-class •*They stayed at a posh hotel.* **2** of a high social class •*She spoke with a posh accent.*

position *NOUN* (**positions**)
1 the place where something is or should be **2** the way in which someone or something is placed or arranged •*He was sleeping in an uncomfortable position.* **3** a person's place in a race or competition **4** a situation or condition •*I am in no position to help you.* **5** a regular job

position *VERB* (**positions**, **positioning**, **positioned**)
to position something somewhere is to place it there

positive *ADJECTIVE*
1 sure or definite •*I am positive I saw him.* •*We need positive proof.* **2** agreeing or saying 'yes' •*We received a positive answer.* **3** a positive number is one that is greater than nought **4** a positive electric charge is one that does not carry electrons
▷ **positively** *ADVERB* in a positive way

positive *NOUN* (**positives**)
a photographic print made from a negative, with light and dark parts as in real life

posse *NOUN* (**posses**) (*say* poss- i)
a group of people that helps a sheriff in the USA

possess *VERB* (**possesses**, **possessing**, **possessed**)
to possess something is to own or have it
▷ **possessor** *NOUN* a person who owns or has something

possessed *ADJECTIVE*
someone is possessed when they are behaving as if they are controlled by an outside force •*He fought like a man possessed.*

possession *NOUN* (**possessions**)
1 a possession is something that you own
2 possession is owning something •*They gained possession of a piece of land.*

possessive *ADJECTIVE*
1 you are being possessive when you want to get and keep things for yourself **2** (*in grammar*) showing that someone owns something •*'His' and 'yours' are possessive pronouns.*

possibility *NOUN* (**possibilities**)
1 possibility is being possible •*Is there any possibility of changing your mind?* **2** a possibility is something that is possible •*There are many possibilities.*

possible *ADJECTIVE*
able to exist, happen, be done, or be used

possibly *ADVERB*
1 in any way •*That cannot possibly be right.*
2 perhaps •*I will arrive at six o'clock, or possibly earlier.*

post [1] *NOUN* (**posts**)
1 an upright piece of wood, concrete, or metal fixed in the ground **2** the starting point or finishing point of a race •*He was left at the post.*

post *VERB* (**posts**, **posting**, **posted**)
to post a notice or poster is to put it in a public place

post [2] *NOUN* (**posts**)
1 the post is the collecting and delivering of letters and parcels **2** post is letters and parcels carried by post; mail **3** a post is a collection or delivery of mail at a particular time •*The last post is at 4 p.m.*

post *VERB* (**posts**, **posting**, **posted**)
to post a letter or parcel is to send it to someone by post

post [3] *NOUN* (**posts**)
1 a regular job **2** the place where a sentry stands
3 a place occupied by soldiers or traders

post *VERB* (**posts**, **posting**, **posted**)
to be posted somewhere is to be sent there for a time as part of your job

post- *PREFIX*
meaning 'after', as in *post-war*

postage *NOUN*
postage is the cost of sending a letter or parcel by post

postage stamp *NOUN* (**postage stamps**)
a stamp for putting on letters and parcels, showing the amount paid

postal *ADJECTIVE*
to do with the post; by post

postal order *NOUN* (**postal orders**)
a voucher you buy at a post office, which can be sent by post and exchanged for money by the person receiving it

postbox *NOUN* (**postboxes**)
a box into which you put letters to be sent by post

postcard *NOUN* (**postcards**)
a card that you can write a message on and post without an envelope

postcode *NOUN* (**postcodes**)
a group of letters and numbers included in an address to help in sorting the post

poster *NOUN* (**posters**)
a large public notice having information or advertising something

postman *NOUN* (**postmen**)
someone who collects and delivers letters and parcels

postmark *NOUN* (**postmarks**)
an official mark stamped on something sent by post, showing when and where it was posted

post-mortem *NOUN* (**post-mortems**)
an examination of a dead body to find the cause of death

post office *NOUN* (**post offices**)
a place where you can post letters and parcels and buy stamps, postal orders, and other official documents

postpone *VERB* (**postpones, postponing, postponed**)
to postpone a meeting or event is to arrange for it to take place later than was originally planned • *The match has been postponed for two weeks.*

> WORD FAMILY
> **Postponement** is when something is arranged to take place later than was originally planned.

postscript *NOUN* (**postscripts**)
something extra added at the end of a letter or book

posture *NOUN* (**postures**)
the way that a person stands, sits, or walks

posy *NOUN* (**posies**)
a small bunch of flowers

pot[1] *NOUN* (**pots**)
1 a deep round container **2** a flowerpot
to go to pot (*informal*) is to become bad or be ruined
pots of money (*informal*) a lot of money

pot *VERB* (**pots, potting, potted**)
1 to pot a plant is to put it into a flowerpot **2** to pot a ball in a game such as snooker or pool is to hit it into a pocket

pot[2] *NOUN*
pot is the drug marijuana

potassium *NOUN*
potassium is a soft silvery-white metallic substance that living things need

potato *NOUN* (**potatoes**)
a vegetable that grows underground

potent *ADJECTIVE*
powerful • *Anne got Marilla a glassful of her potent currant wine.* — L. M. Montgomery, *Anne of Avonlea*
▷ **potency** *NOUN* the potency of something is how powerful it is
▷ **potently** *ADVERB* in a potent way

potential *ADJECTIVE*
capable of happening or becoming important or useful in the future • *She is a potential star.*
▷ **potentially** *ADVERB* as a possibility in the future • *He is potentially one of our best players.*

potential *NOUN*
to have potential is to be capable of becoming important or useful in the future

pothole *NOUN* (**potholes**)
1 a deep natural hole in the ground **2** a hole in a road

potholing *NOUN*
potholing is exploring underground caves by climbing down potholes

> WORD FAMILY
> A **potholer** is someone who goes potholing.

potion *NOUN* (**potions**) (*say* **poh**- shon)
a drink containing medicine or poison

potter[1] *NOUN* (**potters**)
someone who makes pottery

potter[2] *VERB* (**potters, pottering, pottered**)
to potter, or potter about, is to spend time doing little jobs in a relaxed way

pottery *NOUN* (**potteries**)
1 pottery is pots, cups, plates, and other things made of baked clay **2** pottery is also the craft of making pottery **3** a pottery is a place where a potter works

potty[1] *ADJECTIVE* (**pottier, pottiest**)
(*informal*) mad or silly

potty[2] *NOUN* (**potties**)
(*informal*) a small bowl used by young children as a lavatory

pouch *NOUN* (**pouches**)
1 a small bag or pocket **2** a fold of skin in which a kangaroo keeps its young

poultry *NOUN*
poultry are birds such as chickens, geese, and turkeys, kept for their eggs and meat

pounce *VERB* (**pounces, pouncing, pounced**)
to pounce on someone or something is to jump on them or attack them suddenly • *The Pelican opened his gigantic beak and immediately the policemen pounced upon the burglar who was crouching inside.* — Roald Dahl, *The Giraffe and the Pelly and Me*

pound[1] *NOUN* (**pounds**)
1 a unit of money, in Britain equal to 100 pence **2** a unit of weight equal to 16 ounces or about 454 grams

pound[2] *VERB* (**pounds, pounding, pounded**)
1 to pound something is to hit it repeatedly to crush it **2** to pound, or pound along, is to walk with heavy steps **3** your heart is pounding when it beats heavily, making a dull thumping sound • *My heart was pounding with the excitement.*

pour *VERB* (**pours, pouring, poured**)
1 to pour a liquid is to make it flow out of a container **2** to pour is to flow in a large amount • *Blood was pouring from the wound on her leg.* **3** it is

pouring when it is raining heavily **4** to pour in or out is to come or go in large numbers or amounts •*After the programme, letters of complaint poured in.* •*The fans poured out of the stadium.*

SPELLING
Take care not to confuse this word with the verb **pore**; 'pore over' means to study something closely.

pout *VERB* (**pouts**, **pouting**, **pouted**)
you pout when you stick out your lips because you are annoyed or sulking

poverty *NOUN*
poverty is being poor

powder *NOUN* (**powders**)
1 a mass of tiny pieces of something dry, like flour or dust **2** make-up in the form of powder

WORD FAMILY
Something is **powdery** when it is like powder. •*powdery snow*

powder *VERB* (**powders**, **powdering**, **powdered**)
to powder something is to put powder on it •*She powdered her face.*

WORD FAMILY
A **powdered** substance has been made into a powder. •*powdered milk*

power *NOUN* (**powers**)
1 power is strength or great energy **2** power is also control over other people **3** the power to do something is the ability to do it •*Humans have the power of speech.* **4** a power is a powerful country **5** power is also electricity or another form of energy **6** (*in mathematics*) the power of a number is the result obtained by multiplying the number by itself one or more times •*27 is the third power of 3 (3 x 3 x 3 = 27).*

WORD FAMILY
A device is (for example) electric-**powered** or solar-**powered** when it is worked by electricity or by the sun's energy.

powerful *ADJECTIVE*
having a lot of power or influence
▷ **powerfully** *ADVERB* in a powerful way

powerhouse *NOUN* (**powerhouses**)
a power station

powerless *ADJECTIVE*
someone is powerless if they are unable to act or control things

power station *NOUN* (**power stations**)
a building where electricity is produced

practicable *ADJECTIVE*
possible or able to be done •*That is not a practicable plan.*

OTHER WORD
Take care not to confuse **practicable** with **practical**, which is the next word in this dictionary.

practical *ADJECTIVE*
1 someone is practical when they are able to do or make useful things •*She is a very practical person.* **2** something is practical when it is likely to be useful •*That is a practical idea.* **3** concerned with doing or making things •*He has had practical experience.*

practical *NOUN* (**practicals**)
a lesson or examination in which you actually do or make something rather than reading or writing about it

practical joke *NOUN* (**practical jokes**)
a trick played on someone

practically *ADVERB*
1 in a practical way •*He is practically skilled.* **2** almost •*It's practically ready now.*

practice *NOUN* (**practices**)
1 practice is doing something often and regularly so that you get better at it •*I must do my piano practice.* **2** practice is also actually doing something rather than thinking or talking about it •*It's time to put this theory of yours into practice.* •*I hope my plan works in practice.* **3** a practice is the business of a doctor or lawyer

GRAMMAR
Notice that **practice** is a noun, and **practise**, which is the next word in this dictionary, is a verb.

practise *VERB* (**practises**, **practising**, **practised**)
1 to practise something is to do it often so that you get better at it **2** to practise an activity or custom is to do it regularly •*She practises yoga.* **3** to practise (for example) medicine or law is to work as a doctor or lawyer

prairie *NOUN* (**prairies**)
a large area of flat grass-covered land in North America

praise *VERB* (**praises**, **praising**, **praised**)
to praise someone or something is to say that they are good or have done well

praise *NOUN* (**praises**)
praise is words that praise someone or something

pram *NOUN* (**prams**)
a small open carriage for a baby, pushed by a person walking

prance *VERB* (**prances**, **prancing**, **pranced**)
to prance, or prance about, is to jump about in a lively or happy way • *The Scarecrow leaped all over the room, capering and skipping and prancing like a goat.* — Philip Pullman, *The Scarecrow and his Servant*

prank *NOUN* (**pranks**)
a trick played on someone for mischief

prawn *NOUN* (**prawns**)
a shellfish like a large shrimp, used for food

pray *VERB* (**prays**, **praying**, **prayed**)
1 to pray is to talk to God **2** to pray is also to ask earnestly or hope for something • *We are praying for good weather.*

> SPELLING
> Take care not to confuse **pray** with the noun **prey**, which means an animal hunted and eaten by another animal.

prayer *NOUN* (**prayers**)
1 prayer is praying **2** a prayer is what you say when you pray

pre- *PREFIX*
meaning 'before', as in *pre-war*

preach *VERB* (**preaches**, **preaching**, **preached**)
to preach is to give a talk about religion or about right and wrong

> WORD FAMILY
> A **preacher** is someone who preaches.

precarious *ADJECTIVE* (*say* pri- **kair**- i- us)
not at all safe or secure • *That vase is in a precarious position.*
▷ **precariously** *ADVERB* in a precarious way • *Somehow a porter managed to wheel Eddie's huge trunk, with Lady Constance's bags balanced precariously on top, out of the busy station.* — Philip Ardagh, *Terrible Times*

precaution *NOUN* (**precautions**)
something you do to prevent trouble or danger in the future

precede *VERB* (**precedes**, **preceding**, **preceded**)
one thing precedes another when it comes or goes in front of the other thing • *The film was preceded by a short cartoon.*

> WORD FAMILY
> One person or thing takes **precedence** over another when they have the right to go first.

precinct *NOUN* (**precincts**) (*say* **pree**- sinkt)
1 a part of a town where traffic is not allowed • *The town has a large shopping precinct.* **2** the area round a cathedral

precious *ADJECTIVE*
very valuable or loved • *Remembering her precious cordial, Lucy poured a few drops into her brother's mouth.* — C. S. Lewis, *The Lion, The Witch and the Wardrobe*

precipice *NOUN* (**precipices**)
the steep face of a mountain or cliff

précis *NOUN* (**précis**) (*say* **pray**- see)
a brief statement or summary of the main points of something

precise *ADJECTIVE*
1 clear and accurate • *I gave them precise instructions.* **2** exact • *At that precise moment, the doorbell rang.*

> WORD FAMILY
> To do something **precisely** is to do it accurately and carefully; **precision** is being exact or accurate.

predator *NOUN* (**predators**) (*say* **pred**- a- ter)
an animal that hunts other animals

> WORD FAMILY
> **Predatory** animals hunt other animals.

predecessor *NOUN* (**predecessors**) (*say* **pree**- di- ses- er)
an earlier person or thing, such as an ancestor or someone who once did the job you do now

predict *VERB* (**predicts**, **predicting**, **predicted**)
to predict something is to say that it will happen in the future

> WORD FAMILY
> Something is **predictable** when you are able to say what will happen before it actually happens; a **prediction** is something that someone predicts.

predominant *ADJECTIVE*
most important or largest in size or number
▷ **predominance** *NOUN* predominance is being predominant
▷ **predominantly** *ADVERB* mostly; most importantly

predominate *VERB* (**predominates**, **predominating**, **predominated**)
to predominate is to be the largest in size or number, or the most important • *Girls predominate in our class.*

preen *VERB* (**preens**, **preening**, **preened**)
a bird preens when it smoothes and cleans its feathers using its beak

preface *NOUN* (**prefaces**) (*say* **pref**- ass)
an introduction at the beginning of a book

a b c d e f g h i j k l m n o **p** q r s t u v w x y z

prefect *NOUN* (**prefects**)
1 a school pupil who is given authority to help to keep order **2** a local official in some countries

prefer *VERB* (**prefers**, **preferring**, **preferred**)
to prefer one thing to another is to like it better than the other thing

> WORD FAMILY
> Your **preference** is what you prefer.

preferable *ADJECTIVE* (*say* pref- er- a- bul)
something is preferable to something else when it is better or you like it more

> WORD FAMILY
> You use **preferably** to say what you would prefer • *Ring me tomorrow, preferably before 10 o'clock.*

prefix *NOUN* (**prefixes**)
a word or syllable joined to the front of a word to change or add to its meaning, as in *dis*order, *out*stretched, and *un*happy

PREFIXES

Prefix	Meaning
anti-	against
arch-	chief
auto-	self
com-; con-	together; with
contra-	against
de-	removing something
dis-	not; taking away
em-, en-	in; into
ex-	that used to be
extra-	more; outside
fore-	before
il-, im-, in-, ir-	not
il-, im-, in-, ir-, etc-	in; into
inter-	between
mis-	wrong
mono-	one
multi-	many
non-	not
over-	too much
poly-	many
post-	after
pre-	before
pro-	supporting
re-	again
semi-	half
sub-	below
super-	over; beyond
tele-	at a distance
trans-	across
ultra-	beyond
un-	not

pregnant *ADJECTIVE*
a pregnant woman has an unborn baby growing inside her womb

> WORD FAMILY
> **Pregnacy** is being pregnant.

prehistoric *ADJECTIVE*
belonging to a very long time ago, before written records were kept

> WORD FAMILY
> **Prehistory** is the time long ago, before written records were kept.

prejudice *NOUN* (**prejudices**)
a prejudice is when you make up your mind that you don't like someone or something without a good reason or without thinking about it

> WORD FAMILY
> To be **prejudiced** against someone is to dislike them without a good reason or without thinking about it.

preliminary *ADJECTIVE*
coming before something or preparing for it

prelude *NOUN* (**preludes**) (*say* prel- yood)
1 an introduction to a play, poem, or event **2** a short piece of music

premature *ADJECTIVE*
happening or coming before the proper time • *a premature baby*

premier *NOUN* (**premiers**) (*say* prem- i- er)
the leader of a government

> SPELLING
> Take care not to confuse **premier** with **première**, which is the next word in this dictionary.

première *NOUN* (**premières**) (*say* prem- yair)
the first public performance of a play or showing of a film

premises *PLURAL NOUN*
an organization's or business's premises are the building and land it uses

premium *NOUN* (**premiums**) (*say* pree- mi- um)
an amount paid regularly to an insurance company
to be at a premium is to be valued highly and perhaps expensive because of this

Premium Bond *NOUN* (**Premium Bonds**)
a government savings certificate that gives the owner a chance to win a money prize in a draw

premonition *NOUN* (**premonitions**)
a feeling that something bad is going to happen

preoccupied *ADJECTIVE*
you are preoccupied when you are thinking hard about something and don't notice other things

> WORD FAMILY
> A **preoccupation** is something you think about most of the time.

prep *NOUN*
(*informal*) prep is homework

preparation *NOUN* (**preparations**)
1 preparation is getting something ready
2 preparations are things you do in order to get ready for something • *We were making last-minute preparations.*

preparatory *ADJECTIVE* (*say* pri- **pa**- ra- ter- i)
preparing for something

preparatory school *NOUN* (**preparatory schools**)
a school that prepares pupils for a higher school

prepare *VERB* (**prepares, preparing, prepared**)
to prepare something is to get it ready
to be prepared to do something is to be ready or willing to do it

preposition *NOUN* (**prepositions**)
a word you put in front of a noun or pronoun to show how the noun or pronoun is connected with another word, for example *on* in the sentence *Put the flowers on the table* and *with* in the sentence *I'd like some sauce with my food*

PREPOSITIONS
Prepositions are words that tell you how nouns and pronouns are connected with other words. They usually come before nouns or noun phrases. For example, *on* is a preposition in the sentence *Humpty Dumpty sat on a wall*, and *during* is a preposition in the sentence *She fell asleep during the film*. You can sometimes put a preposition at the end of a sentence, like *at* in the sentence *What are you looking at?* Prepositions can show - where something is: *The dog is **in** its basket.* - where something is going: *He was running **towards** us.* - when something happens: *I'll see you **after** lunch.* - how long something lasts: *We stayed there **for** a week.*

prep school *NOUN* (**prep schools**)
a preparatory school

prescribe *VERB* (**prescribes, prescribing, prescribed**)
1 to prescribe a medicine for a patient is to instruct them to take it and give them a prescription for it **2** to prescribe a method or solution is to say what must be done

prescription *NOUN* (**prescriptions**)
a doctor's order for a medicine to be prepared for a patient

presence *NOUN*
your presence somewhere is the fact that you are there • *Your presence is expected.*
in the presence of someone while they are there, in the same place

present[1] *ADJECTIVE* (*say* **prez**- ent)
1 in a particular place; here • *Nobody else was present.* **2** existing or happening now • *Who is the present Queen?*

present *NOUN* (*say* **prez**- ent)
the present is the time now • *Our teacher is away at present.*

present[2] *NOUN* (**presents**) (*say* **prez**- ent)
something that you give to someone or receive from them

present *VERB* (**presents, presenting, presented**) (*say* pri- **zent**)
1 to present something to someone is to give it to them, especially with a ceremony • *Who will present the prizes this year?* **2** to present a play or other entertainment is to perform it or arrange for it to be performed **3** to present a radio or television programme is to introduce it to the audience **4** to present something you have done or made is to show it formally to people • *We are here to present our latest products.*

presentation *NOUN* (**presentations**)
1 a formal talk showing or demonstrating something **2** a ceremony in which someone is given a gift or prize • *I'd like to make a little presentation.*

presenter *NOUN* (**presenters**)
someone who presents something, especially a radio or television programme

presently *ADVERB*
soon; in a while

present participle *NOUN* (**present participles**)
a form of a verb used after *am, are, is* to describe an action that is happening now, or used after *was, were, has been, have been,*
had been to describe an action that went on for some time in the past, for example *looking* in the sentences *I am looking at the pictures* and *I was looking at the pictures*

present tense *NOUN*
a form of a verb used to describe something that is happening now, for example *likes* in the sentence *He likes swimming*

preservative *NOUN* (**preservatives**)
a substance added to food to preserve it

preserve *VERB* (**preserves, preserving, preserved**)
to preserve something is to keep it safe or in good condition

WORD FAMILY
Preservation is preserving something.

preside *VERB* (**presides, presiding, presided**) (*say* pri- **zyd**)
to preside over a meeting or other occasion is to be in charge of it

a b c d e f g h i j k l m n o p q r s t u v w x y z

president *NOUN* (**presidents**)
1 the head of a country that is a republic **2** the person in charge of a society, business, or club

> WORD FAMILY
> The **presidency** is the job of being a president; **presidential** means to do with a president.

press *VERB* (**presses, pressing, pressed**)
1 to press something is to push it firmly or squeeze it • *Press the red button.* **2** to press clothes is to make them flat and smooth with an iron **3** to press someone for something is to urge them to do or give it • *She's pressing me for a decision.*

press *NOUN* (**presses**)
1 the action of squeezing or pushing on something • *Give the bell another press.* **2** the press are newspapers and journalists **3** a machine for printing things **4** a business that prints or publishes books **5** a device for flattening and smoothing things • *a trouser press*

press conference *NOUN* (**press conferences**)
an interview given by a politician or other important person with a group of journalists

press-up *NOUN* (**press-ups**)
an exercise in which you lie face downwards and push down with your hands to lift your body

pressure *NOUN* (**pressures**)
1 pressure is continuous pushing or squeezing • *Apply pressure to the cut to stop it bleeding.* **2** pressure is also the force with which a liquid or gas pushes against something **3** there is pressure on you when someone is trying to persuade or force you to do something

pressurize *VERB* (**pressurizes, pressurizing, pressurized**)
1 to pressurize a place or compartment is to keep it at the same air pressure all the time • *The aircraft is pressurized.* **2** to pressurize someone is to try to force them to do something

prestige *NOUN* (*say* pres- teezh)
prestige is the respect something has because it is important or of a high quality

> WORD FAMILY
> Something is **prestigious** when it is respected for being important or of a high quality.

presumably *ADVERB*
probably; I suppose

presume *VERB* (**presumes, presuming, presumed**)
1 to presume something is to suppose it • *I presumed that he was dead.* **2** to presume to do something is to dare to do it • *I wouldn't presume to advise you.*

> WORD FAMILY
> **Presumption** is supposing that something is probably true; **presumption** is also being too bold or confident.

presumptuous *ADJECTIVE*
too bold or confident

pretence *NOUN* (**pretences**)
a pretence is an attempt to pretend something

pretend *VERB* (**pretends, pretending, pretended**)
1 to pretend is to behave as if something untrue or imaginary is true **2** to pretend something is to claim it dishonestly • *They pretended they were policemen.*

pretender *NOUN* (**pretenders**)
someone who claims a country's throne

pretty *ADJECTIVE* (**prettier, prettiest**)
pleasant to look at or hear; attractive
▷ **prettily** *ADVERB* in a pretty way
▷ **prettiness** *NOUN* prettiness is being pretty

pretty *ADVERB*
(*informal*) quite; moderately • *It's pretty cold outside.*

prevail *VERB* (**prevails, prevailing, prevailed**)
1 to prevail is to be most frequent or general • *The prevailing view is that we were wrong.* **2** to prevail is also to be successful in a battle, contest, or game

prevalent *ADJECTIVE*
most frequent or common; widespread

prevent *VERB* (**prevents, preventing, prevented**)
1 to prevent something is to stop it from happening or make it impossible **2** to prevent someone is to stop them from doing something

> WORD FAMILY
> **Prevention** is stopping something bad from happening; something that is **preventive** is meant to help prevent something. • *preventive medicine*

preview *NOUN* (**previews**)
a showing of a film or play before it is shown to the public

previous *ADJECTIVE*
coming before this; preceding • *I was in London the previous week.*

> WORD FAMILY
> To happen **previously** is to happen before or earlier.

prey *NOUN* (*say* pray)
an animal that is hunted or killed by another animal for food

prey *VERB* (**preys, preying, preyed**) (*say* pray)
to prey on something is to hunt and kill an animal for food • *Owls prey on mice and other small animals.* **to prey on your mind** is to worry you a lot

> SPELLING
> Take care not to confuse **prey** with **pray**, which means to say prayers.

price *NOUN* (**prices**)
1 the amount of money for which something is sold **2** what you have to give or do to get something • *What is the price of peace?*
at any price at any cost

price *VERB* (**prices, pricing, priced**)
to price something is to decide its price

> WORD FAMILY
> Something is **pricey** when it is expensive.

priceless *ADJECTIVE*
1 very valuable **2** (*informal*) very amusing

prick *VERB* (**pricks, pricking, pricked**)
1 to prick something is to make a tiny hole in it **2** to prick someone is to hurt them with something sharp or pointed
to prick up your ears is to start listening suddenly

prick *NOUN* (**pricks**)
a prick is a pricking feeling

prickle *NOUN* (**prickles**)
a sharp point on a plant or animal

> WORD FAMILY
> Something **prickly** is covered in prickles or feels like prickles.

prickle *VERB* (**prickles, prickling, prickled**)
to prickle is to make your skin feel as though lots of little sharp points are sticking into it • *This jumper is prickling me.*

pride *NOUN* (**prides**)
1 pride is a feeling of being very pleased with yourself or with someone else who has done well • *My heart swelled with pride.* **2** pride is also being too satisfied because of who you are or what you have done **3** a pride is something that makes you feel proud • *This stamp is the pride of my collection.* **4** a pride is also a group of lions

priest *NOUN* (**priests**)
1 a member of the clergy **2** someone who conducts religious ceremonies; a religious leader

> WORD FAMILY
> The **priesthood** is the position of being a priest.

priestess *NOUN* (**priestesses**)
a female priest in a non-Christian religion

prig *NOUN* (**prigs**)
someone who is smug and self-righteous

> WORD FAMILY
> A **priggish** person is smug and self-righteous.

prim *ADJECTIVE* (**primmer, primmest**)
liking things to be correct, and easily shocked by anything rude
▷ **primly** *ADVERB* in a prim way
▷ **primness** *NOUN* primness is being prim

primary *ADJECTIVE*
first; most important

> WORD FAMILY
> **Primarily** means mainly or most importantly.

primary colour *NOUN* (**primary colours**)
one of the colours from which all other colours can be made by mixing: red, yellow, and blue for paint, and red, green, and violet for light

primary school *NOUN* (**primary schools**)
a school for the first stage of a child's education, between the ages of 5 and 11

primate *NOUN* (**primates**)
1 an animal of the group that includes human beings, apes, and monkeys **2** an archbishop

prime *ADJECTIVE*
1 chief or most important • *The weather was the prime cause of the accident.* **2** of the best quality

prime *NOUN* (**primes**)
the best part or stage of something • *He was in the prime of life.*

prime *VERB* (**primes, priming, primed**)
1 to prime something is to get it ready for use • *Pour water into the pump to prime it.* **2** to prime a surface is to put a special liquid on it before painting it

prime minister *NOUN* (**prime ministers**)
the leader of a government

prime number *NOUN* (**prime numbers**)
a number that can only be divided exactly by itself and the number one, for example 2, 3, 5, 7, and 11

primer *NOUN* (**primers**)
1 primer is paint used for the first coat on an unpainted surface **2** a primer is a textbook dealing with the first or simplest stages of a subject

primeval *ADJECTIVE* (*say* pry- **mee**- val)
belonging to the earliest times of the world; ancient

primitive *ADJECTIVE*
1 at an early stage of development or civilization • *Primitive humans were hunters rather than farmers.* **2** basic or simple • *Our accommodation was fairly primitive.*

primrose *NOUN* (**primroses**)
a pale yellow flower that comes out in spring

prince *NOUN* (**princes**)
1 the son of a king or queen **2** a man or boy in a royal family

> WORD FAMILY
> A **princely** sum is a large or generous amount of money, although you often mean the opposite when you say this • *I bought a bike for the princely sum of £20.*

princess *NOUN* (**princesses**)
1 the daughter of a king or queen **2** a woman or girl in a royal family **3** the wife of a prince

principal *ADJECTIVE*
chief or most important • *Name the principal cities of Britain.*

> **WORD FAMILY**
> **Principally** means chiefly or mainly.

principal *NOUN* (**principals**)
the head of a college or school

> **SPELLING**
> Take care not to confuse **principal** with **principle**, which is the next word in this dictionary.

principle *NOUN* (**principles**)
1 a general rule or truth • *She taught me the principles of geometry.* **2** someone's principles are the basic rules and beliefs they have about how they should behave
in principle in general, not in detail • *I agree with your plan in principle.*

print *VERB* (**prints, printing, printed**)
1 to print words or pictures is to put them on paper with a machine **2** to print letters is to write them separately and not joined together **3** to print a photograph is to make it from a negative

print *NOUN* (**prints**)
1 print is printed words or pictures **2** a print is a mark made by something pressing on a surface • *Her thumb left a print on the glass.* **3** a print is also a photograph made from a negative

printed circuit *NOUN* (**printed circuits**)
an electric circuit made by pressing thin metal strips on to a board

printer *NOUN* (**printers**)
1 a machine that prints on paper from data in a computer **2** someone who prints books or newspapers

printout *NOUN* (**printouts**)
the information printed on paper from data in a computer

priority *NOUN* (**priorities**) (*say* pry- o- ri- ti)
1 a priority is something that is more urgent or important than other things and needs to be dealt with first • *Repairing the roof is a priority.* **2** priority is the right to go first or be considered before other things • *People in need of urgent medical help will have priority.*

prise *VERB* (**prises, prising, prised**)
to prise something open is to force or lever it open • *He prised open the lid with a screwdriver.* • *Woken by Latch's gargling tooth-brushing sounds, Titus prised his eyes open.* — Debi Gliori, *Pure Dead Wicked*

prism *NOUN* (**prisms**)
1 a piece of glass that breaks up light into the colours of the rainbow **2** (*in mathematics*) a solid object with parallel ends that are equal triangles or polygons

prison *NOUN* (**prisons**)
a place where criminals are kept as a punishment

prisoner *NOUN* (**prisoners**)
someone who is kept in a prison or who is a captive

privacy *NOUN*
privacy is being private or away from other people • *Our new garden fence will give us more privacy.*

private *ADJECTIVE*
1 belonging to a particular person or group of people • *This is a private road.* **2** meant to be kept secret • *These letters are private.* **3** away from other people • *Is there a private place to swim?*
in private where only particular people can see or hear; not in public

> **WORD FAMILY**
> To do something **privately** is to do it away from other people • *Can we speak privately?*

private *NOUN* (**privates**)
a soldier of the lowest rank

privatize *VERB* (**privatizes, privatizing, privatized**)
to privatize a public business or organization is to sell it to private owners to run

> **WORD FAMILY**
> **Privatization** is privatizing businesses and organizations.

privet *NOUN*
privet is an evergreen shrub with small leaves, used to make hedges

privilege *NOUN* (**privileges**)
a special right or advantage given to one person or group of people

> **WORD FAMILY**
> To be **privileged** is to have special advantages that other people don't have.

prize *NOUN* (**prizes**)
1 something you get for winning a game or competition, or for doing well in an examination **2** something taken from an enemy

prize *VERB* (**prizes, prizing, prized**)
to prize something is to value it highly

pro *NOUN* (**pros**)
(*informal*) a professional

pro- *PREFIX*
meaning 'in favour of' or 'supporting', as in *pro-government*

probability *NOUN* (**probabilities**)
the probability of something is how likely it is to happen

probable *ADJECTIVE*
likely to be true or to happen

WORD FAMILY
You say that something will **probably** happen or is **probably** true when you think it is likey to happen or be true.

probation *NOUN*
probation is a time when someone is tried out in a new job to make sure they are suitable for the work **on probation** being supervised by a probation officer
▷ **probationary** *ADJECTIVE* being on probation

probation officer *NOUN* (**probation officers**)
an official who supervises the behaviour of someone convicted of a crime but not sent to prison

probe *NOUN* (**probes**)
1 a long thin instrument used to look closely at something such as a wound **2** an investigation

probe *VERB* (**probes**, **probing**, **probed**)
1 to probe something is to look at it with a probe **2** to probe is to investigate

problem *NOUN* (**problems**)
something difficult to answer or deal with

procedure *NOUN* (**procedures**)
a fixed or special way of doing something

proceed *VERB* (**proceeds**, **proceeding**, **proceeded**) (*say* pro- seed)
to proceed is to go on or continue

proceedings *PLURAL NOUN*
1 things that happen; activities **2** a lawsuit

proceeds *PLURAL NOUN* (*say* proh- seedz)
the proceeds of a sale or event are the money made from it

process *NOUN* (**processes**)
a series of actions for making or doing something **to be in the process of doing something** is to be in the middle of doing it

process *VERB* (**processes**, **processing**, **processed**)
to process something is to treat it or deal with it by a process so that it can be used • *He took the film to the chemist to be processed.*

procession *NOUN* (**processions**)
a number of people or vehicles moving steadily forwards

proclaim *VERB* (**proclaims**, **proclaiming**, **proclaimed**)
to proclaim something is to announce it officially or publicly

WORD FAMILY
A **proclamation** is a public announcement.

prod *VERB* (**prods**, **prodding**, **prodded**)
to prod something or someone is to poke or jab them

prodigal *ADJECTIVE*
wasteful or extravagant
▷ **prodigality** *NOUN* prodigality is being wasteful or extravagant

produce *VERB* (**produces**, **producing**, **produced**)
(*say* pro- **dewss**)
1 to produce something is to make or create it **2** to produce something that is hidden or put away is to bring it out so that people can see it **3** to produce a play or film or other entertainment is to organize the performance of it

produce *NOUN* (*say* prod- yewss)
produce is things produced, especially by farmers

producer *NOUN* (**producers**)
someone who produces a play or film

product *NOUN* (**products**)
1 something someone makes or produces for sale **2** the result of multiplying two numbers • *12 is the product of 4 and 3.*

production *NOUN* (**productions**)
1 production is the process of making or creating something • *The factory is engaged in car production.* **2** production is also the amount someone produces or makes • *Oil production increased last year.* **3** a production is a version of a play or film

productive *ADJECTIVE*
producing a lot of good or useful things

productivity *NOUN*
productivity is the rate at which someone works or produces thing

profession *NOUN* (**professions**)
a type of work for which you need special knowledge and training, for example medicine, law, or teaching

professional *ADJECTIVE*
1 doing a certain type of work to earn money • *He became a professional tennis player.* **2** to do with a profession **3** you can describe something done with great skill and to a high standard as professional

WORD FAMILY
To do something **professionally** is to do it in a professional way.

professional *NOUN* (**professionals**)
someone doing a certain type of work to earn money

professor *NOUN* (**professors**)
a teacher of the highest rank in a university

proficient *ADJECTIVE* (*say* pro- **fish**- ent)
to be proficient at something is to be able to do it well

> WORD FAMILY
> You show **proficiency** at something when you are able to do it well; to do something **proficiently** is to do it well.

profile *NOUN* (**profiles**)
1 a person's profile is a side view of their face **2** a short description of a person's life or character

profit *NOUN* (**profits**)
1 the extra money got by selling something for more than it cost to buy or make **2** an advantage or benefit

profit *VERB* (**profits**, **profiting**, **profited**)
to profit from something is to get an advantage from it

profitable *ADJECTIVE*
making a profit; bringing in money

> WORD FAMILY
> To do something **profitably** is to make a profit doing it.

profound *ADJECTIVE*
1 very deep or intense • *His death had a profound effect on us all.* **2** showing or needing great knowledge or thought • *The poem she wrote was quite profound.*

> WORD FAMILY
> Something **profoundly** affects you when it has a very great effect on you; **profundity** is being very serious or intense.

profuse *ADJECTIVE* (*say* pro- **fewss**)
produced in large amounts; plentiful • *He offered his profuse thanks.*

> WORD FAMILY
> To (for example) apologize **profusely** is to keep apologizing again and again; a **profusion** of something is a very large amount of it.

program *NOUN* (**programs**)
a series of coded instructions for a computer to carry out

program *VERB* (**programs**, **programming**, **programmed**)
to program a computer is to prepare or control it by means of a program

> SPELLING
> This is the American spelling of the word **programme**, and is used when you are talking about computers.

programme *NOUN* (**programmes**)
1 a show, play, or talk on radio or television **2** a list of a planned series of events **3** a leaflet or pamphlet that gives details of a play, concert, or other event

progress *NOUN* (*say* **proh**- gress)
1 progress is forward movement • *The procession made slow progress.* **2** progress is also development or improvement • *You have made a lot of progress this term.*

progress *VERB* (**progresses**, **progressing**, **progressed**) (*say* pro- **gress**)
1 to progress is to move forward **2** to progress is also to develop or improve

> WORD FAMILY
> The **progression** of something is when it develops or moves forward; something is described as **progressive** when it happens or develops steadily.

prohibit *VERB* (**prohibits**, **prohibiting**, **prohibited**)
to prohibit something is to forbid it, especially by law • *Smoking is prohibited.*

> WORD FAMILY
> **Prohibition** is stopping something being done or used.

project *NOUN* (**projects**) (*say* **proj**- ekt)
1 a planned task in which you find out as much as you can about something and write about it **2** a plan or scheme

project *VERB* (**projects**, **projecting**, **projected**) (*say* pro- **jekt**)
1 to project is to stick out **2** to project your voice is to speak loudly and clearly so that it carries a long way **3** to project a picture or film is to show it with a projector on a screen

> WORD FAMILY
> **Projection** is showing a picture or film on a screen with a projector; a **projection** is a part of something that sticks out.

projectionist *NOUN* (**projectionists**)
someone who works a projector

projector *NOUN* (**projectors**)
a machine for showing films or photographs on a screen

prologue *NOUN* (**prologues**) (*say* **proh**- log)
an introduction to a poem or play or long story

prolong *VERB* (**prolongs**, **prolonging**, **prolonged**)
to prolong something is to make it last longer

promenade *NOUN* (**promenades**) (*say* prom- en- **ahd**)
1 a place suitable for walking, especially beside the seashore **2** a leisurely walk

prominent *ADJECTIVE*
1 easily seen; standing out • *She has prominent teeth.* **2** important
▷ **prominence** *NOUN* prominence is being prominent
▷ **prominently** *ADVERB* in a prominent way

promise *NOUN* (**promises**)
1 a promise is a statement that you will definitely do or not do something **2** something shows promise when it shows signs that it will be successful in the future

promise *VERB* (**promises**, **promising**, **promised**)
to promise to do something is to say that you will definitely do it

promising *ADJECTIVE*
likely to be good or successful • *We have several promising pupils.*

promontory *NOUN* (**promontories**) (*say* prom- on- ter- i)
a piece of high land sticking out into the sea • *Beyond the promontory was a wide bay with deep beds of rushes on either side of it.* — Arthur Ransome, *Swallows and Amazons*

promote *VERB* (**promotes**, **promoting**, **promoted**)
1 to be promoted is to be given a more senior or more important job or rank **2** a sports team is promoted when it moves to a higher division or league **3** to promote a product or cause is to make people more aware of it • *He has done much to promote the cause of peace.*
▷ **promoter** *NOUN* someone who promotes something

promotion *NOUN* (**promotions**)
1 promotion is when someone is given a more senior or more important job or rank **2** promotion is also when a sports team moves to a higher division or league **3** a promotion is a piece of publicity or advertising

prompt *ADJECTIVE* (**prompter**, **promptest**)
happening soon or without delay • *We need a prompt reply.*

> WORD FAMILY
> To do something **promptly** is to do it without delay; **promptness** is being prompt.

prompt *VERB* (**prompts**, **prompting**, **prompted**)
1 to prompt someone to do something is to cause or encourage them to do it **2** to prompt an actor is to remind them of their words if they forget them during a play

> WORD FAMILY
> The **prompter** is the person who prompts actors in a play.

prone *ADJECTIVE*
lying face downwards
to be prone to something is to be likely to do it or suffer from it • *He is prone to jealousy.*

prong *NOUN* (**prongs**)
one of the pointed spikes at the end of a fork

pronoun *NOUN* (**pronouns**)
a word used instead of a noun, such as *he*, *her*, *it*, *them*, *those*

> PRONOUNS
> Pronouns are words you use instead of a noun phrase, usually in order that you don't have to repeat a noun phrase you've already used. Instead of saying *Jess was wearing her new hat. Jess bought the hat yesterday.* you could say *Jess was wearing her new hat. She bought it yesterday.* Personal pronouns refer to people and things. They include *I, you, he, she, it, we, they, me, him, her, us, them.* Possessive pronouns show who owns something.
> They include *mine, yours, his, hers, ours, theirs.*

pronounce *VERB* (**pronounces**, **pronouncing**, **pronounced**)
1 to pronounce a word is to say it in a particular way • *'Too' and 'two' are pronounced the same.* **2** to pronounce something is to declare it formally • *I now pronounce you man and wife.*

pronounced *ADJECTIVE*
noticeable; definite • *This street has a pronounced slope.*

pronouncement *NOUN* (**pronouncements**)
something said formally; a declaration

pronunciation *NOUN* (**pronunciations**) (*say* pro- nun- si- **ay**- shon)
the way a word is pronounced

> SPELLING
> Notice the spelling of this word. It is wrong to spell it *pronounciation*.

proof *NOUN* (**proofs**)
1 proof is a fact which shows that something is true or exists • *There is no proof that she stole the money.* **2** a proof is a printed copy of something made for checking before other copies are printed

proof *ADJECTIVE*
giving protection against something • *They wore bullet-proof jackets.*

prop[1] *NOUN* (**props**)
a support, especially one made of a long piece of wood or metal

prop *VERB* (**props**, **propping**, **propped**)
to prop something somewhere is to lean it there so that it doesn't fall over • *The ladder was propped up against the wall.*

prop[2] *NOUN* (**props**)
a piece of furniture or other object used on stage in a theatre

propaganda *NOUN*
propaganda is information, especially false information, that is spread around to make people believe something

propel *VERB* (**propels**, **propelling**, **propelled**)
to propel something is to move it rapidly forward

a b c d e f g h i j k l m n o p q r s t u v w x y z

propellant *NOUN* (**propellants**)
liquid fuel for a rocket

propeller *NOUN* (**propellers**)
a device with blades that spin round to drive an aircraft or ship

proper *ADJECTIVE*
1 suitable or right • *This is the proper way to hold a bat.* **2** respectable • *You must behave in a proper fashion.* **3** (*informal*) complete; great • *He's a proper nuisance.*

> WORD FAMILY
> To do something **properly** is to do it in a way that is correct or suitable.

proper fraction *NOUN* (**proper fractions**)
a fraction that is less than 1, such as $\frac{1}{2}$ or $\frac{3}{5}$

proper noun *NOUN* (**proper nouns**)
the name given to one person or thing, such as *Mary* and *Tokyo*, and usually written with a capital first letter

property *NOUN* (**properties**)
1 a person's property is a thing, or all the things, that belong to them **2** a property is buildings or land belonging to someone **3** a property is also a quality or characteristic that something has • *Rubber has elastic properties.*

prophecy *NOUN* (**prophecies**) (*say* **prof**- i- si)
1 a prophecy is something that someone has said will happen in the future **2** prophecy is saying what will happen in the future

> SPELLING
> Take care not to confuse **prophecy** with **prophesy**, which is a verb and is the next word in this dictionary.

prophesy *VERB* (**prophesies**, **prophesying**, **prophesied**) (*say* **prof**- i- sy)
to prophesy something is to say that it will happen in the future

prophet *NOUN* (**prophets**)
1 someone who makes prophecies **2** a religious teacher who is believed to speak the word of God
the Prophet a name for Muhammad, the founder of the Muslim faith

prophetic *ADJECTIVE*
saying or showing what will happen in the future

proportion *NOUN* (**proportions**)
1 a fraction or share of something • *Water covers a large proportion of the earth's surface.* **2** the proportion of one thing to another is how much there is of one compared to the other • *What is the proportion of oil to vinegar in this salad dressing?* **3** the correct relationship between the size, amount, or importance of two things • *You've drawn the head out of proportion with the body.*
proportions size or scale • *It is a ship of large proportions.*

proportional or **proportionate** *ADJECTIVE*
in proportion; according to a ratio
▷ **proportionally** or **proportionately** *ADVERB* in proportion

propose *VERB* (**proposes**, **proposing**, **proposed**)
1 to propose an idea or plan is to suggest it **2** to propose to someone is to ask them to marry you

proposal *NOUN* (**proposals**)
1 a suggestion **2** when someone asks another person to marry them

proprietor *NOUN* (**proprietors**) (*say* pro- **pry**- et- er)
the owner of a shop or business

propulsion *NOUN*
propulsion is propelling something or driving it forward

prose *NOUN*
prose is writing that is like ordinary speech, not poetry or verse

prosecute *VERB* (**prosecutes**, **prosecuting**, **prosecuted**)
1 to prosecute someone is to make them go to a lawcourt to be tried for a crime

> WORD FAMILY
> **Prosecution** is the process of prosecuting someone; a **prosecutor** is an official who prosecutes people.

prospect *NOUN* (**prospects**) (*say* **pros**- pekt)
1 a possibility or hope; what may happen in the future • *There's not much prospect of the weather improving.* **2** a wide view • *We saw a vast prospect from the top of the hill.*

prospect *VERB* (**prospects**, **prospecting**, **prospected**) (*say* pro- **spekt**)
to prospect is to search for gold or some other mineral

> WORD FAMILY
> A **prospector** is someone who prospects for gold or another mineral.

prosper *VERB* (**prospers**, **prospering**, **prospered**)
to prosper is to be successful or do well

prosperous *ADJECTIVE*
successful or rich

> WORD FAMILY
> **Prosperity** is being successful or rich.

prostitute *NOUN* (**prostitutes**)
someone who takes part in sexual acts for payment

protect *VERB* (**protects**, **protecting**, **protected**)
to protect someone or something is to keep them safe

> WORD FAMILY
> **Protection** is keeping someone or something safe; a **protector** is a person who protects someone or something.

protective *ADJECTIVE*
1 a person is protective when they want to protect someone or something **2** a thing is protective when it is meant to protect something

protein *NOUN* (**proteins**) (*say* **proh**- teen)
protein is a substance found in some types of food, for example meat, eggs, and cheese. Your body needs protein to help you grow and be healthy

protest *NOUN* (**protests**) (*say* **proh**- test)
something you say or do because you disapprove of someone or something

protest *VERB* (**protests**, **protesting**, **protested**) (*say* pro- **test**)
to protest about something is to say publicly that you think it is wrong

> WORD FAMILY
> A **protester** is someone who protests about something.

Protestant *NOUN* (**Protestants**) (*say* **prot**- is- tant)
a member of a western Christian Church other than the Roman Catholic Church

proton *NOUN* (**protons**)
a particle of matter with a positive electric charge

protoplasm *NOUN* (*say* **proh**- to- plazm)
protoplasm is a colourless substance that animal and vegetable cells are made of

prototype *NOUN* (**prototypes**) (*say* **proh**- to- typ)
the first example of something, used as a model for making others

protractor *NOUN* (**protractors**)
a device in the shape of a semicircle, used for measuring and drawing angles on paper

protrude *VERB* (**protrudes**, **protruding**, **protruded**)
to protrude is to stick out • *He had protruding eyes.*

> WORD FAMILY
> A **protrusion** is something that sticks out from a surface.

proud *ADJECTIVE* (**prouder**, **proudest**)
1 very pleased with yourself or with someone else who has done well • *I am proud of my sister.* **2** too satisfied because of who you are or what you have done • *They were too proud to ask for help.*

> WORD FAMILY
> You do something **proudly** when you do it in a way that shows you are proud of something.

prove *VERB* (**proves**, **proving**, **proved**)
1 to prove something is to show that it is true **2** to prove to be something is to turn out to be that way • *The forecast proved to be correct.*

proverb *NOUN* (**proverbs**)
a short well-known saying that states a truth or gives advice, for example *many hands make light work*

proverbial *ADJECTIVE*
1 occurring in a proverb **2** familiar or well-known

provide *VERB* (**provides**, **providing**, **provided**)
1 to provide something is to supply it **2** to provide for something is to prepare for it • *They have provided for all possible disasters.*
provided or **providing** on condition; on condition that • *The jungle, you should know, / Can be a thrilling place to go. / Provided that you do not sin / Against the beasts that live therein.* — Dick King-Smith, *Jungle Jingles*

province *NOUN* (**provinces**)
1 a region or division of a country **2** an area of knowledge or skill
the provinces the part of a country outside the capital

> WORD FAMILY
> A **provincial** town is in a part of a country away from the capital.

provision *NOUN* (**provisions**)
provision is providing something • *the provision of free meals for old people*

provisional *ADJECTIVE*
arranged or agreed on for the time being, but not yet definite • *He has applied for a provisional driving licence.*

provisions *PLURAL NOUN*
supplies of food and drink

provocative *ADJECTIVE*
likely to make someone angry • *That was a provocative remark.*

provoke *VERB* (**provokes**, **provoking**, **provoked**)
1 to provoke someone is to deliberately make them angry **2** to provoke a feeling is to arouse or cause it • *His statement provoked a great deal of criticism.*

> WORD FAMILY
> **Provocation** is saying or doing something to deliberately make someone angry.

prow *NOUN* (**prows**)
the front end of a ship

prowl *VERB* (**prowls**, **prowling**, **prowled**)
to prowl is to move about quietly and secretly, as some animals do when they are hunting

> WORD FAMILY
> A **prowler** is someone who prowls threateningly.

proximity *NOUN*
to be in the proximity of something is to be near it

prudent *ADJECTIVE* (*say* **proo**- dent)
wise and careful; not taking risks

> WORD FAMILY
> **Prudence** is being wise and careful; to act **prudently** is to act in this way.

prune [1] *NOUN* (**prunes**)
a dried plum

prune[2] *VERB* (**prunes**, **pruning**, **pruned**)
to prune a tree or bush is to cut off unwanted parts from it

pry *VERB* (**pries**, **prying**, **pried**)
to pry is to snoop in someone else's business

PS
short for **postscript**

psalm *NOUN* (**psalms**) (*say* sahm)
a religious song, especially one from the Book of Psalms in the Bible

pseudonym *NOUN* (**pseudonyms**) (*say* s'yoo- do- nim)
a false name that an author uses

psychiatrist *NOUN* (**psychiatrists**) (*say* sy- **ky**- a- trist)
a doctor who treats mental illness

psychiatry *NOUN* (*say* sy- **ky**- a- tree)
psychiatry is the treatment of mental illness

> WORD FAMILY
> A (for example) **psychiatric** hospital is for the treatment of mental illness.

psychic *ADJECTIVE* (*say* **sy**- kik)
someone is psychic when they can tell the future or read other people's minds

psychologist *NOUN* (**psychologists**) (*say* sy- **kol**- o- jist)
someone who studies how the mind works

psychology *NOUN*
psychology is the study of the mind and the way people behave

> WORD FAMILY
> **Psychological** means to do with psychology.

PTA
short for *Parent- Teacher Association*, an organization that arranges discussions between teachers and parents about school business, and raises money for the school

pub *NOUN* (**pubs**)
(*informal*) a building where people can buy and drink alcoholic drinks

puberty *NOUN* (*say* **pew**- ber- ti)
puberty is the time when a young person starts to become an adult and their body starts to change

public *ADJECTIVE*
1 belonging to everyone or able to be used by everyone • *I often use public transport.* **2** to do with people in general • *Newspapers can influence public opinion.*

> WORD FAMILY
> To do something **publicly** is to do it in public.

public *NOUN*
the public is people in general
in public openly; where anyone can see or take part

publication *NOUN* (**publications**)
1 a publication is a book or magazine that is printed and sold **2** publication is printing and selling books or magazines

public house *NOUN* (**public houses**)
a pub

publicity *NOUN*
publicity is information or advertising that makes people know about someone or something

publicize *VERB* (**publicizes**, **publicizing**, **publicized**) (*say* **pub**- li- syz)
to publicize something is to make people know about it

public school *NOUN* (**public schools**)
1 (*in England and Wales*) a secondary school that charges fees **2** (*in Scotland and America*) a school run by the State or by a local authority

publish *VERB* (**publishes**, **publishing**, **published**)
1 to publish books or magazines is to print and sell them **2** to publish information is to make it known publicly

> WORD FAMILY
> A **publisher** is a person or company that publishes books or magazines.

puck *NOUN* (**pucks**)
a hard rubber disc used in ice hockey

pucker *VERB* (**puckers**, **puckering**, **puckered**)
to pucker is to form into wrinkles

pudding *NOUN* (**puddings**)
1 a food made in a soft mass, especially with a mixture of flour and other ingredients **2** the sweet course of a meal

puddle *NOUN* (**puddles**)
a small pool, especially of rainwater

puff *VERB* (**puffs**, **puffing**, **puffed**)
1 to puff smoke or steam is to blow it out **2** you puff when you breathe with difficulty • *She was puffing when she got to the top of the hill.* **3** to puff something, or to puff it out, is to inflate or swell it • *He puffed out his chest.*

puff *NOUN* (**puffs**)
a small amount of breath, wind, smoke, or steam • *He vanished in a puff of smoke.*

puffin *NOUN* (**puffins**)
a seabird with a large striped beak

pull *VERB* (**pulls**, **pulling**, **pulled**)
1 to pull something is to get hold of it and make it come towards you or follow behind you **2** to pull is to move with an effort • *She tried to grab the boy but he pulled away.*
to pull a face is to twist your face into a strange expression
to pull in 1 a car pulls in when it stops at the side of the road **2** a train pulls in when it comes into a station and stops
to pull out is to decide to stop taking part in something • *He had to pull out of the race after he*

twisted his ankle.
to pull someone's leg is to tease them
to pull something off is to achieve it
to pull through is to recover from an illness
to pull up is to stop • *A car pulled up and two men got out.*
to pull yourself together is to become calm or sensible

pull *NOUN* (**pulls**)
a pull is an action of pulling • *Give the handle a good pull.*

pulley *NOUN* (**pulleys**)
a wheel with a groove round it to take a rope, used for lifting heavy things

pullover *NOUN* (**pullovers**)
a knitted piece of clothing for the top half of your body, that you put on over your head

pulp *NOUN* (**pulps**)
a soft wet mass of something, especially for making paper

pulp *VERB* (**pulps**, **pulping**, **pulped**)
to pulp something is to make it into a pulp

pulpit *NOUN* (**pulpits**)
a raised platform in a church, from which the preacher speaks to the congregation

pulse[1] *NOUN* (**pulses**)
1 your pulse is the regular beat as your heart pumps your blood through your arteries. You can feel your pulse in your wrist or neck **2** a regular vibration or movement • *The music had a throbbing pulse.*

pulse[2] *NOUN* (**pulses**)
pulses are the edible seeds of certain plants, such as peas, beans, and lentils

pulverize *VERB* (**pulverizes**, **pulverizing**, **pulverized**)
to pulverize something is to crush it into a powder

puma *NOUN* (**pumas**)
a large wild cat of North America

pumice *NOUN* (*say* pum- iss)
pumice is a kind of soft sponge-like stone rubbed on hard surfaces to clean or polish them

pump *NOUN* (**pumps**)
1 a device that forces air or liquid into or out of something, or along pipes **2** a lightweight shoe • *She took off her pumps.*

pump *VERB* (**pumps**, **pumping**, **pumped**)
to pump air or liquid is to force it into or out of something with a pump
to pump something up is to fill something like a balloon or tyre with air or gas

pumpkin *NOUN* (**pumpkins**)
a large round fruit with a hard yellow skin

pun *NOUN* (**puns**)
a joke made by using a word with two different meanings, or two words that sound the same, as in *Choosing where to bury him was a grave decision.*

pun *VERB* (**puns**, **punning**, **punned**)
to pun is to make a pun

punch[1] *VERB* (**punches**, **punching**, **punched**)
1 to punch someone is to hit them with your fist **2** to punch a hole is to make a hole in something • *The guard checked and punched our tickets.* • *The builder punched a hole in the wall.*

punch *NOUN* (**punches**)
1 a punch is a blow or hit with the fist **2** a punch is also a device for making holes in paper, metal, or other things

punch[2] *NOUN* (**punches**)
punch is a hot alcoholic drink

punchline *NOUN* (**punchlines**)
the last part of a joke or story, that makes it funny

punch-up *NOUN* (**punch-ups**)
(*informal*) a fight

punctual *ADJECTIVE*
you are punctual when you arrive exactly on time, not late

> WORD FAMILY
> **Punctuality** is being on time; to do something **punctually** is to do it in good time.

punctuate *VERB* (**punctuates**, **punctuating**, **punctuated**)
to punctuate a piece of writing is to put the commas, full stops, and other punctuation in it

punctuation *NOUN*
punctuation is the set of marks such as commas, full stops, and brackets put into a piece of writing to make it easier to understand

> PUNCTUATION MARKS
> We use punctuation marks to make what we are writing easier to read. We use punctuation to show how a long sentence is divided into units of meaning. You can end a sentence with: a **full stop**: *It's time to go.* a **question mark**: *Can we go now?* or an **exclamation mark**: *Let's go!* You can use these punctuation marks in a sentence: a **comma**: *It was getting late, so we decided to go.* a **colon**: *There are two reasons to go: it's late and I'm tired.* a **dash**: *We had to go— it was already half past eight.* a **semicolon**: *I wanted to stay; however, it was getting late.* **brackets**: *Ben (my brother) couldn't stay long.* **speech marks**: *'I'm going now,' said Ben.* an **apostrophe**: *Ben's gone.* There are separate panels in this dictionary explaining how to use each of these punctuation marks.

puncture *NOUN* (**punctures**)
a small hole made in a tyre by accident

pungent *ADJECTIVE*
smelling or tasting very strong or sharp

punish *VERB* (**punishes, punishing, punished**)
to punish someone is to make them suffer in some way because they have done something wrong

WORD FAMILY
A **punishment** is a way of punishing someone.

punk *NOUN* (**punks**)
a young person who wears black or torn clothes and has spiky or brightly coloured hair, and who likes punk rock

punk rock *NOUN*
punk rock is a kind of loud, simple rock music

punt[1] *NOUN* (**punts**)
a flat-bottomed boat moved by pushing a pole against the bottom of a river while standing in the punt

punt *VERB* (**punts, punting, punted**)
to punt is to use a pole to push a boat along

punt[2] *VERB* (**punts, punting, punted**)
to punt a football is to kick it after dropping it from your hands, before it touches the ground

puny *ADJECTIVE* (**punier, puniest**) (*say* pew-ni)
small and weak • '*Our tribes, if we just whistle them up, will far outnumber your puny forces; so resistance is useless.*' — Edith Nesbit, *Five Children and It*

pup *NOUN* (**pups**)
a puppy

pupa *NOUN* (**pupae**) (*say* pew-pa)
an insect at the stage of development between a larva and an adult insect; a chrysalis

pupil *NOUN* (**pupils**)
1 someone who is being taught by a teacher **2** the opening in the centre of your eye

puppet *NOUN* (**puppets**)
a kind of doll that can be made to move by fitting it over your fingers or hand or by pulling strings or wires attached to it

puppy *NOUN* (**puppies**)
a young dog

purchase *VERB* (**purchases, purchasing, purchased**)
to purchase something is to buy it

WORD FAMILY
A **purchaser** is someone who buys something.

purchase *NOUN* (**purchases**)
1 a purchase is something you have bought
2 purchase is the fact of buying something • *Keep the receipt as proof of purchase.* **3** a purchase is a firm hold or grip • *It was hard to get a purchase on the slippery rocks.*

purdah *NOUN*
purdah is the Muslim or Hindu custom of keeping women from being seen by men or strangers

pure *ADJECTIVE* (**purer, purest**)
1 not mixed with anything else • *Use pure olive oil.*
2 clean or clear • *They washed in a pure cold mountain stream.*

purely *ADVERB*
only, simply • *They did it purely for the money.*

purge *VERB* (**purges, purging, purged**)
to purge people or things is to get rid of them when they are not wanted

purge *NOUN* (**purges**)
an act of purging

purify *VERB* (**purifies, purifying, purified**)
to purify something is to make it pure
▷ **purification** *NOUN* purification is purifying something
▷ **purifier** *NOUN* someone or something that purifies

Puritan *NOUN* (**Puritans**)
a Protestant in the 16th or 17th century who wanted simpler religious ceremonies and strictly moral behaviour

puritan *NOUN* (**puritans**)
someone who believes in leading a strictly moral life

puritanical *ADJECTIVE*
extremely strict in your behaviour and morals

purity *NOUN*
purity is the state of being pure

purple *NOUN* and *ADJECTIVE*
a deep reddish-blue

purpose *NOUN* (**purposes**)
the reason why you do something; what something is for
to do something on purpose is to do it deliberately

purposely *ADVERB*
on purpose

purr *VERB* (**purrs, purring, purred**)
a cat purrs when it makes a gentle murmuring sound because it is pleased

purse *NOUN* (**purses**)
a small bag for holding money

pursue *VERB* (**pursues, pursuing, pursued**)
1 to pursue someone or something is to chase them **2** to pursue an activity is to continue to do it or work at it • *She pursued her studies at college.*

WORD FAMILY
A **pursuer** is a person who chases someone.

pursuit *NOUN* (**pursuits**)
1 pursuit is the action of chasing someone **2** a pursuit is something you spend a lot of time doing

pus *NOUN*
pus is a thick yellowish substance produced in boils and other sore places on your body

push *VERB* (**pushes, pushing, pushed**)
to push something is to move it away from you by pressing against it
to push off (*slang*) is to go away

push *NOUN* (**pushes**)
a pushing movement
to get the push (*informal*) is to be dismissed from a job

pushchair *NOUN* (**pushchairs**)
a small folding chair with wheels, in which a child can be pushed along

puss or **pussy** *NOUN* (**pusses** or **pussies**)
(*informal*) a cat

put *VERB* (**puts**, **putting**, **put**)
1 to put something in a place is to move it there • *Put it over there.* • *Where shall I put it?* **2** to put also means to affect someone or something in a particular way • *They've put me in a bad mood.* **3** to put an idea in a certain way is to express it in words of a special kind • *She put it very tactfully.*
to put someone off is to make them less keen on something • *Seeing you eat so much has put me off my food.*
to put someone up is to give them a place to sleep • *Can we put them up for the night?*
to put something off is to decide to do it later instead of now • *We'll have to put off the party if you're ill.*
to put something on 1 is to switch on an electrical device, for example a light or a television **2** is to start wearing a piece of clothing • *I'll just put on my coat.*
to put something out is to stop something like a fire or light from burning or shining
to put something up is to raise it or make it upright • *Let's put up the tent.*
to put up with something is to be willing to accept it without complaining

putt *VERB* (**putts**, **putting**, **putted**)
to putt a golf ball is to tap it gently towards the hole

putt *NOUN* (**putts**)
when a golfer taps the ball gently towards the hole

putter *NOUN* (**putters**)
a golf club used to putt the ball

putty *NOUN*
putty is a soft paste that sets hard, used by builders to fit windows in their frames

puzzle *NOUN* (**puzzles**)
1 a tricky game that you have to solve **2** a difficult question; a problem

puzzle *VERB* (**puzzles**, **puzzling**, **puzzled**)
1 to puzzle someone is to give them a problem that is hard to understand **2** to puzzle over something is to think hard about it

pygmy *NOUN* (**pygmies**) (*say* **pig**-mi)
an unusually small person or animal

pyjamas *PLURAL NOUN*
a loose lightweight set of jacket and trousers that you wear in bed

pylon *NOUN* (**pylons**)
a metal tower for supporting electric cables. It is made of struts and widens out nearer the ground

pyramid *NOUN* (**pyramids**)
1 an object with a square base and four sloping sides coming to a point **2** an ancient Egyptian monument shaped like this. They were massive and were usually built of huge stone blocks

pyramidal *ADJECTIVE* (*say* pir-**am**-id-al)
shaped like a pyramid • *The house had a pyramidal roof.*

python *NOUN* (**pythons**)
a large snake that crushes its prey

Qq

quack *NOUN* (**quacks**)
the harsh loud sound made by a duck

quack *VERB* (**quacks**, **quacking**, **quacked**)
a duck quacks when it makes a harsh loud sound

quad *NOUN* (**quads**)(*informal*)
1 a quadrangle **2** a quadruplet

quadrangle *NOUN* (**quadrangles**)
a rectangular courtyard with large buildings round it

quadrant *NOUN* (**quadrants**)
a quarter of a circle

quadrilateral *NOUN* (**quadrilaterals**)
a flat shape with four straight sides

quadruple *ADJECTIVE*
1 four times as much or as many **2** having four parts

quadruple *VERB* (**quadruples**, **quadrupling**, **quadrupled**)
1 to quadruple something is to make it four times as much or as many **2** to quadruple is to become four times as much or as many

quadruplet *NOUN* (**quadruplets**)
each of four children born to the same mother at one time

quail[1] *NOUN* (**quails**)
a bird that looks like a small partridge

quail[2] *VERB* (**quails**, **quailing**, **quailed**)
to quail is to feel or show fear

quaint *ADJECTIVE* (**quainter**, **quaintest**)
attractive in an unusual or old-fashioned way

quake *VERB* (**quakes**, **quaking**, **quaked**)
to quake is to tremble or shake

Quaker *NOUN* (**Quakers**)
a member of a religious group called the Society of Friends, founded by George Fox in the 17th century

qualification *NOUN* (**qualifications**)
1 a skill or ability to do a job **2** an examination you have passed or a course you have completed that shows you have a skill or ability **3** something that qualifies a remark or statement

qualify *VERB* (**qualifies**, **qualifying**, **qualified**)
1 to qualify for something such as a job is to be suitable for it or show you have gained the abilities you need to do it • *She qualified as a doctor last year.* **2** to qualify for a competition is to reach a high enough standard to take part in it **3** to qualify a statement or remark is to change it or add to it to make it less strong or less definite

quality *NOUN* (**qualities**)
1 the quality of something is how good or bad it is **2** what something is like • *The paper had a shiny quality.*

quantity *NOUN* (**quantities**)
how much there is of something, or how many things there are of one sort

quarantine *NOUN* (*say* kwo- ran- teen)
quarantine is a period when a person or animal is kept apart from others to prevent a disease from spreading

quarrel *NOUN* (**quarrels**)
a strong or angry argument

quarrel *VERB* (**quarrels**, **quarrelling**, **quarrelled**)
to quarrel with someone is to argue fiercely with them

quarrelsome *ADJECTIVE*
fond of quarrelling or often quarrelling

quarry *NOUN* (**quarries**)
1 a place where stone or slate is dug out of the ground **2** an animal that is being hunted

quart *NOUN* (**quarts**) (*say* kwort)
a measure of liquid, a quarter of a gallon or about 1.136 litres

quarter *NOUN* (**quarters**)
1 each of four equal parts into which something is divided or can be divided **2** three months, one-fourth of a year
at close quarters close together • *They fought at close quarters.*

quarters *PLURAL NOUN*
where someone lives for a time; lodgings

quartet *NOUN* (**quartets**) (*say* kwor- **tet**)
1 a group of four musicians **2** a piece of music for four musicians

quartz *NOUN* (*say* kworts)
quartz is a hard mineral, used in making accurate electronic watches and clocks

quaver *VERB* (**quavers**, **quavering**, **quavered**)
to quaver is to tremble • *Then Cornelius, the oldest of all the elephants, spoke in his quavering voice: 'My good friends, we are seeking a King, why not choose Babar?'* — Jean de Brunhoff, *The Story of Babar*

quaver *NOUN* (**quavers**)
1 a trembling sound **2** a musical note equal to half a crotchet, written ♪

quay *NOUN* (**quays**) (*say* kee)
a harbour wall or pier where ships can be tied up for loading and unloading

queasy *ADJECTIVE* (**queasier**, **queasiest**)
you feel queasy when you feel slightly sick

queen *NOUN* (**queens**)
1 a woman who has been crowned as the ruler of a country **2** a king's wife **3** a female bee or ant that produces eggs **4** a piece in chess, the most powerful on the board **5** a playing card with a picture of a queen

queen mother *NOUN*
a king's widow who is the mother of the present king or queen

queer *ADJECTIVE* (**queerer**, **queerest**)
1 strange or odd **2** ill or unwell • *I feel a bit queer.*

quench *VERB* (**quenches**, **quenching**, **quenched**)
1 to quench your thirst is to drink until you aren't thirsty any more **2** to quench a fire is to put it out

query *NOUN* (**queries**) (*say* kweer- i)
1 a question **2** a question mark

query *VERB* (**queries**, **querying**, **queried**)
to query something is to question whether it is true or correct

quest *NOUN* (**quests**)
a long search, especially for something precious or valuable

question *NOUN* (**questions**)
1 something you ask • *I will try to answer your question.* **2** a problem or subject for discussion
to be out of the question is to be impossible or not even worth considering

question *VERB* (**questions**, **questioning**, **questioned**)
1 to question someone is to ask them questions **2** to question something is to be doubtful about it

> WORD FAMILY
> A **questioner** is someone who asks a question.

questionable *ADJECTIVE*
causing doubt; not certainly true or correct

question mark *NOUN* (**question marks**)
the punctuation mark (?) put at the end of a question

> QUESTION MARKS
> You use a question mark at the end of a sentence which asks a direct question: *What is the largest animal in the world?* Don't use a question mark when you refer to a question in indirect speech *He asked me what the largest animal in the world was.*

questionnaire *NOUN* (**questionnaires**) (*say* kwes- chon- **air**)
a set of questions asked to get information for a survey

queue *NOUN* (**queues**) (*say* kew)
a line of people or vehicles waiting for something

queue *VERB* (**queues**, **queueing**, **queued**) (*say* kew)
people queue, or queue up, when they wait in a queue

quibble *VERB* (**quibbles**, **quibbling**, **quibbled**)
to quibble is to argue or complain about minor details

quibble *NOUN* (**quibbles**)
a quibble is a trivial complaint or objection

quiche *NOUN* (**quiches**) (*say* keesh)
an open tart with a savoury filling

quick *ADJECTIVE* (**quicker**, **quickest**)
1 taking only a short time • *You were quick.* **2** done in a short time • *She gave a quick answer.* **3** able to learn or think quickly **4** (*old use*) alive

quicken *VERB* (**quickens**, **quickening**, **quickened**)
1 to quicken something is to make it quicker • *She quickened her pace.* **2** to quicken is to become quicker

quicksand *NOUN* (**quicksands**)
quicksand is an area of loose wet sand that sucks in anything that falls into it

quid *NOUN* (**quid**)
(*slang*) a pound (£1)

quiet *ADJECTIVE* (**quieter**, **quietest**)
1 silent **2** not loud • *He spoke in a quiet voice.* **3** calm and peaceful • *They lead a quiet life.*

quiet *NOUN*
quiet is a time when it is calm and peaceful • *Let's have a bit of quiet now.*

quieten *VERB* (**quietens**, **quietening**, **quietened**)
1 to quieten something or someone is to make them quiet **2** to quieten is to become quiet

quill *NOUN* (**quills**)
1 a bird's quills are its large feathers **2** a pen made from a large feather **3** a porcupine's quills are its long spines

quilt *NOUN* (**quilts**)
a thick soft cover for a bed

quintet *NOUN* (**quintets**)
1 a group of five musicians **2** a piece of music for five musicians

quit *VERB* (**quits**, **quitting**, **quitted** or **quit**)
1 to quit something is to leave or abandon it
2 (*informal*) to quit doing something is to stop it
• *Quit teasing him!*

> WORD FAMILY
> A **quitter** is someone who quits or gives up.

quite *ADVERB*
1 rather or fairly • *He's quite a good swimmer.*
2 completely or entirely • *I am quite all right.*

quiver[1] *VERB* (**quivers**, **quivering**, **quivered**)
to quiver is to tremble • *He was quivering with excitement.*

quiver[2] *NOUN* (**quivers**)
a container for arrows

quiz *NOUN* (**quizzes**)
a series of questions, especially as an entertainment or competition

quiz *VERB* (**quizzes**, **quizzing**, **quizzed**)
to quiz someone is to ask them a lot of questions

quoit *NOUN* (**quoits**) (*say* koit)
a ring you throw at a peg in the game of **quoits**

quota *NOUN* (**quotas**) (*say* **kwoh**- ta)
a fixed share or amount • *Each school has its quota of equipment.*

quotation *NOUN* (**quotations**)
1 quotation is the action of repeating words that were first written or spoken by someone else
2 a quotation is a set of words taken from a book or speech

quotation marks *PLURAL NOUN*
inverted commas, used to mark a quotation

quote *VERB* (**quotes**, **quoting**, **quoted**)
1 to quote words is to use them in a quotation
2 to quote someone is to quote words first used by them

quotient *NOUN* (**quotients**) (*say* **kwoh**- shent)
the result of dividing one number by another

Rr

rabbi *NOUN* (**rabbis**) (*say* **rab**- I)
a Jewish religious leader

rabbit *NOUN* (**rabbits**)
a furry animal with long ears that digs burrows

rabid *ADJECTIVE* (*say* **rab**- id)
1 a rabid animal is affected with rabies **2** you can say someone is rabid when they are fiercely enthusiastic about something

rabies *NOUN* (*say* **ray**- beez)
rabies is a fatal disease involving madness that affects dogs and cats and can be passed to humans

raccoon *NOUN* (**raccoons**)
a small North American meat-eating animal with greyish-brown fur and a bushy, striped tail

race[1] *NOUN* (**races**)
a competition to be the first to reach a particular place or to do something

race *VERB* (**races**, **racing**, **raced**)
1 to race someone is to have a race against them
2 to race is to move very fast • *The train raced along the track.*

> WORD FAMILY
> A **racer** is a competitor in a race.

race[2] *NOUN* (**races**)
a large group of people who have the same ancestors, and share certain physical features such as the colour of their skin and hair

racecourse *NOUN* (**racecourses**)
a place where horse races are run

racial *ADJECTIVE*
to do with a person's race or with different races

racism *NOUN* (*say* **ray**- sizm)
racism is believing that one race of people is better than all the others and treating people unfairly because they belong to a different race

> WORD FAMILY
> A **racist** is someone who practises racism, and a **racist** attitude or remark is one that shows racism.

rack *NOUN* (**racks**)
1 a framework used as a shelf or container • *a plate rack* **2** an ancient device for torturing people by stretching them

rack *VERB* (**racks**, **racking**, **racked**)
to rack your brains is to think hard to remember something or solve a problem

racket[1] *NOUN* (**rackets**)
a bat with strings stretched across a frame, used in tennis and similar games

racket[2] *NOUN* (**rackets**)
1 to make a racket is to make a loud noise
2 (*informal*) a dishonest business; a swindle

radar *NOUN* (*say* **ray**- dar)
radar is a system that uses radio waves to show the position of ships or aircraft which cannot be seen because of distance or poor visibility

radial *ADJECTIVE*
1 to do with rays or radii **2** having spokes or lines that radiate from a central point

radiant *ADJECTIVE*
1 radiating light or heat **2** you can say someone is radiant when they look happy and beautiful

> WORD FAMILY
> **Radiance** is brightness; to smile **radiantly** is to have a very bright and happy smile.

radiate *VERB* (**radiates**, **radiating**, **radiated**)
1 to radiate heat, light, or other energy is to send it out in rays **2** to radiate is to spread out like the spokes of a wheel • *The city's streets radiate from the central square.*

radiation *NOUN*
1 radiation is heat, light, or other energy given out by something **2** radiation is also energy or particles sent out by something radioactive

radiator *NOUN* (**radiators**)
1 a device that gives out heat, especially a metal container through which steam or hot water flows
2 a device that cools the engine of a motor vehicle

radical *ADJECTIVE*
1 thorough and complete; going right to the roots of something • *The new government made radical changes.* **2** wanting to make changes or reforms • *He is a radical politician.*

> WORD FAMILY
> To be **radically** different is to be completely different.

radical *NOUN* (**radicals**)
someone who is radical

radii
plural of **radius**

radio *NOUN* (**radios**)
1 radio is sending or receiving sound by means of electrical waves **2** a radio is an apparatus for receiving broadcast sound programmes, or for receiving and sending messages

radioactive *ADJECTIVE*
radioactive substances have atoms that break up and send out radiation which produces electrical and chemical effects

> WORD FAMILY
> **Radioactivity** is the state of being radioactive.

radish *NOUN* (**radishes**)
a small hard red vegetable with a hot taste, eaten raw in salads

radium *NOUN*
radium is a radioactive element

radius *NOUN* (**radii**)
1 a straight line from the centre of a circle to the circumference **2** the length of this line

raffle *NOUN* (**raffles**)
a way of raising money by selling numbered tickets, some of which win prizes

raffle *VERB* (**raffles**, **raffling**, **raffled**)
to raffle something is to give it as a prize in a raffle

raft *NOUN* (**rafts**)
a floating platform of logs or barrels tied together

rafter *NOUN* (**rafters**)
each of the long sloping pieces of wood that hold up a roof

rag *NOUN* (**rags**)
1 an old or torn piece of cloth **2** to be dressed in rags is to be wearing very old, torn clothes **3** a piece of ragtime music

rage *NOUN* (**rages**)
great or violent anger
to be all the rage (*informal*) is to be very fashionable or popular

rage *VERB* (**rages**, **raging**, **raged**)
1 to rage is to be very angry **2** to rage is also to be violent or noisy • *The storm was raging outside. Rain lashed against the windows, the wind howled through the telegraph wires.* — Catherine MacPhail, *Granny Nothing*

ragged *ADJECTIVE* (*say* rag- id)
1 torn or frayed **2** wearing torn or old clothes • *a ragged beggar* **3** not smooth • *They gave a ragged performance.*

ragtime *NOUN*
ragtime is a kind of jazz music

raid *NOUN* (**raids**)
1 a sudden attack **2** an unexpected visit from police to search a place or arrest people

raid *VERB* (**raids**, **raiding**, **raided**)
to raid a place is to make a raid on it

> WORD FAMILY
> **Raiders** are people who attack a place in a raid.

rail *NOUN* (**rails**)
1 a bar or rod that you can hang things on or that form part of a fence or banisters **2** a long metal strip that is part of a railway track
by rail on a train

railings *PLURAL NOUN*
a fence made of metal bars

railway *NOUN* (**railways**)
1 the parallel metal strips that trains travel on **2** a system of transport using rails

rain *NOUN*
rain is drops of water that fall from the sky

rain *VERB* (**rains**, **raining**, **rained**)
1 to rain is to come down like rain • *After the explosion fragments of glass rained on them from above.* **2** to rain something is to send it down like rain • *They rained blows on him.*
it is raining when rain is falling

rainbow *NOUN* (**rainbows**)
a curved band of colours that you can sometimes see in the sky when the sun shines through rain

raincoat *NOUN* (**raincoats**)
a waterproof coat

raindrop *NOUN* (**raindrops**)
a single drop of rain

rainfall *NOUN*
rainfall is the amount of rain that falls in a particular place or time

rainforest *NOUN* (**rainforests**)
a dense tropical forest in an area of very heavy rainfall

raise *VERB* (**raises**, **raising**, **raised**)
1 to raise something is to move it to a higher place or to an upright position **2** to raise an amount or number is to increase it • *They raised our pay by 20%.* **3** to raise money is to succeed in collecting it • *They raised $1,000 for the appeal.* **4** to raise your voice is to speak loudly **5** to raise a subject or idea is to mention it for people to think about **6** to raise young children is to bring them up and educate them **7** to raise animals is to breed them **8** to raise a laugh or smile is to make people laugh or smile

raisin *NOUN* (**raisins**)
a dried grape

rake *NOUN* (**rakes**)
a gardening tool with a row of short spikes fixed to a long handle

rake *VERB* (**rakes**, **raking**, **raked**)
1 to rake something is to move it or smooth it with a rake **2** to rake, or rake around, is to search • *I raked around in my desk for the letter.*
to rake something in (*informal*) is to earn it as profit

rally *NOUN* (**rallies**)
1 a large public meeting **2** a competition to test skill in driving **3** a series of strokes and return strokes of the ball in tennis or squash

rally *VERB* (**rallies**, **rallying**, **rallied**)
1 to rally people is to bring them together for a united effort **2** to rally, or rally round, is to come together to support someone **3** to rally is to revive or recover after an illness or setback • *The team rallied when they realized they could win.*

RAM
short for *random-access memory*, a type of computer memory with parts that can be located directly

ram *NOUN* (**rams**)
a male sheep

ram *VERB* (**rams**, **ramming**, **rammed**)
to ram something is to push one thing hard against another

Ramadan *NOUN* (*say* ram- a- **dan**)
Ramadan is the ninth month of the Muslim year, when Muslims do not eat or drink during the daytime

ramble *NOUN* (**rambles**)
a long walk in the country

ramble *VERB* (**rambles**, **rambling**, **rambled**)
1 to ramble is to go for a a long walk in the country **2** to ramble is also to say a lot without keeping to a subject

> WORD FAMILY
> A **rambler** is someone who goes rambling in the country.

ramp *NOUN* (**ramps**)
a slope joining two different levels

rampage *VERB* (**rampages**, **rampaging**, **rampaged**) (*say* ram- **payj**)
to rampage is to rush about wildly or violently

rampage *NOUN*
to go on the rampage is to rush about violently

ran
past tense of **run** *VERB*

ranch *NOUN* (**ranches**)
a large cattle-farm in America

random *NOUN*
at random by chance; without any purpose or plan

a b c d e f g h i j k l m n o p q **r** s t u v w x y z

random *ADJECTIVE*
done or taken at random • *They took a random sample.*

rang
past tense of **ring**[2] *VERB*

range *NOUN* (**ranges**)
1 a collection of different things of the same type • *The shop sells a wide range of games and puzzles.* **2** the limits of something, from the highest to the lowest • *Most of the children here are in the 8-11 age range.* **3** a line of hills or mountains **4** the distance that a gun can shoot, or an aircraft can fly, or a sound can be heard **5** a place with targets for shooting practice **6** a kitchen fireplace with ovens

range *VERB* (**ranges, ranging, ranged**)
1 to range between two limits is to extend from one to the other • *Prices ranged from $1 to $50.* **2** to range people or things is to arrange them in a line • *Crowds were ranged along the streets, hoping to see the Queen go by.* **3** to range is to wander or move over a wide area • *Hens ranged all over the farm.*

Ranger *NOUN* (**Rangers**)
a senior member of the Guides

ranger *NOUN* (**rangers**)
1 someone who looks after a park or forest **2** a mounted police officer in a remote area

rank *NOUN* (**ranks**)
1 a position in a series of people or things • *He was promoted to the rank of captain.* **2** a line of people or things

rank *VERB* (**ranks, ranking, ranked**)
to rank is to have a certain rank or place • *She ranks among the greatest writers.*

ransack *VERB* (**ransacks, ransacking, ransacked**)
to ransack a place is to search it thoroughly, looking for something to steal, and leave it in a mess

ransom *NOUN* (**ransoms**)
money paid so that someone who has been kidnapped can be set free
to hold someone to ransom is to keep them prisoner and demand a ransom

ransom *VERB* (**ransoms, ransoming, ransomed**)
to ransom someone who has been kidnapped is to free them by paying a ransom

rap *VERB* (**raps, rapping, rapped**)
to rap is to knock quickly and loudly

rap *NOUN* (**raps**)
1 a rap is a rapping movement or sound **2** rap is a kind of pop music in which you speak words rapidly in rhythm
to take the rap (*informal*) is to take the blame for something

rapid *ADJECTIVE*
moving or working at speed

> **WORD FAMILY**
> **Rapidity** is speed; to happen **rapidly** is to happen very quickly.

rapids *PLURAL NOUN*
part of a river where the water flows very fast

rare *ADJECTIVE* (**rarer, rarest**)
unusual; not often found or experienced • *She died of a rare disease.*

> **WORD FAMILY**
> Something happens **rarely** when it doesn't happen very often; a **rarity** is a person or thing that is unusual.

rascal *NOUN* (**rascals**)
a dishonest or mischievous person

rash[1] *ADJECTIVE* (**rasher, rashest**)
you are rash when you do something quickly without thinking properly about it • *He tends to be rash.* • *It was a rash decision.*

rash[2] *NOUN* (**rashes**)
1 an outbreak of red spots or patches on the skin **2** a number of unwelcome things happening about the same time • *By the time Hallowe'en arrived, Harry was regretting his rash promise to go to the Deathday Party.* — J. K. Rowling, *Harry Potter and the Chamber of Secrets*

rasher *NOUN* (**rashers**)
a slice of bacon

raspberry *NOUN* (**raspberries**)
a small soft red fruit

Rastafarian *NOUN* (**Rastafarians**) (*say* ras- ta- **fair**- i- an)
a member of a religious group that started in Jamaica

rat *NOUN* (**rats**)
1 an animal like a large mouse **2** you can describe a nasty or treacherous person as a rat

rate *NOUN* (**rates**)
1 how fast or how often something happens • *The train moved at a great rate.* **2** a charge or payment • *What is the rate for a letter to Italy?*
at any rate anyway
at this rate if this is typical or true

rate *VERB* (**rates, rating, rated**)
to rate something or someone is to regard them in a certain way or as having a certain value • *Drivers rate the new car very highly.* • *He rated me among his best friends.*

rather *ADVERB*
1 slightly; somewhat • *It was rather dark.* **2** you would rather do one thing than another thing if you would prefer to do it • *I think I'd rather do this later.* **3** more truly or correctly • *He lay down, or rather fell, on the bed.* **4** (*informal*) as an answer: definitely, yes • *'Will you come?' 'Rather!'*

ratio *NOUN* (**ratios**) (*say* **ray- shi- oh**)
the relationship between two numbers; how many times one number goes into another • *In a group of 2 girls and 10 boys, the ratio of girls to boys is 1 to 5.*

ration *NOUN* (**rations**) (*say* **rash- on**)
the amount of something one person is allowed to have

ration *VERB* (**rations, rationing, rationed**) (*say* **rash- on**)
to ration something is to give it out in fixed amounts because there is not a lot of it to share

rational *ADJECTIVE* (*say* **rash- o- nal**)
reasonable or sensible • *No rational person would do such a thing.*

> WORD FAMILY
> To behave or think **rationally** is to do so in a reasonable or sensible way.

rationalize *VERB* (**rationalizes, rationalizing, rationalized**)
1 to rationalize something complex is to make it logical and regular **2** to rationalize a problem or difficulty is to invent an explanation for it

rat race *NOUN*
the rat race is the continuous struggle for success in a career or business

rattle *VERB* (**rattles, rattling, rattled**)
1 to rattle is to make a series of short sharp hard sounds **2** to rattle something is to make it rattle **3** (*informal*) to rattle someone is to make them nervous and confused

rattle *NOUN* (**rattles**)
1 a rattling sound **2** a baby's toy that rattles

rattlesnake *NOUN* (**rattlesnakes**)
a poisonous American snake that makes rattling sounds with its tail

rave *VERB* (**raves, raving, raved**)
1 to be raving is to be talking wildly **2** to rave about something is to talk very enthusiastically about it

rave *NOUN* (**raves**)
a big party held in a large building with loud electronic music to dance to

raven *NOUN* (**ravens**)
a large black bird

ravenous *ADJECTIVE* (*say* **rav- e- nus**)
very hungry
▷ **ravenously** *ADVERB* in a ravenous way • *The starving dog ate and drank ravenously, then at once settled to sleep.* — Dodie Smith, *The Hundred and One Dalmatians*

ravine *NOUN* (**ravines**) (*say* **ra- veen**)
a very deep narrow gorge

ravioli *NOUN*
ravioli is small squares of pasta filled with meat and served with a sauce

raw *ADJECTIVE* (**rawer, rawest**)
1 raw food is not cooked **2** raw (for example) cotton or sugar is in its natural state before being processed • *What raw materials do you need?* **3** you can say someone is raw when they don't have any experience • *They are just raw beginners.* **4** with the skin removed • *He had a raw wound on his leg.* **5** cold and damp • *There was a raw wind.*

raw deal *NOUN*
a raw deal is being treated unfairly

raw material *NOUN* (**raw materials**)
a natural substance used to make other things

ray[1] *NOUN* (**rays**)
a thin line of light, heat, or other energy

ray[2] *NOUN* (**rays**)
a large sea fish with a flat body and a long tail

razor *NOUN* (**razors**)
a device with a very sharp blade, used for shaving

reach *VERB* (**reaches, reaching, reached**)
1 to reach a place is to go as far as it and arrive there **2** to reach, or reach out, is to stretch out your hand to get or touch something

reach *NOUN* (**reaches**)
1 the distance you can reach with your hand **2** a distance that you can easily travel • *My uncle lives within reach of the sea.*

react *VERB* (**reacts, reacting, reacted**)
to react is to act in response to another person or thing

reaction *NOUN* (**reactions**)
an action or feeling caused by another person or thing

reactor *NOUN* (**reactors**)
an apparatus for producing nuclear power

read *VERB* (**reads, reading, read**)
1 to read something written or printed is to look at it and understand it or say it aloud **2** a gauge or instrument reads a certain amount when that is what it shows • *The thermometer reads 20°.*

> WORD FAMILY
> A **readable** book is enjoyable to read; **readable** writing is clear and easy to read.

reader *NOUN* (**readers**)
1 someone who reads **2** a book that helps you learn to read

readily *ADVERB*
1 willingly or eagerly • *She readily agreed to help.* **2** quickly and without any difficulty • *All the ingredients you need are readily available.*

reading *NOUN* (**readings**)
1 reading is the action of reading a book, magazine, or newspaper **2** a reading is an amount shown on a gauge or instrument

ready *ADJECTIVE* (**readier**, **readiest**)
1 able or willing to do something or to be used at once; prepared **2** quick • *He always has ready answers.*
at the ready ready for action or ready to be used

> WORD FAMILY
> **Readiness** is being ready for something.

ready-made *ADJECTIVE*
made already, and not made specially

real *ADJECTIVE*
1 true or existing; not imaginary **2** genuine; not a copy • *Are those pearls real?*

realism *NOUN*
realism is seeing or showing things as they really are

realist *NOUN* (**realists**)
someone who tries to see things as they really are

realistic *ADJECTIVE*
1 true to life • *It is a very realistic painting.* **2** seeing things as they really are • *She is realistic about her chances of winning.*

> WORD FAMILY
> You say **realistically** when you are talking about what you think can actually be achieved • *Realistically, I don't think we have much hope of winning.*

reality *NOUN* (**realities**)
1 reality is what is real **2** a reality is something that is real • *Cold and hunger are the realities of being homeless.*

realize *VERB* (**realizes**, **realizing**, **realized**)
to realize something is to understand it or accept that it is true

> WORD FAMILY
> **Realization** is realizing something.

really *ADVERB*
truly; certainly; in fact

realm *NOUN* (**realms**) (*say* relm)
1 a kingdom **2** an area of knowledge or activity

reap *VERB* (**reaps**, **reaping**, **reaped**)
1 to reap corn is to cut it down and gather it in when it is ripe **2** to reap a benefit is to gain it

> WORD FAMILY
> A **reaper** is someone who reaps corn.

reappear *VERB* (**reappears**, **reappearing**, **reappeared**)
to reappear is to appear again

> WORD FAMILY
> The **reappearance** of something is when it appears again.

rear [1] *ADJECTIVE*
placed or found at the back • *She had a car with a rear engine.*

rear *NOUN* (**rears**)
the back part of something

rear [2] *VERB* (**rears**, **rearing**, **reared**)
1 to rear young children or animals is to bring them up or help them grow **2** a horse or other animal rears, or rears up, when it rises up on its hind legs so that its front legs are in the air

rearrange *VERB* (**rearranges**, **rearranging**, **rearranged**)
to rearrange something is to arrange it differently

> WORD FAMILY
> **Rearrangement**, or a **rearrangement**, is when something is arranged differently.

reason *NOUN* (**reasons**)
1 the reason for something is why it happens **2** reason is thinking in a clear and logical way • *He wouldn't listen to reason.*

reason *VERB* (**reasons**, **reasoning**, **reasoned**)
1 to reason is to think in a logical way **2** to reason with someone is to try to persuade them of something

reasonable *ADJECTIVE*
1 sensible or logical **2** fair or moderate • *These are reasonable prices for what you get.*

reasonably *ADVERB*
1 in a reasonable way; sensibly • *They were behaving quite reasonably.* **2** fairly; somewhat • *It had taken Mildred several weeks of falling off and crashing before she could ride the broomstick reasonably well.* — Jill Murphy, *The Worst Witch*

reassure *VERB* (**reassures**, **reassuring**, **reassured**)
to reassure someone is to take away their doubts or fears

> WORD FAMILY
> To give someone **reassurance** or **reassurances** is to take away their doubts or fears.

rebel *VERB* (**rebels**, **rebelling**, **rebelled**) (*say* ri-bel)
to rebel is to refuse to obey someone in authority, especially the government

rebel *NOUN* (**rebels**) (*say* reb-el)
someone who refuses to obey or fights against someone in authority

rebellion *NOUN* (**rebellions**)
1 rebellion is when people refuse to obey or fight against someone in authority **2** a rebellion is a fight against someone in authority, especially the government

rebellious *ADJECTIVE*
someone is rebellious when they refuse to obey authority or are likely to rebel

rebound *VERB* (**rebounds**, **rebounding**, **rebounded**)
to rebound is to bounce back after hitting something

rebuild *VERB* (**rebuilds**, **rebuilding**, **rebuilt**)
to rebuild something is to build it again after it has been destroyed

recall *VERB* (**recalls**, **recalling**, **recalled**)
1 to recall someone or something is to remember them **2** to recall someone is to tell them to come back

recap *VERB* (**recaps**, **recapping**, **recapped**)
(*informal*) to recap is to summarize what has been said

recapture *VERB* (**recaptures**, **recapturing**, **recaptured**)
to recapture something or someone is to capture them again, especially after they have escaped

recede *VERB* (**recedes**, **receding**, **receded**)
1 to recede is to go back • *The floods have receded.* **2** a man's hair is receding when he starts to go bald at the front

receipt *NOUN* (**receipts**) (*say* ri- seet)
1 a receipt is a written statement saying that a payment has been received or goods have been delivered **2** receipt is receiving something

receive *VERB* (**receives**, **receiving**, **received**)
1 to receive something is to get it when it is given or sent to you **2** to receive visitors is to greet them formally • *The President was received at Buckingham Palace.*

receiver *NOUN* (**receivers**)
1 someone who receives something **2** someone who buys and sells stolen goods **3** an official who takes charge of a bankrupt person's property **4** a radio or television set **5** the part of a telephone that you hold to your ear

recent *ADJECTIVE*
made or happening a short time ago

> **WORD FAMILY**
> Something happened **recently** when it happened only a short time ago.

receptacle *NOUN* (**receptacles**)
something for holding what is put into it; a container

reception *NOUN* (**receptions**)
1 the sort of welcome that someone gets • *We were given a friendly reception.* **2** a formal party to receive guests • *a wedding reception* **3** a place in a hotel or office where visitors report or check in **4** the quality of the signals your radio or television set receives • *We don't get good reception here.*

receptionist *NOUN* (**receptionists**)
someone whose job is to receive and welcome visitors to a hotel or office

recess *NOUN* (**recesses**)
1 an alcove **2** a time when work or business is stopped for a while

recession *NOUN* (**recessions**)
a reduction in trade or in the wealth of a country

recipe *NOUN* (**recipes**) (*say* ress- i- pi)
a list of ingredients and instructions for preparing or cooking food

reciprocal *ADJECTIVE* (*say* ri- **sip**- ro- kal)
given and received at the same time; mutual • *They gave a reciprocal greeting.*

reciprocal *NOUN* (**reciprocals**)
the amount by which you must multiply a number to obtain the answer 1 • *0.5 is the reciprocal of 2 (0.5 x 2 = 1).*

recital *NOUN* (**recitals**) (*say* ri- **sy**- tal)
a performance of music or poetry by a small number of people

recite *VERB* (**recites**, **reciting**, **recited**)
to recite something such as a poem is to say it aloud

> **WORD FAMILY**
> A **recitation** is something you recite.

reckless *ADJECTIVE*
someone is reckless when they do things without thinking or caring about what might happen
▷ **recklessly** *ADVERB* in a reckless way
▷ **recklessness** *NOUN* recklessness is being reckless

reckon *VERB* (**reckons**, **reckoning**, **reckoned**)
1 to reckon something is to calculate or count it **2** to reckon something is to think it or have an opinion about it • *I reckon it's about to rain.*

reclaim *VERB* (**reclaims**, **reclaiming**, **reclaimed**)
1 to reclaim land is to make it suitable for farming or building on again by clearing or draining it **2** to reclaim something is to get it back, especially after losing it • *I reclaimed my umbrella from the lost property office.*

reclamation *NOUN*
reclamation is making land usable again

recline *VERB* (**reclines**, **reclining**, **reclined**)
to recline is to lean or lie back

a b c d e f g h i j k l m n o p q r s t u v w x y z

recognize *VERB* (**recognizes**, **recognizing**, **recognized**)
1 to recognize someone or something is to know who they are because you have seen them before **2** to recognize a fault or mistake is to admit to it • *We recognize that we may have acted unfairly.*

> WORD FAMILY
> **Recognition** is recognizing someone or something; to be **recognizable** is to be able to be recognized.

recoil *VERB* (**recoils**, **recoiling**, **recoiled**)
to recoil is to move backwards suddenly • *He recoiled in horror.*

recollect *VERB* (**recollects**, **recollecting**, **recollected**)
to recollect something is to remember it

> WORD FAMILY
> **Recollection** is being able to remember something • *I have no recollection of seeing her before*; a **recollection** is something you remember.

recommend *VERB* (**recommends**, **recommending**, **recommended**)
1 to recommend something is to suggest it because you think it is good or suitable • *I recommend the strawberry ice cream.* **2** to recommend an action is to advise someone to do it • *We recommend that you wear strong shoes on the walk.*

> WORD FAMILY
> To give someone a **recommendation** is to recommend something to them.

reconcile *VERB* (**reconciles**, **reconciling**, **reconciled**)
1 to be reconciled with someone is to become friendly with them again after quarrelling or fighting with them **2** you are reconciled to something when you are persuaded to put up with it • *He soon became reconciled to wearing glasses.*

> WORD FAMILY
> **Reconciliation** is becoming friendly with someone again after quarrelling or fighting with them.

reconstruction *NOUN* (**reconstructions**)
1 reconstruction is building something up again **2** a reconstruction is acting out an event that took place in the past • *They did a reconstruction of the bank robbery.*

record *NOUN* (**records**) (*say* **rek**- ord)
1 a disc with recorded sound on it **2** the best performance in a sport or the most remarkable event of its kind • *She broke the record for swimming 100 metres.* **3** a set of facts or information about something that you write down and keep • *Keep a record of all the birds you see in the garden.*

record *VERB* (**records**, **recording**, **recorded**) (*say* ri- **kord**)
1 to record music or sound or a television programme is to store it on a tape or disc **2** to record things that have happened is to put them down in writing

recorder *NOUN* (**recorders**)
1 a tape recorder, video recorder, or other machine for recording sounds and pictures **2** a wooden musical instrument that you play by blowing into one end and covering holes with your fingers **3** someone who records something

record player *NOUN* (**record players**)
a machine that plays records

recount *VERB* (**recount**, **recounting**, **recounted**)
to tell someone about something true that has happened • *We recounted our adventures.*

recount *NOUN* (**recounts**)
a non-fiction text type in which the writer tells the reader about something true that has happened

recover *VERB* (**recovers**, **recovering**, **recovered**)
1 to recover is to get better after being ill **2** to recover something is to get it back after losing it

> WORD FAMILY
> You make a **recovery** when you get better after being ill; the **recovery** of something is getting it back after it was lost.

recreation *NOUN* (**recreations**)
a game, hobby, or other enjoyable pastime you do in your spare time
▷ **recreational** *ADJECTIVE* to do with recreation

recruit *NOUN* (**recruits**)
someone who has just joined the armed forces or a business or club

recruit *VERB* (**recruits**, **recruiting**, **recruited**)
to recruit someone is to get them to join something you belong to

rectangle *NOUN* (**rectangles**)
a shape with four straight sides and four right angles
▷ **rectangular** *ADJECTIVE* in the form of a rectangle

recuperate *VERB* (**recuperates**, **recuperating**, **recuperated**)
to recuperate is to get better after you have been ill

recur *VERB* (**recurs**, **recurring**, **recurred**)
something recurs when it happens again

> WORD FAMILY
> A **recurrence** of something is when it happens again.

recycle *VERB* (**recycles**, **recycling**, **recycled**)
to recycle waste material is to treat it so that it can be used again • *Waste paper can be recycled to make cardboard.*

red *ADJECTIVE* (**redder**, **reddest**)
1 of the colour of blood **2** red hair is orangey-brown in colour **3** (*informal*) to do with Communists; favouring Communism

red *NOUN* (**reds**)
1 a red colour **2** (*informal*) a Communist
to be in the red is to be in debt
to see red is to become suddenly angry

redden *VERB* (**reddens**, **reddening**, **reddened**)
to redden is to become red • *He reddened with embarrassment.*

reddish *ADJECTIVE*
fairly red

redeem *VERB* (**redeems**, **redeeming**, **redeemed**)
1 to redeem something is to get it back by paying for it or handing over a voucher **2** to redeem yourself is to do something good to make up for an earlier mistake **3** to redeem someone is to save them from damnation, as in some religions

> WORD FAMILY
> A **redeemer** is someone who redeems; **redemption** is redeeming or saving someone.

red-handed *ADJECTIVE*
to catch someone red-handed is to catch them while they are actually committing a crime or doing something wrong

redhead *NOUN* (**redheads**)
a person with reddish-brown hair

red herring *NOUN* (**red herrings**)
something that takes attention away from the real point or answer; a false clue

red tape *NOUN*
red tape is all the rules and official forms that make it difficult to get things done quickly

reduce *VERB* (**reduces**, **reducing**, **reduced**)
1 to reduce something is to make it smaller or less **2** to be reduced to something is to be forced to do it • *He was reduced to asking for more money.*

reduction *NOUN* (**reductions**)
1 there is a reduction in something when it becomes smaller or less **2** the amount by which something is reduced • *They gave us a reduction of £5.*

redundant *ADJECTIVE*
1 to be redundant is to be no longer needed **2** someone is made redundant when they lose their job because it is no longer needed

> WORD FAMILY
> **Redundancy** is when someone loses their job because it is no longer needed.

reed *NOUN* (**reeds**)
1 a plant that grows in or near water **2** a thin strip that vibrates to make the sound in some wind instruments, such as a clarinet, saxophone, or oboe

> WORD FAMILY
> A **reedy** voice or sound is high and not very pleasant.

reef *NOUN* (**reefs**)
a line of rocks or sand near the surface of the sea

reef knot *NOUN* (**reef knots**)
a symmetrical double knot for tying two cords together

reek *VERB* (**reeks**, **reeking**, **reeked**)
to reek is to have a strong unpleasant smell

reel *NOUN* (**reels**)
1 a round device on which cotton or thread is wound **2** a lively Scottish dance

reel *VERB* (**reels**, **reeling**, **reeled**)
to reel is to stagger • *The drunk reeled along the road.*
to reel something off is to say a lot very quickly

refer *VERB* (**refers**, **referring**, **referred**)
1 to refer to someone or something is to mention them or speak about them **2** to refer to (for example) a dictionary is to look at it so that you can find something out **3** to refer a question or problem to someone else is to give it to them to deal with

referee *NOUN* (**referees**)
someone who makes sure that people keep to the rules of a game

referee *VERB* (**referees**, **refereeing**, **refereed**)
to referee a game is to act as referee in it

reference *NOUN* (**references**)
1 a mention of something **2** a place in a book or file where information can be found **3** a description of the work someone has done and how well they have done it, used especially when someone is applying for a job
in or **with reference to something** or **someone** concerning them or about them

reference book *NOUN* (**reference books**)
a book that gives information, such as a dictionary or encyclopedia

referendum *NOUN* (**referendums**) (*say* ref- er- en- dum)
a vote on a particular question by all the people in a country

refill *VERB* (**refills**, **refilling**, **refilled**)
to refill something is to fill it again

refill *NOUN* (**refills**)
a container used to replace something that has been used up • *My pen needs a refill.*

refine *VERB* (**refines**, **refining**, **refined**)
to refine something is to purify or improve it

refined *ADJECTIVE*
1 refined (for example) sugar or oil has been made pure by taking other substances out of it **2** someone is refined when they have good manners and are well educated

refinement *NOUN* (**refinements**)
1 refinement is the process of refining something **2** a refinement is something special that improves a thing

refinery *NOUN* (**refineries**)
a factory for refining a product, such as oil

reflect *VERB* **(reflects, reflecting, reflected)**
1 something reflects light or heat or sound when it sends them back from a surface **2** a mirror or other shiny surface reflects something when it forms an image of it **3** you reflect on something when you think seriously about it

reflection *NOUN* **(reflections)**
the image you can see in a mirror or other shiny surface

reflective *ADJECTIVE*
1 sending back light • *The traffic policeman wore a reflective waistcoat.* **2** suggesting or showing serious thought • *The music has a reflective quality.*

reflex *NOUN* **(reflexes)** (*say* **ree**- fleks)
a movement or action that you do without any conscious thought

reflex angle *NOUN* **(reflex angles)**
an angle of between 180 and 360 degrees

reflexive pronoun *NOUN* **(reflexive pronouns)** (*say* ri- **flek**- siv)
(*in grammar*) any of the pronouns *myself, yourself, himself, herself, itself, ourselves, themselves*, which refer back to the subject of the verb, as in *they have hurt themselves*

reforestation *NOUN*
reforestation is the planting of new trees in an area where there used to be a forest

reform *VERB* **(reforms, reforming, reformed)**
1 to reform a person or thing is to improve them by getting rid of their faults **2** someone reforms when they improve their behaviour

reform *NOUN* **(reforms)**
1 reform is changing something to improve it **2** a reform is a change made for this reason

> WORD FAMILY
> **Reformation** is when something is changed to improve it.

Reformation *NOUN*
the Reformation was a movement for change in the Church in the 16th century, leading to the beginning of the Reformed or Protestant Churches

reformer *NOUN* **(reformers)**
someone who makes reforms

refract *VERB* **(refracts, refracting, refracted)**
to refract a ray of light is to change its direction at a point where it enters water or glass at an angle

> WORD FAMILY
> **Refraction** is refracting light.

refrain [1] *VERB* **(refrains, refraining, refrained)**
to refrain from something is to keep yourself from doing it • *Please refrain from talking.*

refrain [2] *NOUN* **(refrains)**
the chorus of a song

refresh *VERB* **(refreshes, refreshing, refreshed)**
to refresh someone who is tired is to make them feel fresh and strong again

refreshments *PLURAL NOUN*
food and drink

refrigerate *VERB* **(refrigerates, refrigerating, refrigerated)**
to refrigerate something is to freeze it so that it keeps in good condition

> WORD FAMILY
> **Refrigeration** is the process of refrigerating food.

refrigerator *NOUN* **(refrigerators)**
a cabinet in which you can store food at a low temperature to keep it fresh

refuel *VERB* **(refuels, refuelling, refuelled)**
to refuel a ship or aircraft is to supply it with more fuel

refuge *NOUN* **(refuges)**
a place where someone can go to be safe from danger

refugee *NOUN* **(refugees)** (*say* ref- yoo- **jee**)
someone who has had to leave their home or country because of war or persecution or disaster

refund *VERB* **(refunds, refunding, refunded)** (*say* ri- **fund**)
to refund money is to pay it back

refund *NOUN* **(refunds)** (*say* **ree**- fund)
money that is paid back to you

refuse *VERB* **(refuses, refusing, refused)** (*say* ri- **fewz**)
to refuse something, or to do something, is to say that you will not accept it or do it • *They refuse to help.*

> WORD FAMILY
> **Refusal**, or a **refusal**, is when someone refuses something.

refuse *NOUN* (*say* **ref**- yooss)
rubbish or waste material

regain *VERB* **(regains, regaining, regained)**
to regain something is to get it back

regard *VERB* **(regards, regarding, regarded)**
1 to regard someone or something as something is to think of them in a certain way • *I regard her as a friend.* **2** to regard someone or something is also to look at them closely

regard *NOUN*
regard is consideration or respect • *They acted without regard for our safety.*
with regard to something about it; in connection with it

regarding *PREPOSITION*
on the subject of; about • *There are rules regarding use of the library.*

regardless *ADJECTIVE*
paying no attention to something • *Buy it, regardless of the cost.*

regards *PLURAL NOUN*
kind wishes you send in a message • *Give your parents my regards.*

regatta *NOUN* (**regattas**) (*say* ri- gat- a)
a meeting for boat or yacht races

reggae *NOUN* (*say* reg- ay)
reggae is a West Indian style of music with a strong beat

regiment *NOUN* (**regiments**)
an army unit consisting of two or more battalions

> WORD FAMILY
> A **regimental** (for example) flag or mascot is one that belongs to a regiment.

region *NOUN* (**regions**)
1 a part of a country **2** a part of the world • *These plants only grow in tropical regions.*

> WORD FAMILY
> A **regional** (for example) accent or TV station is one that belongs to a particular region.

register *NOUN* (**registers**)
1 an official list of names or information, especially of people present each day at a school **2** the range of a voice or musical instrument

register *VERB* (**registers**, **registering**, **registered**)
1 to register something or someone is to put their name on an official list **2** a gauge or instrument registers a certain amount when that is what it shows • *The thermometer registered 25°.* **3** to register a letter or parcel is to have it officially recorded for sending with special care

> WORD FAMILY
> **Registration** is making an official record of something.

registration number *NOUN* (**registration numbers**)
the set of numbers and letters that a motor vehicle has when it is registered

regret *NOUN* (**regrets**)
you feel regret when you feel sorry or sad about something

regret *VERB* (**regrets**, **regretting**, **regretted**)
to regret something is to feel sorry or sad about it

regretful *ADJECTIVE*
feeling sorry or sad about something

> WORD FAMILY
> You say or do something **regretfully** when you do so in a way that shows you feel sorry or sad about something.

> OTHER WORD
> Take care not to confuse **regretful** and **regrettable**, which is the next word in this dictionary.

regrettable *ADJECTIVE*
you say something is regrettable when you wish it hadn't happened

regular *ADJECTIVE*
1 always happening at certain times • *You need regular meals.* **2** even or symmetrical • *She has beautiful regular teeth.* **3** normal or correct • *Do you want a regular or large coffee?* **4** a regular soldier belongs to a country's permanent army

> WORD FAMILY
> To happen with **regularity**, or to happen **regularly**, is to happen again and again or always at certain times.

regulate *VERB* (**regulates**, **regulating**, **regulated**)
to regulate something is to adjust or control it

> WORD FAMILY
> A **regulator** is a device for regulating something.

regulation *NOUN* (**regulations**)
1 a regulation is a rule or law **2** regulation is the adjusting or controlling of something

rehearse *VERB* (**rehearses**, **rehearsing**, **rehearsed**)
to rehearse (for example) a play or piece of music is to practise it before you perform it

> WORD FAMILY
> A **rehearsal** is when you practise something before performing it.

reign *VERB* (**reigns**, **reigning**, **reigned**)
1 to reign is to be king or queen **2** something reigns when it is the most noticeable or important thing • *Silence reigned for a while.*

reign *NOUN* (**reigns**)
the time when someone is king or queen

rein *NOUN* (**reins**)
a strap used by a rider to guide a horse

reindeer *NOUN* (**reindeer**)
a kind of deer that lives in Arctic regions

reinforce *VERB* (**reinforces**, **reinforcing**, **reinforced**)
to reinforce something is to strengthen it

reinforcement *NOUN* (**reinforcements**)
a thing that strengthens something
reinforcements extra troops or equipment sent to strengthen a military force

reject *VERB* (**rejects**, **rejecting**, **rejected**) (*say* ri- jekt)
1 to reject something or someone is to refuse to accept them • *They have rejected my offer of help.* **2** to reject something is to get rid of it • *Faulty parts are rejected at the factory.*

> WORD FAMILY
> **Rejection** is refusing to accept something.

a b c d e f g h i j k l m n o p q **r** s t u v w x y z

reject *NOUN* (**rejects**) (*say* ree- jekt)
a thing that is got rid of, especially because it is faulty or poorly made

rejoice *VERB* (**rejoices**, **rejoicing**, **rejoiced**)
to rejoice is to be very happy or pleased

relate *VERB* (**relates**, **relating**, **related**)
1 things relate to each other when there is a connection between them **2** to relate one thing with another is to compare them **3** to relate a story is to tell it

related *ADJECTIVE*
1 two people are related when they belong to the same family **2** two things are related when they are connected or linked in some way

relation *NOUN* (**relations**)
1 a relation is someone who is related to you **2** relation is the way that one thing is connected or compared with another

relationship *NOUN* (**relationships**)
1 the way people or things are connected with each other **2** the way people get on with one another • *There is a good relationship between the teachers and the children.* **3** a close friendship or connection between two people

relative *NOUN* (**relatives**)
your relatives are the people who are related to you

relative *ADJECTIVE*
1 connected or compared with something
2 compared with the average • *They live in relative comfort.*

relatively *ADVERB*
compared with other people or things; more or less • *Books are relatively cheap.*

relative pronoun *NOUN* (**relative pronouns**)
one of the words *who*, *what*, *which*, or *that*, placed in front of a clause to connect it with an earlier clause. In the sentence *we saw the man who had stolen the car*, the relative pronoun is 'who'

relax *VERB* (**relaxes**, **relaxing**, **relaxed**)
1 to relax is to become less anxious or worried **2** to relax is also to rest or stop working **3** to relax a part of you is make it less stiff or tense • *Try to relax your arm.*

> WORD FAMILY
> **Relaxation** is relaxing.

relay *VERB* (**relays**, **relaying**, **relayed**)
to relay a message or broadcast is to pass it on

relay *NOUN* (**relays**)
1 a race between two teams in which each member of the team runs part of the distance **2** a fresh group taking the place of another • *The firemen worked in relays.* **3** a device for passing on a broadcast

release *VERB* (**releases**, **releasing**, **released**)
1 to release something or someone is to set them free or unfasten them **2** to release a film or record is to make it available to the public

release *NOUN* (**releases**)
1 release is being released **2** a release is something released, especially a new film or record **3** a release is a device that unfastens something • *The seatbelt has a quick release.*

relegate *VERB* (**relegates**, **relegating**, **relegated**) (*say* rel- i- gayt)
1 a sports team is relegated when it goes down into a lower division of a league **2** to relegate something is to put it into a lower group or position than before

> WORD FAMILY
> **Relegation** is being relegated.

relent *VERB* (**relents**, **relenting**, **relented**)
to relent is to be less angry or severe than you were going to be

relentless *ADJECTIVE*
1 never stopping or letting up • *Their criticism was relentless.* **2** showing no pity • *They faced a relentless enemy.*
▷ **relentlessly** *ADVERB* in a relentless way

relevant *ADJECTIVE* (*say* rel- i- vant)
connected with what you are discussing or dealing with

> WORD FAMILY
> The **relevance** of something is how relevant it is.

reliable *ADJECTIVE*
able to be trusted or depended on

> WORD FAMILY
> **Reliability** is being reliable; you are **reliably** informed about something when you are told it by someone you trust.

reliant *ADJECTIVE*
you are reliant on someone or something when you rely on them and can't do without them
▷ **reliance** *NOUN* reliance on someone or something is being reliant on them

relic *NOUN* (**relics**)
something that has survived from an ancient time

relief *NOUN* (**reliefs**)
1 a good feeling you get because something unpleasant has stopped or is not going to happen • *It was such a relief when we reached dry land.* **2** relief is the ending or lessening of pain or suffering **3** aid given to people in need • *The charity is involved in famine relief.* **4** a relief is also a person or thing that takes over or helps with a job **5** relief is also a method of making a map or design that stands out from a flat surface • *The model shows hills and valleys in relief.*

relieve *VERB* (**relieves**, **relieving**, **relieved**)
to relieve pain or suffering is to end or lessen it **to relieve someone of something** is to take it from them

relieved *ADJECTIVE*
feeling good because something unpleasant has stopped or is not going to happen

religion *NOUN* (**religions**)
what people believe about God or gods, and how they worship

religious *ADJECTIVE*
1 to do with religion **2** someone is religious when they they believe in a religion and follow it carefully

religiously *ADVERB*
to do something religiously is to do it with great attention or care • *He wrote up his diary religiously every night.*

reluctant *ADJECTIVE*
you are reluctant to do something when you don't want to do it

> WORD FAMILY
> To show **reluctance** to do something is to show that you don't want to do it; you do something **reluctantly** when you would prefer not to be doing it.

rely *VERB* (**relies, relying, relied**)
to rely on someone or **something** is to trust them or need them to help or support you

remain *VERB* (**remains, remaining, remained**)
1 to remain is to continue in the same place or condition • *It will remain cloudy all day.* **2** to remain is also to be left over • *A lot of food remained after the party.*

remainder *NOUN* (**remainders**)
1 something left over **2** (*in mathematics*) the amount that is left over when you divide one number into another

remains *PLURAL NOUN*
1 something left over **2** ruins or relics **3** a dead body

remark *VERB* (**remarks, remarking, remarked**)
to remark on something is to say something that you have thought or noticed

remark *NOUN* (**remarks**)
something you say

remarkable *ADJECTIVE*
so unusual or impressive that you notice or remember it

> WORD FAMILY
> To do something (for example) **remarkably** well is to do it unusually or noticeably well.

remedial *ADJECTIVE* (*say* ri- **mee**- di- al)
1 helping to cure an illness or problem **2** helping children who learn slowly

remedy *NOUN* (**remedies**)
a cure for an illness or problem

remedy *VERB* (**remedies, remedying, remedied**)
to put something right

remember *VERB* (**remembers, remembering, remembered**)
1 to remember something is to keep it in your mind, or bring it into your mind when you need to **2** to remember someone is to be thinking about them

> WORD FAMILY
> You do something in **remembrance** of someone or something when you do it as a way of remembering them.

remind *VERB* (**reminds, reminding, reminded**)
to remind someone is to help or make them remember something • *The girl in that painting reminds me of you.*

> WORD FAMILY
> A **reminder** of a person or thing is something that makes you think about or remember them.

reminisce *VERB* (**reminisces, reminiscing, reminisced**) (*say* rem- in- **iss**)
to reminisce is to think or talk about things you remember

> WORD FAMILY
> **Reminiscences** are a person's memories of their past life; to be **reminiscent** of something is to remind you of it.

remnant *NOUN* (**remnants**)
a small piece of something left over

remorse *NOUN*
remorse is deep regret for something wrong you have done

remorseful *ADJECTIVE*
feeling remorse
▷ **remorsefully** *ADVERB* in a remorseful way

remorseless *ADJECTIVE*
relentless; not stopping or ending
▷ **remorselessly** *ADVERB* in a remorseless way

remote *ADJECTIVE* (**remoter, remotest**)
1 far away • *He lived on a remote island.* **2** unlikely or slight • *Their chances of winning were remote.*

> WORD FAMILY
> Something is not (for example) **remotely** funny when it is not even slightly funny; **remoteness** is being far away.

remote control *NOUN* (**remote controls**)
1 remote control is controlling something from a distance, usually by means of radio or electricity **2** a remote control is a device for doing this

removal *NOUN* (**removals**)
removing or moving something

remove *VERB* (**removes, removing, removed**)
to remove something is to take it away or take it off

Renaissance *NOUN*
the Renaissance was the revival of art and literature in Europe in the 14th–16th centuries

render *VERB* (**renders**, **rendering**, **rendered**)
1 to render someone (for example) speechless or unconscious is to put them in that condition • *The shock rendered her speechless.* **2** to render help or a service is to provide it

rendezvous *NOUN* (**rendezvous**) (*say* ron- day- voo)
1 a meeting with someone **2** a meeting place • *Exactly one hour later, Pronto arrived in a hired van at the agreed rendezvous.* — Debi Gliori, *Pure Dead Magic*

renew *VERB* (**renews**, **renewing**, **renewed**)
to renew something is to make it as it was before or replace it with something new

> WORD FAMILY
> **Renewal** is when something begins again or is replaced with something new.

renewable *ADJECTIVE*
able to be renewed or replaced; never completely used up

renown *NOUN*
renown is fame • *He is a man of great renown.*

> WORD FAMILY
> To be **renowned** is to be famous • *She is renowned for her generosity.*

rent *NOUN* (**rents**)
a regular payment for the use of something, especially a house or flat

rent *VERB* (**rents**, **renting**, **rented**)
to rent something is to pay money for the use of it

repair *VERB* (**repairs**, **repairing**, **repaired**)
to repair something is to mend it

repair *NOUN* (**repairs**)
1 repair is mending something • *The car is in for repair.* **2** a repair is a mended place • *You can hardly see the repair.*
to be in good repair is to be in good condition

repay *VERB* (**repays**, **repaying**, **repaid**)
1 to repay money is to pay it back **2** to repay someone's kindness is to do something for them in return

> WORD FAMILY
> **Repayment** is paying money back.

repeat *VERB* (**repeats**, **repeating**, **repeated**)
to repeat something is to say it or do it again

repeat *NOUN* (**repeats**)
something that is repeated, especially a television programme

repeatedly *ADVERB*
several times; again and again

repel *VERB* (**repels**, **repelling**, **repelled**)
1 to repel someone or something is to drive or force them away or apart **2** to repel someone is to make them disgusted

> WORD FAMILY
> Something is **repellent** when it is disgusting.

repent *VERB* (**repents**, **repenting**, **repented**)
to repent is to be sorry for what you have done

> WORD FAMILY
> To show **repentance** or feel **repentant** is to be sorry for what you have done.

repetition *NOUN* (**repetitions**)
1 repeating or doing something again **2** something repeated

repetitive *ADJECTIVE*
something is repetitive when it is repeated too much and so becomes boring

replace *VERB* (**replaces**, **replacing**, **replaced**)
1 to replace something is to put it back in its place **2** to replace someone or something is to take their place **3** to replace something is to put a new thing in the place of it • *We will have to replace the old engine with a new one.*

replacement *NOUN* (**replacements**)
1 replacement is when something or someone is replaced for another **2** a replacement is something used or given in place of another

replay *NOUN* (**replays**)
1 a football match played for a second time after the first match has ended in a draw **2** the playing or showing again of a recording

replay *VERB* (**replays**, **replaying**, **replayed**)
to replay a tape is to play it again

replica *NOUN* (**replicas**) (*say* rep- li- ka)
an exact copy

reply *NOUN* (**replies**)
something you say or write to deal with what someone else has asked or said

reply *VERB* (**replies**, **replying**, **replied**)
to reply is to give a reply

report *VERB* (**reports**, **reporting**, **reported**)
1 to report something is to describe something that has happened or something you have studied **2** to report someone is to complain about them to those in charge of them **3** to report to someone is to tell them you have arrived or are available

report *NOUN* (**reports**)
1 a description or account of something **2** a regular statement of how someone has worked or behaved, especially at school **3** an explosive sound • *We heard the report of a gun.*

reported speech *NOUN*
reported speech is when someone's words are given in a changed form reported by someone else, as in *He said that he would come* (reporting the words 'I will come')

reporter *NOUN* (**reporters**)
someone whose job is to collect news for a newspaper or for radio or television

repossess *VERB* (**repossesses**, **repossessing**, **repossessed**)
to repossess goods is to take them back when someone has bought them but cannot finish paying for them

represent *VERB* (**represents**, **representing**, **represented**)
1 to represent something or someone is to be a picture or model or symbol of them **2** to represent something is also to be a typical example of it **3** to represent someone is to support them by speaking or acting on their behalf

> WORD FAMILY
> A **representation** of a thing is something that shows or describes it.

representative *NOUN*
a person or thing that represents others

representative *ADJECTIVE*
typical of a group

repress *VERB* (**represses**, **repressing**, **repressed**)
to repress something or someone is to control or restrain them by force

> WORD FAMILY
> **Repression** is controlling someone by force; a **repressive** government is one that controls people by force.

reprieve *NOUN* (**reprieves**) (*say* ri- **preev**)
someone is given a reprieve when their punishment is postponed or cancelled, especially the death penalty

reprieve *VERB* (**reprieves**, **reprieving**, **reprieved**)
to reprieve someone is to cancel or postpone their punishment

reprimand *VERB* (**reprimands**, **reprimanding**, **reprimanded**)
to reprimand someone is to scold them or tell them off

reprimand *NOUN* (**reprimands**)
a telling-off

reprisal *NOUN* (**reprisals**) (*say* ri- **pry**- zal)
an act of revenge

reproach *VERB* (**reproaches**, **reproaching**, **reproached**)
to reproach someone is to blame them for something and show you are disappointed with them

reproach *NOUN*
reproach is blame or criticism • *His behaviour was beyond reproach.*

reproduce *VERB* (**reproduces**, **reproducing**, **reproduced**)
1 to reproduce something is to make it be heard or seen again • *Sound can be reproduced by discs or magnetic tapes.* **2** to reproduce something is also to copy it **3** animals and people reproduce when they produce offspring
▷ **reproductive** *ADJECTIVE* to do with producing offspring

reproduction *NOUN* (**reproductions**)
1 reproduction is the process of producing offspring **2** a reproduction is a copy of something

reptile *NOUN* (**reptiles**)
a cold-blooded animal that creeps or crawls, such as snakes and lizards

republic *NOUN* (**republics**)
a country ruled by a president and government that are chosen by the people

> WORD FAMILY
> A **republican** is someone who supports the idea of a republic.

Republican *NOUN* (**Republicans**)
a supporter of the Republican Party in the USA

repulsion *NOUN*
1 repulsion is a feeling of disgust **2** repulsion is also repelling something

repulsive *ADJECTIVE*
disgusting

reputation *NOUN* (**reputations**)
what most people think about a person or thing • *He has a reputation for being honest.*

request *VERB* (**requests**, **requesting**, **requested**)
to request something is to ask politely or formally for it

request *NOUN* (**requests**)
1 the action of asking for something **2** what someone asks for

require *VERB* (**requires**, **requiring**, **required**)
1 to require something is to need or want it **2** you are required to do something when you have to do it • *Pedestrians are required to walk on the pavements.*

> WORD FAMILY
> A **requirement** is something that is needed.

reread *VERB* (**rereads**, **rereading**, **reread**)
to reread something is to read it again

rescue *VERB* (**rescues**, **rescuing**, **rescued**)
to rescue someone is to save them from danger or capture

rescue *NOUN* (**rescues**)
when someone is rescued

> WORD FAMILY
> A **rescuer** is a person who rescues someone.

research *NOUN* (**researches**)
research is careful study or investigation to learn more about a subject

> WORD FAMILY
> A **researcher** is someone who does research.

a b c d e f g h i j k l m n o p q r s t u v w x y z

resemblance *NOUN* (**resemblances**)
there is a resemblance between two or more things when they are similar

resemble *VERB* (**resembles**, **resembling**, **resembled**)
to resemble someone or something is to look or sound like them

resent *VERB* (**resents**, **resenting**, **resented**)
to resent something is to feel hurt or angry about it

> WORD FAMILY
> To be **resentful** or to feel **resentment** is to feel hurt or angry about something.

reservation *NOUN* (**reservations**)
1 arranging for (for example) a restaurant table or seat on a train to be kept for you **2** an area of land kept for a special purpose **3** you have reservations about something when you feel doubtful or uneasy about it • *I had reservations about the excuses he made.*

reserve *VERB* (**reserves**, **reserving**, **reserved**)
to reserve something is to keep it or order it for a particular person or for a special use

reserve *NOUN* (**reserves**)
1 a person kept ready to be used if necessary, especially an extra player in a sports team **2** an area of land kept for a special purpose • *This island is a nature reserve.*

reserved *ADJECTIVE*
1 kept for someone • *These seats are reserved.*
2 someone is reserved when they are shy or unwilling to show their feelings

reservoir *NOUN* (**reservoirs**) (*say* rez- er- vwar)
a place where water is stored, especially an artificial lake

reshuffle *NOUN* (**reshuffles**)
a rearrangement, especially an exchange of jobs between people in a group • *The Prime Minister announced a Cabinet reshuffle.*

reside *VERB* (**resides**, **residing**, **resided**)
to reside in a place is to live there

residence *NOUN* (**residences**)
a place where someone lives

resident *NOUN* (**residents**)
someone who lives in a particular place

resign *VERB* (**resigns**, **resigning**, **resigned**)
to resign is to give up your job or position
to resign yourself to something is to accept a difficulty without complaining or arguing

resignation *NOUN* (**resignations**)
1 resignation is accepting a difficulty without complaining **2** a resignation is a letter saying you are resigning a job or position

resin *NOUN* (**resins**) (*say* rez- in)
resin is a sticky substance that comes from plants or is made artificially

resist *VERB* (**resists**, **resisting**, **resisted**)
to resist someone or something is to oppose them or try to stop them

resistance *NOUN*
1 resistance is fighting back or taking action against someone or something • *The troops came up against armed resistance.* **2** resistance is also the ability of a material to hold up the passage of electric current

> WORD FAMILY
> To be **resistant** to something is not to be affected or damaged by it.

resolute *ADJECTIVE* (*say* rez- o- loot)
determined or firm
▷ **resolutely** *ADVERB* in a resolute way

resolution *NOUN* (**resolutions**)
1 resolution is being determined or firm **2** a resolution is something you have decided to do **3** the resolution of a story is the last part where we find out how the story comes to an end and how some of the difficulties faced by the characters are sorted out

resolve *VERB* (**resolves**, **resolving**, **resolved**)
1 to resolve to do something is to decide to do it **2** to resolve doubts or disagreements is to deal successfully with them

resort *NOUN* (**resorts**)
a place where people go for a holiday, especially by the sea
the last resort the only thing you can do when everything else has failed

resort *VERB* (**resorts**, **resorting**, **resorted**)
to resort to something is to make use of it, especially when everything else has failed • *In the end they resorted to violence.*

resound *VERB* (**resounds**, **resounding**, **resounded**)
to resound is to fill a place with sound or to echo

resource *NOUN* (**resources**)
resources are things that you have and are able to use • *The land is rich in natural resources.*

respect *NOUN* (**respects**)
1 respect is admiration for someone's good qualities or achievements **2** respect is also consideration or concern • *Have respect for people's feelings.* **3** a respect is a detail or aspect • *In some respects, he is like his sister.*
with respect to something concerning something

respect *VERB* (**respects**, **respecting**, **respected**)
to respect someone is to have respect for them

respectable *ADJECTIVE*
1 a respectable person has good manners and character **2** something respectable is of a good size or standard
▷ **respectability** *NOUN* respectability is being respectable
▷ **respectably** *ADVERB* in a respectable way

respectful *ADJECTIVE*
showing respect; polite
▷ **respectfully** *ADVERB* in a respectful way • *She listened respectfully.*

respecting *PREPOSITION*
concerning; to do with

respective *ADJECTIVE*
belonging to each one of several • *We went to our respective rooms.*

respectively *ADVERB*
in the same order as the people or things already mentioned • *Emma and I went to London and Paris respectively.*

respiration *NOUN*
respiration is breathing
▷ **respiratory** *ADJECTIVE* to do with breathing

respirator *NOUN* (**respirators**)
a mask or machine for helping with people's breathing

respond *VERB* (**responds**, **responding**, **responded**)
to respond to someone or something is to reply or react to them

response *NOUN* (**responses**)
how you reply or react to something

responsibility *NOUN* (**responsibilities**)
1 responsibility is being responsible for something **2** a responsibility is something for which you are responsible

responsible *ADJECTIVE*
1 looking after something and likely to take the blame if anything goes wrong **2** able to be trusted **3** important and needing trust • *She has a responsible job.* **4** to be responsible for something is to be the cause of it • *Faulty wiring was responsible for the fire.*

> WORD FAMILY
> To behave **responsibly** is to behave in a way that shows you can be trusted.

rest[1] *NOUN* (**rests**)
1 a time when you can sleep or relax **2** a support for something

rest *VERB* (**rests**, **resting**, **rested**)
1 to rest is to sleep or relax **2** to rest on or against something is to lean on it • *The ladder is resting against the wall.* **3** to rest something is to lean or support it somewhere • *Rest the ladder on the roof.*

rest[2] *NOUN*
the rest the part that is left; the others

rest *VERB* (**rests**, **resting**, **rested**)
to rest with someone is to be their responsibility

restaurant *NOUN* (**restaurants**)
a place where you can buy a meal and eat it

restful *ADJECTIVE*
giving a feeling of rest

restless *ADJECTIVE*
you are restless when you can't relax or keep still
▷ **restlessly** *ADVERB* in a restless way
▷ **restlessness** *NOUN* restlessness is being restless

restore *VERB* (**restores**, **restoring**, **restored**)
to restore something is to put it back as it was or make it new again

> WORD FAMILY
> The **restoration** of something is when it is put back as it was or made new again.

restrain *VERB* (**restrains**, **restraining**, **restrained**)
to restrain someone or something is to hold them or keep them tightly controlled

> WORD FAMILY
> **Restraint** is self-control.

restrict *VERB* (**restricts**, **restricting**, **restricted**)
to restrict someone or something is to keep them within certain limits or stop them from acting freely

> WORD FAMILY
> A **restriction** is something that restricts; something is **restrictive** when it stops people doing what they want.

result *NOUN* (**results**)
1 a thing that happens because something else has happened **2** the score or situation at the end of a game or competition or race **3** the answer to a sum or problem

result *VERB* (**results**, **resulting**, **resulted**)
to result is to happen as a result
to result in something is to have it as a result • *The game resulted in a draw.*

resume *VERB* (**resumes**, **resuming**, **resumed**)
to resume, or to resume something, is to start again after stopping

> WORD FAMILY
> The **resumption** of something is when it starts again after stopping.

resuscitate *VERB* (**resuscitates**, **resuscitating**, **resuscitated**) (*say* ri- suss- it- ate)
to resuscitate someone is to revive them after they have been unconscious

retail *NOUN*
retail is the business of selling goods to the public

> WORD FAMILY
> A **retailer** is someone who sells goods to the public, and the business of doing this is **retailing**.

retain *VERB* (**retains**, **retaining**, **retained**)
1 to retain something is to keep it • *Retain your tickets for inspection.* **2** to retain something is to hold it in place

retina *NOUN* (**retinas**) (*say* ret- i- na)
a layer at the back of your eyeball that is sensitive to light

retire *VERB* (**retires**, **retiring**, **retired**)
1 someone retires when they give up regular work at a certain age **2** to retire is also to retreat or withdraw, or to go to bed • *He was so exhausted he had to retire from the race.*

> WORD FAMILY
> **Retirement** is the time when someone gives up regular work.

retiring *ADJECTIVE*
a retiring person is shy and avoids company

retort *VERB* (**retorts**, **retorting**, **retorted**)
to retort is to reply quickly or angrily

retort *NOUN* (**retorts**)
a quick or angry reply

retrace *VERB* (**retraces**, **retracing**, **retraced**)
to retrace your steps is to go back the way you came

retreat *VERB* (**retreats**, **retreating**, **retreated**)
to retreat is to go back when you are attacked or defeated

retrieve *VERB* (**retrieves**, **retrieving**, **retrieved**)
to retrieve something is to get it back or find it again
▷ **retrievable** *ADJECTIVE* able to be got back
▷ **retrieval** *NOUN* retrieval is retrieving something

retriever *NOUN* (**retrievers**)
a dog that can find and bring back birds and animals that have been shot

return *VERB* (**returns**, **returning**, **returned**)
1 to return is to come or go back to a place **2** to return something is to give it or send it back

return *NOUN* (**returns**)
1 when you come back to a place **2** something that is given or sent back **3** profit • *He gets a good return on his savings.* **4** a return ticket • *Do you want a single or return?*

return match *NOUN* (**return matches**)
a second match played between the same teams as an earlier match

return ticket *NOUN* (**return tickets**)
a ticket for a journey to a place and back again

reunion *NOUN* (**reunions**)
a meeting of people who have not met for some time

Rev.
short for **Reverend**

rev *VERB* (**revs**, **revving**, **revved**)
(*informal*) to rev an engine is to make it run quickly

rev *NOUN* (**revs**)
(*informal*) a revolution of an engine

reveal *VERB* (**reveals**, **revealing**, **revealed**)
to reveal something is to show it or make it known

> WORD FAMILY
> A **revelation** is a surprising fact that is made known.

revenge *NOUN*
revenge is harming someone because they have done harm to you

revenue *NOUN* (**revenues**) (*say* rev- e- nyoo)
revenue is money that a business or organization receives

revere *VERB* (**reveres**, **revering**, **revered**) (*say* ri- veer)
to revere someone or something is to respect them deeply or religiously

reverence *NOUN*
reverence is great respect or awe, especially towards God or holy things

> WORD FAMILY
> To be **reverent** is to feel or show awe or respect, especially towards God or holy things.

Reverend *NOUN*
the title of a member of the clergy • *This is the Reverend John Smith.*

reverse *NOUN*
1 the opposite way or side **2** reverse gear
in reverse going in the opposite direction

reverse *VERB* (**reverses**, **reversing**, **reversed**)
1 to reverse something is to turn it round **2** to reverse is to go backwards in a vehicle **3** to reverse a decision is to cancel it

> WORD FAMILY
> A **reversal** is when something is reversed; **reversible** clothing can be worn with either side on the outside.

reverse gear *NOUN*
reverse gear is the gear used to drive a vehicle backwards

review *NOUN* (**reviews**)
1 a published description and opinion of a book or film or play, or a piece of music **2** an inspection or survey of something

review *VERB* (**reviews**, **reviewing**, **reviewed**)
1 to review a book or play or film, or a piece of music, is to write a review of it **2** to review something is to inspect or survey it

> WORD FAMILY
> A **reviewer** is someone who writes a review.

> SPELLING
> Take care not to confuse **review** with the noun **revue**, which means a kind of entertainment.

revise *VERB* (**revises**, **revising**, **revised**)
1 before you do an examination, you revise when you go over work that you have already done **2** to revise something is to correct or change it

> WORD FAMILY
> A **revision** is a change or correction; **revision** is learning work before you do an examination.

revive *VERB* (**revives**, **reviving**, **revived**)
1 to revive something is to start using it again **2** to revive someone is to make them conscious again after fainting

> WORD FAMILY
> A **revival** is when something improves or becomes popular again.

revolt *VERB* (**revolts**, **revolting**, **revolted**)
1 to revolt is to rebel **2** something revolts you when it disgusts or horrifies you

> WORD FAMILY
> Something is **revolting** when it is very unpleasant or disgusting • *What a revolting smell.*

revolt *NOUN* (**revolts**)
a rebellion

revolution *NOUN* (**revolutions**)
1 a rebellion that overthrows the government **2** a complete change **3** one turn of a wheel or engine

revolutionary *ADJECTIVE*
1 to do with a revolution **2** completely new or original

revolutionize *VERB* (**revolutionizes**, **revolutionizing**, **revolutionized**)
to revolutionize something is to change it completely

revolve *VERB* (**revolves**, **revolving**, **revolved**)
something revolves when it goes round in a circle

revolver *NOUN* (**revolvers**)
a pistol that has a revolving store for bullets so that it can be fired several times without having to be loaded again

revue *NOUN* (**revues**)
an entertainment of songs and short sketches

> SPELLING
> Take care not to confuse **revue** with the noun **review**, which means a survey or a piece of writing.

reward *NOUN* (**rewards**)
something given to a person in return for something they have done

reward *VERB* (**rewards**, **rewarding**, **rewarded**)
to reward someone is to give them a reward

rewarding *ADJECTIVE*
pleasing or satisfying

rewind *VERB* (**rewinds**, **rewinding**, **rewound**)
to rewind a cassette or videotape is to wind it back to the beginning

rewrite *VERB* (**rewrites**, **rewriting**, **rewrote**, **rewritten**)
to rewrite something is to write it again or differently

rhetorical question *NOUN* (**rhetorical questions**)
a question that you ask for dramatic effect without expecting an answer, for example 'Who cares?'

rheumatism *NOUN* (*say* **roo**- ma- tizm)
rheumatism is a disease that causes pain and stiffness in the joints and muscles
▷ **rheumatic** *ADJECTIVE* suffering from rheumatism

rhinoceros *NOUN* (**rhinoceroses** or **rhinoceros**) (*say* ry- **noss**- er- os)
a large heavy animal with a horn or two horns on its nose

rhododendron *NOUN* (**rhododendrons**) (*say* roh- do- **den**- dron)
an evergreen shrub with large flowers

rhombus *NOUN* (**rhombuses**)
a shape with four equal sides and no right angles, like a diamond on a playing card

rhubarb *NOUN*
rhubarb is a plant with pink or green stalks used as food

rhyme *NOUN* (**rhymes**)
1 similar sounds in the endings of words, as in *bat* and *mat*, *batter* and *matter* **2** a short rhyming poem

rhyme *VERB* (**rhymes**, **rhyming**, **rhymed**)
1 a poem rhymes when it has rhymes at the ends of its lines **2** one word rhymes with another word when it forms a rhyme with it • *Bat rhymes with hat.*

rhythm *NOUN* (**rhythms**)
a regular pattern of beats, sounds, or movements in music and poetry

> WORD FAMILY
> Something is **rhythmic** or **rhythmical** when it has a rhythm; to do something **rhythmically** is to do it with a rhythm.

rib *NOUN* (**ribs**)
your ribs are the curved bones above your waist

ribbon *NOUN* (**ribbons**)
a strip of nylon, silk, or other material

rice *NOUN*
rice is white seeds from a cereal plant, used as food

rich *ADJECTIVE* (**richer**, **richest**)
1 someone is rich when they have a lot of money or property **2** something is rich when it is full of goodness, quality, or strength **3** costly or luxurious • *The house has rich furnishings.*
▷ **richness** *NOUN* richness is being rich

riches *PLURAL NOUN*
wealth

richly *ADVERB*
thoroughly, completely • *They richly deserved their punishment.*

rick *NOUN* (**ricks**)
a stack of hay or straw

rickety *ADJECTIVE*
a rickety (for example) bridge or chair is unsteady and likely to break or fall down • *The furniture could not have been much simpler: a very old chair, a rickety old bed, and a tumble-down table.* — Carlo Collodi, *The Adventures of Pinocchio*

rickshaw *NOUN* (**rickshaws**)
a two-wheeled carriage pulled by one or more people, used in the Far East

ricochet *VERB* (**ricochets**, **ricocheting**, **ricocheted**) (*say* rik- o- shay)
to ricochet is to bounce off something • *The bullets ricocheted off the wall.*

rid *VERB* (**rids**, **ridding**, **rid**)
to rid a person or place of something unwanted is to free them from it • *He rid the town of rats.*
to get rid of something or **someone** is to cause them to go away • *I wish I could get rid of these spots.*

riddance *NOUN*
good riddance used to show that you are glad that something or someone has gone

riddle *NOUN* (**riddles**)
a puzzling question, especially as a joke

ride *VERB* (**rides**, **riding**, **rode**, **ridden**)
1 to ride a horse or bicycle is to sit on it and be carried along on it **2** to ride is to travel in a vehicle

> WORD FAMILY
> A **rider** is someone who rides a horse.

ride *NOUN* (**rides**)
a journey on a horse or bicycle, or in a vehicle

ridge *NOUN* (**ridges**)
a long narrow part higher than the rest of something • *a mountain ridge*

ridicule *VERB* (**ridicules**, **ridiculing**, **ridiculed**)
to ridicule someone or something is to make fun of them

ridiculous *ADJECTIVE*
extremely silly or absurd
▹ **ridiculously** *ADVERB* in a ridiculous way

rifle *NOUN* (**rifles**)
a long gun. You hold it against your shoulder to fire it

rift *NOUN* (**rifts**)
1 a crack or split **2** a disagreement or a break in a friendship

rig *VERB* (**rigs**, **rigging**, **rigged**)
1 to rig a ship is to fit it with rigging, sails, and other equipment **2** to rig an election or competition is to control the result dishonestly
to rig someone out is to provide them with clothes or equipment
to rig something up is to make it quickly

rigging *NOUN*
rigging is the ropes that support a ship's masts and sails

right *ADJECTIVE*
1 on or towards the east if you think of yourself as facing north **2** correct • *Is this sum right?* **3** fair or honest • *It's not right to cheat.* **4** conservative; not in favour of political reforms

> WORD FAMILY
> The **rightness** of (for example) a decision is the fact that it is correct or fair.

right *ADVERB*
1 on or towards the right • *Turn right.* **2** completely • *Turn right round.* **3** exactly • *She stood right in the middle.* **4** straight; directly • *Go right ahead.*
right away immediately

right *NOUN* (**rights**)
1 the right side **2** what is fair or just; something that people ought to be allowed • *They fought for their rights.*

right *VERB* (**rights**, **righting**, **righted**)
1 to right something is to make it upright • *They learned how to right their canoe.* **2** to right something is also to put it right • *The fault might right itself.*

right angle *NOUN* (**right angles**)
an angle of 90 degrees, like angles in a rectangle

righteous *ADJECTIVE*
morally right or good; doing the right thing
▹ **righteously** *ADVERB* in a righteous way
▹ **righteousness** *NOUN* righteousness is being righteous

rightful *ADJECTIVE*
deserved or proper • *The bike was returned to its rightful owner.*

> WORD FAMILY
> Something is **rightfully** yours when you deserve to have it.

right-hand *ADJECTIVE*
on the right side of something

right-handed *ADJECTIVE*
using the right hand more than the left hand

rightly *ADVERB*
correctly or fairly

rigid *ADJECTIVE* (*say* rij- id)
1 firm or stiff **2** strict or harsh • *The rules are rigid.*

> WORD FAMILY
> **Rigidity** is being stiff or strict; to **rigidly** keep to a rule is to strictly keep to it.

rim *NOUN* (**rims**)
the outer edge of a cup or wheel or other round object

rime *NOUN* (**rimes**)
the part of a syllable that contains the vowel and, if there is one, the final consonant or group of consonants

rind *NOUN* (**rinds**)
the tough skin on bacon, cheese, or fruit

ring[1] *NOUN* **(rings)**
1 something in the shape of a circle • *The children sat in a ring around the clown.* **2** a thin circular piece of metal you wear on a finger **3** the place where a boxing match or other contest is held **4** the space where a circus performs

ring *VERB* **(rings, ringing, ringed)**
to ring something is to put a ring round it • *Ring the answer that you think is the right one.*

ring[2] *VERB* **(rings, ringing, rang, rung)**
1 to ring a bell is to make it sound **2** a bell rings when it makes a clear musical sound **3** to ring someone is to telephone them • *She rang her brother last night.*

ring *NOUN* **(rings)**
a ringing sound
to give someone a ring (*informal*) is to telephone them

ringleader *NOUN* **(ringleaders)**
someone who leads other people in rebellion or mischief or crime

ringlet *NOUN* **(ringlets)**
a long curled piece of hair

ringmaster *NOUN* **(ringmasters)**
the person who is in charge of a performance in the circus ring

ring road *NOUN* **(ring roads)**
a road that goes right round a town

ringworm *NOUN*
a skin disease which makes an itchy rash on the skin

rink *NOUN* **(rinks)**
a place made for skating

rinse *VERB* **(rinses, rinsing, rinsed)**
to rinse something is to wash it in clean water without soap

rinse *NOUN* **(rinses)**
a wash in clean water without soap

riot *NOUN* **(riots)**
wild or violent behaviour by a crowd of people in a public place

riot *VERB* **(riots, rioting, rioted)**
people riot when they run wild and behave violently in a public place

riotous *ADJECTIVE*
wild or unruly

> WORD FAMILY
> To be **riotously** funny is to be very funny indeed.

rip *VERB* **(rips, ripping, ripped)**
to rip something is to tear it roughly
to rip someone off (*slang*) is to charge them too much or swindle them

rip *NOUN* **(rips)**
a torn place

ripe *ADJECTIVE* **(riper, ripest)**
ready to be harvested or eaten
▷ **ripeness** *NOUN* ripeness is being ripe

ripen *VERB* **(ripens, ripening, ripened)**
1 to ripen something is to make it ripe **2** to ripen is to become ripe

rip-off *NOUN* **(rip-offs)**
(*slang*) when someone is cheated by being charged too much for something

ripple *NOUN* **(ripples)**
a small wave on the surface of water

ripple *VERB* **(ripples, rippling, rippled)**
water ripples when it forms small waves on the surface

rise *VERB* **(rises, rising, rose, risen)**
1 to rise is to go upwards • *Smoke was rising from the fire.* • *The sun rises in the east.* **2** to rise is also to get larger or more • *Prices rose this year.* **3** a person rises when they get up from sleeping or sitting • *They all rose as she came in.* **4** people rise, or rise up, when they rebel • *The army rose against the government.* **5** in cooking, a mixture rises when it swells up by the action of yeast

rise *NOUN* **(rises)**
1 an increase, especially in wages **2** an upward slope
to give rise to something is to cause it

risk *VERB* **(risks, risking, risked)**
to risk something is to take a chance of damaging or losing it • *They risked their lives during the rescue.*

risk *NOUN* **(risks)**
a chance that something bad will happen • *There's a risk that the river might flood.*

> WORD FAMILY
> Something is **risky** when doing it is dangerous or involves risk.

risotto *NOUN*
risotto is an Italian dish of rice cooked with vegetables and often with meat

rissole *NOUN* **(rissoles)**
a fried cake of minced meat

rite *NOUN* **(rites)**
a ceremony or ritual

ritual *NOUN* **(rituals)**
a regular ceremony or series of actions

rival *NOUN* **(rivals)**
a person or thing that competes with another or tries to do the same thing

> WORD FAMILY
> A **rivalry** is when two people compete against each other.

rival *VERB* **(rivals, rivalling, rivalled)**
to rival someone or something is to be as good as they are • *Nothing can rival the taste of home-made ice cream.*

river *NOUN* **(rivers)**
a large natural stream of water flowing along a channel

rivet *NOUN* (**rivets**)
a strong metal pin for holding pieces of metal together

rivet *VERB* (**rivets, riveting, riveted**)
1 to rivet something is to fasten it with rivets **2** to rivet someone is to hold them still • *She stood riveted to the spot.* **3** to be riveted by something is to be fascinated by it • *The children were riveted by his story.*

> WORD FAMILY
> Something is **riveting** when it is fascinating and holds your attention.

road *NOUN* (**roads**)
a level way with a hard surface made for traffic to go along

road rage *NOUN*
road rage is angry or violent behaviour by road users

roadroller *NOUN* (**roadrollers**)
a heavy motor vehicle with wide metal wheels used to flatten surfaces when making roads

roadside *NOUN* (**roadsides**)
the side of a road

roadway *NOUN* (**roadways**)
the middle part of the road, used by traffic

roam *VERB* (**roams, roaming, roamed**)
to roam is to wander • *They roamed about the city.* • *For many months, close to starvation, I roamed the hills and glens of the Highlands, hunting and scavenging for my food like some wild beast.* — Michael Morpurgo, *The Last Wolf*

roar *NOUN* (**roars**)
a loud deep sound of the kind that a lion makes

roar *VERB* (**roars, roaring, roared**)
to roar is to make a loud deep sound
to do a roaring trade is to sell a lot of something quickly

roast *VERB* (**roasts, roasting, roasted**)
1 to roast food is to cook it in an oven or over a fire **2** you say you are roasting when you are very hot

rob *VERB* (**robs, robbing, robbed**)
to rob someone or a place is to steal something from them • *He robbed me of my watch.* • *The bank's been robbed.*

> WORD FAMILY
> A **robber** is someone who steals something; a **robbery** is when something is stolen.

robe *NOUN* (**robes**)
a long loose piece of clothing

robin *NOUN* (**robins**)
a small brown bird with a red breast

robot *NOUN* (**robots**)
a machine that imitates the movements of a person or does the work of a person

robust *ADJECTIVE*
tough and strong

rock[1] *NOUN* (**rocks**)
1 a rock is a large stone **2** rock is a large mass of stone **3** rock is also a hard sweet usually shaped like a stick and sold at the seaside

rock[2] *VERB* (**rocks, rocking, rocked**)
1 to rock is to move gently backwards and forwards or from side to side **2** to rock something is to make it do this

rock *NOUN* (**rocks**)
rock music

rock-bottom *ADJECTIVE*
very low • *They're selling mobile phones at rock-bottom prices.*

rocker *NOUN* (**rockers**)
1 a rocking chair **2** a curved support for a chair or cradle
to be off your rocker (*slang*) is to be crazy or mad

rockery *NOUN* (**rockeries**)
part of a garden where people grow flowers between rocks

rocket *NOUN* (**rockets**)
1 a firework that shoots high into the air **2** a pointed tube-shaped vehicle pushed into the air by hot gases, especially as a spacecraft or weapon

rocking chair *NOUN* (**rocking chairs**)
a chair which can be rocked by the person sitting in it

rock music *NOUN*
rock music is popular music with a heavy beat

rocky *ADJECTIVE* (**rockier, rockiest**)
1 a rocky place is full of rocks **2** unsteady or shaky

rod *NOUN* (**rods**)
1 a long thin stick or bar **2** a rod with a line attached for fishing

rode
past tense of **ride** *VERB*

rodent *NOUN* (**rodents**)
an animal that has large front teeth for gnawing things, such as a rat, mouse, or squirrel

rodeo *NOUN* (**rodeos**) (*say* roh- **day**- oh or roh- di- oh)
a display or contest of cowboys' skill in riding and in controlling cattle

rogue *NOUN* (**rogues**)
a dishonest or mischievous person

> WORD FAMILY
> A **roguish** smile is a mischievous one.

role *NOUN* (**roles**)
1 the part that an actor plays in a play, film, or story **2** the purpose something has • *Computers have a role in teaching.*

roll *VERB* (**rolls, rolling, rolled**)
1 to roll is to move along by turning over and over, like a ball or wheel **2** to roll something is to make it do this **3** to roll something, or roll something up, is to form it into the shape of a

cylinder or ball **4** to roll something soft is to flatten it by moving a round heavy object over it **5** a ship rolls when it sways from side to side **6** drums roll when they make a long rumbling sound

roll *NOUN* (**rolls**)
1 a cylinder made by rolling something up **2** a small loaf of bread shaped like a bun **3** a list of names **4** the rumbling sound of drums

roller *NOUN* (**rollers**)
1 a cylinder-shaped object, especially one used for flattening things **2** a long swelling wave in the sea

Rollerblade *NOUN* (**Rollerblades**)
Rollerblades are boots with a line of small wheels fitted underneath, so that you can move smoothly over the ground

roller skate *NOUN* (**roller skates**)
roller skates are boots with two pairs of wheels fitted underneath, so that you can move smoothly over the ground

rolling pin *NOUN* (**rolling pins**)
a heavy cylinder you roll over pastry to flatten it

ROM
short for *read-only memory*, a type of computer memory with information that can be accessed but not changed by the user

Roman *NOUN* (**Romans**)
a person who lived in ancient Rome

Roman *ADJECTIVE*
to do with ancient Rome

Roman candle *NOUN* (**Roman candles**)
a firework that shoots up coloured sparks

Roman Catholic *NOUN* (**Roman Catholics**)
a member of the Church with the Pope in Rome at its head

Romance *ADJECTIVE*
a Romance language belongs to the group of languages which grew out of Latin and which includes French, Italian, Spanish, and Portuguese

romance *NOUN* (**romances**)
1 romance is experiences and feelings connected with love **2** a romance is a love affair or a love story

Roman numerals *PLURAL NOUN*
letters that represent numbers, as used by the ancient Romans (compare *arabic figures*): I = 1, V = 5, X = 10, L = 50, C = 100, and M = 1000

romantic *ADJECTIVE*
1 to do with love or romance **2** to do with emotions or imagination
▷ **romantically** *ADVERB* in a romantic way

Romany *NOUN* (*say* roh- ma- ni)
Romany is the language of the gypsies

romp *VERB* (**romps**, **romping**, **romped**)
to romp is to play in a lively way

romp *NOUN* (**romps**)
a spell of lively play

rompers *PLURAL NOUN*
a piece of clothing for a young child, covering the body and legs

roof *NOUN* (**roofs**)
1 the part that covers the top of a building, shelter, or vehicle **2** the upper part of your mouth

rook *NOUN* (**rooks**)
1 a black bird that looks like a crow **2** a piece in chess, also called a *castle*

room *NOUN* (**rooms**)
1 a room is a part of a building with its own walls and ceiling **2** room is space for someone or something • *Is there room for me?*

roomful *ADJECTIVE* (**roomfuls**)
the amount or number a room will hold

roomy *ADJECTIVE* (**roomier**, **roomiest**)
somewhere is roomy when there is plenty of room or space inside

roost *NOUN* (**roosts**)
the place where a bird rests

root *NOUN* (**roots**)
1 the part of a plant that grows under the ground **2** a source or basis of something • *People say that money is the root of all evil.* **3** a number in relation to the number it produces when multiplied by itself • *9 is the square root of 81.*
to take root is to grow roots or to become established • *The custom never took root in other countries.*

root *VERB* (**roots**, **rooting**, **rooted**)
1 to root is to take root in the ground **2** to root someone is to fix them firmly • *Fear rooted him to the spot.*
to root something out is to find it and get rid of it

root word *NOUN* (**root words**)
a word that you can add prefixes and suffixes to in order to make different words. For example, you can make the words *resting*, *restful*, and *unrest* from the root word *rest*

rope *NOUN* (**ropes**)
a strong thick cord made of strands twisted together
to show someone the ropes is to show them how to do a job

rose [1] *NOUN* (**roses**)
a scented flower with a long thorny stem

rose [2]
past tense of **rise** *VERB*

rosette *NOUN* (**rosettes**)
a large circular badge made of ribbons

rosy *ADJECTIVE* (**rosier**, **rosiest**)
1 pink **2** hopeful or cheerful • *The future looks rosy.*

rot *VERB* (**rots**, **rotting**, **rotted**)
to rot is to go soft or bad so that it is useless • *This wood has rotted.*

rot *NOUN*
1 rot is decay **2** (*informal*) rot is also nonsense •*Don't talk such rot.*

rota *NOUN* (**rotas**)
a list of people who have to do tasks

rotate *VERB* (**rotates**, **rotating**, **rotated**)
1 to rotate is to go round like a wheel **2** to rotate is to take turns at something •*The job of treasurer rotates.*

> WORD FAMILY
> A (for example) **rotary** engine has parts that turn round.

rotation *NOUN*
1 rotation, or a rotation, is when something goes round like a wheel **2** rotation is also taking turns to do something

rotor *NOUN* (**rotors**)
the part of a machine that goes round, especially the large horizontal propeller of a helicopter

rotten *ADJECTIVE*
1 rotted or decayed •*There was rotten fruit on the ground.* **2** (*informal*) nasty or very bad •*We had rotten weather.*
▷ **rottenness** *NOUN* rottenness is being rotten

rottweiler *NOUN* (**rottweilers**)
a large dog with short black and tan hair, often kept as a guard dog

rough *ADJECTIVE* (**rougher**, **roughest**)
1 not smooth; uneven **2** violent; not gentle •*He is a rough boy.* **3** not exact; done quickly •*It's only a rough guess.*
▷ **roughness** *NOUN* roughness is being rough

roughage *NOUN*
roughage is fibre in food, which helps you to digest it

roughen *VERB* (**roughens**, **roughening**, **roughened**)
to roughen something is to make it rough

roughly *ADVERB*
1 approximately; not exactly •*There were roughly a hundred people there.* **2** in a rough way; not gently •*She pushed him roughly out of the way.*

round *ADJECTIVE* (**rounder**, **roundest**)
1 shaped like a circle or ball or cylinder **2** full or complete •*We bought a round dozen.* **3** a round trip is one that returns to the start

round *ADVERB*
1 in a circle or curve; by a longer route •*Go round to the back of the house.* **2** in every direction or to every person •*Hand the cakes round.* **3** in a new direction •*Turn your chair round.* **4** to someone's house or place of work •*Come round at lunchtime.*

round *PREPOSITION*
1 on all sides of •*We'll put a fence round the field.* **2** in a curve or circle about •*The earth moves round the sun.* **3** to every part of •*Show them round the house.*

round *NOUN* (**rounds**)
1 each stage in a competition •*The winners go on to the next round.* **2** a series of visits or calls made by a doctor, postman, or other person **3** a whole slice of bread, or a sandwich made from two whole slices of bread **4** a shot or series of shots from a gun; a piece of ammunition **5** a song in which people sing the same words but start at different times

round *VERB* (**rounds**, **rounding**, **rounded**)
to round a place is to travel round it •*A large car rounded the corner.*
to round a number down is to decrease it to the nearest lower number •*123.4 may be rounded down to 123.*
to round a number up is to increase it to the nearest higher number •*123.7 may be rounded up to 124.*
to round something off is to finish it
to round up people or things is to gather them together

roundabout *NOUN* (**roundabouts**)
1 a road junction at which traffic has to pass round a circular island **2** a merry-go-round

roundabout *ADJECTIVE*
not using the shortest or most direct way •*We went by a roundabout route.*

rounded *ADJECTIVE*
round in shape

rounders *NOUN*
rounders is a game in which players try to hit a ball and run round a circuit

Roundhead *NOUN* (**Roundheads**)
an opponent of King Charles I in the English Civil War of 1642-9

roundly *ADVERB*
thoroughly or severely •*We were roundly told off for being late.*

rouse *VERB* (**rouses**, **rousing**, **roused**)
to rouse someone is to wake them up or make them excited •*I had eaten my hay and was lying down in my straw fast asleep, when I was suddenly roused by the stable bell ringing very loud.* — Anna Sewell, *Black Beauty*

rout *VERB* (**routs**, **routing**, **routed**) (*say* rowt)
to rout an enemy is to defeat them and chase them away

rout *NOUN* (**routs**) (*say* rowt)
a disorganized retreat after being defeated in a battle

route *NOUN* (**routes**) (*say* root)
the way you have to go to get to a place

routine *NOUN* (**routines**) (*say* roo- **teen**)
a regular or fixed way of doing things

rove *VERB* (**roves**, **roving**, **roved**)
to rove is to roam or wander •*The Trunchbull's dangerous glittering eyes roved around the classroom.* — Roald Dahl, *Matilda*
▷ **rover** *NOUN* someone who roves

row [1] *NOUN* (**rows**) (*rhymes with* **go**)
a line of people or things

row [2] *VERB* (**rows**, **rowing**, **rowed**) (*rhymes with* **go**)
to row a boat is to use oars to make it move

> WORD FAMILY
> A **rower** is someone who rows a boat.

row [3] *NOUN* (**rows**) (*rhymes with* **cow**)
1 a great noise or disturbance **2** a quarrel; a noisy argument or scolding

row *VERB* (**rows**, **rowing**, **rowed**)
people row when they have a noisy argument

rowdy *ADJECTIVE* (**rowdier**, **rowdiest**)
noisy and disorderly
▷ **rowdily** *ADVERB* in a rowdy way
▷ **rowdiness** *NOUN* rowdiness is being rowdy

rowing boat *NOUN* (**rowing boats**)
a small boat that you move forward by using oars

royal *ADJECTIVE*
to do with a king or queen

royalty *NOUN*
1 royalty is being royal **2** royalty is also a royal person or royal people • *We will be in the presence of royalty.*

rub *VERB* (**rubs**, **rubbing**, **rubbed**)
to rub something is to move it backwards and forwards while pressing it on something else • *He rubbed his hands together.*
to rub something off or **out** is to make it disappear by rubbing it

rub *NOUN* (**rubs**)
when you rub something • *Give it a quick rub.*

rubber *NOUN* (**rubbers**)
1 rubber is a strong elastic substance used for making tyres, balls, hoses, and other things **2** a rubber is a piece of rubber or soft plastic for rubbing out pencil marks

> WORD FAMILY
> Something is **rubbery** when it looks or feels like rubber.

rubbish *NOUN*
1 rubbish is things that are not wanted or needed **2** rubbish is also nonsense

rubble *NOUN*
rubble is broken pieces of brick or stone

ruby *NOUN* (**rubies**)
a red jewel

rucksack *NOUN* (**rucksacks**)
a bag with shoulder straps that you carry on your back

rudder *NOUN* (**rudders**)
a flat hinged device at the back of a ship or aircraft, used for steering it

ruddy *ADJECTIVE* (**ruddier**, **ruddiest**)
red and healthy-looking • *He had a ruddy face.*

rude *ADJECTIVE* (**ruder**, **rudest**)
1 not polite; not showing respect for other people • *It was rude of me to push in.* **2** indecent or improper • *a rude joke* **3** roughly made • *a rude shelter*
▷ **rudely** *ADVERB* in a rude way
▷ **rudeness** *NOUN* rudeness is being rude

ruffian *NOUN* (**ruffians**)
a violent brutal person

ruffle *VERB* (**ruffles**, **ruffling**, **ruffled**)
1 to ruffle something is to disturb its smoothness • *The bird ruffled its feathers.* **2** to ruffle someone is to annoy them or upset them

rug *NOUN* (**rugs**)
1 a thick piece of material that partly covers a floor **2** a thick blanket

rugby or **rugby football** *NOUN*
rugby is a kind of football game using an oval ball that players may kick or carry

rugged *ADJECTIVE* (*say* **rug**- id)
something rugged has a rough or uneven surface or outline • *His face was rugged.* • *It has a rugged coastline.*

ruin *VERB* (**ruins**, **ruining**, **ruined**)
to ruin something is to spoil it or destroy it completely

ruin *NOUN* (**ruins**)
1 a ruin is a building that has been so badly damaged that it has almost all fallen down **2** ruin is when something is ruined or destoyed
to be in ruins is to be destroyed • *My plans were in ruins.*

> WORD FAMILY
> To be **ruinous** is to cause something to be destroyed.

rule *NOUN* (**rules**)
1 a rule is something that people have to obey **2** rule is ruling or governing • *The country used to be under French rule.*
as a rule usually; normally

rule *VERB* (**rules**, **ruling**, **ruled**)
1 to rule people is to govern them; to rule is to be a ruler **2** to rule something is to make a decision • *The referee ruled that it was a foul.* **3** to rule a line is to draw a straight line with a ruler or other straight edge

ruler *NOUN* (**rulers**)
1 someone who governs a country **2** a strip of wood, plastic, or metal with straight edges, used for measuring and drawing straight lines

ruling *NOUN* (**rulings**)
a judgement or decision • *I will give my ruling tomorrow.*

rum *NOUN* (**rums**)
rum is a strong alcoholic drink made from sugar cane

rumble *VERB* (**rumbles**, **rumbling**, **rumbled**)
to rumble is to make a deep heavy sound like thunder • *His stomach was rumbling.*

a b c d e f g h i j k l m n o p q r s t u v w x y z

rumble *NOUN* (**rumbles**)
a long deep heavy sound • *There was a rumble of thunder in the distance.*

rummage *VERB* (**rummages, rummaging, rummaged**)
to rummage is to turn things over or move them about while looking for something

rummy *NOUN*
rummy is a card game in which players try to form sets or sequences of cards

rumour *NOUN* (**rumours**)
something that a lot of people are saying, although it may not be true

rump *NOUN* (**rumps**)
the back part of an animal, above its hind legs

run *VERB* (**runs, running, ran, run**)
1 to run is to move with quick steps and with both feet off the ground for a time **2** to run is also to move or go or travel • *Tears ran down his cheeks.* **3** a tap or your nose runs when liquid flows from it **4** an engine or machine runs when it is working or functioning • *The engine was running smoothly.* **5** to run something is to manage it or organize it • *She runs a corner shop.* **6** to run someone somewhere is to give them a lift there
to run a risk is to take a chance
to run away is to leave a place quickly or secretly
to run into someone is to meet them unexpectedly
to run out of something is to have used up a supply of it
to run someone over is to knock them down with a car or bicycle

run *NOUN* (**runs**)
1 a spell of running • *Let's go for a run.* **2** a point scored in cricket or baseball **3** a series of damaged stitches in a pair of tights or other piece of clothing **4** a continuous series of events • *They've had a run of good luck.* **5** a place with a fence round it for keeping animals
to be on the run is to be running away, especially from the police

runaway *NOUN* (**runaways**)
someone who has run away from home

rung [1] *NOUN* (**rungs**)
each of the short crossbars on a ladder

rung [2]
past participle of **ring** [2] *VERB*

runner *NOUN* (**runners**)
1 a person or animal that runs in a race **2** the part of a sledge that slides along the ground

runner bean *NOUN* (**runner beans**)
a kind of climbing bean

runner-up *NOUN* (**runners-up**)
someone who comes second in a race or competition

runny *ADJECTIVE* (**runnier, runniest**)
flowing or moving like liquid

runway *NOUN* (**runways**)
a long strip with a hard surface for aircraft to take off and land

rural *ADJECTIVE*
to do with the countryside; in the country

rush [1] *VERB* (**rushes, rushing, rushed**)
1 to rush is to hurry **2** to rush someone is to attack or capture them by surprise

rush *NOUN*
a rush is a hurry • *I can't stop — I'm in a rush.*

rush [2] *NOUN* (**rushes**)
rushes are plants with thin stems that grow in wet or marshy places

rush hour *NOUN*
the rush hour is the time when traffic is busiest

rusk *NOUN* (**rusks**)
a kind of hard dry biscuit for babies to chew

rust *NOUN*
rust is a red or brown substance formed on metal that is exposed to air and dampness

rust *VERB* (**rusts, rusting, rusted**)
metal rusts when it develops rust

rustic *ADJECTIVE*
to do with the countryside

rustle *VERB* (**rustles, rustling, rustled**)
1 to rustle is to make a gentle sound like dry leaves being blown by the wind **2** to rustle horses or cattle is to steal them
to rustle something up (*informal*) is to collect it or provide it quickly

> **WORD FAMILY**
> A **rustler** is someone who rustles horses or cattle.

rusty *ADJECTIVE* (**rustier, rustiest**)
1 coated with rust **2** not as good as it used to be because you have not had enough practice • *My French is a bit rusty.*

rut *NOUN* (**ruts**)
a deep groove made by wheels in soft ground
to be in a rut is to have a dull life with no changes

> **WORD FAMILY**
> A **rutted** road or path is marked with ruts.

ruthless *ADJECTIVE*
someone is ruthless when they are determined to get what they want and don't care if they hurt other people
▷ **ruthlessly** *ADVERB* in a ruthless way
▷ **ruthlessness** *NOUN* ruthlessness is being ruthless

rye *NOUN*
rye is a cereal used to make bread and biscuits

Ss

sabbath *NOUN* (**sabbaths**)
the sabbath is the weekly day for rest and prayer, Saturday for Jews, Sunday for Christians

sabotage *NOUN* (*say* **sab**- o- tah*zh*)
sabotage is deliberately damaging machinery or equipment

sabotage *VERB* (**sabotages**, **sabotaging**, **sabotaged**)
to sabotage machinery or equipment is to deliberately damage it

> WORD FAMILY
> A **saboteur** is someone who commits sabotage.

sac *NOUN* (**sacs**)
any bag-like part of an animal or plant

saccharin *NOUN* (*say* **sak**- a- rin)
saccharin is a very sweet substance used as a substitute for sugar

sachet *NOUN* (**sachets**) (*say* **sash**- ay)
a small sealed packet of something such as shampoo or sugar

sack[1] *NOUN* (**sacks**)
a large bag made of strong material
to get the sack (*informal*) is to be dismissed from your job

sack *VERB* (**sacks**, **sacking**, **sacked**)
(*informal*) to sack someone is to dismiss them from their job

sack[2] *VERB* (**sacks**, **sacking**, **sacked**)
to sack a place is to plunder and destroy it in war

sacred *ADJECTIVE*
to do with God or a god; holy

sacrifice *NOUN* (**sacrifices**)
1 giving up a thing that you value so that something good may happen • *If you want to save some money you might have to make a few sacrifices.* **2** killing an animal or person as an offering to a god
▷ **sacrificial** *ADJECTIVE* offered as a sacrifice

sacrifice *VERB* (**sacrifices**, **sacrificing**, **sacrificed**)
1 to sacrifice something is to give it up so that something good may happen **2** to sacrifice an animal or person is to kill them as an offering to a god

sad *ADJECTIVE* (**sadder**, **saddest**)
unhappy; showing sorrow or causing it

> WORD FAMILY
> To do something **sadly** is to do it in a sad way • *He shook his head sadly*; **sadness** is being sad.

sadden *VERB* (**saddens**, **saddening**, **saddened**)
something saddens you when it makes you sad or unhappy

saddle *NOUN* (**saddles**)
1 a seat that you put on the back of a horse or other animal so that you can ride it **2** the seat of a bicycle

saddle *VERB* (**saddles**, **saddling**, **saddled**)
to saddle an animal is to put a saddle on its back
to be saddled with something is to have it as a burden or problem

sadist *NOUN* (**sadists**) (*say* **say**- dist)
someone who enjoys hurting other people

> WORD FAMILY
> **Sadism** is being a sadist; a **sadistic** person enjoys hurting other people.

safari *NOUN* (**safaris**) (*say* sa- **far**- i)
an expedition to see wild animals or hunt them

safari park *NOUN* (**safari parks**)
a large park where wild animals can roam around freely and visitors can watch them from their cars

safe *ADJECTIVE* (**safer**, **safest**)
1 free from danger; protected **2** not causing danger • *Drive at a safe speed.*

> WORD FAMILY
> To do something **safely** is to do it without risk or danger • *The plane landed safely.*

safe *NOUN* (**safes**)
a strong cupboard or box in which valuable things can be locked away safely

safeguard *NOUN* (**safeguards**)
something that protects you against danger

safeguard *VERB* (**safeguard**, **safeguards**, **safeguarded**)
to safeguard something is to protect it from danger

safety *NOUN*
safety is being safe; protection • *We listened to a talk on road safety.*

safety belt *NOUN* (**safety belts**)
a belt to hold someone securely in a seat

safety pin *NOUN* (**safety pins**)
a curved pin made with a clip that closes to cover the point

sag *VERB* (**sags**, **sagging**, **sagged**)
something sags when it sinks slightly in the middle because something heavy is pressing on it

saga *NOUN* (**sagas**)
a long story with many adventures

sago *NOUN*
sago is a starchy white food used in puddings

said
past tense and past participle of **say** *VERB*

sail *NOUN* (**sails**)
1 a large piece of strong cloth attached to a mast to make a boat move **2** a short voyage • *We went for a sail around the island.* **3** an arm of a windmill
to set sail is to start on a voyage in a ship

sail *VERB* (**sails, sailing, sailed**)
1 to sail somewhere is to travel there in a ship **2** a ship or boat sails when it starts out on a voyage • *What time does the ferry sail?* **3** to sail a ship or boat is to control it

sailboard *NOUN* (**sailboards**)
a flat board with a mast and sail, used for windsurfing

sailor *NOUN* (**sailors**)
1 a member of a ship's crew **2** someone who sails

saint *NOUN* (**saints**)
a holy or very good person

> WORD FAMILY
> A **saintly** person is very good or holy.

sake *NOUN*
for the sake of something in order to do it or get it • *He'll do anything for the sake of money.*
for someone's sake in order to help them or please them • *She went to great trouble for his sake.*

salaam *INTERJECTION*
a word used by Muslims to greet someone

salad *NOUN* (**salads**)
a mixture of vegetables eaten cold and often raw

salami *NOUN* (**salamis**)
salami is a kind of strong spicy sausage

salary *NOUN* (**salaries**)
a regular wage, usually paid every month

sale *NOUN* (**sales**)
1 the selling of something **2** a time when a shop sells things at reduced prices
for sale or **on sale** able to be bought

salesperson *NOUN* (**salespersons**)
someone whose job is to sell things

> OTHER WORDS
> A male salesperson is also called a **salesman** and a female salesperson is also called a **saleswoman**.

saline *ADJECTIVE*
containing salt

saliva *NOUN* (*say* sa- ly- va)
saliva is the natural liquid in your mouth

sally *VERB* (**sallies, sallying, sallied**)
to sally forth or **sally out** is to rush forward or rush ahead

salmon *NOUN* (**salmon**)
a large fish with pink flesh, used for food

salon *NOUN* (**salons**)
a room or shop where a hairdresser or a beauty specialist works

saloon *NOUN* (**saloons**)
1 a motor car with a hard roof **2** a bar in a public house

salt *NOUN*
salt is the white substance that gives sea water its taste and is used for flavouring food

> WORD FAMILY
> **Salty** food or water tastes of salt.

salt *VERB* (**salts, salting, salted**)
to salt food is to use salt to flavour or preserve it

salute *VERB* (**salutes, saluting, saluted**)
to salute is to raise your hand to your forehead as a sign of respect or greeting

salute *NOUN* (**salutes**)
1 the act of saluting **2** when guns are fired as a sign of respect on an official occasion

salvage *VERB* (**salvages, salvaging, salvaged**)
to salvage something such as a damaged ship is to save or rescue it or parts of it • *Jan's treasure box was one of the few things which they had salvaged from the wrecked canoes.* — Ian Serraillier, *The Silver Sword*

salvation *NOUN*
salvation is saving someone or something

same *ADJECTIVE*
not different; exactly equal or alike • *We are the same age.* • *Look, these two leaves are exactly the same.*

samosa *NOUN* (**samosas**)
a small case of crisp pastry filled with a mixture of spicy meat or vegetables

sample *NOUN* (**samples**)
a small amount that shows what something is like

sample *VERB* (**samples, sampling, sampled**)
1 to sample something is to take a sample of it • *Scientists sampled the lake water.* **2** to sample something is also to try part of it • *She sampled the cake.*

sanctuary *NOUN* (**sanctuaries**)
1 a safe place, especially for someone who is being chased or attacked **2** a place where wildlife is protected • *We visited a bird sanctuary.*

sand *NOUN*
sand is the tiny grains of rock that you find on beaches and in deserts

sand *VERB* (**sands, sanding, sanded**)
to sand a surface is to smooth or polish it with sandpaper or rough material

> WORD FAMILY
> A **sander** is a machine for sanding surfaces.

sandal *NOUN* (**sandals**)
a lightweight shoe with straps that go round your foot

sandbag *NOUN* (**sandbags**)
sandbags are bags filled with sand, used to build defences against flood water or bullets

sandpaper *NOUN*
sandpaper is strong paper coated with hard grains, rubbed on rough surfaces to make them smooth

sands *PLURAL NOUN*
a beach or sandy area

sandstone *NOUN*
sandstone is rock made of compressed sand

sandwich *NOUN* (**sandwiches**)
slices of bread with meat, cheese, or some other filling between them

sandy *ADJECTIVE* (**sandier, sandiest**)
1 made of sand; covered with sand **2** sandy hair is yellowish-red

sane *ADJECTIVE* (**saner, sanest**)
having a healthy mind; not mad

sang
past tense of **sing**

sanitary *ADJECTIVE*
free from germs and dirt; hygienic

sanitary towel *NOUN* (**sanitary towels**)
an absorbent pad that a woman uses during menstruation

sanitation *NOUN*
sanitation is arrangements for drainage and the disposal of sewage

sanity *NOUN*
sanity is being sane

sank
past tense of **sink** *VERB*

Sanskrit *NOUN*
Sanskrit is an ancient language of India

sap *NOUN*
sap is the juice inside a tree or plant

sap *VERB* (**saps, sapping, sapped**)
to sap someone's strength or energy is to use it up or weaken it gradually • *The heat had sapped all my energy.*

sapling *NOUN* (**saplings**)
a young tree

sapphire *NOUN* (**sapphires**)
a bright blue jewel

sarcastic *NOUN*
you are being sarcastic when you mock someone or something by saying the opposite of what you mean • *She said she liked the music I was playing but I think she was being sarcastic.*

> WORD FAMILY
> To say something **sarcastically** is to say it in a sarcastic way; **sarcasm** is when someone is being sarcastic.

sardine *NOUN* (**sardines**)
a small sea fish, usually sold packed tightly in tins

sari *NOUN* (**saris**) (*say* sar-i)
a long length of cloth worn as a dress, especially by Indian women and girls

sash *NOUN* (**sashes**)
a strip of cloth worn round the waist or over one shoulder

sash window *NOUN* (**sash windows**)
a window that slides up and down

sat
past tense and past participle of **sit**

satchel *NOUN* (**satchels**)
a bag you wear over your shoulder or on your back, especially for carrying books to and from school

satellite *NOUN* (**satellites**)
1 a spacecraft sent into space to move in an orbit round a planet, in order to get and send information **2** a moon that moves in orbit round a planet

satellite dish *NOUN* (**satellite dishes**)
a dish-shaped aerial for receiving television signals sent by satellite

satellite television *NOUN*
satellite television is television programmes that are broadcast using a satellite

satin *NOUN*
satin is a silky material that is shiny on one side

satire *NOUN* (**satires**)
1 satire is using humour or exaggeration to show the faults of a person or thing, especially the government **2** a satire is a play or piece of writing that does this

> WORD FAMILY
> Something is **satirical** when it uses satire to criticize someone; a **satirist** is someone who writes satire.

satisfaction *NOUN*
1 satisfaction is the feeling of being satisfied
2 satisfaction is also giving someone what they need or want

satisfactory *ADJECTIVE*
good enough; acceptable
▷ **satisfactorily** *ADVERB* in a satisfactory way

satisfy *VERB* (**satisfies, satisfying, satisfied**)
1 to satisfy someone is to give them what they need or want **2** to be satisfied is to be sure of something • *I am satisfied that you have done your best.*

saturate *VERB* (**saturates, saturating, saturated**)
1 to be saturated is to be soaking wet • *My clothes are saturated with rain.* **2** to saturate a place is to make it take in as much as possible or too much of something • *The town is saturated with tourists in the summer.*
▷ **saturation** *NOUN* saturation is being saturated

Saturday *NOUN* (**Saturdays**)
the seventh day of the week

sauce *NOUN* (**sauces**)
1 a sauce is a thick liquid served with food to add flavour **2** (*informal*) sauce is impudence; being cheeky

saucepan *NOUN* (**saucepans**)
a metal cooking pan with a long handle

saucer *NOUN* (**saucers**)
a small curved plate for a cup to stand on

saucy *ADJECTIVE* (**saucier**, **sauciest**)
rude or cheeky

sauna *NOUN* (**saunas**) (*say* saw- na or sow- na)
a room filled with steam where people sit and sweat a lot, used as a kind of bath

saunter *VERB* (**saunters**, **sauntering**, **sauntered**)
to saunter is to walk about in a leisurely way • *The policeman sauntered up to the house about tea time, followed by a damp subdued little pig.* — Beatrix Potter, *The Tale of Pigling Bland*

sausage *NOUN* (**sausages**)
a tube of edible skin or plastic stuffed with minced meat and other ingredients

sausage roll *NOUN* (**sausage rolls**)
a small short roll of pastry filled with meat

savage *ADJECTIVE*
wild and fierce; cruel

WORD FAMILY
To **savagely** attack someone is to attack them in a violent or cruel way; **savagery** is cruel and violent behaviour.

savage *VERB* (**savages**, **savaging**, **savaged**)
an animal savages someone when it attacks them and bites or scratches them fiercely

savannah *NOUN* (**savannahs**) (*say* sa- **van**- a)
a grassy plain in a hot country, with few trees

save *VERB* (**saves**, **saving**, **saved**)
1 to save someone or something is to free them from danger or harm **2** to save something, especially money, is to keep it so that it can be used later **3** to save computer data is to instruct the computer to keep it on its hard disk **4** in football, to save a ball is to stop it going into your goal

WORD FAMILY
A **saver** is someone who saves something, especially money.

savings *PLURAL NOUN*
your savings are the money that you have saved

saviour *NOUN* (**saviours**)
a person who saves someone
our Saviour or **the Saviour** a name for Jesus Christ

savoury *ADJECTIVE*
savoury food is tasty but not sweet

saw [1] *NOUN* (**saws**)
a tool with sharp teeth for cutting wood or other hard materials

saw *VERB* (**saws**, **sawing**, **sawed**, **sawn** or **sawed**)
to saw something is to cut it with a saw

saw [2]
past tense of **see**

sawdust *NOUN*
sawdust is powder that comes from wood when it is cut with a saw

saxophone *NOUN* (**saxophones**)
a wind instrument with a tube that curves upward and a reed in the mouthpiece

say *VERB* (**says**, **saying**, **said**)
to say something is to make words with your voice

say *NOUN*
to have a say or **have your say** is to be able to speak or give your opinion

saying *NOUN* (**sayings**)
a well-known phrase or proverb

scab *NOUN* (**scabs**)
a hard crust that forms over a cut or graze while it is healing

scabbard *NOUN* (**scabbards**)
a cover for a sword or dagger

scaffold *NOUN* (**scaffolds**)
a platform on which criminals are executed

scaffolding *NOUN*
scaffolding is a structure of poles and planks for workers to stand on when building or repairing a house

scald *VERB* (**scalds**, **scalding**, **scalded**)
1 to scald your skin is to burn it with very hot liquid or steam **2** to scald something is to clean it with boiling water

scale [1] *NOUN* (**scales**)
1 a series of units or marks for measuring something • *This ruler has one scale in centimetres and another in inches.* **2** the relationship between the size of something on a map or model and the actual size of the thing in the real world • *The scale of this map is one inch to the mile.* **3** a series of musical notes going up or down in a fixed pattern **4** the relative size or importance of something • *They love organizing parties on a massive scale.*

scale *VERB* (**scales**, **scaling**, **scaled**)
to scale something is to climb up it

scale [2] *NOUN* (**scales**)
1 a scale is one of the thin overlapping parts on the outside of fish, snakes, and other animals **2** scale is the coating that forms on the inside of kettles and pans

WORD FAMILY
Scaly skin is covered in scales.

scales *PLURAL NOUN*
a device for weighing things

scalp *NOUN* (**scalps**)
the skin on the top of your head

scalp *VERB* (**scalps**, **scalping**, **scalped**)
to scalp someone is to cut off their scalp

scamper *VERB* (**scampers**, **scampering**, **scampered**)
to scamper is to run quickly with short steps • *A harvest mouse goes scampering by, / With silver claws and silver eye.* — Walter de la Mare, *Silver*

scampi *PLURAL NOUN*
scampi are large prawns eaten in batter or breadcrumbs

scan *VERB* (**scans**, **scanning**, **scanned**)
1 to scan something is to look at every part of it **2** to scan a piece of writing is to look over it quickly **3** to scan an area, or a part of the body, is to sweep a radar or electronic beam over it in order to find something **4** poetry scans when it has a fixed rhythm

scan *NOUN* (**scans**)
a search or examination using a scanner

scandal *NOUN* (**scandals**)
1 a scandal is a shameful or disgraceful action **2** scandal is gossip that damages someone's reputation

WORD FAMILY
Something is **scandalous** when it is shocking or disgraceful.

Scandinavian *ADJECTIVE*
to do with Scandinavia (Norway, Sweden, and Denmark, and sometimes Finland and Iceland)

scanner *NOUN* (**scanners**)
1 a machine used to examine part of the body, using an electronic beam **2** a machine that converts print and pictures into data that can be read by a computer

scanty *ADJECTIVE* (**scantier**, **scantiest**)
hardly big enough; small

WORD FAMILY
To be **scantily** dressed is to be not wearing very much.

scapegoat *NOUN* (**scapegoats**)
someone who gets all the blame for something that other people have done

scar *NOUN* (**scars**)
a mark left on your skin by a cut or burn after it has healed

scar *VERB* (**scars**, **scarring**, **scarred**)
an injury scars you when it leaves a permanent mark on your skin

scarce *ADJECTIVE* (**scarcer**, **scarcest**)
not enough to supply people • *Wheat was scarce because of the bad harvest.*
to make yourself scarce (*informal*) is to go away or keep out of the way

WORD FAMILY
There is a **scarcity** of something when there is not enough of it.

scarcely *ADVERB*
hardly; only just • *She could scarcely walk.* • *So it was that I found myself at scarcely twelve years of age wandering the world alone and quite destitute.* — Michael Morpurgo, *The Last Wolf*

scare *VERB* (**scares**, **scaring**, **scared**)
to scare someone is to frighten them

scare *NOUN* (**scares**)
a scare is a fright • *You gave me quite a scare.*

scarecrow *NOUN* (**scarecrows**)
a figure of a person dressed in old clothes, that farmers put in a field to frighten birds away from crops

scarf *NOUN* (**scarves**)
a strip of material that you wear round your neck or head

scarlet *ADJECTIVE*
bright red

scary *ADJECTIVE* (**scarier**, **scariest**)
(*informal*) frightening

scatter *VERB* (**scatters**, **scattering**, **scattered**)
1 to scatter things is to throw them in all directions **2** to scatter is to move quickly in all directions • *The crowd scattered when the police arrived.*

scavenge *VERB* (**scavenges**, **scavenging**, **scavenged**)
an animal or bird scavenges when it eats dead animals that have been killed by another animal

WORD FAMILY
A **scavenger** is an animal or bird that scavenges.

scene *NOUN* (**scenes**)
1 the place where something happens • *Here is the scene of the crime.* **2** a part of a play or film **3** a view someone sees **4** an angry or noisy outburst • *They made a scene about the money.*

scenery *NOUN*
1 scenery is the natural features of an area • *We were admiring the scenery.* **2** scenery is also things put on a stage to make it look like a place

scent *NOUN* (**scents**) (*say* sent)
1 a pleasant smell or perfume **2** an animal's smell, that other animals can follow

WORD FAMILY
Something is scented when it has a strong pleasant smell.

scent *VERB* (**scents**, **scenting**, **scented**)
to scent something is to discover it by its scent

sceptic *NOUN* (**sceptics**) (*say* **skep**- tik)
someone who doesn't believe things easily or readily

sceptical *ADJECTIVE* (*say* **skep**- tik- al)
you are sceptical when you don't believe things easily or readily

WORD FAMILY
Scepticism is not believing things easily or readily.

schedule *NOUN* **(schedules)** (*say* **shed-** yool)
a timetable of things that have to be done
to be on schedule is to be on time; not late

scheme *NOUN* **(schemes)**
a plan of what to do

scheme *VERB* **(schemes, scheming, schemed)**
to scheme is to make secret plans

> WORD FAMILY
> A **schemer** is someone who schemes.

scholar *NOUN* **(scholars)**
1 someone who studies a subject thoroughly
2 someone who has been given a scholarship

scholarly *ADJECTIVE*
showing knowledge and learning

scholarship *NOUN* **(scholarships)**
1 a scholarship is a grant of money given to someone for their education **2** scholarship is knowledge and learning

school[1] *NOUN* **(schools)**
1 a place where children go to be taught **2** the children who go there • *The whole school had a holiday.*

school[2] *NOUN* **(schools)**
a group of whales or fish

schoolchild *NOUN* **(schoolchildren)**
a child who goes to school

schoolteacher *NOUN* **(schoolteachers)**
a teacher at a school

schooner *NOUN* **(schooners)** (*say* **skoo-** ner)
a sailing ship with two or more masts

science *NOUN*
science is the study of objects and happenings in the world that can be observed and tested

science fiction *NOUN*
science fiction is stories about imaginary worlds, especially in space and in the future

scientific *ADJECTIVE*
1 to do with science **2** studying things carefully and logically

scientist *NOUN* **(scientists)**
someone who studies science or is an expert in science

scissors *PLURAL NOUN*
a cutting device made of two movable blades joined together

scoff *VERB* **(scoffs, scoffing, scoffed)**
to scoff at someone or something is to make fun of them

scold *VERB* **(scolds, scolding, scolded)**
to scold someone is to tell them off harshly

scone *NOUN* **(scones)** (*say* skon or skohn)
a small plain cake, usually eaten with butter and jam

scoop *NOUN* **(scoops)**
1 a deep spoon for serving soft food such as ice cream or mashed potato **2** a deep shovel
3 (*informal*) an important piece of news that only one newspaper prints

scoop *VERB* **(scoops, scooping, scooped)**
to scoop something, or to scoop it out, is to take it out with a scoop or the palm of your hand

scooter *NOUN* **(scooters)**
1 a kind of motor cycle with small wheels **2** a simple type of bicycle for a child, with two wheels and a narrow platform. You stand on the platform and push on the ground with one foot

scope *NOUN*
1 opportunity or possibility for something • *There is scope for improvement.* **2** the range or extent of something • *Chemistry is outside the scope of the syllabus for this year.*

scorch *VERB* **(scorches, scorching, scorched)**
to scorch something is to make it go brown by slightly burning it

scorching *ADJECTIVE*
very hot

score *NOUN* **(scores)**
1 the number of points or goals made in a game • *What's the score?* **2** (*old use*) a score is twenty • *He reached the age of four-score (= 80) years.*

score *VERB* **(scores, scoring, scored)**
1 to score a goal or point in a game is to get it
2 to score is to keep a count of the score in a game • *I thought you were scoring.* **3** to score a surface is to scratch it

> WORD FAMILY
> A **scorer** is someone who scores a goal or point.

scorn *NOUN*
scorn is treating a person or thing with contempt

scorn *VERB* **(scorns, scorning, scorned)**
to scorn someone or something is to have contempt for them

> WORD FAMILY
> To be **scornful** is to be full of contempt and show no respect.

scorpion *NOUN* **(scorpions)**
an animal related to the spider, with pincers and a poisonous sting in its curved tail

Scot *NOUN* **(Scots)**
a person from Scotland

Scotch *ADJECTIVE*
Scottish

> USING THIS WORD
> Many Scots dislike the use of the word **Scotch**, and prefer to use **Scottish**.

Scotch terrier *NOUN* **(Scotch terriers)**
a small terrier with rough hair

Scottish *ADJECTIVE*
to do with Scotland

scoundrel *NOUN* (**scoundrels**)
a wicked or dishonest person

scour *VERB* (**scours, scouring, scoured**)
1 to scour (for example) a pan or bath is to rub it hard with something rough until it is clean and bright **2** to scour an area is to search it thoroughly

Scout *NOUN* (**Scouts**)
a member of the Scout Association

scout *NOUN* (**scouts**)
someone sent out ahead of a group in order to collect information

scowl *VERB* (**scowls, scowling, scowled**)
to scowl is to look bad-tempered

scowl *NOUN* (**scowls**)
an angry look

scramble *VERB* (**scrambles, scrambling, scrambled**)
1 to scramble is to move quickly and awkwardly • *The women and children scrambled down the hill to get a good view of the standing stones.* — Clive King, *Stig of the Dump* **2** to scramble eggs is to cook them by mixing them and heating them in a pan **3** to scramble for something is to struggle to do it or get it

scramble *NOUN* (**scrambles**)
1 a climb or walk over rough ground **2** a struggle to get something • *There was a scramble for the best seats.* **3** a motorcycle race across rough country

scrap[1] *NOUN* (**scraps**)
1 a scrap is a small piece of something **2** scrap is rubbish, especially unwanted metal

scrap *VERB* (**scraps, scrapping, scrapped**)
to scrap something is to get rid of it when you do not want it

scrap[2] *NOUN* (**scraps**)
(*informal*) a fight

scrap *VERB* (**scraps, scrapping, scrapped**)
to scrap is to fight or quarrel

scrape *VERB* (**scrapes, scraping, scraped**)
1 to scrape something is to rub it with something rough, hard, or sharp **2** to scrape past or through is to only just get past or succeed • *She scraped through her exams.* **3** to scrape something together is to collect it with difficulty • *They scraped together enough money for a holiday.*

> WORD FAMILY
> A **scraper** is a device for scraping something clean.

scrape *NOUN* (**scrapes**)
1 a scraping movement or sound **2** a mark made by scraping something **3** (*informal*) an awkward situation • *He's always getting into scrapes.*

scrappy *ADJECTIVE* (**scrappier, scrappiest**)
done carelessly or untidily

scratch *VERB* (**scratches, scratching, scratched**)
1 to scratch a surface is to damage it by rubbing something sharp over it **2** you scratch your skin when you rub it with your fingers because it itches

scratch *NOUN* (**scratches**)
1 a mark or cut made by scratching **2** the action of scratching • *I need to have a scratch.*
to start from scratch is to begin at the very beginning
to be up to scratch is to be up to the proper standard

scrawl *NOUN* (**scrawls**)
untidy writing • *Can you read my scrawl?*

scrawl *VERB* (**scrawls, scrawling, scrawled**)
to scrawl something is to write it in a hurried or careless way

scream *NOUN* (**screams**)
1 a loud high-pitched cry of pain or fear or anger **2** (*informal*) you can say something is a scream when it is very amusing

scream *VERB* (**screams, screaming, screamed**)
to scream is to make a loud high-pitched cry

screech *NOUN* (**screeches**)
a harsh high-pitched sound • *There was a screech of tyres as the car sped off.*

screech *VERB* (**screeches, screeching, screeched**)
to screech is to make a harsh high-pitched sound • *Baby Thomas screeched. His eyes crossed in horror. Baths were his worst nightmare.* — Catherine MacPhail, *Granny Nothing*

screen *NOUN* (**screens**)
1 a surface on which films or television programmes or computer data are shown **2** a movable panel used to hide or protect something **3** a windscreen

screen *VERB* (**screens, screening, screened**)
1 to screen a film or television programme is to show it **2** to screen something is to hide it or protect it with a screen **3** to screen people is to test them to find out if they have a disease

screw *NOUN* (**screws**)
1 a metal pin with a spiral ridge round it, which holds things by being twisted into them **2** a propeller

screw *VERB* (**screws, screwing, screwed**)
1 to screw something is to fix it with screws **2** to screw something in or on is to fit it by turning it • *Screw the lid on to the jar.* • *I screwed in the light-bulb.*
to screw something up is to twist or squeeze it into a tight ball

screwdriver *NOUN* (**screwdrivers**)
a tool for putting in or taking out screws

scribble *VERB* (**scribbles, scribbling, scribbled**)
to scribble is to write untidily or carelessly, or to make meaningless marks

script *NOUN* (**scripts**)
1 the words of a play, film, or broadcast
2 handwriting **3** something you write, especially the answers you write to exam questions

scripture *NOUN* (**scriptures**)
a sacred book, especially the Bible

scroll *NOUN* (**scrolls**)
a roll of paper or parchment with writing on it

scroll *VERB* (**scrolls, scrolling, scrolled**)
you scroll up or down on a computer screen when you move the text up or down on the screen to see what comes before or after

scrotum *NOUN* (**scrotums** or **scrota**) (*say* skroh- tum)
the pouch of skin behind the penis, containing the testicles

scrounge *VERB* (**scrounges, scrounging, scrounged**)
(*informal*) to scrounge something is to get it without paying for it • *He scrounged a meal from us.*

> WORD FAMILY
> A **scrounger** is someone who tries to get things without paying for them.

scrub[1] *VERB* (**scrubs, scrubbing, scrubbed**)
1 to scrub something is to rub it with a hard brush
2 (*slang*) to scrub a meeting or performance is to cancel it

scrub *NOUN*
the action of scrubbing • *You'll need to give your face a good scrub.*

scrub[2] *NOUN*
scrub is low trees and bushes, or land covered with them

scruffy *ADJECTIVE* (**scruffier, scruffiest**)
shabby and untidy

scrum or **scrummage** *NOUN* (**scrums** or **scrummages**)
(*in rugby football*) a group of players from each side who push against each other and try to win the ball with their feet

scrutinize *VERB* (**scrutinizes, scrutinizing, scrutinized**)
to scrutinize something is to examine it or look at it closely

> WORD FAMILY
> **Scrutiny** is examining or looking at something closely.

scuba diving *NOUN*
scuba diving is swimming underwater, breathing air from a supply carried on your back

scuffle *NOUN* (**scuffles**)
a confused struggle or fight

scuffle *VERB* (**scuffles, scuffling, scuffled**)
people scuffle when they fight in a confused way

scullery *NOUN* (**sculleries**)
a room for washing dishes and other kitchen work

sculptor *NOUN* (**sculptors**)
someone who makes sculptures

sculpture *NOUN* (**sculptures**)
1 a sculpture is something carved or shaped out of a hard material such as stone, clay, or metal
2 sculpture is the art or work of a sculptor

scum *NOUN*
1 scum is froth or dirt on the top of a liquid
2 (*informal and offensive*) people who are thought to deserve contempt or to be worthless

scurry *VERB* (**scurries, scurrying, scurried**)
to scurry is to run or hurry with short steps • *Then a snout appeared, the tip of a tail, and within moments a complete and perfect tiny crocodile had scurried out on to the sand.* — Alexander McCall Smith, *Akimbo and the Crocodile Man*

scurvy *NOUN*
scurvy is a disease caused by lack of fresh fruit and vegetables

scuttle[1] *NOUN* (**scuttles**)
a container for coal, kept by a fireplace

scuttle[2] *VERB* (**scuttles, scuttling, scuttled**)
to scuttle a ship is to sink it deliberately by making holes in the side or bottom

scuttle[3] *VERB* (**scuttles, scuttling, scuttled**)
to scuttle is to run with short quick steps • *'Oh! Oh! Oh!' said Mrs Crabbity, and she turned and scuttled into her cottage like a small frightened spider.* — Vivian French, *Under the Moon*

scythe *NOUN* (**scythes**)
a tool with a long curved blade for cutting grass or corn

sea *NOUN* (**seas**)
1 the salt water that covers most of the earth's surface **2** a large lake or area of water, such as the Mediterranean Sea or the Sea of Galilee **3** a large area of something • *Across the table we saw a sea of faces.*
at sea 1 on the sea **2** unable to understand something or cope with it • *He's completely at sea in his new job.*

seabed *NOUN*
the seabed is the bottom of the sea

seafaring *ADJECTIVE & NOUN*
travelling or working on the sea

> WORD FAMILY
> A **seafarer** is someone who works at sea.

seafood *NOUN*
seafood is fish or shellfish from the sea eaten as food

seagull *NOUN* (**seagulls**)
a sea bird with long wings

sea horse *NOUN* (**sea horses**)
a small fish that swims upright, with a head rather like a horse's head

seal[1] *NOUN* (**seals**)
a furry sea animal that breeds on land

seal[2] *NOUN* (**seals**)
1 something designed to close an opening and stop air or liquid getting in or out **2** a design pressed into a soft substance such as wax or lead

seal *VERB* (**seals**, **sealing**, **sealed**)
to seal something is to close it by sticking two parts together • *He sealed the envelope.*

sea level *NOUN*
sea level is the level of the sea halfway between high and low tide • *The mountain rises 1,000 metres above sea level.*

sea lion *NOUN* (**sea lions**)
a large kind of seal. The male has a kind of mane

seam *NOUN* (**seams**)
1 the line where two edges of cloth join together **2** a layer of coal in the ground

seaman *NOUN* (**seamen**)
a sailor

seamanship *NOUN*
seamanship is skill in sailing a boat or ship

seaplane *NOUN* (**seaplanes**)
an aeroplane that can land on water and take off from water

seaport *NOUN* (**seaports**)
a port on the coast

search *VERB* (**searches**, **searching**, **searched**)
1 to search for something or someone is to look very carefully for them **2** to search a person or place is to look very carefully for something they may have

> WORD FAMILY
> A **searcher** is someone who is trying to find something or someone.

search *NOUN* (**searches**)
1 a very careful look for someone or something **2** when you look for information in a computer database or on the Internet • *Let's do a search for 'Roald Dahl'.*

searching *ADJECTIVE*
a searching question or look is a thorough one that is trying to find out the truth about something

searchlight *NOUN* (**searchlights**)
a light with a strong beam that can be turned in any direction

search party *NOUN* (**search parties**)
a group of people organized to look for someone or something

seashore *NOUN*
the seashore is the land close to the sea

seasick *ADJECTIVE*
someone is seasick when they are sick because of the movement of a ship

> WORD FAMILY
> **Seasickness** is feeling seasick.

seaside *NOUN*
the seaside is a place by the sea where people go on holiday

season *NOUN* (**seasons**)
1 one of the four main parts of the year: spring, summer, autumn, and winter **2** the time of year when a sport or other activity happens • *When does the football season start?*

season *VERB* (**seasons**, **seasoning**, **seasoned**)
to season food is to put salt, pepper, or other strong-tasting things on it to flavour it

seasonal *ADJECTIVE*
happening only at certain times of the year • *Fruit-picking is seasonal work.*

seasoning *NOUN* (**seasonings**)
seasoning is something strong-tasting like salt and pepper, used to season food

season ticket *NOUN* (**season tickets**)
a ticket that you can use as often as you like for a certain period

seat *NOUN* (**seats**)
1 a piece of furniture for sitting on **2** a place in parliament or on a council or a board of a business **3** the place where something is located • *London is the seat of government.* **4** a person's bottom

seat *VERB* (**seats**, **seating**, **seated**)
a place seats a certain number of people when it has that many seats for them • *The theatre seats 3,000.*

seat belt *NOUN* (**seat belts**)
a strap to hold a person securely in the seat of a vehicle or aircraft

seaward or **seawards** *ADVERB*
towards the sea

seaweed *NOUN* (**seaweeds**)
seaweed is plants that grow in the sea

secateurs *PLURAL NOUN* (*say* **sek**- a- terz)
clippers used for pruning plants

secluded *ADJECTIVE*
a secluded place is away from large numbers of people; quiet and hidden • *They found a secluded beach for their picnic.*

> WORD FAMILY
> **Seclusion** is being private or hidden.

second *ADJECTIVE & NOUN*
the next after the first
to have second thoughts is to wonder whether your decision was really right

second *NOUN* (**seconds**)
1 a very short period of time, one-sixtieth of a minute **2** a person or thing that is second **3** someone who helps a fighter in a boxing match or duel **4** something that is not of the best quality

second *VERB* (**seconds**, **seconding**, **seconded**)
1 to second a proposal or motion is to support it formally **2** to second a fighter is to act as their second

secondary *ADJECTIVE*
coming second; not original or essential • *This is of secondary importance.*

secondary colour *NOUN* (**secondary colours**)
a colour made by mixing two primary colours

secondary school *NOUN* (**secondary schools**)
a school for children more than about 11 years old

second-hand *ADJECTIVE & ADVERB*
1 bought or used after someone else has used it • *I can only afford a second-hand car.* **2** that sells used goods • *She runs a second-hand shop.*

secondly *ADVERB*
as the second thing • *Secondly, I'd like to thank my parents.*

second nature *NOUN*
second nature is behaviour that has become a habit • *Lying is second nature to him.*

secrecy *NOUN*
secrecy is being secret

secret *ADJECTIVE*
1 that must not be told or shown to other people **2** that is not known by everyone

> **WORD FAMILY**
> You **secretly** do something when you do it without telling other people. • *Jilly had always secretly thought how marvellous it would be to have a dragon as a pet.* — Helen Cresswell, *Dragon Ride*

secret *NOUN* (**secrets**)
something that is secret
to do something in secret is to do it secretly

secretary *NOUN* (**secretaries**) (*say* **sek**- re- tri)
1 someone whose job is to type letters, keep files, answer the telephone, and make business arrangements for a person or organization **2** the chief assistant of a government minister

secrete *VERB* (**secretes**, **secreting**, **secreted**) (*say* si- **kreet**)
1 to secrete something is to hide it carefully **2** to secrete a substance in the body is to release it • *Saliva is secreted in the mouth.*

> **WORD FAMILY**
> A **secretion** is a substance that is secreted.

secretive *ADJECTIVE* (*say* **seek**- rit- iv)
liking or trying to keep things secret
▷ **secretively** *ADVERB* in a secretive way
▷ **secretiveness** *NOUN* secretiveness is being secretive

secret service *NOUN*
a country's secret service is the government department in charge of spies and espionage

sect *NOUN* (**sects**)
a group of people who have special or unusual religious opinions or beliefs

section *NOUN* (**sections**)
a part of something • *Our school library has a large history section.* • *The tail section of the plane broke off.*

sector *NOUN* (**sectors**)
1 a part of an area or activity **2** a part of a circle made by drawing two straight lines from the centre to the circumference

secure *ADJECTIVE* (**securer**, **securest**)
1 firm and safe • *Is that ladder secure?* **2** not likely to be lost • *I need a secure job.* **3** made safe or protected from attack • *Check that all the doors and windows are secure.*
▷ **securely** *ADVERB* in a secure way

secure *VERB* (**secures**, **securing**, **secured**)
1 to secure something is to make it safe or firmly fixed **2** to secure something is also to get hold of it • *She secured two tickets for the show.*

security *NOUN*
1 security is being secure or safe **2** security is also measures taken to prevent theft, spying, or terrorism **3** you offer something as security when you offer it as a guarantee that you will pay back a loan

sedate *ADJECTIVE* (*say* si- **dayt**)
calm and dignified
▷ **sedately** *ADVERB* in a sedate way • *Children, you are very little, / And your bones are very brittle; / If you would grow tall and stately, / You must try to walk sedately.* — Robert Louis Stevenson, *A Child's Garden of Verses*

sedative *NOUN* (**sedatives**) (*say* **sed**- a- tiv)
a medicine that makes a person calm or helps them sleep

> **WORD FAMILY**
> **Sedation** is giving someone a medicine that makes them calm or helps them sleep.

sediment *NOUN*
sediment is solid matter that settles at the bottom of a liquid

sedimentary *ADJECTIVE* (*say* sed- i- **ment**- er- i)
sedimentary rock is formed from layers of sand, stones, or mud that have settled on the bottom of a lake or river

see *VERB* (**sees**, **seeing**, **saw**, **seen**)
1 to see something or someone is to use your eyes to notice them or be aware of them **2** to see someone is to meet or visit them • *See me after class.* **3** to see something is to understand it • *I see what you mean.* **4** to see someone as something is to imagine them being it • *Can you see yourself as a teacher?* **5** to see that something happens is to make sure of it • *See that the windows are shut.* **6** to see someone somewhere is to escort or lead them • *I'll see you to the door.*
to see through something or **someone** is not to be deceived by them
to see to something is to deal with it

seed *NOUN* (**seeds**)
a tiny part of a plant that can grow in the ground to make a new plant

seedling *NOUN* (**seedlings**)
a very young plant

seek *VERB* (**seeks**, **seeking**, **sought**)
1 to seek a person or thing is to try to find them **2** to seek something is to try to achieve it •*She is seeking fame.*

seem *VERB* (**seems**, **seeming**, **seemed**)
to seem to be something or to have some quality is to appear that way or give that impression •*They seem happy in their new house.*

> WORD FAMILY
> You can say that (for example) a road is **seemingly** endless or a question is **seemingly** stupid when it appears that way but in fact might not be. •*It was a single arch of grey stone, and lying flat upon the bridge was a scarlet alligator, seemingly fast asleep.* — L. Frank Baum, *The Emerald City of Oz*

seen
past participle of **see**

seep *VERB* (**seeps**, **seeping**, **seeped**)
a liquid or gas seeps when it flows slowly through or into or out of something •*Water was seeping into the cellar.*

> WORD FAMILY
> There is **seepage** when something is seeping.

see-saw *NOUN* (**see-saws**)
a plank balanced in the middle so that people can sit at each end and make it go up and down

seethe *VERB* (**seethes**, **seething**, **seethed**)
1 a liquid seethes when it boils or bubbles **2** you are seething when you are very angry or excited

segment *NOUN* (**segments**)
a part that is cut off or can be separated from the rest of something •*He ate a few segments of an orange.*

> WORD FAMILY
> Something is **segmented** when it is divided into segments.

segregate *VERB* (**segregates**, **segregating**, **segregated**) (*say* seg- ri- gayt)
to segregate people of different races or religions is to keep them apart and make them live separately

> WORD FAMILY
> **Segregation** is when people of different races or religions are kept apart and made to live separately.

seismograph *NOUN* (**seismographs**)
a device for detecting the strength of earthquakes

seize *VERB* (**seizes**, **seizing**, **seized**) (*say* seez)
to seize someone or something is to take hold of them suddenly or firmly
to seize up is to become jammed or stuck

seizure *NOUN* (**seizures**)
a seizure is a sudden attack of an illness

seldom *ADVERB*
not often •*I seldom cry.*

select *VERB* (**selects**, **selecting**, **selected**)
to select a person or thing is to choose them carefully

select *ADJECTIVE*
small and carefully chosen •*They have a select group of friends.*

self *NOUN* (**selves**)
the type of person you are; your individual nature •*You'll soon be feeling your old self again.*

self-centred *ADJECTIVE*
selfish; thinking about yourself too much

self-confident *ADJECTIVE*
confident in what you can do

> WORD FAMILY
> **Self-confidence** is being self-confident.

self-conscious *ADJECTIVE*
embarrassed or shy because you know people are watching you

self-contained *ADJECTIVE*
having everything you need in one place •*a self-contained flat*

self-control *NOUN*
self-control is the ability to control your own behaviour or feelings

> WORD FAMILY
> To be **self-controlled** is to be able to control your own behaviour or feelings.

self-defence *NOUN*
1 you act in self-defence when you do something defending yourself against attack **2** self-defence is also skill in defending yourself if someone attacks you

self-employed *ADJECTIVE*
someone who is self-employed works independently and not for an employer

self-evident *ADJECTIVE*
clear or obvious and not needing proof

self-important *ADJECTIVE*
pompous or haughty

selfish *ADJECTIVE*
having or doing what you want without thinking of other people
▷ **selfishly** *ADVERB* in a selfish way
▷ **selfishness** *NOUN* selfishness is being selfish

selfless *ADJECTIVE*
thinking of other people rather than yourself; not selfish

a b c d e f g h i j k l m n o p q r **s** t u v w x y z

self-raising flour *NOUN*
self-raising flour is flour that makes cakes and pastry rise during cooking

self-respect *NOUN*
self-respect is the feeling that you are behaving and thinking in the proper way

self-righteous *ADJECTIVE*
smugly sure that you are behaving virtuously

self-service *ADJECTIVE*
a self-service shop or restaurant is one where customers serve themselves with goods and pay a cashier for what they have taken

self-sufficient *ADJECTIVE*
able to provide what you need without help from others

sell *VERB* (**sells**, **selling**, **sold**)
to sell goods or services is to offer them in exchange for money
to sell out is to sell all your stock of something

semaphore *NOUN*
semaphore is a system of signalling by holding flags out with your arms in positions to indicate letters of the alphabet

semen *NOUN* (*say* see- men)
semen is white liquid produced by males and containing sperm

semi- *PREFIX*
meaning 'half', as in *semicircle*

semibreve *NOUN* (**semibreves**) (*say* sem- i- breev)
the longest musical note normally used, written 𝅝

semicircle *NOUN* (**semicircles**)
half a circle

> WORD FAMILY
> Something is **semicircular** when it is in the form of a semicircle.

semicolon *NOUN* (**semicolons**)
a punctuation mark (;), marking a more definite break in a sentence than a comma does

> SEMICOLON
> You use a semicolon to separate different parts of a sentence before some connectives: *Gorillas are the largest of the apes; nevertheless, they are gentle and shy creatures.* You can use semicolons to join together two sentences which express the same idea in two different ways: *That's a brilliant film; it was the best ever.* You can also use a semicolon when you want to separate each of the items in a long and complicated list of things. A list like this is sometimes introduced by a colon: *There was a jungle mural on his bedroom wall: monkeys leaping from tree to tree; snakes slithering along branches; several brightly-coloured parrots; and a magnificent leopard peeping out through the dense foliage.*

semi-detached *ADJECTIVE*
a semi-detached house is one that is joined to another house on one side

semi-final *NOUN* (**semi-finals**)
a match played to decide who will take part in the final

> WORD FAMILY
> A **semi-finalist** is a contestant in a semi-final.

semitone *NOUN* (**semitones**)
half a tone in music

semolina *NOUN*
semolina is a milk pudding made with grains of wheat

senate *NOUN* (*say* sen- at)
1 the governing council in ancient Rome **2** the higher-ranking section of the parliament in France, the USA, and some other countries

> WORD FAMILY
> A **senator** is a member of a senate.

send *VERB* (**sends**, **sending**, **sent**)
1 to send something somewhere is to arrange for it to be taken there **2** to send someone somewhere is to tell them to go there
to send for something or **someone** is to ask for them to come to you
to send someone up (*informal*) is to make fun of them

senior *ADJECTIVE*
1 older than someone else **2** higher in rank • *He is a senior officer in the navy.*

> WORD FAMILY
> A person's **seniority** is how old or high in rank they are.

senior *NOUN* (**seniors**)
someone is your senior when they are older or higher in rank than you are

senior citizen *NOUN* (**senior citizens**)
an elderly person, especially a pensioner

sensation *NOUN* (**sensations**)
1 a feeling • *We had a sensation of warmth.* **2** a very exciting event or the excitement caused by it • *The news caused a great sensation.*

sensational *ADJECTIVE*
causing great excitement or shock

sense *NOUN* (**senses**)
1 the ability to see, hear, smell, touch, or taste things **2** the ability to feel or appreciate something • *She has a good sense of humour.* **3** the power to think or make good judgements • *He hasn't got the sense to come in out of the rain.* **4** meaning • *The word 'set' has many senses.*
to make sense is to have a meaning you can understand

sense *VERB* (**senses**, **sensing**, **sensed**)
1 to sense something is to feel it or be aware of it • *I sensed that she did not like me.* **2** to sense something is also to detect it • *This device senses radioactivity.*

senseless *ADJECTIVE*
1 stupid; not sensible **2** unconscious

sensible *ADJECTIVE*
wise; having or showing common sense
▷ **sensibly** *ADVERB* in a sensible way

sensitive *ADJECTIVE*
1 affected by the sun or chemicals or something else physical • *I have sensitive skin.* **2** easily offended or upset • *She is very sensitive about her age.* **3** aware of other people's feelings

WORD FAMILY
To deal with something **sensitively** is to do it in a way that shows you are aware of other people's feelings.

sensitivity *NOUN* (**sensitivities**)
1 sensitivity is being sensitive **2** a sensitivity is something you are sensitive about

sensitize *VERB* (**sensitizes**, **sensitizing**, **sensitized**)
to sensitize something is to make it sensitive to light or something else physical

sensor *NOUN* (**sensors**)
a device or instrument for detecting something physical such as heat or light

sent
past tense and past participle of **send**

sentence *NOUN* (**sentences**)
1 a group of words that express a complete thought and form a statement or question or command **2** the punishment given to a convicted person in a lawcourt

SENTENCES
A sentence needs to contain a main verb and most sentences have a subject. Here is a sentence: *The clown ran away from the lion.* In this sentence the subject is *the clown* and the main verb is *ran*. Most sentences are statements like the one above, but there are other kinds of sentence, such as questions *Do you like strawberries?* and commands *Come here!*

sentence *VERB* (**sentences**, **sentencing**, **sentenced**)
to sentence someone is to give them a sentence in a lawcourt • *They were sentenced to two years in prison.*

sentiment *NOUN* (**sentiments**)
1 a sentiment is a feeling or opinion **2** sentiment is a show of feeling or emotion

sentimental *ADJECTIVE*
showing or making you feel emotion, especially too much sad emotion • *That love-story is too sentimental.*
▷ **sentimentality** *NOUN* sentimentality being too sentimental
▷ **sentimentally** *ADVERB* in a sentimental way

sentinel *NOUN* (**sentinels**)
a sentry • *The six black queens stood like silent sentinels on the rocks watching us go.* — Michael Morpurgo, *The Sleeping Sword*

sentry *NOUN* (**sentries**)
a soldier guarding something

separable *ADJECTIVE*
able to be separated from each other

separate *ADJECTIVE* (*say* **sep**- er- at)
1 not joined to anything; on its own **2** not together; not with other people • *They lead separate lives.*

WORD FAMILY
People do something **separately** when they do it on their own, not together • *They arrived together but left separately.*

separate *VERB* (**separates**, **separating**, **separated**) (*say* **sep**- er- ayt)
1 to separate things or people is to take them away from others **2** to separate is to become separate or move away from each other **3** two people separate when they stop living together as a couple

WORD FAMILY
Separation is when people are apart from each other.

September *NOUN*
the ninth month of the year

septic *ADJECTIVE*
a wound goes septic when it becomes infected with harmful bacteria

sequel *NOUN* (**sequels**) (*say* **see**- kwel)
1 a book or film that continues the story of an earlier one **2** something that results from an earlier event

sequence *NOUN* (**sequences**) (*say* **see**- kwenss)
1 a series of things **2** the order in which things should follow each other • *Arrange these playing cards in sequence, the highest first.*

sequin *NOUN* (**sequins**) (*say* **see**- kwin)
sequins are tiny bright discs sewn on clothes to decorate them

serene *ADJECTIVE*
calm and peaceful • *'I'm a-weary of my life; / If you'll come and be my wife, / Quite serene would be my life!' / Said the Yonghy-Bonghy-Bo.* — Edward Lear, *The Courtship of the Yonghy-Bonghy-Bo*
▷ **serenely** *ADVERB* in a serene way
▷ **serenity** *NOUN* serenity is being calm and peaceful

sergeant *NOUN* (**sergeants**) (*say* **sar**- jent)
a soldier or police officer who is in charge of others

a b c d e f g h i j k l m n o p q r s t u v w x y z

sergeant major *NOUN* (**sergeant majors**)
a soldier who is one rank higher than a sergeant

serial *NOUN* (**serials**)
a story that is presented in separate parts over a period, for example week by week

series *NOUN* (**series**)
1 a number of things following each other or connected with each other **2** a set of television or radio programmes with the same title

serious *ADJECTIVE*
1 not funny; important • *We need a serious talk.* **2** thoughtful or solemn • *His face was serious.* **3** very bad • *They've had a serious accident.*
▷ **seriously** *ADVERB* in a serious way
▷ **seriousness** *NOUN* seriousness is being serious

sermon *NOUN* (**sermons**)
a talk given by a preacher

serpent *NOUN* (**serpents**)
a snake

servant *NOUN* (**servants**)
a person whose job is to work in someone else's house

serve *VERB* (**serves, serving, served**)
1 to serve people in a shop is to help them find the things they want to buy **2** to serve food or drink is to give it to people at a meal **3** to serve a person or organization is to work for them **4** to serve is to be suitable for a purpose • *This tree stump will serve as a table.* **5** (*in tennis*) to serve is to start play by hitting the ball to your opponent
it serves you right you deserve it

WORD FAMILY
In tennis, the **server** is the player who starts play by serving.

serve *NOUN* (**serves**)
the action of serving in tennis

service *NOUN* (**services**)
1 service is working for someone or something **2** a service is something that helps people or supplies what they want • *There is a good bus service into town.* **3** a service is also a religious ceremony in a church **4** a service, or dinner service, is a set of plates and crockery **5** a vehicle or machine has a service when someone spends time repairing and maintaining it **6** (*in tennis*) a service is a serve
the services the armed forces of a country

service *VERB* (**services, servicing, serviced**)
to service a vehicle or machine is to repair and maintain it

service station *NOUN* (**service stations**)
a place beside the road where you can buy petrol

serviette *NOUN* (**serviettes**)
a napkin for use at meals

session *NOUN* (**sessions**)
1 a time spent doing one thing • *They were in the middle of a recording session.* **2** a meeting or series of meetings • *The Queen will open the next session of Parliament.*

set *VERB* (**sets, setting, set**) This word has many meanings, depending on the words that go with it:
1 to set something somewhere is to put or place it there • *Set the vase on the table.* **2** to set a device is to make it ready to work • *Have you set the alarm?* **3** to set is to become solid or hard • *The jelly has set now.* **4** the sun sets when it goes down towards the horizon **5** to set someone doing something is to start them doing it • *The news set me thinking.* **6** to set someone a task or problem is to give it to them to do or solve • *Has the teacher set your homework?*
to set about something is to start doing it
to set off or **set out** is to begin a journey
to set something out is to display it or make it known • *She set out her reasons for leaving.*
to set something up is to place it in position or get it started • *We want to set up a playgroup.*

set *NOUN* (**sets**)
1 a group of people or things that belong together **2** a radio or television receiver **3** (*in mathematics*) a collection of things that you treat as a group because they have something in common, such as being odd numbers **4** a series of games in a tennis match **5** the scenery on a stage

set square *NOUN* (**set squares**)
a device in the shape of a right-angled triangle, used for drawing parallel lines and to draw angles

sett *NOUN* (**setts**)
the underground burrow of a badger

SPELLING
You will sometimes see this word spelt *set*.

settee *NOUN* (**settees**)
a sofa

setting *NOUN* (**settings**)
1 the setting of a story is the place and time in which it happens **2** the land and buildings around something • *The house stood in a rural setting.* **3** a set of cutlery or crockery for one person

SETTING
The setting of a story describes where it takes place. This can include, for example: PLACE: *the dark and stormy forest* TIME: *Late that afternoon, in the dark and stormy forest* ATMOSPHERE: *Late that afternoon, in the dark and stormy forest, it was eerily quiet.* SOUND: *Late that afternoon, in the dark and stormy forest, it was eerily quiet, except for the distant howling of wolves.* The more information you can give your reader about a story's setting, the better chance your reader has of appreciating the action in your story.

settle *VERB* (**settles**, **settling**, **settled**)
1 to settle a problem, difficulty, or argument is to solve it or decide about it **2** to settle, or settle down, is to become relaxed or make yourself comfortable • *He settled down in the armchair.* **3** to settle somewhere is to go and live there • *The family settled in Canada.* **4** something light such as dust or snow settles when it comes to rest on something • *The dust was settling on the books.* • *A bird flew down and settled on the fence.* **5** to settle a bill or debt is to pay it

settlement *NOUN* (**settlements**)
1 a settlement is a group of people or houses in a new area **2** a settlement is also an agreement to end an argument

settler *NOUN* (**settlers**)
one of the first people to settle in a new area

set-up *NOUN* (**set-ups**)
(*informal*) the way that something is organized or arranged

seven *NOUN* (**sevens**)
the number 7

seventeen *NOUN* (**seventeens**)
the number 17
▷ **seventeenth** *ADJECTIVE & NOUN* 17th

seventh *ADJECTIVE & NOUN*
the next after the sixth
▷ **seventhly** *ADVERB* in the seventh place; as the seventh one

seventy *NOUN* (**seventies**)
the number 70
▷ **seventieth** *ADJECTIVE & NOUN* 70th

sever *VERB* (**severs**, **severing**, **severed**)
to sever something is to cut or break it off

several *DETERMINER*
more than two but not many

severe *ADJECTIVE* (**severer**, **severest**)
1 strict or harsh; not gentle or kind • *The Mathematical Master frowned and looked very severe, for he did not approve of children dreaming.* — Oscar Wilde, *The Happy Prince* **2** very bad or serious • *a severe cold* • *We're in for some severe weather.*

> WORD FAMILY
> To be (for example) **severely** punished is to be harshly punished; the **severity** of something is its extreme seriousness.

sew *VERB* (**sews**, **sewing**, **sewed**, **sewn** or **sewed**)
(*say* so)
1 to sew cloth or other soft material is to use a needle and cotton to join it or form it into clothing **2** to sew is to work with a needle and thread or with a sewing machine

> SPELLING
> Take care not to confuse this word with **sow**, which means to put seeds in the ground.

sewage *NOUN* (*say* **soo**- ij)
sewage is waste matter carried away in drains

sewer *NOUN* (**sewers**) (*say* **soo**- er)
an underground drain that carries away sewage

sewing machine *NOUN* (**sewing machines**)
a machine for sewing things

sex *NOUN* (**sexes**)
1 a sex is each of the two groups, male or female, that people and animals belong to **2** sex is the instinct that causes members of the two sexes to be attracted to one another **3** sex is also sexual intercourse

sexism *NOUN*
sexism is the unfair or offensive treatment of people of a particular sex, especially women

> WORD FAMILY
> A **sexist** is someone who treats people of a particular sex, especially women, in an unfair or offensive way; a **sexist** remark is offensive to people of a particular sex, especially women.

sextet *NOUN* (**sextets**)
1 a group of six musicians **2** a piece of music for six musicians

sexual *ADJECTIVE*
to do with sex or the sexes
▷ **sexuality** *NOUN* sexuality is feelings to do with sex
▷ **sexually** *ADVERB* in a sexual way

sexual intercourse *NOUN*
sexual intercourse is the act of physical love in which a man puts his penis into a woman's vagina

sexy *ADJECTIVE* (**sexier**, **sexiest**)(*informal*)
1 a sexy person is attractive to people of the opposite sex **2** concerned with sex • *They saw a sexy film.*

shabby *ADJECTIVE* (**shabbier**, **shabbiest**)
1 very old and worn • *The stranger was wearing an extremely shabby set of wizard's robes which had been darned in several places.* — J. K. Rowling, *Harry Potter and the Prisoner of Azkaban* **2** mean or unfair • *What a shabby trick.*
▷ **shabbily** *ADVERB* in a shabby way
▷ **shabbiness** *NOUN* shabbiness is being shabby

shack *NOUN* (**shacks**)
a roughly-built hut

shade *NOUN* (**shades**)
1 shade is an area sheltered from bright sunlight • *We sat down in the shade.* **2** a shade is a colour, or how light or dark a colour is **3** a shade is also a device that decreases or shuts out bright light **4** a shade of something is a slight difference • *This word has several shades of meaning.*

shade *VERB* (**shades**, **shading**, **shaded**)
1 to shade something or someone is to shelter them from bright light **2** to shade a drawing is to make parts of it darker than the rest

> WORD FAMILY
> **Shading** is the parts of a drawing that you make darker than the rest.

shadow *NOUN* (**shadows**)
1 a shadow is a dark shape that falls on a surface when something is between it and the light
2 shadow is an area that is dark because the light is blocked • *His face was in shadow.*

> WORD FAMILY
> A **shadowy** place is dark and full of shadows.

shadow *VERB* (**shadows, shadowing, shadowed**)
1 to shadow someone is to follow them secretly
2 to shadow something is to cast a shadow on it

shady *ADJECTIVE* (**shadier, shadiest**)
1 giving shade • *We sat under a shady tree.*
2 situated in the shade • *Find a shady spot.*
3 dishonest or suspect • *It was a shady deal.*

shaft *NOUN* (**shafts**)
1 a long thin rod or straight part of something **2** a deep narrow hole in a mine or building • *They found an old mine shaft.* • *a lift shaft* **3** a beam of light

shaggy *ADJECTIVE* (**shaggier, shaggiest**)
having long untidy hair

shake *VERB* (**shakes, shaking, shook, shaken**)
1 to shake something is to move it quickly up and down or from side to side • *Have you shaken the bottle?* **2** to shake is to move in this way **3** to shake someone is to shock or upset them • *The news shook her.* **4** to shake is to tremble • *His voice was shaking.*
to shake hands is to clasp someone's right hand as a greeting or as a sign that you agree

shake *NOUN* (**shakes**)
a quick movement up and down or from side to side • *Give the bottle a shake.*
in two shakes very soon • *I'll be there in two shakes.*

shaky *ADJECTIVE* (**shakier, shakiest**)
shaking or likely to fall down
▷ **shakily** *ADVERB* in a shaky way

shall *VERB* (*past tense* **should**)
used with *I* and *we* to refer to the future • *We shall arrive tomorrow.* • *We told them we should arrive the next day.*

shallow *ADJECTIVE* (**shallower, shallowest**)
not deep • *The stream is quite shallow here.* • *We were playing in the shallow end of the pool.*

sham *NOUN* (**shams**)
a person or thing that is not genuine or what they claim to be

shamble *VERB* (**shambles, shambling, shambled**)
to shamble is to walk in an awkward way, dragging your feet along the ground

shambles *NOUN*
you say something is a shambles when it is in great disorder or in a mess

shame *NOUN*
1 shame is a feeling of great sorrow or guilt because you have done something wrong **2** you say something is a shame when it is something that you regret or are sorry about • *What a shame you won't be able to come.*

shame *VERB* (**shames, shaming, shamed**)
to shame someone is to make them feel ashamed

shameful *ADJECTIVE*
causing shame; disgraceful
▷ **shamefully** *ADVERB* in a shameful way

shameless *ADJECTIVE*
feeling or showing no shame
▷ **shamelessly** *ADVERB* in a shameless way

shampoo *NOUN* (**shampoos**)
shampoo is liquid soap for washing things, especially your hair or a carpet

shampoo *VERB* (**shampoos, shampooing, shampooed**)
to shampoo something is to wash it with shampoo

shamrock *NOUN*
shamrock is a small plant rather like clover, with leaves divided in three

shandy *NOUN* (**shandies**)
shandy is a mixture of beer with lemonade or another soft drink

shan't
short for *shall not*

shanty [1] *NOUN* (**shanties**)
a sailor's traditional song

shanty [2] *NOUN* (**shanties**)
a roughly-built hut

shape *NOUN* (**shapes**)
1 the outline of something or the way it looks
2 something that has a definite or regular form, such as a square, circle, or triangle **3** the condition that something is in • *The garden isn't in very good shape.*
to be out of shape is to no longer have the normal shape • *The front wheel was twisted out of shape.*
to take shape is to start to develop properly

shape *VERB* (**shapes, shaping, shaped**)
to shape something is to give it a shape
to shape up is to develop well

shapeless *ADJECTIVE*
having no definite shape • *With these words the Witch fell down in a brown, melted, shapeless mass and began to spread over the clean boards of the kitchen floor.* — L. Frank Baum, *The Wizard of Oz*

shapely *ADJECTIVE* (**shapelier**, **shapeliest**)
having an attractive shape

share *NOUN* (**shares**)
1 one of the parts into which something is divided between several people or things **2** part of a company's money, lent by someone who is then given part of the profits in return

share *VERB* (**shares**, **sharing**, **shared**)
1 to share something, or share it out, is to divide it between several people or things **2** to share something is to use it when someone else is also using it • *She shared a room with me.*

shark *NOUN* (**sharks**)
a large sea fish with sharp teeth

sharp *ADJECTIVE* (**sharper**, **sharpest**)
1 a sharp object has an edge or point that can cut or make holes • *This is a sharp knife.* **2** quick to learn or notice things • *She has sharp eyes.* • *It was sharp of you to spot that mistake.* **3** sudden or severe • *We came to a sharp bend in the road.* • *I felt a sharp pain in my side.* **4** slightly sour • *The apples taste sharp.* **5** above the proper musical pitch

> WORD FAMILY
> To say something **sharply** is to say it in a critical or severe way; **sharpness** is being sharp.

sharp *ADVERB*
1 with a sudden change of direction • *Now turn sharp right.* **2** punctually; exactly • *Be there at six o'clock sharp.*

sharp *NOUN* (**sharps**)
the note that is a semitone above a particular musical note; the sign that indicates this

sharpen *VERB* (**sharpens**, **sharpening**, **sharpened**)
to sharpen something is to make it sharp or pointed

> WORD FAMILY
> A **sharpener** is a device for sharpening a pencil.

shatter *VERB* (**shatters**, **shattering**, **shattered**)
1 to shatter is to break suddenly into lots of tiny pieces **2** to shatter something is to break it in this way **3** to shatter hopes or dreams is to show they are unreal **4** someone is shattered when they are very upset by something • *We were shattered by the news.*

shave *VERB* (**shaves**, **shaving**, **shaved**)
1 someone shaves when they scrape hair from their skin with a razor **2** to shave something is to cut or scrape a thin slice off it

> WORD FAMILY
> A **shaver** is a device for shaving hair from the face.

shave *NOUN* (**shaves**)
the act of shaving the face • *Dad was having a shave.*
a close shave (*informal*) a narrow escape

shavings *PLURAL NOUN*
thin strips that have been shaved off a piece of wood or metal

shawl *NOUN* (**shawls**)
a large piece of material for covering the shoulders or wrapping a baby

she *PRONOUN*
a female person or animal: used as the subject of a verb

sheaf *NOUN* (**sheaves**)
1 a bundle of papers **2** a bundle of corn stalks tied together after reaping

shear *VERB* (**shears**, **shearing**, **sheared**, **shorn** or **sheared**)
to shear a sheep is to cut the wool from it
to shear off is to break off under a force or stress

> WORD FAMILY
> A **shearer** is someone who shears sheep.

> SPELLING
> Take care not to confuse **shear** with **sheer**, which is an adjective meaning complete, vertical, or very thin.

shears *PLURAL NOUN*
a tool like a very large pair of scissors for trimming grass and bushes or for shearing sheep

sheath *NOUN* (**sheaths**)
1 a cover for the blade of a sword or dagger **2** a cover that fits something closely

sheathe *VERB* (**sheathes**, **sheathing**, **sheathed**)
1 to sheathe a sword is to put it into its sheath **2** to sheathe something is to put a protective covering on it

shed[1] *NOUN* (**sheds**)
a simply-made building used for storing things or sheltering animals, or as a workshop

shed[2] *VERB* (**sheds**, **shedding**, **shed**)
to shed something is to let it fall or flow • *The trees are shedding their leaves.* • *He was so badly hurt he was shedding blood.*

she'd
short for *she had, she should,* or *she would*

sheen *NOUN*
a soft shine on a surface

sheep *NOUN* (**sheep**)
a grass-eating animal kept by farmers for its wool and meat

sheepdog *NOUN* (**sheepdogs**)
a dog trained to guard and control sheep

sheepish *ADJECTIVE*
someone looks sheepish when they look shy or embarrassed
▷ **sheepishly** *ADVERB* in a sheepish way

sheer *ADJECTIVE* (**sheerer**, **sheerest**)
1 complete or total • *There was a look of sheer misery on his face.* **2** extremely steep; vertical • *To the right of the road there was a sheer drop.* **3** sheer material is so thin that you can see through it

> SPELLING
> Take care not to confuse **sheer** with **shear**, which is a verb meaning to cut wool off a sheep.

sheet *NOUN* (**sheets**)
1 a large piece of lightweight material put on a bed **2** a whole flat piece of paper, glass, or metal • *You will need two sheets of newspaper.* **3** a wide area of water, snow, ice, or flame

sheikh *NOUN* (**sheikhs**) (*say* shayk)
the leader of an Arab tribe or village

shelf *NOUN* (**shelves**)
1 a flat piece of hard material fitted to a wall or in a piece of furniture so that you can put things on it **2** a flat level surface that sticks out from a cliff or under the sea

shell *NOUN* (**shells**)
1 the hard outer covering round a nut or egg, or round an animal such as a snail or tortoise **2** a metal case filled with explosive, fired from a large gun **3** the walls or framework of a building or ship

shell *VERB* (**shells, shelling, shelled**)
1 to shell something is to take it out of its shell **2** to shell a building, ship, town, etc., is to fire explosive shells at it
to shell out (*slang*) is to pay money

she'll
short for *she will*

shellfish *NOUN* (**shellfish**)
a sea animal that has a shell

shelter *NOUN* (**shelters**)
1 a shelter is a place that protects people from danger or from the weather **2** shelter is being protected from danger or from the weather • *We found shelter from the rain.*

shelter *VERB* (**shelters, sheltering, sheltered**)
1 to shelter somewhere is to stay there because you are protected from danger or from the weather • *We sheltered under the trees.* **2** to shelter something or someone is to protect or cover them • *The hill shelters the house from the wind.*

shelve *VERB* (**shelves, shelving, shelved**)
1 to shelve something is to put it on a shelf or shelves **2** to shelve an idea or piece of work is to reject or postpone it

shepherd *NOUN* (**shepherds**)
someone whose job is to look after sheep

shepherd's pie *NOUN* (**shepherd's pies**)
a baked dish of minced meat covered with mashed potato

sherbet *NOUN* (**sherbets**)
a fizzy sweet powder or drink

sheriff *NOUN* (**sheriffs**)
1 in the USA, the chief law officer in a county **2** the chief judge of a Scottish county

sherry *NOUN* (**sherries**)
a kind of strong wine

she's
short for *she is* and (before a verb in the past tense) *she has*

shield *NOUN* (**shields**)
1 a large piece of metal or wood a person carries to protect their body in fighting **2** a design or trophy in the shape of a shield **3** a protection from harm • *The spacecraft's heat shield protects it as it enters the planet's atmosphere.*

shield *VERB* (**shields, shielding, shielded**)
to shield someone or something is to protect them • *I was shielded from the wind.* • *She shielded her eyes from the sun.*

shift *NOUN* (**shifts**)
1 a change of position or condition **2** a group of workers who start work as another group finishes; the time when they work • *He's on the night shift this month.* **3** a woman's lightweight dress that hangs loosely

shift *VERB* (**shifts, shifting, shifted**)
1 to shift something is to move it **2** to shift is to change position

shilling *NOUN* (**shillings**)
an old British coin that was worth a twentieth of a pound (now 5 pence)

shimmer *VERB* (**shimmers, shimmering, shimmered**)
to shimmer is to shine with a quivering light • *The sea shimmered in the sunlight.* • *Before them the water shimmered, satin smooth and silver grey.* — L. M. Montgomery, *Anne of the Island*

shin *NOUN* (**shins**)
the front of your leg between your knee and your ankle

shine *VERB* (**shines, shining, shone** or, in 'polish' sense, **shined**)
1 to shine is to give out or reflect bright light **2** to shine a torch or light somewhere is to point the light in that direction **3** to shine something is to polish it • *Have you shined your shoes?* **4** to shine is to do well or be excellent • *He does not shine in maths.*

shine *NOUN*
1 shine is brightness **2** a shine is an act of polishing • *Give your shoes a good shine.*

shingle *NOUN*
shingle is pebbles on a beach

shiny *ADJECTIVE* (**shinier, shiniest**)
bright or glossy

ship *NOUN* (**ships**)
a large boat, especially one that goes to sea

ship *VERB* (**ships, shipping, shipped**)
to ship something is to send it on a ship

shipping *NOUN*
1 shipping is all the ships of a country **2** shipping is also the business of carrying goods by ship

shipwreck *NOUN* (**shipwrecks**)
1 when a ship is wrecked in a storm or accident at sea **2** the remains of a wrecked ship

> WORD FAMILY
> Someone is **shipwrecked** when they are left somewhere after their ship has been wrecked at sea.

shipyard *NOUN* (**shipyards**)
a dockyard

shire *NOUN* (**shires**)
a county

shirk *VERB* (**shirks, shirking, shirked**)
you shirk a task or duty when you avoid doing it

shirt *NOUN* (**shirts**)
a piece of clothing you wear on the top half of the body, with a collar and sleeves
to be in your shirtsleeves is to be wearing a shirt but not a jacket over it

shiver *VERB* (**shivers, shivering, shivered**)
you shiver when you tremble with cold or fear

> WORD FAMILY
> You are **shivery** when you can't stop yourself shivering.

shiver *NOUN* (**shivers**)
an act of shivering • *I felt a shiver down my spine.*

shoal *NOUN* (**shoals**)
a large number of fish swimming together

shock[1] *NOUN* (**shocks**)
1 a shock is a sudden unpleasant surprise **2** a shock is also a violent knock or jolt **3** shock is weakness caused by severe pain or injury **4** a shock, or electric shock, is a painful effect caused by a strong electric current passing through your body

shock *VERB* (**shocks, shocking, shocked**)
1 to shock someone is to give them a shock **2** to shock someone is also to make them feel disgusted or appalled

shock[2] *NOUN* (**shocks**)
a shock of hair is a bushy mass of it

shocking *ADJECTIVE*
1 horrifying or disgusting **2** very bad • *The weather's been shocking today.*

shoddy *ADJECTIVE* (**shoddier, shoddiest**)
of poor quality • *This is shoddy work.*

shoe *NOUN* (**shoes**)
1 a strong covering you wear on your foot **2** a horseshoe
to be in someone's shoes is to be in someone's place • *I wouldn't be in your shoes.*

shoelace *NOUN* (**shoelaces**)
a cord for fastening a shoe

shoestring *NOUN*
to do something on a shoestring is to do it with only a small amount of money

shone
past tense and past participle of **shine** *VERB*

shook
past tense of **shake** *VERB*

shoot *VERB* (**shoots, shooting, shot**)
1 to shoot a gun or other weapon is to fire it **2** to shoot a person or animal is to fire a gun at them **3** to shoot somewhere is to move very fast • *The car shot past.* **4** *(in football)* to shoot is to kick or hit a ball at a goal **5** to shoot a film or scene is to film or photograph it • *The film was shot in Africa.*

shoot *NOUN* (**shoots**)
a young branch or new growth of a plant

shooting star *NOUN* (**shooting stars**)
a meteor

shop *NOUN* (**shops**)
1 a building where people buy things **2** a workshop

shop *VERB* (**shops, shopping, shopped**)
to shop is to go and buy things at shops

> WORD FAMILY
> A **shopper** is someone who goes shopping.

shopkeeper *NOUN* (**shopkeepers**)
someone who owns or looks after a shop

shoplifter *NOUN* (**shoplifters**)
someone who steals from shops

> WORD FAMILY
> **Shoplifting** is stealing things from shops.

shopping *NOUN*
1 shopping is buying things at shops • *I like shopping.* **2** shopping is also things that you have bought in shops • *Let me help you carry your shopping.*

shop steward *NOUN* (**shop stewards**)
a trade-union official who represents a group of fellow workers

shore *NOUN* (**shores**)
1 the seashore **2** the land along the edge of a lake

shorn
past tense of **shear**

short *ADJECTIVE* (**shorter, shortest**)
1 not long; not lasting long • *I went for a short walk.* **2** not tall • *He is a short man.* **3** not sufficient; scarce • *Water is short.* **4** bad-tempered • *He was rather short with me.* **5** short pastry is rich and crumbly, and contains a lot of fat

for short as a shorter form of something • *Joanna is called Jo for short.*
short for something a shorter form of something • *Jo is short for Joanna.*
to be short of something is to not have enough of it • *We seem to be short of chairs.*
▷ **shortness** *NOUN* shortness is being short

short *ADVERB*
1 before reaching the point aimed at • *My ball fell just short of the hole.* **2** suddenly • *The horse stopped short.*

shortage *NOUN* (**shortages**)
there is a shortage when there is not enough of something

shortbread *NOUN*
shortbread is a rich sweet biscuit made with butter

shortcake *NOUN* (**shortcakes**)
1 shortbread **2** a light cake usually served with fruit

short circuit *NOUN* (**short circuits**)
a fault in an electrical circuit in which current flows along a shorter route than the normal one

shortcoming *NOUN* (**shortcomings**)
a fault or failure • *He has many shortcomings.*

short cut *NOUN* (**short cuts**)
a route or method that is quicker than the usual one

shorten *VERB* (**shortens, shortening, shortened**)
1 to shorten something is to make it shorter **2** to shorten is to become shorter

shorthand *NOUN*
shorthand is a set of special signs for writing words down as quickly as people say them

short-handed *ADJECTIVE*
to be short-handed is to not have enough people to help you

shortly *ADVERB*
1 soon • *I'll be there shortly.* **2** briefly or sharply • *'Go away,' she said shortly.*

shorts *PLURAL NOUN*
trousers with legs that stop at or above the knee

short-sighted *ADJECTIVE*
1 unable to see things clearly when they are further away **2** not thinking enough about what may happen in the future

shot[1] *NOUN* (**shots**)
1 a shot is the firing of a gun or other weapon **2** shot is lead pellets fired from small guns **3** a good or bad shot is a person judged by their skill in shooting • *She is a great shot.* **4** a shot is a stroke in a game with a ball, such as tennis or snooker **5** a shot is also an injection **6** in photography, a shot is a photograph or filmed sequence **7** a shot is a heavy metal ball thrown as a sport **8** a shot at something is an attempt to do it • *Have a shot at this puzzle.*

shot[2]
past tense and past participle of **shoot** *VERB*

shotgun *NOUN* (**shotguns**)
a gun for firing small lead pellets over a short distance

should *VERB*
used to express **1** what someone ought to do • *You should have told me.* **2** what someone expects • *They should be here soon.* **3** what might happen • *If you should happen to see him, tell him to come.*

shoulder *NOUN* (**shoulders**)
the part of your body between your neck and your arm

shoulder *VERB* (**shoulders, shouldering, shouldered**)
1 to shoulder something is to put it or rest it on your shoulder or shoulders **2** to shoulder blame or responsibility is to accept it

shoulder blade *NOUN* (**shoulder blades**)
each of the two large flat bones at the top of your back

shout *VERB* (**shouts, shouting, shouted**)
to shout is to speak or call very loudly

shout *NOUN* (**shouts**)
a loud cry or call

shove *VERB* (**shoves, shoving, shoved**) (*say* shuv)
to shove something is to push it hard
to shove off (*informal*) is to go away

shovel *NOUN* (**shovels**) (*say* shuv-el)
a tool like a spade with the sides turned up, for lifting and moving coal, earth, sand, snow, and other things

shovel *VERB* (**shovels, shovelling, shovelled**)
to shovel (for example) earth or snow is to move it or clear it with a shovel

show *VERB* (**shows, showing, showed, shown**)
1 to show something is to let people see it • *She showed me her new bike.* **2** to show something to someone is to explain it to them • *Can you show me how to do it?* **3** to show someone somewhere is to guide or lead them there • *I'll show you to your seat.* **4** to show is to be visible • *That stain won't show.*
to show off is to try to impress people
to show something off is to be proud of letting people see it

show *NOUN* (**shows**)
1 an entertainment • *She loves TV game shows.* **2** a display or exhibition • *Have you been to the flower show?*

show business *NOUN*
show business is the entertainment business; the theatre, films, radio, and television

shower *NOUN* (**showers**)
1 a brief fall of rain or snow • *It's only a shower.* **2** a lot of small things coming or falling like rain • *They were met by a shower of stones.* **3** a device or cabinet for spraying water to wash the body; a wash in this

shower *VERB* (**showers, showering, showered**)
1 to shower is to fall like rain **2** to shower someone with things is to give a lot of them • *He showered her with presents.* **3** to shower is to wash under a shower

showery *ADJECTIVE*
raining occasionally

showjumping *NOUN*
showjumping is a competition in which riders make their horses jump over fences and other obstacles

> WORD FAMILY
> A **showjumper** is someone who takes part in showjumping.

showman *NOUN* (**showmen**)
1 someone who presents entertainments
2 someone who is good at attracting attention or at entertaining

> WORD FAMILY
> **Showmanship** is being good at attracting attention or at entertaining.

show-off *NOUN* (**show-offs**)
someone who is trying to impress other people

showroom *NOUN* (**showrooms**)
a large room where goods are displayed for people to look at and to buy

showy *ADJECTIVE* (**showier**, **showiest**)
likely to attract attention; bright or highly decorated
▷ **showily** *ADVERB* in a showy way
▷ **showiness** *NOUN* showiness is being showy

shrank
past tense of **shrink**

shrapnel *NOUN*
shrapnel is pieces of metal scattered from an exploding shell

shred *NOUN* (**shreds**)
1 a tiny strip or piece torn or cut off something • *His cloak had been ripped to shreds.* **2** a very small amount of something • *There's not a shred of evidence for what you say.*

shred *VERB* (**shreds**, **shredding**, **shredded**)
to shred something is to tear or cut it into tiny strips or pieces

shrew *NOUN* (**shrews**)
1 a small animal rather like a mouse **2** a bad-tempered woman

shrewd *ADJECTIVE* (**shrewder**, **shrewdest**)
having common sense and showing good judgement
▷ **shrewdly** *ADVERB* in a shrewd way
▷ **shrewdness** *NOUN* shrewdness is being shrewd

shriek *NOUN* (**shrieks**)
a shrill cry or scream

shriek *VERB* (**shrieks**, **shrieking**, **shrieked**)
to shriek is to give a shrill cry or scream

shrill *ADJECTIVE* (**shriller**, **shrillest**)
a shrill sound is very high and loud • *There was a shrill blast of the whistle.*
▷ **shrilly** *ADVERB* in a shrill way
▷ **shrillness** *NOUN* shrillness is being shrill

shrimp *NOUN* (**shrimps**)
a small shellfish

shrine *NOUN* (**shrines**)
an altar or chapel or other sacred place

shrink *VERB* (**shrinks**, **shrinking**, **shrank**, **shrunk**)
1 to shrink is to become smaller • *My dress has shrunk.* **2** to shrink something is to make it smaller, usually by washing it • *Their jeans have been shrunk.* **3** to shrink from something is to avoid it because you are afraid or embarrassed • *He shrank from meeting strangers.*

shrinkage *NOUN*
shrinkage is the amount that something shrinks

shrivel *VERB* (**shrivels**, **shrivelling**, **shrivelled**)
to shrivel is to become wrinkled and dry

shroud *NOUN* (**shrouds**)
a sheet in which a dead body is wrapped

shroud *VERB* (**shrouds**, **shrouding**, **shrouded**)
1 to shroud a dead body is to wrap it in a shroud
2 to shroud something is to cover or conceal it
• *The mountain was shrouded in mist.*

Shrove Tuesday *NOUN*
the day before Ash Wednesday, when people eat pancakes

shrub *NOUN* (**shrubs**)
a bush or small tree

shrubbery *NOUN* (**shrubberies**)
an area where shrubs are grown

shrug *VERB* (**shrugs**, **shrugging**, **shrugged**)
you shrug when you raise your shoulders slightly as a sign that you don't care or don't know

shrug *NOUN* (**shrugs**)
the act of shrugging

shrunk
past participle of **shrink**

shrunken *ADJECTIVE*
smaller than it used to be because it has shrunk

shudder *VERB* (**shudders**, **shuddering**, **shuddered**)
you shudder when you shake because you are cold or afraid

shudder *NOUN* (**shudders**)
the act of shuddering

shuffle *VERB* (**shuffles**, **shuffling**, **shuffled**)
1 to shuffle is to drag your feet along the ground as you walk **2** to shuffle playing cards is to mix them by sliding them over each other several times

shuffle *NOUN* (**shuffles**)
the act of shuffling • *Give the cards a quick shuffle.*

shunt *VERB* (**shunts**, **shunting**, **shunted**)
to shunt a railway train or wagons is to move them from one track to another

shut *VERB* (**shuts**, **shutting**, **shut**)
1 to shut a door or window, or a lid or cover, is to move it so that it blocks up an opening **2** to shut is to become closed • *The door shut suddenly.*
to shut down is to stop work or business
to shut up (*informal*) is to stop talking
to shut something up is to close it securely

shut *ADJECTIVE*
closed • *Keep your eyes shut.*

shutter *NOUN* (**shutters**)
1 a panel or screen that can be closed over a window **2** the device in a camera that opens and closes to let light fall on the film

shuttle *NOUN* (**shuttles**)
1 a train or bus or aircraft that makes frequent short journeys between two places **2** a space shuttle **3** the part of a loom that carries the thread from side to side

shuttlecock *NOUN* (**shuttlecocks**)
a small rounded piece of cork or plastic with a ring of feathers fixed to it, that you use in the game of badminton

shy *ADJECTIVE* (**shyer**, **shyest**)
timid and afraid to meet or talk to other people

> WORD FAMILY
> To say or do something **shyly** is to say or do it in a shy way; **shyness** is being shy.

SI *NOUN*
an international system of metric units of measurement, including the metre and kilogram

Siamese cat *NOUN* (**Siamese cats**)
a cat with blue eyes and short pale fur with darker patches

Siamese twins *PLURAL NOUN*
twins who are born with their bodies joined together. They are also known as *conjoined twins*

sibling *NOUN* (**siblings**)
your siblings are your brothers and sisters

sick *ADJECTIVE* (**sicker**, **sickest**)
1 ill or unwell • *He looks after sick animals.* **2** you feel sick when you feel that you are going to vomit; you are sick when you vomit
to be sick of something or **someone** is to be tired of them or fed up with them

sicken *VERB* (**sickens**, **sickening**, **sickened**)
1 to sicken someone is to disgust them **2** to sicken is to start feeling ill

sickle *NOUN* (**sickles**)
a tool with a curved blade and a short handle, used for cutting tall grass and crops

sickly *ADJECTIVE* (**sicklier**, **sickliest**)
1 often ill; unhealthy • *a sickly child* **2** making people feel sick • *There was a sickly taste.*

sickness *NOUN* (**sicknesses**)
an illness or disease

side *NOUN* (**sides**)
1 a flat surface, especially one that joins the top and bottom of something **2** a line that forms the edge of a shape • *A triangle has three sides.* **3** the outer part of something that is not the front or the back • *The instructions are on the side of the box.* **4** a position or space to the left or right of something • *There's a window on either side of the door.* **5** your sides are the parts of your body from your armpits to your hips • *I've got a pain down my right side.* **6** a group of people playing, arguing, or fighting against another group • *They are on our side.*

side *VERB* (**sides**, **siding**, **sided**)
to side with someone is to support them in a quarrel or argument

sideboard *NOUN* (**sideboards**)
a long heavy piece of furniture with drawers and cupboards and a flat top

sidecar *NOUN* (**sidecars**)
a small compartment for a passenger, fixed to the side of a motorcycle

sideline *NOUN* (**sidelines**)
something that you do in addition to your normal work or activity

sideshow *NOUN* (**sideshows**)
a small entertainment forming part of a large show, especially at a fair

sideways *ADVERB & ADJECTIVE*
1 to or from the side • *Crabs walk sideways.* **2** with one side facing forward • *We sat sideways in the bus.*

siding *NOUN* (**sidings**)
a short railway line leading off the main line

siege *NOUN* (**sieges**) (*say* seej)
when an army surrounds a place until the people inside surrender

sieve *NOUN* (**sieves**) (*say* siv)
a device made of mesh or perforated metal or plastic, used to separate harder or larger parts from liquid

sift *VERB* (**sifts**, **sifting**, **sifted**)
1 to sift a fine or powdery substance is to pass it through a sieve **2** to sift facts or information is to examine or select them

sigh *NOUN* (**sighs**)
a sound you make by breathing out heavily when you are sad, tired, or relieved

sigh *VERB* (**sighs**, **sighing**, **sighed**)
to sigh is to make a sigh

sight *NOUN* (**sights**)
1 sight is the ability to see • *She has very good sight.* **2** a sight is something that you see • *That sunset is a sight I'll never forget.* **3** the sights of a place are the interesting places worth seeing there • *Visit the sights of Paris.* **4** you can describe something silly or ridiculous to look at as a sight • *What a sight you are!* **5** a sight

on a gun is a device that helps you to aim it
to be in sight is to be able to be seen
on sight as soon as you see someone or something
to be out of sight is to be no longer able to be seen

sight *VERB* (**sights**, **sighting**, **sighted**)
to sight something is to see it or observe it

sightseeing *NOUN*
sightseeing is going round looking at interesting places

WORD FAMILY
A **sightseer** is someone who goes sightseeing.

sign *NOUN* (**signs**)
1 a mark or symbol that stands for something • *a minus sign* **2** a board or notice that tells or shows people something **3** something that shows that a thing exists • *There are signs of rust.* **4** an action or signal giving information or a command • *She made a sign to them to be quiet.*

sign *VERB* (**signs**, **signing**, **signed**)
1 you sign your name when you write your signature on something **2** to sign is to make a sign or signal • *He signed to them to follow him.* **3** to sign someone is to give them a contract for a job, especially in a professional sport • *They have signed three new players.*

signal *NOUN* (**signals**)
1 a device or gesture or sound or light that gives information or a message **2** a series of radio waves sent out or received

signal *VERB* (**signals**, **signalling**, **signalled**)
to signal to someone is to give them a signal
▷ **signaller** *NOUN* someone who gives a signal

signal box *NOUN* (**signal boxes**)
a building from which railway signals and points are controlled

signalman *NOUN* (**signalmen**)
a person who controls railway signals

signature *NOUN* (**signatures**)
your name written by yourself

signature tune *NOUN* (**signature tunes**)
a special tune used to introduce a well-known person on radio or television, or to begin or end a programme

significance *NOUN*
the significance of something is its meaning or importance

significant *ADJECTIVE*
something is significant when it has a meaning or importance
▷ **significantly** *ADVERB* in a way that is important or has a meaning

signify *VERB* (**signifies**, **signifying**, **signified**)
to signify something is to mean it or indicate it

signing or **sign language** *NOUN*
signing is a way of communicating by using movements of your hands instead of sounds, used by deaf people

signpost *NOUN* (**signposts**)
a sign at a road junction showing the names and distances of the places that each road leads to

Sikh *NOUN* (**Sikhs**) (*say* seek)
someone who believes in **Sikhism**, a religion of India having one God and some Hindu and Islamic beliefs

silence *NOUN* (**silences**)
silence is when no sound can be heard

silence *VERB* (**silences**, **silencing**, **silenced**)
to silence someone or something is to make them silent

silencer *NOUN* (**silencers**)
a device designed to reduce the sound made by an engine or a gun

silent *ADJECTIVE*
without any sound; not speaking

WORD FAMILY
To do something **silently** is to do it without speaking or making any sound.

silhouette *NOUN* (**silhouettes**) (*say* sil- oo- **et**)
a dark outline of something seen against a light background

silicon *NOUN*
silicon is a substance found in many rocks and used in making microchips

silk *NOUN*
1 silk is a fine soft thread produced by silkworms for making their cocoons **2** silk is also smooth shiny cloth made from this thread

WORD FAMILY
Silken clothes are made of silk; **silky** hair or fur is soft, smooth, and shiny like silk.

silkworm *NOUN* (**silkworms**)
a kind of caterpillar that covers itself with a cocoon of fine threads when it is ready to turn into a moth

sill *NOUN* (**sills**)
a strip of stone or wood or metal underneath a window or door

silly *ADJECTIVE* (**sillier**, **silliest**)
foolish or unwise
▷ **silliness** *NOUN* silliness is being silly

GRAMMAR
There is no adverb *sillily*, because it would be too difficult to say.

silver *NOUN*
1 silver is a shiny white precious metal **2** silver is also coins made of this metal or a metal that looks like it **3** silver is also a greyish-white colour

WORD FAMILY
Silvery light is shiny and silver in colour. •*On a silvery mushroom was spread the breakfast; little cakes of flower-dust lay on a broad green leaf, beside a crimson strawberry.* — Louisa May Alcott, *Flower Fables*

silver wedding *NOUN* (**silver weddings**)
the 25th anniversary of a wedding

similar *ADJECTIVE*
one thing is similar to another when it is like it in some ways but not exactly the same

WORD FAMILY
The **similarity** between two things is the fact that they are similar; two people are (for example) **similarly** dressed when they are dressed in a similar way.

simile *NOUN* (**similes**) (*say* **sim**- i- li)
a kind of expression in which you describe something by comparing it with something else, such as *bold as brass* or *as brave as a lion*

SIMILES AND METAPHORS
You can use similes and metaphors in your writing to describe people and things in interesting ways. A **simile** is a way of describing something by comparing it with something else. *He was as strong as an ox. Her eyes glinted like blue ice.* You often use a comparing word such as *like* or *as* before a simile. A **metaphor** is a way of describing something as if it really were something else that is similar to it in some way. *He was a lion in battle. She has a heart of gold.* If you say *Robbie eats like a pig*, that's a simile. If you say *Robbie is a pig*, that's a metaphor.

simmer *VERB* (**simmers, simmering, simmered**)
food simmers when it boils very gently over a low heat
to simmer down is to become calm after being anxious or angry

simple *ADJECTIVE* (**simpler, simplest**)
1 easy •*That's a simple question to answer.* **2** not complicated •*It was a simple plan, but it worked.* **3** plain •*She was wearing a simple dress.* **4** not having much sense or intelligence •*Do you think I'm simple or something?*

WORD FAMILY
Simplicity is being simple.

simplify *VERB* (**simplifies, simplifying, simplified**)
to simplify something is to make it simple or easy to understand

WORD FAMILY
Simplification is making something simple.

simply *ADVERB*
1 in a simple way •*Explain it simply.* **2** completely •*It's simply marvellous.* **3** only or merely •*It's simply a question of time.*

simulate *VERB* (**simulates, simulating, simulated**)
1 to simulate something is to reproduce the conditions for it •*The machine simulates a space flight.* **2** to simulate a feeling or state is to pretend to have it •*He simulated illness.*

WORD FAMILY
A **simulation** is when something is simulated or reproduced; a **simulator** is a machine for reproducing the conditions for something, such as flying an aeroplane.

simultaneous *ADJECTIVE* (*say* sim- ul- **tay**- ni- us)
two things are simultaneous when they happen at the same time

WORD FAMILY
Two things happen **simultaneously** when they happen at the same time.

sin *NOUN* (**sins**)
a wicked act that breaks a religious or moral law

sin *VERB* (**sins, sinning, sinned**)
to sin is to commit a sin

WORD FAMILY
A **sinner** is someone who sins.

since *CONJUNCTION*
1 from the time when •*Where have you been since I last saw you?* **2** because •*Since we have missed the bus, we must walk home.*

since *PREPOSITION*
from a certain time •*I have been here since Christmas.*

since *ADVERB*
between then and now •*He has not been seen since.*

sincere *ADJECTIVE* (**sincerer, sincerest**)
you are being sincere when you mean what you say and express your true feelings •*I gave them my sincere good wishes.*

WORD FAMILY
You **sincerely** hope or believe something when you really mean it; **sincerity** is being sincere.

sinew *NOUN* (**sinews**)
strong tissue that joins a muscle to a bone

sinful *ADJECTIVE*
wicked; guilty of sin
▷ **sinfully** *ADVERB* in a sinful way
▷ **sinfulness** *NOUN* sinfulness is being sinful

sing *VERB* (**sings, singing, sang, sung**)
1 to sing is to make musical sounds with your voice **2** birds and insects sing when they make musical sounds

WORD FAMILY
A **singer** is someone who sings.

singe *VERB* (**singes**, **singeing**, **singed**) (*say* sinj)
to singe something is to burn it slightly

single *ADJECTIVE*
1 only one; not double **2** designed for one person • *The bedroom had two single beds.* **3** not married **4** for a journey in one direction only

single *NOUN* (**singles**)
1 a single ticket **2** a record with one song or short piece of music on it **3** you play singles in tennis when you play against only one other person

single *VERB* (**singles**, **singling**, **singled**)
to single someone out is to pick them from other people

single file *NOUN*
in single file in a line, one behind the other

single-handed *ADJECTIVE*
by your own efforts; without any help

single-minded *ADJECTIVE*
thinking only about one thing you are determined to achieve

single parent *NOUN* (**single parents**)
a person who is bringing up a child or children without a partner

single ticket *NOUN* (**single tickets**)
a ticket for a journey you make to a place but not back again

singly *ADVERB*
one at a time or one by one • *These stamps are available singly or in books of twelve.*

singular *NOUN* (**singulars**)
the form of a word meaning only one person or thing, such as *cake* and *child*

singular *ADJECTIVE*
1 in the singular; meaning only one • *'Mouse' is a singular noun.* **2** extraordinary • *She is a woman of singular courage.*

> WORD FAMILY
> To be (for example) **singularly** beautiful is to be remarkably or unusually beautiful.

> SINGULAR AND PLURAL
> If you know the rule for making plurals, you can usually work out the singular form of a word. Exceptions include words like *scissors* and *trousers*, for which there is no singular form. Some words (mass nouns) have no singular or plural form, for example *cheese, milk,* and *money.* If you want to count nouns like these, you have to think of a measurement (*500 grams of cheese)* or a quantity (*more cheese)* because you can't count the thing itself. Look also at the panel on **Plurals.**

sinister *ADJECTIVE*
looking or seeming evil or harmful

sink *VERB* (**sinks**, **sinking**, **sank** or **sunk**, **sunk**)
1 to sink is to go under water • *The ship sank in a storm.* **2** to sink something is to make it go under water • *They fired on the ship and sank it.* **3** to sink, or to sink down, is to go or fall down to the ground • *He sank to his knees.*
to sink in is to be gradually understood

sink *NOUN* (**sinks**)
a fixed basin with taps to supply water

sinus *NOUN* (**sinuses**) (*say* sy- nus)
your sinuses are the hollows in the bones of your skull, connected with your nose • *My sinuses are blocked.*

sip *VERB* (**sips**, **sipping**, **sipped**)
to sip a drink is to drink it slowly in small mouthfuls

siphon *NOUN* (**siphons**)
a bent tube used for transferring liquid from one container to another at a lower level

siphon *VERB* (**siphons**, **siphoning**, **siphoned**)
to siphon liquid is to transfer it with a siphon

sir *NOUN*
a word sometimes used when speaking politely to a man, instead of his name • *Can I help you, sir?*
Sir the title given to a knight • *Sir Francis Drake.*

siren *NOUN* (**sirens**)
a device that makes a loud hooting or screaming sound, usually as a warning signal

sisal *NOUN* (*say* sI-sal)
a fibre made from the leaves of a tropical plant, used for making ropes

sister *NOUN* (**sisters**)
1 your sister is a woman or girl who has the same parents as you **2** a senior nurse in a hospital

sister-in-law *NOUN* (**sisters-in-law**)
a person's sister-in-law is the sister of their husband or wife, or the wife of their brother

sit *VERB* (**sits**, **sitting**, **sat**)
1 to sit is to rest on your bottom, as you do when you are on a chair **2** to sit someone, or to sit someone down, is to put them in a sitting position **3** to sit an examination or test is to do it • *We sit our end-of-year exam this afternoon.* **4** to sit somewhere is to be situated or positioned there • *The house sits on top of a hill.* **5** to sit for someone is to act as a babysitter

> WORD FAMILY
> A **sitter** is someone who is sitting, or a babysitter.

site *NOUN* (**sites**)
1 the place where something has been built or will be built • *They crossed a building site.* **2** a place used for something or where something happened • *We stayed at a camping site.* • *This is the site of a famous battle.*

site *VERB* (**sites**, **siting**, **sited**)
to site something somewhere is to locate or build it there

a b c d e f g h i j k l m n o p q r **s** t u v w x y z

sit-in *NOUN* (**sit-ins**)
a protest in which a lot of people sit down in a place and refuse to move

sitting room *NOUN* (**sitting rooms**)
a room with comfortable chairs for sitting in

situated *ADJECTIVE*
to be situated in a particular place or position is to be placed there • *They lived in a town situated in a valley.*

situation *NOUN* (**situations**)
1 a place or position; where something is **2** all the things that are happening to someone at a particular time; the way things are • *We're now in a difficult situation because we've run out of money.* **3** a job or employment

six *NOUN* (**sixes**)
the number 6

sixpence *NOUN* (**sixpences**)
an old British coin that was worth half a shilling

sixteen *NOUN* (**sixteens**)
the number 16
▷ **sixteenth** *ADJECTIVE & NOUN* 16th

sixth *ADJECTIVE & NOUN*
the next after the fifth
▷ **sixthly** *ADVERB* in the sixth place; as the sixth one

sixty *NOUN* (**sixties**)
the number 60
▷ **sixtieth** *ADJECTIVE & NOUN* 60th

size *NOUN* (**sizes**)
1 how big a person or thing is **2** the measurement something is made in • *I wear a size eight shoe.*

size *VERB* (**sizes**, **sizing**, **sized**)
to size something or **someone up** (*informal*) is to form an opinion about them

sizeable *ADJECTIVE*
fairly large

sizzle *VERB* (**sizzles**, **sizzling**, **sizzled**)
to sizzle is to make a crackling and hissing sound • *The bacon sizzled in the pan.*

skate[1] *NOUN* (**skates**)
1 a boot with a steel blade attached to the sole, used for sliding smoothly over ice **2** a roller skate

skate *VERB* (**skates**, **skating**, **skated**)
to skate is to move around on skates

> WORD FAMILY
> A **skater** is someone who skates.

skate[2] *NOUN* (**skate**)
a large flat sea fish used for food

skateboard *NOUN* (**skateboards**)
a small board with wheels, used for standing and riding on as a sport

skeleton *NOUN* (**skeletons**)
1 the framework of bones in a person's or animal's body **2** the framework or shell of a new building
▷ **skeletal** *ADJECTIVE* to do with a skeleton or like a skeleton

sketch *NOUN* (**sketches**)
1 a quick or rough drawing **2** a short amusing play

sketch *VERB* (**sketches**, **sketching**, **sketched**)
to sketch something or someone is to make a sketch of them

sketchy *ADJECTIVE* (**sketchier**, **sketchiest**)
roughly drawn or described, without any detail • *Reports of what happened are sketchy at the moment.*

skewer *NOUN* (**skewers**)
a long wooden or metal or plastic pin that you push through meat to hold it together while it is being cooked

ski *NOUN* (**skis**) (*say* skee)
a long flat strip of wood or metal or plastic, fastened to each foot for moving quickly over snow

ski *VERB* (**skis**, **skiing**, **skied** or **ski'd**)
to ski is to travel on snow wearing skis

> WORD FAMILY
> A **skier** is someone who skis.

skid *VERB* (**skids**, **skidding**, **skidded**)
to skid is to slide accidentally, especially in a vehicle

skid *NOUN* (**skids**)
a skidding movement • *The car went into a skid on the icy road.*

skilful *ADJECTIVE*
having or showing a lot of skill

> WORD FAMILY
> To do something **skilfully** is to do it in a skilful way.

skill *NOUN* (**skills**)
1 to do something with skill is to do it well **2** a type of work or ability that you learn through training and practice • *He's been learning some new football skills.*

> WORD FAMILY
> To be **skilled** is to have a skill or skills.

skim *VERB* (**skims**, **skimming**, **skimmed**)
1 to skim is to move quickly over a surface **2** to skim something is to remove it from the surface of a liquid, especially to take the cream off milk

> WORD FAMILY
> **Skimmed** milk has had the cream removed.

skimp *VERB* (**skimps**, **skimping**, **skimped**)
to skimp is to use or provide less than is needed for something

skimpy *ADJECTIVE* (**skimpier**, **skimpiest**)
skimpy clothes do not cover much of your body

skin *NOUN* (**skins**)
1 the outer covering of a person's or animal's body **2** the outer covering of a fruit or vegetable **3** a thin firm layer that has formed on the surface of a liquid

skin *VERB* (**skins**, **skinning**, **skinned**)
to skin something is to take the skin off it

skin diving *NOUN*
skin diving is swimming under water with flippers and breathing equipment but without a diving suit

> WORD FAMILY
> A **skin diver** is someone who goes skin diving.

skinny *ADJECTIVE* (**skinnier**, **skinniest**)
very thin

skint *ADJECTIVE*
(*slang*) having no money left

skip[1] *VERB* (**skips**, **skipping**, **skipped**)
1 to skip is to jump or move along by hopping from one foot to the other **2** to skip is also to jump with a skipping rope **3** to skip something is to miss it out or ignore it • *You can skip the last chapter.*

skip *NOUN* (**skips**)
a skipping movement

skip[2] *NOUN* (**skips**)
a large metal container for taking away builders' rubbish

skipper *NOUN* (**skippers**)
the captain of a ship or team

skipping rope *NOUN* (**skipping ropes**)
a length of rope, usually with a handle at each end, that you swing over your head and under your feet as you jump

skirt *NOUN* (**skirts**)
a piece of clothing for a woman or girl that hangs down from her waist

skirt *VERB* (**skirts**, **skirting**, **skirted**)
to skirt something is to go round the edge of it

skirting or **skirting board** *NOUN* (**skirtings** or **skirting boards**)
a narrow board round the wall of a room, close to the floor

skit *NOUN* (**skits**)
a play or sketch or poem that makes fun of something by imitating it

skittish *ADJECTIVE*
lively and excitable

skittle *NOUN* (**skittles**)
a piece of wood or plastic shaped like a bottle, that people try to knock down with a ball in a game of **skittles**

skull *NOUN* (**skulls**)
the framework of bones in your head which contains your brain

skunk *NOUN* (**skunks**)
a black and white furry animal from North America that can make an unpleasant smell

sky *NOUN* (**skies**)
the space above the earth, where you can see the sun, moon, and stars

skylark *NOUN* (**skylarks**)
a small brown bird that sings as it hovers high in the air

skylight *NOUN* (**skylights**)
a window in a roof

skyscraper *NOUN* (**skyscrapers**)
a very tall building

slab *NOUN* (**slabs**)
a thick flat piece of something

slack *ADJECTIVE* (**slacker**, **slackest**)
1 loose; not pulled tight • *The rope was slack.* **2** lazy; not busy or working hard
▷ **slackly** *ADVERB* in a slack way
▷ **slackness** *NOUN* slackness is being slack

slacken *VERB* (**slackens**, **slackening**, **slackened**)
1 to slacken something is to loosen it **2** to slacken is to become slower or less busy • *Her pace gradually slackened.*

slacks *PLURAL NOUN*
loose-fitting casual trousers

slag heap *NOUN* (**slag heaps**)
a heap of waste material from a mine

slain
past participle of **slay**

slam *VERB* (**slams**, **slamming**, **slammed**)
1 to slam (for example) a door is to shut it hard or loudly **2** to slam something is to hit it with great force • *He slammed the ball into the net.*

slang *NOUN*
slang is a kind of colourful language used in less formal writing and speaking

> SLANG WORDS
> Examples of slang words are *dud*, *rip-off*, *skint*, *slosh*. There are also slang phrases such as *up the creek*; and some words with ordinary meanings also have slang meanings, for example *dough*, *jerk*, *lousy*. You will find a lot of other slang words and phrases in this dictionary; they are marked *slang* after the part of speech.

slant *VERB* (**slants**, **slanting**, **slanted**)
1 to slant is to slope or lean **2** to slant news or information is to present it from a particular point of view

slant *NOUN* (**slants**)
1 a sloping or leaning position • *The caravan floor was at a slant.* **2** a way of presenting news or information from a particular point of view

slap *VERB* (**slaps**, **slapping**, **slapped**)
1 to slap someone is to hit them with the palm of your hand **2** to slap something somewhere is to put it there forcefully or carelessly • *We slapped paint on the walls.*

slap *NOUN* (**slaps**)
to give someone a slap is to slap them

slapstick *NOUN*
slapstick is noisy lively comedy, with people hitting each other, throwing things, and falling over

a b c d e f g h i j k l m n o p q r **s** t u v w x y z

slash *VERB* (**slashes**, **slashing**, **slashed**)
1 to slash something is to make large cuts in it **2** to slash prices or costs is to reduce them a lot

slash *NOUN* (**slashes**)
1 a large cut **2** a sloping line (/) used to separate words or letters

slat *NOUN* (**slats**)
a thin strip of wood or plastic, usually arranged to overlap with others, for example in a blind or screen

slate *NOUN* (**slates**)
1 slate is a kind of grey rock that is easily split into flat plates **2** slates are flat pieces of this rock used to cover a roof
▷ **slaty** *ADJECTIVE* like slate

slaughter *VERB* (**slaughters**, **slaughtering**, **slaughtered**) (*say* slor- ter)
1 to slaughter an animal is to kill it for food **2** to slaughter people or animals is to kill a lot of them

slaughter *NOUN*
slaughter is the killing of a lot of people or animals

slaughterhouse *NOUN* (**slaughterhouses**)
a place where animals are killed for food

slave *NOUN* (**slaves**)
a person who is owned by someone else and has to work for them without being paid

slave *VERB* (**slaves**, **slaving**, **slaved**)
to slave over something is to work very hard

> GRAMMAR
> This is an example of a word that is both a noun and a verb, but the verb doesn't mean quite the same as the noun. Other words like this are *sap*, *shield*, and *shoot*. *Slick* is an example of a word that is an adjective and a noun. See if you can find any more words like this in this dictionary.

slavery *NOUN*
slavery is being a slave or the system of having slaves

slay *VERB* (**slays**, **slaying**, **slew**, **slain**)
(*old or poetical use*) to slay someone is to kill them

sledge or **sled** *NOUN* (**sledges** or **sleds**)
a vehicle for travelling over snow, with strips of metal or wood instead of wheels

sledgehammer *NOUN* (**sledgehammers**)
a very large heavy hammer

sleek *ADJECTIVE* (**sleeker**, **sleekest**)
smooth and shiny • *She has lovely sleek hair.*

sleep *NOUN*
1 sleep is the condition in which your eyes are closed, your body is relaxed, and your mind is unconscious • *You need some sleep.* **2** a sleep is a time when you are sleeping • *Did you have a good sleep?*

sleep *VERB* (**sleeps**, **sleeping**, **slept**)
to sleep is to have a sleep

sleeper *NOUN* (**sleepers**)
1 someone who is asleep **2** each of the wooden or concrete beams on which a railway line rests **3** a railway carriage equipped for sleeping in

sleeping bag *NOUN* (**sleeping bags**)
a warm padded bag for sleeping in, especially when you are camping

sleepless *ADJECTIVE*
unable to sleep; without sleep • *We've had a sleepless night.*

sleepwalker *NOUN* (**sleepwalkers**)
someone who walks around while they are asleep

> WORD FAMILY
> **Sleepwalking** is what a sleepwalker does.

sleepy *ADJECTIVE* (**sleepier**, **sleepiest**)
feeling tired and wanting to go to sleep
▷ **sleepily** *ADVERB* in a sleepy way
▷ **sleepiness** *NOUN* sleepiness is being sleepy

sleet *NOUN*
sleet is a mixture of rain with snow or hail

sleeve *NOUN* (**sleeves**)
the part of a piece of clothing that covers your arm

> WORD FAMILY
> A **sleeveless** (for example) jumper or dress is one without sleeves.

sleigh *NOUN* (**sleighs**) (*say* slay)
a large sledge pulled by horses

slender *ADJECTIVE* (**slenderer**, **slenderest**)
1 slim or thin **2** slight or small • *Their chances of winning are slender.*

slept
past tense and past participle of **sleep** *VERB*

slew
past tense of **slay**

slice *NOUN* (**slices**)
a thin flat piece cut off something

slice *VERB* (**slices**, **slicing**, **sliced**)
to slice something is to cut it into slices

slick *ADJECTIVE* (**slicker**, **slickest**)
done quickly and in a clever way, without obvious effort

slick *NOUN* (**slicks**)
a large patch of oil floating on water

slide *VERB* (**slides**, **sliding**, **slid**)
1 to slide is to move smoothly over a flat or polished or slippery surface • *She loved sliding down the bannister.* **2** to slide somewhere is to move there quickly or secretly • *The thief slid behind a bush.*

slide *NOUN* (**slides**)
1 a sliding movement **2** a structure for children to play on, with a smooth slope for sliding down **3** a type of photograph that lets light through and that can be shown on a screen **4** a small glass plate on which you can examine things under a microscope **5** a fastener for keeping your hair tidy

slight *ADJECTIVE* (**slighter**, **slightest**)
very small; not serious or important

slightly *ADVERB*
in a slight way; not seriously • *They were slightly hurt.*

slim *ADJECTIVE* (**slimmer**, **slimmest**)
1 thin and graceful **2** small; hardly enough • *We have a slim chance of winning.*

slim *VERB* (**slims**, **slimming**, **slimmed**)
to slim is to try to make yourself thinner, especially by dieting

> WORD FAMILY
> A **slimmer** is someone who is slimming.

slime *NOUN*
slime is unpleasant wet slippery stuff • *There was slime on the pond.*

> WORD FAMILY
> Something is **slimy** when it is covered in slime.

sling *VERB* (**slings**, **slinging**, **slung**)
1 to sling something somewhere is to throw it there roughly or carelessly • *You can sling your wet clothes into the washing machine.* **2** to sling something is also to hang it up or support it so that it hangs loosely • *He had slung the bag round his neck.*

sling *NOUN* (**slings**)
1 a piece of cloth tied round your neck to support an injured arm **2** a device for throwing stones

slink *VERB* (**slinks**, **slinking**, **slunk**)
to slink somewhere is to move there slowly and quietly because you feel guilty or don't want to be noticed • *He slunk off to bed.* • *The wolf slunk along behind Polly, growling to himself.* — Catherine Storr, *Clever Polly and the Stupid Wolf*

slip *VERB* (**slips**, **slipping**, **slipped**)
1 to slip is to slide without meaning to or to fall over **2** to slip somewhere is to move there quickly and quietly • *He slipped out of the house before anyone was awake.* **3** to slip something somewhere is to put it there quickly and without being seen • *She slipped the letter into her pocket.* **4** to slip something is to escape from it • *The dog slipped its leash.*
to slip up is to make a mistake

slip *NOUN* (**slips**)
1 an accidental slide or fall • *One slip and you could fall into the river.* **2** a small mistake **3** a small piece of paper **4** a piece of women's underwear like a thin dress or skirt
to give someone the slip is to escape from them or avoid them

slipper *NOUN* (**slippers**)
a soft comfortable shoe for wearing indoors

slippery *ADJECTIVE*
smooth or wet so that it is difficult to stand on or hold

slipshod *ADJECTIVE*
a slipshod piece of work is careless or badly done

slit *NOUN* (**slits**)
a long narrow cut or opening

slit *VERB* (**slits**, **slitting**, **slit**)
to slit something is to make a slit in it

slither *VERB* (**slithers**, **slithering**, **slithered**)
to slither is to slip or slide along, often unsteadily • *The snake slithered away.* • *We were slithering around on the ice.*

sliver *NOUN* (**slivers**) (*say* **sli**- ver)
a thin strip of wood, glass, or other material

slog *VERB* (**slogs**, **slogging**, **slogged**)
1 to slog something is to hit it hard or wildly **2** to slog is to work hard • *I'm slogging away at my essay.* **3** to slog is also to walk with effort • *We slogged through the snow.*

slog *NOUN*
a piece of hard work or effort • *Climbing up that hill was a real slog.*

slogan *NOUN* (**slogans**)
a short catchy phrase used to advertise something or to sum up an idea

slop *VERB* (**slops**, **slopping**, **slopped**)
1 to slop liquid is to spill it over the edge of its container **2** liquid slops when it spills in this way

slope *VERB* (**slopes**, **sloping**, **sloped**)
to slope is to go gradually downwards or upwards or to have one end higher than the other

slope *NOUN* (**slopes**)
1 a sloping surface **2** the amount by which a surface slopes • *The hill has a slope of 30°.* **3** the side of a mountain

sloppy *ADJECTIVE* (**sloppier**, **sloppiest**)
1 liquid and spilling easily **2** careless or badly done • *Their work is sloppy.* **3** (*informal*) too sentimental or romantic • *What a sloppy story.*
▷ **sloppily** *ADVERB* in a sloppy way
▷ **sloppiness** *NOUN* sloppiness is being sloppy

slops *PLURAL NOUN*
liquid waste matter

slosh *VERB* (**sloshes**, **sloshing**, **sloshed**) (*slang*)
you slosh liquid, or it sloshes, when it gets splashed in a messy or careless way

slot *NOUN* (**slots**)
a narrow opening to put things in

sloth *NOUN* (**sloths**) (*rhymes with* **both**)
1 sloth is laziness **2** a sloth is a long-haired South American animal that lives in trees and moves very slowly

slot machine *NOUN* (**slot machines**)
a machine that you work by putting a coin in a slot

slouch *VERB* (**slouches**, **slouching**, **slouched**)
to slouch is to move or stand or sit in a lazy way, especially with your head and shoulders bent forwards

slovenly *ADJECTIVE* (*say* sluv- en- li)
careless or untidy

slow *ADJECTIVE* (**slower**, **slowest**)
1 not quick; taking more time than usual **2** a clock or watch is slow when it shows a time earlier than the correct time

slow *ADVERB*
at a slow rate; slowly • *Go slow.*
▷ **slowness** *NOUN* slowness is being slow

slow *VERB* (**slows**, **slowing**, **slowed**)
1 to slow, or to slow down, is to go slower **2** to slow something, or to slow it down, is to make it go slower

slowcoach *NOUN* (**slowcoaches**)
(*informal*) someone who moves or works slowly

slowly *ADVERB*
at a slow rate or speed

sludge *NOUN*
sludge is thick sticky mud

slug *NOUN* (**slugs**)
1 a small slimy animal like a snail without its shell **2** a pellet for firing from a gun

slum *NOUN* (**slums**)
an area of dirty and crowded houses in a city

slumber *NOUN*
slumber is peaceful sleep

slumber *VERB* (**slumbers**, **slumbering**, **slumbered**)
to slumber is to sleep peacefully

slump *VERB* (**slumps**, **slumping**, **slumped**)
to slump is to fall heavily or suddenly

slump *NOUN* (**slumps**)
a slump is a sudden fall in prices or trade

slung
past tense and past participle of **sling** *VERB*

slunk
past tense and past participle of **slink**

slur *NOUN* (**slurs**)
something that harms a person's reputation; an insult

slush *NOUN*
slush is snow that is melting on the ground

> WORD FAMILY
> **Slushy** snow is melting and wet.

sly *ADJECTIVE* (**slyer**, **slyest**)
cunning or mischievous

> WORD FAMILY
> To do something **slyly** is to do it in a sly way • *He glanced at her slyly*; **slyness** is being sly.

smack *VERB* (**smacks**, **smacking**, **smacked**)
to smack someone is to slap them with your hand, especially as a punishment

smack *NOUN* (**smacks**)
a slap with your hand

small *ADJECTIVE* (**smaller**, **smallest**)
not large; less than the normal size

smallpox *NOUN*
smallpox is a serious disease that causes a fever and produces spots that leave scars on the skin

smart *ADJECTIVE* (**smarter**, **smartest**)
1 neat and well dressed **2** clever and quick-thinking **3** fast • *We'll need to walk at a smart pace.*

> WORD FAMILY
> To be **smartly** dressed is to have nice clothes on; to move **smartly** is to do so quickly; **smartness** is being neat and well dressed.

smart *VERB* (**smarts**, **smarting**, **smarted**)
to smart is to feel a stinging pain

smarten *VERB* (**smartens**, **smartening**, **smartened**)
1 to smarten something or someone is to make them smarter • *You need to smarten yourself up a bit.* **2** to smarten is to become smarter

smash *VERB* (**smashes**, **smashing**, **smashed**)
1 to smash is to break into pieces noisily and violently; to smash something is to break it in this way **2** to smash into something is to hit it with great force • *The lorry left the road and smashed into a wall.* **3** (*informal*) to smash something or someone is to destroy them or defeat them completely

smash *NOUN* (**smashes**)
1 the act or sound of smashing **2** a collision between vehicles

smash hit *NOUN* (**smash hits**)
(*informal*) something very successful or popular

smashing *ADJECTIVE*
(*informal*) excellent

smear *VERB* (**smears**, **smearing**, **smeared**)
1 to smear something dirty or greasy is to rub it thickly over a surface **2** to smear someone is to try to damage their reputation

smear *NOUN* (**smears**)
a dirty or greasy mark made by smearing

smell *VERB* (**smells**, **smelling**, **smelt** or **smelled**)
1 you smell something when you use your nose to sense it **2** to smell is to give out a smell • *The cheese smells funny.*

smell *NOUN* (**smells**)
1 a smell is something you can smell, especially something unpleasant **2** smell is the ability to smell things • *I have a good sense of smell.*

> OTHER WORDS
> There are several words for different kinds of smell. A pleasant smell is often an *aroma* or *fragrance* or *scent*; and a nasty smell is often an *odour* or *stench* or *stink*.

smelly *ADJECTIVE* (**smellier**, **smelliest**)
having an unpleasant smell

smelt *VERB* (**smelts**, **smelting**, **smelted**)
to smelt ore is to melt it in order to get metal from it

smile *NOUN* (**smiles**)
an expression on your face that shows you are pleased or amused, with your lips stretched and turning upwards at the ends

smile *VERB* (**smiles**, **smiling**, **smiled**)
to smile is to give a smile

smith *NOUN* (**smiths**)
someone who makes things out of metal

smithereens *PLURAL NOUN*
something is smashed or blown to smithereens when it is broken into lots of tiny fragments

smock *NOUN* (**smocks**)
a loose piece of clothing like a very long shirt

smog *NOUN*
smog is a mixture of smoke and fog

smoke *NOUN*
1 smoke is the grey or blue mixture of gas and particles that rises from a fire **2** to have a smoke is to spend time smoking a cigarette • *He wants a smoke.*

> WORD FAMILY
> A **smoky** place is full of smoke.

smoke *VERB* (**smokes**, **smoking**, **smoked**)
1 something smokes when it gives out smoke • *The fire is smoking.* **2** someone is smoking when they have a lit cigarette in their mouth and are breathing in the smoke from it

> WORD FAMILY
> A **smoker** is someone who smokes cigarettes.

smokeless *ADJECTIVE*
smokeless fuel burns without giving off much smoke

smooth *ADJECTIVE* (**smoother**, **smoothest**)
1 having an even surface without any marks or roughness **2** a smooth liquid or substance has no lumps in it **3** moving without bumps or jolts • *We had a smooth ride.* **4** not harsh; flowing easily • *She spoke in a smooth voice.*

> WORD FAMILY
> Something flows **smoothly** when it does so easily and evenly; something goes **smoothly** when it happens without any problems; **smoothness** is being smooth.

smooth *VERB* (**smooths**, **smoothing**, **smoothed**)
to smooth something is to make it smooth and flat

smother *VERB* (**smothers**, **smothering**, **smothered**)
1 to smother someone is to cover their face so that they can't breathe **2** to smother something is to cover it thickly • *He brought in a cake smothered in icing.* **3** to smother a fire is to put it out by covering it

smoulder *VERB* (**smoulders**, **smouldering**, **smouldered**)
to smoulder is to burn slowly without a flame

smudge *NOUN* (**smudges**)
a dirty or messy mark made by rubbing something

smudge *VERB* (**smudges**, **smudging**, **smudged**)
to smudge paint or ink is to touch it while it is still wet and make it messy

smug *ADJECTIVE* (**smugger**, **smuggest**)
too pleased with yourself
▷ **smugly** *ADVERB* in a smug way
▷ **smugness** *NOUN* smugness is being smug

smuggle *VERB* (**smuggles**, **smuggling**, **smuggled**)
to smuggle something is to bring it into a country secretly and illegally

> WORD FAMILY
> A **smuggler** is someone who smuggles goods.

smut *NOUN*
smut is something rude or indecent

> WORD FAMILY
> **Smutty** jokes or stories are rude or indecent.

snack *NOUN* (**snacks**)
a quick light meal

snag *NOUN* (**snags**)
an unexpected difficulty or obstacle

snag *VERB* (**snags**, **snagging**, **snagged**)
to snag something you are wearing is to catch it on something sharp

snail *NOUN* (**snails**)
a small animal with a soft body in a hard shell

snake *NOUN* (**snakes**)
a reptile with a long narrow body and no legs

snap *VERB* (**snaps**, **snapping**, **snapped**)
1 something snaps when it breaks suddenly with a sharp noise **2** an animal snaps when it bites suddenly or quickly • *The dog snapped at me.* **3** to snap something is to say it quickly and angrily • *There's no need to snap.* **4** to snap your fingers is to make a sharp snapping sound with them **5** to snap something or someone is to take a quick photograph of them

snap *NOUN* (**snaps**)
1 a snap is the act or sound of snapping **2** a snap is also an informal photograph taken quickly **3** snap is a card game in which players shout 'Snap!' when they spot two similar cards

snappy *ADJECTIVE* (**snappier**, **snappiest**)
quick and lively

snapshot *NOUN* (**snapshots**)
an informal photograph taken quickly

snare *NOUN* (**snares**)
a trap for catching animals

snare *VERB* (**snares**, **snaring**, **snared**)
to snare an animal is to catch it in a snare

snarl[1] *VERB* (**snarls**, **snarling**, **snarled**)
an animal snarls when it growls angrily

snarl *NOUN* (**snarls**)
a snarling sound

snarl[2] *VERB*
to be snarled up is to become tangled or jammed • *The motorway was snarled up for several miles.*

snatch *VERB* (**snatches**, **snatching**, **snatched**)
to snatch something is to grab it quickly • *He snatched the bag from me.*

snatch *NOUN* (**snatches**)
1 a short piece of conversation or music **2** (*informal*) a robbery or theft

sneak *VERB* (**sneaks**, **sneaking**, **sneaked**)
1 to sneak somewhere is to move there quietly and secretly **2** (*informal*) to sneak on someone is to tell tales about them

sneak *NOUN* (**sneaks**)
(*informal*) a person who tells tales

sneaker *NOUN* (**sneakers**)
(*in America*) sneakers are trainers

sneaky *ADJECTIVE* (**sneakier**, **sneakiest**)
dishonest or deceitful

sneer *VERB* (**sneers**, **sneering**, **sneered**)
to sneer is to speak or behave in a scornful way

sneeze *VERB* (**sneezes**, **sneezing**, **sneezed**)
you sneeze when you push air through your nose suddenly and uncontrollably • *She was sneezing a lot because of her cold.*
not to be sneezed at (*informal*) valuable or important

sneeze *NOUN* (**sneezes**)
the action or sound of sneezing

sniff *VERB* (**sniffs**, **sniffing**, **sniffed**)
1 to sniff is to make a noise by drawing air in through your nose **2** to sniff something is to smell it with a sniff

sniff *NOUN* (**sniffs**)
the action or sound of sniffing or smelling something

sniffle *VERB* (**sniffles**, **sniffling**, **sniffled**)
to keep sniffing because you have a cold or are crying

snigger *VERB* (**sniggers**, **sniggering**, **sniggered**)
to snigger is to give a quiet sly laugh

snigger *NOUN* (**sniggers**)
a quiet sly laugh

snip *VERB* (**snips**, **snipping**, **snipped**)
to snip something is to cut a small piece or pieces off it

snip *NOUN* (**snips**)
an act of snipping something

sniper *NOUN* (**snipers**)
someone who shoots at people from a hiding place

snippet *NOUN* (**snippets**)
a short piece of news or information

snivel *VERB* (**snivels**, **snivelling**, **snivelled**)
to snivel is to cry or complain in a whining way

snob *NOUN* (**snobs**)
someone who despises people who have not got wealth or power or particular tastes or interests

> WORD FAMILY
> **Snobbery** is despising people who have not got wealth or power or particular tastes or interests; to be **snobbish** is to think or behave like a snob.

snooker *NOUN*
snooker is a game played with long sticks (called *cues*) and 22 balls on a cloth-covered table

snoop *VERB* (**snoops**, **snooping**, **snooped**)
to snoop is to pry or try to find out about someone else's business

> WORD FAMILY
> A **snooper** or **snoop** is someone who snoops.

snore *VERB* (**snores**, **snoring**, **snored**)
to snore is to breathe noisily while you are sleeping

snorkel *NOUN* (**snorkels**)
a tube with one end above the water, worn by an underwater swimmer to get air

snort *VERB* (**snorts**, **snorting**, **snorted**)
to snort is to make a loud noise by forcing air out through your nose

snort *NOUN* (**snorts**)
a snorting noise

snout *NOUN* (**snouts**)
an animal's snout is the front part sticking out from its head, with its nose and mouth

snow *NOUN*
snow is frozen drops of water falling from the sky as small white flakes

snow *VERB* (**snows**, **snowing**, **snowed**)
it is snowing when snow is falling

snowball *NOUN* (**snowballs**)
snow pressed into the shape of a ball for throwing

snowdrop *NOUN* (**snowdrops**)
a small white flower that blooms in early spring

snowflake *NOUN* (**snowflakes**)
a flake of snow

snowman *NOUN* (**snowmen**)
a figure of a person made of snow

snowplough *NOUN* (**snowploughs**)
a vehicle or device for clearing snow from a road or railway track

snowshoe *NOUN* (**snowshoes**)
snowshoes are broad frames with a mesh, that you can attach to your feet so that you can walk over deep snow without sinking in

snowstorm *NOUN* (**snowstorms**)
a storm with snow falling

snowy *ADJECTIVE* (**snowier**, **snowiest**)
1 with snow falling • *We're expecting snowy weather.* **2** covered with snow • *The roofs looked snowy.* **3** brightly white

snub *VERB* (**snubs**, **snubbing**, **snubbed**)
to snub someone is to treat them in a scornful or unfriendly way

snub-nosed *ADJECTIVE*
having a short turned-up nose

snuff *NOUN*
snuff is powdered tobacco that is taken into the nose by sniffing

snug *ADJECTIVE* (**snugger**, **snuggest**)
warm and cosy • *We found a snug corner by the fire.*
▷ **snugly** *ADVERB* in a snug way • *The little ones are tucked up snugly in bed.*

snuggle *VERB* (**snuggles**, **snuggling**, **snuggled**)
to snuggle is to curl up in a warm comfortable place • *She snuggled down in bed.*

so *ADVERB*
1 in this way; to such an extent • *Why are you so cross?* **2** very • *Cricket is so boring.* **3** also • *I was wrong but so were you.*
and so on and other similar things • *They took food, water, spare clothing, and so on.*
or so or about that number • *We need about fifty or so.*
so as to in order to
so far up to now
so what? (*informal*) what does that matter?

so *CONJUNCTION*
for that reason • *They threw me out, so I came here.*

soak *VERB* (**soaks**, **soaking**, **soaked**)
to soak someone or something is to make them very wet or leave them in water
to soak something up is to take in a liquid in the way that a sponge does

so-and-so *NOUN* (**so-and-so's**)(*informal*)
1 a person whose name you don't know or can't remember • *Old so-and-so told me.* **2** an unpleasant person • *He's a real so-and-so.*

soap *NOUN* (**soaps**)
1 soap is a substance you use with water for washing and cleaning things **2** (*informal*) a soap is a soap opera

> WORD FAMILY
> Something is **soapy** when it is full of soap or covered in soap.

soap opera *NOUN* (**soap operas**)
a television serial about the day-to-day life of a group of imaginary people

soar *VERB* (**soars**, **soaring**, **soared**)
1 to soar is to rise or fly high in the air **2** to soar is also to increase a lot • *Prices were soaring.*

sob *VERB* (**sobs**, **sobbing**, **sobbed**)
to sob is to cry with gasping noises

sob *NOUN* (**sobs**)
a sound of sobbing

sober *ADJECTIVE*
1 not drunk **2** calm and serious • *She had a sober expression.* **3** not bright or showy • *The room was painted in sober colours.*

> WORD FAMILY
> To be (for example) **soberly** dressed is to be wearing clothes that are plain and not brightly coloured; **sobriety** is not being drunk.

so-called *ADJECTIVE*
named in what may be the wrong way • *Even the so-called experts couldn't solve the problem.*

soccer *NOUN*
soccer is a game played by two teams which try to kick an inflated ball into their opponents' goal

sociable *ADJECTIVE* (*say* **soh**- sha- bul)
sociable people are friendly and like to be with other people
▷ **sociably** *ADVERB* in a sociable way
▷ **sociability** *NOUN* sociability is being sociable

social *ADJECTIVE* (*say* **soh**- shal)
1 to do with people meeting one another in their spare time • *Let's join a social club.* **2** living in groups, not alone • *Bees are social insects.* **3** to do with society or a community • *They were writing a social history of the area.*

> WORD FAMILY
> To meet people **socially** is to meet them in your spare time, not at work.

socialism *NOUN*
socialism is a political system in which wealth is equally shared and the main industries and resources are controlled by the government

socialist *NOUN* (**socialists**)
someone who believes in socialism

social work *NOUN*
social work is work helping people in a community who have problems

> WORD FAMILY
> A **social worker** is someone who has a job in social work.

society *NOUN* (**societies**)
1 a society is a community of people; society is people living together in a group or nation **2** a society is also a group of people organized for a particular purpose • *He's joined a dramatic society.* **3** society is also company or companionship • *We enjoy the society of our friends.*

sociology *NOUN* (*say* soh- si- **ol**- o- ji)
sociology is the study of how people behave in different societies
▷ **sociological** *ADJECTIVE* to do with sociology
▷ **sociologist** *NOUN* someone who studies sociology

a b c d e f g h i j k l m n o p q r **s** t u v w x y z

sock[1] *NOUN* (**socks**)
a soft piece of clothing that covers your foot and the lower half of your leg
to pull your socks up (*informal*) is to try to do better

sock[2] *VERB* (**socks, socking, socked**)
(*informal*) to sock someone is to hit or punch them hard • *He socked me on the jaw.*

socket *NOUN* (**sockets**)
a device or hole that something fits into, especially the place where an electric plug or bulb is put to make a connection

soda *NOUN*
1 soda is a substance made from sodium, such as baking soda **2** soda is also soda water

soda water *NOUN*
soda water is fizzy water used in drinks

sodium *NOUN* (*say* **soh**- di- um)
sodium is a soft silvery-white metal

sofa *NOUN* (**sofas**)
a long soft seat with sides and a back

soft *ADJECTIVE* (**softer, softest**)
1 not hard or firm; easily pressed or cut into a new shape **2** smooth; not rough or stiff **3** gentle; not loud • *He spoke in a soft voice.*

> **WORD FAMILY**
> To do something **softly** is to do it in a gentle way • *She closed the door softly behind her*; to speak **softly** is to speak quietly; **softness** is being soft.

soft drink *NOUN* (**soft drinks**)
a drink that does not contain alcohol

soften *VERB* (**softens, softening, softened**)
1 to soften something is to make it softer **2** to soften is to become softer

software *NOUN*
(*in computing*) software is programs and data, which are not part of the machinery (the *hardware*) of a computer

soggy *ADJECTIVE* (**soggier, soggiest**)
very wet and heavy

soil[1] *NOUN*
soil is the loose earth that plants grow in

soil[2] *VERB* (**soils, soiling, soiled**)
to soil something is to make it dirty

solar *ADJECTIVE*
to do with the sun or powered by the sun's energy

solar system *NOUN*
the solar system is the sun and the planets that revolve round it

sold
past tense and past participle of **sell**

solder *NOUN*
solder is a soft alloy that is melted to join pieces of metal together

solder *VERB* (**solders, soldering, soldered**)
to solder two pieces of metal is to join them together with solder

soldier *NOUN* (**soldiers**)
a member of an army

sole[1] *NOUN* (**soles**)
1 the bottom part of a shoe or foot **2** a flat sea fish used for food

sole[2] *ADJECTIVE*
single or only • *She was the sole survivor.*

> **WORD FAMILY**
> Someone is (for example) **solely** responsible for something when they are the only one responsible.

solemn *ADJECTIVE*
serious and dignified • *The children could hardly look into the Lion's royal, solemn eyes, for he was both good and terrible at the same time.* — C. S. Lewis, *The Lion, The Witch and the Wardrobe*

> **WORD FAMILY**
> To do something **solemnly** is to do it in a serious and dignified way; **solemnity** is being solemn. • *'In that case,' said the Dodo solemnly, rising to its feet, 'I move that the meeting adjourn.'* — Lewis Carroll, *Alice's Adventures in Wonderland*

solicitor *NOUN* (**solicitors**)
a lawyer who advises clients and prepares legal documents

solid *ADJECTIVE*
1 keeping its shape; not a liquid or gas **2** not hollow; with no space inside • *These bars are made of solid steel.* **3** firm or strongly made • *The house is built on solid foundations.* **4** strong and reliable • *They gave solid support.*

> **WORD FAMILY**
> Something is **solidly** built when it is firmly and strongly built; to rain **solidly** is to rain continuously; the **solidity** of something is how solid it is.

solid *NOUN* (**solids**)
1 a solid thing **2** a three-dimensional shape, such as a cube, sphere, or cone

solidify *VERB* (**solidifies, solidifying, solidified**)
1 to solidify is to change from a liquid into a solid **2** to solidify something is to make it solid

soliloquy *NOUN* (**soliloquies**) (*say* so- **lil**- o- kwi)
a speech expressing deep thoughts, made by an actor alone on the stage and not addressed to anyone else

solitary *ADJECTIVE*
1 alone; on your own • *He lived a solitary life.* **2** single • *This is a solitary example.*

solitude *NOUN*
solitude is being on your own

solo *NOUN* (**solos**)
something sung or performed by one person alone

soloist *NOUN* (**soloists**)
someone who plays or sings a solo

solstice *NOUN* (**solstices**)
either of the two times in the year when the sun is at its furthest point north or south of the equator. The **summer solstice** is about 21 June, and the **winter solstice** is about 22 December, in the northern hemisphere

soluble *ADJECTIVE*
1 a soluble substance is able to be dissolved **2** a soluble problem or puzzle is able to be solved

> **WORD FAMILY**
> **Solubility** is being soluble.

solution *NOUN* (**solutions**)
1 the answer to a problem or puzzle **2** a liquid with something dissolved in it

solve *VERB* (**solves**, **solving**, **solved**)
to solve a problem or puzzle is to find an answer to it

solvent *NOUN* (**solvents**)
a liquid in which other substances can be dissolved

solvent *ADJECTIVE*
to be solvent is to have enough money to pay your debts

sombre *ADJECTIVE*
gloomy or dark • *From their feet the land dropped away into a shallow vale, then rose again to sombre moors inland.* — Rosemary Sutcliff, *Beowulf: Dragonslayer*

some *DETERMINER*
1 a few or a little • *I'd like some biscuits and some sugar.* **2** a certain amount of • *Would you like some cake?* **3** an unknown person or thing • *Some fool left the window open.*

some *PRONOUN*
a certain or unknown number or amount • *Some of them were late.*

somebody *PRONOUN*
someone; some person

somehow *ADVERB*
in some way • *We must finish the work somehow.*

someone *PRONOUN*
some person

somersault *NOUN* (**somersaults**) (*say* sum- er- solt)
a movement in which you turn head over heels and land on your feet

something *PRONOUN*
a certain or unknown thing

sometime *ADVERB*
at some time • *I saw her sometime last year.*

sometimes *ADVERB*
at some times but not always • *We sometimes walk to school.*

somewhat *ADVERB*
to some extent; rather • *He was somewhat annoyed.*

somewhere *ADVERB*
in or to some place

son *NOUN* (**sons**)
a boy or man who is someone's child

sonar *NOUN*
sonar is a system using the echo from sound waves to locate objects underwater

song *NOUN* (**songs**)
1 a song is a tune with words for singing **2** a bird's song is the musical sounds it makes **3** song is singing • *He burst into song.*
to make a song and dance (*informal*) is to make a great fuss

songbird *NOUN* (**songbirds**)
a bird that sings sweetly

sonic *ADJECTIVE*
to do with sound or sound waves

sonnet *NOUN* (**sonnets**)
a kind of poem with 14 lines

soon *ADVERB* (**sooner**, **soonest**)
1 in a short time from now **2** not long after something • *She became ill, but was soon better.* **3** early or quickly • *You spoke too soon.*
as soon as willingly • *I'd just as soon stay at home.*
sooner or later at some time in the future

soot *NOUN*
soot is the black powder left by smoke in a chimney or on a building

> **WORD FAMILY**
> A **sooty** person or thing is covered in soot.

soothe *VERB* (**soothes**, **soothing**, **soothed**)
1 to soothe someone is to make them calm **2** to soothe a pain or ache is to ease it

sophisticated *ADJECTIVE* (*say* sof- **iss**- ti- kay- tid)
1 someone is sophisticated when they are used to a fashionable or cultured life and have experienced a lot of different things **2** something is sophisticated when it is complicated and highly developed • *It is a sophisticated machine.*

> **WORD FAMILY**
> **Sophistication** is being sophisticated.

sopping *ADJECTIVE*
very wet; soaked

soppy *ADJECTIVE* (**soppier**, **soppiest**)
(*informal*) sentimental or silly

soprano *NOUN* (**sopranos**) (*say* so- **prah**- noh)
a woman or young boy with a high singing voice

sorcerer *NOUN* (**sorcerers**)
someone who can do magic

> **WORD FAMILY**
> **Sorcery** is magic or witchcraft.

sorceress *NOUN* (**sorceresses**)
a woman who can do magic

sore *ADJECTIVE* (**sorer**, **sorest**)
1 painful or smarting •*I've got a sore throat.*
2 (*informal*) annoyed or upset
▹ **soreness** *NOUN* soreness is being sore

sore *NOUN* (**sores**)
a red and painful place on your skin

sorely *ADVERB*
seriously; very •*I was sorely tempted to run away.*

MEANING
Notice that the meaning of **sorely** does not have much to do with **sore**. Another adverb like this is **barely**. Can you find any others?

sorrow *NOUN* (**sorrows**)
sorrow is sadness or regret
▹ **sorrowful** *ADJECTIVE* feeling sorrow
▹ **sorrowfully** *ADVERB* in a sorrowful way

sorry *ADJECTIVE* (**sorrier**, **sorriest**)
1 you are sorry that you did something when you regret doing it or want to apologize •*I'm sorry I forgot to send you a birthday card.* **2** you feel sorry for someone when you feel pity for them or are sad that something bad has happened to them •*I'm sorry you've been ill.*

sort *NOUN* (**sorts**)
1 a group of things or people that are similar; a kind •*What sort of fruit do you like?* **2** (*in computing*) putting data in a particular order •*Can you help me do an alphabetical sort of these names?*
sort of (*informal*) rather; to some extent •*I sort of wanted to go*

sort *VERB* (**sorts**, **sorting**, **sorted**)
to sort things is to arrange them in groups or kinds
to sort something out is to organize it or arrange it
to sort someone out (*informal*) is to deal with them or punish them

SOS *NOUN*
an SOS is an urgent appeal for help from someone whose life is in danger

sought
past tense and past participle of **seek**

soul *NOUN* (**souls**)
a person's invisible spirit that some people believe goes on living after the body has died

sound[1] *NOUN* (**sounds**)
1 sound is vibrations in the air that you can detect with your ear **2** a sound is something that you can hear

sound *VERB* (**sounds**, **sounding**, **sounded**)
1 to sound is to make a sound •*The trumpets sounded.* **2** to sound something is to make a sound with it •*Don't forget to sound your horn.* **3** to sound a certain way is to give that impression when heard •*You sound in a good mood.* •*The car sounds as if it needs a service.*

sound[2] *VERB* (**sounds**, **sounding**, **sounded**)
to sound a river or sea is to test the depth of it
to sound someone out is to try to find out what they think or feel about something

sound[3] *ADJECTIVE* (**sounder**, **soundest**)
1 not damaged; in good condition **2** healthy
3 reasonable or correct •*His ideas are sound.*
4 reliable or secure •*They made a sound investment.*
5 thorough or deep •*She has a sound knowledge of the subject.* •*I am a sound sleeper.*

WORD FAMILY
You sleep **soundly** when you sleep deeply; to be **soundly** beaten is to be completely or thoroughly beaten; **soundness** is being reliable or sensible.

sound[4] *NOUN* (**sounds**)
a narrow passage of water

sound barrier *NOUN*
the sound barrier is the resistance of the air to objects moving at speeds near the speed of sound

sound effects *PLURAL NOUN*
special sounds produced to make a play or film more realistic

soundtrack *NOUN* (**soundtracks**)
the sound or music that goes with a film or television programme

soup *NOUN* (**soups**)
a liquid food made from vegetables or meat

sour *ADJECTIVE* (**sourer**, **sourest**)
1 having a sharp taste like vinegar or lemons
2 unpleasant or bad-tempered
▹ **sourly** *ADVERB* in a sour way
▹ **sourness** *NOUN* sourness is being sour

source *NOUN* (**sources**)
1 the place where something comes from **2** the place where a river starts

south *NOUN*
1 the direction to the right of a person facing east
2 the part of a country or city that is in this direction

south *ADJECTIVE & ADVERB*
1 towards the south or in the south **2** coming from the south •*A south wind was blowing.*

south-east *NOUN, ADJECTIVE, & ADVERB*
midway between south and east

southerly *ADJECTIVE* (*say* **suth**- er- lee)
a southerly wind is one that blows from the south

southern *ADJECTIVE* (*say* **suth**- ern)
from or to do with the south

southerner *NOUN* (**southerners**) (*say* **suth**- er- ner)
someone who lives in the south of a country

southward or **southwards** *ADJECTIVE & ADVERB*
towards the south

south-west *NOUN, ADJECTIVE, & ADVERB*
midway between south and west

souvenir *NOUN* (**souvenirs**) (*say* soo- ven- **eer**)
something that you buy or keep to remind you of a person, place, or event

sovereign *NOUN* (**sovereigns**) (*say* **sov**- rin)
1 a king or a queen **2** an old British gold coin that was worth £1

sow [1] *VERB* (**sows, sowing, sowed, sown** or **sowed**) (*rhymes with* **go**)
to sow seeds is to put them into the ground so that they will grow into plants

> WORD FAMILY
> A **sower** is someone who sows seeds.

> SPELLING
> Take care not to confuse this word with **sew**, which means to work with a needle and thread.

sow [2] *NOUN* (**sows**) (*rhymes with* **cow**)
a female pig

soya bean *NOUN* (**soya beans**)
a kind of bean from which edible oil and flour are made

space *NOUN* (**spaces**)
1 space is the whole area outside the earth, where the stars and planets are **2** space is also an area or volume • *There isn't enough space for a car.* **3** a space is an empty area or gap • *There is a space at the back of the cupboard.* • *Leave a space for your name and address.* **4** a space is also a period of time • *They moved house twice in the space of a year.*

space *VERB* (**spaces, spacing, spaced**)
to space things, or space things out, is to arrange them with gaps or periods of time between them

spacecraft *NOUN* (**spacecraft**)
a vehicle for travelling in outer space

spaceman *NOUN* (**spacemen**)
a man who travels in a spacecraft

> USING THIS WORD
> This word usually means a person in a story. In real life, **astronaut** is the normal word.

spaceship *NOUN* (**spaceships**)
a spacecraft

space shuttle *NOUN* (**space shuttles**)
a spacecraft that can travel into space and return to earth

space station *NOUN* (**space stations**)
a satellite which orbits the earth and is used as a base by scientists and astronauts

spacewoman *NOUN* (**spacewomen**)
a woman who travels in a spacecraft

> USING THIS WORD
> This word usually means a person in a story. In real life, **astronaut** is the normal word.

spacious *ADJECTIVE*
large and roomy • *a spacious kitchen*
▷ **spaciously** *ADVERB* in a spacious way
▷ **spaciousness** *NOUN* spaciousness is being spacious

spade *NOUN* (**spades**)
1 a tool with a long handle and a wide blade for digging **2** a playing card with black shapes like upside-down hearts on it

spaghetti *NOUN* (*say* spa- **get**- i)
spaghetti is pasta made in long thin strips

span *NOUN* (**spans**)
1 the length from one end of something to the other **2** the distance between the tips of your thumb and little finger when your hand is spread out **3** a part of a bridge between two supports **4** a period of time

span *VERB* (**spans, spanning, spanned**)
to span something is to reach from one side or end of it to the other • *A wooden bridge spanned the river.*

spaniel *NOUN* (**spaniels**)
a breed of dog with long ears and silky fur

spank *VERB* (**spanks, spanking, spanked**)
to spank someone is to smack them several times on the bottom as a punishment

spanner *NOUN* (**spanners**)
a tool for tightening or loosening a nut

spar [1] *NOUN* (**spars**)
a strong pole used for a mast or boom on a ship

spar [2] *VERB* (**spars, sparring, sparred**)
to spar is to practise boxing • *He was my sparring partner.*

spare *VERB* (**spares, sparing, spared**)
1 to spare something is to afford it or be able to give it to someone • *Can you spare a moment?* **2** to spare someone is to avoid harming them or making them suffer something unpleasant **3** to spare something is to use it or treat it economically • *No expense will be spared.*

spare *ADJECTIVE*
1 not used but kept ready in case it is needed; extra • *Where's the spare wheel?* • *What do you do in your spare time?* **2** thin or lean
to go spare (*slang*) is to become angry

spare *NOUN* (**spares**)
a spare thing or part • *The local garage sells spares.*

sparing *ADJECTIVE*
careful or economical, especially with money

spark *NOUN* (**sparks**)
1 a tiny flash of electricity **2** a tiny glowing piece of something hot

spark *VERB* (**sparks, sparking, sparked**)
to spark is to give off sparks

sparking plug or **spark plug** *NOUN* (**sparking plugs** or **spark plugs**)
a device that makes a spark to explode the fuel in an engine

a b c d e f g h i j k l m n o p q r s t u v w x y z

sparkle *VERB* (**sparkles**, **sparkling**, **sparkled**)
to sparkle is to shine with a lot of tiny flashes of bright light •*The sea sparkled in the sunlight.*

sparkler *NOUN* (**sparklers**)
a firework that sparkles

sparrow *NOUN* (**sparrows**)
a small brown bird

sparse *ADJECTIVE* (**sparser**, **sparsest**)
small in number or amount; thinly scattered •*Vegetation on the island is sparse.*

> WORD FAMILY
> A **sparsely** populated area is one with only a few people; **sparseness** is being sparse.

spat
past tense and past participle of **spit** *VERB*

spatter *VERB* (**spatters**, **spattering**, **spattered**)
to spatter something is to splash it or scatter it in small drops or pieces •*The lorry spattered mud all over the pavement.*

spawn *NOUN*
spawn is the eggs of frogs, fish, and other water animals

spawn *VERB* (**spawns**, **spawning**, **spawned**)
frogs, fish, and other water animals spawn when they lay their eggs

speak *VERB* (**speaks**, **speaking**, **spoke**, **spoken**)
1 to speak is to say something •*I spoke to them this morning.* **2** to speak a language is to be able to talk in it •*Do you speak German?*
to speak up is to say something more clearly or loudly

speaker *NOUN* (**speakers**)
1 a person who is speaking or making a speech **2** the part of (for example) a radio, CD player, or computer that the sound comes out of
the Speaker the person who is in charge of debates in the House of Commons or similar parliaments

spear *NOUN* (**spears**)
a long pole with a sharp point, used as a weapon

spear *VERB* (**spears**, **spearing**, **speared**)
to spear something is to pierce it with a spear or something pointed

special *ADJECTIVE*
1 different from other people or things; unusual **2** meant for a particular person or purpose •*You'll need special training.*

specialist *NOUN* (**specialists**)
an expert in a particular subject

speciality *NOUN* (**specialities**)
1 something that someone specializes in •*Dr Dandiffer is an ethnobotanist. His speciality is the medicinal use of tropical plants.* — Michael Hoeye, *Time Stops for No Mouse* **2** a special product, especially a food

specialize *VERB* (**specializes**, **specializing**, **specialized**)
to specialize is to give particular attention to one subject or thing •*She is specializing in biology.*
▷ **specialization** *NOUN* specialization is specializing in something

specially *ADVERB*
for a special purpose •*I came specially to see you.*

species *NOUN* (**species**) (*say* **spee**- shiz)
a group of animals or plants that have similar features and can breed with each other

specific *ADJECTIVE*
1 definite or precise **2** to do with a particular thing •*The money was given for a specific purpose.*

specifically *ADVERB*
1 in a special way or for a special purpose •*The car is designed specifically for the disabled.* **2** clearly and precisely •*I specifically said we had to go.*

specification *NOUN* (**specifications**)
a detailed list or description of something

specific gravity *NOUN*
the specific gravity of something is its mass compared with the mass of the same volume of water or air

specify *VERB* (**specifies**, **specifying**, **specified**)
to specify a person or thing is to name or mention them precisely •*The recipe specified brown sugar, not white.*

specimen *NOUN* (**specimens**)
1 a small amount or sample of something **2** an example of one kind of plant, animal, or thing •*We saw a fine specimen of an oak.*

speck *NOUN* (**specks**)
1 a tiny piece of something **2** a tiny mark or spot

speckled *ADJECTIVE*
covered with small spots

spectacle *NOUN* (**spectacles**)
1 an exciting sight or display **2** a ridiculous sight

spectacles *PLURAL NOUN*
a pair of lenses in a frame, worn over your eyes to help improve your eyesight

spectacular *ADJECTIVE*
exciting to see •*The exhibition was quite spectacular.* *They went to the Palace of Engineering first, as this was what Grandad wanted to see.* — Theresa Breslin, *Kezzie*

spectator *NOUN* (**spectators**)
a person who watches a game or show

spectre *NOUN* (**spectres**) (*say* **spek**- ter)
a ghost •*'Ghost of the Future,' he exclaimed, 'I fear you more than any spectre I have seen.'* — Charles Dickens, *A Christmas Carol*

spectrum *NOUN* (**spectra**)
1 the band of colours like those in a rainbow **2** a range of things or ideas •*The library caters for a broad spectrum of interests.*

speech *NOUN* (**speeches**)
1 speech is the ability to speak or a person's way of speaking **2** a speech is a talk given to a group of people

speechless *ADJECTIVE*
unable to speak, especially because you are surprised or angry • *For a second, Lloyd was speechless. Then he whirled round. 'It's the Headmaster!' he hissed. 'He's almost here!'*
— Gillian Cross, *The Revenge of the Demon Headmaster*

speech marks *PLURAL NOUN*
inverted commas, used to show that someone is speaking

> SPEECH MARKS
> Speech marks are also called quotation marks or inverted commas. You use them in writing to show that someone is speaking. You put speech marks at the beginning and the end of what someone says, to show the exact words they use. *'I'm going to draw a monster,' said Ruth. David asked, 'What's your name?' 'Help!' he shouted. 'I'm stuck in this tree!'* Speech marks can be either single (' ') or double (" "). It is more usual to use double speech marks in handwriting and single speech marks in print.

speed *NOUN* (**speeds**)
1 the speed of something is the rate at which it moves or happens **2** speed is being quick or fast
at speed fast; quickly

speed *VERB* (**speeds**, **speeding**, **sped** or **speeded**)
to speed is to go very fast or too fast • *Drivers can be fined for speeding.*
to speed up is to become quicker
to speed something up is to make it go or happen faster

speedboat *NOUN* (**speedboats**)
a fast motor boat

speedometer *NOUN* (**speedometers**) (*say* spee- **dom**- it- er)
a device in a vehicle that shows its speed

speedway *NOUN* (**speedways**)
a track for motorcycle racing

speedy *ADJECTIVE* (**speedier**, **speediest**)
quick or fast • *We need a speedy reply.*
▷ **speedily** *ADVERB* fast or quickly

spell[1] *VERB* (**spells**, **spelling**, **spelt** or **spelled**)
to spell a word is to give its letters in the right order

spell[2] *NOUN* (**spells**)
1 a period of time • *We're having a cold spell.* **2** a period of activity • *I must do a spell of work now.*

spell[3] *NOUN* (**spells**)
a set of words that is supposed to have magic power

spellchecker or **spellcheck** *NOUN* (**spellcheckers** or **spellchecks**)
a computer program you use to check your writing to see if your spelling is correct

spelling *NOUN* (**spellings**)
1 the way in which letters are put together to form words **2** how well someone can spell • *Her spelling is poor.*

spend *VERB* (**spends**, **spending**, **spent**)
1 to spend money is to use it to pay for things **2** to spend time is to pass it doing something • *He spent the weekend painting his bedroom.* **3** to spend energy or effort is to use it up • *She spends all her spare energy on gardening.*

sperm *NOUN* (**sperms** or **sperm**)
the male sex cell that joins with an ovum to produce offspring

sphere *NOUN* (**spheres**)
1 a perfectly round solid shape; a globe or ball **2** an area of activity or interest

> WORD FAMILY
> A **spherical** object has the shape of a sphere.

spice *NOUN* (**spices**)
a strong-tasting substance used to flavour food, often made from the dried parts of plants

> WORD FAMILY
> **Spicy** food tastes strongly of spices.

spider *NOUN* (**spiders**)
a small animal with eight legs that spins webs to catch insects on which it feeds

spied
past tense and past participle of **spy** *VERB*

spike *NOUN* (**spikes**)
a pointed piece of metal; a sharp point

> WORD FAMILY
> Something is **spiky** when it is full of spikes or sharp points • *She has short spiky hair.*

spill *VERB* (**spills**, **spilling**, **spilt** or **spilled**)
1 to spill something is to let it fall out of a container by accident • *Careful or you'll spill your juice.* **2** to spill is to fall out of a container • *The coins came spilling out.*

spill *NOUN* (**spills**)
1 when something gets spilt • *There's been an oil spill at sea.*

spin *VERB* (**spins**, **spinning**, **spun**)
1 to spin is to turn round and round quickly **2** to spin something is to make it spin **3** to spin is also to make pieces of wool or cotton into thread by twisting them **4** to spin a web or cocoon is to make it out of threads • *The spider spun a web.*

spin *NOUN* (**spins**)
1 a spinning movement **2** a short outing in a car

spinach *NOUN*
spinach is a vegetable with dark green leaves

spindle *NOUN* (**spindles**)
1 a thin rod on which you wind thread **2** a pin or bar that turns round, or on which something turns round

a b c d e f g h i j k l m n o p q r **s** t u v w x y z

spin-drier *NOUN* (**spin-driers**)
a machine for drying clothes by spinning them round in a drum at high speed

spine *NOUN* (**spines**)
1 the line of bones down the middle of your back **2** a sharp point on an animal or plant • *This cactus has sharp spines.* **3** the back part of a book where the pages are joined together

> **WORD FAMILY**
> A **spinal** injury is one affecting a person's pine; **spiny** animals or plants are covered in spines.

spine-chilling *ADJECTIVE*
frightening and exciting • *We heard a spine-chilling ghost story.*

spinning wheel *NOUN* (**spinning wheels**)
a machine for spinning thread out of wool or cotton

spin-off *NOUN* (**spin-offs**)
something extra produced while you are making something else

spinster *NOUN* (**spinsters**)
a woman who has not married

spiral *ADJECTIVE*
going round and round a central point, getting further from it with each turn

spiral *NOUN* (**spirals**)
something with a spiral shape

spire *NOUN* (**spires**)
a tall pointed part on top of a church tower

spirit *NOUN* (**spirits**)
1 a person's spirit is their soul or their deepest thoughts and feelings **2** a spirit is a ghost or other supernatural being **3** spirit is courage or liveliness **4** a person's spirits are their mood or the way they feel • *She was in good spirits after the exam.* **5** a spirit is also a strong alcoholic drink

spiritual *ADJECTIVE*
1 to do with the human soul and with a person's deepest thoughts and feelings **2** to do with religious beliefs
▷ **spiritually** *ADVERB* in a spiritual way

spiritual *NOUN* (**spirituals**)
a religious song originally sung by Black Americans

spiritualism *NOUN*
spiritualism is the belief that the spirits of dead people communicate with living people

> **WORD FAMILY**
> A **spiritualist** is someone who practises spiritualism.

spit[1] *VERB* (**spits, spitting, spat**)
1 to spit is to send drops of liquid forcibly out of your mouth • *He spat into the basin.* **2** (*informal*) to spit is to rain lightly • *It's only spitting.*

spit *NOUN*
saliva that has been spat out

spit[2] *NOUN* (**spits**)
1 a long thin metal spike put through meat to hold it while it is roasted **2** a narrow strip of land sticking out into the sea

spite *NOUN*
spite is a desire to hurt or annoy someone
in spite of something although something has happened or is happening • *They went out in spite of the rain.*

> **WORD FAMILY**
> Someone is being **spiteful** or behaving **spitefully** when they behave unkindly in order to hurt or annoy someone.

spittle *NOUN*
saliva, especially when it is spat out

splash *VERB* (**splashes, splashing, splashed**)
1 to splash liquid is to make it fly about, as you do when you jump into water **2** to splash is to fly about in drops • *The water splashed all over me.* **3** to splash someone or something is to make them wet by sending drops of liquid towards them • *The bus splashed us as it went past.*

splash *NOUN* (**splashes**)
the action or sound of splashing
to make a splash is to make a big display or effect

splashdown *NOUN* (**splashdowns**)
the landing of a spacecraft in the sea

splendid *ADJECTIVE*
magnificent; very fine
▷ **splendidly** *ADVERB* in a splendid way

splendour *NOUN*
splendour is a brilliant display or appearance • *The children stood for some minutes, held by the splendour of the view.* — Alan Garner, *The Weirdstone of Brisingamen*

splint *NOUN* (**splints**)
a straight piece of wood or metal that is tied to a broken arm or leg to hold it firm

splinter *NOUN* (**splinters**)
a small sharp piece of wood or glass broken off a larger piece

splinter *VERB* (**splinters, splintering, splintered**)
to splinter is to break into splinters

split *VERB* (**splits, splitting, split**)
1 to split is to break into parts **2** to split something is to divide it into parts **3** (*slang*) to split is also to reveal a secret
to split up 1 is to divide into parts **2** is to separate after being together for some time

split *NOUN* (**splits**)
a crack or tear in something, where it has split
the splits a movement in gymnastics with your legs stretched widely in opposite directions

splutter *VERB* (**splutters**, **spluttering**, **spluttered**)
1 to splutter is to make a quick series of spitting or coughing sounds • *The smoke from the bonfire made him splutter.* **2** to splutter is also to speak quickly and unclearly

spoil *VERB* (**spoils**, **spoiling**, **spoilt** or **spoiled**)
1 to spoil something is to damage it and so make it less good or useful • *The rain spoilt our holiday.* **2** to spoil someone is to make them selfish by always letting them have what they want

spoils *PLURAL NOUN*
booty taken in war

spoilsport *NOUN* (**spoilsports**)
someone who spoils other people's fun

spoke[1] *NOUN* (**spokes**)
each of the rods or bars that go from the centre of a wheel to the rim

spoke[2]
past tense of **speak**

spoken
past participle of **speak**

spokesperson *NOUN* (**spokespersons**)
someone who speaks on behalf of a group of people

OTHER WORDS
A male spokesperson is also called a **spokesman** and a female spokesperson is also called a **spokeswoman**.

sponge *NOUN* (**sponges**)
1 a lump of soft material containing lots of tiny holes, used for washing **2** a sea creature from which this kind of material is made **3** a soft lightweight cake or pudding

sponge *VERB* (**sponges**, **sponging**, **sponged**)
1 to sponge something is to wash it with a sponge **2** (*informal*) to sponge is to get money from people without doing anything for them • *He was always sponging off his relatives.*

WORD FAMILY
A **sponger** is someone who gets money from people without doing anything for them.

spongy *ADJECTIVE* (**spongier**, **spongiest**)
soft and absorbent like sponge

sponsor *VERB* (**sponsors**, **sponsoring**, **sponsored**)
1 to sponsor someone is to promise to give them money if they do something difficult and give the money to charity **2** to sponsor something or someone is to provide money to support them

sponsor *NOUN* (**sponsors**)
someone who provides money to support a person or thing, or who supports someone who sets out to do something for charity

WORD FAMILY
Sponsorship is the money someone provides to support a person or thing.

spontaneous *ADJECTIVE* (*say* spon- **tay**- ni- us)
happening or done without being planned; not forced or suggested by someone else • *The assembled company—including young Eddie Dickens—burst into spontaneous applause.* — Philip Ardagh, *Awful End*

WORD FAMILY
You do something **spontaneously** when you do it without planning to; **spontaneity** is being spontaneous.

spooky *ADJECTIVE* (**spookier**, **spookiest**)
(*informal*) frighteningly strange; haunted by ghosts

spool *NOUN* (**spools**)
a rod or reel for winding on something such as thread or film or tape

spoon *NOUN* (**spoons**)
a piece of metal or wood or plastic consisting of a small bowl with a handle, used for lifting food to your mouth or for stirring or measuring

spoon *VERB* (**spoons**, **spooning**, **spooned**)
to spoon something is to lift it or take it with a spoon

spoonful *NOUN* (**spoonfuls**)
as much as a spoon will hold

sport *NOUN* (**sports**)
1 a sport is a game that exercises your body, especially a game you play out of doors • *What sports do you play?* **2** sport is games of this sort • *Are you keen on sport?* **3** (*informal*) a sport is someone who plays or behaves fairly and unselfishly • *Come on, be a sport.*

sporting *ADJECTIVE*
1 connected with sport; interested in sport
2 behaving fairly and unselfishly
a sporting chance a reasonable chance

sports car *NOUN* (**sports cars**)
an open low-built fast car

sports jacket *NOUN* (**sports jackets**)
a man's jacket for informal wear, not part of a suit

sportsman or **sportswoman** *NOUN* (**sportsmen** or **sportswomen**)
a man or woman who takes part in sport

sportsmanship *NOUN*
sportsmanship is behaving fairly and generously in sport and in other ways

spot *NOUN* (**spots**)
1 a small round mark **2** a pimple on your skin **3** a small amount of something • *We've had a spot of bother.* **4** a place • *This is a nice spot.*
on the spot immediately; there and then • *We can repair your bike on the spot.*

spot *VERB* (**spots, spotting, spotted**)
1 to spot someone or something is to notice them or see them • *I suddenly spotted my friend Alex in the crowd.* **2** to be spotted is to be marked with spots

spotless *ADJECTIVE*
perfectly clean

> **WORD FAMILY**
> To be **spotlessly** clean is to be perfectly clean.

spotlight *NOUN* (**spotlights**)
a strong light with a beam that shines on a small area

spotter *NOUN* (**spotters**)
someone who goes to watch or study things that interest them for a hobby • *They are keen trainspotters.*

spotty *ADJECTIVE* (**spottier, spottiest**)
marked with spots

spout *NOUN* (**spouts**)
1 a pipe or opening from which liquid can pour **2** a jet of liquid

spout *VERB* (**spouts, spouting, spouted**)
1 to spout is to come out in a jet of liquid
2 (*informal*) to spout is also to speak for a long time

sprain *VERB* (**sprains, spraining, sprained**)
you sprain your ankle or wrist when you injure it by twisting it

sprain *NOUN* (**sprains**)
an injury by spraining

sprang
past tense of **spring** *VERB*

sprawl *VERB* (**sprawls, sprawling, sprawled**)
1 you sprawl when you sit or lie with your arms and legs spread out **2** to be sprawled is to be spread out loosely or untidily • *There were newspapers sprawled all over the floor.*

spray[1] *VERB* (**sprays, spraying, sprayed**)
to spray liquid is to scatter it in tiny drops over something; to spray something is to cover it with liquid in this way

spray *NOUN* (**sprays**)
1 tiny drops of liquid sprayed on something **2** a device for spraying liquid

spray *NOUN* (**sprays**)
a small bunch of flowers

spread *VERB* (**spreads, spreading, spread**)
1 to spread something is to lay or stretch it out to its full size • *The bird spread its wings and flew away.*
2 to spread something over a surface is to make it cover the surface • *He spread a thick layer of jam on his toast.* **3** to spread news or information is to make it widely known **4** news or information spreads when it becomes widely known • *The story spread quickly round the village.*

spread *NOUN* (**spreads**)
1 something you can spread on bread **2** the breadth or extent of something **3** (*informal*) a large meal

spreadsheet *NOUN* (**spreadsheets**)
(*in computing*) a computer program for arranging figures and other information in a table of rows and columns, and doing calculations

sprightly *ADJECTIVE* (**sprightlier, sprightliest**)
lively and energetic

spring *NOUN* (**springs**)
1 spring is the season of the year when most plants start to grow, between winter and summer **2** a spring is a coil of wire that goes back to its original shape when you bend it or squeeze it and let it go **3** a spring is also a sudden upward movement **4** a spring is also a place where water rises out of the ground and becomes a stream

spring *VERB* (**springs, springing, sprang, sprung**)
1 to spring is to move quickly or suddenly • *He sprang to his feet.* **2** to spring, or spring up, is to develop or come from something • *This squabble has sprung from a misunderstanding.* **3** to spring something on someone is to surprise them with it

springboard *NOUN* (**springboards**)
a springy board from which people jump or dive

spring-clean *VERB* (**spring-cleans, spring-cleaning, spring-cleaned**)
to spring-clean a house is to clean it thoroughly, usually in spring

springtime *NOUN*
springtime is the season of spring

springy *ADJECTIVE* (**springier, springiest**)
able to spring back to its original position when you bend it or squeeze it and let it go • *'I'd like to lie down on this springy heather and watch the stars gradually come sparkling into the sky,' said Anne.* — Enid Blyton, *Five On a Secret Trail*

sprinkle *VERB* (**sprinkles, sprinkling, sprinkled**)
to sprinkle liquid or powder is to make tiny drops or pieces of it fall on something

> **WORD FAMILY**
> A **sprinkler** is a device for sprinkling liquid.

sprint *VERB* (**sprints, sprinting, sprinted**)
to sprint is to run very fast for a short distance

> **WORD FAMILY**
> A **sprinter** is someone who sprints.

sprint *NOUN* (**sprints**)
a short fast race

sprout *VERB* (**sprouts**, **sprouting**, **sprouted**)
1 a plant sprouts when it starts to produce leaves or shoots **2** to grow or start appearing • *When Artemis smiled, as he did now, one almost expected vampire fangs to sprout from his gums.* — Eoin Colfer, *Artemis Fowl*

sprout *NOUN* (**sprouts**)
a Brussels sprout

spruce[1] *NOUN* (**spruces**)
a kind of fir tree

spruce[2] *ADJECTIVE* (**sprucer**, **sprucest**)
neat and smart • *The cats looked very happy and satisfied. Their coats were glossy, their eyes bright and intelligent, their whiskers spruce and clean.* — Ursula Moray Williams, *Gobbolino the Witch's Cat*

sprung
past participle of **spring** *VERB*

spud *NOUN* (**spuds**)
(*informal*) a potato

spun
past tense and past participle of **spin** *VERB*

spur *NOUN* (**spurs**)
1 a sharp device that a rider wears on the heel of their boot to urge a horse to go faster **2** a ridge that sticks out from a mountain
on the spur of the moment on an impulse; without planning

spur *VERB* (**spurs**, **spurring**, **spurred**)
to spur someone, or to spur someone on, is to encourage them

spurt *VERB* (**spurts**, **spurting**, **spurted**)
1 a liquid spurts when it gushes out or up • *Blood was spurting from the cut.*

spurt *NOUN* (**spurts**)
1 a jet of liquid **2** a sudden increase in speed • *He put on a spurt and caught us up.*

spy *NOUN* (**spies**)
someone who works secretly to find out things about another country or person

spy *VERB* (**spies**, **spying**, **spied**)
1 to spy is to be a spy or to watch secretly • *He was spying on us.* **2** to spy someone or something is to see them or notice them • *We spied a house in the distance.*

squabble *VERB* (**squabbles**, **squabbling**, **squabbled**)
people squabble when they quarrel about something unimportant

squabble *NOUN* (**squabbles**)
a minor quarrel or argument

squad *NOUN* (**squads**)
a small group of people working or being trained together

squadron *NOUN* (**squadrons**)
part of an army, navy, or air force

squalid *ADJECTIVE*
dirty and unpleasant • *He lived in a squalid little flat.*
▷ **squalidly** *ADVERB* in a squalid way
▷ **squalor** *NOUN* squalor is being squalid • *They lived in squalor.*

squall *NOUN* (**squalls**)
1 a sudden storm or strong wind **2** a baby's loud cry

> WORD FAMILY
> **Squally** weather is windy and stormy.

squander *VERB* (**squanders**, **squandering**, **squandered**)
to squander money or time is to waste it

square *NOUN* (**squares**)
1 a shape with four equal sides and four right angles **2** in a town, an area surrounded by buildings **3** the result of multiplying a number by itself • *9 is the square of 3.*

square *ADJECTIVE*
1 shaped like a square **2** forming a right angle or having right angles **3** used for units of measurement that give an area, such as a square metre and a square foot. For example, a square metre is the size of a square with each side one metre long **4** equal or even • *The teams are all square with six points each.* • *If you pay for lunch, we'll be square.*
▷ **squareness** *NOUN* squareness is being square

square *VERB* (**squares**, **squaring**, **squared**)
1 to square something is to make it have square edges and corners **2** to square a number is to multiply it by itself • *3 squared is 9.* **3** to square with something is to match it or agree with it • *His story doesn't square with yours.*

square deal *NOUN* (**square deals**)
a deal or agreement that is fair and honest

squarely *ADVERB*
directly or exactly • *The ball hit him squarely in the mouth.*

square meal *NOUN* (**square meals**)
a good satisfying meal

square root *NOUN* (**square roots**)
the number that gives a particular number if it is multiplied by itself • *3 is the square root of 9.*

squash *VERB* (**squashes**, **squashing**, **squashed**)
1 to squash something is to squeeze it so that it loses its shape **2** to squash a person or thing into something is to force them into it when there is not much space • *We squashed ourselves into the minibus.*

squash *NOUN* (**squashes**)
1 a squash is when people or things are pressed together because there is not enough space • *There was a tremendous squash outside the football ground.* **2** squash is a fruit-flavoured drink **3** squash is also a game played with rackets and a small ball in a special indoor court

squat *VERB* (**squats**, **squatting**, **squatted**)
1 to squat is to sit back on your heels **2** to squat in an unoccupied house is to live there without permission

WORD FAMILY
A **squatter** is someone who squats in a house.

squat *ADJECTIVE* (**squatter**, **squattest**)
short and fat

squaw *NOUN* (**squaws**)
a Native American woman or wife

squawk *VERB* (**squawks**, **squawking**, **squawked**)
to squawk is to make a loud harsh cry

squawk *NOUN* (**squawks**)
a loud harsh cry

squeak *VERB* (**squeaks**, **squeaking**, **squeaked**)
to make a short high-pitched sound or cry

squeak *NOUN* (**squeaks**)
a short high-pitched sound or cry

WORD FAMILY
Something is **squeaky** when it makes squeaks. • *a squeaky floorboard*

squeal *VERB* (**squeals**, **squealing**, **squealed**)
to squeal is to make a long shrill sound

squeal *NOUN* (**squeals**)
a long shrill sound

squeeze *VERB* (**squeezes**, **squeezing**, **squeezed**)
1 to squeeze something is to press it from opposite sides, especially so that you get liquid out of it **2** to squeeze somewhere is to force a way into or through a place or gap • *We squeezed into the car.*

WORD FAMILY
A **squeezer** is a device for squeezing fruit.

squeeze *NOUN* (**squeezes**)
1 the action of squeezing **2** a tight fit • *We all got on the bus but it was a bit of a squeeze.* **3** a time when money is difficult to get or borrow

squelch *VERB* (**squelches**, **squelching**, **squelched**)
to squelch is to make a sound like someone treading in thick mud

squelch *NOUN* (**squelches**)
a squelching sound

squid *NOUN* (**squid** or **squids**)
a sea animal with eight short arms and two long ones

squiggle *NOUN* (**squiggles**)
a short curly or wavy line

squint *VERB* (**squints**, **squinting**, **squinted**)
1 to squint at something is to peer at it or look at it with half-shut eyes **2** to squint is to have eyes that look in different directions

squint *NOUN* (**squints**)
a fault in someone's eyesight that makes them squint

squire *NOUN* (**squires**)
1 the man who owns most of the land in a country district **2** in the Middle Ages, a young nobleman who served a knight

squirm *VERB* (**squirms**, **squirming**, **squirmed**)
to squirm is to wriggle about, especially when you feel awkward or embarrassed

squirrel *NOUN* (**squirrels**)
a small animal with grey or red fur and a bushy tail, that lives in trees and eats nuts

squirt *VERB* (**squirts**, **squirting**, **squirted**)
to squirt something is to send it out in a strong jet of liquid; to squirt is to come out like this • *The orange juice squirted in his eye.*

St. or **St**
short for **Saint** or **Street**

stab *VERB* (**stabs**, **stabbing**, **stabbed**)
to stab someone is to pierce or wound them with something sharp • *She stabbed him with a knife.*

stab *NOUN* (**stabs**)
1 the action of stabbing **2** a sudden sharp pain

stability *NOUN*
stability is being stable or firm

stabilize *VERB* (**stabilizes**, **stabilizing**, **stabilized**)
1 to stabilize something is to make it stable **2** to stabilize is to become stable

stabilizer *NOUN* (**stabilizers**)
a device for keeping a vehicle or ship steady

stable [1] *ADJECTIVE* (**stabler**, **stablest**)
steady or firmly fixed
▷ **stably** *ADVERB* in a stable way

stable [2] *NOUN* (**stables**)
a building where horses are kept

stack *NOUN* (**stacks**)
1 a neat pile of things **2** a haystack **3** a large amount of something • *I've got a stack of work to do.* **4** a single small chimney

stack *VERB* (**stacks**, **stacking**, **stacked**)
to stack things is to pile them up neatly

stadium *NOUN* (**stadiums** or **stadia**)
a sports ground surrounded by seats for spectators

staff *NOUN* (**staffs**)
1 the people who work in an office or shop **2** the teachers in a school or college **3** a thick stick for walking with **4** a set of five lines on which music is written

stag *NOUN* (**stags**)
a male deer

stage *NOUN* (**stages**)
1 a platform for performances in a theatre or hall **2** the point that you have reached in a process or journey • *Now for the final stage.*

stage *VERB* (**stages**, **staging**, **staged**)
1 to stage a performance is to present it on a stage **2** to stage an event is to organize it • *They decided to stage a protest.*

stagecoach *NOUN* (**stagecoaches**)
a horse-drawn coach of a kind that used to travel regularly along the same route

stagger *VERB* (**staggers, staggering, staggered**)
1 to stagger is to walk unsteadily **2** to stagger someone is to amaze or shock them • *I was staggered at the price.* **3** to stagger events is to arrange them so that they do not all happen at the same time • *We stagger our holidays so that someone is always here.*

> WORD FAMILY
> Something is **staggering** when it is very surprising or shocking.

stagnant *ADJECTIVE*
stagnant water is not flowing or fresh • *The pond is stagnant.*

stain *NOUN* (**stains**)
1 a dirty mark that is difficult to remove
2 something bad in someone's character or past record

stain *VERB* (**stains, staining, stained**)
1 to stain something is to make a stain on it • *The juice has stained my dress.* **2** to stain material or wood is to colour it

stainless *ADJECTIVE*
without stains

stainless steel *NOUN*
stainless steel is steel that does not rust easily

stair *NOUN* (**stairs**)
each of a series of steps that take you from one floor to another in a building

staircase *NOUN* (**staircases**)
a set of stairs

stake *NOUN* (**stakes**)
1 a thick pointed stick to be driven into the ground **2** the thick post to which people used to be tied for execution by being burnt alive **3** an amount of money you bet on something
to be at stake is to be at risk of being lost

stake *VERB* (**stakes, staking, staked**)
to stake money is to use it on a bet
to stake a claim is to claim something or get a right to it

stalactite *NOUN* (**stalactites**)
a stony spike hanging like an icicle from the roof of a cave

> MEANING
> Notice that **stalactites** come down and **stalagmites** (the next word in this dictionary) go up. One way of remembering which is which is that **stalactite** has a *c* in it, like *icicle*.

stalagmite *NOUN* (**stalagmites**)
a stony spike standing like a pillar on the floor of a cave

stale *ADJECTIVE* (**staler, stalest**)
no longer fresh • *This bread has gone stale.* • *The air in here smells stale.*

stalk [1] *NOUN* (**stalks**)
the main part of a plant, from which the leaves and flowers grow

stalk [2] *VERB* (**stalks, stalking, stalked**)
1 to stalk a person or animal is to follow or hunt them stealthily **2** to stalk is to walk in a proud or stiff way

stall [1] *NOUN* (**stalls**)
1 a table or small open-fronted shop where things are sold, usually in the open air **2** a place for one animal in a stable or shed

stall *VERB* (**stalls, stalling, stalled**)
a vehicle stalls when the engine stops suddenly
• *The car stalled at the traffic lights.*

stall [2] *VERB* (**stalls, stalling, stalled**)
to stall is to delay or hold things up to give yourself more time

stallion *NOUN* (**stallions**)
a male horse

stalls *PLURAL NOUN*
the seats on the ground floor of a theatre or cinema

stamen *NOUN* (**stamens**) (*say* **stay- men**)
the part of a flower that produces pollen

stamina *NOUN* (*say* **stam- in- a**)
stamina is the strength and energy you need to keep doing something for a long time
• *Does she have the stamina to run a marathon?*

stammer *VERB* (**stammers, stammering, stammered**)
to stammer is to keep repeating the sounds at the beginning of words

stammer *NOUN* (**stammers**)
a tendency to stammer

stamp *NOUN* (**stamps**)
1 a small piece of gummed paper with a special design on it; a postage stamp **2** when you bang your foot on the ground **3** a small block with raised letters for printing words or marks on something; the words or marks made with this

stamp *VERB* (**stamps, stamping, stamped**)
1 to stamp is to bang your foot heavily on the ground **2** to stamp an envelope or parcel is to put a postage stamp on it **3** to stamp something is also to put marks on it with a stamp • *The librarian stamped my books.*

stampede *NOUN* (**stampedes**)
a sudden rush of animals or people

stampede *VERB* (**stampedes, stampeding, stampeded**)
animals or people stampede when they rush in a stampede

stand *VERB* (**stands, standing, stood**)
1 to stand is to be on your feet without moving
• *She stood at the back of the hall.* **2** to stand something somewhere is to put it upright there
• *Stand the vase on the table.* **3** something stands somewhere when that is where it is • *The castle stood on the top of a hill.* **4** something stands when

it stays unchanged • *My offer still stands.* **5** to stand a difficulty or hardship is to be able to bear it • *I can't stand the heat.*
it stands to reason it is reasonable or obvious
to stand by is to be ready for action
to stand for something 1 is to tolerate it or put up with it • *She won't stand for any arguments.* **2** is to mean something • *'Dr' stands for 'Doctor'.*
to stand in for someone is to take their place
to stand out is to be clear or obvious
to stand up for someone is to support them or defend them

stand *NOUN* (**stands**)
1 something made for putting things on • *Use a music stand.* **2** a stall where things are sold or displayed **3** a building at a sports ground, that is open at the front with rows of seats for spectators **4** when someone resists an attack or defends their opinion • *She was determined to make a stand for her rights.*

standard *NOUN* (**standards**)
1 how good something is • *They reached a high standard of work.* **2** a thing used to measure or judge something else • *The metre is the standard for length.* **3** a special flag, especially one used by an army

standard *ADJECTIVE*
of the usual or ordinary kind

standardize *VERB* (**standardizes, standardizing, standardized**)
to standardize something is to make it a standard size or type

standard lamp *NOUN* (**standard lamps**)
a lamp on an upright pole that stands on the floor

standard of living *NOUN* (**standards of living**)
the level of comfort and wealth that a person or country has

standby *NOUN* (**standbys**)
something or someone kept to be used if they are needed

standstill *NOUN*
a complete stop • *The blizzard brought traffic to a standstill.*

stank
past tense of **stink** *VERB*

stanza *NOUN* (**stanzas**)
a group of lines in a poem

staple[1] *NOUN* (**staples**)
1 a tiny piece of metal used to fasten pieces of paper together **2** a U-shaped nail

> WORD FAMILY
> A **stapler** is a machine for putting staples in paper.

staple *VERB* (**staples, stapling, stapled**)
to fasten pieces of paper together with a staple

staple[2] *ADJECTIVE*
main or normal • *Rice is their staple food.*

star *NOUN* (**stars**)
1 a large mass of burning gas that you see as a bright speck of light in the sky at night **2** one of the main performers in a film or show; a famous entertainer **3** a shape with five or six points

> WORD FAMILY
> A **starry** sky or night is full of stars.

star *VERB* (**stars, starring, starred**)
1 to star in a film or show is to be one of the main performers **2** a film or show stars someone when it has them as a main performer

starboard *NOUN*
starboard is the right-hand side of a ship or aircraft when you are facing forward

starch *NOUN* (**starches**)
1 starch is a white carbohydrate in bread, potatoes, and other food **2** starch is also a form of this substance used to stiffen clothes

> WORD FAMILY
> **Starchy** food contains a lot of starch; you can say someone is **starchy** when they behave in a very stiff way.

stare *VERB* (**stares, staring, stared**)
to look continuously at someone or something without moving your eyes

stare *NOUN* (**stares**)
a long fixed look • *I gave him a hard stare.*

starfish *NOUN* (**starfish** or **starfishes**)
a sea animal shaped like a star with five points

starling *NOUN* (**starlings**)
a noisy black or brown speckled bird

start *VERB* (**starts, starting, started**)
1 to start something is to take the first steps in doing it **2** to start, or start out, is to begin a journey **3** to start is also to make a sudden movement of surprise • *They all started at the noise outside.*

start *NOUN* (**starts**)
1 the act of starting; the point or place where something starts **2** an advantage that someone starts with • *We gave the young ones 10 minutes' start.* **3** a sudden movement of surprise • *It gave me quite a start when the hooter sounded.*

starter *NOUN* (**starters**)
1 someone who starts a race **2** a device for starting the engine of a vehicle

starting pistol *NOUN* (**starting pistols**)
a pistol fired to signal the start of a race

startle *VERB* (**startles, startling, startled**)
to startle a person or animal is to surprise or alarm them

starve *VERB* (**starves, starving, starved**)
1 someone starves when they suffer or die because they do not have enough food **2** to starve someone is to make them suffer or die in this way • *The prisoners had been starved to death.* **3** to starve someone of something they need is to deprive them of it • *She was starved of love.* **4** (*informal*) to be starving is to be very hungry

> WORD FAMILY
> To die of **starvation** is to die because you do not have enough food.

state *NOUN* (**states**)
1 the quality of a person or thing or their circumstances; the way they are **2** a nation **3** a division of a country **4** you can refer to a government and its officials as the state
to be in a state (*informal*) is to be upset

state *VERB* (**states, stating, stated**)
to state something is to say it clearly or formally

stately *ADJECTIVE* (**statelier, stateliest**)
grand and dignified
▷ **stateliness** *NOUN* stateliness is being stately

stately home *NOUN* (**stately homes**)
a large and splendid house that a noble family has owned for many years

statement *NOUN* (**statements**)
1 words that state something **2** a formal account of something that happened • *A witness to the robbery has given a statement to the police.* **3** a report made by a bank about the money in a person's account

statesman or **stateswoman** *NOUN* (**statesmen** or **stateswomen**)
someone who is important or skilled in governing a state

> WORD FAMILY
> **Statesmanship** is skill in being a statesman or stateswoman.

state school *NOUN* (**state schools**)
a school which gets its money from the government and does not charge fees

static *ADJECTIVE*
not moving or changing

static electricity *NOUN*
static electricity is electricity which is present in something but does not flow as a current

station *NOUN* (**stations**)
1 a set of buildings where people get on or off trains or buses **2** a building for police, firemen, or other workers who serve the public **3** a place from which radio or television broadcasts are made

station *VERB* (**stations, stationing, stationed**)
to station a person somewhere is to place them there for a particular purpose • *He was stationed at the door to take the tickets.*

stationary *ADJECTIVE*
not moving; still • *The car was stationary when the van hit it.*

> SPELLING
> Take care not to confuse **stationary** with **stationery**, which is the next word in this dictionary.

stationery *NOUN*
stationery is paper, envelopes, and other things used for writing or word-processing

statistic *NOUN* (**statistics**)
a piece of information expressed as a number • *These statistics show that the population has doubled.*

> WORD FAMILY
> **Statistical** information is expressed as numbers; to express information **statistically** is to express it by means of statistics.

statistician *NOUN* (**statisticians**) (*say* stat- is- **tish**- an)
an expert in statistics

statistics *NOUN*
statistics is the study of information that is expressed as numbers

statue *NOUN* (**statues**)
a model made of stone or metal to look like a person or animal

status *NOUN* (**statuses**)
1 a person's status is their position or rank in relation to other people • *What is your status in the company?* **2** status is high rank or prestige

staunch *ADJECTIVE*
firm and loyal • *They are the team's most staunch supporters.*

stave *NOUN* (**staves**)
a set of five lines on which music is written

stave *VERB* (**staves, staving, staved** or **stove**)
to stave something is to make a hole or dent in it • *The collision stove in the front of the ship.*
to stave something off is to keep something unwelcome away or delay it • *I ate a banana to stave off my hunger.*

stay *VERB* (**stays, staying, stayed**)
1 to stay somewhere is to continue to be there or to remain there **2** to stay somewhere or with someone is to spend time as a visitor • *We stayed in a little hotel near the sea.*

stay *NOUN* (**stays**)
a period of time spent somewhere • *We didn't have time for a long stay.*

steady *ADJECTIVE* (**steadier, steadiest**)
1 not shaking or moving; firm **2** regular or constant; not changing much • *They kept up a steady pace.*

steady *VERB* (**steadies, steadying, steadied**)
to steady something is to make it steady

a b c d e f g h i j k l m n o p q r **s** t u v w x y z

steak *NOUN* (**steaks**)
a thick slice of meat or fish

steal *VERB* (**steals, stealing, stole, stolen**)
1 to steal something is to take and keep it when it does not belong to you **2** to steal somewhere is to move there stealthily • *He stole out of the room.*

stealthy *ADJECTIVE* (**stealthier, stealthiest**)
moving or doing something secretly and quietly so that you are not noticed

> **WORD FAMILY**
> **Stealth** is being stealthy; to do something **stealthily** is to do it in a stealthy way.

steam *NOUN*
steam is the gas or vapour that comes from boiling water
to run out of steam (*informal*) is to have no energy left

> **WORD FAMILY**
> A **steamy** room is full of steam.

steam *VERB* (**steams, steaming, steamed**)
1 to steam is to give out steam **2** to steam somewhere is to move using the power of steam • *The boat steamed down the river.* **3** to steam food is to cook it with steam • *Let's have a steamed pudding.*
to steam up is to be covered with mist or condensation • *The windows have steamed up.*

steam engine *NOUN* (**steam engines**)
an engine driven by steam

steamer *NOUN* (**steamers**)
a steamship

steamroller *NOUN* (**steamrollers**)
a heavy vehicle with wide metal wheels, used to flatten surfaces when making roads

steamship *NOUN* (**steamships**)
a ship driven by steam

steed *NOUN* (**steeds**)
(*old or poetical use*) a horse

steel *NOUN*
steel is a strong metal made from iron and carbon

> **WORD FAMILY**
> Someone is **steely** when they behave in a strong, hard way, like steel.

steel *VERB* (**steels, steeling, steeled**)
to steel yourself is to find courage to do something difficult

steel band *NOUN* (**steel bands**)
a West Indian band of musicians who play instruments made from oil drums

steep *ADJECTIVE* (**steeper, steepest**)
rising or sloping sharply
▷ **steeply** *ADVERB* in a steep way • *a steeply sloping roof*
▷ **steepness** *NOUN* steepness is being steep

steeple *NOUN* (**steeples**)
a church tower with a spire

steeplechase *NOUN* (**steeplechases**)
a race across country or over hedges and fences

steeplejack *NOUN* (**steeplejacks**)
a person who climbs tall steeples or chimneys to do repairs

steer [1] *VERB* (**steers, steering, steered**)
to steer a vehicle is to make it go in the direction you want

steer [2] *NOUN* (**steers**)
a young bull kept for its beef

steering wheel *NOUN* (**steering wheels**)
a wheel for steering a vehicle

stem *NOUN* (**stems**)
1 the main central part of a plant or tree; a stalk **2** the thin part of a wine glass **3** (*in grammar*) the main part of a word, to which different endings are attached. For example, *call* is the stem of the words *caller*, *called*, *calls*, and *calling*

stem *VERB* (**stems, stemming, stemmed**)
to stem from something is to start there or come from it • *The problem stems from lack of money.*

stench *NOUN* (**stenches**)
a very unpleasant smell

stencil *NOUN* (**stencils**)
a piece of card or metal or plastic with pieces cut out of it, used to produce a picture or design

step *NOUN* (**steps**)
1 a movement you make with your foot when you are walking, running, or dancing **2** the sound of a person putting down their foot when walking **3** each of the level surfaces on a stair or ladder **4** each of a series of actions
to watch your step is to be careful

step *VERB* (**steps, stepping, stepped**)
to step is to tread or walk
to step on it (*slang*) is to hurry
to step something up is to increase it

stepchild *NOUN* (**stepchildren**)
a child that someone's husband or wife has from an earlier marriage. A boy is a **stepson** and a girl is a **stepdaughter**

stepfather *NOUN* (**stepfathers**)
a man who is married to your mother but is not your own father

stepladder *NOUN* (**stepladders**)
a folding ladder with flat treads

stepmother *NOUN* (**stepmothers**)
a woman who is married to your father but is not your own mother

steppe *NOUN* (**steppes**)
a grassy plain with few trees, especially in Russia

stepping stone *NOUN* (**stepping stones**)
stepping stones are a line of stones put in a river or stream to help people walk across

steps *PLURAL NOUN*
a stepladder • *Have you seen my steps?*

stereo *ADJECTIVE*
stereophonic

stereo *NOUN* (**stereos**)
1 stereo is stereophonic sound or recording **2** a stereo is a stereophonic radio or record player

stereophonic *ADJECTIVE* (*say* ste- ri- o- **fon**- ik)
using sound that comes from two different directions to give a natural effect

sterile *ADJECTIVE*
1 clean and free from germs **2** not able to have children or reproduce

> WORD FAMILY
> **Sterility** is being strerile.

sterilize *VERB* (**sterilizes, sterilizing, sterilized**)
1 to sterilize something is to make it free from germs **2** to sterilize a person or animal is to make them unable to bear young
▷ **sterilization** *NOUN* sterilization is sterilizing something or someone

sterling *NOUN*
sterling is British money • *Tourists paid for their meals in sterling.*

stern [1] *ADJECTIVE* (**sterner, sternest**)
strict and severe
▷ **sternly** *ADVERB* in a stern way • *The Lady frowned. 'Is that how you address a queen?' she asked sternly.* — C. S. Lewis, *The Lion, The Witch and the Wardrobe*
▷ **sternness** *NOUN* sternness is being stern

stern [2] *NOUN* (**sterns**)
the back part of a ship

stethoscope *NOUN* (**stethoscopes**) (*say* steth- o- skohp)
a device used by doctors for listening to a patient's heartbeat or breathing

stew *VERB* (**stews, stewing, stewed**)
to stew food is to cook it slowly in liquid

stew *NOUN* (**stews**)
a dish of meat and vegetables cooked slowly in liquid
to be in a stew (*informal*) is to be very worried or agitated

steward *NOUN* (**stewards**)
1 a man whose job is to look after the passengers on a ship or aircraft **2** an official who looks after the arrangements at a public event

stewardess *NOUN* (**stewardesses**)
a woman whose job is to look after the passengers on a ship or aircraft

stick [1] *NOUN* (**sticks**)
1 a long thin piece of wood **2** a walking stick **3** the implement used to hit the ball in hockey, polo, or other ball games **4** a long thin piece of something • *I must get a stick of rock.*

stick [2] *VERB* (**sticks, sticking, stuck**)
1 to stick something sharp into a thing is to push it in roughly or carelessly • *He stuck a pin in her finger.* **2** to stick things is to fasten or join them **3** something sticks when it becomes fixed or jammed • *The door keeps sticking.* **4** (*informal*) you can't stick something when you can't bear it • *I can't stick it any longer.*
to stick out is to come out from a surface or be noticeable
to stick together is to stay loyal to one another
to stick up for someone (*informal*) is to support them or defend them
to be stuck with someone or **something** (*informal*) is to be unable to avoid dealing with them

sticker *NOUN* (**stickers**)
a label or sign for sticking on something

sticking plaster *NOUN* (**sticking plasters**)
a strip of sticky material for covering a cut

stick insect *NOUN* (**stick insects**)
an insect with a long thin body that looks like a twig

stickleback *NOUN* (**sticklebacks**)
a small fish with sharp spines on its back

sticky *ADJECTIVE* (**stickier, stickiest**)
1 able or likely to stick to things **2** (*informal*) unpleasant or nasty • *He came to a sticky end.*
▷ **stickily** *ADVERB* in a sticky way
▷ **stickiness** *NOUN* stickiness is being sticky

stiff *ADJECTIVE* (**stiffer, stiffest**)
1 not able to bend or change its shape easily **2** difficult • *We had a stiff examination.* **3** formal; not friendly **4** strong or severe • *There's a stiff wind outside.*
▷ **stiffly** *ADVERB* in a stiff way
▷ **stiffness** *NOUN* stiffness is being stiff

stiffen *VERB* (**stiffens, stiffening, stiffened**)
1 to stiffen something is to make it stiff **2** to stiffen is to become stiff

stifle *VERB* (**stifles, stifling, stifled**)
1 to be stifled is to find it difficult or impossible to breathe **2** to stifle something is to stop it happening • *She stifled a yawn.* • *John clapped his hands on the ill-fated pirate's mouth to stifle the dying groan.* — J. M. Barrie, *The Adventures of Peter Pan*

stile *NOUN* (**stiles**)
an arrangement of steps or bars for people to climb over a fence

still *ADJECTIVE* (**stiller, stillest**)
1 not moving **2** silent • *In the night, the streets are still.* **3** not fizzy

> WORD FAMILY
> **Stillness** is being quiet and not moving.

still *ADVERB*
1 up to this or that time • *He was still there.* **2** even; yet; in a greater amount • *They wanted still more food.* **3** however • *They lost. Still, they have another game.*

still *VERB* (**stills, stilling, stilled**)
to still something is to make it still

stilts *PLURAL NOUN*
1 a pair of poles on which you can walk high above the ground 2 supports for a house built over water

stimulate *VERB* (**stimulates, stimulating, stimulated**)
1 to stimulate someone is to make them excited or interested 2 to stimulate something is to encourage it to develop • *His new book stimulated an interest in wildlife.*

> WORD FAMILY
> A **stimulant** is a substance, such as coffee, that makes you feel more awake and active for a while; **stimulation** is being stimulated or excited.

stimulus *NOUN* (**stimuli**)
something that encourages a thing to develop or produces a reaction

sting *NOUN* (**stings**)
1 the part of an insect or plant that can cause pain or a wound 2 a painful area or wound caused by an insect or plant

sting *VERB* (**stings, stinging, stung**)
1 an insect or plant stings you when it wounds or hurts you with a sting • *She was stung by a wasp.* 2 part of your body stings when you feel a sharp or throbbing pain there • *My back is stinging from sunburn.* 3 (*slang*) to sting someone is to cheat them by charging them too much

stingy *ADJECTIVE* (**stingier, stingiest**) (*say* **stin**-ji)
mean; not generous

stink *NOUN* (**stinks**)
1 an unpleasant smell 2 (*informal*) an unpleasant fuss or complaint

stink *VERB* (**stinks, stinking, stank** or **stunk, stunk**)
to stink is to have an unpleasant smell

stir *VERB* (**stirs, stirring, stirred**)
1 to stir something liquid or soft is to move it round and round, especially with a spoon 2 to stir is to move slightly or start to move after sleeping or being still • *She didn't stir all afternoon.*
to stir something up is to excite or arouse it • *They are always stirring up trouble.*

stir *NOUN* (**stirs**)
1 an act of stirring • *Give it a stir.* 2 a fuss or disturbance • *The news caused a stir.*

stirrup *NOUN* (**stirrups**)
a metal loop that hangs down on each side of a horse's saddle to support the rider's foot

stitch *NOUN* (**stitches**)
1 a loop of thread made in sewing or knitting 2 a sudden pain in your side caused by running

stoat *NOUN* (**stoats**)
an animal rather like a weasel, also called an ermine

stock *NOUN* (**stocks**)
1 a stock of things is an amount of them kept ready to be sold or used 2 stock is a collection of farm animals, also called livestock 3 a person's stock is the line of their ancestors 4 stock is a liquid used in cooking, made from the juices you get by stewing meat, fish, or vegetables 5 stock is also a number of shares in a company's capital 6 stock is also a garden flower with a sweet smell

stock *VERB* (**stocks, stocking, stocked**)
1 a shop stocks goods when it keeps a supply of them to sell 2 to stock a place is to provide it with a stock of things • *The explorers stocked their base camp with tinned food.*
to stock up is to buy a large supply of something

stockade *NOUN* (**stockades**)
a fence made of large stakes

stockbroker *NOUN* (**stockbrokers**)
someone whose job is to buy and sell stocks and shares for clients

stock car *NOUN* (**stock cars**)
an ordinary car strengthened for use in races in which cars are allowed to bump each other

stock exchange *NOUN* (**stock exchanges**)
a country's central place for selling and buying stocks and shares

stocking *NOUN* (**stockings**)
a piece of clothing that covers the whole of someone's leg and foot

stock market *NOUN* (**stock markets**)
1 a stock exchange 2 the business of buying and selling stocks and shares

stockpile *NOUN* (**stockpiles**)
a large stock of things kept in reserve

stocks *PLURAL NOUN*
a wooden framework with holes for people's legs and arms, in which criminals were locked as a punishment

stocky *ADJECTIVE* (**stockier, stockiest**)
short and solidly built

stodgy *ADJECTIVE* (**stodgier, stodgiest**)
1 thick and heavy; not easy to digest • *The pudding's very stodgy.* 2 dull and boring • *What a stodgy book.*

stoke *VERB* (**stokes, stoking, stoked**)
to stoke a furnace or fire is to add fuel to it

stole [1] *NOUN* (**stoles**)
a wide piece of material worn round the shoulders by women

stole [2]
past tense of **steal**

stolen
past participle of **steal**

stomach *NOUN* (**stomachs**)
1 the part of your body where food starts to be digested 2 the front part of your body that contains your stomach; your abdomen

stomach *VERB* (**stomachs, stomaching, stomached**)
to stomach something is to tolerate it or put up with it • *I can't stomach their awful jokes.*

stone *NOUN* (**stones** or, for the unit of weight, **stone**)
1 stone is the hard solid mineral of which rocks are made **2** a stone is a piece of this mineral **3** a stone is also a jewel **4** a stone is also the hard seed in the middle of some fruits, such as a cherry, plum, or peach **5** a stone is also a unit of weight equal to 14 pounds or about 6.35 kilograms • *She weighs 6 stone.*

stone *VERB* (**stones, stoning, stoned**)
1 to stone someone is to throw stones at them **2** to stone fruit is to take the stones out of it

stone-cold *ADJECTIVE*
extremely cold

stone-deaf *ADJECTIVE*
completely deaf

stony *ADJECTIVE* (**stonier, stoniest**)
1 stony ground is full of stones **2** hard like stone **3** unfriendly or hostile • *Our question was met by a stony silence.*

stood
past tense and past participle of **stand** *VERB*

stool *NOUN* (**stools**)
a small seat without a back

stoop *VERB* (**stoops, stooping, stooped**)
1 to stoop is to bend your body forwards and downwards **2** to stoop to doing something is to lower your standards of behaviour • *I didn't think he'd stoop to cheating.*

stop *VERB* (**stops, stopping, stopped**)
1 to stop something is to finish doing it, or make it finish **2** to stop is to be no longer moving or working or to come to an end **3** to stop something is to prevent it happening or continuing • *I must go out and stop that noise.* **4** to stop a hole or gap, or stop it up, is to fill it **5** to stop at a place is to stay there briefly

stop *NOUN* (**stops**)
1 when something stops or ends • *She brought the car to a stop.* **2** a place where a bus or train stops regularly

stoppage *NOUN* (**stoppages**)
1 an interruption in the work of a business or factory **2** a blockage in something

stopper *NOUN* (**stoppers**)
something that fits into the top of a bottle or jar to close it

stop press *NOUN*
late news printed in a newspaper after printing has started

stopwatch *NOUN* (**stopwatches**)
a watch that you can start or stop, used for timing races

storage *NOUN*
storage is the storing of things

store *VERB* (**stores, storing, stored**)
to store things is to keep them until they are needed

store *NOUN* (**stores**)
1 a place where things are stored **2** things kept for future use **3** a shop, especially a large one
to be in store is to be waiting to happen soon • *There is a treat in store for you.*

storey *NOUN* (**storeys**)
one whole floor of a building

> SPELLING
> Take care not to confuse **storey** with **story**, as in *read me a story*.

stork *NOUN* (**storks**)
a large bird with long legs and a long beak

storm *NOUN* (**storms**)
1 a period of bad weather with strong winds, rain or snow, and often thunder and lightning **2** a violent attack or outburst • *There was a storm of protest.*
a storm in a teacup a big fuss over something unimportant

storm *VERB* (**storms, storming, stormed**)
1 to storm is to move or shout angrily • *He stormed out of the room.* **2** soldiers or police storm a place when they attack it suddenly • *They stormed the castle.*

stormy *ADJECTIVE* (**stormier, stormiest**)
1 likely to end in a storm • *The weather is stormy today.* **2** loud and angry • *We had a stormy meeting.*

story *NOUN* (**stories**)
1 an account of real or imaginary events
2 (*informal*) a lie • *Don't tell stories!*

> SPELLING
> Take care not to confuse **story** with **storey**, which means the floor of a building.

stout *ADJECTIVE* (**stouter, stoutest**)
1 rather fat **2** thick and strong • *She carried a stout stick.* **3** brave • *The defenders put up a stout resistance.*
▷ **stoutly** *ADVERB* in a stout way
▷ **stoutness** *NOUN* stoutness is being stout

stove[1] *NOUN* (**stoves**)
a device that produces heat for warming a room or cooking

stove[2]
past tense and past participle of **stave** *VERB*

stow *VERB* (**stows, stowing, stowed**)
to stow something is to pack it or store it away • *The witch stowed her knitting in her pocket and got up. She followed Lizzie to the mill door and peered in.* — Helen Cresswell, *Lizzie Dripping*
to stow away is to hide on a ship or aircraft so that you can travel without paying

stowaway *NOUN* (**stowaways**)
someone who stows away on a ship or aircraft

straddle *VERB* (**straddles, straddling, straddled**)
1 to straddle something is to sit or stand with your legs either side of it **2** to straddle something is also to be built across it • *A long bridge straddles the river.*

straggle *VERB* (**straggles, straggling, straggled**)
1 to straggle is to walk too slowly and not keep up with the rest of a group **2** to straggle is also to grow or move in an untidy way • *Brambles straggled across the path.*

> WORD FAMILY
> A **straggler** is someone who does not keep up with the rest of a group; **straggly** hair grows or hangs untidily.

straight *ADJECTIVE* (**straighter, straightest**)
1 going continuously in one direction; not curving or bending **2** level • *Is this picture straight?* **3** tidy; in proper order **4** honest or frank • *Give me a straight answer.*

straight *ADVERB*
1 in a straight line • *Go straight on, then turn left.* **2** at once; directly • *I came straight here.*

> SPELLING
> Take care not to confuse **straight** with **strait**, which is a noun meaning a narrow stretch of water.

straightaway *ADVERB*
immediately; at once

straighten *VERB* (**straightens, straightening, straightened**)
1 to straighten something is to make it straight **2** to straighten is to become straight

straightforward *ADJECTIVE*
1 easy to understand or do; not complicated **2** honest or frank

strain *VERB* (**strains, straining, strained**)
1 to strain something is to stretch it or push it or pull it hard or too hard **2** to strain a muscle is to damage it by using it too much **3** to strain is to make a great effort to do something **4** to strain liquid is to put it through a sieve to take out any lumps or other things in it

strain *NOUN* (**strains**)
1 the strain on something is when it is stretched or pulled too hard • *The rope broke under the strain.* **2** a strain is an injury caused by straining **3** strain is the effect on someone of too much work or worry

strainer *NOUN* (**strainers**)
a device for straining liquids

strait *NOUN* (**straits**)
a narrow stretch of water connecting two seas

> SPELLING
> Take care not to confuse **strait** with the adjective **straight**.

straits *PLURAL NOUN*
to be in dire straits is to have severe difficulties

strand *NOUN* (**strands**)
1 each of the threads or wires twisted together to make a rope or cable **2** a lock of hair

stranded *ADJECTIVE*
1 left on sand or rocks in shallow water • *We could see a stranded ship.* **2** left in a difficult or lonely position • *They were stranded in the desert.*

strange *ADJECTIVE* (**stranger, strangest**)
1 unusual or surprising **2** not known or experienced before
▷ **strangely** *ADVERB* in a strange way • *The house was strangely quiet.*
▷ **strangeness** *NOUN* strangeness is being strange

stranger *NOUN* (**strangers**)
1 a person you do not know **2** a person who is in a place they do not know

strangle *VERB* (**strangles, strangling, strangled**)
to strangle someone is to kill them by pressing their throat and so prevent them breathing

> WORD FAMILY
> A **strangler** is a person who strangles someone; **strangulation** is killing someone by strangling them.

strap *NOUN* (**straps**)
a flat strip of leather or cloth or plastic for fastening things together or holding them in place

strap *VERB* (**straps, strapping, strapped**)
to strap something is to fasten it with a strap or straps

strategy *NOUN* (**strategies**)
1 a strategy is a plan to achieve or win something **2** strategy is planning a war or military campaign

> WORD FAMILY
> Something is **strategic** when it is done as part of a plan to achieve or win something; a **strategist** is an expert in strategy.

stratum *NOUN* (**strata**) (*say* **strah**-tum)
a layer or level • *You can see several strata of rock in the cliffs.*

straw *NOUN* (**straws**)
1 straw is dry cut stalks of corn **2** a straw is a narrow tube that you can drink through

strawberry *NOUN* (**strawberries**)
a small red juicy fruit, with its seeds on the outside

stray *VERB* (**strays, straying, strayed**)
to stray is to wander or become lost

stray *ADJECTIVE*
1 wandering around lost • *We found a stray cat.* **2** out of place; separated from all the others • *a stray hair*

stray *NOUN* (**strays**)
a stray dog or cat

streak *NOUN* (**streaks**)
1 a long thin line or mark **2** a streak of something is a trace or sign of it • *He has a cruel streak.*

streak *VERB* (**streaks, streaking, streaked**)
1 to streak something is to mark it with streaks **2** to streak somewhere is to move there very quickly

streaky *ADJECTIVE* (**streakier**, **streakiest**)
marked with streaks

stream *NOUN* (**streams**)
1 a narrow river or brook **2** liquid flowing in one direction **3** a number of things moving in the same direction, such as traffic **4** a group in a school containing children of similar ability

stream *VERB* (**streams**, **streaming**, **streamed**)
1 to stream is to move in a strong or fast flow • *Traffic streamed across the junction.* **2** to stream is also to produce a flow of liquid • *Blood was streaming from her cut hand.* **3** to stream schoolchildren is to organize them in groups of similar ability

streamer *NOUN* (**streamers**)
a long strip of paper or ribbon

streamline *VERB* (**streamlines**, **streamlining**, **streamlined**)
1 to streamline a vehicle or object is to give it a smooth shape that helps it to move easily through air or water **2** to streamline an activity or operation is to make it work more efficiently

street *NOUN* (**streets**)
a road with houses beside it in a city or town

strength *NOUN* (**strengths**)
1 strength is how strong a person or thing is **2** a person's strengths are their good points or the things they are good at • *Patience is your greatest strength.*

strengthen *VERB* (**strengthens**, **strengthening**, **strengthened**)
1 to strengthen something or someone is to make them stronger **2** to strengthen is to become stronger

strenuous *ADJECTIVE*
needing or using great effort and determination

> WORD FAMILY
> To **strenuously** deny something is to do so with energy and determination.

stress *NOUN* (**stresses**)
1 a stress is a force or pressure that pulls or pushes or twists something **2** stress is the effect on someone of too much work or worry or pressure **3** stress is also emphasis, especially the extra force with which you pronounce part of a word or phrase

stress *VERB* (**stresses**, **stressing**, **stressed**)
1 to stress part of a word or phrase is to pronounce it with extra emphasis **2** to stress a point or idea is to emphasize it • *I must stress that this is an unusual problem.* **3** to stress someone is to make them suffer stress

stretch *VERB* (**stretches**, **stretching**, **stretched**)
1 to stretch something is to pull it so that it becomes longer or wider **2** something stretches when it becomes longer or wider when it is pulled **3** you stretch, or stretch out, when you reach out with your arms or extend your arms and legs fully **4** to stretch somewhere is to extend or continue there • *The wall stretches all the way round the park.*

stretch *NOUN* (**stretches**)
1 the action of stretching something • *I got up and had a good stretch.* **2** a continuous period of time or area of land or water

stretcher *NOUN* (**stretchers**)
a framework like a light folding bed with handles at each end, for carrying a sick or injured person

strew *VERB* (**strews**, **strewing**, **strewed**, **strewn** or **strewed**)
to strew things is to scatter them over a surface • *Flowers were strewn over the path.*

stricken *ADJECTIVE*
overcome or strongly affected by a feeling or illness

strict *ADJECTIVE* (**stricter**, **strictest**)
1 demanding that people obey rules and behave well • *The teachers are all fairly strict.* **2** complete or exact • *He's not really a hero in the strict sense of the word.*

> WORD FAMILY
> Something is (for example) **strictly** forbidden when it is completely forbidden; you say something is not **strictly** true when it is not exactly true; **strictness** is being strict.

stride *VERB* (**strides**, **striding**, **strode**, **stridden**)
to stride is to walk with long steps

stride *NOUN* (**strides**)
a long step you take when walking or running
to get into your stride is to settle into a steady rate of work
to take something in your stride is to cope with it easily

strife *NOUN*
strife is fighting or quarrelling

strike *VERB* (**strikes**, **striking**, **struck**)
1 to strike something or someone is to hit them **2** to strike people or a place is to attack them suddenly • *Plague struck the village.* **3** to strike a match is to light it by rubbing it against something rough **4** a clock strikes (for example) seven when it rings seven chimes at seven o'clock **5** workers strike when they stop working as a protest against their pay or conditions **6** to strike oil or gold is to find it by drilling or mining **7** to strike someone in some way is to make them think that way • *The film struck me as rather violent.*
to strike up is to begin playing or singing

strike *NOUN* (**strikes**)
1 a hit **2** when workers refuse to work, as a way of making a protest **3** a find of oil or gold underground
to go on strike is to stop working as a protest

striker *NOUN* (**strikers**)
1 a worker who is on strike **2** in football, an attacking player who tries to score goals

a b c d e f g h i j k l m n o p q r **s** t u v w x y z

striking *ADJECTIVE*
so impressive, interesting, or attractive that you can't help noticing it • *And the most striking pup of all was one who had a perfect horse-shoe of spots on his back – and had therefore been named 'Lucky'.* — Dodie Smith, *The Hundred and One Dalmatians*

string *NOUN* (**strings**)
1 string is thin rope or cord for tying things; a string is a piece of thin rope **2** in music, a string is a piece of stretched wire or nylon used in an instrument to make sounds **3** a string of things is a line or series of them • *There was a string of buses along the High Street.*

string *VERB* (**strings, stringing, strung**)
1 to string something is to hang it on a string **2** to string pearls or beads is to thread them on a string **3** to string beans is to remove the tough fibre from them **4** to string a racket or musical instrument is to put strings on it
to string something out is to spread or stretch it out

stringed *ADJECTIVE*
in music, stringed instruments are ones that have strings, especially members of the violin family

strings *PLURAL NOUN*
the stringed instruments in an orchestra

stringy *ADJECTIVE* (**stringier, stringiest**)
1 long and thin like string **2** stringy meat contains tough fibres

strip[1] *VERB* (**strips, stripping, stripped**)
1 to strip something is to take a covering off it **2** to strip is to take all your clothes off **3** to strip someone of something is to take it away from them

strip *NOUN* (**strips**)
the special outfit worn by a sports team

strip[2] *NOUN* (**strips**)
a long narrow piece of something

strip cartoon *NOUN* (**strip cartoons**)
a series of drawings telling a story; a comic strip

stripe *NOUN* (**stripes**)
1 a long narrow band of colour **2** something worn on the sleeve of a uniform to show the rank of the person wearing it

> WORD FAMILY
> Something is **striped** or **stripy** when it has stripes.

strive *VERB* (**strives, striving, strove, striven**)
to strive to do something is to try hard to do it

strobe *NOUN* (**strobes**)
a light that flickers on and off continuously

strode
past tense of **stride** *VERB*

stroke[1] *NOUN* (**strokes**)
1 a hit or movement made by swinging your arm **2** a swimming style **3** a line drawn by a pen or brush **4** a sudden illness that often causes someone to be paralysed

stroke[2] *VERB* (**strokes, stroking, stroked**)
to stroke something is to move your hand gently along it

stroll *VERB* (**strolls, strolling, strolled**)
to stroll is to walk slowly

stroll *NOUN* (**strolls**)
a short leisurely walk

strong *ADJECTIVE* (**stronger, strongest**)
1 having great power, energy, or effect **2** not easily broken or damaged • *The gate was held by a strong chain.* **3** having a lot of flavour or smell • *Do you like your tea strong?* **4** having a particular number or size • *The game had a crowd 20,000 strong.*

strong *ADVERB*
to be going strong is to be making good progress

stronghold *NOUN* (**strongholds**)
a fortress or other place that is well defended

strongly *ADVERB*
1 in a strong way; with strength • *They fought back strongly.* **2** very much • *The room smelt strongly of perfume.*

strove
past tense of **strive**

struck
past tense and past participle of **strike** *VERB*

structure *NOUN* (**structures**)
1 a structure is something that has been built or put together **2** a thing's structure is the way that it is built or made
▷ **structural** *ADJECTIVE* to do with the way that something is built or made
▷ **structurally** *ADVERB* as regards the structure of something

struggle *VERB* (**struggles, struggling, struggled**)
1 to struggle is to move your body about violently while you are fighting or trying to get free **2** to struggle to do something is to make strong efforts to do it

struggle *NOUN* (**struggles**)
1 fighting or trying to get free **2** a great effort

strum *VERB* (**strums, strumming, strummed**)
to strum a guitar is to sound it by running your finger across its strings

strung
past tense and past participle of **string** *VERB*

strut *VERB* (**struts, strutting, strutted**)
to strut is to walk proudly or stiffly • *Hare began to strut about so that the moon should see what a fine figure of a creature was waiting for her.* — Ted Hughes, *How the Whale Became and Other Stories*

strut *NOUN* (**struts**)
1 a strutting walk **2** a bar of wood or metal that strengthens a framework

stub *VERB* (**stubs, stubbing, stubbed**)
1 you stub your toe when you knock it against something hard **2** to stub, or to stub out, a cigarette or cigar is to put it out by pressing it against something hard

stub *NOUN* (**stubs**)
a short piece of something left after the rest has been used up or worn down

stubble *NOUN*
1 stubble is the short stalks of corn left in the ground after a harvest **2** stubble is also the short stiff hairs growing on a man's chin when he has not shaved

stubborn *ADJECTIVE*
not willing to change your ideas or ways; obstinate
▷ **stubbornly** *ADVERB* in a stubborn way
▷ **stubbornness** *NOUN* stubbornness is being stubborn

stuck [1]
past tense and past participle of **stick** *VERB*

stuck [2] *ADJECTIVE*
unable to move or make progress • *Is anyone stuck?*

stuck-up *ADJECTIVE*
(*informal*) unpleasantly proud or snobbish

stud *NOUN* (**studs**)
a small metal button or knob fixed into something

student *NOUN* (**students**)
someone who studies, especially at a college or university

studio *NOUN* (**studios**)
1 a place where radio or television broadcasts are made **2** a place where cinema or television films are made **3** the room where an artist or photographer works

studious *ADJECTIVE*
fond of studying; studying hard
▷ **studiously** *ADVERB* in a studious way

study *VERB* (**studies, studying, studied**)
1 to study is to spend time learning about something **2** to study something is to look at it carefully

study *NOUN* (**studies**)
1 study is the process of studying **2** a study is a room used for studying or writing

stuff *NOUN*
1 stuff is a substance or material • *What's this stuff at the bottom of the glass?* **2** stuff is also a group of things or a person's possessions • *Will you move your stuff off the table?*

stuff *VERB* (**stuffs, stuffing, stuffed**)
1 to stuff something is to fill it tightly, especially with stuffing • *She stuffed the turkey.* **2** to stuff one thing inside another is to push it in carelessly • *He stuffed the paper into his pocket.*

stuffing *NOUN* (**stuffings**)
1 stuffing is material used to fill the inside of something **2** stuffing is also a savoury mixture you put into meat or poultry before cooking it

stuffy *ADJECTIVE* (**stuffier, stuffiest**)
1 a stuffy room is badly ventilated, without enough fresh air **2** formal and boring
▷ **stuffily** *ADVERB* in a stuffy way
▷ **stuffiness** *NOUN* stuffiness is being stuffy

stumble *VERB* (**stumbles, stumbling, stumbled**)
1 to stumble is to lose your balance or fall over something **2** to stumble when you are speaking is to make mistakes or hesitate
to stumble across something or **stumble on something** is to find it by chance

stump *NOUN* (**stumps**)
1 the bottom of a tree trunk left in the ground when the tree has fallen or been cut down **2** (*in cricket*) each of the three upright sticks of a wicket

stump *VERB* (**stumps, stumping, stumped**)
1 (*in cricket*) to stump the person batting is to get them out by touching the stumps with the ball when they are not standing in the correct place **2** something stumps you when it is too difficult for you • *The last question stumped everyone.*

stun *VERB* (**stuns, stunning, stunned**)
1 to stun someone is to knock them unconscious **2** something stuns you when it shocks or confuses you • *They were stunned by the news.*

stung
past tense and past participle of **sting** *VERB*

stunk
past tense and past participle of **stink** *VERB*

stunt *NOUN* (**stunts**)
1 something daring or dangerous done in a film or as part of a performance **2** something unusual done to attract publicity or attention

stupendous *ADJECTIVE*
amazing; tremendous • *The Iron Man had had the most stupendous idea. The Iron Man would go out, as the champion of the earth, against this monster from space.* — Ted Hughes, *The Iron Man*

stupid *ADJECTIVE* (**stupider, stupidest**)
without reason or common sense; not clever or thoughtful

> WORD FAMILY
> To **stupidly** do something is to do it in a way that shows lack of thought or common sense; **stupidity** is being stupid.

sturdy *ADJECTIVE* (**sturdier, sturdiest**)
strong and solid
▷ **sturdily** *ADVERB* in a sturdy way
▷ **sturdiness** *NOUN* sturdiness is being sturdy

stutter *VERB* (**stutters, stuttering, stuttered**)
to stutter is to keep repeating the sounds at the beginning of words

stutter *NOUN* (**stutters**)
a tendency to stutter

sty[1] *NOUN* (**sties**)
a pigsty

sty[2] or **stye** *NOUN* (**sties** or **styes**)
a sore swelling on your eyelid

style *NOUN* (**styles**)
1 a style is the way that something is done, made, said, or written **2** style is being smart and elegant **3** a style is also a part of the pistil in a flower

style *VERB* (**styles, styling, styled**)
to style something is to give it a special style

stylish *ADJECTIVE*
fashionable and smart
▷ **stylishly** *ADVERB* in a stylish way

stylus *NOUN* (**styluses**)
the device like a needle that travels in the grooves of a record to reproduce the sound

sub *NOUN* (**subs**)(*informal*)
1 a submarine **2** a subscription **3** a substitute, especially in sports

sub- *PREFIX*
meaning 'below', as in *submarine* and *substandard*

subcontinent *NOUN* (**subcontinents**)
a large area of land that forms part of a continent • *the Indian subcontinent*

subdivide *VERB* (**subdivides, subdividing, subdivided**)
to subdivide something that has already been divided is to divide it again into smaller parts

subdue *VERB* (**subdues, subduing, subdued**)
1 to subdue someone is to overcome them or bring them under control **2** to subdue a person or animal is to make them quieter or gentler

subject *NOUN* (**subjects**) (*say* **sub**- jikt)
1 the person or thing that is being talked or written about **2** something that is studied **3** (*in grammar*) the person or thing that is doing the action stated by the verb in a sentence, for example *dog* in the sentence *the dog chewed a bone* **4** someone who must obey the laws of a particular ruler or government

subject *ADJECTIVE*
subject to something depending on it or likely to be affected by it • *Our decision is subject to your approval.*

subject *VERB* (**subjects, subjecting, subjected**) (*say* sub- **jekt**)
to subject someone to something is to make them experience or suffer it • *They subjected him to a string of questions.*

subjective *ADJECTIVE*
1 existing only in a person's mind **2** influenced by a person's own beliefs or ideas • *His account of what happened is rather subjective.*

submarine *NOUN* (**submarines**)
a type of ship that can travel under water

submerge *VERB* (**submerges, submerging, submerged**)
1 to submerge is to go under water **2** to submerge something or someone is to put them under water

> WORD FAMILY
> **Submersion** is when something is submerged.

submission *NOUN* (**submissions**)
1 submission is submitting to someone **2** a submission is something that you submit or offer to someone

submissive *ADJECTIVE*
willing to obey

submit *VERB* (**submits, submitting, submitted**)
1 to submit to someone is to give in to them or agree to obey them **2** to submit something to someone is to hand it in or offer it to be judged or considered

subordinate *ADJECTIVE* (*say* sub- **or**- din- at)
less important, or lower in rank

subordinate *NOUN* (**subordinates**)
someone who is subordinate to someone else

subordinate *VERB* (**subordinates, subordinating, subordinated**) (*say* sub- **or**- din- ayt)
to subordinate something is to treat it as less important than something else
▷ **subordination** *NOUN* subordination is subordinating something

subordinate clause *NOUN* (**subordinate clauses**)
a clause which is added to a main clause, for example *when you arrive* in the sentence *Let me know when you arrive*

subscribe *VERB* (**subscribes, subscribing, subscribed**)
to subscribe to something is to pay money to receive it regularly or to be a member of a club or society

> WORD FAMILY
> A **subscriber** is someone who subscribes to something.

subscription *NOUN* (**subscriptions**)
money you pay to subscribe to something

subsequent *ADJECTIVE*
coming later or after something else • *Subsequent events proved that she was right.*

> WORD FAMILY
> You say something happened **subsequently** when it happened later or afterwards.

subside *VERB* (**subsides, subsiding, subsided**)
1 to subside is to sink • *The house has subsided over the years.* **2** to subside is also to become quiet or normal • *The noise subsided after midnight.*

> WORD FAMILY
> **Subsidence** is when a building or piece of land sinks into the ground.

subsidize *VERB* (**subsidizes**, **subsidizing**, **subsidized**)
to subsidize someone or something is to give them a subsidy

subsidy *NOUN* (**subsidies**)
money paid to keep prices low or to support an industry or activity

substance *NOUN* (**substances**)
1 something that you can touch or see; what something is made of **2** the essential part of something

substantial *ADJECTIVE*
1 large or important **2** strong and solid
▷ **substantially** *ADVERB* mostly • *This story is substantially true.*

substitute *VERB* (**substitutes**, **substituting**, **substituted**)
to substitute one thing or person for another is to use the first one instead of the second • *In this recipe you can substitute oil for butter.*

> WORD FAMILY
> **Substitution**, or a **substitution**, is when one thing or person is used instead of another.

substitute *NOUN* (**substitutes**)
a person or thing that is used instead of another

subtle *ADJECTIVE* (**subtler**, **subtlest**) (*say* sut- el)
1 slight and delicate • *This soup has a subtle flavour.* **2** ingenious but not obvious • *Your jokes are too subtle for me.*
▷ **subtly** *ADVERB* in a subtle way
▷ **subtlety** *NOUN* subtlety is being subtle or delicate

subtract *VERB* (**subtracts**, **subtracting**, **subtracted**)
to subtract one amount from another is to take it away • *If you subtract 2 from 7, you get 5.*

> WORD FAMILY
> **Subtraction** is the process of taking one amount from another.

suburb *NOUN* (**suburbs**)
an area of houses on the edge of a city or large town

> WORD FAMILY
> A **suburban** area or street is in a suburb.

suburbia *NOUN*
suburbia is the suburbs of a place and the people who live in them

subway *NOUN* (**subways**)
an underground passage for pedestrians

succeed *VERB* (**succeeds**, **succeeding**, **succeeded**)
1 to succeed is to do or get what you wanted or intended **2** to succeed someone is to be the next person to do what they did, especially to be king or queen

success *NOUN* (**successes**)
1 success is doing or getting what you wanted or intended **2** a success is a person or thing that does well • *The plan was a great success.*

successful *ADJECTIVE*
having success
▷ **successfully** *ADVERB* in a successful way

succession *NOUN* (**successions**)
1 a series of people or things **2** the right to be the next person to do something, especially becoming king or queen

successive *ADJECTIVE*
following one after another
▷ **successively** *ADVERB* one after another

successor *NOUN* (**successors**)
a person or thing that comes after another • *The headteacher retired and handed over to her successor.*

such *ADJECTIVE*
1 of the same kind • *Cakes and sweets and all such food is fattening.* **2** so great or so much • *That was such fun!*

such-and-such *ADJECTIVE*
one in particular but you are not saying which • *He promises to come at such-and-such a time but is always late.*

suck *VERB* (**sucks**, **sucking**, **sucked**)
1 to suck liquid or air is to take it in through your mouth • *I sucked milk through a straw.* **2** to suck something is to move it around inside your mouth • *She was sucking a sweet.* **3** to suck something is also to draw it in or absorb it • *The boat was sucked into the whirlpool.* • *He sucked in his cheeks.*

suck *NOUN* (**sucks**)
the action of sucking

suction *NOUN*
suction is producing a vacuum so that liquid or air is drawn in • *Vacuum cleaners work by suction.*

sudden *ADJECTIVE*
happening or done quickly and unexpectedly
▷ **suddenness** *NOUN* suddenness is being sudden

suddenly *ADVERB*
quickly and unexpectedly

suds *PLURAL NOUN*
froth on soapy water

sue *VERB* (**sues**, **suing**, **sued**)
to sue someone is to start a claim in a lawcourt to get money from them

suede *NOUN* (*say* swayd)
suede is leather with one side soft and velvety

suet *NOUN*
suet is hard fat from cattle and sheep, used in cooking

a b c d e f g h i j k l m n o p q r s t u v w x y z

suffer *VERB* (**suffers**, **suffering**, **suffered**)
1 to suffer is to feel pain or misery **2** to suffer something unpleasant is to have to put up with it

suffering *NOUN* (**sufferings**)
suffering is pain or misery

sufficient *ADJECTIVE*
enough • *Have we sufficient food?*
▷ **sufficiently** *ADVERB* to a sufficient degree

suffix *NOUN* (**suffixes**)
a word or syllable joined to the end of a word to change or add to its meaning, as in forget*ful*, lion*ess*, and rust*y*

SUFFIXES

Suffix	Meaning
-able, -ible, -uble	able (to be)
-ant; -ent	a doer
-dom	condition; rank; territory
-ee	one who is ...
-er	a doer
-er	more
-esque	in the style of
-ess	used to make feminine forms of words
-est	most
-fold	times
-ful	full of
-hood	state of
-ic	belonging to
-ize; -ise	used to make verbs
-ish	rather like
-ism	belief; system of thought
-ist	a doer
-itis	inflamation of
-less	lacking; free from
-let	small
-ly	used to make adverbs and adjectives
-ment	used to make nouns
-ness	state of being
-oid	like
-or	a doer
-ous	used to make adjectives
-ship	state of being
-some	full of
-ty	showing a condition
-ward(s)	in a particular direction

suffocate *VERB* (**suffocates**, **suffocating**, **suffocated**)
1 to suffocate is to suffer or die because you cannot breathe **2** to suffocate someone is to make it impossible or difficult for them to breathe
▷ **suffocation** *NOUN* suffocation is when someone dies because they cannot breathe

sugar *NOUN*
sugar is a sweet food obtained from the juices of various plants, such as sugar beet or sugar cane

WORD FAMILY
Sugary food or drink has a lot of sugar in it.

suggest *VERB* (**suggests**, **suggesting**, **suggested**)
1 to suggest something is to offer it as an idea or possibility **2** to suggest something is also to give an idea or impression of something • *Your smile suggests that you agree with me.*

suggestion *NOUN* (**suggestions**)
something that you mention to someone as an idea or possibility

suicide *NOUN* (**suicides**)
suicide is killing yourself deliberately • *He committed suicide.*

WORD FAMILY
A person is **suicidal** when they are likely to commit suicide.

suit *NOUN* (**suits**)
1 a matching set of jacket and trousers or jacket and skirt, that are meant to be worn together **2** a set of clothing for a particular activity • *He wore a diving suit.* **3** each of the four sets in a pack of playing cards: spades, hearts, diamonds, and clubs **4** a lawsuit

suit *VERB* (**suits**, **suiting**, **suited**)
1 to suit someone or something is to be suitable or convenient for them **2** a piece of clothing or hairstyle suits you when it looks good on you

suitable *ADJECTIVE*
satisfactory or right for a particular person, purpose, or occasion
▷ **suitability** *NOUN* suitability is being suitable
▷ **suitably** *ADVERB* in a suitable way

suitcase *NOUN* (**suitcases**)
a container with a lid and a handle, for carrying clothes and other things on journeys

suite *NOUN* (**suites**) (*say* sweet)
1 a set of rooms in a hotel **2** a set of matching furniture **3** a set of short pieces of music

suitor *NOUN* (**suitors**)
a man who wants to marry a particular woman

sulk *VERB* (**sulks**, **sulking**, **sulked**)
to sulk is to be silent and bad-tempered because you are not pleased

sulky *ADJECTIVE* (**sulkier**, **sulkiest**)
sulking or inclined to sulk
▷ **sulkily** *ADVERB* in a sulky way
▷ **sulkiness** *NOUN* sulkiness is being sulky

sullen *ADJECTIVE*
sulking and gloomy
▷ **sullenly** *ADVERB* in a sullen way
▷ **sullenness** *NOUN* sullenness is being sullen

sulphur *NOUN*
sulphur is a yellow chemical used in industry and medicine

sulphuric acid *NOUN*
sulphuric acid is a strong colourless acid containing sulphur

sultan *NOUN* (**sultans**)
the ruler of certain Muslim countries

sultana *NOUN* (**sultanas**)
a raisin without seeds

sum *NOUN* (**sums**)
1 a total, or the amount you get when you add numbers together **2** a problem in arithmetic **3** an amount of money

sum *VERB* (**sums, summing, summed**)
to sum up is to give a summary at the end of a discussion or talk

summarize *VERB* (**summarizes, summarizing, summarized**)
to summarize something is to give a short statement of its main points

summary *NOUN* (**summaries**)
a short statement of the main points of something said or written

summer *NOUN* (**summers**)
the warm season between spring and autumn

summertime *NOUN*
summertime is the season of summer

summit *NOUN* (**summits**)
1 the top of a mountain or hill **2** a meeting between the leaders of powerful countries

summon *VERB* (**summons, summoning, summoned**)
to summon someone is to order them to come or appear
to summon something up is to find it in yourself • *He summoned up all his courage for the battle ahead.*

summons *NOUN* (**summonses**)
a command to someone to appear in a lawcourt

sun *NOUN*
1 the star round which the earth travels, and from which it gets warmth and light **2** warmth and light from the sun • *Shall we sit in the sun?*

sun *VERB* (**suns, sunning, sunned**)
to sun yourself is to warm yourself in the sun

sunbathe *VERB* (**sunbathes, sunbathing, sunbathed**)
to sunbathe is to sit or lie in the sun to get a suntan

sunburn *NOUN*
sunburn is the redness of the skin someone gets if they are in the sun for too long

> WORD FAMILY
> To be **sunburned** or **sunburnt** is to be affected by sunburn.

sundae *NOUN* (**sundaes**) (*say* sun- day)
a mixture of ice cream with fruit, nuts, and cream

Sunday *NOUN* (**Sundays**)
the first day of the week

sundial *NOUN* (**sundials**)
a device that shows the time by a shadow made by the sun

sunflower *NOUN* (**sunflowers**)
a tall flower with a large round yellow head

sung
past participle of **sing**

sunglasses *PLURAL NOUN*
dark glasses you wear to protect your eyes from strong sunlight

sunk
past tense and past participle of **sink** *VERB*

sunlight *NOUN*
sunlight is light from the sun

> WORD FAMILY
> A **sunlit** place is lit by sunlight.

sunny *ADJECTIVE* (**sunnier, sunniest**)
1 having a lot of sunshine • *It's a sunny day.* **2** full of sunshine • *What a sunny room.*

sunrise *NOUN* (**sunrises**)
sunrise is the time when the sun first appears; dawn • *They left at sunrise.*

sunset *NOUN* (**sunsets**)
sunset is the time when the sun sets

sunshade *NOUN* (**sunshades**)
a parasol or other device to protect people from the sun

sunshine *NOUN*
sunshine is warmth and light that come from the sun

sunspot *NOUN* (**sunspots**)
a dark patch on the sun's surface

sunstroke *NOUN*
sunstroke is an illness caused by being in the sun for too long

suntan *NOUN* (**suntans**)
a brown colour of the skin caused by the sun

> WORD FAMILY
> A **suntanned** person has a suntan.

super *ADJECTIVE*
(*informal*) excellent or very good

super- *PREFIX*
meaning 'over' or 'beyond', as in *superhuman*

superb *ADJECTIVE*
magnificent or excellent
▷ **superbly** *ADVERB* in a superb way • *He played superbly.*

superficial *ADJECTIVE*
1 on the surface • *It's only a superficial cut.* **2** not deep or thorough • *His knowledge of French is fairly superficial.*
▷ **superficially** *ADVERB* in a superficial way

superfluous *ADJECTIVE* (*say* soo- per- floo- us)
not necessary; no longer needed

superintend *VERB* (**superintends, superintending, superintended**)
to superintend someone or something is to be in charge of them

superintendent *NOUN* (**superintendents**)
1 someone who is in charge **2** a police officer above the rank of inspector

superior *ADJECTIVE*
1 higher or more important than someone else **2** better than another person or thing **3** showing that you think you are better than other people • *The mechanical toys were very superior, and looked down upon everyone else; they were full of modern ideas, and pretended they were real.* — Margery Williams, *The Velveteen Rabbit*

> WORD FAMILY
> **Superiority** is being better than something else; **superiority** is also behaviour that shows you think you are better than other people.

superior *NOUN* (**superiors**)
someone of higher rank or position than another person

superlative *ADJECTIVE* (*say* soo- **per**- la- tiv)
of the highest quality

superlative *NOUN* (**superlatives**)
the form of an adjective or adverb that expresses 'most' • *The superlative of 'big' is 'biggest', and the superlative of 'bad' is 'worst'.*

supermarket *NOUN* (**supermarkets**)
a large self-service shop that sells food and other goods

supernatural *ADJECTIVE*
not belonging to the natural world or having a natural explanation

supersonic *ADJECTIVE*
faster than the speed of sound

superstition *NOUN* (**superstitions**)
a belief or action that is not based on reason or evidence • *It is a superstition that 13 is an unlucky number.*

> WORD FAMILY
> Someone is **superstitious** when they believe in superstitions.

supervise *VERB* (**supervises, supervising, supervised**)
to supervise someone or something is to be in charge of them

> WORD FAMILY
> **Supervision** is being in charge of someone or something; a **supervisor** is a person who does this.

supper *NOUN* (**suppers**)
a meal or snack eaten in the evening

supple *ADJECTIVE* (**suppler, supplest**)
able to bend easily; flexible, not stiff
▷ **supplely** *ADVERB* in a supple way
▷ **suppleness** *NOUN* suppleness is being supple

supplement *NOUN* (**supplements**)
1 something added as an extra **2** an extra section added to a book or newspaper

> WORD FAMILY
> Something is **supplementary** when it is added as an extra.

supply *VERB* (**supplies, supplying, supplied**)
1 to supply something is to give or sell it to people who need it **2** to supply someone is to give them what they need

> WORD FAMILY
> A **supplier** is someone who supplies something.

supply *NOUN* (**supplies**)
1 a supply of something is an amount of it kept ready to be used when needed • *We keep a supply of paper in the cupboard.* **2** supplies are food, medicines, or equipment needed by (for example) an army or an expedition • *The truck was carrying medical supplies.*

support *VERB* (**supports, supporting, supported**)
1 to support something is to hold it so that it does not fall down **2** to support someone or something is to give them help or encouragement **3** to support a sports team is to like them and want them to do well • *Which football team do you support?*

support *NOUN* (**supports**)
1 support is the action of supporting • *You can rely on my support.* **2** a support is a person or thing that supports

supporter *NOUN* (**supporters**)
someone who gives support, especially to a sports team

suppose *VERB* (**supposes, supposing, supposed**)
to suppose something is to think that it is likely or true
to be supposed to do something is to have to do it as an order or duty

> WORD FAMILY
> A **supposition** is something that a person thinks is likely or true.

supposedly *ADVERB*
so people believe or think • *They are supposedly millionaires.*

suppress *VERB* (**suppresses, suppressing, suppressed**)
to suppress something is to keep it hidden or stop it happening • *He managed to suppress a smile.*

> WORD FAMILY
> **Suppression** is suppressing something.

supreme *ADJECTIVE*
highest or greatest; most important

> WORD FAMILY
> **Supremacy** is having more power or a higher position than anyone else; to be (for example) **supremely** happy is to be extremely happy.

sure *ADJECTIVE* (**surer**, **surest**)
1 confident about something; having no doubts • *Are you sure you locked the door?* **2** very likely to happen or do something • *Don't worry, we're sure to win.* **3** completely true or known • *One thing is sure: she is not here at the moment.* **4** reliable • *Visiting places is a sure way of getting to know them.*
to make sure of something is to find out that it is true or right

sure *ADVERB*
(*informal*) certainly; of course • *Sure I'll come with you.*
sure enough (*informal*) certainly; in fact • *I said he'd forget, and sure enough he did.*

surely *ADVERB*
1 certainly or definitely • *'They are evil sailors,' said Jip, 'and their ship is very swift. They are surely the pirates of Barbary.'* — Hugh Lofting, *The Story of Doctor Dolittle* **2** it must be true; I feel sure • *Surely I met you last year.*

surf *NOUN*
surf is the white foam of waves breaking on rocks or the seashore

surf *VERB* (**surfs**, **surfing**, **surfed**)
1 to surf is to go surfing **2** to surf the Internet is to browse through it

surface *NOUN* (**surfaces**)
1 the outside of something **2** each of the sides of something, especially the top part

surface *VERB* (**surfaces**, **surfacing**, **surfaced**)
1 to surface is to come up to the surface from under water • *The submarine slowly surfaced.* **2** to surface a road or path is to give it a hard covering layer

surfboard *NOUN* (**surfboards**)
a board used in surfing

surfing *NOUN*
surfing is the sport of balancing yourself on a board that is carried towards the seashore by the waves

> WORD FAMILY
> A **surfer** is someone who goes surfing.

surge *VERB* (**surges**, **surging**, **surged**)
to surge is to move forwards or upwards like waves • *Back and back retreated the water, surging over rocks, leaving the great steamship exposed to its keel and giant propeller.* — Alan Temperley, *The Brave Whale*

surge *NOUN* (**surges**)
a sudden rush forward or upward

surgeon *NOUN* (**surgeons**)
a doctor who deals with disease or injury by cutting or repairing the affected parts of the body

surgery *NOUN* (**surgeries**)
1 a surgery is a building or room where a doctor or dentist sees patients **2** surgery is the time when patients can see a doctor or dentist • *Surgery will close at 6 o'clock today.* **3** surgery is also the work of a surgeon

surgical *ADJECTIVE*
to do with a surgeon or surgery
▷ **surgically** *ADVERB* by means of surgery

surname *NOUN* (**surnames**)
your last name, which you share with other members of your family

surpass *VERB* (**surpasses**, **surpassing**, **surpassed**)
to surpass someone is to do better or be better than them

surplus *NOUN* (**surpluses**)
an amount left over after you have spent or used what you need

surprise *NOUN* (**surprises**)
1 a surprise is something that you did not expect **2** surprise is the feeling you have when something unexpected happens

surprise *VERB* (**surprises**, **surprising**, **surprised**)
1 to surprise someone is to be a surprise to them **2** to surprise someone is also to catch or attack them unexpectedly

surrender *VERB* (**surrenders**, **surrendering**, **surrendered**)
1 to surrender to someone is to stop fighting them and admit that you have been beaten **2** to surrender something to someone is to give it over to them

surrender *NOUN*
when someone surrenders

surround *VERB* (**surrounds**, **surrounding**, **surrounded**)
to surround someone or something is to be or come all round them

surroundings *PLURAL NOUN*
the things or conditions around a person or place

survey *NOUN* (**surveys**) (*say* ser- vay)
1 a general look at a topic or activity **2** a detailed inspection or examination of a building or area

survey *VERB* (**surveys**, **surveying**, **surveyed**) (*say* ser- vay)
to survey something is to inspect it or make a survey of it

surveyor *NOUN* (**surveyors**)
someone whose job is to survey buildings and land

survive *VERB* (**survives**, **surviving**, **survived**)
1 to survive is to stay alive **2** to survive an accident or disaster is to remain alive in spite of it • *Only two people survived the car crash.* **3** to survive someone is to continue living after they have died

> WORD FAMILY
> **Survival** is staying alive; a **survivor** is someone who survives, especially after an accident or disaster.

suspect *VERB* (**suspects**, **suspecting**, **suspected**) (*say* su- **spekt**)
1 to suspect something unwelcome is to think that it is likely or possible **2** to suspect someone is to think that they have done something wrong or are not to be trusted

suspect *NOUN* (**suspects**) (*say* **sus**- pekt)
someone who is thought to have done something wrong

suspend *VERB* (**suspends**, **suspending**, **suspended**)
1 to suspend something that is happening is to stop it for a time **2** to suspend someone is to take away their job or position for a time • *He was suspended from the team for bad behaviour.* **3** to suspend something is to hang it up

suspense *NOUN*
suspense is an anxious or uncertain feeling you have while you are waiting for something to happen or for news about something • *Don't keep us in suspense—who won?*

suspension *NOUN* (**suspensions**)
1 suspension is suspending something or someone **2** a vehicle's suspension is the set of springs and other devices that make the ride more comfortable

suspension bridge *NOUN* (**suspension bridges**)
a bridge supported by cables

suspicion *NOUN* (**suspicions**)
1 suspicion is feeling that someone has done something wrong or cannot be trusted **2** a suspicion is a slight or uncertain feeling about something or someone

suspicious *ADJECTIVE*
1 making you suspect someone or something • *There are suspicious footprints along the path.* **2** suspecting someone or something • *I'm suspicious about what happened.*
▷ **suspiciously** *ADVERB* in a suspicious way

sustain *VERB* (**sustains**, **sustaining**, **sustained**)
1 to sustain something is to keep it going • *It's difficult to sustain such an effort.* **2** to sustain someone is to give them energy or strength • *We'd packed sandwiches to sustain us on our walk.* **3** to sustain an injury is to be injured

swagger *VERB* (**swaggers**, **swaggering**, **swaggered**)
to walk or behave in a conceited way • *Mr. Toad, arrayed in goggles, cap, gaiters, and enormous overcoat, came swaggering down the steps.* — Kenneth Grahame, *The Wind in the Willows*

swallow [1] *VERB* (**swallows**, **swallowing**, **swallowed**)
to swallow something is to make it go down your throat
to find something hard to swallow is to find it difficult to believe
to swallow something up is to cover or hide it

swallow [2] *NOUN* (**swallows**)
a small bird with a forked tail and pointed wings

swam
past tense of **swim** *VERB*

swamp *VERB* (**swamps**, **swamping**, **swamped**)
1 to swamp something is to flood it **2** to be swamped is to be overwhelmed with a large number of things • *They have been swamped with complaints.*

swamp *NOUN* (**swamps**)
a marsh

> WORD FAMILY
> A **swampy** place is full of swamps.

swan *NOUN* (**swans**)
a large white water bird with a long neck and powerful wings

swank *VERB* (**swanks**, **swanking**, **swanked**)
(*informal*) to swank is to swagger or boast

swap *VERB* (**swaps**, **swapping**, **swapped**)
(*informal*) to swap something is to exchange one thing for another • *After the game they swapped jerseys.*

swap *NOUN* (**swaps**)
1 an act of swapping • *Let's do a swap.* **2** something you swap for something else

swarm *NOUN* (**swarms**)
a large number of insects flying or moving about together

swarm *VERB* (**swarms**, **swarming**, **swarmed**)
1 bees or other insects swarm when they move in a swarm **2** to be swarming is to be crowded with people • *The town is swarming with tourists in summer.*

swastika *NOUN* (**swastikas**) (*say* **swos**- ti- ka)
a sign formed by a cross with its ends bent at right angles, used as a symbol by the Nazis in Germany

swat *VERB* (**swats**, **swatting**, **swatted**) (*say* swot)
to swat a fly or other insect is to hit or crush it

> WORD FAMILY
> A **swatter** is a device for swatting insects.

sway *VERB* (**sways**, **swaying**, **swayed**)
to sway is to move gently from side to side

swear *VERB* (**swears, swearing, swore, sworn**)
1 to swear is to make a solemn promise • *She swore to tell the truth.* **2** to swear someone to secrecy is to make them promise not to tell anyone **3** to swear is also to use very rude or offensive words
to swear by something is to have a lot of confidence in it

swear word *NOUN* (**swear words**)
a word that is very rude or offensive, used especially by someone who is very angry

sweat *VERB* (**sweats, sweating, sweated**) (*say* swet)
you sweat when you give off moisture through the pores of your skin, especially when you are hot or doing exercise

sweat *NOUN* (*say* swet)
sweat is moisture that you give off when you sweat

> WORD FAMILY
> To be **sweaty** is to be covered or damp with sweat.

sweater *NOUN* (**sweaters**) (*say* swet- er)
a jersey or pullover

sweatshirt *NOUN* (**sweatshirts**)
a thick cotton jersey

swede *NOUN* (**swedes**)
a large kind of turnip with purple skin and yellow flesh

sweep *VERB* (**sweeps, sweeping, swept**)
1 to sweep a room or floor is to clean or clear it with a broom or brush • *He swept the floor.* **2** to sweep something away is to move or change it quickly • *The flood has swept away the bridge.* **3** to sweep somewhere is to go there swiftly or proudly • *She swept out of the room.*

sweep *NOUN* (**sweeps**)
1 a sweeping action or movement • *Give this room a sweep.* **2** a chimney sweep

sweeper *NOUN* (**sweepers**)
1 a machine for sweeping floors **2** (*in football*) a defensive player at the back

sweet *ADJECTIVE* (**sweeter, sweetest**)
1 tasting of sugar or honey **2** very pleasant • *There was a sweet smell in the room.* **3** charming or delightful • *What a sweet little cottage.*
▷ **sweetly** *ADVERB* in a very pleasant way • *She smiled sweetly at him.*
▷ **sweetness** *NOUN* sweetness is tasting sweet

sweet *NOUN* (**sweets**)
1 a small shaped piece of sweet food made of sugar or chocolate **2** a pudding; the sweet course in a meal

sweetcorn *NOUN*
sweetcorn is the juicy yellow seeds of maize

sweeten *VERB* (**sweetens, sweetening, sweetened**)
to sweeten something is to make it sweet

> WORD FAMILY
> A **sweetener** is something used to make food or drink taste sweeter.

sweetheart *NOUN* (**sweethearts**)
a person you love very much

sweet pea *NOUN* (**sweet peas**)
a climbing plant with sweet-smelling flowers

swell *VERB* (**swells, swelling, swelled, swollen** or **swelled**)
to swell is to get bigger or louder

> WORD FAMILY
> Something that has swelled a lot is **swollen** • *My wrist is still very swollen where I bumped it.*

swell *NOUN* (**swells**)
the rise and fall of the sea's surface

swelling *NOUN* (**swellings**)
a swollen place on your body

swelter *VERB* (**swelters, sweltering, sweltered**)
to swelter is to be uncomfortably hot

swept
past tense and past participle of **sweep** *VERB*

swerve *VERB* (**swerves, swerving, swerved**)
to swerve is to move suddenly to one side • *The car swerved to avoid the cyclist.*

swerve *NOUN* (**swerves**)
a swerving movement

swift *ADJECTIVE* (**swifter, swiftest**)
quick; moving quickly and easily
▷ **swiftly** *ADVERB* quickly
▷ **swiftness** *NOUN* swiftness is being swift

swift *NOUN* (**swifts**)
a small bird rather like a swallow

swill *VERB* (**swills, swilling, swilled**)
to swill something is to rinse or flush it

swill *NOUN*
swill is a sloppy mixture of waste food given to pigs

swim *VERB* (**swims, swimming, swam, swum**)
1 to swim is to move yourself through the water or to be in the water for pleasure **2** to swim a stretch of water is to cross it by swimming • *She has swum the Channel.* **3** to be swimming in liquid or with liquid is to be covered in it or full of it • *Their eyes were swimming with tears.* **4** your head swims when you feel dizzy

swim *NOUN* (**swims**)
a spell of swimming • *Let's go for a swim.*

swimmer *NOUN* (**swimmers**)
someone who swims • *Are you a good swimmer?*

swimming bath or **swimming pool** *NOUN* (**swimming baths** or **swimming pools**)
a specially built pool with water for people to swim in

swimming costume *NOUN* (**swimming costumes**)
a piece of clothing for swimming in

swimsuit *NOUN* (**swimsuits**)
a one-piece swimming costume

swindle *VERB* (**swindles, swindling, swindled**)
to swindle someone is to get money or goods from them dishonestly

> WORD FAMILY
> A **swindler** is someone who swindles people.

swindle *NOUN* (**swindles**)
a trick to swindle someone

swine *NOUN* (**swine** or **swines**)
1 a pig **2** (*informal*) an unpleasant person or a difficult thing

swing *VERB* (**swings, swinging, swung**)
1 to swing is to move to and fro or in a curve **2** to swing something is to turn it quickly or suddenly • *He swung the car round to avoid the bus.*

swing *NOUN* (**swings**)
1 a swinging movement • *He took a swing at the ball.* **2** a seat hung on chains or ropes so that it can move backwards and forwards **3** the amount that votes or opinions change from one side to the other
to be in full swing is to be full of activity or working fully

swipe *VERB* (**swipes, swiping, swiped**)
1 to swipe someone or something is to give them a hard hit **2** (*informal*) to swipe something is to steal it **3** to swipe a credit card is to pass it through a special reading device when you make a payment

swipe *NOUN* (**swipes**)
a hard hit

swirl *VERB* (**swirls, swirling, swirled**)
to swirl is to move around quickly in circles; to swirl something is to make it do this • *The water swirled down the plug hole.*

swirl *NOUN* (**swirls**)
a swirling movement

swish *VERB* (**swishes, swishing, swished**)
to swish is to make a hissing or rustling sound

swish *NOUN* (**swishes**)
a swishing sound

Swiss roll *NOUN* (**Swiss rolls**)
a thin sponge cake spread with jam or cream and rolled up

switch *NOUN* (**switches**)
1 a device that you press or turn to start or stop something working, especially by electricity **2** a sudden change of opinion or methods

switch *VERB* (**switches, switching, switched**)
1 to switch a device on or off is to use a switch to make it work or stop working **2** to switch something is to change it suddenly

switchboard *NOUN* (**switchboards**)
a panel with switches for connecting telephone lines

swivel *VERB* (**swivels, swivelling, swivelled**)
to swivel is to turn round

swollen
past participle of **swell** *VERB*

swoon *VERB* (**swoons, swooning, swooned**)
(*old use*) to swoon is to faint from fear or weakness

swoop *VERB* (**swoops, swooping, swooped**)
1 to swoop is to dive or come down suddenly • *The eagle swooped down on its prey.* **2** to swoop is also to make a sudden attack or raid

swoop *NOUN* (**swoops**)
a sudden dive or attack • *At last with a glorious swoop like the dive of a wild sea-bird, the witch and her broomstick came down on the Hurricane Mountains.* — Ursula Moray Williams, *Gobbolino the Witch's Cat*

swop *VERB* (**swops, swopping, swopped**)
(*informal*) to swap

sword *NOUN* (**swords**) (*say* sord)
a weapon with a long pointed blade fixed in a handle

swore
past tense of **swear**

sworn
past participle of **swear**

swot *VERB* (**swots, swotting, swotted**)
(*informal*) to swot is to study hard

swot *NOUN* (**swots**)
(*informal*) someone who swots

swum
past participle of **swim** *VERB*

swung
past tense and past participle of **swing** *VERB*

sycamore *NOUN* (**sycamores**)
a tall tree with winged seeds

syllable *NOUN* (**syllables**)
a word or part of a word that has one separate sound when you say it • *'Cat' has one syllable, 'el-e-phant' has three syllables.*
▷ **syllabic** *ADJECTIVE* to do with syllables

syllabus *NOUN* (**syllabuses**) (*say* sil- a- bus)
a list of things to be studied by a class or for an examination

symbol *NOUN* (**symbols**)
1 a mark or sign with a special meaning **2** a thing that stands for something • *The crescent is a symbol of Islam.*

symbolic or **symbolical** *ADJECTIVE*
acting as a symbol of something
▷ **symbolically** *ADVERB* in a symbolic way

symbolism *NOUN*
symbolism is the use of symbols to stand for something

symbolize *VERB* (**symbolizes, symbolizing, symbolized**)
to symbolize something is to be a symbol of it • *Red symbolizes danger.*

symmetrical *ADJECTIVE* (*say* sim- **et**- rik- al)
able to be divided into two halves which are exactly the same but the opposite way round • *Wheels and butterflies are symmetrical.*
▷ **symmetrically** *ADVERB* in a symmetrical way

symmetry *NOUN*
symmetry is the quality of being symmetrical

sympathetic *ADJECTIVE*
feeling sympathy or understanding for someone

> WORD FAMILY
> To do something **sympathetically** is to do it in a way that shows you feel sympathy for someone • *She smiled at me sympathetically.*

sympathize *VERB* (**sympathizes, sympathizing, sympathized**)
to sympathize with someone is to show or feel sympathy for them

sympathy *NOUN* (**sympathies**)
1 sympathy is the sharing or understanding of other people's feelings or opinions **2** sympathy is also the feeling of being sorry for someone's unhappiness or suffering

symphony *NOUN* (**symphonies**)
a long piece of music for an orchestra
▷ **symphonic** *ADJECTIVE* to do with a symphony

symptom *NOUN* (**symptoms**)
something wrong with you that is a sign that you have an illness • *Red spots are a symptom of measles.*
▷ **symptomatic** *ADJECTIVE* being a sign of an illness

synagogue *NOUN* (**synagogues**) (*say* **sin**- a- gog)
a building where Jews meet to worship

synchronize *VERB* (**synchronizes, synchronizing, synchronized**) (*say* **sink**- ro- nyz)
1 to synchronize things is to make them happen at the same time **2** to synchronize watches or clocks is to set them to show the same time
▷ **synchronization** *NOUN* synchronization is making things happen at the same time

syncopated *ADJECTIVE* (*say* **sink**- o- payt- id)
a piece of music is syncopated when the strong beats are played weak and the weak beats are played strong

synonym *NOUN* (**synonyms**) (*say* **sin**- o- nim)
a word that means the same or nearly the same as another word, such as *big* and *large*

> WORD FAMILY
> Two words are **synonymous** when they have the same, or nearly the same, meaning.

> SYNONYMS
> Synonyms are words that have the same or nearly the same meaning as one another. For example, synonyms of *big* include *large, huge, enormous, gigantic, colossal,* and *vast.* Synonyms of *smile* include *grin* and *beam*. In your writing try using new and different words rather than using the same words over and over again. This will make your writing more varied, interesting, and lively. You find synonyms listed in a thesaurus. Look also at the panel on **Antonyms**.

synthesis *NOUN* (**syntheses**)
synthesis is when different things or parts are combined into a whole thing or system

synthesize *VERB* (**synthesizes, synthesizing, synthesized**)
to synthesize something is to make it by combining parts

synthesizer *NOUN* (**synthesizers**)
an electronic musical instrument that can make many different sounds

synthetic *ADJECTIVE*
artificially made; not natural
▷ **synthetically** *ADVERB* in a synthetic way

syringe *NOUN* (**syringes**)
a device for sucking in a liquid and squirting it out

syrup *NOUN* (**syrups**)
a thick sweet liquid

> WORD FAMILY
> Something is **syrupy** when it is thick and sticky like syrup.

system *NOUN* (**systems**)
1 a set of parts or things or ideas that work together • *the digestive system* • *the Solar System* **2** a well-organized way of doing something • *We have a new system for taking books out of the library.*

systematic *ADJECTIVE*
using a system; careful and well planned
▷ **systematically** *ADVERB* in a systematic way

Tt

tab *NOUN* (**tabs**)
a small strip or flap that sticks out

tabby *NOUN* (**tabbies**)
a grey or brown cat with dark streaks in its fur

a b c d e f g h i j k l m n o p q r s **t** u v w x y z

table *NOUN* (**tables**)
1 a piece of furniture with a flat top supported on legs **2** a list of facts or numbers arranged in rows and columns **3** a list of the results of multiplying a number by other numbers • *Do you know your multiplication tables?*

tablecloth *NOUN* (**tablecloths**)
a cloth for covering a table

tablespoon *NOUN* (**tablespoons**)
a large spoon used for serving food

tablespoonful *NOUN* (**tablespoonfuls**)
as much as a tablespoon will hold

tablet *NOUN* (**tablets**)
1 a pill **2** a lump of soap **3** a flat piece of stone or wood with words carved or written on it

table tennis *NOUN*
table tennis is a game played on a table divided in the middle by a net, over which you hit a small ball with bats

tack[1] *NOUN* (**tacks**)
1 a short nail with a flat top
to change tack or **to try a different tack** is to find a different way of doing something

tack *VERB* (**tacks, tacking, tacked**)
1 to tack something is to nail it with tacks **2** to tack material is to sew it together quickly with long stitches **3** to tack is to sail a zigzag course to get full benefit from the wind
to tack something on is to add it as an extra

tack[2] *NOUN*
tack is equipment for horses, such as harnesses and saddles

tackle *VERB* (**tackles, tackling, tackled**)
1 to tackle a task is to start doing it **2** in football or hockey, to tackle a player is to try to get the ball from them or (in rugby) to bring them to the ground

tackle *NOUN* (**tackles**)
1 tackle is equipment, especially for fishing **2** a tackle is when you tackle someone in football or rugby or hockey

tacky *ADJECTIVE* (**tackier, tackiest**)
1 sticky or not quite dry • *The paint is still tacky.*
2 (*informal*) cheaply made and showing poor taste

tact *NOUN*
tact is skill in not offending or upsetting people

tactful *ADJECTIVE*
careful not to offend or upset people by saying something unkind

> WORD FAMILY
> You say something **tactfully** when you say it in a way that avoids offending or upsetting someone.

tactics *PLURAL NOUN*
someone's tactics are the methods they use to achieve or win something

> WORD FAMILY
> A **tactical** action is something you do to help you achieve or win something; to do something **tactically** is to do it as a tactic.

tactless *ADJECTIVE*
likely to offend or upset people; having no tact

> WORD FAMILY
> You say something **tactlessly** when you say it in a way that offends or upsets someone.

tadpole *NOUN* (**tadpoles**)
a young frog or toad at a stage when it has an oval head and a long tail and lives in water

tag[1] *NOUN* (**tags**)
1 a label tied or stuck to something **2** the metal or plastic part at the end of a shoelace

tag *VERB* (**tags, tagging, tagged**)
to tag something is to fix a tag or label on it
to tag along is to go along with other people
to tag something on is to add it as something extra

tag[2] *NOUN*
tag is a game in which one person chases the others

tail *NOUN* (**tails**)
1 the part that sticks out from the rear end of the body of an animal or bird **2** the part at the end or rear of something, such as an aircraft **3** the side of a coin opposite the head

tail *VERB* (**tails, tailing, tailed**)
to tail someone is to follow them without them seeing you
to tail off is to become less and less or smaller and smaller

tailback *NOUN* (**tailbacks**)
a long line of traffic stretching back from an obstruction

tailless *ADJECTIVE*
not having a tail

tailor *NOUN* (**tailors**)
someone whose job is to make clothes

take *VERB* (**takes, taking, took, taken**)
This word has many meanings, depending on the words that go with it: **1** to take something or someone is to get hold of them or bring them into your possession • *He took a cake from the plate.* • *Who do you think took the money?* • *They took many prisoners.* **2** to take someone or something somewhere is to carry or drive or convey them there • *Shall I take you to the station?* • *Take this parcel to the post.* **3** to take something useful or pleasant is to make use of it • *Do you take sugar?* • *You must take a holiday this year.* • *Do take a seat.* **4** to take someone or something is to need them for a purpose • *It will take two people to lift the table.* **5** to take a piece of information is to make a note of

it • *Take their names and addresses.* **6** to take a class for a subject is to teach it to them • *Who takes you for English?* **7** to take one number from another is to subtract it • *Take two from ten and you get eight.* **8** to take an examination is to do it • *I'm taking my maths exam today.* **9** to take a joke is to accept it well**1** to take a photograph or picture is to produce it with a camera
I take it I understand or assume • *I take it that you agree.*
to take off is to leave the ground at the beginning of a flight
to take part in something is to share in doing it
to take place is to happen
to take someone in is to fool or deceive them
to take something off is to remove it
to take something over is to take control of it
to take something up is to start doing it • *I've taken up yoga.*

takeaway *NOUN* (**takeaways**)
1 a place that sells cooked food for customers to take away **2** a meal from a takeaway

takings *PLURAL NOUN*
money that has been received, especially by a shopkeeper

talcum powder or **talc** *NOUN*
talcum powder is a perfumed powder put on the skin to dry it or make it smell pleasant

tale *NOUN* (**tales**)
a story

talent *NOUN* (**talents**)
a natural ability or skill to do something well • *She has a talent for singing.*

> WORD FAMILY
> Someone is **talented** when they have the ability or skill to do something well.

talk *VERB* (**talks, talking, talked**)
to talk is to speak or have a conversation

> WORD FAMILY
> A **talker** is someone who talks, especially someone who talks a lot.

talk *NOUN* (**talks**)
1 a conversation or discussion **2** a lecture

talkative *ADJECTIVE*
someone is talkative when they talk a lot

tall *ADJECTIVE* (**taller, tallest**)
1 higher than the average • *They sat under a tall tree.* **2** measured from the bottom to the top • *The bookcase is two metres tall.*
a tall story is a story that is hard to believe

tally *VERB* (**tallies, tallying, tallied**)
one thing tallies with another when they match or agree • *Do your figures tally with mine?* • *Their answers don't tally.*

Talmud *NOUN*
a collection of writings on Jewish religious law

talon *NOUN* (**talons**)
a strong claw, especially on a bird of prey

tambourine *NOUN* (**tambourines**)
a round musical instrument like a small drum with metal discs fixed around the edge so that it jingles when you shake it or hit it

tame *ADJECTIVE* (**tamer, tamest**)
1 a tame animal is one that is gentle and not afraid of people **2** something is tame when it is dull or uninteresting
▷ **tamely** *ADVERB* in a tame or gentle way
▷ **tameness** *NOUN* tameness is being tame

tame *VERB* (**tames, taming, tamed**)
to tame a wild animal is to make it used to being with people

> WORD FAMILY
> A **tamer** is someone who tames wild animals. • *a lion-tamer*

tamper *VERB* (**tampers, tampering, tampered**)
to tamper with something is to interfere with it or change it so that it will not work properly

tampon *NOUN* (**tampons**)
a plug of soft material that a woman puts into her vagina to absorb the blood during her period

tan *NOUN* (**tans**)
1 a tan is a suntan **2** tan is a yellowish-brown colour

tan *VERB* (**tans, tanning, tanned**)
1 to tan your skin is to make it brown with a suntan **2** to tan the skin of a dead animal is to make it into leather

tandem *NOUN* (**tandems**)
a bicycle for two riders, one behind the other

tang *NOUN*
a strong flavour or smell

tangent *NOUN* (**tangents**) (*say* tan-jent)
a straight line that touches the outside of a curve or circle

tangerine *NOUN* (**tangerines**) (*say* tan-jer-een)
a kind of small orange

tangle *VERB* (**tangles, tangling, tangled**)
1 you tangle something, or it tangles, when it becomes twisted or muddled • *My fishing line has tangled.* **2** something is tangled up when it is twisted together in an untidy mess • *These computer cables are all tangled up.*

tangle *NOUN* (**tangles**)
a twisted or muddled mass of (for example) hair or wire

tank *NOUN* (**tanks**)
1 a large container for a liquid or gas **2** a heavy armoured vehicle used in war

tanka *NOUN* (**tankas**)
a Japanese short poem, with five lines and 31 syllables in the pattern 5,7,5,7,7

tankard *NOUN* (**tankards**)
a large heavy mug for drinking from

tanker *NOUN* (**tankers**)
1 a large ship for carrying oil **2** a large lorry for carrying a liquid

tanner *NOUN* (**tanners**)
someone who tans animal skins to make leather

> WORD FAMILY
> A **tannery** is a place where animal hides are tanned into leather.

tantalize *VERB* (**tantalizes**, **tantalizing**, **tantalized**)
to tantalize someone is to torment them by showing them something good that they cannot have

tantrum *NOUN* (**tantrums**)
an outburst of bad temper

tap[1] *NOUN* (**taps**)
a device for letting out liquid or gas in a controlled flow

tap *VERB* (**taps**, **tapping**, **tapped**)
1 to tap a source of information or supplies is to make use of it **2** to tap a telephone is to fix a device to it so that you can hear someone else's conversation

tap[2] *NOUN* (**taps**)
1 a tap is a quick light hit, or the sound it makes •*I gave him a tap on the shoulder.* **2** tap is tapdancing

tap *VERB* (**taps**, **tapping**, **tapped**)
to tap someone or something is to give them a tap or gentle hit •*I tried tapping on the window.*

tap-dancing *NOUN*
tap-dancing is dancing in hard shoes that make sharp tapping sounds on the floor

> WORD FAMILY
> A **tap-dance** is a dance of this kind; someone who does tap-dancing is a **tap-dancer**.

tape *NOUN* (**tapes**)
1 tape is soft material such as cloth or paper or plastic in a thin strip; a tape is a piece of this **2** tape is also a narrow plastic strip coated with a magnetic substance and used for making recordings; a tape is a cassette •*a video tape*

tape *VERB* (**tapes**, **taping**, **taped**)
1 to tape something is to fasten it by sticking it or tying it with tape **2** to tape music or sound or a television programme is to record it on magnetic tape
to get or **have something taped** (*informal*) is to know or understand it, or be able to deal with it

tape-measure *NOUN* (**tape-measures**)
a long strip marked in centimetres or inches for measuring things

taper *VERB* (**tapers**, **tapering**, **tapered**)
something tapers when it gets narrower towards one end

taper *NOUN* (**tapers**)
a piece of string thinly coated with wax, for lighting things

tape recorder *NOUN* (**tape recorders**)
a machine for recording music or sound on magnetic tape and playing it back

> WORD FAMILY
> A **tape recording** is a recording made with magnetic tape.

tapestry *NOUN* (**tapestries**) (*say* tap- i- stree)
a piece of strong cloth with pictures or patterns woven or embroidered on it

tapeworm *NOUN* (**tapeworms**)
a long flat worm that can live as a parasite in the intestines of people and animals

tapioca *NOUN*
tapioca is a starchy substance consisting of white grains used for making milk puddings

tar *NOUN*
tar is a thick black sticky liquid made from coal or wood and used in making roads

tar *VERB* (**tars**, **tarring**, **tarred**)
to tar something is to cover it with tar

tarantula *NOUN* (**tarantulas**) (*say* ta- **ran**- tew- la)
a large hairy poisonous spider found in warm countries

target *NOUN* (**targets**)
something that you aim at and try to hit or reach

target *VERB* (**targets**, **targeting**, **targeted**)
to target something or someone is to aim at them

tarmac *NOUN*
1 tarmac is a mixture of tar and broken stone, used for making a hard surface on roads and paths and open areas. Tarmac is short for *tarmacadam* **2** the tarmac is an area covered with tarmac, especially on an airfield •*The plane was standing on the tarmac, waiting to take off.*

tarnish *VERB* (**tarnishes**, **tarnishing**, **tarnished**)
1 metal tarnishes when it becomes stained and less shiny **2** to tarnish something is to spoil it •*The scandal tarnished his reputation.*

tarpaulin *NOUN* (**tarpaulins**)
a large sheet of waterproof canvas

tart[1] *NOUN* (**tarts**)
a pie containing fruit or jam

tart[2] *ADJECTIVE* (**tarter**, **tartest**)
sour-tasting •*The apples are tart.*

tartan *NOUN* (**tartans**)
a woollen cloth with a pattern of squares and stripes in different colours, especially as worn in the Scottish Highlands

task *NOUN* (**tasks**)
a piece of work that needs to be done
to take someone to task is to tell them off for doing something wrong

task force *NOUN* (**task forces**)
a group of people, especially soldiers, given a special task to do

tassel *NOUN* (**tassels**)
a bundle of threads tied together at the top and used to decorate something

taste *VERB* (**tastes, tasting, tasted**)
1 to taste food or drink is to eat or drink a small amount to see what it is like **2** food or drink tastes a certain way when it has a particular flavour • *The milk tastes sour.*

taste *NOUN* (**tastes**)
1 the taste of something is the flavour it has when you taste it • *The milk has a strange taste.* **2** taste is the ability to taste things **3** your tastes are the things you like or prefer • *What are your tastes in music?* **4** you show taste when you are able to choose things that are of good quality or go together well • *The way she dresses shows good taste.* **5** a taste is a tiny amount of food • *Can I have a taste of your pudding?*

tasteful *ADJECTIVE*
showing good taste
▷ **tastefully** *ADVERB* in a tasteful way

tasteless *ADJECTIVE*
showing poor taste
▷ **tastelessly** *ADVERB* in a tasteless way

tasty *ADJECTIVE* (**tastier, tastiest**)
tasty food has a strong pleasant taste

tattered *ADJECTIVE*
tattered clothing is badly torn and ragged

tatters *PLURAL NOUN*
in tatters badly torn

tattoo[1] *NOUN* (**tattoos**)
a picture or pattern made on someone's skin with a needle and dye

tattoo *VERB* (**tattoos, tattooing, tattooed**)
someone is tattooed when they have a tattoo on their skin

tattoo[2] *NOUN* (**tattoos**)
1 a drumming sound • *He beat a tattoo on the table with his fingers.* **2** an outdoor entertainment including military music and marching

tatty *ADJECTIVE* (**tattier, tattiest**)
shabby and worn • *The Viking Hotel was beginning to look a bit tatty. What it really needed was a good coat of paint.* — Jeremy Strong, *Viking at School*

taught
past tense and past participle of **teach**

taunt *VERB* (**taunts, taunting, taunted**)
to taunt someone is to jeer at them or insult them • *They taunted. They teased him. / They yelled, 'How Absurd!' / 'Old Horton the Elephant thinks he's a bird!'* — Dr Seuss, *Horton Hatches the Egg*

taunt *NOUN* (**taunts**)
an insulting or mocking remark

taut *ADJECTIVE* (**tauter, tautest**)
stretched tightly
▷ **tautly** *ADVERB* in a taut way
▷ **tautness** *NOUN* tautness is being taut

tavern *NOUN* (**taverns**)
(*old use*) an inn or public house

tawny *ADJECTIVE* (**tawnier, tawniest**)
brownish-yellow

tax *NOUN* (**taxes**)
an amount of money that people and businesses have to pay to the government for public use

tax *VERB* (**taxes, taxing, taxed**)
1 to tax someone is to charge them a tax **2** to tax goods or someone's income is to put a tax on them • *The government taxes alcohol, tobacco, and petrol.*

> WORD FAMILY
> **Taxable** income or profit is money that you have to pay tax on; **taxation** is money that has to be paid as taxes.

taxi *NOUN* (**taxis**)
a car with a driver which you can hire for journeys, with a meter for recording the distance

taxi *VERB* (**taxis, taxiing, taxied**)
an aircraft taxis when it moves slowly along the ground before taking off or after landing

taxpayer *NOUN* (**taxpayers**)
someone who pays taxes

tea *NOUN* (**teas**)
1 tea is a drink made by pouring hot water on the dried leaves of an evergreen shrub **2** tea is also the dried leaves of this shrub **3** tea is also a meal eaten in the late afternoon or early evening

teabag *NOUN* (**teabags**)
a small bag of tea for making tea in a cup

teacake *NOUN* (**teacakes**)
a kind of bun usually eaten toasted and buttered

teach *VERB* (**teaches, teaching, taught**)
1 to teach someone is to show them how to do something or give them knowledge about something **2** to teach a subject is to give lessons in it • *She taught us history last year.*

teacher *NOUN* (**teachers**)
someone who teaches people at a school or college

tea cloth or **tea towel** *NOUN* (**tea cloths** or **tea towels**)
a cloth you use for drying washed dishes and cutlery

teacup *NOUN* (**teacups**)
a cup for drinking tea

teak *NOUN*
teak is a hard strong wood from Asia

a b c d e f g h i j k l m n o p q r s **t** u v w x y z

team *NOUN* (**teams**)
1 a set of players who form one side in a game or sport **2** a group of people who work together

> SPELLING
> Take care not to confuse **team** with **teem**, as in *teeming with rain.*

teapot *NOUN* (**teapots**)
a pot with a handle and spout, for making and pouring out tea

tear[1] *VERB* (**tears, tearing, tore, torn**) (*say* tair)
1 to tear something is to make a split in it or to pull it apart **2** to tear something is also to pull or remove it with force • *He tore the picture off the wall.* **3** to tear is to become torn • *Paper tears easily.* **4** to tear somewhere is to move very quickly there • *He tore down the street.*

tear *NOUN* (*say* tair) (**tears**)
a hole or split made by tearing something

tear[2] *NOUN* (**tears**) (*say* teer)
a drop of water that comes from your eye when you cry

tearful *ADJECTIVE*
in tears; crying easily • *He suddenly became very tearful.* • *Signora Strega-Borgia bid the children a tearful farewell and set off to complete her degree in advanced witchcraft.* — Debi Gliori, *Pure Dead Magic*
▷ **tearfully** *ADVERB* in a tearful way

tear gas *NOUN*
tear gas is a gas that makes people's eyes water painfully

tease *VERB* (**teases, teasing, teased**)
to tease someone is to make fun of them and say things to make them annoyed

teaspoon *NOUN* (**teaspoons**)
a small spoon for stirring tea

teaspoonful *NOUN* (**teaspoonfuls**)
as much as a teaspoon will hold

teat *NOUN* (**teats**)
1 a nipple through which a baby drinks milk **2** the cap of a baby's feeding bottle

tech *NOUN* (**techs**)
(*informal*) a technical college

technical *ADJECTIVE*
1 to do with technology or the way things work
2 using the words that only people who know a lot about a subject will understand • *This article is full of technical terms.*

> WORD FAMILY
> Something is **technically** possible when the technology exists to do it; something is **technically** allowed when it is allowed according to the rules.

technical college *NOUN* (**technical colleges**)
a college where technical subjects are taught

technicality *NOUN* (**technicalities**)
a small detail of the law or a process

technician *NOUN* (**technicians**)
someone whose job is to look after scientific equipment and do practical work in a laboratory

technique *NOUN* (**techniques**) (*say* tek- **neek**)
a particular method of doing something skilfully

technology *NOUN* (**technologies**)
technology is the study of machinery and the way things work
▷ **technological** *ADJECTIVE* to do with technology • *technological developments*

teddy bear *NOUN* (**teddy bears**)
a soft furry toy bear

> **Teddy** is a shortened form of the name *Theodore* and comes from the name of Theodore Roosevelt, who was the American president at the end of the 19th century and was a keen hunter of bears.

tedious *ADJECTIVE* (*say* **tee**- di- us)
annoyingly slow or long; boring
▷ **tediously** *ADVERB* in a tedious way
▷ **tediousness** *NOUN* tediousness is being tedious

tedium *NOUN*
tedium is a dull or boring time or experience • *He hated the tedium of visiting his grandparents.*

teem *VERB* (**teems, teeming, teemed**)
1 to teem with something is to be full of it • *The river was teeming with fish.* **2** to teem, or teem down, is to rain very hard

> SPELLING
> Take care not to confuse **teem** with **team**, as in *football team.*

teenage or **teenaged** *ADJECTIVE*
in your teens; to do with teenagers

teenager *NOUN* (**teenagers**)
a person in their teens

teens *PLURAL NOUN*
the time of your life between the ages of 13 and 19 • *They started playing chess in their teens.*

teeth
plural of **tooth**

teetotal *ADJECTIVE*
never drinking alcoholic drink

> WORD FAMILY
> A **teetotaller** is someone who is teetotal.

telecommunications *PLURAL NOUN*
telecommunications is sending news and information over long distances by telephone, telegraph, fax, television, and radio

telegram *NOUN* (**telegrams**)
a message sent by telegraph

telegraph *NOUN* (**telegraphs**)
telegraph is a way of sending messages by using electric current along wires or by radio
▷ **telegraphic** *ADJECTIVE* using telegraph
▷ **telegraphy** *NOUN* telegraphy is the system of sending messages by telegraph

telepathy *NOUN* (*say* til- **ep**- a- thee)
telepathy is communication of thoughts from one person's mind to another without speaking, writing, or gestures

> WORD FAMILY
> Someone is **telepathic** when they can communicate by telepathy.

telephone *NOUN* (**telephones**)
a device using electric wires or radio to enable someone to speak to another person who is some distance away

telephone *VERB* (**telephones**, **telephoning**, **telephoned**)
to telephone someone is to speak to them by telephone

telephonist *NOUN* (**telephonists**) (*say* til- **ef**- on- ist)
someone who operates a telephone switchboard

telescope *NOUN* (**telescopes**)
a tube with lenses at each end, through which you can see distant objects more clearly because they look closer and larger

telescopic *ADJECTIVE*
1 to do with telescopes **2** folding into itself like a portable telescope

teletext *NOUN*
teletext is a system for displaying news and information on a television screen

televise *VERB* (**televises**, **televising**, **televised**)
to televise an event is to film it and put on television

television *NOUN* (**televisions**)
1 television is a system using radio waves to reproduce pictures on a screen **2** a television, or a television set, is a device for receiving these pictures

tell *VERB* (**tells**, **telling**, **told**)
1 to tell something to someone is to give them information by speaking to them **2** to tell someone to do something is to order them to do it **3** to tell is to reveal a secret • *Promise you won't tell.* **4** to tell something is to recognize it • *Can you tell the difference between butter and margarine?*
all told in all, altogether • *There are ten of them, all told.*
to tell someone off is to scold them
to tell tales is to report someone else's bad behaviour

telling *ADJECTIVE*
having a strong effect or meaning • *It was a telling reply.*

tell-tale *NOUN* (**tell-tales**)
someone who tells tales

tell-tale *ADJECTIVE*
revealing something that is supposed to be secret • *He had a tell-tale spot of jam on his chin.*

telly *NOUN* (**tellies**) (*informal*)
1 telly is television **2** a telly is a television set

temper *NOUN* (**tempers**)
1 a person's mood • *He is in a good temper.* **2** an angry mood • *She was in a temper.*
to lose your temper is to become very angry

temperate *ADJECTIVE*
a temperate climate is neither extremely hot nor extremely cold

temperature *NOUN* (**temperatures**)
1 the temperature of something is how hot or cold it is **2** an unusually high body temperature • *She's feverish and has a temperature.*

tempest *NOUN* (**tempests**)
(*old use*) a violent storm
▷ **tempestuous** *ADJECTIVE* stormy

temple [1] *NOUN* (**temples**)
a building where a god is worshipped

temple [2] *NOUN* (**temples**)
the part of your head between your forehead and your ear

tempo *NOUN* (**tempos**)
the tempo of a piece of music is its speed or rhythm

temporary *ADJECTIVE*
only lasting or used for a short time • *They were using a temporary classroom.*

> WORD FAMILY
> To happen **temporarily** is to happen for a short time.

tempt *VERB* (**tempts**, **tempting**, **tempted**)
to tempt someone is to try to make them do something wrong or unwise

> WORD FAMILY
> **Temptation**, or a **temptation**, is when someone is being tempted; a **tempter** is a person who tempts someone; a woman who does this can be called a **temptress**; something is **tempting** when it is hard to resist.

ten *NOUN* (**tens**)
the number 10

tenant *NOUN* (**tenants**)
someone who rents a house or building or a piece of land from a landlord

> WORD FAMILY
> A **tenancy** is when someone rents a house or building or a piece of land.

tend [1] *VERB* (**tends**, **tending**, **tended**)
something tends to happen when it is likely to happen or is what usually happens • *Prices tend to rise.*

tend[2] *VERB* (**tends**, **tending**, **tended**)
to tend something or someone is to look after them • *Lorna was in her favourite place, the little garden which she tended with such care and diligence.* — R. D. Blackmore, *Lorna Doone*

tendency *NOUN* (**tendencies**)
the way a person or thing is likely to behave • *She has a tendency to be lazy.*

tender[1] *ADJECTIVE* (**tenderer**, **tenderest**)
1 not tough or hard; easy to chew **2** delicate or sensitive • *These are more tender plants.* **3** gentle or loving • *She gave a tender smile.*
▷ **tenderly** *ADVERB* gently or lovingly
▷ **tenderness** *NOUN* tenderness is being tender

tender[2] *VERB* (**tenders**, **tendering**, **tendered**)
to tender something is to give it or offer it • *He tendered his resignation.*

tender *NOUN* (**tenders**)
an offer to do work or supply goods at an agreed price

tendon *NOUN* (**tendons**)
a piece of strong tissue in the body that joins a muscle to a bone

tendril *NOUN* (**tendrils**)
the part of a climbing plant that twists round something to support itself

tennis *NOUN*
tennis is a game played with rackets and a ball on a court with a net across the middle

tenor *NOUN* (**tenors**)
a male singer with a high voice

tenpin bowling *NOUN*
tenpin bowling is a game in which you knock down sets of ten skittles with a ball

tense[1] *ADJECTIVE* (**tenser**, **tensest**)
1 tightly stretched • *tense muscles* **2** to be tense is to be nervous and not able to relax **3** a tense situation makes people feel nervous and unable to relax
▷ **tensely** *ADVERB* in a tense way

tense[2] *NOUN* (**tenses**)
a form of a verb that shows when something happens. The past tense of come is *came*; the present tense is *come*, and the future tense is *will come*

> TENSES
> The tense of a verb tells you when something happens. Verbs have several different forms, depending on their tense. You use the present tense to describe something that is happening now: *I speak, she speaks, they are speaking.* You use the past tense to describe something that has already happened: *I spoke, she was speaking, he has spoken.* You use the future tense to describe something that will happen in the future: *I will speak, they will be speaking.*

tension *NOUN* (**tensions**)
1 tension is a feeling of anxiety or nervousness about something about to happen **2** tension is also how tightly stretched a rope or wire is

tent *NOUN* (**tents**)
a shelter made of canvas or cloth supported by upright poles

tentacle *NOUN* (**tentacles**)
a long bending part of the body of an octopus and some other animals

tenth *ADJECTIVE* & *NOUN*
the next after the ninth
▷ **tenthly** *ADVERB* in the tenth place; as the tenth one

tepid *ADJECTIVE*
tepid liquid is only slightly warm; lukewarm

term *NOUN* (**terms**)
1 the time when a school or college is open for teaching **2** a definite period • *He was sentenced to a term of imprisonment.* **3** a word or expression with a special meaning • *I don't understand these technical terms.* **4** the terms of an agreement are the conditions offered or agreed • *They won't agree to our terms.*
to be on good or **bad terms** is to be friendly or unfriendly with someone

term *VERB* (**terms**, **terming**, **termed**)
to term something is to give it a special name • *This music is termed jazz.*

terminal *NOUN* (**terminals**)
1 a building where passengers arrive or depart • *an airport terminal* **2** a place where a wire is connected to a battery or electric circuit **3** a computer keyboard and screen used for sending data to or from the main computer

terminal *ADJECTIVE*
a terminal illness is one that cannot be cured and that the person will die from

terminate *VERB* (**terminates**, **terminating**, **terminated**)
1 you terminate something, or it terminates, when it ends or stops • *This train terminates here.*

> WORD FAMILY
> **Termination** is ending or stopping something.

terminus *NOUN* (**termini**)
the station at the end of a railway or bus route

termite *NOUN* (**termites**)
a small insect that eats wood and lives in large groups

terrace *NOUN* (**terraces**)
1 a row of houses joined together **2** a level area on a slope or hillside **3** a paved area beside a house

terrapin *NOUN* (**terrapins**)
a kind of small turtle that lives in water

terrible *ADJECTIVE*
awful; very bad

terribly *ADVERB*
awfully; badly • *I'm terribly sorry I kept you waiting.* • *He was missing his parents terribly.*

terrier *NOUN* (**terriers**)
a kind of strong lively small dog

terrific *ADJECTIVE* (*informal*)
1 very good or excellent • *That's a terrific idea.* **2** very great • *They went at a terrific speed.*
▷ **terrifically** *ADVERB* very; greatly

terrify *VERB* (**terrifies**, **terrifying**, **terrified**)
to terrify a person or animal is to make them very frightened

territory *NOUN* (**territories**)
an area of land, especially an area that belongs to a country or person
▷ **territorial** *ADJECTIVE* to do with territory

terror *NOUN* (**terrors**)
terror is great fear

terrorism *NOUN*
terrorism is the use of violence, such as setting off bombs, for political purposes

> WORD FAMILY
> A **terrorist** is someone who takes part in terrorism.

terrorize *VERB* (**terrorizes**, **terrorizing**, **terrorized**)
to terrorize someone is to terrify them with threats

tessellation *NOUN* (**tessellations**)
tessellation is arranging shapes so that they fit together to cover a surface without any gaps in between

> WORD FAMILY
> **Tessellated** shapes are fitted together to cover a surface without any gaps in between.

test *NOUN* (**tests**)
1 a short set of questions to check someone's knowledge, especially in school **2** a series of questions or experiments to get information about someone or something • *They gave her a test for diabetes.* **3** (*informal*) a test match

test *VERB* (**tests**, **testing**, **tested**)
1 to test someone is to give them a test **2** to test something is to use it so that you can find out whether it works properly or find out more about it

testament *NOUN* (**testaments**)
1 a written statement **2** each of the two main parts of the Bible, the **Old Testament** and the **New Testament**

testicle *NOUN* (**testicles**)
each of the two glands in the scrotum of a man or male animal where semen is produced

testify *VERB* (**testifies**, **testifying**, **testified**)
to testify is to give evidence or swear that something is true

testimonial *NOUN* (**testimonials**)
a letter describing someone's abilities and character

testimony *NOUN* (**testimonies**)
evidence; what someone testifies

test match *NOUN* (**test matches**)
a cricket or rugby match between teams from different countries

test tube *NOUN* (**test tubes**)
a tube of thin glass closed at one end, used for experiments in chemistry

testy *ADJECTIVE*
irritable or slightly bad-tempered

tether *VERB* (**tethers**, **tethering**, **tethered**)
to tether an animal is to tie it up so that it cannot move far

tether *NOUN* (**tethers**)
a rope for tying an animal
to be at the end of your tether is to be unable to stand something any more

text *NOUN* (**texts**)
1 the words of something printed or written **2** a text message **3** a short extract from the Bible

text *VERB* (**texts**, **texting**, **texted**)
you text someone when you send them a text message

textbook *NOUN* (**textbooks**)
a book that teaches you about a subject

textiles *PLURAL NOUN*
kinds of cloth; fabrics

text message *NOUN* (**text messages**)
a written message sent using a mobile phone

> WORD FAMILY
> **Text messaging** is sending written messages by mobile phone.

texture *NOUN* (**textures**)
the way that the surface of something feels when you touch it • *Silk has a smooth texture.*

than *CONJUNCTION*
compared with another person or thing • *His sister is taller than him* or *than he is.*

thank *VERB* (**thanks**, **thanking**, **thanked**)
to thank someone is to tell them you are grateful for something they have given you or done for you
thank you words that you say when you thank someone

thankful *ADJECTIVE*
feeling glad that someone has done something for you

> WORD FAMILY
> You say **thankfully** when you are pleased and relieved about something • *Thankfully no one was hurt.*

thankless *ADJECTIVE*
a thankless job or task is one that is not very enjoyable and that you are not likely to get any thanks for

thanks *PLURAL NOUN*
1 words that thank someone **2** (*informal*) a short way of saying 'Thank you'
thanks to someone or **something** because of them • *Thanks to you, we succeeded.*

that *DETERMINER*
the one there • *Whose is that book?*

that *CONJUNCTION*
used to introduce a fact or statement or result • *I hope that you are well.* • *Do you know that it is one o'clock?* • *The puzzle was so hard that no one could solve it.*

that *PRONOUN*
1 the one there • *Whose book is that?* **2** which or who • *This is the book that I wanted.* • *Are you the person that I saw the other day?*

thatch *NOUN*
thatch is straw or reeds used to make a roof

thatch *VERB* (**thatches, thatching, thatched**)
to thatch a roof is to make it with straw or reeds

> WORD FAMILY
> A **thatcher** is someone whose job is thatching roofs.

thaw *VERB* (**thaws, thawing, thawed**)
something thaws when it melts and is no longer frozen • *The snow was beginning to thaw.*

the *DETERMINER* (called the *definite article*)
a particular one; that or those

theatre *NOUN* (**theatres**)
1 a building where people go to see plays or shows **2** a special room where surgical operations are done

theatrical *ADJECTIVE*
to do with plays or acting
▷ **theatrically** *ADVERB* in a theatrical way

thee *PRONOUN*
(*old use*) you, referring to one person and used as the object of a verb

theft *NOUN* (**thefts**)
theft is stealing

their *DETERMINER*
belonging to them • *This is their house.*

theirs *PRONOUN*
belonging to them • *This house is theirs.*

them *PRONOUN*
a word used for *they* when it is the object of a verb, or when it comes after a preposition • *I like them.* • *I gave it to them.*

theme *NOUN* (**themes**)
1 a main idea or subject of (for example) a book or speech **2** a short tune or melody

theme park *NOUN* (**theme parks**)
an amusement park with rides and activities connected with a special subject or theme

themselves *PLURAL NOUN*
them and nobody else, used to refer back to the subject of a verb • *They have hurt themselves.*
by themselves on their own; alone • *They did the work all by themselves.*

then *ADVERB*
1 at that time • *I lived in London then.* **2** after that; next • *Then they came home.* **3** in that case; therefore • *If you are going, then I can stay.*

theology *NOUN*
theology is the study of God and religion

> WORD FAMILY
> A **theologian** is an expert in theology; a **theological** college is one where theology is taught.

theorem *NOUN* (**theorems**)
a statement in mathematics that can be proved

theoretical *ADJECTIVE*
based on theory and not on practice or experience

> WORD FAMILY
> Something is **theoretically** true or possible when it is true or possible in theory.

theory *NOUN* (**theories**)
1 a theory is an idea or set of ideas suggested to explain something **2** the theory of a subject is the ideas and principles behind it, rather than the practice
in theory according to what should happen

therapy *NOUN* (**therapies**)
a way of treating an illness of the mind or the body, usually without using surgery or artificial medicines

> WORD FAMILY
> A **therapist** is an expert in therapy. • *a speech therapist*

there *ADVERB*
1 in or to that place **2** a word that you say to call attention to someone or something or to refer to them • *There's a spider in the bath.* • *There has been a mistake.*

thereabouts *ADVERB*
near there • *They live in York or thereabouts.*

therefore *ADVERB*
for that reason; and so

thermal *ADJECTIVE*
to do with heat; using heat

thermometer *NOUN* (**thermometers**)
a device for measuring temperature

Thermos *NOUN* (**Thermoses**)
(*trademark*) a kind of vacuum flask

thermostat *NOUN* (**thermostats**)
a device that automatically controls the temperature of a room or piece of equipment
▷ **thermostatic** *ADJECTIVE* to do with a thermostat
▷ **thermostatically** *ADVERB* by means of a thermostat

thesaurus *NOUN* (**thesauri** or **thesauruses**)
a kind of dictionary in which words with similar meanings are listed in groups together, instead of one long list in alphabetical order

these *DETERMINER & PRONOUN*
the people or things here

they *PRONOUN*
1 the people or things that someone is talking about **2** people in general • *They say it's a very good film.*

they'd
short for *they had* or *they should* or *they would*

they'll
short for *they will*

they're
short for *they are*

they've
short for *they have*

thick *ADJECTIVE* (**thicker**, **thickest**)
1 measuring a lot from one side to the other • *He cut himself a thick slice of cake.* **2** measured from one side to the other • *The wall is ten centimetres thick.* **3** dense or closely packed together • *The town was in thick fog.* **4** not very runny • *I love thick gravy.* **5** (*informal*) stupid

> WORD FAMILY
> To be **thickly** cut is to be cut in thick pieces; to be **thickly** covered in something is to be covered in a deep layer.

thicken *VERB* (**thickens**, **thickening**, **thickened**)
1 you thicken something, or it thickens, when it becomes thicker • *As he stirred the sauce, it started to thicken.*

thicket *NOUN* (**thickets**)
a group of trees and shrubs growing close together

thickness *NOUN* (**thicknesses**)
the thickness of something is how thick it is

thief *NOUN* (**thieves**)
someone who steals things

thigh *NOUN* (**thighs**)
the part of your leg above your knee

thimble *NOUN* (**thimbles**)
a metal or plastic cover that you put on the end of your finger to protect it when you are sewing

thin *ADJECTIVE* (**thinner**, **thinnest**)
1 measuring a small amount from one side to the other **2** not fat **3** not dense or closely packed together **4** runny or watery

> WORD FAMILY
> To be **thinly** cut is to be cut in thin pieces; to be **thinly** covered in something is to be covered in a thin layer; **thinness** is being thin.

thin *VERB* (**thins**, **thinning**, **thinned**)
1 to thin something, or thin something out, is to make it less thick or less crowded **2** to thin, or thin out, is to become less dense or less crowded • *The crowds had thinned by late afternoon.*

thine *ADJECTIVE*
(*old use*) yours (referring to one person)

thing *NOUN* (**things**)
an object; anything that can be touched or seen or thought about

think *VERB* (**thinks**, **thinking**, **thought**)
1 to think is to use your mind **2** to think something is to have it as an idea or opinion • *I think that's a good idea.* **3** to be thinking of doing something is to be planning to do it

> WORD FAMILY
> A **thinker** is someone who thinks about things.

third *ADJECTIVE & NOUN*
the next after the second
▷ **thirdly** *ADVERB* as the third thing

third *NOUN* (**thirds**)
each of three equal parts into which something can be divided

Third World *NOUN*
the poor or developing countries of Asia, Africa, and South and Central America

thirst *NOUN*
thirst is the feeling that you need to drink

thirsty *ADJECTIVE* (**thirstier**, **thirstiest**)
feeling that you need to drink

thirteen *NOUN* (**thirteens**)
the number 13
▷ **thirteenth** *ADJECTIVE & NOUN* 13th

thirty *NOUN* (**thirties**)
the number 30
▷ **thirtieth** *ADJECTIVE & NOUN* 30th

this *DETERMINER & PRONOUN*
the one here • *Take this pen.* • *This is the one.*

thistle *NOUN* (**thistles**)
a wild plant with prickly leaves and purple or white or yellow flowers

thorn *NOUN* (**thorns**)
a small pointed growth on the stem of roses and other plants

thorny *ADJECTIVE* (**thornier**, **thorniest**)
1 full of thorns; prickly **2** a thorny problem is a difficult one that causes argument or disagreement

thorough *ADJECTIVE*
1 done properly and carefully • *This is a thorough piece of work.* **2** absolute or complete • *Everything was in a thorough mess.*

> WORD FAMILY
> To do something **thoroughly** is to do it properly and carefully; to be **thoroughly** (for example) exhausted or bored is to be completely exhausted or bored; **thoroughness** is doing things properly and carefully.

those *DETERMINER & PRONOUN*
the ones there • *Where are those cards?* • *Those are the ones I want.*

thou *PRONOUN*
(*old use*) you (referring to one person)

though *CONJUNCTION*
in spite of the fact that; even if • *It is not true, though he says it is.*

though *ADVERB*
however; all the same • *She's right, though.*

thought [1] *NOUN* (**thoughts**)
1 a thought is something that you think; an idea or opinion **2** thought is thinking • *I'll give the matter some thought.*

thought [2]
past tense and past participle of **think**

thoughtful *ADJECTIVE*
1 looking or sounding as if you are thinking a lot about something • *There was a long and thoughtful silence and then Pooh, who had been frowning very hard for some minutes, said: 'I make it fifteen.'* — A. A. Milne, *Winnie-the-Pooh* **2** thinking of other people and what they would like
▷ **thoughtfully** *ADVERB* in a thoughtful way
▷ **thoughtfulness** *NOUN* thoughtfulness is being thoughtful

thoughtless *ADJECTIVE*
not thinking of other people and what they would like; reckless
▷ **thoughtlessly** *ADVERB* in a thoughtless way
▷ **thoughtlessness** *NOUN* thoughtlessness is being thoughtless

thousand *NOUN* (**thousands**)
the number 1,000
▷ **thousandth** *ADJECTIVE & NOUN* 1,000th

thrash *VERB* (**thrashes**, **thrashing**, **thrashed**)
1 to thrash someone is to keep hitting them hard with a stick or whip **2** to thrash a person or team is to defeat them completely in a game or sport **3** to thrash, or thrash about, is to fling your arms and legs about wildly

thread *NOUN* (**threads**)
1 a long piece of cotton, wool, nylon, or other material used for sewing or weaving **2** a long thin piece of something **3** the spiral ridge round a screw or bolt

thread *VERB* (**threads**, **threading**, **threaded**)
1 to thread a needle is to put a thread through its eye **2** to thread a long and thin material is to put it through or round something **3** to thread a piece of string is to put beads on it

threadbare *ADJECTIVE*
clothes are threadbare when they are worn thin with threads showing

threat *NOUN* (**threats**)
1 a warning that you will punish or harm someone if they do not do what you want **2** a danger

threaten *VERB* (**threatens**, **threatening**, **threatened**)
1 to threaten someone is to warn them that you will punish or harm them if they do not do what you want **2** to threaten is to be a danger to someone or something • *The quarrel threatened to turn violent.*

three *NOUN* (**threes**)
the number 3

three-dimensional *ADJECTIVE*
having three dimensions: length, width, and height or depth

thresh *VERB* (**threshes**, **threshing**, **threshed**)
to thresh corn is to beat it so that you separate the grain from the husks

threshold *NOUN* (**thresholds**)
1 a slab of stone or board under the doorway of a building; the entrance **2** the beginning of something important • *We are on the threshold of a great discovery.*

threw
past tense of **throw** *VERB*

thrift *NOUN*
thrift is being careful with money and not wasting it

thrifty *ADJECTIVE* (**thriftier**, **thriftiest**)
careful with money and not wasting it
▷ **thriftily** *ADVERB* in a thrifty way

thrill *NOUN* (**thrills**)
1 a sudden feeling of excitement **2** something that gives you this feeling

thrill *VERB* (**thrills**, **thrilling**, **thrilled**)
something thrills you when it gives you a sudden feeling of excitement

> WORD FAMILY
> Something is **thrilling** when it is very exciting.

thriller *NOUN* (**thrillers**)
an exciting story or film, usually about crime or spying

thrive *VERB* (**thrives**, **thriving**, **thrived** or **throve**, **thrived** or **thriven**)
to thrive is to prosper or grow strongly

throat *NOUN* (**throats**)
1 the front of your neck **2** the tube in your neck that takes food and air into your body

throb *VERB* (**throbs, throbbing, throbbed**)
to throb is to beat or vibrate with a strong rhythm • *The ship's engines throbbed quietly.* • *He had a throbbing pain in his head.*

throb *NOUN* (**throbs**)
a throbbing sound or feeling

throne *NOUN* (**thrones**)
1 a special chair for a king or queen **2** the position of being king or queen • *The Prince of Wales is heir to the throne.*

throng *NOUN* (**throngs**)
a large crowd of people

throttle *VERB* (**throttles, throttling, throttled**)
to throttle someone is to squeeze their throat and strangle them

throttle *NOUN* (**throttles**)
a device to control the flow of fuel to an engine

through *ADVERB and PREPOSITION*
1 from one end or side to the other • *I can't get through.* • *Climb through the window.* **2** because of; by means of • *We'll do it through hard work.* **3** (*informal*) finished • *I'm through now.*

through *ADJECTIVE*
1 travelling all the way to a place • *I'm catching a through train to Dover.* **2** having a way through • *This is a no through road.*

throughout *PREPOSITION & ADVERB*
all the way through

throve
past tense of **thrive**

throw *VERB* (**throws, throwing, threw, thrown**)
1 to throw something or someone is to send them through the air **2** to throw something somewhere is to put it there carelessly • *He came in and threw his coat on the chair.* **3** to throw a part of your body is to move it quickly • *She threw her head back and laughed.* **4** to throw someone into a certain state is to put them in that state • *We were thrown into confusion.*
to throw something away is to get rid of it

throw *NOUN* (**throws**)
a throwing action or movement • *That was a good throw.*

thrush *NOUN* (**thrushes**)
a bird that has a white front with brown spots

thrust *VERB* (**thrusts, thrusting, thrust**)
to thrust something somewhere is to push it there with a lot of force • *He thrust his hands into his pockets.*

thud *NOUN* (**thuds**)
the dull sound of something heavy falling

thud *VERB* (**thuds, thudding, thudded**)
to fall with a thud

thumb *NOUN* (**thumbs**)
the short thick finger at the side of each hand
to be under someone's thumb is to be controlled or ruled by them

thump *VERB* (**thumps, thumping, thumped**)
1 to thump someone or something is to hit them heavily **2** to thump is to make a dull heavy sound

thump *NOUN* (**thumps**)
an act or sound of thumping

thunder *NOUN*
thunder is the loud rumbling noise that you hear with lightning during a storm

thunder *VERB* (**thunders, thundering, thundered**)
1 to thunder is to make the noise of thunder
2 someone thunders when they speak with a loud booming voice

thunderous *ADJECTIVE*
extremely loud • *The curtain came down to thunderous applause.*

thunderstorm *NOUN* (**thunderstorms**)
a storm with thunder and lightning

Thursday *NOUN* (**Thursdays**)
the fifth day of the week

thus *ADVERB*
1 in this way • *We did it thus.* **2** therefore • *Thus, we must try again.*

thy *ADJECTIVE*
(*old use*) your (referring to one person)

tick *NOUN* (**ticks**)
1 a small mark, usually ✓, made next to something when checking it as a sign that it is correct or has been done **2** each of the regular clicking sounds that a clock or watch makes **3** (*informal*) a moment • *I won't be a tick.*

tick *VERB* (**ticks, ticking, ticked**)
1 to tick something is to mark it with a tick • *She ticked the correct answers.* **2** a clock or watch ticks when it makes regular clicking sounds
to tick someone off (*informal*) is to scold them or tell them off

ticket *NOUN* (**tickets**)
a piece of paper or card that allows you to do something such as see a show or travel on a bus or train

tickle *VERB* (**tickles, tickling, tickled**)
1 to tickle someone is to keep touching their skin lightly so that they get a tingling feeling that can make them laugh and wriggle **2** to tickle is to have a tickling or itching feeling • *My throat is tickling.* **3** to tickle someone is also to please or amuse them

ticklish *ADJECTIVE*
1 someone is ticklish when they are likely to laugh or wriggle if they are tickled **2** awkward or difficult • *This is a ticklish situation.*

tidal *ADJECTIVE*
to do with tides or affected by tides

tidal wave *NOUN* (**tidal waves**)
a huge sea wave moving with the tide

tiddler *NOUN* (**tiddlers**)
(*informal*) a very small fish

a b c d e f g h i j k l m n o p q r s **t** u v w x y z

tiddlywink *NOUN* (**tiddlywinks**)
a small counter that you flip into a cup with another counter in the game of **tiddlywinks**

tide *NOUN* (**tides**)
the regular rising or falling of the sea, which usually happens twice a day

tide *VERB* (**tides, tiding, tided**)
to tide someone over is to give them what they need, especially money, for the time being

tidy *ADJECTIVE* (**tidier, tidiest**)
1 a tidy place is neat and orderly, with things in the right place • *What a tidy room.* **2** a tidy person keeps things neat and in the right place **3** (*informal*) fairly large • *That's a tidy sum of money.*
▷ **tidily** *ADVERB* in a tidy way • *The bookshelves were tidily arranged.*
▷ **tidiness** *NOUN* tidiness is being tidy

tidy *VERB* (**tidies, tidying, tidied**)
to tidy a place is to make it neat by putting things away in the right place

tie *VERB* (**ties, tying, tied**)
1 to tie something is to fasten it with string, rope, or ribbon **2** to tie a knot or bow is to make one in a strip of material such as a ribbon **3** two players or teams tie when they finish a game or competition with an equal score or position
to be tied up is to be occupied or busy • *I'm tied up all afternoon.*

tie *NOUN* (**ties**)
1 a thin strip of material tied round the collar of a shirt with a knot at the front **2** the result of a game or competition in which two players or teams have the same position or score **3** one of the matches in a competition

tie-break or **tie-breaker** *NOUN* (**tie-breaks** or **tie-breakers**)
an extra game or part of a game, played when the result so far is a tie

tiger *NOUN* (**tigers**)
a large wild animal of the cat family, with yellow and black stripes

tight *ADJECTIVE* (**tighter, tightest**)
1 fitting very closely or firmly fastened • *These shoes are a bit tight.* **2** fully stretched • *Is this string tight enough?* **3** (*informal*) drunk **4** (*informal*) mean or stingy • *He's a bit tight with his money.*

> WORD FAMILY
> Something is fastened or fits **tightly** when it is tight; **tightness** is being tight.

tight *ADVERB*
1 firmly • *Hold on tight.* **2** fully stretched • *Now pull the string tight.*

tighten *VERB* (**tightens, tightening, tightened**)
1 to tighten something is to make it tighter • *These screws need to be tightened.* **2** to tighten is to become tighter

tightrope *NOUN* (**tightropes**)
a tightly stretched rope above the ground, for acrobats to perform on

tights *PLURAL NOUN*
a piece of clothing that fits tightly over the lower parts of the body including the legs and feet

tigress *NOUN* (**tigresses**)
a female tiger

tile *NOUN* (**tiles**)
a thin piece of baked clay or other hard material used in rows to cover roofs, walls, or floors

> WORD FAMILY
> A **tiled** roof, wall, or floor is covered with tiles.

till [1] *PREPOSITION & CONJUNCTION*
until

till [2] *NOUN* (**tills**)
a drawer or box for money in a shop; a cash register

till [3] *VERB* (**tills, tilling, tilled**)
to till soil or land is to plough it ready for cultivation

tiller *NOUN* (**tillers**)
a handle used to turn a boat's rudder

tilt *VERB* (**tilts, tilting, tilted**)
1 to tilt is to slope or lean **2** to tilt something is to tip it or make it slope

tilt *NOUN* (**tilts**)
a sloping position

timber *NOUN* (**timbers**)
1 timber is wood used for building or making things **2** a timber is a beam of wood

time *NOUN* (**times**)
1 time is a measure of the continued existence of everything in years, months, days, and other units **2** you ask the time when you want to know what point in the day it is, as shown on a watch or clock • *What's the time?* **3** a time is a particular moment or period of things existing or happening • *There was a time when I would have agreed with you.* • *Come back another time.* • *There were fields here in past times.* **4** a time is also an occasion • *This is the first time I've been here.* **5** a time is also a period that is suitable or available for something • *Is there time for a drink?* **6** time is the rhythm and speed of a piece of music
at times or **from time to time** sometimes or occasionally
in time or **on time** soon or early enough; not late • *Make sure you get to the station in time.* • *The train left on time.*

time *VERB* (**times, timing, timed**)
1 to time something is to measure how long it takes **2** to time an event or activity is to arrange the time when it will happen • *You timed your arrival perfectly.*

time limit *NOUN* (**time limits**)
a limited amount of time for doing something, or the time by which something must be done

timer *NOUN* (**timers**)
a device for timing things

times *PLURAL NOUN*
multiplied by • *5 times 3 is 15 (5 x 3 = 15).*

time scale *NOUN* (**time scales**)
the length of time that something takes or that you need in order to do something

timetable *NOUN* (**timetables**)
a list of the times when things happen, such as buses and trains leaving and arriving, and when school lessons take place

timid *ADJECTIVE*
nervous and easily frightened
▷ **timidly** *ADVERB* in a timid way
▷ **timidity** *NOUN* timidity is being timid

timing *NOUN*
timing is choosing the right time to do something • *Arriving at lunchtime was good timing.*

timpani *PLURAL NOUN* (*say* timp- a- nee)
kettledrums

tin *NOUN* (**tins**)
1 tin is a soft white metal **2** a tin is a metal container for preserving food

tin *VERB* (**tins, tinning, tinned**)
to tin food is to preserve it in tins

tingle *VERB* (**tingles, tingling, tingled**)
part of your body tingles when you have a slight stinging or tickling feeling there • *The cold water made my skin tingle.*

tingle *NOUN* (**tingles**)
a tingling feeling

tinker *VERB* (**tinkers, tinkering, tinkered**)
to tinker with something is to try to mend or improve it, often without really knowing how to • *He loves tinkering with old clocks.*

tinker *NOUN* (**tinkers**)
(*old use*) someone who travelled around mending pots and pans

tinkle *VERB* (**tinkles, tinkling, tinkled**)
something tinkles when it makes a gentle ringing sound

tinkle *NOUN* (**tinkles**)
a tinkling sound

tinny *ADJECTIVE* (**tinnier, tinniest**)
a tinny sound is thin and high-pitched

tinsel *NOUN*
tinsel is strips of glittering material used for decoration

tint *NOUN* (**tints**)
a shade of a colour, especially a pale one

tint *VERB* (**tints, tinting, tinted**)
to tint something is to colour it slightly

tiny *ADJECTIVE* (**tinier, tiniest**)
very small

tip[1] *NOUN* (**tips**)
the part at the very end of something

tip *VERB* (**tips, tipping, tipped**)
to tip something is to give it a tip • *The parcel was tied in a red ribbon tipped with gold.*

tip[2] *NOUN* (**tips**)
1 a small amount of money given to thank someone who has helped you **2** a quick piece of advice or useful information

tip *VERB* (**tips, tipping, tipped**)
1 to tip someone is to give them a small amount of money to thank them for helping you **2** to tip someone or something is to name them as likely to win or succeed

tip[3] *VERB* (**tips, tipping, tipped**)
1 to tip something is to turn it upside down or tilt it • *She tipped the water out of the bucket.* • *He tipped his head back and laughed.* **2** to tip rubbish is to leave it somewhere

tip *NOUN* (**tips**)
1 a place where rubbish is left **2** a very untidy place

tiptoe *VERB* (**tiptoes, tiptoeing, tiptoed**)
to tiptoe is to walk on your toes very quietly or carefully

tiptoe *NOUN*
on tiptoe walking or standing on your toes

tire *VERB* (**tires, tiring, tired**)
1 to tire someone is to make them tired **2** to tire is to become tired

tired *ADJECTIVE*
feeling that you need to sleep or rest
to be tired of something is to have had enough of it

tireless *ADJECTIVE*
having a lot of energy; not tiring easily

tiresome *ADJECTIVE*
annoying • *Grown-ups never understand anything by themselves, and it is tiresome for children to be always and forever explaining things to them.* — Antoine de Saint-Exupéry, *The Little Prince*

tissue *NOUN* (**tissues**)
1 tissue, or tissue paper, is thin soft paper **2** a tissue is a piece of this **3** tissue is also the substance of which an animal or plant is made

tit[1] *NOUN* (**tits**)
a kind of small bird

tit[2] *NOUN*
tit for tat something equal given in return

titbit *NOUN* (**titbits**)
a small piece of something

title *NOUN* (**titles**)
1 the name of something such as a book, film, painting, or piece of music **2** a word that shows a person's position or profession, such as • *Sir, Lady, Dr, Mrs.* **3** a legal right to something, especially land or property

titter *VERB* (**titters, tittering, tittered**)
to titter is to giggle or laugh in a silly way

to *PREPOSITION*
1 towards • *They set off to London.* **2** as far as; so as to reach • *I am soaked to the skin.* **3** compared with; rather than • *She prefers cats to dogs.*

> GRAMMAR
> You use **to** with a verb to make an infinitive, for example *I want to see him.* You also use it to show purpose, for example *he does that to annoy us*, and sometimes to stand for the verb when it is left out, for example the second *to* in the sentence *we meant to ask but we forgot to.*

to *ADVERB*
to the usual or closed position • *Push the door to.*
to and fro backwards and forwards

toad *NOUN* (**toads**)
an animal like a large frog, that lives on land

toad-in-the-hole *NOUN*
toad-in-the-hole is sausages baked in batter

toadstool *NOUN* (**toadstools**)
a fungus that looks like a mushroom, and is often poisonous

toast *VERB* (**toasts**, **toasting**, **toasted**)
1 to toast food is to cook it by heating it under a grill or in front of a fire **2** to toast someone or something is to have a drink in their honour

toast *NOUN* (**toasts**)
1 toast is toasted bread **2** a toast is when people are asked to toast someone or something with a drink • *Let's drink a toast to the bride and groom.*

toaster *NOUN* (**toasters**)
an electrical device for toasting bread

tobacco *NOUN*
tobacco is the dried leaves of certain plants prepared for smoking in cigarettes, cigars, or pipes

tobacconist *NOUN* (**tobacconists**)
a shopkeeper who sells cigarettes, cigars, and tobacco

toboggan *NOUN* (**toboggans**)
a small sledge for sliding downhill

> WORD FAMILY
> **Tobogganing** is sliding downhill on a toboggan.

today *NOUN*
this day • *Today is Monday.*

today *ADVERB*
1 on this day • *I saw him today.* **2** nowadays • *Today we don't have slaves.*

toddler *NOUN* (**toddlers**)
a young child who is just learning to walk

toe *NOUN* (**toes**)
1 each of the five separate parts at the end of each foot **2** the part of a shoe or sock that covers your toes

toffee *NOUN* (**toffees**)
1 toffee is a sticky sweet made from butter and sugar **2** a toffee is a piece of this

toga *NOUN* (**togas**)
a long loose piece of clothing worn by men in ancient Rome

together *ADVERB*
with another person or thing; with each other • *They went to school together.* • *Now glue the two parts together.*

toil *VERB* (**toils**, **toiling**, **toiled**)
1 to toil is to work hard **2** to toil is also to move slowly and with difficulty • *The village carpenter had fixed up a bench upon which panting grown-ups could sit and rest themselves after they had toiled up the hill.* — Elizabeth Goudge, *The Little White Horse*

toilet *NOUN* (**toilets**)
1 a large bowl with a seat that you use for getting rid of waste from your body **2** a room with a toilet in it

toilet paper *NOUN*
toilet paper is paper for cleaning yourself after you have used a toilet

token *NOUN* (**tokens**)
1 a card or voucher that you can exchange for goods in a shop **2** a piece of metal or plastic you use instead of money to pay for something **3** a sign or signal of something • *Please accept these flowers as a small token of my gratitude.*

told
past tense and past participle of **tell**

tolerable *ADJECTIVE*
able to be tolerated; bearable

> WORD FAMILY
> To do something **tolerably** well is to do it fairly well.

tolerant *ADJECTIVE*
accepting or putting up with other people's behaviour and opinions when you don't agree with them

> WORD FAMILY
> You show **tolerance** when you are willing to accept other people's behaviour and opinions; to do something **tolerantly** is to do it in a tolerant way.

tolerate *VERB* (**tolerates**, **tolerating**, **tolerated**)
to tolerate something is to allow it or put up with it although you do not approve of it

toll [1] *NOUN* (**tolls**)
1 a payment charged for using a bridge or road **2** an amount of loss or damage • *The death toll in the earthquake is rising.*

toll [2] *VERB* (**tolls**, **tolling**, **tolled**)
to toll a bell is to ring it slowly

tom or **tomcat** *NOUN* (**toms** or **tomcats**)
a male cat

tomahawk *NOUN* (**tomahawks**)
an axe used by Native Americans

tomato *NOUN* (**tomatoes**)
a soft round red fruit with seeds inside it, eaten as a vegetable

tomb *NOUN* (**tombs**) (*say* toom)
a place where a dead body is buried; a grave

tomboy *NOUN* (**tomboys**)
a girl who enjoys rough noisy games and activities

tombstone *NOUN* (**tombstones**)
a memorial stone set up over a grave

tommy-gun *NOUN* (**tommy-guns**)
a small machine-gun

tomorrow *NOUN* and *ADVERB*
the day after today

tom-tom *NOUN* (**tom-toms**)
a type of drum that you beat with the palms of your hands

ton *NOUN* (**tons**)
1 a unit of weight equal to 2,240 pounds or about 1,016 kilograms **2** (*informal*) a large amount • *There's tons of room.* **3** (*slang*) a speed of 100 miles per hour

tonal *ADJECTIVE*
to do with tone
▷ **tonally** *ADVERB* as regards tone

tone *NOUN* (**tones**)
1 a sound in music or speech **2** each of the five larger intervals between two notes in a musical scale **3** a shade of a colour **4** the quality or character of something

tone *VERB* (**tones, toning, toned**)
to tone something down is to make it softer or quieter
to tone in is to blend or fit in well, especially in colour

tone-deaf *ADJECTIVE*
unable to tell the difference between musical notes

tongs *PLURAL NOUN*
a tool with two arms joined at one end, used to pick things up or hold them

tongue *NOUN* (**tongues**)
1 the long soft part that moves about inside your mouth **2** a language **3** the flap of material under the laces of a shoe **4** the part inside a bell that makes it ring

tongue-tied *ADJECTIVE*
to be tongue-tied is to feel too shy or embarrassed to speak

tongue-twister *NOUN* (**tongue-twisters**)
a sentence or phrase that is very difficult to say

tonic *NOUN* (**tonics**)
something that makes a person healthier or stronger

tonight *ADVERB & NOUN*
this evening or night

tonne *NOUN* (**tonnes**)
a metric ton, a unit of weight equal to 1,000 kilograms

tonsillitis *NOUN*
tonsillitis is a disease that makes your tonsils extremely sore

tonsils *PLURAL NOUN*
your tonsils are two small masses of soft flesh inside your throat

too *ADVERB*
1 also • *Take the others too.* **2** more than is wanted or allowed or wise • *Don't drive too fast.*

took
past tense of **take**

tool *NOUN* (**tools**)
a device that you use to help you do a particular job, such as a hammer or saw

toolbar *NOUN* (**toolbars**)
a row of symbols on a computer screen that show the different things that you can do with a particular program

tooth *NOUN* (**teeth**)
1 each of the hard white bony parts that grow in the gums, used for biting and chewing **2** each in a row of sharp points on a saw or comb
to fight tooth and nail is to fight very fiercely

> WORD FAMILY
> A **toothed** (for example) animal or tool has teeth.

toothache *NOUN*
toothache is a pain in one of your teeth

toothbrush *NOUN* (**toothbrushes**)
a small brush on a long handle, for brushing your teeth

toothpaste *NOUN* (**toothpastes**)
toothpaste is a creamy paste for cleaning your teeth

top [1] *NOUN* (**tops**)
1 the highest part of something **2** the upper surface of something **3** the covering or stopper of a jar or bottle **4** a piece of clothing you wear on the upper part of your body

top *ADJECTIVE*
highest or most important • *They were travelling at top speed.*

top *VERB* (**tops, topping, topped**)
1 to top something is to put a top on it • *The cake was topped with icing.* **2** to top something is also to be at the top of it • *She tops the class in maths.*
to top something up is to fill it to the top when it is already partly full

top [2] *NOUN* (**tops**)
a toy that can be made to spin on its point

top hat *NOUN* (**top hats**)
a man's tall stiff black or grey hat worn with formal clothes

topic *NOUN* (**topics**)
a subject that you are writing or talking or learning about

topical *ADJECTIVE*
to do with things that are happening or in the news now • *The film we saw was very topical.*
▷ **topicality** *NOUN* topicality is being topical
▷ **topically** *ADVERB* in a topical way

topic sentence *NOUN* (**topic sentences**)
the sentence that tells you what the main topic of a paragraph is. It is usually the first sentence

topless *ADJECTIVE*
not wearing any clothes on the top half of your body

topmost *ADJECTIVE*
highest • *Jay, Magpie, and Parrot went along at dawn and sat in the topmost twigs of Cat's old tree.* — Ted Hughes, *How the Whale Became and Other Stories*

topping *NOUN* (**toppings**)
food that is put on the top of (for example) a cake or pizza

topple *VERB* (**topples**, **toppling**, **toppled**)
1 to topple, or topple over, is to fall over **2** to topple something is to make it fall over **3** to topple someone in power is to overthrow them

top secret *ADJECTIVE*
extremely secret

topsy-turvy *ADVERB & ADJECTIVE*
upside-down; muddled

torch *NOUN* (**torches**)
1 a small electric lamp that you hold in your hand **2** a stick with burning material on the end, used as a light

tore
past tense of **tear** *VERB*

toreador *NOUN* (**toreadors**)
a bullfighter

torment *VERB* (**torments**, **tormenting**, **tormented**)
1 to torment someone is to make them suffer or feel pain **2** to torment someone is also to keep annoying them deliberately

> WORD FAMILY
> Someone's **tormentor** is the person who is tormenting them.

torment *NOUN* (**torments**)
torment is great suffering

torn past participle of **tear** *VERB*

tornado *NOUN* (**tornadoes**) (*say* tor- **nay**- doh)
a violent storm or whirlwind

torpedo *NOUN* (**torpedoes**)
a long tube-shaped missile sent under water to destroy ships and submarines

torpedo *VERB* (**torpedoes**, **torpedoing**, **torpedoed**)
to torpedo a ship is to attack it with a torpedo

torrent *NOUN* (**torrents**)
a very strong stream or fall of water • *Then a great storm came up, with thunder and lightning. The wind howled, the rain came down in torrents, and the waves got so high, they splashed right over the boat.* — Hugh Lofting, *The Story of Doctor Dolittle*

> WORD FAMILY
> **Torrential** rain pours down very heavily.

torso *NOUN* (**torsos**)
the main part of the human body, not including the head, arms, or legs

tortoise *NOUN* (**tortoises**) (*say* **tor**- tus)
a slow-moving animal with a shell over its body

torture *VERB* (**tortures**, **torturing**, **tortured**)
to torture someone is to make them feel great pain, especially so that they will give information

torture *NOUN* (**tortures**)
torture is something done to torture a person

> WORD FAMILY
> A **torturer** is someone who tortures people.

Tory *NOUN* (**Tories**)
a Conservative

toss *VERB* (**tosses**, **tossing**, **tossed**)
1 to toss something is to throw it into the air **2** to toss a coin is to throw it in the air and see which side lands uppermost, as a way of deciding something **3** to toss is to move about restlessly in bed • *She was tossing and turning all night.*

total *NOUN* (**totals**)
the amount you get by adding everything together

total *ADJECTIVE*
1 complete; including everything • *What is the total amount?* **2** complete • *There was total darkness outside.*
▷ **totally** *ADVERB* completely • *Now I'm totally confused.*

total *VERB* (**totals**, **totalling**, **totalled**)
1 to total something is to add it up **2** to total an amount is to reach it as a total • *Sales totalled over £50,000 this month.*

totalitarian *ADJECTIVE* (*say* toh- tal- i- **tair**- i- an)
using a form of government with only one political party

totem pole *NOUN* (**totem poles**)
a large pole carved or painted by Native Americans

totter *VERB* (**totters**, **tottering**, **tottered**)
to totter is to walk unsteadily or wobble

toucan *NOUN* (**toucans**)
a tropical bird with a large brightly-coloured beak

touch *VERB* (**touches**, **touching**, **touched**)
1 you touch something when you feel it lightly with your hand or fingers **2** to touch something is to come into contact with it or hit it gently **3** to be

touching something is to be next to it so that there is no space in between **4** to touch something is also to interfere or meddle with it • *Don't touch anything in this room.* **5** to touch an amount is to just reach it • *His temperature touched 104 degrees.* **6** to touch someone is to affect their emotions • *We were touched by his sad story.*
to touch down is to land in an aircraft or spacecraft
to touch something up is to improve it by making small changes or additions

touch *NOUN* (**touches**)
1 a touch is an act of touching • *You can find any train timetable you want at the touch of a button.* **2** touch is the ability to feel things by touching them **3** a touch is also a small thing that greatly improves something • *We're just putting the finishing touches to it.* **4** touch is also communication with someone • *We have lost touch with them.* **5** touch is also the part of a football or rugby pitch outside the playing area • *He kicked the ball into touch.*

touch and go *ADJECTIVE*
uncertain or risky

touchy *ADJECTIVE* (**touchier**, **touchiest**)
easily or quickly offended

tough *ADJECTIVE* (**tougher**, **toughest**)
1 strong; hard to break or damage • *You'll need tough shoes for the climb.* **2** tough food is hard to chew **3** rough or violent • *The police were dealing with tough criminals.* **4** firm or severe • *It's time to get tough with football hooligans.* **5** difficult • *It was a tough decision.*
▷ **toughly** *ADVERB* in a tough way
▷ **toughness** *NOUN* toughness is being tough

toughen *VERB* (**toughens**, **toughening**, **toughened**)
to toughen someone or something, or toughen them up, is to make them tougher

tour *NOUN* (**tours**)
a journey in which you visit several places

tourist *NOUN* (**tourists**)
someone who is travelling or on holiday abroad

> WORD FAMILY
> **Tourism** is travelling or being on holiday abroad.

tournament *NOUN* (**tournaments**)
a competition in which there is a series of games or contests

tow *VERB* (**tows**, **towing**, **towed**) (*rhymes with* **go**)
to tow a vehicle or boat is to pull it behind you in another vehicle • *They towed our car to a garage.*

tow *NOUN*
an act of towing

toward or **towards** *PREPOSITION*
1 in the direction of • *She walked towards the sea.* **2** in relation to • *He behaved kindly towards his children.* **3** as a contribution to • *Put the money towards a new bicycle.*

towel *NOUN* (**towels**)
a piece of soft cloth that you use for drying yourself

> WORD FAMILY
> **Towelling** is material that towels are made of.

tower *NOUN* (**towers**)
a tall narrow building or part of a building

tower *VERB* (**towers**, **towering**, **towered**)
to tower above or over things is to be taller than them • *The skyscrapers towered above the city.*

tower block *NOUN* (**tower blocks**)
a tall building containing offices or flats

town *NOUN* (**towns**)
a place with many houses, shops, schools, offices, and other buildings

town hall *NOUN* (**town halls**)
a building with offices for the local council and usually a hall for public events

towpath *NOUN* (**towpaths**)
a path beside a canal or river

toxic *ADJECTIVE*
poisonous

toy *NOUN* (**toys**)
something to play with

toy *VERB* (**toys**, **toying**, **toyed**)
to toy with an idea is to think about it casually or idly

toyshop *NOUN* (**toyshops**)
a shop that sells toys

trace *NOUN* (**traces**)
1 a mark or sign left by a person or thing • *He vanished without a trace.* **2** a very small amount of something • *They found traces of blood on the carpet.*

trace *VERB* (**traces**, **tracing**, **traced**)
1 to trace someone or something is to find them after a search • *Police are trying to trace one of the witnesses.* **2** to trace a picture or map is to copy it by drawing over it on thin paper you can see through

traceable *ADJECTIVE*
able to be traced or found

track *NOUN* (**tracks**)
1 a path made by people or animals **2** tracks are marks left by a person or thing **3** a set of rails for trains or trams to run on **4** a road or area of ground prepared for racing **5** a metal belt used instead of wheels on a heavy vehicle such as a tank or tractor
to keep track of something or **someone** is to know where they are or what they are doing

track *VERB* (**tracks**, **tracking**, **tracked**)
1 to track a person or animal is to follow them by following the signs they leave **2** to track something is to follow or observe it as it moves

> WORD FAMILY
> A **tracker** is someone who tracks people or animals.

tracksuit *NOUN* (**tracksuits**)
a warm loose suit of a kind worn by athletes for jogging and warming up

tract[1] *NOUN* (**tracts**)
1 an area of land **2** a series of connected parts in the body

tract[2] *NOUN* (**tracts**)
a short pamphlet or essay, especially about religion

traction *NOUN*
1 traction is the ability of a vehicle to grip the ground • *The car's wheels lost traction in the mud.* **2** traction is also a medical treatment in which an injured arm or leg is pulled gently for a long time by means of weights and pulleys

traction engine *NOUN* (**traction engines**)
a heavy steam or diesel engine used for pulling a heavy load

tractor *NOUN* (**tractors**)
a motor vehicle with large rear wheels, used for pulling farm machinery or heavy loads

trade *NOUN* (**trades**)
1 trade is the business of buying or selling or exchanging things **2** a trade is a job or occupation, especially a skilled craft

trade *VERB* (**trades**, **trading**, **traded**)
to trade is to buy or sell or exchange things
to trade something in is to give it towards the cost of something new • *He traded in his motorcycle for a car.*

trademark *NOUN* (**trademarks**)
a symbol or name that only one manufacturer is allowed to use

trader *NOUN* (**traders**)
someone who buys and sells things in trade

tradesman *NOUN* (**tradesmen**)
someone who sells or delivers goods

trade union *NOUN* (**trade unions**)
an organization of workers in a particular industry, set up to help improve pay and work conditions

tradition *NOUN* (**traditions**)
1 tradition is the passing down of customs and beliefs from one generation to the next **2** a tradition is a custom or belief passed on in this way

traditional *ADJECTIVE*
1 passed down from one generation to the next • *It is a book of traditional stories from all round the world.* **2** of a kind that has existed for a long time • *We go to a very traditional school.*

> WORD FAMILY
> Something is **traditionally** done a certain way when that is what has been done for generations.

traffic *NOUN*
1 traffic is vehicles, ships, or aircraft moving along a route **2** traffic is also trade, especially in something illegal or wrong • *They were involved in traffic in drugs.*

traffic *VERB* (**traffics**, **trafficking**, **trafficked**)
to traffic in something is to trade in it illegally

traffic lights *PLURAL NOUN*
a set of coloured lights used to control traffic at road junctions and other hazards

traffic warden *NOUN* (**traffic wardens**)
an official whose job is to make sure that vehicles are parked legally

tragedy *NOUN* (**tragedies**)
1 a play with unhappy events or a sad ending
2 a very sad event

tragic *ADJECTIVE*
1 very sad or distressing **2** to do with tragedy
▷ **tragically** *ADVERB* in a way that is very sad or distressing

trail *NOUN* (**trails**)
1 a path or track through the countryside or a forest **2** the scent and marks left behind by an animal as it moves **3** marks left behind by something that has passed

trail *VERB* (**trails**, **trailing**, **trailed**)
1 to trail an animal is to follow the scent or marks it has left behind **2** you trail something, or it trails, when it drags along the ground behind you **3** to trail behind someone is to follow them more slowly or at a distance • *A few walkers trailed behind the others.* **4** to trail is also to hang down or float loosely • *She wore a long trailing scarf.*

trailer *NOUN* (**trailers**)
1 a truck or other container that is pulled along by a car or lorry **2** a short film advertising a film or television programme that will soon be shown

train *NOUN* (**trains**)
1 a group of railway coaches or trucks joined together and pulled by an engine
2 a number of people or animals moving along together, especially in a desert • *a camel train*
3 a series of things • *The train of events began in London.* **4** a long part of a dress that trails on the ground

train *VERB* (**trains**, **training**, **trained**)
1 to train someone is to give them skill or practice in something **2** to train is to learn how to do a job • *He's training to be a doctor.* **3** to train is also to practise for a sporting event • *She was training for the race.* **4** to train a plant is to make it grow in a particular direction • *Roses can be trained up walls.* **5** to train a gun is to aim it at a target • *He trained his rifle on the bridge.*

trainer *NOUN* (**trainers**)
1 a person who trains people or animals **2** a soft shoe with a rubber sole, worn for running and sport

traitor *NOUN* (**traitors**)
someone who betrays their country or friends

tram *NOUN* (**trams**)
a passenger vehicle that runs along rails set in the road

tramp *NOUN* (**tramps**)
1 a person without a home or job who walks from place to place **2** a long walk **3** the sound of heavy footsteps

tramp *VERB* (**tramps**, **tramping**, **tramped**)
1 to tramp is to walk with heavy footsteps **2** to tramp is also to walk for a long distance

trample *VERB* (**tramples**, **trampling**, **trampled**)
to trample something, or to trample on it, is to crush it by treading heavily on it

trampoline *NOUN* (**trampolines**) (*say* tramp- o- leen)
a large piece of canvas joined to a frame by springs, used by gymnasts for jumping on

trance *NOUN* (**trances**)
a dreamy or unconscious condition like sleep

tranquil *ADJECTIVE*
quiet and peaceful

> WORD FAMILY
> **Tranquillity** is being quiet and peaceful.

tranquillizer *NOUN* (**tranquillizers**)
a drug used to make a person feel calm and relaxed

trans- *PREFIX*
meaning 'across' , as in *transatlantic*

transaction *NOUN* (**transactions**)
a piece of business that involves buying and selling something

transatlantic *ADJECTIVE*
across the Atlantic Ocean or on the other side of it

transfer *VERB* (**transfers**, **transferring**, **transferred**) (*say* trans- **fer**)
1 to transfer someone or something is to move them from one place to another **2** to transfer something is to give it or pass it on to someone else

transfer *NOUN* (**transfers**) (*say* **trans**- fer)
1 the process of moving a person or thing from one place to another **2** a piece of paper with a picture or design that can be transferred to another surface by soaking or heating the paper

transferable *ADJECTIVE*
a ticket is transferable when it can be used by someone other than the person who bought it

transform *VERB* (**transforms**, **transforming**, **transformed**)
to transform a person or thing is to change their form or appearance to something quite different • *The caterpillar is transformed into a butterfly.*

> WORD FAMILY
> A **transformation** is a complete change in the form or appearance of something.

transformer *NOUN* (**transformers**)
a device used to change the voltage of an electric current

transfusion *NOUN* (**transfusions**)
putting blood taken from one person into another person's body

transistor *NOUN* (**transistors**)
1 a tiny electronic device that controls a flow of electricity **2** a portable radio that uses transistors to strengthen the signal it receives

transition *NOUN* (**transitions**)
a change from one thing to another

> WORD FAMILY
> A **transitional** period or process is one during which there is a change from one thing to another.

transitive *ADJECTIVE*
(*in grammar*) a verb is transitive when it is used with a direct object, for example *ran* in *they ran a paper shop* (but not in *they ran away*)

translate *VERB* (**translates**, **translating**, **translated**)
to translate something said or written in one language is to say or write it in another language

> WORD FAMILY
> A **translation** is something translated from another language; a **translator** is someone who translates language.

translucent *ADJECTIVE*
something is translucent when it allows light to shine through, without being fully transparent

transmission *NOUN* (**transmissions**)
1 transmission is transmitting something
2 a transmission is a radio or television broadcast
3 a vehicle's transmission is the gears that transmit power from the engine to the wheels

transmit *VERB* (**transmits**, **transmitting**, **transmitted**)
1 to transmit a broadcast or signal is to send it out **2** to transmit something is to send it or pass it from one person or place to another

transmitter *NOUN* (**transmitters**)
a device for transmitting radio signals

transparency *NOUN* (**transparencies**)
1 transparency is being transparent **2** a transparency is a type of transparent photograph that you can project on a screen

transparent *ADJECTIVE*
something is transparent when you can see through it

transpire *VERB* (**transpires**, **transpiring**, **transpired**)
1 to transpire is to become known • *It transpired that she had known nothing about it.* **2** to transpire is also to happen • *This is what transpired.* **3** plants and animals transpire when they emit moisture through their leaves or skin

transplant *VERB* (**transplants**, **transplanting**, **transplanted**)
1 to transplant a body organ is to remove it from one person and put it in another **2** to transplant a plant is to move it from one place to another
▷ **transplantation** *NOUN* transplantation is transplanting something

a b c d e f g h i j k l m n o p q r s **t** u v w x y z

transplant *NOUN* (**transplants**)
1 when a body organ is removed from one person and put in another • *a heart transplant* **2** something that is transplanted

transport *VERB* (**transports**, **transporting**, **transported**) (*say* trans- port)
to transport people or things is to take them from one place to another

> WORD FAMILY
> **Transportation** is taking people or things from one place to another.

transport *NOUN* (*say* **trans**- port)
1 transport is the process of transporting people or things **2** transport is also vehicles used to do this

transporter *NOUN* (**transporters**)
a heavy vehicle for transporting large objects, such as cars

trap *NOUN* (**traps**)
1 a device for catching and holding animals **2** a plan or trick to capture, detect, or cheat someone **3** a two-wheeled carriage pulled by a horse **4** a bend in a pipe, filled with liquid to prevent air or gas escaping

trap *VERB* (**traps**, **trapping**, **trapped**)
1 to trap a person or animal is to catch them in a trap **2** to trap someone is to capture, detect, or cheat them **3** to be trapped is to be stuck in a dangerous situation you can't escape from • *They were trapped in the burning building.*

trapdoor *NOUN* (**trapdoors**)
a door in a floor, ceiling, or roof

trapeze *NOUN* (**trapezes**)
a bar hanging from two ropes, used as a swing by acrobats

trapezium *NOUN* (**trapeziums**)
a four-sided figure that has only two parallel sides, which are of different length

trapezoid *NOUN* (**trapezoids**)
a four-sided figure with no two sides parallel

trapper *NOUN* (**trappers**)
someone who traps animals, especially for their fur

trash *NOUN*
trash is rubbish or nonsense

> WORD FAMILY
> Something is **trashy** when it is worthless or rubbish.

travel *VERB* (**travels**, **travelling**, **travelled**)
to travel is to go from one place to another

travel *NOUN*
travel is going on journeys • *Do you enjoy travel?*

travel agent *NOUN* (**travel agents**)
a person or business whose job is to arrange travel and holidays for people

traveller *NOUN* (**travellers**)
1 someone who is travelling or who often travels **2** a person who lives in a vehicle and does not settle in one place

traveller's cheque *NOUN* (**traveller's cheques**)
a cheque for a fixed amount of money that is sold by banks and that can be exchanged for money in other countries

trawler *NOUN* (**trawlers**)
a fishing boat that pulls a large net behind it

tray *NOUN* (**trays**)
a flat piece of wood or metal or plastic, used for carrying food, cups, plates, and other household things

treacherous *ADJECTIVE*
1 betraying someone; not loyal **2** dangerous or unreliable • *It's been snowing and the roads are treacherous* .

> WORD FAMILY
> To **treacherously** do something is to betray someone by doing it; **treachery** is doing something that betrays someone.

treacle *NOUN*
treacle is a thick sweet sticky liquid made from purified sugar

tread *VERB* (**treads**, **treading**, **trod**, **trodden**)
to tread on something is to walk on it or put your foot on it

tread *NOUN* (**treads**)
1 the sound someone makes when they walk • *He had a heavy tread.* **2** the part of a staircase or ladder that you put your foot on **3** the part of a tyre that touches the ground

treason *NOUN*
treason is betraying your country

treasure *NOUN* (**treasures**)
1 treasure is a collection of valuable things like jewels or money **2** a treasure is a precious thing

treasure *VERB* (**treasures**, **treasuring**, **treasured**)
to treasure something is to think that it is very precious

treasure hunt *NOUN* (**treasure hunts**)
a game in which people try to find a hidden object

treasurer *NOUN* (**treasurers**)
an official who is in charge of the money of an organization or club

treasury *NOUN* (**treasuries**)
a place where treasure is stored
the Treasury the government department in charge of a country's income

treat *VERB* (**treats**, **treating**, **treated**)
1 to treat someone or something in a certain way is to behave towards them in that way • *She treats her friends very kindly.* **2** to treat a person or animal is to

give them medical care • *He was treated for sunstroke.* **3** to treat someone is to pay for their food or drink or entertainment • *I'll treat you to an ice cream.*

treat *NOUN* (**treats**)
1 something special that gives someone pleasure **2** the act of treating someone by paying for them • *This is my treat.*

treatment *NOUN* (**treatments**)
1 your treatment of someone is the way you treat them **2** treatment is medical care

treaty *NOUN* (**treaties**)
a formal agreement between two or more countries

treble *ADJECTIVE*
three times as much or three times as many

treble *NOUN* (**trebles**)
1 treble the amount of something is three times as much or as many **2** a treble is a boy with a high singing voice

treble *VERB* (**trebles**, **trebling**, **trebled**)
1 to treble something is to make it three times as big **2** to treble is to become three times as big

tree *NOUN* (**trees**)
a tall plant with leaves, branches, and a thick wooden stem called a trunk

trek *VERB* (**treks**, **trekking**, **trekked**)
to trek is to make a long walk or journey

trek *NOUN* (**treks**)
a long walk or journey

trellis *NOUN* (**trellises**)
a framework of crossing wooden or metal bars, used to support climbing plants

tremble *VERB* (**trembles**, **trembling**, **trembled**)
to tremble is to shake gently, especially because you are afraid

tremble *NOUN* (**trembles**)
a trembling movement or sound

tremendous *ADJECTIVE*
1 very large or very great • *A tremendous banging noise was coming from inside the Pelican's beak. It sounded as though someone was using a sledgehammer against it from the inside.* — Roald Dahl, *The Giraffe and the Pelly and Me* **2** excellent

WORD FAMILY
You can say you are (for example) **tremendously** excited or **tremendously** grateful when you are very excited or grateful indeed.

tremor *NOUN* (**tremors**)
1 a shaking or trembling **2** a small earthquake

trench *NOUN* (**trenches**)
a long hole or ditch dug in the ground

trend *NOUN* (**trends**)
the general direction in which something is going or developing

trendy *ADJECTIVE* (**trendier**, **trendiest**)
(*informal*) fashionable; trying to be up to date
▷ **trendily** *ADVERB* in a trendy way
▷ **trendiness** *NOUN* trendiness is being trendy

trespass *VERB* (**trespasses**, **trespassing**, **trespassed**)
to trespass is to go on someone's land or property without their permission • *The sign said 'No Trespassing'.*

WORD FAMILY
A **trespasser** is someone who is trespassing • *Trespassers will be prosecuted.*

trestle *NOUN* (**trestles**)
each of a set of supports on which you place a board to make a table

trial *NOUN* (**trials**)
1 trying or testing something to see how well it works **2** the process of hearing all the evidence about a crime in a lawcourt is to find out whether someone is guilty of it
by trial and error by trying out different methods until you find one that works
on trial being tried out, or being tried in a lawcourt

triangle *NOUN* (**triangles**)
1 a flat shape with three straight sides and three angles **2** a percussion instrument made from a metal rod bent into a triangle

WORD FAMILY
Something is **triangular** when it is in the shape of a triangle.

tribe *NOUN* (**tribes**)
a group of families living together, ruled by a chief
▷ **tribal** *ADJECTIVE* to do with tribes or a tribe • *a tribal leader*

tribesman *NOUN* (**tribesmen**)
a man who belongs to a particular tribe

tributary *NOUN* (**tributaries**)
a river or stream that flows into a larger river or a lake

tribute *NOUN* (**tributes**)
1 something said or done as a mark of respect or admiration for someone **2** money that people in one country used to have to pay a powerful ruler in another country

trick *NOUN* (**tricks**)
1 something done to deceive or fool someone **2** a clever or skilful action • *a card trick.* **3** the winning of one round of a card game such as whist

trick *VERB* (**tricks**, **tricking**, **tricked**)
to trick someone is to deceive or fool them

WORD FAMILY
Trickery is doing something to deceive or fool someone; a **trickster** is someone who plays tricks on people.

trickle *VERB* (**trickles**, **trickling**, **trickled**)
liquid trickles when it flows slowly in small quantities

trickle *NOUN* (**trickles**)
a slow gradual flow

tricky *ADJECTIVE* (**trickier**, **trickiest**)
1 difficult or awkward • *There were a couple of tricky questions in the quiz.* **2** cunning or deceitful

tricycle *NOUN* (**tricycles**)
a vehicle like a bicycle with three wheels

tried
past tense and past participle of **try** *VERB*

trifle *NOUN* (**trifles**)
1 a pudding made of sponge cake covered with custard, fruit, and cream **2** a very small amount of something **3** something that has little importance or value

trifle *VERB* (**trifles**, **trifling**, **trifled**)
to trifle with someone or something is to treat them without seriousness or respect

trifling *ADJECTIVE*
very small or unimportant

trigger *NOUN* (**triggers**)
a lever that is pulled to fire a gun

trigger *VERB* (**triggers**, **triggering**, **triggered**)
to trigger something, or trigger it off, is to start it happening

trillion *NOUN* (**trillions**)
a million million (1,000,000,000,000)

> BRITISH AND AMERICAN
> In Britain, but not in America, **trillion** can also mean a million million million (1,000,000,000,000,000,000). People often say **trillions**, meaning very many, and then the exact number is not important.

trilogy *NOUN* (**trilogies**)
a group of three books or films about the same characters

trim *ADJECTIVE* (**trimmer**, **trimmest**)
neat and tidy

trim *VERB* (**trims**, **trimming**, **trimmed**)
1 you trim something when you cut the edges or unwanted parts from it **2** to trim clothing is to decorate its edges • *The gown was trimmed with fur.* **3** in a boat, to trim the sails is to arrange them to suit the wind

trim *NOUN*
an act of trimming • *My hair needs a quick trim.*
to be in trim is to be in good condition

Trinity *NOUN*
the Trinity in Christianity, the union of Father, Son, and Holy Spirit in one God

trio *NOUN* (**trios**)
1 three people or things **2** a group of three musicians **3** a piece of music for three musicians

trip *VERB* (**trips**, **tripping**, **tripped**)
1 to trip, or trip over, is to catch your foot on something and fall or stumble **2** to trip someone, or trip them up, is to make them fall or stumble **3** to trip, or trip along, is to move with quick gentle steps

trip *NOUN* (**trips**)
1 a short journey or outing **2** the action of tripping or stumbling

tripe *NOUN*
1 tripe is part of the stomach of an ox used as food **2** (*informal*) tripe is also nonsense

triple *ADJECTIVE*
1 three times as much or three times as many **2** consisting of three parts or involving three people or groups

triple *VERB* (**triples**, **tripling**, **tripled**)
to triple something is to make it three times as big

triple jump *NOUN*
an athletics event in which athletes try to jump as far as possible with a hop, step, and jump

triplet *NOUN* (**triplets**)
each of three children or animals born at the same time to the same mother

tripod *NOUN* (**tripods**) (*say* **try**- pod)
a stand with three legs, for supporting a camera or other instrument

triumph *NOUN* (**triumphs**)
1 a triumph is a great success or victory **2** triumph is a feeling of victory or success • *They returned home in triumph.*

triumph *VERB* (**triumphs**, **triumphing**, **triumphed**)
to triumph is to win or succeed

triumphant *ADJECTIVE*
enjoying a victory or celebrating one
▷ **triumphantly** *ADVERB* in a triumphant way • *'Now do you believe in witches?' cried Lizzie's witch triumphantly.* — Helen Cresswell, *Lizzie Dripping*

trivial *ADJECTIVE*
not important or valuable
▷ **trivially** *ADVERB* in a trivial way
▷ **triviality** *NOUN* triviality is being unimportant

trod
past tense of **tread** *VERB*

trodden
past participle of **tread** *VERB*

troll *NOUN* (**trolls**)
a creature in Scandinavian mythology, either a dwarf or a giant

trolley *NOUN* (**trolleys**)
1 a basket on wheels, used in supermarkets **2** a small table on wheels, used for serving food and drink

trombone *NOUN* (**trombones**)
a large brass musical instrument with a sliding tube

troop *NOUN* (**troops**)
an organized group of people, especially soldiers or Scouts

troop *VERB* (**troops, trooping, trooped**)
people troop when they move along in large numbers

troops *PLURAL NOUN*
soldiers

trophy *NOUN* (**trophies**)
a cup or other prize you get for winning a competition

tropic *NOUN* (**tropics**)
a line of latitude about $23\frac{1}{2}°$ north of the equator (**Tropic of Cancer**) or about $23\frac{1}{2}°$ south of the equator (**Tropic of Capricorn**)
the tropics the hot regions between these two latitudes

WORD FAMILY
A **tropical** (for example) plant, bird, or rainforest is one found in the tropics.

trot *VERB* (**trots, trotting, trotted**)
1 a horse trots when it runs gently without cantering or galloping **2** a person trots when they run gently with short steps

trot *NOUN* (**trots**)
a trotting run
on the trot (*informal*) one after another

trouble *NOUN* (**troubles**)
trouble is something that causes worry or difficulty
to be in trouble is to be likely to get punished because of something you have done
to take trouble is to take great care in doing something

trouble *VERB* (**troubles, troubling, troubled**)
1 to trouble someone is to cause them worry or difficulty **2** to trouble someone is also to bother or disturb them • *Sorry to trouble you, but can you spare a minute?* **3** to trouble to do something is to make an effort to do it • *Nobody troubled to ask us what we wanted.*

troublesome *ADJECTIVE*
causing trouble or worry

trough *NOUN* (**troughs**) (*say* trof)
1 a long narrow box for animals to eat or drink from **2** an area of low pressure between two areas of high pressure

trousers *PLURAL NOUN*
a piece of clothing worn over the lower half of your body, with two parts to cover your legs

trout *NOUN* (**trout**)
a freshwater fish

trowel *NOUN* (**trowels**)
1 a tool for digging small holes or lifting plants **2** a tool with a flat blade for spreading cement or mortar

truant *NOUN* (**truants**)
a child who stays away from school without permission
to play truant is to stay away from school without permission

WORD FAMILY
Truancy is being absent from school without permission.

truce *NOUN* (**truces**)
an agreement to stop fighting for a while

truck *NOUN* (**trucks**)
1 a lorry **2** an open railway wagon for carrying goods **3** a cart

trudge *VERB* (**trudges, trudging, trudged**)
to trudge is to walk slowly and heavily

true *ADJECTIVE* (**truer, truest**)
1 real or correct; telling what actually exists or happened • *This is a true story.* **2** genuine or proper • *He was the true heir.* **3** loyal and faithful • *You are a true friend.*
to come true is to actually happen • *I hope your dreams come true.*

truly *ADVERB*
1 truthfully **2** sincerely or genuinely • *We are truly grateful.* **3** loyally or faithfully

trump *NOUN* (**trumps**)
a playing card of a suit that ranks above the others for one game or round of play

trump *VERB* (**trumps, trumping, trumped**)
to trump a card is to beat it by playing a trump

trumpet *NOUN* (**trumpets**)
a brass musical instrument with a narrow tube that widens at the end

WORD FAMILY
A **trumpeter** is someone who plays the trumpet.

trumpet *VERB* (**trumpets, trumpeting, trumpeted**)
1 an elephant trumpets when it makes a loud sound **2** to trumpet something is to shout it out or announce it loudly

truncheon *NOUN* (**truncheons**)
a short thick stick carried as a weapon by a police officer

trundle *VERB* (**trundles, trundling, trundled**)
to trundle is to move along heavily, especially on wheels • *A lorry trundled across the bridge.* • *The little wooden horse trundled up the garden path and battered on the door with his wooden wheels, making a fearful din.* — Ursula Moray Williams, *Adventures of the Little Wooden Horse*

trunk *NOUN* (**trunks**)
1 the main stem of a tree **2** an elephant's long flexible nose **3** a large box with a hinged lid, for carrying or storing clothes and other things **4** the human body except for the head, legs, and arms

trunk call *NOUN* (**trunk calls**)
a long-distance telephone call

trunk road *NOUN* (**trunk roads**)
a main road

trunks *PLURAL NOUN*
shorts worn by men and boys for swimming, boxing, and other activities

trust *VERB* (**trusts, trusting, trusted**)
1 to trust someone or something is to believe that they are good or truthful or reliable **2** to trust that something is so is to hope it • *I trust that you are well.*
to trust someone with something is to let them use it or look after it

trust *NOUN*
1 trust is the feeling that a person or thing can be trusted **2** trust is also responsibility or being trusted • *Our pet dog was left in the trust of our next-door neighbour.*

trustful *ADJECTIVE*
trusting people
▷ **trustfully** *ADVERB* in a trustful way

trustworthy *ADJECTIVE*
able to be trusted; reliable

trusty *ADJECTIVE*
trustworthy or reliable

truth *NOUN* (**truths**)
1 truth is the quality of being true; the facts about something **2** a truth is something that is true

truthful *ADJECTIVE*
1 telling the truth • *They are truthful children.* **2** true • *They gave a truthful account of what happened.*
▷ **truthfully** *ADVERB* in a truthful way
▷ **truthfulness** *NOUN* being truthful

try *VERB* (**tries, trying, tried**)
1 to try to do something is to make an effort to do it or to see if you can do it • *Try to keep still.* **2** to try something is to use it to see if it works or taste it to see if you like it • *Try this can opener.* **3** to try someone in a lawcourt is to find out whether they are guilty of a crime, by hearing all the evidence about it **4** to try someone is also to annoy them over a long time • *You really do try me with your constant complaining.*
to try something on is to put on clothes to see if they fit or look good
to try something out is to use it to see if it works

try *NOUN* (**tries**)
1 a go at trying something; an attempt • *Have another try.* **2** (*in rugby football*) putting the ball down on the ground behind your opponents' goal to score points

T-shirt *NOUN* (**T-shirts**)
a shirt or vest with short sleeves

tub *NOUN* (**tubs**)
a round container for liquids or soft stuff such as ice cream

tuba *NOUN* (**tubas**) (*say* tew- ba)
a large brass musical instrument that makes a deep sound

tube *NOUN* (**tubes**)
1 a tube is a long thin hollow piece of material such as metal, plastic, rubber, or glass **2** a tube is also a long hollow container for something soft such as toothpaste **3** the tube is the underground railway in London • *She goes to work by tube.*

tuber *NOUN* (**tubers**)
a thick rounded plant root or stem that produces buds

tubing *NOUN*
tubing is a length or piece of tube

tubular *ADJECTIVE*
shaped like a tube

tuck *VERB* (**tucks, tucking, tucked**)
to tuck something somewhere is to push a loose edge of it there so that it is tidy or hidden • *Now tuck in the flap of the envelope.* • *She tucked her hair under her cap.*
to tuck in (*informal*) is to eat heartily
to tuck someone up is to put the bedclothes snugly round them

tuck *NOUN* (**tucks**)
1 a tuck is a flat fold stitched in a piece of clothing **2** (*slang*) tuck is food, especially the kind which children enjoy eating

tuck shop *NOUN* (**tuck shops**)
a shop that sells tuck to children

Tuesday *NOUN* (**Tuesdays**)
the third day of the week

tuft *NOUN* (**tufts**)
a bunch of soft or fluffy things such as threads, grass, hair, or feathers, held or growing together

tug *VERB* (**tugs, tugging, tugged**)
to tug something is to pull it hard

tug *NOUN* (**tugs**)
1 a hard or sudden pull **2** a small powerful boat used for towing ships

tug-of-war *NOUN*
a contest between two teams pulling a rope from opposite ends

tulip *NOUN* (**tulips**)
a large bright cup-shaped flower that grows on a tall stem from a bulb

tumble *VERB* (**tumbles, tumbling, tumbled**)
1 to tumble is to fall over or fall down clumsily **2** to tumble to something is to suddenly realize it or be aware of it

tumble *NOUN* (**tumbles**)
a clumsy fall

tumble-drier *NOUN* (**tumble-driers**)
a machine that dries washing in a rotating drum with heated air passing through

tumbler *NOUN* (**tumblers**)
1 a drinking glass with no stem or handle **2** an acrobat

tummy *NOUN* (**tummies**)
(*informal*) your stomach

tumour *NOUN* (**tumours**) (*say* tew- mer)
an abnormal growth on or in your body

tumult *NOUN* (*say* tew- mult)
an uproar or state of great confusion

tumultuous *ADJECTIVE*
noisy and excited • *The teams walked onto the pitch to tumultuous applause.* — J. K. Rowling, *Harry Potter and the Chamber of Secrets*

tuna *NOUN* (**tuna** or **tunas**) (*say* tew- na)
a large sea fish used for food

tundra *NOUN*
tundra is a large area of flat land in cold regions (especially northern Canada and Siberia) with no trees and with soil that is frozen for most of the year

tune *NOUN* (**tunes**)
a short piece of music; a pleasant series of musical notes
to be in tune is to be at the correct musical pitch

tune *VERB* (**tunes, tuning, tuned**)
1 to tune a musical instrument is to adjust it to be in tune **2** to tune a radio or television is to adjust it to receive a particular broadcasting station **3** to tune an engine is to adjust it so that it works smoothly

tuneful *ADJECTIVE*
having a pleasant tune
▷ **tunefully** *ADVERB* in a tuneful way

tunic *NOUN* (**tunics**) (*say* tew- nik)
1 a jacket that is part of some uniforms **2** a loose piece of clothing with no sleeves

tunnel *NOUN* (**tunnels**)
a passage made underground or through a hill

tunnel *VERB* (**tunnels, tunnelling, tunnelled**)
to tunnel is to make a tunnel

turban *NOUN* (**turbans**)
a covering for the head made by wrapping a long strip of cloth round it, worn especially by Sikh, Hindu, or Muslim men

turbine *NOUN* (**turbines**)
a machine or motor that is driven by a flow of water or gas

turbulent *ADJECTIVE*
moving violently; heaving • *The seas in March can be turbulent.*

WORD FAMILY
Turbulence is violent and uneven movement of air or water.

turf *NOUN* (**turfs** or **turves**)
1 turf is short grass with the soil it is growing in **2** a turf is a piece of grass and soil cut out of the ground

turkey *NOUN* (**turkeys**)
a large bird kept for its meat

Turkish bath *NOUN* (**Turkish baths**)
a bath in steam or hot air

Turkish delight *NOUN*
Turkish delight is a sweet consisting of lumps like jelly covered in powdered sugar

turmoil *NOUN*
turmoil is a great disturbance or confusion

turn *VERB* (**turns, turning, turned**)
1 to turn is to move round or move to a new direction; to turn something is to make it move in this way **2** to turn (for example) pale is to change appearance and become pale **3** to turn into something is to change into it • *The frog turned into a prince.* **4** to turn something into something else is to change it • *You can turn milk into cheese.* **5** to turn a device on or off is to use a switch to make it work or stop working; to turn (for example) a radio or television up or down is to make it louder or softer
to turn out is to happen a certain way • *The weather's turned out fine.*
to turn something down is to refuse it
to turn something out is to empty it
to turn up is to appear or arrive suddenly or unexpectedly

turn *NOUN* (**turns**)
1 the action of turning; a turning movement • *Give the key three turns.* **2** a place where a road bends; a junction • *Take the next turn on the left.* **3** a task or duty that people do one after the other • *It's your turn to wash up.* **4** a short performance in a show **5** (*informal*) an attack of illness; a nervous shock • *It gave me a nasty turn.*
a good turn is a favour you do for someone
in turn first one and then the other; following one after another

turncoat *NOUN* (**turncoats**)
someone who changes sides or changes what they believe

turnip *NOUN* (**turnips**)
a plant with a large round white root used as a vegetable

turnover *NOUN* (**turnovers**)
a small pie made of pastry folded over fruit or jam

turnstile *NOUN* (**turnstiles**)
a revolving gate that lets one person through at a time

turntable *NOUN* (**turntables**)
a revolving platform or support, especially the part of a record player that you put the record on

turpentine *NOUN* (*say* ter- pen- tyn)
turpentine is a kind of oil used to make paint thinner and to clean paintbrushes

turquoise *NOUN* (*say* ter- kwoiz)
1 a sky-blue or greenish-blue colour **2** a blue jewel

turret *NOUN* (**turrets**)
1 a small tower in a castle **2** a revolving structure containing a gun

turtle *NOUN* (**turtles**)
a sea animal that looks like a tortoise
to turn turtle is to capsize

tusk *NOUN* (**tusks**)
one of a pair of long pointed teeth that stick out of the mouth of an elephant or walrus or boar

a b c d e f g h i j k l m n o p q r s t u v w x y z

tussle *NOUN* (**tussles**)
a hard struggle or fight

tussle *VERB* (**tussles, tussling, tussled**)
to tussle is to struggle or fight over something

tutor *NOUN* (**tutors**)
a teacher who teaches one person or a small group at a time

TV
short for **television**

tweak *VERB* (**tweaks, tweaking, tweaked**)
to tweak something is to twist it or pull it sharply

tweak *NOUN* (**tweaks**)
a tweaking movement

tweed *NOUN*
tweed is a thick rough woollen cloth

tweezers *PLURAL NOUN*
a small tool for gripping or picking up small things like stamps and hairs

twelve *NOUN* (**twelves**)
the number 12
▷ **twelfth** *ADJECTIVE & NOUN* 12th

twenty *NOUN* (**twenties**)
the number 20
▷ **twentieth** *ADJECTIVE & NOUN* 20th

twice *ADVERB*
1 two times; on two occasions **2** double the amount

twiddle *VERB* (**twiddles, twiddling, twiddled**)
to twiddle something is to turn it round or over and over in an idle way • *He was twiddling a knob on the radio.*

twiddle *NOUN* (**twiddles**)
a twiddling movement

twig [1] *NOUN* (**twigs**)
a short thin branch or shoot

twig [2] *VERB* (**twigs, twigging, twigged**)
(*informal*) to twig something is to realize what it means • *I suddenly twigged what she was talking about.*

twilight *NOUN*
twilight is the time of dim light just after sunset

twin *NOUN* (**twins**)
1 each of two children or animals born at the same time from one mother **2** each of two things that are exactly alike

twin *VERB* (**twins, twinning, twinned**)
one city or town is twinned with one in another country when they have an arrangement involving exchange visits and other cultural events that they do together

twine *NOUN*
twine is strong thin string

twinge *NOUN* (**twinges**)
a sudden pain or unpleasant feeling

twinkle *VERB* (**twinkles, twinkling, twinkled**)
to twinkle is to sparkle or shine with flashes of bright light

twinkle *NOUN* (**twinkles**)
a twinkling light

twirl *VERB* (**twirls, twirling, twirled**)
to twirl is to turn round and round quickly; to twirl something is to make it do this

twirl *NOUN* (**twirls**)
a twirling movement

twist *VERB* (**twists, twisting, twisted**)
1 to twist something is to turn its ends in opposite directions **2** to twist is to turn round or from side to side • *The road twisted through the hills.* **3** to twist something is to bend it out of its proper shape • *My bicycle's front wheel is twisted.* • *I think I've twisted my ankle.* **4** (*informal*) to twist someone is to swindle them

twist *NOUN* (**twists**)
a twisting movement or action

twister *NOUN* (**twisters**)
(*informal*) someone who swindles people

twitch *VERB* (**twitches, twitching, twitched**)
to twitch is to jerk or move suddenly and quickly; to twitch something is to make it do this

twitch *NOUN* (**twitches**)
a twitching movement

twitter *VERB* (**twitters, twittering, twittered**)
birds twitter when they make quick chirping sounds

two *NOUN* (**twos**)
the number 2
to be in two minds is to be undecided about something

two-dimensional *ADJECTIVE*
having two dimensions: length and width; flat

two-faced *ADJECTIVE*
dishonest or deceitful

tying
present participle of **tie** *VERB*

type *NOUN* (**types**)
1 a type is a group or class of similar people or things; a kind or sort **2** type is letters and figures designed for use in printing

type *VERB* (**types, typing, typed**)
to type something is to write it with a typewriter or computer

typewriter *NOUN* (**typewriters**)
a machine with keys that you press to print letters or figures on a sheet of paper

WORD FAMILY
A **typewritten** document or text is written with a typewriter.

typhoid *NOUN*
a serious disease caused by harmful bacteria in food or drinking water

typhoon *NOUN* (**typhoons**)
a violent windy storm

typical *ADJECTIVE*
1 having the usual qualities or features of a particular type of person or thing • *They are typical schoolchildren.* **2** as you would expect from a particular person or thing • *She worked with typical thoroughness.*

> WORD FAMILY
> Something **typically** happens a certain way when that is what usually happens.

typist *NOUN* (**typists**)
a person who types, especially as their job

tyranny *NOUN* (**tyrannies**) (*say* **ti**- ra- nee)
tyranny is a cruel or unjust way of ruling people

> WORD FAMILY
> A **tyrannical** ruler uses their power in a cruel or unjust way.

tyrant *NOUN* (**tyrants**) (*say* **ty**- rant)
someone who rules people cruelly or unjustly

tyre *NOUN* (**tyres**)
a covering of rubber fitted round the rim of a wheel to make it grip the road and run smoothly

Uu

udder *NOUN* (**udders**)
the bag-like part of a cow, goat, or ewe, from which milk is taken

UFO *NOUN* (**UFOs**)
short for *unidentified flying object*

ugly *ADJECTIVE* (**uglier**, **ugliest**)
1 not beautiful; unpleasant to look at **2** threatening or dangerous • *The crowd was in an ugly mood.*
▷ **ugliness** *NOUN* ugliness is being ugly

ulcer *NOUN* (**ulcers**)
a sore on the inside or outside of your body

ultimate *ADJECTIVE*
furthest in a series of things; final
▷ **ultimately** *ADVERB* finally or eventually

ultra- *PREFIX*
meaning 'beyond', as in *ultraviolet*

ultraviolet *ADJECTIVE*
ultraviolet light is light beyond the violet end of the spectrum, that causes your skin to tan

umbilical cord *NOUN* (**umbilical cords**)
the tube through which a baby receives nourishment in the mother's womb, connected to the baby's navel

umbrella *NOUN* (**umbrellas**)
a mushroom-shaped piece of cloth stretched over a folding frame, which you open to protect yourself from rain

umpire *NOUN* (**umpires**)
someone who makes sure that people keep to the rules in cricket, tennis, and some other games

un- *PREFIX*
meaning 'not', as in *uncommon*, or added to verbs to make the action of the verb opposite to normal, as in *undo*

> GRAMMAR
> There are so many words beginning with **un-** that only the most common and interesting ones can be included here. They are the ones you will most often hear people use and read in books, and want to use yourself. You can make many more words, especially by adding un- to an adjective, for example *unexplained*, *unripe*, *unsociable*.

unable *ADJECTIVE*
not able • *She was unable to hear.*

unaided *ADJECTIVE*
without any help

unanimous *ADJECTIVE* (*say* yoo- **nan**- i- mus)
a unanimous decision or vote is one where everyone agrees

> WORD FAMILY
> There is **unanimity** when everyone agrees; to decide or vote for something **unanimously** is to do it with everyone agreeing • *She was elected unanimously.*

unarmed *ADJECTIVE*
without weapons • *unarmed combat.*

unavoidable *ADJECTIVE*
not able to be avoided; bound to happen
▷ **unavoidably** *ADVERB* in an unavoidable way

unaware *ADJECTIVE*
not knowing about something • *Blissfully unaware that his fate was being decided, Paddington was sitting in the middle of the bathroom floor drawing a map of South America with a tube of Mr Brown's shaving cream.* — Michael Bond, *A Bear Called Paddington*

unawares *ADJECTIVE*
unexpectedly; without someone knowing • *His question caught me unawares.*

unbearable *ADJECTIVE*
something is unbearable when it is so painful or unpleasant that you cannot bear or endure it
▷ **unbearably** *ADVERB* in an unbearable way • *It was unbearably hot.*

unbelievable *ADJECTIVE*
1 difficult to believe **2** amazing

> WORD FAMILY
> To be **unbelievably** (for example) good or stupid is to be so good or stupid that it is difficult to believe.

a b c d e f g h i j k l m n o p q r s t u v w x y z

unblock *VERB* (**unblocks**, **unblocking**, **unblocked**)
to unblock something is to clear it of a block or obstruction

unborn *ADJECTIVE*
not yet born

uncalled for *ADJECTIVE*
not justified or necessary • *Your rudeness is uncalled for.*

uncanny *ADJECTIVE* (**uncannier**, **uncanniest**)
strange and mysterious • *There was an uncanny silence.*

uncertain *ADJECTIVE*
1 not certain • *He is uncertain about what to do.* **2** not reliable • *The weather is uncertain at the moment.*

> WORD FAMILY
> To do something **uncertainly** is to do it in an uncertain way; **uncertainty** is being uncertain about something.

uncle *NOUN* (**uncles**)
1 the brother of your father or mother **2** your aunt's husband

uncomfortable *ADJECTIVE*
not comfortable
▷ **uncomfortably** *ADVERB* in an uncomfortable way

uncommon *ADJECTIVE*
not common; unusual

unconscious *ADJECTIVE*
1 not awake or knowing what is happening around you because you have fainted or been knocked out **2** not aware of something • *I was unconscious of doing anything wrong.*

> WORD FAMILY
> To do something **unconsciously** is to do it without being aware of doing it; **unconsciousness** is being unconscious.

uncontrollable *ADJECTIVE*
unable to be controlled
▷ **uncontrollably** *ADVERB* in an uncontrollable way

uncountable *ADJECTIVE*
unable to be counted; too many to count

uncouth *ADJECTIVE* (*say* un- **kooth**)
rude and rough in manner

uncover *VERB* (**uncovers**, **uncovering**, **uncovered**)
1 to uncover something is to take the cover or top off it **2** to uncover a secret or something unknown is to discover it • *The police have uncovered a huge fraud.*

undecided *ADJECTIVE*
you are undecided about something when you have not made up your mind about it

undeniable *ADJECTIVE*
impossible to deny; certainly true

> WORD FAMILY
> Something is **undeniably** true when it is certainly true.

under *PREPOSITION*
1 lower than; below • *Hide it under the desk.* **2** less than • *They are under 5 years old.* **3** ruled or controlled by • *The army is under his command.* **4** in the process of; undergoing • *The road is under repair.* **5** using; moving by means of • *The machine moves under its own power.*

under *ADVERB*
in or to a lower place • *Slowly the diver went under.*

underarm *ADJECTIVE & ADVERB*
with the arm kept below shoulder level and moving forward and upwards

undercarriage *NOUN* (**undercarriages**)
an aircraft's undercarriage is its landing wheels and the parts that support them

underclothes *PLURAL NOUN* or **underclothing** *NOUN*
underwear

underdeveloped *ADJECTIVE*
1 not fully developed or grown **2** an underdeveloped country is one that is poor and lacks modern industrial development

underdog *NOUN* (**underdogs**)
the person or team in a contest that is expected to lose

underdone *ADJECTIVE*
not properly done or cooked

underfoot *ADVERB*
1 on the ground where you are walking • *It was slippery underfoot.* **2** under someone's feet • *The flag fell to the ground and was trampled underfoot.*

undergo *VERB* (**undergoes**, **undergoing**, **underwent**, **undergone**)
to undergo something is to experience something or be subjected to it • *He underwent several operations on his leg.*

undergraduate *NOUN* (**undergraduates**)
a student at a university who has not yet taken a degree

underground *ADJECTIVE & ADVERB*
1 under the ground **2** done or working in secret

underground *NOUN* (**undergrounds**)
a railway that runs through tunnels under the ground

undergrowth *NOUN*
undergrowth is bushes and other plants growing closely under tall trees

underhand *ADJECTIVE*
secret and deceitful

underlie *VERB* (**underlies**, **underlying**, **underlay**, **underlain**)
to underlie something is to be the cause or basis of it • *Hard work underlies the team's success this season.*

> WORD FAMILY
> An **underlying** cause of something is one that is important but not easy to notice.

underline *VERB* (**underlines**, **underlining**, **underlined**)
1 to underline something you have written is to draw a line under it **2** to underline a fact is to emphasize it or show it clearly • *This accident underlines the need to be careful all the time.*

undermine *VERB* (**undermines**, **undermining**, **undermined**)
1 to undermine someone's efforts or plans is to weaken them gradually **2** to undermine something is to make a hollow or tunnel beneath it

underneath *PREPOSITION & ADVERB*
below or beneath

underpants *PLURAL NOUN*
a piece of men's underwear worn under trousers

underpass *NOUN* (**underpasses**)
a place where one road or path goes under another

underprivileged *ADJECTIVE*
people who are underprivileged don't have the same opportunities or standard of living as most people

understand *VERB* (**understands**, **understanding**, **understood**)
1 to understand something is to know what it means or how it works **2** to understand something is also to have heard about it • *I understand you've not been well.* **3** to understand someone is to know what they are like and why they behave the way they do

understandable *ADJECTIVE*
1 able to be understood **2** reasonable or normal • *He replied with understandable delight.*

> WORD FAMILY
> To be (for example) **understandably** disappointed is to be disappointed in a way that seems normal and reasonable.

understanding *NOUN*
1 understanding is the power to understand or think; intelligence **2** an understanding is when people have an agreement **3** understanding is also sympathy or tolerance

understanding *ADJECTIVE*
sympathetic and helpful • *He was very understanding when I was ill.*

understudy *NOUN* (**understudies**)
an actor who learns a part in a play so that they can play the part if the usual actor isn't able to perform

undertake *VERB* (**undertakes**, **undertaking**, **undertook**, **undertaken**)
to undertake something is to agree or promise to do it

undertaker *NOUN* (**undertakers**)
someone whose job is to arrange funerals

undertaking *NOUN* (**undertakings**)
something that someone agrees to do

underwater *ADJECTIVE*
placed or used or done below the surface of water

underwear *NOUN*
underwear is clothes you wear next to your skin, under other clothes

underworld *NOUN*
1 in legends, the underworld is the place for the spirits of the dead; hell **2** the underworld is also people who are regularly involved in crime

undesirable *ADJECTIVE*
not wanted or liked

undeveloped *ADJECTIVE*
not yet developed

undo *VERB* (**undoes**, **undoing**, **undid**, **undone**)
1 to undo something is to unfasten or unwrap it • *Can you undo this knot?* **2** to undo something already done is to cancel the effect of it • *He has undone all our careful work.*

undoubted *ADJECTIVE*
definite or certain
▷ **undoubtedly** *ADVERB* certainly

undress *VERB* (**undresses**, **undressing**, **undressed**)
1 to undress is to take your clothes off **2** to undress someone is to take their clothes off

unearth *VERB* (**unearths**, **unearthing**, **unearthed**)
1 to unearth something is to dig it up **2** to unearth something is also to find it after searching for it

unearthly *ADJECTIVE*
supernatural; strange and frightening

uneasy *ADJECTIVE* (**uneasier**, **uneasiest**)
anxious or worried • *Noah had been studying the sky since dawn yesterday, and he had looked uneasy all morning.* — Richard Platt, *Pirate Diary*

> WORD FAMILY
> To do something **uneasily** is to do it in a way that shows you are anxious or worried.

uneatable *ADJECTIVE*
not fit for eating

unemployed *ADJECTIVE*
to be unemployed is to be without a job

> WORD FAMILY
> **Unemployment** is being without a job; **unemployment** is also the number of people without a job.

a b c d e f g h i j k l m n o p q r s t u v w x y z

uneven *ADJECTIVE*
1 not level, flat, or regular • *The path was uneven.* **2** not of the same quality throughout • *It was an uneven performance.*
▷ **unevenly** *ADVERB* in an uneven way
▷ **unevenness** *NOUN* unevenness is being uneven

unexpected *ADJECTIVE*
not expected; surprising

> WORD FAMILY
> To happen **unexpectedly** is to happen when you are not expecting it.

unfair *ADJECTIVE*
not fair; unjust
▷ **unfairly** *ADVERB* in an unfair way
▷ **unfairness** *NOUN* unfairness is being unfair

unfaithful *ADJECTIVE*
not faithful or loyal

unfamiliar *ADJECTIVE*
not familiar

unfasten *VERB* (**unfastens, unfastening, unfastened**)
to unfasten something is to open it when it has been fastened

unfavourable *ADJECTIVE*
not favourable or helpful
▷ **unfavourably** *ADVERB* in an unfavourable way

unfinished *ADJECTIVE*
not finished

unfit *ADJECTIVE*
1 someone is unfit when they are not fit or fully healthy **2** to be unfit for something is to be not suitable • *He is unfit for the job.* • *Next day there was a dead calm, most unfit for war.* — Arthur Ransome, *Swallows and Amazons*

unfold *VERB* (**unfolds, unfolding, unfolded**)
1 to unfold something is to open it or spread it out • *She unfolded the map.* **2** to unfold a story or plan is to make it known gradually **3** a story unfolds when it becomes known gradually

unforgettable *ADJECTIVE*
impossible to forget

unforgivable *ADJECTIVE*
not able to be forgiven

unfortunate *ADJECTIVE*
1 unlucky **2** you say something is unfortunate when you wish it hadn't happened; regrettable • *It was an unfortunate remark.*

> WORD FAMILY
> You say **unfortunately** when you are sad about something • *Unfortunately he wasn't able to come to the party.*

unfreeze *VERB* (**unfreezes, unfreezing, unfroze, unfrozen**)
1 to unfreeze something is to make it no longer frozen **2** to unfreeze is to become no longer frozen

unfriendly *ADJECTIVE*
not friendly
▷ **unfriendliness** *NOUN* unfriendliness is being unfriendly

ungrateful *ADJECTIVE*
not grateful
▷ **ungratefully** *ADVERB* in an ungrateful way

unhappy *ADJECTIVE* (**unhappier, unhappiest**)
1 not happy or pleased **2** you say something is unhappy when you wish it hadn't happened; regrettable • *It was an unhappy choice of words.*
▷ **unhappily** *ADVERB* in an unhappy way
▷ **unhappiness** *NOUN* unhappiness is being unhappy

unhealthy *ADJECTIVE* (**unhealthier, unhealthiest**)
1 not in good health **2** not good for you • *She has an unhealthy diet.*

unheard-of *ADJECTIVE*
never known or done before; extraordinary

unicorn *NOUN* (**unicorns**) (*say* yoo-ni-korn)
an imaginary animal in stories, like a horse with a long straight horn growing out of the front of its head

uniform *NOUN* (**uniforms**)
the special clothes worn by members of an army or school or organization

uniform *ADJECTIVE*
always the same; not changing
▷ **uniformly** *ADVERB* in a way that does not change

uniformed *ADJECTIVE*
wearing a uniform

uniformity *NOUN*
uniformity is being uniform or the same

unify *VERB* (**unifies, unifying, unified**)
to unify several things, especially countries, is to join them into one thing; to unify is to join together

> WORD FAMILY
> **Unification** is when several things are joined together into one thing.

unimportant *ADJECTIVE*
not important
▷ **unimportance** *NOUN* unimportance is being unimportant

uninhabited *ADJECTIVE*
a place is uninhabited when there is nobody living there

unintentional *ADJECTIVE*
not done deliberately

> WORD FAMILY
> To do something **unintentionally** is to do it by accident.

uninterested *ADJECTIVE*
not interested

> USING THIS WORD
> Take care not to confuse **uninterested** with **disinterested**, which means 'impartial'.

uninteresting *ADJECTIVE*
not interesting

union *NOUN* (**unions**)
1 the joining of things together; a united thing **2** a trade union

Union Jack *NOUN* (**Union Jacks**)
the flag of the United Kingdom

unique *ADJECTIVE* (*say* yoo- **neek**)
something is unique when it is the only one of its kind • *Everyone's fingerprints are unique.* • *This jewel is unique.*
▷ **uniquely** *ADVERB* in a unique way
▷ **uniqueness** *NOUN* uniqueness is being unique

unisex *ADJECTIVE*
designed to be suitable for either men or women

unison *NOUN* (*say* **yoo**- ni- son)
in unison said or done by people together at the same time

unit *NOUN* (**units**)
1 an amount used in measuring or counting, such as a centimetre or a pound **2** a single person or thing **3** a group of people or things that belong together

unite *VERB* (**unites**, **uniting**, **united**)
1 to unite several people or things is to form them into one thing or group **2** people or things unite when they join together

unity *NOUN* (**unities**)
1 unity is being united or having agreement **2** a unity is a complete thing

universal *ADJECTIVE*
including everyone and everything

> WORD FAMILY
> To be (for example) **universally** known or accepted is to be known or accepted by everyone.

universe *NOUN*
the universe is everything that exists, including the earth and living things and all the stars and planets

university *NOUN* (**universities**)
a place where people go to study for degrees after they have left school

unjust *ADJECTIVE*
not fair or just
▷ **unjustly** *ADVERB* in an unjust way

unkind *ADJECTIVE* (**unkinder**, **unkindest**)
cruel and not kind
▷ **unkindly** *ADVERB* in an unkind way
▷ **unkindness** *NOUN* unkindness is being unkind

unknown *ADJECTIVE*
not known

unleaded *ADJECTIVE*
unleaded petrol does not contain lead

unless *CONJUNCTION*
except when; if not • *We cannot go unless we are invited.*

unlike *PREPOSITION*
not like • *Unlike me, she enjoys sport.*

unlike *ADJECTIVE*
not alike; different • *The two children are very unlike.*

unlikely *ADJECTIVE* (**unlikelier**, **unlikeliest**)
not likely to happen or be true

unload *VERB* (**unloads**, **unloading**, **unloaded**)
to unload a container or vehicle is to take off the things it carried

unlock *VERB* (**unlocks**, **unlocking**, **unlocked**)
to unlock a door or container is to open it with a key

unlucky *ADJECTIVE* (**unluckier**, **unluckiest**)
not lucky

> WORD FAMILY
> Something **unluckily** happens when it is the result of bad luck.

unmistakable *ADJECTIVE*
not likely to be mistaken for something or someone else; clear and definite
▷ **unmistakably** *ADVERB* in a way that is unlikely to be mistaken for something else • *His accent was unmistakably French.*

unnatural *ADJECTIVE*
not natural or normal
▷ **unnaturally** *ADVERB* in an unnatural way

unnecessary *ADJECTIVE*
not needed

> WORD FAMILY
> To do something **unnecessarily** is to do it when it is not needed.

unoccupied *ADJECTIVE*
a house is unoccupied when it is empty, with no one living there

unpack *VERB* (**unpacks**, **unpacking**, **unpacked**)
to unpack a suitcase or bag is to take out the things in it

unpleasant *ADJECTIVE*
not pleasant
▷ **unpleasantly** *ADVERB* in an unpleasant way
▷ **unpleasantness** *NOUN* unpleasantness is being unpleasant

unplug *VERB* (**unplugs**, **unplugging**, **unplugged**)
to unplug an electrical device is to disconnect it by taking its plug out of the socket

unpopular *ADJECTIVE*
not liked or enjoyed by people

> WORD FAMILY
> The **unpopularity** of a person or thing is the fact that they are unpopular.

unravel *VERB* (**unravels**, **unravelling**, **unravelled**)
1 to unravel something is to unwind it or disentangle it **2** to unravel a problem or mystery is to investigate it and solve it

unreal *ADJECTIVE*
not real; existing only in the imagination

unreasonable *ADJECTIVE*
not reasonable or fair

unrest *NOUN*
unrest is a discontented feeling among a group of people, or the trouble caused by it

unroll *VERB* (**unrolls**, **unrolling**, **unrolled**)
to unroll something is to open it when it has been rolled up

unruly *ADJECTIVE* (**unrulier**, **unruliest**) (*say* un- **roo**- lee)
badly behaved and difficult to control
▷ **unruliness** *NOUN* unruliness is being unruly

unsafe *ADJECTIVE*
not safe; dangerous

unscrew *VERB* (**unscrews**, **unscrewing**, **unscrewed**)
to unscrew something is to undo it by turning it or by removing screws

unseemly *ADJECTIVE*
not proper or suitable; indecent

unseen *ADJECTIVE*
not seen or noticed •*He managed to slip out of the room unseen.*

unselfish *ADJECTIVE*
not selfish; not thinking only about yourself
▷ **unselfishly** *ADVERB* in an unselfish way
▷ **unselfishness** *NOUN* unselfishness is being unselfish

unsightly *ADJECTIVE*
not pleasant to look at; ugly

unskilled *ADJECTIVE*
not having or not needing special skill or training

unsound *ADJECTIVE*
not sound or reliable

unsteady *ADJECTIVE* (**unsteadier**, **unsteadiest**)
shaking or wobbling or likely to fall
▷ **unsteadily** *ADVERB* in an unsteady way
▷ **unsteadiness** *NOUN* unsteadiness is being unsteady

unsuccessful *ADJECTIVE*
not successful
▷ **unsuccessfully** *ADVERB* in an unsuccessful way

unsuitable *ADJECTIVE*
not suitable
▷ **unsuitably** *ADVERB* in an unsuitable way

unthinkable *ADJECTIVE*
too bad or unlikely to be worth thinking about

untidy *ADJECTIVE* (**untidier**, **untidiest**)
messy and not tidy
▷ **untidily** *ADVERB* in an untidy way
▷ **untidiness** *NOUN* untidiness is being untidy

untie *VERB* (**unties**, **untying**, **untied**)
to untie something is to undo it when it has been tied

until *PREPOSITION & CONJUNCTION*
up to a particular time or event •*The shop is open until 8 o'clock.* •*We will stay with you until the train comes.*

untimely *ADJECTIVE*
happening too soon or at an unsuitable time

unto *PREPOSITION*
(*old use*) to

untold *ADJECTIVE*
too great to be counted or measured •*The hurricane caused untold damage.*

untoward *ADJECTIVE*
inconvenient or unfortunate •*I hope nothing untoward happens.*

untrue *ADJECTIVE*
not true

untruthful *ADJECTIVE*
not telling the truth
▷ **untruthfully** *ADVERB* in an untruthful way

unused *ADJECTIVE* (*say* un- **yoozd**)
not yet used
unused to something (*say* un- **yoost**) not familiar with something •*He is unused to eating meat.*

unusual *ADJECTIVE*
different from what is usual or normal; strange or rare

> **WORD FAMILY**
> To be (for example) **unusually** cold is to be colder than is usual or normal.

unwanted *ADJECTIVE*
not wanted

unwell *ADJECTIVE*
not well; ill

unwilling *ADJECTIVE*
you are unwilling to do something when you don't want to do it
▷ **unwillingly** *ADVERB* in an unwilling way
▷ **unwillingness** *NOUN* unwillingness is being unwilling

unwind *VERB* (**unwinds**, **unwinding**, **unwound**)
(*rhymes with* **find**)
1 to unwind something is to unroll it **2** to unwind is to become unrolled **3** (*informal*) to unwind is also to relax after you have been working hard

unworthy *ADJECTIVE*
not deserving something; not good enough for something

unwrap *VERB* (**unwraps**, **unwrapping**, **unwrapped**)
to unwrap something is to take it out of its wrapping

unzip *VERB* (**unzips**, **unzipping**, **unzipped**)
to unzip something is to undo it when it is zipped up

up *ADVERB*
1 in or to a standing or upright position • *Stand up.* **2** in or to a high or higher place or level • *Put it up on the shelf.* • *Prices are going up.* **3** completely • *Eat up your carrots.* **4** out of bed • *It's time to get up.* **5** finished • *Your time is up.* **6** (*informal*) happening • *Something is up.*
to be up against something is to be faced with difficulties or dangers
ups and downs changes of luck, sometimes good and sometimes bad
to be up to something is to be doing something mysterious or suspicious • *What are they up to?*
up to date 1 modern or fashionable **2** having the latest information

up *PREPOSITION*
in or to a higher position on something • *Let's climb up the mountain.*

upbringing *NOUN*
your upbringing is the way you have been brought up

update *VERB* (**updates**, **updating**, **updated**)
to update something is to bring it up to date

upgrade *VERB* (**upgrades**, **upgrading**, **upgraded**)
to upgrade a machine is to improve it by installing new parts in it

upheaval *NOUN* (**upheavals**)
a sudden violent change or disturbance

uphill *ADJECTIVE & ADVERB*
1 sloping upwards; going up a slope **2** difficult • *It was an uphill job.*

uphold *VERB* (**upholds**, **upholding**, **upheld**)
to uphold a decision or belief is to support it or agree with it

upholstery *NOUN*
upholstery is covers and padding for furniture

upkeep *NOUN*
the upkeep of something is the cost of looking after it and keeping it in good condition

uplands *PLURAL NOUN*
the highest part of a country or region

upon *PREPOSITION*
on

upper *ADJECTIVE*
higher in position or rank

upper case *NOUN*
upper case is capital letters

upper class *NOUN* or **upper classes** *PLURAL NOUN*
the highest class in society, especially the aristocracy

WORD FAMILY
Upper-class people belong to the upper class.

upright *ADJECTIVE*
1 standing straight up; vertical **2** honest

upright *NOUN* (**uprights**)
an upright post or support

uprising *NOUN* (**uprisings**)
a rebellion or revolt against the government

uproar *NOUN*
uproar is a loud or angry noise or disturbance • *The room was in uproar.*

upset *ADJECTIVE* (*say* up- set)
unhappy or anxious about something

upset *VERB* (**upsets**, **upsetting**, **upset**) (*say* up- set)
1 to upset someone is to make them unhappy or anxious **2** to upset something is to knock it over and spill its contents

upset *NOUN* (**upsets**) (*say* **up**- set)
1 a slight illness • *He's got a stomach upset.* **2** an unexpected result or setback • *Losing the game on Saturday was a real upset.*

upshot *NOUN*
what happens in the end • *The upshot was that we had to stay behind.*

upside down *ADJECTIVE & ADVERB*
1 with the upper part underneath instead of on top; the wrong way up **2** in disorder or confusion • *The thieves turned the place upside down.*

upstairs *ADVERB & ADJECTIVE*
to or on a higher floor in a house or other building

upstart *NOUN* (**upstarts**)
someone who quickly reaches a position of power and behaves arrogantly

upstream *ADJECTIVE & ADVERB*
in the direction opposite to the flow of a river or stream

uptake *NOUN*
to be quick on the uptake is to be quick to understand
to be slow on the uptake is to be slow to understand

uptight *ADJECTIVE*
(*informal*) upset or nervous about something

up-to-date *ADJECTIVE*
1 modern or fashionable **2** having the latest information

upward *ADJECTIVE & ADVERB*
going towards what is higher

upwards *ADVERB*
towards what is higher

a b c d e f g h i j k l m n o p q r s t **u** v w x y z

uranium *NOUN* (*say* yoor- **ay**- ni- um)
uranium is a radioactive metal used as a source of atomic energy

urban *ADJECTIVE*
to do with a town or city

urbanize *VERB* (**urbanizes**, **urbanizing**, **urbanized**)
to urbanize a place is to make it more like a town
▷ **urbanization** *NOUN* urbanization is being urbanized

urchin *NOUN* (**urchins**)
a dirty or mischievous child

Urdu *NOUN*
Urdu is a language related to Hindi, spoken in northern India and Pakistan

urge *VERB* (**urges**, **urging**, **urged**)
1 to urge someone to do something is to try to persuade them to do it **2** to urge people or animals is to drive them forward

urge *NOUN* (**urges**)
a sudden strong desire or wish • *She felt an urge to go for a swim.*

urgent *ADJECTIVE*
needing to be done or dealt with immediately

> WORD FAMILY
> **Urgency** is when something needs to be done or dealt with immediately; something is needed **urgently** when it is needed immediately.

urinate *VERB* (**urinates**, **urinating**, **urinated**) (*say* **yoor**- i- nayt)
to urinate is to pass urine out of your body
▷ **urination** *NOUN* urination is passing urine

urine *NOUN* (*say* **yoor**- in)
urine is the waste liquid that collects in your bladder and is passed out of your body
▷ **urinary** *ADJECTIVE* to do with the passing of urine

urn *NOUN* (**urns**)
1 a large metal container with a tap, in which water is heated **2** a kind of large vase for holding the ashes of a person who has been cremated

US or **USA**
short for *United States of America*

us *PRONOUN*
a word used for *we*, usually when it is the object of a sentence, or when it comes after a preposition • *She likes us.* • *She gave it to us.*

usable *ADJECTIVE*
that you can use

usage *NOUN* (**usages**) (*say* **yoo**- sij)
the way that something is used, especially the way that words and language are used

use *VERB* (**uses**, **using**, **used**) (*say* yooz)
to use something is to perform an action or job with it • *Are you using my pen?*
used to did in the past • *I used to live in Glasgow.*
to be used to something or **someone** is to know them well or be familiar with them • *We're used to hard work.*
to use something up is to use all of it, so that none is left

use *NOUN* (**uses**) (*say* yooss)
1 the action of using something or being used
2 the purpose or value of something • *Can you find a use for this box?* • *This knife is no use to us.*

used *ADJECTIVE* (*say* yoozd)
not new; second-hand • *We're buying a used car.*

useful *ADJECTIVE*
able to be used a lot or do something that needs doing
▷ **usefully** *ADVERB* in a useful way
▷ **usefulness** *NOUN* usefulness is being useful

useless *ADJECTIVE*
1 not having any use **2** (*informal*) not very good at something • *I'm useless at drawing.*
▷ **uselessly** *ADVERB* in a useless way
▷ **uselessness** *NOUN* uselessness is being useless

user *NOUN* (**users**)
someone who uses something

user-friendly *ADJECTIVE* (**user-friendlier**, **user-friendliest**)
designed to be easy to use

usher *NOUN* (**ushers**)
someone who shows people to their seats in a church or cinema or theatre

usher *VERB* (**ushers**, **ushering**, **ushered**)
to usher someone is to lead them in or out of a place • *Hal ushered the children inside a dim room with a low ceiling – so low that Hal's grey hair almost brushed against the top.* — Lemony Snicket, *A Series of Unfortunate Events*

usherette *NOUN* (**usherettes**)
a woman who shows people to their seats in a cinema or theatre

usual *ADJECTIVE*
as happens often or all the time; expected • *He sat in his usual chair by the fire.* • *She was late as usual.*

> WORD FAMILY
> Something **usually** happens when it happens on most occasions or normally.

usurp *VERB* (**usurps**, **usurping**, **usurped**) (*say* yoo- **zerp**)
to usurp power or a position is to take it by force from someone else

> WORD FAMILY
> A **usurper** is someone who usurps power.

utensil *NOUN* (**utensils**) (*say* yoo- **ten**- sil)
a tool or device, especially one you use in the house

uterus *NOUN* (**uteri**)
a woman's uterus is her womb

utilize *VERB* (**utilizes**, **utilizing**, **utilized**)
to utilize something is to make use of it
▷ **utilization** *NOUN* utilization is making use of something

utmost *ADJECTIVE*
greatest •*Look after it with the utmost care.*

utopia *NOUN* (**utopias**)
an imaginary place where everyone is happy and everything is perfect

utter[1] *VERB* (**utters, uttering, uttered**)
to utter something is to say it clearly, or to make a sound with your mouth •*He uttered a loud yell.* •*Sheltered under a clump of Scots pine, the beasts gazed up at the moonlit sky in a state of utter contentment.* — Debi Gliori, *Pure Dead Wicked*

> WORD FAMILY
> An **utterance** is something that someone says.

utter[2] *ADJECTIVE*
complete or absolute •*It was utter misery.*

> WORD FAMILY
> To be (for example) **utterly** different or ridiculous is to be completely different or ridiculous.

U-turn *NOUN* (**U-turns**)
1 a turn a vehicle makes when it is driven round in one movement to face the opposite direction **2** a complete change of ideas or policy

Vv

vacancy *NOUN* (**vacancies**)
a job, or a room in a guest house, that is available and not taken

vacant *ADJECTIVE*
1 empty; not filled or occupied •*There were no vacant seats.* **2** not showing any expression •*He gave a vacant stare.*

> WORD FAMILY
> To look or stare **vacantly** is to do it without showing any expression.

vacate *VERB* (**vacates, vacating, vacated**)
to vacate a place is to leave it empty

vacation *NOUN* (**vacations**) (*say* vay- **kay**- shon)
a holiday, especially between the terms at a university

vaccinate *VERB* (**vaccinates, vaccinating, vaccinated**) (*say* **vak**- si- nayt)
to vaccinate someone is to protect them from a disease by injecting them with a vaccine

> WORD FAMILY
> **Vaccination**, or a **vaccination**, is when you are vaccinated against a disease.

vaccine *NOUN* (**vaccines**) (*say* **vak**- seen)
a type of medicine injected into people to protect them from disease

vacuum *NOUN* (**vacuums**)
a completely empty space; a space without any air in it

vacuum *VERB* (**vacuums, vacuuming, vacuumed**)
to clean something using a vacuum cleaner

vacuum cleaner *NOUN* (**vacuum cleaners**)
an electrical device that sucks up dust and dirt from the floor

vacuum flask *NOUN* (**vacuum flasks**)
a container with double walls that have a vacuum between them, for keeping liquids hot or cold

vagina *NOUN* (**vaginas**) (*say* va- **jy**- na)
the passage in a woman's female body that leads from the outside of her body to her womb

vague *ADJECTIVE* (**vaguer, vaguest**)
not definite or clear •*I only have a vague memory of his face.*

> WORD FAMILY
> You **vaguely** remember something when you don't remember it clearly; **vagueness** is being vague.

vain *ADJECTIVE* (**vainer, vainest**)
1 too proud of yourself, especially of how you look **2** unsuccessful or useless •*They made vain attempts to save him.*
in vain with no result; without success •*I tried in vain to call for help.*

> WORD FAMILY
> You **vainly** do something when you do it without success.

valentine *NOUN* (**valentines**)
1 a card sent on St Valentine's Day (14 February) to someone you love **2** the person you send a valentine to

valiant *ADJECTIVE*
brave or courageous
▷ **valiantly** *ADVERB* in a brave or courageous way

valid *ADJECTIVE*
able to be used or accepted; legal •*Your passport is not valid.*

> WORD FAMILY
> The **validity** of something is the fact that it is acceptable or legal.

valley *NOUN* (**valleys**)
an area of low land between hills

valour *NOUN*
valour is bravery, especially in a battle

valuable *ADJECTIVE*
1 worth a lot of money **2** very useful or important •*She gave me valuable advice.*

valuables *PLURAL NOUN*
things that are worth a lot of money

value *NOUN* (**values**)
1 the amount of money that something could be sold for **2** how useful or important something is

value *VERB* (**values**, **valuing**, **valued**)
1 to value something is to think that it is important or worth having • *I value her friendship.* **2** to value something is also to work out how much it could be sold for • *The estate agent is coming to value the house.*

> WORD FAMILY
> A **valuation** of something is an estimate of what it is worth; a **valuer** is someone who values something.

valueless *ADJECTIVE*
having no value

valve *NOUN* (**valves**)
1 a device used to control the flow of gas or liquid **2** a device that controls the flow of electricity in older electrical equipment

vampire *NOUN* (**vampires**)
in stories, a creature that sucks people's blood

van *NOUN* (**vans**)
1 a small lorry with a covered area for goods at the back **2** a railway carriage used for goods or for the train's guard

vandal *NOUN* (**vandals**)
someone who deliberately breaks or damages things, especially buildings

> WORD FAMILY
> **Vandalism** is the doing deliberate damage to something, especially a building.

vane *NOUN* (**vanes**)
1 a pointer that shows which way the wind is blowing **2** the blade or surface of a propeller, sail of a windmill, or other device that moves through air or water

vanilla *NOUN*
vanilla is a flavouring made from the pods of a tropical plant

vanish *VERB* (**vanishes**, **vanishing**, **vanished**)
to vanish is to disappear completely

vanity *NOUN*
vanity is being too proud of yourself, especially of how you look

vanquish *VERB* (**vanquishes**, **vanquishing**, **vanquished**)
to vanquish someone is to win a victory over them

vaporize *VERB* (**vaporizes**, **vaporizing**, **vaporized**)
to vaporize is to turn into vapour

vapour *NOUN* (**vapours**)
a visible gas, such as mist or steam, which some liquids and solids can be turned into by heat

variable *ADJECTIVE*
able or likely to change

variable *NOUN* (**variables**)
something that varies or can vary, especially a variable quantity

variation *NOUN* (**variations**)
1 a variation in something is a change in it • *There have been slight variations in temperature.*
2 variation is the process of changing something
3 a variation is a different form of something

varied *ADJECTIVE*
of various kinds; full of variety • *She has varied interests.*

variety *NOUN* (**varieties**)
1 a variety is a number of different kinds of the same thing • *There was a variety of cakes to choose from.* **2** a variety is a particular kind of something • *There are many rare varieties of butterfly.* **3** variety is a situation where things are not always the same • *We have a life full of variety.* **4** variety is also a form of entertainment made up of short performances of singing, dancing, and comedy

various *ADJECTIVE*
1 of different kinds • *They came for various reasons.*
2 several • *We met various people.*
▷ **variously** *ADVERB* in several different ways

varnish *NOUN* (**varnishes**)
a liquid that dries to form a hard shiny surface on wood or other surfaces

varnish *VERB* (**varnishes**, **varnishing**, **varnished**)
to varnish wood or another surface is to put varnish on it

vary *VERB* (**varies**, **varying**, **varied**)
1 to vary is to keep changing • *The weather varies a lot here.* **2** things vary when they are different from each other • *The cars are the same, although the colours vary.* **3** to vary something is to make changes to it

vase *NOUN* (**vases**) (*say* vahz)
a jar used for holding flowers or as an ornament

vast *ADJECTIVE*
very large or wide • *Vast stretches of land flashed by; grassland, mountains, grassland again. Naledi suddenly felt very small.* — Beverley Naidoo, *Journey to Jo'burg*

> WORD FAMILY
> To be **vastly** superior or different is to be greatly superior or very different; **vastness** is being very large or wide.

VAT
short for *value-added tax*, a tax on goods and services

vat *NOUN* (**vats**)
a very large container for holding liquid

vault *VERB* (**vaults**, **vaulting**, **vaulted**)
you vault something, or vault over it, when you jump over it, using your hands to support you or with the help of a pole

vault *NOUN* (**vaults**)
1 a jump done by vaulting **2** an arched roof **3** an underground room for storing money and valuables

VCR
short for **video cassette recorder**

VDU
short for **visual display unit**

veal *NOUN*
veal is the meat from a calf

vector *NOUN* (**vectors**)
(*in mathematics*) a quantity that has size and direction, such as velocity (which is speed in a certain direction)

Veda *PLURAL NOUN*
the ancient writings of the Hindu religion

veer *VERB* (**veers**, **veering**, **veered**)
to veer is to swerve or change direction suddenly • *No sooner had we returned to the deck when the wind veered rapidly round.* — Richard Platt, *Pirate Diary*

vegan *NOUN* (**vegans**) (*say* **vee**- gan)
someone who does not use or eat any products made from animals

vegetable *NOUN* (**vegetables**)
a plant that can be used as food

vegetarian *NOUN* (**vegetarians**) (*say* vej- i- **tair**- i- an)
someone who does not eat meat

vegetate *VERB* (**vegetates**, **vegetating**, **vegetated**)
to vegetate is to lead a dull life doing nothing interesting

vegetation *NOUN*
vegetation is plants that are growing

vehicle *NOUN* (**vehicles**)
a means of carrying people or things, especially on land. Cars, buses, trains, and lorries are vehicles

veil *NOUN* (**veils**)
a piece of thin material to cover a woman's face or head

veil *VERB* (**veils**, **veiling**, **veiled**)
1 to veil something is to cover it with a veil **2** to veil something such as a hint or a threat is to suggest it without being clear about it

vein *NOUN* (**veins**)
1 your veins are the tubes in your body that carry blood towards your heart **2** a line or streak on a leaf or rock or insect's wing **3** a long deposit of a mineral in the middle of rock

velocity *NOUN* (**velocities**) (*say* vil- **os**- i- tee)
velocity is speed in a particular direction

velvet *NOUN*
velvet is a soft material with short furry fibres on one side

> WORD FAMILY
> Something is **velvety** when it feels soft, like velvet.

vendetta *NOUN* (**vendettas**)
a long-lasting quarrel or feud

vending machine *NOUN* (**vending machines**)
a machine that you can buy food, drinks, or other things from

vendor *NOUN* (**vendors**)
someone who is selling something

venerable *ADJECTIVE*
worthy of respect or honour because of being so old

venereal disease *NOUN* (**venereal diseases**)
(*say* vin- **eer**- i- al)
a disease that is passed on by sexual intercourse

venetian blind *NOUN* (**venetian blinds**)
a blind for a window, made of thin horizontal slats which you can move to control the amount of light that comes through

vengeance *NOUN*
vengeance is harming or punishing someone because they have done harm to you
with a vengeance very strongly or effectively

> WORD FAMILY
> A **vengeful** person wants to punish someone who has harmed them.

venison *NOUN*
venison is the meat from a deer

Venn diagram *NOUN* (**Venn diagrams**)
(*in mathematics*) a diagram using circles to show how sets of things relate to one another

venom *NOUN*
1 venom is the poison of snakes **2** venom is also a feeling of bitter hatred for someone

> WORD FAMILY
> A **venomous** snake is poisonous.

vent *NOUN* (**vents**)
an opening in something, especially to let out smoke or gas
to give vent to something is to express your feelings openly • *He gave vent to his anger.*

ventilate *VERB* (**ventilates**, **ventilating**, **ventilated**)
to ventilate a place is to let fresh air come into it and move around it

> WORD FAMILY
> **Ventilation** is letting fresh air move freely around a place; a **ventilator** is something that does this or that helps someone to breathe.

ventriloquist *NOUN* (**ventriloquists**) (*say* ven- **tril**- o- kwist)
an entertainer who speaks without moving their lips, making it appear that a dummy is speaking

> WORD FAMILY
> **Ventriloquism** is what a ventriloquist does.

venture *NOUN* (**ventures**)
something new that you decide to do that is risky or daring

venture *VERB* (**ventures**, **venturing**, **ventured**)
to venture somewhere is to go there even though you know it might be dangerous or difficult • *They seldom ventured up Blackford Hill these days. Even muffled in woollens, it was far too cold and blowy there.* — Aileen Paterson, *Maisie Meets Her Match*

venue *NOUN* (**venues**)
a place where an event is held

veranda *NOUN* (**verandas**) (*say* ver- **an**- da)
an open terrace with a roof along the outside of a house

verb *NOUN* (**verbs**)
a word that shows what someone or something is doing, such as *be*, *go*, *sing*, *take*

> VERBS
> All sentences must contain a verb. Some verbs describe actions or feeling. For example: *I* ***came***. *She* ***ate***. *They* ***know***. A very common verb is the verb 'to have': *I* ***have*** *a cat. He* ***has*** *a cat.* The most common verb in English is the verb 'to be' which has many different forms including:
> *I* ***am***, *you* ***are***, *he* ***was***, *we* ***were***. Verbs have several different forms, depending on which tense they are in. These include the present tense (*she walks* or *she is walking*), the past tense (*she walked* or *she was walking*), and the future tense (*she will walk*).

verbal *ADJECTIVE*
spoken rather than written • *We had a verbal agreement.*

> WORD FAMILY
> To **verbally** agree or express something is to do it in spoken words, not in writing.

verdict *NOUN* (**verdicts**)
the decision reached by a judge or jury about whether someone is guilty of a crime

verge *NOUN* (**verges**)
a strip of grass beside a road or path

verge *VERB* (**verges**, **verging**, **verged**)
to verge on something is to be nearly something • *His remark verged on the absurd.*

verify *VERB* (**verifies**, **verifying**, **verified**)
to verify something is to find or show whether it is true or correct
▷ **verification** *NOUN* verification is verifying something

vermin *NOUN*
vermin are animals or insects that damage crops or food or carry disease, such as rats and fleas

verruca *NOUN* (**verrucas**) (*say* ver- **oo**- ka)
a kind of wart on the sole of your foot

versatile *ADJECTIVE* (*say* **ver**- sa- tyl)
able to do or be used for many different things

> WORD FAMILY
> **Versatility** is being able to do or be used for many different things.

verse *NOUN* (**verses**)
1 verse is writing in the form of poetry **2** a verse is a group of lines in a poem or song **3** a verse is also each of the short numbered sections of a chapter in the Bible

version *NOUN* (**versions**)
1 someone's account of something that has happened • *His version of the accident is different from mine.* **2** a different form of a thing • *I don't like their version of the song.*

versus *PREPOSITION*
against or competing with, especially in sport • *The final will be Brazil versus Germany.*

vertebra *NOUN* (**vertebrae**) (*say* **ver**- ti- bra)
each of the bones that form your backbone

vertebrate *NOUN* (**vertebrates**) (*say* **ver**- ti- brit)
an animal with a backbone

vertex *NOUN* (**vertices**)
the highest point of a hill, or of a cone or triangle

vertical *ADJECTIVE*
going directly upwards, at right angles to something level or horizontal
▷ **vertically** *ADVERB* in a vertical direction

vertigo *NOUN*
vertigo is feeling dizzy because you are high up

very *ADVERB*
to a great amount; extremely • *It is very cold.*

very *ADJECTIVE*
1 exact or actual • *That's the very thing we need!*
2 extreme • *We've reached the very end.*

Vesak *NOUN* (*say* **ves**- ak)
Vesak is an important festival of Buddhism, held in April to May

vessel *NOUN* (**vessels**)
1 a boat or ship **2** a container for liquids **3** a tube inside an animal or plant, carrying blood or some other liquid

vest *NOUN* (**vests**)
a piece of underwear you wear on the top half of your body

vested interest *NOUN* (**vested interests**)
you have a vested interest in something when you have a strong reason for wanting it to happen, because it will help you

vestment *NOUN* (**vestments**)
a piece of outer clothing worn by the clergy or choir at a church service

vestry *NOUN* (**vestries**)
a room in a church where the vestments are kept and the clergy and choir prepare for a service

vet *NOUN* (**vets**)
a person trained to treat sick animals

veteran *NOUN* (**veterans**)
1 a person with long experience of something **2** a soldier who has returned from a war

veteran car *NOUN* (**veteran cars**)
a car made before 1916

veterinary *ADJECTIVE* (*say* vet- rin- ree)
to do with the medical treatment of animals

veto *NOUN* (**vetoes**) (*say* vee- toh)
1 a refusal to let something happen **2** the right to stop something from happening

veto *VERB* (**vetoes**, **vetoing**, **vetoed**)
to veto something is to refuse to let it happen

vex *VERB* (**vexes**, **vexing**, **vexed**)
to vex someone is to annoy them or cause them worry
▷ **vexation** *NOUN* vexation is vexing someone

VHF
short for *very high frequency*

via *PREPOSITION* (*say* vy- a)
going through; stopping at • *This train goes from Edinburgh to London via York.*

viaduct *NOUN* (**viaducts**) (*say* vy- a- dukt)
a long bridge with many arches, carrying a road or railway over low ground

vibrate *VERB* (**vibrates**, **vibrating**, **vibrated**)
to vibrate is to move quickly from side to side and with small movements • *Every time a train went past the walls vibrated.*

WORD FAMILY
You can feel **vibration** or **vibrations** when something moves quickly from side to side and with small movements.

vicar *NOUN* (**vicars**)
a member of the clergy who is in charge of a parish

vicarage *NOUN* (**vicarages**)
the house of a vicar

vice [1] *NOUN* (**vices**)
1 a vice is a bad or evil habit **2** vice is evil or wickedness

vice [2] *NOUN* (**vices**)
a device with jaws for holding something tightly in place while you work on it

vice-president *NOUN* (**vice-presidents**)
a deputy to a president

vice versa *ADVERB* (*say* vys- ver- sa)
the other way round • *'We talk about them and vice versa' means 'We talk about them and they talk about us'.*

vicinity *NOUN* (**vicinities**)
the area near or surrounding a particular place • *Are there any parks in the vicinity?*

vicious *ADJECTIVE* (*say* vish- us)
1 cruel and aggressive **2** severe or violent
▷ **viciously** *ADVERB* in a vicious way
▷ **viciousness** *NOUN* viciousness is being vicious

victim *NOUN* (**victims**)
1 a person who suffers from something • *He is a polio victim.* **2** someone who is killed, injured, or robbed • *The murderer lay in wait for his victim.*

victimize *VERB* (**victimizes**, **victimizing**, **victimized**)
to victimize someone is to treat them unfairly

victor *NOUN* (**victors**)
the winner of a battle or contest

Victorian *ADJECTIVE*
belonging to the time when Queen Victoria reigned (1837-1901)

victory *NOUN* (**victories**)
winning a battle or contest or game

WORD FAMILY
Someone is **victorious** when they win a battle or contest or game.

video *NOUN* (**videos**) (*say* vid- i- oh)
1 video is the recording on tape of pictures and sound **2** a video is a video recorder **3** a video is also a television programme or a film recorded on a video cassette

video *VERB* (**videoes**, **videoing**, **videoed**)
to video something is to record it on videotape

video recorder or **video cassette recorder** *NOUN* (**video recorders** or **video cassette recorders**)
a machine for recording television programmes and playing them back

videotape *NOUN* (**videotapes**)
videotape is magnetic tape used for video recording

view *NOUN* (**views**)
1 what you can see from one place • *There's a fine view from the top of the hill.* **2** someone's opinion • *She has strong views about smoking.*
in view of something because of it
on view shown for people to see

view *VERB* (**views**, **viewing**, **viewed**)
1 to view something is to look at it carefully **2** to view something or someone in a certain way is to think about them in that way • *He viewed us with suspicion.*

viewer *NOUN* (**viewers**)
someone who watches something, especially a television programme

viewpoint *NOUN* (**viewpoints**)
your viewpoint is your opinion about something

a b c d e f g h i j k l m n o p q r s t u v w x y z

vigilant *ADJECTIVE* (*say* vij- i- lant)
someone is vigilant when they are watching carefully for something
▷ **vigilantly** *ADVERB* in a vigilant way
▷ **vigilance** *NOUN* vigilance is watching carefully for something

vigorous *ADJECTIVE*
full of strength and energy
▷ **vigorously** *ADVERB* in a vigorous way

vigour *NOUN*
vigour is strength and energy

Viking *NOUN* (**Vikings**)
a Scandinavian pirate or trader in the 8th to 10th centuries

vile *ADJECTIVE* (**viler**, **vilest**)
disgusting or bad • *What a vile smell.*

villa *NOUN* (**villas**)
a house, especially a large one in its own grounds, or one used for holidays abroad

village *NOUN* (**villages**)
a group of houses and other buildings in the country, smaller than a town

> WORD FAMILY
> A **villager** is someone who lives in a village.

villain *NOUN* (**villains**)
a wicked person or criminal

> WORD FAMILY
> A **villainous** person is very wicked; **villainy** is being wicked.

vine *NOUN* (**vines**)
a plant on which grapes grow

vinegar *NOUN*
vinegar is a sour liquid used to flavour food

vineyard *NOUN* (**vineyards**) (*say* vin- yard)
an area of land where vines are grown to produce grapes for making wine

vintage *NOUN* (**vintages**)
1 all the grapes that are harvested in one season, or the wine made from them **2** the period from which something comes • *The furniture is of 1920s vintage.*

vintage car *NOUN* (**vintage cars**)
a car made between 1917 and 1930

vinyl *NOUN* (*say* vy- nil)
vinyl is a kind of plastic

viola *NOUN* (**violas**) (*say* vee- oh- la)
a stringed instrument rather like a violin but slightly larger and with a lower pitch

violate *VERB* (**violates**, **violating**, **violated**)
1 to violate a rule or law is to break it **2** to violate a person or place is to treat them without respect

> WORD FAMILY
> The **violation** of a rule or law is when it is broken.

violence *NOUN*
1 violence is when someone uses force to hurt or kill people **2** violence is also force that damages things • *We weren't prepared for the violence of the storm.*

> WORD FAMILY
> To be **violent** is to use violence; something such as a storm or a dislike is **violent** when it is strong and forceful; to do something **violently** is to do it with great force.

violet *NOUN* (**violets**)
1 a bluish-purple colour **2** a small plant that usually has purple flowers

violin *NOUN* (**violins**)
a musical instrument with four strings, played with a bow

> WORD FAMILY
> A **violinist** is someone who plays a violin.

VIP
short for *very important person*

viper *NOUN* (**vipers**)
a small poisonous snake

virgin *NOUN* (**virgins**)
a person who has never had sexual intercourse
▷ **virginity** *NOUN* virginity is being a virgin

virtual *ADJECTIVE*
1 amounting to the real thing in effect • *His silence was a virtual admission of guilt.* **2** using virtual reality • *Click here to go on a virtual tour of the gallery.*

virtually *ADVERB*
in effect; nearly • *She virtually admitted it.*

virtual reality *NOUN*
virtual reality is an image or environment created by a computer that imitates the real world and that you can be part of

virtue *NOUN* (**virtues**)
1 a virtue is a good quality in a person's character • *Honesty is a virtue.* **2** virtue is moral goodness

> WORD FAMILY
> A **virtuous** person behaves in a very good way; you **virtuously** do something when you are being good doing it.

virus *NOUN* (**viruses**) (*say* vy- rus)
1 a microscopic creature that can cause disease **2** a disease caused by a virus • *The doctor said I had a virus.* **3** a hidden set of instructions in a computer program that is designed to destroy data

visa *NOUN* (**visas**)
an official mark put on someone's passport by officials of a foreign country to show that the holder of the passport has permission to enter that country

visibility *NOUN*
visibility is how far you can see clearly • *Visibility is down to 20 metres.*

visible *ADJECTIVE*
able to be seen • *The ship was visible on the horizon.*

> WORD FAMILY
> To be **visibly** (for example) shocked is to be shocked in a way that is easy to notice.

vision *NOUN* (**visions**)
1 vision is the ability to see **2** a vision is something that you see or imagine, especially in a dream **3** vision is also imagination and understanding • *They need a leader with vision.*

visit *VERB* (**visits**, **visiting**, **visited**)
to visit a place or person is to go to see them or stay there

visit *NOUN* (**visits**)
a short stay at a place or with a person

visitor *NOUN* (**visitors**)
someone who is visiting or staying at a place

visor *NOUN* (**visors**) (*say* vy- zer)
the clear part of a helmet that closes over the face

visual *ADJECTIVE*
to do with seeing; used for seeing
▷ **visually** *ADVERB* to do with your ability to see

visual aid *NOUN* (**visual aids**)
a picture or film or video used in teaching

visual display unit *NOUN* (**visual display units**)
a screen on which a computer displays information

visualize *VERB* (**visualizes**, **visualizing**, **visualized**)
to visualize something is to form an image of it in your mind

vital *ADJECTIVE*
1 extremely important; essential • *It is vital that we get there on time.* **2** connected with life; needed in order to live

> WORD FAMILY
> Something is **vitally** important when it is extremely important.

vitality *NOUN*
vitality is liveliness or energy

vitamin *NOUN* (**vitamins**)
each of several substances which are present in some foods and which you need to stay healthy

vivid *ADJECTIVE*
bright and clear • *The colours are very vivid.* • *She gave a vivid description of the storm.*

> WORD FAMILY
> To remember something **vividly** is to remember it very clearly; **vividness** is being bright and clear.

vivisection *NOUN*
vivisection is doing experiments on live animals as part of scientific research

vixen *NOUN* (**vixens**)
a female fox

vocabulary *NOUN* (**vocabularies**)
1 the vocabulary of a language is all the words used in it **2** a person's vocabulary is the words that they know and use

vocal *ADJECTIVE*
to do with the voice; using your voice
▷ **vocally** *ADVERB* using your voice

vocalist *NOUN* (**vocalists**)
a singer in a band

vocation *NOUN* (**vocations**)
1 a job or activity that you feel strongly you want to do **2** a strong feeling that you want to do a particular job

vocational *ADJECTIVE*
teaching you the skills you need for a particular job • *They are going to have some vocational training.*

vodka *NOUN* (**vodkas**)
vodka is a strong alcoholic drink especially popular in Russia

voice *NOUN* (**voices**)
1 the sound you make when you speak or sing **2** the ability to speak or sing • *She has lost her voice.* **3** the right to say something • *Do I get a voice in the decision?*

voice *VERB* (**voices**, **voicing**, **voiced**)
to voice something is to say it clearly and strongly • *He voiced their objections to the plan.*

volcano *NOUN* (**volcanoes**)
a mountain with a hole at the top formed by molten lava which has burst through the earth's crust

> WORD FAMILY
> A **volcanic** rock or eruption is caused or produced by a volcano.

vole *NOUN* (**voles**)
a small animal rather like a rat

volley *NOUN* (**volleys**)
1 a number of bullets or shells fired at the same time **2** in ball games, hitting or kicking the ball back before it touches the ground

volleyball *NOUN*
volleyball is a game in which two teams hit a large ball to and fro over a net with their hands

volt *NOUN* (**volts**)
a unit for measuring the force of an electric current

voltage *NOUN* (**voltages**)
voltage is electric force measured in volts

volume *NOUN* (**volumes**)
1 the amount of space filled by something **2** the strength or power of sound • *Turn down the volume!* **3** an amount • *The volume of work has increased.* **4** a book, especially one of a set

voluntary *ADJECTIVE*
done or doing something because you want to, not for pay

> WORD FAMILY
> To do something **voluntarily** is to do it because you want to.

volunteer *VERB* (**volunteers**, **volunteering**, **volunteered**)
1 to volunteer is to offer to do something that you do not have to do **2** to volunteer (for example) information or time is to provide it willingly without being asked for it • *Several people generously volunteered their time.*

volunteer *NOUN* (**volunteers**)
someone who volunteers to do something

vomit *VERB* (**vomits**, **vomiting**, **vomited**)
to vomit is to bring food back from the stomach through your mouth

vote *VERB* (**votes**, **voting**, **voted**)
1 to vote for someone or something is to show which you prefer by putting up your hand or making a mark on a piece of paper **2** to vote to do something is to say that you want to do it • *I vote we go away this weekend.*

vote *NOUN* (**votes**)
1 a way of choosing someone or something by getting people to put up their hand or make a mark on a piece of paper **2** a choice you make by voting **3** the right to vote

voter *NOUN* (**voters**)
someone who votes, especially in an election

vouch *VERB* (**vouches**, **vouching**, **vouched**)
to vouch for something or **someone** is to say they are genuine or reliable

voucher *NOUN* (**vouchers**)
a piece of paper showing that you are allowed to pay less for something or that you can get something in exchange

vow *VERB* (**vows**, **vowing**, **vowed**)
to vow is to make a solemn promise to do something

vow *NOUN* (**vows**)
a solemn promise

vowel *NOUN* (**vowels**)
any of the letters a, e, i, o, u, and sometimes y

voyage *NOUN* (**voyages**)
a long journey by ship or in a spacecraft

> WORD FAMILY
> A **voyager** is someone who goes on a voyage.

vulgar *ADJECTIVE*
rude; without good manners

vulgar fraction *NOUN* (**vulgar fractions**)
a fraction shown by numbers above and below a line (such as $\frac{1}{2}$ and $\frac{7}{8}$), not a decimal fraction

vulnerable *ADJECTIVE*
able to be harmed or attacked easily

vulture *NOUN* (**vultures**)
a large bird that eats dead animals

vulva *NOUN* (**vulvas**)
the outer parts of the female genitals

Ww

wad *NOUN* (**wads**)
a pad or bundle of soft material or pieces of paper

waddle *VERB* (**waddles**, **waddling**, **waddled**)
to waddle is to walk with short steps, rocking from side to side, like a duck • *Aunt Sponge, fat and pulpy as a jellyfish, came waddling up behind her sister to see what was going on.* — Roald Dahl, *James and the Giant Peach*

waddle *NOUN* (**waddles**)
a waddling walk

wade *VERB* (**wades**, **wading**, **waded**)
to wade through water or mud is to walk through it

wafer *NOUN* (**wafers**)
a thin kind of biscuit, often eaten with ice cream

waffle *NOUN* (**waffles**)
1 a waffle is a crisp square pancake with a pattern of squares on it **2** waffle is talking for a long time without saying anything important or interesting

wag *VERB* (**wags**, **wagging**, **wagged**)
1 a dog wags its tail when it moves it quickly from side to side because it is happy or excited **2** you wag your finger when you move it up and down or from side to side

wag *NOUN* (**wags**)
a wagging movement

wage *NOUN* or **wages** *PLURAL NOUN*
the money paid to someone for the job they do

wage *VERB* (**wages**, **waging**, **waged**)
to wage a war or campaign is to fight it

wager *NOUN* (**wagers**) (*say* way-jer)
a bet

wager *VERB* (**wagers**, **wagering**, **wagered**)
to wager someone is to make a bet with them

waggle *VERB* (**waggles**, **waggling**, **waggled**)
to waggle something is to move it quickly to and fro

wagon *NOUN* (**wagons**)
1 a cart with four wheels, pulled by a horse or ox **2** an open railway truck

wagtail *NOUN* (**wagtails**)
a small bird with a long tail that it moves up and down when it is standing still

wail *VERB* (**wails**, **wailing**, **wailed**)
to wail is to make a long sad cry

wail *NOUN* (**wails**)
a sound of wailing

waist *NOUN* (**waists**)
the narrow part in the middle of your body

waistcoat *NOUN* (**waistcoats**)
a close-fitting jacket without sleeves, worn over a shirt and under a jacket

wait *VERB* (**waits**, **waiting**, **waited**)
1 to wait, or to wait for someone or something, is to stay in a place or situation until something happens **2** to wait is also to be a waiter

wait *NOUN* (**waits**)
a time spent waiting • *We had a long wait for the bus.*

waiter *NOUN* (**waiters**)
a man who serves people with food in a restaurant or hotel

waiting list *NOUN* (**waiting lists**)
a list of people waiting for something to become available

waiting room *NOUN* (**waiting rooms**)
a room provided for people who are waiting for something

waitress *NOUN* (**waitresses**)
a woman who serves people with food in a restaurant or hotel

waive *VERB* (**waives**, **waiving**, **waived**)
to waive a right or privilege is to say you do not need it • *She waived her right to a first-class seat.*

> SPELLING
> Take care not to confuse **waive** with **wave**, as in *they waved goodbye*.

wake[1] *VERB* (**wakes**, **waking**, **woke**, **woken**)
1 you wake, or wake up, when you stop sleeping **2** to wake someone, or wake them up, is to make them stop sleeping • *You have woken the baby.*

wake[2] *NOUN* (**wakes**)
1 the trail left on the water by a ship or boat **2** what is left when something is gone, or when something unusual has happened • *The storm left a lot of damage in its wake.*
in the wake of someone or **something** following or coming after them

waken *VERB* (**wakens**, **wakening**, **wakened**)
to waken someone is to wake them

walk *VERB* (**walks**, **walking**, **walked**)
to walk is to move along on your feet at an ordinary speed

walk *NOUN* (**walks**)
1 a journey on foot **2** the way that someone walks • *He has a funny walk.* **3** a path or route for walking • *There are some lovely walks near here.*

walkabout *NOUN* (**walkabouts**)
an informal stroll among a crowd by an important visitor

walker *NOUN* (**walkers**)
someone who goes for a walk, especially a long one

walkie-talkie *NOUN* (**walkie-talkies**)
a small portable radio transmitter and receiver

walking stick *NOUN* (**walking sticks**)
a stick a person carries or uses as a support while walking

walk of life *NOUN* (**walks of life**)
a person's walk of life is the job or occupation they have

wall *NOUN* (**walls**)
1 a structure built of brick or stone and forming one of the sides of a building or room, or going round a garden or other space **2** the outer surface of something, such as the stomach

wall *VERB* (**walls**, **walling**, **walled**)
to wall something, or wall it in, is to surround or enclose it with a wall

wallaby *NOUN* (**wallabies**) (*say* **wol**- a- bee)
a kind of small kangaroo

wallet *NOUN* (**wallets**)
a small flat folding case for holding banknotes, credit cards, and small documents

wallflower *NOUN* (**wallflowers**)
a sweet-smelling garden plant

wallop *VERB* (**wallops**, **walloping**, **walloped**)
(*informal*) to wallop someone is to hit or beat them

wallow *VERB* (**wallows**, **wallowing**, **wallowed**)
1 to wallow is to roll about in water or mud **2** to wallow in something is to get great pleasure from it • *They are wallowing in luxury.*

wallpaper *NOUN* (**wallpapers**)
wallpaper is paper used to cover the walls of rooms

walnut *NOUN* (**walnuts**)
a kind of nut with a wrinkled surface

walrus *NOUN* (**walruses**)
a large Arctic sea animal that looks like a large seal and has two long tusks

waltz *NOUN* (**waltzes**)
a dance with three beats to a bar

waltz *VERB* (**waltzes**, **waltzing**, **waltzed**)
to waltz is to dance a waltz

wand *NOUN* (**wands**)
a short thin rod used by a magician, wizard, or fairy

wander *VERB* (**wanders**, **wandering**, **wandered**)
1 to wander is to go about without trying to reach a particular place **2** to wander, or wander off, is to stray or get lost • *Don't let the sheep wander.*

> WORD FAMILY
> A **wanderer** is someone who keeps travelling from place to place.

wane *VERB* (**wanes**, **waning**, **waned**)
1 the moon wanes when its bright area gets gradually smaller **2** to wane is to become less or smaller or less strong • *His popularity was waning.*

a b c d e f g h i j k l m n o p q r s t u v **w** x y z

wangle *VERB* (**wangles, wangling, wangled**)
(*informal*) to wangle something is to get it or arrange it by trickery or clever planning • *I'll see if I can wangle you a ticket to the première.*

want *VERB* (**wants, wanting, wanted**)
1 to want something is to feel that you would like to have it or do it **2** to want something is also to need it • *Your hair wants cutting.*

want *NOUN* (**wants**)
1 a want is a wish to have something **2** want of something is a lack of it • *They died for want of water.*

wanted *ADJECTIVE*
someone is wanted when they are being looked for by the police as a suspected criminal • *He was a wanted man.*

war *NOUN* (**wars**)
1 war is fighting between nations or armies; a war is a period of fighting **2** a war is also a serious struggle or effort against an evil such as crime or disease

warble *VERB* (**warbles, warbling, warbled**)
to warble is to sing gently, the way some birds do

warble *NOUN* (**warbles**)
a warbling sound

warbler *NOUN* (**warblers**)
a kind of small bird

ward *NOUN* (**wards**)
1 a long room with beds for patients in a hospital **2** a child looked after by a guardian **3** an area of a town or city represented by a councillor

ward *VERB* (**wards, warding, warded**)
to ward something off is to keep it away • *He put his arms up to ward off the blows.*

-ward or **-wards** *SUFFIX*
an ending for words such as *backward* and *homewards*, which show direction

warden *NOUN* (**wardens**)
1 an official in charge of a hostel or college, or who supervises something **2** a traffic warden

warder *NOUN* (**warders**)
an official in charge of prisoners in a prison

wardrobe *NOUN* (**wardrobes**)
1 a cupboard to hang your clothes in **2** a stock of clothes or costumes

warehouse *NOUN* (**warehouses**)
a large building where goods are stored

wares *PLURAL NOUN*
goods offered for sale

warfare *NOUN*
warfare is fighting or waging war

warhead *NOUN* (**warheads**)
the explosive head of a missile

warlike *ADJECTIVE*
warlike people are fond of fighting or are likely to start a war

warm *ADJECTIVE* (**warmer, warmest**)
1 fairly hot; not cold or cool **2** warm clothes are thick and keep you warm **3** a warm person is enthusiastic or friendly • *They gave us a warm welcome.* **4** (*informal*) close to the right answer, or to something hidden • *You're getting warm now.*

> WORD FAMILY
> You are **warmly** dressed when you are dressed in warm clothes; to **warmly** welcome or greet someone is to do it in a very friendly way.

warm *VERB* (**warms, warming, warmed**)
1 to warm something or someone is to make them warm **2** to warm, or warm up, is to become warm **to warm up** is to do gentle exercises to prepare yourself before playing sport

warm-blooded *ADJECTIVE*
having blood that does not change temperature according to the surroundings

warmth *NOUN*
1 warmth is being warm or keeping warm • *The cattle huddled together for warmth.* **2** warmth is also being friendly and enthusiastic • *She was touched by the warmth of their welcome.*

warn *VERB* (**warns, warning, warned**)
to warn someone is to tell them about a danger or difficulty that might affect them

warning *NOUN* (**warnings**)
something said or written to warn someone

warp *VERB* (**warps, warping, warped**) (*say* worp)
1 to warp, or be warped, is to become bent or twisted out of shape because of dampness or heat **2** to warp someone's ideas or judgement is to distort them • *Jealousy warped his mind.*

warp *NOUN*
the warp is the lengthwise threads in weaving, crossed by the weft

warrant *NOUN* (**warrants**)
a document that gives the police the right to arrest someone or search a place

warrant *VERB* (**warrants, warranting, warranted**)
to warrant something is to justify or deserve it • *Nothing warrants such rudeness.*

warren *NOUN* (**warrens**)
a piece of ground where there are many rabbit burrows

warrior *NOUN* (**warriors**)
someone who fights in battles; a soldier

warship *NOUN* (**warships**)
a ship designed for use in war

wart *NOUN* (**warts**)
a small hard lump on your skin

wary *ADJECTIVE* (**warier, wariest**)
cautious and careful • *I gave the tiger a wary glance.*
▷ **warily** *ADVERB* cautiously
▷ **wariness** *NOUN* wariness is being cautious

was
1st and 3rd person singular past tense of **be**

wash *VERB* (**washes**, **washing**, **washed**)
1 to wash something is to clean it with water **2** you wash when you clean yourself with water **3** to wash is to flow over or against something • *Waves washed over the beach.* **4** to be washed somewhere is to be carried along by the force of moving water • *The boxes were washed overboard.* **5** (*informal*) an explanation or excuse won't wash when it is not acceptable or believable • *That story just won't wash.*
to wash up is to wash the dishes and cutlery after a meal

wash *NOUN* (**washes**)
1 the action of washing **2** the disturbed water behind a moving ship **3** a thin coating of colour or paint

washable *ADJECTIVE*
able to be washed without being damaged

washbasin *NOUN* (**washbasins**)
a small basin with taps, holding water for washing your hands and face

washer *NOUN* (**washers**)
1 a small ring of metal or rubber placed between two surfaces, especially under a bolt or screw, to fit them tightly together **2** a washing machine

washing *NOUN*
washing is clothes that need to be washed or have been washed

washing machine *NOUN* (**washing machines**)
a machine for washing clothes

washing-up *NOUN*
washing-up is washing the dishes and cutlery after a meal

wash-out *NOUN* (**wash-outs**)
(*slang*) a complete failure

wasn't
short for *was not*

wasp *NOUN* (**wasps**)
a stinging insect with black and yellow stripes across its body

wastage *NOUN*
wastage is losing something by waste

waste *VERB* (**wastes**, **wasting**, **wasted**)
1 to waste something is to use more of it than you need to, or to use it without getting much value from it **2** to waste something is also to fail to use it • *You are wasting a good opportunity.*
to waste away is to become thinner and weaker

waste *ADJECTIVE*
1 left over or thrown away because it is not wanted • *What shall we do with all this waste paper?* **2** not used or usable • *We came to an area of waste land.*

waste *NOUN* (**wastes**)
1 a waste is wasting something or not using it well • *It's a waste of time.* **2** waste is things that are not wanted or used **3** a waste is also an area of desert or frozen land • *We flew over the wastes of Alaska.*

wasteful *ADJECTIVE*
wasting things or not using them well
▷ **wastefully** *ADVERB* in a wasteful way

watch *VERB* (**watches**, **watching**, **watched**)
1 to watch someone or something is to look at them for some time **2** to watch, or watch out, is to be on guard or ready for something to happen • *Watch for the light to change.* **3** to watch something is also to take care of it • *His job is to watch the sheep.*
to watch out is to be careful about something
▷ **watcher** *NOUN* someone who watches something

watch *NOUN* (**watches**)
1 a device like a small clock, usually worn on a person's wrist **2** a period of being on guard or on duty

watchdog *NOUN* (**watchdogs**)
a dog kept to guard buildings

watchful *ADJECTIVE*
alert and watching carefully
▷ **watchfully** *ADVERB* in a watchful way
▷ **watchfulness** *NOUN* watchfulness is being alert

watchman *NOUN* (**watchmen**)
someone whose job is to guard a building at night

water *NOUN* (**waters**)
1 water is a transparent colourless liquid that is a compound of hydrogen and oxygen **2** a water is a sea or lake **3** water is also the state of the tide • *The sea is at high water.*
to pass water is to urinate

water *VERB* (**waters**, **watering**, **watered**)
1 to water a plant is to sprinkle water over it • *Have you watered the flowers?* **2** to water an animal is to give it water to drink **3** your eyes or mouth water when they produce tears or saliva • *The smell of toast makes my mouth water.*
to water something down is to dilute it or make it weaker

water closet *NOUN* (**water closets**)
a lavatory with a pan that is flushed by water

watercolour *NOUN* (**watercolours**)
1 a paint that can be mixed with water **2** a painting done with this kind of paint

watercress *NOUN*
a kind of cress that grows in water

water cycle *NOUN*
the process by which water falls to the ground as rain and snow, runs into rivers and lakes, flows into the sea, evaporates into the air and forms clouds, and then falls to the ground again

waterfall *NOUN* (**waterfalls**)
a place where a river or stream flows over a cliff or large rock

watering can *NOUN* (**watering cans**)
a container with a long spout, for watering plants

waterlogged *ADJECTIVE*
waterlogged ground is so wet it cannot soak up any more water

watermark *NOUN* (**watermarks**)
1 a mark showing the level of water **2** a faint design in some types of paper, which you can see if you hold it up to the light

watermelon *NOUN* (**watermelons**)
a large melon with a smooth green skin and red juicy flesh.

waterproof *ADJECTIVE*
able to keep water out • *a waterproof jacket*

water-skiing *NOUN*
the sport of skimming over the surface of water on flat boards (**water-skis**) while being towed by a motor boat

watertight *ADJECTIVE*
1 made so that water cannot get into it **2** a watertight (for example) excuse or plan is carefully prepared so that it has no mistakes or weaknesses • *He has a watertight alibi.*

waterway *NOUN* (**waterways**)
a river or canal that ships can travel on

waterworks *NOUN* (**waterworks**)
a place with pumping machinery for supplying water to a district

watery *ADJECTIVE*
1 like water **2** full of water • *You have watery eyes.*

watt *NOUN* (**watts**)
a unit of electric power

wave *VERB* (**waves**, **waving**, **waved**)
1 to wave is to move your hand from side to side, usually to say hello or goodbye **2** you wave something, or it waves, when it moves from side to side or up and down • *Flags were waving in the wind.* **3** to wave hair is to make it curl

wave *NOUN* (**waves**)
1 a moving ridge on the surface of water, especially on the sea **2** a curling piece of hair **3** (*in science*) one of the to-and-fro movements in which sound and light and electricity travel **4** the action of waving your hand • *He gave us a little wave.* **5** a sudden build-up of something strong • *She felt a wave of anger.*

> SPELLING
> Take care not to confuse **wave** with **waive**, as in *she waived her rights.*

waveband *NOUN* (**wavebands**)
the wavelengths between certain limits

wavelength *NOUN* (**wavelengths**)
the size of a sound wave or electric wave

waver *VERB* (**wavers**, **wavering**, **wavered**)
1 to waver is to be unsteady or uncertain • *They wavered between two choices.* **2** to waver is also to move unsteadily

wavy *ADJECTIVE* (**wavier**, **waviest**)
full of waves or curves

wax[1] *NOUN* (**waxes**)
wax is a soft substance that melts easily, used for making candles, crayons, and polish

> WORD FAMILY
> Something is **waxy** when it looks or feels like wax.

wax *VERB* (**waxes**, **waxing**, **waxed**)
to wax something is to cover it with wax

wax[2] *VERB* (**waxes**, **waxing**, **waxed**)
the moon waxes when its bright area gets gradually larger

waxwork *NOUN* (**waxworks**)
a model made of wax, especially a full-size model of a person

way *NOUN* (**ways**)
1 how something is done; a method or manner **2** the way to a place is how you get there **3** a road or path leading from one place to another **4** a distance • *Is it a long way?* **5** a respect • *It's a good idea in some ways.* **6** a condition or state • *Things are in a bad way.*
to get your own way is to make people let you have what you want
in the way blocking something or stopping something from progressing
no way (*informal*) that is impossible; that is not true

WC
short for **water closet**, used especially on a plan or a sign showing where a lavatory is

we *PRONOUN*
a word used by someone to mean 'I and someone else' or 'I and others'

weak *ADJECTIVE* (**weaker**, **weakest**)
1 without much strength or energy **2** easy to break, bend, or defeat **3** poor at doing something

> WORD FAMILY
> You (for example) smile **weakly** when you do it without much enthusiasm; **weakness** is being weak; a **weakness** a person has is one of their faults or something they don't do well.

weaken *VERB* (**weakens**, **weakening**, **weakened**)
1 to weaken something is to make it weaker **2** to weaken is to become weaker

weakling *NOUN* (**weaklings**)
a weak person

wealth *NOUN*
1 wealth is a lot of money or property **2** a wealth of something is a lot of it • *The book has a wealth of illustrations.*

wealthy *ADJECTIVE* (**wealthier**, **wealthiest**)
someone is wealthy when they have a lot of money or property

weapon *NOUN* (**weapons**)
something used to harm or kill people in a battle or fight

wear *VERB* (**wears**, **wearing**, **wore**, **worn**)
1 to wear something is to be dressed in it **2** to wear something is to damage it by rubbing or using it; to wear is to become damaged like this • *The carpet has worn thin.* **3** to last • *This cloth wears well.*
to wear off is to become less strong or intense
to wear out is to become weak or useless
to wear someone out is to make them very tired
▷ **wearer** *NOUN* someone who wears something

wear *NOUN*
1 wear is clothes • *Where can I find men's wear?*
2 wear is gradual damage done by rubbing or using something

weary *ADJECTIVE* (**wearier**, **weariest**)
very tired

> WORD FAMILY
> To do something **wearily** is to do it in a way that shows you are very tired; **weariness** is being very tired.

weasel *NOUN* (**weasels**)
a small fierce animal with a slender body

weather *NOUN*
weather is the rain, snow, wind, sunshine, and temperature at a particular time or place
to be under the weather is to feel ill or depressed

weather *VERB* (**weathers**, **weathering**, **weathered**)
1 to weather is to become worn because of being exposed to the weather **2** to weather something is to make it suffer the effects of the weather • *The wind and rain have weathered the cliffs.* **3** you weather a difficulty when you come through it successfully • *They weathered the storm.*

weathercock *NOUN* (**weathercocks**)
a pointer, often shaped like a cockerel, that turns in the wind and shows which way the wind is blowing

weave *VERB* (**weaves**, **weaving**, **wove**, **woven**)
1 to weave material or baskets is to make them by crossing threads or strips over and under each other **2** to weave is to twist and turn • *He wove skilfully through the traffic.*

> WORD FAMILY
> A **weaver** is someone who weaves material.

web *NOUN* (**webs**)
1 a net of thin sticky threads that spiders spin to catch insects **2** something complicated • *We were caught up in a web of lies.* **3** a computer network, especially the Internet

webbed or **web-footed** *ADJECTIVE*
webbed feet have toes joined by pieces of skin, as ducks' feet do

website *NOUN* (**websites**)
a place on the Internet where you can get information

wed *VERB* (**weds**, **wedding**, **wedded** or **wed**)
to wed someone is to marry them

we'd
short for *we had* or *we should* or *we would*

wedding *NOUN* (**weddings**)
the ceremony when a man and woman get married

wedge *NOUN* (**wedges**)
1 a piece of wood or metal or plastic that is thick at one end and thin at the other, pushed between things to force them apart or to hold them tight **2** something shaped like a wedge • *a wedge of cheese*
the thin end of the wedge a situation which is not bad yet but might get worse

wedge *VERB* (**wedges**, **wedging**, **wedged**)
to wedge something is to hold it in place, especially with a wedge

Wednesday *NOUN* (**Wednesdays**)
the fourth day of the week

weed *NOUN* (**weeds**)
a wild plant that grows where it is not wanted

weed *VERB* (**weeds**, **weeding**, **weeded**)
to weed the ground is to remove weeds from it

weedy *ADJECTIVE* (**weedier**, **weediest**)
1 full of weeds **2** thin and weak

week *NOUN* (**weeks**)
1 a period of seven days, especially from Sunday to the following Saturday **2** the part of the week that doesn't include the weekend

weekday *NOUN* (**weekdays**)
any day except Saturday and Sunday

weekend *NOUN* (**weekends**)
Saturday and Sunday

weekly *ADJECTIVE & ADVERB*
every week

weep *VERB* (**weeps**, **weeping**, **wept**)
to weep is to cry or shed tears

weeping willow *NOUN* (**weeping willows**)
a kind of willow tree that has drooping branches

weft *NOUN*
the weft is the threads on a loom that are woven across the warp

weigh *VERB* (**weighs**, **weighing**, **weighed**)
1 to weigh something is to find out how heavy it is **2** to weigh a certain amount is to have that as its weight • *How much do you weigh?*
to weigh anchor is to raise the anchor and start a voyage
to weigh someone down is to depress or trouble them
to weigh something down is to hold it down with something heavy
to weigh something up is to think about it carefully before deciding what to do

weight *NOUN* (**weights**)
1 weight is the measure of how heavy something is **2** a weight is a piece of metal of known weight, used on scales to weigh things **3** a weight is also a heavy object, used to hold things down

> WORD FAMILY
> Astronauts are **weightless** when they float around because there is no gravity.

weightlifting *NOUN*
weightlifting is the sport or exercise of lifting heavy weights

weighty *ADJECTIVE* (**weightier**, **weightiest**)
1 heavy **2** important • *These are weighty matters.*

weir *NOUN* (**weirs**) (*say* weer)
a small dam across a river or canal to control the flow of water

weird *ADJECTIVE* (**weirder**, **weirdest**) (*say* weerd)
very strange or unnatural
▷ **weirdly** *ADVERB* in a very strange or unnatural way
▷ **weirdness** *NOUN* weirdness is being weird

welcome *NOUN* (**welcomes**)
a kind or friendly greeting or reception

welcome *ADJECTIVE*
1 that you are glad to get or see • *This is a welcome surprise.* **2** allowed or free to do or take something • *You are welcome to use my bicycle.*

welcome *VERB* (**welcomes**, **welcoming**, **welcomed**)
to welcome someone or something is to show that you are pleased when they arrive

weld *VERB* (**welds**, **welding**, **welded**)
to weld pieces of metal or plastic together is to join them by using heat or pressure

> WORD FAMILY
> A **welder** is someone who welds things together.

welfare *NOUN*
welfare is people's health, happiness, and comfort

welfare state *NOUN*
a system of paying for health care and other social services from public funds

well[1] *NOUN* (**wells**)
a deep hole dug or drilled to get water or oil out of the ground

well[2] *ADVERB* (**better**, **best**)
1 in a good or successful way • *He can play the piano quite well now.* **2** thoroughly • *Wash your hands well.* **3** actually; probably • *It may well be our last chance.*
as well also
to be well off is to be fairly rich or fortunate

well *ADJECTIVE*
1 in good health • *She is not well.* **2** good or satisfactory • *All is well.*

we'll
short for *we shall* or *we will*

well-being *NOUN*
well-being is health or happiness

well-disposed *ADJECTIVE*
to be well-disposed towards someone is to have friendly feelings for them

wellington boots or **wellingtons** *PLURAL NOUN*
rubber or plastic waterproof boots

well-known *ADJECTIVE*
known to many people

well-mannered *ADJECTIVE*
having good manners

went
past tense of **go** *VERB*

wept
past tense and past participle of **weep**

were
plural and 2nd person singular past tense of **be**

we're
short for *we are*

werewolf *NOUN* (**werewolves**)
in stories, a person who sometimes changes into a wolf

west *NOUN*
1 the direction where the sun sets **2** the part of a country or city that is in this direction

west *ADJECTIVE & ADVERB*
1 towards the west or in the west **2** coming from the west • *There was a west wind blowing.*

westerly *ADJECTIVE*
a westerly wind is one that blows from the west

western *ADJECTIVE*
from or to do with the west

western *NOUN* (**westerns**)
a film or story about the people of western America in the 19th century and early 20th century

westward or **westwards** *ADJECTIVE & ADVERB*
towards the west

wet *ADJECTIVE* (**wetter**, **wettest**)
1 covered or soaked in water or other liquid **2** not yet set or dry • *Watch out for wet paint.* **3** rainy • *It's been wet here all day.*
▷ **wetness** *NOUN* wetness is being wet

wet *VERB* (**wets**, **wetting**, **wetted**)
to wet something is to make it wet

wet blanket *NOUN* (**wet blankets**)
someone who is gloomy and who prevents other people from enjoying themselves

wet suit *NOUN* (**wet suits**)
a rubber suit that clings to the skin, worn by skin divers and windsurfers to keep them warm and dry

we've
short for *we have*

whack *VERB* (**whacks**, **whacking**, **whacked**)
to whack someone or something is to hit them hard

whack *NOUN* (**whacks**)
a hard hit or blow

whale *NOUN* (**whales**)
a very large sea animal
to have a whale of a time (*informal*) is to enjoy yourself

whaler *NOUN* (**whalers**)
a person or ship that hunts whales

whaling *NOUN*
whaling is hunting whales

wharf *NOUN* (**wharves** or **wharfs**) (*say* worf)
a quay where ships are loaded or unloaded

what *ADJECTIVE*
1 used to ask the amount or kind of something • *What kind of bike have you got?* **2** used to say how strange or great a person or thing is • *What a fool you are!*

what *PRONOUN*
1 what thing or things • *What did you say?* **2** the thing that • *This is what you must do.*
what's what (*informal*) what is important or useful • *She knows what's what.*

whatever *PRONOUN*
1 anything or everything • *Do whatever you like.*
2 no matter what • *I'll be there whatever happens.*

whatever *ADJECTIVE*
of any kind or amount • *Get whatever help you can.*

wheat *NOUN*
wheat is a cereal plant from which flour is made

wheel *NOUN* (**wheels**)
1 a round device that turns on an axle passing through its centre. Wheels are used to move vehicles or work machinery **2** a horizontal revolving disc on which clay is made into a pot

wheel *VERB* (**wheels, wheeling, wheeled**)
1 to wheel a bicycle or cart is to push it along on its wheels **2** to wheel is to move in a curve or circle • *The column of soldiers wheeled to the right.*

wheelbarrow *NOUN* (**wheelbarrows**)
a small cart with one wheel at the front and two handles at the back

wheelchair *NOUN* (**wheelchairs**)
a chair on wheels for a person who cannot walk

wheel clamp *NOUN* (**wheel clamps**)
a device that can be locked around a vehicle's wheel to prevent it from being driven away

wheeze *VERB* (**wheezes, wheezing, wheezed**)
to wheeze is to make a whistling or gasping noise as you breathe

whelk *NOUN* (**whelks**)
a shellfish that looks like a snail

when *ADVERB*
at what time • *When can you come to tea?*

when *CONJUNCTION*
1 at the time that • *The bird flew away when I moved.*
2 because; considering that • *Why do you smoke when you know it is dangerous?*

whenever *CONJUNCTION*
at any time; every time • *Whenever I see him, he's smiling.*

where *ADVERB & CONJUNCTION*
1 in or to what place • *Where have you put the glue?*
2 in or to that place • *Leave it where it is.*

whereabouts *ADVERB*
roughly where; in what area • *Whereabouts is Timbuktu?*

whereabouts *NOUN*
the place where something is • *Have you any idea of her whereabouts?*

whereas *CONJUNCTION*
but on the other hand • *Some people like sailing, whereas others hate it.*

whereupon *ADVERB*
after that; and then

wherever *ADVERB & CONJUNCTION*
in or to whatever place; no matter where

whether *CONJUNCTION*
used to introduce more than one possibility • *I don't know whether they are here or not.*

whey *NOUN* (*say* way)
whey is the watery liquid left when milk forms curds

which *ADJECTIVE*
what particular • *Which way did he go?*

which *PRONOUN*
1 what person or thing • *Which is your desk?* **2** the person or thing just mentioned • *Here's my book, which you asked me to bring.*

whichever *PRONOUN & ADJECTIVE*
that or those which; any which • *Take whichever you like.*

whiff *NOUN* (**whiffs**)
a slight smell of something • *He caught a whiff of perfume as she walked past him.*

while *CONJUNCTION*
1 during the time that; as long as • *She was singing while she worked.* **2** but; although • *She is fair, while her sister is dark.*

while *NOUN*
a period of time • *We have waited all this while.*

while *VERB* (**whiles, whiling, whiled**)
to while away time is to pass it doing something leisurely • *It poured all that afternoon, and the little company in the lighthouse whiled away the time playing cards.* — Enid Blyton, *Five Go to Demon's Rocks*

whilst *CONJUNCTION*
while

whim *NOUN* (**whims**)
a sudden desire to do or have something

whimper *VERB* (**whimpers, whimpering, whimpered**)
to whimper is to cry with a low trembling

whimper *NOUN* (**whimpers**)
a sound of whimpering

whine *VERB* (**whines, whining, whined**)
1 to whine is to make a long high piercing sound
2 to whine is also to complain in an annoying way

whine *NOUN* (**whines**)
a whining sound

whinny *VERB* (**whinnies**, **whinnying**, **whinnied**)
a horse whinnies when it neighs gently

whip *NOUN* (**whips**)
a cord or strip of leather fixed to a handle and used for hitting people or animals

whip *VERB* (**whips**, **whipping**, **whipped**)
1 to whip a person or animal is to beat them with a whip **2** to whip cream is to beat it until it becomes thick and frothy **3** (*informal*) to whip something is to steal it
to whip something out (*informal*) is to take it out quickly or suddenly
to whip something up is to stir up people's feelings • *They quickly whipped up support for the idea.*

whirl *VERB* (**whirls**, **whirling**, **whirled**)
you whirl something round, or it whirls, when it turns or spins very quickly

whirl *NOUN* (**whirls**)
when something turns or spins very quickly

whirlpool *NOUN* (**whirlpools**)
a strong current of water going round in a circle and pulling things towards it

whirlwind *NOUN* (**whirlwinds**)
a very strong wind that whirls around or blows in a spiral

whirr *VERB* (**whirrs**, **whirring**, **whirred**)
to whirr is to make a continuous buzzing sound

whirr *NOUN* (**whirrs**)
a continuous buzzing sound

whisk *VERB* (**whisks**, **whisking**, **whisked**)
1 to whisk cream or eggs is to beat them until they are thick or frothy **2** to whisk something somewhere is to move it there very quickly • *A waiter whisked away my plate.*

whisk *NOUN* (**whisks**)
1 a device for whisking eggs or cream **2** a whisking movement

whisker *NOUN* (**whiskers**)
1 whiskers are the long stiff hairs on the face of a cat or other animal **2** you can refer to the hair growing on a man's face as his whiskers

whisky *NOUN* (**whiskies**)
a kind of very strong alcoholic drink

whisper *VERB* (**whispers**, **whispering**, **whispered**)
to whisper is to speak very softly or secretly

whisper *NOUN* (**whispers**)
a very soft voice or sound

whist *NOUN*
whist is a card game usually for four people

whistle *VERB* (**whistles**, **whistling**, **whistled**)
1 you whistle when you make a shrill or musical sound by blowing through your lips **2** something whistles when it makes a shrill sound • *The kettle was whistling away.*

whistle *NOUN* (**whistles**)
1 a whistling sound **2** a device that makes a shrill sound when you blow into it

white *ADJECTIVE* (**whiter**, **whitest**)
1 of the very lightest colour, like snow or milk **2** having light-coloured skin **3** white coffee is coffee with milk

> WORD FAMILY
> **Whiteness** is being white; something is **whitish** when it is fairly white in colour.

white *NOUN* (**whites**)
1 a white colour **2** the substance round the yolk of an egg, which turns white when it is cooked

white elephant *NOUN* (**white elephants**)
a useless possession

white-hot *ADJECTIVE*
something is white-hot when it is extremely hot, or so hot that heated metal looks white

whiten *VERB* (**whitens**, **whitening**, **whitened**)
1 to whiten something is to make it white **2** to whiten is to become white

whitewash *NOUN*
whitewash is a white liquid made from lime and chalk and painted on walls and ceilings

whitewash *VERB* (**whitewashes**, **whitewashing**, **whitewashed**)
to whitewash a wall or ceiling is to coat it with whitewash

Whitsun *NOUN*
Whitsun is Whit Sunday, or the period around it

Whit Sunday *NOUN*
Whit Sunday is the seventh Sunday after Easter

whiz *VERB* (**whizzes**, **whizzing**, **whizzed**)
1 to whiz is to move very quickly **2** to whiz is also to sound like something rushing through the air

who *PRONOUN*
1 which person or people • *Who threw that?* **2** the person or people spoken about • *These are the boys who did it.*

whoever *PRONOUN*
any person who • *Whoever comes is welcome.*

whole *ADJECTIVE*
1 all of something • *Could you eat a whole pizza?* **2** not broken or damaged

whole *NOUN* (**wholes**)
a complete thing; all the parts of something
on the whole considering everything; mainly

wholefood *NOUN* (**wholefoods**)
wholefood is food that has not been processed or produced with artificial fertilizers

wholemeal *ADJECTIVE*
wholemeal flour or bread is made from the whole grain of wheat

whole number *NOUN* (**whole numbers**)
a number without a fraction

wholesale *ADJECTIVE & ADVERB*
1 sold in large quantities to be sold again by others **2** on a large scale; including everybody or everything • *There has been wholesale destruction.*

wholesome *ADJECTIVE*
healthy and good for you • *We all need wholesome food.*

wholly *ADVERB*
completely or entirely

whom *PRONOUN*
a word used for **who** when it is the object of a verb or comes after a preposition, as in *the boy whom I saw* or *the boy to whom I spoke*

whoop *NOUN* (**whoops**) (*say* woop)
a loud excited cry

whoopee *INTERJECTION* (*say* **wuup**- ee)
a cry of joy

whooping cough *NOUN* (*say* **hoop**- ing- kof)
whooping cough is an illness that makes you cough and gasp

who's
short for *who has* or *who is*

whose *ADJECTIVE & PRONOUN*
1 belonging to what person • *Whose bike is that?* **2** of which; of whom • *The girl whose party we went to.*

why *ADVERB*
for what reason or purpose

wick *NOUN* (**wicks**)
1 the string that goes through the middle of a candle and is lit to give a flame **2** the strip of material that you light in a lamp or heater that uses oil

wicked *ADJECTIVE* (**wickeder**, **wickedest**)
1 very bad or cruel; doing things that are wrong **2** mischievous • *He gave a wicked smile.* **3** (*slang*) very fine or good • *That's a wicked goal!*

WORD FAMILY
To do something **wickedly** is to do it in a cruel or mischievous way; **wickedness** is doing bad things.

wicker or **wickerwork** *NOUN*
wicker or wickerwork is reeds or canes woven together to make baskets and furniture

wicket *NOUN* (**wickets**)
1 in cricket, each set of three stumps with two bails on top of them **2** the part of a cricket ground between or near the wickets

wicketkeeper *NOUN* (**wicketkeepers**)
the fielder in cricket who stands behind the batsman's wicket

wide *ADJECTIVE* (**wider**, **widest**)
1 measuring a lot from one side to the other • *The river was wide.* **2** from one side to the other • *The room is 4 metres wide.* **3** covering a large range • *She has a wide knowledge of birds.*

wide *ADVERB* (**wider**, **widest**)
1 you are wide awake when you are completely or fully awake **2** to open or spread something wide is to open or spread it as far as possible **3** far from the target • *The shot went wide.* **4** over a large area • *She travelled far and wide.*

widely *ADVERB*
commonly; among many people • *They are widely admired.*

widen *VERB* (**widens**, **widening**, **widened**)
to widen something is to make it wider; to widen is to become wider

widespread *ADJECTIVE*
existing or found in many places; common

widow *NOUN* (**widows**)
a woman whose husband has died

widower *NOUN* (**widowers**)
a man whose wife has died

width *NOUN* (**widths**)
the width of something is how much it measures from one side to the other

wield *VERB* (**wields**, **wielding**, **wielded**) (*say* weeld)
to wield a weapon or tool is to hold it and use it • *a picture of a knight wielding a sword.*

wife *NOUN* (**wives**)
the woman that a man has married

wig *NOUN* (**wigs**)
a covering of false hair worn on the head

wiggle *VERB* (**wiggles**, **wiggling**, **wiggled**)
to wiggle something is to move it from side to side

wiggle *NOUN* (**wiggles**)
a wiggling movement

wigwam *NOUN* (**wigwams**)
the tent of a Native American

wild *ADJECTIVE* (**wilder**, **wildest**)
1 wild animals and plants live or grow in their natural state and are not looked after by people **2** wild land is in its natural state and has not been changed by people **3** not controlled; violent or angry • *His behaviour became more and more wild.* • *She went wild when she saw the mess.* **4** very foolish or unreasonable • *They do have wild ideas.*

WORD FAMILY
To do something **wildly** is to do it in a way that is not controlled • *My heart was beating wildly;* **wildness** is being wild.

wild *NOUN* (**wilds**)
1 animals live in the wild when they live in their natural environment **2** the wilds are areas of a country far from towns and cities, where there are few people

wilderness *NOUN* (**wildernesses**)
an area of wild country; a desert

wildlife *NOUN*
wildlife is wild animals in their natural setting

a b c d e f g h i j k l m n o p q r s t u v w x y z

wilful *ADJECTIVE*
1 someone is wilful when they are determined to do exactly what they want • *What a wilful child.* **2** something is wilful when it is done deliberately • *This is wilful disobedience.*
▷ **wilfully** *ADVERB* in a wilful way
▷ **wilfulness** *NOUN* wilfulness is being wilful

will[1] *VERB* (*past tense* **would**)
used to refer to the future • *I will be there at 12 o'clock.*

will[2] *NOUN* (**wills**)
1 will is the power to use your mind to decide and control what you do **2** someone's will is what they choose or want • *He was forced to write the letter against his will.* **3** someone's will to do something is their determination to do it • *She has a strong will to succeed.* **4** a will is a legal document saying what is to be done with someone's possessions after they die

willing *ADJECTIVE*
ready and happy to do what is wanted • *Are you willing to help?*

> WORD FAMILY
> You do something **willingly** or show **willingness** to do it when you are happy to do it.

willow *NOUN* (**willows**)
a tree with thin flexible branches, often growing near water

wilt *VERB* (**wilts, wilting, wilted**)
a plant wilts when it loses freshness and droops • *'A fairy flower bracelet doesn't wilt until all the fairy dust wears off,' Flora explained.* — Gwyneth Rees, *Fairy Dust*

wily *ADJECTIVE* (**wilier, wiliest**)
crafty or cunning
▷ **wiliness** *NOUN* being crafty or cunning

wimp *NOUN* (**wimps**)
(*informal*) a feeble or timid person

win *VERB* (**wins, winning, won**)
1 to win a contest or game or battle is to do better than your opponents **2** to win something is to get it by using effort or in a competition • *She won second prize.*

win *NOUN* (**wins**)
a success or victory

wince *VERB* (**winces, wincing, winced**)
to wince is to make a slight movement because you are in pain or embarrassed

winch *NOUN* (**winches**)
a device for lifting or pulling things, using a rope or cable that goes round a wheel or drum

winch *VERB* (**winches, winching, winched**)
to winch something is to lift it or pull it with a winch

wind[1] *NOUN* (**winds**) (*rhymes with* **tinned**)
1 wind, or a wind, is a current of air **2** wind is gas in the stomach or intestines that makes you uncomfortable **3** wind is also breath used for a purpose, such as running **4** in an orchestra, the wind is the wind instruments
to get or **have the wind up** (*slang*) is to be scared

wind[2] *VERB* (**winds, winding, wound**) (*rhymes with* **find**)
1 something like a road or river winds when it twists and turns • *The river winds down the valley.* **2** to wind something is to wrap or twist it round something else • *She wound her scarf round her neck.* **3** to wind, or wind up, a watch or clock is to tighten its spring so that it works
to wind up somewhere is to end up there • *They wound up in gaol.*

windfall *NOUN* (**windfalls**)
1 a fruit blown down from a tree **2** a piece of unexpected good luck, especially a sum of money

wind instrument *NOUN* (**wind instruments**)
a musical instrument played by blowing, such as a trumpet or clarinet

windmill *NOUN* (**windmills**)
a mill with four long arms called *sails* which are turned by the wind

window *NOUN* (**windows**)
1 an opening in a wall or roof to let in light and air, usually filled with glass **2** the glass in a window opening **3** (*in computing*) an area on a computer screen used for a particular purpose

window shopping *NOUN*
window shopping is browsing in shop windows without buying anything

windpipe *NOUN* (**windpipes**)
the tube through which air reaches your lungs

windscreen *NOUN* (**windscreens**)
the window at the front of a motor vehicle

> BRITISH AND AMERICAN
> In America, the word **windshield** is normally used.

windsurfing *NOUN*
windsurfing is surfing on a board with a sail fixed to it

> WORD FAMILY
> A **windsurfer** is someone who goes windsurfing.

windward *ADJECTIVE*
facing the wind, especially on a ship

windy *ADJECTIVE* (**windier, windiest**)
with a lot of wind • *It's a windy day today.*

wine *NOUN* (**wines**)
1 an alcoholic drink made from grapes or other plants **2** a dark red colour

wing *NOUN* (**wings**)
1 a bird's or insect's wings are the parts it uses for flying **2** an aircraft's wings are the long flat parts that stick out from its sides and support it in the air

3 a part of a building that extends from the main part **4** each side of a theatre stage, out of sight of the audience **5** the part of a motor vehicle's body above a wheel **6** each of the players in football and other ball games whose place is at the side of the field **7** a section of a political party, having particular views
on the wing flying
to take wing is to fly away

> WORD FAMILY
> **Winged** insects or other creatures have wings •*Pegasus was a mythical winged horse*; **wingless** insects have no wings.

wing *VERB* (**wings**, **winging**, **winged**)
1 to wing someone is to wound them in the side **2** a bird wings its way when it flies a long way

wingspan *NOUN* (**wingspans**)
the distance across the wings of a bird or aeroplane

wink *VERB* (**winks**, **winking**, **winked**)
1 you wink when you close and open one of your eyes quickly **2** a light winks when it flickers or twinkles •*It looked like Aladdin's cave. Necklaces and bracelets hung winking from the roof of the shelter.* — Clive King, *Stig of the Dump*

wink *NOUN* (**winks**)
1 when you close and open one of your eyes quickly **2** a short period of sleep •*I didn't sleep a wink.*

winkle *NOUN* (**winkles**)
a shellfish that is used for food

winkle *VERB* (**winkles**, **winkling**, **winkled**)
to winkle something out is to find it with a lot of effort

winner *NOUN* (**winners**)
1 a person who wins something **2** (*informal*) something very successful •*Her new book is a winner.*

winnings *PLURAL NOUN*
the money someone wins in a game or by betting

winter *NOUN* (**winters**)
the coldest season of the year, between autumn and spring

> WORD FAMILY
> **Wintry** weather is cold, like winter; a **wintry** smile is cold and unfriendly.

wintertime *NOUN*
wintertime is the season of winter

wipe *VERB* (**wipes**, **wiping**, **wiped**)
to wipe something is to rub it gently to dry it or clean it
to wipe something out is to destroy it or cancel it •*He's wiped out his debt.*

wipe *NOUN* (**wipes**)
the action of wiping •*Give it a quick wipe.*

wiper *NOUN* (**wipers**)
a device for wiping something, especially on a vehicle's windscreen

wire *NOUN* (**wires**)
a thin length of metal used to carry electric current or for making fences

wire *VERB* (**wires**, **wiring**, **wired**)
to wire something, or wire it up, is to connect it with wires to carry electricity

wireless *NOUN* (**wirelesses**)
(*old use*) a radio set

wiring *NOUN*
wiring is the system of wires carrying electricity in a building or in a device

wiry *ADJECTIVE* (**wirier**, **wiriest**)
1 a wiry person is lean and strong **2** wiry hair is tough and stiff

wisdom *NOUN*
1 wisdom is being wise **2** wisdom is also wise sayings or writings

wisdom tooth *NOUN* (**wisdom teeth**)
a molar tooth that may grow at the back of your jaw much later than the other teeth

wise *ADJECTIVE* (**wiser**, **wisest**)
knowing or understanding many things and so able to make sensible decisions
to be none the wiser is to not know any more about something than you did before

> WORD FAMILY
> Someone **wisely** does something when it is the sensible thing to do •*He wisely decided to tell the truth.*

wish *VERB* (**wishes**, **wishing**, **wished**)
1 to wish something, or wish to do something, is to think or say that you would like it **2** to wish someone something is to say that you hope they will get it •*They wished us luck.*

wish *NOUN* (**wishes**)
1 something you want **2** when you wish for something •*Make a wish.* •*We send you our best wishes.*

wishbone *NOUN* (**wishbones**)
a forked bone from the breast of a chicken or other bird

wisp *NOUN* (**wisps**)
a thin piece or line of something light or fluffy, such as hair or smoke

> WORD FAMILY
> **Wispy** hair or smoke is in the form of wisps.

wistful *ADJECTIVE*
thinking sadly about something you can no longer have •*Pollyanna laughed again, but she sighed, too; and in the gathering twilight her face looked thin and wistful.*
— Eleanor H. Porter, *Pollyanna*
▷ **wistfully** *ADVERB* in a wistful way
▷ **wistfulness** *NOUN* wistfulness is being wistful

a b c d e f g h i j k l m n o p q r s t u v **w** x y z

a b c d e f g h i j k l m n o p q r s t u v w x y z

wit *NOUN* (**wits**)
1 wit is intelligence or cleverness **2** wit is also a clever kind of humour **3** a wit is a witty person
to keep your wits about you is to stay alert

witch *NOUN* (**witches**)
a woman who is believed to use magic

witchcraft *NOUN*
witchcraft is using magic, especially to make bad things happen

witch doctor *NOUN* (**witch doctors**)
a magician who belongs to a tribe and is thought to heal people

with *PREPOSITION*
there are many meanings, of which the most important are: **1** having •*I saw a man with a wooden leg.* **2** in the company of or accompanied by •*I came with a friend.* **3** using •*Hit it with a hammer.* **4** against •*They fought with each other.* **5** because of •*He shook with laughter.* **6** towards or concerning •*Be careful with that.*

withdraw *VERB* (**withdraws, withdrawing, withdrew, withdrawn**)
1 to withdraw something is to take it away or take it back •*She withdrew her offer.* **2** to withdraw is to retreat or drop out of something •*The troops have withdrawn from the frontier.* •*His injury meant he had to withdraw from the race.*

> WORD FAMILY
> **Withdrawal** is when someone withdraws something or withdraws from a place; a **withdrawal** is an amount of money someone takes out of their bank account.

wither *VERB* (**withers, withering, withered**)
a plant withers when it shrivels or wilts

withhold *VERB* (**withholds, withholding, withheld**)
to withhold something is to refuse to give it to someone •*He has withheld his permission.*

within *PREPOSITION & ADVERB*
inside; not beyond something •*Is the top shelf within your reach?*

without *PREPOSITION*
not having; free from •*It is difficult to live without money.*

withstand *VERB* (**withstands, withstanding, withstood**)
to withstand something is to resist it or put up with it successfully •*The bridge is designed to withstand high winds.*

witness *NOUN* (**witnesses**)
1 a person who sees something happen and can describe it •*There were no witnesses to the accident.* **2** a person who gives evidence in a lawcourt

witty *ADJECTIVE* (**wittier, wittiest**)
clever and amusing
▷ **wittily** *ADVERB* in a witty way

wizard *NOUN* (**wizards**)
1 a man who has magic powers **2** a person who is very good at something •*He's a wizard on the accordion.*

> WORD FAMILY
> **Wizardry** is the clever and impressive things that a computer or other machine can do.

wobble *VERB* (**wobbles, wobbling, wobbled**)
to wobble is to move unsteadily from side to side

wobble *NOUN* (**wobbles**)
a wobbling movement

> WORD FAMILY
> Something is **wobbly** when it moves unsteadily from side to side.

woe *NOUN* (**woes**)
1 someone's woes are their troubles and misfortunes **2** woe is great sorrow

> WORD FAMILY
> A **woeful** person is very sad; you can say something is **woeful** when it is very bad or serious; to look or say something **woefully** is to do it very sadly.

wok *NOUN* (**woks**)
a deep round-bottomed frying-pan used in Chinese cookery

woke
past tense of **wake** *VERB*

woken
past participle of **wake** *VERB*

wolf *NOUN* (**wolves**)
a wild animal like a large fierce dog

woman *NOUN* (**women**)
a grown-up female human being

womb *NOUN* (**wombs**) (*say* woom)
the part of a female's body where babies develop before they are born

won
past tense and past participle of **win** *VERB*

wonder *VERB* (**wonders, wondering, wondered**)
1 to wonder about something is to be trying to decide about it •*I wonder what we should do next.* **2** to wonder at something is to feel surprise and admiration about it

wonder *NOUN* (**wonders**)
1 wonder is a feeling of surprise and admiration **2** a wonder is something that makes you feel surprised and admiring
no wonder it is not surprising

wonderful *ADJECTIVE*
marvellous or excellent
▷ **wonderfully** *ADVERB* extremely; very well

won't
short for *will not*

wood *NOUN* (**woods**)
1 wood is the substance that trees are made of **2** a wood is a lot of trees growing together

wooded *ADJECTIVE*
a wooded area is covered with growing trees

wooden *ADJECTIVE*
1 made of wood **2** stiff or awkward • *His movements were wooden.*

woodland *NOUN* (**woodlands**)
land covered with trees

woodlouse *NOUN* (**woodlice**)
a small crawling creature with seven pairs of legs, living in rotten wood or damp soil. It rolls itself into a ball if it is alarmed

woodpecker *NOUN* (**woodpeckers**)
a bird that taps tree trunks with its beak to find insects

woodwind *NOUN*
in an orchestra, the woodwind is the wind instruments that are usually made of wood or plastic, such as the clarinet and oboe

woodwork *NOUN*
1 woodwork is making things with wood
2 woodwork is also things made out of wood

woodworm *NOUN* (**woodworm** or **woodworms**)
the larva of a beetle that bores into wood

woody *ADJECTIVE* (**woodier**, **woodiest**)
1 like wood or made of wood **2** full of trees

wool *NOUN*
1 wool is the thick soft hair of sheep or goats **2** wool is also thread or cloth made from this hair

woollen *ADJECTIVE*
made of wool

woollens *PLURAL NOUN*
clothes made of wool

woolly *ADJECTIVE* (**woollier**, **woolliest**)
1 covered with wool **2** made of wool or like wool **3** vague and not clear • *He has woolly ideas.*
▷ **woolliness** *NOUN* woolliness is being woolly

word *NOUN* (**words**)
1 a set of sounds or letters that has a meaning and is written with a space before and after it **2** a brief talk with someone • *Can I have a word with you?* **3** your word is when you promise to do something • *He cannot keep his word.* **4** a command or signal to do something • *Run when I give the word.* **5** a message or piece of news • *We sent word that we had arrived safely.*

word *VERB* (**words**, **wording**, **worded**)
to word something is to express it in words

word class *NOUN* (**word classes**)
each of the groups (also called **parts of speech**) into which words can be divided in grammar: noun, adjective, pronoun, adverb, preposition, determiner, conjunction, interjection

> WORD CLASSES
> Words can be put into sets called word classes, or parts of speech. The main ones are: *noun, pronoun, verb, adjective, adverb, preposition, conjunction, determiner*. There are separate panels in this dictionary telling you about each of these word classes.

wording *NOUN*
the wording of something is the words used to say it

word processing *NOUN*
word processing is using a computer for writing and editing letters and documents, and for printing them out

> WORD FAMILY
> A **word processor** is a computer used for word processing.

wordy *ADJECTIVE* (**wordier**, **wordiest**)
using too many words • *We heard a wordy speech.*

wore
past tense of **wear** *VERB*

work *VERB* (**works**, **working**, **worked**)
1 to work is to spend time doing something that needs effort or energy **2** to work is also to have a job or be employed • *She works in a bank.* **3** something works when it operates correctly or successfully • *Is the lift working?* **4** to work something is to make it act or operate • *Can you work the lift?* **5** to work (for example) loose is to become gradually loose • *The screw had worked loose.*
to work out is to succeed or reach the right answer
to work something out is to find the answer to it

work *NOUN* (**works**)
1 work is something that you have to do that needs effort or energy • *Digging is hard work.* **2** a person's work is their job • *What work do you do?* **3** at school, your work is something you write or produce • *Please get on with your work quietly.* **4** (in science) work is the result of applying a force to move an object **5** a work is a piece of writing or music or painting • *The book has all the works of Shakespeare.*
to be at work is to be working

workable *ADJECTIVE*
a workable plan is able to be carried out

worker *NOUN* (**workers**)
1 someone who works **2** a member of the working class **3** a bee or ant that does the work in a hive or colony but does not produce eggs

workforce *NOUN* (**workforces**)
the number of people who work for a business or factory

working class *NOUN* or **working classes** *PLURAL NOUN*
people who do paid manual or industrial work

> WORD FAMILY
> **Working-class** people belong to the working class.

workman *NOUN* (**workmen**)
a man who does manual work

workmanship *NOUN*
workmanship is skill in making something

workout *NOUN* (**workouts**)
a session of physical exercise or training

works *PLURAL NOUN*
1 the moving parts of a machine **2** a factory or industrial site

worksheet *NOUN* (**worksheets**)
a sheet of paper with a set of questions about a subject for students

workshop *NOUN* (**workshops**)
a place where things are made or mended

world *NOUN* (**worlds**)
1 the world is the earth with all its countries and peoples **2** a world is a planet • *The film is about creatures from another world.* **3** everything to do with a particular subject or activity • *He knows a lot about the world of sport.*

worldly *ADJECTIVE* (**worldlier**, **worldliest**)
1 to do with life on earth **2** only interested in money and possessions
▷ **worldliness** *NOUN* worldliness is being worldly

world war *NOUN* (**world wars**)
a war involving many countries all over the world

worldwide *ADJECTIVE & ADVERB*
over the whole world

World Wide Web *NOUN*
the system for keeping information on computers all over the world so that people can use it by using the Internet

worm *NOUN* (**worms**)
1 a small thin wriggling animal without legs, especially an earthworm **2** (*informal*) an unimportant or unpleasant person

worm *VERB* (**worms**, **worming**, **wormed**)
to worm your way somewhere is to get there by wriggling or crawling
to worm something out of someone is to get them to tell you something secret

worn [1]
past participle of **wear** *VERB*

worn [2] *ADJECTIVE*
damaged because it has been rubbed or used so much
to be worn out is to be very tired

worry *VERB* (**worries**, **worrying**, **worried**)
1 to worry is to feel anxious or troubled about something **2** to worry someone is to make them feel anxious or troubled about something **3** an animal worries its prey when it holds it in its teeth and shakes it

> WORD FAMILY
> To be **worried** is to be anxious or troubled about something; someone is a **worrier** if they worry a lot.

worry *NOUN* (**worries**)
1 worry is worrying or being anxious **2** a worry is something that makes you anxious

worse *ADJECTIVE & ADVERB*, comparative of **bad** and **badly**
more bad or more badly; less good or less well

worsen *VERB* (**worsens**, **worsening**, **worsened**)
1 to worsen is to become worse **2** to worsen something is to make it worse

worship *VERB* (**worships**, **worshipping**, **worshipped**)
to worship God or a god is to give them praise or respect

> WORD FAMILY
> A **worshipper** is someone who worships.

worship *NOUN*
worship is worshipping; religious ceremonies or services

worst *ADJECTIVE & ADVERB* superlative of **bad** and **badly**
most bad or most badly; least good or least well

worth *ADJECTIVE*
1 having a certain value • *This stamp is worth £100.* **2** deserving something; good or important enough for something • *That book is worth reading.*

worth *NOUN*
a thing's worth is its value or usefulness

worthless *ADJECTIVE*
having no value; useless

worthwhile *ADJECTIVE*
important or good enough to be worth doing

worthy *ADJECTIVE* (**worthier**, **worthiest**)
deserving respect or support • *The sale is for a worthy cause.*
to be worthy of something is to deserve or be good enough for something • *This charity is worthy of your support.*
▷ **worthily** *ADVERB* in a worthy way
▷ **worthiness** *NOUN* worthiness is being deserving or good enough for something

would *VERB*
1 past tense of the verb **will** • *We said we would do it.* • *He said he would come if he could.* **2** used in polite questions or requests • *Would you like some tea?*

wouldn't
short for *would not*

wound [1] *NOUN* (**wounds**) (*say* woond)
an injury done to a part of a person's or animal's body, especially one in which the skin is cut

wound *VERB* (**wounds**, **wounding**, **wounded**)
1 to wound a person or animal is to give them a wound **2** to wound someone is to hurt their feelings

wound [2] (*say* wownd)
past tense and past participle of **wind** *VERB*

wove
past tense of **weave**

woven
past participle of **weave**

wrap *VERB* (**wraps**, **wrapping**, **wrapped**)
to wrap something is to put paper or some other covering round it

wrap *NOUN* (**wraps**)
a shawl or cloak worn to keep you warm

wrapper *NOUN* (**wrappers**)
a piece of paper or plastic that something is wrapped in

wrapping *NOUN* (**wrappings**)
wrapping is material used to wrap something, especially a present

wrath *NOUN* (*rhymes with* **cloth**)
(*old-fashioned use*) anger
▷ **wrathful** *ADJECTIVE* angry
▷ **wrathfully** *ADVERB* angrily

wreath *NOUN* (**wreaths**) (*say* reeth)
flowers and leaves and branches bound together to make a circle

wreathe *VERB* (**wreathes**, **wreathing**, **wreathed**) (*say* reeth)
to be wreathed in something is to be covered in it or decorated with it • *Her face was wreathed in smiles.*

wreck *VERB* (**wrecks**, **wrecking**, **wrecked**)
to wreck something is to damage or ruin it so badly that it cannot be used again

> WORD FAMILY
> A **wrecker** is someone who wrecks something.

wreck *NOUN* (**wrecks**)
a badly damaged ship or car

wreckage *NOUN*
wreckage is the pieces of something that has been wrecked

wren *NOUN* (**wrens**)
a very small brown bird

wrench *VERB* (**wrenches**, **wrenching**, **wrenched**)
to wrench something is to pull or twist it suddenly or violently • *He wrenched the door open.* • *But at the Faun's cave a terrible surprise awaited them. The door had been wrenched off its hinges and everything lay smashed on the floor.* — C. S. Lewis, *The Lion, The Witch and the Wardrobe*

wrench *NOUN* (**wrenches**)
1 a wrenching movement **2** a tool for gripping and turning bolts or nuts

wrestle *VERB* (**wrestles**, **wrestling**, **wrestled**)
1 to wrestle with someone is to fight them by grasping them and trying to throw them to the ground **2** to wrestle with a problem or difficulty is to struggle to solve it

> WORD FAMILY
> A **wrestler** is someone who wrestles for sport, and the sport is **wrestling**.

wretch *NOUN* (**wretches**)
someone who is unhappy, poor, or disliked

wretched *ADJECTIVE* (*say* **rech**- id)
1 poor and unhappy • *a wretched beggar* **2** not satisfactory or pleasant • *This wretched car won't start.*

wriggle *VERB* (**wriggles**, **wriggling**, **wriggled**)
to wriggle is to twist and turn your body
to wriggle out of something is to avoid doing something you do not like

wriggle *NOUN* (**wriggles**)
a wriggling movement

> WORD FAMILY
> A **wriggly** creature wriggles a lot.

wring *VERB* (**wrings**, **wringing**, **wrung**)
1 to wring something wet, or to wring it out, is to squeeze or twist it to get the water out of it **2** to wring something is to squeeze it violently • *I'll wring your neck!*
wringing wet very wet; soaked

wrinkle *NOUN* (**wrinkles**)
1 wrinkles are the small lines and creases that appear in your skin as you get older **2** a small crease or line on the surface of something

wrinkle *VERB* (**wrinkles**, **wrinkling**, **wrinkled**)
something wrinkles when wrinkles appear in or on it

> WORD FAMILY
> **Wrinkled** skin or clothing has wrinkles.

wrist *NOUN* (**wrists**)
the joint that connects your hand to your arm

wristwatch *NOUN* (**wristwatches**)
a watch that you wear on your wrist

write *VERB* (**writes**, **writing**, **wrote**, **written**)
1 to write words or signs is to put them on paper or some other surface so that people can read them **2** to write a story or play or a piece of music is to be the author or composer of it **3** to write to someone is to send them a letter
to write something off is to think it is lost or useless

writer *NOUN* (**writers**)
a person who writes; an author

writhe *VERB* (**writhes**, **writhing**, **writhed**) (*say* ryth)
to writhe is to twist your body about because you are in pain or discomfort

writing *NOUN* (**writings**)
1 writing is something you write **2** your writing is the way you write

> WRITING
> Every piece of writing needs to have an audience and a purpose. Different audiences and purposes need particular kinds of vocabulary, sentence structure, level of formality, shape and structure of text. For example:
> In **discursive writing**, you are writing a balanced discussion, trying to put both sides of an argument fairly.
> In **persuasive writing**, you are trying to persuade your reader to do or believe something. You only need to set out one side of the argument, although you can refer to the other.
> In **journalistic writing**, you are writing as if for a newspaper. Different newspapers have different styles and purposes of writing.
> In **procedural writing**, you are writing instructions to help someone to make or do something.
> In **report writing**, you are describing what something is or does.
> In **explanatory writing**, you are explaining how something works.
> In the different kinds of **narrative writing**, you are telling a story.
> In **informal writing**, you may be writing a chatty letter to a friend.
> In **formal writing**, you need to use language carefully because formal writing is often for legal and official purposes.
> There are many other kinds of writing and purposes for writing. It is important to think about what you are writing before you begin.

wrong *ADJECTIVE*
1 not fair or morally right • *It is wrong to cheat.* **2** incorrect • *Your answer is wrong.* **3** not working properly • *There's something wrong with the engine.*

> WORD FAMILY
> To **wrongly** do something is to do it in a way that is unfair or incorrect.

wrong *ADVERB*
wrongly • *You guessed wrong.*

wrong *NOUN* (**wrongs**)
something that is wrong
to be in the wrong is to have done or said something wrong

wrong *VERB* (**wrongs**, **wronging**, **wronged**)
to wrong someone is to do wrong to them

wrote
past tense of **write**

wrung
past tense and past participle of **wring**

wry *ADJECTIVE* (**wryer**, **wryest**)
slightly mocking or sarcastic • *He gave a wry smile.*

Xx

xenophobia *NOUN*
xenophobia is a strong dislike of foreigners

Xmas *NOUN* (**Xmases**)
(*informal*) Christmas

X-ray *NOUN* (**X-rays**)
a photograph of the inside of something, especially a part of the body, made by a kind of radiation that can pass through something solid

X-ray *VERB* (**X-rays**, **X-raying**, **X-rayed**)
to X-ray something is to make an X-ray of it

xylophone *NOUN* (**xylophones**) (*say* zy- lo- fohn)
a musical instrument made of wooden bars of different lengths, that you hit with small hammers

yacht *NOUN* (**yachts**) (*say* yot)
1 a sailing boat used for racing or cruising **2** a private ship

yachtsman or **yachtswoman** *NOUN* (**yachtsmen** or **yachtswomen**)
a man or woman who sails in a yacht

yam *NOUN* (**yams**)
a tropical vegetable that grows underground

yank *VERB* (**yanks**, **yanking**, **yanked**)
to yank something is to pull it strongly and suddenly

yap *VERB* (**yaps, yapping, yapped**)
a small dog yaps when it makes a shrill barking sound

yap *NOUN* (**yaps**)
a shrill barking sound

yard [1] *NOUN* (**yards**)
a measure of length, 36 inches or about 91 centimetres

yard [2] *NOUN* (**yards**)
a piece of ground beside a building, or one used for a special purpose, such as a railway yard

yarn *NOUN* (**yarns**)
1 yarn is thread spun by twisting fibres together **2** (*informal*) a yarn is a tale or story

yashmak *NOUN* (**yashmaks**)
a veil covering most of the face, worn by some Muslim women

yawn *VERB* (**yawns, yawning, yawned**)
1 you yawn when you open your mouth wide and breathe in deeply because you are tired or bored **2** to yawn is also to form a wide opening • *The chasm yawned in front of them.*

yawn *NOUN* (**yawns**)
an act of yawning

ye *PRONOUN*
(*old use*) you (referring to more than one person)

year *NOUN* (**years**)
the time that the earth takes to go right round the sun, about $365\frac{1}{4}$ days or twelve months

yearly *ADJECTIVE & ADVERB*
every year

yearn *VERB* (**yearns, yearning, yearned**)
to yearn for something is to long for it

yeast *NOUN*
yeast is a substance used in baking bread and in making beer and wine. It causes alcohol and carbon dioxide to form

yell *NOUN* (**yells**)
a loud cry or shout

yell *VERB* (**yells, yelling, yelled**)
to yell is to cry or shout loudly

yellow *NOUN*
the colour of ripe lemons and buttercups

yellow *ADJECTIVE* (**yellower, yellowest**)
1 yellow in colour **2** (*informal*) cowardly

yelp *VERB* (**yelps, yelping, yelped**)
to yelp is to make a shrill bark or cry, as a dog does when it is hurt

yelp *NOUN* (**yelps**)
a yelping sound

yen [1] *NOUN* (**yens**)
a longing for something

yen [2] *NOUN* (**yen**)
a Japanese unit of money

yeoman *NOUN* (**yeomen**) (*say* **yoh-man**)
(*old use*) a man who owns and runs a small farm

Yeoman of the Guard *NOUN* (**Yeomen of the Guard**)
a guard at the Tower of London; a beefeater

yes *INTERJECTION*
a word used for agreeing to something

yesterday *NOUN & ADVERB*
the day before today

yet *ADVERB*
1 up to now; by this time • *Has the postman called yet?* **2** eventually; still • *I'll get even with him yet.* **3** in addition; even • *She became yet more excited.*

yet *CONJUNCTION*
nevertheless • *It is strange, yet it is true.*

yeti *NOUN* (**yetis**) (*say* **yet-ee**)
a very large hairy creature thought to live in the Himalayas

yew *NOUN* (**yews**)
an evergreen tree with red berries and dark leaves like needles

yield *VERB* (**yields, yielding, yielded**)
1 to yield is to surrender or give in • *He yielded to persuasion.* **2** to yield a crop or profit is to produce it • *These trees yield good apples.*

yield *NOUN* (**yields**)
an amount produced by something • *What is the yield of wheat per acre?*

yippee *INTERJECTION*
a shout of joy

yodel *VERB* (**yodels, yodelling, yodelled**)
to yodel is to sing or shout with your voice going rapidly from low to high notes

yoga *NOUN*
yoga is a Hindu system of exercise, meditation, and self-control

yoghurt *NOUN* (**yoghurts**) (*say* **yog-ert**)
yoghur is milk made thick by the addition of bacteria, giving it a sharp taste

yoke *NOUN* (**yokes**)
a curved piece of wood put across the necks of animals pulling a cart

yoke *VERB* (**yokes, yoking, yoked**)
to yoke animals is to harness them or link them by means of a yoke

yolk *NOUN* (**yolks**) (*rhymes with* **coke**)
the yellow part of an egg

Yom Kippur *NOUN*
the Day of Atonement, an important Jewish religious festival

yonder *ADVERB & ADJECTIVE*
(*old use*) over there

Yorkshire pudding *NOUN* (**Yorkshire puddings**)
a pudding made of batter and usually eaten with roast beef

you *PRONOUN*
1 the person or people someone is speaking to • *Who are you?* **2** people; anyone • *You can never be too sure.*

you'd
short for *you had* or *you should* or *you would*

you'll
short for *you will*

young *ADJECTIVE* (**younger**, **youngest**)
having lived or existed only a short time; not old

young *PLURAL NOUN*
an animal's or bird's young are its babies

youngster *NOUN* (**youngsters**)
a young person or child

your *DETERMINER*
belonging to you

you're
short for *you are*

yours *PRONOUN*
belonging to you • *Is this house yours?*
Yours faithfully, Yours sincerely, Yours truly formal ways of ending a letter before you sign it

yourself *PRONOUN* (**yourselves**)
you (referring to one person) and nobody else, used to refer back to the subject of a verb • *Have you hurt yourself?*
by yourself or **yourselves** on your own • *Did you do the work all by yourself?*

youth *NOUN* (**youths**)
1 youth is being young, or the time when you are young **2** a youth is a young man **3** youth also means young people • *What do you think of today's youth?*

WORD FAMILY
Someone is **youthful** when they are young or seem to be young.

youth club *NOUN* (**youth clubs**)
a club providing leisure activities for young people

youth hostel *NOUN* (**youth hostels**)
a hostel where young people can stay cheaply when they are on holiday

you've
short for *you have*

yo-yo *NOUN* (**yo-yos**)
a round wooden or plastic toy that moves up and down on a string which you hold

yuppie *NOUN* (**yuppies**)
(*informal*) a young middle-class person with a professional job, who earns a lot of money and spends it on expensive things

Zz

zany *ADJECTIVE* (**zanier**, **zaniest**)
funny in a crazy kind of way

zap *VERB* (**zaps**, **zapping**, **zapped**)(*slang*)
1 to zap something or someone is to attack or destroy them, especially in a computer game **2** to zap between television channels is to use a remote control to quickly change from one to another

WORD FAMILY
A **zapper** is a remote control for changing television channels.

zeal *NOUN*
zeal is keenness, especially in doing what you believe to be right

zealous *ADJECTIVE* (*say* **zel**- us)
very enthusiastic
▷ **zealously** *ADVERB* very enthusiastically

zebra *NOUN* (**zebras**)
an African animal like a horse with black and white stripes

zebra crossing *NOUN* (**zebra crossings**)
part of a road marked with broad white stripes for pedestrians to cross

zenith *NOUN*
1 the part of the sky directly above you • *The south wind began to blow and the June sunset reddened the sky to the zenith.* — Richard Adams, *Watership Down* **2** the highest point of something

zero *NOUN* (**zeros**)
nought; the figure 0

zest *NOUN*
zest is great enjoyment or enthusiasm

zigzag *NOUN* (**zigzags**)
a line or route full of sharp turns from one side to the other

zigzag *VERB* (**zigzags**, **zigzagging**, **zigzagged**)
to zigzag is to move in a series of sharp turns from one side to the other • *The tunnel veered to the left, zigzagged violently, and came to an end on a ledge overlooking a great void.* — Alan Garner, *The Weirdstone of Brisingamen*

zinc *NOUN*
zinc is a white metal

zip *NOUN* (**zips**)
1 a zip, or zip fastener, is a device with two rows of small teeth that fit together, used to join two pieces of material **2** a zip is also a sharp sound like a bullet going through the air **3** zip is liveliness or energy

zip *VERB* (**zips**, **zipping**, **zipped**)
1 to zip something, or zip it up, is to fasten it with a zip **2** to zip, or zip along, is to move quickly with a sharp sound

zodiac *NOUN* (*say* **zoh**- di- ak)
an area of the sky divided into twelve equal parts, called **signs of the zodiac**, each named after a constellation

zombie *NOUN* (**zombies**)
(*informal*) someone who seems to be doing things without thinking, often through tiredness

zone *NOUN* (**zones**)
a district or area set aside for a particular use • *This is a no-parking zone.*

zoo *NOUN* (**zoos**)
a place where wild animals are kept so that people can look at them or study them

zoology *NOUN* (*say* zoh- **ol**- o- jee)
zoology is the study of animals

WORD FAMILY
Something **zoological** is to do with zoology; a **zoologist** is an expert in zoology.

zoom *VERB* (**zooms**, **zooming**, **zoomed**)
to zoom is to move very quickly, especially with a buzzing sound

zoom lens *NOUN* (**zoom lenses**)
a camera lens that can be adjusted continuously to focus on things that are close up or far away

OXFORD
Dictionaries and Thesauruses for home and school

Oxford Very First Dictionary

Oxford First Dictionary
Oxford First Thesaurus

Oxford Junior Illustrated Dictionary
Oxford Junior Illustrated Thesaurus

Oxford Junior Dictionary
Oxford Junior Thesaurus

Oxford Primary Dictionary
Oxford Primary Thesaurus

Oxford Children's Dictionary
Oxford Children's Thesaurus

Oxford Concise School Dictionary
Oxford Concise School Thesaurus

Oxford School Dictionary
Oxford School Thesaurus

Oxford Pocket School Dictionary
Oxford Pocket School Thesaurus

Oxford Mini School Dictionary
Oxford Mini School Thesaurus

Oxford Student's Dictionary

Large print

Oxford Young Readers' Dictionary
Oxford Young Readers' Spelling Dictionary